Foreword to the First Edition

by THE HON SIR LAURENCE STREET, KCMG, K StJ
Chief Justice of New South Wales

An age-old problem confronting students in the common law has been the mastering of an ever increasing volume of decided cases and cognate material. Since the earliest times it has been an accepted and respected province of legal scholarship to select and distil the essential substance of these basic sources and to marshall this substance with explanatory text within the manageable confines of a single work.

The earliest extant Abridgement of the English Year Books was published in 1490. During the following century the use by students of "commonplace" books or abridgements became well established. Rolle's Abridgement, compiled in the early seventeenth century, is, perhaps, the precursor of the modern books of cases and materials containing, as it does, not only digests and extracts from case law, but also Parliamentary records and Statutes. Smith's Leading Cases and White and Tudor have become standard textbooks, running through many editions since their first publication in 1837 and 1849 respectively.

During the post World War II years there has been an enormous expansion in both the mass of cases and basic source material as well as the number of teaching institutions in the common law world. This has led to renewed interest in and use of the casebook as a vehicle for teaching and studying the law. In these years many have been published dealing with various specialised topics.

Professor Peden has recognised and set out to fill the need to provide students with a collection within one volume of the leading cases and related materials within the field of commercial law. He has brought to bear upon this task a happy combination of research, teaching experience and scholarship. The cases and materials are comprehensive and wide ranging. More importantly from the student's point of view, they have been linked together in a logical overall framework and set within the fabric of an instructive text. The author has used hypothetical situations to exemplify the operation of the principles deducible from the basic sources quoted. He has challenged the student's understanding of the essential points by formulating precise questions. Above all he has covered the complex field of commercial law in a manner that shows up its inter-relation and its consistency with fundamental common law principles.

The resulting work is a teaching aid which is at once both sound and clear. I welcome it as a valuable addition to the teaching literature of the law. Its advent is timely inasmuch as the future prosperity of this country is to no small extent dependent upon the continuing development and expansion of our trade and commerce. An indispensable adjuvant in this development and expansion is a legal profession soundly instructed and well-versed in the substance and the operation of commercial law. Professor Peden is to be commended for bringing out a textbook which will aid in the training of lawyers to fill this requirement.

Chief Justice's Chambers L W STREET
Sydney

Acknowledgments

The author acknowledges with gratitude permission by the following authors and publishers to reproduce extracts from cases, statutes and other materials in this book:

Butterworths Law Publishers Pty Ltd—cases reported in the All England Reports and Law Times Reports.

Butterworths Pty Ltd—cases reported in the Australian Law Reports.

Butterworths of New Zealand Ltd—cases reported in the New Zealand Law Reports.

The Incorporated Council of Law Reporting for England and Wales—cases reported in the Law Reports and Weekly Law Reports.

Council of Law Reporting in Victoria—cases reported in the Victorian Law Reports and Victorian Reports.

Lloyd's, London—cases reported in Lloyd's Law Reports.

The Law Book Company Ltd—cases reported in the Commonwealth Law Reports, Federal Law Reports, Australian Law Journal Reports, Australian Bankruptcy Cases, New South Wales State Reports and Weekly Notes, New South Wales Law Reports, South Australian State Reports, Tasmanian Law Reports, and Queensland State Reports.

Attorney-General for Western Australian—cases reported in the Western Australian Reports.

The Commercial Law Association of Australia Ltd—extract from article "Bank Credit Cards" by Chappenden.

National Commercial Banking Corporation of Australia Ltd—extract from *Finance of International Trade,* 4th ed, 1979.

The Yale Law Journal—extracts from articles "Legal Realism: Its Cause and Cure" by Gilmore, vol 70, pp 1042-3; "What Price Contract?—An Essay in Perspective", by Llewellyn, vol 40, pp 746-8.

Sweet & Maxwell Ltd—extracts from article "Codification of Mercantile Law" by Chalmers. Law Quarterly Review, vol 19, pp 10-11, and Temperley, *Carriage of Goods by Sea Act 1924,* 4th ed, pp 1-4.

Martinus Nijhoff, extract from Clarke, *Aspects of the Hague Rules, 1976.*

The Attorneys-General for the Commonwealth, New South Wales, Victoria, South Australia and Tasmania—sections from various statutes.

The Permanent Editorial Board for the Uniform Commercial Code—extracts from the Code and Official Comments.

The International Chamber of Commerce—extracts from *Incoterms 1980* and *The Uniform Customs and Practice for Documentary Credits.*

Contents

	Page
Foreword	iii
Acknowledgments	iv
Preface	vii
Table of Cases	ix
Comparative Table of Sale of Goods Acts	xxvi

Introduction	1

Chapter

1 THE NATURE AND SOURCES OF COMMERCIAL LAW	3
1 The Origins of Modern Commercial Law	3
2 The Subject Matter of Commercial Law	4
3 Policy Considerations and Law Reform	6
4 Commercial Law Practice	7
5 A Prototype Transaction	8

2 SALE OF GOODS: SCOPE, DEFINITION AND FORMAL REQUIREMENTS	10
1 The Contract of Sale in its Commercial Context	11
2 The Purpose and Scope of the Sale of Goods Act	15
3 What is a Contract for Sale of Goods?	19
4 Formal Requirements: Is the Statute of Frauds Necessary?	27

3 IMPLIED CONDITIONS IN CONTRACTS OF SALE	35
1 Implied Conditions in General	35
2 Implied Terms: Title and Freedom from Encumbrances	37
3 Implied Conditions: Conformity, Fitness and Quality	40

4 PERFORMANCE OF THE SALES CONTRACT AND REMEDIES FOR BREACH	83
1 Events Prior to Delivery: The Passing of Property and Risk	83
2 Performance by Delivery and Acceptance of Goods and Payment	111
3 Remedies for Breach	130

5 IMPORT AND EXPORT SALES	143
1 The Significance and Characteristics of International Sales	143
2 Special Forms of Import and Export Contracts	144
3 Related Contracts of Carriage	163
4 An International Law of Sales	193

Teaching Materials and Cases on Commercial Transactions

Chapter	Page
6 CONTRACTS OF INSURANCE	197
1 The Function of Insurance Contracts	197
2 The Uberrimae Fidei Doctrine and Construction of Insurance Contracts	207
3 Insurable Interest	243
4 The Indemnity Principle and its Applications	250
5 Insurance Claims	262
7 FINANCING TRANSACTIONS: LENDING ON THE SECURITY OF GOODS	265
1 The Function of Credit Transactions	265
2 Types of Security Interests in Personal Property	268
3 Perfection of Security Interests in Goods	278
4 The Insolvent Debtor and Bankruptcy Proceedings	286
5 Fraudulent Dispositions, Preferences and Floating Charges	300
6 Money-lending, Hire-purchase and Consumer Credit Legislation	327
8 PRIORITIES IN RELATION TO CHATTEL SECURITIES	335
1 The Nemo Dat Rule and Protection of Bona Fide Purchasers	335
2 Priority Conflicts between Competing Secured Creditors	355
3 Financing Farm Products	377
9 LENDING ON THE SECURITY OF PROCEEDS: ASSIGNMENT OF CHOSES IN ACTION AND CHATTEL PAPER; CREDIT CARDS	381
1 An Overview of Credit Practices involving Proceeds	381
2 Requirements for Valid Assignments	383
3 Priorities between Competing Claims	405
4 Financing through Chattel Paper	410
5 Arrangements with Credit Cards	416
10 FINANCING THROUGH NEGOTIABLE INSTRUMENTS, PROMISSORY NOTES AND LETTERS OF CREDIT	423
1 The Origin, Purpose and Function of Negotiable Instruments	423
2 Transfer and Negotiation of Bills of Exchange	425
3 Rights and Liabilities of Parties and Discharge	440
4 Financing International Transactions: Letters of Credit	457
11 THE BANKER-CUSTOMER RELATIONSHIP AND THE BANKING SYSTEM	482
1 The Australian Banking System, and the Use of Cheques	482
2 Duties of Paying Bank and its Customer at Common Law	491
3 Duties of Collecting and Paying Banks and Pt III Bills of Exchange Act	502
Index	529

Preface

There have been a number of textbooks available for some years dealing with commercial law, but apart from collections of cases prepared for distribution within individual faculties, there has been no satisfactory published set of teaching materials. It is hoped that this publication will fill that gap.

The choice of topics has been designed to meet the curriculum requirements of students of commercial and business law in university faculties of law, commerce and economics, as well as commerce and accounting students in colleges of advanced education. These materials have been prepared in the conviction that students cannot fully understand the purpose and effect of commercial law rules without some appreciation of the nature and form of the transactions upon which those rules operate. Without some prior experience in the world of business they often flounder with the legal rules as if in a vacuum. Again, the commercial transactions of contract, sale, carriage, insurance, loan, security, assignment, and payment must appear to students as unrelated pieces in some strange commercial jig-saw. This book attempts to alleviate these problems by adopting a number of teaching techniques which I have found helpful in teaching these subjects during the past 15 years. A fuller statement of these methods is set out in the Introduction at p 1.

Three basic points should be made at the outset:

(1) The book contains an integrated set of teaching materials;

(2) It adopts a transactional approach: ie, it emphasises the purpose and operation of commercial transactions as they occur in practice;

(3) In selecting cases and other materials, preference has been given wherever possible to Australian and New Zealand authorities, with reference to English and American sources to fill gaps or to demonstrate alternative approaches to policy issues.

Since the previous edition published in 1979, a number of significant changes have taken place in areas covered by this book. The more important are:

(1) The enactment in Victoria of the package of three new Acts in the consumer credit area: The Credit Act 1981, Chattel Securities Act 1981 and Goods (Sales and Leases) Act 1981. The New South Wales equivalent Consumer Credit Act 1981 has been enacted but has not yet come into force. The result of this legislation will be the end of hire-purchase transactions as such in Victoria and New South Wales as has been the position in South Australia since 1973. These changes are reflected in the materials in Chapters 3, 7, 8 and 9.

(2) Important changes introduced by the Bankruptcy Amendment Act 1980, which are taken into the text of Chapter 7.

(3) The uniform adoption of the National Companies Code 1981, which has made necessary significant changes in Chapters 7 and 8 in relation to floating charges, and the rules governing priorities and tacking.

(4) A number of important cases, the most significant of which include:

    (a) The Privy Council judgment in *Port Jackson Stevedoring Pty Ltd v Salmon & Spraggon (Australia) Pty Ltd,* upholding Barwick CJ's

dissenting opinion in the High Court: see p 184, *infra*;
(b) the House of Lords decision in *United City Merchants (Investments) Ltd v Royal Bank of Canada* (p 472, *infra*) which involved fraud in relation to a documentary letter of credit transaction;
(c) the High Court decision in *Commonwealth Trading Bank of Australia v Sydney Wide Stores Pty Ltd* (p 492, *infra*) which resolved an earlier conflict of authority between the High Court and House of Lords regarding the duties of banker and customer in relation to alterations of cheques.

The law is stated as at 30 June 1983.

I should like to thank a number of people who have provided valuable assistance toward production of the second edition of this book. Mark Jackson, Christine Tomasich, David Wilkie and Alan Worsley, all Macquarie law students, helped to collect materials and check references required to bring the book up to date. I am most grateful to my secretary, Mrs Joan Rattray, for the most competent manner in which she typed the manuscript and prepared the Table of Cases. Alan Worsley also helped with the Subject Index, and a number of other Macquarie students helped with the arduous task of proof reading. I was greatly encouraged by the helpful comments, suggestions and corrections received from many students who have used the first edition of the Casebook over the past five years.

I acknowledge once again the unfailing support of my wife Jean and our children during the preparation of this book.

Macquarie University JOHN R PEDEN
Sydney
1 September 1983

Table of Cases

References in bold type indicate where cases are extracted in detail

A A Radio Taxi Trucks Ltd v Curyer [1965] 168
Abbott v Wolsey [1895] 29
Adelphi Bank v Edwards 494
Adler v Dickson (1955) 181, 182, 183, 184
Akron Tyre Co Pty Ltd v Kittson (1951) **273**, 279, 371, 402
Albacora SRL v Westcott & Laurence Line Ltd (1966) 176, 178
Albazero, The [1974] 90, 102
Albemarle Supply Co Ltd v Hind Co [1928] **362**, 364, 366, 367, 368
Alexander v Thomas (1851) 430
Allester Ltd, Re [1922] 477
Allied Mills Ltd v Gwydir Valley Oilseeds Pty Ltd (1978) **109**
Allison v Bristol Marine Insurance Co Ltd 247, 248
Amco Enterprises Pty Ltd v Wade [1968] 21
Anchor Products Ltd v Hedges (1966) 167
Anderson v Fitzgerald (1853) 221
Anderson v Morice (1874) 106
Anderson v Pacific Fire and Marine Insurance Co (1872) 234
Anglo-African Merchants Ltd v Bayley [1970] **205**, 213
Anning v Anning (1907) 387, 388, 392
Ant Jurgens Margarinefabrieken v Louis Dreyfus & Co [1914] 133
Arab Bank Ltd v Ross 427, **444**
Arcos Ltd v E A Ronaasen & Son [1933] 54
Arden v Arden (1885) 408
Aristoc Industries Pty Ltd v Wenham (Builders) Pty Ltd [1965] 34, 138
Armaghdown Motors Ltd v Gray Motors Ltd [1963] 88
Armco (Aust) Pty Ltd v Federal Commissioner of Taxation (1948) 451
Arnhold Karberg & Co v Blythe, Green, Jourdain & Co (1915) ... 98, 154, 159
Asfar & Co v Blundell [1896] 103
Ashington Piggeries Ltd v Christopher Hill Ltd [1972] 35, 43, **50**
A-G for NSW v Hills & Halls Ltd (1923) 378, 379
Australasian Brokerage Ltd v Australian and New Zealand Banking Corp
   Ltd (1934) 202
Australian & International Insurances Ltd v Workers' Compensation Commission
   of NSW (1972) 199
Australian Independent Distributors Ltd v Winter & Others (1965) 484
Australian Knitting Mills Ltd v Grant (1933) 43, 45, 76
Australian Mutual Provident Society v Derham (1979) 524
Australian Provincial Assurance Association v Producers and Citizens Co-operative
   Assurance Co of Australia Ltd (1931) 234
Australian Provincial Assurance Co Ltd v Coroneo (1938) 22, **369**
Automatic Tube Co Pty Ltd v Adelaide Steamship (Operations) Ltd (1966) ... 178
Automobile & General Finance Co Ltd v Cowley-Cooper (1948) 89
Automobile Finance Co of Australia Ltd v Henderson (1928) 449
Automobile Finance Co Ltd v Law 427, **451**, 454
Ayers v Moore [1940] 443

B & H Constructions Pty Ltd v Campbell [1963]	**27**, **91**, 112
Babatsikos v Car Owners' Mutual Insurance Co Ltd [1970]	**208**, 218, 235
Baines v Swainson (1863)	345
Baker v Barclays Bank Ltd [1955]	522
Baldry v Marshall [1925]	**72**
Bank of Australasia v Hall (1907)	316, 317
Bank of England v Vagliano Bros [1891]	**16**, 435, 436, 437, 446, 493, 497
Bank of Ireland v Trustees of Evans' Charities (1855)	493, 494
Bank of NSW v The Commonwealth (1948)	483
Bank of NSW v The Northern British and Mercantile Insurance Co (1882)	245
Bank of Victoria Ltd v Langlands Foundry Co Ltd (1898)	279
Barclays Bank Ltd v Astley Industrial Trust Ltd [1970]	**509**
Barnes, Re; Ex parte Stapleton; Barnes & Anor (1961)	**301**
Barnett Ltd v National Insurance Co of New Zealand Ltd [1965]	264
Barr v Gibson (1838)	41
Barrow, Lane & Ballard Ltd v Phillip Phillips & Co [1929]	**103**
Barton v Deputy Commissioner of Taxation (1974)	**293**
Batos v Hewitt (1867)	215
Bawden v London, Edinburgh and Glasgow Assurance Co [1892]	230, 231, 232, 236
Baxendale v Bennett (1878)	494
Bayley v Manchester, Sheffield and Lincolnshire Railway Co (1872)	202
Beale v Taylor [1967]	82
Beecham (H) & Co v Francis Howard & Co (1921)	47, 48
Beer v Walker (1877)	46
Behrend & Co v Produce Brokers' Co [1920]	103
Belfast Ropework Co Ltd v Bushell [1918]	168
Bellamy v Marjoribanks (1852)	514
Belshaw v Bush (1851)	443
Benaim & Co v L S Debono (1924)	123
Benger v Quartermain [1934]	369
Bergmann v Macmillan (1881)	400
Bergougman v British Motors Ltd (1929)	373
Bettini v Gye (1876)	225
Biddell Brothers v E Clemens Horst Co [1911]	**150**, 161
Biggar v Rock Life Assurance Co [1902]	230, 231, 235, 236
Bird & Co v Thomas Cook & Son Ltd [1937]	445
Bird, Re (as Trustee of the Estate of Arcadiou); Ex parte M & G Casabene & Sons	**319**
Bishopsgate Motor Finance Corp Ltd v Transport Brakes Ltd [1949]	338
Black v Elliott (1859)	46
Blackwood's Ltd v Chartres (1931)	415
Blakely Ordinance Co, Re; Ex parte New Zealand Banking Corp (1867)	406, 411
Blyth Shipbuilding and Dry Docks Co Ltd, Re [1926]	90, **94**
Boag v Standard Marine Insurance Co Ltd [1937]	260
Boehm v Bell (1799)	247
Boileau v Heath [1898]	20
Bond v Barrow Haematite Steel Co [1902]	396
Bonior v A Siery Ltd [1968]	444
Booth Steamship Co Ltd v Cargo Fleet Iron Co Ltd [1916]	131
Boston Fruit Co v British & Foreign Marine Insurance Co Ltd [1906]	248
Bottomgate Industrial Co-operative Society, Re The (1891)	484, 485
Bowes v Shand (1877)	51
Bowmaker Ltd v Wycombe Motors Ltd [1946]	368
Boydell v James (1936)	**25**, 284
Boys v Rice (1908)	41
Brady v Stapleton (1952)	305

Table of Cases

Braithwaite v W A McArthur Ltd (1898) 279
Brennan v Pitt Son and Badgery Ltd (1899) 448, 449
Brice v Bannister (1878) 386, 395, 400
Bristol Tramways & Carriage Co v Fiat Motors Ltd (1910) 48, 75, 76
British Traders' Insurance Co Ltd v Monson (1964) 244, 249, **254**, 258
British Tramways Co v Fiat Motor Ltd [1910] 16
Brooklyn Lodge Pty Ltd v Ryan (1972) 42
Brooks Robinson Pty Ltd v Rothfield [1951] **21**, 31
Brown v Davies (1789) 446
Brown v Edgington (1841) 46, 58, 67, 68
Brown (BS) & Son Ltd v Craiks Ltd [1970] 67, **77**
Browne v Hare (1858) 107
Brownlie v Campbell (1880) 220
Bruce v Jones (1863) 256
Brunker v Perpetual Trustee Co Ltd (1937) 389, 392
Burnand v Rodocanachi (1882) 253
Burnby v Bollet (1847) 58, 67
Burns v McFarlane (1940) 319, 322
Burns v Stapleton (1959) 310, 311, 314, 322
Burrows v Smith (1894) 46
Business Computers Ltd v Anglo-African Leasing Ltd [1977] 406
Butterworth v Kingsway Motors Ltd [1954] 39

Cameron v Campbell and Worthington Ltd [1930] 137
Cameron & Co v Slutzkin Pty Ltd (1923) 44
Cammell Laird & Co v Manganese Bronze and Brass Co [1934] 48, 56, 59, 61, 71, 74, 75, 76
Canada Atlantic Grain Export Co v Eilers (1929) 75, 76
Capri Jewellers Pty Ltd v Commonwealth Trading Bank of Australia (1973) (unreported) 526
Car and Universal Finance Co Ltd v Caldwell [1965] **346**
Carlos v Fancourt (1794) 429
Carpenters' Co v British Mutual Banking Co Ltd [1938] 512, 524
Carter v Boehm (1766) 211
Castellain v Preston (1883) 244, 246, 249, **251**, 255, 256, 258, 260
Catip, Re; Malick v Lloyd (1913) 281
Cavalier v Pope (1906) 180
Celthene Pty Ltd v WKJ Hauliers Pty Ltd (1981) 189, 196
Chamberlain v Young (1893) 99
Channon v English Scottish & Australian Bank (1918) 525
Chanter v Dickinson (1843) 22
Chao (trading as Zung Fu Co) v British Traders and Shippers Ltd [1954] 116, 123
Chapman v Pole (1870) 256
Chaproniere v Mason (1905) 46
Charter v Sullivan [1957] **137**
Chubu Asahi Cotton Spinning Co Ltd v The Ship Tenos (1968) 178
City Motors (1933) Pty Ltd v Southern Aerial Super Service Pty Ltd (1961) 26
City Taylors Ltd v Evans (1922) 260
Clark v Bulmer (1843) 22
Clarke v Spence (1836) 95
Claude R Ogden & Co Pty Ltd v Reliance Fire Sprinkler Co Pty Ltd and Others; Davies (First Third Party); Stenhouse (NSW) Ltd (Second Third Party) [1973] **201**
Clay v Yates (1856) 24
Clayton's case (1816) 324

Cleland v London General Insurance Co Ltd (1935)... 215
Clemens (E) Horst Co v Biddell Bros (1912)... 158, 159
Club Development & Finance Corp Pty Ltd v Bankers' & Traders' Insurance
  Co Ltd [1971]... 240
Clutton v Attenborough & Son [1897].. 435, 436, 437
Clyne v Deputy Commissioner of Taxation (1981)... 405
Coggs v Bernard (1703).. 165
Colledge v H C Curlett Construction Co Ltd [1932]... 369
Collier, Re; Ex parte Dan Rylands Ltd (1891)... 296
Collins Trading Co Pty Ltd v Maher [1969]... 34
Collyer v Isaacs (1881).. 275
Colonial Bank of Australasia Ltd v Marshall [1906]....................... 492, 496, 497
Commercial Bank of Australia Ltd v Flannagan (1932)....................................... 511
Commercial Bank of Australia Ltd v Younis [1979]... 528
Commercial Banking Co of Sydney Ltd v Jalsard Pty Ltd [1973]....................... 471
Commission Car Sales (Hastings) Ltd v Saul [1957].. 142
Commissioner of Taxation v Australia & New Zealand Banking Group Ltd
  (1979)... 501
Commissioner of Taxation v Everett (1979).. 401, 403
Commissioners of State Savings Bank v Permewan, Wright & Co (1914)...... 484,
                                                                                           489, 504, 505, 511, **512**
Commissioners of Taxation v E S & A Bank Ltd [1920]............. 487, 504, 511, 519
Commonwealth, The v Temple (1949)... 167
Commonwealth Homes and Investment Co Ltd [1943]..................................... 244
Commonwealth Trading Bank v Reno Auto Sales Pty Ltd [1967].................... **499**
Commonwealth Trading Bank of Australia v Sydney Wide Stores Pty Ltd
  and Another (1981)... 492, 528
Compagniedes Messageries Maritimes v Wilson (1954)........................... 173, 263
Comptoir D'Achat v Luis de Ridder LTDA (The Julia) [1911]......................... 153
Comptroller of Stamps (Vic) v Howard-Smith (1936).. 390
Condogianis v Guardian Assurance Co Ltd (1921).. 212
Connolly Brothers Ltd, Re (No 2) [1912]... 357
Cooper, Ex parte; Re Baum (1878)... 280
Cosmas Fish Processors International Pty Ltd v Hofmann Nominees Pty Ltd
  [1982].. 325
Cotter v Luckie [1918].. 86
Couturier v Hastie (1856)... 103
Craine v The Colonial Mutual Fire Insurance Co Ltd (1920)........................... 262
Crane (G E) Sales Pty Ltd v Commissioner of Taxation (1971)....................... 383
Crawcour, Ex parte; Re Robertson (1878).. 280
Crears v Hunter (1887).. 443
Crumplin's case... 518, 519
Cunningham Ltd (J & J) v Robert A Munro & Co Ltd (1922).......................... 461
Curran v Newpark Cinemas Ltd [1951]... 387
Currie v Misa (1875).. 509
Curtice v London City & Midland Bank Ltd [1908]... 500
Cutter v Powell... 22
Czarnikow (C) Ltd v Koufos [1969].. 63

Da Costa v Cockburn Salvage & Trading Pty Ltd (1970).................................. 167
Dalby v India and London Life Assurance Co (1854).. 249
Dalgety & Co Ltd v AMP Society [1908]............................... 209, 211, 213, 235
Dane v Mortgage Insurance Corp [1894].. 255
Darrell v Tibbitts (1880).. 254, 256
Darrell Lea (Vic) Pty Ltd v Union Assurance Co [1969].................................... 215
Davey & Co v Williamson & Sons Ltd [1898].. 324
David Jones Ltd v Willis (1934)... 50

Table of Cases

Davis v Miller (1894) ... 46
Davjoyda Estates Pty Ltd v National Insurance Co of New Zealand Ltd (1967) ... 249
Dawsons Ltd v Bonnin [1922] ... 209, 212, **222**
Day v Bank of NSW (1978) ... 511, 512
Dearle v Hall (1828) ... 402, **406**, 408, 410, 415, 424
Deaves v CML Fire and General Insurance (1979) ... **232**, 242
De Bernardy v Harding (1853) ... 22
Debtor, Re a [1914] ... 298
Debtor, Re a [1930] ... 292
Debtor, Re a [1939] ... 296
Debtor, Re a; Ex parte The Debtor v Bowmaker Ltd [1951] ... 296
Demby Hamilton & Co Ltd v Barden [1949] ... 109
Denbigh Cowan & Co and R Atcherley & Co, Re (1921) ... 155
Deta Nominees Pty Ltd v Viscount Plastic Products Ltd (1979) ... 34
Diamond v Graham [1968] ... 444
Diamond Alkali Export Corp v Bourgeois (1916) ... 99, 154
Discovery Books Pty Ltd, Re (1972) ... 314
District Savings Bank Ltd, Re; Ex parte Coe (1861) ... 485
Dittmer Gold Mines Ltd, Re (No 1) [1954] ... 323
Docker's case (1938) ... 316
Dominion Motors Ltd v Grieves [1936] ... 137
Donald v Suckling (1868) ... 276
Donoghue v Stevenson (1932) ... 45, 50, 79
Doolan v Midland Railway Co (1877) ... 167
Doughan v Ley and Another (1946) ... **138**
Douglas v Tiernan (1931) ... **449**
Downs Distributing Co Pty Ltd v Associated Blue Star Stores Pty Ltd (1948) ... 312, 314, 320, 322
Drummond v Van Ingen (1887) ... 71
Dublin City Distillery v Doherty [1914] ... 282
Duche (TM) & Sons (UK) Ltd v Walworth Industries (Aust) Pty Ltd [1962] ... 479
Dudgeon v Chie (1955) ... 30
Duncan v Blundell (1820) ... 24
Dunlop Pneumatic Tyre Co Ltd v Selfridge & Co Ltd (1915) ... 180
Durham Bros v Robertson [1898] ... **385**

Earl (G & T) (1925) Ltd v Hemsworth RDC (1928) ... 389
Eastern Distributors Ltd v Goldring (Murphy, Third Party) [1957] ... 341, 342, 343, 350
Eastwood and Holt v Studer (1926) ... 98
Ebert v Union Trustee Co of Australia Ltd (1960) ... 298
Eclipse Motors Pty Ltd v Nixon [1940] ... 142
Edinburgh Ballarat Gold Quartz Mine Co v Sydney (1891) ... 437
Edward Owen Engineering Ltd v Barclays Bank International Ltd [1978] ... 474
Elcock v Thomson [1949] ... 256
Elder Dempster case [1924] ... 180, 181, 182, 183
Elder Smith Goldsbrough Mort Ltd v McBride, Palmer (Third Party) (1976) ... **41**
Ellenborough, Re [1903] ... 389, 393
Ellershaw v Magniac (1851) ... 98
English, Scottish and Australian Bank Ltd v Bank of South Africa (1922) ... 471, 517, 518
English & Scottish Mercantile Investment Co v Brunton Ltd [1892] ... 357, 406
Esmail (trading as H M H Esmail & Sons) v J Rosenthal & Sons Ltd [1964] ... 116

Establissment Esefka International Austalt v Central Bank of Nigeria [1979] 477
Eurymedon, The [1975] 189
Evans v Rival Granite Quarries Ltd [1910] 324

FAI Insurances Ltd v Custom Credit Corp Ltd (1980) **244**
Fairbairn v Miller [1918] 166
Fairlie, Re (1969) 297
Fankhauser v Mark Dykes Pty Ltd [1960] 167
Farnsworth v Federal Commissioner of Taxation (1949) 370
Federal Commissioner of Taxation v Betro Harrison Constructions
  Pty Ltd (1978) 403
Fisher v Automobile Finance Co of Australia Ltd [1928] 364, 365, 366, 367
Florance, Re (1979) 297
Forbes v Marshall (1855) 446
Fouldes v Willoughby (1841) 375
Fowler v Hollins (1872) 375
Fox v Devonshire (1759) 265
Frank v Grosvenor Motor Auctions Pty Ltd [1960] 72
Frank Hammond Pty Ltd v Huddart Parker Ltd (1956) 178
Franov v Deposit & Investment Co Ltd (1962) 358
Freeman v Pope (1870) 304
Frost v Aylesbury Dairy Co (1905) 46
Fullwood v Hurley [1928] 206

Gabarron v Kreeft (1875) 98, 107
Gallagher v Shilcock [1949] 134
Gardiner v Gray (1815) 23, 44, 74
Gas Light Improvement Co v Terell (1870) 325
General Distributors Ltd v Paramotors Ltd [1962] 344
General Motors Acceptance Corp v Credit Tribunal (1977) 128, 412
General Trading Co's case (1911) 158
George Wills & Co Ltd v Davids Pty Ltd (1957) 73
German v Yates (1915) 392
Gian Singh & Co Ltd v Banque de l'Indochine [1974] 471, 474
Gibbons v Westminster Bank Ltd [1939] 499
Gilbert, Stokes & Kerr Pty Ltd v Dalgety & Co Ltd (1948) 181, 182, 183
Gilchrist Watt & Sanderson Pty Ltd v York Products Pty Ltd
  (1970) 163, 166
Gillett v Hill (1834) 89
Ginner v King (1890) 44
Glasgow Assurance Corp v Symondson & Co (1910) 210
Glegg v Bromley [1912] 304, 311, 314
Glendarroch, The (1894) 178
Glicksman v Lancashire & General Assurance Co [1927] 212, 214, 218, 235
Global Dress Co Ltd v Boase & Co Ltd [1966] 166
Godfrey v Brittanic Assurance Co Ltd [1963] 209, 211, 215
Goldberger, Re; Ex parte JJ Williams (Murwillumbah) Pty Ltd [1908] 297
Goldring v Royal London Auxiliary Insurance Co Ltd (1914) 236
Goodwin v Robarts (1875) 3
Goole & Hall Steam Towing Co Ltd v Ocean Marine Insurance Co Ltd
  [1928] 260
Gosford Meats Pty Ltd v Queensland Insurance Co Ltd (1970) 263
Goss v Lord Nugent (1833) **44**
Governments Stock Co Ltd v Manila Railway Co Ltd [1897] 324, 357
Graham v Freer (1980) 18
Graham v Wright (1872) 212
Grant v Australian Knitting Mills Ltd [1936] **48**, 73, 75, 76, 78, 79

Table of Cases

Grantham Homes Pty Ltd v Interstate Permanent Building Society Ltd (1979) ... 512
Great Eastern Railway v Lord's Trustee [1909] ... 283
Great Western Railway Co v London and County Banking Co [1901] ... 488
Green v All Motors Ltd [1917] ... 365, 366, 367
Greenhill v Federal Insurance Co Ltd [1927] ... 204
Greenwood v Martins Bank Ltd [1933] ... **433**, 492
Grey v Australian Motorists & General Insurance Co Ltd [1976] ... 387
Griffiths v G W J Blackman & Co Pty Ltd (1972) ... 322
Griffiths v Peter Conway Ltd [1939] ... **64**
Grigor v International Harvester Co of Australia Pty Ltd [1942] ... 369
Guaranty Trust Co of New York v Hannay & Co (1918) ... 430
Guardian Assurance Co Ltd v Condogianis (1919) ... 211, 212, 213, 214, 215
Guardian Assurance Co Pty Ltd v Underwood Constructions Pty Ltd (1974) ... 197
Gulf Refining Co v Williams Roofing Co (1945) ... 420
Gurr v Esanda Ltd (1982) ... 353

Hadley v Baxendale (1854) ... **135**, 140
Hadley v Henry (1896) ... 445
Halliday v Holgate (1808) ... 386
Hall's case (1875) ... 181
Hamilton, Fraser & Co v Pandorf & Co (1887) ... 178
Hamilton's Windsor Ironworks, Re (1879) ... 407
Hammer & Barrow v Coca-Cola & Ors [1962] ... 113, 117, **122**
Hamzeh Malas & Sons v British Imex Industries Ltd [1958] ... 460, 467
Hansson v Hamel & Harley Ltd (1922) ... 158
Hardman v Booth (1862) ... 345, 346
Hardwick Game Farm v Suffolk Agricultural Poultry Producers Association [1969] ... 62, 63, 64, 66, **69**, 73
Hardy & Co v Hillerns & Fowler [1923] ... 120, 121, 123
Harman v Bennett (1958) ... 46
Harman v Reeve (1856) ... 31
Harvey v MacDonald [1927] ... 28
Hasell v Bagot, Shakes & Lewis Ltd and Others (1911) ... 140, 141
Heilbutt v Hickson ... 86
Heimann v Commonwealth of Australia (1938) ... 202
Helby v Matthews [1895] ... 25, 274, 351
Helson v McKenzies (Cuba Street) Ltd [1950] ... 512
Helstan Securities Ltd v Hertfordshire CC [1978] ... 411
Henry Dean & Sons (Sydney) Ltd v P O'Day Pty Ltd (1927) ... 153, **156**, 457
Henry Kendall & Sons v William Lillico & Sons Ltd [1968] ... **69**, 73
Hepburn v A Tomlinson (Hauliers) Ltd [1966] ... 245, 251, 254, 260
Herrick v Leonard and Dingley Ltd Charter Travel Co Ltd and Anor (Third Parties) [1975] ... 184, 193, 194
Heyman v Darwins Ltd [1942] ... 186, 263
Hickox v Adams (1876) ... 158
Higgs v Assam Tea Co (1869) ... 406
Hilton v Westminster Bank Ltd (1926) ... 500
Hircock v Farrelly [1960] ... 310
Hobbs v Marlow [1977] ... 264
Hobbs v Petersham Transport Pty Ltd (1971) ... **163**, 168
Hobson v Gorringe [1897] ... 369
Hocking v Western Australian Bank (1909) ... 401, 402
Hoel v Flour City Fuel and Transfer Co (1919) ... 166
Hoeper v Neldner [1932] ... 30, 130
Holland v Hodgson (1872) ... 20, 369
Hollins v Fowler (1875) ... 345

Case	Page
Holmes, Re (1885)	407
Holroyd and Others v Marshall and Others (1861)	270, 275
Hookway, (F E) & Co Ltd v Alfred Isaacs & Sons [1954]	53
Hopkinson v Rolt (1861)	361
Hordern v Federal Mutual Insurance Co of Australia Ltd (1924)	258
Horwood v Millar's Timber and Trading Co Ltd [1917]	389
Houghland v R R Low (Luxury Coaches) Ltd [1962]	166
House Property Co of London Ltd v London County and Westminster Bank (1915)	505
Howes, Re; Ex parte Hughes [1892]	297
Hubbard, Ex parte; Re Hardwick (1886)	283
Hughes v Pump House Hotel Co Ltd [1902]	387, 400
Ian Stach Ltd v Baker Bosley Ltd [1958]	459, 465, 467
Inglis v Stock (1885)	89
Ingram v Little [1961]	346
Insurance Commissioner v Associated Dominions Assurance Society Pty Ltd (1953)	199
International Leasing Corp (Vic) Ltd v Aiken (1966)	387
Ipswich Gaslight Co v King & Co (1886)	68
Ipswich Permanent Money Club Ltd v Arthy [1920]	408
Ireland v Livingston (1872)	158, 497
Irving v Manning (1847)	255
Irving v Richardson (1931)	247
Jackson, Re v Bassford Ltd (1906)	325
Jackson v Rotax Motor and Cycle Co [1910]	48, 125
Jackson v Watson & Sons (1909)	46
James v Abrahams (1981)	298
James v The Commonwealth (1939)	85, 90, **97**, 149
James v Thomas H Kent & Co Ltd [1950]	23
James O'Mara, Re (1924)	284
Jansz v GMB Imports Pty Ltd (1979)	85
Jeffcott and Another v Andrew Motors Ltd [1960]	130, **131**
Joachimson v Swiss Bank Corp [1921]	485, 492
Joel v Law Union and Crown Insurance Co [1908]	214, **219**
Johann Plischke & Sohne v Allison Brothers, Ltd [1936]	**132**
John v Bacon (1870)	167
John Edwards & Co v Motor Union Insurance Co Ltd [1922]	260
John F Goulding Pty Ltd v Victorian Railways Commissioners (1932)	164
John's Period Furniture Pty Ltd v Commonwealth Savings Bank of Australia (1980)	526
Johnson v Guardian Assurance Co Ltd (1931)	240
Johnson v Stear (1863)	276
Johnstone & Wilmot Pty Ltd v Kaine (1928)	26
Jones v Bright (1829)	23, 46, 58, 68
Jones v Gordon [1877]	**447**
Jones v Just (1868)	58, 75
Jones (RE) Ltd v Waring & Gillow Ltd [1926]	444
Joseph v Lyons (1884)	275
Joseph Reid Pty Ltd v Schultz (1949)	85, **88**
Joseph Travers & Sons v Cooper [1915]	166
Joseph Travers & Sons Ltd v Longel Ltd (1948)	41
Joubert and Joubert v Corona Manufacturing Co [1922]	153
Joyce v Swann (1864)	107
Judd, Re (1924)	298
Jumna Khan v The Bankers and Traders Insurance Co Ltd (1926)	235, 236, 237

Table of Cases

Kargotich v Mustica [1973]......**136**
Karinjee Jivanjee & Co v William F Malcolm & Co (1926)......155
Karlshams Oljefabriker v Eastport Navigation Corp (The Elafi) (1982)......**91**
Kay's Leasing Corp Pty Ltd v CSR Provident Fund Nominees Pty Ltd [1962]......369
Kazacos v Fire and All Risks Insurance Co Ltd (1970)......**215**
Keane v Australian Steamships Pty Ltd (1929)......188
Keech v Sandford (1726)......40
Keene v Thomas [1905]......365, 367
Keighley Maxsted & Co v Durant [1901]......248
Kekewich v Manning (1851)......393, 394
Kendall v Lillico [1968]......78
Kendall v London Bank of Australia (1918)......488, 489, 511
Kennedy v Panama, etc, Mail Co [1867]......17, 18
Kent v Parer [1922]......281
Kepitagalla Rubber Estates Ltd v The National Bank of India Ltd [1909]......**497**
King v Greig [1931]......273, 281
Kirk v Blurton (1841)......446
Koch v Dicks (1933)......453
Kolokytuas & Anor v Federation Insurance Ltd (1980)......226
Koon v Brinkerhoff......108
Kwei Tek Chao v British Traders and Shippers Ltd [1954]......113, 116, **120**, 123, 127, 130, 140

Kwik Hoo Tong case (1929)......121

Ladbroke & Co v Todd (1914)......519
Lake v Simmons [1927]......345
Laney v Gates (1935)......441
Langmead v Thyer Rubber Co Ltd [1947]......351
Learoyd Bros & Co v Pope & Sons Ltd [1966]......166
Lee v Butler [1893]......25, 351
Lee v Griffin (1861)......21, 24
Leeds Bank v Walker (1883)......451
Lency & Sons Ltd v Callingham and Thompson (1908)......139
Leonard v Wilson (1834)......445
Leppard, Re (1974)......297
L'Estrange v L'Estrange (1850)......391
Lett v Morris (1831)......395
Levine, Re (1942)......310
Levy v Scottish Employers' Insurance Co (1901)......230
Lewis v Andrews and Rowley Pty Ltd (1956)......373
Lewis v Averay [1972]......335
Lickbarrow v Mason (1794)......179
Lister v Romford Ice and Cold Storage Co Ltd [1957]......260
Liverpool & London and Globe Insurance Co v Hartley & Ford [1927]......393
Lloyds & Scottish Finance Ltd v Williamson [1965]......344
Lloyds Bank Ltd v Bank of America National Trust and Savings Association [1938]......477
Lloyds Bank Ltd v The Chartered Bank of India, Australia and China [1929]......503
Lloyds Bank Ltd v E B Savory & Co [1932]......522
Lombard Australia Ltd v Wells Park Motor Pty Ltd [1960]......**364**
London and South Western Bank v Wentworth (1880)......493
London Bank of Australia Ltd v Kendall (1920)......517, 525
London Joint Stock Bank Ltd v Macmillan [1918]......492, 493
London Joint Stock Bank v Simmons [1892]......425, 446

Long, Re; Ex parte Fraser Confirming Pty Ltd (1975) ... 295
Lucena v Craufurd (1806) ... 244
Lumsden & Co v London Trustee Savings Bank [1971] ... 512
Lunn v Thornton (1845) ... 275, 389
Lupton v White (1808) ... 372

McArdle (dec'd), Re [1951] ... 393
McCormack v J B & L Nominees Pty Ltd (1981) ... 34
Macdonald v Law Union Fire and Life Insurance Co (1874) ... 217
McEntire v Crossley Bros Ltd [1895] ... 25, 280
MacKay, Re (1972) ... 284
MacKay v Commercial Bank of New Brunswick (1874) ... 202
Mackay v London General Insurance Co Ltd (1935) ... 212
McKay Massey Harris Pty Ltd v Icianz Ltd and Others; The Mahia (No 2) [1960] ... **147**, 163
McLean v Clydesdale Banking Co (1883) ... 509
McLeay v Commissioner of Inland Revenue [1963] ... 400, 402
Macpherson Train & Co Ltd v Howard Ross & Co Ltd [1955] ... 54
McRae v Commonwealth Disposals Commission (1951) ... 103
Macaura v Northern Assurance Co Ltd [1925] ... 258
Machu v London and South-Western Railway Co (1848) ... 167
Magnussen v Flanagan [1981] ... 346
Mahia, The (No 2) [1960] ... **147**
Malmberg's case (1924) ... 158, 159
Manbre Saccharine Co v Corn Products Co (1919) ... 160, 161
Manchester Liners Ltd v Rea Ltd (1922) ... 46, 51, 63, 64, 70
Manchester, Sheffield and Lincolnshire Railway Co v North Central Wagon Co (1888) ... 280
Manchester Trust v Furness [1895] ... 231, 336, 357
Mangles v Dixon (1849) ... 406
Mann, Re [1958] ... 292
Maple Flock Co v Universal Furniture Products (Wembley) Ltd [1934] ... 113, 118
Marcus Clark (Victoria) Ltd v Brown (1928) ... 26
Marene Knitting Mills Pty Ltd v Greater Pacific General Insurance Ltd (1976) ... 264
Marfani & Co Ltd v Midland Bank Ltd [1968] ... 504, 511, **520**
"Marlborough Hill" (Ship) v Cowan & Sons (1921) ... 99
Marsden v Meadows (1881) ... 280
Martineau v Kitching (1872) ... 106, 108
Mash & Murrell Ltd v Joseph I Emanuel Ltd [1961] ... 63, 78, 105
Matthes v Carter (1955) ... 29
Maye v Colonial Mutual Life Assurance Society Ltd (1924) ... 237
Mayne Nickless Ltd v Pegler and Another [1974] ... **238**
Mayor, The, Constables & Co of Merchants of the Staple of England v Governor of Bank of England (1887) ... 493
Medway Oil and Storage Co v Silica Gel Corp (1928) ... 46, 48
Melachrino and Another v Nickoll and Knight [1920] ... 140
Melbourne Corp v The Commonwealth (1947) ... 483, 484
Mercantile Bank of India Ltd v Central Bank of India Ltd [1938] ... 477
Mercantile Credits Ltd v F C Upton & Sons Pty Ltd (1974) ... 351
Meres v Ansell ... 44
Mersey Shipping & Transport Co v Rea Ltd (1925) ... 181, 183
Mersey Steel and Iron Co Ltd v Naylor, Benzon & Co (1884) ... 161
Metropolitan Knitting and Hosiery Co Ltd (in liq) v Thomas Burnley & Sons Ltd (1924) ... 29
Meyer v Everth (1814) ... 43, 44

Table of Cases

Case	Page
Microbeads AG v Vinhurst Road Markings Ltd [1975]	39
Midland Bank Ltd v Reckit [1933]	510
Miida Electronics Inc v Mitsui OSK Lines Ltd (1981)	189
Millars' Karri and Jarrah Co (1902) v Weddel, Turner & Co (1908)	118
Miller (R W) & Co Pty Ltd v Australian Oil Refining Pty Ltd (1967)	173
Mills v Stokman (1966)	20
Milroy v Lord (1862)	**388**, 400
Minnesota Mining & Manufacturing (Australia) Pty Ltd v The Ship "Novoaltaisk" [1972]	178
Mirabita v Imperial Ottoman Bank (1878)	98, 107, 149, 151
Mitchell v Jones (1905)	349
Mogg v Baker	272
Moorcock, The (1889)	151
Moraitis v Harvey Trinder (Qld) Pty Ltd [1969]	208
Morelli v Fitch & Gibbons (1928)	47, 48
Morgan v Price (1849)	256
Morgan v Russell & Sons [1909]	20
Morison's case [1914]	503
Morison v London County and Westminster Bank [1914]	488, 514
Morris v C W Martin & Sons Ltd [1966]	164, 166
Mortgage Loan & Finance Co of Australia Ltd v Richards (1932)	344
Moss v Old Colony Trust Co (1923)	469
Motor Credits (Hire Finance) Ltd v Pacific Motor Auctions Pty Ltd (1963)	**338**
Motor Credits Ltd v Wollaston (1929)	415
Mount (D F) Ltd v Jay and Jay (Provisions) Co Ltd [1960]	133
Mulliner v Florence [1878]	277, 363
Mutual Life Assurance Society v Langley (1886)	407
Mutual Life Insurance Co of New York v Ontario Metal Products Co Ltd [1925]	212, 213, 218, 240
National Bank of New Zealand Ltd v Walpole and Patterson Ltd [1975]	498
National Provincial Bank v Harle (1881)	386
Neill v Hewens (1953)	310
Newsholme Brothers v Road Transport and General Insurance Co Ltd [1929]	208, **228**, 236
Newtons of Wembley Ltd v Williams [1965]	352
New York Life Insurance Co v Fletcher (1886)	231
New Zealand Shipping Co Ltd v A M Satterthwaite & Co Ltd [1974]	184–7
Niblett Ltd v Confectioners Materials Co Ltd [1921]	77
Nichols, Ex parte (1883)	386
Nirens v Fowler Asphalt Pty Ltd (1966)	293
Norman v Federal Commissioner of Taxation (1963)	387, 388, **389**, 398, 399, 400, 402, 403, 408
North v Great Northern Railway Co (1860)	139
North and South Insurance Corp v National Provincial Bank Ltd (1936)	99
North and South Trust Co v Berkeley [1971]	207, 208, 264
North and South Wales Bank v Macbeth [1908]	437
Norton and Steele v Davison [1899]	**29**, 33
Norwich Fire Insurance Society Ltd v Brennans (Horsham) Pty Ltd [1981]	264
Norwich Winterthur Insurance (Australia) Ltd v Con-Stan Industries of Australia Pty Ltd [1981]	264
Oatway, Re [1903]	372
Odessa, The [1916]	**276**

Official Assignee of Madras v Mercantile Bank of India Ltd [1935] 477
Ogden's case [1973] 227
Oliver v Davis [1949] 443
Olsson v Dyson (1969) 389
Oppenheimer v Frazer and Wyatt [1907] 345
Orbit Mining & Trading Co Ltd v Westminster Bank Ltd [1963] 511
O'Reilly v Commissioners of the State Bank of Victoria (1983) 501
Orr & Barber v Union Bank of Scotland (1854) 493
Oughtred v Internal Revenue Commissioners [1960] 402
Owens v Harris Bros (1932) 336

Pacific Motor Auctions Pty Ltd v Motor Credits (Hire Finance) Ltd (1965) **348**
Pacific Trading Co Ltd v Wiener (1923) 54
Page v Commonwealth Life Assurance Society Ltd (1936) 286
Pain, Re; Gustavson v Haviland [1919] 402
Palmer v Carey [1926] 310
Palmer v Pratt (1824) 430
Panda OHG v Circle Products Ltd [1970] 150
Parchim, The [1918] **106**, 149
Parr v Rural Agents Pty Ltd [1975] 263
Parsons v Sexton (1847) 42
Parsons, Ex parte (1886) 283
Paterson v Tash (1743) 345
Patrick, Re [1891] 394
Patten v Thomas Motors Pty Ltd [1965] 39
Patullo, Re; Ex parte Official Receiver (1931) 307
Pavia & Co, SPA v Thurmann-Nielsen [1952] **458**, 461, 469
Performing Right Society Ltd v London Theatre of Varieties Ltd [1924] 393
Phillips v Brooks [1919] 346
Photo Production Ltd v Securicor Transport Ltd (1980) 186
Pickering v Busk (1812) 345
Picturesque Atlas Co Ltd, The, v Phillipson [1890] 17, 18
Pinfold, Re (1961) 293
Pinnock Brothers v Lewis & Peat Ltd [1923] 51
Plaimar Ltd v Waters Trading Co Ltd (1945) **153**, 163, 189
Planche v Colburn (1831) 22
Plischke & Sohne v Allison Bros Ltd [1936] 130
Polenghi v Dried Milk Co (1904) 156
Polgardy v Australian Guarantee Corp Ltd (1981) 128
Pollard v Bank of England (1871) 500
Poole v Smith's Car Sales (Balham) Ltd [1962] 90
Portavon Cinema Co Ltd v Price and Century Insurance Co Ltd [1939] 258
Port Jackson Stevedoring Pty Ltd v Salmon & Spraggon (1978) **184**, 196
Port Line Ltd v Ben Line Steamers Ltd [1958] 336
Postmaster-General v W H Jones & Co (London) Ltd [1957] 131, 133
Preist v Last (1903) 46
Price v Parsons (1936) 25, **279**, 327
Price's case (1952) 316
Provident Finance Corp Pty Ltd v Hammond [1978] 406
Pukuweka Sawmills Ltd v Winger [1917] 369
Pulley v Public Trustee [1956] 393
Pyrene Co Ltd v Scindia Navigation Co Ltd [1954] 83, 147, 148

Quan Yick v Hinds (1904) 4
Queensland Bacon Pty Ltd v Rees (1966) 306, 307, 308, 311, 312, 313, 320, 321

Table of Cases

R v Manchester Profiteering Committee; Ex parte Lancashire and Yorkshire
  Railway Co (1920) 46
R V Ward Ltd v Bignall [1967] **133**
Radio Corp Pty Ltd v Bear (1961) 84, 310, 314
Raffoul v Esanda Ltd (1970) 346
Rayner v Hambros Bank (1943) 471
Readhead v Midland Railway Co (1869) 167
Redgrave v Hurd [1881] 17
Rees v Bank of NSW (1964) 305, 307, 309, **314**, 320
Reeves v Barlow (1884) 275
Reeves v Capper (1838) 362
Regina Chevrolet Sales Ltd v Riddell [1942] 374
Reid v Fairbanks (1853) 372
Reid v Macbeth & Gray [1904] 96
Reid v Smith (1905) 369
Rekstin v Severo Sibirsko and Bank of Russian Trade Ltd [1933] ... 387
Rendall v Associated Finance Pty Ltd [1957] **370**
Reynolds v Ashby & Son [1904] 369
Richards (S) & Co Ltd v Lloyd (1933) 319
Richardson v Commercial Banking Co of Sydney Ltd (1952) 306, 307, 308, 316
Riddiford v Warren [1901] 17, 18
Riverstone Meat Co Pty Ltd v Lancashire Shipping Co Ltd [1961] ... 167
Roache v Australian Mercantile Land & Finance Co Ltd (No 2) (1966) ... **345**
Robarts v Tucker [1851] 493
Robbie (N W) & Co Ltd v Witney Warehouse Co Ltd [1963] 324
Robertson v Grigg (1932) 305, 322, 403
Robertson v Hamilton (1811) 247
Robertson (J S) (Aust) Pty Ltd v Martin (1956) **68,** 127
Robinson v Dunmore (1801) 165
Robinson v Graves [1935] 21
Robinson v Macdonnell 272
Rolfe Lubell v Keith [1979] 441
Rose, Re; Midland Bank Executor and Trustee Co Ltd v Rose
  [1949] 388, 390, 392
Rose, Re; Rose v Inland Revenue Commissioners [1952] 388, 390
Rosenhain and Another v Commonwealth Bank of Australia (1922) ... **429**
Rosenthal (J) & Sons Ltd v Esmail [1965] **113**
Ross v London County Westminster and Parr's Bank (1919) 519
Roumeli Food Stores (NSW) Pty Ltd v The New India Assurance Co
  Ltd [1972] 241
Rowe (H) & Co Pty Ltd v Pitts (1973) 441
Rowland v Divall [1923] **38,** 40
Roxburghe v Cox (1881) 405, 406
Royal Insurance Co v Mylius (1926) 244
Rozanes v Bowen (1928) 205, 218
Rozenbes v Kronhill (1956) 292
Ruben (E & S) Ltd v Faire Brothers & Co Ltd [1949] 113, **119,** 122, 123, 124
Russell, Ex parte; Re Butterworth (1882) 316
Ryan v Bank of New South Wales [1978] 528

Salmon & Spraggon (Australia) Pty Ltd v Joint Cargo Services Pty Ltd
  and Port Jackson Stevedoring Pty Ltd [1977] 189
Samuel McCausland Ltd v Railton [1931] 162
Samuels v Davis [1943] 24
Sandell v Porter (1966) 305
Sandeman & Sons v Tyzack & Branfoot Steamship Co Ltd [1913] ... 370, 372
Sanders v Maclean (1883) 151, 160

Satterthwaite's case 184–7
Saunders v Queensland Insurance Co Ltd (1931) 211, 212, 213, 215, 218,
                                                                                      227, 234
Scanlan's New Neon Ltd v Tooheys Ltd (1943) 13, 202
Scarf v Jardine (1882) 348
Scholfield v Earl of Londesborough [1896] 494, 495
Schoolman v Hall (1951) 212, 215
Schroeder v Central Bank of London Ltd (1876) 500
Schroeder (A) Music Publishing Co Ltd v Macaulay [1974] 145
Scott v Avery and Ors (1856) 263
Scottish Loan & Finance Co Ltd v Payne (1935) 449
Scruttons Ltd v Midland Silicones Ltd [1962] 185
Seath v Moore (1886) 95
Sharp v Batt (1930) 105, **107**
Sharp v Ellis; Re Edward Love & Co Pty Ltd [1972] 444
Shepherd v Federal Commissioner of Taxation (1965) 387, **396**, 402, 408
Shepherd v Harrison (1871) 97, 99
Shield's Estate, Re; Bank of Ireland (Governor & Co), Petitioners
    [1901] 485
Shipping Corp of India Ltd v Gamlen Chemical Co (A/Asia) Pty Ltd
    (1981) **174**
Shipton Anderson & Co, Re, v Harris & Co (1915) 103
Shipton Anderson & Co Ltd v Weil Bros Ltd [1912] 112
Shirlaw v Southern Foundries Ltd [1939] 13
Sidney Raper Pty Ltd v Commonwealth Trading Bank of Australia [1975] ... 526
Sinason-Teicher Inter-American Grain Corp v Oilcakes and Oilseeds
    Trading Co Ltd [1954] 460, 461
Singer Manufacturing Co v London & South Western Railway Co
    [1894] 366, 368
Sir James Laing & Sons v Barclay, Curle & Co [1908] 95, 96
Skandia Insurance Co Ltd v Skoljarev (1979) 178
Sky Petroleum Ltd v VIP Petroleum Ltd [1974] 138, **139**
Slingsby v District Bank Ltd [1932] 446, 496, 524
Smith v Commercial Banking Co of Sydney Ltd (1910) 431
Smith v Union Bank of London (1875) 515, 516
Smith, Re (1901) 392
Snelling v Lord Huntingfield (1834) 22
Societe Generale v The Metropolitan Bank (Ltd) (1873) 494
Sorley and Stirling v Surawski [1953] 353
Southern British National Trust Ltd (in liq) v Pither (1937) 405
Southern Cross Assurance Co Ltd v Australian Provincial Assurance
    Association Ltd (1935) 201, 207, 240, 249, 251
Speedway Safety Products Pty Ltd v Hazell & Moore Industries Pty Ltd
    (1982) 82
Spyer v Phillipson [1931] 369
Staffs Motor Guarantee Ltd v British Wagon Co Ltd
    [1934] 342, 343, 349, 350
Standing v Bowring (1885) 387
Stanley Thompson Investments Pty Ltd v Nock & Kirby Finance Co
    Pty Ltd [1969] 369
Startup v Macdonald (1843) 151
State Savings Bank of Victoria Commissioners v Permewan Wright & Co
    Ltd (1915) 485
Steadfast Insurance Co Ltd, The, v F & B Trading Co Pty Ltd (1971) ... 240, 262
Steel Wing Co Ltd, Re [1921] 392, 400, 402
Steels & Busks Ltd v Bleecker Bik & Co Ltd [1956] 53
Stein Forbes & Co v County Tailoring Co (1916) 98

Table of Cases

Stenning v Radio & Domestic Finance Ltd [1961] ... 427, **447**
Sterns Ltd v Vickers Ltd [1923] ... **89**, 90, 93, 105
Stock Motor Ploughs Ltd v Forsyth (1932) ... 425, 426, 427
Stokman v Mills (1966) ... **19**
Stokvis, Re (1934) ... 298
Stone v Reliance Mutual Insurance Society Ltd [1972] ... 264
Stoneleigh Finance Ltd v Phillips [1965] ... 284
Storey v Lane (1981) ... 286
Suisse Atlantique Société D'Armement Maritime SA v NV Rotterdamsche Centrale [1967] ... 169, 179, 186
Suttons Motors Pty Ltd v Hollywood Motors Pty Ltd [1971] ... 346
Swan, Ex parte (1859) ... 493
Swan v The North British Australasian Co (1863) ... 493
Sydney Hydraulic and General Engineering Co v Blackwood & Son (1908) ... 22
Sykes v Stratton [1972] ... 479
Sztejn v J Henry Schroder Banking Corp (1941) ... 473

T C Industrial Plant Pty Ltd v Robert's Queensland Pty Ltd (1963) ... 141
TNT (Melbourne) Pty Ltd v May & Baker (Australia) Pty Ltd (1966) ... 163, 186
Tailby v Official Receiver (1888) ... 273, 275, 389, 390
Talga Ltd v M B C International Ltd (1976) ... 479
Tamvaco v Lucas (1861) ... 157, 161
Tancred v Delagoa Bay and East Africa Railway (1889) ... 386
Tappenden v Artus and Rayleigh Garage Ltd (1964) ... 368
Tatam v Haslar (1889) ... 449
Taylor v Combined Buyers Ltd [1924] ... **85**
Taylor v Deputy Commissioner of Taxation (1969) ... 389
Taylor v Oakes, Roncoroni & Co (1922) ... 161
Taylor v White (1964) ... 311, 314
Tebb v Hodge (1869) ... 310
Teheran-Europe Co Ltd v S T Belton (Tractors) Ltd [1968] ... 63
Thirkell v Cambi [1919] ... 30
Thompson (W L) Ltd v Robinson (Gunmakers) Ltd [1955] ... 137
Thomson v McInnes (1911) ... 30
Thomson v Weems (1884) ... 212, 217, 221, 224, 225
Thorne (L G) & Co Pty Ltd v Thomas Borthwick & Sons (A/Asia) Ltd (1956) ... 43
Thornett and Fehr v Beers & Son [1919] ... 42, 72
Tilley v Official Receiver in Bankruptcy (1960) ... 451, 500
Torkington v Magee [1902] ... 5
Tournier v National Provincial and Union Bank of England [1924] ... 501
Tregelles v Sewell (1862) ... 152
Turner v Mucklow (1862) ... 68
Tweddle v Atkinson (1861) ... 180
Twyne's case (1601) ... 305
Tye v Fynmore (1813) ... 44

Underwood (A L) Ltd v Bank of Liverpool and Martins [1924] ... 503, 505
United City Merchants (Investments) Ltd v Royal Bank of Canada [1982] ... **472**
United Dominions Trust Ltd v Kirkwood [1966] ... 485
United Railways of the Havana and Regla Warehouses Ltd, Re [1960] ... 193
Universal Guarantee Pty Ltd v National Bank of Australasia Ltd (1965) ... 505, 511, 524, 525
Urquhart Lindsay & Co Ltd v Eastern Bank Ltd [1922] ... **466**, 468

Valletort Sanitary Steam Laundry Co Ltd, Re [1903] ... 336
Van Casteel v Booker (1848) ... 98, 99, 107

Varley v Whipp (1900) **42, 47, 51, 54**
Vaudeville Electric Cinema Ltd v Muriset [1923] 369
Vic Mill Ltd, Re [1913] 138
Vigers Brothers v Sanderson Brothers (1901) 124
Vinden v Hughes [1905] **435**
Vital Learning Aids Pty Ltd and the Companies Act, Re [1979] **281**
Voyle v Hughes (1854) 393

Wade v Waldon (1909) 225
Waight v Waight and Walker [1952] 282
Wait v Baker (1848) 97, 107, 159
Wait & James v Midland Bank (1926) 91
Wait, Re [1927] **16**
Walker v Bradford Old Bank Ltd (1884) 395
Wallace v Woodgate (1824) 131
Wallis v Russell (1902) 46
Walsh, Spriggs, Nolan and Finney v Hoag & Bos Pty Ltd [1977] **442**
Walter v James (1871) 443
Walton & Sullivan Ltd v J Murphy & Sons Ltd [1955] 402
Wardar's (Import & Export) Co Ltd v W Norwood & Sons Ltd [1968] 90, **92**
Warman v Southern Counties Car Finance Corp Ltd [1949] 38
Warrington v Early (1853) 429
Washington Diamond Mining Co, Re [1893] 317
Waters v Monarch Fire & Life Assurance Co (1856) 245, 246, 248
Waters Trading Co case (1951) 182, 183
Watson Re; Ex parte Official Receiver in Bankruptcy (1890) 280
Watt v Westhoven [1933] **17**, 18
Webb v Cassidy (1907) 167
Webb v Stenton (1883) 384
Weiner v Gill [1906] 90
Weiner v Harris [1910] 90
Weiss, Re; Ex parte White v John Vicars & Co Ltd [1970] **306**, 314
West v Williams [1899] 361
Western Australian Bank v Royal Insurance Co (1908) 244
Western Australian Insurance Co Ltd v Dayton (1924) 211, 213, 237
Westminster Bank Ltd v Hilton (1926) 500
Westminster Bank Ltd v Zang [1966] 511
Wetherill, Re (1907) 281
Wheelton v Hardisty (1858) 217
Whiteley Ltd v Hilt [1918] 372
Wiggins Teape Australia Pty Ltd v Baltica Insurance Co Ltd [1970] 228
William Brandt's Sons & Co v Dunlop Rubber Co [1905] 392
Williams v Atlantic Assurance Co [1933] 392, 402
Williams v Commissioner of Inland Revenue [1965] 400
Williams v Commissioner for Main Roads (1940) 181
Williams v Lloyd (1934) 304
Williamson (J C) Ltd v Lukey and Mulholland (1931) 10
Wilson v Avec Audio-Visual Equipment Ltd [1974] 264
Wilson v Darling Island Stevedoring Ltd (1956) 178, **179**
Wilson v Kelland [1910] 357
Wilson v New Zealand Express Co Ltd (No 3) [1924] 166
Wilson, Holgate & Co v Belgian Grain and Produce Co (1920) 158
Wilton v Commonwealth Trading Bank of Australia [1973] 512
Wimble Sons & Co Ltd v Rosenberg & Sons [1913] 148
Winkfield, The [1902] 248
Wong v Hutchison (1951) 140
Wood v Bell 95

Table of Cases

Woodgate v Godfrey (1879)......280
Woods v Russell......95
Woollatt v Stanley (1928)......451
Wragge v Sims Cooper & Co (Australia) Pty Ltd (1933)......442, 443
Wren v Holt (1903)......47
Wren v Mahoney (1972)......292
Wrightson v McArthur and Hutchisons (1919) Ltd [1921]......282

Xantho, The (1887)......178

Y Z Finance Co Pty Ltd v Cummings (1964)......426
Yango Pastoral Co Pty Ltd v First Chicago Australia Ltd (1978)......528
Yearworth v Pierce (1647)......20
Yeovil Glove Co Ltd, Re [1965]......323
York Products Pty Ltd v Gilchrist Watt & Sanderson Pty Ltd [1968]......166
Yorkshire Insurance Co v Campbell [1917]......226
Yorkshire Insurance Co Ltd v Nisbet Shipping Co Ltd [1962]......256
Yorkshire Woolcombers' Association Ltd, Re [1903]......276, 324
Young v Grote (1827)......493, 494, 495
Young & Marten Ltd v McManus Childs Ltd [1969]......23

Ziel Nominees Pty Ltd and Anor v VACC Insurance Co Ltd and Anor (1976)......258

Comparative Table of Sale of Goods Acts

NSW	Vic	Qld	SA	WA	Tas	ACT	NZ
3	2	60	58	58	—	4	1(2),(3)
4	4, 5	61	59	59	5	62	60
5	3	3	—	60	3	5	2
6	6	4	1	1	6	6	3
7	7	5	2	2	7	7	4
8	8	6	3	3	8	8	5
9	9	—	4	4	9	—	—
10	10	8	5	5	10	10	7
11	11	9	6	6	11	11	8
12	11	10	7	7	12	12	9
13	12	11	8	8	13	13	10
14	13	12	9	9	14	14	11
15	14	13	10	10	15	15	12
16	15	14	11	11	16	16	13
17	16	15	12	12	17	17	14
18	17	16	13	13	18	18	15
19	18	17	14	14	19	19	16
20	19	18	15	15	20	20	17
21	21	19	16	16	21	21	18
22	22	20	17	17	22	22	19
23	23	21	18	18	23	23	20
24	24	22	19	19	24	24	21
25	25	23	20	20	25	25	22
26	26, 27	24	21	21	26	26	23
—	28	—	22	22	27	—	24
27	29	25	23	23	28	27	25
—	83	26	24	24	29	28	26
28	30, 31	27	25	25	30	29	27
29	82	28	26	26	31	30	28
30	34	29	27	27	32	31	29
31	35	30	28	28	33	32	30
32	36	31	29	29	34	33	31
33	37	32	30	30	35	34	32
34	38	33	31	31	36	35	33
35	39	34	32	32	37	36	34
36	40	35	33	33	38	37	35
37	41	36	34	34	39	38	36
38	42	37	35	35	40	39	37
39	43	38	36	36	41	40	38
40	44	39	37	37	42	41	39
41	45	40	38	38	43	42	40
42	46	41	39	39	44	43	41
43	47	42	40	40	45	44	42
44	48	43	41	41	46	45	43
45	49	44	42	42	47	46	44
46	50	45	43	43	48	47	45
47	51	46	44	44	49	48	46
48	52	47	45	45	50	49	47
49	53	48	46	46	51	50	48
50	54	49	47	47	52	51	49
51	55	50	48	48	53	52	50
52	56	51	49	49	54	53	51
53	57	52	50	50	55	54	52
—	58	53	51	51	56	55	53
54	59	54	52	52	57	56	54
55	60	55	53	53	58	57	55
56	—	—	—	—	—	—	—
57	61	56	54	54	59	58	56
58	62	57	55	55	60	5(2)(b)	57
59	63	58	56	56	61	59	58
60	64	59	57	57	62	60	59

Introduction

Purpose. The purpose of these materials is to provide Australian teachers and students of Commercial Law with an interesting presentation of the law and practice of the most common and important business transactions. In doing so we will trace the movement of goods from manufacturer to the ultimate consumer; this distribution system accounts for a huge proportion of today's international and domestic trade. A number of transactions are encountered along this route and will be integrated in order to present a full picture. These include the transactions of sale, insurance, carriage, security and payment. Special treatment is also given to methods of enforcement and the developing principles of consumer protection.

Method of treatment. The materials are designed for teaching, not as a text for professional lawyers. Materials have been chosen for the maximum educative and stimulative value for students rather than to cover every legal rule. The emphasis is upon typical transactions as they recur in the real business world rather than upon abstruse legal doctrine.

Students will only be able fully to understand the principles of commercial law and apply them to problems if they have a knowledge of the nature of the transactions involved. Unfortunately, at the time when they are studying commercial law, most students have little first-hand knowledge of the business world. Therefore each major topic has been prefaced with some material explaining the underlying policy or business purpose of a particular relationship, transaction, practice or legal principle.

Although much of commercial law is statutory, results very often depend on the facts of the case and particularly the contents of written documents. In order to bring alive the statute and case law for students, there are included a number of typical commercial documents, with which again most would have little, if any, prior acquaintance.

In order to make the material more realistic and to integrate the series of transactions, there is presented in Chapter 1 a basic prototype transaction which thereafter will be constantly referred to and developed for purposes of illustration. This prototype and its variations and additions as well as its dramatis personae are intended to stimulate and hold student interest. It will also be used as the basis for a number of the problems which are included throughout the book. These problems are essential teaching tools because legal rules are meaningless to students unless they can apply them to fact situations. A conscious effort has also been made to stimulate interest by raising policy issues and questioning whether the present law is functional and responsive to commercial needs.

CHAPTER 1

The Nature and Sources of Commercial Law

"In the good old days, commercial law was made not by the courts but by the merchants... The primary task of commercial law is to maintain a fair balance between competing interests. No principle can be pressed beyond a certain point without disturbing that balance. It is not possible to guarantee justice in the individual case; the best that the law can hope to achieve is a set of solutions to typical problems which will commend themselves to the business community as producing a fair result in the generality of cases."

Professor R M Goode
(1982) 13 *Camb LR* 14, 22

Section 1: The Origins of Modern Commercial Law
Section 2: The Subject Matter of Commercial Law
Section 3: Policy Considerations and Law Reform
Section 4: Commercial Law Practice
Section 5: A Prototype Transaction

SECTION 1: THE ORIGINS OF MODERN COMMERCIAL LAW

ENGLISH ANCESTRY

The ancestry of Australian commercial law dates back to the English law merchant. During the Middle Ages, England was an important trading nation but neither the King's Courts nor parliament concerned themselves greatly with facilitating or regulating commerce and the common law was ill-adapted to mercantile needs. Prior to the seventeenth century, the enforcement of commercial transactions was left largely to the courts of boroughs, local fairs and markets, and Staple Courts for transactions with foreign merchants. Maritime disputes were settled by the courts of seaport towns.

The nature of the rules applied by these courts is illustrated in the following passage from *Goodwin v Robarts* (1875) 10 Ex 337 at 346:

> The law merchant is sometimes spoken of as a fixed body of law, forming part of the common law, and, as it were, coeval with it. But as a matter of legal history, this view is altogether incorrect. The law merchant thus spoken of with reference to bills of exchange and other negotiable securities, though forming part of the general body of the *lex mercatoria*, is of comparatively modern origin. It is neither more nor less than the usages of merchants and traders in the different departments of trade, ratified by the decisions of courts of law, which, upon such usages being proved before them, have adopted them as settled law with a view to the interests of trade and the public convenience, the court proceeding herein on the well-known principle of law that, with reference to transactions in the different departments of trade, courts of law, in giving effect to the contracts and dealings of the parties, will assume that the latter have dealt with one another on the footing of any custom or usage prevailing generally in the particular department. By this process, what before was usage only

unsanctioned by legal decision, has become engrafted upon, or incorporated into, the common law, and may thus be said to form part of it.

The trend towards recognition of mercantile usages which began with Chief Justices Coke and Holt reached its full flowering under Lord Mansfield so that by 1750, the law merchant had been incorporated into the common law. Although initially mercantile customs had to be proved in court in suits between merchants, towards the end of the seventeenth century the common law courts treated these customs as part of the common law and applied them in cases involving non-merchants. Since the law merchant tended to reflect the customs of merchants in international trade, it offered a generally uniform basis for settling disputes and minimised conflict of laws problems.

Conflict continued into the nineteenth century over which of the King's Courts, Admiralty or Common Law, should exercise various aspects of maritime jurisdiction. That conflict was finally resolved when the Judicature Act 1873 incorporated the Admiralty Court in the High Court of Justice. However, commercial suits are still referred to particular jurisdictions of the state Supreme Courts in Australia, although under the Judicature system broad jurisdiction is conferred on all divisions of these courts.

RECEPTION IN AUSTRALIA

The common law principle of reception is stated by Blackstone in his *Commentaries* (Introduction, Section 4):

> It hath been held that if an uninhabited country be discovered and planted by English subjects all the English laws then in being, which are the birthright of every English subject, are immediately in force. But this must be understood with very many and very great restrictions. Such colonists carry with them only so much of the English law as is applicable to their new situation and the condition of an infant colony...

Despite some uncertainty as to the application of this rule to the conditions of the original convict colony, the English statute 9 Geo IV, c 83 stipulated that all laws and statutes in force in England on 25 July 1828, should be applied "so far as the same could be applied within those [Australian] colonies": see *Quan Yick v Hinds* (1904) 2 CLR 345. Accordingly, the colonies received the English mercantile law of that date. Later variations between English and Australian law in this field have generally resulted from statute rather than from differences of custom or judicial decision.

SECTION 2: THE SUBJECT MATTER OF COMMERCIAL LAW

HOW WOULD YOU DEFINE COMMERCIAL LAW?

Your answer to this question will probably depend upon your viewpoint: there is no hard and fast definition. It certainly includes mercantile law or the rules governing transactions between merchants. Many of these rules were devised specifically for mercantile transactions before the advent of a consumer class. Nevertheless, these same rules have been applied by the common law courts in transactions where one or both parties were not merchants.

While Maine's statement that "the movement of progressive societies has hitherto seen a movement from status to contract" has been recognised as basically true in relation to private dealings in property, Holdsworth points out that "the growth in progressive societies of the complexity of social, commercial, and industrial relations has led to the growth of new varieties of status": *A History of English Law,* 5th ed, Vol II, p 455. The corporation is a new juristic person and the status of a company director carries with it new duties; there is a growing awareness that different rules should apply to transactions between a merchant and consumer than to those between two merchants. Can you think of other examples where commercial law recognises special status?

REAL AND PERSONAL PROPERTY

Another means of delimiting commercial law is by reference to the subject matter of the transaction. Transactions concerning land are usually dealt with in courses in real property or conveyancing, while commercial law is usually regarded as dealing with personal property which is a broad term describing all interests of money value other than those protected by the law of real property. There is a woolly area in between which is classified as fixtures, and is generally dealt with in courses on real property. In what situations will it be important to determine whether a particular piece of property is real or personal property?

CHOSES IN POSSESSION AND CHOSES IN ACTION

Within the genus of personal property, there exist a number of species. The most common examples of personal property are goods, which because of their inherent tangible usefulness are the main subject of commercial transactions. They are sometimes described as chattels or *choses in possession.*

However, there are also valuable "properties" forming the subject matter of commercial transactions which are intangible, and often incapable of being possessed in a physical sense. These are called *choses in action.* Important examples include company shares, debentures and other securities; book debts and other account receivables; bills of exchange, cheques and promissory notes; copyrights, patents, trademarks and industrial designs; technical know-how, insurance policies and interests under deceased estates and trusts. Each has an important role in the business world, requiring the protection of the law. They are distinguished from choses in possession (chattels) in that they can only "be claimed or enforced by [court] action and not by taking physical possession": *Torkington v Magee* [1902] 2 KB 427 at 430. Ownership of choses in action is often evidenced by documents since possession of an intangible right is impossible. Although you own this book the copyright in the manuscript is a separate chose in action.

Why does the law draw distinctions between real and personal property, choses in possession and in action, and different types of choses in action? Just as we suggested that the status of the person entering a contract should be reflected in the legal rules governing the transaction, so the type or characteristics of the property involved sometimes demand differential treatment.

RELATED AREAS

This discussion is intended to impress upon you the importance of commercial transactions in today's world. The volume of trade and investment in goods, and technical know-how at the national and international level is staggering. Without minimising the importance of land development and the law of real property, including its place in the solicitor's practice, the broad trend in investment and legal development is towards commerce and commercial law as described above.

The main transactions with which we are concerned are: sale, hire, carriage, insurance, security and payment. However, there are no watertight compartments insulating commercial law. Revenue legislation, particularly income tax and sales tax, and stamp duty have a pervasive impact upon most commercial transactions and the businessman and lawyer ignore them at their peril.

The federal structure of legislative powers in Australia also affects commercial law. Although specific powers are conferred upon the Commonwealth with an undefined residuum left to the states, the current trend is towards greater exercise of federal power. A few of the Commonwealth's powers are exclusive; eg, posts and telegraphs, customs and export duties and export bounties: Constitution ss 52, 69, 90. However, most Commonwealth legislative powers may be exercised concurrently by the states, but "when a law of a State is inconsistent with a law of the Commonwealth, the latter shall prevail, and the former shall, to the extent of the inconsistency, be invalid": Constitution s 109. The most important Commonwealth powers in the commercial area are interstate trade and commerce, taxation, customs, banking, insurance, weights and measures, bills of exchange, bankruptcy, copyrights, patents and trademarks, corporations, territories: see s 51. This leaves quite a large area of intrastate commerce within the exclusive power of the states, although the impact of Commonwealth legislation may still prevail in some situations. For example, state legislation regulating priorities between competing securities must give place to any inconsistent provision in the Commonwealth Bankruptcy Act. Can you think of any other examples of constitutional conflict in the commercial law area?

SECTION 3: POLICY CONSIDERATIONS AND LAW REFORM

A teacher of commercial law is only doing half his job if his students acquire merely a knowledge of the law as it is. The future of the legal system is at least partly dependent on informed criticism of the law and adequate reform. Against what criteria should commercial law be judged? What are its goals and purposes? Answers will vary according to political and economic viewpoints and must also take account of varying economic and commercial conditions.

In Australia, the following factors seem relevant: our economy is based upon free enterprise but competition is curtailed in some areas by oligopolies; we have an abundance of natural resources but limited capital and labour with which to exploit them; there are huge unpopulated distances between our major industrial centres, and we are divided by great oceans from our nearest export markets. We have adopted a federal system of government and the English judicial system. What other factors do you think are relevant?

In the light of these and other relevant factors, consider the following possible criteria for measuring our commercial law.

(1) Absence of artificial restrictions upon the free flow of goods and services.

(2) Classification of transactions along functional lines to take account of the type of property and the circumstances of the parties to it.

(3) Relatively simple procedures for making credit available, and providing adequate security for repayment.

(4) An equitable balance between the freedom to make any contract and the need to provide adequate protection for parties in the weaker position. Can you give examples?

(5) Adequate sanctions to enforce compliance with commercial standards. What kind of sanctions would you envisage?

(6) Clear formulations of the legal rules to promote certainty in commercial transactions.

(7) Uniformity in order to simplify interstate commerce. How best can this be achieved?

Can you think of additional criteria? As we proceed, measure the law as you find it against your criteria.

Commercial law is undergoing a period of considerable growth and change. Consumerism is making a strong challenge to the use by business interests of standard form contracts and the maxims of *caveat emptor* and *nemo dat quod non habet*. Environmental protection is the political catchcry of the eighties and this emergent area of legal activity is finding new sanctions to curb industrialists. The goal of uniform state legislation in commercial law has received some recent impetus in Australia although the federal structure with its seven separate legislatures continues as a barrier to uniformity.

Because the commercial environment, business methods and technology are undergoing constant and rapid change, there is a pressing need for continuing review of the laws regulating business enterprises and transactions. Unless the law is kept up-to-date and responsive to business needs, the free flow of commerce will be restricted. How are these needs to be ascertained, and reforms implemented? There has been too little empirical enquiry and insufficient exchange of information between business interests, lawyers and law reform bodies. Law reform is a full-time job and Australia needs more permanent law reform commissions, with the staff and facilities to conduct the necessary surveys, and prepare thorough comprehensive reports and draft legislation.

SECTION 4: COMMERCIAL LAW PRACTICE

There is no fully adequate substitute for experience, whether in commerce or in legal practice. Unfortunately, students, and many lawyers, lack a realistic understanding of the commercial world. We can only suggest some few examples of the pitfalls likely to beset the commercial lawyer and the characteristics and skills to which he should aspire.

Even experienced businessmen often have a corresponding difficulty in recognising the symptoms of a legal problem in their business. While it is not suggested that businessmen should become their own bush lawyers, an acquaintance with the materials in this book should assist tomorrow's business executives to the early recognition of legal issues and of the need for professional advice.

The lawyer who has a knowledge of commercial methods generally, and who is willing to devote time to enquire into the particular market conditions confronting his individual clients will be better prepared to advise them as well as winning their confidence. Two examples will suffice. At the general level, how many lawyers can really understand a balance sheet? A more specific example is the realisation of the possible impact of currency revaluations upon long-term export contracts which will assist the lawyer to advise upon the drafting of provisions facilitating renegotiation of prices.

Pure legal knowledge will never alone make a good lawyer. Legal rules regulate the consequences of fact situations. An ability to sift the relevant facts from a complicated series of events and to analyse their significance is also essential. In some areas, such as trade practices and industrial arbitration, the lawyer must also be able to direct the marshalling of economic and other empirical data.

In the commercial and revenue fields, the traditional lawyers' role of advising *after the event* and in litigious contexts is giving way to what one writer has called "prophylactic planning". This refers to the creation and structuring of legal relationships so as to obtain maximum protection and minimise taxation imposts of various kinds. Lawyers who advise on such structures or negotiate and draft important commercial contracts are in a sense creating the fabric of the law.

The modern commercial lawyer also faces the increasing problem of keeping up-to-date. On the one hand, he must be aware of the detail of recent amendments in statutes and regulations and case law developments. On the other, the growing complexity of commercial dealings is throwing up broader issues involving the possibility of constitutional challenges and the application of conflict of law rules. There is a real danger that these possibilities will be overlooked in the day-to-day attention to detail.

Commercial law problems do not present themselves in neat packages marked simply contracts, trade practices or income tax. Aspects of all three and other areas may be involved in the one transaction. The good commercial lawyer must have the necessary breadth to pull together these strands, both common law and statutory, substantive and procedural, and assess their effect on complex fact situations.

Further characteristics of the good commercial lawyer are:
 (a) he foresees problems and assists his clients to avoid or overcome them at an early stage;
 (b) he keeps his clients informed of progress with their dealings or cases;
 (c) he maintains a balance between legal niceties and commercial needs;
 (d) he keeps an open mind as to alternative methods of settling disputes.

Two illustrations of the last two points are worth noting. It is often not worth litigating a valid claim if the cost will outweigh the likely proceeds of the action: a speedy negotiated settlement may be better. A full-scale court case may also be undesirable if it could result in adverse publicity; therefore an arbitration clause inserted in the original contract may be a wise precaution. Again, rather than embark on lengthy litigation of a claim for damages, resort may be had to the speedy remedies of injunction or a declaratory order so that the contract can proceed to the mutual benefit of both parties.

The modern tendency in law schools is to raise questions of professional responsibility at appropriate points in substantive courses rather than only in a separate subject of Legal Ethics. Examples of such questions facing the commercial lawyer include: Should he act for both parties to a transaction? Should he disclose his interest in a company which is a party to a transaction with a client? Should he plead a technical defence based upon a sly but lawful practice? Should he make the first approach to an existing client to appraise him of a change in the law necessitating lucrative legal work for himself? Opportunities to discuss some of these questions will be provided by specific examples later in this book.

SECTION 5: A PROTOTYPE TRANSACTION

As mentioned above, a major problem with students (and lawyers alike) is to communicate the commercial significance of the legal rules he is using and to appreciate the way in which a particular transaction fits into the total commercial framework. Although a single transaction, for example, a retail sale, is often considered in isolation, it is beneficial to keep in mind a picture of the general flow of goods from manufacturer through distribution outlets to the ultimate consumer. Therefore, the following prototype has been developed as a basis for constant reference and discussion at appropriate points throughout the book.

Jim Handy developed a new carburettor capable of revolutionising the motor industry. Because of its potential for profit Jim decided to undertake its manufacture and distribution himself. Thus, Jim became the instigator of a broad network of commercial transactions. Jim decided to incorporate as a company—Carb Pty Ltd.

Subsequently, Carb appointed Midco of Tokyo as its sole agent, and entered into export contracts for its carburettors to overseas car manufacturers such as Mitzi Co of Tokyo. Carb entered into two further contracts, for the transportation of the goods with an international carrier Trans Shipping Co, and for insurance in transit with Coverall Insurance Ltd. Carb also sought to integrate the financing of its imports and purchases of raw materials with the moneys receivable from Mitzi for its export sales. This could be arranged by means of a documentary letter of credit through Carb's banker, City Bank.

Carb also sold carburettors to Australian manufacturers such as Greatparts Ltd and individual consumers such as Driver. Assuming carburettors supplied by Carb proved defective, the remedies available to Mitzi, Greatparts and Driver require analysis. Assuming that a finance company such as Easy Finance, finances Driver's purchase of a defective carburettor, can Driver seek recovery from Easy Finance as well as from Carb? Conversely, if Carb's customers fail to pay, what are Carb's rights under the contract of sale, or under a bill of exchange or cheque given by a buyer in payment?

As Carb expanded its operations it required further loan financing and therefore established a continuing line of credit through City Bank on the security of a floating charge over Carb's present and future assets. Subsequently Carb sought additional finance through Easy Finance on the security of a further charge and also from Factors Ltd by means of an assignment of the book debts owing to it. Carb also acquired some of its raw materials from various suppliers such as Comp Co on credit terms. Assuming Carb defaulted under these various transactions, the respective rights of its secured and unsecured creditors will require resolution.

These and other questions will be raised in numerous examples and problems throughout this book. Most of them relate to the above prototype, so keep the basic framework in mind.

QUESTIONS

Question 1

(1) Why did English merchants avoid litigating their claims in the medieval common law courts?

(2) To what extent are the law merchant and commercial customs part of the Australian law?

Question 2

(1) Should the same rules govern contracts between
(a) two businessmen?
(b) a company and an individual?
(c) two private individuals?

(2) Consider the distinguishing characteristics of the following types of property and what differences should be made in the legal rules governing their disposition in order to accommodate those characteristics?
(a) land
(b) goods being imported into Australia
(c) new goods
(d) second-hand goods
(e) farm produce
(f) motor vehicles
(g) company shares
(h) book debts
(i) cheques
(j) copyrights and patents
(k) insurance policies.

Question 3

(1) Can you think of examples of potential conflict between federal and state legislative powers in the commercial law area?

(2) What are the advantages and disadvantages of codifying commercial law?

CHAPTER 2

Sale of Goods: Scope, Definition and Formal Requirements

"No amount of human ingenuity will ever make a code that will not require exposition."

Earl of Halsbury LC
Introduction to *Halsbury's Laws of England*, 1st ed

"The Statute of Frauds must not ... be used as an instrument of fraud."

Mr Justice Evatt
J C Williamson Ltd v Lukey and Mulholland (1931) 45 CLR 282 at 308

Section 1: The Contract of Sale in its Commercial Context
Section 2: The Purpose and Scope of the Sale of Goods Act
Section 3: What is a Contract for Sale of Goods?
Section 4: Formal Requirements: Is the Statute of Frauds Necessary?

In the first edition of this casebook, three chapters were devoted to principles of contract law which are relevant to contracts in general, but which were illustrated in the main by reference to contracts relating to goods. These chapters have been deleted from the current edition solely for reasons of space and cost. Students who have already studied a course on contract law should be able to recall and apply the doctrines they have covered where appropriate. For present purposes, it is therefore necessary to point out the topics which have been purposely omitted from this edition, namely:

(1) The requirements of offer and acceptance, consideration and intention to create a binding relationship which are basic requirements for any valid contract.

(2) The means of identifying the express terms of the contract which involve the distinction between
    (a) contractual promises or terms, which form part of the contract; and
    (b) mere representations about the goods sold or other aspects of the contract which are not intended to form part of the contract, but which may give rise to legal liability if made fraudulently or negligently.

(3) The "parol (oral) evidence rule" which precludes the admission of evidence to vary or contradict the terms of a written contract, and the judicial device of recognising a collateral warranty or contract to circumvent that rule.

(4) The distinction between
    (a) express terms resulting from the parties' written or oral statements;
    (b) terms implied by trade custom or usage, a previous course of dealing between the parties, or in exceptional cases by the court to give the contract business efficacy; and
    (c) terms implied in an increasing number of contracts by statute particularly in

the consumer area. It is this third category of implied terms with which we are primarily concerned in Chapter 3.

(5) The further distinction drawn by the courts and the legislature between conditions and warranties and the important consequences which flow from that distinction.

(6) The phenomenon of standard form contracts with their characteristic exclusion clauses, and the judicial and legislative devices employed to counter them such as strict rules of construction, the so-called but now discredited doctrine of fundamental breach, the doctrine of unconscionability and the Contracts Review legislation.

Chapters 2 to 5 are concerned with the most common commercial transaction—the sale of goods. There are two facets of the commercial contract of sale that mark it out for special consideration.

First, it is the central transaction in world and domestic trade being the essential lifeblood of the entire distribution chain for primary produce and manufactured goods. Accordingly, in Chapters 2 to 4 attention is focused on commercial sales between merchants, with appropriate emphasis given to the special features of consumer sales and legislation affecting them where appropriate. Transactions involving international elements are considered in Chapter 5.

Second, the law relating to sale of goods was one of the first (shortly after negotiable instruments) to be codified in England, and that "code" has been the basis for similar legislation throughout the common law world. Accordingly, in this and the following two chapters, emphasis is placed upon the statutory provisions and their interpretation.

SECTION 1: THE CONTRACT OF SALE IN ITS COMMERCIAL CONTEXT

The second of the policy considerations suggested in Chapter 1 was that transactions should be classified along functional lines to take account of the type of property and circumstances of the parties to it. In Question 2 at the end of that chapter you considered some factors which distinguish commercial transactions from other dealings.

Professor Karl Llewellyn was the major architect of the modern American law of sales, comprised in art 2 of the Uniform Commercial Code. He was also regarded as a legal realist.

Karl N Llewellyn: Through Title to Contract and a Bit Beyond
(1938) 15 *NYULQR* 159 at 163–5

One caveat is vital. In an effort to get and stay close enough to typical facts to make discussion meaningful, I shall confine this paper to *mercantile* phases of Sales. The situations and results described and the judgments expressed lie primarily in the realm of the dealer-seller, and again primarily in the realm of dealer-to-dealer or of factorage transaction. They have no application to a farmer's horse trade, and almost none to the purchase by Mrs Sweeney of a fountain pen or of a new oil burner. They do not touch the questions raised when a boardinghouse keeper turns her furniture over to her landlord for back rent just before the sheriff arrives with an attachment for the coal bill. All these and many other nonmercantile or hardly even semimercantile situations raise problems to which the "general" law of Sales *purports* to have been more or less adequately applied. I suspect that a closer examination of those "Sales" problems in which farmers, consumers, corner retailers other than chain stores, and the like other-than-major-mercantile types dominate the picture would turn up a series of interesting discrepancies, in patterns of outcome as well as in need, between some or all of such situations and the more purely mercantile ones. For the traditional lump-concept "Seller", in terms of which the Uniform Sales Act is cast, has lost working value not only in the measure in which sellers, and selling units, and business units which have sales units as adjuncts, have come to vary in complexity and power; but has lost value also as growing economic differentiation has channeled the activities and interests of significantly different types of seller (or buyer) into different lines. For example, the utter dominance of contract for sale over present sale is today not only largely limited to the mercantile phases of Sales law, but it is unequally developed in various of those mercantile phases. In consequence, and in test of the thesis that the concepts basic to the "general law of Sales" are in many aspects not only too general but in their lines of generality poorly adjusted to the facts, I concentrate upon a single portion of the material, itself manifold enough: the mercantile...

What, then, are the problems with which it is the business of the mercantile law of Sales to cope? They turn chiefly about occasional hitches in the process known to economists as distribution (which includes assembling), to business-school men as marketing (which includes purchasing), to lawyers as formation and performance of contract (which includes sale; which includes also single deals, long-run deals, and legally queer running arrangements of various complexion). A group of men have had a lawyer arrange a number of semimagical rituals of corporation-creating, by virtue of which a whole group can thenceforth be known as "*the* seller"; they have engaged some capital in a business enterprise. They make a series of bargains with other groups, somewhat similarly organised. The bargains include descriptions, general or in finespun precision, of goods to be delivered, often enough leaving much to be filled in later: "Specifications to follow". There are commonly indications of price, time, manner of delivery, manner of packaging, and the like. In most lines the delivery is agreed to be on credit; in some (notably agricultural produce and automobiles sold to dealers) the seller insists on cash.

Let us take the case of one peculiarly significant type of hitch: *"The buyer" goes back on "his" bargain*. The question is whether "the seller" can recover the price, or only damages. The issue is real, narrow, and, under our law, important. But it is also, as we pose it technically, silly. To a silly issue no sane answer is possible. This one we currently pose thus: Has Title passed? and solve by locating a mythical—or should I say more accurately "mystical"?—essence known as Title, which is hung over the buyer's head or the seller's like a halo. Halos are, it appears, indivisible. And there is only one halo for buyer and seller to make out with. This does not, as our orthodox doctrine goes, require explanation. It simply is so.

THE STAGES OF A COMMERCIAL SALE

Obeying Llewellyn's injunctions to concentrate on commercial sales and realistically to examine the transaction in context, the following prototype has been designed to focus attention on the stages of most importance and potential conflict between buyer and seller. A businessman or lawyer who can see the whole picture is more likely to be able to identify the correct place for an individual piece of the jigsaw puzzle. As we unfold the picture, the relevant sections of the Sale of Goods Act (SGA) will be plotted in their appropriate positions. Citation is to the New South Wales Act, and corresponding sections in other states can be ascertained from the table on p xxvi.

Stage 1: formation. Through the contact made by Midco, Carb Pty Ltd negotiated a sale of 20,000 carburettors to the Japanese car manufacturer Mitzi Co. Several questions arise immediately.

Q—How does Carb ensure that it obtains a binding and enforceable contract?

A—(1) It is commercially prudent to check Mitzi's commercial and credit standing since an enforceable contract with a straw man may be worse than useless.

(2) It is a prudent legal precaution to check that Mitzi is properly incorporated, and that if the goods are for export, any necessary import and export licences and exchange control approval can be obtained.

(3) If the agreement happens to be made in Japan or requires performance in Japan, it is necessary to determine whether the formation of the contract and its performance is to be governed by the law of an Australian state or of Japan. We shall assume for present purposes that New South Wales law applies.

(4) The requirements for a *binding* contract, namely, certainty, intention to enter

legal relations, offer and acceptance and consideration must be satisfied. These are common law requirements and are not specified in the Act.

(5) However, assuming the contract comes within the definitions of "contract for sale" of "goods" in ss 5 and 6 it will attract the provisions of the SGA.

Accordingly, in states retaining the Statute of Frauds provisions such as New South Wales, a contract, though binding may not be *enforceable* unless the formalities of the Act are satisfied: s 9.

Stage 2: terms of the contract. Carb and Mitzi will agree upon a number of specific terms of the contract. This is largely a matter of commercial negotiation on items such as specifications, price and delivery dates. It is important that these be set out in unambiguous language and any doubts resolved before the contract is made: differences as to the intended meaning of specific terms are one of the commonest sources of dispute when a contract turns sour.

Q—How are the terms of the contract interpreted? How are gaps in the contract filled?

A—(1) If the language of the contract is clear and unambiguous, it will be given its ordinary meaning. Where special trade terms are used they will attract the special meaning according to the usage of the trade provided the usage is well known, certain and reasonable. This common law principle is preserved by SGA ss 19(3) and 57. Similarly, the terms used may be interpreted in the light of a previous course of dealing between the parties: see s 57.

(2) The terms of the contract will fall into the categories of conditions or warranties: s 16. The distinction is the basis for important consequences in the event of breach (see below).

(3) Gaps will not normally be filled in the contract except in very limited circumstances: see eg *The Moorcock* (1889) 14 PD 64; *Shirlaw v Southern Foundries Ltd* [1939] 2 KB 206; *Scanlan's New Neon Ltd v Tooheys Ltd* (1943) 67 CLR 169.

(4) A number of conditions as to title, quality and fitness will be implied by law into the contract: ss 17-20. However, these may be excluded (s 57) provided an appropriate form of exclusion is used and it does not attempt to destroy the very basis of the contract: see doctrine of fundamental breach on p 179, *infra*. Similar conditions implied by the Sale of Goods Act 1923 (NSW) Pt VIII, Trade Practices Act 1974 Pt V, Goods (Sales and Leases) Act 1981 (Vic) and the uniform Hire-Purchase Acts Pt III in respect of consumer transactions cannot be excluded except within closely defined circumstances.

Stage 3: events prior to delivery of goods. Now that Carb and Mitzi have made a binding and enforceable contract including appropriate terms and conditions, the onus falls initially upon Carb to produce the carburettors. However, a number of "accidents" can occur along the way.

Q—What happens if Carb is prevented from performing by strikes or a change in government policy concerning exports, or through a fire which destroys the consignment in course of production or when it is ready for shipment, or en route to Mitzi?

A—(1) In very limited circumstances, the common law doctrine of frustration or Frustrated Contracts Act 1959 (Vic), 1978 (NSW) may apply; otherwise see ss 10-12 where the answer may depend on whether the carburettors are specific goods: see s 5 definition.

(2) The commercial reality of passing of risk from Carb to Mitzi is made to depend on the legal concept of passing of property: ss 21-23 and 25.

Q—If Mitzi fails to pay for the goods can Carb reclaim them from Mitzi? What if Mitzi has already resold or encumbered them?

A—The answer will depend again on whether property has passed, or whether Mitzi has obtained possession of the goods or documents representing the goods and upon the bona fides of the sub-buyer or encumbrancee: ss 23, 24, 26–28.

Q—If Carb learns that Mitzi is insolvent, can it refuse delivery after manufacture or after shipping?

A—The answer will again depend in part on whether property has passed, whether Carb has reserved its right of disposal, and whether the goods are still in the course of transit: ss 24, 46–48.

Stage 4: delivery and acceptance of the goods and payment. Carb will be obliged to deliver the carburettors, but this may mean delivery at Carb's own factory door (ie Mitzi must collect them) or that Carb must send them to Mitzi.

Q—What are Carb's obligations in relation to delivery?

A—(1) As indicated above, the contract may particularise Carb's obligation and if Carb delivers late, or in the incorrect manner it will be in breach of contract, and Mitzi may be entitled to reject the goods or sue for damages: ss 31–35.

(2) If the contract provides for delivery by instalments, a defective delivery of one or more instalments may entitle Mitzi to refuse future instalments as well: s 34.

(3) If Carb is obliged to deliver to Mitzi in Japan, Carb must make proper arrangements for shipment and insurance: ss 35–36.

(4) If the goods are lost or damaged in transit, Mitzi should be able to claim compensation from the carrier (if at fault) or from the insurance company.

Q—What are Mitzi's obligations in relation to acceptance?

A—(1) Mitzi is obliged to accept delivery of goods which conform to the contract, and to pay in accordance with the contract: s 31.

(2) Mitzi is entitled to a reasonable opportunity to examine the goods before deciding whether it will accept them as conforming to the contract. However, if Mitzi resells after delivery of the goods it will be deemed to have accepted the goods: ss 37–38.

(3) If the contract calls for payment by Mitzi on receipt of documents representing the goods but before their physical delivery, or if Mitzi has arranged to sub-sell the goods in transit, it may be stuck with the goods even if they do not conform to the contract.

Stage 5: remedies for breach. Either Carb or Mitzi may be guilty of breaching the contract at any time after it has been formed. If either party renounces the contract either by express refusal to perform or by acting in such a way as to indicate an intention not to perform the contract, the other can immediately treat itself as discharged and sue for breach.

Q—What are Carb's remedies for breach by Mitzi?

A—(1) If Mitzi has failed to pay for the goods, Carb may be able to withhold delivery, or stop the goods in transit, and in either case, resell the goods: ss 41–50. In any event, Carb can sue Mitzi for damages for any loss resulting from Mitzi's wrongful refusal to accept and pay for the goods: ss 52 and 55.

(2) Alternatively, Carb can sue Mitzi for the contract price: s 51.

Q—What are Mitzi's remedies for breach by Carb?

A—(1) If the breach is of a condition of the contract, Mitzi can rightfully refuse to accept the goods, and need not return them to Carb provided it advises Carb of its refusal to accept: ss 16(2) and 39. However, if Mitzi has accepted the goods, or property in specific goods has passed to it, Mitzi will lose its right to reject for breach of condition and can only sue Carb for damages: ss 16(3), 23 and 38.

(2) If the breach is of a warranty only, or Mitzi has lost its right to reject for breach of condition as above, or decides to accept despite a breach of condition,

Sale of Goods

Mitzi can set up the breach in diminution or extinction of the price, or sue Carb for damages: ss 16(2), 54 and 55.

(3) If Carb fails or refuses to deliver, Mitzi can sue for damages: ss 53 and 55.

QUESTION

Question 1

In the light of the prototype transaction outlined above, identify the points at which the relationship or rights of the parties are likely to differ in the following different situations:

(a) commercial sales between merchants;
(b) commercial sales between merchants in an international setting;
(c) consumer sales.

In answering the question consider the effect of various statutory provisions on the different transactions.

SECTION 2: THE PURPOSE AND SCOPE OF THE SALE OF GOODS ACT

The primary source of present Australian law of sale of goods is the Sale of Goods Acts, enacted almost uniformly in the respective states and territories and all derived from the English Sale of Goods Act 1893. That Act, prepared by the renowned draftsman Sir Mackenzie Chalmers, formed with the Bills of Exchange Act 1882, Factors Act 1889, Partnership Act 1890, and Marine Insurance Act 1906, a pattern of statutory formulation of common law principles which has been described as the age of commercial codification. Each of these Acts has been widely followed in Australia and other common law countries.

As suggested in the previous section, the Act was designed to follow the chronological sequence of a contract from formation through to remedies for breach.

Sir Mackenzie Chalmers: Codification of Mercantile Law
(1903) 19 *LQR* at 10–11

A practical and working code cannot spring from the head of the draftsman, as Pallas Athene is fabled to have sprung, fully equipped, from the head of her father Zeus. In legislation, as in other sciences, the *a priori* road is a dangerous one to tread. When the principles of the law are well settled, and when the decided cases that accumulate are in the main mere illustrations of accepted general rules, then the law is ripe for codification. A code can usefully settle disputed points, and fill up small lacunae in the law, but it should always have its feet on the ground. If you go above and beyond experience, you are codifying in the air, and will probably do more harm than good to commerce and mercantile law. No service is done to the cause of codification by putting the case for it too high. The province of a code, I venture to think, is to set out, in concise language and logical form, those principles of the law which have already stood the test of time. It co-ordinates and methodises, but does not invent, principles.

Compare the following description of a code from one of the principal draftsmen of the Uniform Commercial Code.

Grant Gilmore: Legal Realism: Its Cause and Cure
(1961) 70 *Yale LJ* 1037 at 1042–3

We may pause to consider what we mean by the ambiguous term: codification. "Code" is often used as a loose synonym for "Statute"; when the legislature passes a statute which regulates an area previously left to the decisional law, lawyers are apt to say that the area has been "codified". I think that we can make a better use of the two terms: A "statute", let us say, is a legislative enactment which goes as far as it goes and no further: that is to say, when a case arises which is not within the precise statutory language, which reveals a gap in the statutory scheme or a situation not foreseen by the draftsmen (even though the situation is within the general area covered by the statute), then the court should put the statute out of mind and reason its way to decision according to the basic principles of the common law. A "code", let us say, is a legislative enactment which entirely pre-empts the field and which is assumed to carry within it the answers to all possible questions: thus when a court comes to a gap or an unforeseen situation, its duty is to find, by extrapolation and analogy, a solution consistent with the policy of the codifying law; the pre-code common law is no longer available as an authoritative source. We may take another, subsidiary distinction between "statute" and "code". When a "statute", having been in force for a time, has been interpreted in a series of judicial opinions, those opinions themselves become part of the statutory complex: the meaning of the statute must now be sought not merely in the statutory text but in the statute *plus* the cases that have been decided under it. A "code", on the other hand, remains at all times its own best evidence of what it means: cases decided under it may be interesting, persuasive, cogent, but each new case must be referred for decision to the undefiled code text.

THE EFFECT OF THE SALE OF GOODS ACT ON PREVIOUS LAW

Refer to the Sale of Goods Act 1923 (NSW) s 4(2).
How is s 4(2) to be interpreted?
In *British Tramways Co v Fiat Motor Ltd* [1910] 2 KB 831 at 836 Cozens-Hardy MR answered:

The object and intent of the [English] statute of 1893 was, no doubt, simply to codify the unwritten law applicable to the sale of goods, but in so far as there is an express enactment, that alone must be looked at and must govern the rights of the parties, even though the section may to some extent have altered the prior common law.

The classic statement of how a codifying Act, in this case the Bills of Exchange Act 1882 is to be interpreted, is in:

Bank of England v Vagliano Brothers
House of Lords [1891] AC 107

Lord Herschell (at 144–5): I think the proper course is in the first instance to examine the language of the statute and to ask what is its natural meaning, uninfluenced by any considerations derived from the previous state of the law, and not to start with inquiring how the law previously stood, and then, assuming that it was probably intended to leave it unaltered, to see if the words of the enactment will bear an interpretation in conformity with this view.

If a statute, intended to embody in a code a particular branch of the law, is to be treated in this fashion, it appears to me that its utility will be almost entirely destroyed, and the very object with which it was enacted will be frustrated. The purpose of such a statute surely was that on any point specifically dealt with by it, the law should be ascertained by interpreting the language used instead of, as before, by roaming over a vast number of authorities in order to discover what the law was ...

Does s 4(2) exclude the previous rules of equity, as well as of common law?
In referring to the exclusion of the prior "rules of common law", is s 4(2) using "common law" in its broad sense of non-statutory law so that it excludes rules of equity as well, or do the words refer only to the common law rules in contrast to equitable rules?

Re Wait
Court of Chancery [1927] 1 Ch 606

Atkin LJ (at 635): The code [English Sale of Goods Act 1893] was passed at a time when the principles of equity and equitable remedies were recognised and given effect to in all our courts, and the particular equitable remedy of specific performance is specially referred to in s 52.[1] The total sum of legal relations (meaning by the word "legal" existing in equity as well as in common law) arising out of the contract for the sale of goods may well be regarded as defined by the code. It would have been futile in a code intended for commercial men to have created an elaborate structure of rules dealing with the rights at law, if at the same time it was intended to leave, subsisting with the legal rights, equitable rights inconsistent with, more extensive, and coming into existence earlier than the rights so carefully set out in the various sections of the code.

Watt v Westhoven
Supreme Court of Victoria (Full Court) [1933] VLR 458

[The plaintiff sold and delivered to the defendant a car and received payment of part of the price. He sued for the balance and the defendant counterclaimed for rescission and repayment of the purchase money paid on the grounds that she was induced to purchase by misrepresentation as to the age and original cost of the car. The jury found the representations were false, but not fraudulent, and that each of them formed part of the inducement to purchase.]

Lowe J (at 464): ... The question asked by the learned County Court judge for the opinion of this court may be said shortly to be, whether a sale of a chattel can be rescinded on the ground that it was induced by innocent misrepresentation as to the condition of that chattel. In the statement of this question I am using the word "sale" in the sense attributed to it by s 6(3) of the Goods Act 1928, and in contradistinction to the words "agreement to sell"; and the question affirms that the buyer received the very chattel she bargained for but that at the time of sale the condition of the chattel in fact differed from the condition represented. The representation, moreover, was one which in an action of deceit would be regarded as material, but it was not one which went, as the phrase is, "to the substance of the contract". Had such a question arisen before the Judicature Acts, it is plain from the decision in *Kennedy v Panama Mail Co* (1867) LR 2 QB 580 at 587, the answer must have been in the negative. It is boldly asserted, however, that this decision is no longer law. It is said that the rule in equity in relation to the effect of innocent misrepresentation on a contract was much more liberal than the common law rule enunciated in *Kennedy's* case, as appears from the judgment of Jessel MR in *Redgrave v Hurd* (1881) 20 Ch D 1, and that since the Judicature Acts the equitable rule has become the rule in all courts and relates to all contracts without exception, and operates in the present case to give an affirmative answer to the question raised. The argument so stated raises a matter of the greatest importance and warrants close consideration, but after such consideration I am of opinion that the argument cannot be accepted ...

Assuming, however, that the rule in equity was as Jessel MR stated it, it did not, in my opinion, at any time apply, and does not now apply, to the sale of goods. The argument for the general application of the equitable rule rests on the provision of the Judicature Acts (which has been copied into our own Supreme Court Act) that in all matters in which there was before the passing of the Judicature Acts any conflict or variance between the rules of equity and the rules of the common law with reference to the same matter, the rules of equity shall prevail. Courts of equity did not entertain jurisdiction (with exceptions not material to the present discussion) in the case of sale of goods. There was in such a case no conflict or variance between the rules of the common law and of equity. The provision referred to never operated, and the rule of common law was not affected. I need not discuss the matter in detail, since it is fully dealt with, in a manner which I respectfully adopt, in the New Zealand case of *Riddiford v Warren* (1901) 20 NZLR 572. Our own Full Court had also, in 1890, arrived at the conclusion that the rule laid down in *Kennedy's* case was the rule governing cases of innocent misrepresentation inducing contracts for the sale of goods—*The Picturesque Atlas Co Ltd v Phillipson* (1890) 16 VLR 675—a decision some years after the coming into operation in this state of the Judicature Act.

In this state of the law the Sale of Goods Act 1896 was passed, and by s 5(2) (now s 4(2) of the Goods Act 1928) it was provided that "the rules of the common law including the law merchant save in so far as they are inconsistent with the express provisions of this Part and

---

[1] This section is not included in the NSW Act, but was copied in Vic, s 58; SA, s 51; WA, s 51; Qld, s 53; Tas, s 56; ACT, s 55.

in particular the rules relating to the law of principal and agent and the effect of fraud misrepresentation duress or coercion mistake or other invalidating cause shall continue to apply to contracts for the sale of goods". I feel clear that it was the common law rule as laid down in *Kennedy's* case which was in cases of misrepresentation to continue to apply. This matter is discussed generally in *Riddiford v Warren,* and I refrain from further discussing it. I may, however, add that I think there is a narrow and particular ground on which the same result follows in Victoria. *The Picturesque Atlas Publishing Co v Phillipson* had, before the Sale of Goods Act, settled the law for Victoria, and it was this law which the Sale of Goods Act preserved. In fact the decision of the court is in line with the general reasoning referred to, and the general and the particular grounds lead to the same result . . .

The conclusion at which I have arrived renders it unnecessary to enter upon a discussion of the particular difficulties involved in the further question argued, viz, that in any event the contract for the sale of the motor car had been so far executed as now to preclude the remedy of rescission. For the above reasons I think that the first question in the special case should be answered No . . .

[**Mann ACJ** and **Gavan Duffy J** delivered judgments to the like effect.]

As *Watt v Westhoven* illustrates, the question of the survival of equitable rules is not of merely academic interest. More recently the Full Court of South Australia refused to follow that decision and allowed rescission for innocent misrepresentation in a sale of goods case: *Graham v Freer* (SA Supreme Court, 23 December 1980) Law Society Judgment Scheme 125. At common law, rescission was only available for innocent misrepresentation where the subject matter of the contract turned out to be *totally different* from that represented so that there was a total failure of consideration. In equity, however, rescission was more readily available. Accordingly, the applicability of the above decisions in other states is of some continuing importance. In England and in South Australia, the issue has been put to rest by the enactment of a Misrepresentation Act which confers a right to rescind in circumstances where rescission in equity would previously have been allowed.

In New South Wales two further provisions must be considered:

(1) Supreme Court Act 1970 Pt IV, which finally achieved fusion of law and equity, includes:

57 The Court shall administer concurrently all rules of law, including rules of equity.

64 In all matters in which there was formerly or is any conflict or variance between the rules of equity and the rules of the common law with reference to the same matter, the rules of equity shall prevail.

(2) Sale of Goods Act 1923 (NSW) includes s 56 which is not found in other jurisdictions:

56 Nothing in this Act shall affect any remedy in equity of the buyer or the seller in respect of any breach of a contract of sale or any breach of warranty.

The Sale of Goods Act of a particular jurisdiction will only apply if that is the law deemed appropriate under the conflict of law rules. The question of what law is appropriate may arise in relation to the formation of the contract or its performance. In international sales, the parties will often stipulate which law they intend to govern their contract. If they do not do so, the courts may have to select the law with which the contract has the closest and most real connection.

In Chapter 5 on Import and Export Sales:
(a) the above questions which properly form part of a course on conflict of laws, will be covered in further detail; and
(b) attention will be focused on the efforts of international agencies to create a uniform regime of international private law for adoption by trading nations and their merchants in relation to their international transactions.

Sale of Goods

QUESTION

Question 2

(1) Can a buyer who has been induced to purchase goods as the result of an innocent misrepresentation by the seller rescind such a contract? Compare statutory provisions in the different states which may affect your answer.

(2) In what circumstances may the courts justifiably have regard to decisions in sale of goods cases decided prior to the enactment of the Sale of Goods Act?

SECTION 3: WHAT IS A CONTRACT FOR SALE OF GOODS?

Reference was made in Chapter 1 to situations where the distinction between real and personal property is important. Similarly, it may be important to distinguish a sale of goods from other transactions. Some of the reasons are:

(1) Sales of goods, wares and merchandise are generally exempted from stamp duty, whereas sales of interests in land and retail hire-purchase agreements are not: see eg, Stamp Duties Act 1920 (NSW) ss 41, 66, 75A-E.

(2) Formal requirements differ according to whether the contract relates to land, goods or services.

(3) The conditions implied by various statutes will vary according to whether the contract is a sale or hire-purchase agreement, and whether it relates to goods, services or an interest in land.

CONSUMER SALES

Legislation in most states and the Trade Practices Act 1974 make special provisions for transactions described variously as "consumer sales" (NSW SGA s 62) "consumer contracts" (SA Consumer Transactions Act s 5) and "contracts to supply goods or services to a consumer" (Trade Practices Act ss 68–74). The definitions of these consumer transactions also vary between the statutes. Both the Credit Act (Vic) and the Consumer Credit Act (NSW) provide for credit sale contracts to consumers: see ss 5 and 14. Other specific forms of consumer transactions are further regulated by special statutes in each state: eg, NSW, Lay-By Sales Act 1943; Book Purchasers' Protection Act 1899; Door-to-Door Sales Act 1967.

Sale of Goods Act 1923 (NSW)

The SGA s 5 contains these definitions:

"Contract of sale" includes an agreement to sell as well as a sale.

"Goods" includes all chattels personal other than things in action and money. The term includes emblements and things attached to or forming part of the land which are agreed to be severed before sale or under the contract of sale.

Stokman v Mills
New South Wales Court of Appeal [1966] 1 NSWR 612

[Mr and Mrs Mills owned land near Goulburn, New South Wales, on which was a heap of slate left some years before by a quarrying company. They agreed to sell the slate *in situ* to Warren for £400 and further agreed not to sell the land without making the sale subject to the prior agreement with Warren. Warren resold the slate still *in situ* to Stokman and subsequently the Mills sold the land to Mr Mills' mother, Mrs Daphne Mills. Mrs Mills disputed Stokman's right to come onto the property to load and remove the slate. One of the questions for the court was whether the sale of the slate was governed by the Sale of Goods Act.]

Asprey JA (Wallace P and **Holmes JA** concurring) (at 619): . . . So far I have been considering the position of the parties to this suit apart from statute but in s 5(1) of the Sale of Goods

Act 1923, as amended, the word "goods" is defined as including "all chattels personal other than things in action and money. The term includes emblements and things attached to or forming part of the land which are agreed to be severed before sale or under the contract of sale", and "contract of sale" includes "an agreement to sell as well as a sale". This definition effected an important change in the common law by declaring that "goods" also "include 'things attached to or forming part of the land' not only when they are to be severed before sale (which was the law before the Act) but also when they are agreed to be severed under the contract of sale": *Benjamin on Sale,* 8th ed, p 186. To bring the thing in question within the definition, it must be a separate entity or thing though, in a conveyancing sense, it may at the time of the contract form part of the land (see *Yearworth v Pierce* (1647) Aleyn 31; 82 ER 900, with which contrast *Morgan v Russell & Sons* [1909] 1 KB 357, where, in the latter case, upon the facts found, "the cinders and slag, the subject of the contract, had become part of the ground or soil itself and were not separate and detached heaps resting, so to speak, upon the ground"). In the present case the slate, which was comprised in a separate and defined pile or dump, had originally been severed from the realty by quarrying and by the process of separating it from the other slate considered to be suitable for the manufacture of roofing tiles. If it subsequently became part of the realty, it only did so by resting upon the land of its own weight. It was a distinct and separate entity (in contradistinction to the cinders and slag in *Morgan v Russell & Sons*). It was in a deliverable state. It was inanimate and had ceased to benefit the land or to obtain any benefit from the land upon which it was situated. Upon the assumption that it was part of the realty, it was agreed to be severed under the contract dated 14 November 1955 and, as between the parties to the contract, in these circumstances, the slate, in my opinion, would fall within the definition of "goods" in the Act. Having regard to the provisions of the contract and to the operation of ss 22 and 23 r 1 of the Act it would appear to me that, as between the plaintiff Warren and D A and W K Mills, the property in the slate passed to the plaintiff Warren: see generally *Benjamin on Sale,* 8th ed, pp 186-8; *Blackburn on Contract of Sale,* 3rd ed, p 16.

On appeal this decision was varied by the High Court of Australia:

Mills v Stokman
High Court of Australia (1966) 116 CLR 61

Barwick CJ (at 71): I have come to think that the proper inference from what is known by evidence in the suit is that the heap represented unwanted dross cast on one side with the intention that it should remain on the land indefinitely, and, by implication, that it should form part of it. In my opinion, the proper inference from its continuous association with the land in the meantime is that it had been dealt with as realty by succeeding owners. Those inferences are enough within the authorities to warrant the conclusion that the heap of dross was on 14 November 1955 part of the realty. Reference to *Holland v Hodgson* (1872) LR 7 CP 328 is sufficient to indicate the relevant principles in this connection; for my part, I find no need to rely on or to discuss particular instances such as *Boileau v Heath* [1898] 2 Ch 301, whose differentiating circumstances may need to be regarded. In my respectful opinion, it is not correct to regard this heap of dross as comparable to some separate substance attached to the land by no more than its own weight. In the course of time, like a heap of earth, it had no doubt become integrated at its base with the subjacent soil. Nor, in my opinion, is it correct to ignore the intention which the quarrying company must have had of abandoning to the land the unwanted and worthless dross of its operations.

So far as the reasons of the Supreme Court founded on the Sale of Goods Act are concerned, it is sufficient, in my respectful opinion, to point out that there was in truth no agreement on the part of either D A or W K Mills or of the respondent Warren to sever the slate from the land. The agreement of 1955 went no further than to purport to sell the slate to that respondent and to give him a right to enter and remove it. He did not agree to do so. No doubt it is implicit in the terms of the agreement that both parties thought that the slate was already severed: they did purport to deal with it as if it were a chattel interest. But an agreement to sever cannot be constructed out of that assumption on the part of the parties. In my respectful opinion, the Supreme Court was in error in regarding s 5(1) and ss 22 and 23 r 1 of the Sale of Goods Act as applicable to the slate or the agreement of 1955.

It follows that the declaration as to the ownership of the heap of dross made by the Supreme

Court cannot be sustained. However, so to decide does not dispose of the case. As in my opinion the heap formed part of the land, the agreement of 1955, supported by consideration, is capable of creating an equitable *profit ā prendre*. It contains an express grant of the right to enter and to remove the slate in the heap.

[The other judges delivered judgments to similar effect.]

Decision of New South Wales Court of Appeal varied.

Compare *Amco Enterprises Pty Ltd v Wade* [1968] St R Qd 445.

CONTRACTS FOR WORK AND LABOUR, OR TO SUPPLY AND ERECT A STRUCTURE OR EQUIPMENT

In other cases, the result of A's efforts may be that B ends up with a portrait, dentures, built-in furniture or a piece of equipment *in situ*. However, will these constitute contracts for sale of goods?

Brooks Robinson Pty Ltd v Rothfield
Supreme Court of Victoria (Full Court) [1951] VLR 405

Dean J (at 407): Plaintiff brought an action in the County Court for the sum of 91*l*. Its particulars of demand were: The plaintiff demands of you payment for work done and materials supplied at your request for the manufacture of a cocktail cabinet. The only defence was that the contract was one for the sale of goods above 10*l* in value and, being wholly oral, was unenforceable by reason of s 9 of the Goods Act 1928. The learned County Court judge upheld this defence and entered judgment for the defendant. The plaintiff now appeals and relies on two grounds: (a) that the contract was not a contract of sale; (b) that, if it was a contract of sale, defendant has repudiated the contract, plaintiff has accepted such repudiation, and is entitled to recover upon a *quantum meruit* because the contract no longer subsists.

Before considering these two points, it is necessary to refer to the facts, which were not in dispute.

Plaintiff was doing work on doors and glass fittings at defendant's home. Defendant's wife, who, it was not disputed, acted with his authority, asked plaintiff to undertake the construction of a cocktail cabinet in accordance with blueprints prepared by an architect, except for some wrought iron work and a pivot which defendant was having executed by another firm. The cabinet was designed to occupy a doorway in a curved wall between two rooms, to revolve upon a pivot and to be carried on wheels. Plaintiff agreed to construct the cabinet as desired upon a "cost plus" basis. Plaintiff began the work of constructing the cabinet upon its own premises, and upon receiving the pivot from the manufacturer, assembled the cabinet upon it. Eventually, after plaintiff had made several attempts to get in touch with defendant, his wife telephoned and said, "This job has been going on for so long that we have decided to wipe our hands of the whole matter." Further attempts to interview the defendant failed, and letters written to him were unanswered. The plaintiff expended money in labour and materials for which defendant refused to pay. The cabinet is still on the plaintiff's premises and is of no value for any other purpose. The wrought iron doors, to be obtained by defendant, were not obtained, but otherwise the cabinet is complete. The total value of plaintiff's labour and materials plus profit is 91*l*, the amount claimed.

The first ground of appeal was that the contract was not one for the supply of goods, but was a contract for work and labour. The distinction has been so recently and authoritatively stated by the Court of Appeal in *Robinson v Graves* [1935] 1 KB 579 that it is unnecessary to refer to earlier cases. At 587, Greer LJ said: "If you find, as they did in *Lee v Griffin* (1861) 1 B & S 272, that the substance of the contract was the production of something to be sold by the dentist to the dentist's customer, then that is a sale of goods. But if the substance of the contract, on the other hand, is that skill and labour have to be exercised for the production of the article and that it is only ancillary to that that there will pass from the artist to his client or customer some materials in addition to the skill involved in the production of the portrait, that does not make any difference to the result, because the substance of the contract is the skill and experience of the artist in producing the picture." In my opinion, if the contract was to manufacture and supply a cabinet according to the plan, it was plainly a contract for the sale of goods.

But appellant contends that it was a contract which required it not only to manufacture but to install the completed cabinet in the house in such a manner that it became a fixture, and that no property passed until it was so installed. If this be correct, it is clear that the contract would be for work and labour and would not be a contract of sale: *Clark v Bulmer* (1843) 11 M & W 243; *Chanter v Dickinson* (1843) 5 Man & G 253; *Sydney Hydraulic and General Engineering Co v Blackwood & Son* (1908) 8 SR (NSW) 10; *Benjamin on Sale,* 7th ed, p 177. The question is thus one of fact: what was it that plaintiff had to do in order to complete its part of the contract? In response to a request for further particulars, plaintiff set out the terms of the request on which he sued. These were that plaintiff should make and "install" the cabinet. In evidence, plaintiff's witnesses did not make any reference to the installation of the cabinet, but said that the obligation of the plaintiff was to undertake construction of the cabinet in accordance with the blueprint—other than the wrought iron work. In answer to an interrogatory put in by plaintiff, defendant swore that plaintiff had been requested to "manufacture and install" the cabinet in accordance with the blueprint. No evidence was given as to the nature of the installation except such as can be gathered from the blueprint, a photostat copy of which was in evidence. It does appear from the evidence that the wrought iron work was to be supplied to plaintiff by another manufacturer, that the wrought iron included the pivot on which the cabinet revolved and also the cabinet doors, and that the cabinet was designed so as to occupy a doorway in a curved wall between two rooms. The plaintiff received the pivot from the manufacturer after some delay and assembled the partly completed cabinet on the pivot and completed its construction so far as possible without the doors, which were not received from the other manufacturers.

The blueprint was not explained by any evidence, but as it was the basis of plaintiff's instructions, it is important. From the drawings, it appears that the pivot was attached to or let into the ceiling or some projection therefrom, and it would appear that it was attached to or let into the floor. The pivot was seated in a shaft mounted on ball bearings. This called for some attachment to the floor. It appears that the front of the cabinet could occupy either of two positions. In one position it was swung into the hall, and in another into a room. It revolved on the pivot and was carried on rubber wheels. It served as a wall between the room and the hall.

Meagre as the evidence is, I think sufficient does appear to establish that the cabinet was not a piece of furniture capable of being moved from room to room or from house to house, but was part of the structure of the house. When installed it served as a wall, and was part of the house itself. It was really an elaborate sort of door, serving the additional purpose of a receptacle. It was made to conform to the precise measurements of the space for its situation in the house. It was attached to the structure for the better enjoyment of the house itself. It did not rest merely by its own weight so as to be prima facie not a fixture, but was attached to the structure, and is prima facie a fixture: see *Australian Provincial Assurance Co Ltd v Coroneo* (1938) 38 SR (NSW) 700 (FC). Even if it were not attached but were resting merely by its own weight it could not have been intended to be placed in position temporarily, but it was intended as a permanent part of the house. As between a devisee of the house and a residuary legatee it would pass to the former. In my opinion, it sufficiently appears that plaintiff had, as part of its contract, to affix it to the house, that no property passed until it had done so, and that it was accordingly not a contract of sale of goods and s 9 of the Goods Act 1928 is no defence.

Plaintiff cannot sue upon the basis of having performed the contract, for it has not in fact done so. Nor does it sue for damages for breach of the contract. It has sued for work and labour done and materials supplied, and claims payment upon a *quantum meruit* for work done and materials supplied. When the defendant has repudiated the contract and plaintiff has accepted such repudiation, the contract is rescinded. Plaintiff then cannot sue on the special contract, but the special contract is no bar to its claim based upon a *quantum meruit,* and it is no answer to such a claim that full performance would not have been profitable: *Lodder v Slowey* [1904] AC 442; *Snelling v Lord Huntingfield* (1834) 1 Cr M & R 20; *De Bernardy v Harding* (1853) 8 Exch 822; *Planche v Colburn* (1831) 8 Bing 14. See notes to *Cutter v Powell* 2 Sm LC, 13th ed, p 23: "... it is an invariably true proposition, that, whenever one of the parties to a special contract not under seal has, in an unqualified manner, refused to perform his side of the contract, or has disabled himself from performing it by his own act, the other party has, thereupon, a right to elect to treat it as rescinded, and may, on so electing, immediately sue on a *quantum meruit* for anything which he had done under it before the rescission." Reference may be made to articles by the present Lord Justice Denning in the *Law Quarterly Review* Vol 41, p 79; Vol 55, p 54, and to His Lordship's judgment in *James v Thomas H Kent & Co Ltd* [1950] 2 All ER 1099 at 1103; and to *Cheshire & Fifoot on Contracts,* pp 391-2, 424-6. It is unnecessary to consider the effect upon this principle of s 9 of the Goods Act 1928, if contrary to the opinion already expressed, the contract was rendered unenforceable by that section. Although the contrary was contended, I think it clear on the evidence that the defendant had repudiated the contract and that plaintiff, by not proceeding to complete the work and by suing for work already done and materials already supplied, had accepted such repudiation.

In my opinion, the appeal should be allowed; the judgment of the County Court must be set aside and judgment entered for plaintiff for the amount claimed with costs to be taxed. Respondent must pay the costs of the appeal which are to be taxed.

[**Sholl** and **Martin JJ** both concurred.]

Appeal allowed.

Young & Marten Ltd v McManus Childs Ltd
House of Lords [1969] 1 AC 454

[McManus Childs, house builders, employed subcontract tilers Young & Marten to supply and lay a specified brand Somerset 13 red tiles on a number of houses which McManus Childs were building. The subcontractors obtained those tiles from the only manufacturer and laid them as required. Owing to an undetectable manufacturing defect, the tiles broke in frosty weather and the purchasers of the houses sued the builders who in turn sued the subcontractors. They were too late under the Limitation Act to sue the manufacturer. The primary question concerned the obligations of the subcontractors to the builders.]

Lord Upjohn (at 471): My Lords, the sole, though important, question in this appeal is as to the extent of the implied warranty (if any) imposed by law upon a contractor who agrees to do work and supply materials. The appellants, experienced in supplying and laying roofing materials, were employed by the respondents on a contract admittedly for work and materials to supply and lay Somerset 13 red tiles to the roofs of certain houses being built on an estate at Gerrards Cross. Did they thereby impliedly make any warranty that the tiles supplied by them were (a) of good quality and (b) reasonably fit for the purpose for which they were supplied?

Had the contract been one for sale of goods, then it is not in dispute that s 14(2) of the Sale of Goods Act 1893 would have applied and entitled the respondents to succeed in their claim for breach of warranty that the tiles were of good quality; for it was common ground that, though Somerset 13 tiles are in general a high grade tile of good quality fit for the purpose for which they were supplied, this particular batch was deficient, though the deficiency was latent and not discernible on reasonable examination by a person of skill and experience, as was agreed before the learned Official Referee.

Your Lordships were properly referred to authorities in the nineteenth century, for s 14(2) only put the common law as it had been established into a statutory code. The departure of the common law in relation to sale of goods from the old principle of *caveat emptor* (which still applies fundamentally to sale of real estate) was recognised as long ago as 1815 by Lord Ellenborough CJ in *Gardiner v Gray* (1815) 4 Camp 144. He stated the principle that where there was a sale by description the purchaser has a right to expect a saleable article answering to the description in the contract and that is an implied term in every such contract. Where there was no opportunity to inspect, the principle of *caveat emptor* did not apply. Your Lordships need not consider any question of an opportunity to inspect, because, as Park J in effect recognised much later in *Jones v Bright* (1829) 5 Bing 533 at 548, in the case of latent defects (with which alone your Lordships are concerned) there cannot be an opportunity to inspect.

There are many later cases developing Lord Ellenborough's principle until we find Best CJ in the case I have just mentioned saying (at 544): "If a man sells an article, he thereby warrants that it is merchantable." Curiously enough, however, there was no equal body of decision at common law in the nineteenth century to support, in express terms, a similar implied warranty in the case of contracts for work and materials.

But that a man who supplies his labour or his labour and materials is subject to the same basic obligation cannot be doubted. In *Duncan v Blundell* (1820) 3 Stark 6 at 7 in 1820 Bayley J in his usual direct language said of a case where the defendant had undertaken to supply and fit a stove: "Where a person is employed in a work of skill, the employer buys both his labour and his judgment; he ought not to undertake the work if it cannot succeed, and he should know whether it will or not. Of course it is otherwise if the party employing him choose to supersede the workman's judgment by using his own."

The distinction between a contract for the sale of goods and a contract for the provision of work and materials is one which depends on the particular nature of each individual contract, as was said as long ago as 1856 in *Clay v Yates* (1856) 1 H & N 73, and it is frequently a question of fine distinction. It would be most unsatisfactory, illogical, and indeed a severe blow to any idea of a coherent system of common law, if the existence of an implied obligation depended upon such a distinction. That there are distinctions between the two types of contracts is undoubted; questions of pleading (in the old days), passing of property, and so on. But, of course, the real distinction upon which so many decisions were focused depended upon the fact that for 277 years until 1954 a contract of sale above a small value required evidence in writing to be enforceable, whereas a contract for work and materials did not.

In such cases the question whether any terms should be implied in the case of the one type of contract rather than the other seldom arose. The exception, however, did arise in *Samuels v Davis* [1943] KB 526; [1943] 2 All ER 3 (CA) where a dentist sued for a denture which he had made and supplied for which his patient refused to pay because it did not fit his gums. The County Court judge held that the denture was not reasonably fit for the purpose for which it was supplied. In the leading case of *Lee v Griffin* (1861) 1 B & S 272, it had been held that such a contract was one of sale. As du Parcq LJ (as he then was) said, [1943] KB 526 at 529: "In *Lee v Griffin* the court was not directing its attention to the question whether there were any incidents in the case of a contract for the sale of a denture which were different from those in the case of a contract for the work and labour expended on the making of a denture. I have no doubt that, if the question had arisen for decision, whether it made any difference whether the contract was described as one of sale or one of work and labour, the answer for the present purpose would have been: 'None whatever.'"

In the same case, delivering the first judgment of the Court of Appeal, Scott LJ had said that it was a matter of legal indifference whether the contract was one for the supply of goods, or one of service to do work and supply materials.

So I cannot see any logical distinction between the obligations which ought in general to be implied with regard to quality and fitness between a sale of goods and a contract for work and materials. Indeed, for my part I think, as a matter of common sense and justice, one who contracts to do work and supply materials ought to be under at least as high, if not a higher, degree of obligation with regard to the goods he supplies and the work that he does than a seller who may be a mere middleman or wholesaler.

[The other judges delivered judgments to like effect.]

SPECIFIC AND UNASCERTAINED GOODS

The Act draws a distinction between these two types of goods which carry important consequences under other sections. "Specific goods" are defined as "goods identified and agreed upon at the time the contract is made". Thus, if Carb buys a "1982 Holden panel van Reg No JIM007" the van is specific goods, but "a Fastcut 303 lathe manufactured by Biltwell" is not specific goods and any lathe meeting that description can be delivered. The distinction is important in relation to loss where the goods have perished (ss 11, 12), the right to reject for breach of condition (s 16(3)), the passing of property (ss 21–24) and of risk (s 25).

RELATIONSHIP TO HIRE-PURCHASE AND CONSUMER CREDIT AGREEMENTS

Hire-purchase agreements were devised by legal draftsmen in the nineteenth century as a means of protecting the title of the seller or financier of goods until the balance of the purchase price was paid. Typically the goods were hired to the consumer who was given an option of purchasing them for a nominal consideration at the end of the hiring period provided all instalments of hiring charges had been paid. The device received judicial recognition in *Helby v Matthews* [1895] AC 471, in which it was held that the agreement was not an agreement to buy, and therefore the hirer could not pass title by resale or pledge under the equivalent of s 27(2) Sale of Goods Act (Qld). However, where the seller not only gave the hirer an *option* to purchase but also *obliged* him to do so, the agreement was treated as a conditional sale agreement, and the buyer could pass title to a bona fide purchaser under the Sale of Goods Act s 27(2): eg, *Lee v Butler* [1893] 2 QB 318. This position was reversed in three states which have abolished hire-purchase and replaced it by the concept of a credit sale and deemed mortgage back to the seller: see Consumer Transactions Act 1972 (SA) ss 5, 24; Credit Act 1981 (Vic) s 14; Consumer Credit Act 1981 (NSW) s 14.

Similarly, the seller's title was protected from the hirer's assignees or trustee in bankruptcy and the agreement was not necessarily void for non-registration under the Bills of Sale legislation: *McEntire v Crossley Bros Ltd* [1895] AC 457. However, where an existing owner of goods sells and takes them back under hire-purchase in a refinancing arrangement, the transaction is likely to be regarded as a sham for a secured loan and avoided by the Bills of Sale legislation: *Price v Parsons* (1936) 54 CLR 332; *Boydell v James* (1936) 36 SR (NSW) 620.

The above distinctions can be blurred in some situations. First, when Australian legislatures moved to protect consumers under hire-purchase, they did not confine their definition of hire-purchase agreements to the classic form of hiring plus option to purchase typified in *Helby v Matthews*: see eg Hire-Purchase Act 1959 (Qld) s 2.

Thus, a *Helby v Matthews* agreement will not be a sale of goods and an unconditional sale (or a wholesale hire-purchase arrangement) will not be a hire-purchase agreement within the statutory definition. However, in between these two situations, a conditional sale agreement (of the *Lee v Butler* variety) is clearly caught by the Hire-Purchase Act definition, but also remains, at least for some purposes, a contract of sale, since SGA (Qld) s 4(2) expressly contemplates a conditional as well as an absolute sale. The question whether one or both Acts applies to an agreement of this hybrid type may be of importance in relation to:

(a) the requirements as to contents and form: see Section 4 of this chapter;
(b) the conditions of fitness and quality implied under the respective Acts: see Chapter 3;
(c) the application of SGA (Qld) s 27(2), whereby "a person having bought or agreed to buy goods" who is in possession of them but has not acquired title nor completed paying for the goods, can confer a good title on a bona fide purchaser or encumbrancee.

In relation to the first two issues, it is arguable that both Acts can apply simultaneously. On the third, two opposing views have been suggested:

(1) Since the buyer is given a statutory right under Hire-Purchase Act s 12 to return the goods without paying the full price, he has not agreed to *buy* the goods and therefore cannot pass title under Sale of Goods Act (Qld) s 27(2): see Else-Mitchell & Parsons, *Hire-Purchase Law,* 4th ed, 1968, p 215.

(2) The contract remains a contract of sale, albeit conditional as contemplated under s 6(2), subject to the condition subsequent of a right to return under Hire-Purchase Act s 12. In South Australia, Victoria and New South Wales title to the goods vests in the buyer under a consumer credit contract when the contract is made or the goods are delivered subject to a mortgage back to the seller: Consumer Transactions Act 1972 (SA) s 25; Credit Act 1981 (Vic) s 14; Consumer Credit Act 1981 (NSW) s 14. The Sale of Goods Act then applies to this contract of sale on credit in the same manner as to a cash sale.

A second situation where there can be confusion between the classifications of sale and hire-purchase is where an agreement to sell is negotiated, the buyer pays a deposit or leaves a trade-in and takes possession of the goods on the understanding that he will obtain finance on hire-purchase terms. A number of issues can arise in this situation. Is there a sale in the first instance which is novated when the hire-purchase agreement is consummated, or is the prospective hirer merely a bailee pending signing of the hire-purchase agreement? The question can be critical if the "hirer" never obtains finance but refuses to return the goods, or alternatively finds the goods unsuitable: *City Motors (1933) Pty Ltd v Southern Aerial Super Service Pty Ltd* (1961) 106 CLR 477. Can the original agreement be attacked as an unregistered bill of sale which is implemented through the hire-purchase agreement as a security device? And will the answer differ depending upon whether the hire-purchase agreement is made with the original dealer or an independent finance company? See *Johnstone & Wilmot Pty Ltd v Kaine* (1928) 23 Tas LR 43; *Marcus Clark (Victoria) Ltd v Brown* (1928) 40 CLR 540.

QUESTIONS

Question 3

What advantage was there to the plaintiffs in *Stokman v Mills* in arguing that the sale of the slate was governed by the Sale of Goods Act? Would it have made any difference to the result if Mr and Mrs Mills had agreed to load the slate on to Warren's (or Stokman's) trucks?

Question 4

What factors will determine whether a contract is for sale of goods or for work and labour? What is the significance of the distinction? How would non-compliance with any formal requirements in relation to such a contract affect the obligations of the supplier? If the formal requirements of the Sale of Goods Act are not complied with, will the supplier be left without any remedy in all circumstances?

Question 5

Carb Pty Ltd required an acid bath for its factory. As general manager of Carb, Jim Handy approached Forge, an equipment wholesaler and asked if it would supply and install a Dipit 1411 acid bath manufactured by Wellbilt Ltd. Forge quoted an inclusive price of $14,000 and on receiving Forge's assurance that the bath would never corrode or leak, Jim ordered the bath from Forge.

Forge delivered the bath and installed it by cementing the bath to Carb's factory floor and attaching it with special plumbing to the factory's waste disposal.

Two months later, Carb used a new and very strong acid solution in the bath which had only just come on the market. The acid corroded the bath which commenced leaking and could not be repaired.

(1) What statutes should be considered in relation to the above situation?
(2) If Carb has not paid the $14,000 to Forge, is it obliged to do so?
(3) Advise Carb generally.
(4) In what respects would your advice change in the following alternative situations:
   (a) Forge has now been made bankrupt; or
   (b) Carb had purchased the bath directly from Wellbilt Ltd; or
   (c) the bath rested by its own weight on the floor without being cemented?

Sale of Goods

SECTION 4: FORMAL REQUIREMENTS: IS THE STATUTE OF FRAUDS NECESSARY?

The *raison d'être* of formal requirements for contracts derived from the English Statute of Frauds 1677 was, according to its title, "the prevention of many fraudulent practices which are commonly endeavoured to be upheld by perjury and subornation of perjury". First, in earlier times, the jury performed the role of witnesses and jurors, and decided cases on their own knowledge and not necessarily in accordance with the evidence. Second, very often the best evidence was not admissible because of the rule which precluded an interested party or his/her spouse from testifying. Third, mutual promises had been recognised since the sixteenth century as sufficient consideration for an executory contract, and the unstable social and political conditions of the time encouraged the unscrupulous to manufacture evidence in support of spurious claims.

Accordingly, the statute required that there be some signed document or other external evidence of the existence of unperformed contracts of various kinds for them to be enforceable. The contracts affected included those in respect of land (see now, eg, Conveyancing Act (NSW) s 54A), goods to the value of £10 (now NSW SGA s 9), contracts of guarantee and contracts not to be performed within a year. The statute has been criticised on a number of grounds, and with changing social and economic conditions, a number of the provisions have been repealed or modified: see, eg Law Reform (Statute of Frauds) Act 1962 (WA) s 2. The provision dealing with contracts for sale of goods was repealed in England (1954), Queensland (1972) and South Australia (1982). It remains in the other Australian states. It has been re-enacted in modified form in the United States in the Uniform Commercial Code.

Other statutes regulating consumer sales specify their own formal requirements, and sanctions, for non-compliance. For example, the uniform Hire Purchase Act 1960 (Qld) s 3 requires every hire-purchase agreement to be in writing, signed by all parties, and containing detailed information regarding the terms of hire. Non-compliance by the owner is a statutory offence and entitles the hirer to avoid all interest charges: s 3(3) and (4). An unwritten agreement is not enforceable by the finance company: s 3(5). Compare the requirements under NSW, Lay-By Sales Act 1943 s 5, Consumer Credit Act 1981 ss 30, 46, Door-to-Door Sales Act 1967 s 3; Vic, Credit Act 1981 ss 30, 46; SA, Consumer Transactions Act 1972 s 20, Consumer Credit Act 1972 ss 40, 41.

For present purposes, we will concentrate attention on the formulation in Sale of Goods Act 1923 (NSW) s 9. Before reaching your own conclusion as to whether s 9 has outlived its usefulness, consider the following cases dealing with its interpretation and application.

ACCEPTANCE AND RECEIPT

B & H Constructions Pty Ltd v Campbell
Supreme Court of New South Wales in Commercial Causes [1963] NSWR 333

[B & H Constructions tendered a quotation of £2230 to supply fabricated steelwork to Campbell and Duggan (C and D) who were constructing the Coogee Aquarium. Campbell orally accepted the quotation during a conversation with Langham of B & H. After B & H had fabricated and was ready to deliver the steel, C and D refused to take delivery, but did receive delivery of nuts and bolts supplied by B & H through Mercator Supply Co. There was no written note of the contract and no deposit. B & H sued C and D for the purchase price and C and D pleaded inter alia that the contract was unenforceable by virtue of the Sale of Goods Act s 9.]

Walsh J (at 334): ... On the facts, I hold that an agreement was made orally between the plaintiff and the defendants, and this was made either on 27 or 28 October 1960, but more probably on 27 October. I accept Langham's evidence on this matter as being substantially correct. The plaintiff had sent a written quotation to Green [an architect, as agent for defendants] which had been passed on by him to Campbell. The offer which this contained was one which, by its terms, called for a written acceptance. If there had been merely a verbal acceptance of that offer without more, this would not have brought about a binding contract, since the plaintiff could have said truly that it was not bound. But this circumstance did not prevent the parties from making, if they were willing to do so, a concluded oral contract in their conversation about the matter. I hold that this is what they did ...

[His Honour then concluded that the measurements made on the site and the drawings that were afterwards made indicated that both parties acted on the footing that a contract had been made and that it was, to the knowledge of the defendants, being actively carried out by the plaintiffs. His Honour continued:]

It has been suggested that the plaintiff cannot maintain an action for the price, and that its remedy, if any, is an action for damages for breach of contract. But it is my opinion that the property in the floor level steelwork passed to the purchasers when the fabrication of it had been completed and it was ready for delivery. I think that this ought to be regarded, in the circumstances of the case, as representing the intention of the parties as to when the property should pass. If it was necessary, in accordance with r 5(1) in s 23 of the Act that there should have been appropriation of the steel by the plaintiff with the assent of the defendants, I think that it can be concluded that when the contract was made the defendants assented impliedly to a subsequent appropriation by the plaintiff, and that the property passed when the plaintiff, having completed the steelwork, appropriated it to the contract with the defendants. In any event, there is evidence which I accept, that later on one of the defendants inspected the steelwork, which was pointed out as being that which had been prepared under this contract, whereupon the defendants made a proposal about the plaintiff buying back the steel. This was an assent to the appropriation which had been earlier made by the plaintiff, with the result that that appropriation was effective to pass the property ...

I must now consider the plea based on s 9 of the Sale of Goods Act. The first thing to be said is that this was a contract for the sale of goods within the meaning of the Act. It was somewhat faintly suggested for the plaintiff that it was a contract for work and labour and so did not fall within the Act. I think that upon consideration of the discussion of the cases in *Benjamin,* 8th ed, pp 156–8, it must be concluded that this was a contract to which the Act applies. See also *Harvey v MacDonald* [1927] St R Qd 50, a case very similar to the present one so far as this point is concerned.

There was no note or memorandum in writing of the contract, signed by the defendants or their agent. But I have reached the conclusion that, within the meaning of s 9(1) the defendants did "accept part of the goods so sold and actually receive the same", and that therefore the defence fails.

The evidence shows that a carter took to the premises of the defendants, on 7 November 1960, a bag containing certain bolts and nuts. These were left there and Duggan signed a delivery docket which referred to them. They were not afterwards returned to the plaintiff or to Mercator Supply Co Pty Ltd, this being the company from which they came. So far as appears, they are still in the possession of the defendants. The evidence shows that in its quotation, and therefore in the contract later made, the plaintiff had undertaken to supply holding down bolts which would be necessary for the work of erecting the steel which the plaintiff was to supply. Therefore, it would have been part of the duty of the plaintiff to deliver the holding down bolts to the Coogee Aquarium site. The plaintiff ordered bolts and nuts from the Mercator Company and asked it to deliver them to that site instead of to the plaintiff's premises. The delivery dockets were made out to B & H Constructions, but on them was written, "One bag to Mr Campbell, Coogee Baths".

The evidence shows then that the goods left at the place to which the plaintiff would have to make delivery, were part of the goods which were the subject matter of the sale. There is no doubt that, in a physical sense, the buyer accepted these goods and actually received them. But it is contended that, in the circumstances, this did not occur in such a way as to satisfy the requirements of the provisions in s 9(1). It is said that it did not show any recognition of an existing agreement for sale. It is said that it does not appear that the defendants received those goods as vendees, and that the view is at least equally open that they received them as bailees for B & H Constructions Pty Ltd, to which they were addressed. But the defendant Duggan does not give evidence which explains satisfactorily the receipt and retention of the bolts for some other purpose than to have them in readiness for use on the site when the bulk of the steel should be delivered and its erection commenced. Theories that he received them as bailee for B & H Constructions, intending either to hand them over when a representative of that company should call, or alternatively, to retain them in the capacity of bailee until the time when the bulk of the steel should be delivered, so that they might then be available along with it, seem to have little relationship to the facts. It is more natural to refer the receipt of the goods to some contract which the defendants had made as purchasers. It has not been suggested, of course, that they had themselves ordered any such goods from Mercator Supply Co Pty Ltd, and if what was done was indicative of a contract of sale, it should be regarded as indicating a contract to which the plaintiff was a party.

To satisfy the requirements of the section, it is necessary only that what is done should point to some contract of sale, and it is not essential that it should be indicative of the terms of that contract. See *Benjamin,* 8th ed, p 206; *Metropolitan Knitting and Hosiery Co Ltd (in liq) v Thomas Burnley & Sons Ltd* (1924) 35 CLR 232 at 242.

I think that the correct conclusion on the evidence is that the defendants received and retained the goods in the character of vendees, that is, in circumstances showing a recognition of some contract of sale.

The contract which was made did not necessarily require that all the goods to which the first part of it referred (that is, the part relating to the floor level steel) should be delivered at the same time. No doubt if the seller had afterwards refused to deliver the bulk of the steel, the buyers would have been entitled to return the bolts and nuts, assuming that they had already taken them under a contract of sale. They would not become liable to pay for portion of the goods if the contract to supply the whole of them was not fulfilled by the seller. In this sense, there was not a final "acceptance" of the goods as being in performance of the contract. But this does not matter. It is not to acceptance in that sense that s 9 refers.

I do not think it makes any difference to the operation of s 9 if the part of the goods accepted and actually received is a small part only. The language of the section contains no such restriction on its operation.

In the circumstances, it is not necessary for me to express any opinions on two other submissions by which Mr Yeldham for the plaintiff, sought to show that it was entitled to succeed even if the contract, as such, was unenforceable because of s 9. One of these was a submission that he could succeed in an action for money due on accounts stated...

The other submission, which was alternative to counsel's main arguments, was that the original contract had ceased to exist because it had been repudiated by the defendants, and this repudiation had been accepted by the plaintiff and that, in these circumstances, the plaintiff could succeed on a *quantum meruit* claim, on the principles discussed in *Matthes v Carter* (1955) 55 SR (NSW) 357. It is not necessary to examine this argument. On the view of the facts which I take, it does not apply. By that I mean that I do not think the contract did cease to operate, in the sense required for the application of that argument.

For the reasons stated, there should be a verdict for the plaintiff for £2230, and I direct that judgment may be entered accordingly.

It is useful to compare the concept of acceptance under s 9 with that under s 38: see s 9(3). What justification is there for the different meanings of acceptance? What is the effect of acceptance under the respective sections? Compare *Abbott v Wolsey* [1895] 2 QB 97.

EARNEST OR PART PAYMENT

An earnest is some item of value which is given, in the same way as a cash deposit, as a guarantee that the buyer means business. If the buyer defaults it is not refundable. A cash deposit may serve two purposes, as a guarantee and as part payment of the price. The earnest or part payment must be acknowledged by the seller to be effective under s 9. In *Norton and Steele v Davison* [1899] 1 QB 401, an amount of £1 overpaid on a previous order by the defendant buyer was agreed to be applied as a part payment on the contract in question which was wholly oral. The agreement to apply the credit to the contract was held not to satisfy the requirements of the Sale of Goods Act. What questions of policy are raised by this decision? Do you consider it to be sound law?

NOTE OR MEMORANDUM

The note need not take any special form, but it must contain sufficient information to recognise unequivocally the pre-existence of the contract and indicate expressly or by reference to another document the essential terms of parties, names, description of goods and price. Where the only compliance with s 9 is a note signed by one party, the contract can be enforced *against* that party but *not by* him.

A statement of the terms of an oral contract included in a signed document such as an affidavit prepared for litigation can be relied upon provided it was in existence prior to commencement of the action to enforce the contract: *Dudgeon v Chie* (1955) 55 SR (NSW) 450.

The note can be signed by an agent on behalf of a party, including a postal clerk who signs a telegram for one of the parties. How is the connection between the telegram and the contract established?

Hoeper v Neldner
South Australia Supreme Court in Banco [1932] SASR 173

[Hoeper ordered chaff from Neldner by telephone. Neldner confirmed the order in writing but Hoeper refused to proceed. After many letters Neldner telegraphed: "No reply to my letters to you 20, 27 January and 5 February. When are you sending bags for January portion chaff contracts with me? Neldner." Hoeper retelegraphed in reply: "Waiting to see you personally re misunderstanding on your part re contract. Hoeper."

Neldner sued Hoeper for damages for non-acceptance of the chaff. Hoeper pleaded non-compliance with Sale of Goods Act 1895 (SA) s 4(1) (NSW) s 9(1)). The magistrate gave judgment for Neldner for £476/19/6. Hoeper appealed.]

Richards J (at 179–81): I do not consider that it could properly be held that the telegram by using the expression "misunderstanding re contract" necessarily recognised the existence of a contract, although, if it did recognise any contract, it may be conceded that it was the contract in question. It might, I think, refer to a disputed contention that there was a contract. But even if the proper interpretation of the telegram is that it recognised the contract sued on, that, although necessary (*Thirkell v Cambi* [1919] 2 KB 590), is not all that is required. It is necessary for the memorandum itself to be referred to. This principle appears to be recognised, expressly or impliedly, in all the reported cases. It was stated emphatically by Griffith CJ in *Thomson v McInnes* (1911) 12 CLR 562 at 569: "The reference, therefore, in the document signed must be to some other document as such, and not merely to some transaction or event in the course of which another document may or may not have been written." Indeed, it is difficult to see how otherwise it could be held that there is a note or memorandum in writing of the contract signed by the party to be charged or his agent. In the present case the only writing signed by the appellant or his agent is his telegram of 10 February, and unless that, in effect, incorporates some other document it is not a note or memorandum of the contract. How can it be said to incorporate the letter of 5 September 1930 merely by referring to the contract?

The natural meaning of the word "contract" is not a document, but a transaction; and an examination of the extrinsic evidence in this case, assuming that it is admissible for the present purpose, shews, I think, that such is its actual meaning in the telegram. Certainly, it does not establish that the sender of the telegram intended to refer to any documents . . . the evidence going to shew that "misunderstanding," if any, there was, seems clearly to disclose that the reference in the telegram relied on is to the contract itself and not to any memorandum of it, which, therefore, cannot be said to be incorporated in the telegram, or connected with it, by reference. It follows that there is no memorandum signed by the appellant or his agent of the contract sued on.

Sale of Goods

With regret I have to agree that the order should be made absolute and the appeal be allowed.

[**Murray CJ** and **Piper J** delivered judgments to the same effect.]

Appeal allowed.

SEVERABILITY AND THE ACTION OF QUANTUM MERUIT

The harshness of s 9 as illustrated by the above cases can sometimes be averted. For example:

(1) A contract may provide for the sale of goods and other services which are not covered by s 9. If the contract is severable because a number of separate items are designated with separate prices assigned to each, the part providing for services may be separately enforced though the sale itself is unenforceable under s 9.

(2) Even where the contract for sale and other services is entire because, for example, separate prices have not been specified, the court will ascertain the value of the goods sold in order to determine whether s 9 applies. If it does apply, and renders the contract of sale unenforceable, the other part can still be enforced on the basis of *quantum meruit* for the reasonable value of the services actually performed: *Harman v Reeve* (1856) 18 CB 587; 139 ER 1500.

(3) Where the contract is solely to manufacture goods for the buyer, it may be construed as a contract for work and labour and not subject to s 9. What test is to be applied? See *Brooks Robinson Pty Ltd v Rothfield*, p 21, *supra*. If it is held to be an unenforceable contract for sale of goods, can the manufacturer nevertheless recover on the basis of *quantum meruit*? Clearly he cannot simply sue for the contract price, or his profit margin if he has not performed the contract, since this would directly circumvent s 9. However, if the manufacturer has expended labour and materials in partially or wholly completing the work before the buyer repudiates, and the manufacturer rescinds the contract, he should be entitled to recover in *quantum meruit* the reasonable value of his services without relying on the unenforceable contract.

SHOULD S 9 BE REPEALED OR AMENDED?

C Grumfeld: Comment on Law Reform (Enforcement of Contracts) Act 1954
(which repealed inter alia Sale of Goods Act 1893 (UK) s 4)

(1954) 17 *MLR* 451

Few statutes in English law have been so consistently criticised for so long a period of time as the Statute of Frauds 1677. The principal result of its technical, procedural requirements was to afford an opportunity for technical, unmeritorious defences. Both the Judiciary and plaintiffs' counsel laboured hard to restrict the scope of its spacious working... After the mid-nineteenth century, its irrelevance to the realities of proof and procedure in the courts became quite spectacular. In all these circumstances, its persistence paid an impressive tribute to the inadequacy of law reform machinery in England.

Karl N Llewellyn: What Price Contract? — An Essay in Perspective
(1931) 40 *Yale LJ* 704 at 746–8

Prophylactic form

But just as no system of promise-enforcement can do its work without taking account of the fact that existence of forms commonly sufficient to enforcement may be produced by illicit means, so no system may ignore the value of forms as records and vouchers and reckonable evidence of what was agreed upon in that deal. Contracts are transactions, not mere events; and, as deliberate transactions, are capable of prophylactic regulation; since they are transactions relied upon, men have an interest in predictable security as to their legal effects. Hence for a variety of transactions, and by no means an ill-chosen assortment, the Statute of Frauds requires for enforceability a memorandum of the essential terms, signed by the borrower.

That statute is an amazing product. In it de Leon might have found his secret of perpetual youth. After two centuries and a half the statute stands, in essence better adapted to our needs than when it first was passed. By 1676 literacy (which need imply no great consistency in spelling) may well have been expected in England of such classes as would be concerned in the transactions covered by the statute's terms. Certainly, however, we had our period here in which that would hardly hold — we counted our men of affairs, in plenty, who signed by mark. But schooling has done its work. The idea, which must in good part derive from the statute, that contracts at large will do well to be in writing, is fairly well abroad in the land. "*His* word is as good as his bond" contains a biting innuendo preaching caution. Meantime the modern developments of business — large units requiring internal written records if files are to be kept straight, and officers informed, and departments coordinated, and the work of shifting personnel kept track of; the practice of confirming oral deals in writing, the use of typewriters, of forms — all these confirm the policy of the statute; all these reduce the price in disappointments exacted for its benefits.

[After referring to the pros and cons of the parol evidence rule, which precludes the proof of oral terms to vary a written contract which is in itself complete Llewellyn concluded:]

Yet the net effect of the two rules together, as they work into lay practice, and viewed simply in their effects outside of litigation, is almost certainly wholesome; both in encouraging permanent trustworthy record of agreements, and in inducing care in the making of that record.

THE POSITION UNDER THE UNIFORM COMMERCIAL CODE

The following extract from the Uniform Commercial Code now in force in virtually all American states contains some interesting points of difference.

2-201 Formal Requirements; Statute of Frauds (1) Except as otherwise provided in this section a contract for the sale of goods for the price of $500 or more is not enforceable by way of action or defense unless there is some writing sufficient to indicate that a contract for sale has been made between the parties and signed by the party against whom enforcement is sought or by his authorized agent or broker. A writing is not insufficient because it omits or incorrectly states a term agreed upon but the contract is not enforceable under this paragraph beyond the quantity of goods shown in such writing.

(2) Between merchants if within a reasonable time a writing in confirmation of the contract and sufficient against the sender is received and the party receiving it has reason to know its contents, it satisfies the requirements of subsection (1) against such party unless written notice of objection to its contents is given within 10 days after it is received.

(3) A contract which does not satisfy the requirements of subsection (1) but which is valid in other respects is enforceable
   (a) if the goods are to be specially manufactured for the buyer and are not suitable for sale to others in the ordinary course of the seller's business and the seller, before notice of repudiation is received and under circumstances which reasonably indicate that the goods are for the buyer, has made either a substantial beginning of their manufacture or commitments for their procurement; or
   (b) if the party against whom enforcement is sought admits in his pleading, testimony or otherwise in court that a contract for sale was made, but the contract is not enforceable under this provision beyond the quantity of goods admitted; or
   (c) with respect to goods for which payment has been made and accepted or which have been received and accepted (s 2-606).

A useful commentary on this section is contained in Sutton, "The Uniform Commercial Code and the Law of Contract" (1967) 5 *Syd LR* 398 at 414-15.

In Australia, Queensland and South Australia are the only states which have repealed the formal requirements section of their Sale of Goods Acts. It is interesting to note that in the 1972 parliamentary debate on the amendments to the Queensland Sale of Goods Act the only amendment which the state Labor opposition opposed was the repeal of this section. Their argument was that, from the viewpoint of the consumer, the existing provision provided some protection. They conceded that the main defect in that provision was the low limit of $20 and advocated its amendment to a commercially realistic figure of $100 rather than total repeal of the section: see (1973) 47 *ALJ* 111. The recommendation of the Law Reform Commission of New South Wales in its *Working Paper on The Sale of Goods* (1975) that the section should be repealed has not been implemented in that state.

Those who support the retention of Statute of Frauds requirements usually rely at least in part on the argument that the exceptions within the statute and those created by the courts are adequate to cover the hard cases. Much of the debate and litigation has focused on the scope of these exceptions. The situation varies somewhat between the various sections of the original statute. For example, the doctrine of part performance was developed by the equity courts to enable a plaintiff to prove by oral evidence and to enforce a contract where the defendant had induced or allowed the plaintiff to perform acts in fulfilment of, or referable only to, the contract where it would be unconscionable to allow the defendant to plead the statute. However, the doctrine is not recognised in relation to sales of goods, apparently because of its equitable origins and the fact that specific performance of a contract for sale of goods is rarely granted. In contrast, past performance is a recognised exception to the equivalent provisions regarding land transactions. See eg, Conveyancing Act 1919 (NSW) ss 54$_A$(2) and 23$_E$(d) and corresponding provisions in other states.

QUESTIONS

Question 6

What are the advantages and disadvantages of retaining s 9 of the Sale of Goods Act? What policy issues are raised by the retention of this provision in today's market place? Should it be amended or repealed? In answering the question consider similar provisions in other jurisdictions.

Question 7

(1) Carb Pty Ltd accepted a written but unsigned order from Handel Barr, a motor bike enthusiast, to supply five carburettors of Carb's own design for use by Barr in his racing bikes. The total price was $800. Is the contract enforceable?

(2) What difference (if any) would it make if
(a) Barr had supplied the design to Carb? or
(b) the number of carburettors ordered had been two? Or sixty?

(3) Assume that the contract provided that the five carburettors were to be built according to Barr's own design and, after Carb had manufactured the carburettors, Barr inspected them at Carb's factory, and said: "This is not how I designed them — I will not pay."
(a) Can Carb enforce the contract?
(b) Has Barr any available defence?
(c) Assume Barr had merely telephoned Carb and said "I am no longer interested in your carburettors". Carb had spent $400 tooling up to manufacture according to Barr's design. Advise Carb as to remedy and how much it can recover.

Question 8

(1) Do you agree with the decision in *Norton & Steele v Davison* [1899] 1 QB 401?
(2) Would it have made any difference if either
(a) the parties had agreed to treat Norton and Steele as having repaid the credit of £1 to Davison who then repaid the same amount as a deposit on the new contract without any money having actually changed hands; or

(b) the agreement for the set-off had been made after the contract of sale; or
(c) at the time the contract was made Steele had given Davison a signed receipt for £1.

FURTHER READING

For a general reference work on sale of goods, see Sutton, *Sales and Consumer Law in Australia and New Zealand,* 3rd ed, 1983.

The most comprehensive review of the present Sale of Goods legislation and proposals for reform is Law Reform Commission of New South Wales, *Working Paper on Sale of Goods,* 1975.

Students seeking a source of comparative or alternative approaches to sales could examine Uniform Commercial Code art 2.

Section 2: The Purpose and Scope of the Sale of Goods Act

Atiyah & Treitel, "Misrepresentation Act 1967" (1967) 30 *MLR* 369.
Greig, "Misrepresentation and Sales of Goods" (1971) 87 *LQR* 179.
Starke, "A Restatement of the Australian Law of Contract as a First Step Towards an Australian Uniform Contract Code" (1975) 49 *ALJ* 234.
Uniform Commercial Code art 1–102, 1–103.

Section 3: What is a Contract for Sale of Goods?

Aristoc Industries Pty Ltd v Wenham (Builders) Pty Ltd [1965] NSWR 581 at 586–7.
Collins Trading Co Pty Ltd v Maher [1969] VR 20.
Davies, "Implied Conditions as to Fitness in a Contract of Hire: An Anglo-Australian Conflict" (1964) 38 *ALJ* 277.
Deta Nominees Pty Ltd v Viscount Plastic Products Ltd [1979] VR 167.
Turner, "Common Law Implied Terms of Fitness in Contracts of Simple Hire and Hire-Purchase: An Analysis" (1972) 46 *ALJ* 560, 619.

Section 4: Formal Requirements: Is the Statute of Frauds Necessary?

Deta Nominees Pty Ltd v Viscount Plastic Products Ltd, supra.
McCormack v J B & L Nominees Pty Ltd [1981] WAR 198.
"The Statute of Frauds and the Business Community: A Re-appraisal in Light of Prevailing Practices" (1957) 66 *Yale LJ* 1038.
"The Statute of Frauds in Queensland" (1973) 47 *ALJ* 111.

CHAPTER 3

Implied Conditions in Contracts of Sale

"I do not believe that the Sale of Goods Act was designed to promote metaphysical discussions as to the nature of what is delivered, in comparison with what is sold. The test of description ... is intended to be a broader, more commonsense, test of a mercantile character."

Lord Wilberforce
Ashington Piggeries Ltd v Christopher Hill Ltd [1972] AC 441 at 489

Section 1: Implied Conditions in General
Section 2: Implied Terms: Title and Freedom from Encumbrances
Section 3: Implied Conditions: Conformity, Fitness and Quality

In this chapter, we focus upon conditions implied in sales and hiring contracts by the Sale of Goods Act (SGA). Comparisons are drawn to those implied by the Hire-Purchase Act (HPA) and Trade Practices Act (TPA). Section 1 provides an overview of the function of implied conditions and of the general scope of consumer legislation. Section 2 deals with the implied conditions as to the seller's title. In Section 3, the vital implied conditions of conformity with description and sample, and of fitness for purpose and merchantable quality are considered in depth. Because the operation of these conditions is interrelated, they are dealt with together in one section rather than being singled out for separate analysis.

SECTION 1: IMPLIED CONDITIONS IN GENERAL

Terms can be implied into a contract of sale or hire or for services by virtue of the common law or usage except to the extent precluded by statute: see eg SGA ss 19(1), (2), (3), 57. However, the most important sources of implied terms are the SGA, HPA and TPA. The English Sale of Goods Act 1893 set out primarily to codify the conditions which the common law already implied into every contract of sale but left the parties entirely free to vary or totally exclude these terms. For half a century these statutory terms formed the basis on which courts developed a matrix of interpretation and attempted to balance the rights of seller and buyer in both commercial and consumer transactions.

Since the introduction of the HPA and TPA, and special provisions for consumer sales in some states, the categories of commercial sales and consumer sales have been regulated under separate sets of rules. The overriding differences have been the stricter conditions imposed upon suppliers and restrictions upon the freedom to vary or exclude those conditions in the case of consumer transactions.

For present purposes, it is therefore intended to concentrate attention upon the implied conditions under SGA with comparisons to the HPA and TPA.

Teaching Materials and Cases on Commercial Transactions

The following schedule is intended only as a road map for finding the various provisions. It is obvious that detailed comparison of the various provisions demands careful perusal of every word of the sections themselves.

Implied Condition/ Warranty as to	Sale of Goods Act (NSW)	Hire-Purchase Act (Qld)	Trade Practices Act (Cth)
Title			Part V — *Consumer Transactions Only*
Right to sell	s 17(1) Can be excluded	s 5(1)(b) ⎫ non-	s 69(1)(a) — excludable under s 69(3)
Quiet possession	(2) expressly or by implication	(a) ⎬ excludable	(b) ⎫ can be qualified
Freedom from charge/encumbrance	(3) in all cases: s 57	(c) ⎭ s 33(1)	(c) ⎭ under s 69(3)
			Otherwise non-excludable: s 68.
Conformity			
Correspondence with description	s 18 — requires sale by description — can be excluded, but (i) not in a consumer sale: s 64(1) (ii) may be an express term (iii) may be a fundamental term		s 70 requires sale by description — does not apply to a sale by auction; otherwise non-excludable s 70(2) not excludable by self-selection
Correspondence with sample	s 20 — requires sale by sample; — can be excluded, but not in a consumer sale: s 64(1).		s 72 — requires sale by reference to sample in the course of business — does not apply to a sale by auction; otherwise non-excludable: s 68, subject to limitation in s 68A.
Quality			
Merchantable quality	s 19(2) requires: (a) purchase by description from (b) seller dealing in similar goods *Proviso* for defects where buyer has examined. Definition of "Merchantable Quality": s 64(3) Can be excluded, but not in a consumer sale: s 64(1) In consumer sale: (a) not applicable to defects brought to buyer's notice: s 64(4) (b) liability of seller of second-hand goods limited to cash price of the goods: s 64(9)	s 5(2) Need not be sold by description or by dealer *Proviso* for defects where hirer has examined Non-excludable except for second hand goods with hirer's written acknowledgement of exclusion: ss 5(2)(b), 33(1).	s 71(1) requires sale in course of business Need not be sold by description *Provisos* for (a) defects drawn to customer's attention (b) defects where hirer has examined. Definition of "Merchantable Quality": s 66(2) does not apply to a sale by auction; otherwise non-excludable: s 68, subject to limitation in s 68A.
Fitness for purpose	s 19(1) requires: (a) express/implied making known (b) reliance on seller's skill (c) seller deals in similar goods *Proviso* for specified goods sold under patent/trade name. Can be excluded, but not in a consumer sale: s 64(1).	s 5(3) requires express/implied making known by owner/dealer/servant/agent; Need not rely on dealer's skill and owner/dealer need not deal in similar goods; No proviso for goods sold under patent/trade name. Non-excludable except for second-hand goods with hirer's written acknowledgement of exclusion.	s 71(2) requires: (a) sale in the course of business (b) express/implied making known *Proviso* where no reliance or unreasonable to rely on seller's skill. Seller need not deal in similar goods. No proviso for goods sold under patent/trade name. Does not apply to a sale by auction; otherwise non-excludable: s 68, subject to limitation in s 68A.

SCOPE OF CONSUMER LEGISLATION

Although consumerism became one of the catchcries of the 1960s and '70s, the legislative framework is still emerging. A uniform pattern applies throughout Australia under Commonwealth TPA Pt V, and under state HPA and Consumer Credit Acts in South Australia, New South Wales and Victoria. While the respective SGA remain uniform in relation to commercial sales, some states have made special provisions for consumer sales: eg Sale of Goods Act 1923 (NSW) Pt VIII and Consumer Transactions Act 1972 (SA) Pt II. TPA Pt V Div 1 also regulates misleading advertising, and misrepresentation of goods or services. A variety of provisions strike at false trade descriptions, misleading advertising, inadequate standards in goods and information under a plethora of different state Acts: see eg Consumer Protection Act 1969 (NSW); Consumer Affairs Act 1970 (Qld); Trade Descriptions and False Advertisements Act 1936 (WA). The Consumer Credit Act (NSW) and Credit Act (Vic) provide for liability of credit providers and linked credit providers: s 24.

APPLICATION OF TRADE PRACTICES ACT PT V

The application of Pt V of the Act is limited in two different ways. First, because of the limited constitutional powers of the Commonwealth parliament, TPA concentrates its attention upon contracts in which the supplier is a corporation (relying upon s 51(xx) of the Constitution). However, by s 6(2)(c) and (h) the Act is given an extended operation to transactions in which the supplier is a person rather than a corporation subject to the restriction that the contract for the supply of goods or services is confined to a contract in the course of, or in relation to, trade or commerce:

(a) between Australia and places outside Australia (relying on trade and commerce power: Constitution s 51(i));
(b) among the states (relying on s 51(i));
(c) within a territory, between two territories (relying on the territories power: Constitution s 122).

The Act also applies to conduct engaged in by *persons* (as well as corporations) in the course of the supply of goods or services to the Commonwealth government or its instrumentalities (relying on Constitution s 52(1)) or by use of post, telegraph, telephone, radio or television (relying on posts and telegraphic power: Constitution s 51(v)).

Second, the terms implied by Pt V are deliberately limited:
(a) to transactions in which the corporation (or person in the situations outlined above) supplies goods or services *in the course of a business* (the one exception is s 69 regarding title, encumbrances and quiet possession);
(b) to transactions with consumers which are delimited under s 4B. The definition in this section deserves careful study.

The HPA provisions are also limited to consumer transactions in that the definition of "hire-purchase agreement" in s 2(1) excludes sales to persons engaged in selling goods of the same nature or description (wholesalers or retailers).

The diversity between definitions of consumer transactions may be further illustrated by the definition of "consumer sale" in the Sale of Goods Act (NSW) Pt VIII.

SECTION 2: IMPLIED TERMS: TITLE AND FREEDOM FROM ENCUMBRANCES

The Sale of Goods Act s 17 implies:
(a) a condition that the seller has a right to sell the goods;

(b) a warranty that the buyer shall have and enjoy quiet possession of the goods; and
(c) a warranty that the goods shall be free of any charge or encumbrance not declared or known to the buyer.

THE RIGHT TO SELL

The first of these is the most likely to raise difficulties.

Rowland v Divall
English Court of Appeal [1923] 2 KB 500

[The plaintiff, a motor dealer, bought a car for £334 from the defendant and used it for several months before reselling it. It was then discovered that the car had been stolen at some previous time and the plaintiff and his purchaser were compelled to surrender the car to the true owner. The plaintiff refunded the purchase price to his purchaser, and sued the defendant for £334 purchase price he had paid.]

Atkin LJ (at 506–7): ... It seems to me that in this case there has been a total failure of consideration, that is to say that the buyer has not got any part of that for which he paid the purchase money. He paid the money in order that he might get the property, and he has not got it. It is true that the seller delivered to him the de facto possession, but the seller had not got the right to possession and consequently could not give it to the buyer. Therefore the buyer, during the time that he had the car in his actual possession had no right to it, and was at all times liable to the true owner for its conversion. Now there is no doubt that what the buyer had a right to get was the property in the car, for the Sale of Goods Act expressly provides that in every contract of sale there is an implied condition that the seller has a right to sell; and the only difficulty that I have felt in this case arises out of the wording of s 11, sub-s 1(c) [NSW s 16(3)], which says that: "Where a contract of sale is not severable, and the buyer has accepted the goods ... the breach of any condition to be fulfilled by the seller can only be treated as a breach of warranty, and not as a ground for rejecting the goods and treating the contract as repudiated, unless there be a term of the contract, express or implied, to that effect." It is said that this case falls within that provision, for the contract of sale was not severable and the buyer had accepted the car. But I think that the answer is that there can be no sale at all of goods which the seller has no right to sell. The whole object of a sale is to transfer property from one person to another. And I think that in every contract of sale of goods there is an implied term to the effect that a breach of the condition that the seller has a right to sell the goods may be treated as a ground for rejecting the goods and repudiating the contract notwithstanding the acceptance, within the meaning of the concluding words of sub-s (c); or in other words that the sub-section has no application to a breach of that particular condition. It seems to me that in this case there must be a right to reject, and also a right to sue for the price paid as money had and received on failure of the consideration, and further that there is no obligation on the part of the buyer to return the car, for *ex hypothesi* the seller had no right to receive it. Under those circumstances can it make any difference that the buyer has used the car before he found out that there was a breach of the condition? To my mind it makes no difference at all. The buyer accepted the car on the representation of the seller that he had a right to sell it, and inasmuch as the seller had no such right he is not entitled to say that the buyer has enjoyed a benefit under the contract. In fact the buyer has not received any part of that which he contracted to receive—namely, the property and right to possession—and, that being so, there has been a total failure of consideration. The plaintiff is entitled to recover the £334 which he paid.

[**Bankes** and **Scrutton LJJ** delivered judgments to the same effect.]

Appeal allowed.

For a similar situation relating to a hire-purchase agreement, see *Warman v Southern Counties Car Finance Corp Ltd* [1949] 2 KB 576.

Where the person purporting to sell does not have title at that time (eg a hirer under an uncompleted hire-purchase agreement), but subsequently acquires title (eg by paying off the balance owing to the owner) the seller's completed title then "feeds" or cures the buyer's defective title. If the buyer gives notice of rescission before the seller perfects his title, the rescission is effective because there remains no contract to feed. Conversely the buyer cannot reject for breach of condition after the seller perfects his title which then vests automatically in the buyer: *Patten v Thomas Motors Pty Ltd* [1965] NSWR 1457; (1965) 83 WN (Pt 2) (NSW) 378. Compare *Butterworth v Kingsway Motors Ltd* [1954] 1 WLR 1286; [1954] 2 All ER 694.

A final question concerns what circumstances would indicate an intention of the parties that s 17(1) was not intended to apply. It has been held that this intention is implied in the case of a sheriff selling goods taken in execution of a judgment debt. In practice he should make the intention explicit by expressly stating that he is selling the "right title and interest (if any) of the judgment debtor" thereby clearly casting on the buyer the risk of adverse claims.

WARRANTY OF QUIET POSSESSION

This warranty would appear only to protect the buyer against interference by the seller himself or a third party with a lawful claim to possession. The warranty is not often utilised since most interferences with possession arise because of a defect in title for which s 17(1) is available. An interesting exception is *Microbeads AG v Vinhurst Road Markings Ltd* [1975] 1 WLR 218. Vinhurst purchased a road marking machine from Microbeads. The purchasers were dissatisfied with the machine and refused to pay the balance of purchase money. Subsequent to the sale, a third company Prismo obtained a patent which it claimed was infringed by the machine and sought an injunction to prevent Vinhurst using the machine. When sued for the outstanding purchase price, Vinhurst raised defences alleging breach of the implied condition as to title and quiet possession under English Sale of Goods Act ss 12(1) and (2) (NSW ss 17(1) and (2)). The Court of Appeal held that there was no breach of the implied condition as to title and right to sell under s 12(1) because the seller had the right to sell at the time when property was to pass. However, there was a breach of the implied warranty as to quiet possession under s 12(2) even though the patent was only granted and the claim for infringement made subsequent to the sale.

Under the HPA, similar terms are implied, although the owner only undertakes to have a right to sell and that the goods will be free from encumbrances at the time when the property is to pass. These terms cannot be excluded.

TPA s 69 follows the revised version of the English Sale of Goods Act s 12. It cannot be excluded from a consumer sale. However, where the contract or circumstances indicate that the seller intends to transfer only such title as he or a third person may have:

(a) the condition of right to sell does not apply;
(b) the warranty of freedom from encumbrances is limited to a warranty that all encumbrances known to the supplier have been disclosed to the consumer prior to contract; and
(c) the warranty of quiet possession is limited to the actions of the supplier or other person whose title he is transferring or anyone claiming through them.

QUESTIONS

Question 1

Under what conditions may s 17 SGA (NSW) and its implied terms be excluded? How does this section compare with other similar legislation? Can a seller who has no title to the goods which he purports to transfer to the buyer rectify the situation and avoid an action for breach of contract? Where the seller has title, under what conditions would he be in breach of s 17(1) or (2)?

Question 2

(1) Upon what basis was *Rowland v Divall* decided? Could it have been decided upon any other basis? Was the length of the use of the car by the purchaser relevant in deciding the case?

(2) Should the purchaser have been required to pay for the use of the car during that period?

(3) Would it have made a difference if the seller had known of the defective title when he purported to sell?

(4) Do the implied conditions of s 17 apply where the seller has no title whatsoever? Consider the definition in s 5(1).

SECTION 3: IMPLIED CONDITIONS: CONFORMITY, FITNESS AND QUALITY

These implied conditions determine the type and quality of goods which the seller must deliver to fulfil his contractual obligations. They go to the root of the contract in the commercial sense, and have generated much legal dispute and litigation. Before examining the fine print of the statutory provisions, it may be helpful to provide an overview of the position by reference to our basic example.

CONFORMITY

Sale by description. Carb Pty Ltd contracted to sell 20,000 carburettors to Mitzi Co. The contract, even if oral, would describe or identify the goods in some way. Even in a supermarket sale, goods are generally described on the label. Commonsense and the realities of the market place indicate that Carb should supply goods which conform to the contract. The common law rule is the same and is now codified in SGA s 18 and TPA s 70.

Sale by sample. Mitzi may have requested a sample carburettor and then ordered 20,000 on the basis of the sample. The Sale of Goods Act s 20 and TPA s 72 require that the bulk conforms to the sample in quality, and that Mitzi shall have a reasonable opportunity of comparing the bulk with the original sample. The bulk should have no defects which were not apparent from a reasonable examination of the sample.

Merchantable quality. If Carb supplies carburettors which just barely comply with the contractual description but are poorly finished or otherwise of inferior quality, Mitzi may be very disappointed but have no remedy for non-conformity. The respective Acts therefore imply conditions requiring that goods be of merchantable quality. The case law (and more recently the consumer protection provisions of the statutes) have been concerned with the meaning of merchantable quality. On the other hand, the legislature has provided some protection for a seller such as Carb where, for example, prior to contract, Mitzi examines the carburettors which have patent defects or Carb specifically draws them to Mitzi's attention. Note the varying formulations in SGA ss 19(2) and 64(3), (4); TPA ss 66(2) and 71 ; and HPA s 6(2).

Fitness for purpose. Prior to contract Mitzi may have indicated to Carb that it required the carburettors for a particular purpose, and expressly or impliedly relied on Carb's skill and judgment to supply goods suitable for that purpose. Carb's obligation in that situation is to supply goods which are suitable for that purpose.

The various conditions described above are not mutually exclusive. Some or all may apply to the one contract. Carb may sell carburettors by description and by sample to Mitzi who also relied on Carb's skill to choose or manufacture goods which will fulfil Mitzi's declared purpose. Carb may breach in one sale one or all of the implied conditions. Although these conditions may have an overlapping effect in a given situation, they each have their own exclusive area covering situations not covered by the other. For example, Carb may supply carburettors which conform to description and sample, are perfectly made, merchantable and suitable for most engines, but are wholly unsuitable for Mitzi's declared purpose: only SGA s 19(1) will have been breached.

To this point we have been discussing the question of what terms are implied in a contract. In some circumstances these implied terms will be excluded. Assuming that one or more of these terms are implied into the contract, the next question is whether they have been breached. This is a factual issue, requiring the physical attributes of the goods to be measured against the abstract legal language in the various sections. Questions of value and degree arise. How closely must goods conform to their description, or the sample? What do "merchantable" and "reasonably fit for that purpose" mean? What defects ought an examination reveal? Assuming breach of an implied condition, a final question is whether the buyer can reject the goods or only sue for damages, which will be considered in Chapter 4.

In examining these and other questions in the following cases, remember that some cases will involve more than one condition. However, the general order of treatment is in line with the above outline.

SALE BY DESCRIPTION: SGA s 18

SGA s 18 should be compared with TPA s 70; HPA has no corresponding provision. Note that the same phrase "by description" is used in SGA s 19(2) and that cases dealing with this aspect of the two sections tend to be cited interchangeably.

WHEN IS A SALE BY DESCRIPTION?

Elder Smith Goldsbrough Mort Ltd v McBride, Palmer (Third Party)
Supreme Court of New South Wales [1976] 2 NSWLR 631

[The defendants Dr and Mrs McBride purchased a bull at an auction sale of stud cattle conducted by the plaintiff company on behalf of the owners Mr and Mrs Palmer who were joined as third parties to the action. The defendants refused to pay the purchase price of $21,000 because the bull proved to be infertile. The plaintiff sued the defendants for the price, and the defendants sought indemnity against the vendors Mr and Mrs Palmer.]

Sheppard J (at 640): The learned authors of *Benjamin on Sale*, 8th ed, p 615, say as to sales by description: "Sales by description may, it seems, be divided into sales:

"1. Of unascertained or future goods, as being of a certain kind or class, or to which otherwise a 'description' in the contract is applied.

"2. Of specific goods, bought by the buyer in reliance, at least in part, upon the description given, or to be tacitly inferred from the circumstances, and which identifies the goods.

"So far as any descriptive statement is a mere warranty or only a representation, it is no part of the description ... It is clear that there can be no contract for the sale of unascertained or future goods except by some description ... It follows that the only sales not by description are sales of specific goods *as such*. See *Boys v Rice* (1908) 27 NZLR 456 where the subject is considered. Specific goods may be sold as such when they are sold without any description, express or implied; or where any statement made about them is not essential to their identity; or where, though the goods are described, the description is not relied upon, as where the buyer buys the goods such as they are."

The passage, as it was set out on p 641 of the seventh edition of *Benjamin on Sale*, was adopted by Sellers J, as he then was, as being "a concise and convenient summary of the law to be applied" in *Joseph Travers and Sons Ltd v Longel Ltd* (1948) 64 TLR 150 at 153.

A sale of specific goods will not usually be a sale by description, where the buyer has had an opportunity of inspecting the goods. Neither the ship in *Barr v Gibson* (1838) 3 M & W

390, nor the reaping machine in *Varley v Whipp* [1900] 1 QB 513 was able to be inspected by the buyer. And see *Parsons v Sexton* (1847) 136 ER 763. But there are cases where, despite the availability of the article to be sold for inspection, there will nevertheless be a sale by description: *Thornett & Fehr v Beers & Son* [1919] 1 KB 486; *Chalmers' Sale of Goods*, 17th ed, p 119. At that page in Chalmers the learned authors say: "Where goods are described by the contract, and the buyer contracts in reliance on that description, there is a sale by description even if the goods be specific ... And it may apply even where he (the buyer) has seen and selected the goods, if the deviation of the goods from the description is not apparent": [1900] 1 KB 513.

It is true that in *Varley v Whipp* Channell J, referring to the English counterpart of s 18 of the Act, said that the most usual application of the section was to the case of unascertained goods, but thought that it must also be applied to cases such as the one before him where there was no identification otherwise than by description. But this absolute statement is criticised by *Benjamin* in a note at p 614: see also *Brooklyn Lodge Pty Ltd v Ryan*, Court of Appeal, 27 June 1972, unreported.

Here the bull was made available for inspection, but the evidence of the two veterinary surgeons satisfies me that no inspection of the bull able to be made by or on behalf of the defendants at or about the time of the sale would have revealed the bull's condition. It was in every sense a latent defect. Even if it had been possible to take a sample of the bull's semen, which the evidence does not suggest was so, the fact that the sample was unsatisfactory would not itself have necessarily indicated the condition. It may simply have been due to the fact that the bull had been prepared for the show and was in show condition, and not to the more serious and underlying problem which the subsequent tests have revealed. The veterinary surgeons were only able to reach their conclusions after a number of tests over a period of months, and after substantial numbers of cows had been put to the bull without result. No examination of the bull by a veterinary surgeon on behalf of the defendants would, therefore, have availed them anything, and the fact that there was provided to them an opportunity to inspect the animal does not prevent the sale from being one by description if the description goes to such a matter as its fertility.

The description which is alleged is that the bull was sold as a breeding, or stud, or stud breeding bull. A consideration of the entirety of the circumstances of the sale, particularly that it was a sale of stud stock, that it was so described in a catalogue issued on behalf of the third parties and which distinguished between this sale and a sale of fat cattle to be held on another day, and the substance of the conversation or conversations between McBride and Crowe before the sale (not because of what was actualy said, but because of the underlying assumption on which it or they were held) lead me to conclude that, although the sale was of specific goods it was nevertheless a sale by description, the description being "a breeding bull". That was what the third parties, by their agent, the plaintiff, put up for sale at the auction; not simply a bull, but a breeding bull. In reaching this conclusion I have borne in mind that there is, as Channell J said in *Varley v Whipp* [1900] 1 KB 513 at 515 a fine line between something which identifies what is sold and something which amount to a mere collateral warranty. Here, as what I have so far said indicates, I have come to the conclusion that what was sold was a breeding bull, that there was a sale of Midgeon Supreme by that description and that there was, therefore, by virtue of s 18 of the Act, an implied condition in the contract which was made between the third parties and the defendants that the bull would correspond with that description.

[His Honour then considered whether there was an express condition that the bull was a breeding or stud bull, and continued:]

Without overlooking any distinction which there may be between the actual implication of a condition into a contract (a matter controlled by the provisions of the Act) and the ascertainment of a description of goods, not from express words but from surrounding circumstances and that description so derived giving rise to an express condition, I think the better view here is that the sale was one by description within the meaning of s 18 of the Act giving rise to the necessity, by reason of that section, to imply the term.

[His Honour then found a breach by the third parties (who had tendered the bull to auction) of the implied condition to deliver a breeding or fertile bull and that there should be a verdict for the defendants against them and continued at 650:]

Implied Conditions in Contracts of Sale

The defendants still have the bull, and there is evidence that its value for slaughtering purposes is $500. The defendants have otherwise lost the entirety of the sum of $21,000 which they are liable to pay to the plaintiff. There will, therefore, be a verdict for the defendants against the third parties upon the first count in the sum of $20,500, and judgment accordingly.

Note the other cases extracted below, which also deal with the question of sale by description: *Australian Knitting Mills Ltd v Grant*—judgment of Dixon J in the High Court, and Lord Wright for the Privy Council; and *Ashington Piggeries Ltd v Christopher Hill Ltd*.

SALES IN SELF-SERVICE STORES

Final Report of the Committee on Consumer Protection, 1962

[The Molony Committee considered the uncertain position under the English Sale of Goods Act 1893 (para 441):]

The shop counter across which the customer asks for what he wants has ceased to be the prominent feature of retail establishments it once was. The customer is now encouraged to make his choice unaided by a sales assistant. A very considerable proportion of consumer goods are selected from shelves in self-service stores or from open counters or racks in shops that still maintain some sales staff. It is questionable whether these sales are "by description" and if not, the customer has no shred of right in law to complain of a defective purchase. This form of trading is on the increase and may well extend to a much wider range of article with the growth of discount houses. ...

The English Act has now been amended and the following provision inserted in the corresponding TPA s 70.

70 (2) A supply of goods is not prevented from being a supply by description for the purposes of sub-section (1) by reason only that, being exposed for sale or hire, they are selected by the consumer.

SALE BY SAMPLE: SGA s 20

SGA s 20 should be compared with TPA s 72. Does the phrase "by reference to a sample" indicate a change in scope from SGA s 20?

SGA s 20(2)(c) and TPA s 72(c) should be considered in conjunction with SGA s 19(2) and TPA s 71(1).

HPA has no provision equivalent to SGA s 20.

LG Thorne & Co Pty Ltd v Thomas Borthwick & Sons (A/asia) Ltd
Supreme Court of New South Wales in Banco (1956) 56 SR (NSW) 81

[The plaintiff purchased 50 drums of neatsfoot oil from the defendant. The written documents contained a complete contract and made no reference to samples; however, samples had been shown by the defendant to the seller during negotiations prior to signing the documents. The trial judge held the contract was a sale by sample and that the bulk did not correspond with the sample. The defendant appealed.]

Street CJ (at 87): ... The substantial matter which has been argued is whether the contract proved between the two parties amounted to a contract for a sale by sample. If it was such a sale, then there would be an implied term that the bulk should correspond with the sample, and the plaintiff company, having established on uncontradicted evidence that the bulk did not so correspond, would be entitled to recover.

But the mere fact that a sample has been shown by the intending vendor to the prospective purchaser during the course of negotiations leading up to a sale does not necessarily make the final contract a contract of sale by sample. If the contract is reduced to writing after the sample has been shown and makes no reference to this fact, then the written contract, if it be a complete contract, cannot have the added term incorporated in it. In *Meyer v Everth* (1814) 4 Camp 22; 171 ER 8 the sale concerned 50 hogsheads of sugar loaves, a sample of sugar having been produced and shown by the defendants to the plaintiff. No reference, however, was made to this fact in the bought note, and Lord Ellenborough held that the plaintiff was not entitled to recover because the sugar supplied was not equal in quality to the sample. Lord

Ellenborough said: "It was no part of the contract that the sugar should be equal to the sample. Where goods are sold in this way, I think evidence might be admissible to show that, at the time of the sale, a sample was fraudulently exhibited to deceive the buyers, whereby the plaintiff has been induced to purchase the commodity, which turned out of greatly inferior quality and value. But when the sale note is silent as to the sample, I cannot permit it to be incorporated into the contract. This would be contrary to *Meres v Ansell* 3 Wils 275 and would amount to an admission of parol evidence to contradict a written document": Camp at 23; ER at 8.

The law was laid down to the same effect in *Tye v Fynmore* (1813) 3 Camp 462; 170 ER 1446, *Gardiner v Gray* (1815) 4 Camp 144; 171 ER 46, and *Ginner v King* (1890) 7 TLR 140. All these were cases where, after a sample had been shown, a note was made of the contract without reference to the sample, and in each case it was held that there could not be incorporated in the contract a term that the bulk should correspond with the sample. These cases are of some antiquity, but are still cited for the general proposition that the exhibition of a sample during negotiations for the contract "does not of itself render it a sale by sample, and if there be a sale note which does not refer to the sample, this is not a sale by sample": *Chitty on Contracts*, 21st ed, 1955, Vol 2, p 632. The law is laid down to the same effect and the same cases are cited in *Benjamin on Sale*, 8th ed, 1950, p 653 *et seq*.

The general rule concerning the use of parol evidence to add to or vary a written contract is clear: "By the general rules of the common law, if there be a contract which has been reduced into writing, verbal evidence is not allowed to be given of what passed between the parties, either before the written instrument was made, or during the time that it was in a state of preparation, so as to add to or subtract from, or in any manner to vary or qualify the written contract.": per Denman CJ in *Goss v Lord Nugent* (1833) 5 B & Ad 58 at 64, 65; 110 ER 715.

If the written agreement in question, signed after due consideration, contains on its face a complete contract with provision for all matters relevant to the particular transaction involved, then the court will not, in general, allow evidence to be given for the purpose of establishing that some additional term agreed upon between the parties has been omitted. There are, of course, exceptions to this rule. Thus, in *Cameron & Co v Slutzkin Pty Ltd* (1923) 32 CLR 81, a sample was submitted before the contract was made, and evidence was held to be properly admissible for the purpose of identifying the subject matter of the contract. The object of this evidence was to show the sense which the parties themselves had attached to the name they had used in the description of the goods which were the subject matter of the sale. Another exception exists in cases where it is claimed that the full agreement is not contained in the writing but the document in question only contains part of the contract between the parties. In such cases the contract may be found partly in the written document and partly in the oral or written communications of the parties leading up to the written document. But if the written document is clear on its face and contains all terms appropriate to the transaction, and is signed by the parties as the record of their agreement, then further evidence is not admissible.

In the present case the document sent by the defendant company to the plaintiff company and confirmed by the latter, and referred to in the letter of 31 July 1952, sets out the arrangement with a considerable degree of particularity ... In my view, the parties appear to have set down all the terms which they regarded as necessary to be incorporated in the contract between them, although undoubtedly in the preliminary discussions and negotiations the plaintiff company had insisted upon having a sample and obviously entered into the contract in the belief that the bulk would correspond with the samples which had been analysed. But none the less, when the written contract provided for the analysis of the oil which was to be the subject matter of the contract, it did no more than refer to it as refined neatsfoot oil, with a limit on the free fatty acid content. I am not able to distinguish this case from those to which I have earlier referred, and of which *Meyer v Everth* may be taken as an example. There would seem little doubt that the purchaser in that case only bought after seeing the sample, and bought in the expectation of getting in bulk sugar similar to the sample, but none the less evidence was not allowed to be given for the purpose of adding to the sale note a further term that the sale was a sale by sample. In the present case, in view of the fact that the document contains a clear description of the oil in question, fixes the price and method of delivery, and makes provision for other contingencies which might possibly arise in the carrying out of the contract, I find it difficult to hold, on the authorities, that it is open to the plaintiff to prove that there was a further term agreed upon between the parties, namely, that the bulk should comply with the sample.

I reach this conclusion with some reluctance, for I am confident that it was the common understanding of both parties that the plaintiff was buying as a result of its inspection of the samples and would not have bought unless they had been satisfactory and complied with its requirements. The defendant, in the correspondence which took place after the plaintiff refused to accept the goods, never suggested that it was not a sale by sample, but asserted that the oil supplied was in fact equivalent to the sample, and only raised this answer to the plaintiff company's claim after litigation had been entered upon. That, however, does not seem to me to be sufficient to overcome the general rule with regard to parol variations of written contracts, and with some regret I think that his Honour fell into error in this regard and the appeal must therefore be allowed.

I think, however, that in all the circumstances of this case a new trial should be ordered rather than judgment entered for the defendant. As I have pointed out, it appears to me that the parties clearly contemplated that a satisfactory sample was an essential preliminary to any contract being entered into, and it was also understood that the bulk, when supplied, would correspond with the sample.

[**Herron J** (dissenting) held that the parties intended that the sale be by sample, and that the written contract did not contain the whole of the terms of the contract. The whole of the facts and circumstances, oral and written, should be examined as the trial judge did, and his finding that there was a sale by sample ought not to be disturbed. The appeal should be dismissed.

Roper CJ in Eq delivered a judgment agreeing with Street CJ.]

Appeal allowed.

MERCHANTABLE QUALITY AND FITNESS FOR PURPOSE: SGA s 19

Australian Knitting Mills and John Martin & Co Ltd v Grant
High Court of Australia (1933) 50 CLR 387

Dixon J (at 412): The respondent has recovered damages for personal injuries against the manufacturer and the retailer of undergarments which have been found to be the cause of a serious disorder of his skin. The judgment against them was joint and both appeal against it. The manufacturer was sued in tort; the retailer, in contract. The retailer is a shopkeeper which in the ordinary way sold to the plaintiff two pairs of underpants and two singlets of the other defendant's manufacture. The plaintiff has obtained a finding by the learned Chief Justice of South Australia that the underpants were in an improper condition because the webbing at the ends of the legs contained sodium sulphite so as to be unfit for the purpose of wearing. This finding of fact was attacked on behalf of the appellants. But on their behalf it was also contended that, even if the finding stood, neither of them was liable for the damages suffered by the plaintiff. The manufacturer was held liable upon the ground that in undertaking the manufacture of underclothes, which it sold to retailers put up in a form in which they were expected to sell them to their customers, the manufacturer incurred a duty to exercise reasonable care that they should contain nothing likely to harm the wearer, a duty which it was inferred had not been fulfilled. The manufacturer, besides denying any want of care in fact, maintained that in point of law no such duty existed towards the plaintiff. In this court, the question whether the contention is well founded must depend upon the interpretation of the decision of the House of Lords in *Donoghue v Stevenson* [1932] AC 562. On the one side it is said that, in the case of a thing not of its own nature dangerous and not known to be dangerous because of some special property, the manufacturer's duty of care to users of the article who have not acquired it immediately from him was, by that decision, held to exist only when he establishes a "special relation" with them by putting up the article in such a form that until the consumer or user is about to consume or use it all reasonable opportunity of examining, testing or judging of its condition is excluded and all likelihood of alteration of or interference with it by intermediaries is removed. On the other side it is said that it is at least enough if the manufacturer shows, by labelling, tying or otherwise, that he contemplates the consumer's or user's receiving the article exactly as it left the manufacturer.

But for reasons which will appear I find it unnecessary to decide whether the manufacturer incurred a duty of care to the plaintiff.

The plaintiff based his case against the retailer upon each of two conditions said to be implied under s 14 of the Sale of Goods Act 1895 (SA) which transcribes s 14 of the English Act. The learned Chief Justice considered that in the sale of the underclothes, a condition was implied under this provision that they should be reasonably fit for the purpose of wearing. He held that, in requesting to be supplied with underclothes for himself, the plaintiff had made known to the seller the particular purpose for which the goods are required so as to show that the buyer relied on the seller's skill or judgment. It is settled that the purpose for which goods are supplied may be "particular" within the meaning of this provision although it is the sole use for which goods of that kind are adapted. The purpose need not be some special use or requirement: *Priest v Last* [1903] 2 KB 148 (CA); (1903) 89 LT 33, per Walton J; *Wallis v Russell* (1902) 2 LR 585. Thus in the case of food where the supplier is commonly considered responsible for seeing to the quality, state or freshness of the article little difficulty seems to have been felt in implying a condition upon a sale by a shopkeeper or retailer that it is reasonably fit for eating or drinking: compare *Frost v Aylesbury Dairy Co* [1905] 1 KB 608; *Jackson v Watson & Sons* [1909] 2 KB 193 at 202, per Farwell LJ; *Chaproniere v Mason* (1905) 21 TLR 633; and *R v Manchester Profiteering Committee; Ex parte Lancashire and Yorkshire Railway Co* (1920) 84 JP 177 at 181; 36 TLR 593 at 594, per Bankes LJ.

When an article is sold for immediate consumption or use and the purpose to which it is to be put enters in to the very description under which it is sold, to imply a condition that it is fit to be so consumed or used is or, apart from the statute, would be an ordinary application of the general principles of contract. But the basis of the implication would be found in the nature of the transaction rather than in the buyer's reliance or appearance of reliance upon the seller's skill or his judgment. Thus, in 1829, in *Jones v Bright* (1829) 5 Bing 533 at 544; 130 ER 1167 at 1172, Best CJ considered it to be "a broad principle: If a man sells an article, he thereby warrants that it is merchantable,—that it is fit for some purpose ... If he sells it for a particular purpose, he thereby warrants it fit for that purpose": compare *Brown v Edgington* (1841) 2 Man & G 279; 133 ER 751; *Black v Elliot* (1859) 7 F & F 595; 175 ER 868; *Harman v Bennett* (1858) 1 F & F 400; 175 ER 781; *Beer v Walker* (1877) 37 LT 278; *Burrows v Smith* (1894) 10 TLR 246; and *Davis v Miller* (1894) 10 TLR 286. It has been authoritatively declared that sub-s 1 of s 14 made no change in the common law: *Manchester Liners Ltd v Rea Ltd* [1922] 2 AC 74. But it does not follow that the form in which the provision is expressed may now be disregarded or given an application which its natural meaning would not suggest. It is true that in *Rea's* case at 85, 86 Lord Atkinson formulated propositions or presumptions which may tend to produce a result less easily reached if affirmative proof were exacted that the buyer did in fact so make known the purpose as actually to show that he relied on the seller's skill or his judgment. But Lord Sumner at 89, 90 said: "The buyer has to make known, expressly or by implication, the particular purpose for which the goods are required. He has to do this, so as to show that he trusts the seller's skill and judgment to supply something reasonably fit for the purpose ... The words of s 14(1) are 'so as to show', not 'and also shows'. They are satisfied, if the reliance is a matter of reasonable inference to the seller and to the court."

In *Medway Oil and Storage Co v Silica Gel Corp* (1928) 33 Com Cas 195 Lord Sumner, in a judgment delivered for a House consisting of himself, Lord Atkinson and Lord Warrington, made a pronouncement upon s 14(1) which apparently was intended as an authoritative exposition. He said: "On a scrutiny of s 14(1) of the Sale of Goods Act, I think these propositions may be stated upon it: (a) The buyer's reliance is a question of fact to be answered by examining all that was said or done with regard to the proposed transaction on either side from its first inception to the conclusion of the agreement to purchase. (b) The section does not say that the reliance on the seller's skill or judgment is to be exclusive of all reliance on anything else, on the advice, for example, of the buyer's own experts or the use of his own knowledge or commonsense. Indeed it would never be possible to be sure that the element of reliance on the seller entered into the matter at all unless the buyer made some statement to that effect. It follows that the reliance in question must be such as to constitute a substantial and effective inducement which leads the buyer to agree to purchase the commodity. (c) This warranty, though no doubt an implied one, is still contractual; and, just as a seller may refuse to contract except upon the terms of an express exclusion of it, so he cannot be supposed to consent to the liability which it involves unless the buyer's reliance on him, on which the liability rests, is shown, and shown to him. The Tribunal must decide whether the circumstances brought to his knowledge showed this to him as a reasonable man or not; but there must be evidence to bring it home to his mind before the case for the warranty can be launched against him.

"My Lords, I would like to add a few commonplace observations. One naturally asks, why should any buyer ever be supposed not to rely on the seller's skill or judgment? It can do him no harm to do so, and may do him some good. Till the seller refuses to deal at all unless any such reliance is renounced surely a man of sense must be deemed to want to get for himself all that the law allows ... In this case I rather think that this may have been the view present to the mind of Rowlatt J ... He would appear to have thought that reliance on the buyer's part follows almost as a matter of course from the communication of his purpose whenever he knows less than the seller does about the substance which he is minded to buy. My Lords, I think this will in most cases be a question of degree. To go into a chemist's shop for something for your toothache; to order milk for your baby from a dairy; to write to a coal merchant that your ship is lying in his port and to ask him to bunker her, are simple cases in which reliance is not indeed presumed in law but is obvious in fact. But reliance on another and not on yourself is not a course which is always either obvious or probable; it may be so far from what prudence would dictate as to be neither."

In the present case, I think the difficulty in implying the conditions arises from the necessity which this statement emphasises of an actual reliance upon the skill or judgment of the seller as a material inducement to the buyer. If the circumstances of the sale did exhibit such a reliance, it was exhibited to the seller. But, in respect of underclothing sold by a retailer under a well-known manufacturer's brand, it may be doubted whether the ordinary buyer takes any account of the skill or the judgment of the retailer. Indeed, there is some inconsistency between the argument that the manufacturer by the form in which the underclothing is put up brings himself into a special relation with the ultimate purchaser or user, and the argument that the purchaser relies on the intermediaries' skill or judgment in selecting or purveying it for the purpose of wear. But, as the plaintiff relies upon another condition, which, I think, must be implied, the case cannot, I think, be disposed of on the ground that the condition of reasonable fitness is not made out, and, in these circumstances, it is the better course to refrain from forming a concluded view upon a matter of such general application. It must be remembered in connection with the implication of the condition of reasonable fitness that s 14 of the Sale of Goods Act provides that there is no implied warranty or condition as to the quality or fitness for any particular purpose of goods supplied under a contract of sale except in the cases stated in the section. If, therefore, promises which, upon previous authorities, would be contained in a sale of some common kind cannot be referred to the exceptions stated in the provision, the statute has made important changes in the rights springing from everyday transactions.

It is the second of these exceptions upon which the plaintiff also relies. The exception is as follows: "Where goods are bought by description from a seller who deals in goods of that description (whether he be the manufacturer or not), there is an implied condition that the goods shall be of merchantable quality. Provided that if the buyer has examined the goods, there shall be no implied condition as regards defects which such examination ought to have revealed."

Specific or ascertained goods may be "bought by description" within the meaning of this provision; it is not limited to unascertained goods: *Varley v Whipp* [1900] 1 QB 513; *Wren v Holt* [1903] 1 KB 610; *Boys v Rice* (1908) 27 NZLR 1038; *H Beecham & Co v Francis Howard & Co* [1921] VLR 428; *Morelli v Fitch & Gibbons* [1928] 2 KB 636. Further, as appears from the proviso, the buyer may, at or before the time of sale, have examined the goods and so established their identity independently of the description. When identified goods are sold, it is obvious that they remain the subject of the sale whether they do, or do not, correspond with the description which the parties have given them. But, however certainly the identity of the goods may be established, the parties must, since the intention is expressed or communicated, refer in some way to the goods. They must use some "description" to refer to them. A difficulty, therefore, cannot but arise in determining when the sale is "by" the description and when not. Apparently the distinction is between sales of things sought or chosen by the buyer because of their description and of things of which the physical identity is all important. When the ground upon which the goods are selected or identified is their correspondence to a description and when, therefore, it may be said that the buyer primarily relies upon their classification or possession of attributes, then, notwithstanding that they are bought as specific goods ascertained and identified, the goods are bought by description. In the ordinary case of a sale over the counter by a shopkeeper to a customer, who calls for an article of a given description, inspects the specimens produced, and buys one, the transaction is a sale by description. There is in such a case a condition that the goods are of merchantable quality but a condition which, because of the examination, is qualified by the proviso to the sub-section and extends only to defects not reasonably discoverable by such an examination.

The condition that goods are of merchantable quality requires that they should be in such an actual state that a buyer fully acquainted with the facts and, therefore, knowing what hidden defects exist and not being limited to their apparent condition would buy them without abatement of the price obtainable for such goods if in reasonably sound order and condition and without special terms. See *Bristol Tramways & Carriage Co v Fiat Motors Ltd* [1910] 2 KB 831 at 840; *Jackson v Rotax Motor and Cycle Co* [1910] 2 KB 937 at 950; *Morelli v Fitch & Gibbons* [1928] 2 KB 636; *H Beecham & Co v Francis Howard & Co* [1921] VLR 428.

The plaintiff, in my opinion, in buying the underclothing in the ordinary course "over the counter" obtained the benefit of such a condition. This conclusion makes it necessary, at any rate for the purpose of ascertaining the liability of one of the appellants, the retailer, to consider the question of fact, namely, whether any of the underwear when supplied to the plaintiff was in an improper condition because of the presence of harmful chemical agents. The ultimate statement of this issue of fact may not, perhaps, be precisely identical for the purpose of all three causes of action set up by the plaintiff. But, in the circumstances of the case, it is, I think, correct in substance that the plaintiff fails to establish negligence in the manufacturer and to establish a breach of the condition that the clothing should be reasonably fit for the purpose of his wear unless he has proved that the legs of the underpants contained some sulphur compound of such a strength or of such an amount that a real likelihood of their proving a source of injury to some wearer existed at the time of sale ... [His Honour then considered the factual claim against the manufacturer in negligence and concluded that it had not been established.

Starke and **McTiernan JJ** delivered judgments to the similar effect.

Evatt J (dissenting) held that the plaintiff was entitled to recover from the retailer for breach of the implied condition that the underwear was reasonably fit for the purpose of wear, and from the manufacturer for negligent breach of his duty of care to the plaintiff.]

Appeal allowed. Judgment for the defendants.

[The plaintiff then appealed to the Privy Council.]

Grant v Australian Knitting Mills Ltd
Privy Council [1936] AC 85

[The judgment of their Lordships was delivered by Lord Wright.]

Lord Wright (at 97): ... So far as concerns the retailers, Mr Green conceded that if it were held that the garments contained improper chemicals and caused the disease, the retailers were liable for breach of implied warranty, or rather condition, under s 14 of the South Australia Sale of Goods Act 1895, which is identical with s 14 of the English Sale of Goods Act 1893. [His Lordship then set out the terms of the section.]

He limited his admission to liability under exception (ii), but their Lordships are of opinion that liability is made out under both exception (i) and exception (ii) to s 14, and feel that they should so state out of deference to the conflicting views expressed in the court below. Section 14 begins by a general enunciation of the old rule of *caveat emptor*, and proceeds to state by way of exception the two implied conditions by which it has been said the old rule has been changed to the rule of *caveat venditor*: the change has been rendered necessary by the conditions of modern commerce and trade. The section has been recently twice discussed by the House of Lords, once in *Medway Oil and Storage Co v Silica Gel Corp* (1928) 33 Com Cas 195 and again in *Cammell Laird & Co v Manganese Bronze and Brass Co* [1934] AC 402. There are numerous cases on the section, but as these were cited below it is not necessary to detail them again. The first exception, if its terms are satisfied, entitles the buyer to the benefit of an implied condition that the goods are reasonably fit for the purpose for which the goods are supplied, but only if that purpose is made known to the seller "so as to show that the buyer relies on the seller's skill or judgment". It is clear that the reliance must be brought home to the mind of the seller, expressly or by implication. The reliance will seldom be express: it will usually arise by implication from the circumstances: thus to take a case like that in question, of a purchase from a retailer, the reliance will be in general inferred from the fact that a buyer goes to the shop in the confidence that the tradesman has selected his stock with skill and judgment: the retailer need know nothing about the process of manufacture: it is immaterial whether he be manufacturer or not: the main inducement to deal with a good retail shop is the expectation that the tradesman will have bought the right goods of a good make: the goods sold must be, as they were in the present case, goods of a description which it is in the course of the seller's business to supply: there is no need to specify in terms the particular purpose for which the buyer requires the goods, which is none the less the particular purpose within the meaning of the section, because it is the only purpose for which any one would ordinarily want the goods. In this case the garments were naturally intended, and only intended, to be worn next the skin. The proviso does not apply to a case like the sale of Golden Fleece-make such as is here in question, because Golden Fleece is neither a patent nor a trade name within the meaning of the proviso to exception (i). With great deference to Dixon J, their Lordships think that the requirements of exception (i) were complied with. The conversation at the shop in which the appellant discussed questions of price and of the different makes did not affect the fact that he was substantially relying on the retailers to supply him with a correct article.

The second exception in a case like this in truth overlaps in its application the first exception; whatever else merchantable may mean, it does mean that the article sold if only meant for one particular use in ordinary course, is fit for that use; merchantable does not mean that the thing is saleable in the market simply because it looks all right; it is not merchantable in that event if it has defects unfitting it for its only proper use but not apparent on ordinary examination: that is clear from the proviso, which shows that the implied condition only applies to defects not reasonably discoverable to the buyer on such examination as he made or could make. The appellant was satisfied by the appearance of the underpants; he could not detect, and had no reason to suspect, the hidden presence of the sulphites: the garments were saleable in the sense that the appellant, or any one similarly situated and who did not know of their defect, would readily buy them: but they were not merchantable in the statutory sense because their defect rendered them unfit to be worn next the skin. It may be that after sufficient washing that defect would have disappeared; but the statute requires the goods to be merchantable in the state in which they were sold and delivered; in this connection a defect which could easily be cured is as serious as a defect that would not yield to treatment. The proviso to exception (ii) does not apply where, as in this case, no examination that the buyer could or would normally have made would have revealed the defect. In effect, the implied condition of being fit for the particular purpose for which they are required, and the implied condition of being merchantable, produce in cases of this type the same result. It may also be pointed out that there is a sale by description even though the buyer is buying something displayed before him on the counter: a thing is sold by description, though it is specific, so long as it is sold not merely as the specific thing but as a thing corresponding to a description, eg, woollen undergarments, a hot-water bottle, a second-hand reaping machine, to select a few obvious illustrations.

The retailers, accordingly, in their Lordships' judgment are liable in contract: so far as they are concerned, no question of negligence is relevant to the liability in contract. But when the position of the manufacturers is considered, different questions arise: there is no privity of contract between the appellant and the manufacturers: between them the liability, if any, must be in tort, and the gist of the cause of action is negligence. The facts set out in the foregoing show, in their Lordships' judgment, negligence in manufacture. According to the evidence, the method of manufacture was correct: the danger of excess sulphites being left was recognised and was guarded against: the process was intended to be fool proof. If excess sulphites were left in the garment, that could only be because someone was at fault. The appellant is not required to lay his finger on the exact person in all the chain who was responsible, or to specify what he did wrong. Negligence is found as a matter of inference from the existence of the defects taken in connection with all the known circumstances: even if the manufacturers could by apt evidence have rebutted that inference they have not done so.

On this basis, the damage suffered by the appellant was caused in fact (because the interposition of the retailers may for this purpose in the circumstances of the case be disregarded) by the negligent or improper way in which the manufacturers made the garments. But this mere sequence of cause and effect is not enough in law to constitute a cause of action in negligence, which is a complex concept, involving a duty as between the parties to take care, as well as a breach of that duty and resulting damage. It might be said that here was no relationship between the parties at all: the manufacturers, it might be said, parted once and for all with the garments when they sold them to the retailers, and were therefore not concerned with their future history, except in so far as under their contract with the retailers they might come under some liability: at no time, it might be said, had they any knowledge of the existence of the appellant: the only peg on which it might be sought to support a relationship of duty was the fact that the appellant had actually worn the garments, but he had done so because he had acquired them by a purchase from the retailers, who were at that time the owners of the goods by a sale which had vested the property in the retailers and divested both property and control from the manufacturers. It was said there could be no legal relationships in the matter save those under the two contracts between the respective parties to those contracts, the one between the manufacturers and the retailers and the other between the retailers and the appellant. These contractual relationships (it might be said) covered the whole field and excluded any question of tort liability: there was no duty other than the contractual duties.

This argument was based on the contention that the present case fell outside the decision of the House of Lords in *Donoghue's* case [1932] AC 562. Their Lordships, like the judges in the courts in Australia, will follow that decision, and the only question here can be what that authority decides and whether this case comes within its principles. [His Lordship stated the facts of that case and continued:]

Their Lordships think that the principle of the decision is summed up in the words of Lord Atkin at 599: "A manufacturer of products, which he sells in such a form as to show that he intends them to reach the ultimate consumer in the form in which they left him with no reasonable possibility of intermediate examination, and with the knowledge that the absence of reasonable care in the preparation or putting up of the products will result in an injury to the consumer's life or property, owes a duty to the consumer to take that reasonable care."

Compare also the High Court's decision in *David Jones Ltd v Willis* (1934) 52 CLR 110.

Ashington Piggeries Ltd v Christopher Hill Ltd: Norsildmel (Third Party)
House of Lords [1972] AC 441; [1971] 1 All ER 847

[The plaintiffs Christopher Hill, food compounders, agreed to supply the defendants Ashington Piggeries (controlled by Mr Udall), mink breeders, with mink food known as "King Size". Hill prepared animal foods as a regular part of its business but had never prepared food for and knew nothing about mink. Ashington provided the formula for "King Size" to Hill who suggested the substitution of one ingredient, herring meal, in lieu of the more expensive fish meal. Hill purchased its herring meal from Norsildmel under a contract for "300 to 350 tons of NORWEGIAN HERRING MEAL fair average quality of the season."

King Size killed Ashington's mink because the ingredient herring meal contained the toxic chemical DMNA which it was later discovered caused liver disease in mink and it appeared was also toxic to other animals.

Ashington refused to pay Hill for the contaminated feed and Hill sued for the purchase price. Ashington counterclaimed for breach of the implied conditions of conformity with description (s 13; NSW s 18), fitness for purpose (s 14(1); NSW s 19(1)), and merchantable quality (s 14(2), NSW s 19(2)). Hill joined its supplier Norsildmel and sought indemnity from it under ss 13 and 14(1).

Because of the large number of issues involved and the differing views of the members of the House of Lords, the judgments have been edited and rearranged under the headings: (a) Sale by description; (b) Fitness for purpose; and (c) Merchantable quality.

As Lord Wilberforce stated at 489: "Because of the way in which the Sale of Goods Act has slotted the pre-existent common law remedy into compartments, it is necessary to consider separately the three relevant provisions. It is well known that there is a good deal of overlapping between them, so that this subdivision is artificial and gives rise to difficulty. But there is no avoiding this procedure."]

Sale by description (Ashington Piggeries v Christopher Hill)
Lord Hodson (at 466): ... The language used is directed to the identification of goods. The point is made by Channell J in *Varley v Whipp* [1900] 1 QB 513 at 516: "The term 'sale of goods by description' must apply to all cases where the purchaser has not seen the goods, but is relying on the description alone." This is not to say that it may not apply even where the purchaser has seen the goods if the deviation from the description is not apparent, but this has no bearing on the facts of the instant case. The essential point is that identification of the goods is that with which the section is concerned. The defendants rely on the oft quoted decision of Roche J in *Pinnock Brothers v Lewis & Peat Ltd* [1923] 1 KB 690. This related to the sale of East African copra cake. The goods were so adulterated with castor seed as to be poisonous to cattle. It was held that the goods were not properly described as copra cake at all and that the sellers were not protected by a clause in the contract that: "The goods are not warranted free from defect rendering same unmerchantable which would not be apparent on reasonable examination, any statute or rule of law to the contrary notwithstanding."

The relevant breach of description relates only to the herring meal element in the formula. The defendants say this was not herring meal, it was herring meal plus DMNA which is not an authorised ingredient of the formula. I agree with the Court of Appeal in arriving at the conclusion that the evidence does not support the view that DMNA was something added to the herring meal, as the castor seed was to the copra cake. One of the defendants' own witnesses (Dr Pearson) was disposed to agree that DMNA was something in the herring meal which had gone wrong. As the Court of Appeal pointed out, sodium nitrite was used as a preservative just as salt had been previously used. It produced a chemical reaction in some cases which produced DMNA. In my opinion, it is working the word "description" too hard to say that "herring meal" was a misdescription. The herring meal was contaminated but no poisonous substance was added to it so as to make the description "herring meal" erroneous.

The distinction between "description" of goods and their quality is made by Lord Dunedin in *Manchester Liners Ltd v Rea Ltd* [1922] 2 AC 74 at 80: "The tender of anything that does not tally with the specified description is not compliance with the contract. But when the article tendered does comply with this specific description, and the objection on the buyer's part is an objection to quality alone, then I think s 14(1) settles the standard, and the only standard by which the matter is to be judged."

The claim based on s 13 accordingly must, in my opinion, fail.

Viscount Dilhorne (at 484): ... In *Chalmers' Sale of Goods Act*, 3rd ed, 1893, p 27, the author, who drafted the Act, cites the following passage from the judgment of Lord Blackburn in *Bowes v Shand* (1877) 2 App Cas 455 at 480: "If the description of the article tendered is different in any respect it is not the article bargained for, and the other party is not bound to take it."

In *Pinnock Brothers v Lewis & Peat Ltd* it was only after the cake had been fed to animals and they had been made ill that it was analysed and found to contain castor beans in so large a proportion as to make it poisonous. Roche J held that there was a failure of the goods to comply with the description.

"Herring meal does not normally contain a poison": Milmo J [1968] 1 Lloyd's Rep 457 at 481. Did the presence of DMNA merely affect the quality of the herring meal or did it make a difference in kind? If the former, then there was no failure to deliver in accordance with the description. If the latter, there was. In view of the fact that herring meal is not normally poisonous to animals, I think that, as in the *Pinnock* case, there was a difference in kind. Whether such a difference is brought about by the admixture of other substances or by the effect of manufacture when a particular preservative has been used, seems to me immaterial. True it is that the presence of DMNA could not have been detected on a visual examination of the meal and that the presence of castor beans in the copra cake was only discovered on analysis, but the fact that the adulteration or contamination is not discoverable on inspection does not, in my opinion, prevent a buyer from establishing that goods bought by description do not comply with the description.

The line between a difference in quality and a difference in kind may in many instances be difficult to draw. Here, where the distinction is between poisonous and non-poisonous herring meal, that was, in my opinion, more than a difference in quality, and I agree with Milmo J in thinking that there was difference in kind and so a breach of s 13.

Lord Wilberforce (at 489): *Section 13 of the Act*: The question is whether the compound mink food sold by the respondents (under the name "King Size") corresponded with the description. The appellants' case was that the food was to be made up according to a formula which identified generically the ingredients and specifically the chemical additives, quantifying precisely the proportions of each ingredient. One of these ingredients was herring meal. The food delivered in certain relevant months, it was claimed, did not correspond with the description because it contained a significant quantity of DMNA. The proposition is that "King Size" made partly of herring meal which contains DMNA does not correspond with the description "King Size". This can be reduced to the proposition that the herring meal ingredient did not correspond with the description because it contained DMNA. The analogy was invoked, inevitably, by the appellants of copra cake with castor seed; the respondents invoked that of oxidised iron. The learned judge accepted the former, the Court of Appeal the latter.

Whether in a given case a substance in or upon which there has been produced by chemical interaction some additional substance can properly be described or, if one prefers the word, identified, as the original substance qualified by the addition of a past participle such as contaminated or oxidised, or as the original substance plus, or intermixed with, an additional substance, may, if pressed to analysis, be a question of an Aristotelian character. Where does a substance with a quality pass into an aggregate of substances? I do not think that it can be solved by asking whether the chemical interaction came about by some natural or normal process, eg, preservation by the addition of salt (sodium chloride), or by some alien intrusion by the production of DMNA from sodium nitrite through a heating effect. I cannot see any distinction in principle in this difference. Further I do not believe that the Sale of Goods Act was designed to provoke metaphysical discussions as to the nature of what is delivered, in comparison with what is sold. The test of description, at least where commodities are concerned, is intended to be a broader, more commonsense, test of a mercantile character. The question whether that is what the buyer bargained for has to be answered according to such tests as men in the market would apply, leaving more delicate questions of condition, or quality, to be determined under other clauses of the contract or sections of the Act. Perhaps this is to admit an element of impression into the decision, but I think it is more than impression which leads me to prefer the answer, if not all of the reasoning, of the Court of Appeal that the defect in the meal was a matter of quality or condition rather than of description. I think that buyers and sellers and arbitrators in the market, asked what this was, could only have said that the relevant ingredient was herring meal and, therefore, that there was no failure to correspond with description. In my opinion, the appellants do not succeed under s 13.

Lord Diplock (at 504): . . . Udall bases his claim against Hill in the first instance on s 13 of the Act. The goods, he submits, did not correspond with the description by which they were sold. The contract was oral. The subject matter was unascertained goods, and it is common ground that the description by which they were sold was contained in Udall's formula which set out in detail the ingredients of the feeding-stuff to be compounded by Hill. One of the described ingredients was "herring meal". Udall contended that the description also included the expression "mink food"—but for the purposes of the claim under s 13 I do not think this matters . . .

Udall's formula was commercial not chemical. The ingredient described as "herring meal" did not cease to comply with that description because it was manufactured from herrings to which a preservative had been added to prevent them from deteriorating. The most usual preservative is common salt (sodium chloride) but the evidence showed that another salt of sodium, sodium nitrite, had been used in Norway for several years before 1961. In certain conditions which can occur during the normal process of manufacture of herring meal the amino acids naturally present in the herring break down into an organic chemical, dimethylamine, which can react with sodium nitrite to form DMNA (dimethylnitrosamine). The occurrence of this reaction may affect the quality of the meal. It does not alter its identity as "herring meal".

[**Lord Guest** (at 473) agreed substantially with the judgment of Lord Hodson that the fact that the herring meal was contaminated by DMNA did not result in a different substance from the herring meal in the description. There was no loss of identity and no breach of s 13.]

Sale by description (Christopher Hill v Norsildmel)
Lord Hodson (at 469): ... I come now to the second appeal, that is to say the appeal of the plaintiffs against the third parties, who were exonerated in the Court of Appeal. The third parties, called Norsildmel, are the successors of a Norwegian body being the Export Committee for Herringmeal and Herringoil from whom they took over in 1964. It is not necessary to draw any distinction between these two bodies for the purposes of this case. C T Bowring & Co Ltd called "Bowrings", were the exclusive selling agents of the third parties in the United Kingdom.

The contract of sale between the plaintiffs and the third parties was made in writing in the English language on the third parties' printed form with typed insertions and is set out in some detail in the judgment of Milmo J, but it will be sufficient to refer to a few portions in order to appreciate the issues which arise under s 13 of the Sale of Goods Act. Against the marginal words in block capitals QUANTITY & DESCRIPTION appear the words: "About 300/350 ... tons at sellers' option of 2240 lb/1016 kilos of NORWEGIAN HERRING MEAL fair average quality of the season, expected to analyse not less than 70 per cent protein, not more than 12 per cent fat and not more than 4 per cent salt."

The price clause concluded with a paragraph reading: "In the event of any surpluses of fat and/or salt, sellers will make an allowance to buyers at the rate of 1 per cent surplus = 1 per cent of the contract price, fractions pro rata. If the fat contents exceed 13 per cent or the salt contents exceed 5 per cent, the buyers will have the right of rejection." Shipment was to be from Norway during March 1961. There was provision for sampling and analysis and general conditions, of which No 3 reads: "The goods to be taken with all faults and defects, damaged or inferior, if any, at valuation to be arranged mutually or by arbitration."

The plaintiffs base their claim against the third parties under s 13 solely on a breach of the terms to be implied under s 13, that the goods shall correspond with the description. The contest on description has been as to whether "fair average quality of the season" is part of the description of the goods or whether, as the third parties contend, it is a warranty of quality. From the layout of the document it seems clear that the third parties are right on this matter. Looking at the photograph of the original contract and bearing in mind that a term ought not to be regarded as part of the description unless it identifies the goods sold, one sees that the words "Norwegian Herring Meal" appear in the printed form in capital letters and are sufficient to satisfy the marginal requirement of description. The words following, faq as it is called in brief, beginning "expected to analyse" etc, clearly do not form part of the description and cannot therefore be used to embrace, so to speak, the faq phrase and make it part of the description in that way. It is also to be noticed that general condition No 3 has nothing to bite on unless faq falls for consideration under this rejection clause dealing with breach of warranty.

Although quality could be used, no doubt, as part of a description it is, I think, not so used in this case; there is a warranty of quality but no more. It is natural so to read it where it may be expected that there will perhaps be divergences in the goods supplied from the samples submitted. The reference to faults and defects in general condition 3 leads to this conclusion. I have used the word "sample" although this is not a case of sale by sample, agreeing with your Lordships that the use of the faq term performs the same function as sale by sample, cf per Devlin J in *F E Hookway & Co Ltd v Alfred Isaacs & Sons* [1954] 1 Lloyd's Rep 491, and per Sellers J in *Steels & Busks Ltd v Bleecker Bik & Co Ltd* [1956] 1 Lloyd's Rep 228.

I am content to accept the formulation of the third parties accepted by the Court of Appeal [1969] 3 All ER 1496 at 1520-1: "In essence, it relates, and relates only, to such qualities as are apparent on an ordinary examination or analysis of the goods, such as is usually done in the trade in relation to such goods." Before leaving the construction of the contract I should add that I agree with the Court of Appeal that general condition 3 is to be read as purporting to exclude the buyer's right to reject goods for faults and defects but not as purporting to exclude his right to recover from the sellers compensation for any consequential damage which he may sustain by reason of acceptance of goods which thereafter turn out to be defective and cause loss or damage by reason of that defect. The plaintiff's claim against the third parties based on s 13 must accordingly fail.

Lord Guest (at 475): *Section 13 of the Sale of Goods Act 1893*: The primary argument for Hill was that the whole of the clause "Quantity and Description" was "the description" of the goods within the meaning of s 13, the terms of which have already been quoted. It was said that "fair average quality of the season" (faq) must be part of the description because on what has been conveniently described as the "sandwich principle" that part of the clause dealing with expected analysis of the meal was part of the description. It therefore followed that the intervening words faq must also be part of the description. In my view, the fallacy of this argument lies in the fact that the "expected analysis" is not part of the description. Where goods are unascertained, "description" implies a specification whereby the goods can be identified by the buyer. Such a case was *Arcos Ltd v E A Ronaasen & Son* [1933] AC 470 where the timber contracted for was precisely specified as to length, breadth and thickness. Neither faq not the expected analysis provision identifies the goods. They prima facie indicate the quality of the goods: see *Pacific Trading Co Ltd v Wiener* (1923) 14 Lloyd LR 51 at 54, Roche J. There is a case where the contract was for goods "afloat per SS *Morton Bay* due London approximately June 8"; these words were held to be part of the description: *Macpherson Train & Co Ltd v Howard Ross & Co Ltd* [1955] 1 WLR 640. But that is a different case from the present. It enabled the goods to be identified. I do not dispute that there may be cases where a qualitative description of the goods may come within the section. The case of *Varley v Whipp* [1900] 1 QB 513 is an example of such a case. It concerned the sale of a reaping machine stated to have been new the previous year and to have been used to cut only fifty or sixty acres. This was held to be a sale by description. But in that case the description would have identified the goods as a nearly new machine.

I have reached the conclusion without much difficulty that faq is not part of the description of "Norwegian herring meal" contained in the contract, nor is the expected analysis part of the description. Apart from the side note "Quantity and Description" in the sales contract, I can find no justification whatever for importing faq into the description of the goods. The sidenote by itself cannot control the clause where the rest of the clause is clear and unambiguous.

If faq is not part of the description of the goods, then it becomes unnecessary to consider the question whether the herring meal was faq and whether, if it was, it covers latent defects. These questions were extensively debated before the House. On the assumption that only the words "Norwegian herring meal" were part of the description, then the question whether there was a breach of s 13 is the same as that raised in the principal appeal and I would, accordingly, hold that there was no breach of s 13.

General Condition 3: I agree with the rest of your Lordships in thinking that this clause is no bar to Hill's action for indemnity. This was the view of both courts below and I see no reason to differ from them.

Viscount Dilhorne (at 485): ... I now turn to the respondents' claim against the third party.

On 14 February 1961 the respondents entered into a contract with Sildemelutvalget, the export committee for Herringmeal and Herringoil, to whom the third party is the successor, through C T Bowring & Co of Leadenhall Street, for the purchase of herring meal. [His Honour referred to the "Quantity and Description" paragraph and continued:]

The sale was thus of goods by description. There was considerable controversy as to what was the description, the respondents contending that it included the words "fair average quality of the season"; the third party that it did not.

Where a sale is by description, the description identifies the goods. In my opinion, the words "fair average quality of the season" do not do so. They do not assist in the identification of the goods and merely relate to the quality of the herring meal. I do not think that the fact that this paragraph of the contract has the words "Quantity and Description" beside it suffices to justify the conclusion that the words were intended to be part of the description of the goods, though I appreciate that there may be cases where a reference to quality may be part of the description identifying the goods the subject of the sale.

In my opinion, the description of the goods the subject of the sale was Norwegian herring meal, and nothing more. The expectation that on analysis it would not have less than 70 per cent protein or more than 12 per cent fat and 4 per cent salt cannot be part of the description identifying the goods.

The respondents alleged that there was a breach of s 13 of the Sale of Goods Act by the third party. Whether or not there was depends on whether the meal supplied could properly be described as Norwegian herring meal. Norwegian herring meal does not normally contain a poison. The meal delivered contained DMNA in sufficient quantities to kill mink and, as I have said, in my opinion, to be harmful to other animals.

The same question arises for decision in relation to the respondents' claim under s 13 as arose on the appellants' claim against the respondents. For the reasons I have already stated, and which I need not repeat, in my opinion the difference between Norwegian herring meal, which is normally harmless to animals, and Norwegian herring meal containing DMNA in sufficient quantities as to be harmful to animals is not just a difference of quality but one of kind and I would, therefore, find in favour of the respondents on this issue.

Lord Diplock (at 511): ... So I come once more to s 13 of the Sale of Goods Act 1893, upon which Hill in turn founds his claim against the Norwegians.

Since the contract was in writing the description by which the goods were sold must be determined by construing the words used by the parties in the contract. [His Honour referred to the "Quantity and Description" paragraph and continued:]

I agree with your Lordships that the description by which the goods were sold is limited to the words "Norwegian herring meal". That is what identifies the subject matter of the contract. Where a contract contains an express statement about the quality of the goods to be supplied the prima facie inference is that this was intended by the parties not as an identification of the kind of goods that are alone the subject matter of the contract, but as an express stipulation as to the standard of quality to which goods of that kind supplied under the contract shall conform. Such an express stipulation may be intended as a condition or as a warranty. Which it is, depends upon the construction of the contract. This, in turn, depends upon what can be inferred, from the whole of the terms of the contract and the circumstances in which it was negotiated, as to the importance that the parties attached to it. Did they regard exact conformity with the stipulated standard as so vital to the contract that no distinction was to be drawn between a minor divergence or one which was great? Or did they intend to differentiate according to the magnitude of the divergence? If the former, the stipulation is a condition and the consequence of a breach of it would be the same as if the stipulation did form part of the description by which the goods were sold, though it would be classified under s 11 as an express condition and not as an implied condition under s 13. If the latter, the stipulation is an express warranty, but does not exclude reliance upon the implied condition of merchantable quality under s 14(2) if the divergence is so great as to make the goods not reasonably fit for any purpose for which they are normally used.

In a contract, such as that between Hill and the Norwegians, for the sale of a commodity in which there is an established market and for which there is more than one normal use, a divergence from the stipulated standard of quality which falls short of rendering them useless for every normal use, would be reasonably expected by both parties to affect the value of the goods according to the magnitude of the divergence, and prima facie to amount only to a warranty, a breach of which would not entitle the buyer to reject the goods as being *dehors* the contract. That such was the intended effect of the stipulation "fair average quality of the season" is, in my view, confirmed by general condition 3: "The goods to be taken with all faults and defects damaged or inferior, if any, at valuation to be arranged mutually or by arbitration." I construe this clause as excluding any right of the buyer to reject the goods for any non-conformity with the stipulation as to quality which falls short of rendering them unmerchantable.

Hill did not allege any express warranty or quality in his pleading. He relied upon the words "fair average quality of the season" as being part of the description by which the goods were sold. I will, however, come back to their effect as an express warranty of quality later.

[His Lordship later concluded (at 514) that this warranty related only to such qualities as are apparent on an ordinary trade examination or analysis of the goods. The presence of DMNA in the herring meal was not such a quality and no breach of the express warranty of quality had been established by Hill. Lord Wilberforce (at 495) agreed with Lord Diplock on this aspect of the case.]

Fitness for purpose (Ashington Piggeries v Christopher Hill)
Lord Wilberforce (at 490): *Section 14(1) of the Act*: I do not think it is disputed or in any case disputable, that a particular purpose was made known by the buyers so as to show that they relied on the sellers' skill and judgment. The particular purpose for which "King Size" was required was as food for mink.

Equally I think it is clear (as both courts have found) that there was reliance on the respondents' skill and judgment. Although the Act makes no reference to partial reliance, it was settled, well before the *Cammell Laird* case [1934] AC 402 was decided in this House, that there may be cases where the buyer relies on his own skill or judgment for some purposes and on that of the seller for others. This House gave to that principle emphatic endorsement.

The present is certainly such a case. In the words of Milmo J [1968] 1 Lloyd's Rep 457 at 480: "On the one hand Mr Udall was relying on his own judgment as to what his formula should contain and the levels at which the various ingredients in it should be included. On the other, he was relying, and had no alternative but to rely, upon the [respondents] to obtain the ingredients, to see they were of good quality and not to use ingredients which, as a result of contamination, were toxic."

The word "toxic" will require some examination but, subject to this, I consider that this passage correctly states the position as regards reliance.

The field thus left to the sellers can be described in terms of their responsibility as merchants, to obtain and deliver ingredients, and relevantly herring meal, not unfit by reason of contamination, to be fed to animals, including mink. The field reserved to the buyers, on the other hand, was that of particular or specific suitability for mink. There was no doubt that herring meal, as such, was suitable for mink; on the other hand, the particular consignments supplied in 1961 were unsuitable because of the presence of DMNA. What, then, was the nature of this unsuitability?

If mink possessed an idiosyncrasy, which made the food as supplied unsuitable for them though it was perfectly suitable for other animals, this would be the buyers' responsibility, unless, as is not the case here, they had made this idiosyncrasy known to the sellers so as to show reliance on them to provide for it. But any general unsuitability would be the sellers' responsibility. Although the evidence was not very complete, it is sufficiently shown, in my opinion, that mink are more sensitive to DMNA than most other animals to whom compound foods would be sold. Chicken and pigs are among the least sensitive, next cattle and then sheep, with mink at the top of the scale. So the question arises, what does the buyer, alleging unfitness, have to prove? If the fact were that the herring meal supplied, while damaging to mink, was perfectly harmless to all other animals to whom it might be fed, it would be unjust to hold the sellers liable. If, on the other hand, the herring meal was not only lethal to mink but also deleterious, though not lethal, to other animals, the sellers' responsibility could be fairly engaged. A man can hardly claim that the product he sells is suitable, especially if that is a foodstuff, merely because it fails to kill more than one species to which it is fed.

In this case, because of the difficulty of tracing the lethal element, the evidence as to its presence, its strength and its effect was not scientifically complete. It was not until 1964 that DMNA was identified. By that time all the infected herring meal had been disposed of, and all other animals to which it had been fed had died. The critical question in this part of the appeal is whether the buyers proved enough to show that their mink died because of some general, that is, non-specific, unsuitability of the herring meal through contamination. The burden was upon the buyers to show that this was so.

The Court of Appeal, who decided against the buyers on this point, based their decision on a conclusion regarding the balance of the contaminated herring meal which was not used for mink food. The consignment which killed the appellants' mink was part (8½ tons) of a total of 333½ tons, the rest of which was sold by the respondents for inclusion in feeding-stuffs in the normal way. The Court of Appeal [1969] 2 Lloyd's Rep 425 at 462 found that this balance was "perfectly suitable" as a feeding-stuff for animals for whom the respondents normally compounded foods, and from this drew the conclusion that the deaths of the mink were due to some specific idiosyncrasy. I cannot accept that this conclusion was justified. The evidence certainly showed that no complaints were received from any person who received meal from the balance of the consignment, but that was all. There was no evidence in what quantities, or over what period, any of this meal was fed, not even, accepting that no deaths resulted (and premature deaths may have occurred), was there any evidence that the animals in question were not adversely affected in weight, fertility or in damage to their livers. The absence of complaint is insufficient by itself to establish perfect suitability.

But the matter does not end with rejection of the Court of Appeal's finding: the basic difficulty remains. Given that the buyers had to show general unsuitability and not merely specific unsuitability for mink, did they do so? It is here that the concept of toxicity becomes relevant.

[His Lordship then reviewed the factual evidence and concluded:] The equation is, therefore, this: that DMNA is inherently and generally toxic: that as included in the relevant herring meal it poisoned the appellants' mink: that this poisoning was not due to any specific indiosyncrasy among mink: that its effect on other species or sub-species is not accurately known beyond that it is potentially deleterious at least to the liver and that most normal species are more tolerant of it than mink.

In my opinion, the appellants made good their case: they proved the cause of their losses to lie in the inclusion of a generally (viz non-specific as regards mink) toxic ingredient in the food. It was not for them to show that this same food killed, or poisoned, other species. So to require would place far too high a burden on a buyer. The buyer may have no means of ascertaining what the effect on other species may be. The whole of the contaminated consignment may have been fed to the buyer's animals; is the buyer to fail because he cannot show that this particular consignment killed, or at least injured, other animals? He must, I think, carry his proof to the point of showing that the guilty ingredient has some generally (as opposed to specifically) toxic quality. But once he has done this, has he not shown, at least with strong prima facie force, that a feeding-stuff which contained it was unsuitable? Is he not entitled to throw on to the seller the burden of showing, if he can, that the damage to the buyer's animals was due to some factor within the field of responsibility reserved to the buyer? I would answer yes to these questions. In the end, it is for the judge to decide whether, on the evidence, the buyers have proved their case. Milmo J's conclusions are expressed in three passages, one in the main action, the others in the third party proceedings (the whole case was heard together): "Herring meal does not normally contain a poison. The herring meal which killed the English mink contained DMNA which is a poison, and it contained it at a level sufficiently high to be lethal to mink, which are animals to which herring meal can properly be fed. All animals are sensitive to DMNA poisoning, though mink are more sensitive than most": [1968] 1 Lloyd's Rep 457 at 481.

"I find that the meal which poisoned the English mink was not reasonably fit for use as an ingredient in animal foodstuffs because of the fact that it contained in substantial and significant quantities DMNA which is a toxic substance to which all animals are sensitive": at 487.

"While I accept that there was no evidence that the meal *had a deleterious effect* upon any animal or other type of livestock other than mink, I do not consider that it was proved affirmatively that the meal which killed the mink *could have been fed with impunity* to all other types of livestock": at 486—emphasis supplied.

This is precisely the position: coupled with the general finding as to toxicity (something to which all animals are sensitive, ie, liable to suffer liver damage) it amounts to a rejection of the only line of defence open to the respondents—namely, that the relevant consignment was fit to be fed to all normal animals and only unfit to be fed to mink.

In my opinion, these finding were justified and correct.

So much for the facts, but there remains one legal argument on this part of the case. Section 14(1) contains the words "and the goods are of a description which it is in the course of the seller's business to supply". The respondents relied on these words and persuaded the Court of Appeal to decide that the requirement was not satisfied because, briefly, the respondents were not dealers in mink food. A similar argument was put forward on the words in s 14(2) "where goods are bought by description from a seller who deals in goods of that description". The Court of Appeal decided this point, too, in the respondents' favour. The respondents, they held, did not deal in mink food, or "King Size", before Mr Udall placed with them the orders which produced the defective goods. I have some doubt whether this argument is even correct on the facts, because Mr Udall had been ordering "King Size" for several months before he ordered the fatal consignment. But we must deal with the legal argument because it is clearly of general importance. It appears never previously to have been accepted and it substantially narrows the scope of both sub-sections. It rests, in the first place, upon a linguistic comparison of the meaning of the word "description" in the three places where it appears and on the argument that it must mean the same in each place.

I do not accept that, taken in its most linguistic strictness, either sub-section bears the meaning contended for. I would hold that (as to sub-s (1)) it is in the course of the seller's business to supply goods if he agrees, either generally, or in a particular case, to supply the goods when ordered, and (as to sub-s (2)) that a seller deals in goods of that description if his business is such that he is willing to accept orders for them. I cannot comprehend the rationale of holding that the sub-sections do not apply if the seller is dealing in the particular goods for the first time or the sense of distinguishing between the first and the second order for the goods or for goods of the description. The Court of Appeal offered the analogy of a doctor sending a novel prescription to a pharmacist, which turns out to be deleterious. But as often happens to arguments of this kind, the analogy is faulty: if the prescription is wrong, of course the doctor is responsible. The fitness of the prescription is within his field of responsibility. The relevant question is whether the pharmacist is responsible for the purity of his ingredients and one does not see why not.

But, moreover, consideration of the preceding common law shows that what the Act had in mind was something quite simple and rational: to limit the implied conditions of fitness of quality to persons in the way of business, as distinct from private persons. Whether this should be the law was a problem which had emerged, and been resolved, well before 1893. The first indication of the point arose in *Jones v Bright* (1829) 15 Bing 533 (copper sheathing). Two of the judges regarded it as an essential allegation that the defendant should have been the manufacturer of the defective copper. Park J in fact, as 546, used the words "distinguishing, as I do, between the manufacturer of an article and the mere seller". In *Brown v Edgington* (1841) 2 Man & G 279 at 291 (the crane rope) we find a description of the defendant by Bosanquet J as "a dealer in articles of that description", clearly a reason for holding him liable though he was not the manufacturer. The distinction between the dealer and the private seller is clearly brought out in *Burnby v Bollet* (1847) 16 M & W 644, where a man bought a carcase in the market but later sold it to another farmer. His exemption from liability for defects in the carcase was explicily based on his private character; he was "not clothed with any character of general dealer in provisions" (at 649), he was "not dealing in the way of a common trade" (at 655). And finally in the forerunner case of *Jones v Just* (1868) LR 3 QB 197 we find Mellor J in his fourth and fifth categories, which anticipate respectively s 14(1) and 14(2) of the Sale of Goods Act 1893, referring to a manufacturer or dealer contracting to supply an article which he manufactures or produces, or in which he deals, and to a manufacturer undertaking to supply foods manufactured by himself or in which he deals, so clearly following and adopting the prior accepted division between sales by way of trade and private sales.

One asks, therefore, what difference the insertion in the Sale of Goods Act of the word "description" made to these well-accepted rules. It seems at least clear that the words now appearing in s 14(1) "and the goods are of a description which it is the seller's business to supply" cannot mean more than "the goods are of a kind . . .". "Description" here cannot be used in the sense in which the word is used when the Act speaks of "sales by description", for s 14(1) is not dealing with sales by description at all. If this is so, I find no obstacle against reading "goods of that description" in a similar way in s 14(2). In both cases the word means "goods of that kind" and nothing more. Moreover, even if this is wrong, and "description" is to be understood in a technical sense, I would have no difficulty in holding that a seller deals in goods "of that description" if he accepts orders to supply them in the way of business; and this whether or not he has previously accepted orders for goods of that description.

So, all other elements being present as I have tried to show, I would hold that s 14(1) applies to the present case. [His Lordship then held that s 14(2) also applied.]

[**Lord Hodson** (at 467–9), **Lord Guest** (at 473) and **Viscount Dilhorne** (at 485) delivered judgments substantially agreeing with Lord Wilberforce on this aspect of the case. In his judgment extracted below Lord Diplock combined his analysis of sub-ss (1) and (2) of s 14 (NSW s 19).]

Lord Diplock (at 504): . . . Alternatively Udall sought to bring his claim under s 14(1) or 14(2).

Implied Conditions in Contracts of Sale

These two sub-sections are interrelated. Unlike s 13 they are not concerned with the identity of the goods which are the subject matter of the contract, but with their "quality" or their "fitness for any particular purpose".

All goods which are sold finish up by being used for some purpose or another by the ultimate user, consumer or converter. This is not necessarily the actual buyer under the contract of sale. He may intend to pass them on by sale or otherwise to the person who actually puts them to that use. But the purpose for which they will be used by the ultimate consumer or converter is the "purpose for which the goods are required" within the meaning of s 14(1).

The only condition as to "quality" which is to be implied under s 14(2) is that the goods shall be of "merchantable quality". This is likewise concerned with use. Goods are of merchantable quality if they are fit for use for any purpose for which goods which correspond with the description by which they were sold would normally be used.

The dichotomy between the two sections is thus between fitness for use for a "particular purpose" and fitness for use for one of several purposes for which goods which correspond with the description by which they were sold would normally be used. But if there is only one purpose for which goods of that description would normally be used, the condition to be implied under each of the sub-sections is the same. In such a case one would expect to find some common principle which links the circumstances which give rise to the implied condition under sub-s (1) and the circumstances which give rise to the implied condition under sub-s (2).

So far as concerns the conduct of the buyer, the circumstances which give rise to the implied condition under sub-s (1), are, first, that he should make known expressly or by implication to the seller what is the particular purpose for which the goods are required and, secondly, that he should do so in such a way as to make the seller reasonably understand that he is relying upon the seller to exercise sufficient skill or judgment to ensure that the goods are fit for that particular purpose. This he generally does by selecting a seller who makes it his business to supply goods which are used for purposes of that kind. It does not matter that the seller does not possess the necessary skill or judgment nor does it matter that in the then state of knowledge no one could by exercise of skill or judgment detect the particular characteristic of the goods which rendered them unfit for that purpose. This may seem harsh upon the seller, but its harshness is mitigated by the requirement that the goods must be of a description which it is in the course of the seller's business to supply. By holding himself out to the buyer as a manufacturer or dealer in goods of that kind he leads the buyer reasonably to understand that he is capable of exercising sufficient skill or judgment to make or to select goods which will be fit for the particular purpose for which he knows the buyer wants them.

I have used the word "kind" as meaning the same as the word "description" in the sub-section. The sub-section applies to all types of contracts for the sale of goods: to contracts for the sale of specific goods or for sale by sample, which are not contracts of sale of goods "by description", as well as to contracts which are. Where the contract is not one for the sale of goods by description the expression in the sub-section "goods of a description which it is in the course of the seller's business to supply" can only mean that the seller does deal in goods of a kind that can be verbally identified by a description that is wide enough to include goods which are intended for use for the particular purpose for which the buyer requires the goods which are the subject matter of the contract. I do not think that this expression bears any different meaning when the contract is one for sale of goods by description. I agree with the Court of Appeal that it is not limited to the "description" by which the actual goods that are the subject matter of the contract are sold. It would have been no defence to the sellers in *Cammell Laird & Co Ltd v Manganese Bronze and Brass Co Ltd* [1934] AC 402 to say that they had never previously supplied a ship's propeller of the particular dimensions ordered although these did form part of the description by which the goods which were the subject matter of that contract were sold. It was sufficient that it was in the course of their business to supply ships' propellers.

In contrast to sub-s (1) the corresponding conduct of the buyer which gives rise to the implied condition under sub-s (2) is that he should have bought the goods "by description". The sub-section does not apply to any other type of contract for the sale of goods. By describing the goods that are to be the subject matter of the contract the buyer makes it known to the seller by implication that the goods are required for, at any rate, one of the purposes for which the goods of that description are normally required—or, if there is only one such purpose, that they are required for that purpose. But, as in the case of sub-s (1), the mere ordering of goods by description does not suffice to show the buyer's reliance upon the seller's knowledge of the purposes for which goods of that description are normally used or of the characteristics needed to make then fit for any of those purposes. It is only by selecting a seller who makes it his business to supply goods of the *same* description as that by which the goods which are the subject matter of the contract are bought, that the buyer shows his reliance upon the skill and judgment of the seller to supply goods which are reasonably fit for one of the purposes disclosed by the description by which the buyer has bought the goods. For this description constitutes the only information which the buyer has given the seller about the purpose for which the goods are required.

It follows that I agree with the Court of Appeal that in the phrase in sub-s (2): "Where goods are bought by description from a seller who deals in goods of that description", the words "that description" refer to and mean the actual description by which the goods which are the subject matter of the contract were bought. Not only is it impossible to ascribe any other meaning to it grammatically but also, as I have endeavoured to explain, it makes good commercial sense. The expression "that description" in sub-s (2) as referring to goods in which the seller deals, is thus narrower in meaning than the expression "a description" in sub-s (1) as referring to goods which it is in the course of the seller's business to supply.

The key to both sub-sections is reliance—the reasonable reliance of the buyer upon the seller's ability to make or select goods which are reasonably fit for the buyer's purpose coupled with the seller's acceptance of responsibility to do so. The seller has a choice whether or not to accept that responsibility. To enable him to exercise it he must be supplied by the buyer with sufficient information to acquaint him with what he is being relied upon to do and to enable him to appreciate what exercise of skill or judgment is called for in order to make or select goods which will be fit for the purpose for which the buyer requires them.

This consideration, in my view, throws light upon two matters arising under s 14. The first is the meaning of "particular purpose" in sub-s (1). The second is the application of the doctrine of "partial reliance" under both sub-s (1) and sub-s (2).

To attract the condition to be implied by sub-s (1) the buyer must make known the purpose for which he requires the goods with sufficient particularity to enable a reasonable seller, engaged in the business of supplying goods of the kind ordered, to identify the characteristics which the goods need to possess to fit them for that purpose. If all that the buyer does make known to the seller is a range of purposes which do not all call for goods possessing identical characteristics and he does not identify the particular purpose or purposes within that range for which he in fact requires the goods, he does not give the seller sufficient information to enable him to make or to select goods possessing a characteristic which is needed to make them fit for any one of those purposes in particular, if the same characteristic either is not needed to make them fit, or makes them unfit, for other purposes within the range.

A "range of purposes" case thus poses a stark question of legal policy as to whether the seller's responsibility ought to be to supply goods which are fit for at least one of the purposes within the range or to supply goods which are fit for all of those purposes unless he expressly disclaims responsibility for their fitness for any one or more of them. The answer to this question of policy has, in my view, been pre-empted by sub-s (2) of s 14 of the Sale of Goods Act 1893.

The commonest way in which a buyer makes known to the seller a range of purposes for which the goods are required is by the description by which he buys them and by nothing more. This is the case that is contemplated by sub-s (2). This, as it has been authoritatively construed by the courts, provides that the only condition to be implied as to the responsibility of the seller is that the goods should be reasonably fit for one of the purposes within the range.

To supplement the description by which the goods are bought, or to replace it if they are not bought by description, the buyer may identify with greater precision the purpose for which the goods are required, by making it known to the seller in some other way. This is the case contemplated by sub-s (1). He may do this expressly or by implication. At any rate, if he does so expressly he can make it known to the seller that he relies upon the seller to supply goods that are fit for more than one purpose or, indeed, for all possible purposes which lie within a range. But the mere fact that the seller knows that the buyer is engaged in a business in which goods of the description by which they are bought *may* be needed for any one of a number of purposes within the range of those for which goods of that description are normally used, adds nothing to what he might reasonably infer from the fact that the buyer ordered the goods by a description which covers goods fit for a range of purposes, without particularising which of those purposes he requires goods for. It might be otherwise if the seller knew that the buyer was engaged in a business in which goods of the description by which they were bought were needed for one or more only of the purposes within the whole range.

It would, in my view, conflict with the principle of reliance which underlies s 14(1) and (2) and would be a misuse of a statutory code of this kind, to treat a range of purposes for any one of which the buyer *may* require the goods, on the one hand, as constituting "the particular purpose for which the goods ar required" and so giving rise to an implied condition under sub-s (1) that they shall be reasonably fit for all purposes within the range, if the seller's knowledge of the *range* is derived in whole or in part from some circumstance other than the description by which the goods are ordered; and, on the other hand, as giving rise to an implied condition under sub-s (2) that the goods need only be fit for one of the purposes within the range, if the seller's knowledge of the *range* is derived solely from the description by which the goods are ordered. So to construe the code would for practical purposes deprive sub-s (2) of any effect.

I turn next to "partial reliance". The actual words of sub-s (1) appear to contemplate two classes of contracts only; one, where the buyer does not rely at all upon the skill or judgment of the seller to see to it that the goods supplied are reasonably fit for a particular purpose; the other where the buyer does so rely and the other requirements of the sub-section are satisfied. As a matter of linguistics it is possible to construe the expression "so as to show that the buyer relies" as referring to a reliance which was only partial, in the sense that the reliance was not the only or even the determinative factor which induced the buyer to enter into the contract. But it is not possible to extract from the language of the sub-section any qualification upon the implied undertaking by the seller, if there is such reliance, that the goods supplied by him shall be reasonably fit for the particular purpose for which they are required by the buyer. Yet as a result of technological advances since 1893 there are an increasing number of cases where the preparation of goods fit for a particular purpose calls for the exercise of more than one kind of expertise. The buyer may himself possess one of the kinds of expertise needed but lack another and may choose a seller who has led him to believe that he, the seller, possesses it. The only reliance by the buyer upon the skill or judgment of the seller is that in the preparation or selection of the goods he will exercise that kind of expertise which he has led the buyer reasonably to believe that he possesses. The goods supplied may then be unfit for the particular purpose for which both parties knew they were required, either because of a defect which lay within the sphere of expertise of the seller or because of a defect which lay within the sphere of expertise of the buyer himself.

The way in which the principle of reliance which underlies sub-ss (1) and (2) should be applied to a more complex contract of this kind, which was not in the immediate contemplation of the draftsman of the code, poses another stark question of legal policy. In large part this decision was made by your Lordships' House in 1934 in the *Cammell Laird* case [1934] AC 402. It was there laid down that if the defect in the goods which rendered them unfit for their purpose was due to a characteristic which it lay within the sphere of expertise of the seller to detect and avoid, the responsibility for their unfitness lay with the seller. The *ratio decidendi* leads ineluctably to the corollary that if the defect was due to a characteristic which it lay within the sphere of the expertise of the buyer to detect and avoid, the seller was not contractually responsible for it. It did not attract the implied condition under sub-s (1). The field of the seller's undertaking as to the fitness of the goods for the purpose corresponded with the field of the buyer's reliance upon the skill and judgment of the seller.

My Lords, this seems to me to be consistent with commonsense and business honesty. It was accepted as the correct principle by both courts below and by all parties to the appeals in this House. But the *Cammell Laird* case leaves open for decision an ancillary question of legal policy which your Lordships are now called upon to decide for the first time. That question is whether, in a case of partial reliance of this kind, once the goods have been proved to be unfit for the purpose for which they were required the onus lies upon the buyer to prove that the defect was due to a characteristic which it lay within the field of expertise of the seller to detect and avoid; or does it lie upon the seller to prove that the defect was due to a characteristic which lay within the sphere of expertise of the buyer.

I do not think that there is anything in the Sale of Goods Act 1893 or in hitherto accepted law which inhibits your Lordships from deciding this question whichever way commends itself to the majority. The choice depends largely upon one's personal view as to whether the swing of the pendulum since 1893 from *caveat emptor* to *caveat venditor* has now gone far enough and ought to be arrested, or whether it should be given a further impetus, albeit a minor one, upon its current course. For my part I would have been in favour of arresting it. But I recognise that a decision to the contrary is simply one of policy and, as it commends itself to the majority of your Lordships, I accept it with good grace as now forming part of the law of contracts for the sale of goods.

Once it is accepted, it is decisive of the first appeal. Hill's sphere of expertise upon which Udall relied lay in the selection of ingredients for "King Size" mink food which would be of a quality suitable for use in compound feeding-stuffs for domestic animals and poultry other than mink. The particular purpose, known to both parties, for which Udall required the "King Size" mink food was as a feeding-stuff for mink. Udall proved that it was unsuitable for that purpose and that its unsuitability was due to the quality of an ingredient, herring meal, selected by Hill. Upon the findings of fact of Milmo J, Hill failed to prove affirmatively that the herring meal was of a quality suitable for use in compound feeding-stuffs for domestic animals and poultry other than mink. Therefore, Udall is entitled to succeed upon his claim for damages for breach of the condition to be implied under s 14(1) of the Sale of Goods Act 1893.

On the other hand, I do not think that the contract between Udall and Hill was one which attracted any implied condition as to merchantable quality under s 14(2) of the Act. The expression "merchantable quality" in relation to goods implies that at the time of the contract of sale there already exists a market in goods of the kind described from which it is possible to identify a standard of comparison or norm with which the goods should correspond in order to be acceptable to a reasonable buyer of such goods in that market. There was no existing market in "King Size" mink food. It was an entirely new product in which Hill made plain to Udall he had never dealt before. The contract was for the sale of goods by description; but whether the description was limited to what was stated in Udall's formula as to the ingredients and their proportions or whether it also included a reference to the goods as a feeding-stuff for mink the description was not one of goods in which Hill dealt within the meaning of s 14(2).

To hold the contrary would, in my view, conflict with the principle of reliance which underlies both sub-ss (1) and (2) of s 14. If the "King Size" compound had been unsuitable as a feeding-stuff for mink solely because any food compounded in accordance with Udall's formula would have been unsuitable for mink, it would have been unmerchantable for there was no other purpose for which it could be used in commerce. Yet it would be contrary to commonsense and business honesty if Hill, who had done precisely that which Udall had reasonably relied upon him to do, were liable for a defect in the goods in a respect in which no reliance had been placed upon Hill.

Fitness for purpose (Christopher Hill v Norsildmel)
Lord Guest (at 476): *Section 14(1) of the Sale of Goods Act 1893*: [After quoting the section, his Lordship continued:] The courts below differed as to the application of this section and I have found this the most difficult part of the case.

If I set out the argument for Norsildmel it will focus the issue. Mr Lloyd argued that the purpose which was made known to the seller was the purpose of compounding for animal feeding-stuffs and that this was not a particular purpose within the meaning of s 14(1). It was not so particular as to show that the buyer relied on the seller's skill or judgment. The expressed purpose of compounding for animal feeding-stuffs did not give the seller an opportunity of deciding whether he would contract with the buyer. It was further contended that the feeding of herring meal to mink had not been shown to be a normal use of herring meal in Norway or Great Britain. Reference was made to certain passages in the speeches in *Hardwick Game Farm v Suffolk Agricultural Poultry Producers Association* [1969] 2 AC 31. If I select one typical passage from the speech of my noble and learned friend, Lord Reid, it must not be thought that I have not had in my mind other similar passages from the other judgments. I quote from p 80: "It was argued that, whenever any purpose is stated so as to bring this sub-section into operation, the seller must supply goods reasonably fit to enable the buyer to carry out his purpose in any normal way. But that can only be right if the purpose is stated with sufficient particularity to enable the seller to exercise his skill or judgment in making or selecting appropriate goods."

But before I proceed I must refer to another passage in the speech of my noble and learned friend. After referring to *Manchester Liners Ltd v Rea Ltd* [1922] 2 AC 74, he says at 81: "I do not think that this case is any authority for the view which has sometimes been expressed that if the seller knows the purpose for which the buyer wants the goods it will be presumed that the buyer relied on his skill and judgment."

In *Teheran-Europe Co Ltd v S T Belton (Tractors) Ltd* [1968] 2 QB 545 at 554 Lord Denning MR said that this passage in Lord Reid's speech had dealt a "knock-out blow" to the idea that where a particular purpose was made known to the seller there is a presumption that the buyer relies on his skill or judgment. None of the others of their Lordships in *Hardwick* referred to this point. In fact Lord Pearce at 115 says that: "The whole trend of authority has inclined towards an assumption of reliance wherever the seller knows the particular purpose." I do not understand my noble and learned friend, Lord Reid, to be saying that the presumption can never be drawn from the mere fact that a particular purpose is made known to the seller. He emphasises that the question is whether in the whole circumstances the inference can properly be drawn that a reasonable man in the shoes of the seller would realise that he was being relied upon.

The whole of s 14(1) so far as relevant must be read together: "Where the buyer, expressly or by implication, makes known to the seller the particular purpose for which the goods are required, so as to show that the buyer relies on the seller's skill or judgment, . . ." The purpose must be a "particular" purpose. It must be a definite purpose. In *Hardwick Game Farm* the purpose of compounding into feeding-stuffs for pigs and poultry was held sufficiently particular (see my noble and learned friend, Lord Morris of Borth-y-Gest at 93). "A communicated purpose, if stated with reasonably sufficient precision, will be a particular purpose. It will be the given purpose." (See also Lord Pearce at 114.)

In the present case the purpose was for compounding into animal feeding-stuffs, which would seem sufficiently definite. It distinguishes it from use as fertiliser. The knowledge of the seller need not be expressly communicated: it may be by implication, as the section provides. If the seller knows the purpose for which the buyer requires the goods, then no express intimation by the buyer is necessary. It will be implied: see *Mash & Murrell Ltd v Joseph I Emanuel Ltd* [1961] 1 WLR 862 at 866 and *Manchester Liners Ltd v Rea Ltd* [1922] 2 AC 74.

The question in the present case therefore resolves itself into this: Whether in all the circumstances it is proper to draw the inference that there was reliance by the buyer on the seller's skill or judgment—in other words, whether the particular purpose of the herring meal for compounding into animal feeding-stuffs having been made known, the sellers knew that it was likely that it would be fed to mink. Whether the test is "likely", "not unlikely", or "liable to" is a matter of taste, but all these tests are comprised in the speeches in *C Czarnikow Ltd v Koufos* [1969] 1 AC 350. If the proper inference from all the evidence is that Norsildmel knew that herring meal was used as food for mink, then, in my view, it is sufficient to show the reliance required by the section. If the particular purpose is shown, then it is an easy step to draw the inference of reliance.

Hill start off with the undoubted advantage that they have a finding in their favour by the trial judge: Milmo J [1968] 1 Lloyd's Rep 457 at 484, 490.

[His Lordship then quoted the judge's findings to the effect that herring meal was at the time a perfectly normal and well-known ingredient of the diet of mink kept in captivity both in Europe, America, Scandinavia and Norway; and that Norsildmel must have known of the practice of feeding herring meal to mink.]

The Court of Appeal, for reasons which they gave, disturbed this finding of fact and held that there was not sufficient evidence to establish that Norsildmel knew before the contract was entered into that herring meal was being fed to mink.

In my view, the Court of Appeal were not entitled to disturb what was essentially a finding of fact by the trial judge. It depended not only on documentary evidence but also upon the evidence of witnesses. Milmo J did not accept the evidence of Norsildmel's two witnesses, Arnesen and Voldnes, who said they did not know of this fact before 1957. I find that there was sufficient evidence upon which the trial judge could make a finding as to the requisite knowledge on the part of Norsildmel.

Herring meal is an international commodity dealt with throughout the world as animal feeding-stuff. The most significant fact is that from 1957–61 there were recurrent outbreaks of a liver disease in mink in Norway where herring meal was being fed to mink. These were investigated. It was not known then what was the cause of the disease or that it came from herring meal. But the fact that herring meal was being fed to mink must have been known to Norsildmel who were so heavily involved in the sale of that commodity. Mr Voldnes admitted that they knew that from 1957 Norwegian mink farmers were feeding herring meal to mink.

[His Lordship then quoted further evidence of the use of herring meal in feeding mink.]

If Norsildmel had knowledge that herring meal was being fed to mink in Norway and elsewhere I see no reason why it was necessary for Hill to prove use in Great Britain.

Mr Lloyd for Norsildmel relied very strongly on *Griffiths v Peter Conway Ltd* [1939] 1 All ER 685. In that case a lady purchased a Harris tweed coat. After wearing it she developed dermatitis. She made a claim under s 14(1) of the Sale of Goods Act. The evidence revealed that the plaintiff's skin was abnormally sensitive and that there was nothing in the cloth which would have affected the skin of a normal person. The abnormality of the plaintiff's skin was not made known to the retailer. The plaintiff failed on the ground of the abnormality of her skin, which no seller would assume to exist. I regard this as a highly special case which has no application to the present. All animals are sensitive to DMNA. Whether it is lethal depends on the animal and the quantity of meal supplied in the food. Mink may be more sensitive than other animals but the tweed coat in *Griffiths v Peter Conway Ltd* would not have harmed a normal person.

Lord Wilberforce (at 496): ... The scope and applications of s 14(1) of the Sale of Goods Act 1893 was fully considered by this House in *Hardwick Game Farm v Suffolk Agricultural Poultry Producers Association Ltd* [1969] 2 AC 31. The opinion expressed in that case endorsed a tendency which other cases (such as *Manchester Liners Ltd v Rea Ltd* [1922] 2 AC 74) had shown, to expand the scope of s 14(1) so as to cover territory which might otherwise, on a first reading, have been thought to belong to s 14(2). I think that this tendency essentially reflects a reversion to the more general approach to questions of the seller's liability under implied warranty adopted by the common law, as contrasted with the compartmentalisation into separate, but inevitably overlapping, provisions adopted by the Sale of Goods Act. *Naturam expellas furca* is a maxim which tends to apply to codifications. At any rate it is clear that this House in the *Hardwick* case accepted that the "making known" so as to show reliance which the section requires is easily deduced from the nature and circumstances of the sale, and that the word "particular" means little more than "stated" or "defined". As Lord Pearce said in *Hardwick* at 115: "There is no need for a buyer formally to 'make known' that which is already known": and here there is no doubt that the third parties, through their selling agents C T Bowring & Co Ltd and also directly, knew what the herring meal was required for, namely, for inclusion in animal feeding-stuffs to be compounded by the buyers, and no special purpose in relation to mink was relied on. The third parties were, moreover, a committee, or co-operative, of manufacturers of herring meal: in this case, whether one speaks of implication or presumption, the conclusion can hardly be otherwise than that of reliance by the buyers to produce a product reasonably fit for the purpose. I observe, indeed, that my noble and learned friend, Lord Guest, who felt difficulty in *Hardwick* as to the application of s 14(1) against persons who were dealers in the market, said that he could well understand, where the sale is by a manufacturer to a customer, that the inference (sc of reliance) can easily be drawn: at 106. I agree with Milmo J that it ought to be drawn in this case.

Then was the purpose, to be used for inclusion in animal feeding-stuffs to be compounded by the buyers, a particular purpose? In my opinion, certainly yes. It is true that the purpose was wide, wider even than the purpose accepted as particular in *Hardwick* (for compounding into food for cattle and poultry), and, if one leaves aside a possible alternative use as fertiliser,

Implied Conditions in Contracts of Sale

on which there was some indefinite evidence, the purpose so made known covers a large part of the area which would be within s 14(2). But I do not think, as the law has developed, that this can be regarded as an objection or that in accepting a purpose so defined, as a "particular purpose", the court is crossing any forbidden line. There remains a distinction between a statement (express or implied) of a particular purpose, though a wide one, with the implied condition (or warranty) which this attracts, and a purchase by description with no purpose stated and the different condition (or warranty) which that attracts. Moreover, width of the purpose is compensated, from the seller's point of view, by the dilution of his responsibility: and to hold him liable under an implied warranty of fitness for the purpose of which he has been made aware, wide though this may be, appears as fair as to leave him exposed to the vaguer and less defined standard of merchantability. After all, the seller's liability is, if I may borrow the expression of my noble and learned friend, Lord Morris of Borth-y-Gest, no more than to meet the requirement of a buyer who is saying to him "that is what I want it for, but I only want to buy if you sell me something that will do". I think that well expresses the situation here.

The next point is whether, when the meal turned out to be unsuitable for feeding to mink, this was a matter to be treated as within the seller's responsibility. There are two distinct points here: the first is whether feeding to mink was a normal use, within the general purpose of inclusion in animal feeding-stuffs: the second is whether, assuming that the seller's implied warranty did not extend beyond that of general suitability for animals, including possibly mink, the buyers were able to show a breach of that warranty.

The first point involves an issue of fact which received lengthy examination in the courts below. The decision on it depended to a great extent upon the view taken of two Norwegian witnesses called by the third parties, who were the assistant director of the third parties and the chief executive of a Norwegian herring oil factory at the relevant time. These witnesses were called to show that the third parties did not know in 1961 that herring meal might be fed to mink.

Unfortunately the courts below reached different conclusions. Milmo J did not accept the disclaimer of the Norwegian witnesses. He found that both were aware in or before 1961 that herring meal was being fed to mink in Norway and that herring meal was a normal and well-known ingredient of the diet of mink kept in captivity in Norway and (he added) in other countries. On this basis he found that Sildmelutvalget knew of the practice of feeding herring meal to mink.

The Court of Appeal reached an opposite conclusion. They held that the respondents had failed to establish that at the date of the contract the third party should reasonably have contemplated that it was not unlikely that the herring meal, the subject matter of the contract, might be fed to mink. On the contrary, they found on the evidence that the result of such contemplation would have been that it was highly unlikely that the herring meal would be fed to mink, and they added (though this would appear to be both an irrelevant matter and, since the meal was not known to be toxic, also factually incorrect) to which alone it would be harmful.

On this issue, the careful re-examination of the evidence which took place in this House, convinced me that the Court of Appeal was not justified in reversing in this matter the findings of fact of the trial judge. The latter were supported by the impression made on him by the two Norwegian witnesses in the witness box, by some important letters written by the third parties in late 1960 on the subject of herring meal and its potentiality as mink food, and by the general probabilities of the case, the fact being that there were numerous mink and fox farms in Norway to which herring meal had been fed. In my opinion, we must reinstate the judge's conclusion, that feeding to mink was a normal user in 1961 and known as such to the third parties. That the relevant consignment or part of it might be fed to mink was also known to the respondents.

I should add that some, but slight, reliance was placed on the fat content of the meal supplied. The argument was that herring meal with a high fat content is unsuitable for mink, that the herring meal in question had a high fat content and that this showed that the buyers could not be relying on the seller's judgment. There are several answers to this. In the first place, the actual fat content (9.6 per cent) was below that fixed by the contract (12–13 per cent) which seems to show that the buyer regarded the herring meal as in this respect suitable. And, secondly, even if it were excessive, this could be a matter within the buyer's responsibility quite consistently with the purity of the meal being within the seller's responsibility. The argument is, in my opinion, conclusive.

If I am right so far on the question of suitability and reliance, similar considerations arise on the question whether the consignment was in fact unsuitable, so as to involve a breach of warranty, to those already discussed as between the appellants and the respondents, and for the same reasons the conclusion follows, in my opinion, that a breach of warranty under s 14(1) was proved. The respondents did not, in this part of the appeal, pursue a claim under s 14(2).

Finally, any question as to remoteness of damage is disposed of by the finding that feeding to mink was a normal user and contemplated as such by both parties to the contract.

I would allow both appeals.

[**Lord Hodson** and **Viscount Dilhorne** agreed substantially with the judgment of Lord Wilberforce on this aspect of the case.]

Lord Diplock (at 512): ... I turn next to s 14(1) upon which Hill also relies. The most that Hill made known to the Norwegians about the purposes for which the herring meal was required was what I have previously termed a "range of purposes". The extent of that range was limited to what their agent in London had learnt from Hill in the course of previous dealings as to the nature of Hill's business. The range so made known included use as an ingredient in feeding-stuffs for many kinds of domestic animals and poultry. What it did not include was use as an ingredient in feeding-stuffs for mink. This seems to me to be conclusive that even if the Norwegians knew that Norwegian herring meal was a commodity which might be used as an ingredient in the diet of mink, use for that purpose can neither be nor form any part of the particular purpose for which the goods were required which was *made known by the buyer to the seller*, so as to give rise to the implied condition under s 14(1) that they should be reasonably fit for feeding mink.

My Lords, it will already be apparent that, for the reasons which I have already advanced in discussing "range of purposes", the decision of this House in *Hardwick Game Farm v Suffolk Agricultural Poultry Producers Association* [1969] 2 AC 31 that the fourth parties were liable to the third parties for breach of the condition implied under s 14(1) in my view goes to the utmost limit of what can be held to be a "particular purpose" within the meaning of that section without amending the Act itself. However desirable it may be to make such an amendment, to do so lies beyond the competence of this House of Parliament acting alone — even in its judicial capacity. I myself would distinguish that part of the decision in the *Hardwick Game Farm* case whenever I can. I do not think that it is open to your Lordships to extend it.

There are at least two relevant distinctions between the facts in the second appeal and those in the appeal between the third and fourth parties in the *Hardwick Game Farm* case. The first I have already mentioned. Neither expressly not by implication had Hill ever made known to the Norwegians that the range of purposes for which he required the herring meal included use as an ingredient in the diet of mink, whereas in the *Hardwick Game Farm* case the third party had at least by implication made known to the fourth party that his range of purposes did include use as an ingredient in the diet of pheasants, for which it proved to be unsuitable.

The second distinction is that at the time of the relevant contract between the third and fourth parties in the *Hardwick Game Farm* case it was not known that there could be any characteristics of the commodity sold, Brazilian groundnut extractions, which might render them unsuitable for feeding to pheasants that would not also render them unsuitable for feeding to all other species of animals and birds. As was pointed out by Lord Reid, at 83, the information that the goods were required for feeding to pheasants as well as to other animals and birds would not in fact have enabled the fourth parties to exercise any skill or judgment which they then possessed other than that which was called for in selecting goods fit for the purpose of feeding to all kinds of animals and birds. In the instant appeal it was known that there were some characteristics of Norwegian herring meal, in particular the fat content, which might render it unsuitable for feeding to mink though not unsuitable for feeding to other animals and birds. The information that the herring meal was required for feeding to mink would in fact have enabled the Norwegians to exercise skill and judgment in selecting goods fit for this particular purpose and had they been given this information it is unlikely that, because of its high fat content, they would have selected the particular consignment of herring meal for delivery under the contract. It is true that, at the time, the reason for their not doing so would not have been the presence of DMNA in the consignment, of which they knew nothing, but its fat content which was much higher than was then thought to be suitable in a food for mink. But the fact that to their knowledge there was at least one characteristic which distinguished herring meal which was suitable for feeding to mink from herring meal which was suitable for feeding to some other animals was, in my view, sufficient to displace any inference that Hill, who did not make it known to them that he required the herring meal for feeding to mink, showed that he relied upon their skill and judgment to supply a meal which was suitable for that purpose.

I recognise that, unlike the first, the second distinction is fortuitous. Fat content bears no necessary relationship to DMNA content. But if, as I have suggested earlier, the key to s 14(1) is reliance, mere knowledge by the seller that the goods *may* be required for use for feeding to mink is not enough. Unless they know that the goods *are* required for that purpose and the source of their knowledge is the buyer himself, there is no ground for any reasonable inference that the buyer was relying on the skill or judgment of the seller to select herring meal which is fit for feeding to mink, if there is any characteristic which distinguishes herring meal which is fit for that purpose from herring meal which is fit for feeding to other animals or birds.

Merchantable quality (Ashington Piggeries v Christopher Hill)
Lord Guest (at 473): . . . *Section 14(2) of the Sale of Goods Act 1893*: This section provides that where goods are bought by description from a seller who deals in goods of that description there is an implied condition that the goods shall be of merchantable quality. There is an admission by Hill that the goods were not of merchantable quality. So that the only issue which arises is on the first limb of this section.

The argument for Hill was that as the goods bought were "King Size" mink food and as Hill had not previously dealt in goods of that contractual description the section did not apply. Such was the approach of the Court of Appeal. This is a plausible and possible construction of the sub-section. But, in my view, such a strict construction would lead to absurd results. Suppose a customer goes to a tobacconist's shop and orders a box of Larañaga cigars in which the tobacconist had not previously dealt. If the cigars were not fit for smoking, there would be no liability on the tobacconist as he had not previously dealt in goods of that particular description, namely, Larañaga cigars. I cannot believe that the section bears such a restricted meaning. Some support for the view which I have expressed is to be found in observations of my noble and learned friend, Lord Reid, in *B S Brown & Son Ltd v Craiks Ltd* [1970] 1 WLR 752 at 755: "The appellants mainly relied on the contention that, whereas cloth of this description had been commonly used for making dresses, there was no evidence that such cloth had ever been put to any industrial use. There is, I think, some ambiguity in saying that goods are of the same description where the contract description is a precise and detailed specification for their manufacture. One may mean of the same precise and detailed description, and that may be novel: or one may mean of the same general description, and that may be common. In most of the authorities the latter meaning seems to have been adopted."

Mr Guest for Ashington Piggeries gave the House an elaborate examination of the common law before the passing of the Sale of Goods Act 1893. He argued that as the Sale of Goods Act was a codifying statute, it should in large measure represent the law on the subject before the passing of the Act. As Sir Mackenzie Chalmers put it in the introduction to his first edition of *The Sale of Goods Act*, p iv: "The Bill is almost entirely a reproduction of common law", and the changes in the Act were very slight. Mr Guest referred to a number of cases in the nineteenth century which he said made it clear that there was no distinction between the word "description" at common law and as it subsequently appeared in s 14(1) and (2). The word "description" in s 14(1) clearly had a wide import. The principles he argued, embodied in these sections applied where goods were supplied by a manufacturer or dealer in way of his business as opposed to where the seller sold goods in a private capacity. It is true that the distinction can be drawn between the case of *Brown v Edgington* (1841) 2 Man & G 279 where the seller of a piece of rope put himself forward as the manufacturer, although the rope was manufactured by an independent contractor, and was held liable, and the case of *Burnby v*

Bollett (1847) 16 M & W 644, where trading was done in an individual capacity and there was no liability for defective goods. These may be but straws in the wind. But there is the classic passage in *Jones v Just* (1868) LR 3 QB 197 at 202-3 of Mellor J which is supposed to be the basis of the enactment of s 14 of the Sale of Goods Act 1893, which I quote: "Fourthly, where a manufacturer or a dealer contracts to supply an article which he manufactures or produces, or in which he deals, to be applied to a particular purpose, so that the buyer necessarily trusts to the judgment or skill of the manufacturer or dealer, there is in that case an implied term or warranty that it shall be reasonably fit for the purpose to which it is to be applied: *Brown v Edgington* (1841) 2 Man & G 279; *Jones v Bright* (1829) 15 Bing 533. In such a case the buyer trusts to the manufacturer or dealer, and relies upon his judgment and not upon his own. Fifthly, where a manufacturer undertakes to supply goods, manufactured by himself, or in which he deals, but which the vendee has not had the opportunity of inspecting, it is an implied term in the contract that he shall supply a merchantable article ...".

This case is referred to in the note to s 14(1) in *Chalmers*, 1st ed. If this be the principle lying behind s 14, I see no reason why the scope of the dealer's business in s 14(2) should be restricted to the contract description of the goods.

If the purpose of the qualifying words "deals in goods of that description" was to confine the section to a dealer in the way of business as opposed to a private capacity, then I think a fair interpretation of the words would be "who deals in goods of that kind". If this is the proper interpretation of s 14(2) then the conditions are satisfied because Hill had dealt before in goods of that kind, namely, animal feeding-stuffs. In my view, Hill are in breach of the implied condition as the goods were not of merchantable quality.

[**Lord Wilberforce** (at 495) extracted above (p 58) and **Viscount Dilhorne** (at 485) agreed with **Lord Guest** that the respondent Christopher Hill did deal in goods of the contractual description and therefore s 14(2) was applicable. **Lord Hodson** (at 469) agreed with the Court of Appeal that Christopher Hill did not deal in goods of that description, namely, the mink food called "King Size", and that s 14(2) did not apply. **Lord Diplock** (at 509) in his judgment extracted above (p 62) agreed with the Court of Appeal and Lord Hodson that s 14(2) did not apply.

The implied condition of merchantable quality under s 14(2) was not relied upon by Christopher Hill in its action for indemnity against Norsildmel.]

APPLICATION OF ASHINGTON PIGGERIES CASE TO AUSTRALIA

Of particular concern to Australian courts will be the questions of (a) when are goods of a description which it is in the course of a seller's business to supply under s 19(1), and (b) when does a seller deal in goods of that description under s 19(2). For example, compare the following statement of Dixon CJ in the High Court of Australia in:

J S Robertson (Aust) Pty Ltd v Martin
High Court of Australia (1956) 94 CLR 30

Dixon CJ (at 43): ... In my opinion [the plaintiff buyer] failed to show that the circumstances were such that the condition that the goods should be of merchantable quality was implied in the contract they alleged. It failed to show that Arnos Supplies Co dealt in goods of the description forming the subject of the contract.

There is very little authority upon the precise application of the expression "who deals in goods of that description" in s 14(2) of the Sale of Goods Act 1893 (Imp) or upon the previous law it codifies. Little assistance is given by *Turner v Mucklow* (1862) 6 LTNS 690 or *Ipswich Gaslight Co v King & Co* (1886) 3 TLR 100. These cases treat residual products of a manufacturing process as not necessarily goods of a description in which the manufacturer deals. There are more cases upon the words in s 14(1) "goods of a description which it is in the course of the seller's business to supply". But the nature of the condition to be implied under s 14(1) and the other necessary factors required make cases under that provision of little use as guides under s 14(2). The present case is singular and the question turns on unusual facts, so far as they are proved. Apparently Arnos Supplies Co manufactured metal goods in which the process of manufacture depended on impress stamping. It seems that they did not manufacture electrical goods. There is no evidence that they imported goods for sale or indented goods or contracted to sell goods to be imported. So far as appears the transaction now in question was an isolated one springing from the facts that Martin had brought the specimens of the trouser press back to Australia with many other things with a view to considering manufacturing them or procuring them to be manufactured, that the plaintiff's chairman had his interest attracted by the novelty, that Martin decided against attempting its manufacture but agreed, according to the hypothesis demanded by the plaintiff's case, to sell 5000 of the presses of Driver's manufacture to the plaintiff.

It may be that the point depends on want of evidence but on the whole I think that on these facts the plaintiff has failed to establish that an essential part existed of the basis on which the application of s 14(2), ie s 19(ii) of the Victorian Act, rests.

It is significant that the requirements that:
(a) goods are of a description which it is in the course of the seller's business to supply—in the implied condition of fitness for purpose (s 19(1)); and
(b) goods are bought by description from a seller who deals in goods of that description—in the implied condition of merchantable quality (s 19(2)), were never contained in HPA s 5, have been deleted from the English Sale of Goods Act (see Sale of Goods (Implied Terms) Act 1973) and have not been included in TPA s 71.

OTHER ASPECTS OF CONDITION OF FITNESS

There remain two aspects of s 19(1) which require further treatment: the element of reliance and the proviso of sale of a specified article under its patent or other trade name.

Hardwick Game Farm v Suffolk Agricultural Poultry Producers Association
House of Lords [1969] 2 AC 31; [1968] 2 All ER 444
(Also cited as *Henry Kendall & Sons v William Lillico & Sons Ltd*.)

[The plaintiffs bought from the defendant association compounded meals for feeding to their pheasants and partridges, which they reared for stock and sale. The meal contained Brazilian groundnut extraction which was contaminated by fungus and the birds died or became deformed. Actions between the plaintiffs and defendants and between them and the suppliers of the groundnut extraction were brought on appeal to the House of Lords where various aspects of SGA s 14(1) and (2) (NSW ss 19(1) and (2)) were considered.]

Lord Reid (at 79): ... On the face of it s 14(1) has a narrower scope [than s 14(2)]. It requires that the buyers shall have required the goods for a particular purpose, and that purpose shall have been made known to the seller, and that it shall have been made known to him in such circumstances that he realised or ought to have realised that the buyer was relying on his using his skill or judgment to select goods fit for that purpose. Many cases in which the seller has been held liable under this sub-section might equally well and more logically have been decided under sub-s (2). But there has been a tendency to construe sub-s (2) too narrowly and to compensate for that by giving a wide construction to sub-s (1).

If the object of the disclosure of the particular purpose is, as I think it must be, to give to the seller an opportunity to exercise his skill or judgment in making or selecting appropriate goods, then it is difficult to see how a stated purpose can be a "particular" purpose if it is stated so widely that it would cover different qualities of goods, because carrying out the purpose in one way would only require a lower quality of goods whereas carrying it out in another way would require a higher quality. Different qualities normally sell at different prices. If a customer sought from a manufacturer or dealer cloth for the purpose of making overcoats the dealer could not know what quality was required. A cut-price tailor would not want to pay the price of cloth used in Savile Row, and the tailor in Savile Row would not use the quality which the cut-price tailor wants. Unless the seller knew the nature of the buyer's business his only clue to the quality which the buyer wanted would be the price which the buyer was prepared to pay. If a high price was offered it might no doubt be right to hold that he must supply goods suitable for high quality coats. But it could not be right that if the cloth was sold at a price appropriate for the lower quality, the dealer would have to supply a higher quality simply because the buyer had stated that his purpose was to make overcoats and the lower quality would not always be reasonably fit for making every kind of overcoat.

It was argued that, whenever any purpose is stated so as to bring this sub-section into operation, the seller must supply goods reasonably fit to enable the buyer to carry out his purpose in any normal way. But that can only be right if the purpose is stated with sufficient particularity to enable the seller to exercise his skill or judgment in making or selecting appropriate goods. The seller may know or be told that the merchant who is buying from him is buying for the purpose of reselling the goods in the course of his business. That may be sufficient to enable the seller to select appropriate goods or it may not. If the buyer's trade is such that some of his customers will want goods of the description which he is buying from the seller for one purpose or of one quality, and others of his customers will want goods of that description of another quality for another purpose, it could not be right that the buyer, merely by stating that he wants the goods for resale in the course of his business, could impose on the seller the obligation to supply goods reasonably fit for resale to every ordinary customer of the buyer no matter what his requirements might be.

Perhaps the solution of this problem is to be found in the application of the requirement of the section that the particular purpose must be made known "so as to show that the buyer relied upon the seller's skill or judgment". A buyer who is buying for the purpose — known to the seller — of reselling in the course of his business may want superior goods for which some of his customers will pay a high price, or he may want goods of lower quality to sell to less demanding customers. If he does not say which he wants, or at least indicate which he wants by the price which he is offering, how can he be relying on the seller to supply something reasonably fit for his purpose?

The leading case is *Manchester Liners Ltd v Rea Ltd* [1922] 2 AC 74. But it is not a very satisfactory source from which to extract general principles. Lord Buckmaster began his speech by saying, at 77: "... when the circumstances in which this appeal has arisen are examined, it will be found that its determination really depends upon the proper aspect of the facts rather than on an examination of uncertain principles of law." Rea were coal merchants and the shipowner's order was for "500 tons South Wales coal for the steamship *Manchester Importer*". It might seem from Lord Buckmaster's speech that there was something unusual about the furnaces in this ship, but Lord Atkinson, at 83, quoted the finding of the trial judge that the "coal actually delivered was not reasonably fit for an ordinary average Manchester steamer like the *Manchester Importer* in the hands of average officers and crew". So one would assume that coal merchants could easily have found out if they did not know already what kind of coal was needed. Lord Dunedin said at 82: "It was not the buyer who was going to find the coal. He says to the seller 'I want 500 tons for a special purpose, will you give it me?' The seller could easily have guarded himself, but he merely answered 'yes', by confirming the proposal as made. Not only so, but he came into court asserting that he did supply Welsh coal of suitable quality."

The passages in Lord Buckmaster's speech at 79 usually quoted are: "It is plain that the order was expressed for the use of a particular steamship, and it must, therefore, be assumed that the respondents knew the nature of her furnaces and the character of the coal she used, for it was this coal they contracted to supply ... If goods are ordered for a special purpose, and that purpose is disclosed to the vendor, so that in accepting the contract he undertakes to supply goods which are suitable for the object required, such a contract is, in my opinion, sufficient to establish that the buyer has shown that he relies on the seller's skill and judgment."

I think that importance was attached to the fact that the seller was expressly told for what ship the coal was wanted. It is certainly not necessary in many cases that the buyer should state his purpose expressly, but in a doubtful case it is much easier to infer that the seller ought to have realised that the buyer was relying on him if the purpose is stated expressly. I am not at all convinced that that inference would have been drawn if Rea had merely happened to know — still less if he had merely assumed — that the coal was wanted for the *Manchester Importer*. I do not think that this case is any authority for the view which has sometimes been expressed that if the seller knows the purpose for which the buyer wants the goods it will be presumed that the buyer relied on his skill and judgment. Lord Sumner said, at 90: "The words of s 14(1) are 'so as to show', not 'and also shows'. They are satisfied, if the reliance is a matter of reasonable inference to the seller and to the court, and in this case I think the evidence supports the finding of Salter J that the inference ought to be drawn.''

Lord Wright might appear to be going further when he said in *Cammell Laird* [1934] AC 402 at 423: "Such a reliance must be affirmatively shown; the buyer must bring home to the mind of the seller that he is relying on him in such a way that the seller can be taken to have contracted on that footing. The reliance is to be the basis of a contractual obligation.''

But I do not think that he meant more than that in the whole circumstances a reasonable man in the shoes of the seller would have realised that he was being relied on. In *Grant's* case [1936] AC 85 at 99, he said: "It is clear that the reliance must be brought home to the mind of the seller, expressly or by implication. The reliance will seldom be express: it will usually arise by implication from the circumstances: thus to take a case like that in question, of a purchase from a retailer, the reliance will be in general inferred from the fact that a buyer goes to the shop in the confidence that the tradesman has selected his stock with skill and judgment: the retailer need know nothing about the process of manufacture: it is immaterial whether he be manufacturer or not: the main inducement to deal with a good retail shop is the expectation that the tradesman will have bought the right goods of a good make ..."

A shopkeeper's goodwill consists largely in his reputation of being reliable — the better the shop the easier it is to draw this inference.

Drummond v Van Ingen (1887) 12 App Cas 284 was decided at a time when there was no clear distinction between the two implied conditions which are now set out in sub-ss (1) and (2) of s 14. The contract was for "mixt worsted coatings" equal in quality and weight to samples. The goods were exported by Van Ingen but rejected by the buyers, returned and resold at a loss. Van Ingen claimed damages on the ground that the goods were not merchantable. The trial judge found that there was an implied warranty that the cloth should be merchantable generally as worsted coatings, should be properly manufactured and should be suitable to be made up into coats in the ordinary course of tailor's work, but that the cloth was not merchantable as worsted coating and was not properly manufactured and suitable to be made up into coats in the ordinary course of tailoring. The Earl of Selborne said, at 287: "I think your Lordships must ... take the existence of the defect, in a degree sufficient to render the cloth unmerchantable for the purposes for which goods of the same general class had previously been used in the trade, to have been sufficiently established."

He went on (at 288) to discuss the degree of knowledge of the trade to be expected of the manufacturer — but still I think in connection with merchantability — for he said (at 289) that the respondents had "a right to assume that the appellants, accepting the order, could and would produce and deliver a good article, having the weight and all the other apparent qualities of the samples, which would be as merchantable for coatings as other articles of the same class previously known in the trade".

Lord Herschell and Lord Macnaghten come nearer to applying the condition now set out in s 14(1). Indeed Lord Macnaghten says, at 296: "But the question is not were they saleable, but were they fit for the purpose for which they were known to have been ordered."

This was a case of the goods being bought from the manufacturer. It can only be in unusual circumstances that a buyer does not rely in part at least on the skill or judgment of the manufacturer, or that a manufacturer is entitled to assume that the buyer is not relying on him at least to some extent.

Note that TPA s 71(2) retains the concept of reliance but raises a presumption that where the consumer's particular purpose is made known the condition of fitness will be implied except where the circumstances show that the consumer does not rely, or that it is unreasonable for him to rely. The onus is cast on the seller to disprove reliance, and the objective test would effectively negate an exclusion clause stating that the consumer did not rely if that was inconsistent with the circumstances.

Does a buyer rely on a seller's skill and judgment where he orders goods by reference to their trade name or does the proviso to SGA s 19(1) apply? There is no equivalent proviso in HPA s 5(3) or TPA s 71(2).

Baldry v Marshall
English Court of Appeal [1925] 1 KB 261

Bankes LJ (at 266): ... The mere fact that an article sold is described in the contract by its trade name does not necessarily make the sale a sale under a trade name. Whether it is so or not depends upon the circumstances. I may illustrate my meaning by reference to three different cases. First, where a buyer asks a seller for an article which will fulfil some particular purpose, and in answer to that request the seller sells him an article by a well-known trade name, there I think it is clear that the proviso does not apply. Secondly, where the buyer says to the seller, "I have been recommended such and such an article"—mentioning it by its trade name—"will it suit my particular purpose?" naming the purpose, and thereupon the seller sells it without more, there again I think the proviso has no application. But there is a third case where the buyer says to a seller, "I have been recommended so and so"—giving its trade name—"as suitable for the particular purpose for which I want it. Please sell it to me". In that case I think it is equally clear that the proviso would apply and that the implied condition of the thing's fitness for the purpose named would not arise. In my opinion the test of an article having been sold under its trade name within the meaning of the proviso is: Did the buyer specify it under its trade name in such a way as to indicate that he is satisfied, rightly or wrongly, that it will answer his purpose, and that he is not relying on the skill or judgment of the seller, however great that skill or judgment may be?

OTHER ASPECTS OF CONDITION OF MERCHANTABLE QUALITY

The cases extracted above have not called for discussion of two further aspects of the condition as to merchantable quality, namely, the proviso regarding examination by the buyer, and, when the condition is found applicable, the criteria for testing merchantable quality.

PROVISO REGARDING EXAMINATION

This proviso does not oblige the buyer actually to examine the goods, but if he does so, he cannot later complain under SGA s 19(2) of defects which *such examination ought to have revealed*. The proviso may appear illogical in that it penalises a buyer who takes the trouble to actually examine (but who is careless) while protecting the buyer who has ample *opportunity* to examine but refrains, perhaps purposely, from doing so. The precise meaning of the phrase "such examination ought to have revealed" is not self-evident. Is the buyer entitled to rely on SGA s 19(2) where he makes:

(a) the appropriate kinds of examinations and tests for discovering the defects, but does so carelessly so that he fails to observe the defects? or

(b) an examination, but of a kind which no reasonable person would make because, for example, it could never reveal any defects however carefully it was done?

In (a) the answer is clearly "no".

In (b) a literal interpretation of the language suggests the answer is "yes": see *Frank v Grosvenor Motor Auctions Pty Ltd* [1960] VR 607 at 609; but compare *Thornett and Fehr v Beers & Son* [1919] 1 KB 486 at 489. Does the change of language in HPA (Qld) s 5(2)(a) ("*the* examination"), or TPA s 71(1)(b) ("*that* examination") suggest any different result?

Under SGA s 19(2), once the requirements of the section are fulfilled, the seller's liability is absolute in the sense that it is no defence that he was not aware, or could not have been expected to be aware of the defects. Similarly under SGA s 19(1) it is no defence for the seller to prove that he took reasonable steps to ensure that the goods were fit for the buyer's purpose even where it was impossible for the seller to discover the defects. The position is the same under TPA s 71(1) and (2).

Implied Conditions in Contracts of Sale

WHAT IS "MERCHANTABLE QUALITY"?

The courts have attempted various formulations in applying the test of merchantable quality, and recently statutory definitions have been enacted in the consumer protection legislation. First, the judicial versions, of which you should re-read the judgments of Dixon J and Lord Wright in *Grant's* case extracted earlier. They have been the subject of some critical comments in later cases.

George Wills & Co Ltd v Davids Pty Ltd
High Court of Australia (1957) 98 CLR 77

[The plaintiff, Davids, purchased a number of cases of canned beetroot from George Wills & Co which upon examination 14 to 16 months later was found to have deteriorated. The plaintiff sued for breach of SGA s 19(2). The contract described the goods as canned beetroot but the parties knew that the contract was for beetroot *canned in vinegar*. Beetroot canned in brine was shown to have a longer life than beetroot canned in vinegar. On appeal to the High Court.]

Dixon CJ, McTiernan, Williams, Fullagar and **Taylor JJ** (at 89): The expression "merchantable quality", in relation to goods the subject of a contract of sale, must, obviously constitute a reference to their condition or quality. Consequently, goods are said to be of merchantable quality "if they are of such a quality and in such a condition that a reasonable man, acting reasonably, would, after a full examination, accept them under the circumstances of the case in performance of his offer to buy them, whether he buys them for his own use or to sell again": *Benjamin on Sale*, 8th ed, 1950, p 645, and cases there cited. Now, if as the learned District Court judge found, the normal life of beetroot canned in vinegar is 12 months, how can evidence that more than 12 months after its purchase it was found to have deteriorated in the manner previously described be taken as proof that it was defective when it was supplied? Or, perhaps it may be asked, if the contract called for the supply of beetroot canned in vinegar, how could the vendor have discharged its obligation under the contract by supplying canned beetroot which would keep for a longer period? Or, indeed, having been supplied with beetroot canned in vinegar, could the purchaser have rejected it merely because it had then ascertained that its normal life was 12 months only? The answer to these questions is provided by saying that, if the contract called for the supply of beetroot canned in vinegar, the parties were bound to deliver and accept goods of this description and, if the condition and quality of the goods were normal for goods of this description, the purchaser could have no complaint on the ground of their merchantability. It would be nothing to the point, on any such complaint, to show that beetroot canned in vinegar would not keep for as long a period as canned peas or canned beans or, indeed, beetroot canned in brine or for as long as other canned foodstuffs. Nor would it be material to show that a wholesaler, who had purchased such goods might still have them in his store more than twelve months later. Indeed, evidence as to the keeping quality of other goods and as to the practice of the wholesale grocery trade would not be admissible in such circumstances.

Hardwick Game Farm v Suffolk Agricultural Producers Association
House of Lords [1969] 2 AC 31; [1968] 2 All ER 444
(Also cited as *Henry Kendall & Sons v Lillico & Sons Ltd*: see facts extracted earlier.)

Lord Reid (at 75): ... Merchantable can only mean commercially saleable. If the description is a familiar one it may be that in practice only one quality of goods answers that description—then that quality and only that quality is merchantable quality. Or it may be that various qualities of goods are commonly sold under that description—then it is not disputed that the lowest quality commonly so sold is what is meant by merchantable quality: it is commercially saleable under that description. I need not consider here what expansion or adaptation of the statutory words is required where there is a sale of a particular article or a sale under a novel description. Here the description groundnut extractions had been in common use.

The novel feature of this case is that whereas in 1960 there appears to have been thought to be only one quality of this product, subject to minor variations, it has now been discovered that particular parcels though apparently of the usual quality may really be of a very different quality because they are contaminated by minute quantities of a powerful poison. So the question at once arises — do you judge merchantable quality in light of what was known at the time of the sale or in light of later knowledge?

It is quite clear that some later knowledge must be brought in for otherwise it would never be possible to hold that goods were unmerchantable by reason of a latent defect. By definition a latent defect is something that could not have been discovered at the time by any examination which in light of then existing knowledge it was reasonable to make. But there is a question as to how much later knowledge ought to be brought in. In the present case it had become well known before the date of the trial that the defect was that these Brazilian groundnut extractions were contaminated by poison: but it had also become well known that, while this poison made the goods unsuitable for inclusion in food for poultry, it was generally regarded as proper to include such extractions in cattle food, provided that the proportion included did not exceed 5 per cent of the whole. The question is whether this latter fact should be taken into account in deciding whether these goods were of merchantable quality in 1960.

I think it would be very artificial to bring in some part of the later knowledge and exclude other parts. In this case it is quite true that there was a period, after the nature and effect of this contamination had been discovered but before it had become accepted that small quantities of contaminated goods could safely be included in cattle foods, during which contaminated groundnut extractions were virtually unsaleable. But suppose that in this case it had been discovered at an early stage that these goods could be used for cattle food, so that there never was a period during which they were unsaleable. In that case I would not think it possible to take into account the nature of the defect but to exclude from consideration the effect which knowledge of the defect had on the market ...

A statement with regard to the meaning of s 14(2) which has been commonly accepted is that of Lord Wright in *Cammell Laird & Co v The Manganese Bronze and Brass Co* [1934] AC 402. In that case the respondents contracted to supply two specially designed ship's propellers. They first supplied propellers which were unsatisfactory and it was only at a third attempt that they supplied propellers which were satisfactory. Cammell Laird sued for damages caused by the delay. They succeeded on the terms of the contract and under s 14(1). But Lord Wright went on to consider the application of s 14(2). Apart from a short general statement at the end of the speech of Lord Tomlin, at 413, none of the other noble and learned lords said anything about s 14(2) or Lord Wright's gloss on it. Lord Wright said, at 430: "In earlier times, the rule of *caveat emptor* applied, save only where an action could be sustained in deceit on the ground that the seller knew of the defect, or for breach of express warranty (warrantizando vendidit). But with the growing complexity of trade, dealings increased in what are now called 'unascertained or future goods', and more generally 'goods sold by description'. As early as 1815 in *Gardiner v Gray* (1815) 4 Camp 144, Lord Ellenborough stated the rule. Goods had been sold as waste silk; a breach was held to have been committed on the ground that the goods were unfit for the purpose of waste silk and of such a quality that they could not be sold under that denomination. What sub-s (2) now means by 'merchantable quality' is that the goods in the form in which they were tendered were of no use for any purpose for which such goods would normally be used and hence were not saleable under that description."

I feel sure that Lord Wright did not really mean this to be a test of universal application in the form in which he stated it. If he did I disagree for reasons which I shall state. In the *Cammell Laird* case, if the propellers were of no use for the ship for which they had been designed it was true to say that they were of no use for any other ship and therefore unsaleable as propellers. But there are many cases in which different qualities of a particular kind of goods are commonly sold under different descriptions. Suppose goods are sold under the description commonly used to denote a high quality and the goods delivered are not of that high quality but are of a lower quality which is commonly sold under a different description, then it could not possibly be said that the goods in the form in which they were tendered were of no use for any purpose for which those goods would normally be used. They would be readily saleable under the appropriate description for the lower quality. But surely Lord Wright did not mean to say that therefore they were merchantable under the description which was appropriate for the higher quality. They plainly were not. Lord Wright said, at 430, "no use for any purpose for which *such goods* would normally be used". Grammatically "such goods" refers back to "the goods in the form in which they were tendered". But what he must have meant by "such goods" were goods which complied with the description in the contract under which they were sold. Otherwise the last part of the sentence "and hence were not saleable under that description" involves a non sequitur. If I now set out what I am sure he meant to say I think it would be accurate for a great many cases though it would be dangerous to say that it must be universally accurate. The amended version would be: "What sub-s (2) now means by 'merchantable quality' is that the goods in the form in which they were tendered were of no use for any purpose for which goods which complied with the description under which these goods were sold would normally be used, and hence were not saleable under that description." This is an objective test: "were of no use for any purpose ..." must mean "would not have been used by a reasonable man for any purpose ..."

That would produce a sensible result. If the description in the contract was so limited that goods sold under it would normally be used for only one purpose, then the goods would be unmerchantable under that description if they were of no use for that purpose. But if the description was so general that goods sold under it are normally used for several purposes, then goods are merchantable under that description if they are fit for any one of these purposes: if the buyer wanted the goods for one of those several purposes for which the goods delivered did not happen to be suitable, though they were suitable for other purposes for which goods bought under that description are normally bought, then he cannot complain. He ought either to have taken the necessary steps to bring sub-s (1) into operation or to have insisted that a more specific description must be inserted in the contract.

That would be in line with the judgment of Mellor J in *Jones v Just* (1868) LR 3 QB 197 which has always been regarded as high authority. He said, at 205: "It appears to us that, in every contract to supply goods of a specified description which the buyer has no opportunity to inspect, the goods must not only in fact answer the specific description, but must also be saleable or merchantable under that description."

The buyer bought manilla hemp: on arrival the goods were found to be damaged to such an extent as not to be saleable under that description and the buyer resold under the description "Manilla hemp with all faults" and received about 75 per cent of what merchantable manilla hemp would have fetched. So it certainly could not be said that the goods were of no use. But the buyer recovered, as damages for breach of the implied warranty, the difference between what the hemp would have been worth if merchantable as manilla hemp and what he was able to get for it when sold "with all faults".

It would also be in line with what Lord Wright said in *Canada Atlantic Grain Export Co v Eilers* (1929) 35 Lloyd LR 206 at 213: "... if goods are sold under a description which they fulfil, and if goods under that description are reasonably capable in ordinary use of several purposes, they are of merchantable quality within s 14(2) of the Act if they are reasonably capable of being used for any one or more of such purposes, even if unfit for use for that one of those purposes which the particular buyer intended."

There is another statement by Lord Wright regarding s 14(2) in *Grant v Australian Knitting Mills Ltd* [1936] AC 85 at 99: "The second exception (ie, s 14(2)) in a case like this in truth overlaps in its application the first exception (ie, s 14(1)); whatever else merchantable may mean, it does mean that the article sold, if only meant for one particular use in ordinary course, is fit for that use; merchantable does not mean that the thing is saleable in the market simply because it looks all right."

That too appears to me to be in line with my amended version of what he said in the *Cammell Laird* case at 413.

Another explanation of the phrase "merchantable quality" which has frequently been quoted is that of Farwell LJ in *Bristol Tramways Carriage Co Ltd v Fiat Motors Ltd* [1910] 2 KB 831 at 841 (CA): "The phrase in s 14(2) is, in my opinion, used as a meaning that the article is of such quality and in such condition that a reasonable man acting reasonably would after a full examination accept it under the circumstances of the case in performance of his offer to buy that article whether he buys for his own use or to sell again." I do not find this entirely satisfactory. I think what is meant is that a reasonable man in the shoes of the actual buyer would accept the goods as fulfilling the contract which was in fact made. But if the description was so wide that goods required for different purposes were commonly bought under it and if these goods were suitable for some of those purposes but not for the purpose for which the buyer bought them, it would have to be a very reasonable buyer indeed who admitted that the goods were merchantable, and that it was his own fault for not realising that goods might be merchantable under that description although unsuitable for his particular purpose.

There was also another explanation brought to our attention. In *Australian Knitting Mills Ltd v Grant* (1933) 50 CLR 387 at 413, Dixon J said: "The condition that goods are of merchantable quality requires that they should be in such an actual state that a buyer fully acquainted with the facts and, therefore, knowing what hidden defects exist and not being limited to their apparent condition would buy them without abatement of the price obtainable for such goods if in reasonable sound order and condition and without special terms."

I would only qualify this by substituting "some buyers" for "a buyer". "A buyer" might mean any buyer: but for the purposes for which some buyers wanted the goods the defects might make the goods useless, whereas for the purposes for which other buyers wanted them the existence of the defects would make little or no difference. That is in fact the position in the present case. I think that it must be inferred from the evidence that buyers who include groundnut extractions in their cattle foods are prepared to pay a full price for goods which may be contaminated. But buyers who only compound poultry foods would obviously not be prepared to buy contaminated goods at any price. Nevertheless contaminated groundnut extractions are merchantable under the general description of groundnut extractions because, rather surprisingly, some buyers appear to be ready to buy them under that description and to pay the ordinary market price for them ...

Lord Pearce (at 117): ... Were these goods merchantable? Merchantability is concerned not with purpose but with quality. The judge found that the groundnut meal was of merchantable quality and the Court of Appeal has upheld this finding. That finding does not, as it happens, affect the result of the case. Therefore, no purpose could be served by a detailed investigation of the complicated evidence and considerations involved. But in my opinion the judge arrived at this conclusion on an erroneous view of the principles applicable. He found ([1964] 2 Lloyd's Rep 227 at 271) that the goods "were capable in their ordinary user of being ultimately compounded into food for cattle (including a wide variety of animals under that description) or into food for poultry (including a wide variety of birds under that description). As compounded into food for cattle, certainly older cattle, it has been used without harm, though some of it has been injurious to calves and pigs. There was, at any rate, a limited market in this country after the troubles arose in 1960, inasmuch as BOCM sold some of their Brazilian groundnut meal which they had left on their hands for food for cattle, but not for poultry." Again, "On the other hand, since the trouble in 1960, the London cattle food trade market has not imported any groundnut meal into this country from Brazil, and ... the word 'Brazilian', as applied to groundnut meal in this country, is a dirty word. As a compound food for poultry, quantities of it have been proved to be lethal to very young birds, such as day-old ducklings, turkey poults, and pheasant chicks and poults and injurious to chickens in a much less degree. The plaintiff's breeding hen pheasants, however, suffered no ill effects. Though the meal was unfit for use for one purpose, as a compound food for poultry, I cannot find that the meal, in the form in which it was tendered, *was of no use for any purpose for which* the meal *would normally be used and hence was unsaleable under that description.*"

The words which I have underlined come from Lord Wright's opinion in *Cammell Laird & Co v Manganese Bronze and Brass Co* [1934] AC 402 at 430. He used similar expressions in *Canada Atlantic Grain Export Co v Eilers* (1929) 35 Lloyd LR 206 at 213, where he upheld a finding of merchantability with which he was obviously out of sympathy and in *Grant v Australia Knitting Mills Ltd* [1936] AC 85 at 99, Havers J preferred these dicta to the definition of Farwell LJ in *Bristol Tramways Carriage Co Ltd v Fiat Motors Ltd* [1910] 2 KB 831 at 840 that a merchantable article is "of such quality and in such condition that a reasonable man acting reasonably would after a full examination, accept it under the circumstances of the case in performance of his offer to buy that article whether he buys for his own use or to sell again". [His Honour then referred to Dixon J's price abatement test in *Australian Knitting Mills Ltd v Grant* (1933) 50 CLR 387 at 418 and continued:]

In my opinion, the definition of Farwell LJ ([1910] 2 KB 831 at 840) as amplified by Dixon J ((1933) 50 CLR 387 at 418) is to be preferred to that of Lord Wright ([1934] AC 402 at 430) which has, I think, the following weakness. The suggestion, without more, that goods are merchantable unless they are no use for any purpose for which they would normally be used and hence would be unsaleable under that description may be misleading, if it contains no reference to price. One could not say that a new carpet which happens to have a hole in it or a car with its wings buckled are of no use for their normal purposes and hence would be unsaleable under that description. They would no doubt, if their price was reduced, find a ready market. In return for a substantial abatement of price a purchaser is ready to put up with serious defects, or use part of the price reduction in having the defects remedied. In several classes of goods there is a regular retail market for "seconds", that is, goods which are not good enough in the manufacturer's or retailer's view to fulfil an order and are therefore sold off at a cheaper price. It would be wrong to say that "seconds" are necessarily merchantable.

Sir Owen Dixon was clearly right in saying (above) that in order to judge merchantability one must assume a knowledge of hidden defects, although these do not manifest themselves or are not discovered until some date later than the date of delivery which is the time as at which one must estimate merchantability (see also Atkin LJ in *Niblett Ltd v Confectioners Materials Co Ltd* [1921] 3 KB 387 at 404: "No one who knew the facts would buy them in that state or condition; in other words they were unsaleable and unmerchantable.") But what additional after-acquired knowledge must one assume? Logic might seem to indicate that the court should bring to the task all the after-acquired knowledge which it possesses at the date of trial. But I do not think that this is always so. For one is trying to find what market the goods would have had if their subsequently ascertained condition had been known. As it is a hypothetical exercise, one must create a hypothetical market. Nevertheless the hypothetical market should be one that could have existed, not one which could *not* have existed at the date of delivery. Suppose goods contained a hidden deadly poison to which there was discovered by scientists two years after delivery a simple, easy, inexpensive antidote which could render the goods harmless. They would be unmarketable at the date of delivery if the existence of the poison was brought to light, since no purchaser could then have known the antidote to the poison. Hypothesis is no reason for complete departure from possibility. One must keep the hypothesis in touch with the facts as far as possible. But I do not think that the point is important on the present facts.

In the present case, if on the day of delivery one had immediately compounded from it and fed the mixture from it to turkeys or young chickens or young pheasants it appears from the evidence that the birds would have died. One would then have had to label the goods for the market "This food contains toxin so that if compounded in normal proportions it is fatal to turkeys, young chickens, or young pheasants or ducklings." And also, I think, "The nature of and strength of the toxin are unknown." I find it hard to believe that there was on the date of delivery a market for it so labelled without abatement of price, even without the addition of the last sentence. On such evidence as there is it seems unlikely ...

B S Brown & Son Ltd v Craiks Ltd
House of Lords [1970] 1 All ER 823

[The appellants gave the respondents two orders for quantities of cloth at 36.25d per yard. There was no dispute that the goods were bought by description and that the respondent dealt in goods of that description. However, the appellants claimed that the cloth was not of merchantable quality because they could not use it for dress material, and they eventually resold it for 15d per yard. The trial judge found that there was a basic misunderstanding between the parties since the appellants thought they were purchasing material suitable for dresses and the respondents thought that the material was required for industrial purposes. The appellants had not made known to the respondents, either expressly or by implication, the purpose for which the goods were required. He further held that there was no evidence that cloth answering the whole of the description had ever been used for industrial purposes, but that the cloth was reasonably capable of being used and was saleable for a number of industrial purposes at a price of at least 30d per yard.]

Lord Guest (at 828): Passing now to the question of price, this does not seem to have bulked very largely in the arguments before the courts below. In my view, this case must be approached on the basis that the goods were not one-purpose-only goods but goods which were reasonably capable of being used for more than one purpose, as the Lord Ordinary has found. In the case of such dual purpose goods it is not, in my opinion, legitimate for the purpose of deciding whether the goods are of merchantable quality to compare the contract price too closely with the price at which the goods were sold for the secondary purpose. There will always be a discrepancy in cases of breach of contract; otherwise there could be no claim of damages. The assumption is that the goods are merchantable for a secondary purpose and unless the price is what has been described as a "throw-away price" the discrepancy sheds little or no light on the question of merchantable quality. "Commercially saleable" suggests that the price must not be unreasonably low. The Lord Ordinary has disposed of the question of price on the footing that it only arises where there is a case of latent defect, which was the case in *Kendall v Lillico* [1968] 2 All ER 444; [1969] 2 AC 31. I am not satisfied that this is a sound distinction. I cannot, for my part, see that the question of latent defect makes any difference. I would hold to the view I expressed in *Kendall v Lillico* All ER at 477; AC at 108 that price cannot be omitted entirely but, on mature reconsideration, I think that the test of Dixon J in *Grant v Australian Knitting Mills Ltd* (1933) 50 CLR 387 at 408; on appeal [1936] AC 85; [1935] All ER Rep 209 which I approved was expressed too broadly. The expression he used—"without abatement of the price obtainable" cannot be construed strictly. It cannot be a necessary requirement of merchantability that there should be no abatement of price. If the difference in price is substantial so as to indicate that the goods would only be sold at a "throw-away price," then that may indicate that the goods were not of merchantable quality. In the present case the difference in price of 6.25d on 36.25d is not, in my view, so material as to justify any such inference. The Lord Ordinary found [1969] SLT at 108: "The price of 36.25d per yard was higher than would have been normal for it as an industrial fabric, but not unreasonably high for the [respondents] constructing it for such a purpose. On the other hand, this price of 36.25d per yard was low for a dress fabric, and the [respondents'] price for constructing it as a dress fabric would have been higher."

In my view, the Lord President (Lord Clyde) and Lord Guthrie dealt adequately with this branch of the appellants' argument.

I would dismiss the appeal.

[**Lord Reid** and **Viscount Dilhorne** delivered judgments to a similar effect. **Lord Hodson** and **Lord Wilberforce** concurred in the judgment of Lord Guest.]

Appeal dismissed.

In *Mash & Murrell Ltd v Joseph I Emanuel Ltd* [1961] 1 All ER 485, the plaintiffs purchased a consignment of Cyprus potatoes to be shipped from Limassol in Cyprus C & F Liverpool from the defendant sellers who were potato importers and knew the nature of the plaintiffs' business and that they required the potatoes for use in England.

The potatoes were proved to be unfit for human consumption on their arrival in England. On the assumption that the sea voyage on the vessel *Ionian* was a normal one, Diplock J found the defendants liable for breach of the implied condition of merchantable quality under s 14(2) SGA (UK). He held that in the case of goods sold CIF and C & F merchantability means that the goods should remain from the time of delivery (that is, under a CIF contract the time of shipment) in a merchantable condition until arrival at destination and a reasonable time thereafter for disposal. Since the potatoes were unfit on arrival, he implied that they were in breach of the condition since they were not capable of standing a normal voyage to Liverpool so as to be of merchantable quality at the time of arrival. He gave judgment for the plaintiffs.

The defendants appealed to the Court of Appeal on the ground inter alia that Diplock J drew a wrong inference from the facts proved before him and that the voyage was not a normal voyage.

The Court of Appeal (Ormrod, Harman and Pearson LJJ), as reported in [1962] 1 All ER 77, assumed for the purposes of the appeal that the alleged warranty was implied in the contract, viz, a warranty that the potatoes when put on board were in such a state that, after a normal voyage, they would on arrival be in such a condition as to be suitable for the purpose for which the plaintiffs required them, ie, sale to retailers for human consumption. The court held, however, that the proper inference on the facts proved and on the balance of probability was that the potatoes remained unventilated probably continuously for five days and nights in hot summer weather while the *Ionian* was at Famagusta and that heat asphyxiation resulting was the initial cause of their deterioration. The voyage was therefore not a normal voyage and there was no sufficient ground for inferring that the potatoes when put on board at Limassol were not fit to travel on a normal voyage so as to constitute a breach of the assumed warranty. The appeal was allowed.

THE LAW COMMISSION AND LEGISLATORS TRY THEIR HANDS

Following these diverse judicial formulations the Law Commission in England formulated a definition of merchantability upon which the statutory definitions in English SGA s 62(1A) and TPA s 66(2) are based. See also TPA s 66(1). It appears that the definition in s 66(2) was intended to be exclusive of the previous common law formulations. Compare the similar definitions applicable to consumer sales under SGA s 64(3) and (9) (NSW). Compare also the equivalent provision under art 2 of the Uniform Commercial Code:

2-314(2) Goods to be merchantable must be at least such as:—
  (a) pass without objection in the trade under the contract description; and
  (b) in the case of fungible goods, are of their average quality within the description; and
  (c) are fit for the ordinary purposes for which such goods are used; and
  (d) run, within the variations permitted by the agreement of even kind, quality and quantity within each unit and among all units involved; and
  (e) are adequately contained, packaged, and labelled as the agreement may require; and
  (f) conform to the promises or affirmations of fact made on the container or label if any.

THE MANUFACTURER'S LIABILITY

The subject of the liability of manufacturers to the ultimate users of their products, or to those injured by defective goods, is commonly described as products liability law. It traces its modern origins to the famous case of *Donoghue v Stevenson* [1932] AC 562 in which the House of Lords laid down the principle that a manufacturer owes a duty of care to any person whom he ought reasonably to have in contemplation as being affected by his acts or omissions. See passage from Lord Atkins' speech quoted in *Grant's* case, p 79, *supra*. This subject generally is discussed in torts rather than contracts courses because there is normally no contract between manufacturer and ultimate consumer, and therefore the general provisions of SGA do not apply (although s 19(1) and (2) cover sales by manufacturers). Similarly there is no contract between manufacturer (or retailer) and the spouse, children or donees of the consumer who may be injured by the product.

The inadequacy of the common law rules is further illustrated by the difficulty in some cases of proving negligence, the limitation of damages to what was reasonably foreseeable with the result that consequential economic loss is often not recoverable. There is also some doubt whether so-called "guarantees" given by manufacturers are of much value to consumers because they often (a) are couched in very qualified terms, (b) contain provisions exempting the manufacturer from liability for negligence resulting in consequential loss, and (c) are made dependent upon the prompt return by the consumer to the manufacturer of a warranty card.

Since consumer protection has become a political catchcry, a number of statutory provisions have bridged the contractual lacunae between manufacturer and consumer by imposing direct liability on the manufacturer for defective products. A number of different approaches have been adopted:

(1) The imposition of direct non-excludable statutory warranties by the manufacturer, together with a right of indemnity against the manufacturer by a

retailer who is obliged to compensate a consumer for breach of a condition or warranty as to quality can be found in the Manufacturers Warranties Act 1974 and Law Reform (Manufacturers Warranties) Ordinance 1977 (ACT).

(2) The conferring on the consumer of a direct statutory right to compensation against a manufacturer or importer who has supplied goods to a distributor or retailer for the purpose of resupply: TPA Pt V Div 2A.

(3) The imposition of statutory warranties to remedy defects in goods: eg, Motor Dealers Act 1974 (NSW) s 27.

(4) The granting to courts dealing with consumer transactions power to join and order manufacturers to remedy the defect or pay the estimated cost of doing so: eg, SGA s 64(5); HPA s 5.

(5) The imposition of general obligations of fair dealing and the prohibition of unfair trade practices under Consumer Protection Acts of the various states: eg, Consumer Protection Act 1969 (NSW) Pt III. The most important provisions are those contained in TPA Pt V Div 1 dealing with misleading conduct, product safety standards, etc.

(6) The granting of a general right to damages for loss resulting from a breach of the provisions of TPA Pt V by s 82.

QUESTIONS

Question 3

(1) What effect did the enactment of SGA s 18 have on sales by description? Did it improve the buyer's position?

(2) Can words describing the quality of goods sold ever form part of the description to which s 18 will apply?

(3) What distinction can be drawn between the *Elder Smith* and *Ashington Piggeries* cases on the issue of sale by description, to justify the decisions in each case? Is the reasoning in both cases consistent on this issue?

Question 4

(1) Carb Pty Ltd sold two carburettors for $150 to Splash who intended to use them in his speedboat.

(2) Jim Handy sold 500 carburettors for $35,000 to Mitzi Co for use in manufacturing speedboats.

In both situations what remedies are available to the buyers if the carburettors prove defective? Which buyer would find it easier to establish a breach of any implied condition? In answering these questions assume all negotiations and signing of the contracts took place at Jim's home in Sydney and the contract was wholly performed in New South Wales.

Question 5

Where goods purchased have more than one purpose for which they can normally be used, how should the courts determine whether their quality satisfies the conditions of the contract? What factors will be relevant? In what respects have various legislatures assisted in providing criteria of merchantable quality and how useful are those criteria?

Question 6

TPA s 71(2) has omitted the proviso regarding sales of goods under patent or other trade name which is included in the equivalent SGA condition. What effect is this omission likely to have on the scope of the TPA section?

Implied Conditions in Contracts of Sale

Question 7

In the context of s 19(1) and 19(2) SGA when will the seller be responsible for the fact that the goods sold by him are unsuitable for the buyer's purpose? Illustrate your answer by reference to any cases you consider relevant.

Question 8

Carb Pty Ltd wrote to Yo Co Rubber Co asking for details of its synthetic gaskets. Carb required the gaskets for carburettors which it intended to use in aeroplane and snowplough engines which would be operating in sub-zero termperatures; however, Carb did not advise Yo Co of this fact and Yo Co had never previously manufactured gaskets specifically for use in cold climates.

Yo Co sent Carb a rubber gasket for inspection. Carb did not test this gasket at low temperatures before ordering "10,000 synthetic gaskets" from Yo Co.

Some months after receiving the full consignment of gaskets, Carb found that the gaskets were not synthetic but natural rubber and cracked when exposed to sub-zero temperatures, although they worked effectively in temperate climates.

Advise Carb of its rights.

How would your advice differ in each of the following alternative fact situations:

(1) At the time of ordering the gaskets Carb had notified Yo Co that it required the gaskets for use in aeroplanes and snowploughs.

(2) Carb had notified Yo Co as in (1) above and Yo Co had manufactured Carb's gaskets of a synthetic material supplied to it by another manufacturer who specialised in such material and had assured Yo Co of its suitability in freezing temperatures.

(3) Carb had supplied Yo Co with a sample of a synthetic gasket which was effective at sub-zero temperatures and the contract referred to "10,000 gaskets as per sample".

(4) The contract referred to "aeroplane gaskets".

Question 9

Jim Handy was establishing a small sheep stud as a hobby and for tax purposes. He heard a radio advertisement for the sale of stud rams by Stampede Pty Ltd, from whose yards he then purchased a Border Leicester ram named Prolific. Advise Jim fully as to his possible remedies in each of the following alternative situations:

(1) Jim selected Prolific from a pen which bore the sign "Healthy Rams" and paid $12,000 without discussion. Prolific was in excellent condition but was a wether.

(2) Jim selected Prolific from a pen which bore a sign "Fat Stock" and paid $12,000 for the ram without discussion. Prolific died five days later.

(3) The same facts as in (2) but the radio advertisement had described the sheep as "prime healthy beasts".

(4) A salesman handed Jim a sale catalogue headed "Stampede's Best Breeding Stock", from which he selected Prolific and paid $12,000 for him. Prolific proved to be a healthy ram but lazy and impotent.

(5) Stampede did not have a sale catalogue, but Jim stated to Stampede's salesman, "I want a good breeding ram. I believe Border Leicesters are very fertile. I'll buy Prolific". The salesman replied simply, "Write out your cheque and I'll give you a receipt". Prolific was a Border Leicester ram with an excellent pedigree. His general condition and wool were good but he was impotent.

FURTHER READING
Section 1: Implied Conditions in General
United Kingdom
Final Report of the Committee on Consumer Protection (The Molony Committee Report) 1962, Cmnd 1781.
Report of the Committee on Consumer Credit (Crowther Report) 1971, Cmnd 4596.
The Law Commission and the Scottish Law Commission:
  (1) Exemption Clauses in Contracts; First Report: Amendments to the Sale of Goods Act 1893 (1969) which resulted in the enactment of the United Kingdom Supply of Goods (Implied Terms) Act 1973 and also formed the basis for the implied terms in Trade Practices Act, Pt V.
  (2) Exemption Clauses: Second Report, 1976.
  (3) Liability for Defective Products, 1977.
Twelfth Report of the Law Reform Committee (Transfer of Title to Chattels) 1966, Cmnd 2958.

Australia
Law Reform Commission of New South Wales, Working Paper on Sale of Goods, 1975.
Report on Fair Consumer Credit Laws (Molomby Committee Report) 1972.
Report on the Law relating to Consumer Credit and Moneylending (Rogerson Committee Report) 1969.

Section 2: Implied Terms: Title and Freedom from Encumbrances
Battersby & Preston, "The Concepts of Property, Title and Owner used in the Sale of Goods Act 1893" (1972) 35 *MLR* 268.
Ellinger, "Buyer's Remedies when Seller does not have the Right to Sell the Goods" (1969) 5 *Victoria Uni Well LR* 168.

Section 3: Implied Conditions: Conformity, Fitness and Quality
Sale by Description
Beale v Taylor [1967] 1 WLR 1193.

Quality and Fitness
Davies, "Implied Conditions as to Fitness in a Contract of Hire: An Anglo-Australian Conflict" (1964) 38 *ALJ* 277.
Davies, "Merchantability and Fitness for Purpose: Implied Conditions of the Sale of Goods Act 1893" (1969) 85 *LQR* 74.
Franzi, "Merchantable Quality and Particular Purposes: Questions of Overlap" (1977) 51 *ALJ* 298.
Greig, "A Slight Case of Additives" (1971) 2 *A Curr LR* 237.
Hudon, "Time and Terms as to Quality in Sale of Goods" (1978) 94 *LQR* 566.
Note (1973) 47 *ALJ* 742.
Speedway Safety Products Pty Ltd v Hazell & Moore Industries Pty Ltd [1982] 1 NSWLR 255.
Sutton, "Let Sellers and Manufacturers Beware" (1980) 54 *ALJ* 146.
Turner, "Common Law Implied Terms of Fitness in Contracts of Simple Hire and Hire-Purchase: An Analysis" (1972) 46 *ALJ* 560.
Walton, "Implied Warranties in the Sale of Goods" (1976) 7 *Syd LR* 463.

CHAPTER 4

Performance of the Sales Contract and Remedies for Breach

"The ship's rail has lost much of its nineteenth-century significance. Only the most enthusiastic lawyer could watch with satisfaction the spectacle of liabilities shifting uneasily as the cargo sways at the end of a derrick across a notional perpendicular projecting from the ship's rail."

Mr Justice Devlin
Pyrene Co Ltd v Scindia Navigation Co Ltd
[1954] 2 QB 402 at 419

Section 1: Events Prior to Delivery: The Passing of Property and Risk
Section 2: Performance by Delivery and Acceptance of Goods and Payment
Section 3: Remedies for Breach

In this chapter, we turn to the final three stages of our prototype transaction as outlined at the beginning of Chapter 2. Turn back to pp 13–15 and note the questions under:

Stage 3: Events prior to Delivery of Goods.
Stage 4: Delivery and Acceptance of the Goods and Payment.
Stage 5: Remedies for Breach.

SECTION 1: EVENTS PRIOR TO DELIVERY: THE PASSING OF PROPERTY AND RISK

As the questions set out under Stage 3 indicate, most of the events we are concerned with might be described as accidents resulting in non-performance or loss to one or other of the parties. In simple commercial terms the main question will be: "who must bear responsibility for this non-performance or accept the risk of loss?" However, the legal answers have not been simple. The traditional legal base point for answering many of the questions has been to ascertain whether at the critical time the title to the goods has passed from seller to buyer, and detailed rules have been developed for finding the answer.

In Chapter 2 we noted Karl Llewellyn's dissatisfaction with the "passing of title" concept, and as the principal architect of Article 2 of the Uniform Commercial Code, he presided over its retrenchment. In the following extract, he described the pre-Code law under the Uniform Sales Act which largely corresponded to the Anglo-Australian Sale of Goods Acts.

Karl N Llewellyn: Through Title to Contract and a Bit Beyond
(1938) 15 *NYULQR* 159 at 165–70

The essence of the Sales transaction is dynamic. Lump-title fits only in that rare case in which our economy resembles that of three hundred years ago: where the whole transaction can be accomplished at one stroke, shifting possession along with title, no strings being left behind — as in cash purchase of an overcoat worn home. But the contract for sale on credit, the shifting of goods to market via a factor, the shipment against draft, the instalment sale, the delivery or shipment on approval, the agreement to sell goods lying in warehouse under non-negotiable receipt — these are not one-stroke transactions. They involve, each one, a complicated *series* of actions of varying significance. They involve a period, often an extended period, during which matters are in temporary suspension or are in active flux between the parties; over considerable periods of time there is no such Title in *either* party as the static picture of Title suggests. Take non-commercial shipbuilding. Admit that the builder has much or most of what we know as ownership. Yet is he *"free* to use", if buyer's inspector is on the job, checking on what goes on? Or if a possible action for specific delivery, or injunction against sale to another, is in the offing? Should the buyer who makes contract payments as building proceeds be regarded as bare of interest simply because the time has not yet come when the transaction will be wholly over and the vessel "his" and his alone? One needs no passing of Title to the vessel, plank by plank, nor does one need a vessel that is buyer's up to six feet from the keel, and seller's in what has been built since. One needs only, on the price and security side, a concept akin to equitable charge. But I do not want to linger on one illustration. The important point is to see the seller-buyer relation, save where a single stroke severs it utterly, as dynamic movement to which the Whole-Title concept applies on *neither* side. What other meaning have such concepts as specification, assent of seller and assent of buyer to appropriation, lien, stoppage in transit, goods not readily remarketable, delay in delivery, instalment, severability? Where the transaction proceeds in a series of lesser actions, often long-drawn-out, no static legal whole-hog concept can fit comfortably, unless some almost violently vital step in the series can be seen to shift the whole scene — as perhaps when a letter of acceptance drops into the mailbox. Such a violently vital step, in Sales transactions, is almost nonexistent ... De facto, then, Sales questions move much along the motto of the most orthodox of modern economists: *Natura non facit saltum*. Which can be rendered: It takes legal fiat to give little facts huge meaning ... And *so,* for sound solution. The approach of prevailing Sales doctrine, before or apart from the Act and in it, is this: Unless cogent reason be shown to the contrary, the location of Title will govern every point which it can be made to govern. It will govern, between the parties, risk, action for the price, the applicable law in an interstate transaction, the place and time for measuring damages, the power to defeat the other party's interest, or to replevy, or to reject; it will govern, as against outsiders, leviability, rights against tort-feasors, infraction of criminal statutes about sales, incidence of taxation, power to insure. The burden is put upon any individual issue to show why it should be honored by being severed from the Title-lump in any particular, and given individualised treatment. Now this would be an admirable way to go at it if the Title concept (or other basic integrated concept used) had been tailored to fit the normal course of a *going or suspended situation during its flux or suspension*. But Title was not thus conceived, nor has its environment of buyers and sellers had material effect upon it. It remains, in the Sales field, an alien lump, undigested. It even interferes with the digestive process.

What is to be striven for, if it can be produced, is some other and different integrated baseline concept which does fit the normality of the seller-buyer relation. I greatly doubt that such a single concept can be produced; today I find too many kinds of seller in contact with too many kinds of buyer in too many kinds of transaction. But what I am clear on is that we *can* isolate *types,* either of transaction, or of party, or of issue, and get light on how better to deal with those *types*. The retailer, the individual consuming-purchaser, the dealer-purchaser, the industrial purchaser have already been suggested and somewhat studied in the literature.

Under the present law, the question whether property has passed from Carb to Mitzi remains of considerable importance as it will be at least a factor, and sometimes the exclusive factor, in determining:

   (a) whether the creditors or liquidator of either Carb or Mitzi can claim the goods, eg *Radio Corp Pty Ltd v Bear* (1961) 108 CLR 414;

   (b) whether a sub-buyer can obtain a good title to the goods;

   (c) who is to bear the loss in the event of the destruction, damage or deterioration of the goods;

(d) whether Mitzi can reject the goods for breach of a condition or is only entitled to sue for damages: SGA s 16(3);
(e) whether Carb can sue Mitzi for the purchase price: SGA s 51(1);
(f) who is entitled to sue for the conversion or detention of the goods by a third party: eg *James v The Commonwealth* (1939) 62 CLR 339; *Joseph Reid Pty Ltd v Schultz* (1949) 49 SR (NSW) 231.

Atiyah has argued that the "passing of property" concept is of less significance in practice than the above list would indicate: Atiyah, *The Sale of Goods*, 6th ed, 1980, Ch 17.

There is some confusion between the use in SGA of the terms "property" and "title". "Property" is defined in s 5 as "the general property in goods and not merely a special property" (ie not a limited interest by way of security as under a mortgage or pledge). However, in the concept of "property passing from seller to buyer" it means the particular title to the interest in the goods which the seller has agreed to transfer. This will normally be an absolute interest except where the seller only purports to sell the right title and interest (if any) of X as in the case of sales by sheriffs or pawnbrokers.

Sections 21-25 headed "Transfer of *property* as between seller and buyer" deal with the passing of property in the sense described above. These sections are not always conclusive so far as the rights of third parties are concerned because of the effect of the succeeding ss 26-29 headed "Transfer of *Title*". The latter sections, together with SGA s 50(2), the Factors Act provisions and the common law estoppel principle, constitute exceptions to the *nemo dat* rule that a non-owner cannot pass title. For example, Carb may have agreed to sell goods to Mitzi and under SGA ss 21-23 property may have passed; however, if Carb has obtained possession and resells or pledges to X who takes in good faith and without notice of Mitzi's purchase, X will acquire under SGA s 28(1) a good *title* as against Carb and Mitzi, although Carb will be liable to Mitzi for breach of contract and conversion of Mitzi's goods. Conversely, where Mitzi has obtained possession with Carb's consent but property has not passed to it under SGA ss 21-23, resale or pledge by Mitzi to Y will pass title to Y under SGA s 28(2) even though Mitzi may have defaulted in paying Carb for the goods. The *nemo dat* rule and the exceptions to it will be considered in more detail in Chapter 7.

WHEN DOES PROPERTY PASS TO THE BUYER?

Sections 21-24 codify the answers to this question. They should be read carefully with the definitions of "specific goods" (explained at p 24, *supra*), "future goods" and of goods in a "deliverable state": s 5(1) and (4). Section 21 precludes any property passing in unascertained goods until they have been ascertained and appropriated to the contract in a manner binding upon both seller and buyer: *Jansz v GMB Imports Pty Ltd* [1979] VR 581. Section 22 establishes the primary criterion of the parties' intention, but the rules in s 23 have been important in determining that intention.

Section 23 r 1. Note the requirements of unconditional contract, specific goods and deliverable state. The rule is appropriate enough for "over-the-counter" sales where payment and delivery coincide with passing of property and risk. However, should the time of delivery and payment be ignored in other cases?

Taylor v Combined Buyers Ltd
Supreme Court of New Zealand [1924] NZLR 627

[The plaintiff purchased from the defendant a new motor car. After using it for three months he brought an action for rescission or damages on the grounds inter alia of breach of the implied condition of merchantable quality.]

Salmon J [held that the implied condition had been breached and then considered whether the buyer could reject the goods under s 13 (NSW s 16) or if he was precluded from doing so on the basis that property in specific goods had passed to the buyer or that he had accepted them under s 37 (NSW s 38):]

It remains to consider the remedy to which the plaintiff is entitled. He claims the right to reject and return the car, and if this cannot be had he claims damages. The normal consequence of a breach of condition, as opposed to a mere breach of warranty, is that the property in the goods so conditionally sold does not pass to the buyer, and that he can therefore reject and return the goods. This general rule is applicable when the sale is of specific goods, no less than in the case of unascertained goods. If I go into a bookseller's shop to buy a copy of *Chitty on Contracts* and find on opening the parcel delivered to me that it contains instead a copy of *Addison on Torts,* the property has not passed to me, and I can forthwith return the book on the ground of a breach of the implied condition of conformity with the description. And so with any other condition — as, for example, that of merchantable quality. This rule, however, is subject to the important exceptions indicated by s 13 of the Act. The first sub-section provides that "Where a contract of sale is subject to any condition to be fulfilled by the seller, the buyer may waive the condition, or may elect to treat the breach of such condition as a breach of warranty." The third sub-section provides that: "Where a contract of sale is not severable, and the buyer has accepted the goods or part thereof, or where the contract is for specific goods the property in which has passed to the buyer, the breach of any condition to be fulfilled by the seller can only be treated as a breach of warranty, and not as a ground for rejecting the goods and treating the contract as repudiated, unless there is a term of the contract, express or implied, to that effect." As pointed out in *Benjamin on Sales,* 6th ed, p 645, this provision as to the passing of the property on a sale of specific goods raises a difficulty of interpretation. Strictly speaking, if specific goods are sold subject to a condition, the property cannot be held to pass until this condition has either been fulfilled or waived. What is meant, then, by saying that if the property has passed the condition can only be treated as a warranty and not as a ground for rejecting the goods? Conceivably the provision may mean that if the contract is such that the property would have passed to the buyer but for the condition, a breach of the condition cannot be treated as such, but must be treated as a mere breach of warranty. If this is the true meaning, a specific article could never be rejected for any breach of the conditions as to description, fitness, or merchantable quality at any time after the property in that article would have passed to the buyer if these conditions had not existed or had been duly fulfilled. This interpretation, however, is not in conformity with the words of the section, which speaks of cases in which the property has actually passed, not of cases in which it would have passed but for the condition. It is also inconsistent with the judgment of this court in *Cotter v Luckie* [1918] NZLR 811; [1918] GLR 583, in which case the purchaser of a bull at auction, who had taken delivery of the animal, and who on examination discovered that it did not conform with the description under which it was sold, was held entitled to return it to the seller. In that case the circumstances were such that the property in the bull would certainly have passed to the buyer but for the breach of the condition. Nevertheless s 13 of the Sale of Goods Act was not regarded as excluding the right of rescission in favour of a right of action for damages as for breach of warranty. I conclude, therefore, that on the sale of a specific article the buyer is entitled to reject the article for any breach of the implied condition of conformity with the description, fitness for the purpose, or merchantable quality, notwithstanding the circumstance that but for the breach of that condition the property in the article would have already passed to the buyer. If this is so, the reference in s 13 to the passing of the property as excluding the right of rejection must be read as limited to cases in which the property has passed to the buyer, notwithstanding the breach of condition, in consequence of waiver, or acceptance, or otherwise *ex post facto.*

I have to consider, therefore, whether the plaintiff's right of rejecting the motor car has been lost by acceptance of the goods within the meaning of s 13(3). "Acceptance" is defined by s 37, which provides that a buyer is deemed to have accepted the goods in three cases: (i) When he intimates to the seller that he has accepted them; (ii) when he does any act in relation to them inconsistent with the ownership of the seller; and (iii) when, after the lapse of a reasonable time, he retains the goods without intimating to the seller that he has rejected them.

The antecedent and equivalent common law on this question is thus stated in *Heilbutt v*

Hickson LR 7 CP 438 at 451: "In cases of executory contracts where there is a warranty of quality the purchaser is not only not bound to receive the goods unless they correspond with the warranty, but even after they have been delivered by the vendor may reject them on discovering the defect. It is, however, generally necessary, in order to enable the purchaser to recover back the price which he may have paid for the goods, that he should not have done more than was necessary for a fair trial of them, or for the purpose of examination and comparison, and also that he should reject the goods within a reasonable time, and that he should not have done any act to alter the position of the vendor ... If the purchaser has exercised acts of dominion over the goods, as by parting with the property in them, or has prevented the vendor being placed in the same situation, then, generally speaking, he will not be entitled to return or reject them."

The commonest instances of the application of this doctrine as to the effect of acceptance in destroying the right of rejection for breach of condition are cases of the sale of unascertained goods followed by delivery of goods not in accordance with the contract. If, however, I am correct in the foregoing conclusion that the right of rejection extends even to specific goods purchased under such circumstances that the property would have already passed to the buyer were it not for some breach of the implied condition as to description, fitness, or merchantable quality, then this right of rejection must be subject to the doctrine of acceptance, as established by s 37 of the Act, in the same way as in the case of sales of unascertained goods. The right of rejection of specific goods on the ground that they are not in conformity with the description, or are not fit for the buyer's purpose, or are not of merchantable quality, must therefore be exercised in due time before it has been destroyed either (i) by intimation of acceptance, or (ii) by unreasonable delay, or (iii) by acts of dominion inconsistent with the rights of the vendor as owner of the goods.

I have to determine, therefore, whether in any such manner the plaintiff has lost the right of rejection in the present case. He purchased the car on the 20 January 1923 and, after having been taught to drive it by the defendant's servants, he took possession a few days later. He rescinded the contract on 21 April, three months later, by a letter from his solicitors to the defendant company. In the meantime he had driven the car from Wellington to Napier and back, and also used it frequently on short journeys in Wellington and its vicinity. During this period the car had progressively developed numerous defects, and had required repairs and adjustments on several occasions. The car must have been driven by the plaintiff for some hundreds of miles altogether. On behalf of the vendor it is contended that this delay of three months was unreasonable, and that user to the extent indicated amounted to an exercise of dominion by the buyer inconsistent with the ownership of the vendor, and therefore that the right of rejection has been lost. It is contended on behalf of the purchaser that the nature of the car's defects could only be made manifest by a somewhat extended period of use, and therefore that user during a period of three months amounted to nothing more than a reasonable examination of the car for the purpose of ascertaining whether it was in conformity with the contract. What amounts to reasonable examination, and to reasonable delay for the purpose of examination, is a question of fact which depends on the nature of the article sold and the nature of the defects alleged. There are cases in which these defects are discoverable at once or on a mere cursory inspection. There are other cases in which the defects are so far latent that some form of investigation, or even user, and some consequent delay, may be essential for their discovery. But if such user or such delay exceeds what is reasonably necessary for this purpose it amounts to an acceptance which destroys the right of rejection and relegates the purchaser to his right to damages as for a breach of warranty. This, I think, is what has occurred in the present case. The purchaser has done more than merely try the car for the purpose of ascertaining its defects. He has used the car for his own purposes to a substantial extent and for a substantial period, and has thereby obtained for himself the benefit of part of the consideration for which he paid the purchase-money to the vendor. He cannot now return the car and recover the purchase-money ... Even, however, if the defects were so far latent as to be undiscoverable except by the process of extended use, I am not prepared to say that this circumstance would have saved the buyer's right of rejection. There may be articles whose failure to conform to the contract may be undiscoverable until they have been so far used that the purchaser has obtained a substantial part of the benefit of his purchase. I am not prepared to say that in such a case the purchaser can still reject and recover the purchase-money on the plea that he did no more than was necessary for the effective inspection of the goods. In such cases it may be that the purchaser is necessarily limited to a claim for damages, inasmuch as he cannot avoid the operation of s 37 in taking away his right of rejection.

I consider accordingly that it is now too late for the plaintiff to reject the car, but that he is entitled to recover damages. The measure of damages is the difference between the value of the car as it actually was at the date of purchase and the value which it would have possessed had it actually conformed to the warranty of fitness and merchantable quality.

Plaintiff awarded damages.

See also *Armaghdown Motors Ltd v Gray Motors Ltd* [1963] NZLR 5.

Section 23 r 2. The goods must also be specific, but the seller is required to do something to put them in a deliverable state. What is the purpose of the further requirement of notification to the buyer before property can pass and how important is it in practice?

Joseph Reid Pty Ltd v Schultz
Supreme Court of New South Wales in Banco (1949) 49 SR (NSW) 231

[Freeman entered an agreement under seal with the plaintiff company whereby he agreed to sell to the plaintiff "all the millable hardwood timbers standing or being on [Freeman's] land on the following terms and conditions namely:

"(1) The owner [Freeman] shall fell at least 100,000 superficial feet of the said timber each calendar month and place same on ramps on the said land."

Under the agreement the plaintiff was regularly to take delivery of the timber, measure same at its mill and notify Freeman of the quantity taken. The defendant Schultz (apparently in pursuance of an arrangement with Freeman) took from one of the ramps some logs which Freeman had cut from trees on the land. The plaintiff sued Schultz for conversion of its timber.

The judgment of the court was delivered by Jordan CJ.]

Jordan CJ [after stating the above facts, continued (at 232):] The ground of appeal relied on is that there was no evidence that the logs were the property of the plaintiff company or that it was entitled to possession of them when the defendant took them, because on the true construction of the contract it was one for the sale of unascertained or future goods (within s 23 r 5 of the Sale of Goods Act) and there had been no unconditional appropriation with the necessary assent. In support of this ground it was submitted that upon the true construction of the deed of 25 June 1942, the logs had not become the property of the plaintiff company because admittedly they had not been measured and their price ascertained.

I think it clear that the recital in the deed that the owner Freeman had agreed to sell and the plaintiff company to purchase "all the millable marketable hardwood timbers growing standing or being on the said land" operated as an agreement to sell and purchase all trees on the land answering to that description, subject to cl 8. A recital in a deed may operate as a covenant where it appears to have been the intention of the parties that it should so operate: *Norton on Deeds,* 2nd ed, pp 215, 537. I think also that what was agreed to be sold was "specific goods", that is, goods identified and agreed upon at the time the contract of sale was made, within the meaning of s 5 of the Sale of Goods Act 1923, as amended. But by the contract of sale the seller was bound to do something to the goods for the purpose of putting them into a deliverable state, namely, fell the trees, put them into such a condition that they could be placed on ramps, and place them on ramps. Hence, it followed from s 23 r 2 that, unless a different intention appeared, property in any particular millable marketable hardwood tree did not pass until (in the case of a tree felled and ramped by the owner Freeman) it had been felled and ramped and the buyer had notice that this had been done. I think, however, from the frame of the contract read as a whole that it was intended that property should pass to the plaintiff as soon as the logs had been placed on a ramp, without the necessity for notification to the buyer that this had been done. But, however this may be, the contentions before the learned trial judge were that the contract between the plaintiff and Freeman was one for the sale of unascertained or future goods within s 23 r 5 of the Sale of

Goods Act, that property therefore did not pass to the plaintiff until the timber was unconditionally appropriated to the contract by the plaintiff with the assent of Freeman or by Freeman with the assent of the plaintiff, and that it was necessary that the logs should be not only ramped but taken away and measured or branded before property passed. The learned judge made no error in law in rejecting these contentions, and this is the ground of law now relied on in the appeal. The defendant cannot rely now upon a point of law unless it was raised at the trial and the judge's decision obtained on it: *Automobile & General Finance Co Ltd v Cowley-Cooper* (1948) 66 WN (NSW) 5. I may add that I see no reason for supposing that his Honour made any mistake of law.

For the reasons which I have stated, I am of opinion that the appeal fails and should be dismissed with costs.

Appeal dismissed with costs.

Sterns Ltd v Vickers Ltd
English Court of Appeal [1923] 1 KB 78

Scrutton LJ (at 83): The judgment below seems to have been based on the assumption that the plaintiffs had contracted to purchase a certain quantity of spirit of a particular specific gravity and had had delivered to them a spirit of a different specific gravity from that contracted for. But that assumption does not fit the facts, which were as follows: Messrs Vickers, the vendors in the present case, were themselves purchasers from the Admiralty of 200,000 gallons then lying in the London and Thames Haven Oil Company's tank. That purchase they had made on 3 January and on 17 January they resold to the plaintiffs 120,000 gallons, part of the 200,000 gallons "now lying in tank known as 78 at Thames Haven". I think Mr Thorn Drury is right in saying that as at the material time there had been no severance of the quantity purchased from the larger bulk there were no specific 120,000 gallons in which the property passed. The question as to the effect of such a sale of an undivided portion of a larger bulk has frequently arisen in the courts, and was much discussed in the well-known case of *Inglis v Stock* (1885) 10 App Cas 263, where a similar argument to that which was addressed to us here was addressed to the court for the purpose of showing that a person who had bought a certain number of tons of sugar, part of a larger stock, had no insurable interest in the quantity bought, because no specific bags had been appropriated to the contract and consequently the property in them had not passed. But as Lord Blackburn there pointed out, although the purchaser did not acquire the property in any particular number of tons of sugar he did acquire an undivided interest in the larger bulk and that undivided interest the House of Lords held to be insurable. The acquisition of an undivided interest in a larger bulk clearly will not suffice to pass the property when the appropriation to the contract has to be made by the vendor himself. As Bayley B said in *Gillett v Hill* (1834) 2 Cr & M 530 at 535: "Where there is a bargain for a certain quantity" of goods "ex a greater quantity, and there is a power of selection in the vendor to deliver which he thinks fit, then the right to them does not pass to the vendee until the vendor has made his selection, and trover is not maintainable before that is done". Nor probably will the acquisition of such an undivided interest pass the property, so as to entitle the purchaser to sue for a conversion, in a case where the power of appropriation is, as here, in a third party. But in that latter case, whether the property passes or not, the transfer of the undivided interest carries with it the risk of loss from something happening to the goods, such as a deterioration in their quality, at all events after the vendor has given the purchaser a delivery order upon the party in possession of them, and that party has assented to it. The vendor of a specified quantity out of a bulk in the possession of a third party discharges his obligation to the purchaser as soon as the third party undertakes to the purchaser to deliver him that quantity out of the bulk. In the present case, what happened was that at the date of the contract there was a bulk larger than the quantity sold, and it was of the contract quality according to sample. A delivery warrant was issued by the Thames Haven Co undertaking to deliver that quantity from the bulk which at that time corresponded with the sample. That warrant was accepted by the purchaser and by their sub-purchaser, Lazarus, who proceeded to pay rent for the storage from the date of the warrant. In those circumstances I come clearly to the conclusion that as between the plaintiffs and the defendants the risk was on the plaintiffs the purchasers. The vendors had done all that they undertook to do. The purchasers had the right to go to the storage company and demand delivery, and if they had done so at the time they would have got all that the defendants had undertaken to sell them. What the purchasers here are trying to do is to put the risk after acceptance of the warrant upon persons who had then no control over the goods, for it seems plain that after the acceptance of that warrant the vendors would have had no right to go to the storage company and request them to refuse delivery to the purchaser. For these reasons, treating the matter as a question rather of the transfer of risk than of the passing of property—for strictly I do not think the property passed, but only a right to an undivided share in the bulk to be selected by a third person—I think the view taken by the judge below was erroneous. He seems to have considered the question of transferring the risk, and thought there was no evidence of it. With that view I cannot agree. I think the only conclusion to be drawn from the evidence is that the risk did pass. The appeal must be allowed.

[**Bankes LJ** and **Eve J** agreed.]

Appeal allowed.

Section 23 r 3 is similar to r 2 in that it is based upon further action by the seller but is more artificial and less necessary, since the weighing or testing could presumably be done at a later stage or by the buyer or a third party without affecting the commercial aspects of the transaction.

Section 23 r 4 involves a number of issues including: when are goods sold "on approval" or "on sale or return", by what kind of acts may the buyer be deemed to have "adopted the transaction" under sub-r (a), and the factual determination of a reasonable time under sub-r (b).

In *Poole v Smith Car Sales (Balham) Ltd* [1962] 2 All ER 482 the plaintiff left his car with the defendants on a "sale or return" basis indicating to the defendants that they were to sell it for not less than £325. Three months later the plaintiff demanded payment for the car or its return within three days. Almost a month later the car was returned in a deteriorated and damaged condition and the plaintiff refused to accept it. The Court of Appeal held the transaction was one of sale or return notwithstanding that the defendant's purpose in acquiring the car was for resale to one of their customers. The court took judicial notice of the falling seasonal market for second-hand cars and, applying r 4(b), held property had passed to the defendants because a reasonable time had expired. The defendant dealers were therefore liable for the purchase price of £325.

Compare *Weiner v Gill* [1906] 2 KB 574, and *Weiner v Harris* [1910] 1 KB 285.

Section 23 r 5. The central issue under this rule is when are the goods unconditionally appropriated: see eg *Wardar's (Import & Export) Co Ltd v W Norwood & Sons Ltd* below. Where the goods are being carried to the buyer by a carrier, r 5(2) has the effect that they are deemed to have been unconditionally appropriated unless the seller reserves his right of disposal. He can do this either in the contract or in the arrangements for carriage. But will it make a difference if the carrier is not engaged by the buyer? See *James v The Commonwealth*, p 97, *infra*.

Under s 24 the seller Carb Pty Ltd may reserve its right of disposal either in the contract of sale or by the manner in which it consigns the goods, in particular the way in which the bill of lading is issued: *James v The Commonwealth*, p 97, *infra*, and *The Albazero* [1974] 2 All ER 906.

Other questions arise under r 5 where the contract requires Carb to manufacture goods such as a ship to Mitzi's specification to be paid for by instalments: see *In re Blyth Shipbuilding and Dry Docks Co Ltd*, p 94, *infra*.

And will r 5(1) be applied where the goods agreed to be sold are part of a larger bulk which is in the hands of a third party? See *Sterns Ltd v Vickers Ltd*, p 89, *supra*.

Rule 5(1) requires the buyer's assent to the appropriation. Can this be implied?

Performance of the Sales Contract

Can it be given in advance of the appropriation? See eg *B & H Constructions Pty Ltd v Campbell* extracted at p 27, *supra*.

Karlshams Oljefabriker v Eastport Navigation Corp (The Elafi)
Queens Bench Division (Commercial Court) [1982] 1 All ER 208

The buyers purchased, under four identical cif contracts, a total of 6000 metric tons of copra which was being shipped from the Philippines to Sweden. Shipping documents relating to the four contracts were exchanged between the buyers and the sellers during the voyage. The consignment was part of a cargo of 22,000 tons of copra loaded on the shipowners' vessel in the Philippines, the balance of 16,000 tons being off-loaded at Hamburg and Rotterdam before the vessel proceeded to Sweden with the buyers' consignment. After the vessel had sailed from the Philippines it was discovered that more copra had been loaded onto the vessel than that for which bills of lading had been issued. No further bills of lading were issued for the additional quantity, but a parcel of 500 tons of it was sold by the sellers to an intermediary Frank Fehr who resold it to the buyers. During discharge of the buyers' consignment in Sweden some 825 tons were damaged by water entering a hold as the result of the shipowners' negligence. The buyers accepted the total consignment, including the damaged copra, and then claimed from the shipowners in respect of the damage. The shipowners denied liability and the dispute was referred to arbitration. The arbitrators found that the shipowners were responsible to the buyers for the damage and further that, notwithstanding the quantity stated in the contract, the parties intended that all the copra remaining on board after discharge at Hamburg should pass through the intermediary to the buyers. On appeal by a special case stated by the arbitrators the question arose whether at the time the damage occurred the buyers were the owners of the cargo and therefore entitled to sue the shipowners in tort. The shipowners contended that the property in the copra did not pass to the buyers until it was discharged in Sweden, by which time the damage had already occurred.

[On the issue of ascertainment, for the purpose of s 16 (NSW s 21), in regard to both the copra purchased directly under the four separate contracts and the copra purchased through the intermediary, it was held the goods were ascertained by a process of exhaustion, after prior deliveries to others, when discharge was completed at Hamburg, since the buyers could then say that all the copra remaining on board was theirs. On the issue of appropriation, s 18 r 5(1) (NSW s 23 r 5(1)) was considered.]

Mustill J (at 216): The question of appropriation is less straightforward, and here I think there may be a difference from the simpler case, where all the contracts are made with the same seller, since the attribution of the cargo to individual contracts may have a real practical significance. For example, if it had unexpectedly been found, when the time came for discharge, that there was a shortage rather than a surplus, the question would have arisen whether the claimants should sue Frank Fehr for non-delivery or the carriers under the bill of lading. The only way to deal with this question would be to look for some event happening at or after the moment of discharge which could be treated as an appropriation by the sellers, the carrier or the claimants. The same analysis must, I believe, apply if there is over- not under-delivery, so that if r 5 were to make an appropriation a pre-condition of the transfer of property the claimants would not acquire title until the completion of discharge.

Rule 5 does not, however, have this effect. It merely creates a rebuttable presumption that an appropriation is necessary for the transfer of title. Ultimately, the question is one of intent. It is true that the property in an undivided bulk will not normally pass before appropriation. But this is because in most cases the act of ascertainment is simultaneous with the act of appropriation, and without ascertainment there can be no transfer of title. The present case is, however, an exception, for if the reasoning of *Wait & James v Midland Bank* (1926) 31 Com Cas 172 is applicable here there was an ascertainment during the voyage. This released the inhibition on the passing of property, and all that remains to be considered is the intention of the parties. Did they intend that the transfer of title should be held up until the completion of discharge, or did they intend that the claimants should be able to say of the cargo "That is all ours", from the moment at Hamburg when the interests of all the other buyers had been satisfied?

The answer to this question may be reached by two stages. First, as regards the goods purchased direct from International Copra. These were the subject of a cif sale. I can see nothing to displace the ordinary presumption that property under such a sale is intended to pass on the negotiation of the documents. This happened during the ocean voyage. It is true that the intention of the parties could not immediately be fulfilled, since the goods were not yet ascertained. As soon as this happened, however, on the completion of discharge at Hamburg, there was no longer anything to prevent the presumed intention from taking effect. Second, as regards the Frank Fehr portion, the award supplies the answer to the question; for the arbitrators have found that, as between the respective parties to the purchase from International Copra and the resale to the claimants, the intention was that on completion of the discharge of the cargo destined for Hamburg there should pass to the buyers the property in whatever surplus goods then remained on board the vessel. There is nothing surprising in such a finding nor any ground for believing that the arbitrators may have misdirected themselves by (for example) giving insufficient weight to r 5 ...

In the result, therefore, I agree with the conclusion of the arbitrators that the claimants became owners of the goods on the completion of discharge of the Hamburg consignment, and that they accordingly had title to sue in tort in respect of the damage caused during discharge at Karlshamn.

Answer in favour of the claimants.

Wardar's (Import & Export) Co Ltd v W Norwood & Sons Ltd
English Court of Appeal [1968] 2 All ER 602

[The facts are set out in the following judgment.]

Harman LJ: This is an appeal from a judgment of Danckwerts LJ, sitting in the Queen's Bench, on 24 October 1967. I sympathise heartily with Danckwerts LJ, when he starts by saying that he had a very difficult task in finding out what the facts were. So have we. In fact I am not sure that we know them very well now, and there is a good deal of speculation.

The story begins when the defendant sellers, who are meat importers, bought two consignments of kidneys from the Argentine in the autumn of 1964. The consignments were delivered in London and put into cold storage by the sellers, who presumably then advertised them for sale. On 13 October 1964, there was a telephone conversation between them and the plaintiff buyers at which there was an agreement to sell 600 out of the 1500 cartons to the buyers, who already, I gather, had subsold to their own purchasers. On that same day the buyers made some inspection of the cartons, which were presumably at that time in good condition, and indeed there was some outside evidence that apart from the 600 cartons with which we are here concerned these goods were of merchantable quality.

Some carriers were thereupon instructed to pick up the goods and take them to Scotland, in pursuance of the subsale to a firm called Drummond in Glasgow. One McBeath, who had come down from Scotland with a lorry-load of fresh meat, apparently called on some agents called McKay's on the evening of 13 October and was told that he would be taking back to Scotland the next day these 600 cartons. He attended apparently early in the morning of 14 October at McKay's office, and was there given what was described as a delivery note, which was his authority to pick up these 600 cartons and load them on his lorry and take them off. His lorry was a refrigerated lorry, but it was not cool because it had brought down fresh, unchilled meat from Scotland and did not need to be chilled for that purpose.

Mr McBeath apparently arrived at 8 am at the warehouse in Smithfield and there he found the goods already outside the cold store and waiting on the pavement to be picked up. He delivered his authority, that is to say his delivery note, and the cold storage firm directed Smithfield porters who were on the spot to put the goods on the lorry. That process took from first to last from 8 am till about noon, and Mr McBeath got off at noon. There was in the course of it what was called a tea-break, of unknown length, said by some people to stretch for an hour but whether that is a libel or not it is not for me to say. Anyhow by the time these goods were loaded on to the lorry there was a good deal of evaporation of the freezing to which they had been subject when they were in the cold store, and Mr McBeath had never turned on his refrigerating machinery; he did that during this tea-break, which was said to be at about 10 am or a little after. He admitted that it would take three hours anyhow from then before the cooling process really spread to the insulation surrounding the lorry; so that the goods were in an unchilled lorry for several hours or at least the great part of that time. He signed for them and added the words at the bottom "In soft condition". He presumably signed towards 12 noon, just before he got off, so they were by then noticeably becoming unfrozen. He took them to Scotland. He had a night stop on the way, but he kept his refrigeration on all the time. He delivered them in Glasgow; and almost at once there were protests. The goods were condemned by the medical officer of health—or at least 470 out of the 600 cartons were —and the whole consignment, I gather was treated as unfit for human consumption. The question is, on whom is the loss to fall; and that depends on when the property in the goods passed from seller to buyer.

Section 16 of the Sale of Goods Act 1893 provides: "Where there is a contract for the sale of unascertained goods, no property in the goods is transferred to the buyer unless and until the goods are ascertained." That applies here because the 1500 cartons did not have any note or indication on them which were selected by the buyer: he simply bought 600 out of the 1500 and, therefore, there was no ascertainment at that point. Therefore there must be, for a transfer of the property, an ascertainment of the goods. Section 18 deals with intention: it deals with the sale of specific goods. Section 20 provides: "Risk prima facie passes with property. Unless otherwise agreed, the goods remain at the seller's risk until the property therein is transferred to the buyer, but when the property therein is transferred to the buyer, the goods are at the buyer's risk whether delivery has been made or not ..." Section 29(3) provides: "Where the goods at the time of sale are in the possession of a third person, there is no delivery by seller to buyer unless and until such third person acknowledges to the buyer that he holds the goods on his behalf ..." Therefore as soon as the cold storage official (who was the third person in question) acknowledged to Mr McBeath that the goods were his, the property seems to me to have passed, and I think that that moment must be the time when Mr McBeath took delivery under his delivery note and that is acknowledged by the owner of the cold store as entitling Mr McBeath to take the goods away.

Consequently, it seems to me that the property in the goods passed and the risk passed as soon as the goods already taken out of the cold store were acknowledged to be the goods of the buyer. If that is so, it seems to me that on the balance of probability it is fairly clear that the damage was done after and not before that moment and that therefore the risk was on the buyer. The counterclaim should succeed accordingly, and I would therefore allow the appeal.

Salmon LJ [stated the facts and continued (at 605):] At the time of the sale it was a sale of unascertained goods: 600 cartons were bought out of a total of 1500 cartons. This case really turns on when the property passed to the buyers. It is plain that as a rule the goods remain at the sellers' risk until the property does pass to the buyers. After the property passes, then the goods are at the buyers' risk: s 20 of the Sale of Goods Act 1893. There are special circumstances (of which *Sterns Ltd v Vickers Ltd* [1922] All ER Rep 126; [1923] 1 KB 78 is an example) when the risk may pass to the buyers even before the property has passed to them; but there are no such special circumstances here. The case, as I say, depends entirely on when it was that the property passed.

Under r 5 of s 18, the property passes to the buyers in the case of unascertained goods such as these when the goods are unconditionally appropriated to the contract. At 8 am the carrier arrived; and the carrier was the buyers' agent. There were the goods, which had been left on the pavement by the sellers' agent for the purpose of fulfilling the contract. The carrier handed over the delivery note with the clear intention that those goods should be accepted for loading; and the loading commenced.

It is unnecessary to decide the point whether there was an unconditional appropriation to the contract at the moment when the goods were put on to the pavement, which is perhaps fortunate, because we do not know precisely when that was; but in my view there can be no doubt that there was a clear, unconditional appropriation when the delivery order was handed over in respect of the goods which had been deposited on the pavement for loading. There is certainly no evidence that they were not then of merchantable quality. It would seem from the evidence of Mr McBeath, the driver of the lorry, that at some stage the porters wished to take a tea-break. The driver was apparently concerned at the goods being left standing on the pavement, but he was told, according to his evidence, that the tea-break would take only five minutes. It appears that it took about an hour; and it was after the tea-break, according to Mr McBeath that he first noticed that some of the cartons were dripping, which would be a strong indication that the goods had by then started to deteriorate. Meantime, however, a good many of the cartons—we do not know how many—had already been loaded into the lorry. Since, however (as I think), the goods were appropriated to the contract when the delivery order was handed over and accepted in respect of the goods standing on the pavement, any deterioration that occurred thereafter was at the risk of the buyers. We know that when the goods arrived at their destination the vast bulk of them were not of merchantable quality. We also know from the driver of the lorry that he did not turn on the refrigeration, so he says, until the tea-break was taken. At any rate, the refrigeration did not become effective until 3 pm. It may not be very material, but it does not seem to me to be at all unlikely, if the goods were left in a stuffy lorry, as they were, for some hours, that the deterioration may have occurred during that time. The driver said that this was a hot day. Unless it was a very exceptional day for 14 October in this country, I cannot think that the sun had much strength in it by 8 am. In any event, none of this, I think, matters, because at 8 am these goods were appropriated to the contract and the risk of deterioration then fell on the buyers; and there is no evidence that there was any deterioration before eight o'clock in the morning.

Accordingly, I agree with Harman LJ that this appeal should be allowed.

[**Phillimore J** agreed.]

Appeal allowed.

Re Blyth Shipbuilding and Dry Docks Co Ltd
Chancery Division [1926] 1 Ch 494

[Blyth Co agreed to build a ship for an Italian company under a contract providing for payment by instalments at various stages of the vessel's construction, which was to take place under the inspection of the purchasers' surveyor, who had the right to approve or reject the quality of materials and workmanship. Clause 6 provided: "From and after the payment by the purchasers to the builders of the first instalment on account of the purchase price the vessel and all materials and things appropriated for her shall thenceforth, subject to the lien of the builders for unpaid purchase money including extras, become and remain the absolute property of the purchasers."

After the vessel was partly constructed and two instalments of the purchase money paid, debenture holders sought to enforce their security by appointing a receiver and manager over Blyth Co's assets and undertaking. They laid claim to (a) the partly completed vessel; (b) worked material assembled in the company's yard, ready and approved by the purchasers' surveyor for incorporation in the vessel's hull but not yet incorporated; and (c) unworked material in the company's yard intended to be used in the vessel but not yet approved by the surveyor.]

Romer J [after stating the facts at 499:] At the hearing before me it was not seriously contended that the property in the unworked material had passed to the Italian company, but this company does claim that the property in the uncompleted vessel and in the worked material has passed to it. Whether it has or has not is the question that I now have to determine.

The agreement of 24 November 1924, was unquestionably a contract for the sale of future goods within the meaning of the Sale of Goods Act 1893, this expression being defined by s 62 sub-s 1, of the Act as meaning goods to be manufactured or acquired by the seller after the making of the contract of sale. By s 16 of that Act it is provided that "where there is a contract for the sale of unascertained goods," which expression I understand to mean or include future goods, "no property in the goods is transferred to the buyer unless and until the goods are ascertained". Section 18, so far as material, is as follows: "Unless a different intention appears, the following are rules for ascertaining the intention of the parties as to the time at which the property in the goods is to pass to the buyer ... Rule 5(1): Where there is a contract for the sale of unascertained or future goods by description and goods of that description and in a deliverable state are unconditionally appropriated to the contract, either by the seller with the assent of the buyer, or by the buyer with the assent of the seller, the property in the goods thereupon passes to the buyer. Such assent may be express or implied, and may be given either before or after the appropriation is made." Goods are in a deliverable state within the meaning of the Act when they are in such a state that the buyer would under the contract be bound to take delivery of them: see s 62 sub-s 4. In the case therefore of a contract for the sale of a thing to be made, such as a ship, the property in the thing does not

Performance of the Sales Contract

pass as a general rule until it has been completed and appropriated to the contract with the assent of both buyer and seller. And this would seem to have been the law before the passing of the Act. But before the Act it was competent to the parties to agree that the thing in its various stages of construction might be appropriated to the contract, and that the property in the thing as it existed from time to time should pass before completion of the whole. I do not understand that in this respect the Act has made any alteration of the law. For s 18 is expressly qualified by the words: "Unless a different intention appears," and in the case of *Sir James Laing & Sons v Barclay, Curle & Co* [1908] AC 35 at 43, a case relating to a contract for the construction of a ship entered into in the year 1907, Lord Halsbury said: "There is no doubt that a contract might be so framed as to give the purchaser power to claim the property in those parts which, when they are put together, make the complete ship." Section 16 is not indeed qualified in any way. But in the cases to which I am referring, I apprehend that the contract is not in strictness merely a contract for the sale of a complete ship. It is in truth a contract for the sale from time to time of a ship in its various stages of construction or of materials to be used in the construction of a ship, the seller, however, being under an obligation of working up the things sold into a complete ship for the purpose of putting them into a deliverable state. It is therefore a contract for the sale of unascertained goods which by appropriation with consent are from time to time ascertained, and there is nothing in s 16 to prevent the property from thereupon passing. They are not, however, in a deliverable state. Until they are, the property will not, therefore, pass, having regard to the terms of s 18, unless a different intention appears. Such an intention may be expressed or it may be inferred. Cases in which the intention has been inferred are *Woods v Russell* (1822) 5 B & Al 942; *Clarke v Spence* (1836) 4 Ad & E 448; and *Wood v Bell* (1856) 5 E & B 772; 6 E & B 355. It is unnecessary for me to consider these cases in detail, because the effect of them has been summarised by Lord Watson in the case of *Seath v Moore* (1886) 11 App Cas 350 at 380, 384. After referring to the three cases Lord Watson said this: "The English decisions to which I have referred appear to me to establish the principle that, where it appears to be the intention, or in other words the agreement, of the parties to a contract for building a ship, that at a particular stage of its construction, the vessel, so far as then finished, shall be appropriated to the contract of sale, the property of the vessel as soon as it has reached that stage of completion will pass to the purchaser, and subsequent additions made to the chattel thus vested in the purchaser will, *accessione,* become his property. It also appears to me to be the result of these decisions that such an intention or agreement ought (in the absence of any circumstances pointing to a different conclusion) to be inferred from a provision in the contract to the effect that an instalment of the price shall be paid at a particular stage, coupled with the fact that the instalment has been duly paid, and that until the vessel reached that stage the execution of the work was regularly inspected by the purchaser, or someone on his behalf. I do not think it is indispensable, in order to sustain that inference, that there shall be a stipulation for payment of an instalment in the original contract, or that the stipulated instalment shall have been actually paid. The absence of these considerations, which are, in themselves, of great importance, might, in my opinion, be supplied by other circumstances. At all events, whenever during the currency of a contract which contains no such stipulation, the parties in good faith agree that the purchaser shall pay a sum to account of the price, and that the vessel, so far as constructed at the date of that payment, shall be appropriated to the contract, I see no reason to doubt that the new covenant so made ought to have the same effect as if it had been a term of the original contract. I am, however, of opinion that, by the law of England, in order to pass the property as sold, there must always be facts proved or admitted sufficient to warrant the inference that the purchaser has agreed to accept the corpus so far as completed as in part implement of the contract of sale. There is another principle which appears to me to be deducible from these authorities and to be in itself sound, and that is, that materials provided by the builder and portions of the fabric, whether wholly or partially finished, although intended to be used in the execution of the contract, cannot be regarded as appropriated to the contract, or as "sold", unless they have been affixed to or in a reasonable sense made part of the corpus.

Later he said, in further reference to an incomplete corpus, that the property might have passed to the purchaser if at the time when a payment was made under the contract, or at the time when the incomplete corpus was appropriated by mutual consent to the contract, the parties intended and agreed that the contract work so far as then completed and existing in *forma specifica* should be sold to the purchaser. He then added: "But in order to constitute an agreement to that effect, it must appear that the purchaser consented to accept of the subject in the same condition in which it then was as part of the completed subject which was to be subsequently delivered to him by the seller under the contract of sale."

[His Honour then considered *Reid v Macbeth & Gray* [1904] AC 223 and *Sir James Laing & Sons v Barclay, Curle & Co* [1908] AC 35 and continued at 507:] In many respects the contract which the House of Lords had to consider in the case last cited closely resembles that with which I have to deal, and, were it not for cll 6 and 8 of the present contract, would practically be indistinguishable. It becomes, therefore, necessary to ascertain what is the true construction and effect of those clauses. Are they clauses which, like cll 4 and 5 in the contract in *Reid v Macbeth & Gray* [1904] AC 223, were merely intended by the parties to form a security, or are they clauses which indicate the intention of the parties that the property should pass? In my opinion, according to their true construction, they do indicate an intention that the property in the uncompleted vessel should pass. That would appear to be the natural meaning of the words used, and there is nothing in the earlier part of the agreement to indicate that the words were not intended by the parties to bear their natural meaning. On the contrary. The fact that the ship was to be paid for by instalments and was constructed under the inspection of the purchasers (though such facts are not conclusive in themselves) strongly points to the conclusion that the property in the uncompleted vessel was intended to pass. I say advisedly "the property in the uncompleted vessel" because, in my opinion, cl 6 does not, according to its true construction, deal with the property in materials not affixed to, and so made part of, the vessel, even though such materials had been inspected by and approved of by the surveyor of the Italian company.

I am led to this conclusion by the following considerations. Although such materials and things may have been passed by the surveyor, it was necessary, before they could be considered as finally appropriated to the vessel, that they should be fixed to the vessel in a manner approved of by the surveyor, and, until this had been done, I cannot think that the materials and things were appropriated for the vessel within the meaning of cl 6. Confirmation of this view is to be found, I think, in cll 8 and 10. Under the former clause, in the event of default in payment of any instalment, the company could by notice in writing rescind the agreement, and thereupon the clause provides that the Italian company should cease to have any interest or property in the vessel, no reference being made to materials and things. The object of cl 8 would appear to be, in the event mentioned, to revest in the company the property which had become vested in the Italian company under the provisions of cl 6. If this be so, it would appear that the word "vessel" in cl 8 was treated as being wide enough to include materials and things appropriated for her within the meaning of cl 6, and this could not well be the case unless the materials and things had been so appropriated as to form part of the uncompleted vessel. By cl 10 it is provided that during the construction of the vessel, and until it shall be delivered to the Italian company, the company should at their own expense insure the vessel and all materials and things built into the vessel. Here again it seems to me that the object of the clause was to compel insurance of everything the property in which had passed to the Italian company, and if this be so it is another indication that by the phrase "materials and things appropriated for her" used in cl 6 the parties meant materials and things built into the vessel.

I therefore come to the conclusion that the property in the uncompleted vessel has passed to the Italian company, and the reasoning that has led me to this conclusion also leads me to the conclusion that the property in the materials not actually built into the vessel has not so passed. For, until these materials were so built into the vessel, they were not to be paid for by the Italian company, and the only fact in any way tending to show that the parties intended the property in them to pass is the fact that they were inspected and passed by the surveyor of the Italian company. This circumstance, however, can have no weight in view of the fact that, according to the construction which I have put upon the contract, the parties have expressly agreed that the property in the uncompleted vessel should pass to the Italian company, but have made no express provision as to the passing of the property in the loose materials.

[The Italian company appealed from the decision in relation to the worked and unworked materials intended for the vessel. The Court of Appeal (Pollock MR, Warrington and Sargant LLJ) affirmed Romer J and dismissed the appeal.]

In reading the next case, it may be of assistance to understand that a bill of lading is at the same time: (a) a receipt issued by a shipping company to the consignor acknowledging having received the goods consigned for shipment; (b) a document of title to those goods which will be issued in accordance with the consignor's directions either in his own name or that of his agent or of the consignee (buyer). The person to whom it is issued (eg the seller) may then assign the bill of lading by endorsing and delivering it to another person (eg the buyer); (c) the contract of carriage which sets out the conditions on which the shipping company agrees with the consignor (and his assignees) to carry the goods.

James v The Commonwealth
High Court of Australia (1939) 62 CLR 339

[The plaintiff sued the Commonwealth inter alia for conversion by Commonwealth officers of five specific parcels of dried fruit which the plaintiff had consigned to interstate buyers. The officers had seized the fruit in enforcement of the Dried Fruits Act 1928-1935 which the Privy Council had declared invalid as being in contravention of the constitutional guarantee of freedom of interstate trade and commerce under s 92 of the Commonwealth Constitution: [1936] AC 578; 55 CLR 1.

The first four consignments were sent by sea from Port Adelaide to an interstate port by ships carrying general cargo pursuant to sales contracts which required the seller to arrange for the sea-carriage of the goods to the port nominated by the buyer. In each case the Commonwealth officers seized the goods before the buyers received possession. The fifth consignment of goods was seized at the end of an overland journey upon which they were carried by the plaintiff's servant for delivery to the buyer's warehouse.]

Dixon J [after dealing with the effects of s 92 and the authority of the Commonwealth officers at 377:] In transactions of such a description the final test of the time or stage when the transfer of property in the goods takes place is the intention of the parties or more strictly, of the seller. The provisions of the English Sale of Goods Act 1893 were in force in all the states the law of which might be considered to govern the passing of property in any of the five cases (New South Wales, No 1 of 1923; Victoria, No 3694; Queensland, 60 Vict No 6; South Australia, No 630 (1895)). That legislation expresses the rules or presumptions of law which had long guided the courts in determining when the property passed in goods shipped by a seller in fulfilment of a contract for the sale of unascertained goods to be forwarded to the buyer by sea. They are to be found in ss 16, 18, r 5, and 19 of the English Act. It is unnecessary to set them out textually.

The seller in shipping a definite parcel of goods in performance of a contract for the sale of unascertained goods by description ascertains the goods, and prima facie he appropriates them to the contract. The terms of the contract import the prior assent of the buyer to his doing so, and accordingly, if the appropriation is unconditional, the presumption is that he intended that the property should pass without more. If he does not reserve the right of disposal of the goods, as it is called, his delivery of the goods to the shipowner as a carrier for the purpose of transmission to the buyer is deemed an unconditional appropriation of the goods to the contract. But he may reserve the right of disposal until certain conditions are fulfilled, and then, notwithstanding shipment for transmission to the buyer, property in the goods will not pass to the buyer until fulfilment of the conditions. If by the bill of lading which the seller obtains from the shipowner the goods are deliverable to his order or that of his agent, then he is deemed prima facie to have reserved the right of disposal.

The older cases show the reason for this. Shipment is not a delivery to the buyer by the seller. It is delivery to a bailee, the shipowner or the master of the ship, for delivery to the person indicated by the bill of lading, the person for whom they are to be carried: *Wait v Baker* (1848) 2 Ex 1 at 8; 154 ER 380 at 383; *Shepherd v Harrison* (1871) LR 5 HL 116 at 128. It was for this reason that Bramwell B expressed the view that the act of shipment is not completed until the giving of the bill of lading; because it remains uncertain on whose account the goods are shipped till the bill of lading is given and they are not shipped on the buyer's account till a bill is given by the terms of which the goods are deliverable to him: *Gabarron v Kreeft* (1875) LR 10 Ex 274 at 281. But the taking of a bill in which the goods are expressed to be deliverable to the seller is not incompatible with the passing of the property to the buyer; for he may act, although in his own name, as the agent of the buyer and he may by indorsing the bill of lading put the buyer in the same situation as if he were named therein: see *Van Casteel v Booker* (1848) 2 Ex 691 at 708, 709; 154 ER 668 at 675. "When the vendor on shipment takes the bill of lading to his own order, he has the power of absolutely disposing of the cargo, and may prevent the purchaser from ever asserting any right of property therein ... So, if the vendor deals with or claims to retain the bill of lading in order to secure the contract price, as when he sends forward the bill of lading with a bill of exchange attached, with directions that the bill of lading is not to be delivered to the purchaser till acceptance of payment of the bill of exchange, the appropriation is not absolute, but, until acceptance of the draft, or payment, or tender of the price, is conditional only, and until such acceptance, or payment, or tender, the property in the goods does not pass to the purchaser": per Cotton LJ in *Mirabita v Imperial Ottoman Bank* (1878) 3 Ex D 164 at 172.

In the course of an often quoted passage in *The Parchim* [1918] AC 157 at 170, 171, Lord Parker says: "The prima facie presumption in such a case appears to be that the property is to pass only on the performance by the buyer of his part of the contract and not forthwith subject to the seller's lien. Inasmuch, however, as the object to be attained, namely, securing the contract price, may be attained by the seller merely reserving a lien, the inference that the property is to pass on the performance of a condition only is necessarily somewhat weak, and may be rebutted by the other circumstances of the case." But in *Stein Forbes & Co v County Tailoring Co* (1916) 115 LT 215 at 216, Atkin J, as he then was, said: "I doubt whether goods are appropriated unconditionally if the seller does not mean the buyer to have them unless he pays for them." A positive statement, which I imagine represented an almost daily application of the law, had been made by Scrutton J in *Arnhold Karberg & Co v Blythe Green Jourdain & Co* [1915] 2 KB 379 at 387. Speaking of the judgments in *Mirabita v Imperial Ottoman Bank*, he said: "I understand the effect of those judgments to be that where the seller by taking the bill of lading in his own name or to his own order has reserved the *jus disponendi* or power of dealing with the goods, the property does not pass on shipment, but is vested in the vendor until he receives payment from the buyer in exchange for the documents of title. If the seller has taken the bill of lading in the purchaser's name, but retains it as security for the price, the property appears to vest on the buyer's tendering the price": at 387. And later Lord Roche as he now is, said: "ordinarily, although as Lord Parker said in *The Parchim* ... the presumption of the reservation of a right of disposal that is derived from the retention of documents until payment is made is a presumption which may be rebutted, yet the general and natural conclusion from the retention of documents is that the right of disposal of the goods is thereby retained. That depends now upon statute. Rule 5 of s 18 of the Sale of Goods Act provides that where the contract is for the sale of unascertained goods the property passes upon unconditional appropriation to the contract. Section 19 says that where there is a contract for the sale of specific goods or where goods are subsequently appropriated to the contract, the seller may by the terms of the contract or appropriation reserve the right of disposal of the goods until certain conditions are fulfilled. That is a description of what is not an unconditional appropriation to the contract but a conditional appropriation; and ordinarily—and in my view this case falls within the ordinary rule—when documents are only to be handed over when payment is made that imports that a right of disposal is reserved": *Eastwood and Holt v Studer* (1926) 31 Com Cas 251 at 255.

To the foregoing account of the general principles which must be applied in determining whether the property in the dried fruit seized had already passed from the plaintiff to his buyers, it is necessary to add an observation upon the form in which bills of lading may be issued. Bills of lading are often so filled in that, after mentioning the consignor or shipper by name as the person from whom the goods have been received, they express the obligation to deliver the goods at the port of discharge not as an obligation to deliver to a named or specified person but to deliver to order or to order or assigns.

Where in this way the goods are consigned to order without expressly stating whose order, the document operates to make the goods deliverable to the order of the consignor or to his order or assigns: see *Ellershaw v Magniac* (1851) 6 Ex 570 n at 571, 572; 155 ER 670 at 671,

672; *Van Casteel v Booker* (1848) 2 Ex at 692, 698 and 707; 154 ER at 669, 671 and 675; *Shepherd v Harrison* (1869) LR 4 QB 196 at 199, 207, 495; (1871) LR 5 HL 116 at 128, 131; cf *Chamberlain v Young* [1893] 2 QB 206 and *North and South Insurance Corp v National Provincial Bank Ltd* [1936] 1 KB 328 at 334, 335.

The bills of lading or shipping receipts by which the plaintiff consigned the goods seized were made out according to this practice, which is a very old one.

In three of the four cases where the goods seized were carried by sea the contract of carriage was expressed as an acknowledgment that the goods had been received to be forwarded to the port of delivery by a named ship or any other ship. That is to say, they were shipping receipts or "received for shipment" bills of lading and not "shipped" bills of lading. It does not appear to be completely settled whether the transfer of such documents is enough to transfer property in the goods while in the hands of the carrier: see *Diamond Alkali Export Corp v Fl Bourgeois* [1921] 3 KB 443; *"Marlborough Hill" (Ship) v Cowan & Sons* [1921] AC 444.

Section 7 of the Commonwealth Sea-Carriage of Goods Act 1924 must have been aimed at giving to shipping receipts of this kind the same effect as shipped bills of lading, but the drafting is very obscure and its effectiveness may be doubted: cf New Zealand Act No 25 of 1922 s 3(4). But, for the purpose of determining when under a sale of unascertained goods to be sent by sea the property passes to the buyer, it is the seller's intention as manifested by his conduct that must be considered rather than the legal effect upon the title to the goods of a transfer of the document expressing the contract of sea-carriage. The things to be looked at in connection with the document are, first, the name the seller has caused to be inserted as the person to whom or to whose order the goods are to be delivered at the end of the transit, and, next, how the document has been indorsed, forwarded and otherwise dealt with in fulfilment of the contract of sale. There is no reason to doubt that the same significance should be given to such matters whether the document is a shipping receipt or a shipped bill of lading. In dealing with the particular facts relating to each seizure, to which it is now necessary to turn, it must be steadily borne in mind that the intention of the seller is paramount, that is, assuming that the terms of the contract of sale leave it to him to make the appropriation.

The first seizure for which the plaintiff sues as a conversion was made in Sydney some time during the day of 5 October 1932. The seizure was made by a person authorised by the New South Wales Dried Fruits Board, a "prescribed authority"; but that board acted upon the express authority of the Commonwealth Minister of Commerce communicated by the secretary of the department. The goods seized consisted of 50 cases of dried lexias, white muscatel grapes. They had been discharged from the SS *Time* on 20 September on her arrival from Adelaide and had not been removed from the wharf. The value is agreed at £80 10s 6d.

The lexias had been shipped in Adelaide by A H Landseer Ltd, shipping agents acting on the instructions of the plaintiff. They had been shipped in partial fulfilment of an order given some months before by a merchant named D Clarton for 250 boxes of seeded raisins. The terms of the agreement to sell were that they should be packed in seventy 1 1b cartons to the case at 6s a dozen cartons, less three per cent; freight paid to Sydney, cash against shipping documents. There is some doubt whether the cartons were supplied by Clarton or by the plaintiff, though the original order contemplated that the former should supply his own cartons. The shipping receipt or bill of lading acknowledged the receipt of the goods for shipment from A H Landseer Ltd to be forwarded by the SS *Time* or any other ship to Sydney and there the owner to take delivery; consigned to order; freight payable at Sydney.

A H Landseer Ltd indorsed the shipping receipt in blank and handed it to the plaintiff. The evidence is by no means distinct as to how the plaintiff dealt with the document, but it would appear that he drew a bill of exchange for the price and cost of insurance and transmitted the bill of exchange, the shipping receipt and some form of insurance cover through a bank, for presentation to Clarton. Apparently Clarton on the morning of the seizure paid a cheque to the bank in respect of the draft and obtained the documents. Assuming that the goods had not already been seized, I think that the property in the goods clearly passed to Clarton at this point, if it had not already done so.

[His Honour then considered evidence that on receiving notice of the government's intention to seize the goods, the buyer Clarton attempted to stop payment of his cheque, and subsequently the plaintiff refunded the purchase price to him, and continued at 384:]

None of these circumstances appears to me to be opposed to the conclusion that the payment to the bank was made before the seizure. In my opinion the plaintiff has not in respect of this parcel established his cause of action in conversion.

No assignment of Clarton's right to sue for the seizure was obtained from him. I do not think that the rescission of the contract of sale implied in the repayment involved an implied assignment, nor could it, in my opinion, revest the goods in the plaintiff. They may have gone out of existence by 11 November, but in any case Clarton had at best a thing in action.

The second seizure complained of as a conversion took place five days later, that is, on 10 October 1932. This seizure also was made on the express authority of the Commonwealth Minister of Commerce communicated by the secretary of the department on the same occasion. It was carried out by an officer authorised by the New South Wales Dried Fruits Board as a prescribed authority. The goods seized were described in the notice of seizure as 20 cases of dried lexias. They were seized on the wharf where they had been discharged from the SS *Milora* on 7 October on her arrival from Adelaide. They had been shipped, consigned to Sydney, by A H Landseer Ltd as agents for the plaintiff. The shipment was in part fulfilment of a contract with H Hooper & Co for the sale by the plaintiff of 100 cases each containing seventy 1 lb packets of seeded raisins at 6s per dozen net fob Port Adelaide, insurance under an open policy, terms net demand draft. The shipping receipt or bill of lading acknowledged shipment of the goods from A H Landseer Ltd to be forwarded by the SS *Milora* or any other ship to Sydney and there the owner to take delivery; consigned to order; freight payable at Sydney. A H Landseer Ltd indorsed the shipping receipt in blank and handed it to the plaintiff, who made out an invoice for the price, the cost of the bill of lading and stamp, and exchange, drew a bill of exchange upon Hooper & Co for the amount and lodged the shipping receipt, the invoice and probably some insurance certificate and the draft with a bank for presentation.

The goods were seized before presentation, and Hooper & Co refused them, writing across the back of the draft "Documents not in order. Goods seized no licences attached," that is, no owner's licence under the Dried Fruits (Inter-State Trade) Regulations. On these facts I do not think the property in the goods had passed to Hooper & Co before the seizure. In a fob contract "prima facie the property passes to the buyer upon shipment, but as in a cif contract the inference may be rebutted and the moment of the passing of the property postponed, as for instance where the seller deals with the bill of lading in such a manner as to show that he did not intend to appropriate the goods to the contract, or that he has reserved a right of disposal until performance of the contract terms of payment, whether they be payment in cash or by acceptance of a bill of exchange": Halsbury, *Laws of England*, 2nd ed, Vol 29, p 226.

Here, I think, the object of the plaintiff in dealing as he did with the shipping receipt or bill of lading was to secure payment of the price before he gave up the title to the goods, and this means a reservation of the *jus disponendi*. The bill of lading was taken, or put, in a condition in which delivery of the instrument might give title to the goods. But, though this is consistent with the absence of any intention to reserve control and disposition, there seems no reason to doubt that the understanding of the parties was that until payment the vendor should retain, and upon payment the purchaser should obtain, all the *indicia* of title and the title itself to the goods. I attach little or no weight to the plaintiff's request to Hooper & Co that they should join him in his suit against the Commonwealth or to the assertion by which he backed it that ownership passed to them on shipment. Risk perhaps did, but ownership, in my opinion, did not.

The value of the goods is agreed at £35 1s 7d, and, in my opinion, the plaintiff is entitled to recover this sum for conversion of the seeded muscatels or lexias.

[His Honour then considered the seizure of the third consignment in respect of which the plaintiff's agent retained control of the bill of lading for goods shipped from Adelaide to Launceston and reconsigned to Melbourne where they were seized. The buyers did not intend to pay until the bills of lading were handed over and it was therefore to be inferred that property was not intended to pass prior to their seizure. Accordingly, the plaintiff was entitled to damages for their conversion.]

[His Honour then considered the fourth seizure, of 268 cases of sultanas consigned from Adelaide to Sydney through the agents Youngs Ltd for forwarding on to the buyer J L Irwin & Co in Brisbane. The buyer in fact had requested that the sultanas be shipped on a through bill of lading direct to Brisbane but the ship did not go further than Sydney. The goods were seized in Sydney.]

Dixon J (at 391): The bill of lading acknowledged that the goods were received for shipment by A H Landseer Ltd on board the *James Cook* to be delivered at Sydney unto order or his, its or their assigns, freight charges to be paid by the owner of the goods at Adelaide. A H Landseer Ltd indorsed the bill of lading in blank and handed it to the plaintiff's representative. By them it was sent by post to Youngs Ltd with directions to forward the goods on to Irwin & Co, Brisbane, by the first available steamer, stating that the goods were shipped on their instructions. A letter of advice was sent to Irwin & Co, Brisbane, informing them that, as the *James Cook* went only to Sydney, the sultanas had been sent care of Youngs Ltd, Sydney, with a request to forward them on the first steamer. In their reply Irwin & Co wrote: "You do not state where the bill of lading is. Are you posting this direct to us or are you sending it to Youngs Ltd, Sydney?" A draft for the price and charges was drawn and sent through a bank for presentation to Irwin & Co, but in fact the seizure took place before it was presented and instructions were sent to the bank for its withdrawal. On the shipment of the goods a marine insurance from Adelaide to Sydney was obtained in the plaintiff's name, probably through A H Landseer Ltd under an open policy of the plaintiff. How the insurance slip was dealt with does not appear, but it seems likely that it was attached to the bill of lading and was sent to Youngs Ltd, Sydney. The value of the goods was agreed at £309 13s 3d.

Upon the facts of this transaction I think there is much difficulty in determining when the property in the goods was meant to pass. The form in which the bill of lading was taken and the indorsement are consistent with the conclusion that the plaintiff retained the *jus disponendi* in the goods. They were clearly appropriated to the contract, but I do not think that the shipment was itself an unconditional appropriation. The difficulties experienced in transhipping goods had led the plaintiff, in effect, to place the entire control of the goods in the hands of Youngs Ltd, Sydney, and to authorise them to act upon instructions from the buyer. It may be said that for payment by the buyer the plaintiff was content to rely on J L Irwin & Co's personal credit. He made the draft payable seven days after sight to allow for the arrival of the goods in Brisbane. But, on the other hand, this course was taken as a matter of convenience because of the transhipment and the necessity of using a Sydney shipping agent for that purpose. It was a substitute for the practice under which ownership was transferred when the bill of lading was delivered up in exchange for acceptance of a draft or payment. It seems quite clear that neither party supposed that, if the goods were seized before they reached Brisbane, the loss would fall on the buyer, and this appears to me to be a material consideration. Section 18 r 5(2) of the Sale of Goods Act 1893 (Eng) says that, where, in pursuance of the contract, the seller delivers the goods to the buyer or to a carrier or other bailee for the purpose of transmission to the buyer and does not reserve the right of disposal, he is deemed to have unconditionally appropriated the goods to the contract. If these conditions are fulfilled, then, according to sub-r (1) of the same rule, the result is that the property passes to the buyer. But, in common with other rules of the section, r 5 is only a rule for ascertaining the intention of the parties unless a different intention appears. The real question is whether, looking at the manner in which the course of the particular transaction arose, prior practice, the expectation of the buyer that another course might have been followed and the manifest belief of both parties that seizure meant that the loss would fall on the plaintiff and the price would not be payable, an intention to the contrary should not be imputed. A difficulty is to fix on another point at which the property should pass. Did they intend it to pass on payment? That might take place before arrival and the goods might be seized on the wharf, though, no doubt, they hardly thought there would be much danger once they reached Brisbane. Receipt of the bill of lading would be no better. Yet removal from the wharf could scarcely have been the condition contemplated. It is, I think, necessary to recognise that both parties regarded the transaction as necessarily outside the course of ordinary commercial dealing. But, up to the point when the goods would arrive in Sydney, the plaintiff proceeded in accordance with practice. At that point he looked to Youngs Ltd to do what they should think proper for the purpose of getting the goods into the hands of the buyer. It is hardly conceivable that Youngs Ltd, a company forming part of an organisation employed by James, were unaware that they had been invoked in the course of avoiding the dried fruits boards. They were, no doubt, at liberty to act on the buyer's instructions. But they might not receive any instructions from him. I think that, on the whole, the proper inference is that there was no intention that the property in the goods should pass, at all events up to the time when Youngs Ltd should, either by the manner in which they reshipped the goods and dealt with the bill of lading on reshipment, or by shipping the goods in accordance with special instructions from the buyer or otherwise, place the goods at the disposal or under the control of the buyer. So far as the parties adverted to the relation between payment of the price and ownership of the goods, they were actually concerned only with the fact that the price would not be payable if the goods were seized. There was, therefore, no intention to pass the property immediately on shipment, or at any earlier time than was usual or than the exigencies of the transaction might require. I think that the truth was that Youngs Ltd were put in the place of the seller to carry out the work of reshipment, acting, just as the seller would, under the buyer's instructions, if he gave any. When the bill of lading was sent to them by the plaintiff's representative it was the plaintiff's bill of lading. The goods were conceived as still at the plaintiff's risk, the chief risk being that of seizure.

My conclusion is that, at the time of seizure, the property in the parcel of dried fruit had not passed from the plaintiff, who, therefore, is entitled to recover the value, £309 13s 3d, in conversion.

The fifth case in which the plaintiff complains of a seizure of his goods is relatively simple.

Campbell & Sutton Ltd, merchants, of Broken Hill in New South Wales, gave orders to the plaintiff for the delivery of dried fruit to them in Broken Hill from Berri in South Australia. The orders were fulfilled by the plaintiff sending the fruit on his own motor lorries. On 15 April 1936 they ordered 180 cases of dried fruit which they specified in a letter requesting the plaintiff to get it away as soon as possible by road from Berri. The cases were dispatched on 22 April loaded on a lorry of the plaintiff. On 21 April the secretary of the South Australian Dried Fruits Board had a conversation over the long-distance telephone with the secretary of the federal Department of Commerce upon the subject of the plaintiff's consignment of dried fruit to Broken Hill, and, on 22 April, he received a telegram from the secretary of the Department of Commerce telling him that, if the fruit could be definitely identified and no licence had been issued, the board, as a prescribed authority, should issue instructions to an inspector to seize the fruit immediately it crossed the border. The fruit on the plaintiff's lorry was accordingly seized at Broken Hill by an inspector authorised by the board as a prescribed authority. The officer wrote a receipt for the fruit upon the cart note held by the plaintiff's driver.

The value of the fruit, plus cartage to Broken Hill, is agreed at £303 6s 8d.

In my opinion it is quite clear that the property had not passed to Campbell & Sutton Ltd, but remained with the plaintiff, and that the Commonwealth is responsible for the seizure. The plaintiff is entitled to recover in conversion upon this cause of action.

Judgment for the plaintiff for the value of goods seized except for the first consignment.

This case may be compared with the more recent English decision in *The Albazero* [1974] 2 All ER 906, in which Brandon J discussed the presumption in the equivalent section to SGA s 24(2) (NSW) that the seller is deemed to reserve the right of disposal by having the bill of lading issued to his own order. On the particular facts of that case, the property in the goods was held to have passed when the seller endorsed and posted the bill of lading to the buyer.

WHEN DOES RISK PASS TO THE BUYER?

Before examining the relevant SGA provisions and some of the cases, it is necessary to describe what is meant by risk in relation to a sale of goods. In fact it can mean a number of different things. It is not defined in the Act, but is dealt with in five sections: 11, 12, 25, 35(3) and 36. In most cases these sections are concerned with the risk that the goods may perish, or be stolen, lost or damaged, or in some instances that they may deteriorate without the fault of the seller or buyer. They are not concerned with the risk that a buyer may become insolvent, the seller may fail to deliver, or with a defect in title, or with fluctuations in market price even though events result in loss to one or both parties.

Sections 11 and 12 deal with a situation more akin to frustration than a normal commercial risk because in each case, the seller is precluded from delivering specific goods which have perished. In each case the seller bears the loss resulting from the goods perishing, but is excused from performance of the contract or damages for non-delivery.

Section 11 seems at first sight to be a reasonable rule to cover a situation where the seller is precluded from performing the contract because of his mistake as to the existence of the goods. It is based upon *Couturier v Hastie* (1856) 5 HL Cas 673. However, it leaves some unanswered questions including:

(1) Should the section allow the seller to avoid all liability if the goods have never in fact existed, or if he has warranted their existence?: see *McRae v Commonwealth Disposals Commission* (1951) 84 CLR 377.

(2) What is meant by "perish"? Is it confined to complete destruction or does it also include theft, compulsory acquisition by government authority, or such deterioration as to render the goods unmerchantable? See *Asfar & Co v Blundell* [1896] 1 QB 123; *Re Shipton Anderson & Co v Harris & Co* [1915] 3 KB 676; and *Barrow, Lane & Ballard Ltd v Phillip Phillips & Co Ltd,* below.

Section 12 likewise leaves the loss with the seller but excuses him from performance as under the common law doctrine of frustration where a contract is rendered incapable of performance through causes outside the parties' control.

Both sections are confined to specific goods. Why is there no need for them in the case of a contract to sell unascertained goods? Would they apply to quasi-specific goods (ie an unascertained part of a specific whole)?

Both Victoria and New South Wales have enacted legislation based upon the Law Reform (Frustrated Contracts) Act 1943 (UK). See Frustrated Contracts Act 1959 (Vic) and Frustrated Contracts Act 1978 (NSW) which regulate aspects of frustrated contracts such as the return of moneys paid.

Barrow, Lane & Ballard Ltd v Phillip Phillips & Co
King's Bench Division [1929] 1 KB 574

[The plaintiffs entered an oral contract to sell to the defendants "700 bags marked ECP and known as Lot 7 of Chinese groundnuts in shell then lying at the National Wharves in London at the price of £28 per ton". The plaintiffs accepted payment on 12 October by two bills of exchange. Subsequently National Wharves delivered 591 bags to the defendants but the remaining 109 bags were found to have been fraudulently disposed of or irregularly delivered prior to 12 October. Accordingly, the defendants dishonoured the bills of exchange. The plaintiffs sued on the bills and, in the alternative, for the price of goods sold and delivered.]

Wright J (at 580): This is one of those unfortunate cases in which one of two innocent parties has to suffer by the fraud of a third party. The trouble has arisen because certain goods deposited in the ordinary course of business with a firm of wharfingers in London, the National Wharves and Warehousing Co Ltd, had been fraudulently abstracted while in their possession. This is the first case in my experience in which wharfingers in London, in whom great confidence has always been reposed, have failed in their trust. I do not know what individuals were guilty of the fraudulent transaction, nor does it concern me. The wharfingers are now in liquidation, and it appears from statements in a letter from them dated 13 December 1927 that any assets which they have are in the hands of the debenture holders. The result is that whoever has to suffer by the loss of these goods will, so far as I can see, have no redress from the wharfingers ... These bills of exchange were handed over to the plaintiffs on 12 October 1927, in return for a delivery order.

At the last mentioned date, in my judgment, it was intended that the property in the 700 bags should pass from the plaintiffs to the defendants. I regard this parcel as an indivisible parcel of goods within the description given by Bailhache J in the case of *Behrend & Co v Produce Brokers' Co* [1920] 3 KB 530; 25 Com Cas 286. In that case the parcel was a parcel of 200 tons of Egyptian cotton seed and the learned judge there held, and I think rightly, that in commerce that was an indivisible parcel of goods. The same is certainly true, in my judgment, *a fortiori* of this specific parcel of 700 bags, the location of which was expressly defined in the contract. The defendants on 12 October 1927, presented their delivery order to the wharf, and as no question was there raised they thereupon assumed that the matter was in order ...

If the whole 700 bags had remained in the wharf on 11 October 1927, the fraudulent abstraction being subsequent to that date, and the parcel intact on that date, there could be no question, I think, that the property must have passed on 12 October from the plaintiffs to the defendants. But that in fact was not so. When the contract of 11 October was made, there was not in existence any parcel such as is described in the contract. There was a parcel of 591 bags, but there was not a parcel of 700 bags.

If, on the other hand, the whole 700 bags had been stolen on 11 October 1927, without the knowledge of either party, or if it had been destroyed by fire—if for any such reason it did not exist as a parcel at all on 11 October there can be no doubt that s 6 of the Sale of Goods Act 1893 [NSW s 11] would have applied. [His Lordship read that section.] The section says that as the contract has reference to specific goods and as those goods, without the knowledge of the seller, are not in existence at the date of the contract, there is nothing on which the contract can operate and it is void. In other words, because the parties are contracting about something which, unknown to them, has no existence in fact, the intention of both of them is completely frustrated and there is no contract between them. The rule has been established for many years that, where a contract relates to specific goods which do not then exist, the case is not to be treated as one in which the seller warrants the existence of those specific goods, but as one in which there has been a failure of consideration and mistake.

This case raises a further problem, which, so far as I know, and so far as learned counsel have been able to ascertain, has never hitherto come before the court. The problem is this: Where there is a contract for the sale of specific goods, such as the parcel of goods in this case, and some, but not all, of the goods have then ceased to exist for all purposes relevant to the contract because they have been stolen and taken away and cannot be followed or discovered anywhere, what then is the position? Does the case come within s 6 of the Sale of Goods Act, so that it would be the same as if the whole parcel had ceased to exist? In my judgment it does. The contract here was for a parcel of 700 bags, and at the time when it was made there were only 591 bags. A contract for a parcel of 700 bags is something different from a contract for 591 bags, and the position appears to me to be in no way different from what it would have been if the whole 700 bags had ceased to exist. The result is that the parties were contracting about something which, at the date of the contract, without the knowledge or fault of either party, did not exist. To compel the buyer in those circumstances to take 591 bags would be to compel him to take something which he had not contracted to take, and would in my judgment be unjust.

There is, as I have said, no authority so far on the point. There are, however, certain expressions of weight which have been referred to during the argument. In particular in Sir Mackenzie Chalmers' book on the *Sale of Goods Act 1893*, 10th ed, p 31, in a note to s 6 of the Act there is this passage: "But if a man contracts to sell five dozen of a particular brand of champagne, it would be immaterial if unknown to him his whole stock of wine had been destroyed by fire. He must procure five dozen of that champagne elsewhere or pay damages. A mixed case might arise which is not covered by the section. Suppose a man contracts to sell to B 'five dozen of the '74 champagne now in my cellar,' not knowing that all but three dozen had been destroyed by fire. The question has not been decided, but probably the contract would be void." I agree with that expression of opinion and adopt it in my judgment, although, in my opinion, the case put by the learned author is not so strong as the present case, because the contract here was for a parcel of goods which was indivisible and described in every particular ...

The result is that in my judgment the plaintiffs fail in their claim on the bills of exchange ...

Judgment for the defendants.

In contrast to the above cases, if risk has passed to the buyer Mitzi before the goods are lost, destroyed, damaged or deteriorated, Mitzi (or its insurer) must bear that loss, since it will be obliged to pay the full purchase price even though it receives no goods or damaged goods. Accordingly, the primary question is: Has risk passed to the buyer? Under SGA s 25 this will generally correspond with the passing of property but the following qualifications on that correspondence should be noted:

(1) Section 25 recognises the right of the parties to reach a contrary agreement.

(2) The first proviso to s 25 throws the risk upon the party through whose fault delivery is delayed if the loss might not otherwise have occurred: see *Sharp v Batt*, p 107, *infra*.

(3) The second proviso to s 25 leaves the liability of either party as a bailee for the other where it would stand under the general law of bailment: see *Sharp v Batt*, p 107, *infra*.

(4) Where the contract requires Carb to send the goods to Mitzi, failure by Carb to make a reasonable contract of carriage with the carrier (say, Trans Co) will entitle Mitzi to refuse to treat this as proper delivery, or to hold Carb responsible in damages for any loss occurring during transit: s 35(2). Similarly, Carb must give Mitzi adequate notice of intended shipment to enable Mitzi to insure or the goods will remain at Carb's risk: s 35(3).

(5) If Carb agrees to deliver at its own risk, Mitzi may nevertheless incur the risk of deterioration due to normal causes: s 36. Carb however remains liable if the goods deteriorate during a normal voyage because of defects inherent in them at the time of shipment: see *Mash & Murrell Ltd v Joseph I Emmanuel Ltd*, p 78, *supra*.

In addition to the above rules allocating risk between seller and buyer, there will often be a remedy available against a carrier, stevedoring company, or warehouseman who is negligent in carrying, handling or storing the goods. Again, the parties will in most instances insure against loss through varying causes and questions as to passing of risk are sometimes really battles between the companies which have insured the respective parties.

The following cases deal with the rules as to passing of risk. You should also refer back to *Sterns Ltd v Vickers Ltd*, p 89, *supra*, and *James v The Commonwealth*, p 97, *supra*. In reading the cases consider whether the rules are commercially appropriate. And compare the results with those suggested by the following sections of art 2 of the Uniform Commercial Code:

§ 2-509 Risk of Loss in the Absence of Breach

(1) Where the contract requires or authorises the seller to ship the goods by carrier
  (a) if it does not require him to deliver them at a particular destination, the risk of loss passes to the buyer when the goods are duly delivered to the carrier even though the shipment is under reservation (Section 2-505); but
  (b) if it does require him to deliver them at a particular destination and the goods are there duly tendered while in the possession of the carrier, the risk of loss passes to the buyer when the goods are there duly so tendered as to enable the buyer to take delivery.

(2) Where the goods are held by a bailee to be delivered without being moved, the risk of loss passes to the buyer
  (a) on his receipt of a negotiable document of title covering the goods; or
  (b) on acknowledgment by the bailee of the buyer's right to possession of the goods; or
  (c) after his receipt of a non-negotiable document of title or other written direction to deliver, as provided in subsection (4)(b) of Section 2-503.

(3) In any case not within subsection (1) or (2), the risk of loss passes to the buyer on his receipt of the goods if the seller is a merchant; otherwise the risk passes to the buyer on tender of delivery.

(4) The provisions of this section are subjct to contrary agreement of the parties and to the provisions of this Article on sale on approval (Section 2-327) and on effect of breach on risk of loss (Section 2-510).

§ 2–510 Effect of Breach on Risk of Loss

(1) Where a tender or delivery of goods so fails to conform to the contract as to give a right of rejection the risk of their loss remains on the seller until cure or acceptance.

(2) Where the buyer rightfully revokes acceptance he may to the extent of any deficiency in his effective insurance coverage treat the risk of loss as having rested on the seller from the beginning.

(3) Where the buyer as to conforming goods already identified to the contract for sale repudiates or is otherwise in breach before risk of their loss has passed to him, the seller may to the extent of any deficiency in his effective insurance coverage treat the risk of loss as resting on the buyer for a commercially reasonable time.

The Parchim
Privy Council [1918] AC 157

[The appellants were a Dutch company which had bought a cargo of nitrate on the ship *Parchim* from German sellers. The British government had seized the cargo in transit shortly after the outbreak of World War I on the grounds that it was enemy property. The bills of lading had been issued in the sellers' name. Under the contract payment was to be made within 90 days of receipt of the first bill of lading and the sellers were to arrange insurance on behalf of the buyers. The first bill of lading duly indorsed was deposited with the sellers' bank in Amsterdam on 9 September for the buyers' inspection and an invoice was sent to the buyers calling for payment by 9 December. The British government seized the cargo on 6 December. The President of the Prize Court held that property remained in the German sellers as at 6 December because the presumption that they had reserved the right of disposal was not rebutted. The Dutch Company appealed. The judgment of the Privy Council was delivered by Lord Parker of Waddington.]

Lord Parker (at 168): According to the authorities, it is beyond doubt that the fact that the cargo was at the buyers' risk from the moment it was placed on board points to the property having been intended to pass at that time. The general principle subsequently embodied in the Sale of Goods Act 1893 s 20, was as early as 1873 laid down by Blackburn J in *Martineau v Kitching* (1872) LR 7 QB 436 at 453, 454, where he says: "As a general rule, *res perit domino*, the old civil law maxim, is a maxim of our law; and when you can shew that the property passed the risk of the loss, prima facie, is in the person in whom the property is. If, on the other hand, you go beyond that, and shew that the risk attached to the one person or the other, it is a very strong argument for shewing that the property was meant to be in him. But the two are not inseparable. It may be very well that the property shall be in the one and the risk in the other." It is true that in that same case and in others there are dicta of judges that an express clause stating at whose risk the subject matter is to be at any particular time is to be construed as indicating that at that time the property is in someone else, otherwise the clause would be unnecessary; but that is an application of the maxim *expressio unius,* and the point does not arise in the present case. There is here no express clause dealing with the risk; it is on the whole tenor of the contract that it appears that the goods are at the buyers' risk after shipment, as they then become bound to pay the price at the end of an agreed period of credit. This fact is a strong argument, as Blackburn J says, to show that it was meant that the property should then pass. Further, there is here a contract for the sale of the whole cargo of a named ship on a particular voyage. The cargo was not on board, so that when the contract was made it was a contract for the future sale of a sufficient but then unascertained part of the bulk then at the disposal of the seller and ready for shipment ...

[His Lordship then discussed the case of *Anderson v Morice* (1874) LR 10 CP 58; (1875) LR 10 CP 609; (1876) 1 App Cas 713 and continued at 169:] In cases such as that was, and such as this is, as soon as a full cargo has been shipped the particular bags on board become ipso facto the cargo of the ship, and thereby become the subject matter which has been agreed to be sold. The sellers' representatives here were clearly authorised to select the particular bags of the description in the contract which were to go on board; no question arises here of the description and quality, as the certificates and analysis when tendered were accepted, a small rebate being made in respect of a slight variation which appears to have been justified by the contract; at any rate, it was not objected to. The shipment under such circumstances seems such an unqualified and decisive appropriation that it would require something very clear and express in the way of a reservation to make the appropriation a conditional one.

The English cases, however, on which the Sale of Goods Act was founded seem to show that the appropriation would not be such as to pass the property if it appears or can be inferred that there was no actual intention to pass it. If the seller takes the bill of lading to his own order and parts with it to a third person, not the buyer, and that third person, by possession of the bill of lading, gets the goods, the buyer is held not to have the property so as to enable him to recover from the third party, notwithstanding that the act of the seller was a clear breach of the contract: *Wait v Baker* (1848) 2 Ex 1; *Gabarron v Kreeft* (1875) LR 10 Ex 274. This seems to be because the seller's conduct is inconsistent with any intention to pass the property to the buyer by means of the contract followed by the appropriation. On the other hand, if the seller deals with the bill of lading only to secure the contract price, and not with the intention of withdrawing the goods from the contract, he does nothing inconsistent with an intention to pass the property, and therefore the property may pass either forthwith subject to the seller's lien or conditionally on performance by the buyer of his part of the contract: *Mirabita v Imperial Ottoman Bank* (1878) 3 Ex D 164; *Van Casteel v Booker* (1848) 2 Ex 691; *Browne v Hare* (1858) 3 H & N 484; *Joyce v Swann* (1864) 17 CB (NS) 84. The prima facie presumption in such a case appears to be that the property is to pass only on the performance by the buyer of his part of the contract and not forthwith subject to the seller's lien. Inasmuch, however, as the object to be attained, namely, securing the contract price, may be attained by the seller merely reserving a lien, the inference that the property is to pass on the performance of a condition only is necessarily somewhat weak, and may be rebutted by the other circumstances of the case ...

Their Lordships have come to the conclusion, after carefully considering all the facts, that it was the intention of the parties to the contract that the property in the cargo should pass to the buyer upon shipment, but that the buyer was not intended to have possession of the cargo, or of the bills of lading which represented the cargo, until actual payment at due date of the purchase price. With the exception of the form of the bills of lading, everything points to this conclusion. The contract is for the sale of the whole cargo of a named ship. On shipment, or at any rate on notification of shipment, the cargo is at the risk of the buyer, who has to pay for it whether it arrives or not. The cargo is to be insured for buyer's account and benefit and insured at its arrived value, including profit, which the buyer alone could make ...

Their Lordships will therefore humbly advise His Majesty that this appeal should be allowed with costs, and that the cargo be released to the appellants.

Sharp v Batt
Supreme Court of Tasmania (1930) 25 Tas LR 32

[A Tasmanian orchardist Sharp contracted to sell 1650 cases of apples to Batt including 2 consignments of 100 cases of a variety known as Geeveston Fannies. The apples were picked and ready for delivery but Batt requested Sharp to delay delivery for approximately one month during which time some of the apples developed "Black Spot", which therefore Sharp did not deliver. Sharp sued for non-payment of part of the price which Batt admitted but counterclaimed for breach of contract by short delivery.]

Clark J [dealing with this aspect of the case at 54:] On the evidence which I have referred to earlier I find (1) that the "Geeveston Fanny" apples were picked for some weeks at least before they were packed; (2) that the plaintiff knew that there was a risk of unwrapped apples developing "Black Spot", and that there was no such risk in the case of wrapped apples, and (3) that he saw some of the "Geeveston Fanny" apples from time to time before they were packed, and observed that they were developing "Black Spot"; (4) that if he had packed the 135 cases of the "Geeveston Fanny" variety when they were first picked, he would have obtained 100 cases of standard fruit—the plaintiff stated this in his evidence.

According to the evidence of the plaintiff and his wife and Mr Nicholas, it is not at all uncommon for orchardists to leave picked apples unwrapped, and they stated that sometimes it is not reasonably practicable to do otherwise, as the packers cannot always keep up with the pickers. But the evidence did not show that it was not reasonably practicable to wrap these "Geeveston Fanny" apples almost immediately after they were picked, and I am satisfied that they could have been wrapped long before the "Black Spot" developed. I therefore find that the plaintiff did not do all that he reasonably could have done to have prevented the "Black Spot" from developing on the 135 cases of the "Geeveston Fanny" variety, and that if he had done what he could have, that is to say, wrapped the apples, he would have prevented the "Black Spot" from attacking the 135 cases. This finding means that the shortage of 100 cases of the "Geeveston Fanny" variety was not occasioned by an act of God.

But in dealing with the case of the 100 cases of the "Geeveston Fanny" variety it becomes necessary to consider the fifth ground of defence.

Section 25 of The Sale of Goods Act 1896, reads [His Honour read the section.]

At the time these apples developed "Black Spot", the property in them had not passed under the contract—it would have passed on delivery—and on the facts I have found if the apples had been delivered soon after they were picked, the loss not only "might" not have occurred, but certainly would not have.

The first question then is, was the delivery of the 100 cases delayed by the fault of the defendant? The contract provided that the apples were to be delivered in accordance with the defendant's shipping instructions. The defendant gave instructions to ship the "Geeveston Fannies" on 22 April, and then on 23 April he altered the shipping date to about 20 May. The contract does not expressly assign any limit to the shipping dates which the defendant could appoint, but the nature of the contract and the circumstances, I think, show plainly that both parties contemplated that the dates to be appointed by the shipping instructions would be the times at which the apples became fit for picking, or within a reasonable time thereafter, and that it was not to be in the right of the defendant to appoint such a late date as would require the plaintiff to keep the apples for a month after they had been picked. The date originally fixed for the shipment of the "Geeveston Fannies" was just about the date at which they would become fit to pick, and an instruction to ship them at any time during April or early in May would, I think, have been within the right of the defendant under the contract, but I do not think that an instruction to ship on 20 May was.

I am therefore of opinion that the delivery of the 100 cases of "Geeveston Fannies" was delayed through the fault of the defendant. But does the proviso to the second clause of s 25 include the case of a delay in delivery where the property does not pass until delivery, or is it confined to the case of the property having passed, but the goods not having been delivered and the delivery being delayed? I think it includes the former case, as well as the latter: see *Martineaux v Kitchen* (1872) LR 7 QB 436 at 456; and *Benjamin on Sale,* 6th ed, p 464.

Therefore these 100 cases were at the defendant's risk.

But I have found on the facts, that the plaintiff knew that there was a risk of the 135 cases, which he set aside to provide the 100 cases, developing "Black Spot", and that, if they were wrapped right away, there would be no such risk, and that he saw some of the apples in the 135 cases from time to time during the period that they were standing in the sheds awaiting packing, and noticed that some of them were developing "Black Spot".

Then what do the words "at the risk" in s 25 of The Sale of Goods Act 1896 mean?

Do they, in such a case as this, mean that the vendor need not do anything to protect or preserve the goods although he knows that there is not only a risk that they will perish if certain precautions which he could take are not taken, but actually sees that the perishment has commenced, or if not, what is the responsibility of the vendor in such a case?

The responsibility of a vendor in such a case is, I think, that which is stated in *Benjamin on Sale,* 6th ed, p 466, where 3 Salkeld 61, and the American case of *Koon v Brinkerhoff* 39 Hun 130, are cited. In 3 Salkeld 61, it is said that "the seller shall deliver the thing sold, and he shall keep it safe till it is delivered, which he is bound to do with the same care as if it were a thing lent to him: for the seller had or is presumed to have a benefit by the sale; but this care of keeping is only for a reasonable time, for after a fault neglect of the buyer if the thing be lost the seller is not liable unless it was lost *dolo malo*". In *Koon v Brinkerhoff,* Haight J, said that after the passing of the property the seller "is bound to that degree of care and diligence which men of common prudence generally bestow on their own property. The rule, however, is limited to cases where the buyer is under no obligation to remove the goods. For if a time be fixed for actual delivery and it has elapsed, or if no time having been fixed for actual delivery, the vendee receives notice to take away the goods, the obligation of the seller is simply to observe good faith, and he is responsible only in case of fraud or gross negligence simulated to fraud ... he is only liable in like manner as a depository or mandatory in case of fraud or gross negligence, the custody of the goods being solely for the advantage of the vendee."

These observations were made with respect to a case where the property had passed, but I think the same rule applies to the case where the transfer of the property had been delayed by the fault of the buyer.

Then was the plaintiff guilty of gross negligence? That he was guilty of negligence I have no doubt. He saw the apples from time to time between the date they were picked (about middle of April) and 13 May and he saw them developing "Black Spot"; but although he knew he could prevent any more of them developing the disease by wrapping, he left them as they were, and did not advise the defendant or the T.O.P. of the position until about 13 May. But his evidence and that of his wife is that orchardists do not wrap apples until they are required for shipment, and the plaintiff knew that he had 135 cases from which to pick out the 100 cases to be delivered. This evidence, that orchardists never wrap until just before shipment, must surely mean unless it is seen that "Black Spot" has set in, for it is inconceivable that an orchardist would sit by and see his apples destroyed when he could save them by wrapping them.

But the plaintiff knew that he had 135 cases, and he no doubt thought that there would not be so much "Black Spot" that he could not get 100 cases out of the 135 cases. On the whole, I do not think that I can find that he was guilty of such gross negligence, as would throw the risk back on him ...

Judgment for plaintiff on his claim, and for defendant on his counterclaim.

Allied Mills Ltd v Gwydir Valley Oilseeds Pty Ltd
Court of Appeal [1978] 2 NSWLR 26

Hutley JA: This is an appeal by the defendant from a verdict and judgment of Coates DCJ, given on 25 November 1977.

The appellant was the seller and the respondent was the buyer, of 130 tonnes of linseed meal in store at the seller's place of business in Moree. His Honour found that the contract was for the unconditional sale of specific goods in a deliverable state, so that the property passed on the making of the contract, on or prior to 4 February 1975.

The terms of the contract were embodied in two documents. There was a purchase order which was signed by the seller, followed by a written contract in the seller's form. The only difference is that the seller's form of contract contained the following clause: "Sellers shall not be liable in any respect for failure or delay in fulfilment and performance of this contract or any part thereof if hindered or prevented directly or indirectly by an Act of God, Riots, Rebellion, Strikes, Lockouts or by any cause beyond their control."

Delivery was to take place during February 1975, and the goods were to be picked up by the buyer's agent. In breach of contract, and for its own purposes, the seller declined to deliver 100 tonnes during February, and on 21 March 1975 there was a fire in the shed in which it was stored.

The buyer had resold the linseed meal. It was forced to enter the market to obtain other meal to satisfy its contracts, and bought this meal at a higher price, $85 per tonne, that is $30 per tonne higher than the sale price. It sued to recover the sum of $3000, being the extra expense to which it was put in buying linseed meal at a higher price. It recovered this sum.

[His Honour then referred to s 25 SGA (NSW) and *Demby Hamilton & Co Ltd v Barden* [1949] 1 All ER 435 and continued at 28:] The first submission for the seller is that the judgment under appeal was wrong, because the proviso quoted above only exonerated the buyer from the necessity of paying for the goods which were burnt, and did not give him a cause of action in damages. This conclusion does not follow from the above case; the most which can be said is that it provides no authority in a case such as the present.

Some support is provided for this contention by the second proviso which preserves the law of bailment, and it may be that it is in the relationship of bailor and bailee that the relevant rights of these parties is to be found. It is not, in my opinion, necessary to decide this question as even, on this basis, I consider the judgment under appeal plainly right.

The appellant submitted that the seller was the bailee, and the buyer the bailor. This is correct. The first proviso which reversed the risk by reason of the fault of the seller did not, however, alter their respective titles, as it is not necessary in law for the risk and the ownership to be coincidental. As Benjamin, *Sale of Goods*, 1974 ed, p 197, para 417 says: "If the property has passed to the buyer under the contract of sale, but the seller remains in possession of the goods, it appears that he does so as a bailee for reward until the time for delivery has arrived."; and the learned author further states at p 198, para 418: " . . . if the risk has passed to the buyer, but delivery is delayed due to the seller's fault, the seller must assume the risk of any loss which might not have occurred but for such fault, and in addition must take reasonable care of the goods."

It would seem clear to me that, where a seller who is a bailee for reward does not deliver the goods in accordance with the contract, as here, he cannot take advantage of his own wrong and contend that he has a lower degree of responsibility than he had pursuant to the contract itself. The bailee here, having failed to deliver the goods, is liable to the buyer, unless it is able to establish that it had taken reasonable care of the goods which, in this case, means it had established that it had not stored them under conditions under which they might be damaged: see Paton, *Bailment in the Common Law*, p 168.

There is no evidence which would justify a finding that it had discharged its burden. Even though his Honour found the evidence which was called by the plaintiff (the buyer) unhelpful, the burden lay upon the seller (the defendant) to establish affirmatively that the damage which was suffered was not its fault.

The conditions of sale above referred to did not help the defendant, because its failure to fulfil the performance of this contract was not due to a cause beyond its control. It was due to a cause within its control. If it had complied with the terms of the contract, the goods would not have been in the place where the fire occurred and, further, it failed to establish that it had no responsibility for the occurrence of the fire.

[**Moffitt P** agreed with Hutley JA and **Mahoney JA** decided the case in favour of the plaintiffs on the grounds that the goods were at risk of the seller because of the first proviso to s 25.]

Appeal dismissed.

CAN THE SELLER RECLAIM THE GOODS?

Although in the original outline of "Events Prior to Delivery of Goods" we included for chronological purposes questions concerning Carb's right to reclaim the goods in the event of Mitzi failing to pay for them or becoming insolvent, the legal aspects of the questions will be examined in Section 3 "Remedies for Breach".

QUESTIONS

Question 1

Jim Handy found a used workbench at a clearance sale and agreed to purchase it on "cash on delivery" terms for $150. When will property pass to Jim?

Question 2

On 22 November Jim Handy agreed to buy a 1978 second-hand Rover sedan from Prestige Cars which agreed to overhaul the gearbox and replace a body panel before delivery which was promised by 15 December. Jim paid a deposit of $500 and agreed to collect the car on 15 December.

Prestige Cars completed the work by 15 December but failed to notify Jim that the car was ready before it was destroyed in a fire at Prestige Cars' premises on 17 December. Advise Jim whether he can recover his deposit or if he is obliged to pay the balance of the purchase price.

Would your advice differ if the work had not been completed by 17 December when the car was destroyed?

Question 3

To what circumstances is s 12 SGA (NSW) directed? Does the section leave any situation unprovided between a seller and buyer of goods? Under what circumstances is the conduct of both parties relevant when considering whether the goods perish "without any fault on the part of the seller or buyer"? How satisfactory is the section and how can it be improved? In answering the question consider cases, statutes and any other recommendations you may consider relevant.

Question 4

Carb Pty Ltd contracted to sell 40,000 carburettors to Mitzi Co. The contract required Carb to send them by ship to Tokyo. Mitzi was to arrange its own insurance. The purchase price of $500,000 was payable on or before delivery of the bill of lading for the goods. Carb shipped the goods on *Titanic II* and obtained the bill of lading in its name. Carb then endorsed the bill in blank and sent it to its Tokyo agent Midco with instructions to hand it over to Mitzi on receipt of $500,000. Before the bill of lading reached Tokyo, *Titanic II* sank.

Advise Carb if it is entitled to keep the $500,000 purchase price.

What difference would there be in your answer in the following alternative situations:

(1) Carb had the bill of lading issued in Mitzi's name, notified Mitzi of this and Mitzi sent $500,000 to Carb before Carb sent the bill of lading and *Titanic II* sank.

(2) Due to a wharf strike Carb had been forced to delay shipment for six months during which time the carburettors rusted in the damp shipping terminal.

(3) Carb had not notified Mitzi that the goods had been shipped and Mitzi, as a result, had not insured the goods; or if all the goods had been shipped and the contract implied or required that Carb insure on Mitzi's behalf and Carb insured against fire but not marine risks.

(4) Without Carb's knowledge, stevedores had stolen 2000 carburettors prior to Carb and Mitzi making their contract and a further 10 after the contract was made.

(5) Carb owned *Titanic II*.

Question 5

(1) Why have the courts been loath to apply r 1 of SGA s 23 and how have they avoided doing so? Should the rule be changed, and if so, in what way?

(2) Is the manner in which the SGA deals with the passing of risk from seller to buyer the most commercially desirable? To which other aspects of the transaction could risk be related, and what practical considerations do you consider relevant to the question of the passing of risk?

SECTION 2: PERFORMANCE BY DELIVERY AND ACCEPTANCE OF GOODS AND PAYMENT

It is intended in this section to briefly outline the obligations of seller and buyer under SGA Pt IV by reference to our basic example, and then to concentrate attention on the following particular aspects: contracts to deliver by instalments; the buyer's obligation to accept the goods; the relationship of this obligation to the buyer's right to examine the goods; and the consequences of acceptance.

DELIVERY

Carb's basic duty as seller is to deliver conforming goods to the buyer Mitzi in the manner, and at the time and place, stipulated or contemplated under the contract. Mitzi has a correlative duty to accept and pay for them: s 30. To the extent that the contract is silent on any of the details of these obligations, the gaps may be filled by reference to the rules contained in the other relevant sections of SGA Pt IV. For example, the correlative duties to deliver and pay are deemed to be concurrent conditions unless otherwise agreed: s 31.

Delivery is used here in its technical sense of "voluntary transfer of possession from one person to another": s 5(1) definition. Accordingly, if Carb undertakes to sell and deliver to Mitzi it does not follow that Carb is obliged to dispatch the goods to Mitzi which may have to arrange for their collection at its own expense and risk. In the absence of express or implied agreement, the place of delivery is the seller's place of business or residence (s 32(1)) which means that the buyer must collect the goods.

A common commercial transaction is a string contract where the same goods, usually a fungible commodity such as wheat or oil, are the subject of a succession of sales between exporters, importers, agents and middlemen. In such cases, sellers may not personally deliver the goods but will arrange for their delivery by third parties. In other cases, the goods may not be moved physically at all but may be the subject of a symbolic or constructive delivery. For example, Carb's carburettors may be held in transit to Tokyo or in the warehouse of Carb's Tokyo agent Midco. When Carb wishes to deliver them to Mitzi, it will send Mitzi the bill of lading or delivery order or a direction addressed to Midco to hand over goods to Mitzi or Mitzi's nominee. If Mitzi sub-sold the same goods, it could effect delivery by transferring the bill of lading or delivery order to its sub-buyer: see s 32(3).

The contract may stipulate a time for delivery. Slight delays in delivery will not entitle Mitzi to rescind unless the contract makes time of delivery of the essence or it is implied because, eg, the goods are perishable. Where Mitzi is required to do something to enable Carb to deliver, eg, advise the place for delivery or arrange a contract of carriage, Carb is not obliged to deliver until Mitzi does so.

Section 33 deals with the question of non-conforming delivery, ie, where the seller delivers too much or too little, or the goods are mixed with other goods. Sometimes the contract will allow for variations in the quantity, particularly in the case of fungible bulk goods and the courts will allow very minor variations under the *de minimis* principle: eg *Shipton Anderson & Co Ltd v Weil Bros Ltd* [1912] 1 KB 574 which involved a 55 lb discrepancy in a contract for 4950 tons. The test appears to be whether the excess or deficiency is such as would influence the mind of a reasonable buyer.

Where the buyer Mitzi sends a carrier to collect the goods, it will be important to determine whether delivery to the carrier constitutes delivery under the contract. If the carrier is in fact Carb's servant, delivery will not take place until the goods reach Mitzi or *its* agent. However, if the carrier is Mitzi's servant, delivery may be effected when he collects the goods with the result that property and risk pass to Mitzi, and also Carb will lose its unpaid seller's lien and right of stoppage in transit: ss 45–47; see Section 3. However, delivery to an independent carrier even though nominated by Mitzi, will pass property and risk to Mitzi, while Carb will still retain its right of stoppage, and lien if it reserves its right of disposal: s 45(1).

ACCEPTANCE

Note that acceptance here is used in the sense of acceptance of goods in performance of the contract: see s 9(3) and compare *B & H Constructions Pty Ltd v Campbell*, p 27, *supra*.

The buyer's obligations are to accept goods which conform to the contract and to pay for them: s 30. However, as suggested in the original questions under Stage 4 of the sequence of events, this simple proposition can be complicated in several ways:

(1) If the contract provides for Carb to deliver the goods to Mitzi by instalments, or there are several separate contracts to make separate deliveries of similar goods,

does the failure of Carb to deliver conforming goods under one instalment or contract entitle Mitzi to reject not only that delivery but future ones as well? This question can be broken down into a number of legal issues. The first question is whether there is one contract or several contracts. If there is only one, then a further question is whether it is severable into parts, so that by acceptance of part of the goods, Mitzi will lose its right to reject the residue if it does not comply with the contract: s 16(3) and *J Rosenthal & Sons Ltd v Esmail* [1965] 2 All ER 860, below. In addition, what test is to be applied to decide whether Carb's failure to deliver conforming goods under one instalment indicates a repudiation of the entire contract entitling Mitzi to terminate? See *Maple Flock Co v Universal Furniture Products (Wembly) Ltd* [1934] 1 KB 148; *Hammer and Barrow v Coca-Cola & Ors* [1962] NZLR 723, p 117, *infra*.

(2) If Mitzi accepts the whole or part of the goods, or, in most jurisdictions, if property in specific goods passes to it, Mitzi may lose its right to reject the goods even though (a) they do not conform to the contract: s 16(3); and (b) it has not examined the goods as it is entitled to do under s 37. This problem arises in relation to specific goods because of the interrelationship of s 16(3) with s 23 r 1 whereby property can pass to Mitzi in specific goods before it has had an opportunity to examine them. A further question is whether s 37 is to be interpreted so as to prevail over s 38; ie can Mitzi be deemed to have accepted goods under s 38 before it has had a reasonable opportunity of examining them under s 37. The apparent harshness of s 38 in this situation has been moderated by judicial interpretation and, in some instances, by recent legislation: see generally, *E & S Ruben Ltd v Faire Brothers & Co Ltd* [1949] 1 KB 254, p 119, *infra*; *Kwei Tek Chao v British Traders and Shippers Ltd* [1954] 2 QB 459, p 120, *infra*; and *Hammer and Barrow v Coca-Cola*, p 122, *infra*. Trade Practices Act 1974 s 75A; Misrepresentation Act 1971-72 (SA) s 12; Sale of Goods Ordinance 1975 (ACT) s 4; Goods (Sales & Leases) Act 1981 (Vic) s 3 and Goods Act 1958 (Vic) s 99: see p 128, *infra*.

(3) Section 38 deems a buyer Mitzi to have accepted goods in three situations:
(a) if Mitzi advises Carb that it has accepted them;
(b) when the goods have been delivered to it, and it does any act in relation to them which is inconsistent with Carb's ownership; or
(c) when after a lapse of a reasonable time it retains the goods without intimating to Carb that it has rejected them.

In practical terms (a) and (c) will not usually create any problems because Mitzi can avoid (a) by not advising Carb of acceptance until satisfied that the goods do comply with the contract; and under (c) Mitzi should examine the goods within the reasonable time allowed. If the goods are of a kind which can only be tested over a period of time or will only reach the promised level of performance after a "running-in period", Mitzi should negotiate for special provision of a specific trial period before final acceptance.

The situation in (b) will create problems if the goods are *constructively* delivered to Mitzi without being physically received so that no opportunity to examine arises, and Mitzi pledges the goods to obtain finance to pay for the goods or resells them, for example, under a string contract: see the cases cited under (2) above.

J Rosenthal & Sons Ltd v Esmail
House of Lords [1965] 2 All ER 860

[Esmail, a Hong Kong exporter contracted to sell cotton cloth to the buyer J Rosenthal & Sons Ltd under the following contract.

"HMH ESMAIL & SONS
PO Box 551,
HONG KONG

Teaching Materials and Cases on Commercial Transactions

SALE CONTRACT No JRS/114
Hong Kong 19 November 1960

To Messrs J Rosenthal & Sons Ltd, Manchester 14, England.

As buyers.

From Messrs HMH Esmail & Sons, Hong Kong.

As sellers.

Payment: Against irrevocable letter of credit at sight through our bankers.
Shipments: February 1961.
Terms and conditions:
(1) Claims, if any, to be settled amicably, or through arbitration. All claims must be supported by reputable chamber of commerce certificate.
(2) Difference of slight nature in quality, designs, shades, dimensions, etc is allowed.
(3) In case of 'force majeure' sellers are allowed to ship late.
(4) A grace of 21 days is allowed in each and every shipment.
(5) Each shipment under this contract shall be deemed as a separate contract.
(6) Draft shall be accepted on presentation irrespective of any claim whatsoever. Claim, if any, must be lodged within 14 days of the delivery of the goods after which no claim will be entertained.
(7) The date of bill of lading shall be accepted as conclusive date of shipment.
(8) If documents are received late the sellers or their agents are not responsible for any wharf demurrage or any charge whatsoever on goods for that reason.
(9) This indent is between the buyers and sellers as between principals and principals.
Reference: Your cable dated 12.11.60
One hundred sixty seven thousand, one hundred forty six (167,146) yards cotton grey poplin, 'A' Grade.
Construction: 98×62 32/30s.
Width: $37\frac{1}{2}$ in $\times$ 120 yds.
Price: Twenty one and a half ($21\frac{1}{2}$d) pence per yd.
   cif Liverpool.

HMH ESMAIL & SONS
For J ROSENTHAL & SONS LTD.
Director.
25 November 1960."

The other relevant facts appear from the following judgment of **Lord Pearson** (at 866):] The other main issue in the appeal is whether at the material time the contract was severable, so as to allow the buyers having accepted one part of the goods, to reject the remainder. The seller contends that the contract was not severable, and accordingly that, even if there was a breach of condition in respect of the yarn counts, the buyers, having accepted one part of the goods, were not entitled to reject the remainder. The contract provided for "shipments: February, 1961" and No 5 of the terms and conditions provided that "Each shipment under this contract shall be deemed as a separate contract". It seems clear, and is not disputed, that the respondent, as the seller and shipper, had an option to make one shipment or two or more shipments, but there is a question of how he should be held to have exercised his option. The answer to that question must, I think, depend, mainly at any rate, on the terms of the contract and the communications made by the seller to the buyers rather than on the physical nature of the operation carried out by the stevedores at the port of loading, of which the buyers would not have knowledge and would not be expected to enquire.

At the material times in 1960 and 1961 there was a quota system for regulating exports of cotton cloth from Hong Kong to the United Kingdom. The seller, having initially offered his own quota of 83,573 yards of the cloth to the buyers, was able to arrange with his suppliers for their quota of the same amount to be added. He then offered to sell the total quantity of 167,146 yards to the buyers and they accepted the offer, and the contract, to which I have referred, was made in November 1960. There was soon afterwards a falling market, and the buyers put forward several proposals for alteration of the contract to make it less onerous for them, but the seller refused to have any alteration. There was, however, an implied alteration. The buyers, notwithstanding repeated enquiries and protests from the seller, failed to open the letter of credit required by the contract, and the seller nevertheless shipped the goods. As the learned judge found, and counsel on both sides have agreed, the effect was to substitute for the original payments provision a new implied provision for payment against documents in Manchester.

The whole quantity of the cloth (167,146 yards) was placed on board one ship, the *Benrinnes*, on one day, 28 February 1961[1]. But as there were two quotas involved, there were two sets of documents, one set relating to bales numbered 1-70, covered by invoice No 8854, and the other set relating to bales numbered 71-140, covered by invoice No 8855. Initially there were separate certificates of origin and exporter's certificates, and later there were added separate packing lists, bills of lading, insurance policies, invoices and sight drafts. On the other hand, it seems to me that in the correspondence the predominant emphasis is on the unity of the loading operation and the unity of the total quantity of goods ...

[His Lordship then dealt with the correspondence between the parties culminating in the buyer's acceptance of the documents relating to the first half of the shipment comprising bales Nos 1-70 on invoice No 8854 and rejection of the documents relating to the balance comprising bales Nos 71-140 on invoice No 8855 and continued at 868:]

The goods, or most of them had been resold: those which had been accepted were resold by the buyers, and those which had been rejected were resold by the seller through a bank. As the market was still falling, the proceeds of the resales were substantially less than the contract price.

The seller sued the buyers for damages for non-acceptance of bales Nos 71-140, the subject of invoice No 8855. The damages claimed were equal to the contract price less the amounts realised on resale. The buyers resisted the seller's claim, pleading that the goods were not in conformity with the contract and so their refusal to accept and pay for them was justified. The buyers had a counterclaim, which, was in substance for the return of the price which they had paid for bales Nos 1-70, the subject of invoice No 8854, but as they had plainly accepted these goods the counterclaim failed at the trial and there has been no appeal in respect of it.

The basic issue has been throughout whether the buyers, who admittedly have the burden of proof on this issue, have succeeded in proving that the goods which were shipped by the seller were not in conformity with the contract description. In this respect no distinction is drawn between different parcels of the goods: it is assumed that they were all alike. The learned trial judge Roskill J [1964] 2 Lloyd's Rep at 457 found against the buyers on this issue, and Davies LJ [1964] 2 Lloyd's Rep at 462 would have agreed with him, but the majority of the Court of Appeal, Danckwerts LJ and Salmon LJ [1964] 2 Lloyd's Rep at 462, 465 held in favour of the buyers that the disconformity had been proved. The seller contends that the decision of Roskill J on this issue should be restored. If this contention succeeds, the appeal should be dismissed ...

[His Lordship then considered the evidence and concluded that the buyers had not proved the alleged failure of the goods to correspond with the contract and continued at 869:]

On the second main issue the Court of Appeal [1964] 2 Lloyd's Rep 447 decided in favour of the seller on the ground that there was only one shipment and that the contract was not severable, and accordingly the buyers by their acceptance of the one lot of goods covered by invoice No. 8854 debarred themselves from lawfully rejecting the other lot of goods covered by invoice No 8855. On this point they agreed with the learned trial judge. I have found the point difficult, but in the end I am not inclined to differ from their conclusion. The decision turns on the facts of the particular case rather than on general rules of law.

As I see the position, there are broadly three main points:

(i) The fact that all the goods were shipped in the same ship on the same day and the seller informed the buyers that this had been done tends strongly to show that the seller was exercising his option in favour of an entire contract. The provision that "Each shipment under this contract shall be deemed as a separate contract", is, I think, primarily designed to enable a seller to make delivery by instalments with a series of shipments in different ships. As the seller did not do this, there is a prima facie inference that he was choosing to make one shipment and keep the contract undivided.

(ii) On the other hand, by forwarding to the buyers two sets of documents the seller was giving an apparent indication of an intention to divide the contract into two transactions. The

---

[1] 28 February seems to have been the date when the ship sailed from Hong Kong.

documents tendered or offered to the buyers included two separate bills of lading. That fact in some other case might be highly important, or even conclusive, as evidence of severability of the contract, because the two separate bills of lading would enable, and might be said to invite, the buyers to sell the two lots of goods separately to different persons, sub-buyer A and sub-buyer B. In that event the buyers, having conditionally obtained the property in the goods by paying the price and taking the bills of lading (*Chao (Trading as Zung Fu Co) v British Traders and Shippers Ltd* [1954] 1 All ER 779 at 795, 796; [1954] 2 QB 459 at 487, per Devlin J) would conditionally pass the property to the sub-buyers. Then, if sub-buyer A found his lot of goods, though defective, suitable for his purpose and accepted them, but sub-buyer B found his lot of goods defective and unsuitable for his purpose and rightly rejected them, what, then, is the position of the buyers in relation to the seller? They ought to be able to accept the one lot of goods and reject the other lot, and this they cannot do unless the contract is severable. However, on the particular facts of this case that point loses much of its force, because there had been a long course of dealing between the parties, and the seller was likely to know that the buyers were buying the grey cloth for conversion and not for resale in the same state. When the seller forwarded the separate bills of lading and other documents to the buyers, he would not reasonably be regarded as inviting them to resell the two lots of goods separately. The buyers had been told that there were two quotas, which accounted for the two sets of documents. On the particular facts of this case I do not think that the seller's forwarding of the two sets of documents is conclusive to show that he was electing to divide the contract into two transactions, in other words to make the contract severable.

(iii) I have set out above some extracts from the correspondence. I think the general effect of the correspondence is to show that both parties understood, and were saying to each other, that there was one shipment and there was one undivided contract. The buyers were protesting that there ought as a matter of fairness and according to previous practice to have been several shipments over a period, but they were recognising that there had been in fact only one shipment.

I think therefore that, although the question is difficult, on balance the evidence shows that the seller elected to make one shipment and to keep the contract undivided. There has been in this appeal much discussion as to the meaning and effect of s 11(1)(c) of the Sale of Goods Act 1893 [NSW s 16(3)] both in itself and when read in conjunction with s 30, s 34 and s 35 [NSW ss 33, 37, 38]. I think that as a result of the discussion the meaning of s 11(1)(c) as it applies to this case has become plain. It has to be considered whether the contract of sale is severable at the material time in the material respect. In this case the seller had an option to make the contract one transaction or divide it into two or more transactions by his mode of performance. The contract is not severable merely because the seller had that option: one has to see how he has exercised his option in the performance of the contract: if he has by his mode of performance divided the contract into two or more transactions, the contract is "severable" within the meaning of the section. The material time is the time at which the buyer has to decide how he is to treat the seller's breach of condition. Be it assumed that the buyer has accepted part of the goods. If the seller by his mode of performing the contract has made the sale and purchase of that part of the goods a separate transaction, the buyer is entitled to treat the sale and purchase of the remainder of the goods as a separate transaction, and if there has been a breach of condition by the seller the buyer is entitled to reject the remainder of the goods notwithstanding his acceptance of the part. On the other hand, if (as appears to be the case here) the seller has, by his mode of performing the contract, made it an entire contract—not severable—the buyer, having accepted part of the goods, is not entitled to reject the remainder. There is nothing in s 30, or s 34 or s 35 which invalidates this view as to the effect of s 11(1)(c) in the present case ... I would dismiss the appeal.

Lord Hodson (at 862): My Lords, I have had the advantage of reading the opinion of my noble and learned friend, Lord Pearson, in which he has expressed the conclusion that the appellant buyers have failed to prove that the goods in question disconformed to contract so as to justify rejection. I agree and have nothing to add in this respect so that the appeal must, in my opinion, be dismissed.

There was, however, a second point vital to the decision of the Court of Appeal [1964] 2 Lloyd's Rep 447, *sub nom Esmail (trading as HMH Esmail & Sons) v J Rosenthal & Sons Ltd*, which by a majority found in favour of the buyers on the question of fact but dismissed their appeal nevertheless. This point depends on the construction and operation of s 11(1)(c) of the Sale of Goods Act 1893 ...

On the one hand, the consecutive numbering of the two parcels, 1–70 and 71–140, and the fact that the two parcels were put on the same ship point to the conclusion that the option was never exercised and the contract remained entire. On the other hand, the fact that there were two sets of documents, and in particular two bills of lading, albeit explained by the goods being covered by two separate export quotas, points to the option having been exercised. The cases which are relied on by the seller go to show that shipment is independent of the bill of lading and may precede it in a cif contract, but they do not detract from the peculiar position of the bill of lading, delivery of which is symbolic of the delivery of the goods themselves, and I have reached the same conclusion as my noble and learned friend, Lord Guest, that is to say, that the two parcels of goods became two shipments when separate bills of lading were taken out in respect of each notwithstanding the fact that both shipments were carried in the same ship. By making two shipments the seller, in my opinion, exercised his option to sever the contract.

[**Lord Reid** and **Lord Upjohn** agreed with Lord Pearson. **Lord Guest** agreed with Lord Hodson on the question of the severability of the contract.]

Appeal dismissed.

Hammer and Barrow v Coca-Cola & Ors
New Zealand Supreme Court [1962] NZLR 723

Action for damages arising out of a contract made between the plaintiff and the first defendant for the manufacture of 200,000 wooden yoyos.

The plaintiff company (referred to as "Hammer & Barrow") was a company which, at all material times, was carrying on business at Christchurch as a manufacturer of various forms of wooden articles. The company was substantially owned and controlled by a Mr Jenkins. The factory foreman was a Mr Pulley.

The first defendant, the Coca-Cola Export Corp (referred to as "Coca-Cola") was a corporation incorporated in the United States of America and carrying on business in New Zealand. It did not itself carry on the business of bottling the beverage known as Coca-Cola but operated in conjunction with various companies in New Zealand who carry out the bottling operations. The executives of Coca-Cola in New Zealand concerned in one way or another with the present contract were (a) Mr Brennan (one of the two general managers), (b) Mr Burge (the other general manager), and (c) Mr Chapman (the advertising manager). A Mr Stevens was in charge of the regional operations of Coca-Cola in Australia and New Zealand.

The second defendant, the Northern Bottling Co Ltd, was a company incorporated in New Zealand and carrying on business at Auckland. It was one of the several bottling companies already referred to. The manager of this company (referred to as "Northern Bottling") is a Mr Cave.

The third party, Duncan Russell and Ives Sa (referred to as "Duncan Russell") was a company registered in Venezuela. It carried on business throughout the world as a promoter of advertising campaigns. It owned one or more trademarks including the mark "Genuine Duncan YoYo". The president of Duncan Russell was Mr J Russell who controls the business of the company from its head office in Florida. The Vice-President of the company responsible in the field for the company's operations in Australia, New Zealand and the East was a Mr Murray. The advertising campaigns promoted by Duncan Russell were largely based on the promotion and sale of yoyos in conjunction with some client who wished to advertise his own products. Coca-Cola (prior to the events which led to this action) had availed itself of the type of advertising promoted by Duncan Russell and had carried out successful promotions in many parts of the world.

After some preliminary correspondence and discussions between Duncan Russell and Coca-Cola Mr Chapman, on behalf of Coca-Cola, wrote the following letter to the plaintiff:

"We have pleasure in enclosing our official purchase order for 200,000 YoYos strung and packed 24 to a box, boxes packed 24 to a carton.

"Each article to be produced to the requirements of the Duncan Yo-Yo organisation and to be finished in a red lacquer as per the attached sample, and carrying the slogan 'Drink Coca-Cola Ice Cold' on one side and 'Drink Coca-Cola Ice Cold, Genuine Duncan Yo-Yo' on the other side, also for 200,000 packets each containing two Yo-Yo strings stapled in one dozen packet lots, again to specifications satisfactory to the Duncan Yo-Yo Organisation.

"Delivery as manufactured, commencing with 30,000 by August 10, 1960 as per your quotation of 9 June. We are enclosing a Yo-Yo which is to be regarded as a sample for colour only, and is not intended in any way to be a guide for the shaping of the Yo-Yo itself.

"We are also enclosing the art work for the two sides. Set out below are the names of Bottlers and quantities to be dispatched to each, and we would be pleased if you would arrange dispatch to these Bottlers in the order listed, completing one Bottler's requirements before commencing on another's."

There followed a list of the respective bottlers with numbers of yoyos to be sent to each and the dates by which delivery was required. The number to be sent to Northern Bottlers was 85,000 ...

Some 85,248 yoyos were delivered to Northern Bottling by the plaintiff but of these 114 cartons each containing four gross, a total of 65,664 were returned to the plaintiff as defective. Between 22 and 23 cartons were sent by Northern Bottlers to retailers, and the remainder were opened for examination.

On 14 October 1960 Coca-Cola purported to rescind the whole contract for the purchase of 200,000 yoyos. No further yoyos were subsequently delivered although the plaintiffs had in hand a further 29,376 yoyos packed ready for delivery and 32,953 in process of manufacture. They now sued Coca-Cola and Northern Bottling for damages for breach of contract, and Duncan Russell was joined as third party.

Richmond J [after setting out the facts and making the findings as above:] I turn now to consider the following questions:

(1) Was Coca-Cola entitled to rescind the contract *in futuro,* as it purported to do by letter of 14 October 1960?

(2) To what extent, if at all, was Coca-Cola entitled to reject the yoyos actually delivered to Auckland?

I have already mentioned that a total of 85,248 yoyos was delivered to Auckland. I have also mentioned the fact that by letter of 14 October 1960 Coca-Cola, by its solicitors, purported to rescind the entire contract for the manufacture of 200,000 yoyos, and that no further yoyos were thereafter delivered under the contract. A substantial portion of the plaintiff's claim for damages (namely the sum of £6887) relates to the refusal of Coca-Cola to accept any further deliveries under the contract.

The principles governing the rights of a buyer, in the case of a contract for the delivery of goods by instalments, to refuse to accept delivery of further instalments are conveniently and authoritatively set out in the judgment of the Court of Appeal in *Maple Flock Co v Universal Furniture Products (Wembley) Ltd* [1934] 1 KB 148; [1933] All ER Rep 15. It was there laid down (KB at 157; All ER at 18) that the main tests to be considered are, first, the ratio quantitatively which the breach bears to the contract as a whole, and secondly, the degree of probability or improbability that such breach will be repeated. It was also pointed out (KB at 155, 156; All ER at 18) that the test "whether the acts and conduct of the party evince an intention no longer to be bound by the contract" is to be decided, in general, not by reference to the subjective mental state of the defaulting party, but objectively by reference to the relation in fact of the default to the whole purpose of the contract. The court referred with approval to the following passage occurring in the judgment of Bigham J in *Millars' Karri and Jarrah Co (1902) v Weddel, Turner & Co* (1908) 14 Com Cas 25 at 29: "Thus, if the breach is of such a kind, or takes place in such circumstances as reasonably to lead to the inference that similar breaches will be committed in relation to subsequent deliveries, the whole contract may there and then be regarded as repudiated and may be rescinded. If, for instance, a buyer fails to pay for one delivery in such circumstances as to lead to the inference that he will not be able to pay for subsequent deliveries; or if a seller delivers goods differing from the requirements of the contract, and does so in such circumstances as to lead to the inference that he cannot, or will not, deliver any other kind of goods in the future, the other contracting party will be under no obligation to wait to see what may happen; he can at once cancel the contract and rid himself of the difficulty."

In the present case the ratio quantitatively which the breach bore to the contract as a whole was very considerable as it affected some 80 per cent of the 85,000 yoyos delivered to Auckland out of a total contract quantity of 200,000. The whole history of the matter was, in my opinion, extremely unsatisfactory and disquieting from point of view of Coca-Cola. In this connection the early failure of Hammer & Barrow to produce yoyos of the size and appearance called for by the original contract is highly relevant. The unsatisfactory appearance of the yoyos and the fact that they would not run down the string freely was made the subject of a sharp complaint by Mr Murray to Mr Jenkins in Mr Murray's letter of 29 September 1960. By telegram of 10 October Northern Bottling requested Hammer & Barrow to send 20 cartons of replacement stock as per sample submitted by Mr Jenkins in Auckland on Friday 7 October. Mr Jenkins did nothing either in reply to this telegram, or as a result of Mr Murray's earlier complaints to send good replacement stock to Auckland. It is no doubt true that he was arranging for improvements in production in the factory and that a time lag was involved in bringing these improvements into effect. Nevertheless, the situation from the point of view of Coca-Cola was that notwithstanding complaints from Mr Murray and a request for replacement stock by Northern Bottling, Mr Jenkins did nothing to correct the situation so far as the Auckland campaign was concerned.

I attach great importance to the fact that the yoyos had been ordered for the purpose of a special form of advertising campaign. This campaign involved the expenditure of considerable time and effort on the part of Coca-Cola and its several bottling companies, and on the part of Duncan Russell. Moreover, the campaign involved the prestige of Coca-Cola as between itself and its bottling companies, retailers, and the public. The yoyos were not articles which could be readily and speedily acquired elsewhere should Hammer & Barrow fail in future deliveries to produce articles in accordance with the contract. In spite therefore of the efforts which were being made by Hammer & Barrow to improve the quality of the yoyos, I am of the opinion that the whole circumstances and history of the matter, as at 14 October 1960, justified Coca-Cola in rescinding the contracts so far as future deliveries were concerned, rather than submit to the risk of having put upon them further unsatisfactory deliveries. It follows that the plaintiff's claim for damages for non-acceptance of further deliveries under the contract must fail.

[His Honour then considered the second question, namely, the extent, if any, to which Coca-Cola was entitled to reject the yoyos and strings actually delivered in Auckland. That part of the judgment is reproduced on p 122, *infra*, after the earlier decisions in *E & S Ruben Ltd v Faire Brothers & Co Ltd*, and *Kwei Tek Chao v British Traders and Shippers Ltd*.]

E & S Ruben Ltd v Faire Brothers & Co Ltd
King's Bench Division [1949] 1 KB 254

[The plaintiff sellers E & S Ruben Ltd contracted to sell to Faire Brothers 10 tons of vulcanised rubber Linatex material in rolls measuring 41 × 5 feet, six ounces to the square yard fit for use in the manufacture of soles for footware, and similar in all respects to two samples supplied by the sellers to the buyers.

Faire were buying the rubber for resale to Skelmersdale Shoes Co Ltd footwear manufacturers, and ordered the rubber from Ruben after contracting to resell 5 tons to Skelmersdale on the basis of the sample supplied by Ruben. At Faire's request Ruben agreed to dispatch the 5 tons to Skelmersdale. The action was tried before Hilbery J who held that, as a matter of reasonable inference, after Faire had placed the order in writing with Ruben, they confirmed their contract of resale to Skelmersdale and sent Ruben instructions to address the goods to that company, and Ruben acted for Faire in so delivering the goods.

When the rubber was delivered to them, Skelmersdale rejected it on the grounds that it was delivered not in rolls but in small lengths, and not in lengths of 41 feet as ordered, that it was hard and crinkly and was useless for manufacture of footwear and was not in accordance with sample.]

Hilbery J [after stating the facts at 258:] I think it clear that the buyers did in fact purport to reject the goods, saying in effect that they were not of the description, or in accordance with the sample given, and that they would not pay. True, they do not actually use the word "reject"; or say that "the goods are lying here awaiting your collection"; things which are generally said ...

The next question is whether the buyers had lost their right to reject. If they resold to the Skelmersdale company after making their contract with the sellers and after delivery of the goods to them, even constructive delivery, that is strong evidence that they have acted in a way which is inconsistent with their right to reject. By s 35 of the Sale of Goods Act 1893: "The buyer is deemed to have accepted the goods when he intimates to the seller that he has accepted them, or when the goods have been delivered to him, and he does any act in relation to them which is inconsistent with the ownership of the seller ... " When the buyers' representative intimated to the sellers that he would take ten tons of the rubber offered, five tons to be delivered at once and five tons later, and asked them to act for him and send the goods direct to the Skelmersdale company and they agreed, the buyers were taking delivery constructively at the sellers' premises when the sellers set aside goods against the contract. Thereafter the sellers were acting for the buyers as agents in putting the goods on the lorry and dispatching them on their journey to Lancashire. If that is so, then as Atkin LJ pointed out in *Hardy & Co v Hillerns & Fowler* [1923] 2 KB 498, "we have here to face the problem whether the act of the buyers in reselling and dispatching the goods was inconsistent with the ownership of the sellers. If it was, they must be deemed to have accepted them ... all the words of the section [35] must have effect given to them. The words are: 'when the goods have been delivered to him' — that is to the buyer — 'and he does any act' of the kind specified. That means that the buyer must have got delivery before he does the 'act'."

Here, I think, the buyers took delivery at the sellers' premises when the goods were set aside against the contract. Thereafter the handling of the goods by passing them on to the carrier was an act done for the buyers with their goods by the sellers; an act done by the sellers for the buyers with the buyers' goods. That being so, it appears to me that the buyers lost their right to reject and must be driven back on to their plea of breach of warranty. Whether that will give them the whole amount of the sellers' claim or not, I do not know; but even if the buyers had been able to establish that they had not lost their right to reject and did reject, I am not satisfied by the evidence that they could recover their loss of profit on the resale, because such evidence as I have of the resale to the Skelmersdale company seems to indicate the sale of an article on totally different terms and of a totally different description, though on the same sample ...

In the circumstances, the goods were in my opinion in accordance neither with the description nor with sample. While the buyers did, in fact, intend to convey to the sellers that they rejected the goods, and the sellers understood that the buyers were rejecting, nevertheless, for the reasons given, the buyers have lost their right to reject and must treat the matter on the basis of breach of warranty. Therefore, on the claim, subject to the counterclaim and to set-off of any amount due on it, there must be judgment for the sellers. The counterclaim can be determined, when particulars of the alleged damage have been given, either by arrangement between the parties or by a Master in the King's Bench Division. That would be a cheap and simple way of disposing of the matter.

Judgment for the plaintiffs.

Kwei Tek Chao v British Traders and Shippers Ltd
Queen's Bench Division [1954] 2 QB 459

[The defendant company, exporters based in London, contracted under a cif contract to sell to the plaintiff Hong Kong merchants a quantity of Rongalite chemical. The contract specified that shipment must take place not later than 31 October 1951 and payment was to be by drawing against a letter of credit on production of "shipped" bills of lading at the buyers' bank. The buyers and their sub-buyer Nam Hua in Hong Kong refused to extend the shipment date because the price of Rongalite was falling. The goods were not shipped until 3 November, but on 10 November the sellers presented to the buyers bank bills of lading altered by the sellers' agents, but without the sellers' knowledge to show shipment had been made on 31 October. The bank paid the price, and the buyers subsequently accepted the bills of lading. When the buyers lost their contract of resale because it was discovered that shipment did not take place in October and Nam Hua refused to accept the documents or goods because of the fall in market value, the plaintiff buyers sued the defendant company for return of the price or alternatively for damages for breach of contract. In the course of his judgment **Devlin J** said (at 484):]

There is one other matter on this aspect of the case with which I should also deal, although it arises only indirectly. In view of the conclusion at which I have arrived that I am dealing with two separate breaches, each with their separate remedies, it is not relevant to consider whether the buyers lost their right to reject the goods. In my view they lost their right to reject the documents, and their right to reject the goods was something different which they could exercise one way or the other whichever way they chose. If there had been only one right to reject it would have been material to ascertain whether the buyers had in any event lost their right to reject by any action taken by them in relation to the documents. Had they handled the documents in such a way as to amount to an acceptance under s 35 of the Sale of Goods Act 1893, and if they had committed that act before they had knowledge of the true position, then Mr Roskill would have been faced with the argument that when the goods were landed the buyers were in any event obliged to accept them, having already lost their right to reject them, so that no distinction could properly be drawn between that and the *Kwik Hoo Tong* case [1929] 1 KB 400.

One of the matters which was therefore canvassed in the course of the argument was whether the buyers, by pledging the documents to their bank as they did immediately upon receipt of them, had not in any event dealt with the goods in such a way as to amount to an acceptance under s 35 and had thereby lost their right to reject. On the view which I have taken, this point no longer arises. What I have to say about it is, therefore, merely obiter dictum, but in view of the fact that it is a matter of some importance and that I have had considerable assistance from the researches of Mr Roskill and Mr Honeyman on the point, I think it desirable that I should state, if only so that those who may be concerned in the future may know that the problem arises and has to be solved, what I think is the right answer to it. Clearly, it would create a great deal of embarrassment and inconvenience in the ordinary forms of credit in these transactions if the normal act of pledging goods to the bank, which is done in ninety-nine cases out of a hundred, resulted in the buyer losing his right to reject. Yet, on the face of it, it seems that by pledging the goods he is doing an act, inconsistent with the ownership of the seller, which amounts to an acceptance under s 35.

[His Honour then considered *Hardy & Co (London) Ltd v Hillerns & Fowler* [1923] 2 KB 490 and continued at 487:]

Atkin LJ, in the course of his judgment in *Hardy & Co (London) Ltd v Hillerns and Fowler* [1923] 2 KB 490, dealt with the situation which is always a little puzzling under the cif contract: if the property passes when the documents are handed over, by what legal machinery does the buyer retain a right, as he undoubtedly does, to examine the goods when they arrive, and to reject them if they are not in conformity with the contract? Atkin LJ put forward two views for consideration. One was that the property in the goods, notwithstanding the tendering of the documents, did not pass until the goods had been examined or until an opportunity for examination had been given. The other was that it passed at the time of the tendering of the documents, but only conditionally and could be revested if the buyer properly rejected the goods. Mr Roskill argues (and I think rightly) that for the first possible view indicated by Atkin LJ no other authority can be found, and it would clearly create considerable complications. If there is no property in the goods, how can the buyer pledge them? It would provide a simple answer to the point had it arisen in this case, since there could not be a pledge. I think that the true view is that what the buyer obtains, when the title under the documents is given to him, is the property in the goods, subject to the condition that they revest if upon examination he finds them to be not in accordance with the contract. That means that he gets only conditional property in the goods, the condition being a condition subsequent. All his dealings with the documents are dealings only with that conditional property in the goods. It follows, therefore, that there can be no dealing which is inconsistent with the seller's ownership unless he deals with something more than the conditional property. If the property passes altogether, not being subject to any condition, there is no ownership left in the seller with which any inconsistent act under s 35 could be committed. If the property passes conditionally the only ownership left in the seller is the reversionary interest in the property in the event of the condition subsequent operating to restore it to him. It is that reversionary interest with which the buyer must not, save with the penalty of accepting the goods, commit an inconsistent act. So long as he is merely dealing with the documents he is not purporting to do anything more than pledge the conditional property which he has. Similarly, if he sells the documents of title he sells the conditional property. But if, as was done in *Hardy & Co (London) Ltd v Hillerns and Fowler* [1923] 2 KB 490, when the goods have been landed, he physically deals with the goods and delivers them to his sub-buyer, he is doing an act which is inconsistent with the seller's reversionary interest. The seller's reversionary interest entitles him immediately upon the operation of the condition subsequent, that is, as soon as opportunity for examination has been given, to have the goods physically returned to him in the place where the examination has taken place without their being dispatched to third parties. The dispatch to a third party is an act, therefore, which interferes with the reversionary interest. A pledge or a transfer of documents such as that which takes place on the ordinary string contract does not.

[His Honour then held that loss of profit on the sale under the Nam Hua contract was not recoverable because there was no evidence that the defendants had any knowledge that the plaintiffs intended to resell those very goods, and therefore the amount of damages was only the market value of similar goods.]

Judgment for the plaintiffs.

Hammer & Barrow v Coca-Cola & Ors
New Zealand Supreme Court [1962] NZLR 723

[For facts see extract on p 117, *supra*.]

Richmond J [continued at 727:] The next question which has to be decided is the extent, if any, to which Coca-Cola was entitled to reject the yoyos and strings which were delivered to Auckland. As a preliminary to this inquiry I should deal with a submission made by Mr Mahon to the effect that Coca-Cola did not, in fact, at any time reject these yoyos ...

[His Honour considered the evidence and concluded:]

At the latest therefore, Coca-Cola did, by letter of 14 October 1960 purport to reject all yoyos (other than those actually sold) which had been delivered to Auckland.

The real question is how far, if at all, this rejection was effective. The answer to this question depends upon whether or not Coca-Cola has "accepted" the goods within the provisions of s 37 of the Sale of Goods Act 1908 ...

It will be seen that s 37 contemplates three ways in which a buyer may "accept" goods which do not correspond with the requirements of the contract. First, the buyer may intimate to the seller that he has accepted the goods. It was not suggested that any such intimation was given in the present case. Secondly, the buyer is deemed to have accepted the goods "when the goods have been delivered to him, and he does any act in relation to them which is inconsistent with the ownership of the seller". Finally, the buyer is deemed to have accepted the goods when, after a lapse of a reasonable time he retains the goods, without intimating to the seller that he has rejected them. For the plaintiff, Mr Mahon relied strongly upon the submission that the present case is governed by one or other, or both of the two types of conduct secondly and finally referred to in the section as constituting acceptance.

The first submission made by Mr Mahon was to the effect that the resale of the yoyos by Coca-Cola to Northern Bottling carried with it the result that Coca-Cola had no right of rejection at all. In this connection Mr Mahon relied upon the decision of Hilbery J in *E & S Ruben Ltd v Faire Bros & Co Ltd* [1949] 1 KB 254; [1949] 1 All ER 215. [His Honour referred to the facts of that case and continued:]

Hilbery J held that when the buyers asked the sellers to act for them and send the goods direct to the footwear company, and the sellers agreed to do so, the buyers were taking delivery constructively at the sellers' premises when the sellers set aside goods against the contract, and that thereafter the sellers were acting for the buyers as agents in putting the goods on the lorry and dispatching them on their journey to the footwear company. Accordingly, the act of the sellers in sending on the goods to the footwear company was in reality an act of the buyers (through their agents, the sellers). That act was "inconsistent with the ownership of the seller" within the meaning of s 35 of the Sale of Goods Act 1893, *22 Halsbury's Statutes of England*, 2nd ed, p 985 (corresponding with s 37 of the New Zealand Sale of Goods Act 1908). It occurred *after* the buyers had taken constructive delivery of the goods and accordingly the requirements of the section as pointed out by Atkin LJ were satisfied.

The decision in *E & S Ruben Ltd v Faire Brothers and Co Ltd* does not appear to have been the subject of later judicial consideration. It was however reviewed by Professor Gower in 12 *MLR* 368. Professor Gower adverted to the apparent uncertainty which exists as to the meaning of the phrase "delivery to him" as used in s 35 of the English Act. He pointed out that in *Hardy & Co v Hillerns and Fowler* both the Court of Appeal and Greer J in the court below ([1923] 1 KB 658) appear to have accepted the finding of the arbitrator that delivery took place when the goods themselves were handed over to the consignee on arrival of the ship, in other words, to the place where it was contemplated that examination of the goods should take place. He pointed out that in *Ruben v Faire* this point does not appear to have been considered and suggests that it might have been argued in that case that the parties had agreed that the sub-purchaser's address was the place for examination. It is to be noted in this connection that in *Benaim & Co v L S Debono* [1924] AC 514 at 520; [1924] All ER Rep 103, the Privy Council seems to have attached importance to the way in which the purchaser dealt with the goods in question after their arrival at Malta, although the facts of the case disclose (AC at 517; All ER at 105) that after shipment of the goods in Gibraltar, and before their arrival in Malta, the consignee had resold all the goods to other purchasers. While adverting to the view apparently taken in the matter in *Hardy v Hillerns*, Professor Gower expressed the view that "one would have thought that 'delivery' must be used in the same sense as elsewhere in the Act and s 32(1) applied so that delivery to a carrier would prima facie be sufficient delivery to the buyer". This particular problem has subsequently been the subject of a dictum by Devlin J in *Chao v British Traders Ltd* [1954] 1 All ER 779 at 795. Devlin J was discussing the position in relation to a cif contract. He was, however, concerned with the meaning of the words "delivery to him" as used in s 35 of the Sale of Goods Act. It had been suggested by counsel that in that section the word "delivered" means physical delivery of the goods from the ship. Devlin J said "I cannot take that view of it. I think that 'delivery' means, as s 62(1) of the Act defines it, a 'voluntary transfer of possession' and therefore it means transfer of possession under the contract of sale".

The second question adverted to by Professor Gower is the meaning of the phrase "any act in relation to them which is inconsistent with the ownership of the seller". I take the opportunity of quoting *in extenso* Professor Gower's observations in this connection. His comments are as follows:

"Secondly, there seems to be some slight obscurity as to what acts will be deemed to be 'inconsistent with the ownership of the seller'. In both *Hardy v Hillerns* and *Ruben v Faire* the act was the onward delivery of the goods themselves to a sub-purchaser, and the judgment of Greer J implies that nothing less than the physical movement of the goods will suffice. He pointed out that under s 36 the buyer who rejects is not bound to return the goods to the seller but the seller has to collect. He said, at 644: 'If the buyer was entitled to reject them when they had been sent 100 miles, or it may be 500 miles, away from the place where they were delivered, it would, in my judgment, be for the seller to take the goods back to the place of delivery. I think that supports the view that if the buyer for his own purposes sends the goods away from the place of delivery, it is not likely that the statute would put upon the seller the obligation of bringing them back to the place where he had sent them? Similarly Bankes LJ said in the Court of Appeal ([1923] 2 KB at 496): 'Where under a contract of sale goods are delivered to the buyer which are not in accordance with the contract, so that the buyer has a right to reject them, the seller upon receipt of notice of rejection is entitled to have the goods placed at his disposal so as to allow of his resuming possession forthwith, and if the buyer has done any act which prevents him from so resuming possession that act is necessarily inconsistent with his right? It would therefore appear that the mere sub-sale, even though accompanied by transfer of the documents of title, will not take away the buyer's right of rejection; there must be a dealing with the goods themselves and perhaps, as we have seen, this must take place not merely after delivery to the buyer in the normal sense but after delivery to the place contemplated for examination."

In *Chao v British Traders Ltd* Devlin J (at 796) expressed the view that under a cif contract, when the documents of title are given to the buyer, he obtains the property in the goods, subject to the condition that the property revests if on examination he finds the goods not in accordance with the contract. Devlin J thought that the "ownership of the seller", for the purposes of s 35 of the Sale of Goods Act [NSW s 38], is in such cases his right (in the event of rejection after an opportunity for examination has been made) "to have the goods physically returned to him in the place where the examination has taken place and without being dispatched to third parties". The learned judge then went on to express the view that neither a pledge of the goods nor a sale of documents by the buyer would conflict with the "ownership of seller" as thus described.

In the present case I am not, of course, concerned with a cif contract. Nevertheless I find the observations of Devlin J and the comments made by Professor Gower of the greatest assistance in the present case. In the present case it was one of the original terms of the contract (contained in a letter of 24 June from Coca-Cola to Hammer & Barrow) that Hammer & Barrow would arrange dispatch to the various bottlers in the order listed. Later, Coca-Cola stated that "we are therefore prepared to accept your first delivery of 35,000 to 40,000 yoyos in Auckland not later than Monday, 12 September". Mr Jenkins in a letter to Coca-Cola said: "A shipment to Auckland of over 12,000 yoyos was made on 31 August and this will be followed up with shipments of 8,000 yoyos each two working days. We have instructed W Whittaker Ltd to attend to transport and insurance on your behalf." The original prices quoted for yoyos and packets of strings was expressed to be "factory door" in a letter of 9 June 1960 written by Mr Jenkins to Mr Murray. Prices were similarly described in the purchase order. In these circumstances it seems to me that W Whittaker Ltd received the various consignments of yoyos as agents for Coca-Cola and that delivery of the goods to Coca-Cola, within the meaning of s 37 of the Sale of Goods Act (NZ), probably took place in Christchurch when the yoyos were handed over by Hammer & Barrow to W Whittaker Ltd. I also consider that in the circumstances of the present case the place for the examination of the goods contemplated by the contract was the premises of Northern Bottling in Auckland. For the purposes of s 37 of the Sale of Goods Act (NZ) the "ownership of the seller", once the goods were delivered to W Whittaker Ltd, consisted essentially in the right of Hammer & Barrow to have the goods returned to it, at the premises of Northern Bottling in Auckland, in the event of their being rejected by Coca-Cola. Hammer & Barrow would of course be entitled to the return of the goods in the same condition as on the arrival of those goods in Auckland subject only to such interference with that state and condition as would necessarily arise from a reasonable examination.

The material question then is whether Coca-Cola, *after* delivery of the goods in Christchurch to W Whittaker Ltd acted in a manner inconsistent with the "ownership" of Hammer & Barrow.

It seems quite clear in the first place that the arrangements for resale of the yoyos by Coca-Cola to Northern Bottling were made in June 1960. There is a purchase order of 20 June 1960 and a covering letter of the same date on the file of documents put in in evidence. By this purchase order Northern Bottling ordered 469 gross of yoyos from Coca-Cola. This is a lesser number than the eventual quantity ordered for Auckland, but there is no evidence establishing that the increase in number was arranged between Coca-Cola and Northern Bottling *after* the deliveries began in Christchurch. The onus of proof of any "acceptance" by Coca-Cola must lie on Hammer & Barrow. In the absence of evidence to the contrary I therefore conclude that the agreement for resale was concluded between Coca-Cola and Northern Bottling prior to the commencement of deliveries by Hammer & Barrow.

It also seems to me that the act of W Whittaker Ltd in delivering yoyos to the premises of Northern Bottling in Auckland, even though W Whittaker Ltd be regarded as the agent of Coca-Cola, cannot be considered as an act of Coca-Cola inconsistent with the ownership of Hammer & Barrow. It was merely the carriage of the goods to the place contemplated for examination by the buyer and was not therefore inconsistent with the right of the seller, in the event of rejection, to have the goods returned to him at the place of examination.

I think that the facts of the present case are distinguishable from those in *E and S Ruben v Faire Brothers and Co Ltd*. In that case the special arrangements between the plaintiff and the defendant led Hilbery J to the conclusion that the sellers were acting as agents of the buyers when they handed over the goods to the carrier for onward transit to the sub-purchaser. In the present case I consider that Hammer & Barrow were acting solely in their own capacity as vendors when they handed over the goods to W Whittaker Ltd. I think that up to the stage where the goods arrived at the premises of Northern Bottling in Auckland there was no such dealing with the goods on the part of Coca-Cola as would be inconsistent with the right of Hammer & Barrow to have the goods returned to them at those premises in Auckland in the event of rejection.

In the present case I have held that the goods dispatched to Auckland were not in accordance with the contract description. It follows that the property in the goods did not pass to Coca-Cola when the goods were delivered to W Whittaker Ltd: *Vigers Brothers v Sanderson*

Brothers [1901] 1 KB 608; and Sale of Goods Act s 20 r 5. The ownership of the goods was capable therefore of passing only as a result of acceptance by Coca-Cola and pending any such acceptance could not vest in Northern Bottling as sub-purchaser by virtue of the agreement for sale between that company and Coca-Cola. In like manner, I think that any possession of the goods on the part of Northern Bottling must be regarded as subject to the exercise by Coca-Cola of its rights of examination and rejection. In effect, and whether the matter be regarded from the point of view of the ownership in the goods or the possession of the goods, I do not think that Coca-Cola had (at the point of time when the goods arrived into the Northern Bottling store) divested itself of the power to return the goods to Hammer & Barrow in the event of those goods being rejected.

In the result I have come to the conclusion that the broad submission made by Mr Mahon to the effect that Coca-Cola had lost any right to reject the goods by virtue of the resale of those goods to Northern Bottling cannot succeed.

I turn now to consider the events subsequent to the arrival of the goods in Auckland, in order to decide whether those subsequent events constituted an acceptance, either in whole or in part, of the yoyos delivered to Auckland.

The evidence is silent as to any arrangements which may have been made between Coca-Cola and Northern Bottling regarding the examination of the goods in Auckland. It is clear however that Duncan Russell (by virtue of an agreement between that company and Coca-Cola), undertook "to supervise the proper manufacture of the said yoyos to the correct specifications". Mr Murray was in Auckland at all material times during the delivery of the yoyos and was actively engaged in their examination and in efforts (by way of sorting and sanding) to render some of them fit for the purposes of the yoyo campaign. There is no suggestion in the evidence of any member of the staff of Coca-Cola taking any active part in the examination of the yoyos on their arrival in Auckland. In the circumstances, the only reasonable inference which I can draw is that Mr Murray was in fact the representative of Coca-Cola in Auckland to examine the yoyos on arrival and that Coca-Cola must accept as its own acts, any acts of Mr Murray amounting in law to an acceptance of the whole or any part of the goods delivered.

It is also necessary to decide whether the yoyos delivered to Auckland were one entire and indivisible instalment within the framework of the contract for 200,000 yoyos, or whether the deliveries made to Auckland constituted separate instalments within the framework of the total number of yoyos ordered for delivery to that city.

The original contract between Coca-Cola and Hammer & Barrow provided for delivery "as manufactured". Whatever ambiguity existed in this expression was, I think, resolved by the conduct of the parties when deliveries commenced. As is apparent from the table of deliveries prepared by Mr Matson, consignments of yoyos were dispatched on various dates between 31 August and 29 September 1960, and each consignment was followed up by a separate invoice. This procedure had the full approval of Coca-Cola as appears from the evidence of Mr Arkley, who is the chief accountant on the staff of Coca-Cola. A similar problem arose for determination in *Jackson v Rotax Motor and Cycle Co* [1910] 2 KB 937, and reference may also be made to 34 *Halsbury's Laws of England*, 3rd ed, p 101, para 148. I have come to the conclusion that it was the intention of the parties in the present case that each separate consignment of yoyos dispatched by Hammer & Barrow to Auckland should constitute a separate instalment.

I turn now to consider to what extent these individual instalments were accepted.

The evidence shows that a considerable number of yoyos were, with the knowledge and consent of Mr Murray, delivered by Northern Bottling to various retailers for purposes of resale. [His Honour then discussed the evidence and continued:] I find as a fact that the defendant accepted 51 cartons and accordingly lost its right of rejection in respect of those cartons.

As regards the remaining consignments (comprising in all a total of 97 cartons) I am not satisfied by the evidence that the defendant did more than make some, certainly not excessive, examination of these. In particular, I am not satisfied by the evidence that they were removed from the premises of Northern Bottling or dealt with in any way which was inconsistent with the ownership of Hammer & Barrow.

It remains therefore to consider, in relation to these latter consignments, whether the defendant retained them after the lapse of a reasonable time without intimating to Hammer & Barrow that it had rejected them. If it did so retain the goods then by virtue of s 37 of the Sale of Goods Act it is deemed to have accepted them. The approximate dates of arrival in Auckland, and the number of cartons involved in each consignment (making up the total of 97 cartons with which I am now concerned) are as follows:

19 September	22 cartons
22 September	17 cartons
26 September	14 cartons
29 September	12 cartons
4 October	12 cartons
7 October	20 cartons

If I take the letter of 14 October 1960 as the actual notice of rejection of the goods by Coca-Cola (as opposed to the slightly earlier notice of rejection given by Northern Bottling on 10 October) then the period during which the goods were retained was, in the case of the earliest consignment with which I am concerned, a total period of 25 days. The question which I have to decide is whether, in all the circumstances of the case, this was more than a "reasonable time". Section 57 of the Sale of Goods Act [NSW s 58] provides that "where by this Act any reference is made to a 'reasonable time', the question what is a reasonable time is a question of fact". Goods in the present case were manufactured for a special purpose and there could accordingly be no question of the vendor being seriously prejudiced by a moderate delay, as there could be no suggestion that he thereby lost an opportunity of reselling the goods—a matter which would normally be of considerable importance in determining the question of reasonable time for rejection, particularly where there might be a risk of the vendor having to resell goods on a falling market.

...

The question whether the goods were retained for an unreasonable time is not one as regards which I have been able to derive any real assistance from the few reported cases which deal with the problem of acceptance arising from retention of goods without notification of rejection. It is essentially a question of fact and in the particular and peculiar circumstances of the present case I am not satisfied that the delay was unreasonable, and in the result I find that the 97 cartons of yoyos delivered in Auckland on varying dates between 19 September and 7 October were not "accepted" by the defendant.

It follows from my finding that Coca-Cola accepted 51 cartons of yoyos and strings that Hammer & Barrow is prima facie entitled to recover from Coca-Cola the contract price of the goods so accepted. In its defence however, Coca-Cola relies on the provisions of s 54 of the Sale of Goods Act whereby a buyer who is compelled as a result of acceptance to treat any breach of condition on the part of the seller as a breach of warranty, is entitled to set up the breach of warranty in diminution or extinction of the price. The same claim is made in a different way in a counterclaim filed by Coca-Cola. In that counterclaim Coca-Cola claims as damages for breach of warranty the total amount of the price claimed by Hammer & Barrow.

Where the breaches of warranty are, as in this case, breaches of warranty of quality, then s 54(3) provides that the measure of damages is prima facie the difference between the value of the goods at the time of delivery to the buyer, and the value they would have had if they had answered to the warranty. That rule is discussed in some detail in *Mayne & McGregor on Damages*, 12th ed, paras 400, 401 and 402. It is there pointed out that the value of the goods is to be determined by reference to market value, and no doubt the reason for this is that in the ordinary way a purchaser who receives goods which are not up to contract description can go into the market and purchase goods which do answer to the warranty and at the same time dispose of the goods delivered under the contract at whatever their market value may be. In the present case the goods, to the knowledge of all parties, were ordered for a special purpose and were not of a type which could have been replaced from other sources—at any rate in time for the campaign which had been organised in Auckland to commence on 19 September 1960. Moreover, the get-up of the goods including the printed matter appearing on boxes, packages and instruction sheets, meant they could not be resold in the ordinary way.

The present case is therefore one in which the value of the goods as warranted, and their "unsound" value, must be determined by some other means.

The only evidence which I have of the value of the goods as warranted is the contract price, and I accept the contract price in the present case accordingly ... In the circumstances of the present case I think that the measure of the unsound value of the yoyos and strings must be the price which Coca-Cola, acting reasonably, did or could have obtained for the yoyos and strings by selling them.

Reasonable efforts were in fact made to sell the goods in the particular market for which they were designed, and those efforts included attempts to sort the yoyos and to sandpaper the grooves once the true condition of the yoyos became known to Mr Murray and Mr Cave...

In the result, the purchase price of the yoyos and strings in the 51 cartons is diminished by way of damages for breach of warranty to a figure of £753 6s 7d. This amount was in fact paid by Coca-Cola to Hammer & Barrow by cheque forwarded under cover of a letter of 13 December 1960. Its payment is acknowledged in the Statement of Claim. There is, therefore, nothing presently owing by Coca-Cola to Hammer & Barrow for the price of yoyos and strings sold and delivered under the contract, and the plaintiff's action accordingly fails completely as against Coca-Cola...

Judgment for the defendant.

J S Robertson (Aust) Pty Ltd v Martin
High Court of Australia (1956) 94 CLR 30

[In this case extracted on p 68, *supra*, Dixon CJ and Williams J both held that a buyer who insures goods and claims on the insurance policy in respect of pillage in transit has not acted inconsistently with the sellers' ownership.]

Williams J (at 59): ... Section 40 of the Act [Goods Act (Vic); NSW s 38] provides that the buyer is deemed to have accepted the goods ... when the goods have been delivered to him and he does any act in relation to them which is inconsistent with the ownership of the seller. As has already been said when two of the cases of presses reached Sydney they were found to have been pillaged and the plaintiff made a claim under the insurance policy for the loss sustained and was paid for this loss. It was submitted that this was an act of the plaintiff in relation to the presses shipped to Sydney that was inconsistent with the ownership of the seller. A buyer who takes delivery of goods which he has not previously examined has the right under s 39 of the Goods Act [NSW s 37] to examine the goods for the purpose of ascertaining whether they are in conformity with the contract. Pending the exercise of this right he has the property in the goods subject to the condition that they shall revest in the seller if upon the examination he finds them to be not in accordance with the contract: *Kwei Tek Chao v British Traders & Shippers Ltd* [1954] 2 QB 459 at 487. A purchaser who has this conditional property in goods for which he has paid the price and of which he has taken delivery must have the right to insure the goods without forfeiting his right to reject the goods under s 39. By insuring the goods, he does nothing which is inconsistent with the ownership of the seller. If a loss occurs and he makes a claim on the insurance company for the loss and receives payment, the payment takes the place of the goods that have been lost and, if the buyer subsequently became entitled to reject the goods, he would have to credit the seller with the insurance moneys. It is simply an illustration of the principle that a person must do everything he can to mitigate the damage flowing from a breach of contract. A buyer who acts in this way does nothing inconsistent with the ownership of the seller. His actions are completely consistent with that ownership ...

In its Tenth Report: *Innocent Misrepresentation*, 1962, the English Law Reform Commission stated (para 15):

Where there has been a genuine acceptance of goods by a buyer who has been able to form an opinion of their quality, it is not unreasonable that he should have no right to reject them, just as the right to rescind for misrepresentation is lost if the buyer affirms the contract with full knowledge of the facts. But in many cases the Sale of Goods Act appears to deprive the buyer of any right to reject defective goods before he has had an opportunity of examining them. This is plainly unsatisfactory. We accordingly suggest, first, that it should be made clear that acts which would amount to acceptance within the meaning of s 35 should not be held to do so until the buyer has had a reasonable opportunity of examining the goods as contemplated by s 34; secondly, that in the case of specific goods the right to reject for breach of condition should depend not on the passing of the property (which is the test under s 11(1)(c) but, as it does in the case of other goods, on acceptance by the buyer. The evidence we have received indicates that this is of particular importance in connection with the practice of selling goods in sealed containers, where acceptance ought not to be a bar to rescission until the buyer has had an opportunity of examining the goods.

This recommendation has been implemented by the Misrepresentation Act 1967 (UK) s 4 and the Misrepresentation Act 1971–1972 (SA) ss 11 and 12, so that in the relevant sections of the South Australian SGA the words shown below in square brackets have been deleted and those in italics have been added:

11(3) Where a contract of sale is not severable, and the buyer has accepted the goods, or a part thereof, [or where the contract is for specific goods the property in which has passed to the buyer] the breach of any condition to be fulfilled by the seller can only be treated as a breach of warranty, and not as a ground for rejecting the goods and treating the contract as repudiated, unless there be a term of the contract express or implied to that effect.

35 The buyer is deemed to have accepted the goods when he intimates to the seller that he has accepted them, or *(subject to section 34 of this Act)* when the goods have been delivered to him, and he does any act in realtion to them which is inconsistent with the ownership of the seller, or when, after the lapse of a reasonable time, he retains the goods without intimating to the seller that he has rejected the goods.

These amendments have been followed in the ACT (Sale of Goods Ordinance 1957 s 4) and Victoria (Goods (Sales and Leases) Act 1981 s 3).

The Trade Practices Act 1974 (Cth) s 75A and Goods Act 1958 (Vic) s 99 (inserted in 1981) go further by conferring on the buyer a specific right to rescind the contract and return the goods within a reasonable time after he has received and had a reasonable opportunity to inspect the goods. Note the safeguards that the goods must be defective at the time of delivery (a fact which may be difficult to prove); and the buyer must not have damaged the goods by abnormal use.

Does TPA s 75A raise questions of inconsistency with the position under state law? The decision in *General Motors Acceptance Corp v Credit Tribunal* (1977) 137 CLR 545 may have some bearing on this question; see also *Polgardy v Australian Guarantee Corp Ltd* (1981) 34 ALR 391 on the question of jurisdiction.

Compare the corresponding provisions of the Uniform Commercial Code:

§ 2-602(1) Rejection of goods must be within a reasonable time after their delivery or tender. It is ineffective unless the buyer seasonably notifies the seller.

§ 2-606(1) Acceptance of goods occurs when the buyer
  (a) after a reasonable opportunity to inspect the goods signifies to the seller that the goods are conforming or that he will take or retain them in spite of their non-conformity; or
  (b) fails to make an effective rejection (sub-section (1) of section 2-602), but such acceptance does not occur until the buyer has had a reasonable opportunity to inspect them; or
  (c) does any act inconsistent with the seller's ownership, but if such act is wrongful as against the seller it is an acceptance only if ratified by him.
  (2) Acceptance of a part of any commercial unit is acceptance of that entire unit.

§ 2-607(2) Acceptance of goods by the buyer precludes rejection of the goods accepted and if made with knowledge of non-conformity cannot be revoked because of it unless the acceptance was on the reasonable assumption that the non-conformity would be seasonably cured but acceptance does not of itself impair any other remedy provided by this article for non-conformity.

§ 2-608(1) The buyer may revoke his acceptance of a lot or commercial unit whose non-conformity substantially impairs its value to him if he has accepted it:
  (a) on the reasonable assumption that its non-conformity would be cured and it has not been seasonably cured; or

(b) without discovery of such non-conformity if his acceptance was reasonably induced either by the difficulty of discovery before acceptance or by the seller's assurances.

(2) Revocation of acceptance must occur within a reasonable time after the buyer discovers or should have discovered the ground for it and before any substantial change in condition of the goods which is not caused by their own defects. It is not effective until the buyer notifies the seller of it.

QUESTIONS

Question 6

(1) What is the purpose of SGA s 16(3)? How successfully does it achieve that purpose? Does s 16(3) (in conjunction with other sections) over-achieve in some circumstances?

(2) If you are not satisfied with the present operation of s 16(3), what amendments would you recommend to it or other related sections of SGA? What useful lessons might the Australian law reformer learn from other jurisdictions in relation to the buyer's right to reject non-conforming goods?

(3) Is there conflict between Trade Practices Act (Cth) s 75A and Sale of Goods Act (NSW) s 16(3)? If so, how might it be resolved?

Question 7

Greatparts Ltd, a Wollongong wholesaler of automotive parts, placed an order by telephone with Carb Pty Ltd for the supply of 5000 carburettors at a price of $120,000. During the conversation it was agreed that delivery would be made at Carb's Sydney factory, but that Carb would dispatch carburettors in crates containing a minimum of 100 carburettors to sub-purchasers' premises on the south coast if so directed by Greatparts. The contract was not confirmed in writing.

Before delivery of any carburettors, Greatparts contracted to resell 1000 carburettors to each of three south coast motor dealers and verbally requested Carb to dispatch 1000 carburettors to each dealer, and the remaining 2000 to Greatparts' warehouse in Wollongong. When the first consignment of 1000 carburettors reached the first dealer Bestcars Ltd, 600 of the carburettors proved to be faulty, and Bestcars notified Greatparts that it was returning the entire consignment. The 2000 carburettors received by Greatparts direct from Carb were then examined and 1100 were also found to be faulty.

The consignments of 1000 carburettors to the two remaining dealers were not due to be dispatched by Carb until the following week, but Greatparts decided that it would prefer to reject the entire order including the consignments dispatched or to be dispatched to dealers.

Advise Greatparts.

What difference would it make to your advice in the following *alternative* situations:

(1) The order by Greatparts had been in writing.

(2) It was agreed between Greatparts and Carb that delivery would take place at Greatparts' warehouse.

(3) It was agreed between Carb and Greatparts that the carburettors for delivery to the sub-buyers were to be packed 100 to the crate but the crates as actually delivered contained only 90 carburettors.

(4) Of the 2000 carburettors delivered to Greatparts' warehouse, 300 had only minor faults which Greatparts immediately rectified.

SECTION 3: REMEDIES FOR BREACH

The buyer Mitzi's right of rejection of non-conforming goods is of course a very effective remedy which may amount to a rescission of the contract. It is a self-help remedy not requiring the intervention of the courts, although the question whether the goods do or do not conform to the contract, and hence whether Mitzi was entitled to reject, may be subsequently litigated. If Mitzi's rejection was unfounded, it will itself be in breach of contract for non-acceptance. In cases of doubt the parties may agree to accept the verdict of an impartial arbitrator or seek a declaratory order from the court.

As already noted in cases such as *Hoeper v Neldner*, p 30, *supra*, and *Kwei Tek Chao v British Traders and Shippers Ltd*, p 120, *supra*, the motivation to reject goods may sometimes be provided or strengthened by external factors, such as loss of sub-purchaser or a movement in market prices, which are really unrelated to the formation or performance of the contract. It may sometimes appear that the remedies available to the aggrieved party do not adequately take account of the motives of the party refusing to perform.

SELLERS' REMEDIES

In examining remedies available to the seller Carb in the event of Mitzi's default as set out in Stage 5 at the beginning of Chapter 2, note that Carb's remedies may be divided into:

(a) self-help remedies in respect of the goods: withholding delivery (lien), stopping the goods in transit, and resale; and
(b) those requiring court action: suing for the price, or for damages for non-acceptance.

UNPAID SELLERS' RIGHTS AGAINST THE GOODS

An unpaid seller is defined in SGA s 41(1). His rights against the goods are:

42(1) Subject to the provisions of this Act and of any statute in that behalf, notwithstanding that the property in the goods may have passed to the buyer, the unpaid seller of goods as such has by implication of law—
  (a) a lien on the goods for the price while he is in possession of them;
  (b) in the case of the insolvency of the buyer a right of stopping the goods *in transitu* after he has parted with possession of them;
  (c) a right of resale as limited by this Act.

If under their contract property has not passed from the unpaid seller Carb to Mitzi, the lien is really redundant since Carb, as owner, is entitled to retain possession, but s 42(2) gives it similar rights in that situation. Section 43 sets out the situations in which Carb is entitled to exercise its lien by retaining possession. Being a possessory remedy, Carb's lien will terminate if it delivers the goods to a carrier, eg, Trans Shipping Co (not being Carb's servant) or other bailee for transmission to Mitzi, or Mitzi or its agent lawfully obtains possession of the goods: s 45(1) and see *Jeffcott v Andrew Motors Ltd*, p 131, *infra*.

During the course of the transit of the goods from Carb to Mitzi, Carb's lien is ended but Carb can exercise its right of stoppage and regain possession if Mitzi becomes insolvent: s 46. If Carb regains possession in this way it can reassert its lien. The course of transit is described in s 47. It does not refer to carriage by air, except in amendments made to the Sale of Goods Ordinance in the ACT. While ss 46 and 47 set out the law clearly enough, difficult factual questions will arise as to whether the goods remain in transit or have come into the possession of the buyer or its agent: see, eg, *Ex parte Miles; Re Isaacs* (1885) 15 QBD 39; *Plischke & Sohne v Allison Bros Ltd*, p 132, *infra*. Is the necessary relationship established with a carrier when goods are posted by mail so that the unpaid seller can stop them in transit? See *Postmaster-General v W H Jones & Co (London) Ltd*, p 133, *infra*.

When Carb exercises its right of stoppage in the manner described in s 48, Trans Shipping must obey. The carrier's position was fully considered by the English Court of Appeal in *Booth Steamship Co Ltd v Cargo Fleet Iron Co Ltd* [1916] 2 KB 570. The effect of the decision may be paraphrased:

(1) If Trans Shipping fails to obey Carb's stop notice it will be liable in conversion.

(2) Although Carb is entitled under SGA s 48(2) to order redelivery to itself or in accordance with its directions, Trans Shipping's claim to a lien on the goods for its freight costs takes priority over Carb's claim.

(3) Although Trans should not hand over the goods to Mitzi it is entitled to perform its part of the contract of carriage which it made with Mitzi and thereby earn its freight by carrying the goods to their agreed destination.

Jeffcott and Another v Andrew Motors Ltd
Court of Appeal of New Zealand [1960] NZLR 721

[The case involved the typical facts of a fraudulent rogue buying a car from a private seller, the plaintiffs, with a valueless cheque and reselling to an innocent purchaser the defendant. The Court of Appeal held that the defendant acquired a good title as a bona fide purchaser for value from the original buyer who had obtained possession with the consent of the original seller under s 27(2) (NSW SGA s 28(2)). McCarthy J at first instance and one of the Appeal Court judges, Hutchinson J, also considered the plaintiff's claim to an unpaid seller's lien under ss 41 and 42 (NSW ss 42 and 43).]

Hutchinson J (at 730): ... As recorded in the judgment of the learned judge in the court below, the only submission ultimately relied on for the appellants in this case was that they were entitled under ss 40 to 44 of the Sale of Goods Act to an unpaid seller's lien on the car.

Under s 41(1) the unpaid seller of goods has, by implication of law: "(a) a lien on the goods, or right to retain them for the price, while he is in possession of them." That right exists notwithstanding that the property in the goods may have passed to the buyer. Under sub-s (2) the seller has a similar and co-extensive right where the property in goods has not passed to the buyer. Nothing therefore turns, in connection with this argument, as applied to this case, on any question whether or not the property in the motor car passed to Stevens. The important words there for the purpose of this case are the words "while he is in possession of them".

Section 42 sets out the cases in which the unpaid seller of goods has this lien, but it is only the unpaid seller "who is in possession of them" who has it. At no time since Stevens obtained possession of the car by fraud have the appellants been in possession of it. In particular, they were not in possession of it when they commenced their proceedings against the respondent. There may in some cases be a question of fact, or mixed fact and law, as to whether an unpaid seller is in possession of goods... There is no such question here; the fact that the appellants were not in possession of the car when they took their action is plain and undisputed.

Under s 44(1)(b) [NSW s 45(1)(b)] an unpaid seller loses his lien "when the buyer or his agent lawfully obtains possession of the goods". It was contended for the appellants that the buyer in this case, Stevens, did not obtain possession of the car lawfully, but obtained it unlawfully. This appears to be in accordance with the view stated in *Benjamin on Sale*, 8th ed, p 849, where it is said, on the authority of *Wallace v Woodgate* (1824) Ry & Mood 193; 171 ER 990 that the addition of the qualifying adverb "lawfully" shows that the possession must not be obtained tortiously as against the seller; but the view has been expressed that, to read the paragraph consonantly with other sections of the Act, "lawfully" must mean "with the consent of the seller". Whether that contention for the appellants is correct or not, I am prepared to assume its correctness for the purpose of the argument for the appellants based on s 44(1)(b). The argument was that, as that paragraph provides that an unpaid seller loses his lien when the buyer lawfully obtains possession of the goods, he does not lose the lien when the buyer unlawfully obtains possession of them. That argument assumes that, if a certain proposition is sound, the converse proposition is sound also; it is what is sometimes called a "back-handed" argument, and its soundness depends on an accurate ascertainment of what the alternative is to the known proposition. The alternative put forward here is not the only alternative is to the known proposition. The alternative put forward here is not the only alternative to what appears in s 44(1)(b), nor is it, in my opinion, the true alternative to it. It is clear from ss 41 and 42 that the unpaid seller's lien is a possessory lien only; indeed that is emphasised in s 44 itself, where the words "right of retention" are twice used as equivalent to the word "lien". The only sound inference, in my opinion, in relation to a buyer's unlawfully obtaining possession of the goods, which may be taken from s 44(1)(b), is that the unpaid seller's lien will not then be finally lost, but may revive if he again obtains possession of them...

Mr Harding contended that, even though the appellants did not have possession of the car, they could claim that the court make a declaration that they have a lien upon the car and are entitled to have possession of it restored to them and order the return of the car, this as sought in para 2(a) and (b) of the prayer of their statement of claim. But, in my opinion, the court cannot declare that they have such a lien for the simple reason that the existence of such a lien depends on possession. Nor can it, in my opinion, simply because they would have such a lien if they were in possession of the car, order its return to them, for such a lien, like common-law possessory liens—as to which see 24 *Halsbury's Laws of England*, 3rd ed, p 145, para 265—is a shield, not a sword, giving a defence not a right of action.

Appeal dismissed.

Johann Plischke & Sohne v Allison Brothers Ltd
King's Bench Division [1936] 2 All ER 1009

Branson J (at 1010): ... The action arises in the following way. In September 1934, the plaintiffs, who are manufacturers of linen goods, accepted an order placed by a firm, Napier Bros, for a quantity of hemstitched linen goods, and, according to the confirmation of the order, the terms were "Free house, London, exclusive of 90 days' acceptance," and in pursuance of that contract the plaintiffs shipped the goods through Karl Prior of Hamburg, on the steamer *Awk* to Allison Bros, London. The *Awk* arrived on 14 January 1935. According to the evidence which has been given by the shipping clerk of the defendants and the accountant of the firm of Napiers, Napiers instructed Allisons to warehouse these goods and to hold them pending further instructions. On 14 January or within a few days of it, Napiers found themselves so embarrassed financially that they called a meeting of their creditors and executed a deed of arrangement. As soon as this got to the knowledge of the plaintiffs, they cabled to Prior, of Hamburg, to prevent delivery, and Prior on the same day cabled the defendants not to deliver.

The question arises whether the plaintiff has succeeded in exercising the unpaid vendor's right of stopping goods *in transitu*. That is the real issue in this case. It has been strenuously argued by Mr Davis for the plaintiffs that the *transitus* of these goods did not end until they were delivered, not at any warehouse or other place in London, but at the premises of Messrs Napiers; and he says the goods were never delivered and consequently the *transitus* was not concluded when on 18 January the order to stop delivery was given and received.

In the first place the question turns on what was the meaning of the contract, and it is urged that the term "Free house, London," indicates that the goods have to be delivered at the named place which was the premises of Messrs Napiers. But I think that all that means is that the buyer has a right to demand that the property shall be delivered to him, and that it does not exclude the ordinary right of the purchaser to indicate that they should be delivered to some other place than his own private premises; and I cannot construe this contract as meaning that the transit cannot come to an end unless the goods are delivered at Messrs Napiers. If it means that Napiers were prepared to take delivery at any antecedent stop in the *transitus*, there is no reason in law or in commonsense why they should not be able to say "leave them in the Regent's Canal Dock and we will take delivery of them there". What happened, there is no doubt, is that before the ship arrived, Allisons, who had acted as forwarding agents, inquired of Napiers where they wanted the goods delivered, and Napiers said: "Put them into the warehouse of the Regent's Canal Dock and leave them there for further instructions." It is quite plain that Allisons had no authority as agents for the sellers to put them in dock, and it is obvious that they must have done so as agents for the purchasers. The moment these goods, having been landed in the ordinary course and put in the warehouse pending payment of the duty, the goods have come into the hands of Napiers' agents, the *transitus* has ended, and that is the end of the matter. It is said by Mr Davis that *transitus* cannot finish until the duty has been paid and the goods properly received into this country. That would be true if Napiers were still insisting upon the delivery of the goods at 12 Wilson Street. But it is not true if Napiers are prepared to say "we do not want these goods except where they are now".

I think on the true view of this case that the *transitus* finished when the goods were collected from the steamer by Allisons. The *transitus* ended by the end of 14 January or at all events long before 18 January. That decides this case in my view. But even if I am wrong on this point, the Sale of Goods Act 1893 s 45(2) [NSW s 47(2)] dealing with the question of stoppage *in transitu* which enacts "If the buyer or his agent in that behalf obtains delivery of the goods before their arrival at the appointed destination, the transit is at an end", operates to put an end to this transit when the goods were being held by Allisons as agents for Napiers. Some question has been raised as to the correctness of the argument that Allisons were acting as agents for Napiers in this matter. This is, however, quite consistent with the letters they wrote at the time.

It seems to me that the plaintiffs must fail in this action, and I give judgment for the defendant with costs.

See also *Postmaster-General v W H Jones & Co (London) Ltd* [1957] NZLR 829 where it was held that for the purpose of s 47(1) goods are not delivered to a carrier or other bailee for the purpose of sending the goods to the buyer and that therefore goods sent by post cannot be stopped in transit because no contract arises between the seller and the Post Office.

RESALE BY BUYER OR SELLER

Under SGA s 49 a resale by the buyer Mitzi will not defeat the unpaid seller Carb's right of lien or stoppage *in transitu* unless:
  (a) Carb has assented thereto (eg, *D F Mount Ltd v Jay and Jay (Provisions) Co Ltd* [1960] 1 QB 159); or
  (b) Mitzi has obtained possession of a document of title to the goods which it lawfully transfers to a buyer or pledgee who takes in good faith and for value (eg, *Ant Jurgens Margarinefabrieken v Louis Dreyfus & Co* [1914] 3 KB 40).

SGA s 50 deals with Carb's power to resell the goods as against Mitzi's default. If property has not passed to Mitzi, or Carb has validly rescinded, as contemplated under s 50(4), Carb resells as owner. However, where property has passed to Mitzi and Carb has not reserved a right to resell, its entitlement to resell will rest on s 50(3), although the second buyer will be protected by s 50(2). There remain the questions as to whether a resale under s 50(3) is on behalf of Carb or Mitzi, who is entitled to any profit arising on such resale, and as to the application of any deposit paid on the first sale:

R V Ward Ltd v Bignall
English Court of Appeal [1967] 1 QB 534

[The defendant Bignall, a motor dealer, contracted to buy a Ford Zodiac and a Vanguard from the plaintiff company for a total price of £850. He paid a deposit of £25. The defendant then refused to take delivery or pay the balance purchase price. The plaintiff had not reserved any express right of resale in the event of the defendant's default. The plaintiff subsequently resold the Vanguard for £350, but was unable to resell the Zodiac. The plaintiff sued for "damages, being the balance of the contract price, £825, less the £350 received from the sale of the Vanguard, plus £22 10s advertising expenses in respect of the two cars since the date of contract, a total of £497 10s".]

Sellers LJ [after stating the facts at 540:] The action in the lower court followed, as I think, the statement of claim and was, in substance, for damages for non-aceptance. That was the plaintiffs' proper claim, in my view, but no questions arose about the Zodiac. What had happened to it since 6 May was not investigated except that the plaintiffs had advertised it for sale unavailingly on some seven occasions between 13 May and 10 August 1965. No value was placed on it at the trial. By the letter of 12 October 1965, it had been offered to the defendant for £475, and he had refused it.

Throughout the trial it was assumed, as I see it, that the property had not passed to the defendant on 6 May 1965, notwithstanding the plaintiffs' solicitors' statement to the contrary. If reference had been made to the issue, which it was not, the court would have had to have regard to ss 17 and 18 of the Sale of Goods Act 1893 [NSW ss 22, 23]. In this court counsel for the plaintiffs stressed s 18 r 1, but that only applies "unless a different intention appears". In accordance with s 17(2), the court has to have regard in finding the intention of the parties "to the terms of the contract, the conduct of the parties, and the circumstances of the case". The fact that the defendant after inspection agreed to buy the two vehicles on the morning of 6 May 1965 and paid £25 in cash at the time goes but a little way to establishing that the parties intended the vehicles then and there to become the buyer's property. There was not even a payment by cheque. The buyer went to his bank to get cash, and that was to be handed over to Mrs Ward. He had not even seen the log book or inquired of its existence. No mention was made of the removal of the vehicles or of their insurance, although it is possible (no evidence was adduced) that the defendant as a dealer had some floating insurance cover.

I would hold that the property had not passed to the buyer; all that has happened since 6 May 1965, fits in with that view, and is not in harmony with the two vehicles having been transferred to the buyer when the bargain was made. The plaintiffs' remedy was rightly pursued below as damages for non-acceptance.

I need not develop that further, as, in my view, the result of this case would be the same whether the property had passed as the time of the sale or not ...

As a binding contract has been established the plaintiffs were unpaid sellers and by s 39(1)(c) of the Act [NSW s 42(1)(c)] they had a right of resale as limited by the Act. [His Honour then quoted s 48 (NSW s 50) and continued:]

The question on this part of the appeal is whether, if the property passed on the sale, the Zodiac car which has not been sold remains the buyer's property so that the action of the plaintiffs is for the price, or whether by the sale of the Vanguard the plaintiffs have rescinded the whole contract on the buyer's breach of it so that the ownership of the Zodiac reverted back to the plaintiffs and their remedy is in damages under the statute, or, in effect, damages for non-acceptance, giving credit for what they have received from the sale of the goods or part thereof.

Sub-sections (1) and (2) of s 48 speak clearly. Sub-section (4) expressly provides: "the original contract of sale is thereby rescinded". That was necessary because, where the seller "expressly reserves right of re-sale in case the buyer should make default", a seller who resold under such a contract would be applying and affirming the contract, and his action would be consistent with it. Under sub-s (3) no such provision of rescission is necessary, for, if an unpaid seller resells, he puts it out of his power to perform his contract and his action is inconsistent with a subsisting sale to the original buyer. Once there is a resale in accordance with s 48 by an unpaid seller in possession of the contractual goods the contract of sale is rescinded, whether the resale be of the whole of the goods or of part of them, and in this respect sub-ss (3) and (4) fall into line.

As the property in the goods reverts on such a resale, the seller retains the proceeds of sale whether they be greater or less than the contractual price. The probability in normal trade is that the price would be less, giving rise to a claim for damages, as for non-acceptance of the goods.

That was the view taken in *Benjamin on Sale*, 7th ed, 1931, edited by Judge Kennedy KC, and the second edition of *Halsbury's Laws of England*, 3rd ed, Vol 29, 1960, p 185, para 249, which states: "When the buyer, by his words or conduct, repudiates the contract, the seller, even where the property has passed, is entitled to treat the contract of sale as rescinded, and to resell the goods as an owner thereof, but without prejudice to his right to damages in respect of any loss caused to him by the buyer's default."

Since those editions, Finnemore J has interpreted s 48(3) in *Gallagher v Shilcock* [1949] 2 KB 765; [1949] 1 All ER 921. He held (I read from the headnote) that:

"Having regard to the express provision for rescission in s 48(4) ... where the right of resale has been reserved in the contract of sale, the true construction of sub-s (3) is that, where an unpaid seller, in the absence of such a reservation, exercises his right of resale under sub-s (3), that exercise does not operate to rescind the contract, for the seller, in so acting, is affirming the contract and ensuring that he receives the contract price."

With all respect to that learned and very experienced judge, I think the construction works the other way round. The express reservation in a contract would permit the unpaid seller to resell without acting inconsistently or in conflict with his obligations. His conduct would not evidence a rescission by him on the buyer's breach. Nevertheless, sub-s (4) makes the resale operate as a rescission and leaves the remedy, if any loss ensues, in damages. That brings it into harmony with sub-s (3), which also gives a claim for damages for any loss occasioned by the original buyer's breach of contract. If the unpaid seller resells the goods, he puts it out of his power to perform his obligation under the original contract, that is, to deliver the contractual goods to the buyer. By the notice to the buyer, the seller makes payment of the price "of the essence of the contract", as it is sometimes put. It requires the buyer to pay the price or tender it within a reasonable time.

If he fails to do so, the seller in possession of the goods may treat the bargain as rescinded and resell the goods. The suit for damages becomes comparable to a claim for damages for non-acceptance of the goods where the property never has passed. The property has reverted on the resale, and the second buyer gets a good title. The seller resells as owner. Sub-section (2) expressly gives the buyer a good title thereto as against the original buyer.

On this view of the law the plaintiffs cannot recover the price of the Zodiac, which is in the circumstances their property. They can, however, recover any loss which they have sustained by the buyer's default. The parties have sensibly agreed that the value of the Zodiac in May 1965 was £450. The total contract price was £850, against which the plaintiffs have received £25 in cash and £350 in respect of the Vanguard, and have to give credit for £450 for the Zodiac. To the loss of £25 must be added the sum for advertising, which was admittedly reasonably incurred—£22 10s. The plaintiffs' loss was, therefore, £47 10s.

I would allow the appeal and enter judgment for £47 10s in favour of the plaintiffs in substitution for the award of the deputy judge.

[**Diplock LJ** delivered judgment to the similar effect. **Russell LJ** agreed.]

Appeal allowed.

UNPAID SELLERS' PERSONAL RIGHTS OF ACTION

Under SGA s 51 Carb may sue Mitzi for the contract price of the goods if Mitzi wrongfully neglects to pay provided that either (a) property in the goods has passed to Mitzi, or (b) the contract stipulates for payment on a particular day irrespective of delivery and Carb is ready to perform all its obligations under the contract. Why is Carb not entitled to sue for the price where Mitzi has defaulted but property has not passed to it?

Where Mitzi refused to accept and pay for the goods, the more usual remedy is for Carb to sue for damages for non-acceptance under s 52(1), which simply confirms the common law action for breach of contract. Sections 52(2) and 55 merely preserve the common law rules for assessing damages, which were stated in the leading case of *Hadley v Baxendale* (1854) 9 Ex 341 at 354–5; 156 ER 151:

Where two parties have made a contract which one has broken, the damages which the other party ought to receive in respect of such breach of contract should be:

[1st rule] such as may fairly and reasonably be considered either arising naturally, ie, according to the usual course of things, from such breach of contract itself, or:

[2nd rule] such as may reasonably be supposed to have been in the contemplation of both parties, at the time they made the contract, as the probable result of the breach of it.

[The court continued:] Now, if the special circumstances under which the contract was actually made were communicated by the plaintiff to the defendants, and thus known to both parties, the damages resulting from the breach of such contract, which they would reasonably contemplate, would be the amount of injury which would ordinarily follow from a breach of contract under these special circumstances so known and communicated. But, on the other hand, if these special circumstances were wholly unknown to the party breaking the contract, he, at the most, could only be supposed to have had in his contemplation the amount of injury which would arise generally, and in the great multitude of cases not affected by any special circumstances, from such a breach of contract. For, had the special circumstances been known, the parties might have specially provided for the breach of contract by special terms as to the damages in that case; and of this advantage it would be very unjust to deprive them.

SGA s 52(2) incorporates the first rule, while s 55 ensures that the second rule remains available. Section 52(3) adopts a special rule for assessing damages where there is an "available market" for the goods in question. It can be viewed as a specific application of the first rule coupled with seller Carb's duty to act reasonably to mitigate its loss, in this case by going into the market to recoup its loss by resale against Mitzi's breach. There has been some confusion in the cases as to the meaning of the phrase "available market". It will obviously be in Mitzi's interest to establish that there was an available market so that Carb's damages will be restricted by s 52(3) to the difference between the contract price and the current price at the time Mitzi ought to have accepted the goods. If s 52(3) does not apply, Carb would be entitled to recover for loss of the profit which it would have made on the completed sale to Mitzi.

Kargotich v Mustica
Supreme Court of Western Australia (Full Court) [1973] WAR 167

Wallace J: This is an appeal from the decision of Stipendiary Magistrate Zempilas delivered at the local court, Perth, on 23 May 1972. In the action in the lower court the appellant, an authorised dealer in New Holland farm machinery claimed damages for loss of profit arising out of the respondents' refusal to take delivery of a New Holland 1010 Stackliner ordered by the respondents. The defence to the appellant's claim was that the stackliner which the appellant proposed to deliver to the respondents was not a new machine and the respondents were therefore justified in not taking delivery thereof.

The learned magistrate found as a fact that the machine (stackliner) offered to the respondents was in fact a new machine and that the respondents had no right to reject it. His Worship further found that on the question of loss of one out of two sales there was a duty on the appellant to mitigate his own damage and he found as a fact that the respondent V Mustica offered the appellant's sales manager to take a new machine if one was delivered within two weeks and that had this machine been supplied the appellant would have effected two sales. The failure to effect two sales was due to the appellant's failure to mitigate his loss by supplying a new machine to the respondents.

The appellant's grounds of appeal are:
(1) that upon the facts as found by the learned magistrate the appellant is entitled to judgment for the sum of $959.56;
(2) that the finding of the learned magistrate that the appellant failed in his duty to mitigate his loss is wrong and against the evidence and the weight of the evidence;
(3) that the finding of the learned magistrate that the appellant had a duty to enter into the second contract with the respondents was wrong in law.

With respect, I agree with the appellant that the learned magistrate was wrong in finding that the appellant failed in his duty to mitigate his loss and that the appellant's failure to effect two sales was due to his failure to supply a new machine to the respondents. This, however, does not conclude the matter.

The evidence before the learned magistrate was that upon the respondents' refusal to take delivery of the New Holland stackliner, the appellant was successful in selling that machine to L C Kentish & Co of Keysbrook on 19 November. It was sold as a new machine but at a somewhat lesser margin of profit than the appellant would have made had the respondents taken delivery thereof. Hence the magistrate's award of $90 damages to the appellant. In the proceedings before the lower court, most of the evidence seems to have been devoted to the question as to whether or not the stackliner which the appellant was about to deliver to the respondents was in fact new. No regard seems to have been paid to the question as to whether or not another machine would have been readily available to the appellant to have sold to L C Kentish & Co assuming that the respondents had taken delivery of the first machine or, alternatively, to supply to the respondents within the 14 days' limitation which they specified. In my view the respondents were not entitled to specify any period of limitation and it was

Performance of the Sales Contract

not encumbent upon the appellant to provide the respondents with another machine within that period of time.

There is some evidence as to the availability of another machine even though it take the form more of inference than direct evidence. I refer to the evidence of Kargotich, who is a dealer, to the effect that he was familiar with the type of machine, that he had sold several, that he had no machine in stock at the time it was ordered by the respondents, that he simply wrote out an order form for the transaction providing for delivery before 1 November, had a discussion in May with the New Holland people as a result of which he was assured that the machine would be available for November and that in due course he was told that delivery thereof would be made from Busselton. In addition there is the evidence of Ronald Young, former sales manager for New Holland, as to the method by which the machine in question was supplied to New Holland agents on extended credit and consignment and that when a sale was effected anywhere in the state a machine held by an agent anywhere within the state would be made available for sale.

The appellant through its counsel sought to rely on a circular form of sales letter, Exhibit D, which seems to have been put in evidence for the purpose of identifying the sale price of the machine in question and which is dated 22 June 1971. That sales letter referred to limited stocks of the machine having arrived from overseas and at present being prepared for shipment by New Holland's manufacturing department. In my view it has little or no value if it is meant to prove the availability of additional stackliners. On the other hand, the learned magistrate's finding that the appellant failed to effect two sales was due to his failure to mitigate his loss by supplying a new machine to the respondents, carries with it the inference that such a machine was available but it is only an inference.

It is for the appellant to prove his loss. He may do that in the way in which it was achieved in *Cameron v Campbell and Worthington Ltd* [1930] SASR 402, where the Chief Justice of South Australia held that a dealer in motor truck chassis was entitled to recover as damages his loss of profit on a sale frustrated by a purchaser's refusal to take delivery where it was "notorious that purchasers are not readily to be found". Or in the case of *W L Thompson Ltd v Robinson (Gunmakers) Ltd* [1955] Ch 177; [1955] 1 All ER 154, wherein the agent of Vanguard motor cars was successful in recovering loss of profit suffered by a purchaser's refusal to take delivery of a Vanguard motor car because Vanguard motor cars were not easy to sell in East Riding and the plaintiff's loss of bargain represented the loss of one more sale that it would have made had the defendant not refused to take delivery. Again the plaintiff may succeed as in the case of *Dominion Motors Ltd v Grieves* [1936] NZLR 766, wherein the plaintiff recovered loss of profit arising out of the defendant's failure to accept delivery of a motor chassis suitable for omnibus work on the principle that the plaintiff company as a dealer was in business for the purpose of making a profit on every transaction in which it engaged. It lost its transaction through the default of the purchaser, lost the opportunity of making a certain amount of profit and had still on its hands the article which it acquired which it may sooner or later sell but to somebody who would have bought, in any event, such an item. The plaintiff, in other words, was deprived of a second profit.

On the other hand, the appellant could well fail as did the plaintiff in *Charter v Sullivan* [1957] 2 QB 117; [1957] 1 All ER 809, where the plaintiff admitted that Hillman Minx motor vehicles were in heavy demand, the demand exceeding the supply. In other words the court of appeal in that case came to the conclusion that the plaintiff failed to prove that he had sustained the loss of profit claimed because he could have sold the vehicle to another customer and conversely could not have obtained enough vehicles to satisfy the demand.

It all depends upon where the onus lies. In *Dominion Motors Ltd v Grieves* counsel for the plaintiff company said that the onus lay upon the defendant to establish that there was an available market in the sense conveyed by sub-s (3) of s 49 of the Sale of Goods Act. Without deciding the question of onus the trial judge commented that whilst this assertion may be so, on the evidence he found that it had been established to his satisfaction that there was not any available market for the goods in question. I think the inference to be gained from the judgment of Callan J in *Dominion Motors Ltd v Grieves* as to onus is supported by the judgments in the court of appeal decision in *Charter v Sullivan* where it was held that the plaintiff had failed to prove his loss of profit claimed because of his acknowledgment that the demand for Hillman Minx vehicles exceeded the supply. It seems wrong in principle that a defaulting purchaser should not have cast upon him the onus of satisfying the court in circumstances such as these that the plaintiff would have been able to effect a second sale because a second machine was available for that purpose.

However I am bound by the authority of *Charter v Sullivan*. The inferences to be drawn from the evidence and the learned magistrate's findings are insufficient to discharge the onus which rests upon the appellant to have proved his damages and therefore this appeal should fail.

[**Burt** and **Wickham JJ** delivered judgments to the same effect.]

Appeal dismissed.

The same general approach has been adopted in cases involving contracts for the manufacture of specific items for the buyer where the test adopted is whether supply exceeds demand (ie no available market) so that the effect of the buyer's default is that the resale of the goods will be to an additional rather than a substituted customer with consequent loss of profit: *Re Vic Mill* [1913] 1 Ch 465.

BUYERS' REMEDIES

We have already noted in the previous section that if Carb tenders delivery of non-conforming goods, Mitzi's most effective initial remedy is to refuse to accept and pay for them. In that case Mitzi would also be entitled to buy alternative goods from another source of supply and to sue Carb for damages: s 53. Alternatively, Mitzi can accept the goods and set up the breach of warranty in diminution or extinction of the price, or if it has paid for the goods, sue Carb for damages: s 54.

If Carb fails to deliver specific goods, or possibly unascertained goods, Mitzi may be able to have the contract specifically enforced in special circumstances where damages would be an inadequate remedy: s 56.

SPECIFIC PERFORMANCE

In most instances, damages for non-delivery will provide Mitzi with an adequate remedy. In the SGA in England and Australian states except New South Wales the following provision appears to give such a right: Goods Act 1958 (Vic).

58 In any action for breach of contract to deliver specific or ascertained goods the court may if it thinks fit on the application of the plaintiff by its judgment direct that the contract shall be performed specifically without giving the defendant the option of retaining the goods or payment of damages...

In its place the Sales of Goods Act 1923 (NSW) s 56 provides:

Nothing in this Act shall affect any remedy in equity of the buyer or the seller in respect of any breach of a contract of sale or any breach of warranty.

As the result of these provisions, it would appear important to ascertain:
(a) the circumstances in which the courts will grant specific performance of a contract of sale of goods apart from the provision in Goods Act (Vic) s 58: *Doughan v Ley* below, and see *Cook v Rogers* (1946) 46 SR (NSW) 229; *Aristoc Industries Pty Ltd v Wenham (Builders) Pty Ltd* [1965] NSWR 581; and
(b) whether the courts would grant specific performance of a contract for sale of unascertained goods: *Sky Petroleum Ltd v VIP Petroleum Ltd* [1974] 1 All ER 954, p 139, *infra*.

Dougan v Ley and Another
High Court of Australia (1946) 71 CLR 142

[The plaintiffs Ley and Nash contracted to buy from the defendant Dougan a taxicab Reg No 1155 with its associated licence under the Transport Act 1930 (NSW). Taxi licences were in short supply and constantly diminishing. The plaintiffs' claim for specific performance was granted by the Supreme Court of NSW. The defendant appealed.]

Williams J (at 153): ... It is clear that the Court of Equity will not decree specific performance of a contract where a money payment, or in other words damages, will afford an adequate remedy for the breach, and that this is the position in the case of most forms of personal property, such as goods which can be readily purchased in the market and government stock and shares in listed companies which can be readily purchased on the Stock Exchange. But it is equally clear that the Court of Equity will decree specific performance of contracts for the sale of chattels which are unique or have for some other reason a special or peculiar value. The contract of 2 November was not a mere contract for the purchase of a chattel. It was a contract for the purchase of a chattel adapted to carry on a particular business, and of the registration and licence without which that business could not be carried on. It was therefore a contract of a composite character. The evidence shows that if the purchase money had been apportioned, the greater sum would have been attributable to the purchase of the registration and licence. This registration and licence were both capable of being renewed annually and of being transferred to another vehicle which replaced the existing taxicab.

The Court of Equity can intervene to protect the rights of persons who have interests in licences which are necessary to enable them to carry on business: *Lency & Sons Ltd v Callingham and Thompson* [1908] 1 KB 79 at 85. It can also intervene where chattels are of special value to a person in order to carry on his business: *North v Great Northern Railway Co* (1860) 2 Giff at 68; 66 ER at 30. The present composite contract incorporates both these features. The fact that there were a number of other taxicabs whose registrations and licences were still capable of being transferred at the date of the suit and that the respondents might have purchased one of these cabs in lieu of the appellant's vehicle is immaterial. It is equally immaterial that the respondents, after suit brought, managed to purchase another taxicab. If personal property is of such a nature that it can be the subject matter of a suit for specific performance, the subsequent purchase of similar property could no more affect the rights of the purchaser to specific performance than the subsequent purchase of another block of entirely comparable land in a subdivision adjoining the block already purchased could affect the right of the purchaser to have the previous contract specifically performed. I agree with His Honour's statement that "this particular chattel, with the rights which come from registration and the licence as a taxicab, is of such a nature that this court can properly entertain a suit for specific performance in regard to this sale".

[**Dixon J** and **McTiernan J** delivered judgments to the same effect.]

Appeal dismissed.

Sky Petroleum Ltd v VIP Petroleum Ltd
Chancery Division [1974] 1 All ER 954

[The facts appear from the following judgment.]

Goulding J: This is a motion for an injunction brought by the plaintiff company, Sky Petroleum Ltd, as buyer, under a contract dated 11 March 1970 made between the defendant company, VIP Petroleum Ltd, as seller, of the one part and the plaintiff company of the other part. That contract was to operate for a period of 10 years, subject to certain qualifications, and thereafter on an annual basis unless terminated by either party giving to the other not less than three months written notice to that effect. It was a contract at fixed prices, subject to certain provisions which I need not now mention. Further, the contract obliged the plaintiff company—and this is an important point—to take its entire requirement of motor gasoline and diesel fuel under the contract, with certain stipulated minimum yearly quantities.

After the making of the agreement, it is common knowledge that the terms of trade in the market for petroleum and its different products changed very considerably, and I have little doubt that the contract is now disadvantageous to the defendant company. After a long correspondence, the defendant company, by telegrams dated 15 and 16 November 1973, has purported to terminate the contract under a clause therein providing for termination by the defendant company if the plaintiff company fails to conform with any of the terms of the bargain. What is alleged is that the plaintiff company has exceeded the credit provisions of the contract and has persistently been, and now is, indebted to the defendant company in larger amounts than were provided for. So far as that dispute relates, as for the purposes of this motion it must, to the date of the purported termination of the contract, it is impossible for me to decide it on the affidavit evidence. It involves not only a question of construction of the contract, but also certain disputes on subsequent arrangements between the parties and on figures in the accounts. I cannot decide it on motion and the less I say about it the better.

What I have to decide is whether any injunction should be granted to protect the plaintiff company in the meantime. There is trade evidence that the plaintiff company has no great prospect of finding any alternative source of supply for the filling stations which constitute its business. The defendant company has indicated its willingness to continue to supply the plaintiff company, but only at prices which, according to the plaintiff company's evidence, would not be serious prices from a commercial point of view. There is, in my judgment, so far as I can make out on the evidence before me, a serious danger that unless the court interferes at this stage the plaintiff company will be forced out of business. In those circumstances, unless there is some specific reason which debars me from doing so, I should be disposed to grant an injunction to restore the former position under the contract until the rights and wrongs of the parties can be fully tried out.

It is submitted for the defendant company that I ought not to do so for a number of reasons...

Now I come to the most serious hurdle in the way of the plaintiff company which is the well-known doctrine that the court refuses specific performance of a contract to sell and purchase chattels not specific or ascertained. That is a well-established and salutary rule and I am entirely unconvinced by counsel for the plaintiff company when he tells me that an injunction in the form sought by him would not be specific enforcement at all. The matter is one of substance and not of form and it is, in my judgment, quite plain that I am for the time being specifically enforcing the contract if I grant an injunction. However the ratio behind the rule is, as I believe, that under the ordinary contract for the sale of non-specific goods, damages are a sufficient remedy. That, to my mind, is lacking in the circumstances of the present case. The evidence suggests, and indeed it is common knowledge, that the petroleum market is in an unusual state in which a would-be buyer cannot go out into the market and contract with another seller, possibly at some sacrifice as to price. Here, the defendant company appears for practical purposes to be the plaintiff company's sole means of keeping its business going, and I am prepared so far to depart from the general rule as to try to preserve the position under the contract until a later date. I therefore propose to grant an injunction...

ACTION FOR NON-DELIVERY OR LATE DELIVERY

Mitzi's right of action for non-delivery is codified under SGA s 53 (which is the mirror image of s 52) with the convenient rule in s 53(3) where there is an available market, and the general *Hadley v Baxendale* formulation in s 53(2) to fall back on where the buyer cannot mitigate his loss by buying against Carb's breach. Factual issues will arise as to the extent to which Mitzi may reasonably be expected to search or incur further risks in attempting to mitigate its loss: see, eg, *Hasell v Bagot Shakes & Lewis Ltd* (1911) 13 CLR 374. Other questions arise if Carb gives advance notice that it will not deliver on due date. Is Mitzi obliged to accept this anticipatory breach? Is the market price to be that current at the date of notification or when the goods ought to have been delivered? See *Melachrino v Nickoll and Knight* [1920] 1 KB 693. One of the results of Mitzi being unable to obtain alternative supplies may be its inability to fulfil commitments to a sub-purchaser thereby incurring damages. Whether Mitzi can recover these damages from Carb in turn will depend on whether Carb ought to have had in contemplation the fact that Mitzi might resell: *Wong v Hutchison* (1951) 68 WN (NSW) 55; and *Kwei Tek Chao v British Traders and Shippers Ltd* [1954] 2 QB 459, p 120, *supra*.

If Carb delivers goods after the due date for delivery and Mitzi accepts them, Mitzi can nonetheless recover damages for breach of warranty as to the delivery date. Where there is an available market this damage may be measured by comparing market values at the date stipulated for delivery and at the date of actual delivery. If the goods would have been used by Mitzi to earn income and Carb ought to have foreseen this result, as in the case of machinery, then Mitzi can recover damages for loss of profit under the second rule in *Hadley v Baxendale*.

Performance of the Sales Contract

OTHER BREACHES OF WARRANTY

Recovery of damages for goods accepted despite a breach of warranty is governed by s 54 which also allows such damages to be set up in direct diminution of the purchase price as the buyer did in *Hasell v Bagot, Shakes & Lewis Ltd* (1911) 13 CLR 374. The general principles of contract law apply to such assessment of damages: see, eg, *TC Industrial Plant Pty Ltd v Robert's Queensland Pty Ltd* [1964] ALR 1083; (1963) 37 ALJR 289.

QUESTIONS

Question 8

Under what conditions can a seller exercise his power of resale? If a deposit has been paid by the buyer, under what circumstances can the seller keep the deposit and/or any additional profit received on resale? In your answer refer to relevant statutory provisions and cases.

Question 9

Under a written contract Carb Pty Ltd agreed to manufacture for Mitzi Co 500 carburettors according to Mitzi's specifications at $20 each—a total contract price of $10,000. Carb's manufacturing costs including overheads amounted to $6000 but when the order was ready for delivery Mitzi refused to accept it. At this time Carb's factory was not operating at full capacity and business was rather slow. However, immediately Mitzi defaulted Jim Handy contacted Greatparts Ltd and explained Carb's predicament. Greatparts had an interstate subsidiary which required carburettors urgently and agreed to buy 400 provided delivery was made immediately. However, Greatparts would only pay $15 per carburettor because it would have to make modifications to the carburettors which had been built to Mitzi's specifications. Carb sold the 400 carburettors to Greatparts for $6000. It was unable to resell the remaining 100. Advise Carb of its rights against Mitzi and what damages, if any, it might expect to recover.

Would it make any difference to your advice if Greatparts had bought the full 500 carburettors at $15 each?

Question 10

(1) Greatparts Ltd was a wholesale distributor of motor parts accessories at Wollongong. On 1 February it contracted to purchase from Carb Pty Ltd 1000 carburettors at $20 each for delivery 1 May. On 1 March, Carb advised Greatparts that due to production difficulties it would not be able to fulfil the contract. Greatparts immediately sought alternative supplies, and found that the ruling price was now $25 due to wage adjustments. Fearing further increases, Greatparts purchased 1000 carburettors on 5 March from AMP Industries for $25 each for immediate delivery. By 1 May, the price had fallen to $18 due to falling metal prices.

Advise Greatparts what damages it might anticipate recovering from Carb.

(2) Assume that after Carb defaulted, Greatparts had not bought any carburettors from other sources. What damages could it recover:

(a) on the above facts? or

(b) if the price had risen further to $30 by 1 May?

(3) Assume further that in reliance upon Carb's contract, Greatparts had on 10 February entered a contract to supply Bestcars during May with 300 carburettors at $30 each. Following Carb's default Greatparts had sought for alternative supplies but due to general shortages in the industry had only been able to procure:

(a) 100 carburettors at $25 each;

(b) 100 carburettors (heavy duty) at $40 each.

Greatparts delivered these carburettors to Bestcars and obtained an additional $3 for each of the 100 heavy duty carburettors (ie $33 per carburettor).

Greatparts discovered that it could procure carburettors in Hong Kong but the only way to obtain them in time to meet its contract with Bestcars would have been by airfreight at a landed cost of $100 per carburettor. Greatparts decided not to do this and Bestcars sued it for breach of contract.

Discuss the measure of damages recoverable by Greatparts from Carb.

FURTHER READING

Section 1: Events Prior to Delivery: Passing of Property and Risk

Battersby & Preston, "The Concepts of Property, Title and Owner used in the Sale of Goods Act, 1893" (1972) 35 *MLR* 268.

"Frustrated Contracts" (1979) 11 *Comm Law Assoc Bull* 91.

Law Reform Commission of NSW, "Report on Frustrated Contracts" *LRC* 25 (1976).

Lawson, "The Passing of Property and Risk in Sale of Goods — A Comparative Study" (1949) 65 *LQR* 352.

Nicol, "The Passing of Property in Part of a Bulk" (1979) 42 *MLR* 129.

Sealy, "'Risk' in the Law of Sale" (1972) 31 *Camb LR* 225.

Section 2: Performance by Delivery and Acceptance of Goods and Payment

Gower, "Sale of Goods — Right of Rejection" (1949) 12 *MLR* 368.

Section 3: Remedies for Breach

Commission Car Sales (Hastings) Ltd v Saul [1957] NZLR 144.

Eclipse Motors Pty Ltd v Nixon [1940] VLR 49.

Lawson, "An Analysis of the Concept of Available Market" (1969) 43 *ALJ* 52.

CHAPTER 5

Import and Export Sales

"The notion dies hard that in some way exports are patriotic but imports are immoral."
Lord Harlech

Section 1: The Significance and Characteristics of International Sales
Section 2: Special Forms of Import and Export Contracts
Section 3: Related Contracts of Carriage
Section 4: An International Law of Sales

In Chapter 1 it was suggested that transactions between parties at a distance, and especially international sales, generate different characteristics and problems from domestic or consumer transactions and therefore warrant special treatment. This chapter is devoted to that purpose. It will build upon the materials in Chapters 2 to 4 and also pave the way for examination of other transactions involved in international trade. These include insurance, bills of exchange and letters of credit which are considered in Chapters 6 and 10. Contracts of carriage form an integral part of an export/import sale and so they are considered in this chapter. The contract of insurance is also a vital element in the international sale, but its special characteristics and application in other contexts call for separate consideration — in Chapter 6.

In this chapter, Section 1 will emphasise the importance of international sales in world trade and for the Australian economy. It will also provide an overview of a total international sale transaction including the associated contracts of carriage and insurance and modes of payment; this factual sketch will be used also as a focus for discussion in subsequent chapters.

Section 2 concentrates on the characteristics and legal incidents of typical export/import contracts such as cif and fob, and will lead into specific treatment of contracts of carriage by land, sea and air in Section 3. Section 4 focuses on the problems created by the international nature of many export/import transactions resulting from different legal rules in the respective countries associated with the transaction.

SECTION 1: THE SIGNIFICANCE AND CHARACTERISTICS OF INTERNATIONAL SALES

The volume of international trading in goods has expanded greatly since the beginning of this century. It has enormous implications for world peace and politics. Economic conditions among the major trading nations have vital effects upon the economies, balance of payments and currency values of their trading partners. Developments in international trade law have not kept pace with the complex problems created by this expansion. It is particularly important for Australian lawyers and businessmen involved in international trade to understand the importance to Australia of her international trade.

Until comparatively recent times, Australia's exports were largely confined to rural products while a large proportion of imports were industrial and farm equipment and consumer goods. The picture of limited manufacturing for local consumption within each colony changed after Federation which resulted in the removal of interstate trade barriers (Constitution s 92) and a uniform protective tariff stimulated Australian manufacturing. The expanding transportation system gradually matched the great distances separating the industrial centres of each state; and the world wars created a demand for increased quantity and variety in manufactures. However, it was not until the post-war era that the industrial structure moved forward substantially, especially in the engineering and motor vehicle sectors.

Although industrial production now exceeds the value of rural products, and the export of minerals and manufactured goods have expanded in recent years, rural production (primarily wool, wheat and meat) still accounts for approximately 35 per cent of Australia's export income, which is substantially above the world average for other developed nations. Conversely, Australian imports are composed mainly of manufactured goods. Concurrent changes have taken place with Australia's major trading partners, and the previously overwhelming nexus with Britain and the United States is now overshadowed by trade with Japan. Australia's surplus raw materials, and dependence on foreign capital for major manufacturing together with her isolated geographic position will ensure international trade remains of vital importance to her economy.

Many of the important characteristics and issues related to international sales can best be illustrated by reference to a factual example. The following is based upon our original outline involving a sale by Carb Pty Ltd of Sydney to Mitzi Co of Tokyo of 20,000 carburettors for $200,000. We shall introduce two new characters—an international multimodal carrier, Trans Shipping Co, and Coverall Insurance Ltd. The international nature of the sale raises immediately the threshold question of whether the creation of the contract is to be governed by New South Wales or Japanese law (ie, does SGA s 9 have to be complied with?). Again is the performance of the contract to be governed by New South Wales or Japanese law? The need for certainty and the desirability of a uniform regime of international rules to govern the transaction become apparent and will be considered in Section 4.

The contract should make clear who is to arrange for carriage and insurance of the goods in transit, when risk passes from Carb to Mitzi and whether the freight and insurance premium are included in the price. Special terms such as cif and fob are useful here and are considered in Section 2. The contract should also make provision for any necessary export or import licences and certificates of inspection.

It may be necessary for the goods to be carried by several different carriers, eg, by land and sea, and they may be held in a warehouse pending shipment. What are the responsibilities of each carrier and warehouse-keeper? Will it make a difference if the goods are carried in a sealed container throughout the transit? Against what risks should Carb or Mitzi insure? These legal aspects of the contracts of carriage and insurance will be examined in Section 3 and Chapter 6 respectively. The sale contract should also make clear who is responsible for obtaining any government approvals such as export and import licences, exchange control approval, certificates of inspection and origin where necessary.

How is Mitzi to pay for the goods and in what currency? Who must bear the risk of fluctuations in currency exchange rates? Is Carb willing and able to extend credit to Mitzi until the shipment reaches Tokyo? If not, is Mitzi expected to pay before sighting the goods, or how else can this time gap be bridged? The use of negotiable instruments and letters of credit to finance such transactions is examined in Chapter 10.

SECTION 2: SPECIAL FORMS OF IMPORT AND EXPORT CONTRACTS

International trade has developed to such an extent that considerable steps have been taken by interested parties and governments to achieve standardised forms and terms. In this area, standard contract forms are usually achieved only after long consultation between representatives of sellers' and buyers' groups often in conjunction with shipping and insurance interests. They come within the first rather than the second category of standard form contracts described by Lord Diplock in *A Schroeder Music Publishing Co Ltd v Macaulay* [1974] 3 All ER 616 at 624. Examples include the separate forms of standard contracts and conditions prepared by the United Nations Economic Commission for Europe in respect of specific commodities including cereals, citrus fruit, timber, coal, plant and machinery, and consumer durables. The purpose here is to reach a fair balance between the parties, eliminate legal terms which may have particular or different connotations in a particular legal system, and create a contract which carries its own law with it in the sense that it does not require a particular set of legal rules such as the Sale of Goods Act to define the parties' rights. However, such contracts do not have the force of law in the way the Sale of Goods Act implies non-excludable conditions into a consumer sale. It will only apply when the parties adopt the standard contract form with or without modifications. In order to enforce such a contract or recover damages for its breach, resort would be necessary to a court or arbitrator which had jurisdiction in the matter. Other standard contract forms are adopted by trade associations of buyers and sellers such as the London Corn Trade Association and the Incorporated Oil Seeds Association (London).

At a more general level, the International Chamber of Commerce (ICC) has developed in its publication Incoterms 1980, uniform rules of interpretation for the trade terms most commonly used in international sales. The advantage here is that the parties can incorporate these rules into their contract by use of the shorthand term, for example a sale can be made "cif Tokyo, Incoterms 1980", or "fob Sydney, Incoterms 1980".

Incoterms 1980 stipulates the obligations under a cif clause as follows:

A The seller must:
(1) Supply the goods in conformity with the contract of sale, together with such evidence of conformity as may be required by the contract.

(2) Contract on usual terms at his own expense for the carriage of the goods to the agreed port of destination by the usual route, in a seagoing vessel (not being a sailing vessel) of the type normally used for the transport of goods of the contract description, and pay freight charges and any charges for unloading at the port of discharge which may be levied by regular shipping lines at the time and port of shipment.

(3) At his own risk and expense obtain any export licence or other governmental authorisation necessary for the export of the goods.

(4) Load the goods at his own expense on board the vessel at the port of shipment and at the date or within the period fixed or, if neither date nor time has been stipulated, within a reasonable time, and notify the buyer, without delay, that the goods have been loaded on board the vessel.

(5) Procure, at his own cost and in a transferable form, a policy of marine insurance against the risks of carriage involved in the contract. The insurance shall be contracted with underwriters or insurance companies of good repute on FPA terms, and shall cover the CIF price plus 10 per cent. The insurance shall be provided in the currency of the contract, if procurable.[1]

Unless otherwise agreed, the risks of carriage shall not include special risks that are covered in specific trades or against which the buyer may wish individual protection. Among the special risks that should be considered and agreed upon between seller and buyer are theft, pilferage, leakage, breakage, chipping, sweat, contact with other cargoes and others peculiar to any particular trade.

---

[1] CIF A(5) provides for the minimum terms (FPA) and period of insurance (warehouse to warehouse). Whenever the buyer wishes more than the minimum liability to be included in the contract, then he should take care to specify that the basis of the contract is to be "Incoterms" with whatever addition he requires.

When required by the buyer, the seller shall provide, at the buyer's expense, war risk insurance in the currency of the contract, if procurable.

(6) Subject to the provisions of article B(4) below, bear all risks of the goods until such time as they have effectively passed the ship's rail at the port of shipment.

(7) At his own expense furnish to the buyer without delay a clean negotiable bill of lading for the agreed port of destination, as well as the invoice of the goods shipped and the insurance policy or, should the insurance policy not be available at the time the documents are tendered, a certificate of insurance issued under the authority of the underwriters and conveying to the bearer the same rights as if he were in possession of the policy and reproducing the essential provisions thereof. The bill of lading must cover the contract goods, be dated within the period agreed for shipment, and provide by endorsement or otherwise for delivery to the order of the buyer or buyer's agreed representative. Such bill of lading must be a full set of "on board" or "shipped" bills of lading, or a "received for shipment" bill of lading duly endorsed by the shipping company to the effect that the goods are on board, such endorsement to be dated within the period agreed for shipment. If the bill of lading contains a reference to the charter-party, the seller must also provide a copy of this latter document.

Note: A clean bill of lading is one which bears no superimposed clauses expressly declaring a defective condition of the goods or packaging.

The following clauses do not convert a clean into an unclean bill of lading:
(a) clauses which do not expressly state that the goods or packaging are unsatisfactory, eg "second-hand cases", "used drums", etc; (b) clauses which emphasise the carrier's non-liability for risks arising through the nature of the goods or the packaging; (c) clauses which disclaim on the part of the carrier knowledge of contents, weight, measurement, quality, or technical specification of the goods.

(8) Provide at his own expense the customary packing of the goods, unless it is the custom of the trade to ship the goods unpacked.

(9) Pay the costs of any checking operations (such as checking quality, measuring, weighing, counting) which shall be necessary for the purpose of loading the goods.

(10) Pay any dues and taxes incurred in respect of the goods up to the time of their loading, including any taxes, fees or charges levied because of exportation, as well as the costs of any formalities which he shall have to fulfil in order to load the goods on board.

(11) Provide the buyer, at the latter's request and expense (see B(5)), with the certificate of origin and the consular invoice.

(12) Render the buyer, at the latter's request, risk and expense, every assistance in obtaining any documents, other than those mentioned in the previous article, issued in the country of shipment and/or of origin and which the buyer may require for the importation of the goods into the country of destination (and, where necessary, for their passage in transit through another country).

B The buyer must:

(1) Accept the documents when tendered by the seller, if they are in conformity with the contract of sale, and pay the price as provided in the contract.

(2) Receive the goods at the agreed port of destination and bear, with the exception of the freight and marine insurance, all costs and charges incurred in respect of the goods in the course of their transit by sea until their arrival at the port of destination, as well as unloading costs, including lighterage and wharfage charges, unless such costs and charges shall have been included in the freight or collected by the steamship company at the time freight was paid.

If war insurance is provided, it shall be at the expense of the buyer (see A(5)).

Note: If the goods are sold "CIF landed", unloading costs, including lighterage and wharfage charges, are borne by the seller.

(3) Bear all risks of the goods from the time when they shall have effectively passed the ship's rail at the port of shipment.

(4) In case he may have reserved to himself a period within which to have the goods shipped and/or the right to choose the port of destination, and he fails to give instructions in time, bear the additional costs thereby incurred and all risks of the goods from the date of the expiration of the period fixed for shipment, provided always that the goods shall have been

duly appropriated to the contract, that is to say, clearly set aside or otherwise identified as the contract goods.

(5) Pay the costs and charges incurred in obtaining the certificate of origin and consular documents.

(6) Pay all costs and charges incurred in obtaining the documents mentioned in article A(12) above.

(7) Pay all customs duties as well as any other duties and taxes payable at the time of or by reason of the importation.

(8) Procure and provide at his own risk and expense any import licence or permit or the like which he may require for the importation of the goods at destination.

As will be seen in cases extracted hereunder some care must be taken in using these convenient shorthand terms for more complex obligations. The cases also show that there is no mandatory magic in the terms or the contracts which bear their names since the parties are free to vary their contract from the classic form. The fob contract has become a very flexible instrument: see Devlin J in *Pyrene Co Ltd v Scindia Navigation Co Ltd* [1954] 2 QB 402 at 424 quoted in *"The Mahia" (No 2)*, p 148, *infra*.

Incoterms also contains descriptions of the obligations of sellers and buyers under other types of contract including ex works, free on rail (for), and free alongside ship (fas). In each case the descriptions follow closely the meanings recognised in trade and by the courts but offer the advantage of simple yet comprehensive statement.

The following cases should be read to obtain an understanding of the commercial realities underlying these transactions and to appreciate the legal incidents of the respective contracts including the respective obligations of sellers and buyers, when property and risk pass, and what the contract price covers.

FOB CONTRACTS

McKay Massey Harris Pty Ltd v Icianz Ltd and Others: "The Mahia" (No 2)

Supreme Court of Victoria (Full Court) [1960] 1 Lloyd's Rep 191

[The facts appear from the following judgment.]

O'Bryan J: The steamship *Mahia* from Montreal, Canada, arrived at the port of Melbourne at about 5.30 pm on 6 August 1947, and berthed at No 6 Victoria Dock. She was carrying as deck cargo to be discharged at Melbourne, 1199 drums (66 tons) of sodium chlorate which Captain Startup, who at the time was assistant harbour-master for the Melbourne Harbour Trust Authority, said was classified in a list of dangerous cargoes which they had as B class dangerous cargo. The off-loading of this cargo began at about 9 am on 7 August ...

This cargo was taken on board at Montreal on 29 May 1947, consigned to Imperial Chemical Industries of Australia & New Zealand Ltd (whom I will refer to hereafter as ICI) for delivery at ship's tackle at Melbourne ...

The unloading of drums proceeded without mishap until about 11.20 am. In that time, 390 drums had been landed and carted off to the ICI premises at Yarraville. At 11.20 am, as the stevedores were handling drums preparatory to putting them on a tray to be carried over the ship's side, a flame of fire was observed coming either from the inside of a drum or from its side. In a remarkable short space of time the stack was ablaze, and there followed a devastating and uncontrollable fire and explosions in the course of which great damage was done to the ship and other cargo on board.

The plaintiff was the owner and consignee of a number of internal combustion gasoline engines being carried in one of the ship's holds. As a result of the fire and explosions, damage was done to these engines and the plaintiff suffered loss in consequence thereof. The plaintiff, together with other cargo-owners, was called upon by the ship to pay a sum of money by way of general average contribution for repairs to the ship to remedy what were claimed to be salvage operations carried out during the fire to save both ship and cargo, the plaintiff's share being £572 5s 6d. The plaintiff sought to recover this loss from four parties: two companies incorporated under the law of the Dominion of Canada, viz, the Electric Reduction Co of Canada Ltd and the Electric Reduction Sales Co Ltd, who were sued as the manufacturers and distributors respectively of the said sodium chlorate; ICI, who was the consignee of the cargo; and the United Stevedoring Proprietary Ltd (hereinafter referred to as the "Stevedoring Company"), which was the company engaged in off-loading the goods from the *Mahia* when the fire broke out.

Neither of the Canadian companies entered an appearance to the writ and judgment was obtained against them by default. As neither company seems to have any residential or other connection with this country or to have any assets here, the judgment against them may be of little value to the plaintiff. However, we have nothing to do with that. The action proceeded before Lowe J, against ICI and the Stevedoring Company. In the result, his Honour directed that judgment be entered for ICI against the plaintiff, but that there should be judgment for the plaintiff against the Stevedoring Company for the sum of £7174 10s 7d. Included in that sum is the sum of £572 5s 6d, the general average item to which I have already referred.

Against that judgment the Stevedoring Company has appealed, claiming first that judgment should have been entered in its favour against the plaintiff, and secondly that if the plaintiff was entitled to any judgment against it there should not have been included in the amount of such judgment the said sum of £572 5s 6d. The plaintiff has also appealed against that part of the judgment which was in favour of ICI. I propose first to deal with the claim against the Stevedoring Company ..

[His Honour then considered the plaintiff's claim against the Stevedoring Company and concluded that negligence had not been established and accordingly the Stevedoring Company's appeal should be allowed. He then outlined the basis of the plaintiff's claim against ICI and its appeal against the decision of Lowe J in favour of ICI. He continued at 214:]

The contention that ICI is responsible for what happened in Canada is based upon the proposition that the consignor in putting these goods on board the *Mahia* and in arranging for their carriage by sea as deck cargo, was acting as the agent of ICI, and that ICI is vicariously responsible for the negligence (if any) of the consignor in relation to these matters. I put aside the question whether the consignor was guilty of negligence in arranging for the shipping of these 1199 drums as deck cargo, without at least warning the ship that the drums were not watertight and of the possible consequences thereof. Dr Coppel's submission was that the property in the sodium chlorate passed to ICI when the goods were loaded on rail at Buckingham, and that from thenceforward the property and the control of the goods were with ICI, whose responsibility it was to exercise by its servants or agents reasonable care in relation to the shipping and stowage of the goods as cargo on the *Mahia*. Dr Coppel agreed, as I understood his argument, that it was essential to this part of his case to show that property in the goods passed to ICI before the goods were shipped on board the *Mahia* ..

As is pointed out by Schmitthoff in *The Export Trade*, 2nd ed, p 49: "... the five specific presumptions laid down in s 18 [NSW s 23] are not appropriate to the particular circumstances of an export sale."

It is important also to bear in mind the provision of s 24, that when goods are appropriated to a contract the seller may reserve the right of disposal of the goods until certain conditions are fulfilled. In such a case, notwithstanding the delivery of the goods to the buyer or to a carrier or other bailee for the purpose of transmission to the buyer, the property in the goods does not pass to the buyer until the conditions imposed by the seller are fulfilled. Moreover, when goods are shipped and by the bill of lading the goods are deliverable to the order of the seller or his agent, the seller is prima facie deemed to reserve the right of disposal; there is also a rebuttable presumption that the appropriation of the goods to the contract was intended to be conditional and that the property should not pass, where the seller has drawn on the buyer for the purchase price and transmits the bill of exchange and the bill of lading to the buyer together to secure acceptance or payment of the bill of exchange. These propositions apply to fob and cif contracts alike.

As was pointed out by Devlin J in *Pyrene Co Ltd v Scindia Navigation Co Ltd* [1954] 2 QB 402 at 424; [1954] 1 Lloyd's Rep 321 at 332:

"... The fob contract has become a flexible instrument. In what counsel called the classic type as described, for example, in *Wimble Sons & Co Ltd v Rosenberg & Sons* [1913] 3 KB 743, the buyer's duty is to nominate the ship, and the seller's to put the goods on board for account of the buyer and procure a bill of lading in terms usual in the trade. In such a case the seller is directly a party to the contract of carriage at least until he takes out the bill of lading in the buyer's name. Probably the classic type is based on the assumption that the ship nominated will be willing to load any goods brought down to the berth or at least those of which she is notified. Under present conditions, when space often has to be booked well in advance, the contract of carriage comes into existence at an earlier point of time. Sometimes the seller is asked to make the necessary arrangements; and the contract may then provide for his taking the bill of lading in his own name and obtaining payment against the transfer, as in a cif contract. Sometimes the buyer engages his own forwarding agent at the port of loading to book space and to procure the bill of lading; if freight has to be paid in advance this method may be the most convenient. In such a case the seller discharges his duty by putting the goods on board, getting the mate's receipt and handing it to the forwarding agent to enable him to obtain the bill of lading ..."

In *James v The Commonwealth* (1939) 62 CLR 339 at 377, Dixon J, speaking of contracts for the sale of unascertained goods on either fob or cif terms said:

"In transactions of such a description the final test of the time or stage when the transfer of property in the goods takes place is the intention of the parties or, more strictly, of the seller ..."

[His Honour then quoted from Dixon J's judgment at 378-9 the passages cited by him from *Mirabita v Imperial Ottoman Bank, The Parchim* and *Arnold Karberg & Co v Blythe, Green, Jourdain & Co.* He then examined the facts and continued at 218:]

But it is from this material that the court is asked to determine what were the terms of the contract of sale in relation to these shipments, and in particular when the parties intended that the property in the goods should pass. It is impossible to say in respect of either the missing order No 2 or order No 3 whether it was an offer to buy or the acceptance of an offer to sell. No doubt in each case a contract of sale was ultimately made in regard to both the 399 drums and the 800 drums and that the price was agreed to be fob Buckingham and that the terms of payment were to be by telegraphic transfer. But in neither case was it an fob contract of the "classic type" as described in the judgment of Devlin J cited above. Here, it was not contemplated that the buyer should nominate a ship, but it is to be inferred from the way in which the transactions were carried out that it was the seller's obligation to make the necessary arrangements as to shipment. The goods were not only put on rail at Buckingham, but in each case freight to Melbourne had already been arranged by the seller, and when the goods were put on rail a through bill of lading was issued to the seller providing for the carriage of the goods by sea to Melbourne. By the bill of lading it was the seller who entered into the contract of carriage with the carrier. It was the seller who paid the inland freight and who undertook with the shipping company to prepay direct to it the ocean freight. It is true that the agreement was to deliver to the consignee, ie, ICI, or its agents from the ship's tackle at the port of Melbourne, but the bill of lading was issued to the contracting party to whom the promises were made, viz, the seller of the goods. In the case of the 399 drums the seller notified the buyer that the goods had been shipped and required telegraphic transfer of the price in accordance with contract, and in the same cable advised the buyer that the documents had been airmailed that day. The buyer immediately in reply telegraphed the necessary funds to the seller in Canada. In the case of the 800 drums, after cable advice was sent by the seller that the goods had been shipped, the buyer by telegraphic transfer sent funds to Canada in payment for the goods. It was only thereafter that the "documents", ie, bill of lading, insurance policy and invoice, were sent on by the seller to the buyer. The manner in which payment was arranged and carried out in both cases is very much like the case in which the seller has drawn on the buyer for the purchase price and transmits the bill of exchange and the bill of lading to the buyer together to secure acceptance or payment of the bill of exchange. In such a case it is generally inferred that the property was not intended to pass until the buyer honours the bill.

So, here, in relation to the 399 drums the seller cabled a request for telegraphic transfer of the price in accordance with contract, and at the same time announced that he was sending by airmail the documents (which I take to be the invoice, the bill of lading and the policy of insurance). This was apparently done on the faith of the buyer honouring his contract to pay by telegraphic transfer. If the buyer did not do so, it should have returned the bill of lading. This and what took place in regard to the 800 drums suggest strongly that the parties did not intend property to pass until payment had been made, and this was long after the seller had placed the goods on rail at Buckingham and long after the last act was done by the seller which resulted in them being received and stowed as deck cargo on the *SS Mahia*. In any event, whatever may be the true view as to when the property in these two consignments passed, I am of the opinion that the plaintiff has failed to prove that anything the seller did in relation to arranging for the shipment of these goods on board the *Mahia* was done by it otherwise than in its capacity as seller. For these reasons, I am of the opinion that everything that was done in Canada in relation to the shipping of these goods on the *Mahia* was done by the seller in its capacity as seller and pursuant to its contract of sale and not as agent for the buyer.

The appeal of the plaintiff against the judgment in favour of ICI should therefore, in my opinion, be dismissed.

[**Herring CJ** and **Smith J** delivered judgments to the same effect.]

Appeal dismissed.

It is instructive to compare the decision of the English Court of Appeal in *Panda OHG v Circle Products Ltd* [1970] 1 Lloyd's Rep 499.

CIF CONTRACTS

As discussed above, the fob and cif contracts are flexible instruments which are varied according to the requirements of the parties. There are also a number of defined variants of the cif contract:

c and f (named port of destination) — as is clear from the omission of the "i", this contract does not require the seller to arrange insurance, which is the concern of the buyer if he desires it.

cifc (cost, insurance, freight and commission);

cife (cost, insurance, freight and exchange);

cifc and i (cost, insurance, freight, commission and interest).

For a more detailed discussion of the variants of the cif contract, see Schmitthoff, *The Export Trade*, 7th ed, Ch 2, p 39.

Biddell Brothers v E Clemens Horst Co
English Court of Appeal [1911] 1 KB 934

[The plaintiffs contracted to purchase from the defendants 100 bales Pacific Coast hops to be shipped from the United States to England and to "pay for the said hops at the rate of ninety (90) shillings sterling per 112 lbs, cif to London, Liverpool or Hull. Terms net cash". The contract did not specify whether the buyers were obliged to pay against the shipping documents.]

Kennedy LJ [after stating the facts at 954, dissenting:] ... The plaintiffs' — that is the appellants' — argument, apart from a reference to certain subordinate and subsidiary printed clauses to which I shall advert after dealing with the main question, hangs upon considerations arising from (a) the absence, after the words "net cash", of such words as "against documents", or "in exchange for documents"; (b) the provisions of s 28 and s 34 of the Sale of Goods Act 1893 [NSW ss 31, 37] in respect of the buyer's rights to have delivery in exchange for the price and to have an opportunity to examine goods tendered for acceptance.

[His Lordship then considered the effect of the absence from the cif contract of the words "against documents" and concluded that their omission did not change the nature of the cif contract. He continued at 955:] The application of the principles and rules of the common law, now embodied in the Sale of Goods Act 1893, to the business transaction embodied in the cif contract appears to me to be decisive of the issue between these parties. Let us see, step by step, how according to those principles and rules the transaction specified in such a cif contract as that before us is and, I think, must be carried out in order to fulfil its terms.

At the port of shipment — in this case San Francisco — the vendor ships the goods intended for the purchaser under the contract. Under the Sale of Goods Act 1893 s 18 [NSW s 23] by such shipment the goods are appropriated by the vendor to the fulfilment of the contract and by virtue of s 32 [NSW s 35] the delivery of the goods to the carrier — whether named by the purchaser or not — for the purpose of transmission to the purchaser is prima facie to be deemed to be a delivery of the goods to the purchaser. Two further legal results arise out of the shipment.

Import and Export Sales

The goods are at the risk of the purchaser, against which he has protected himself by the stipulation in his cif contract that the vendor shall, at his own cost, provide him with a proper policy of marine insurance intended to protect the buyer's interest, and available for his use, if the goods should be lost in transit; and the property in the goods has passed to the purchaser, either conditionally or unconditionally. It passes conditionally where the bill of lading for the goods, for the purpose of better securing payment of the price, is made out in favour of the vendor or his agent or representative: see the judgments of Bramwell LJ and Cotton LJ in *Mirabita v Imperial Ottoman Bank* (1878) 3 Ex D 164. It passes unconditionally where the bill of lading is made out in favour of the purchaser or his agent or representative, as consignee. But the vendor, in the absence of special agreement, is not yet in a position to demand payment from the purchaser; his delivery of the goods to the carrier is, according to the express terms of s 32, only "prima facie deemed to be a delivery of the goods to the buyer"; and under s 28 of the Sale of Goods Act, as under the common law (an exposition of which will be found in the judgments of the members of the Exchequer Chamber in the old case of *Startup v Macdonald* (1843) 6 Man & G 593), a tender of delivery entitling the vendor to payment of the price must, in the absence of contractual stipulation to the contrary, be a tender of possession. How is such a tender to be made of goods afloat under a cif contract? By tender of the bill of lading, accompanied in case the goods have been lost in transit by the policy of insurance. The bill of lading in law and in fact represents the goods. Possession of the bill of lading places the goods at the disposal of the purchaser. "A cargo at sea", says Bowen LJ in *Sanders v Maclean* (1883) 11 QBD 327 at 341, "while in the hands of the carrier, is necessarily incapable of physical delivery. During this period of transit and voyage, the bill of lading by the law merchant is universally recognised as its symbol, and the indorsement and delivery of the bill of lading operates as a symbolical delivery of the cargo. Property in the goods passes by such indorsement and delivery of the bill of lading, whenever it is the intention of the parties that the property should pass, just as under similar circumstances the property would pass by an actual delivery of the goods. And for the purpose of passing such property in the goods and completing the title of the indorsee to full possession thereof, the bill of lading, until complete delivery of the cargo has been made on shore to some one rightfully claiming under it, remains in force as a symbol, and carries with it not only the full ownership of the goods but also all rights created by the contract of carriage between the shipper and the shipowner. It is a key which in the hands of a rightful owner is intended to unlock the door of the warehouse, floating or fixed, in which the goods may chance to be." The meaning of "delivery" under the Sale of Goods Act is defined by s 62 [NSW s 5(1)] to be "voluntary transfer of possession from one person to another". Such delivery, as the learned draftsman of the Act and its editor remarks in his note to this section, may be either actual or constructive: see *Chalmers' Sale of Goods Act, 1893,* 7th ed, p 140; and, as Bowen LJ has pronounced, in the case of seaborne goods, the delivery of the bill of lading operates as a symbolical delivery of goods. But then I understand it to be objected on behalf of the plaintiffs: "Granted that the purchaser might, if he pleased, take this constructive delivery and pay against it the price of the goods; what is there in the 'cost freight and insurance' contract which compels him to do so? Why may he not insist on an option of waiting for a tender of delivery of the goods themselves after having had an opportunity of examining them after their arrival?"

There are, I think, several sufficient answers to such a proposition. In the first place, an option of a time of payment is not a term which can be inferred, where the contract itself is silent. So far as I am aware, there is no authority for the inference of an option as to times of payment to be found either in the law books or in the Sale of Goods Act. Secondly, if there is a duty on the vendor to tender the bill of lading, there must, it seems to me, be a corresponding duty on the part of the purchaser to pay when such tender is made. Very relevant on this point is the language of Brett LJ in his judgment in *Sanders v Maclean* at 337, which applies to this class of contract the same principle as was expounded by Bowen LJ in *The Moorcock* (1889) 14 PD 64. He said: "The stipulations which are inferred in mercantile contracts are always that the party will do what is mercantilely reasonable"; and, if it be the duty implied in the cif contract, as held by Brett LJ in that case, that the vendor shall make every reasonable exertion to send forward and tender the bill of lading as soon as possible after he has destined the cargo to the particular vendee, it is, I venture to think, "mercantilely reasonable" that the purchaser should be held bound to make the agreed payment when delivery of the goods is constructively tendered to him by the tender of the bill of lading, either drawn originally in his favour or indorsed to him, and accompanied in case of loss by the policy of insurance. For thereunder, as the bill of lading with its accompanying documents comes forward by mail, the purchaser obtains the privilege and absolute power of profitably dealing with the goods days or weeks, or, perhaps, in the case of shipments from a distant port, months, before the arrival of the goods themselves. This is, indeed, the essential and peculiar advantage which the buyer of imported goods intends to gain under the cif contract according to the construction which I put upon it.

But, in truth, the duty of the purchasers to pay against the shipping documents, under such a contract as the present, does not need the application of that doctrine of the inference in mercantile contracts that each party will do what is "mercantilely reasonable", for which we have the great authority of Lord Esher. The plaintiffs' assertion of the right under a cost freight and insurance contract to withhold payment until delivery of the goods themselves, and until after an opportunity of examining them, cannot possibly be effectuated except in one of two ways. Landing and delivery can rightfully be given by the shipowner only to the holder of the bill of lading. Therefore, if the plaintiff's contention is right, one of two things must happen. Either the seller must surrender to the purchaser the bill of lading, whereunder the delivery can be obtained, without receiving payment, which, as the bill of lading carries with it an absolute power of disposition, is, in the absence of a special agreement in the contract of sale, so unreasonable as to be absurd; or, alternatively, the vendor must himself retain the bill of lading, himself land and take delivery of the goods, and himself store the goods on quay (if the rules of the port permit), or warehouse the goods, for such time as may elapse before the purchaser has an opportunity of examining them. But this involves a manifest violation of the express terms of the contract "90s per 112 lbs cost freight and insurance". The parties have in terms agreed that for the buyer's benefit the price shall include freight and insurance, and for his benefit nothing beyond freight and insurance. But, if the plaintiffs' contention were to prevail, the vendor must be saddled with the further payment of those charges at the port of discharge which *ex necessitate rei* would be added to the freight and insurance premium which alone he has by the terms of the contract undertaken to defray.

Finally, let me test the soundness of the plaintiff's contention that according to the true meaning of this contract their obligation to pay arises only when delivery of the goods has been tendered to them after they have had an opportunity of examination, in this way. Suppose the goods to have been shipped, the bill of lading taken, and the insurance for the benefit of the buyer duly effected by the seller, as expressly stipulated in the contract. Suppose the goods then during the ocean transit to have been lost by the perils of the sea. The vendor tenders the bill of lading, with the insurance policy and the other shipping documents (if any) to the purchaser, to whom from the moment of shipment the property has passed, and at whose risk, covered by the insurance, the goods were at the time of loss. Is it, I ask myself, arguable that the purchaser could be heard to say, "I will not pay because I cannot have delivery of and an examination of the goods"? But it is just this which is necessarily involved in the contention of these plaintiffs. The seller's answer, and I think conclusive answer, is, "You have the bill of lading and the policy of insurance." It is noticeable that in the course of the argument in *Tregelles v Sewell* (1862) 7 H & N 574 at 579 Martin B observes, "The purchaser was to have a policy of insurance, which is usually considered as equivalent to the goods," and earlier in the same argument Wilde B (at 578) asked, "If the meaning is 'to be delivered at Harburgh', what necessity is there for insurance?" The contract in that case was a contract in the fuller form, namely, against documents, but it does not seem to me that that affects the value of those observations as to the relative rights of the buyer and seller.

I have only to add as to this, the main question in the present case, a few words in regard to ss 28 and 34 of the Sale of Goods Act. As I have already said, my own view as to s 28 is that the section is satisfied by the readiness and willingness of the seller to give possession of the bill of lading. I am, however, far from saying that the view which is suggested in the course of the judgment of Hamilton J, namely, that when the parties have entered into a cif contract they have "otherwise agreed", is not one which could be supported, as I hold that a similar view is the true view also in regard to s 34, sub-s 2. As to s 34, sub-s 1, there is no difficulty. No one suggests that the plaintiffs, if they pay against documents, become thereby precluded from rejecting the goods if, on examination after their arrival, they are found to be not goods in accordance with the contract, or from recovering damages for breach of contract if they prefer that course ...

[After considering some other points in relation to the subsidiary printed clauses of the cif contract, his Lordship concluded that the judgment of Hamilton J in favour of the defendant sellers was right and the plaintiffs' appeal should be dismissed.

The majority judges **Vaughan Williams** and **Farwell LJJ** held however, that the buyers were not bound to pay on tender of the shipping documents but were entitled to refuse payment until, upon arrival of the hops, they had been given an opportunity for inspection of them.]

Appeal allowed.

[The defendant sellers appealed to the House of Lords which upheld the appeal in a very short judgment which specifically adopted the dissenting opinion of Kennedy LJ: [1911] AC 18.]

The judgment of Kennedy LJ has been applied in Australian cases: see eg *Joubert and Joubert v Corona Manufacturing Co* [1922] VLR 644; *Henry Dean & Sons (Sydney) Ltd v P O'Day Pty Ltd* (1927) 39 CLR 330.

A seller such as Carb sometimes finds it more convenient to ship goods under one bill of lading and a single floating insurance cover in fulfilment of obligations under several contracts with different purchasers. Since Carb cannot deliver the one bill of lading and insurance policy to Mitzi and other purchasers as well, it should provide in its contract to tender in lieu a delivery order and a certificate of insurance.

In *Comptoir D'Achat v Luis de Ridder Ltda (The Julia)* [1949] AC 293, the House of Lords dealt with a contract described as cif but which provided for payment on presentation of delivery orders and certificates of insurance. It was held that the term cif referred to the components of costs, insurance and freight; that the printed form of contract used was one suitable for an orthodox cif contract but could also be used for other transactions, and hence the use of the label cif did not determine the rights and obligations of the parties in relation to the performance of the contract and passing of property.

Plaimar Ltd v Waters Trading Co Ltd
High Court of Australia (1945) 72 CLR 304

Rich, Dixon and **McTiernan JJ:** This appeal concerns the liability to the seller of a buyer of goods, to be shipped late in 1941 from Zanzibar to Fremantle, which, it is conjectured, were lost at Singapore while awaiting transhipment to Fremantle.

The buyer, a manufacturing company carrying on business in Perth, had been accustomed to purchase Zanzibar clove oil from the seller, a company carrying on a merchant's business in Sydney and elsewhere. The transaction now in question depends upon a written contract, dated 22 September 1941. The seller claims that it amounts to a cif contract, or, if not that, at least one which places upon the buyer the risk of loss or damage to the goods during transit. Having tendered to the buyer, who rejected them, a bill of lading, insurance policy and invoice in respect of the lost goods, the seller sued in the Supreme Court of Western Australia for the price, for which it recovered judgment before Wolff J. From that judgment, the present appeal comes.

The contract is expressed in a letter from the seller confirming the buyer's order. It describes the order as one for four tons of Zanzibar clove oil packed in drums each approximately five hundredweights. Then under "price" it proceeds as follows: "eight shillings and a penny (stg) per lb. Nett landed weight Cost Insurance Freight Fremantle, Bank exchange Australia/London to buyers' account. This price is based on the current rate of freight and marine insurance, any variation to buyers' account."

Under "shipment" there is the statement: "Per steamer during October/November/December 1941 from original port." Then follow references to "insurance" and "war risk insurance." "WPA for not exceeding the above value plus 10 per cent. If it can be arranged by sellers war risk insurance is to be covered and charged to buyers' account."

Next comes: "Terms: nett cash against delivery order or bill/lading." The contract then concludes: "Sellers not responsible for any loss or delay caused by strikes—direct or indirect—fire force majeure and other circumstances beyond their control."

A contract for the sale of goods upon cif terms places upon the seller an obligation to ship goods of the contract description to a destination, from a port and at a time indicated by the contract, to obtain a proper bill of lading and a customary insurance covering the ocean transit, to make out an invoice for the price showing what sum, if any, the consignee must pay for freight and giving the buyer credit for the amount, and, as soon as reasonably practicable, to tender these documents to the buyer in exchange for payment of the amount shown on the invoice, or acceptance of a bill of exchange therefor, as the contract may provide.

It is "a contract for the sale of goods to be performed by the delivery of documents, and what those documents are must depend upon the terms of the contract itself": per Bankes LJ, *Arnhold Karberg & Co v Blythe, Green, Jourdain & Co* [1916] 1 KB 495 at 510. "It is not a contract that goods shall arrive, but a contract to ship goods complying with the contract of sale, to obtain, unless the contract otherwise provides, the ordinary contract of carriage to the place of destination, and the ordinary contract of insurance of the goods on that voyage, and to tender these documents against payment of the contract price. The buyer then has the right to claim the fulfilment of the contract of carriage, or, if the goods are lost or damaged, such indemnity for the loss as he can claim under the contract of insurance": per Scrutton J in *Arnhold Karberg & Co v Blythe, Green, Jourdain & Co* [1915] 2 KB 379 at 388. "The condition of the goods at the time of the tender of the shipping documents is not material, nor is the value of the documents at the time of the tender material. In all such matters the risk is on the buyer. He may be obliged to pay for goods although they may be at the bottom of the sea, or although through some unforseen circumstance they may never arrive, or although they may have been lost owing to some cause not covered by the agreed form of policy": per Bankes LJ [1916] 1 KB at 510. "In my view, therefore, the relevant question will generally be not 'what at the time of declaration or tender of documents is the condition of the goods?' ... but 'what, at the time of tender of documents, was the condition of those documents as to compliance with the contract ...?' ": per Scrutton J [1915] 2 KB at 388.

The leading terms of the contract under our consideration are characteristic of a sale on cif terms and raise a presumption that it falls within that category. But it is claimed that a close examination of its terms show that some of them conflict with the basal conception and change the character of the contract into one in which the arrival of the goods is essential and the risk of their loss in transit is not accepted by the buyer.

In the first place, the words following the statement of money price "nett landed weight" are relied upon as showing that the price is only ascertainable after the goods are landed and that, at all events, risks of loss of weight, as by leakage, fall on the seller. Then, the use of the expression "not exceeding the above value plus 10 per cent" in stating the amount of the insurance is used as an indication that, since the choice of amount lies with the seller, insurance must be his protection, not the buyer's, and since the clause fixes a maximum, the object of all the references to insurance must simply be to put the burden of the cost of it upon the buyer. In the third place, it is contended that, if payment may be against delivery order, the theory of the cif transaction is destroyed. Lastly, the *force majeure* clause is relied upon as another indication that the seller takes the risk and needs to be relieved in exceptional circumstances.

It is convenient to deal with these points in reverse order. The argument upon the *force majeure* clause is fallacious because it is referable to the obligations of the seller whatever they may be and throws no light on their extent or duration. It is entirely consistent with its terms to treat it as relieving him in circumstances beyond his control from the obligation of shipping the goods and forwarding and tendering the documents. It is comparable with the clause, a clause differently worded however, in *Diamond Alkali Export Corp v Bourgeois* [1921] 3 KB 443.

The reference to the delivery order gives the seller a choice. If he finds it more convenient, because for example the bill of lading includes other goods, he can await the ship's arrival, obtain a delivery order and tender that instead of a bill of lading. It does not alter the conditions which the seller must fulfil if he chooses to tender a bill of lading and the obligations of the buyer, if that course is taken. The use of the words "not exceeding" does appear illogical for, if insurance is to protect the buyer, the naming not of a maximum but a definite amount would be expected. The reference, however, to war risk that immediately follows, is plainly on the footing that insurance is to protect the buyer and the clause making variations in insurance rates an affair of the buyer looks in the same direction. The addition of 10 per cent, or some other percentage, to cover the buyer's profit or the increased value to him is a not uncommon practice, and, on the whole, it looks as if the clause is to express a limit of the amount of the responsibility of the seller to insure but, subject to that limit, to leave him under the same obligation of effecting a reasonable insurance as well as to amount as to other terms.

There is more cogency in the argument founded on the words "nett landed weight". If the landing of the goods must be awaited, how can the conditions imported by cif terms be complied with and how can the responsibility for risks ever arise?

The provision is, of course, based on the assumption that the purpose of the contract will be fulfilled and the goods will be available for weighing. The real question is whether it imports an indispensable condition into the contract. It seems clear that one way open to the seller of performing his obligations under the contract is to hand over a bill of lading against payment. The goods could not be weighed before delivery to the consignee which, of course, means that the bill of lading is spent, even if not surrendered. It is evident that the weighing may be after payment of the price has been made against the bill of lading. In other words, just as under a cif contract examination of the goods for condition and quality must take place after the delivery of the bill of lading, so under this contract may the final computation of the quantity and adjustment of the price. It is a fair inference that arrival and weighing were not intended to be a condition of or precedent to liability. In *Re Denbigh Cowan & Co and R Atcherley & Co* (1921) 125 LT 388 the particular contract there in question was held to be on cif terms, notwithstanding that it provided for "net landing weights" and specified — "payment: cash (before delivery if required) against documents or delivery order". The Court of Appeal decided, accordingly, that the buyers were entitled to receive a policy of insurance, even although the goods arrived and the sellers chose to tender, not a bill of lading, but a delivery order. The purpose, according to counsel in that case, of giving the seller the choice of presenting a delivery order and not a bill of lading was to free him from difficulties when goods comprised in one bill of lading were sold in different parcels and so, too, with goods covered by one insurance. The Court of Appeal, however, on the terms of the particular form of contract, rejected the view that, if the seller chose to use a delivery order, that dispensed him from tendering a policy of insurance. In *Karinjee Jivanjee & Co v William F Malcolm & Co* (1926) 25 Lloyd LR 28, in dealing with a contract containing another divergence from what otherwise were cif terms, Roche J said at 30: "There are many contracts of a mixed nature which contain elements proper to cif contracts and proper to contracts for actual delivery of goods; but in its general scope this contract partakes far more of the elements and character which belong to cif contracts than to any other form of contract." This observation applies to the present case, in which the proper conclusion from the whole document appears to be that, in spite of the variations from type, the contract is in essence a sale upon cif terms, and that it casts an obligation on the buyer to pay the price on a tender in due time of proper shipping documents independently of the arrival of the goods.

It is, therefore, necessary to decide whether the seller did so tender proper shipping documents.

It was objected on behalf of the buyer that neither the bill of lading nor the insurance gave him adequate protection; that a policy had not been obtained until after the loss of the goods; that reasonable expedition had not been shown in forwarding and tendering the documents; and that, at the trial, proof of actual shipment, at a proper port, of the contract goods had not been given . . .

In the language of the Sale of Goods Act 1895 (WA), the seller must make such contract with the carrier as may be reasonable, having regard to the nature of the goods and the other circumstances of the case. "The obligation is satisfied if the contract of carriage is in a form current in the trade or on the contemplated route. The seller is not called upon to procure a contract on more favourable terms than those usually contained in the ordinary bill of lading in use in the trade or on the route concerned. In any given case the test to be applied is whether it is in accordance with the usage and practice in the trade to carry goods of the contractual description shipped from and to the places in the contract under a contract of carriage such as that in question": *Kennedy on CIF Contracts*, 2nd ed, 1928, p 41.

The buyer, in the particulars under its defence, has set out a number of objections to the conditions of the bill of lading. They are all governed by the consideration that, on the particular route, the shipper could not be expected to obtain a more favourable bill of lading . . . [His Honour then referred to the facts and argument and concluded:]

The evidence shows that there is no direct shipping available from Zanzibar to Fremantle, that the only practicable course was that adopted and that it involved the acceptance of the bill of lading in question as that of the only shipping line carrying cargo from Zanzibar to Singapore on through bills of lading to Fremantle. It also appears that, in a number of prior transactions, the sellers had shipped by the same route and, for what it is worth, under the same bill of lading.

[His Honour then held that the sellers had done what was reasonable with respect to insurance during transhipment and that they had done all that would be reasonably done in tendering the bill of lading.]

Appeal dismissed.

The above cases establish that a cif contract between Carb and Mitzi is in effect a sale of goods which is performed by Carb delivering documents which Mitzi is obliged to accept and pay for in accordance with the contract. It is no excuse that the goods have been lost or destroyed at sea. But what is the position where the goods themselves do not comply with the contract?

Henry Dean & Sons (Sydney) Ltd v O'Day Pty Ltd
High Court of Australia (1927) 39 CLR 330

[The defendant seller P O'Day Pty Ltd agreed to sell and the plaintiff to buy, "150 bales, first selection Liverpool wheat sacks ... turned mended and sound 9s per dozen cif & e, Sydney. Delivery during November 1925. Terms — net cash against bill of lading or ship's order which will enable buyers to obtain delivery of the goods." The defendant shipped the sacks in Melbourne for delivery in Sydney. They were not first selection wheat sacks but were rejects including malt, flour, pea and potato bags. The description in the seller's invoice was "150 bales Liverpool sacks". The plaintiff refused to accept and pay for the documents on the grounds that they did not indicate that the goods satisfied the contract description, and sued the defendant for damages for non-delivery. One of the defendant's pleas was that the plaintiff was not ready and willing to perform the contract. The defendant also counterclaimed damages against the plaintiff for refusal to accept and pay for the goods. At the trial in the NSW Supreme Court Gordon J found for the plaintiff and dismissed the cross-action. On appeal the Full Court reversed the decision of Gordon J and ordered a verdict for the defendant. The plaintiff buyer appealed to the High Court.]

Isaacs J: In my opinion the unanimous judgment of the Full Court of New South Wales was correct and should be affirmed.

When resolved into its simplest elements this case is, as I think, of an elementary character. It ultimately raises no question but this: Is the buyer of goods cif who on tender of proper shipping documents persistently refuses to receive them and pay the stipulated price except on inspection of the goods, or other proof of their compliance with the contract, entitled to recover damages from the seller because it is afterwards discovered that the goods shipped were not in accordance with the contract? However great the failure of the vendor to perform his primary duty, the question I have stated must, in my opinion, be answered in the negative. Cross-actions were brought: seller sued buyer for non-acceptance, and properly failed; buyer sues seller for non-delivery and claims that the seller's breach of his duty to ship the goods, not only disentitles the seller to recover damages for the buyer's refusal above stated, but also prevents that refusal from being wrongful. This is a rather novel and, from a mercantile standpoint, a somewhat disturbing contention, and so needs a little careful examination. First, it is said that, where under a cif contract the seller fails to ship goods in conformity with the contract, the "documents" can never be proper, because they cannot in the nature of things represent contractual goods, and therefore, whatever reason actuates the buyer in refusing to pay, that refusal is rightful within the contemplation of the contract. No authority was, or could be cited for that position. No doubt the formal accuracy of the documents would be unavailing to the seller if, after provisional acceptance and payment, the buyer found that the goods were not in fact in conformity with the contract and had exercised its undoubted right to reject the goods and demand a return of the money paid: see s 37(1) of the Sale of Goods Act 1923 (No 1 of 1923) (NSW); and *Polenghi v Dried Milk Co* (1904) 10 Com Cas 42. In that sense, the main provision being broken by the seller, the documents would be worthless. But that is not the same as saying they were defective as "ordinary and usual shipping documents" (see per Cockburn CJ, in

Tamvaco v Lucas (1861) 1 B & S 185 at 197), and therefore not the documents contracted for. I am very distinctly of opinion that to say so is wholly inconsistent with the true notion of a cif contract. Doubtless any refusal by the buyer to accept and pay on receipt of the shipping documents may escape pecuniary consequences, if it be shown that the seller by his own breach has disentitled himself from complaining. But that does not divest the buyer's failure of any wrongfulness which it may have, when judged by the standard of the obligations he has assumed. The propriety of the documents as documents must be judged of apart from such a consideration. If, on their face, they show a departure from the contract, they are not such as are contemplated by the bargain. If they are in the usual form of such documents, and would be proper if the contract were so far performed as to ship goods in conformity with the contract, then no objection can be made on the ground only that the documents are not those stipulated. Any objection made to the documents must be considered on its own footing. An objection may be to something which a reasonable man might fairly question and require to be cleared up—as, for instance, an apparent alteration. Or, if the invoice were such that a merchant buyer could, according to mercantile practice, reasonably require it to be more explicit and he did require it to be made more explicit, no one would regard such objections as any evidence of want of readiness and willingness on the part of the buyer to perform the contract.

But here the position is wholly different. First of all, there was nothing wrong, or even apparently wrong, with the documents. Even now no particulars of disconformity with the contract are pointed to with respect to the policy and the bill of lading. The invoice is the only possible source of complaint. The contract was for "150 bales, first selection Liverpool wheat sacks. When new 41 in × 23 in 8 porter 9 shot. 300 to the bale. Original weight about 2¼ lbs shipped at Calcutta fair average. Turned mended and sound". Now that is the description of the sacks, all of which could be insisted on by the buyer. Then the contract said: "Price—9 s per dozen cif & e Sydney." "Terms—net cash against bill of lading or ship's order which will enable buyers to obtain delivery of the goods." The invoice said— "To 150 bales Liverpool sacks at 9s cife £1687 10s—Per SS *Suva*." That invoice was enclosed in a letter the first paragraph of which was:— "We enclose herewith invoice amounting to £1687 10s, for 150 bales Liverpool sacks which have been shipped to Sydney per SS *Suva* in fulfilment of your esteemed order through Messrs C H Wood & Co." As no challenge was made and no evidence was given with respect to the necessity of saying in the invoice "first selection", I am not, nor can a court possibly be, in a position to say whether those words were essential according to mercantile custom, or whether they would have been sufficient. No such issue was raised. So far as I can see, even apart from the appellant's failure to raise it at the trial, the invoice was sufficient for its purpose. It indicated the class of goods, it connected up with the other documents, and, reading it and the letter, there is no doubt in my mind—in the absence of mercantile evidence to the contrary— that the seller indicated and represented to the buyer that the sacks shipped were in accordance with their contract. That was tacitly admitted by the buyer in its reply letter of 12 November. That letter began the *ultra* demand by asking for the original invoice. The seller would not comply, and the buyer refused payment. On 16 November the seller threatened to sell against buyer. Then the buyer telegraphed that "documents do not identify goods as being according to contract". And it added, "Draft will be accepted as soon as goods *proved* equal description purchased ... We wrote you for oversea invoices which you have not provided." I have italicised the word "proved" for a reason which will be presently apparent. Refusal continued, the ship arrived, the goods were examined, found not to be in accordance with contract and rejected on that ground. The letter of refusal said (inter alia): "Your refusal to give us *the evidence we asked for*, namely, the overseas invoices describing the pack," etc.

[His Honour referred to the trial judge's decision and continued at 343:]

I have first to test the contention that documents are necessarily defective if the goods turn out to be in disconformity with the contract. To test that, we must assume the goods themselves were, when shipped, in conformity with the contract. If they were, there is no question the bill of lading protected the buyer throughout, and would have entitled the buyer to obtain them, pursuant to his contract, the identification of the goods shipped with those described in the bill of lading not being challenged. Nor is there any suggestion that if the goods as shipped were lost, the buyer would have met with any obstacle in recovering on the insurance policy. The invoice, as it seems to me, described the goods in a manner that no merchant could misunderstand or fail to see that they had reference to the goods contracted for, for there is no suggestion of any other contract to which they could be referable. If it did not as a matter of law, then it must be because the goods must be fully described, for in law one part of the description is as vital as another, and every particle of the description of the goods should have been inserted. In short, but for the fact that the goods as shipped did not answer to the contractual description, the seller must have succeeded in its action. This conclusion is so important to the mercantile community that I venture to refer to some legal authorities, including some cases already mentioned by the Supreme Court.

[His Honour referred to *Ireland v Livingston* (1872) LR 5 HL 395; *E Clemens Horst Co v Biddell Bros* [1912] AC 18; *Hansson v Hamel & Horley Ltd* [1922] 2 AC 36 and continued:]

This particular contract contains two relevant express statements. First, it declares the price is "cif & e Sydney". Next, it states: "Net cash against bill of lading or ship's order which will enable buyers to obtain delivery of the goods." I will assume—since it is not necessary to do more—that the combined effect of these two provisions is that the ordinary cif documents are required, with one possible variation at the option of the seller, namely, the substitution of a ship's order for the bill of lading. The primary result of that is that "the ordinary shipping documents" were to be delivered to the purchaser: per Lord Cairns LC in *Hickox v Adams* (1876) 34 LT 404 at 407. The modified result is that, in the absence of any express stipulation and in the absence also of any proved mercantile usage to the effect that any other documents are deliverable for the purpose (see *Wilson, Holgate & Co v Belgian Grain and Produce Co* [1920] 2 KB 1 at 8; and per Scrutton LJ and Atkin LJ in *Malmberg v H J Evans & Co (1924)* 41 TLR 38 at 39, 40), the documents required to be delivered are (says Bailhache J in *Wilson, Holgate & Co v Belgian Grain and Produce Co* at 7) "a bill of lading, an invoice and a policy of insurance, and it is well understood that under a contract of that kind these are the documents which the seller is required to tender". Naturally, the invoice is for purposes which are confined to the personal relations of buyer and seller, which are already definitely settled by the terms of the contract itself. But the other two documents have probably other purposes and may have to bring the buyer into possible relations with other persons. It is as to these that Lord Sumner, in his judgment in *Hansson v Hamel & Horley Ltd* at 46, refers in a passage of importance. His Lordship says: "When documents are to be taken up the buyer is entitled to documents which substantially confer protective rights throughout. He is not buying a litigation, as Lord Trevethin (then A T Lawrence J) says in the *General Trading Co's* case (1911) 16 Com Cas 95 at 101. These documents have to be handled by banks, they have to be taken up or rejected promptly and without any opportunity for prolonged inquiry, they have to be such as can be re-tendered to sub-purchasers, and it is essential that they should so *conform to the accustomed shipping documents* as to be reasonably and readily fit to pass current in commerce." There is not a word there about any assurance in the shipping documents that the goods are in conformity with the contract between buyer and seller. Such an assurance, even by description, would be out of place between shipowner and seller, or between insurer and seller, and equally so between buyer and his sub-purchaser. In each of those cases the description of the goods must be relative to the particular contract it is connected with. As between the buyer and seller the shipping documents must give the proper protection to the seller in respect of the dangers of carriage and the perils insured against, and of course, they must not be inconsistent with the buyer's rights. The documents must be such as are customary as between the shipowner or insurer on the one hand, and the owner of the goods on the other. But by the nature of the contract of sale the buyer must trust to the seller's promise that the proper goods will be shipped and to whatever is customarily included in the documents to show they have been shipped. If he mistrusts the seller, then he may take the risk of refusing to pay on presentation of documents in proper form. The refusal may turn out to be actionable or to be non-actionable by the fault of the seller. But even if non-actionable for that reason, it may be a refusal that affords answerable evidence of inability or unwillingness to pay, whatever the seller has done. Suppose, for instance, the present appellant on presentation of the documents had said expressly: "We are neither in a position to pay, nor are we willing to pay, and therefore we refuse acceptance of the documents." Then, suppose they discovered a week afterwards that the seller's goods were not up to the contract. No doubt the seller must fail, as it has failed, in a claim for damages. But could the buyer succeed in a cross-action? And if not, why can it succeed now? Gordon J, as I have shown, has found as a fact why the buyer refused: not because it found any fault in the documents, not because the goods shipped were not in accordance with the contract, but because, as the goods *might* not be in accordance with the contract, the buyer required inspection of the goods themselves. This attitude was maintained for many days, and although the vendor made more than one attempt to overcome the refusal it was adhered to; and finally the vendor declared the transaction at an end. At that time there was no knowledge that the goods were not in accordance with the contract, and therefore there must have been some other reason for the buyer's persistent attitude. The reason was that stated, namely, insistence on inspection of goods that might or might not be up to contract. That was legally unjustifiable: *E Clemens Horst Co v Biddell Bros* [1912] AC 18 and per Scrutton LJ in *Malmberg's* case (1924) 41 TLR 38 at 40. Ultimately the seller terminated the contract, as it had a right to do. On a turn of the market the buyer demanded performance, but, in the circumstances, necessarily without relation to the document tendered and refused. I see no escape from the conclusion that the refusal, which became irrevocable, cannot be regarded in law as anything but want of readiness and willingness on the buyer's part to perform an essential obligation on its part — the most characteristic duty of a buyer under such a contract — even though the seller had not done all that the contract demanded of it. The subsequent demand for performance, besides being a pure afterthought and deserving no consideration, was utterly ineffectual to influence the contract or its performance.

The appeal, in my opinion, should be dismissed.

Higgins J: [His Honour referred to the facts and continued:]

It seems to be assumed that under what is called a cif contract — costs, insurance, freight — there is an absolute duty on the part of the purchaser to pay the purchase-money and take up the documents sent by the vendor when they arrive at the destination, whether the goods contracted for are sent or not. It must follow that even if the purchaser learn by accident that the goods shipped are not the goods contracted for, he is not at liberty to refuse to pay and to take up the documents. No case has been cited which directly establishes such an extraordinary result; but there are cases which show that delivery of the goods to the master of the ship on behalf of the purchaser is delivery to the purchaser, and that it is the duty of the purchaser, under ordinary circumstances, to pay when he is advised of the consignment. But these cases apply only on the assumption that the proper goods, the goods the subject of the contract, have been put on board.

[His Honour referred to *Wait v Baker* (1848) 2 Ex 1 where Parke B had held that it is necessary that the goods should agree with the contract.]

The same qualification of the rule appears in *Benjamin on Sale*, 5th ed, p 743: "When delivery is to be made by a bill of lading, the rule is that the seller makes a good delivery if he forward to the buyer, as soon as he reasonably can after the shipment, a bill of lading, duly indorsed and effectual to pass the property in the goods, purporting to represent goods in accordance with the contract, *and which are in fact in accordance therewith.*" As for the case of *E Clemens Horst Co v Biddell Bros* [1911] 1 KB 214, 934; [1912] AC 18 on which so much reliance has been placed, it is absolutely consistent with these statements of the law. The primary judge, Hamilton J (now Lord Sumner), laid down the five duties of the vendor on cif terms who claims payment on tender of the documents; and he puts in the forefront, as an essential condition, his duty "to ship at the port of shipment *goods of the description contained in the contract*": KB at 220. "Such terms", he adds, "constitute an agreement that the delivery of the goods, *provided they are in conformity with the contract*, shall be delivery on board ship at the port of shipment". The case turned on the fact that no time was specified in the contract when the cash price was to be paid. Section 28 of the (English) Sale of Goods Act says that payment is to be against delivery; and it was held in the House of Lords, which accepted the views of Hamilton J, and in the Court of Appeal of Kennedy LJ, that the delivery of the bill of lading *when the goods are at sea* can be treated as delivery of the goods themselves. In that case there was no question as to the goods at sea answering the description in the contract; but the phrase used by Lord Loreburn, "when the goods are at sea", does not apply when other goods than *the* goods are being sent to the destination. The case of *Arnhold Karberg & Co v Blythe, Green, Jourdain & Co* [1916] 1 KB 495, before the Court of Appeal, was a war case. War had broken out between Germany and England. The bill of sale had been made void by the war; and it was held that it was not a sufficient compliance with the usual cif rule to tender such a bill of sale; for the documents tendered must be valid and *effective* documents — that is to say, valid and effective to pass to the purchaser the goods contracted for. In the present case, the documents, if taken up by the purchaser, would not have been valid and effective to pass to the purchaser the goods for which he had contracted. If the proper goods have been shipped, and if they have been lost at sea, the purchaser has to look to his policy of insurance to secure to him payment for the value; "if the vendor fulfils his contract *by shipping the appropriate goods* in the appropriate manner under a proper contract of carriage, and if he also obtains the proper documents for tender to the purchaser, I am unable to see how the rights or duties of either party are affected by the loss of the ship or goods": per McCardie J in *Manbre Saccharine Co v Corn Products Co* [1919] 1 KB at 203.

That the shipping of the proper goods is a condition precedent to the right of the vendor under a cif contract to claim the price is quite clear. But what is the position when the purchaser for some reason has become suspicious that goods of the description for which he contracted are not on their way, but other goods, and documents which *on their face* are consistent with the contract, are presented to him? If he decline to pay when the documents are tendered, he takes the risk of breaking his contract if the goods turn out to be right; but he cannot be treated as not ready and willing to perform his contract if the goods turn out to be wrong. The goods here have turned out to be wrong. This is clearly laid down in *Sanders v Maclean* (1883) 11 QBD 327. In that case, there were three bills of lading from Russia, and two only were presented to the purchaser in London. Cotton LJ said at 339: "If the purchaser chooses to refuse to accept the cargo, because he does not know whether in fact the tender does comply with the terms of the contract, and whether the other part of the bill of lading has been parted with or not, ... and if it should turn out on investigation that in fact what was tendered to him was an effectual bill of lading effectual to pass the property in the cargo then he broke his contract by not paying the money and by refusing to accept the cargo when such effectual bill of lading was tendered to him." In that case, the third bill of lading was in the hands of the shipper, unendorsed and ineffective; and it was held that the tender of the only effective originals of the set was a sufficient tender, and put the purchaser in the wrong. As Bowen LJ said at 343: "The person who rejects effective and adequate documents of title on the ground that another document may possibly be outstanding, does so at his own risk. If his surmise turns out to be well founded, his rejection of the tender would be justified. But if it is a mere surmise and has no foundation in fact, he has chosen, by excess of caution, to place himself in the wrong."

Now, in the present case, the purchaser, when the invoice was sent to him, and he was asked to honour the draft through the Commercial Bank, and to take up the bill of lading and the insurance policy, did suspect that something was wrong. The invoice was certainly consistent with the description in the contract; but it spoke of "$150 bales Liverpool sacks", and did not say "150 bales *first selection* Liverpool *wheat* sacks", as the contract said. In acknowledging the letter of the vendor with the invoice, before the boat reached Sydney, the purchaser wrote: "We would *like* you to send us the original invoice" (the goods came from England) "showing that they are first selection bags packed by Messrs Martin and Levy Bros & Knowles according to our purchase." The vessel reached Sydney on 16 November, and payment of the draft was refused; and the vendor telegraphed that unless the documents were "accepted and paid for before three same will be sold against you". This threat led the purchaser to telegraph immediately (16 November): "We have not refused payment your draft. Your documents do not identify goods as being according contract. Draft will be accepted soon as goods proved equal description purchased. Boat due today. Expect examine tomorrow. We wrote you for oversea invoices which you have not provided." The vendor telegraphed at once to the purchaser that its action was a breach of contract, and that the vendor was "selling documents unless our conditions of today complied with". On the 17th the goods on the vessel were inspected, and were found not to be "first selection" bags, but rejections from the "first selection", including, as it appears, malt bags, flour bags, pea bags, potato bags. The trial was before a judge, without a jury, who found for the plaintiff; it is our duty to weigh the evidence; and, so far as I can see, the purchaser never wavered from the position which it took up in its telegram of 16 November. It wanted to carry out the contract. The vendor had, under the contract, all the month of November in which to deliver; and in a letter of 26 November the purchaser said: "We still require you to complete your contract and delivery to us 150 bales first selection Liverpool wheat sacks. Unless you deliver us these sacks in accordance with the contract, we shall be compelled to claim upon you for damages for breach of contract ... as there are only three working days left now in November, and we may have to go on the market and buy to complete our engagements."

There is no doubt that the plaintiff right through the transaction was ready and willing to perform the contract in the ordinary sense of the words, and that the contract was not performed because of the defendant's fault in sending the wrong goods. The defendant contends, however, that it was the duty of the plaintiff to pay the draft and to take up the bill of lading and documents, and that, if the goods supplied were wrong, the plaintiff had a remedy only in an action to recover the money. No case has been cited which supports this contention; the shipping of goods of the description in the contract is, in my opinion, a condition precedent to the liability to pay.

It may be taken for granted that the plaintiff had no right to demand to see the overseas invoice, or to demand inspection of the goods before payment. I do not regard the letter of 12 November as a demand, but merely as an expression of what the plaintiff would "like" in view of the ambiguity of the invoice; but counsel for the defendant, by an ingenious cross-examination, led the plaintiff's managing director to admit that "nothing short of the overseas invoice or an inspection of the goods would have satisfied him *at that period*" (after the ambiguous invoice). But it is not a question as to the state of mind of the managing director: it is a question as to what the plaintiff or the defendant did; or failed to do; or, finally, was the plaintiff ready and willing to perform the contract. There certainly was no repudiation of the contract in the sense of *Mersey Steel and Iron Co v Naylor Benzon & Co* (1884) 9 App Cas 434, and the vendor had no right to treat the contract as at an end after the 16 November. Mr Mitchell has put his client's case frankly and fairly before us; but, in my opinion, the plaintiff has amply satisfied the burden of proof that he was always ready and willing to perform the contract; and the appeal should be allowed, and the judgment of Gordon J restored.

Starke J: Under a cif contract a seller is bound to ship goods according to the contract description, and a buyer is bound to pay the price on tender of the usual or customary mercantile documents. It is sometimes a question of fact whether particular documents are, or are not, usual or customary in relation to the contract: *Tamvaco v Lucas* (1862) 31 LJ QB 296.

In the present case the seller did not ship goods of the contract description, but tendered to the buyer documents for the goods it had in fact shipped. If the buyer had paid for the goods on the presentation of these documents, it would not have been precluded from subsequently rejecting the goods, and recovering the moneys paid and damage for the breach of contract: *Biddell Bros v E Clemens Horst Co* [1911] 1 KB 934, per Kennedy LJ; [1912] AC 18. If the buyer had rejected the goods on tender of the documents for an untenable reason, it might still justify its act "on other and valid grounds": *Tamvaco v Lucas* (1859) 1 E & E 592; *Manbre Saccharine Co v Corn Products Co* [1919] 1 KB 198 at 202 *et seq; Taylor v Oakes, Roncoroni & Co* (1922) 38 TLR 349, 517; *Kennedy on Cif Contracts*, pp 168-9.

Owing to the form of invoice in this case, the buyer, I gather, suspected that goods had not been shipped in accordance with the contract description and it rejected the documents tendered unless it had an inspection of the goods shipped. By the terms of the contract, however, the buyer was not entitled to insist upon inspection before payment: *Biddell Bros v E Clemens Horst Co* [1911] 1 KB 934.

Nevertheless, it is clear upon the authorities that the buyer can, upon the facts proved in this case, justify its rejection of the documents, and that the seller cannot succeed in an action against the buyer for the price or for damages.

It is said, however, that the acts of the buyer establish the fact that it was not ready and willing on its part to pay for the goods on tender of documents, in accordance with its obligation under the contract ...

The question is, in truth, one of fact. The goods the subject of the contract of sale were 150 bales first selection Liverpool wheat sacks. "First selection" is a most material part of that description. The invoice tendered with the bill of lading and policy of insurance was as follows: "To 150 bales Liverpool sacks at 9s cife £1687 10s." In my opinion, any reasonable businessman would regard that description with well-grounded suspicion, and be uncertain whether the documents tendered to him represented goods in conformity with the contract...

[His Honour then considered the evidence and concluded that the plaintiff buyer had not refused to perform the contract, but as it was uncertain whether the documents tendered to it related to goods of the contract description it required assurance of this before payment. Accordingly the plaintiff was ready and willing to perform the contract and its appeal should be allowed.

Knox CJ agreed substantially with Higgins J. Powers J agreed substantially with Isaacs J.]

Appeal allowed.

[Leave to appeal to the Privy Council was refused: (1929) 42 CLR 595.]

The above decision was considered and distinguished in *Samuel McCausland Ltd v Railton* [1931] VLR 247.

QUESTIONS

Question 1

What different duties arise for both buyer and seller under cif and fob contracts? What would be the effect of either the buyer or seller failing to fulfil any of their respective obligations? To what extent can the parties modify either of these forms of sale? What other types of contract are used in international trade and how do they differ from cif and fob contracts?

Question 2

When will property pass under a cif contract? What is the effect of a seller under such a contract having the bill of lading made out in the buyer's name but retaining possession of it?

When will risk normally pass under a cif contract? What are the parties' obligations under such a contract when the goods are lost in transit?

Question 3

What advantages are afforded to both international buyer and seller by adopting provisions from the ICC Incoterms in their contract of sale? Is this procedure preferable to agreeing on their own particular contractual terms? Give your reasons.

Question 4

Carb Pty Ltd made a contract in April to sell "35,000 hard steel carburettors cif Yokohama for $550,000 net cash against documents August delivery". Carb shipped the goods on *Titanic II* owned by Trans Shipping Co which reached Yokohama where the goods were unloaded safely. Carb arranged through its Tokyo agents for tender of shipping documents to Mitzi including an invoice which referred to "35,000 carburettors: $550,000".

Mitzi had received warning from a third party that the carburettors might be made of a composition plastic casing covered with soft steel alloy, and is unwilling to accept the shipment until satisfied on this point. However, Carb refused to allow Mitzi an inspection before payment.

Advise Mitzi generally in relation to the present situation and how the problem could be averted in future.

Question 5

What difference would it make to your advice in Question 4 if *Titanic II* had hit a coral reef and sank with all cargo three days after leaving Sydney and one of the following alternatives applied:

(1) The contract had provided for sale of "35,000 carburettors delivery per *Titanic II* afloat cif Yokohama $550,000 net cash on presentation of delivery order and certificate of insurance at Yokohama or arrival of *Titanic II* with goods at Yokohama whichever first occurs". After *Titanic II* sank, Carb tendered to Mitzi a delivery order, certificate of insurance from Coverall Insurance Ltd covering theft and breakage but not loss at sea;

(2) Carb had based its price on a quotation for freight obtained from Trans Shipping Co, but when Carb obtained the bill of lading in August the freight had increased

by $20,000 in line with general increases in the industry. After *Titanic II* sank, Carb presented proper shipping documents to Mitzi with an invoice for $570,000;

(3) The contract had provided for sale of "35,000 carburettors for $500,000 fob *Titanic II* departing Sydney in August". In addition Carb agreed to obtain the bill of lading and insurance cover for the voyage to Yokohama. After *Titanic II* sank Carb presented proper shipping documents to Mitzi with an invoice for $520,000, representing contract price plus the $20,000 freight increase.

SECTION 3: RELATED CONTRACTS OF CARRIAGE

Every export transaction necessarily involves carriage of goods which will also be insured while in transit. It is impossible to cover adequately in this text all aspects of contracts of carriage and insurance, but the export transaction will be used to illustrate some of the more important principles and issues.

In developed countries today, up to one-third of GNP is spent on transport, and competition between various sectors of the industry for a larger share of this market is fierce. Three major factors will influence the commercial user's choice of transport: cost, convenience and speed. Additional cost of air transport or individual delivery is often justified by speed and convenience where goods are perishable or income producing—eg fresh fruit, newspapers or a vital part for a machine. The main convenience factor is whether the goods are carried door-to-door which may also be related to reliability; and container transport has been developed to fulfil this objective. The "fast carrier" which loses or misdirects the goods in transit may be compared to the hare in its race with the tortoise. Road transport offers the advantage of door-to-door carriage. Conversely, some industries are located on rail sidings or beside wharves. However, road transport is not always direct as major road carriers often use local carriers to bring goods to depots for classification, reassignment and carriage to the next break-bulk depot prior to delivery to individual destinations. Thus the goods may be handled by a number of individual carriers with resulting problems in allocation of responsibility for loss: see, eg *TNT (Melbourne) Pty Ltd v May & Baker (Australia) Pty Ltd* (1966) 115 CLR 353; *Hobbs v Petersham Transport Pty Ltd, infra*. Similarly, goods carried by sea are sometimes transhipped: *Plaimar Ltd v Waters Trading Co Ltd*, p 153, *supra*. Again, goods may be damaged while in the custody of stevedores (*McKay Massey Harris Pty Ltd v ICIANZ Ltd*, p 147, *supra*) or in storage with warehousekeepers while awaiting shipment or collection: *Gilchrist Watt & Sanderson Pty Ltd v York Products Pty Ltd* [1970] 3 All ER 825; 44 ALJR 269 (PC).

General principles of bailment

In many of these illustrations the carrier or custodian of the goods is a bailee under a contract of bailment. The relationship of bailment occurs when the bailor of goods (usually the owner or owner's agent) passes possession of them to a bailee upon his undertaking to keep, and then return or deliver the specific goods to the bailor or according to his directions. The bailee owes a duty to the owner of the goods which exists independently of any contract although it can be modified by contract. It is important to appreciate what circumstances give rise to a bailment, the nature of the bailee's duties and what the bailor must prove in order to establish a breach of those duties.

Hobbs v Petersham Transport Co Pty Ltd; Petersham Transport Co Pty Ltd v ASEA Electric (Australia) Pty Ltd
High Court of Australia (1971) 124 CLR 220; [1971] ALR 675

[The plaintiff ASEA engaged the defendant Petersham Transport to carry valuable electrical equipment by road from Sydney to northern New South Wales. The defendant employed the third party, a firm of carriers, Hobbs Bros, to actually carry the goods. While the goods were on Hobbs' vehicle which was travelling at about 25 mph on level ground, the axle broke, causing the vehicle to overturn and damaging the goods. The evidence showed that Hobbs' vehicle was in good condition and suitable to the task, the driver was competent, and the axle broke cleanly with no indication of prior defect which reasonable inspection might have revealed.

The plaintiff sued the defendant (1) for breach of the contract of carriage, and (2) for failure as a carrier to safely carry the goods and for damaging them by its negligence. The plaintiff did not sue Hobbs, but the defendant claimed against Hobbs as a third party for breach of contract and for negligence. The trial judge Nagle J gave judgment for the plaintiff and for the defendant against the third party. The New South Wales Court of Appeal dismissed the appeal by the defendant and third parties, who then appealed to the High Court of Australia.

Barwick CJ delivered a judgment substantially to the same effect as that of Windeyer J below.

McTiernan J agreed with Menzies J and concurred in his reasons.]

Menzies J: The critical decision to be made here, as it seems to me, is whether the evidence established affirmatively that the fracture of the axle of the bogie of the trailer which caused the vehicle to overturn happened without any negligent act or omission of the defendant or any servant of the defendant.

It is common ground that the defendant was a bailee for reward of the equipment being carried. It was not under an absolute duty to deliver. It was a qualified duty and, to use the language of Starke, Dixon and McTiernan JJ in *John F Goulding Pty Ltd v Victorian Railways Commissioners* (1932) 48 CLR 157 at 166, "it would not be broken if the defendants were disabled from delivery through destruction or loss of the goods which reasonable care and skill on their part could not avoid". To escape liability for non-delivery the onus of proving that the non-delivery, however caused, was without fault on its part, rested upon it. A modern statement of the position is to be found in the judgment of Lord Denning MR in *Morris v C W Martin & Sons Ltd* [1966] 1 QB 716 at 726 as follows:

"Once a man has taken charge of goods as a bailee for reward, it is his duty to take reasonable care to keep them safe; and he cannot escape that duty by delegating it to his servant. If the goods are lost or damaged, whilst they are in his possession, he is liable unless he can show — and the burden is on him to show — that the loss or damage occured without any neglect or default or misconduct of himself or of any of the servants to whom he delegated his duty."

These well-established rules, which I think should be accepted without qualification or gloss, do not constitute a carrier, such as the defendant, an insurer; he escapes liability if he can show that non-delivery of goods entrusted to him for carriage was not due to his fault, notwithstanding that he does not show how the loss actually occurred. In this, his obligation is less onerous than that imposed by law upon a common carrier who is, of course, responsible for the safety of the goods entrusted to him, except for loss arising solely from act of God or the Queen's enemies or inherent vice in the goods carried or from the fault of the consignor. If the defendant had been a common carrier he could not have hoped to escape from liability in the circumstances of this case.

His Honour the learned trial judge was not satisfied that the onus of disproving negligence had been discharged. The problem for this court is whether he should have been so satisfied.

The defendant made a strong case but there was an omission, the significance of which is, I think, of critical importance. It did not prove that, in the course of servicing its vehicle, the axle which broke had been inspected periodically, or, indeed, at all. The driver's evidence was to the effect that he had not inspected the axles of the vehicle and that the checking of the axles was the duty of a mechanic in the defendant's employment at its Leichhardt depot. This mechanic, one Looker, as the driver said, "did the checking of the axles if necessary — any services". Mr Looker was not called.

Had there been anything in the appearance of the axle at the point of fracture to indicate that the fracture was otherwise than a completely new break, I would have thought that the defendant's attempted proof that it was free from blame would, by reason of the foregoing omission, have been incomplete. It is the convincing evidence that the fracture was clean and fresh — which it seems His Honour accepted — upon which the defendant had to rely to complete its case and to negative the existence of any prior defect in the axle which broke that reasonable inspection might have revealed.

Not without hesitation, I have come to the conclusion that the inference which the evidence required is that the fracture did happen all at once and without there being any prior fault, such as a hairline crack, which reasonable examination of the axle might have revealed. The lack of evidence of inspection of the axle had, therefore, no significance because, had there been such an examination, it would have revealed nothing that could have contributed to the accident. The defendant did, I think, prove inter alia that the breaking of the axle of the bogie happened without any fault on its part or on the part of its servants.

I have therefore come to the conclusion that the learned trial judge should have found affirmatively that the non-delivery of the goods was not due to default on the part of the defendant.

It is for this reason that I am of the opinion that the defendant's appeal should be allowed.

Windeyer J [after stating the facts at 237:] A person who is not a common carrier but who undertakes to carry goods for reward is commonly called a private carrier. It was in 1703 firmly established as the rule of our law by the great judgment of Holt CJ in *Coggs v Bernard* (1703) 1 Salkeld 26; 91 ER 25; 2 Ld Raym 909; 92 ER 107, that a private carrier is a bailee of goods delivered to him. If he is to carry them for reward, he is a bailee for reward and as such bound to use due care and diligence to keep the goods safely and to deliver them undamaged. The standard of care and diligence is that which a careful and vigilant man would exercise in respect of goods of his own of the same kind in similar circumstances. A bailment comes into existence upon a delivery of goods of one person, the bailor, into the possession of another person, the bailee, upon a promise, express or implied, that they will be redelivered to the bailor or dealt with in a stipulated way. A carrier to whom goods are delivered for carriage is a bailee. But a person who undertakes that he will carry goods is not a bailee of them unless they be actually delivered to and received by him.

The case has been conducted on the assumption that neither the defendant nor the Hobbs brothers was a common carrier. In the ordinary way of their businesses, each was no doubt a private carrier. But on a document dated 12 August 1957 setting out the terms on which the Hobbs brothers agreed "as a sub-contractor to perform contracts of carriage" for the defendant, this appeared: "I accept the responsibility of that of a Common Carrier at Law." This document was signed by one Johnson who was a servant of the Hobbs brothers. He was the driver of the vehicle on which the goods were being carried at the time of the accident. He gave evidence. Under cross examination by counsel for the Hobbs brothers he said that he had no instructions from them to do anything but pick up goods as directed by a representative of the defendant: but it was not disputed that he had signed the document and handed it to the defendant; and the learned trial judge rightly, I think, admitted it as evidence "against the third party". In the result it may be that the Hobbs brothers should, as between themselves and the defendant, be regarded as common carriers with respect to the journey in question for private carriers can assume the responsibilities of a common carrier for a particular transaction: *Robinson v Dunmore* (1801) 2 B & P 416; 126 ER 1359. However, as will appear, I do not think that the character of the Hobbs brothers is a decisive element in the case.

It has been assumed throughout the argument that the defendant was a bailee of goods of which the plaintiff was bailor and that the liability of the defendant is to be measured accordingly. This proposition has not been questioned. Nevertheless I think that it is mistaken, and that the mistake is critical. The plaintiff's declaration alleged that the defendant "was a carrier of goods for hire and the plaintiff delivered to the defendant and the defendant received as such carrier certain goods of the plaintiff . . ." But, as I understand the case, there was no evidence that the plaintiff ever delivered the goods to the defendant. They were delivered by representatives of the plaintiff company directly to Johnson, the servant of the Hobbs brothers. They had been lying on a wharf at Pyrmont, Sydney. They were loaded directly from the wharf on to the lorry belonging to the Hobbs brothers, of which Johnson was the driver. Johnson had been told by one of the Hobbs to go to the wharf and there report to a Mr Howe, who was the manager of the defendant company, and take directions from him. Johnson met Howe at the wharf. Howe pointed out the cases to be loaded on Johnson's vehicle. They had been unshipped and put upon the wharf earlier in the day. The actual loading on to Johnson's vehicle was done by a crane operated, it seems, by a wharfinger or stevedore. The articles in question were part of a shipment of electrical goods that the plaintiff had imported from abroad. These were over a period of some days being taken from the wharf by different carriers. These carriers had, it seems, all been engaged by the defendant. In each case Howe supervised the loading, including the loading of Johnson's vehicle. He did this in association with a Mr Badman, an employee of the plaintiff who was at the wharf throughout and who checked the delivery of the plaintiff's goods to the various carriers. When the goods were on the wharf they were apparently in the custody of the plaintiff's shipping agents. They were never, so far as the evidence shews, in the custody of the defendant.

The Hobbs brothers were sub-contractors of the defendant to perform its contract with the plaintiff. They were strangers to that contract. They had no contract with the plaintiff. But the common law, deriving its concept of bailment largely from the civil law, has never subsumed bailment under the general law of contract. It is now beyond dispute that the relationship of bailor and bailee of a chattel can arise and exist independently of contract. By taking the plaintiff's goods into their physical possession when they were loaded on to their lorry the Hobbs brothers undertook the duties and obligations of a bailee for reward. Whether or not a sub-contractor of a bailee is himself properly called a bailee is a debatable question of terminology. But it is I think not a relevant question in this case because, as I have said, the evidence does not shew that the defendant itself ever became a bailee. However, whether that were so or not, the Hobbs brothers unquestionably became directly liable to the plaintiff if they, by their servants and agents, failed to take due care of the goods. This, the doctrine expounded in *Morris v C W Martin & Sons Ltd* [1966] 1 QB 716, was made firmly binding for us by a judgment of the Privy Council last year: *Gilchrist Watt & Sanderson Pty Ltd v York Products Pty Ltd* [1970] 1 WLR 1262; (1970) 44 ALJR 269 affirming the decision of the Supreme Court of New South Wales: *York Products Pty Ltd v Gilchrist Watt & Sanderson Pty Ltd* [1968] 3 NSWR 551. I need not elaborate this. I merely refer, as a pertinent statement of the rule, to passages in the judgment of Sachs J in *Learoyd Bros & Co v Pope & Sons Ltd* [1966] 2 Lloyd's Rep 142 at 147-8.

The obligation of a carrier as bailee is to exercise due care, skill and diligence for the safety of chattels entrusted to him. If he fails to deliver them safely at the end of the bailment, that is evidence of a failure to perform his duty to exercise due care of them. He can rebut this by shewing that their loss or damage was not the result of any default on his part. But to escape liability he must establish that. The burden lies on him. That this is the rule of the common law has been asserted in many cases in England extending now over more than a century. I need not cite them all. Cogent statements are that of Lord Halsbury, which Buckley LJ quoted in *Joseph Travers & Sons v Cooper* [1915] 1 KB 73 at 88:

"It appears to me that here there was a bailment made to a particular person, a bailment for hire and reward, and the bailee was bound to show that he took reasonable and proper care for the due security and proper delivery of that bailment; the proof of that rested upon him."

And the words of Buckley LJ himself in that case: "The defendant as bailee of the goods is responsible for their return to their owner. If he failed to return them it rested upon him to prove that he did take reasonable and proper care of the goods, and that if he had been there he could have done nothing, and that the loss would still have resulted. He has not discharged himself of that onus."

Recent statements by the Court of Appeal of this rule may be found in *Houghland v R R Low (Luxury Coaches) Ltd* [1962] 1 QB 694, and in *Global Dress Co Ltd v Boase & Co Ltd* [1966] 2 Lloyd's Rep 72. Australian decisions to the same effect are cited in the judgments in the Supreme Court in this case and I need not cite them all here. *Fairbairn v Miller* [1918] VLR 615 is a good example. The same rule has been applied in New Zealand: *Wilson v New Zealand Express Co Ltd (No 3)* [1924] NZLR 890, and in some jurisdictions in the United States: see especially *Hoel v Flour City Fuel and Transfer Co* (1919) 175 NW 300.

This rule has been seen as an anomaly. It is suggested that a carrier's failure to deliver goods in accordance with his contract is simply an illustration of a *res ipsa loquitur*: that it is an evidentiary fact from which, in the absence of an explanation, an inference can be drawn of default on the part of the carrier, but that the ultimate onus is upon the plaintiff and that it never shifts. This proposition would be irrefutable if the rights of the parties depended simply on a contract to carry with due care. But that, it seems, is not so when goods having been delivered into his custody, the carrier has assumed the duties of a bailee for reward. An explanation of the apparent anomaly may well be that the duty of a bailee to use due care does not arise from contract or from tort. It could in former times have been asserted in either assumpsit or in case: but it is now generally recognised as sui generis. If the matter be put in terms of an implied undertaking or promise by the bailee, it is that he will redeliver the goods to the bailor or whoever he appoints to receive them, except he, the bailee, be prevented from doing so by events not caused by negligence on his part, proof of the exception being upon him. Seen in this way, the burden that is put upon a bailee of exonerating himself when he fails to redeliver the goods is simply a peculiar incident of the law of bailment. I accept the analysis that Sholl J made after a survey of the authorities in his judgment in *Fankhauser v Mark Dykes Pty Ltd* [1960] VR 376. I appreciate that the second count of the plaintiff's declaration tenders an issue of fact to be proved by the plaintiff. I realise too that to say that the bailee must exonerate himself when the facts raise a prima facie inference of negligence may well seem anomalous when set alongside the doctrine that this court has established for Australia of the onus of proof in cases when *res ipsa loquitur* is put forward: as in *Anchor Products Ltd v Hedges* (1966) 115 CLR 493 ... One explanation that has been put forward is that an inference of negligence arises if the loss be not explained by the bailee, the burden of adducing explanatory evidence being on him because the facts are peculiarly within his knowledge and not within the knowledge of the bailor. However, despite all these countervailing considerations I think that the rule as to the onus, being an incident of the law of bailment, is too firmly established to be shaken by demands for logical consistency with the consequences of *res ipsa loquitur* in other circumstances.

If I thought that the defendant had become a bailee of the goods, I would, for the reasons I have given, agree with the learned judges of the Supreme Court that it was for it, the defendant, to negative negligence as the cause of the accident; and then, because for reasons that I gave in *Da Costa v Cockburn Salvage & Trading Pty Ltd* (1970) 124 CLR 192, I would gravely hesitate to say that the learned trial judge was wrong, especially as two other members of the Supreme Court were of the same opinion. The question would be whether anything which would have avoided the accident, and which ought reasonably to have been done, was not done. If that was left in doubt the bailee would be liable. But, as I do not think that the defendant was a bailee, this is in my view irrelevant. It would be the relevant onus if the plaintiff had sued the Hobbs brothers directly as bailees, or had sought to amend this action to sue them in the alternative. But neither of these courses was pursued. It is now presumably too late for either, as any claim by the plaintiff against the Hobbs brothers is statute barred: see *The Commonwealth v Temple* (1949) 49 SR (NSW) 373 at 376-7 and cases there cited. The Hobbs brothers are therefore only liable if the defendant be liable, and then only to indemnify it. I therefore turn back to the position of the defendant under the contract it made with the plaintiff.

Although the Hobbs brothers were independent contractors, the defendant is, by well-established common law rules, liable for their negligence in relation to the carriage of the plaintiff's goods. That is because the defendant impliedly promised the plaintiff that the goods would be carried to their destination with due care. If it procured someone else to perform the carriage for it, it became liable for his, the sub-contractor's negligence: *Doolan v Midland Railway Co* (1877) 2 App Cas 792; *John v Bacon* (1870) LR 5 CP 437; *Machu v London and South-Western Railway Co* (1848) 2 Ex 415; 154 ER 554. The rationale of this may be debatable. But I think that Professor Atiyah, who discusses it in his book *Vicarious Liability in the Law of Torts*, 1967, pp 361-2, rightly describes it as a form of vicarious liability. In *Riverstone Meat Co Pty Ltd v Lancashire Shipping Co Ltd* [1961] AC 807 at 865 Lord Radcliffe spoke of it as "the carrier's responsibility for the diligence of all those whom he employs to discharge his own primary duty". I think therefore that the plaintiff would be entitled to recover damages from the defendant if it proved that the accident occurred by negligence for which the Hobbs brothers were responsible either because their vehicle was negligently driven, or because there had been negligence in maintaining it so that it was not in a serviceable condition. But to establish liability on the part of the defendant it would be necessary for the plaintiff to prove this negligence. The onus was on it. It could not found its case on the onus that a bailee has; for the defendant was not a bailee. It could claim that the fact that the vehicle ran off the road spoke for itself of negligence, and called for an explanation. But the explanation of the accident in a broken axle left it upon the plaintiff to prove that this was the result of negligence. The mere fact that the mechanism of a vehicle fails does not itself shew that the owner or driver was negligent. No doubt a failure to maintain a vehicle in good order may in some cases amount to negligence. But even a common carrier of passengers is not to be held responsible for the consequences of a latent defect in his vehicle not discoverable by reasonable inspection: *Readhead v Midland Railway Co* (1869) LR 4 QB 379; *Webb v Cassidy* (1907) 27 NZLR 489. I need not rehearse the evidence. It makes it abundantly clear that, the onus being on the plaintiff to prove negligence, the plaintiff's case failed. The appeal should therefore be allowed.

[**Owen J** held that the evidence established that non-delivery of the goods was not due to any negligence on the part of the carrier and that the appeal should be allowed.]

Appeals by the defendant and third parties allowed.

Comparison may be made with other decisions in *Fankhauser v Mark Dykes Pty Ltd* [1960] VLR 376; *A A Radio Taxi Trucks Ltd v Curyer* [1965] SASR 110.

CARRIAGE OF GOODS BY LAND

The above cases amply illustrate the nature of a contract of carriage by road. In *Hobbs v Petersham Transport Pty Ltd* (1971) 124 CLR 220, Menzies and Windeyer JJ refer to the liability of a common carrier. Whether Trans Shipping is a common carrier is a question of fact, the main determinant being whether it reserves the right to refuse carriage. A common carrier is one who holds himself out as willing to carry for hire as his public business. The test has been stated:

Did the defendant, while inviting all and sundry to employ him, reserve to himself the right of accepting or rejecting their offers of goods for carriage whether his lorries were full or empty, being guided in his decision by the attractiveness or otherwise of the particular offer and not by his ability or inability to carry having regard to his other engagements?: *Belfast Ropework Co Ltd v Bushell* [1918] 1 KB 210 at 215, per Bailhache J.

If Trans Shipping is a common carrier, it commits a common law offence punishable by indictment if it refuses to carry the goods of any member of the public provided the goods are properly packed and of the type it normally carries and the destination is within its normal area of operation. As indicated in Menzies J's judgment, Trans' liability to the consignor Carb is much stricter than that of a private carrier, although this has been qualified by legislation in the case of a carrier by land: see Common Carriers Act 1902 (NSW) ss 3, 4, 7, 9; Carriers and Innkeepers Act 1958 (Vic) ss 3, 4, 6, 8; Carriage of Goods by Land (Carriers Liabilities) Act of 1967 (Qld) ss 5, 6, 7; The Carriers Act 1891 (SA) ss 2, 5, 10, 11; Carriers Act 1920 (WA) ss 2, 7, 9; Common Carriers Act 1874 (Tas) ss 3, 8, 10. In return Trans is entitled at common law to insist on payment in advance, to be informed by consignor Carb if the goods are dangerous and to a lien over the goods carried for the freight. Since these rights can be obtained as against the consignor by express contract, it is not surprising that carriers will often attempt to avoid holding themselves out as common carriers.

In Australia, the government railways are common carriers (see, eg, Government Railways Act 1912 (NSW) s 33) although their position has been affected by legislation. The Public Transport Commission of New South Wales offers two rates: owner's risk rate which limits the commission's liability to $50, and Commission's Risk Rate, where for an extra fee (similar to an insurance premium) the commission accepts the liability of a common carrier. Three copies of the waybill are issued, for the consignor, the commission, and to accompany the goods to the consignor.

CARRIAGE OF GOODS BY AIR

Goods, other than passengers' baggage, consigned for carriage by air whether within Australia or on international routes, are carried pursuant to an air consignment note or air waybill. Like rail waybills these are issued in triplicate but, unlike bills of lading, they do not constitute documents of title (see *infra*). The speed of air transport is such that there is virtually no need for a negotiable air waybill being used as security for financing the purchase of goods consigned by air, and in practice air waybills are printed as "not negotiable" documents. Accordingly, the carrier is not precluded from delivering except on production of the air waybill, but must deliver to the consignee upon request.

Some aspects of air carriage are regulated by the Commonwealth Civil Aviation (Carriers' Liability) Act 1959 which adopted the 1929 Warsaw Convention on International Carriage by Air and the 1955 Hague Protocol to the Convention. Although these conventions set out contents and procedure for issuance of air waybills, they are primarily concerned with liability for death or bodily injury to passengers and loss or damage to their baggage. The Commonwealth adopting Act does not purport to regulate carriage of general air cargoes which remains a matter for common law and the terms of the contract. Accordingly, the carrier can limit its liability by appropriate exclusion clauses.

CARRIAGE OF GOODS BY SEA

Notwithstanding the increase in air cargoes, and the swing from rail to road transport, by far the greatest volume of Australia's and the world's international trade is carried by sea, and this aspect of the export/import transaction continues to be of vital importance.

The two basic forms of contract by which goods are carried by sea are the charterparty and bill of lading. A cif contract will always require, and an fob contract will often involve, issuance of a bill of lading and a charterparty may also be involved. For example, the Australian Wheat Board in selling wheat to overseas buyers typically sells on fob terms (sometimes with extended credit) from a designated Australian port. The fob contract requires the buyers to arrange the carriage of large wheat consignments in ships which are chartered for the purpose.

CHARTERPARTIES

A *charterparty* is similar to a lease in that the shipowner agrees to place the entire ship or a specified part of it at the disposal of the charterer. In a charter by demise, the charterer takes possession and control of the ship, supplying the fuel and crew. In other cases, the owner retains possession and general control of the vessel but places it at the disposal of the charterer who agrees to load a full cargo and pay freight thereon, or "dead" freight on the space he fails to use. The charterparty may be for a particular voyage or for a fixed period of time: eg *Suisse Atlantique Societe D'Armement Maritime SA v NV Rotterdamsche Kolen Centrale* [1967] 1 AC 361. In either case the ship owner depends upon the charterer making full use of its vessel in order to maximise the owner's return from the charter freight. Accordingly, the charterparty will normally specify a particular time schedule (*lay days*) for loading and discharging cargo at each port and will stipulate liquidated damages in the form of a rate of *demurrage* for any additional time taken, and conversely will award the charterer payment of *dispatch* for loading etc in a shorter period than the agreed lay days. Much litigation on charterparties involves construction and application of standard clauses concerning dead freight, demurrage, dispatch and other specific clauses. Charterparties are not subject to statutory regulation.

BILLS OF LADING

A *bill of lading* is the other main shipping document. It would be issued in triplicate by Trans Shipping as the operator of the ship (ship owner or charterer) by way of a contract of carriage and signed by the Master or Agent of the ship. As explained earlier, the bill of lading is also a receipt for and a document of title to the goods consigned. See sample bill of lading on p 170.

As a receipt for the goods, the bill of lading will describe the quantity and type of goods and sometimes give their weight. It will also indicate whether the goods are actually shipped (ie, received on board) or only received for shipment, and are in apparent good order and condition. This information is important to the consignee Mitzi under a cif contract when required to accept shipping documents without seeing

Teaching Materials and Cases on Commercial Transactions

BILL OF LADING

B/L No. **3-3**

Shipper: **Carb Pty. Limited, 10 Gearway, Ryde. N.S.W.**

Reference No. **MITZI-42**

Consigned to order of: **Mitzi Co, Tasumi-Ku, Tokyo**

Notify address:

Local vessel: — from —

Vessel: **Titanic II** Port of loading: **Sydney**

THE TRANS LINE

Port of discharge	Final destination (if on-carriage)	Freight payable at	Number of original Bs/L
Yokohama	Tokyo	Sydney	Three (3)

Marks & Nos.	Number and kind of packages; description of goods	Gross weight	Measurement
MIT YOKOHAMA 1-200	200 cases automotive carburettors	50,000 kg	

Particulars above declared by Shipper

Freight	
Charges	
Collection Charges	
Bills of Lading	

SHIPPED on board in apparent good order and condition and to be discharged at the above port or place of discharge or so near thereto as the vessel may safely get, remain and leave always afloat.
Weight, measurement, quality, quantity, contents, condition, marks, numbers and value although declared by the Shipper in this Bill of Lading shall be considered as unknown to the Carrier unless expressly recognised and agreed to the contrary. The signing of this Bill of Lading shall not be considered as such an agreement.
One original Bill of Lading must be surrendered duly endorsed in exchange for the goods.
Freight, charges and primage whether prepayable or not and whether paid or not shall be considered as fully earned upon shipment and shall be paid vessel and/or cargo lost or not lost. Freight, charges and primage shall not be returned vessel and/or cargo lost or not lost.
In accepting this Bill of Lading the Merchant expressly accepts and agrees to all the stipulations, conditions and exceptions whether written, stamped, printed or otherwise incorporated and whether the Bill of Lading be signed by the merchant or not.
IN WITNESS whereof the Master or the Agent of the above vessel has signed the number of original Bills of Lading stated above, all of this tenor and date, one of which being accomplished the others shall be void.

Agents at port of destination: **Midco, Misagi-Cho, Yokohama**

Place and date of issue: **Sydney, 1 May, 1984**

Signed (for the Master) by **O. L. D. Salt.**

the goods. As a document of title a negotiable bill of lading can be transferred from Carb to Mitzi. This symbolic method of transferring possession and title forms the crucial link in the international sales and financing of goods afloat.

As a contract of carriage, the bill of lading has become the focus for determining the rights and liabilities of consignors, consignees, shipowners, charterers and stevedores. The bill of lading is a standard form contract of adhesion which will contain or incorporate by reference a number of provisions protective of the shipowner or charterer. The Australian Wheat Board's bill of lading in fact incorporates by reference the terms of the associated charterparty.

THE HAGUE RULES

In order to obtain a fair balance between these parties the International Law Association in 1921 drafted a set of rules relating to bills of lading which are known as the Hague Rules. These have been adopted in Australia and by at least 80 nations.

R Temperley: Carriage of Goods By Sea Act 1924
4th ed, 1932, pp 1-4

With the development of overseas commerce in the last decades of the nineteenth century, the forms of bill of lading used for general cargo shipments in the liner services gradually became overloaded with an accumulation of various and obscure terms, conditions and exceptions, designed to relieve the carriers from almost every conceivable liability. In consequence, not only the shippers, who might possibly have an opportunity of examining the contents of such documents before the shipment, but still more the subsequent holders, or other parties interested, eg, bankers, receivers of cargo, and cargo underwriters, who have no such opportunity, were quite unable to understand the extent of their rights against the carrier or to estimate the value of the security which they held.

The liner companies, limited in number and thus capable of effective organisation, were for all practical purposes in the position of monopolists, and therefore able to dictate the terms of their bills of lading. On the other hand, owing to their great numbers and to the diversity of the goods shipped by them, the merchants, in many cases, were unable by organisation or otherwise to negotiate on equal terms with the shipowners. Moreover, the fact that the primary interest of the shippers (as opposed to the consignees) of goods was directed to the rate of freight rather than to the conditions of carriage contributed to the same result. Nor could bankers and underwriters, not being parties to the contracts of carriage, intervene effectually.

In these circumstances, agitation arose for legislative action. This led, in 1893, to the passing of the well-known Harter Act in the United States, which had the effect of fixing by law many important conditions for the carriage of goods by sea from and to that country.

This example was followed by certain British Dominions, viz, Australia, in the Sea Carriage of Goods Act 1904; Canada, in the Water-Carriage of Goods Act 1910; and New Zealand, in a series of Acts. But these Dominion Acts were not uniform in their provisions; and, this having caused inconvenience, the Imperial Shipping Committee, which was appointed by the Imperial government in 1920 at the instance of the British Dominions for the purpose of (among other things) inquiring into complaints with regard to conditions in the inter-Imperial trades, in its report, dated February 1921, recommended the introduction of uniform legislation throughout the British Empire on the lines of the Canadian Water-Carriage of Goods Act 1910. The British government accordingly pledged its word, apparently on the occasion of a Conference of Prime Ministers of the Empire in 1921, to take steps to this end.

But the shipping community in this country viewed with apprehension the introduction of any measure which would replace the existing liberty of contract by a statutory code of conditions for the carriage of goods by sea, particularly a measure prepared and introduced by a government department, and steps were accordingly taken to formulate, in co-operation with the other interests concerned, a set of rules for the standardising of bills of lading which might be generally adopted as a voluntary international code.

The aid of the International Law Association was secured, and, in consultation with representatives of various interests, the Maritime Law committee of that association drew up a code of rules for this purpose, known as the Hague Rules 1921. This code was settled at the meeting of the International Law Association held at The Hague in September 1921, and was thereupon issued for the consideration of the commercial public.

It was hoped that the Hague Rules would be approved by all concerned and generally adopted without delay, and that the promised statutory unification of the law throughout the British Empire would thus become unnecessary.

But this hope was disappointed. Although the Hague Rules were voluntarily incorporated in the forms of bills of lading used by certain lines of steamships, and were re-issued with some amendment as the Hague Rules 1922, there was little evidence of any strong movement towards their early general adoption throughout the British Empire or abroad. The agitation for legislation persisted, and led to the holding of the Diplomatic International Conference on Maritime Law in Brussels in 1922, referred to in the preamble to the Act.

The delegates at that conference, as mentioned in the preamble to the Act, unanimously recommended the adoption of a draft Convention, which in effect embodied the Hague Rules, as the basis of a Convention between the participating States, and on the 25 August, 1924, the "International Convention for the Unification of certain Rules of Law relating to Bills of Lading" was signed at Brussels by the representatives of a large number of countries. The scheme contemplated was that each State would, on the Convention becoming effective, give the rules statutory force with respect to all outward bills of lading...

In an interesting work comparing English and French Law, Clarke estimates that four-fifths of all carriage of goods by sea is governed by the Hague Rules. He also provides the following insights into the background to the Convention:

M A Clarke: Aspects of the Hague Rules
1976, pp 3-7

In the nineteenth century, freedom to contract for the shipment of goods had become freedom for powerful carriers to impose the bondage of unfair terms on those shippers, the majority, in a position of commercial inferiority. This was true of all trading states. In France, the courts were deaf to pleas that carriers by sea should share the liability of other carriers for their servants under art 1384 c civ: sea carriers could not supervise the acts of their maritime servants, and the range of persons from whom these servants could be chosen was restricted by law. However, the real guarantee of the carriers' position lay in two related factors. Firstly, their commercial interests reflected those of dominant elements in national and political life. Secondly, commercial piracy could still be conducted under the flag of free trade which was respected by prevalent liberalism. Thus, it was in a nation of shippers that the first reforms were passed, the United States. Thus, when in 1913 de Monzie proposed similar reforms in France, reforms which satisfied the ostensible objections of the carriers, they were not even discussed. This was one of many attempts to institute legislative reform.

The shippers complained that the carriers took advantage of their weak bargaining position and that the equality prerequisite to true freedom to contract was lacking; that the carriers' immunity made insurance costly and that the risk of carriers' negligence was borne by the shippers, either directly or indirectly through inflated premiums; that immunity to suit became in practice indifference to the conduct of maritime servants which was often negligent or theftuous. The shippers could point to similar reforms at home and abroad. The shippers were latterly supported by the insurers and bankers. An attempt to bring pressure on carriers by boycotting contracts weighted in favour of the latter failed. But this new lobby brought a change in the nature of the debate during and after the First World War; the concern was now the value of the bill of lading as a commercial document, as a security for advances on documentary credit. The carriers replied that domestic reforms would compel the carriers of the state in question to increase their freight charges, that experience showed that, notwithstanding the greater security offered, too many shippers would prefer to risk their goods and save their money by contracting with foreign carriers able to charge a lower freight. The carriers of that state would thus suffer a competitive disadvantage on their own doorstep. Reform could only be acceptable at international level.

The ILA, at its Hague Conference of 1921, drew up the agreement known as the Hague Rules, intended for voluntary adoption by carriers in their bills of lading. The only sanction was to be commercial pressure by bankers and insurers. But the carriers did not comply for fear and distrust of their competitors which, in turn, reinforced the distrust of the shipping interests which had pressed for legislation. The rules were further discussed by the ILA at Buenos Aires in October 1922 and by the CMI in London shortly afterwards, and it was clear that any reform must be binding and thus instituted at diplomatic level ... Although the matter had not been subject to the usual preparation by the CMI, a large degree of agreement, obtained with difficulty, was embodied in the rules. Thus their form was retained as the basis for a convention, notwithstanding the protests of some delegations, and it was provided that this draft might, subject to the deliberations of the Subcommission and to certain amendments, become the final convention without further submission to the Conference. This is what happened in 1924 on the 25 August.

By the Carriage of Goods by Sea Act 1924, the United Kingdom gave effect to the Convention as it existed in 1922, and this Act differed slightly from the text signed in 1924 ...

On the basis of these investigations Clarke suggests the following lessons of history:

The objectives of the 1924 Convention lay not only in the general advantages offered by uniformity of law, but particularly in the removal of certain defects in the previous situation. The main object was to secure the bill of lading as a commercial document, and this could only be achieved by —

(1) redressing the imbalance of bargaining power between shipper and carrier, by placing the weight of legislation behind the shipper where necessary; this imbalance remains a problem today in developing areas of the world;

(2) clarifying the nature and scope of the minimum obligations imposed: buyers and banks need to know their rights without painful scrutiny of each bill of lading.

The lessons of the past were that, to achieve these objects, the Convention must have binding force and must regulate both domestic and international contracts. It must be binding

(1) because experience had shown that a voluntary system would not work in so controversial a matter;

(2) lest carriers of states with parallel domestic legislation be at a disadvantage vis-à-vis carriers of states without such legislation;

(3) to provide sufficient momentum for the abrogation of binding domestic rules in conflict with the Convention.

The Convention must apply to both domestic and international contracts

(1) to promote competitive equality between carriers;

(2) because the security of bills of lading was important in both domestic and international spheres. [Footnotes omitted.]

Australia adopted the Hague Rules in the Commonwealth Sea-Carriage of Goods Act 1924. The Act applies to carriage of goods under bills of lading *from* any Australian port to either an interstate or overseas destination. It does not apply to purely intrastate shipment which is covered by state legislation; eg Sea-Carriage of Goods Act 1921 (NSW) which is, like the previous Commonwealth Sea-Carriage of Goods Act 1904, on which it is based, more restricted in scope and protective of shippers rather than shipowners when compared to the Hague Rules. Although the Commonwealth Act does not apply to the importation of goods, where shipment originates in another country which has adopted the Hague Rules they will still apply. The rules can in any event be incorporated by express intention of the parties either in a bill of lading covering the import of goods or in a charterparty: eg, *R W Miller & Co Pty Ltd v Australian Oil Refining Pty Ltd* (1967) 117 CLR 288. A bill of lading issued in Australia which is covered by the rules must contain an express statement that it is to have effect subject to the rules: s 6. Any attempt to exclude the operation of the Act or the jurisdiction of Australian courts is void: s 9 and *Compagniedes Messageries Maritimes v Wilson* (1954) 94 CLR 577. The Hague Rules were modernised by a 1968 Brussels Protocol (which has not been adopted in Australia) and are known as the Hague-Visby Rules.

The interpretation of these rules has created a large body of case law and the uniform nature of the rules also makes the numerous decisions of English courts of great relevance to Australia. One of the major areas of dispute has been the reconciliation of the carrier's obligations under art III rr 1 and 2 with its immunity under art IV r 2.

Shipping Corp of India Ltd v Gamlen Chemical Co (A/Asia) Pty Ltd
High Court of Australia (1981) 55 ALJR 88

Mason and Wilson JJ: In June 1972 the respondent's goods were shipped aboard the appellant's ship under a clean bill of lading for carriage from Sydney to Indonesia. While crossing the Great Australian Bight the vessel experienced heavy weather. Upon its arrival at the Port of Fremantle on 9 July 1972, it was discovered that the goods had broken adrift from their rope lashings and sustained extensive damage.

The respondent sued the appellant in the Supreme Court of New South Wales claiming damages for negligence. The alleged negligence consisted of the failure to use due and proper care in the stowage of the goods. The appellant relied upon the exception contained in r 2(c) of art IV of the Hague Rules (the rules) contained in the Schedule to the Sea-Carriage of Goods Act 1924 (Cth), asserting that the loss or damage to the goods arose from "perils dangers and accidents of the sea, namely heavy weather". The appellant contended that the heavy weather experienced during the voyage constituted a peril of the sea within the terms of the paragraph and that therefore it was not liable for the damage regardless of any negligence by it in stowing the goods ...

In the result, his Honour held that the weather conditions did amount to a peril of the sea notwithstanding that they could have been foreseen and guarded against, and that that peril together with the inadequate stowage of the goods was a concurrent cause of the damage. He held that it was not necessary that the exception upon which the appellant relied should have been the sole cause of the damage, and he therefore dismissed the claim.

On appeal to the Court of Appeal of the Supreme Court, Samuels JA, with Moffitt P and Reynolds JA concurring, held that the rules have not altered the common law principle that an exception in a bill of lading as to perils of the sea is not available where negligence of the carrier is established. Reynolds JA summed up the conclusion of the court in the following words:

"Loss or damage does not arise or result from perils of the sea where negligence is a concurrent cause. Where negligence allows or facilitates the perils of the sea to inflict damage on cargo, then in all relevant respects the loss or damage arises or results from the negligence. The perils of the sea must be guarded against by the use of due care."

The appeal was allowed, and the appellant carrier now appeals by special leave to this court.

[Their Honours referred to rules of construction and the history of the Hague Rules and continued at 93:]

It is convenient to set out the relevant provisions of the Rules:

"*Article II*
Risks

Subject to the provisions of Article VI, under every contract of carriage of goods by sea, the carrier, in relation to the loading, handling, stowage, carriage, custody, care and discharge of such goods, shall be subject to the responsibilities and liabilities, and entitled to the rights and immunities hereinafter set forth.

"*Article III*
Responsibilities and Liabilities

1. The carrier shall be bound before and at the beginning of the voyage, to exercise due diligence to —
   (a) make the ship seaworthy;
   (b) properly man, equip and supply the ship; and
   (c) make the holds, refrigerating and cool chambers, and all other parts of the ship in which goods are carried, fit and safe for their reception, carriage and preservation.

2. Subject to the provisions of Article IV, the carrier shall properly and carefully load, handle, stow, carry, keep, care for and discharge the goods carried.

...

8. Any clause, covenant or agreement in a contract of carriage relieving the carrier of the ship from liability for loss or damage to or in connection with goods arising from negligence, fault or failure in the duties and obligations provided in this Article or lessening such liability otherwise than as provided in these rules, shall be null and void and of no effect.

A benefit of insurance or similar clause shall be deemed to be a clause relieving the carrier from liability.

"*Article IV*
Rights and Immunities

1. Neither the carrier nor the ship shall be liable for loss or damage arising or resulting from unseaworthiness unless caused by want of due diligence on the part of the carrier to make the ship seaworthy, and to secure that the ship is properly manned, equipped and supplied, and to make the holds, refrigerating and cool chambers and all other parts of the ship in which goods are carried fit and safe for their reception, carriage and preservation in accordance with the provisions of paragraph 1 of Article III.

Whenever loss or damage has resulted from unseaworthiness, the burden of proving the exercise of due diligence shall be on the carrier or other person claiming exemption under the section.

2. Neither the carrier nor the ship shall be responsible for loss or damage arising or resulting from—
   (a) act, neglect or default of the master, mariner, pilot or the servants of the carrier in the navigation or in the management of the ship;
   (b) fire, unless caused by the actual fault or privity of the carrier;
   (c) perils, dangers and accidents of the sea or other navigable waters;
   (d) act of God;
   (e) act of war;
   (f) act of public enemy;
   (g) arrest or restraint of princes, rulers or people, or seizure under legal process;
   (h) quarantine restrictions;
   (i) act or omission of the shipper or owner of the goods, his agent or representative;
   (j) strikes or lock-outs or stoppage or restraint of labour from whatever cause, whether partial or general;
   (k) riots and civil commotions;
   (l) saving or attempting to save life or property at sea;
   (m) wastage in bulk or weight or any other loss or damage arising from inherent defect, quality or vice of the goods;
   (n) insufficiency of packing;
   (o) insufficiency or inadequacy of marks;
   (p) latent defects not discoverable by due diligence;
   (q) any other cause arising without the actual fault or privity of the carrier, or without the fault or neglect of the agents or servants of the carrier, but the burden of proof shall be on the person claiming the benefit of this exception to show that neither the actual fault or privity of the carrier nor the fault or neglect of the agents or servants of the carrier contributed to the loss or damage.

. . .

4. Any deviation in saving or attempting to save life or property at sea, or any reasonable deviation shall not be deemed to be an infringement or breach of these rules or of the contract of carriage, and the carrier shall not be liable for any loss or damage resulting therefrom.

5. Neither the carrier nor the ship shall in any event be or become liable for any loss or damage to or in connection with goods in an amount exceeding One hundred pounds per package or unit, or the equivalent of that sum in other currency, unless the nature and value of such goods have been declared by the shipper before shipment and inserted in the bill of lading.

This declaration if embodied in the bill of lading shall be prima facie evidence, but shall not be binding or conclusive on the carrier.

By agreement between the carrier, master or agent of the carrier and the shipper another maximum amount than that mentioned in this paragraph may be fixed, provided that such maximum shall not be less than the figure above named.

Neither the carrier nor the ship shall be responsible in any event for loss or damage to or in connection with goods if the nature or value thereof has been knowingly misstated by the shipper in the bill of lading.

6. Goods of an inflammable, explosive or dangerous nature to the shipment whereof the carrier, master or agent of the carrier, has not consented, with knowledge of their nature and character, may at any time before discharge be landed at any place or destroyed or rendered

innocuous by the carrier without compensation, and the shipper of such goods shall be liable for all damages and expenses directly or indirectly arising out of or resulting from such shipment.

If any such goods shipped with such knowledge and consent shall become a danger to the ship or cargo, they may in like manner be landed at any place or destroyed or rendered innocuous by the carrier without liability on the part of the carrier except to general average, if any."

It is not necessary to have regard to art V beyond mentioning that it recognises that a carrier may surrender all or any of his rights and immunities or he may increase any of his responsibilities and liabilities that are contained under the rules. Likewise, art VI does not need to receive any special attention save to note that it allows for a limited contracting out of the obligations and immunities provided by the rules but only in the case of special situations other than "ordinary commercial shipments made in the ordinary course of trade".

Article II provides an important and relevant background to a consideration of arts III and IV in that it declares that the carrier in relation to the loading, handling, stowage, carriage, custody, care and discharge of goods pursuant to a contract of carriage of goods by sea "shall be subject to the responsibilities and liabilities, and entitled to the rights and immunities hereinafter set forth". The Article contemplates the dual operation, side by side, of responsibilities and liabilities on the one hand and rights and immunities on the other.

Coming to art III, the appellant places reliance on the fact that while r 2 opens with the words "Subject to the provisions of Article IV" there is no similar preface to r 1. The distinction may be significant. On the one hand, it furnishes an expectation that the obligation imposed by r 2 is to be qualified in some respects by the provisions of art IV. On the other hand, it also makes plain the intention that there is to be no qualification of the obligation imposed by r 1, whereby the carrier is "bound . . . to exercise due diligence" to prepare the ship in the manner described.

With regard to r 2 of art III, the obligation is not expressed in terms of "due diligence"; it is to "properly and carefully" perform a wide range of operations, namely, load, handle, stow, carry, keep, care for and discharge the goods. In *Albacora SRL v Westcott & Laurance Line Ltd* [1966] 2 Lloyd's Rep 53 at 63-4, Lord Pearson makes several observations to the following effect about this rule:

(1) there is a prima facie obligation under the rule which may be displaced or modified by some provision of art IV;

(2) the obligation is not to achieve the desired result, that is, the arrival of the goods in an undamaged condition at their destination. It is an obligation to carry out certain operations properly and carefully;

(3) the word "properly" adds something to "carefully", it "carefully" has a narrow meaning of merely taking care. The element of skill or sound system is required in addition to taking care; and

(4) Article IV contains many and various provisions, which may have different effects on the prima facie obligation arising under art III r 2 . . .

There is no doubt on the findings in this case that the appellant failed to properly and carefully stow the goods, and was therefore prima facie in breach of the obligation imposed, "subject to Article IV", by art III r 2.

The appellant argued that it is not responsible for the damage because it resulted from a peril of the sea: art IV r 2(c). But is this an accurate statement of the findings of the learned trial judge? Those findings were that the goods were not adequately stowed, that the ship encountered heavy weather which constituted a peril of the sea, that if the goods had been properly stowed the damage would not have occurred, and that the negligence of the carrier and the peril of the sea were concurrent causes of the damage. It seems to us that an accurate reflection of these findings requires one to treat the two concurrent causes of the loss as inseparable, and therefore joint. The loss would not have occurred but for the faulty stowage, but on the other hand, the faulty stowage did not cause the loss by itself. On this view, and treating the matter strictly as a matter of construction of the rule, it cannot be said that the damage resulted from a peril of the sea, and the appellant fails. The conclusion is strengthened by the consideration that on the findings of the trial judge there would have been no loss if it had not been for the negligence of the carrier.

But let us take a broader view, testing the proposition by reference to other paras of art IV r 2. It seems to us that the effect of the appellant's argument is that the rules reflect the intention that even though a carrier has occasioned damage to goods through his negligence in circumstances which prima facie constitute a breach of the obligation imposed by art III r 2, nevertheless he will be relieved of responsibility for that damage in every case except where the damage results from:

(i) fire caused by the actual fault or privity of the carrier (art IV r 2(b));
(ii) latent defects in the goods which were discoverable by due diligence (art IV r 2(p)); or
(iii) any cause other than those listed in art IV rr 1, 2(a) to (p) inclusive, which is occasioned by the actual fault or privity of the carrier, or the fault or neglect of the agents or servants of the carrier (r 2(q)).

With great respect, we think that such an extraordinary result has only to be stated to suggest that the argument is untenable. It would denude the obligation imposed by art III r 2 of much of its substance. There is a more persuasive answer ready to hand to explain why art IV r 2 does not expressly preserve liability for negligence in all cases. It is that paras (c) to (o) inclusive, with the exception of (l), are all matters which in themselves are beyond the control of the carrier or his servants. Any reference in that context to negligence is inappropriate, because they are events which of their nature occur independently of negligence on the part of the carrier. For example, one would not expect to see the rule relieve the carrier from responsibility for damage resulting from "act of God, unless caused by the fault or neglect of the carrier, his agents or servants". The remaining paras of r 2 carry their own explanation. Paragraph (a) has its origin in s 3 of the Harter Act, and has attracted a particular history: cf *Gosse Millard* [1929] AC 223 at 230, 236. Paragraph (b) relates to fire and reflects its own particular statutory history: see the Merchant Shipping Act 1894 (UK) s 502. Paragraph (l) deals with deviation to save life and property, and receives fuller treatment in art IV r 4. Paragraph (q) is of the greatest assistance in the task of construction, because in our opinion it expresses the fundamental scheme of the rules. That scheme is to impose certain responsibilities and liabilities on the carrier of goods by sea, from which he cannot contract out (cf art III r 8), but to give him immunity in respect of loss or damage caused otherwise than by negligence for which he is responsible, save in the special cases to which we have referred. To the extent to which art III r 2, by using the word "properly" imposes on the carrier a more onerous duty than an absence of negligence then clearly to that extent the immunities described in art IV r 2 operate to qualify the liability otherwise resting on the carrier; indeed, if this is not the case then as Temperley points out in his monograph, Carriage of Goods by Sea Act 1924, 3rd ed, 1932, p 48, para (q) is not an immunity at all, for it would do no more than shift the onus of proof on to the carrier. On the other hand, if such a line of reasoning seeks to extract a greater symmetry of purpose than the rules viewed in their entirety will admit, then the proper observation is simply that it must not be thought that the effect of the prefatory words to art III r 2 is to compel some impact on the scope and operation of the obligation imposed by that rule from every provision in art IV. Ample justification for the preface is to be found in the presence in art IV of r 2(a) and (b), and rr 4, 5 and 6. Each of these provisions adds a significant qualification to either the scope of the obligation or the consequences of a breach. There is then nothing surprising in the fact that those paras of art IV r 2 which do not depend on any conduct of the carrier, his agents or servants, have nothing to say to art III r 2. Other rules in art IV also provide the carrier with important immunities: the right to deviate in certain circumstances (r 4), the right to deal with dangerous goods (r 6), and a limitation on the quantum of damage for which he is liable (r 5).

It follows then, in our opinion, that the question whether the carrier is entitled to rely upon art IV r 2(c) to protect him from loss or damage will require to be answered by reference to all the circumstances of a particular case. While this would be so irrespective of the exception upon which the carrier relied, it is particularly so in the case of perils of the sea, a term which is apt to cover such a wide range of mishaps at sea. There is a difference between the Anglo-Australian conception of "perils of the sea" and the United States-Canadian conception. According to the latter, "perils of the sea" include losses to goods on board which are peculiar to the sea and "are of extraordinary nature or arise from irresistible force or overwhelming power, and which cannot be guarded against by the ordinary exertion of human skill and prudence": *The Guilia* (1914) 218 F 744, adopting *Story on Bailments*, 1856 ed, s 512(a). In the United Kingdom and Australia it is not necessary that the losses or the cause of the losses should be "extraordinary": *Carver, Carriage by Sea,* 12th ed, 1971, s 161; *Skandia Insurance*

Co Ltd v Skoljarev (1979) 53 ALJR 683 at 686-7. Consequently sea and weather conditions which may reasonably be foreseen and guarded against may constitute a peril of the sea.

What is important for present purposes is that Story's description of "perils of the sea" excludes losses which could be avoided by the carrier's skill and prudence. Despite the broader concept of "perils of the sea" which prevailed in the United Kingdom and Australia a similar result was achieved in cases in which the loss or damage to the goods brought about by the action of the sea would not have occurred but for negligence on the part of the carrier or those for whom he was responsible. It was held, looking beyond the proximate cause, that the effective cause of loss was the carrier's negligence and that accordingly he could not take advantage of the "perils of the sea" exception in the bill of lading: *The Xantho* (1887) 12 App Cas 503 at 510; *Hamilton, Fraser & Co v Pandorf & Co* (1887) 12 App Cas 518 at 525. The United States decisions turn on a narrower concept of "perils of the sea" whereas the English decisions turn rather on the issue of causation, looking more to the requirement that the exception is for loss or damage which results from or arises from "perils of the sea". But in each case the decisions give effect to the language of the bills of lading that constituted the contract of carriage ...

It remains for us to mention the reliance by the appellant on the decision of the House of Lords in *Albacora*. As we have already made clear, the essence of Mr Beaumont's argument is that the fact of negligence by the carrier is irrelevant in a case where the carrier can establish that a peril of the sea was a contributing or concurrent cause of the damage. In such a case the carrier is entitled to the full benefit of the immunity conferred by art IV r 2. Mr Beaumont found support for his submission in the following passage in the judgment of Lord Pearson in *Albacora* [1966] 2 Lloyd's Rep 53 at 64:

"There is no express provision, and in my opinion there is no implied provision in the Hague Rules that the shipowner is debarred as a matter of law from relying on an exception unless he proves absence of negligence on his part. But he does have to prove that the damage was caused by an excepted peril or excepted cause, and in order to do that he may in a particular case have to give evidence excluding causation by his negligence. It was proved in this case that the shipowner was not negligent."

With respect we think that the appellant misconceives the thrust of the observation of Lord Pearson. The key to the statement is to be found in the phrase "unless *he proves* absence of negligence on his part". His Lordship in our opinion is dealing with the question of onus of proof and taking up a position in opposition to the much debated statement by Wright J in *Gosse Millard*, which is described in one of the texts as "heresy": cf *Carver, Carriage by Sea* 12th ed, 1971, Vol 1 para 226A. The point was of no relevance in *Albacora* because, as his Lordship observes, it was proved in the case that the shipowner was not negligent; nor is it relevant in this case because it has been proved that the shipowner was negligent. We may say, in passing, that we agree with Samuels JA in the Court of Appeal when he points out that the correct sequence of pleading is set out in the judgment of Lord Esher in *The Glendarroch* [1894] P 226 at 231, 233. We are unable to draw any support from Lord Pearson's statement for the proposition advanced for the appellant.

For these reasons, the appellant, in our opinion, has failed to make out its case.

We would dismiss the appeal.

[**Aicken** and **Gibbs JJ** agreed with Mason and Wilson JJ. **Stephen J** substantially agreed with the joint judgment.]

Appeal dismissed.

Other typical cases on the relationship of aspects of art III rr 1 and 2 with art IV r 2 include *Chubu Asahi Cotton Spinning Co Ltd v The Ship "Tenos"* (1968) 12 FLR 291; 88 WN (Pt 1) (NSW) 395 and *Minnesota Mining & Manufacturing (Australia) Pty Ltd v The Ship "Novoaltaisk"* [1972] 2 NSWLR 476. Other provisions of the Hague Rules have also been considered by Australian courts in *Wilson v Darling Island Stevedoring and Lighterage Co Ltd*, p 179, *infra*, *Automatic Tube Co Pty Ltd v Adelaide Steamship (Operations) Ltd* (1966) 9 FLR 130 (liability of carrier limited to actions brought within one year of delivery: art III r 6 and meaning of delivery); *Frank Hammond Pty Ltd v Huddart Parker Ltd* [1956] VLR 496 (meaning of knowing misstatement of contents under art IV r 5).

As previously noted, charterparties and bills of lading are generally contracts of adhesion containing exclusion clauses favouring the shipowner, and sometimes the charterer: eg, *Suisse Atlantique* case, p 169, *supra*. It was in the context of such cases regarding deviation from the usual and customary route that the doctrine of fundamental breach developed. A person seeking to obtain the benefit of a contract or to protect himself from liability by reliance upon an exclusion clause contained in it usually must establish that he was a party to the contract.

QUESTIONS OF PRIVITY

A bill of lading will normally be issued to the consignor of goods (eg, Carb). As it has been held to be a transferable document, Carb can readily transfer it to the buyer Mitzi by indorsement and delivery, provided Trans Shipping has drawn it in a form indicating that intention, eg, requiring delivery "to Carb or order," "to Carb or assigns," or "to bearer": *Lickbarrow v Mason* (1794) 5 TR 683; 101 ER 380. Any problem of privity for Mitzi as consignee or buyer is removed by statutory provisions conferring on the consignee or indorsee the same rights as the consignor Carb had. For example, Usury, Bills of Lading, and Written Memoranda Act 1902 (NSW) s 5 provides:

5   Every consignee of goods named in a bill of lading, and every indorsee of a bill of lading to whom the property therein mentioned shall pass upon or by reason of such consignment or indorsement, shall have transferred to and vested in him all rights of suit and be subject to the same liabilities in respect of such goods, as if the contract contained in the bill of lading had been made with himself.

A *transferable* bill is not a fully *negotiable* instrument comparable to a bill of exchange (see Chapter 10) since Mitzi as indorsee takes subject to equities and any defects in Carb's previous title. However, in addition to the exceptions to the *nemo dat* rule available to Mitzi as the buyer of goods (eg, NSW SGA s 28(1) and (2), Factors (Mercantile Agents) Act 1923 s 5), as assignee of a bill of lading Mitzi receives a further degree of protection from SGA s 49 and Usury, Bills of Lading, and Written Memoranda Act 1902 (NSW) s 7:

7   Every bill of lading in the hands of a consignee or indorsee for valuable consideration representing goods to have been shipped on board a vessel shall be conclusive evidence of such shipment as against the master or other person signing the same, notwithstanding that such goods or some part thereof may not have been so shipped, unless such holder of the bill of lading has had actual notice, at the time of receiving the same, that the goods had not been in fact laden on board.

The position is more complicated where a third party, typically a stevedoring company, not being a party to the bill of lading, seeks to use its provisions, which often incorporate the Hague Rules, as a shield against the consignee's claim for negligent handling of the cargo.

Wilson v Darling Island Stevedoring and Lighterage Co Ltd
High Court of Australia (1955) 95 CLR 43

[The facts appear from the following judgment.]

Fullagar J (at 65): The plaintiff is a merchant carrying on business in Sydney. The defendant is a company incorporated in New South Wales and carrying on in the port of Sydney and elsewhere the business of stevedoring. On 20 November 1953 a case of *tulle soie* and *tulle rayonne* was shipped by F J Hawkes & Co Ltd of London by the motor vessel Tremayne to be carried from Marseilles to Sydney under a bill of lading signed on behalf of the master of the ship. The goods were consigned "to order", and at some stage the bill of lading was indorsed in blank and presumably delivered to the plaintiff Wilson. The goods arrived in the port of Sydney on board the vessel in January 1954. Paragraphs 5, 6, 7 and 8 of the case stated should be set out in full. They are as follows: "5. The defendant company was engaged by Messrs

Macdonald Hamilton & Co, agents of the owners of the said vessel, to act as stevedore for the said ship, and to discharge, sort, stack and store all of its cargo. 6. In pursuance of such engagement the defendant discharged the said goods from the said vessel on or about the 20 January 1954, and proceeded to sort, stack and store the said goods in the shed at No 9 berth, Woolloomooloo Bay in the port of Sydney. 7. It was at all material times the practice in the port of Sydney for the stevedores engaged by the ship to handle and store cargo pending the removal of the goods of the consignee, and this practice was at all material times known to the parties. 8. On or about 21 January 1954, and whilst acting in pursuance of the said engagement and whilst continuing to sort stack and store the said goods, and before delivery of the said goods to the plaintiff, a mobile crane owned and negligently operated by the defendant company its servants and agents struck and fractured the main pipe of the overhead water sprinkler system in such shed." The result of this exploit was that the plaintiff's goods were soaked with water and rendered worthless. The amount of the plaintiff's loss is agreed at £394 19s 4d.

On the facts above stated it is clear that the defendant is prima facie liable in damages to the plaintiff. The defendant, however, relies on certain provisions indorsed on the bill of lading, under which the goods were shipped, and which is annexed to the case stated. Several of these provisions were referred to in argument, but in the view which I take, it is necessary only to set out one clause. That clause is as follows: "Period of responsibility. The carrier has no responsibility whatsoever for the goods prior to the loading on and subsequent to the discharge from the vessel. Goods in the custody of the carrier or his agents or servants before loading and after discharge whether being forwarded to or from the vessel or whether awaiting shipment, landed, or stored, or put into hulk or craft belonging to the carrier or not, or pending transhipment at any stage of the whole transport, are in such custody at the sole risk of the owners of the goods and the carrier shall not be liable for loss or damage arising or resulting from any cause whatsoever."

The clause which I have quoted raises, or may raise, questions of construction, but it is convenient to defer these until consideration has been given to the legal basis of the argument for the defendant company and to certain decisions on which it relies. The argument is that this clause in the bill of lading exempts the defendant company from liability for the damage caused to the plaintiff's goods by the negligence of its servants. The obvious answer to that argument is that the defendant is not a party to the contract evidenced by the bill of lading, that it can neither sue nor be sued on that contract, and that nothing in a contract between two other persons can relieve it from the consequences of a tortious act committed by it against the plaintiff. The general principle has been applied in many cases, of which *Tweddle v Atkinson* (1861) 1 B & S 393; 121 ER 762; *Cavalier v Pope* [1906] AC 428 and *Dunlop Pneumatic Tyre Co Ltd v Selfridge & Co Ltd* [1915] AC 847 are well-known examples.

[His Honour then considered cases in which the promisee was held to have contracted as trustee for a third party and continued at 68:] The defendant company in the present case does not rely upon any trust. It says that there is a rule of the common law which entitles it to rely on the exceptions from liability contained in the bill of lading. This rule, it says, was laid down by the House of Lords in *Elder, Dempster & Co Ltd v Paterson, Zochonis & Co Ltd* [1923] 1 KB 420; [1924] AC 522. In this case Elder, Dempster & Co had chartered a ship named the *Grelwen* on time charter from the owners. The plaintiff company shipped a number of casks of palm oil by this ship from West African ports to Hull. The casks were crushed by other cargo negligently laid over them, and a large part of the oil escaped. The bill of lading contained a clause which provided that "the shipowners, hereinafter called the company, shall not be liable for" inter alia "any loss or damage arising from stowage". The plaintiff company sued both the charterers and the owners. The major question in the case was whether the damage should be attributed to unseaworthiness (which was outside the exemption clause) or to bad stowage (which was within that clause). It was ultimately decided in the House of Lords that it was due to bad stowage. It was then held that the exemption clause protected both the charterers and the owners. The exemption clause in terms exempted "the shipowners, hereinafter called the company", and there is a footnote in the report of the case in the Court of Appeal which says: "It was not disputed that this term included the defendants Elder Dempster & Co the time charterers of the *Grelwen*" [1923] 1 KB at 422. From this footnote and from the whole treatment of the case both in the Court of Appeal and in the House of Lords it seems plain that the actual contract of carriage was treated as having been made between the shippers and the charterers, but that the terms on which the shipowners handled the goods were the terms set out in the bill of lading, so that the exemption clause therein protected them, as well as the charterers, against liability for negligent stowage of cargo.

A conceivable ground of the decision in the *Elders Dempster* case is that the master of the ship, although for many purposes the servant of the owners, took possession of the goods not on behalf of the owners but on behalf of the charterers. On this view the owners would not be responsible for the negligent stowing, and they would have no need to rely on the exemption clause in the bill of lading. Lord Sumner (with whose judgment Lord Dunedin and Lord Carson agreed) mentioned this view as a possible view, but observed that the charterparty recognised the shipowners as having a possessory lien for hire, and said that he preferred to base his decision on the ground that: "... in the circumstances of this case the obligations to be inferred from the reception of the cargo for carriage to the United Kingdom amount to a bailment upon terms, which include the exceptions and limitations of liability stipulated in the known and contemplated form of bill of lading": [1924] AC at 564. It is not, I think, profitable to pursue the question whether the view of Lord Cave ([1924] AC at 534) or the view of Lord Finlay ([1924] AC at 548) differed in substance from that of Lord Sumner. Lord Carson agreed both with Lord Cave and with Lord Sumner, but the important thing, to my mind, is that he agreed with Lord Sumner. The passage which I have quoted from Lord Sumner's judgment must, in my opinion, be regarded as stating the *ratio decidendi* of the *Elder Dempster* case.

Before proceeding further I would make two general observations. In the first place, Lord Sumner's view, as expressed, clearly does not go beyond the case of the owner of a chartered ship. On the other hand, the view expressed by Scrutton LJ, in the Court of Appeal ([1923] 1 KB at 441) although it also does not in terms go beyond a case of owner and charterer of a ship, was (without the concurrence of Bankes LJ) in *Mersey Shipping & Transport Co v Rea Ltd* (1925) 21 Lloyd LR 375 at 378 expanded into a wide general rule to the effect that, if A agrees to do work for B on condition that he is not to be liable for negligence, and C is engaged by A (whether as a servant of A or as an independent contractor with A) to do the work, C will not be liable to B in tort if his own personal negligence causes damage to B. There is, in my opinion, no foundation whatever for suggesting that there is any such general rule of law. Owen J in *Gilbert, Stokes & Kerr Pty Ltd v Dalgety & Co Ltd* (1948) 48 SR (NSW) 435; 65 WN (NSW) 196 said: "I would have thought that no such general principle was to be found in the law of agency, and would have agreed entirely with the statement to that effect by Jordan CJ in *Williams v Commissioner for Main Roads* (1940) 40 SR (NSW) 472 at 478; 57 WN (NSW) 169": (1948) 48 SR (NSW) at 443; 65 WN (NSW) at 198. I also would agree with that statement. According to Denning LJ in *Adler v Dickson* [1955] 1 QB 158 at 184-5 a distinction is to be drawn, and, if A stipulates with B that he will not be liable for the negligence of his servants or agents, his servants and agents are not protected, but, if A stipulates with B that neither he nor his servants or agents are to be liable for negligence, his servants and agents will be protected. I should have thought it clear that, unless from special circumstances (such as existed in *Hall's* case (1875) LR 10 QB 437) a contract including the exempting clause could be inferred between B and a particular servant or agent of A, the servants and agents of A would not be protected in either case.

I cannot leave this subject without observing that the word "agent" appears to me to be often misused in this connection, and one cannot help feeling that this misuse is largely responsible for at least one of the views which have been entertained of the *Elder Dempster* case [1924] AC 522. It seems to me quite wrong to say that a stevedoring company engaged by a shipowner to load or unload a ship is an "agent" of the shipowner, just as it would be wrong to say that a builder is an "agent" of a building owner. If A engages B to lay out a garden for him, and B engages C to do the actual work, C is not in any intelligible legal sense B's agent. B is an independent contractor, and C is either A's servant or an independent contractor with A. Agency in the legal sense simply does not come into the matter.

The second observation I would make is this. What has been supposed to be a principle involved in the *Elder Dempster* case (although there is a conspicuous lack of unanimity as to what that principle really is) has, as will be seen, been extended so as to give to a stevedore exemption from liability for negligence by virtue of a provision in a bill of lading to which the stevedore is not a party, and which is really no concern whatever of the stevedore. This appears to me to be a "development" of the common law which is altogether out of character, and which is exactly the opposite of what one would have expected and felt to be justified. It is all the more remarkable in view of the fact that the modern tendency has been to expand the field of liability in tort. The common law has, I think, from quite early times — consistently with its general policy of freedom of contract — allowed the validity of provisions in a contract which limit or exclude liability for negligence. But it has always frowned upon such provisions and insisted on construing them strictly.

[His Honour then considered several English cases as well as *Gilbert, Stokes & Kerr Pty Ltd v Dalgety & Co Ltd* (1948) 48 SR (NSW) 435; 65 WN (NSW) 196 and continued at 73:]

The *Gilbert Stokes* case was approved and applied by the Full Court of New South Wales in *Waters Trading Co Ltd v Dalgety & Co Ltd* (1951) 52 SR (NSW) 4; 69 WN (NSW) 23. The facts in that case are not distinguishable from those in the present case, and the decision is, as I have said directly challenged. It purports to apply the *Elder Dempster* case, but the difficulty felt about formulating the true rule is indicated by such expressions as that used by Herron J: "Whatever may be the precise legal ground on which the immunity of the agent can be supported . . .": (1951) 52 SR (NSW) at 15; 69 WN (NSW) 23. When no precise legal ground for supporting an immunity can be found, there must be strong reason for suspecting that the immunity cannot be supported at all . . .

I have now to consider for myself the effect of the *Elder Dempster* case. [His Honour then identified and rejected three main interpretations of the *Elder Dempster* case, namely, a general principle of the law of agency; a general rule of the law of bailment; or a new general principle of the law of contract to the effect that a third party could have the benefit of an exemption clause inserted in a contract for his benefit. He continued at 75:]

I find myself quite unable to accept any of the variously expressed generalisations which have been made about the *Elder Dempster* case. None of them appears to me to have any sound legal basis and I suspect that they would have filled Lord Sumner with amazement. My own views are generally in accord with those expressed by Jenkins LJ in *Adler v Dickson* [1955] 1 QB at 186 *et seq*, and I read the shorter judgment of Morris LJ in the same case as expressing substantially the same views.

After stating the facts to be assumed for the purposes of the case Jenkins LJ proceeded to deal with the general position at law. He said: "If the contract with the company had contained no exempting provisions, the plaintiff would, as I understand the law, have had separate and distinct rights of action (a) against the company for breach of contract or, alternatively, in tort, on the principle of '*respondeat superior*', and (b) against the defendants as the persons actually guilty of the tortious acts or omissions which caused the damage. The plaintiff's right of action against the company is clearly taken away by the exempting provisions of the contract, but I fail to see how that can have the effect of depriving her also of her separate and distinct right of action against the defendants as the actual tortfeasors. There is certainly no express provision purporting so to deprive her, and in the absence of any express provision to that effect I see no justification for implying one. The exempting provisions in terms apply only to the liability of the company, without any reference to the liability of servants of the company for the consequences of their own tortious acts. *Even if these provisions had contained* words purporting to exclude the liability of the company's servants, *non constat* that the company's servants could successfully rely on that exclusion in proceedings brought against them by some party injured by their tortious conduct, for the company's servants are not parties to the contract": [1955] 1 QB at 186.

A little later his Lordship said: "A good deal was said in the course of the argument before us about the absurdity of a stipulation relieving an employer of his liability for the negligence of his servant while leaving untouched the servant's liability for that same negligence. I do not follow this . . . To my mind, it is far more absurd to impute to a passenger on a ship, who has contracted with a shipowner for a given voyage in terms which exempt the shipowner from liability for his servant's negligence, an intention thereby to deprive himself of all right to redress against the servants of the shipowner for any and every negligent act or omission which may be committed by such servants in the course of their duties, however gross the negligence and however grave the resulting damage to the passenger may be": [1955] 1 QB at 186, 187.

Jenkins LJ then referred to the *Elder Dempster* case [1924] AC 522. He said: It "is relied on for the defendants as establishing the general proposition that where A contracts to render services to B on terms that A is not to be liable to B for damage caused by the negligence of A's servants or agents, and in the course of the performance of the contract A's servant or agent is guilty of negligence causing damage to B, A's servant or agent is entitled to the same immunity from suit as is accorded to A, his master or principal, by the exempting condition, and this notwithstanding that the negligence of the servant or agent is such as would clearly have entitled B to maintain an action against him in tort apart from the exempting condition. It would seem that the only limit to be placed on this sweeping proposition is that the negligence of the servant or agent must consist in something done or omitted by him in the course of the performance of the contract, a limit the precise scope of which is by no means easy of definition": [1955] 1 QB at 189, 190.

Jenkins LJ then examined in detail what was said in the *Elder Dempster* case and concluded: "The *Elder Dempster* case can well be explained by reference to its own facts without ascribing to their Lordships any intention to lay down any such general principle as the defendants here contend for, nor do I think that their Lordships' language, carefully directed as it was to the particular facts of the case then before the House, can fairly be construed as doing so": [1955] 1 QB at 195. Finally his Lordship referred to *Mersey Shipping & Transport Co v Rea Ltd* (1925) 21 Lloyd LR at 375, in which divergent views as to the effect of the *Elder Dempster* case were expressed by Bankes LJ and Scrutton LJ. Bankes LJ said: "But the court there held that, under the circumstances of the vessel being chartered to form one of the owners' regular line, the proper inference to draw was that the goods were shipped under conditions which would cover both charterer and shipowner": (1925) 21 Lloyd LR at 377. Scrutton LJ deduced a far wider proposition from the case. Jenkins LJ said: "I prefer the view of Bankes LJ to that of Scrutton LJ": [1955] 1 QB at 195. I respectfully agree.

I have quoted at some length from the judgment of Jenkins LJ in *Adler v Dickson* [1955] 1 QB 158, because I respectfully and entirely agree with the views expressed by his Lordship. I do not think that anybody has yet succeeded in satisfactorily formulating any new and far-reaching principle as being involved in the *Elder Dempster* case and the simplest explanation of this fact is that there is no such principle involved. As Jenkins LJ said, it can well be explained by reference to its own facts: [1955] 1 QB at 195. It turned, in my opinion, on the very special and peculiar relationships which are created when goods are consigned to be carried on a chartered ship. Those relationships differ widely, and give rise to questions of great variety. [His Honour then referred to Carver, *The Law of Carriage of Goods by Sea*, 9th ed, 1952, pp 285, 286 and continued at 78:]

The present case is not a case of a chartered ship, and it is not a case in which the owner of cargo shipped seeks to make the shipowner liable in tort. The *Elder Dempster* case appears to me to have nothing whatever to do with it. There is no basis for any such inference as that on which the *Elder Dempster* case rests. The stevedore is a complete stranger to the contract of carriage, and it is no concern of his whether there is a bill of lading or not, or, if there is, what are its terms. He is engaged by the shipowner and by nobody else, and the terms on which he handles the goods are to be found in his contract with the shipowner and nowhere else. The shipowner has no authority whatever to bind the shipper or consignee of cargo by contract with the stevedore, and there is, in my opinion, no principle of law—deducible from the *Elder Dempster* case or from any other case—which compels the inference of any contract between the shipper or consignee and the stevedore. If the stevedore negligently soaks cargo with water and ruins it, I can find neither rule of law nor contract to save him from the normal consequences of his tort. The *Gilbert Stokes* case (1948) 48 SR (NSW) 435; 65 WN (NSW) 196 and the *Waters Trading Co* case (1951) 52 SR (NSW) 4; 69 WN (NSW) 23 were, in my opinion, wrongly decided, and I think that they should be overruled.

In the view which I take, nothing turns on the construction of the particular bill of lading in this case, and on that matter I will say only two things. The first is that it may well be arguable (the cases are numerous and difficult to reconcile) that the material clause in the bill of lading ought not to be regarded as exempting from liability for negligence. The second is that, if I thought (as I do not) that the distinction drawn by Denning LJ in *Adler v Dickson* [1955] 1 QB 158 at 184-5 was sound, I should have held that, as a matter of construction, the shipowner only was protected by the material clause in the bill of lading.

In my opinion, the appeal should be allowed, and the judgment below set aside. The questions in the case stated should be answered: (1) No (2) It is unnecessary to answer this question. In accordance with the agreement of the parties, there should be judgment for the plaintiff for £394 19s 4d.

Dixon CJ: I have had the advantage of reading the judgment of Fullagar J and entirely agree in it.

[**Kitto J** delivered a judgment substantially agreeing with Fullagar J.

Williams and **Taylor JJ** (dissenting) held that the respondent stevedoring company was entitled to rely on the limitation provisions contained in the bill of lading since it was carrying out its duties by way of performance of that contract.]

Appeal allowed.

See also *Herrick v Leonard and Dingley Ltd Charter Travel Co Ltd and Anor* [1975] 2 NZLR 566.

Port Jackson Stevedoring Pty Ltd v Salmond & Spraggon (Australia) Pty Ltd "The New York Star"
Privy Council [1980] 3 All ER 257.

[Lord Wilberforce delivered the judgment of the Board which consisted of Lord Diplock, Lord Fraser of Tullybelton, Lord Scarman and Lord Roskill.]

Lord Wilberforce: This is an appeal, by special leave, from a judgment of the High Court of Australia dated 3 April 1978 which, by a majority, dismissed an appeal from the Court of Appeal of the Supreme Court of New South Wales. That court had allowed an appeal from a decision of Sheppard J sitting in commercial causes by which he dismissed the action.

The action was brought by the respondent ("the consignee") in respect of a consignment of razor blades in 37 cartons, shipped from Canada to Australia on the *New York Star*, a ship of the Blue Star Line. The relevant bill of lading dated 27 March 1970 was issued in Montreal, Quebec; the port of loading was St John, New Brunswick; and the port of discharge was Sydney. The shipper named in the bill of lading was Schick Safety Razor Co Division of Eversharp of Canada Ltd; the respondent was named as consignee. The bill of lading was issued to the consignor and was transmitted to and accepted by the consignee.

The appellant ("the stevedore") carried on business as stevedore in the port of Sydney; 49 per cent of its capital was owned by Blue Star Line Australia Ltd and it commonly acted as stevedore in Sydney for the Blue Star Line.

The *New York Star* arrived at Sydney on 10 May 1970. On her arrival (and there was evidence that this was in accordance with the normal practice in the port) the packages of razor blades were discharged from the ship and placed by the stevedore in part of a shed (called "the dead house") on the wharf which was under its control. Later the goods were stolen from the wharf, having been delivered by servants of the stevedore to persons who had no right to receive them, so that when the consignee presented the bill of lading they were unavailable. The consignee brought this action against the stevedore and against the ship's agent, Joint Cargo Services Pty Ltd, alleging negligence in failing to take proper care of the goods, delivery of the goods to an unauthorised person and non-delivery to the consignee. The action against the ship's agent failed at first instance and has not been the subject of appeal. The trial judge, however, found that the stevedore had been negligent in the care of the goods that there had been a misdelivery; these findings have not been disputed.

The bill of lading contained, in cl 2, a Himalaya clause (see *Adler v Dickson* [1954] 3 All ER 397; [1955] 1 QB 158) extending the benefit of defences and immunities conferred by the bill of lading on the carrier to independent contractors employed by the carrier, and also, in cl 17, a time bar (similar to that contained in the Hague Rules) barring any action if not brought within one year after the delivery of the goods or the date when the goods should have been delivered; this action was not so brought. These provisions were in substance identical with those considered by this Board in *New Zealand Shipping Co Ltd v Satterthwaite & Co Ltd* [1974] 1 All ER 1015; [1975] AC 154, an appeal from the Court of Appeal in New Zealand. The stevedore relied on these provisions as affording a defence to this action.

It is now necessary to state in detail the issues which were contested, and the decisions which were given in the three courts in Australia.

Before Sheppard J it was contended by the consignee (i) that there had been a fundamental breach by the stevedore of its obligations as bailee of the goods (the "fundamental breach" point), (ii) that one of the necessary conditions for applying the Himalaya clause had not been satisfied, in that it had not been shown that the carrier had authority to act on the stevedore's behalf in accepting the bill of lading (the "agency" point), (iii) that the bill of lading ceased to have any operation after the goods passed over the ship's rail (the "capacity" point). Sheppard J rejected all these contentions, though he found that the necessary agency was established only by ratification. He gave judgment for the stevedore.

In the Court of Appeal the same three contentions were put forward, and were rejected by the court. The court found that the necessary agency was directly established by the evidence, so that reliance on ratification was not necessary. In addition, however, the consignee was given leave to take a fresh point, namely (iv) that there was no proof of consideration moving from the stevedore so as to entitle it to the benefit of defences and immunity clauses in the bill of lading (the "consideration" point). The Court of Appeal accepted that contention, allowed the appeal and gave judgment for the consignee for $14,684.98 damages.

In the High Court of Australia the "agency" point and the "consideration" point were again argued, but rejected by the majority of the court (Barwick CJ, Mason and Jacobs JJ). There was also argument on the "fundamental breach" point, but this was not dealt with in the judgments. As to the "capacity" point, senior counsel for the consignee expressly disclaimed reliance on it (not surprisingly since Glass JA in the Court of Appeal had described it as "without substance") and argument on it was not heard. However, the majority of the court (Barwick CJ dissenting) decided the appeal in favour of the consignee on this point.

Finally, it should be mentioned that the Board's decision in *Satterthwaite's* case was followed without question by the trial judge and by the Court of Appeal. Their Lordships understand that there was no argument in the High Court on the correctness of this decision. However two members of the majority (Stephen and Murphy JJ) expressed disagreement with it.

It was in this situation that their Lordships decided, exceptionally, to grant special leave to appeal to Her Majesty in Council.

It will be seen from the foregoing that the point which calls for decision by their Lordships is the "capacity" point. This was fully argued by both sides to the appeal. Before dealing with it, their Lordships must briefly state their position on the other points, on which argument was addressed by the consignee.

First, as to the Board's decision in *Satterthwaite's* case. This was a decision, in principle, that the Himalaya clause is capable of conferring on a third person falling within the description "servant or agent of the Carrier (including every independent contractor from time to time employed by the Carrier)" defences and immunities conferred by the bill of lading on the carrier as if such persons were parties to the contract contained in or evidenced by the bill of lading. But the decision was not merely a decision on this principle, for it was made clear that in fact stevedores employed by the carrier may come within it, and moreover that they normally and typically will do so. It may indeed be said that the significance of *Satterthwaite's* case lay not so much in the establishment of any new legal principle as in the finding that, in the normal situation involving the employment of stevedores by carriers, accepted principles enable and require the stevedore to enjoy the benefit of contractual provisions in the bill of lading. In the words of Mason and Jacobs JJ in the High Court:

"When the circumstances described by Lord Reid [sc in *Scruttons Ltd v Midland Silicones Ltd* [1962] 1 All ER 1 at 10; [1962] AC 446 at 474] exist, the stevedore will on the generally accepted principles of the law of contract be entitled to his personal contractual immunity. The importance of [*Satterthwaite's* case] is the manner in which on the bare facts of the case their Lordships were able to discern a contract between the shipper and the stevedore, and, we would add, to do so in a manner which limited the approach to those commercial contexts in which immunity of the stevedore was clearly intended in form and almost certainly known by both the shipper and the stevedore to be intended."

Although, in each case, there will be room for evidence as to the precise relationship of carrier and stevedore and as to the practice at the relevant port, the decision does not support, and their Lordships would not encourage, a search for fine distinctions which would diminish the general applicability, in the light of established commercial practice, of the principle. As regards its applicability in Australia, their Lordships are content to leave the matter as it was left by the Australian courts, including the High Court. They are the more satisfied to do so in view of the reasoned analysis of the legal principles involved which appears in the judgment of Barwick CJ. Their Lordships find, as Barwick CJ himself declares, this to be in substantial agreement with and indeed to constitute a powerful reinforcement of one of the two possible bases put forward in the Board's judgment.

The applicability of the decision was accepted in their joint judgment by Mason and Jacobs JJ although they reached a decision adverse to the stevedore on the "capacity" point.

Second, as to the factual ingredients needed to confer on the stevedore the benefit of the contract. From what has already been said it follows that this issue requires no prolonged discussion. Not only is the factual situation in the present case in all respects typical of that which the Board, in *Satterthwaite's* case, thought sufficient to confer that benefit, but each relevant ingredient has, in fact, been found to exist. Agency has been found, as a fact, by all three courts, with only the qualification as regards the judgment of Sheppard J already mentioned. The provision of consideration by the stevedore was held to follow from this Board's decision in *Satterthwaite's* case and in addition was independently justified through Barwick CJ's analysis.

Third, as to "fundamental breach". The proposition that exemption clauses may be held inapplicable to certain breaches of contract as a matter of construction of the contract, as held by the House of Lords in *Suisse Atlantique Société d' Armement Maritime SA v NV Rotterdamsche Kolen Centrale* [1966] 2 All ER 61; [1967] 1 AC 361 and *Photo Production Ltd v Securicor Transport Ltd* [1980] 1 All ER 556; [1980] 2 WLR 283, and indorsed in Australia by Windeyer J in *Thomas National Transport (Melbourne) Pty Ltd v May & Baker (Australia) Pty Ltd* (1966) 115 CLR 353 at 376, was not disputed. But counsel for the consignee put forward a special, and ingenious, argument that, because of the fundamental nature of the breach, the stevedore had deprived itself of the benefit of cl 17 of the bill of lading, the time bar clause. A breach of a repudiatory character, which he contended that the breach in question was, entitles the innocent party, unless he waives the breach, to claim to be released from further performance of his obligations under the contract. So far their Lordships of course agree. One of these obligations, counsel proceeded to argue, was to bring any action on the breach within a period of one year, and the innocent party was released from this obligation. An alternative way of putting it was that the bringing of suit within one year was a condition with which the innocent party was obliged to comply; the repudiatory breach discharged this condition. A further point made was that cl 17 applied at most to actions for breach of contract; the stevedore's negligence as bailee, however, gave rise to an action in tort which was not governed by the time bar.

Their Lordships' opinion on these arguments is clear. However adroitly presented, they are unsound, and indeed unreal. Clause 17 is drafted in general and all-embracing terms:

"In any event the Carrier and the ship shall be discharged from all liability in respect of loss or damage unless suit is brought within one year after the delivery of the goods or the date when the goods should have been delivered. Suit shall not be deemed brought until jurisdiction shall have been obtained over the Carrier and/or the ship by service of process or by an agreement to appear."

The reference to delivery of the goods shows clearly that the clause is directed towards the carrier's obligations as bailee of the goods. It cannot be supposed that it admits of a distinction between obligations in contract and liability in tort; "all liability" means what it says.

Moreover it is quite unreal to equate this clause with those provisions in the contract which relate to performance. It is a clause which comes into operation when contractual performance has become impossible, or has been given up; then, it regulates the manner in which liability for breach of contract is to be established. In this respect their Lordships found it relevantly indistinguishable from an arbitration clause, or a forum clause, which, on clear authority, survive a repudiatory breach: see *Heyman v Darwins Ltd* [1942] 1 All ER 337; [1942] AC 356; *Photo Production Ltd v Securicor Transport Ltd* [1980] 1 All ER 556 at 567; [1980] 2 WLR 283 at 295. Counsel for the consignee appealed for support to some observations by Lord Diplock in *Photo Production Ltd v Securicor Transport Ltd* All ER at 566-7; WLR at 294-5, where reference is made to putting an end "to all primary obligations ... remaining unperformed". But these words were never intended to cover such "obligations", to use Lord Diplock's word, as arise when primary obligations have been put an end to. There then arise, on his Lordship's analysis, secondary obligations which include an obligation to pay monetary compensation. Whether these have been modified by agreement is a matter of construction of the contract. The analysis, indeed, so far from supporting the consignee's argument, is directly opposed to it. Their Lordships are of opinion that, on construction and analysis, cl 17 plainly operates to exclude the consignee's claim.

Their Lordships now deal with the "capacity" argument. This rather inapposite word has been used, for convenience, in order to indicate the general nature of the submission. More fully, this was that, at the time when the loss occurred, the goods had been discharged and were no longer in the custody of the carrier. Consequently, the stevedore was acting not as an independent contractor employed by the carrier to perform the carrier's obligations under the bill of lading, but as a bailee. His liability, in that capacity, was independent of and not governed by any of the clauses of the contract. This point enables a distinction to be made with *Satterthwaite's* case, for there, since the goods were damaged in the course of discharge, the capacity of the stevedore as a person acting on behalf of the carrier was not contested.

Their Lordships can at this point dispose of one question of fact. It appears to have been the view both of Stephen J and of Mason and Jacobs JJ in the High Court that the stevedore was remunerated for his services in stacking and storing the goods on the wharf by the consignee; this, if correct, might be an argument for finding that it was not, in respect of these matters, acting in the course of employment by the carrier. In fact, however, the evidence, including the actual account, showed that these charges were paid by the ship's agent on behalf of the carrier, thus, if anything, giving rise to an inference the other way. Their Lordships put this matter aside and proceed to deal with the point on the construction of the relevant provisions of the bill of lading.

On its face, the document stated that delivery would be effected "by the Carrier or his Agents" in exchange for the bill of lading, and the preamble provided that the goods were: "to be transported subject to all the terms of this bill of lading ... to the port of discharge ... and there, to be delivered or transhipped on payment of the charges thereon ..." and further — "It is agreed that the custody and carriage of the goods are subject to the following terms on the face and back hereof which shall govern the relations, whatsoever they may be, between the shipper, consignee, and the Carrier, Master and ship in every contingency, wheresoever and whatsoever occurring ..."

Clause 5 was as follows: "The Carrier's responsibility in respect of the goods as a carrier shall not attach until the goods are actually loaded for transportation upon the ship and shall terminate without notice as soon as the goods leave the ship's tackle at the Port of Discharge from Ship or other place where the Carrier is authorised to make delivery or end its responsibility. Any responsibility of the Carrier in respect of the goods attaching prior to such loading or continuing after leaving the ship's tackle as aforesaid, shall not exceed that of an ordinary bailee, and, in particular, the Carrier shall not be liable for loss or damage to the goods due to — flood: fire, as provided elsewhere in this bill of lading: falling or collapse of wharf, pier or warehouse: robbery, theft or pilferage: strikes, lockouts or stoppage or restraint of labor from whatever cause, whether partial or general: any of the risks or causes mentioned in paragraphs (a), (e) to (l) inclusive and (k) to (p) inclusive, of sub-div 2 of s 4 of the Carriage of Goods by Sea Act of the United States; or any risks or causes whatsoever, not included in the foregoing, and whether like or unlike those hereinabove mentioned, where the loss or damage is not due to the fault or neglect of the Carrier. The Carrier shall not be liable in any capacity whatsoever for any non-delivery or mis-delivery, or loss of or damage to the goods occurring while the goods are not in the actual custody of the Carrier."

Clause 8 was as follows: "Delivery of the goods shall be taken by the consignee or holder of the Bill of Lading from the vessel's rail immediately the vessel is ready to discharge, berthed or not berthed, and continuously as fast as vessel can deliver notwithstanding any custom of the port to the contrary. The Carrier shall be at liberty to discharge continuously day and night, Sundays and holidays included, all extra expenses to be for account of the Consignee or Receiver of the goods notwithstanding any custom of the port to the contrary. If the Consignee or holder of the Bill of Lading does not for any reason take delivery as provided herein, they shall be jointly and severally liable to pay the vessel on demand demurrage at the rate of one shilling and sixpence sterling per gross register ton per day or portion of a day during the delay so caused: such demurrage shall be paid in cash day by day to the Carrier, the Master or Agents. If the Consignee or holder of the Bill of Lading requires delivery before or after usual hours he shall pay any extra expenses incurred in consequence. Delivery ex ship's rail shall constitute due delivery of the goods described herein and the Carrier's liability shall cease at that point notwithstanding consignee receiving delivery at some point removed from the ship's side and custom of the port being to the contrary. The Carrier and his Agents shall have the right of nominating the Berth or Berths for loading and discharging at all ports and places whatsoever any custom to the contrary notwithstanding. The Carrier shall not be required to give any notification of disposition or arrival of the goods."

Clause 14 was as follows: "Neither the Carrier nor any corporation owned by, subsidiary to or associated or affiliated with the Carrier shall be liable to answer for or make good any loss or damage to the goods occurring at any time and even though before loading on or after discharge from the ship, by reason or by means of any fire whatsoever, unless such fire shall be caused by its design or neglect."

These provisions must be interpreted in the light of the practice that consignees rarely take delivery of goods at the ship's rail but will normally collect them after some period of storage on or near the wharf. The parties must therefore have contemplated that the carrier, if it did not store the goods itself, would employ some other person to do so. Furthermore a document headed "Port Jackson Stevedoring Pty Ltd Basic Terms and Conditions for Stevedoring at Sydney, NSW" showed that it was contemplated that the stevedore would be so employed. These practical considerations, which are developed in the judgment of Barwick CJ, explain the somewhat intricate interrelation of cll 5 and 8.

It is convenient to start with cl 8. This, in the first sentence, creates an obligation on the consignee to take delivery from the ship's rail the moment that the ship is ready to discharge; if he does not he must pay demurrage. This provision, which is in line with the decision in *Keane v Australian Steamships Pty Ltd* (1929) 41 CLR 484, is a valuable protection for the carrier, which he may, or may not, insist on. The bill of lading takes account of both possibilities. The first sentence of cl 5, quite consistently, provides that the carrier's responsibility *as a carrier* terminates as soon as the goods leave the ship's tackle. But, since the carrier may not have insisted that the consignee take delivery at this point, the rest of cl 5 continues by recognising that the carrier may continue to have some responsibility for the goods after discharge. He cannot after all dump them on the wharf and leave them there. So to suppose would be commercially unreal and is not contemplated by the bill of lading. Clause 5 in terms attributes responsibility to the carrier as bailee and defines the period in express terms as 'continuing after leaving the ship's tackle'. There is nothing in the latter part of cl 8 that is inconsistent with this. It merely provides that *delivery* ex ship's rail shall constitute *due delivery* and that the carrier's liability shall cease at that point. But this leaves open the option not to insist on delivery ex ship's rail, and leaves, to be governed by cl 5, his responsibility if he does not.

The question may be asked: what is the carrier's position if he acts as his own stevedore and himself stacks and stores the goods? In the High Court, Stephen J did not provide an answer to this, but, in view of the provisions referred to above, their Lordships think that the answer is clear, namely that he would be liable for them, as bailee, under the contract. If that is so, it seems indisputable that if, instead, the carrier employs a third party to discharge, stack and store that person would be acting in the course of his employment, performing duties which otherwise the carrier would perform under the bill of lading, and so would be entitled to the same immunity as the carrier would have. Their Lordships would add that both cl 5, in references to theft or pilferage (which may be expected to occur, if it does occur, on the wharf) and cl 14, referring to fire occurring after discharge, also recognise that the carrier may have responsibilities after this event. It is made clear by cl 5 that, irrespective of the period of carriage defined by the contract, the immunity of the carrier is not coextensive with this period but extends both before and after it. The stevedore's immunity extends, by virtue of cl 2, over the same period.

On this point (and indeed on the appeal as a whole) their Lordships are in agreement with the judgment of Barwick CJ. They will humbly advise Her Majesty that the appeal be allowed. The costs order of the High Court of Australia will remain undisturbed and the costs of this appeal will be borne by the stevedore in accordance with the undertaking which it gave.

Appeal allowed.

The principles of *"The Eurymedon"* and *Salmon & Spraggon* cases have now been applied to a situation involving carriage of goods by land: see *Celthene Pty Ltd v WKJ Hauliers Pty Ltd* [1981] 1 NSWLR 606; they have also been applied in Canada: *Miida Electronics Inc v Mitsui OSK Lines Ltd* (1981) 124 DLR (3d) 33.

LEGAL PROBLEMS OF CONTAINERISATION

The rapid expansion of container transport has raised new issues in relation to the law of sea-carriage. The basic aim of container transport is to carry goods door-to-door in full container loads without unpacking and repacking. However, some goods are carried to central depots and there combined with other consignments in mixed containers. In both cases, container transport offers the advantages of reduced handling, quicker mechanised loading and unloading, less damage and pilferage in transit, and the prospect of lower freights.

Some of the more important legal issues raised are:

A single contract of carriage. The traditional international sale transaction involved typically as many as three sets of transport documents for the three distinct stages of the transit. Carb's Ryde factory to port of loading; sea-transit; and port of discharge Yokohama to Mitzi's Tokyo premises. We have already seen that *through bills of lading* are used where transhipment is necessary as in *Plaimar Ltd v Waters Trading Co Ltd*, p 153, *supra*. Similarly, the main carrier Trans Shipping would act as agent for the consignor Carb arranging for the onward carriage by road or rail from Yokohama. The original bill of lading would contain a clause to the following effect:

> The freight received is inclusive of the cost of forwarding to Tokyo which will be arranged through the present carrier Trans Shipping Co acting as agent for the shipper and/or consignees of the goods without any liability whatsoever, the conditions of such forwarding to be the current lawful forms of contract. To avoid the tendering of separate documents at each stage of the journey delivery at destination will be given only on one of these sets of bills of lading unto Trans Shipping Co or its assigns and notice to this effect shall be included in the oncarrier's bill of lading or other freight contracts.

With container transport the same approach has been extended to all phases of the transit, with the main container shipping company undertaking responsibility for the through carriage, but in practice arranging collection and on-carriage through its agents. Where the container is collected at Carb's factory, the container bill of lading issued by Trans Shipping can only be a *received for shipment* bill and not a *received on board* bill. Since the container will be sealed, it will probably describe the cargo as "one container packed by shipper Carb and said by shipper to contain 20,000 carburettors in apparent good order and condition". Since both these qualifications would not satisfy the normal requirements under a contract to deliver a valid bill of lading, Carb would need to qualify its contract with Mitzi, which in turn would need to refer to the qualifications in any of its documentation with a sub-buyer or bank.

Liability of the carrier. This critical issue involves such questions as whether:
(a) the Hague Rules apply to a container *received for shipment* bill of lading;
(b) the rules apply to land transit covered by the container bill;
(c) the container itself or the individual boxes inside it are to be regarded as "a package or unit" for the purposes of the limitation clause in art IV r 5 of the Hague Rules.

Given the international nature of container transport, these matters should be covered by international convention and the Visby Protocol to the Hague Rules attempted to do so, for example, by providing:

> Where a container, pallet or similar article of transport is used to consolidate goods, the number of packages or units enumerated in the bill of lading as packed in such article of

transport shall be deemed the number of packages or units for the purpose of this paragraph, as far as these packages or units are concerned. Except as aforesaid such article of transport shall be considered the package or unit.

The Protocol has not been adopted in Australia.

Insurance arrangements. Container companies have advocated that container documentation can be streamlined by combining the container bill of lading with an appropriate certificate of insurance as in the specimen below. While this might promote efficiency, it could be used as a tying device to preclude the shipper from arranging independent insurance and thereby reduce competition. Would this arrangement constitute the practice of exclusive dealing and infringe Trade Practices Act 1974 s 47, or is it exempted if covered by a conference agreement in relation to overseas cargo shipping under Pt X of the Act?

For further consideration of the legal problems of containerisation, see Schmitthoff, *The Export Trade*, 7th ed, 1980, Ch 24.

COMBINED TRANSPORT BILL OF LADING AND CERTIFICATE OF INSURANCE

SPECIMEN

Total No. of Packages

See Reverse for qualifications and conditions

LLOYD'S CERTIFICATE OF INSURANCE

THIS IS TO CERTIFY that the Container Contents particularised above have been declared for insurance on Policies effected with Underwriters at LLOYD'S and British Marine Insurance Companies (in the proportions shown on the back hereof). These Policies are on the Standard Form of LLOYD'S and Companies Marine Policy, stamped in accordance with British Revenue Law, and subject to the special conditions stated hereon.

TERMS OF INSURANCE: The current Institute or Trade Clauses indicated above and on the back hereof and as more fully described in the*...Tariff, available at .... Including the conditions of the Institute War clauses and the Institute Strikes, Riots and Civil Commotions clauses.

PERIOD OF INSURANCE .... as ☐ below

[1.] From time of arrival at Place of Acceptance until time of leaving the Place of Delivery hereunder.

[2.] From time of commencement of transit, whilst in the ordinary course of transit, and until termination in accordance with relevant clauses referred to under "TERMS OF INSURANCE".

INSURED VALUE: As declared and stated above.

CLAIMS: In the event of loss or damage which may result in a claim under this insurance, immediate notice must be given to* .... or its authorised agent nearest to the place where the loss or damage is discovered and a survey thereafter held as and when required by them.

Documents in support of claim, including Invoice Survey/Discrepancy Report and Bill of Lading, should be forwarded as directed by*... or its authorised agents.

SIGNATURE ....
For the Committee of Lloyd's

Place of Acceptance	Place of Delivery (or Options)	
		In witness of the Contracts of Carriage herein .... ( ) originals have been issued one of which being accomplished the other to be void.
		For ....
	For other terms see back	Issued at .... on ....

Continued next page

Import and Export Sales

COMBINED TRANSPORT BILL OF LADING AND CERTIFICATE OF INSURANCE
—*continued*

Shipper	*Bill of Lading and Certificate of Insurance No.* .... *Shipper's Reference*		
	OCL OVERSEAS CONTAINERS LTD. (Incorporated in the United Kingdom)	OR	**ACT** ASSOCIATED CONTAINER TRANSPORTATION LIMITED (Incorporated in the United Kingdom)
Consignee or Order	An asterisk*..........indicates where the appropriate carrier (OCL or ACT) in practice would be named in this document. ACCEPTED BY*......... from the Shipper in apparent good order and condition (save as may be stated hereon or on the reverse hereof): The goods specified below, The Container(s) detailed below packed by or on behalf of the Shipper and said by Shipper to contain the goods specified below in apparent good order and condition. for transportation subject to all the terms hereof (including the terms on the reverse hereof) from the Place of Acceptance to the Place of Delivery by any conveyance and by any vessel(s) whether as specified below or substitute(s) and with or without transhipment and via the intended port of loading or other port(s) and by any route at*..............................option and subject to all the terms thereof. On presentation of this document (duly endorsed) to*............ or to its authorised Agents at any of its or their places of business by or on behalf of any person (hereinafter called the Holder) to whom the property in the Goods has passed upon or by Reason of the consignment thereof or the endorsement hereof or otherwise and without prejudice to the rights and liabilities of the Shipper, Holder and*....................... at common law or under any statute, the terms hereof shall in all respects become binding between*......and the Holder as though the contract contained herein or evidenced hereby had been made between them.		
Notify Party			

Intended Vessel	Intended Port of Loading	Total Insured Value (in words) } Currency .... Figs:			
Intended Port of Discharge	Freight & Charges Where Paid/Due	Aust. Inland Haulage	U.K. Inland Haulage	Basic Service Charge	Insurance

Details of cargo as declared by Shipper

Marks and Numbers	Number and kind of packages; description of goods	Insurance Conditions	Container No(s).	Gross Weight lbs.	Measurement cu. ft.

SPECIMEN

QUESTIONS

Question 6

(1) What duty does a bailee for reward owe as a carrier of goods? Can this duty be avoided by delegation? Where a carrier sub-contracts the carriage of goods, does he owe a duty to the owner if he has never received possession of the goods?

(2) What is the meaning of common carrier and what difference would it make to the duties and liabilities of a carrier for reward if he is a common carrier?

Question 7

What is the purpose of a "Himalaya" clause? What are the legal and commercial justifications for such a clause? To what extent have the courts modified the principles of contract law when considering such a clause? In answering the question refer to any relevant cases as well as any policy issues you consider relevant.

Question 8

Carb Pty Ltd arranged for Transhaul Ltd to transport a crate of 500 carburettors from Sydney to Brisbane. At Transhaul's request, Carb signed a consignment note to cover the carriage of the goods by Transhaul, which included the following provisions:

"1. Carrier means Transhaul Ltd and any other person or company with whom the carrier may arrange for the carriage of the goods including any servant, agent, employee or sub-contractor.

"2. The consignor hereby authorises the carrier to arrange with a sub-contractor(s) for the carriage of the goods. Any such arrangement shall be deemed to be satisfied by the consignor upon delivery of the goods to the sub-contractor(s) who shall thereupon be entitled to the full benefit of these conditions; and to this end the carrier is deemed to enter this contract as agent for the sub-contractor(s).

"3. The goods remain at the risk of the consignor and the carrier shall not be liable in tort or contract for any loss or damage to the goods either in transit or storage from any cause including the negligence of the carrier."

Transhaul sub-contracted to Col Lydde the carriage of the crate from Carb's factory to Transhaul's depot. While in transit Col Lydde's vehicle hit a lamp post and caught fire, and the carburettors were destroyed.

Advise Carb of its rights against Transhaul Ltd and Col Lydde.

Question 9

Mitzi Co purchased 1500 generators from Carb Pty Ltd. Terms of sale were cif Yokohama $150,000 cash against documents, provided Mitzi should pay the freight on delivery and deduct same from the price.

Because the generators were exceptionally heavy Carb arranged with the shipping company Crateships Ltd for the five containers holding the generators to be secured to the deck of the vessel *Glenelg* by special locking bolts. Crateships issued a bill of lading to "Carb Pty Ltd or order" stating that 1500 generators were received on board as container cargo for shipment Sydney to Yokohama and provided:

"(1) The carrier shall not be responsible for any loss, damage or spoilage of the goods except to the extent provided by the Hague Rules and this bill of lading shall have effect subject to those rules.

"(2) In issuing this bill the carrier contracts for itself and on behalf of those who may be engaged by it from time to time in loading or unloading cargo on or from its vessels and also such persons shall be deemed to be parties to this contract."

Two weeks after leaving Sydney the *Glenelg* encountered a heavy storm during which three of Carb's containers broke loose from the deck and were lost overboard.

It was later established that the special locking bolts had not been used to secure the containers.

During the course of unloading cargo in Yokohama, stevedores engaged by Crateships through the Yokohama Port Authority negligently tipped over one of the remaining two containers intended for Mitzi, badly damaging all generators packed in it. It was later established that this container had also come away from its fastenings during the storm but had been secured again without loss.

Crateships had never previously sent ships to Yokohama nor had any prior dealings with the Yokohama Port Authority.

Mitzi Co seeks your advice as to:
(a) What law governs the contract of carriage with Crateships;
(b) whether Crateships can sue Mitzi for the freight;
(c) whether Mitzi can recover damages from Crateships and/or Yokohama Port Authority.

SECTION 4: AN INTERNATIONAL LAW OF SALES

One of the characteristics of an international sale is that it often involves parties from two or more countries whose domestic law of sales differ. Difficulties have been minimised in relation to trade between many common law countries by the similarity of their Sale of Goods legislation inherited from the English Act of 1893. However, differences still occur, and are magnified in transactions with European or Japanese traders. This situation has resulted in the preparation of international conventions for the unification of international sales law which are discussed below.

CONFLICT OF LAW RULES

In the absence of an applicable international law, the traditional approach to these conflict of laws issues has been that the so-called "proper law of the contract" applies. The parties can nominate that law in the contract itself as eg in *Herrick v Leonard and Dingley Ltd* [1975] 2 NZLR 566 unless the proper law is prescribed by statute as the Sea-Carriage of Goods Act 1924 s 9 does for Australian export bills of lading. If the parties fail to nominate the applicable law, the courts will decide which law is to apply:

In an inquiry as to what is the proper law of a contract in which the parties have not expressed their own selection of the law to be applied, many matters have to be taken into consideration. Of these, the principal are the place of contracting, the place of performance, the place of residence or business of the parties respectively, and the nature and subject matter of the contract. But ... the most satisfactory formulation is the one "with which the transaction has the most real connection": *Re United Railways of the Havana and Regla Warehouses Ltd* [1960] Ch 52 at 91.

For a full treatment of this subject see P E Nygh, *Conflict of Laws in Australia*, 3rd ed, 1976, Ch 15, or *Benjamin's Sale of Goods*, 2nd ed, 1981, Ch 25.

Thus, where Mitzi in Japan sends a telegram to Carb in Sydney accepting Carb's offer to sell carburettors fob Sydney, the court must choose between the place of contracting, ie where the offer is accepted, namely Japan and the place of performance, namely Sydney. If New South Wales and Japanese law differ on the requirements for a valid contract, such as offer, acceptance and consideration, these questions will usually also be determined by the proper law of the putative contract. However, the requirements as to the contract being evidenced by writing or otherwise are regarded as merely evidentiary, and are determined according to the law of the forum. Thus, if Carb sues Mitzi in a New South Wales court, which determines that the proper law of the contract is Japanese law, Carb will still have to prove compliance with NSW SGA s 9 in order to enforce the contract. If satisfied on that score, the New South Wales court would then ascertain the Japanese law on the basis of expert witnesses and agreed translations of Japanese statutes, and apply that law to the interpretation and performance of the contract in the same way that the New Zealand court applied English law to the interpretation of the bill of lading in *Herrick's* case.

Choice of law is also important in relation to the title to goods. If Mitzi becomes insolvent, and Carb exercises its right of stoppage *in transitu* and resells the goods in Singapore, the buyer's title will be determined according to the law of the situs of the goods, namely Singapore: see generally *Benjamin, supra*, pp 1295-306. Another issue concerns the appropriate jurisdiction in which to commence proceedings on an international sale. For example, a New South Wales court will not accept jurisdiction to hear Carb's case against Mitzi unless Mitzi is served with the writ within the jurisdiction, voluntarily submits to the jurisdiction, or the court grants leave under its statutory jurisdiction to serve Mitzi outside the jurisdiction. Leave may be granted where the contract was made in New South Wales, is governed by New South Wales law or was broken in New South Wales.

UNIFORM INTERNATIONAL SALES LAWS

Notwithstanding the above rules for resolving conflict of law questions, there are definite advantages for world trade in the unification of the law governing international sales. In addition to the role of the ICC and the UN Economic Commission for Europe in promoting uniform terms of sale referred to earlier, the International Institute for the Unification of Private Law at Rome (UNIDROIT) prepared two uniform model laws on international sales. These were accepted at an international conference at The Hague in 1964 and are known as the 1964 Hague Conventions on (a) Uniform Law on the International Sale of Goods (ULIS), and (b) Uniform Law on the Formation of Contracts for the International Sale of Goods. Each is open for accession by all nations and has been ratified by UK and some Western European countries: see, eg, Uniform Laws on International Sales Act 1967 (UK) operative from August 1972, which permits parties to "opt into" ULIS but does not make its application compulsory to all international sales. Since its creation in 1968, the United Nations Commission on International Trade Law (UNCITRAL) of which Australia is a member, has done much work to revise and improve ULIS for wider adoption as well as other projects directed to the unification and simplification of international transactions.

ULIS, if accepted unconditionally, would displace national sales laws in relation to an international sale between parties having their places of business in different countries where both countries have adopted ULIS. The Convention also allows a country to adopt ULIS on the basis that (a) it would only apply to contracts if ULIS was specifically chosen by the parties; and/or (b) it would only apply if each of the parties had its place of business or habitual residence in a different country which had also ratified the Convention. As mentioned above, the United Kingdom has chosen method (a) which severely limits the usefulness of the Convention.

Each Convention has attempted to reconcile the differences in substantive law between existing common law and civil law systems. If widely adopted the uniform laws have the potential to minimise conflicts in international trade.

INTERNATIONAL TRADE IN PRACTICE

Most lawyers, and many businessmen who have not previously been involved in international trade, find the conceptual and practical aspects difficult. The risks involved are greater than in a domestic transaction in that

(a) the buyer will often not have the opportunity to inspect the goods before becoming obliged to pay for them;
(b) the seller may have difficulty collecting payment from a buyer in a foreign country;
(c) each party may not be aware of legal rules or practices in the foreign country, or changes in the economic or political climate in that country;
(d) fluctuations in the rate of currency exchange may expose either party to unexpected cost.

Information relating to the practical operation of export and import transactions is available in publications produced by the major trading banks. One of the best is The National Bank of Australasia's (now National Commercial Bank) *Finance of International Trade*, 4th ed, 1979, from which the following passage is taken (pp 99-100):

Risks in import transactions

Except where goods are being paid for on "open account", or are being received on consignment, it is unlikely that the importer will have the opportunity to inspect the goods prior to the seller receiving payment, or the importer incurring a commitment to pay apart from the contract of sale eg where a drawing is made under a documentary credit or the importer accepts a term bill and receives the documents on acceptance. Hence if the goods are not in accordance with samples, or quality is not as specified, or they are otherwise unsatisfactory and amicable arrangements cannot be made with the supplier, or there is no agreed upon arbitration procedure, there is left the question of legal action based on the contract of sale to secure damages. Whether such action is warranted depends upon the amount involved, the national law applicable, where legal action must be taken, the costs of the action, and whether a judgment against the supplier, if obtained, can be enforced.

The need to take legal action, with its cost and uncertainties, is one to be avoided, and importers should consider what measures can be taken to ensure that the need does not arise. If the importer has an agent in the supplier's country it may be possible for closer supervision to be maintained over shipments. In some cases, where the type of goods and amount involved so warrant, it is generally possible to arrange for an independent superintendence company (specialising in such work) to inspect the goods prior to shipment and provide their certificate that the quality etc is in accordance with the contract of sale.

One of the best safeguards is a thorough investigation of the reputation and standing of the supplier prior to placing orders.

Where similar goods are available from other suppliers in the same overseas country, or from suppliers in other countries, the prices and terms offered competitively will be closely considered by the importer. However, other factors besides competitive prices enter into the picture—the reliability of the supplier, his quality standards, and his ability to meet delivery dates. Importers should always seek reports from banks and other sources on the standing of suppliers with whom they are considering dealing to ensure their reliability and commercial standing. The value of overseas visits by importers for "on the spot" enquiries cannot be overstressed.

If the date by which goods are shipped is a vital aspect (eg goods ordered for Christmas trade) the contract of sale should be specific so that the importer has clear legal grounds for refusing payment, should he wish to do so, if it is apparent that goods have not been shipped by the specified shipment date. Where an importer is paying for goods by means of a documentary credit he can instruct the issuing bank to include a "latest date for shipment" in the terms of the credit.

This risk of damage to, or loss of, the goods in transit can be covered by normal marine insurance. Where the supplier has the responsibility of taking out insurance cover it is desirable that the contract of sale sets out the agreement between the parties as to the type of cover to be obtained. This enables the importer to make sure that his interests are adequately protected.

If an importer has contracted to make payment in Australian currency he avoids an exchange risk. However, if payment to the supplier is to be made in an overseas currency then an exchange risk exists from the date of the contract of sale until Australian currency is paid by the importer to obtain the overseas currency to pay the supplier. Forward exchange contracts with an Australian bank provide the means of covering this risk.

Financing of import transactions, insuring against the buyer's default under an export sale transaction, and exchange control requirements are all considered in Chapter 10.

QUESTION

Question 10

Identify some of the problems which face the Australian exporter and importer respectively. Discuss the ways in which legal rules and practices have been used to overcome or minimise these problems.

FURTHER READING

Section 2: Special Forms of Import and Export Contracts

Sassoon, *CIF and FOB Contracts*, 2nd ed, 1975.

Schmitthoff, *The Export Trade*, 7th ed, 1980.

Section 3: Related Contracts of Carriage

Celthene Pty Ltd v WKJ Hauliers Pty Ltd & Anor [1981] 1 NSWLR 606.

Edwards, "Some Aspects of the Liability of Airline Operators in Australia" (1961) 34 *ALJ* 142.

Goldring, "Carriage by 'Combined Transport' " (1978) 6 *ABLR* 151.

Goldring, "The Container as a 'Package or Unit' under the Hague Rules" (1974) 2 *ABLR* 127.

O'Hare, "Allocating Shipment Risk and the UNCITRAL Convention" (1977) 4 *Monash ULR* 117.

O'Hare, "Shipping Documentation for the Carriage of Goods and the Hamburg Rules" (1978) 52 *ALJ* 415.

Powles, "The Himalaya Clause" (1979) *Lloyd's Mar & Com LQ* 331.

Reynolds, "The Negligent Stevedore Yet Again" (1980) 96 *LQR* 506.

Salter, "Transport Note" (1981) 9 *ABLR* 142.

Tedeschi, "Consideration, Privity and Exemption Clauses: *Port Jackson Stevedoring Pty Ltd v Salmon and Spraggon (Australia) Pty Ltd*" (1981) 55 *ALJ* 876.

"The Himalaya Clause Upheld" (1981) *J Bus L* 65.

Section 4: An International Law of Sales

Department of Trade and Resources, "Standardised Export Documents for Australia".

CHAPTER 6

Contracts of Insurance

"The policy is made up of a jumble of ill-assorted documents expressed in that distinctive style which insurance companies have made their own."

Mr Justice Mason
Guardian Assurance Co Pty Ltd v Underwood Constructions Pty Ltd
(1974) 48 ALJR 307 at 308

Section 1: The Function of Insurance Contracts
Section 2: The Uberrimae Fidei Doctrine and Construction of Insurance Contracts
Section 3: Insurable Interest
Section 4: The Indemnity Principle and its Applications
Section 5: Insurance Claims

Insurance is a very big worldwide industry today and it pervades every type of commercial and many domestic transactions and relationships. It warrants several volumes and a law course to itself. Within the confines of this book and a commercial law course, one can only attempt to outline the essentials. This aim will be assisted by using the basic fact situation outlined at the beginning of Chapter 5 in which Carb Pty Ltd insured with Coverall Insurance Ltd a consignment of carburettors in transit to Mitzi Co in Tokyo. In Section 1 the commercial and social functions of insurance are explained, and types of available insurance cover illustrated. The relationship between insurer Coverall Insurance Ltd, its representative Jinx, insurance broker Premium Brokerage Co, and proponent Carb are examined.

In Section 2, we focus on the relationship between the proposal form signed by Carb and the policy issued by Coverall. What is the effect of an incorrect answer in the proposal? Is Carb obliged to disclose additional information not requested on the form? What is the effect of a "basis of the contract" clause in the policy? How is the policy to be construed? The effect of some other common provisions in insurance contracts are also considered.

Section 3 deals with the concept of insurable interest, explains why the proponent Carb is required to have such an interest, and considers the relationship between insurable interest and the indemnity principle. This principle is the main topic in Section 4. Is Carb entitled to recover under its policy with Coverall the full amount of the policy or the amount of its loss or some other sum? A number of specific applications of the indemnity principle will be illustrated, including salvage, contribution and subrogation. Section 5 deals briefly with the procedure for making a claim under a policy, and the effect of procedural requirements in the policy including a submission to arbitration.

SECTION 1: THE FUNCTION OF INSURANCE CONTRACTS

The chief function of insurance is to share the burden of individual risks of loss amongst a group. This process has been institutionalised as Ackerman suggests in the following definition:

Ackerman: Insurance: Its Meaning and Significance
(1950) March *Insurance LJ* 171

If, for clarity, we must define the word insurance, care should be taken to include the following: (1) a social system, method, scheme or device; (2) restoration of capital or economic loss due to hazards of the commercial or economic world; (3) a common fund provided by a group or groups of society; (4) an administrative body to take care of the fund; (5) a method of distributing the fund when the risk assumed becomes a reality and loss occurs.

Companies and individuals buy insurance policies, paying premiums which are small compared with the potential losses. Premiums are based upon the nature and size of the risk insured against, and certain characteristics of the proponent for insurance. The probability and size of a potential claim under the policy are assessed on the basis of the insurer's knowledge and experience, and information supplied by the proponent. For example, Coverall's decision to insure Carb, and its calculation of the premium will be affected by:

(a) the nature of the risk: premium will differ between theft and fire cover;
(b) the subject matter: timber is more combustible than steel and is more expensive to insure against fire;
(c) Carb's past record: a history of claims under policies of the proposed type may result in rejection of the proposal or a weighted premium.

It is therefore not surprising that Carb is obliged to disclose to Coverall all material facts (ie those which will be relevant to Coverall's acceptance and assessment of Carb's proposal for insurance).

By sharing the risk of loss through insurance, the proponent replaces uncertainty with security which is important—both in a commercial and a domestic context. However, insurance has its social costs: the administrative expenses of government schemes and insurance companies' expenses and profits. Insurance companies have suggested that the very security provided by insurance may result in less care being taken against the occurrence of the insured hazard but there is little concrete evidence to support this view. Various devices are used to combat carelessness and the other moral hazard that the insured may fraudulently seek to profit by deliberately causing the loss. For example, Coverall may offer a reduced premium on Carb's factory if Carb installs a fire sprinkler system; or it may insert an excess clause in the policy requiring Carb to pay the first $500 of any claim. Coverall will certainly be unwilling to overinsure Carb.

TYPES OF INSURANCE RISKS

A basic classification of risks is that between general (sometimes called fundamental) risks and particular risks. General risks have general causes and consequences. Thus, Cyclone Tracy caused widespread devastating damage, and war, floods and earthquakes result in similar national emergencies for which governments grant a degree of assistance. In contrast, particular risks have individual causes and localised effects such as the theft of Carb's consignment or a fire in its factory. The dividing line between the two types of risks can be viewed in social and political terms as based upon the distinction between laissez-faire individualism and a social welfare system. In this century the trend has been to extend the umbrella of government assistance over a number of risks which were once regarded as particular only and therefore the responsibility of the individual. These include sickness and unemployment benefits, aged and disability pensions, compulsory third party and motor vehicle and workmen's compensation insurance.

The role of governments in Australia in relation to insurance has been along three main lines. First, they have legislated for compulsory insurance in some areas, notably, state laws requiring insurance against liability for personal injuries to third parties through use of a motor vehicle, and workmen's compensation insurance. The state-owned government insurance offices, for example in New South Wales and Queensland, carry a large proportion of this insurance. A degree of compulsory cover was likewise involved in the federal Medibank scheme. In some overseas jurisdictions compulsory third party insurance has been replaced by a no-fault scheme of compensation for motor vehicle accident victims which removes the need to prove that the defendant was negligent.

Second, by the Export Payments Insurance Corporations Act 1956 (now replaced by the Export Finance and Insurance Corporation Act 1974) the Commonwealth government established a statutory corporation for the purpose of encouraging and expanding Australian export trade by providing a specialised range of insurance and guarantee facilities not normally obtainable from commercial insurers. These include insurance against the risk of non-payment by overseas buyers, and guarantees of loans made by commercial lending institutions to finance Australian exports. The Housing Loans Insurance Corporation offers in return for a single premium an analogous guarantee of home loans made by building societies and other housing financiers: Housing Loans Insurance Act 1965.

Third, the federal and to a lesser degree state governments have legislated to protect policy holders. Under the Australian Constitution s 51(xiv) the Commonwealth government has power to legislate with respect to "insurance, other that State insurance; also State insurance extending beyond the limits of the State concerned" (ie, with respect to all insurance, except insurance conducted by a state government instrumentality wholly within its own state). The Commonwealth has acted to regulate marine and life insurance under the Marine Insurance Act 1909 and the Life Insurance Act 1945. It has also provided for controls over insurance companies other than life companies under the Insurance Act 1973 and Insurance (Deposits) Act 1932. The main purpose of these Acts is to ensure the stability and solvency of insurance companies. Since premium income must be calculated to cover claims which under some types of insurance may arise many years in the future, the risks of insolvency are high. This is particularly true in relation to third party motor vehicle, accident and product liability insurance where verdicts for personal injury claims are difficult to predict.

To this end the Life Insurance Act s 15 provides that only companies registered with the Insurance Commissioner can carry on life insurance business in Australia. Part III of the Act also provides for the lodgment of substantial deposits by life companies with the commissioner, restricts the mixing of premium and other income, and provides for audit and actuarial investigation of companies' affairs and the furnishing of reports to the commissioner. A similar approach is taken in relation to general non-life insurance (including marine insurance) under the Insurance Act 1973.

Although the Commonwealth has power to further regulate insurance companies, it has not provided for their incorporation. Again the form and some of the details of life policies are prescribed but not the requirements for making a valid contract. These and other matters remain for determination under state law. For a discussion of the constitutional ambit of the Commonwealth insurance power, see *Insurance Commissioner v Associated Dominions Assurance Society Pty Ltd* (1953) 89 CLR 78; *Australian & International Insurances Ltd v The Workers' Compensation Commission of NSW* (1972) 125 CLR 470; [1972-73] ALR 260; and G Sawer, "Administrative Control of Companies—The Life Insurance Example" (1970) 44 *ALJ* 303.

An illustration of state legislation affecting insurance contracts is the Insurance Act 1902 (NSW) ss 18–20 (inserted by Commercial Transactions (Miscellaneous Provisions) Act 1974 s 6, which also changed the title of the Act from Life, Fire and Marine Insurance Act to its new short title): see p 226, *infra*.

Within the category of particular risks referred to above there is a great variety of types of insurance cover. These range from home and automobile insurance, television breakdown, accommodation expenses when stranded by an airline strike to a large number of business risks including theft of payroll, loss of profits from machinery breakdown, product liability, contractor's all risks insurance and death of key employees. Cover can be sought against virtually any risk which may result in financial loss, including, for example, damage to Marlene Dietrich's legs. The parties in a lengthy and expensive commercial litigation insured the judges' life lest his death during the case might result in the expense of a new trial. Insurance cover for personal accidents and to a greater extent for sickness and disabilities has become a major growth area for Australia's life insurance industry. Liability insurance is an expanding area: it includes insurance against liability of doctors, lawyers, etc for professional negligence, of manufacturers for defective products and of homeowners for dangerous dogs and garden tools.

However, there are some legal limitations upon the ambit of insurance contracts. First, a contract which purports to be an insurance contract but is really a wager or gaming contract is void. For example, Gaming and Betting Act 1912 (NSW) s 16 provides:

16 All contracts or agreements, whether by parole or in writing, by way of gaming or wagering shall be null and void, and no suit shall be brought or maintained for recovering any sum of money ... upon any wager ...

Both insurance and wagers are based upon future contingencies: what is the point of distinction between them? Second, the statutory requirements in relation to life and marine insurance that the proponent have an insurable interest preclude insurance in certain cases. These provisions which are considered in Section 3 should be compared with the prohibition on wagers. Third, in addition to these legal requirements, the moral hazard will mean that in practice an insurance company will decline to cover some risks which it is lawfully permitted to insure.

Various risks can be covered in the same policy and the scope of the cover offered will vary between competing insurance companies even though they may apply the same general label to their respective policies. Accordingly, the terms of each policy should be read carefully to ensure that the appropriate hazards are covered rather than extraneous ones. It may be desirable to consult an insurance broker in this regard. Particular attention should be paid to the schedule of contingencies and exclusions, which will contain many terms of art. These are effectively shorthand descriptions of various hazards or qualifications thereto which have received judicial interpretation over the years.

A final general point is that when we say Coverall Insurance insured Carb's goods or Jim Handy's life, the statement is misleading if taken literally since Coverall does not promise that the goods will not be lost at sea or destroyed by fire or that Jim will not die. Rather, it promises to compensate Carb for its loss arising out of these occurrences. There are several important consequences which flow logically from this point:

(1) If Carb insures a lathe for a period of one year, and one week later it is totally destroyed by fire, Carb can claim on the policy but cannot argue that the contract is frustrated as a basis for claiming a rebate of the premium for the unexpired period of 51 weeks.

(2) Carb may insure goods belonging to someone else if their destruction would involve Carb in financial loss.

(3) Carb can insure goods for their cost price plus freight and insurance charges so that if they are lost, the amount recovered will indemnify Carb for its total loss even though this exceeds the value of the goods.

RELATIONSHIP OF INSURER, REPRESENTATIVE, BROKER AND PROPONENT

Insurance companies normally operate through representatives, agents and brokers. These intermediaries are often authorised by the companies to issue interim protection in the form of cover notes and to submit proposals for insurance from proponents. For example, Coverall Insurance Ltd may send a canvasser Jinx to offer Carb insurance, or Carb may approach a broker such as Premium Brokerage Co to obtain quotations for appropriate cover for its business activities. The necessary proposal forms may be filled in by either Jinx or Premium prior to signature by Carb and submission to Coverall. In the course of negotiations, Carb may make pertinent disclosures to Jinx or Premium. In each case it will be important to determine whether they are acting at this point as agents for Carb or for Coverall since an agent generally has power to bind its principal within the scope of its authority. In practice Jinx and Premium would be remunerated not by Carb but by Coverall for any insurance cover sold.

Claude R Ogden & Co Pty Ltd v Reliance Fire Sprinkler Co Pty Ltd and Others; Davies (First Third Party); Stenhouse (NSW) Ltd (Second Third Party)
Supreme Court of New South Wales [1973] 2 NSWLR 7

[The plaintiff sued the defendant Reliance for negligent installation of an automatic fire sprinkler system in the plaintiff's factory which it alleged resulted in its destruction by fire and a loss in excess of $1 million. The defendant and associated companies ("the group") had previously held public and products liability insurance policies with Sun Alliance Insurance Co. A number of claims had been made by the group's customers in respect of defective products or workmanship and some had been paid or settled and indemnity obtained from Sun Alliance, which advised the Group that it would not renew its policies.

The Group then arranged similar insurance cover through the insurance broker Stenhouse (NSW) Ltd with BMW Payne Liability Agencies Pty Ltd ("PLA") as agent of a Lloyd's syndicate represented by F W Davies. The group's directors Hedley and Buckmaster verbally advised Laird and Singleton of Stenhouse that Sun Alliance had decline to renew the group's insurance and of the prior claims. Stenhouse prepared and signed a proposal for insurance on behalf of the group, in which questions 1 and 2 relating to prior claims and cancellations of policies were answered "Not known to brokers."

Following the plaintiff's claim against the Group, the latter sought indemnity in respect of any liability it might incur to the plaintiff by joining as third parties in the action:

(a) the underwriter Davies for indemnity under the policies; and

(b) Stenhouse for negligence in its capacity as broker and in completing the proposal.

The report deals only with the third party proceedings, which, by consent, were heard first as a commercial cause without a jury.]

Macfarlan J: ... It is perhaps important that I should first refer very briefly to the principles of law in accordance with which decisions should be made about the materiality of facts. These principles have been stated many times, but for present purposes it is sufficient to refer to two judgments of high authority. In *Southern Cross Assurance Co Ltd v Australian Provincial Assurance Association Ltd* (1939) 39 SR (NSW) 174 at 187, Jordan CJ and Nicholas J said: "Since the contract of assurance is *uberrimae fidei* the assured is subject to an obligation (which is a common law obligation and not a contractual obligation) ... to disclose to the assurance company every material fact known to him which a reasonable man would realise to be material ... A fact is material if it would induce a reasonable assurance company to refuse the risk or to stipulate terms as to premiums or otherwise more favourable to itself than it would require if the fact did not exist ... The questions whether the fact exists and if so whether it was material to be disclosed are both questions of fact for the jury if they are disputed ..."

I will first consider the misrepresentations which learned counsel for PLA submitted had been made and it should be noted that his primary argument was based upon their existence.

[His Honour then considered the evidence regarding disclosure of past claims history, amount of premium previously paid to Sun Alliance, the circumstances in which Sun Alliance did not wish to renew the policy and the answers to questions 1 and 2 in the proposal. He continued at 19:] As I have already said, in whatever manner the proposal is contrued, it misrepresented the knowledge of Stenhouse, and therefore of Reliance, about prior claims and cancellations. In my opinion these were misrepresentations of material facts.

It is necessary to notice at this point an argument that was submitted by learned counsel who appeared for Reliance. He sought to avoid certain obvious consequences for his client of some of the misrepresentations that had been made. To this end he argued that, because at the time of the meeting between Singleton and Payne on 20 May 1968, Stenhouse had not been appointed broker for the Group, it, therefore, had no authority to make any representations. In my opinion this argument does not give proper weight to the evidence or to certain principles of law. The evidence was that the Group authorised Stenhouse to obtain a quotation and to give the information that was necessary to obtain it. I think that this appears in the evidence of Buckmaster, Laird and Singleton. As part of the process of obtaining the quotation it was necessary to disclose, among other things, the nature of the claims history and the relations of the intending insured with previous insurers. This authority in my opinion also carried with it authority to disclose facts which might cause the premiums to be lower, and I also think that the amount being paid for premiums in the current policy would properly be included among such facts. It is, in my opinion, not an answer for learned counsel for the Group to argue that Stenhouse was never authorised to misrepresent any facts. In my opinion his point is made clear by the judgment of Dixon J, Evatt J and McTiernan J in *Australasian Brokerage Ltd v Australian and New Zealand Banking Corp Ltd* (1934) 52 CLR 430 at 450, 451. [His Honour then referred to *Bayley v Manchester, Sheffield & Lincolnshire Railway Co* (1872) LR 7 CP 415 at 420 and *Mackay v Commercial Bank of New Brunswick* (1874) LR 5 PC 394 at 410, 411 and continued at 21:]

These authorities in my opinion mean that Reliance is not entitled to assert in support of its general argument that, if Stenhouse in its negotiations with PLA misrepresented material facts, such misrepresentations were made without its authority and were, therefore, not binding upon it. The true situation was that Stenhouse had been authorised by Reliance to obtain quotations from underwriters and had also been authorised, in aid of the principal mandate, to make statements of such facts as were necessary to obtain the quotations. It follows, in my opinion, that Reliance having "confided the conduct of the negotiations" ((1934) 52 CLR 430 at 450) is bound by and is also responsible for all statements made by Stenhouse which concern the subject matter of quotations by underwriters. Nor is Reliance entitled to obtain exoneration if the statements are untrue because, as Willes J said ((1872) LR 7 CP 415 at 420) it is "answerable for the wrong of the person so intrusted either in the manner of doing such an act, or in doing such an act under circumstances in which it ought not to have been done ..."

It follows therefore that, independently of my decision with respect to waiver and estoppel on the first and third misrepresentations, I must decide that PLA was entitled to avoid the policy.

[His Honour considered various arguments advanced by counsel for Reliance and Stenhouse that the underwriters Davies had waived their right to full disclosure or were estopped from avoiding the policy and rejected both arguments. He then moved to the claim of Reliance against Stenhouse. After considering the claim that Stenhouse was in breach of its contract to use reasonable care and skill in performing its functions as broker for Reliance, he concluded at 30:] In the result I am of the opinion that by the terms of its contract Stenhouse did promise to complete the necessary proposal forms, and it is in my opinion, inescapable that that obligation also carried with it an obligation to complete them with reasonable care and skill. If this were not so the contract made between Reliance and Stenhouse would be devoid of any business efficacy: cf *Heimann v The Commonwealth* (1938) SR (NSW) 691 at 695; 55 WN (NSW) 235 at 237; *Scanlans New Neon Ltd v Tooheys Ltd* (1943) 67 CLR 169 at 197.

[His Honour then considered Stenhouse's denial that it failed to exercise reasonable care as brokers. He concluded that the Group's requirements of its broker were fully communicated to and understood by Stenhouse. He continued at 32:] I have formed the opinion that it follows from what I have said that the relationship of Reliance and Stenhouse was that of lay client and expert and professional broker. I think also that that relationship was fully understood by both parties, and also that, as part of the relationship, Reliance was entitled to rely on the wide experience and considerable expertise that Stenhouse claimed to have. In this situation it is apparent, in my opinion, that it was inappropriate, because it was not necesary, for the lay client to suggest to the expert professional broker what ought or ought not to be done; what inquiries ought or ought not be made; or how negotiations should be conducted with the underwriter. Although Buckmaster had by November 1970 become a non-practising barrister and no doubt in May 1968 was making favourable progress towards the climax of his legal studies and perhaps the zenith of his career as a lawyer, I cannot regard this circumstance as altering the relationship I have just stated or as increasing the responsibility of Reliance or diminishing that of Stenhouse.

The matters I have discussed make plain that Stenhouse undertook, and indeed was anxious, to effect proper insurances for Reliance. If this were to be done it is my opinion that Stenhouse then incurred two further obligations which can be expressed as follows: (a) an obligation to collect such information regarding the nature of the company's business and its claims history as the underwriters could properly require, and, (b) an obligation to pass on that information to the underwriters. I will consider each of these obligations separately.

Learned counsel who appeared for Stenhouse argued with great earnestness that it was the contractual obligation of Reliance to collect relevant facts concerning the company's business and claims history, to collate and then to give to the broker every such relevant detail. The soundness of this argument must be considered not only with the words of the written agreement but also having regard to the circumstances which existed before and when the agreement was made. I have already, at an earlier place in this judgment, stated by opinion that Buckmaster and Hedley had made it clear to Laird and to Singleton that the character of the Group's business was such that claims were inevitably made from time to time and that, indeed, such claims had been made; that Buckmaster and Hedley also told Stenhouse of the Fiberglass claim and mentioned it by name; that they also told it of the difficulties it was having in negotiating with Sun Alliance a settlement of another claim that had been made, and that Sun Alliance had decided not to renew the Group's public and product liability insurance. I do not intend to state again my reasons for these opinions, but there may well and significantly be added to them some astonishing evidence given by Singleton and Laird, that they did not have to worry about giving claims histories to underwriters. Singleton gave the following evidence: "Q—And is what you tell his Honour this, that unless the underwriter requested information as to the past claims history, you would not concern yourself with ascertaining whether the past claims history had been a disastrous one? A—Yes."

Having regard to the evidence I have quoted, I am not at all surprised that Laird and Singleton, to express the matter most favourably to them, do not remember being told by Buckmaster and Hedley the facts which I have decided they were told. In my opinion the overwhelming inference of all the acceptable evidence is that Singleton did not bother about getting a claims history. He simply, in my opinion, was not concerned about a claims history, unless specifically asked to be so by PLA ...

But I have decided that Stenhouse was itself obliged to collect such information about the company's business and its claims history as should be disclosed to the underwriters, and, curiously, the evidence is quite specific that the only prudent course for Stenhouse to have adopted was to have sought a claims history from past insurers ...

I conclude my examination of this point by saying that there is not any acceptable evidence in this case that Stenhouse ever asked the Group to provide a claims history. The only evidence relating to the point was that given by Singleton of the telephone conversation he said that he had on 20 May 1968 with Buckmaster at the time when Payne was in his office. I have already rejected this evidence and explained my reasons for doing so.

I have already expressed the opinion that one of the contractual obligations imposed upon Stenhouse was to pass on to the underwriters a proper claims history and a description of the company's business. In my opinion it is beyond doubt that PLA was never told the Group's claims history. Certainly it was never told it in any oral conversation and it was not argued that it was done in the proposal.

I have just examined the contractual obligation of Stenhouse to tell PLA of relevant information it had received. A particular aspect of this obligation concerns the manner in which that should be done. In answer to the questions in the proposal concerning claims history and cancellations Stenhouse wrote, as is now so well known: "Not known to brokers." In the circumstances in which this answer was given I am of the opinion that it was a further breach of the contractual duty of Stenhouse to exercise reasonable care and skill. The answer divorced from the anterior circumstances to which I have already referred was, of course, untrue. Secondly, in its character as an untrue statement it exposed the client, Reliance, and the validity of the policy thereafter to be issued to the risk, as should have been well known to an experienced broker, that the policy would be avoided. In *Greenhill v Federal Insurance Co Ltd* [1927] 1 KB 65 at 85, 86 the law was restated in these words by Scrutton LJ: "I have always understood the proper line that an underwriter should take, except in matters that he is bound to know, is absolutely to abstain from asking any questions, and to leave the assured to fulfil his duty of good faith, and make full disclosure of all material facts, without being asked. And it seems to me to be of great importance to the general duty of disclosure that that position of the underwriter should be maintained, and not whittled away by alleged waiver."

But the serious quality of the two breaches of this contractual obligation to which I have just referred is emphasised and made more serious by the circumstance that Reliance was never told that the proposal, or any of the other 39 proposals, had been submitted with these unhappy answers. If indeed, as was argued on behalf of Stenhouse, Reliance was contractually obliged to collect, select, prepare and then give to its broker a complete claims history, I am of the opinion that Stenhouse ought, before the proposal was submitted to PLA, to have told Reliance the form the answers took. It never did. Let it be argued, contrary to the fact, that, before Stenhouse had been appointed broker, Reliance had been devious and had deliberately made misleading statements as, perhaps, Laird and Singleton suggested. It was at least, in my opinion, obligatory on Stenhouse, after it had been appointed broker, to tell Reliance that it intended to submit a proposal with the answer "Not known to brokers". By this failure Stenhouse prevented Reliance from giving the claims history to the underwriter. On this point the evidence of Laird is of great significance. He said: "Q — Would you agree that it would be a safe procedure in every case for the broker to ask the client to check the proposal form before it is submitted to the underwriter? A — Was your question that it would be a safer procedure? Q — Would you agree that it would be a safe procedure for a broker to ask a client to check a proposal form before it is submitted to an underwriter? A — Yes. It would be a safe procedure, yes."

This was not done and I have no doubt that if it had been done neither Buckmaster nor Hedley would have agreed that the proposal should go forward in that form.

For the reasons I have given I am of the opinion that Stenhouse failed in its duty to exercise reasonable care and skill when it submitted the proposal in the form it did . . .

I will now consider another defence that was made by Stenhouse. This defence alleged that Reliance would disclose to Stenhouse "all information in its possession with respect to fire claims". I think it is implicit in the form in which this defence was stated, and I certainly think it was expressed in the form it was argued, that the contention was that a term was to be implied in the contract made by Reliance with Stenhouse that the former would search through all the records of all its subsidiaries over an innominate number of years for the purpose of compiling a list of information concerning prior claims and, having made this collection, give it to Stenhouse. Whether or not this term is to be implied it is interesting to record part of the evidence given by Mr Singleton. That witness said: "Q — But from your experience wouldn't you expect that any insurer who has been given only claims paid in respect of a three year period, and who understood that he was being given only claims paid as distinct from outstanding claims — from your experience, wouldn't you consider that as a matter of course the insurer would ask for outstanding claims? A — Sometimes it is very difficult to get outstanding claims and even an accurate knowledge from a large group of companies. The company secretary on most occasions probably does not know about them." But the very nature of the relationship which had been established between the parties before the contract was made, in my opinion, is evidenced in the contract when it was made, and was a recognition that Stenhouse was the expert who knew the information which ought to be disclosed. If indeed the relationship were not thus, and were as Stenhouse contended, the duty of making a decision about what was relevant to be disclosed would rest with the client. That is one of the very situations that Reliance sought to avoid and, in my opinion, one on which Stenhouse, by the words of its contract, undertook to give advice. It is true that Buckmaster knew it would be necessary to make disclosures of past claims, and, for evidence of his knowledge on this point if it is necessary, a reference need only be made to what he and Hedley said at the meeting on 24 May 1968, and what Buckmaster said to Singleton on 10 July 1968. "Do they know of our past claims?" was the question that Buckmaster asked Singleton. The reply was: "Yes", but significantly it was not: "You have not told us anything about past claims or given us a written list of your claims history." Indeed Buckmaster had authorised Singleton to speak to the past insurers to get any assistance that he wanted.

In the case of the instant contract it is not, in my opinion, necessary to imply a term that the client will volunteer its past claims experience in order to give the contract appointing the broker a business efficacy. For the broker can still carry out that contract by taking alternative courses which are either to ask the client or refer to past insurers. Indeed Singleton, but only after the fire and in May 1969, did refer to Sun Alliance and did obtain a two-year claims history as he requested. If he had asked, and he did not do so, Buckmaster for information or help Buckmaster would have co-operated, as indeed both Laird and Singleton acknowledged. But in my opinion it is not necessary for the purposes of the contract to rely on the client in the manner that learned counsel argued. It may well be imprudent to do so ...

[His Honour then referred to the Group's alternative claim against Stenhouse in negligence and indicated, without deciding the point that since the only formal relationship between the parties lay in contract, the Group would not be entitled to sue for negligence arising out of the same subject matter.

In the result, his Honour pronounced the following orders:
(1) Verdict for the first-named third party Davies.
(2) A declaration that in the event that the defendant in the action (Reliance Group) is held to be legally liable to pay damages claimed by the plaintiff the defendant is entitled to recover damages from the second-named party Stenhouse in an amount equal to the amount of the indemnity to which the defendant would have been entitled had it been entitled to be indemnified in respect of the said claim under the policy issued by PLA together with an amount equal to the sum to which the defendant would have been entitled in respect of law costs, charges and expenses.]

The role of the insurance representative or broker in completing the proposal form will be considered further in Section 2 in connection with the doctrine of *uberrimae fidei*. The broker is an intermediary between the assured and the insurer or underwriter. This can lead to a conflict of interest. To whom does the broker owe his primary duty? In *Anglo-African Merchants v Bayley* [1970] 1 QB 311 at 322-4; [1969] 2 All ER 421 at 428-30, Megaw J said:

Counsel for the defendant conceded that, in all matters relating to the placing of the insurance, the insurance broker is the agent of the assured, and of the assured only. I do not think that this proposition of law has ever been in doubt amongst lawyers. I hope it is not in doubt amongst insurance brokers or insurers. More than 40 years ago Scrutton LJ said: "I agree, that in the case of marine insurance there is not the slightest doubt, and never has been the slightest doubt, that the broker is not the agent of the underwriter." He then went on to say that in his experience it would be quite wrong to say that this applies merely to marine insurance: see *Rozanes v Bowen* (1928) 32 Lloyd LR 98 at 101.

Counsel for the defendant, however, submitted, on instructions, that while this principle applies to the placing of the policy (be it noted that Scrutton LJ expressed no such limitation), yet when a claim arises under a policy the insurance broker who placed the policy may thereupon become an agent of both parties in certain respects. This, says counsel, is not merely the practice at Lloyd's; it is the practice also in the non-Lloyd's insurance market in this country; indeed, it is said, it is worldwide practice in the insurance business. When a claim arises, it is asserted, the insurer—Lloyd's underwriters or other insurers—may, and commonly does, instruct the insurance broker who placed the insurance to obtain a report from assessors as to the claim. The broker is, apparently, entitled to accept these instructions without a by-your-leave from his principal, the assured, and without the principal being told by the agent that he is accepting instructions from the adverse, or potentially adverse, party. The assessors' report, unless it contains allegations of fraud, goes from the assessors to the insurer via the broker. The broker sees the report and keeps a copy on his file. But the broker may not disclose the contents of the report to the assured or to the assured's legal advisers, without the express consent of the insurer. The report is the insurer's document.

That practice was followed in the present case. There was a copy of such a report in Garthwaites' file relating to this insurance. It was not made available by Garthwaites to the assured. Privilege was claimed in respect of it against the assured. That claim was persisted in until a very late stage of the hearing. Indeed, though the document was at last made available to the plaintiffs out of their agent's file, this was, I think, claimed to be done as a matter of grace only.

The law, again, has been stated with clarity and precision in the judgment of Scrutton LJ in *Fullwood v Hurley* [1928] 1 KB 498 at 502: "No agent who has accepted an employment from one principal can in law accept an engagement inconsistent with his duty to the first principal ... unless he makes the fullest disclosure to each principal of his interest, and obtains the consent of each principal to the double employment."

The principle is expressed in this way in *Bowstead on Agency*, 13th ed, p 144: "... he may not act for both parties to a transaction unless he ensures that he fully discloses all the material facts to both parties and obtains their informed consent to his so acting ... Any custom to the contrary will not be upheld."

If an insurance broker, before he accepts instructions to place an insurance, discloses to his client that he wishes to be free to act in the way suggested, and if the would-be assured, fully informed as to the broker's intention to accept such instructions from the insurers and as to the possible implications of such collaboration between his agent and the opposite party, is prepared to agree that the broker may so act, good and well. In the absence of such express and fully informed consent, in my opinion it would be a breach of duty on the part of the insurance broker so to act.

The potential dangers and undesirable consequences are obvious in any case where, as here, an agent permits himself, without the express consent of his principal, to make a compact with the opposite party whereby he is supplied with information which he is, or may be, precluded from passing on to his principal. Such a relationship with the insurer inevitably, even if wrongly, invites suspicion that the broker is hunting with the hounds whilst running with the hare. It readily leads to consequences such as occurred in this case where a broker refused to comply with a proper request from his principal's solicitors, but sought or accepted advice from the adverse party's solicitors as to how he should act vis-à-vis his principal. If the insurer desires to obtain an assessor's report, he can obtain it through some other channel than the assured's agent, the broker who has placed the insurance. If the insurer thinks it would be helpful in arriving at a fair and proper settlement of a claim that the assured's broker should see the whole or part of the assessor's report, he can disclose it to the broker; but not, in the absence of the express consent of the assured, subject to a condition that the agent shall withhold relevant information from his principal.

It was said by counsel, on instructions, that the practice which he described is common knowledge, not only as being the practice of Lloyd's brokers, but as being general practice in the insurance market. I find it remarkable, if so, that there is no reference to it—none so far as I am aware, and none to which counsel could refer me—in any decided case or in any of the well-known textbooks dealing with insurance law, some which deal at length with the practice of the insurance market and the position of insurance brokers. Even if it were established to be a practice well known to persons seeking insurance—not merely to insurers and brokers—I should hold the view, in conformity with the passage which I have cited from *Bowstead*, that a custom will not be upheld by the courts of this country if it contradicts the vital principle that an agent may not at the same time serve two masters—two principals—in actual or potential opposition to one another: unless, indeed, he has the explicit, informed, consent of both principals. An insurance broker is in no privileged position in this respect.

Contracts of Insurance

See also *North and South Trust Co v Berkeley* [1971] 1 WLR 47; [1971] 1 All ER 980.

Reference should be made in this section to one other relationship of considerable importance in insurance business, namely between the original insurer and a reinsurer. Insurance is based upon the statistical probability that premiums received for a large number of risks will be sufficient to meet the claims made when some of those risks come home to roost. The statistical probabilities can be upset if a single event is insured for an amount which is totally out of proportion with the other policies. Therefore, the insurer may reinsure with another insurer. For example, Coverall may be pleased to have Trans Shipping Co's insurance business, but may not wish to underwrite the total liability for the loss of *Titanic II* valued at say $200 million. Like a bookmaker laying off his bets to square his book, Coverall may share the risk by reinsuring its own liability with a Lloyd's syndicate. The practice of reinsurance is illustrated in *Southern Cross Assurance Co Ltd v Australian Provincial Assurance Association Ltd* (1935) 53 CLR 618.

QUESTIONS

Question 1

Explain the purpose and function of insurance contracts. Consider the following schemes and arrangements as well as any others you find helpful to illustrate your answer:
(1) Carb Pty Ltd takes out three policies with Coverall Insurance Ltd against:
 (a) more than 30 points of rain falling at Ryde during its annual outdoor motor accessories display;
 (b) negligence claims against it for defective automotive components;
 (c) Jim Handy's death while he remains managing director of the company.
(2) Carb decides to cancel all its insurances because they are too expensive and to invest annually the amount of premiums previously paid to Coverall in long-term Commonwealth bonds.
(3) Compulsory third-party motor vehicle insurance schemes.

Question 2

Is Coverall Insurance obliged to insure Carb once it has received Carb's proposal form? What relevant matters will affect Coverall's assessment of the appropriate premium to charge Carb? In answering the question consider any factors specifically applicable to Carb or any actions which Carb may take which would affect the premium.

Question 3

Consider to whom the insurance broker owes his primary duty. What degree of skill is imputed to an insurance broker and what degree of care is required in explaining a contract of insurance to a proponent? If the insurance broker is involved in a Lloyd's scheme, will any difficulties arise as to his primary duty? To what extent are surrounding circumstances used to indicate the nature of the relationships involved? How adequate are the existing legal rules in responding to the situations raised in this question?

SECTION 2: THE UBERRIMAE FIDEI DOCTRINE AND CONSTRUCTION OF INSURANCE CONTRACTS

In Chapter 1 it was suggested that legal transactions should be critically examined in the context of their commercial function so as to ascertain whether the legal rules are responsive to commercial needs. The function of an insurance contract has been outlined in the previous section: in what ways does it differ from a contract of sale or carriage? In *Newsholme Brothers v Road Transport and General Insurance Co Ltd* [1929] 2 KB 356 at 362, Scrutton LJ said:

> The contract of insurance requires the utmost good faith; the insurer knows nothing; the assured knows everything about the risk he wants to insure and he must disclose to the insurer every fact material to the risk.

This requirement of disclosure under the principle of *uberrimae fidei* (utmost good faith) is in stark contrast to the normal rule in commercial transactions between parties at arm's length, namely, *caveat emptor* (let the buyer beware). The justification appears to be the proponent's inherent advantage of knowing all the facts about the risk to be insured. On the other hand, the insurance policy itself will normally be a contract of adhesion with terms drawn exclusively by the insurer, who no doubt conceives a need for self-protection against fraud. In the cases extracted below, consider whether the insurers and the courts have taken that protection to unnecessary lengths to the detriment of bone fide proponents. Is there a need for reform by legislative intervention?

The insured must also avoid falsehood and fraud in carrying out the terms of the policy and in making claims: *Moraitis v Harvey Trinder (Q'land) Pty Ltd* [1969] Qd R 226 at 236. The insurer has a corresponding duty of good faith in the sense that it must not make misrepresentations and should avoid conflict of duty situations: see *North and South Trust Co v Berkeley* [1971] 1 WLR 47; [1971] 1 All ER 980. However in each case this duty requires only fair dealing and avoidance of falsehood and fraud; it does not involve unsolicited disclosures as does the *uberrimae fidei* principle.

In examining the insured Carb's duty of disclosure it may be helpful to break the issues into three broad headings, although each overlaps the others. First, what information must the insured disclose in every case? Second, what is the effect of provisions in the proposal form or policy which purport to require disclosure of additional information? Third, how, when and to whom must disclosure be made?

THE TEST OF MATERIALITY

Issues under the first heading include:

(1) Must Carb disclose information which it considers material or which Coverall Insurance Ltd considers material?

(2) Are Coverall's internal decisions as to what factors should influence premium rates relevant?

(3) Is Carb obliged to disclose relevant information of which it is unaware, or has forgotten?

(4) Upon whom rests the onus of proving materiality?

Babatsikos v Car Owners' Mutual Insurance Co Ltd
Supreme Court of Victoria [1970] VR 297

[The complainant, Babatsikos, sued the defendant insurer in the Melbourne Court of Petty Sessions to recover $591.15 under a comprehensive motor vehicle insurance policy in respect of the cost of repairs to his vehicle. The defendant argued that it was entitled to refuse indemnity because the complainant made certain misrepresentations and/or non-disclosures in his proposal form, and alternatively that it was entitled to avoid the policy whether or not the misrepresentations were material since the proposal was expressed to form the basis of the contract. The magistrate entered judgment for the complainant. The defendant obtained an order *nisi* to review this decision.]

Pape J: ... The proposal form which the complainant admitted having signed was tendered in evidence by the defendant during the cross-examination of the complainant. It contained the following questions and answers by the complainant: Question 4(c) "How long have you held a driver's licence?" Answer: "Three years and four months."

Question 6(c) "Will any person holding a learner's permit or a provisional licence ever drive the vehicle?" Answer: "No."

The proposal concluded with these words: "I do hereby declare and warrant that the answers given above are in every respect true and correct, and I have not withheld any information likely to affect the acceptance of this proposal, and I agree that this proposal and declaration shall be the basis of the contract between the company and myself and I further agree to accept the company's policy subject to the terms and conditions to be contained therein."

The complainant's signature followed these words, together with the date, 21 June 1968.

The evidence of the complainant as disclosed in the affidavits in support of the order *nisi* and in the answering affidavit showed that he was involved in an accident in which his vehicle was damaged on 25 February 1969. It also showed that he had one year and nine months' driving experience in Victoria, but that he had previously driven in Germany for about 15 months, and that although he had never held a driver's licence in Germany, he was not obliged to hold such a licence because (being a foreigner) he was entitled to drive a motor car if he held a social security card which he did hold. He also swore that he had driven a motor car in Greece for about one year as a driver under instruction ...

[After referring to the argument addressed to him his Honour summarised the issues at 300:] The stipendiary magistrate gave the following reasons for judgment: "I have to consider only two questions here, that is question 6(c) — will any person holding a learner's permit or a provisional licence ever drive this vehicle? I hold that the complainant is not the holder of a provisional licence and would not hold a provisional licence in other states. The next question 4(c) — how long have you held a driver's licence? The answer given was three years and four months — but the defendant in fact had only held the licence for one year and nine months. On the authority which has been cited to me on behalf of the complainant (*Godfrey v Brittanic Assurance Co Ltd* [1963] 2 Lloyd's Rep 515) it is for the defendant to show that the representation was material, and upon the evidence before me I am not prepared to say that the insurance company has discharged this burden. There will, therefore, be an order in favour of the complainant." After argument the amount of the order was fixed at $591.15 the cost of repair.

On 5 June 1969 Master Jacobs granted an order *nisi* to review this decision on the following grounds:

(1) That the magistrate was in error in holding that the onus was upon the defendant to adduce evidence to show that the misrepresentation constituted by the complainant's answer to question 4(c) was material.

(2) That the magistrate should have formed his own opinion of the materiality of the said representation irrespective of whether any evidence was given at all as to such materiality.

(3) That even if there was such an onus upon the defendant upon the evidence given to the magistrate he was bound to have found that the said representation was material.

(4) That the magistrate ought to have found that the failure by the complainant to disclose the fact that he was the holder of a probationary licence amounted to a non-disclosure of a material fact sufficient to entitle the defendant to avoid the contract of insurance ...

Grounds 1 and 2 I think ought to be considered together. Ground 1, I think, proceeds upon a misunderstanding of what the stipendiary magistrate said in giving his reasons for judgment. It assumes that he held that there was an onus on the defendant to prove that the misrepresentation contained in the answer was material, and that he then held that this onus could be discharged only if the defendant adduced evidence of materiality. I do not think the stipendiary magistrate so held. What he did hold was that it was for the defendant to show that the representation was material, and that upon the evidence before him he was not prepared to say that this burden had been discharged. There can be no doubt that the burden of proving materiality was on the defendant: Instruments Act 1958 s 25; *Dawsons Ltd v Bonnin* [1922] 2 AC 413, per Viscount Finlay at 429; [1922] All ER Rep 88; *Godfrey v Brittanic Assurance Co* [1963] 2 Lloyd's Rep 515, per Roskill J at 518; *Davies v National Fire & Marine Insurance Co* [1891] AC 485, per Lord Hobhouse at 489; *Dalgety & Co Ltd v AMP Society*

[1908] VLR 481, per Cussen J at 497; 14 ALR 299; *Preston & Colinvaux*, 2nd ed, p 89; *McGillivray*, 5th ed, Vol 1, paras 810, 819 and 920. I did not understand Mr Merralls to contest this proposition.

But the magistrate did not hold that materiality could only be established if the defendant adduced evidence on that issue. Evidence having in fact been adduced the magistrate was bound to give consideration to it and assign to it such weight as he thought proper. But, as I shall subsequently show, the defendant was not required to adduce evidence, for some circumstances are so obviously material and some are so obviously not material that evidence would be superfluous. But there are other circumstances which involve questions of novelty or doubt, and if a defendant does not call evidence to show that such circumstances would be regarded as material by a prudent insurer, or if the evidence which is called is insufficient to satisfy the tribunal that those representations were material and the tribunal is unable to feel satisfied that they were material, then the burden of proof has not been sustained. The magistrate did not say that materiality could only be established if the defendant called evidence which satisfied him of the materiality.

Ground 2 which was that "The magistrate should have formed his own opinion of the materiality of the said representation irrespective of whether any evidence was given at all as to such materiality" is allied to the first ground and seems to suggest that the magistrate was bound to ignore any evidence given by or on behalf of the defendant and act upon his own opinion. I cannot believe that this is what was intended, for such evidence as there was was led by the defendant and was relied upon by it. Such a proposition could, of course, not be sustained. What I think the ground means is that since the magistrate said that upon the evidence before him he was not satisfied that the defendant had discharged the burden of proving materiality, he must be taken as having failed to apply his own mind to the question. I do not think on a fair reading of his reasons for judgment this was the case. It is true that he did not say: "The evidence of the witness, De Graaf, has not satisfied me that this matter was material, and since I am unable to say for myself whether the question would have been regarded as material by a prudent underwriter, I hold that the defendant has not discharged the burden of proof." But in my view this is the true effect of what he said. I do not think that it can be maintained that when the magistrate said "It is for the defendant to show that the representation was material and upon the evidence before me I am not prepared to say that the insurance company has discharged that burden", he was intending merely to say that he was not prepared to act on De Graaf's evidence without having turned his own mind to the question. What he meant to convey by his words was that the evidence given did not convince him that the matter would have been material to a prudent insurer, and that in these circumstances he himself was not satisfied that it was material. That is a view which, in my opinion, was quite open to him having regard to the fact that the answer to this question was not self evident or obvious and to the deficiencies in the evidence which was led by the defendant ostensibly to assist him to arrive at an informed judgment. I think, therefore, that neither ground 1 nor ground 2 is made out.

[His Honour then referred to authorities regarding the admissibility of evidence as to the practice of insurers in determining whether particular facts or circumstances are material, and continued at 305:] It would thus appear that such evidence is admissible, but is not essential, unless the question of materiality is not obvious to the tribunal, in which case if no evidence is called the defendant may be held liable because he has not discharged the burden of proof. This is made plain by what was said by Scrutton J, in *Glasgow Assurance Corp v Symondson & Co* (1910) 16 Com Cas 109, where at 119 his Lordship said: "Although in recent practice evidence has frequently been admitted of underwriters to state whether in their opinion certain facts would influence the judgment of a prudent assurer, no such evidence was tendered by either party in this case. I am, therefore, left to form my own judgment on the question from such knowledge as I have of insurance matters."

But although the cases establish that the evidence of experts other than the parties may be given, it is less clear that the insurer himself, or if it be a company, the officers of the company, are entitled to give evidence as to the practice of the insurer in regard to a particular class of risk, for the question is (as is pointed out in the passage from *Halsbury* to which I have just referred) not what the particular insurer would regard as material, but what a prudent insurer would so regard and it does not always follow that a particular insurer is necessarily a prudent insurer. There would seem to be little doubt that an officer of a defendant company (if he were qualified to do so) could give evidence of the general practice of other insurers, and in *Dalgety & Co Ltd v AMP Society*, Cussen J was disposed to think that he could. But the learned judge thought that such officers of a defendant ought not be allowed to state that a particular representation or nondisclosure by the assured was material to the risk they were invited to insure against. Nevertheless, there are statements in Australian cases which support the view that they may do so. In *Guardian Assurance Co Ltd v Condogianis* (1919) 26 CLR 231 at 245; 25 ALR 185 Isaacs J (in a dissenting judgment), said: "It is to be noted that ... no witness is called from the Guardian Assurance Co to say either that they had no actual knowledge of the fact, (that there had been an earlier fire) or that it was the practice of that company to attach importance to such fires, or that the company was induced as alleged, to issue the policy by its ignorance of that fact. No doubt it is not incumbent on the company to prove as a matter of law that it was so induced, but in the circumstances the defendant's complete absence from the witness box weighs with me upon the question of what a reasonable assurance company might have done in the circumstances of the case."

In *Western Australian Insurance Co Ltd v Dayton* (1924) 35 CLR 355 at 379; 30 ALR 106 Isaacs ACJ (with whom Gavan Duffy J agreed), said: "As to materiality, that is always a question of fact, dependent on 'all the circumstances at the time the contract was made'. See *Carter v Boehm* (1766) 3 Burr 1905; [1588-1774] All ER Rep 183. The test of materiality is whether in view of 'all the circumstances at the time' which include, of course, the full circumstances of the fact undisclosed, that fact would have influenced the company as a prudent insurer in fixing the premium or in determining to accept the risk. But it must not be forgotten that 'the circumstances' include the knowledge, the practice and the proved conduct of the insurer. If for instance, it were the known practice of a company to disregard a certain class of facts, the non-disclosure of such a fact would not prima facie qua that company be material, however it might be with regard to another company." See also *Saunders v Queensland Insurance Co Ltd* (1931) 45 CLR 557, per Evatt J at 571; [1932] ALR 60, and *Godfrey v Brittanic Assurance Co Ltd*, where Roskill J permitted an officer of the defendant company to give evidence as to its practice.

These cases seem to establish that upon the issue of materiality evidence may be given by the defendant as to its practice. But although such evidence is admissible as part of the circumstances existing at the time of the proposal, it does not of itself establish materiality, although it may assist the tribunal of fact to come to a conclusion on the issue. In truth it goes only part of the way — it at least establishes that the defendant regarded it as material (and so negatives any suggestion that the defendant did not regard it as of importance), but it does not of necessity establish that a prudent insurer would have regarded it as material. It is conceivable that a particular insurance company may decide as a matter of policy not to insure proponents of a certain religion or faith, and so regard it as material to be informed by the answer to a question in the proposal of the religion of the proponent. But the mere asking of the question would not make the matter material unless it were established that a prudent insurer would so regard it. Prima facie such a matter would not be material, but evidence might show that it was material and could be so regarded by a prudent insurer, as might be the case if the intended insurance was against fire and the subject matter of the insurance within an area where religious dissension had caused rioting and arson.

I turn, therefore, to ground 3, which attacks the magistrate's finding that although the answer to question 4(c) was false, nevertheless, he was not satisfied that it was material to the risk.

In considering ground 3 (which relates solely to the complainant's answer to question 4(c) in the proposal) it is first of all necessary to examine the effect of s 25 of the Instruments Act 1958. That section was first enacted by s 2(1) of the Instruments (Insurance Contracts) Act 1936 (No 4464). It reads as follows: "No contract of insurance (other than a contract of life insurance) shall be avoided by reason only of any incorrect statement made by the proponent in any proposal or other document on the faith of which such contract was entered into revived or renewed by the insurer unless the statement so made was fraudulently untrue or material in relation to the risk of the insurer under the contract." It is to be observed that this section is confined to statements made by the proponent in any proposal or other document, and has thus no application to questions of nondisclosure unless the nondisclosure renders the statement untrue: cf *Guardian Assurance Co Ltd v Condogianis* (1919) 26 CLR 231; 25 ALR 185; and on appeal *sub nom Condogianis v Guardian Assurance Co Ltd* (1921) 29 CLR 341; 27 ALR 238; [1921] 2 AC 125. It is not easy at first reading of this section to ascertain what the legislature had in mind in enacting it for (apart from cases of nondisclosure) before the passing of the Act contracts of insurance could only be avoided if a false representation was made fraudulently or if made innocently, it was material to the risk. In *Dawsons Ltd v Bonnin* [1922] 2 AC 413 at 422; [1922] All ER Rep 88, Viscount Haldane said: "In England it was always possible to set aside a contract for misrepresentation, but the representation, although sufficient for the jurisdiction, even though perfectly innocent, had to be material. Moreover, at common law it was no defence to an action on a contract that there had been misrepresentation, unless the misrepresentation were fraudulent or of a recklessness analogous to fraud." It cannot be assumed that in enacting this section the legislature intended merely to restate the common law relating to misrepresentations. What then was its object? I think that what the legislature was directing its mind to was the class of case where in the proposals for insurance or the policy the proponent warranted the truth of his answers to the questions put to him and the statements made therein and agreed that the answers or the statements were to be the basis of the contract. Where the proponent made his answers or statements part of the contract it was a matter of no consequence whether they were material or not: *MacGillivray*, 5th ed, Vol 1, p 385, para 794. In *Thomson v Weems* (1884) 9 App Cas 671, Lord Blackburn said at 683: "It is competent to the contracting parties, if both agree to it and sufficiently express their intention so to agree, to make the actual existence of anything a condition precedent to the inception of any contract; and if they do so the non-existence of that thing is a good defence. And it is not of any importance whether the existence of that thing was or was not material; the parties would not have made it a part of the contract if they had not thought it material, and they have a right to determine for themselves what they shall deem material."

In *Glicksman v Lancashire & General Assurance Co* [1927] AC 139, Viscount Dunedin said at 143: "A contract of insurance is denominated a contract *uberrimae fidei*. It is possible for persons to stipulate that answers to certain questions shall be the basis of the insurance, and if that is done then there is no question as to materiality left, because the persons have contracted that there should be materiality in those questions; but quite apart from that, and alongside of that, there is the duty of no concealment of any consideration which would affect the mind of the ordinary prudent man in accepting the risk." See also *Anderson v Fitzgerald* (1853) 4 HL Cas 484; 10 ER 551; *Condogianis v Guardian Assurance Co* [1921] 2 AC 125 at 129; *Schoolman v Hall* [1951] 1 Lloyd's Rep 139 at 142; *Mackay v London General Insurance Co Ltd* (1935) 51 Lloyd LR 201, and *Graham v Wright* (1872) 3 VR (L) 79.

The point is well illustrated by *Dawsons Ltd v Bonnin* where although a statement as to where a motor vehicle would usually be garaged was held to be immaterial, nevertheless the policy was avoided because it provided that the proposal should be the basis of the contract. A similar result followed in *Mackay v London & General Insurance Co Ltd*.

It has further been held that the mere fact that a question is asked about certain matters in the proposal is some evidence of the materiality of that matter: *Glicksman v Lancashire & General Assurance Co* at 144, and *Saunders v Queensland Insurance Co Ltd* (1931) 45 CLR 557, per Evatt J at 571: [1932] ALR 60. Where the parties have agreed that the proposal is to be the basis of the contract (as is the case here) and where questions are asked in a proposal form even if there be no agreement that the proposal is to be the basis of the contract, the result under the law existing before this section was passed was that what I might call "constructive materiality" was or might be established — it was established by the agreement of the parties, if the proposal was made the basis of the contract, and it might by the asking of a question tend to show that the matter was material if there were no such provision.

In my view, what s 25 was designed to do was to abrogate these principles, and to provide that in future cases where it is sought to avoid insurance contracts on the ground of incorrect statements in proposals or other documents, fraud or materiality in fact had to be shown, and that materiality imputed or inferred by contract or by the asking of the question was no longer sufficient. [His Honour then referred to *Mutual Life Insurance Co v Ontario Metal Products Co Ltd* [1925] AC 344 which involved the consideration of s 156 of the Ontario Insurance Act 1914 and continued at 309:]

I, therefore, am of opinion that neither the provision in the proposal making it the basis of the contract, nor the fact that a question was asked, are relevant matters to be considered in deciding the question of materiality, and that this must be treated as question of fact for the magistrate to determine having regard to all the circumstances disclosed in the evidence.

What then is the test of materiality? Mr Merralls argued that it was whether a prudent insurer would have been influenced in his acceptance of the risk or in his assessment of the premium had the question been answered correctly. Mr Duggan, who appeared to show cause, was disposed to suggest that the test was whether a reasonable proponent would, having regard to all the circumstances, consider the matter material.

In my opinion the test propounded by Mr Merralls is the correct test. I think the position is correctly set out in *Preston & Colinvaux's Law of Insurance*, 2nd ed, pp 89, 90. The learned authors there say: "Everything is material which will guide a prudent insurer in determining whether he will take the risk and, if so, at what premium and on what conditions. In determining the question whether a particular fact is one which ought to be disclosed, the test to be applied is not what the assured thinks, nor even what the insurers think, but whether a prudent and experienced insurer would be influenced in his judgment if he knew of it. There are dicta to suggest that the test is 'What would a reasonable assured consider material'?" (and the authors there set out the cases where this has been said, and continue:) "but s 18(2) of the Marine Insurance Act 1906 (s 24(2) of the Commonwealth Marine Insurance Act 1909) adopts the test of the judgment of a prudent insurer, and since marine and non-marine insurance law is identical in this respect, this test may be regarded at the proper one ... It does not matter whether the omission to communicate a material fact arises from intention, or indifference, or mistake, provided the assured knew of the fact in question. What is regarded as material by the 'more experienced and intelligent insurers' carrying on the business in question at the time is what matters, and the general practice of insurers is relevant in this respect."

It has sometimes been said in Australian cases that the test is what a reasonable assured would consider material: see for example per Isaacs J in *Guardian Assurance Co Ltd v Condogianis* (1919) 26 CLR 231 at 246; 25 ALR 185; and recently Megaw J in *Anglo-African Merchants v Bayley* [1969] 2 WLR 686 at 691; [1969] 2 All ER 421, suggested that such might be the case, although he admitted that the position might be more favourable to insurers than as he had stated. Cussen J on the other hand, in *Dalgety & Co v AMP Society* [1908] VLR 481; 14 ALR 299, adopted the prudent insurer test (see VLR at 500).

But I think the position is determined for Australian courts by the judgment of the Judicial Committee of the Privy Council in *Mutual Life Insurance Co of New York v Ontario Metal Products Co Ltd* [1924] AC 344, which is binding upon me, for in that case Lord Salvesen at 350, 351 said: "The main difference of judicial opinion centres around the question what is the test of materiality? Mignault J (in the Supreme Court of Canada from which the appeal came) thought that the test is not what the insurers would have done but for the misrepresentation or concealment, but 'what any reasonable man would have considered material to tell them when questions were put to the insurer.' Their Lordships are unable to assent to this definition." It would thus appear that the Judicial Committee rejected the test suggested by Mr Duggan. Furthermore, in *Saunders v Queensland Insurance Co Ltd* (1931) 45 CLR 557 at 563; [1932] ALR 60, Starke J said: "It is an absolute duty at common law on the part of a person proposing assurance to disclose all facts within his knowledge material to the risk."

The question the magistrate had to determine was thus, whether the defendant had satisfied him on a balance of probabilities that the length of time that the complainant had held a licence was a matter that a prudent insurer would have been influenced by in deciding whether to accept the risk or in relation to the premium he would ask had he decided to accept the risk. This, as the cases cited show (particularly *Western Australian Insurance Co v Dayton*), was entirely a question of fact for the magistrate to decide ...

In my view the magistrate was not bound by the evidence to decide that this matter was material to the risk. He first of all held that the complainant's answer to question 4(c) was false, in that he said that he had held a licence for three years and four months, whereas the magistrate found that he had held such a licence for only one year and nine months. Mr Duggan made a valiant effort to induce me to say that the magistrate's finding was wrong.

He contended that as a matter of construction question 4(c) was not directed to the period of time during which the complainant had held a licence in Victoria, but that it comprehended the period of time during which the complainant held a licence in any country. I am disposed to agree with this contention, and Mr Merralls did not contend for a more restricted interpretation. There is, I think, with respect, much force in the observation of Lord Atkinson, in the House of Lords in *Glicksman's* case [1927] AC 139 at 144 that "it is a lamentable thing that insurance companies will abstain from shaping the questions they put to intending insurers in clear and unambiguous language". Since the question was framed by the defendant it must be construed *contra proferentem*.

[His Honour then considered the meaning of the words "driver's licence" in question 4(c) and concluded that the complainant had only held a licence in that sense for one year and nine months and therefore his answer was a clear misrepresentation. He continued at 311:] But in considering the materiality of the representation it must not be overlooked that the representation with which we are now concerned related to the period of time during which the complainant had held a licence to drive, and not to whether he held a probationary licence. What is said to be a material fact is that the complainant did not disclose that he had held a licence for only one year and nine months. But the defendant's evidence disclosed that it was not directly interested in this matter, but only in the question whether he had a probationary licence. In these circumstances, I think the magistrate was justified in taking the view that the complainant did not misrepresent a material fact, but misrepresented something which, had it been correctly stated, would have enabled the defendant to ascertain what it contends was a material fact, namely, that he held a probationary licence, for a true answer would have put the defendant on enquiry as to the nature of the licence which the complainant held: see *Joel v Law Union & Crown Insurance Co* [1908] 2 KB 863, per Buckley LJ at 897; and *Guardian Assurance Co Ltd v Condogianis* (1919) 26 CLR 231 at 246; 25 ALR 185 where Isaacs J says: "And it must be remembered that unless the matter itself is directly material it is not open to the company to say that it might have been indirectly material as leading to the discovery of other matters." Although this was said in a dissenting judgment which was not upheld by the Judicial Committee of the Privy Council, I do not apprehend that this particular point was decisive against the view taken by the majority of the court or by the Judicial Committee ...

It seems to me that the evidence of De Graaf did no more than establish as a matter of general policy that the defendant company would not insure drivers holding probationary licences, but that apart from the possession of such a licence it would insure any driver of limited experience such as the proponent had. So regarded, it is difficult to see that the question asked was material to the risk, for the representation related to the period during which the proponent had held a licence and not to the type of licence held, and the evidence was that the defendant would have insured the complainant but for the possession by him of a probationary licence.

One other matter leads me to conclude that the magistrate was entitled to say that he had not been satisfied that materiality had been shown, and it is this. I have endeavoured to show that evidence by the defendant's own officer, although admissible, provided only part of the material on which a finding of materiality might be made. Such evidence showed that the defendant regarded the possession of a probationary licence as material (if that be to the point of this aspect of the case, which I am disposed to think it was not). But even if that had been a relevant consideration, the evidence takes the defendant only part of the way it must travel, for it must show that the holding of a probationary licence would have affected a prudent insurer. De Graaf was unable to give evidence of the practice of other insurers, and therefore the magistrate was left to make up his own mind on this matter. The materiality of this representation (whether it relates to the length of time the licence had been held or to the possession of a probationary licence) is not a question of a kind that answers itself, as would be the case if the failure to disclose previous fires in cases of fire insurance or the failure to disclose previous illnesses in the case of a life insurance would involve.

Although the authorities I have referred to show that a defendant is not bound to call expert evidence of materiality to a prudent insurer, yet if he does not do so but relies on his convincing the court that it was material and the court is unable to come to a conclusion whether a particular fact would affect the prudent insurer or not, he must accept the position that the court might find itself bound to hold against him on the burden of proof. That seems to me to be exactly what the magistrate has done, and the supplementary affidavit and the answering affidavit show that it was put to him that he should take this course, and I must confess that had I been in his position and faced with the very unsatisfactory evidence presented in this case, I should have been disposed to say that I had not been satisfied that materiality had been established. I think, therefore, that ground 3 has not been sustained.

Ground 4 is that "the magistrate ought to have found that the failure by the complainant to disclose the fact that he was the holder of a probationary licence amounted to a nondisclosure of a material fact sufficient to entitle the defendant to avoid the contract of insurance".

According to the affidavits, it was argued by the defendant that even if the magistrate held that question 6(c) had been answered truthfully, the proponent was still under a duty to disclose matters which might affect the mind of a prudent insurer, and he had failed to disclose that he was the holder of a probationary licence. Before me it was argued that the fact that the defendant asked a question about learners' licences and provisional licences should have alerted the complainant to the fact that the defendant was interested to know if the complainant held a restricted licence. But it seems to me that this is immaterial, for the duty to disclose material facts does not depend upon whether the proponent believes the matter to be material: *Batos v Hewitt* (1867) LR 2 QB 595, per Cockburn CJ at 607; *Saunders v Queensland Insurance Co Ltd* (1931) 45 CLR 557, per Starke J at 563; [1932] ALR 60; and *Darrell Lea (Vic) Pty Ltd v Union Assurance Co* [1969] VR 401, per Lush J at 404.

That the duty of disclosure of material facts exists along with the duty to answer questions correctly and thereby not to make misrepresentations is demonstrated by what Lord Dunedin said in *Glicksman's* case in the passage which I have already cited from his judgment. It is also clear from cases such as *Godfrey v Brittanic Assurance Co Ltd* [1963] 2 Lloyd's Rep 515 at 527; *Guardian Assurance Co v Condogianis* (1919) 26 CLR at 246; 25 ALR 185, and in [1921] AC at 128-9; *Cleland v London General Insurance Co Ltd* (1935) 51 Lloyd LR 156; *Schoolman v Hall* [1951] 1 Lloyd's Rep 139 at 142, and from *MacGillivray*, 5th ed, Vol 1, paras 863, 864 and 873; *Preston & Colinvaux*, 2nd ed, p 95, and *Halsbury*, 3rd ed, Vol 122, p 186, para 356, that the mere fact that a question such as question 6(c) is answered correctly does not relieve the proponent from making a full disclosure of material facts. Nevertheless "it is unquestionably plain that questions in a proposal form may be so framed as necessarily to imply that the underwriter only wants information on certain subject matters or that within a particular subject matter their desire for information is restricted within the narrow limits indicated by the terms of the question, and in such a case they may *pro tanto* dispense the proposer from what otherwise at common law would have been a duty to disclose everything material": see per Asquith LJ in *Schoolman v Hall* at 143.

[His Honour then concluded that the magistrate had intended his finding that materiality had not been established to cover both the representation and the non-disclosure; and after considering all the evidence agreed with that finding. He concluded at 317-18:] I, therefore, think that ground 4 is not made out, and that this order *nisi* should be discharged. The defendant has only itself to blame for this result. It has accepted the complainant's premium, and the trouble that has occurred is largely due to its careless use of a New South Wales form in connection with Victorian business ...

If the defendant desires (as it is entitled to do) to decline as a matter of policy to refuse to insure all holders of probationary licences, it ought in my view to provide in its policies that no indemnity will attach under the policy if the vehicle insured is being driven by the holder of a licence on probation. Had it done so, doubtless it would not have secured the complainant's business, but even if he had accepted a policy in that form, all this litigation would have been avoided.

Order nisi discharged.

Kazacos v Fire and All Risks Insurance Co Ltd
Supreme Court of New South Wales in Commercial Causes
(1970) 92 WN (NSW) 397

[The facts appear from the following judgment.]

Taylor J: The plaintiff in this action seeks to recover under two policies for insurance effected by him with the defendant company on the premises wherein he carried out the business of a chemist at Lakemba Railway Station.

The risk covered by both policies was the damage or destruction by fire of the premises, fittings and stock in trade. The first policy, described as the fire insurance policy, insured the building, including the landlord's fixtures and fittings, occupied by the insured as a pharmacy situate at the station at Lakemba for $3000, the stock in trade and merchandise for $8000, the business furniture, fixtures and fittings for $3000. The policy was dated 6 December 1966, the proposal for it was dated 23 November 1966. The policy does not contain any express provisions incorporating into the policy the proposal or the questions and answers in the proposal or the declaration at the end thereof. The second policy is described as a consequential fire loss policy. It is dated the same day, the proposal for it is dated 23 November 1966. It indemnifies the insured against loss of gross profits as by the policy to be ascertained. The total sum insured was $15,000. This policy provided: "Whereas the insured has delivered to the company a proposal dated as shown in the schedule herein which it is agreed shall be the basis of this contract of insurance."

The plaintiff had carried on business in this pharmacy for some years. He met a Mr Morris, an inspector of the defendant company, and the insurances were agreed upon. He signed two proposals in which the answers to certain questions were written in by Mr Morris from information furnished to him by the insured. The proposals provided that the person filling out the proposal form in whole or in part should be his agent and not that of the company. The relevant questions and answers in the proposal for the fire policy are:

"(1) By whom is the bulding owned? A. Insured.

"(2) Is the property proposed for insurance in any way mortgaged or otherwise encumbered? A. No.

"(4) Is any power used? If so state particulars. A. No."

It is claimed by the defendant that the answers to all three questions are untrue. Nothing turns on the answers to the questions in the second proposal.

The premises wherein the plaintiff carried on his business were in fact owned by the Commissioner for Railways. The plaintiff was the lessee of these premises for a term of five years from 1 January 1966. the plaintiff had given a trader's bill of sale in November 1963 to Deposit & Investment Co Ltd in the sum of $5250 secured on the personal chattels belonging to the mortgagor of the premises: Railway Ramp, Lakemba.

The chemist shop had in it, inter alia, a power point and a cash register electrically operated.

The questions that arise for determination may be thus summarised:

"In respect of the Fire Policy,

"(1) Were the answers to the questions earlier set out true?

"(2) Were the answers to the questions warranted to be true, that is, was it a term of the contract between the plaintiff and the defendant that they were true?

"If no,

"(3) Were the answers to the questions or any of them a misrepresentation, misdescription or non-disclosure in any material particular?

"In respect of the Consequential Fire Loss Policy,

"(1) Did the plaintiff answer the questions earlier referred to untruthfully and incorrectly?

"(2) Did the plaintiff fail to disclose to the defendant company:

    (a) That he did not own the premises to which the insurance was to apply?

    (b) That there was a mortgage over certain of the furniture, fittings and effects the subject of the insurance?

    (c) That power was used on the subject premises?

"(3) Was this a failure to disclose material matters?"

On 9 January 1967, at night there was a fire on the premises, the building was partially destroyed and there was considerable damage to the stock, fittings and fixtures and there was a disruption of the plaintiff's business. In due course the insurance company claimed to avoid both policies and returned to the plaintiff a cheque for the premiums.

Coming now to the answers to the questions, I hold that the answer to the first question, "By whom is the building owned?", is untrue, though not intentionally so. In the context in which it is used the answer to the question means, I believe, that the insured is saying that he is the owner of the freehold, and he was not. The answer to the second question is partially untrue, not intentionally so, and it is incorrect. The property proposed for insurance, so far as it consisted of the building, was not mortgaged, but what was also proposed to be insured were the business furniture, fittings and fixtures other than those belonging to the Commissioner for Railways, and moveable utensils, and these were the subject of a trader's bill of sale.

The answer to the third question, "Is any power used?", is true. The word "power" in this question, in my opinion, having regard to the context, means power capable of driving machinery and would not cover power that could be used for radiators or power to operate the electrically operated till.

The question then is what is the effect of the answers to these questions being untrue? Mr Campbell, for the insurance company, contended that the effect of the contract was that the truth of these statements was warranted by the terms of the proposal, that they are in fact untrue and this entitled the insurance company, without more, to avoid the fire policy. In respect of the second policy he contended that they were untrue statements of material matters and, equally, the defendant was entitled to avoid the policy. He also relied on a provision in the consequential fire loss policy to this effect: "The company will not be liable for any loss under this policy unless the insured's property destroyed or damaged at the premises is insured against such damage and the company by which such property is insured shall have paid for or admitted liability in respect of such damage." If the company was entitled to avoid and had in fact avoided the first policy, then this clause would operate to relieve it from liability under the consequential fire loss policy.

For the plaintiff, Mr Milne contended that there was no warranty in respect of the answers to the questions in the proposal for the fire policy; if they were untrue they did not amount to material misrepresentations; the defendant was not entitled to avoid either policy.

As to the statements in the proposals, in the third edition of MacGillivray, *Insurance Law*, para 941, it is said: "Statements and promises in the proposal may be warranties if they are incorporated into the contract. The proposal becomes part of the policy when it is expressly stated in the policy to be so, or where it is expressed to be the basis of the contract, but a mere reference to the proposal for a further description of the risk or a statement that a proposal was delivered and that the policy was issued in consideration thereof will not incorporate it as part of the policy. If the proposal is incorporated all express warranties and declarations therein will have the same force as if they were contained in the body of the policy."

Paragraph 942: "If a policy has been issued and the proposal is not made part of it the nominal warranties in the proposal and declarations have the force of representations only and the warranty must be found, if at all, in the policy itself."

This I accept as an accurate statement of the law in accordance with the principle and authority. It is to be remembered that it is the policy that is the contract between the parties and it is a written contract. The proposal is an offer to accept a policy together with the information which the company required so that it may decide to insure or not to insure. If the proposal is accepted and the policy issues then the contract of insurance between the parties is contained in the policy. What is in the proposal can only be contractual between the parties if it is incorporated by reference or otherwise as part of the concluded written contract, the policy: *Macdonald v Law Union Fire and Life Insurance Co* (1874) LR 9 QB 328; see also *Wheelton v Hardisty* (1858) 27 LJ QB 241; 120 ER 106; *Thomson v Weems* (1884) 9 App Cas 671; *Halsbury's Laws of England*, 3rd ed, Vol 22, pp 194–5.

Mr Campbell contended that it was sufficient to constitute a warranty of the truth of the answers if the proposal itself so provided, and he relied upon passages from *General Principles of Insurance Law*, 2nd ed, by E R Hardy Ivamy, p 132: "The usual declaration at the foot of the proposal form that the answers are true, that they are to be the basis of proposed contract of insurance, makes the truth of the answers a condition precedent and the proposed assured by signing it signifies his agreement thereto. The condition may, however, appear for the first time in the policy, in which case the assured signifies his agreement by suing on the policy." At p 241 of the same work the learned author, speaking of conditions, says this: "The mere fact that the stipulation appears on the face of the policy does not necessarily render it a condition precedent. In this respect fire insurance appears to resemble life insurance and to differ from marine insurance, where it has long been held the rule that statements bearing on the risk introduced into the policy are to be construed as warranties. On the other hand, the stipulation is not prevented from being a condition precedent by the fact that it does not appear upon the face of the policy. It may be endorsed upon the policy or may be contained in another and separate document, such as a proposal, provided that it is incorporated into the policy by express words or otherwise."

Mr Campbell much pressed me with a passage from the judgment of Scrutton LJ in *Rozanes v Bowen* (1928) 32 Lloyd LR 98 at 103: "The second point, as I understand it, was that the answers were not in any way incorporated with the policy so that the correct answering was a condition precedent. The answer to that appears to be at the bottom of the form: 'This proposal is to serve as the basis of the contract' and if so, the truth of the statement in it is equally the basis of the contract." The point at issue in the case was the right of Lloyds to avoid this policy because in the proposal there was a question, "Have you already had losses? If 'Yes' kindly answer them summarily, shortly", and the answer was "Yes. My employee lost some months ago a little necklace worth 4000 francs." In fact he had suffered numerous other losses by theft. Scrutton LJ dealt with the case as a failure to disclose material circumstances. He went on to deal in his judgment with the question of materiality.

If the answers to the questions had been warranted to be true and they were in fact false no question of materiality arose, and I cannot read this statement in the judgment of Scrutton LJ as meaning that it is sufficient to constitute a contractual warranty if the statement appears in the proposal without it being incorporated into the contract itself.

For these reasons I am of opinion that the truth of the answers to the questions was not warranted as a term of the fire policy. The question then is, do either or both of the questions and answers constitute a misrepresentation in a material particular? Since I have already held that the answer to each question is untrue, then the only remaining question is, were either or both of these untrue statements material so as to entitle the insurer to avoid the policy? Materiality of a particular fact, subject to proper direction on the test to be applied, is a question of fact: *Halsbury's Laws of England*, 3rd ed, Vol 22, p 188, para 260.

The authorities on the question of materiality of untrue statements in a proposal were recently considered by Pape J of the Supreme Court of Victoria in *Babatsikos v Car Owners' Mutual Insurance Co Ltd* [1970] VR 297. I would adopt the test laid down by His Honour, which was taken from *Mutual Life Insurance Co of New York v Ontario Metal Products Co Ltd* [1925] AC 344: "When statements made by an insured person upon his application for a policy of life insurance are not made the basis of the contract but are to be treated merely as representations, an inaccurate statement is material so as to vitiate the policy if the matters concealed or misrepresented, had they been truly disclosed, would have influenced a reasonable insurer to decline the risk, or to have stipulated for a higher premium; it is not sufficient that they would merely have caused delay in issuing the policy while further inquiries were being made." I also agree with his Honour's judgment that the burden of proving materiality is on the defendant and that he may do this either by calling evidence or by convincing the tribunal of the fact of materiality.

[His Honour then referred to *Babatsikos'* case at 308 and concluded that in the absence of any statutory provision he had to determine the case on principles laid down by the common law authorities.]

I do not think that the fact that the insurers asked the question in the proposal is decisive of the question. It affords, no doubt, a reason for holding that the insurance company itself thought the matter was material. Whether a reasonable insurer in the circumstances would have so thought is a different matter.

[His Honour cited *Glicksman's* case [1927] AC 139 and *Saunders v Queensland Insurance Co Ltd* (1931) 45 CLR 557 and concluded:] Neither of these cases is, in my opinion, authority for the proposition that a question asked in a proposal establishes necessarily that the answer to that question is material.

In the present case no evidence was called and it is left to me to determine the question of materiality of the untrue answers to the questions. My finding would be that I am not prepared to say that either of them is material, and for these reasons: the misrepresentation contained in the first question and answer is that he owned the building. In fact he held a lease for five years of the property from the Commissioner for Railways. If a reasonable insurer had been told that he had a lease for five years, I cannot see how this would have made any difference to its accepting the risk of the premises being destroyed by fire or seeking any increased premium. The plaintiff's title to the premises is not a matter which affects in any way the likelihood or otherwise of their being burnt or damaged by fire.

There is not any question involved of a moral hazard and the only suggestion that could be made as to why the acceptance of the risk would be influenced is that a person who owned the premises would be more likely to have financial stability than a person who merely leased them. I do not think this necessarily follows. Still less do I think it would have anything to do with a reasonable insurer declining the risk.

As to the second misrepresentation, that there was no mortgage on the premises insured, had it been disclosed that the insured had in fact for many years had a trader's bill of sale over his stock and trade, book debts and fixtures, I cannot see how this would to a reasonable insurer have afforded a ground for declining the risk or stipulating for a higher premium ...

In the absence of any evidence, I am not prepared to hold that the answer to either question was material. This finding determines the matter. The parties have agreed on the value of the damage to the building at $2060, the furniture $3000, stock $8000 and consequential loss $1500, a total of $14,560.

[His Honour then considered the plaintiff's contention that he should be awarded interest on the amount of the verdict under s 141 Common Law Procedure Act 1899 (see now Supreme Court Act 1970 s 94). Interest was awarded on the verdict amount at seven per cent from the date of purported avoidance of the policy to the date of judgment. At 404 he added:] Before I part with this case I think it is proper to draw attention to the fact that there may well be need in this state for a provision comparable to s 25 of the Instruments Act of Victoria. The present tendency in insurance contracts is to make the answers to the questions in the proposal and the proposal itself part of the policy. The effect of this is that if there is an untrue or incorrect statement made in the proposal, then, no matter how trivial or how immaterial it is, the insurance company may avoid the policy, since the truth of the matter is warranted. This, coupled with the usual provision in proposals that the person filling in the answers to the questions is deemed to be the agent of the insured and not of the insurance company (whose agent he in fact is in most cases), could well result in contracts being avoided on the incorrectness of matters where there has been no fraud and where the misrepresentation is on a matter quite immaterial to the risk.

Verdict for the plaintiff for $14,560, together with $3666 interest, a total of $18,226.

Joel v Law Union and Crown Insurance Co
English Court of Appeal [1908] 2 KB 863

[The plaintiff was the executrix of the will of Robina Morrison, deceased, who sued the defendant for £3000 being the amount of a policy issued by the defendant on Morrison's life on 4 November 1902. The policy was issued pursuant to a proposal form dated 27 October 1902 which contained answers to standard questions regarding place and date of birth, occupation, habits, etc. There was no dispute as to the accuracy of these answers.

On 31 October 1902, Morrison was interviewed by Dr Bernard Scott on behalf of the defendant insurer. He asked her further questions on a second printed form and filled in her answers including:

(7) What medical men have you consulted? When? And what for? Dr T B Scott, Bournemouth; rarely; colds. Dr Hodson, Brighton; last spring, measles.

(9) Have you at any time had, and if so, when, any of the following ailments, viz:

(b) apoplexy, palsy, fits of any kind, mental derangement, brain fever, or other disease of the brain? No.

Morrison signed the following declaration at the end of the form: "I, the said Robina Morrison, do hereby declare, with reference to the proposal for assurance on my life, and my declaration 30 October (? 27) 1902, that the answers to the foregoing questions are true."

The policy contained no reference to the proposal or other declarations.

The plaintiff admitted that in 1894 the assured had suffered from nervous depression for which she was treated by a Dr Morgan; that she had suffered acute mania and was certified by Dr Morgan with the result that for six months in 1895 she was confined in a sanatorium of Dr Leach. It appeared that she was ignorant of the facts that she had been insane and had been under restraint on that account, and that she had been led to believe that she had been sent away for a rest cure on account of nervous breakdown. The assured committed suicide, while of unsound mind, in March 1906.

Lord Alverston CJ, on the basis of the jury's findings of fact, held that the policy was void for non-disclosure. The plaintiff appealed to the Court of Appeal.]

Fletcher Moulton LJ: ... The contract of life insurance is one *uberrimae fidei*. The insurer is entitled to be put in possession of all material information possessed by the insured. This is authoritatively laid down in the clearest language by Lord Blackburn in *Brownlie v Campbell* (1880) 5 App Cas 925 at 954: "In policies of insurance, whether marine insurance or life insurance, there is an understanding that the contract is *uberrima fides* [sic] that, if you know any circumstances at all that may influence the underwriter's opinion as to the risk he is incurring, and consequently as to whether he will take it, or what premium he will charge, if he does take it, you will state what you know. There is an obligation there to disclose what you know, and the concealment of a material circumstance known to you, whether you thought it material or not, avoids the policy." There is, therefore, something more than an obligation to treat the insurer honestly and frankly, and freely to tell him what the applicant thinks it is material he should know. That duty, no doubt, must be performed, but it does not suffice that the applicant should bona fide have performed it to the best of his understanding. There is the further duty that he should do it to the extent that a reasonable man would have done it; and, if he has fallen short of that by reason of his bona fide considering the matter not material, whereas the jury, as representing what a reasonable man would think, hold that it was material, he has failed in his duty, and the policy is avoided. This further duty is analogous to a duty to do an act which you undertake with reasonable care and skill, a failure to do which amounts to negligence, which is not atoned for by any amount of honesty or good intention. The disclosure must be of all you ought to have realised to be material, not of that only which you did in fact realise to be so.

But in my opinion there is a point here which often is not sufficiently kept in mind. The duty is a duty to disclose, and you cannot disclose what you do not know. The obligation to disclose, therefore, necessarily depends on the knowledge you possess. I must not be misunderstood. Your opinion of the materiality of that knowledge is of no moment. If a reasonable man would have recognised that it was material to disclose the knowledge in question, it is no excuse that you did not recognise it to be so. But the question always is, Was the knowledge you possessed such that you ought to have disclosed it? Let me take an example. I will suppose that a man has, as is the case with most of us, occasionally had a headache. It may be that a particular one of those headaches would have told a brain specialist of hidden mischief. But to the man it was an ordinary headache undistinguishable from the rest. Now no reasonable man would deem it material to tell an insurance company of all the casual headaches he had had in his life, and, if he knew no more as to this particular headache than that it was an ordinary casual headache, there would be no breach of his duty towards the insurance company in not disclosing it. He possessed no knowledge that it was incumbent on him to disclose, because he knew of nothing which a reasonable man would deem material or of a character to influence the insurers in their action. It was what he did not know which would have been of that character, but he cannot be held liable for non-disclosure in respect of facts which he did not know.

Insurers are thus in the highly favourable position that they are entitled not only to bona fides on the part of the applicant, but also to full disclosure of all knowledge possessed by the applicant that is material to the risk. And in my opinion they would have been wise if they had contented themselves with this. Unfortunately the desire to make themselves doubly secure has made them depart widely from this position by requiring the assured to agree that the accuracy, as well as the bona fides, of his answers to various questions put to him by them or on their behalf shall be a condition of the validity of the policy. This might be reasonable in some matters, such as the age and parentage of the applicant, or information as to his family history, which he must know as facts. Or it might be justifiable to stipulate that these conditions should obtain for a reasonable time — say during two years — during which period the company might verify the accuracy of the statements which by hypothesis have been made bona fide by the applicant. But insurance companies have pushed the practice far beyond these limits, and have made the correctness of statements of matters wholly beyond his knowledge, and which can at best be only statements of opinion or belief, conditions of the validity of the policy. For instance, one of the commonest of such questions is, "Have you any disease?" Not even the most skilled doctor after the most prolonged scientific examination could answer such a question with certainty, and a layman can only give his honest opinion on it. But the policies issued by many companies are framed so as to be invalid unless this and many other like questions are correctly — not merely truthfully — answered, though the insurers are well aware that it is impossible for any one to arrive at anything more certain than an opinion about them. I wish I could adequately warn the public against such practices on the part of insurance offices. I am satisfied that few of those who insure have any idea how completely they leave themselves in the hands of the insurers should the latter wish to dispute the policy when it falls in. In the case of the question to which I have referred, if it can be shewn, even by the aid of the contemporaneous examination of the medical referee of the office itself, that the insured had at the time some disease, the policy is void. The disease may have been unknown, and even undiscoverable; it may have been transient, and have had no effect on his future life, or on the cause of his death. These things are immaterial. If the company choose to dispute the policy, and establish a single inaccuracy in these statements, which are thus made conditions, the policy is void, and usually all that has been paid thereon is forfeit. Hence I fully agree with the words used by Lord St Leonards in his opinion in the case of *Anderson v Fitzgerald* (1853) 4 HLC 484 at 507 to the effect that in this way provisions are introduced into policies of life assurance which, "unless they are fully explained to the parties, will lead a vast number of persons to suppose that they have made a provision for their families by an insurance on their lives, and by payment of perhaps a very considerable proportion of their income, when in point of fact, from the very commencement, the policy was not worth the paper upon which it was written."

Under these circumstances it is plainly the duty of the court to require the insurers to establish clearly that the insured consented to the accuracy, and not the truthfulness, of his statements being made a condition of the validity of the policy. No ambiguous language suffices for this purpose. The applicant can be and is called on to answer all questions relevant to the matter in hand. But this is merely the fulfilment of a duty — it is not contractual. To make the accuracy of these answers a condition of the contract is a contractual act, and, if there is the slightest doubt that the insurers have failed to make clear to the man on whom they have exercised their right of requiring full information that he is consenting thus to contract, we ought to refuse to regard the correctness of the answers given as being a condition of the validity of the policy. In other words, the insurers must prove by clear and express language the *animus contrahendi* on the part of the applicant; it will not be inferred from the fact that questions were answered, and that the party interrogated declared that his answers were true. This is only what a witness does when he declares he has given true evidence. He is stating his belief, and not making a contract ...

It is evident, therefore, that the case turns mainly on the status and meaning of the paper signed by her on the occasion of her visit to the doctor. I entertain the strongest opinion that the accuracy of the replies to the doctor who examined her was not a contractual limitation or condition of the contract, but that these replies were, and were intended by both parties to be, only statements made by her to the best of her knowledge for the purpose of assisting the medical referee and the company to judge of the goodness of her life, ie, of the risk they were taking. In the first place, the occasion and the circumstances of the statement raise a strong probability that this was so. As Lord Blackburn says with regard to a similar case in *Thomson v Weems* (1884) 9 App Cas 671 at 683, "There was very strong ground for saying that it was not shewn that the assured contracted that her answers to a medical man selected by the company, who was to examine her alone and report to them confidentially the conclusion to which he came, were warranted to be accurate; the very object of the examination would be frustrated if the patient was not to answer frankly and without reserve to the questions she was asked." Next, the nature of the questions shews that they must have been regarded as between the interlocutor and the answerer as relating to belief only.

[His Lordship then referred to the circumstances of the assured's interview with Dr Scott and the answers to the questions on the printed form, and continued at 892:] I am therefore of opinion that the paper signed by the applicant before the doctor does not support the case of the defendants. Taken by itself, without any evidence of the explanations given by the medical referee in putting the questions, it does not to my mind afford any evidence of non-disclosure of the fact of the applicant having been attended by Dr Kinsey Morgan, still less does it shew that the applicant answered untruthfully the questions put to her on behalf of the company as explained to her by the examining doctor. There is nothing in the paper which leads me to think that she acted at that interview otherwise than as an honest person, genuinely desirous to perform her duty to the company, might reasonably have been expected to do. I therefore put this declaration aside as insufficient to support the defence.

But I now come to the point which has occasioned me the greatest difficulty. Over and above the two documents signed by the applicant, and in my opinion unaffected by them, there remained the common law obligation of disclosure of all knowledge possessed by the applicant material to the risk about to be undertaken by the company, such materiality being a matter to be judged of by the jury and not by the court. Here the jury have found that the applicant foolishly but not fraudulently concealed from the defendants that she had consulted Dr Kinsey Morgan in the year 1894 for nervous depression, and that the fact that she had so consulted him was material for the company to know in considering whether they would insure her life. I have no hesitation in coming to the conclusion that we cannot act upon these findings so as to support the judgment for the defendants, because the declaration signed by her was allowed to go to the jury as, and taken by the judge to be, a concealment of the fact which made her liable as for non-disclosure. For the reasons I have given I am of opinion that no such case can be based on that declaration. But I cannot say that, taking the whole of the evidence together, the jury might not have come to the conclusion that in fact there was non-disclosure of the knowledge that she had in this respect, and that she ought to have realised that such knowledge was material. The fact that her own doctor — the ordinary medical referee of the company — seems to have been fully aware of as much as she herself knew about her having consulted Dr Kinsey Morgan, and shews by his report that he attached no importance to it, makes me wonder that the jury should have returned a finding that they did to the fourth question, and makes me believe that they meant by it to say, not that she had any knowledge that a reasonable person would have considered material to impart to the company, but that the fact, if imparted and followed up by them, would have led to the discovery of matters unknown to her which would have been material. This does not, in my opinion, suffice to support defence of non-disclosure. But the findings exist, and, though for the above reasons I am of opinion that the judgment for the defendants must be set aside, I cannot say that even with proper directions there may not be evidence for the jury to consider on these issues, and I therefore am of opinion that the case ought to be sent down for a new trial.

[**Vaughan Williams** and **Buckley LJJ** gave judgments to similar effect.]

New trial ordered.

The Marine Insurance Act 1909 contains its own provisions as to materiality: see, eg, ss 23–27; compare also Life Insurance Act 1945 (Cth) s 83.

In all other types of policy the common law precedents must be reconciled and applied which is not an easy task: see generally O'Hare, "Materiality and the Insurance Contract" (1971) 2 *ACLR* 230.

Terms of the Policy and Materiality

You will have gathered from reading the cases extracted above that it is common practice for insurance companies to ask questions in proposal forms and seek to convert the answers into contractual terms. This practice raises further issues:

(1) Does the fact that Coverall asks a particular question in the proposal form automatically make an untrue answer material? If not, can the answer be regarded as a misrepresentation entitling Coverall to avoid the policy?

(2) Is there a distinction between non-disclosure and misrepresentation?

(3) Is it competent for Coverall to stipulate that an untrue, but immaterial answer, shall form the basis of the contract?

(4) Is there a need for legislative intervention on these issues?

Dawsons Ltd v Bonnin and Others
House of Lords [1922] 2 AC 413

[The facts appear from the following judgment.]

Viscount Haldane: My Lords, this is an appeal from a judgment of the Second Division of the Court of Session, which affirmed a decision of the Lord Ordinary who had tried the action, but varied the reasons on which that decision was based. The action was brought by the appellants to recover a sum of £500 and interest against the respondents, with whom they had insured a motor lorry against fire and also any claims for damages made by the public. The vehicle had been in fact destroyed by fire. The question in the appeal is whether the respondents were freed from liability under the policy by reason of inaccuracy in a statement made by the appellants in the proposal submitted when the policy was issued, to the effect that the motor would usually be garaged at a certain address, whereas it was garaged elsewhere.

My Lords, the policy was issued to the appellants on 8 February 1917, by the agent in Glasgow of the respondents, who were Lloyd's underwriters. The transaction was initiated by a proposal form, signed on behalf of the appellants, who were furniture removal contractors carrying on business at 46 Cadogan Street, Glasgow. They used motor cars and lorries in this business, which they had been in the habit of insuring. Among others with whom they had had transactions of this kind was a Mr Hamilton, an insurance broker, who acted for various insurance societies. He appears to have called on them and to have offered a quotation for the insurance in question, which was accepted. He then filled in a form of proposal from information he thought he had obtained from them, and this when signed became the proposal form as to which the question had arisen. It commenced by setting out the particulars of the motor vehicle intended to be insured, the make being of what was called the Halley lorry type, and of the scope of the indemnity desired, confined to fire and to claims by the public. There then followed 10 questions (to each of which a statement in answer was given), relating to the proposer's name and address, 46 Cadogan Street, Glasgow, and the purpose for which the vehicle was to be used. The fourth of these statements was made in response to a request for a statement of the full address at which the vehicle would usually be garaged. The answer given was "above address", that is to say, 46 Cadogan Street. There was a subsequent question as to the district in which the vehicle would be used, to which the answer was "Glasgow and district". The rest of the 10 questions and answers are not material. Following on the proposal form and in the same document came the policy itself. It proceeded on the narrative that the insured (the appellants) had subscribed and delivered to the insurers the proposal form, dated 22 January 1917, "which proposal shall be the basis of the contract and be held as incorporated herein". The policy then stated that the premium had been paid for an insurance for 12 months, and it set forth the terms of the insurance as including inter alia indemnity to the extent of £500 against loss or damage caused by fire. Appended to the policy and qualifying it there was a statement of "conditions of insurance". The fourth condition was in these terms: "Material misstatement or concealment of any circumstance by the insured material to assessing the premium herein, or in connection with any claim, shall render the policy void."

What happened was this. On 27 December 1917, the vehicle insured was garaged, not at 46 Cadogan Street, but at Dovehill Farm, which had been a farmsteading at Newlands, on the outskirts of Glasgow, but was within the city of Glasgow area. On that date it was burned accidentally ...

The question which arises is whether, under these circumstances, the respondents are liable under the policy they had issued. They contend that the fourth of the answers in the proposal form was untrue. They say that the vehicle insured was not intended to be usually garaged at 46 Cadogan Street but at Dovehill, and that the answer actually given to the fourth question was not accurate, inasmuch as it amounted either to a misrepresentation of intention as to present and future storing or to a contract as to storing in the future which was broken. They also argue that the fourth of the conditions appended to the policy was that any material misstatement or concealment of any circumstance material to assessing the premium was by express provision to render the policy void, and that there was actually misstatement or concealment of the circumstance that the vehicle was to be garaged at Dovehill, a garage which they allege was in such a situation and of such a character that if disclosure had been made the assessment of the premium would have been affected.

My Lords, the reply of the appellants, the insured, on this point was that the question whether the motor vehicle was to be stored at Dovehill or at Cadogan Street was not a material one. The chief risks covered by the policy were in the main wholly unconnected with fire at the garage, and the percentage of the premium to be allocated to that risk was very small. The respondents called evidence to prove that they did consider that the question was one of importance, and the learned judges in the court below appear to have given credence to that evidence and to have attached weight to it. This is an important fact, and I am reluctant to differ from them. But I think that, notwithstanding some differences in the way in which they cross-examined the witnesses called for the respondents, the appellants have sufficiently proved by testimony which commends itself that in all probability no importance would have been attached to any answer to the fourth question in the proposal form to the effect that Dovehill was to be the place of garage.

But that does not dispose of the case. For if the respondents can show that they contracted to get an accurate answer to this question, and to make the validity of the policy conditional on that answer being accurate, whether the answer was of material importance or not, the fulfilment of this contract is a condition of the appellants being able to recover.

My Lords, for this reason it appears to me that the question which really lies at the root of the matter in dispute is one of construction simply. I do not look on the fourth condition appended to the policy as what is important for this purpose, for that condition extends to classes of possible misstatements and concealments which go beyond those to which the proposal statements are confined. On the other hand, they relate to any such as may be actually material in assessing the premium, as distinguished from such as are made by special stipulation as to accuracy conditions of the validity of the general contract of insurance. If there are statements in the answers to the questions in the proposal form which are in this way constituted by special stipulation conditions, they are therefore unaffected by the subsequent and independent condition dependent on materiality.

[His Lordship then referred to the development of the distinction between conditions, warranties and representations and continued:] As Lord Blackburn observed in *Thomson v Weems* (1884) 9 App Cas 683 at 684: "It is competent to the contracting parties, if both agree to it and sufficiently express their intention so to agree, to make the actual existence of anything a condition precedent to the inception of any contract; and if they do so the non-existence of that thing is a good defence. And it is not of any importance whether the existence of that thing was or was not material; the parties would not have made it a part of the contract if they had not thought it material, and they have a right to determine for themselves what they shall deem material." He goes on to point out that in policies of marine insurance it is settled that any statement of a fact bearing on the risk is, "by whatever words and in whatever place, to be construed as a warranty, and, prima facie, at least, that the compliance with that warranty is a condition precedent to the attaching of the risk". Without going so far as to hold that this rule is also applicable to the construction of life policies generally, he thought that it applied to the life policy before him, and "when we look at the terms of this contract, and see that it is expressly said in the policy, as well as in the declaration itself, that the declaration shall be the basis of the policy, that it is hardly possible to avoid the conclusion that the truth of the particulars (which, I think, include his statement that he was of temperate habits) is warranted".

My Lords, Lord Blackburn lays stress in these words on the expression "basis" ... I do not think that it matters whether the representation which is made "basic" is as to a state of present fact or to something to be carried out in the future, such as garaging at a particular place. What is important in the latter alternative is that the insured cannot recover unless he can show that he has performed his part, for his performance has been made the condition of performance by the other party.

My Lords, with these principles of construction in view I turn to the contract before us. As to the fourth of the appended conditions, this, as I have already observed, extends to matters which go beyond in some respects, and are outside in other respects, those dealt with specifically in the proposal form. Moreover, the fourth condition is limited to what is "material to assessing the premium", and I will assume for present purposes that nothing material in this sense was misstated or concealed. If so, that fourth condition does not apply. But on the other hand I do not find in the language used in it anything which cuts down or interferes with the effect of the fourth of the answers in the proposal form, if this in itself imports a condition. If it does import by itself a condition, then I think that, as Lord

Contracts of Insurance

Blackburn laid down in the passage quoted, it imports a condition which must be shown to have been complied with, whether material from an ordinary business standpoint or not. It is clear that the answer was textually inaccurate. I think that the words employed in the body of the policy can only be properly construed as having made its accuracy a condition. The result may be technical and harsh, but if the parties have so stipulated we have no alternative, sitting as a court of justice, but to give effect to the words agreed on. Hard cases must not be allowed to make bad law. Now the proposal, in other words the answers to the questions specifically put in it, are made basic to the contract. It may well be that a mere slip, in a Christian name, for instance, would not be held to vitiate the answer given if the answer were really in substance true and unambiguous. *Falsa demonstratio non nocet*. But that is because the truth has been stated in effect within the intention shown by the language used. The misstatement as to the address at which the vehicle would usually be garaged can hardly be brought within this principle of interpretation in construing contracts. It was a specific insurance, based on a statement which is made foundational if the parties have chosen, however carelessly, to stipulate that it should be so. Both on principle and in the light of authorities such as those I have already cited, it appears to me that when answers, including that in question, are declared to be the basis of the contract this can only mean that their truth is made a condition exact fulfilment of which is rendered by stipulation foundational to its enforceability.

My Lords, for these reasons I feel myself compelled to assent to the general conclusion arrived at by all the learned judges in the Court of Session.

[His Lordship then stated that he preferred to base his decision on the untrue answer in the proposal form rather than on the fourth of the appended conditions.

Viscount Cave gave judgment to the similar effect.]

Lord Dunedin: My Lords, I have found this case one of difficulty. Had I been able to take the view that was taken of the evidence by the learned judges of the Court of Session it would have been easy. That view is embodied in the finding: "Find that the policy is void because the answer to the fourth question in the proposal form contains a material misstatement of a circumstance by the insured material to the assessing of the premium under the policy."

I think that the evidence shows that the misstatement was not in fact material to the assessment of the premium. I cannot therefore decide the case upon the ground of the application of the fourth section of the conditions of assurance, which provides that "material misstatement or concealment of any circumstance by the insured material to assessing the premium herein, or in connection with any claim, shall render the policy void". The same view of the evidence disposes of what I may call the common law doctrine in insurance cases as to disclosure of facts material to the risk. Nor am I able to say that the series of cases, of which *Weems* (1884) 9 App Cas 671 may be taken as a type, enable me to find direct authority. In each of these cases—they are cited by the Lord Ordinary in his opinion—there was either a statement signed by the proposer that his answers to the questions put to him were true, and that he warranted them to be true; or there was a clause in the policy that if any of the statements were untrue the policy was to be void.

Was then the statement as to the usual place of garage material? I pointed out in the case of *Wade v Waldon* 1909 SC 571 at 576 that there may be in contracts certain stipulations which go to the root of the contract, a breach of which entitles the other party to hold the contract at an end; and that there are other stipulations which do not go to the root and only give rise, if broken, to actions of damages. At the same time I quoted Lord Watson, who in his turn quoted the judgment of Blackburn J in *Bettini v Gye* (1876) 1 QBD 183, and pointed out that it was within the power of parties to contract that particular matters, however trivial, might form conditions precedent. Have the parties so contracted in this case? That raises the pure question, as yet I think undecided, when certain statements are said to be the "basis of the contract and incorporated therewith", is that equivalent to saying that these statements are held to be contractually material?

After much consideration, unwillingly in the circumstances of the case, and contrary to my first impression, I have come to the conclusion that it is. I think that "basis" cannot be taken as merely pleonastic and exegetical of the following words, "and incorporated therewith". It must mean that the parties held that these statements are fundamental—ie, go to the root of the contract—and that consequently if the statements are untrue the contract is not binding.

And therefore I come to the same conclusion as has been come to by the noble Viscount who has preceded me [Viscount Cave] and for essentially the same reasons.

I ought, in justice to the learned judges of the Court of Session, to say that I find that they had proposed to follow what Lord Sumner said in the *Yorkshire Insurance Co* case [1917] AC 218 but by the finding quoted they put the judgment on the other ground. I am of the opinion that the appeal must be dismissed with the variation proposed.

[**Lord Wrenbury** and **Viscount Finlay**] dissented, holding that the question whether the car was to be garaged in a building of brick, stone or wood made no difference in assessing the premium, and that therefore there was no misstatement material to assessing the premium within condition 4.

The House of Lords by majority refused the appeal, and affirmed the decision of the Second Division of the Court of Session in Scotland subject to a variation.]

In considering the effect of clauses purporting to constitute the "basis of the contract" you should also refer back to *Babatsikos'* case, p 208, *supra*, and note the effect of Instruments Act 1958 s 25 which is quoted by Pape J. With it should be compared Marine Insurance Act 1909 ss 24 and 26, and the following provisions:

Life Insurance Act 1945 (Cth)

84 A policy shall not be avoided by reason only of any incorrect statement (other than a statement as to the age of the life insured) made in any proposal or other document on the faith of which the policy was issued or reinstated by the company unless the statement—
   (a) was fraudulently untrue; or
   (b) being a statement material in relation to the risk of the company under the policy, was made within the period of three years immediately preceding the date on which the policy is sought to be avoided or the date of the death of the life insured, whichever is the earlier.

Insurance Act 1902 (NSW)

18 (1) In any proceedings taken in a court in respect of a difference or dispute arising out of a contract of insurance, if it appears to the court that a failure by the insured to observe or perform a term or condition of the contract of insurance may reasonably be excused on the ground that the insurer was not prejudiced by the failure, the court may order that the failure be excused.

(2) Where an order of the nature referred to in subsection (1) has been made, the rights and liabilities of all persons in respect of the contract of insurance concerned shall be determined as if the failure the subject of the order had not occurred.

These provisions give rise to several matters of interpretation as well as important policy questions of freedom of contract and consumer protection: see Question 8, *infra*.

Kolokytuas & Anor v Federation Insurance Ltd

Supreme Court of New South Wales Common Law Division. Reported in CCH Australian and New Zealand Insurance Cases (1980) Vol 1, 60-412

Rogers J: A proposal bearing date 18 May 1978 was made by the plaintiffs to the defendant. The proposal set out the usual kinds of questions to be answered which appear in documents of this nature, and then concluded with the following: "I hereby declare that the Answers given above are in every respect true, and that I have not withheld any information likely to affect the acceptance of this Proposal; and I undertake to exercise all ordinary and reasonable precaution for the safety of the said Property; and I agree that the Proposal and Declaration shall be the Basis of the Contract between the Company and myself and shall be taken as part of the Policy, and the particulars supplied in this Proposal shall be deemed express and continuing warranties furnished by me or on my behalf and I further agree ... I make this Proposal subject to the terms and conditions as printed and written in the policy to be issued hereon, which I hereby accept and agree to pay the premium required by the Company."

On 21 March 1978 a cover note was issued in respect of the property and covered the property until a policy issued bearing date 18 May 1978. The policy made no reference whatsoever to the proposal as being part of the policy conformably with the intimation in that vein contained in the proposal. Condition (1) provided: "This Policy shall be voidable in the event of misrepresentation, misdescription or non-disclosure in any material particular."

It appears to me, guided as I am by authority, that there remains the common law obligation to disclose material facts over and above the width of the contractual obligation, even if the declaration in the proposal is part of the contract of insurance. For present purposes it is necessary to look in a little more detail at the decision of the High Court in *Saunders v Queensland Insurance Co Ltd* (1931) 45 CLR 557. The headnote sufficiently sets out the relevant facts when it states that the appellant effected insurance on certain premises with the respondent company. The policy contained a provision that the insurance should be subject to particulars in the proposal for insurance which, it was agreed, should constitute the basis of the insurance and be incorporated in, and form part of, the policy. The proposal was filled in by an agent of the proponent and the declaration made by the proponent's agent in the proposal declared that the proponent had not "withheld any information likely to affect the acceptance of this proposal". The words are the same as in the proposal in the present case.

For various reasons which it is unnecessary to consider, the trial judge gave judgment for the defendant company and discharged the jury. In the context of the appeal to the High Court, Starke and Dixon JJ expressed the view to which I have already referred, that the duty of disclosure is one which arises at common law. Further, and relevantly to the present issue, Starke J said at 563-4: "The pleadings raise other issues. One is the respondent company's allegation that the appellant withheld from it information that was likely to affect the acceptance of the proposal. It will be remembered that one of the matters warranted by the appellant in her declaration was that she had not withheld any information likely to affect the acceptance of the proposal. In fact she had previously had a fire and made a claim under a policy, and this was not disclosed to the company. It is an absolute duty at common law on the part of a person proposing assurance to disclose all facts within his knowledge material to a risk ... But a warranty not to withhold any information involves, I think, a narrower obligation, namely, an obligation not to make a conscious omission — that is, not to omit to state any fact present to the mind of the insured. The fact of the previous fire and claim was within the knowledge of the appellant, but whether she withheld the information in the sense last mentioned is a fact upon which a jury must pass its verdict, as also is the question whether the information was likely to affect the acceptance of the proposal. Again, the company has pleaded that the appellant concealed material facts from it, namely, the fire and the claim, which were within her own knowledge. This issue has not been decided. It involves a consideration of the absolute duty of disclosure already mentioned, and of the question whether the facts that were concealed were material to the risk."

A similar view to that of Starke J was expressed by Dixon J at 568.

The decision of Macfarlan J in *Ogden's* case [1973] 2 NSWLR 7 seems to point to the same view. It appears that, in that case also, it was a term of the proposal that the person preparing it had "not withheld any information likely to affect acceptance of (the) proposal". It was in the light of a proposal in those terms that his Honour expressed the conclusion that the obligation was one which arose in absolute terms as a result of the application of the relevant principles of common law.

In the result, I am of the view that, even if the proposal and the declaration are part of the policy of insurance, there continues to subsist a duty of disclosure on the part of the insured which is not supplanted or destroyed by the terms of the declaration. That duty cannot be described as a "term or condition of the contract of insurance" and accordingly, s 18 [of the Insurance Act 1902 (NSW)] does not deal with the consequence of failure to discharge that duty.

In his recent book, *Insurance Law in Australia and New Zealand*, Professor Sutton addressed himself to the problem presently under consideration. Basing his comment on the decision of the High Court in *Saunders'* case the learned author at p 59, para 2.81 said: "A warranty by the proponent that he has not withheld any information within his knowledge material to the decision of the insurer in respect of the proposal is narrower than the duty of non-disclosure and has its basis in contract, whereas the duty of non-disclosure is a common law duty. It follows from this that s 18 of the Insurance Act 1902 (NSW) will have no application where the duty of non-disclosure is broken because that is a breach of an obligation arising at common law and is not a failure to observe a term of the contract."

In the circumstances, I am of the view that, for the reasons given, I do not have any power to relieve the plaintiffs from the consequences of what I hold to be a failure on their part to disclose material facts. It is, therefore, unnecessary for me to deal with the application to strike out the reply or to delve further into any question of fact which may be sought to be relied upon to excuse the failure I have found to have been committed.

The consequence is that, in the action as a whole, there must be a verdict for the defendant, and that I must order the plaintiffs to pay the defendant's costs.

Judgment for the defendant.

Insurance policies usually contain many other provisions in addition to the so-called "basis of the contract" clause. These conditions exemplify several features of standard form contracts. First, in the great majority of cases they are contracts of adhesion whose terms are non-negotiable and tend to protect the underwriter. Second, the standard conditions have been settled for many years, and have acquired a degree of certainty as the result of innumerable judicial decisions. Insurance companies are therefore loath to change them. However, they are also subject to the criticism that they are couched in very legal and specialised language which is unintelligible to many businessmen and to the uninitiated majority of private policy holders.

A convenient example of a standard form policy is the Lloyd's SG policy contained in Second Schedule to the Marine Insurance Act 1909. It is not a compulsory form but does comply with the mandatory requirements of ss 28 and 29 of the Act, and forms the basis for most marine policies. It can be adapted to suit the circumstances of a particular marine insurance by using appropriate provisions from the Institute Cargo Clauses issued by the London Institute of Marine Underwriters. (See, eg, *Wiggins Teape Australia Pty Ltd v Baltica Insurance Co Ltd* [1970] 2 NSWR 77.) The Lloyd's SG Policy will be construed in accordance with the rules for construction set out in the Second Schedule to the Act: see s 36(2). In each case these standard provisions offer the advantage of increased certainty of meaning derived from previous judicial decisions.

THE MODE OF DISCLOSURE

We have noted above that not only should Carb answer the questions on Coverall's proposal form, but it also has an overriding duty to take the initiative in making a full disclosure of all material facts whether or not Coverall has asked the pertinent questions. Further issues include: (a) To whom should such disclosure be made? (b) Is it sufficient to advise Premium Brokerage or Coverall's representative Jinx who then fails to record the information on the proposal form? (c) What difference does it make if the proposal form is signed by Carb after the incorrect information is inserted? or if the proponent is blind or illiterate?

Newsholme Brothers v Road Transport and General Insurance Co Ltd
English Court of Appeal [1929] 2 KB 356

Scrutton LJ: This appeal from Rowlatt J raises the kind of troublesome question which inevitably arises from the course of business of accident and life insurance companies, as contrasted with that of marine insurance companies. The contract of insurance requires the utmost good faith; the insurer knows nothing; the assured knows everything about the risk he wants to insure and he must disclose to the insurer every fact material to the risk. The marine underwriter sits still and asks no question; a proposal for insurance is brought to him by a broker, to whom he pays commission, but who is the agent of the assured. The assured and his broker must disclose everything they know material to the risk. The knowledge of the broker is not the knowledge of the underwriter, and the broker is bound to communicate it to the underwriter. I deal hereafter with his duty to his own principal.

Contracts of Insurance

The practice of life and accident insurers is different; they employ an agent to canvass and procure proposals for them. In general, he cannot make contracts binding them, but only submits proposals for their consideration. Unlike the marine underwriter, they do ask questions; they give their agent a proposal form containing a number of questions on matters which they think material; and he is expected to submit that proposal form with the answers of the proposed assured filled in and signed by the assured. The proposal form contains a promise, a warranty, that the truth of the proposer's answers shall be the basis of the contract, and is signed by the proposer. It is inevitable in such a course of business that the agent employed to get proposals will sometimes fill in or assist in filling in the answers on the form, and if they are inaccurate, the proposer, though he has signed the promise that those answers are true, alleges that the fault is that of the agent of the insurance company who filled in the answers, and claims, not that he can rescind the contract, but that he can rely on it without being prejudiced by the inaccuracy of the answers he has signed as true. There then comes a conflict, which is visible in the authorities cited to us. Between the desire to hold the insurer, who employs an agent to bring him business, liable for anything that agent does in procuring business, and, on the other hand, the contention that a man who signs a promise that certain written statements are true and the basis of his contract, which statements, if he read them before signing, he would know to be untrue, cannot claim to vary his contract by omitting that promise and misstatement. The insurance companies also run the risk of the contention that matters they do not ask questions about are not material, for, if they were, they would ask questions about them.

The facts in the present case appear in an award stated by an arbitrator in the form of a special case, as supplemented by further information given by the arbitrator as the result of a reference back to him by the court. Messrs Newsholme Brothers are motor-bus proprietors; Mr Willey is an agent of the insurance company. On 18 January 1927, Mr A Newsholme, a partner in the firm, signed a proposal for an insurance of a motor-omnibus. The proposal form contained a warranty: "We hereby warrant that the answers stated above are true, that we have withheld no information which might influence the acceptance of this proposal, and that the warranty hereby given shall be held to be promissory, and shall be the basis of the contract between us and the company. We agree to accept a policy in the current form now issued by the company to cover risks of the nature insured, and subject to the terms, conditions and exceptions contained in such current form of policy whereof we shall be deemed to have notice, and we agree to pay the premium thereon." The form also contained 14 questions to be answered and answers were included in the form signed by A Newsholme. The arbitrator finds that the answers to questions 7, 8 and 14, "were not true or correct, and thereby information was withheld from the insurance company which might have influenced the acceptance of the proposal". That finding is in the terms of the warranty. The questions and answers were as follows: "(7) Have you previously been insured for motor risks? If so, give name of company." Answer: "Atlas". "(8) Have any insurers at any time in respect of any motor vehicle: (a) declined your proposal, or cancelled or not invited renewal of your policy." Answer: "No". (b) "required increased premium or special conditions on renewal, or required you to carry the first amount of each loss?" Answer: "No". "(14) State hereunder particulars of all claims made or accidents which have occurred in connection with any motor vehicles owned by you, or under your control, during the past two years, whether insured or not," and then a schedule is filled in stating certain accidents. The arbitrator does not find what the true answers would have been; the case must proceed on the basis that these answers were untrue in material respects. The arbitrator finds that the answers were in the handwriting of Willey, the insurance agent, and that Newsholme apparently left the matter entirely in the hands of Willey. He finds that Willey was told the true facts by Newsholme, and that the reason for his not writing down the true facts did not appear. It must be either (1) that he unintentionally wrote untruths, because (a) he did not understand Newsholme's communication to him, or (b) forgot what he was told, or (c) did not understand the questions asked; or (2) that he intentionally wrote down untrue facts to earn his commission. Whichever alternative is the truth, Willey was writing the answers as the amanuensis of Newsholme, whose answers they were to be; and after Willey had written the answers, Newsholme signed the proposal, and must be taken to have promised the truth of what he signed. I do not understand how in receiving the information as to the answers and in writing those answers, Willey can be taken to be anything else than the agent of the person whose answers they are to be, and he must be taken to have written them and promised they were true. I can understand a contention that Newsholme was induced to sign by the representation of Willey, that these answers were what the insurance company required, though such a contention would be difficult to sustain in view of Newsholme's knowledge that the answers were untrue; but the result of such a contention, if sustained would be rescission of the contract, not its enforcement with the omission of the untrue answers.

The arbitrator's view is expressed in para 13 of the case, and appears to rest on waiver of the untruth by acceptance of the premium, with knowledge of the untruth, the knowledge of Willey being the knowledge of the insurance company. This requires a consideration of the position of Willey, as to which the original case contained para 12: "The facts as to the position of the said J Willey are as follows: He was appointed an agent by writing under the hand of the Agency Manager of the insurance company and was supplied by the insurance company with proposal forms. His duties were to procure persons to take out insurance policies with the insurance company and to obtain from them duly filled in and signed proposal forms. He was authorised by the insurance company to receive premiums on their behalf. He was not authorised to give a cover note or enter into any policy of insurance. I do not find that the insurance company authorised Willey to fill in the proposal forms, or that they were aware that he had in fact done so." ...

[His Lordship then referred to the court's request to the arbitrator for further information including what he meant by the agent Willey's authority to obtain proposal forms duly filled in and signed. He continued at 366:] Asked to explain what he means by "duly", he gives an explanation that he meant that the agent must, as far as he can, see that the answers were sound and correct, but he is not to investigate them; the answers must be regular, as far as the agent knows. As a matter of law, I do not understand this; the proposal is the proposal of the assured, the responsibility of declaring it true is his; how can it be the duty of the company, through their directors or agents, to the assured, to see that the assured makes correct statements of fact, when he promises them they are true, especially when the arbitrator declines to find that the agent had authority from the company to fill in the form, or what in fact the usual conditions of his appointment in this matter were.

On the case as originally stated, without the subsequent explanations, Rowlatt J took the view that Willey was the agent of Newsholme in filing up the proposal, and that Newsholme promised in writing that what Willey wrote and Newsholme signed was to be the basis of the contract, and that under these circumstances the contract could not be varied by oral statements from Newsholme to Willey. He therefore decided that the arbitrator came to a wrong decision in law when he held that the knowledge of Willey was the knowledge of the company. Newsholme Brothers appeal.

The difficulty on the authorities arises from the alleged conflict between the decisions of the English Court of Appeal in *Bawden v London, Edinburgh and Glasgow Assurance Co* [1892] 2 QB 534 and the decisions of Wright J in *Biggar v Rock Life Assurance Co* [1902] 1 KB 516, and of Wills and Phillimore JJ in *Levy v Scottish Employers' Insurance Co* (1901) 17 TLR 229.

The facts in *Bawden's* case were as follows: Bawden was an illiterate man, almost unable to read or write, but able to write his name. He had only one eye. Quin was a local agent of the insurance company. No evidence was given as to the extent of his authority, but the court "gathered from what he did" that he had no authority to make contracts, but that he had authority to negotiate and settle the form of the assured's proposal for insurance, and he was supplied with forms for that purpose. Lord Esher used the phrase "negotiate and settle the terms of the proposal"; Lindley LJ: "He was the person deputed by the company to receive the proposal, and to put it into shape"; Kay LJ: "It was his duty to get the form of proposal filled up and signed by the proposer, and to see that this was done correctly." It is not clear on what evidence the learned Lords Justices came to this finding. The proposal form contained a number of questions, the answers to which were filled in by Quin at the dictation of Bawden, and these answers were all correct. It also contained a printed declaration, the material words of which were: "I ... have no physical infirmity, nor are there any circumstances that render me peculiarly liable to accidents ... I agree that the statements contained in this proposal shall form the basis of the contract between me and the company."
It also contained a marginal note against this clause: "If not strictly applicable, particulars

of any deviation must be given at back." No particulars as to his one-eyed condition were given at back by either Quin or the assured, but Bawden signed his name to the proposal, and Quin forwarded it to the company who accepted it. Quin knew, at the time he did so, that Bawden had only one eye. The policy was renewed from time to time, and Bawden met with an accident which destroyed the sight of the remaining eye. The court held that Quin's knowledge was the knowledge of the company, who must, therefore, be taken to have contracted with a man who, to their knowledge, was a one-eyed man. The policy insured £500 "if the direct effect of [the injury by accident] shall, within three calendar months from the occurrence of such injury, occasion ... permanent total disablement," eg "irrecoverable loss of sight in both eyes"; and £250 if it caused complete and irrecoverable loss of sight in one eye. The court gave the plaintiff £500, though it is difficult to see how the accident within three months caused loss of sight in both eyes; the loss of sight in one eye had been caused long before the accident. The court held that the knowledge of the agent was the knowledge of the company and that the company, therefore, could not rely on the declaration of the assured that he had no physical infirmity, and that this was the basis of the contract. It will be noted that the agent made no inaccuracy in filling up the proposal, unless it was that he did not enter particulars of deviation on the back. Kay LJ says that it was his duty to the company to do this, but the other two judges do not mention the point. Kay LJ is also the only judge who says that it was Quin's duty to see that the proposal was filled up "correctly"; Lindley LJ uses the phrase "put it into shape", and Lord Esher says "negotiate and settle". I find considerable difficulty in seeing how a person who fills up the proposal can be the agent of the person to whom the proposal is made. A man cannot contract with himself. A makes a proposal to B by signing it, and communicating it to B. If A gets some one — C — to fill up the form for him before he signs it, it seems to me that C in doing so must be the agent of A who has to make the proposal, not of B who has to consider whether he will accept it. If C is also the agent of B to procure proposals, and induces A to make a proposal by representing that a certain form of proposal contains the particulars that B wants to know, when it does not, the remedy seems to be to rescind the written contract procured by misrepresentation, not to alter the written contract and claim the benefit of it as altered.

[His Lordship then considered a number of Scottish and Irish cases as well as the US Supreme Court decision, *New York Life Insurance Co v Fletcher* (1886) 117 US 519, the reasoning of which was applied in *Biggar's* case [1902] 1 KB 516. In that case the agent of the company filled in answers, false to his knowledge, in the proposal form and the assured signed the form without reading it and without knowledge of the untrue answers. Wright J held that the agent in filling up the form was the agent of the proposer and the proposer having agreed that the truth of the statements in the form was the basis of the contract, could not recover against the company if they were untrue. He continued at 373:]

These cases and *Bawden's* case [1892] 2 QB 534 have been in a number of reported cases before judges of first instance, discussed and followed, sometimes on the lines of *Bawden's* case, sometimes on the lines of *Biggar's* case ...

In my view, the important question for the decision of this case is whether the knowledge of the agent, acquired in filling up the proposal for the assured, is to be taken as the knowledge of the company. If the person having authority to bind the company by making a contract in fact knows of the untruth of the statements and yet takes the premium, the question may be different. Even then I see great difficulty in avoiding the effect of the writing signed by the proposer that the truth of the statements is the basis of the contract. But where the person contracting for the company has no actual knowledge, but only constructive notice, the difficulties of the proposer are greater. In commercial matters, the doctrine of constructive notice is not favoured: see the explanation by Lindley LJ in *Manchester Trust v Furness* [1895] 2 QB 539 at 545 ... Now in *Bawden's* case the agent did not fill up any answer incorrectly. He did not put on the back of the proposal any statement that the assured was a one-eyed man; one member of the court held that by reason of the note on the form, it was his duty to do this. There is no such note here. The court had no evidence as to the actual authority, but found what it was from what the agent did. The assured who signed the declaration was an illiterate man who could hardly read. In the present case the arbitrator produces the actual authority, but will not find that Willey had authority from the company to fill up the form and will not find what the usual terms and conditions are. The inaccuracy relied on is on the form as filled up for the proposer by Willey, and not on the form as signed by the proposer, Willey taking no part in the inaccuracy except that he knows of it by his own observation, apart from statements made to him by the proposer to enable him to complete the proposer's form for the proposer. It appears to me that the facts in this present case are not substantially similar with those in *Bawden's* case so as to make the conclusions of law drawn from them in the latter case binding on this court, even if those conclusions are not inconsistent with the two decisions in the House of Lords to which I have referred.

In my view the decision in *Bawden's* case is not applicable to a case where the agent himself, at the request of the proposer, fills up the answers in purported conformity with information supplied by the proposer. If the answers are untrue and he knows it, he is committing a fraud which prevents his knowledge being the knowledge of the insurance company. If the answers are untrue, but he does not know it, I do not understand how he has any knowledge which can be imputed to the insurance company. In any case, I have great difficulty in understanding how a man who has signed, without reading it, a document which he knows to be a proposal for insurance, and which contains statements in fact untrue, and a promise that they are true, and the basis of the contract, can escape from the consequences of his negligence by saying that the person he asked to fill it up for him is the agent of the person to whom the proposal is addressed.

In my view the judgment of Rowlatt J was right and the appeal must be dismissed with costs.

[**Green** and **Russell LJJ** delivered judgments to similar effect.]

Appeal dismissed.

Deaves v CML Fire and General Insurance
High Court of Australia (1979) 23 ALR 539; 53 ALJR 382

Stephen J: In 1974 Mr and Mrs Deaves were the owners of a service station at Amberley, in Queensland. Early in that year they decided to increase the amount of existing insurance cover on their service station. Mr Deaves visited the local office of their fire and public risk insurers, the SGIO, and was told that a representative would call to arrange for an increased cover. No one called, despite a second visit by Mr Deaves to the SGIO office, but a representative from another insurance company, the CML, did call, for a quite different purpose: to see if Mr Deaves wished to increase the amount of a policy on his life issued by the CML. Mr Deaves declined but, being dissatisfied with the lack of response from the SGIO, he asked the CML representative whether his company had "fire cover and that sort of thing for the shop", mentioning the SGIO's failure to send a representative to see him. According to Mr Deaves the CML representative replied that his company did "have fire policies and public risk and that" but that he personally attended only to life insurance; however he would get another representative who did deal with such policies to call on the Deaves.

A week or so later another CML representative called at the service station, armed with a fire insurance proposal form and other forms, and talked to Mr Deaves about insurance cover. Mr Deaves told him of his wish to increase the total amount of his existing fire and public risk cover on the service station and of the SGIO's failure to attend to his request that someone from that office call to arrange for an increase in the cover afforded by his existing SGIO policies. They discussed the allocation of cover and several proposal forms were then filled in by the representative.

Contained in the fire insurance proposal was the following request for information: "Give particulars of sum already insured with this and other Insurers on identical property proposed to be insured under this proposal." In the space provided in the proposal for a response to this request the representative wrote "N/A", an abbreviation for "not applicable". What caused the representative to so describe this request for particulars does not expressly appear from the evidence. The CML called no evidence about any aspect of the transaction and Mr Deaves, who did give evidence, could only say that while the representative was filling in the proposals he questioned Mr Deaves from time to time about the particulars to be inserted in them, Mr Deaves supplying answers to those questions and then signing the proposals when they had been completed by the representative. He had no recollection of that particular item in the fire insurance proposal or of any question about it. Mr Deaves said to the representative "Am I covered from today because I would like to go in and cancel the policies at the SGIO?"

He was told he would be covered by CML from that day. He then and there paid the premiums for the policies to be issued by CML and received a receipt. It does not appear whether then or later he received any cover note from CML. The SGIO fire policy which Mr Deaves intended to cancel showed as the insured Mr and Mrs Deaves as joint owners and a Mr and Mrs Willis as mortgagees but Mr Deaves does not appear to have appreciated this fact or at least to have attached any significance to it. He did not mention it to the CML representative. Mr and Mrs Willis were in fact mortgagees of the service station property.

Some time after the visit by the CML representative, perhaps as long as a month afterwards, perhaps only a day or so later, Mr Deaves called at the SGIO office again, said that he wished to cancel the SGIO policies and signed forms presented to him for that purpose. In the form he signed relating to the fire policy he wrote "Please cancel above policy any refund to above address". The form bears date, in another's hand, "31 May 1974" and contains a reference, in its heading, to the fire policy here in question. Because he did not subsequently receive any return of part premium from SGIO in respect of this policy, as he did for other of the cancelled policies, he later spoke to the SGIO office by telephone and was told that SGIO had to get permission from the mortgagees of the service station property before that policy could be cancelled. He was neither asked nor did he do anything himself about obtaining the mortgagees' consent, nor did he inform CML about any of this. Whatever SGIO may have sought to do about obtaining the consent of the mortgagees, it proved abortive since Mr and Mrs Willis in fact heard nothing from SGIO.

Some months later the Deaves' service station burnt down and they immediately claimed on their CML fire policy. Then followed many months' delay while the CML, although not rejecting the claim, neither paid under it nor accepted any liability in respect of it. What appears to have concerned the CML was the concurrent existence of two fire policies over the property, their own and the original SGIO policy, coupled with the fact that the SGIO policy insured not only the Deaves' interest but also that of the mortgagees. This latter fact was, in a sense, the cause of the former since it was the existence of the mortgagees' interest that caused the SGIO to refrain from giving immediate effect to Mr Deaves' notice of cancellation of the SGIO policy. Ultimately, almost a year and a half later, the CML asserted, apparently for the first time, that the Deaves lacked an insurable interest in the service station because the amount of indebtedness owed by them to Mr and Mrs Willis, and secured by mortgage over the service station, exceeded the value of the property insured. Although persisted in for some time, this contention seems later to have been abandoned in favour of other grounds for resisting the Deaves' claim to indemnity. These new grounds ultimately became the defences upon which the CML relied when sued by the Deaves.

The action against CML which is the subject of this appeal was the second of two which, in 1976, the Deaves instituted in the Supreme Court of Queensland. Earlier that year they and Mr and Mrs Willis joined in proceedings against SGIO, claiming under the fire policy issued by it, that is to say, under the original policy in respect of which Mr Deaves had given the purported cancellation notice. The two actions were heard together, CML being joined by SGIO as a third party in the action against it, seeking contribution from CML. The Deaves and Mr and Mrs Willis succeeded in their action againt SGIO but the Deaves failed in their action against CML which was also successful in its defence of the third party claim made against it. Appeals by SGIO and by the Deaves were dismissed by the Full Court and it is from the dismissal of the Deaves' appeal in their action against CML that they now appeal to this court. SGIO has not appealed from the order of the Full Court and the Deaves' judgment against it has been satisfied by payment.

As mentioned earlier, two main grounds of defence are relied upon by CML. The first relies upon the response of "N/A", not applicable, made to the request in the proposal for particulars of other sums insured on the service station. The second, not wholly unconnected since it also relates to the continued existence of the SGIO policy, relies upon condition 3 of the CML policy, under which all benefit is declared forfeit if default be made in notification to CML of any other insurances upon the property insured. I go first to the question raised by the response "N/A", appearing in the proposal.

The first step must be to determine what was conveyed by "not applicable" when inserted, in abbreviated form, in the CML proposal, and for this purpose I put aside for the moment the fact that it was the CML's own representative who was the author of the phrase. The words themselves are a simple, although unexplained, assertion that the request for particulars does not apply to the Deaves' proposal for fire insurance. Being unexplained, they convey no more than that, although they necessarily give rise to speculation, not as to their meaning, which is clear, but as to what lies behind it: as to why this request for particulars should be inapplicable to the proposal in question.

Be that as it may, the response "not applicable" did not, in my view, amount to a negative response either in form or in substance. It did not convey the meaning that no sum was already insured on the property. That fact was, no doubt, one of the several possible reasons which, as a matter of speculation, might be thought to lie behind the stated inapplicability but it is no more than that. In fact, of course, it is clear that the author of the phrase, the CML representative, cannot have had that in mind as constituting the reason for inapplicability: on the contrary, a fact uppermost in his mind must have been the existence of SGIO's insurance cover, which he now had the opportunity of replacing with cover provided by his own company.

The response "not applicable" not itself amounting to the negative statement that there was no sum already insured on the property, the question arises whether the response may nevertheless be deemed to be such a negative statement. In the margin of the proposal appears, in large type, the words "Any questions on this proposal not replied to are to be deemed answered in the negative". Even assuming in favour of the respondent that these words extend not only to questions duly phrased in interrogative terms, but also to a request for information worded, as here, in the imperative, this is not a case of a question "not replied to". A reply was in fact provided and the form which it took left no room for the operation of this deeming provision, which would have reulted in a deemed response bearing a quite different meaning: *Saunders v Queensland Insurance Co Ltd* (1931) 45 CLR 557 at 563 per Starke J, at 567 per Dixon J and at 569-70 per Evatt J. I may add that it is, in any event, by no means clear what would be the effect of any deemed "answer in the negative" when what is in issue is a request for particulars rather than a direct question. To say this is, perhaps, only to suggest that it may be unduly generous to CML to make the assumption in its favour to which I have referred in the opening words of this paragraph.

The result is, therefore, that neither expressly nor by a process of deeming can it be said that the response "not applicable" amounted to a statement that no other insurance existed in respect of the Deaves' service station. Accordingly it did not constitute a misrepresentation to that effect. Nor was it any misrepresentation according to the meaning which it truly bears; that is, as a statement that the particulars sought were, for some unspecified reason, not applicable to the Deaves' proposal for insurance. To the extent that Mr Deaves was in any way competent to declare that the particular information sought by CML was inapplicable, he can but have been expressing his own view as to its applicability, a view which CML might not, of course, have shared, although its representative, who supplied the answer, no doubt did. The statement seems to me, from its very nature, to be no more than an expression of opinion, capable of involving a misrepresentation only if the opinion so expressed was not honestly held: *Anderson v Pacific Fire and Marine Insurance Co* (1872) LR 7 CP 65, per Willes J at 69. In fact the statement appears to have reflected quite accurately Mr Deaves' state of mind; nothing in the evidence would support a view to the contrary; the policies enquired about were, after all, policies which, as he then thought, he was about to cancel.

It should not pass unnoticed that if the response, "N/A", attracted any attention when the proposal found its way to the offices of CML, the slightest inquiry from its representative would have revealed the reason for the alleged inapplicability. Whether any such inquiry was made must remain unknown since CML chose to call no evidence on any aspect of the transaction.

If the response "not applicable" involved no misrepresentation it matters not whether, as a result of the declaration and warranty clause appearing in the proposal and despite the absence of any "basis clause" in the policy itself, that response in fact became a contractual condition of the policy of insurance. If it did, it was not untrue and gave rise to no breach of condition. Accordingly it is unnecessary for me to say anything concerning the seeming divergence between English authority and that represented by the decision of this court in *Australian Provincial Assurance Association Ltd v Producers and Citizens Co-operative Assurance Co of Australia Ltd* (1932) 48 CLR 341.

In my view, the statement that the seeking of particulars as to other insurance was "not applicable" did not become any the less true when, some considerable time after the proposal was furnished to CML, it became known to the Deaves that there was some hold-up in the cancellation of the SGIO fire policy, due to the need for the mortgagees' consent. It is clear from Mr Deaves' evidence that he did not appreciate the very real interest which the mortgagees had in retaining insurance, in their names, over the mortgaged premises. Consequently, to him the news that their consent to the cancellation of the SGIO fire policy was necessary appears to have represented no real impediment to his plan to cancel the SGIO policy but only a factor which explained the delay in his receipt from SGIO of the refund of part premium.

No doubt one element which went to make up the unspecified reason lying behind the response "not applicable" was the belief of the Deaves that it lay within their power to cancel the SGIO policy. On the view which I take of the representation involved in the Deaves' response it matters not whether that belief was in fact correct in law, since it formed no part of the response itself, being no more than an element going to make up the reason which prompted that response.

Misrepresentation aside, there remains the question of non-disclosure. Since this was a proposal for insurance the Deaves were obliged to disclose all matters material to the acceptance of the risk or to the fixing of the premium. In the present case any doubt as to the materiality of the existence of other insurance is, I think, answered by the fact that CML in its proposal expressly made its existence the subject of a request for particulars: *Glicksman v Lancashire and General Assurance Co Ltd* [1925] 2 KB 593, per Scrutton LJ at 609 and, on appeal, per Viscount Dunedin in [1927] AC 139 at 144. While this may not be conclusive (see *Babatsikos v Car Owners' Mutual Insurance Co Ltd* [1970] VR 297, per Pape J at 306-7), it is enough in the present case: as Cussen J said in *Dalgety & Co Ltd v AMP Society* [1908] VLR 481 at 512, one may be one's own juryman in obvious cases of materiality and this is such a case. No evidence is necessary to establish that, whatever be the appropriate criterion of materiality and whether involving the prudent insurer or the reasonable proponent for insurance, the existence of a substantial degree of double insurance is a material circumstance.

Most relevant to the issue of non-disclosure is, of course, the fact that, far from there having been either active concealment or passive failure to disclose on the part of the Deaves, they went out of their way to thrust upon CML knowledge of the relevant fact, that the service station was already insured by SGIO. Mr Deaves first informed the CML's life policy representative of the fact in explaining why he was seeking fire cover from CML. That this information found its way to the administration of CML may be inferred in the absence of evidence suggesting an alternative explanation, from the subsequent visit by the second CML representative. To him a disclosure of the existence of the SGIO cover was also made. Its details may not have been conveyed but at least the fact that it was for a lesser amount than was to be sought from CML is made clear. Indeed, it may be inferred that the response "not applicable" which that representative supplied in filling in the proposal was occasioned by his knowledge of the SGIO cover combined with his knowledge of the Deaves stated intention of cancelling that cover after cover with CML had been established.

In these circumstances the evidence refutes the suggestion that there was non-disclosure by the Deaves of the existence of insurance cover provided by the SGIO policy. To say this is not, I think, to run counter to the findings of fact of the primary judge. As I read his judgment his Honour did not direct his mind to the question of the authority of the CML representatives to receive on behalf of CML relevant information from Mr Deaves. His Honour set out passages from Mr Deaves' evidence and said of them that they constituted no proof that the CML's fire policy representative was other than the Deaves' agent "for the purpose of filling in answers to questions in the proposal form". His Honour had earlier observed that the onus lay on the Deaves of showing that the CML representative "was in fact acting on behalf of CML so as to bind it" and so as to make his knowledge that of CML itself, adding that proof of "authority to issue cover notes, waive payment of premiums and issue receipts, does not alone, discharge such an onus". His Honour relied upon *Jumna Khan v Bankers and Traders Insurance Co Ltd* (1926) 37 CLR 451 at 454 and *Biggar v Rock Life Assurance Co* [1902] 1 KB 516 at 524-5 in support of these propositions. On appeal, Hoare J who alone dealt with this aspect, seems to have taken a somewhat similar view, saying that no inference might be drawn that the representative was "in effect the agent for the insurer as to the knowledge of the insurer relating to the existing insurance" because there was not sufficient evidence to that effect.

Jumna Khan's case is no authority for the proposition for which it is thus cited. In that case the insurance company's agent obtained the appellant's signature to a blank form of proposal and, having sent him away without asking him any questions at all, then had his own clerk fill in the blank proposal. As filled in, it answered in the negative questions concerning previous fires and concerning fire risk having previously been declined. On both counts the answers were untrue. The policy which issued stated that the particulars in the proposal, to which the insurance was made subject, should be deemed to have been inserted or furnished by the assured. Both in this court and when the case was earlier on appeal in the Full Court of the New South Wales Supreme Court ((1925) 25 SR (NSW) 422), no question arose of whether knowledge of the agent, gained from the appellant, might be attributed to the insurer and this for the good reason that the agent had gained no relevant knowledge but, as Higgins J observed, at 454, had simply put into the proposal "some statement as having been made by the plaintiff which was not made by him". The case was in no way concerned with an agent's authority to receive, on behalf of the insurer, information from the applicant for insurance relevant to the risk. It turned rather upon the question whether the agent or his clerk might be the insurer's agent in filling in the proposal form. It decided, consistently with much earlier authority, that in doing so they acted as the appellant's agent, so that the insurer could not itself be fixed with responsibility for false statements in the proposal.

Jumna Khan's case is just a case as those discussed in *MacGillivray and Parkington on Insurance Law*, 6th ed, 1975, para 946-8, of which *Biggar's* case is a leading example. A conflict of authority, represented on the one hand by *Bawden v London Edinburgh and Glasgow Assurance Co* [1892] 2 QB 534 and on the other by *Biggar's* case and by Scottish and United States decisions to the like effect, for some time existed concerning insurers' agents who, while having knowledge of the true position, incorrectly fill in for an intending insured a proposal form which the latter signs. In *Newsholme Brothers v Road Transport and General Insurance Co Ltd* [1929] 2 KB 356 these cases were analysed in detail by Scrutton LJ and by Greer LJ. They may be seen to turn on the fact that the assured had signed the proposal containing the untrue information. Because of this fact the agent's knowledge of the truth could not be imputed to the insurer, if for no other reason than because, having signed the proposal "which contains statements in fact untrue, and a promise that they are true, and the basis of the contract (the applicant for insurance cannot thereafter) escape the consequences of his negligence by saying that the person he asked to fill it up for him is the agent of the person to whom the proposal is addressed" per Scrutton LJ at 376. Greer LJ said of such a case, at 382, "notice to the agent whose duty was to obtain a signed proposal form and send it to the company, was not notice to the company of anything inconsistent with the signed proposal form, and that in filling up the form, whether he mistook the instructions of the insured, or whether he intentionally filled in something different from what he was told, he was not acting as the agent of the company, but as the agent of the insured".

In the present case there was communication to the CML representative of the facts relating to the SGIO policy and that communication was unaffected by any untruthful statement contained in the proposal signed by Mr Deaves. While the agent may have lacked authority from the CML to fill up the proposal on behalf of the Deaves he nevertheless received, as a part of his function as a representative of CML, information from them relevant to the risk. Having received such information, and the signed proposal not being contradictory of it, the CML is to be treated as itself possessing that knowledge: an applicant for insurance, having made a disclosure to the insurer's agent, "has a right to expect that the agent will transmit to the insurers all that he has been told and that the agent will do so accurately": Ivamy, *General Principles of Insurance Law*, 3rd ed, 1975, p 520.

The position in a case such as the present is illustrated by *Golding v Royal London Auxiliary Insurance Co Ltd* (1914) 30 TLR 350, a case typical of the fact situation encountered in the *Jumna Khan* class of cases but with one added ingredient sufficient to differentiate it from them: after the agent had incorrectly filled in the proposal (in doing which he was held to be acting as the applicant's agent), the applicant noted the error and informed the agent of it before issue of the policy. The agent forgot to pass on this factual correction to the insurer, yet the insurer was held to be fixed with knowledge of the truth because it was one of the duties of the agent to convey the applicant's answers, including a corrected answer, to the insurer. That was enough to prevent the insurer from relying upon the falsity of the original answer which appeared in the proposal, despite the fact that answers in the proposal formed the basis of the policy and if untrue would, regardless of their materiality, avoid the policy.

This not being a case in which the response written into the proposal by the CML representative was either untrue or otherwise contradictory of what the intending assured told him, the difficulties for a plaintiff who has signed such a proposal, either in blank or after it is completed, and has thereby adopted as his own the incorrect information which it conveys, do not arise. The contrast between such cases and the present case is made by Ivamy, op cit, p 523, when, after dealing with such cases, he says, "Different considerations apply where the proposal, as filled up by the agent, contains no false statements, but the insurers seek to avoid the policy on the ground that some further fact ought to have been disclosed. In this case, the basis of the contract, so far as it rests upon the proposal, is not affected. If the fact has been disclosed to the agent by the proposed assured, or has otherwise come to the agent's knowledge in the course of his employment, there does not seem to be any valid reason why the agent's knowledge should not be imputed to the insurers. Though the agent, in filling up the proposal, may go outside the scope of his authority and become for that purpose the agent of the proposed assured, he remains for all the purposes of his employment the agent of the insurers. The proposed assured is entitled to assume that the agent knows what ought to be stated and what may be omitted, and it is submitted that the proposed assured is not responsible for the agent's failure to pass on the information to the insurers, notwithstanding the fact that the proposal has been filled up by the agent".

It follows, in my view, that CML must be treated as having knowledge of the existence of a policy issued by SGIO and providing fire cover in respect of the service station. That knowledge was, it is true, coupled with knowledge of the intention on the part of the Deaves to cancel the SGIO fire policy. But no change ever occurred in the subsequent intentions of the Deaves such as might require to be communicated to the other contracting party. At all times until the happening of the fire the Deaves intended to cancel the SGIO policy, all that ever changed was their expectation of early implementation of that intention. The need for the mortgagees' consent was understood by them as a delaying factor, but as no more than that.

For the foregoing reasons I conclude that there was here no want of disclosure of material information by the Deaves to the CML such as would provide any answer to the Deaves' claim under the CML policy. Although never to the forefront of the respondent's submissions, it was contended on its behalf that failure to reveal the existence of the Willis mortgage also amounted to non-disclosure. As to this, it is enough to say that the CML proposal called for no such disclosure, that there is no suggestion that Mr Deaves was ever asked about the matter and that, in the absence of inquiry, the existence of a mortgage does not appear of itself to be a fact calling for unsolicited disclosure by an applicant for fire insurance: *MacGillivray and Parkington on Insurance Law*, 6th ed, 1975, para 783; Ivamy, op cit, p 121.

[His Honour then considered the question of condition 3 of the CML policy, which required the appellants to give written notice to the insurer of any other insurances upon the property. He held that the SGIO policy was still in force, and that the breach of condition 3 entitled the respondent to rely upon that breach to avoid any liability under the policy.

Gibbs ACJ agreed with Stephen J on the above issues.

Mason J held that the answer "N/A" was an incorrect answer to the material question of existing insurances and entitled the respondent to avoid liability.

Jacobs and **Murphy JJ** dissented.]

Appeal dismissed.

With the above cases may be compared *Maye v Colonial Mutual Life Assurance Society Ltd* (1924) 35 CLR 14 (illiterate proponent for life insurance disclosed to canvasser that he had been refused insurance as a first class life but agent filled in proposal untruthfully); *Western Australian Insurance Co Ltd v Dayton* (1924) 35 CLR 355 (proposal for renewal of motor vehicle policy signed by proponent in blank under pressure from insurer's representative without disclosure of previous claims raised issue of estoppel); *Jumna Khan v The Bankers and Traders Insurance Co Ltd*

(1926) 37 CLR 451 (illiterate proponent signed blank proposal for fire insurance relying upon agent to complete it); *Stone v Reliance Mutual Insurance Society Ltd* [1972] 1 Lloyd's Rep 469 (CA) (agent instructed by company to fill in forms for proponent did so without asking proponent any questions).

In relation to life insurance policies which come within the definition of "industrial policies" the following provision applies:

Life Insurance Act 1945 (Cth)

126 (1) Where any agent or servant of a company writes or fills in or has before the commencement of this Act written or filled in any particulars in a proposal for an industrial policy with the company, then, notwithstanding any agreement to the contrary between the proponent and the company, any policy issued in pursuance of the proposal shall not be avoided by reason only of any incorrect or untrue statement contained in any such particulars so written or filled in unless the incorrect or untrue statement was in fact made by the proponent to the agent or servant for the purposes of the proposal.

(2) The burden of proving any such statement was so made shall lie upon the company.

(3) Nothing in this section shall be deemed to allow of the avoidance of any policy for any reason or in any circumstances for or in which the policy could not have been avoided apart from the provisions of this section.

...

In s 4(1) "industrial policy" is defined as "a policy in respect of which the premiums are contracted to be paid at intervals of less than two months and are contracted to be received, or are usually received, by means of collectors ..."

A further issue concerns the time at which Carb is obliged to make disclosure to Coverall. It is common practice for insurance companies to offer insurance protection in the form of a cover note in response to telephoned instructions pending completion of a proposal form and issuance of a formal policy. Must full disclosure take place (a) prior to issuance of the cover note, or (b) prior to issuance of the policy? Is Carb under a continuing duty to disclose additional material facts which come to its knowledge after completion of the proposal form, after issuance of the policy, or prior to renewal of an existing policy?

Mayne Nickless Ltd v Pegler and Another
Supreme Court of New South Wales [1974] 1 NSWLR 228

Samuels J: On or about 3 June 1968, one George Klokas, hereinafter called "the deceased", bought a motor vehicle from Friendly Motors. On the same day a representative of Friendly Motors telephoned the second defendant, NRMA Insurance Ltd, hereinafter called "the company", and arranged for a cover note over the vehicle to be issued in the sum of $900. The cover note, dated 3 June 1968, was duly issued and was, so far as is material, in these terms: "You are hereby covered from 2 pm 3/6/1968 to midnight 3/7/1968 (unless notice of cancellation be given in the meantime) for an amount of $900 on your motor vehicle." There followed details of the vehicle in question and then: "Subject to the conditions of this company's comprehensive motor car/vehicle insurance policy and a satisfactory proposal for your insurance."

On 5 June 1968, the deceased, driving the vehicle in question, collided with and severely damaged a truck owned by the plaintiff. It is agreed between the parties to the present proceedings that the collision was due solely to the negligent driving of the deceased, who received injuries whereof he later died.

On 4 July 1968, Penelope Klokas, the deceased's widow, completed a motor car insurance proposal form and forwarded it to the company. This form contained a number of questions (which must be regarded as directed to the deceased) of which it is necessary to mention only one. The question was: "11 Have you ... (a) had an accident or fire happen to a motor vehicle and/or made a claim against any insurance company?" The question was answered "No".

This answer was in fact untrue, because on 12 February 1968, the deceased, while the holder of a learner's permit, was involved in an accident in Paddington in which his and two other vehicles were damaged, and had made a claim for indemnity under a comprehensive policy upon his then insurers. They rejected it for the reason that in breach of the conditions of the policy, the deceased, while holding a learner's permit, had not been accompanied by a licensed driver.

There followed correspondence between the Public Solicitor, acting for Mrs Klokas, and the company and the company's solicitors. The Public Solicitor sought indemnity under the cover note and the indemnity was refused on 1 October 1968. At this time, leaving aside one ground which plainly had no substance, the basis of the refusal was expressed to be that the proposal form was not satisfactory within the terms of the cover note. On 18 November 1968, the company's solicitors, having been asked to elaborate upon their first statement, took the ground that the answer to question 11 in the proposal was untrue. Hence it was said that, the proposal being the basis of the contract, and the deceased having thus warranted that the answers given were true and correct, the false answer rendered the proposal unsatisfactory and unacceptable to the company.

Towards the end of 1969, the solicitors for the plaintiff entered the fray, seeking to recover the damage to the plaintiff's truck. Again, the company denied liability to indemnify the deceased. On 9 November 1970, Helsham J granted letters of administration to Mr Pegler, the first defendant, as nominee of the plaintiff, for the purposes of representing the deceased in any actions or proceedings brought by the plaintiff against the deceased for damages claimed to arise out of the accident on 5 June 1968, and of enforcing any rights of the deceased or his estate under any contract of insurance ...

The plaintiff then took out a summons in the Equity Division seeking a declaration against Mr Pegler and the company that the company was bound to indemnify Mr Pegler as the administrator of the deceased in respect of any verdict recovered against him by the plaintiff in the action to which I have referred: provided, that is, that arbitration proceedings were commenced by Mr Pegler against the company as stipulated in the policy. Following the issue of that summons a statement of claim was filed in the Common Law Division, but what I have before me now is the summons which has been transferred from the Equity Division to the Common Law Division, and transferred to the commercial list.

Mr K R Handley, leading counsel for the company, argued these principal submissions. First, the duty of disclosure which binds any applicant for insurance applies in respect of a cover note. The fact of the deceased's accident in February 1968 was material. He did not disclose it prior to the issue of the cover note. Hence, the contract of insurance constituted by the cover note was voidable at the company's option and the company duly avoided it. Accordingly there was no contract of insurance in force on 5 June 1968, when the deceased met his death.

Secondly, the indorsement on the cover note introduced by the words "subject to" constitutes a condition precedent to valid cover. Since the proposal was not satisfactory, because it contained a statement in fact untrue, the company was again entitled to avoid the cover note *ab initio* which it in due course did.

There appears to be no authority which distinctly establishes that the duty of disclosure binds an applicant for a cover note as it does the proponent for a policy. The use of a cover note is of course both general and familiar. In the present case, it was issued at the request of the vendor of the vehicle acting as the deceased's agent in order that the deceased might have indemnity pending the completion of a formal proposal and the issue of a policy. It is, I suppose, true, as Mr D M J Bennett for the plaintiff contends, that a cover note is an informal way of obtaining insurance cover. But it is plainly a contract of insurance. In Welford, *The Law Relating to Accident Insurance*, 1923 ed, p 58, this appears: "The cover note ... operates as a provisional acceptance, protecting the proposed assured from the time of its issue ... until the insurers have definitely decided whether to accept or decline the proposal ...

"The cover note is in itself a contract of insurance, governing the rights and liabilities of the parties in the event of a loss taking place during its currency. The assured is, therefore, entitled to enforce the contract contained in the cover note, provided that he has complied with its conditions; ..."

Hence, it must be arguable without more that, since a cover note is a contract of insurance, the ordinary incidents which apply during the formation of such a contract apply to a cover note also, so that the duty of disclosure exists unimpaired.

This is indeed the conclusion which is stated in *Halsbury's Laws of England*, 3rd ed, Vol 22, p 208, para 391. There, dealing with interim insurance, in which term a cover note is included, the learned authors say: "There must of course be a contract for the grant of such an interim insurance, however informally or even colloquially it may be made, and being a contract of insurance, stringent attention will be paid to the duty on the proposer to make full and frank disclosure of material facts if the grant is being made without the proposer signing anything."

No authority is quoted in support of this proposition. But, even in the absence of direct authority, I would be inclined to accept the principle, because I can see no reason why the duty of disclosure should apply to one type of contract of insurance and not to another, notwithstanding that that other may be less formal and of an interim kind.

However, it seems to me that Mr Handley's argument derives some support from the decision of the Full Court in *Johnson v Guardian Assurance Co Ltd* (1931) 31 SR (NSW) 386; 48 WN (NSW) 124. There, a cover note was issued and extended, and during the extended period the premises insured were destroyed by fire. The insurers declined to indemnify on the grounds that the plaintiff assured had failed to disclose his nationality of origin and his true name, or that there had previously occurred fires on premises occupied by the plaintiff or his wife. It seems that at the trial it was agreed between the parties that the duty of disclosure applied. Hence, the issue for the jury was whether or not the facts which were not disclosed were material. The jury found for the plaintiff. On appeal by the insurers, it was argued that a cover note, being an insurance contract, was *uberrimae fidei* so that there was a duty on the plaintiff to disclose all material facts, the absence of a proposal and the failure of the insurer to ask questions being immaterial. Halse-Rogers J (SR (NSW) at 391; WN (NSW) at 126), delivering a judgment in which Street CJ and Harvey CJ in Eq concurred, said: "It being conceded that there was such a duty on the plaintiff to disclose all material matters, and it being also conceded that it was for the jury to decide as to whether any information omitted was material, the question for our determination is whether the evidence as to materiality was all one way, or whether there was evidence which entitled the jury to refuse to accept what was referred to as the unchallenged evidence of the insurance managers."

In *Club Development & Finance Corp Pty Ltd v Bankers' & Traders' Insurance Co Ltd* [1971] 2 NSWLR 541, Macfarlan J had before him a claim upon two cover notes to which the defence was non-disclosure of material facts before the contracts of insurance created by the cover notes came into existence. In his judgment, his Honour refers to *Johnson's* case, to *Southern Cross Assurance Co Ltd v Australian Provincial Assurance Association Ltd* (1939) 39 SR (NSW) 174; 56 WN (NSW) 77 and to *Mutual Life Insurance Co of New York v Ontario Metal Products Co Ltd* [1925] AC 344. His Honour ultimately rejected the defence, because he was of the opinion that the plaintiff did not fail to disclose to the insurers any fact which was material, but his Honour plainly accepted the proposition that the duty of disclosure applied, notwithstanding that the contracts of insurance were contained in cover notes and not in a formal policy. Both *Johnson's* case and the *Club Development* case finally turned upon the question of materiality and not upon the duty to disclose what was in fact material, but I regard each of them as lending support to Mr Handley's submission which, in any event, is well founded on principle, and is further sustained by dicta in the recently reported decision of the High Court in *The Steadfast Insurance Co Ltd v F & B Trading Co Pty Ltd* (1971) 125 CLR 578 at 583, 586.

Mr Bennett's attractive argument to the contrary seems to me to overlook or misconceive the true character of a cover note. A cover note is an interim arrangement designed to protect the assured against the consequences of the delay necessarily involved in the completion of a proposal and its consideration by the insurers. Application for a cover note is invariably made to the insurers to whom it is intended to propose for a policy. The cover note is normally (and was here) subject to terms and conditions (such as are applicable) of the insurers' standard form of policy covering the relevant risk. Most importantly, the cover note, during its currency, at once puts the insurers on the same risk they will undertake by issuing the policy. It may be conceded that a cover note is commonly of short duration and usually issued without the formality of a proposal or any questions or inquiries from the insurers. But it is in every sense a contract upon which the assured may sue and upon which the insurers may be liable to the full extent of the indemnity which the subsequent policy will confer. I can see no reason, therefore, either in principle or in good commercial sense, why insurers should be expected, by entering into such an engagement, to expose themselves to the hazards which the doctrine of disclosure is intended to avert.

I am of the opinion that the deceased, prior to the issue of this cover note, was bound to disclose all facts material to the insurance.

Mr Bennett then contends that, if there was a duty of disclosure, it was merely to disclose "those matters which would create a situation where no reasonable person would believe that an insurer knowing those facts would grant cover". I may say at once that, granted the existence of a duty to disclose, I can see no ground for diluting that duty when a cover note rather than a policy is in question. It is in each case a duty to disclose all facts material to the risk to be covered. But Mr Bennett's proposition, by framing the criterion of materiality in terms of the belief of the reasonable person (that is, the reasonable assured), harks back to a test which has been advanced as the determinant of materiality. What then is the proper test of materiality?

[His Honour then considered the test of materiality, and held that:]

(1) the facts relating to the previous accident were material and should have been disclosed at least to a sufficient extent to enable the insurer to inquire into them in detail (*Roumeli Food Stores (NSW) Pty Ltd v The New India Assurance Co Ltd* [1972] 1 NSWLR 227);

(2) the words "subject to ... a satisfactory proposal" indicated that a satisfactory proposal was intended to be a basis of the availability of indemnity thereunder;

(3) since the proposal contained a misstatement of fact which would amount to a breach of warranty and concealed a fact material to the risk it was not a satisfactory proposal in that it was reasonably open to a prudent insurer to regard it as unsatisfactory; and

(4) the insurance company was therefore entitled to avoid the insurance cover *ab initio*.

[He therefore refused the declaration sought and dismissed the summons with costs.]

QUESTIONS

Question 4

In considering whether Carb has omitted a material fact in filling out the proposal form, what is the true test of materiality? Is it the subjective opinion of Carb or of Coverall? Or is it the objective view of the reasonable man in the position of the proponent, or of the prudent insurer? Would it matter if Coverall did not consider the fact material? Upon whom does the onus of proof rest? What evidence will the court consider most relevant in determining whether a fact is material?

Question 5

Is there any practical difference between a finding by a court that prior to issuance of a policy by Coverall Insurance Ltd, Carb Pty Ltd:

(a) made an innocent but material misrepresentation to Coverall; or
(b) innocently omitted to disclose material facts to Coverall?

Question 6

Carb Pty Ltd submitted a proposal to Coverall Insurance Ltd for comprehensive insurance on the company's delivery van. One of the questions in the proposal form was "where will the vehicle be garaged?" Mary Handy filled in the form in her capacity as company secretary, inadvertently inserting her home address in the outlying rural fringe of Sydney. Unbeknown to Mary, Jim had decided, prior to her filling in the form, that the utility would be garaged at the Ryde factory. Due to her heavy workload, Mary forgot to tell Jim the manner in which she had completed the form. On receipt of the proposal form, Coverall issued a policy to Carb. Some time later the van was damaged beyond repair in a collision near the Handy's house. Will Carb Pty Ltd be entitled to recover under the following *alternative* circumstances:

(a) The premiums set by Coverall for vans garaged,

     (i) in the suburbs of Sydney are higher than those for the rural fringe because of the increased risk of an accident occurring in the suburbs, or
     (ii) in the suburbs and the rural areas are the same, or
- (b) As in (a) but either
  - (i) the accident occurred in Ryde? or
  - (ii) the policy stated that "It is agreed that this policy is issued on the faith of the proposal form signed on behalf of Carb Pty Ltd and the truth of the answers in that form shall be the basis of this contract of insurance", or
- (c) Mary had deliberately inserted her home address, knowing that the van was to be garaged at Ryde, or
- (d) Mary inadvertently omitted to answer the question regarding the address. Coverall made no enquiry but inserted Mary's residential address in the space on the proposal form, and charged the lower premium applicable to rural locations as in (a)(ii) above, or
- (e) As in (d) except assume that the policy states: "This policy and all claims thereunder shall be governed by Victorian law", or
- (f) Immediately after the policy was issued, Mary discovered the van was to be garaged at the Ryde factory, she recalled that she had inserted her home address, but she did not notify Coverall of the change.

Question 7

Compare *Deaves v CML Fire & General Insurance Co Ltd, supra,* with other relevant cases. Can you identify any divergent lines of authority amongst these cases, and where does *Deaves* case stand in relation to them? Are these lines of authority reconcilable on their own particular facts, or are there wider considerations being taken into account by the courts?

Question 8

In 1978 the Australian Law Reform Commission proposed that both life and general insurance be subject to the same general provisions:

• An insurer should not be entitled to avoid a claim by reliance upon a basis of contract clause.
• An insurer should not be entitled to avoid a claim by reliance upon innocent non-disclosure or innocent material misrepresentation.
• An insurer should be entitled to avoid a claim where the insured was guilty of concealment or deliberate misrepresentation at the time of entry into the contract, provided:
  (a) the matter concealed or misrepresented was material to the particular insurer;
  (b) the insured knew or suspected that the matter concealed or misrepresented was material to that insurer; and
  (c) the onus of proof in respect of the insured's knowledge or suspicion should be on the insured himself.
• A court should have a general discretion to adjust the rights of the parties where rejection of a claim would be permitted by the above rules but would result in clear injustice to the insured.

What were the aims of the Commission in making these proposals and to what extent have they been adopted by Australian courts and legislatures?

Question 9

In 1978 the Australian Law Reform Commission recommended the prohibition of stipulations that a cover note is to be subject to the completion of a satisfactory or acceptable proposal form. What policy issues are raised by such a stipulation and how would it affect the interim period of cover between the issuing of the cover note and the completion of the proposal form? Under what circumstances should a cover note become ineffective?

SECTION 3: INSURABLE INTEREST

In Section 1 we noted that wagers are generally prohibited whereas insurance contracts are lawful provided the insured has an insurable interest. This raises a number of questions:
(1) What is the definition of insurable interest and how is it distinguished from a wager?
(2) What is the justification for requiring an insurable interest and where is the requirement laid down?
(3) What is the relationship between insurable interest and the indemnity principle?
The requirement of insurable interest is entirely statutory but the definition of what constitutes such an interest will depend upon the type of policy, the language of the particular statute and its judicial interpretation.

MARINE INSURANCE

The English Marine Insurance Act 1745 first introduced the requirement of insurable interest. The present Australian provisions are contained in the Commonwealth Marine Insurance Act 1909. See particularly ss 10–14. Similar provisions in state legislation are based upon the original English Acts: eg NSW, Imperial Acts Application Act 1969, ss 24–28; Vic, Instruments Act 1958 ss 15, 16.

LIFE INSURANCE

In eighteenth century England the practice had developed of individuals taking contracts of insurance on the lives of other persons and events which bore no direct relationship to the interests of the insured party. In that respect they resembled wagers. The legislative response was:

Life Assurance Act 1774 (14 Geo III c 48)

An Act for regulating Insurances upon Lives, and for prohibiting all Such Insurances except in Cases where the Persons insuring shall have an Interest in the Life or Death of the Persons insured.

WHEREAS it hath been found by Experience, that the making Insurances on Lives, or other Events, wherein the Assured shall have no Interest, hath introduced a mischievous Kind of Gaming: For Remedy whereof, be it enacted by the King's most Excellent Majesty, by and with the Advice and Consent of the Lords Spiritual and Temporal, and Commons, in this present Parliament assembled, and by the Authority of the same, That from and after the passing of this Act, no Insurance shall be made by any Person or Persons, Bodies Politic or Corporate, on the Life or Lives of any Person or Persons, or on any other Event or Events whatsoever, wherein the Person or Persons for whose Use, Benefit, or on whose Account such Policy or Policies shall be made, shall have no Interest, or by way of Gaming or Wagering; and that every Assurance made contrary to the true Intent and meaning hereof, shall be null and void, to all Intents and Purposes whatsoever.

2 And it shall not be lawful to make any Policy or Policies on the Life or Lives of any Person or Persons or other Event or Events, without inserting in such Policy or Policies the Person or Persons' Name or Names interested therein, or for whose Use, Benefit, or on whose Account, such Policy is so made or underwrote.

3 And in all Cases when the Insured hath Interest in such Life or Lives, Event or Events, no greater Sum shall be recovered or received from the Insurer or Insurers than the Amount or Value of the Interest of the Insured in such Life or Lives, or other Event or Events.

4 Provided always, That nothing herein contained shall extend, or be construed to extend, to Insurances *bona fide* made by any Person or Persons, on Ships, Goods, or Merchandises;

but every such Insurance shall be as valid and effectual in the Law, as if this Act had not been made.

This Act was received as part of English law upon settlement of the Australian colonies, and still applies in most states. In New South Wales and Victoria it has been repealed and re-enacted: in Victoria in the Instruments Act ss 21-24, and in New South Wales by Imperial Acts Application Act 1969 ss 22 and 23.

Each of the above Acts applies not only to life policies but also to general accident and fire policies other than those specifically excluded in s 4 and s 23(4) respectively. However, the state legislation would yield to the Commonwealth Life Insurance Act 1945 which lays down an expanded definition of insurable interest in relation to life insurance but does not exclude the previous common law interpretations:

Life Insurance Act 1945 (Cth)

86 (1) An insurable interest shall be deemed to be had by—
   (a) a parent of a child under twenty-one years of age, or a person *in loco parentis* of such a child—in the life of the child;
   (b) a husband—in the life of his wife;
   (c) a wife—in the life of her husband;
   (d) any person—in the life of another upon whom he is wholly or in part dependent for support or education;
   (e) a corporation or other person—in the life of an officer or employee thereof; and
   (f) a person who has a pecuniary interest in the duration of the life of another person—in the life of that person.

(2) This section shall apply to policies whether effected before or after the commencement of this Act.

(3) This section shall not be construed to limit or restrict in any way the meaning of insurable interest as understood at the commencement of this Act

OTHER TYPES OF INSURANCE

In relation to insurances not covered by the above provisions the requirement of insurable interest will be based upon legislation outlawing gaming and wagering in general, such as the Gaming and Betting Act 1912 (NSW) s 16 quoted on p 200, *supra*. What is the rationale for the requirement of insurable interest?

FAI Insurances Ltd v Custom Credit Corp Ltd
Federal Court of Australia (1980) 44 FLR 431

Fisher J (at 439): Essentially insurance is an indemnity or payment of a sum to cover an injury, in circumstances where there is, because of the element of risk, the possibility of loss: *Re Commonwealth Homes and Investment Co Ltd* [1943] SASR 211 at 231. However, even though not all contracts of insurance are contracts of indemnity, a policy of insurance on property is such a contract: *Castellain v Preston* (1883) 11 QBD 380 at 386 and *British Traders' Insurance Co Ltd v Monson* (1964) 111 CLR 86. Where a mortgagee insures, or, pursuant to an arrangement with his mortgagor, is insured against the risk of fire, what is insured is not the debt but the security, and the mortgagee is insured as the holder of the security for the debt: *Royal Insurance Co v Mylius* (1926) 38 CLR 477 at 489. Thus the insurable interest is the security for a debt and a mortgagee, whether legal or equitable, has an insurable interest in the mortgaged property: *Western Australian Bank v Royal Insurance Co* (1908) 5 CLR 533 at 550, 557; and per Bowen LJ in *Castellain v Preston* at 398. A lender may have an insurable interest in a property even though it cannot be technically said that it holds a mortgage in law or in equity, for an insurable interest has been categorised as "any legal or equitable estate, or any right which may be prejudicially affected or any responsibility which may be brought into operation by fire": *Western Australian Bank v Royal Insurance Co* at 556-7. However, there cannot be any "prejudice" unless a debt exists. The classic definition of an insurable interest is that of Lord Eldon in *Lucena v Craufurd* (1806) 2 Bos & Pul (NR) 269; 127 ER 630, namely "a right in the property or a right derivable out of some contract about the property". Somewhat more recently in New South Wales to have an insurable interest has been defined as follows: "to be interested in the preservation of a thing is to be so circumstanced with respect to it as to have benefit from its existence, prejudice from its destruction": *Bank of New South Wales v The North British and Mercantile Insurance Co* (1882) 3 NSWLR 60 at 76. It would appear to follow that a lender of money has an insurable interest in a property if there is a presently existing indebtedness in respect of which the property is in some manner charged or obligated.

Because a policy of insurance on property, or more specifically a contract of insurance against fire, is a contract of personal indemnity, it is necessary that at all relevant times the insurer have an insurable interest in the property the subject of the insurance. If it were otherwise, the contract would in essence be a contract of wager, Joske & Brooking, *Insurance Law*, p 60. Thus the rationale for the necessity to ensure that the insurer has an insurable interest is the need to establish that the contract is not by way of wager.

Hepburn v A Tomlinson (Hauliers) Ltd
House of Lords [1966] AC 451

[The respondents, carriers, held an all risks insurance policy on tobacco manufactured goods and/or machinery of Imperial Tobacco Co under which the appellant underwriter agreed to indemnify the respondents against all loss, damage or liability.

When this policy was effected there was in force between the tobacco company and the respondents an agreement whereby the respondents were obliged to "insure and keep insured with full comprehensive cover against loss of goods in transit or otherwise from the said vehicles with an approved insurance company ...".

The respondents carried a quantity of cigarettes belonging to Imperial Tobacco in lorries which were hired to that company but driven by the respondents' servants, to Imperial Tobacco's warehouse in London where they were stored overnight pending unloading next morning. During the night the goods were stolen without any negligence on respondents' part. Roskill J and the Court of Appeal both held the respondents were entitled to recover under their policy. The underwriter appealed to the House of Lords.]

Lord Reid [stated the facts, and continued:] There can be no doubt that a bailee has an insurable interest in goods entrusted to him, and it has not been denied that the respondents were bailees of the cigarettes when they were stolen. I think that the law was accurately stated by Lord Campbell CJ in *Waters v Monarch Fire & Life Assurance Co* (1856) 5 E & B 870 at 880-1. In that case a bailee, a wharfinger, had insured against fire, not only his own goods, but also goods "in trust or on commission" in his warehouse and this was held to include goods of customers which he held there. Lord Campbell said: "They were so entrusted with the goods deposited on their wharfs; I cannot doubt the policy was intended to protect such goods; and it would be very inconvenient if wharfingers could not protect such goods by a floating policy. Then, this being the meaning of the policy, is there anything illegal in it? It cannot now be disputed that it would be legal at common law; and Mr Lush properly admits that it is not prohibited by the terms of any statute. And I think that a person entrusted with goods can insure them without orders from the owner, and even without informing him that there was such a policy. It would be most inconvenient in business if a wharfinger could not, at his own cost, keep up a floating policy for the benefit of all who might become his customers. The last point that arises is, to what extent does the policy protect those goods. The defendants say that it was only the plaintiffs' personal interest. But the policies are in terms contracts to make good 'all such damage and loss as may happen by fire at the property hereinbefore mentioned'. That is a valid contract; and, as the property is wholly destroyed, the value of the whole must be made good, not merely the particular interest of the plaintiffs. They will be entitled to apply so much to cover their own interest, and will be trustees for the owners as to the rest."

In no case cited to us has there been any adverse criticism of that passage. A bailee can if he chooses merely insure to cover his own loss or personal liability to the owner of the goods either at common law or under contract and if he does that of course he can recover no more under the policy than sufficient to make good his own personal loss or liability. But equally he can if he chooses insure up to his full insurable interest — up to the full value of the goods entrusted to him. And if he does that he can recover the value of the goods though he has suffered no personal loss at all. But in that case the law will require him to account to the owner of the goods who has suffered the loss or, as Lord Campbell says, he will be trustee for the owners. I need not consider whether this is a trust in the strict sense or precisely on what ground the owner can sue the bailee for the money which he has recovered from the insurer. A similar situation would arise if a bailee sued a wrongdoer for the full value of goods converted or destroyed by him; there is no doubt that such an action can succeed and equally I would think that there can be no doubt that the bailee must then account to the true owner. The fact that a bailee has an insurable interest beyond his own personal loss if the goods are destroyed has never been regarded as in any way inconsistent with the overriding principle that insurance of goods is a contract of indemnity. The question is whether the bailee has insured his whole insurable interest — in effect has taken out a goods policy — or whether he has only insured against personal loss — has taken out a personal liability policy.

The answer to that question must depend on the true construction of the policy ... [His Honour considered the policy and continued at 469:]

This case has been complicated by the supposed existence of a rule that, if the insured has only a limited interest in the subjects insured, he cannot recover more than sufficient to indemnify him against his own personal loss, unless it is shewn that he intended to insure for the benefit of the owner of those subjects. It is said that under this supposed rule that intention need not appear from the terms of the policy and need not have been communicated to the insurer, but that the intention can be proved by evidence. But it is a fundamental principle that the construction of a contract cannot be governed or affected by the intention or belief of one of the parties not communicated to the other: and for very good reason. It would be most unfair if one party were to find his apparent rights under the contract altered by reason of some state of mind of the other party of which he was not and could not be aware. The supposed rule appears to have been deduced by text writers from obiter dicta of Bowen LJ in *Castellain v Preston* (1883) 11 QBD 380 at 397-9 (CA) and it appears to me to have arisen from failure to distinguish cases where the assured insures his own insurable interest from cases where, as in marine insurance policies, he is insuring on behalf of undisclosed principals. Under the ordinary law of principal and agent an undisclosed principal cannot come in to take advantage of a contract unless the agent intended to act on his behalf. The law of marine insurance may not correspond in all respects with the ordinary law of principal and agent, but I see nothing really anomalous in it. It is however a very different matter when the insurer is insuring on his own behalf. In the present case Players are not coming in as undisclosed principals and there is no room for the introduction of a requirement that the respondents must have intended to act as their agents or on their behalf. If there were any question whether the policy is a wagering policy, intentions would be relevant, but no such question arises in this case and it could hardly arise in a case of this character ...

But then, says counsel for the appellant, a decision that an assured, entering into a contract of indemnity on his own behalf, can recover more than sufficient to indemnify himself personally, would conflict with the principle that parties to a contract cannot confer enforceable rights on a third party: here if the respondents can recover more than sufficient for their own indemnity and if Players can require them to account for the surplus, in effect the result is that this contract does so operate as to confer enforceable rights on Players who are not a party to it. Let me assume that in strict logic there is some ground for his argument. No doubt the principle preventing *jus quaesitum tertio* has been firmly established for at least half a century. But it does not appear to me to be a primeval or necessary principle of the law of England. We must uphold it until it is altered. But I do not think that we are bound to be astute to extend it on a logical basis so as to cut down an exception, if it be an exception, which has stood unchallenged since the decision of *Waters'* case (1856) 5 E & B 870 more than a century ago.

In my judgment, this policy on its true construction must be held to be a policy on goods, and the respondents are entitled to recover under it the value of the goods up to the limits expressed in the policy. But the law will require them to account to Players, the owners of the goods, for what they do not require for their own indemnification.

I would therefore dismiss this appeal.

[**Lord Pearce** considered the construction of the policy and reached similar conclusions to those of Lord Reid. He continued at 476:]

Undoubtedly there has been some lack of clarity in the law, as stated in the textbooks and in some of the cases, with regard to the part played by the unilateral intention of the assured who has either no personal interest or only a part interest in the ownership of goods.

Mr Littman is, I think, right in saying that the question of the assured's unilateral intention came into this branch of the law by way of public policy and marine insurance. One need not here consider s 26(3) of the Marine Insurance Act 1906; which certainly appears to enact that in certain marine policies the unilateral intention of the assured may widen or narrow the scope of a policy of assurance effected by him. It is not, I think, a guide to the general law, but it does appear to be based on a dictum of Brett J in *Allison v Bristol Marine Insurance Co Ltd* (1876) 1 App Cas 209 at 216.

Insurance policies can be gaming transactions if they are effected on goods in which the assured has no interest. In the eighteenth century such policies were common, particularly in marine insurance, and they were enforceable (but without any judicial enthusiasm) at common law. In 1745, however, an Act (19 Geo 2 c 37) to regulate insurance on ships referred in its preamble to the "mischievous kind of gaming or wagering, under the pretence of assuring the risk on shipping", and enacted that no assurances should be made on any goods on board any British ships, "interest or no interest, or without further proof of interest than the policy, or by way of gaming or wagering ... and that every such assurance shall be null and void to all intents and purposes". Thereafter various statutes, down to the Marine Insurance (Gambling Policies) Act 1909, dealt with this matter.

The Life Assurance Act 1774 extended similar principles to other contracts of insurance without interest, but excepted insurance on goods against land risks. These, although made without interest, were enforceable until 1845 when the Gaming Act was passed. That Act rendered void all contracts which in substance are wagers made without interest in the subject matter of the insurance. Thus, if insurance was effected by a person without an insurable interest he could not recover.

In *Boehm v Bell* (1799) 8 Term Rep 154 at 162 Lawrence J said: "The case turns on this short question, whether or not the insured had an interest which they might insure? Did they mean to game? or was not there a loss against which they might indemnify themselves, by a policy of insurance?"

There have been many cases dealing with circumstances where it is doubtful whether an assured has an insurable interest, and questions have arisen when he is seeking to recover moneys where the loss falls on others. It may be that he is insuring as agent or as trustee. Even though he is not strictly the one or the other, the circumstances may be such that he has only a limited interest in the goods but that commercial convenience makes it reasonable for him to insure the whole property in the goods and to recover the whole of the moneys, holding the balance in trust for those whose loss it represents. In such a case he is not gaming and there is no reason why he should not so act.

In *Robertson v Hamilton* (1811) 14 East 522 at 532-3, Lord Ellenborough CJ said: "The plaintiffs, having an insurable interest in the whole mass of the property restored, may recover upon this policy as trustees for those who are interested with themselves in the whole; though they may be afterwards called upon to divide it amongst the several claimants in the proportions due to each; and a recovery in this action will not exclude any of the parties from unravelling the account in equity. If we were not accustomed in this place to handle questions among the *apices juris*, it would appear extraordinary that this should be considered as a gambling policy within the statute, in which the plaintiffs had no real interest, when it is stated in the case that they are the owners of one of the captured ships, and that after the mass of the captured property had been redeemed by the sacrifice of a part for the benefit of the whole, they expended their own money in securing the whole concern, which had been brought into hotchpot. In what sense can we consider the plaintiffs as gamblers?"

In *Irving v Richardson* (1831) 2 B & Ad 193, however, where a mortgagee of a ship (under a then recent statute the mortgagor did not cease to be owner) insured it, it was held that the question whether he could recover the value of the mortgagor's interest as well as his own fell to be decided by the question whether he had intended to insure the mortgagor's interest. Littledale J there said (at 196): "Before the late Registry Act the mortgagee of a ship was, in point of law, the owner, and might insure to the full extent of the ship's value to the mortgagor as well as to himself. But by the statute the interests of mortgagor and mortgagee are more distinctly severed than they formerly were. The mortgagor, now, does not cease to be an owner.

In order, therefore, that the defendant in this case" (the mortgagee) "might not keep possession of a sum exceeding not only the value stated in the policies, but also the amount of his interest, it became necessary to ascertain what it was that he had in reality insured; and with this veiw it was rightly put to the jury whether, in effecting the policies, he intended to insure the whole interest in the vessel, or merely the amount of his own as mortgagor."

It appears clear from that case that a mortgagee who had the normal rights of a mortgagee in the property of the goods mortgaged could have recovered the whole proprietary interest in the goods without expressly proving his unilateral intention, holding in trust for the mortgagor the proportionate part of the sum recovered. And it was only the fact that a recent Act had taken away his rights in the property that made it necessary for him to show his intention. Since, however, that Act left him with no ownership or property in the goods, I infer that he was treated by the court as a person who had no proprietary interest in the goods, and who, if he was merely insuring as an agent, must prove his intention when insuring on another's behalf. Otherwise I have some doubt as to the validity of that case.

This case was relied on by Brett J in *Allison v Bristol Marine Insurance Co Ltd* (1876) 1 App Cas 209 at 216 when he said that "by reason of the general understanding of merchants, which has been sufficiently made known to the courts, it is to be held, as matter of law, without further proof, that wherever the subject matter of a policy is described in it in general terms, it is to be taken to cover the interest, which is within its terms, which the assured has at risk, unless the contrary appears to have been the intention of the assured from other parts of the policy, or other proof".

If and in so far as this dictum is intended to say that the unilateral intention of the assured can extend or narrow the interest which the policy covers there is force in Lord Atkinson's remarks in *Boston Fruit Co v British & Foreign Marine Insurance Co Ltd* [1906] AC 336 at 343; 22 TLR 571 (HL): "Under the old authorities the governing factor in determining the person or class of persons who came within such a clause, or was or were entitled to ratify and take advantage of the contract contained in it, was apparently the intention, disclosed or undisclosed, existing in the mind of the person who effected the policy with the underwriters at the time he effected it. The underwriter, it would seem, was held to have insured those whom the person who dealt with him intended should be insured though that intention was never communicated to him. I doubt very much whether that doctrine can long survive the decision of your Lordships' House in *Keighley, Maxsted & Co v Durant* [1901] AC 240; 17 TLR 527 (HL) or whether the rule of construction thus adopted in the case of marine policies from earlier times is not inconsistent with the root principle which lies at the foundation of all the law of contract, namely, that there must always be the consent ad diem of the two contracting minds to make a valid contract." But so far as concerns an agent who has no interest and is effecting an insurance for others, his unilateral intention is of importance to this extent that, unless he intends to effect the insurance on behalf of his principal, he is simply wagering and there is nothing which an undisclosed principal can ratify.

The bailee of goods, however, is in a very different position. He has a right to sue for conversion, holding in trust for the owner such of the damages as represent the owner's interest. He may likewise sue in negligence for the full value of the goods, though he would have had a good answer to an action by the bailor for the loss of the goods bailed: *The Winkfield* [1902] P 42; 18 TLR 178 (CA).

It would seem irrational, therefore, if he could not also insure for their full value. Both those who have the legal title and those who have a right to possession have an insurable interest in the real or personal property in question. There seems, therefore, no reason in principle why they should not be entitled to insure for the whole value and recover it. They must, however (like plaintiffs in actions of trover or negligence), hold in trust for the other parties interested so much of the moneys recovered as is attributable to the other interests. But is proof of an intention to insure for the interests of others a necessary condition precedent for a plaintiff seeking to recover on an insurance policy in such circumstances? I do not think so.

In the case of *Waters* (1856) 5 E & B 870 at 881 Lord Campbell CJ said: "I think that a person entrusted with goods can insure them without orders from the owner, and even without informing him that there was such a policy. It would be most inconvenient in business if a wharfinger could not, at his own cost, keep up a floating policy for the benefit of all who might become his customers ... as the property is wholly destroyed, the value of the whole must be made good, nor merely the particular interest of the plaintiffs. They will be entitled to apply so much to cover their own interest, and will be trustees for the owners as to the rest. The authorities are clear that an assurance made without orders may be ratified by the owners of the property, and then the assurers become trustees for them", and Crompton J said (at 882): "The parties meant to insure those goods with which the plaintiffs were entrusted, and in every part of which they had an interest, both in respect of their lien and in respect of their responsibility to their bailors. What the surplus after satisfying their own claim might be, could only be ascertained after the loss, when the amount of their lien at that time was determined; but they were persons interested in every particle of the goods."

There is no suggestion in the judgments that the unilateral intention of the assured was relevant ...

In *Castellain v Preston* (1883) 11 QBD 380 however, Bowen LJ, having referred to mortgagees and bailees and admitted their right to recover, made observations to the effect that no part owner could recover for more than the interest which he had intended to insure. Taken in their full meaning his words create some difficulty, but the judgment was not reserved and his remarks were obiter. His real point was that a part owner could not recover for himself (so as to put into his own pocket) more than the value of his interest; for if he intended to do that he would simply be wagering.

A bailee or mortgagee, therefore (or others in analogous positions), has, by virtue of his position and his interest in the property, a right to insure for the whole of its value, holding in trust for the owner or mortgagor the amount attributable to their interest. To hold otherwise would be commercially inconvenient and would have no justification in commonsense. In my opinion, there is no burden on him to prove his intention to insure their interest on their behalf. If, however, the defendants can affirmatively prove that he had an intention not to do so, his insurance quoad that other interest is gaming and he cannot recover. But the burden of proving that is on the defendants.

In the present case the plaintiffs were bailees and there was nothing in the pleadings that could amount to an assertion that the policy was a wager in that unilaterally the plaintiffs had an intention not to insure the owners' interest in the goods for them and not to hold on the owners' behalf any moneys which they might recover. The only issue, therefore, was one of construction, namely, did the policy cover the whole property in the goods. Any discussion of the unilateral intention of the assured was irrelevant ...

I would therefore dismiss the appeal.

[**Lord Hodson** delivered a judgment to the same effect. **Lord Guest** and **Lord Wilberforce** agreed with Lord Reid.]

Appeal dismissed.

With the above case may be compared the following Australian cases: *British Traders' Insurance Co Ltd v Monson*, p 254, *infra*; and *Davjoyda Estates Pty Ltd v National Insurance Co of New Zealand Ltd* (1967) 69 SR (NSW) 381 (purchaser of property on trust for another has an insurable interest as soon as contract is exchanged with vendor).

A further issue concerns the time at which the insured must possess an insurable interest and whether that interest must continue throughout the term of the policy: see *Dalby v India and London Life Assurance Co* (1854) 15 CB 365; 139 ER 465; and *The Southern Cross Assurance Co Ltd v The Australian Provincial Assurance Association Ltd* (1935) 53 CLR 618.

The consequence of Carb obtaining insurance from Coverall without having the requisite insurable interest is that the contract is unlawful and void *ab initio*. If Carb repents of the unlawful contract while it is still wholly executory, that is, before the risk has begun to run, it will be entitled to recover any premium it has paid. Similarly, if Coverall or its agent induced Carb to enter the contract by a fraudulent misrepresentation that it was lawful, the premium can be recovered. In other cases, where both parties are *in pari delicto*, the courts will not assist Carb in rescinding an unlawful contract. Having received the premium Coverall might still meet a claim on the policy on an *ex gratia* basis but again the courts would not enforce a claim under an unlawful insurance contract.

QUESTIONS

Question 10

How would you distinguish between a wager and a contract to insure an insurable interest? Does the nature of an insurable interest vary depending on the type of insurance and, if so, how? What relationship is necessary for the insurer to establish an insurable interest (a) at common law and (b) under statute? What is the purpose and function of the requirement of insurable interest?

Question 11

Discuss whether Coverall Insurance Ltd would be obliged to honour the following:

(1) Carb Pty Ltd obtained an all risks policy on the metal press used by it for manufacturing, which it had borrowed from Rival Co. The metal press was insured for its full market value of $75,000, although Carb paid only $20,000 for its use for one year, when it was to be returned to Rival Co. Carb did not advise Coverall that the press was owned by Rival Co. The press was destroyed by fire while in Carb's possession.

(2) On 10 July, Carb obtained a marine insurance policy in respect of a tool die it was negotiating to buy. On 20 July it contracted to buy the die which was lost at sea on 30 August.

(3) Carb's best customer was Greatparts Ltd. It had no legal obligation to continue buying carburettors from Carb, but Carb believed that because of the close friendship between Jim Handy and its manager Lever, Greatparts would continue to do so while Lever remained manager. Carb insured Lever's life with Coverall; Lever died shortly thereafter.

(4) Carb was owed $50,000 by a customer, Windup Ltd, being the unpaid balance of purchase-money owed on a consignment of carburettors already delivered to Windup Ltd. Fearing that it might not be paid, Carb took out an insurance policy for $50,000 on Windup's entire stock-in-trade, its factory and the life of its chief executive.

(5) Carb obtained an insurance policy for $2 million on the life of Jim Handy, its Managing Director. His annual salary was $50,000. While Jim was overseas the company needed cash urgently and sold the policy to an entrepreneur Hood. Shortly after his return Jim was killed by an unidentified hit-and-run driver.

SECTION 4: THE INDEMNITY PRINCIPLE AND ITS APPLICATIONS

This section involves the meaning of indemnity insurance and its relationship to the requirement of insurable interest considered above. We will also be concerned with the following issues.

(1) Does the indemnity principle apply uniformly to all types of insurance or can it vary or be modified in some instances?

(2) How is the principle applied where Carb Pty Ltd has:
(a) overinsured;
(b) underinsured;
(c) insured the same risk with several insurance companies;
(d) retained the residue of the insured assets after the loss has occurred; or
(e) suffered loss at the hands of a third party wrongdoer.

INSURABLE INTEREST AND INDEMNITY

In *Hepburn v A Tomlinson (Hauliers) Ltd*, p 246, *supra*, Lord Reid said:

> The fact that a bailee has an insurable interest beyond his own personal loss if the goods are destroyed has never been regarded as in any way inconsistent with the over-riding principle that insurance of goods is a contract of indemnity.

The High Court applied the same principle to a reassurance contract in the *Southern Cross Assurance Co* case (1935) 53 CLR 618. Thus the two principles are not inconsistent. In many cases they will overlap since if Carb has no insurable interest either at the time of taking out insurance on its own behalf or at the time of the loss, it would be defeated by both principles. In other cases the rules complement each other; eg, if Carb has contracted to sell goods to Mitzi but retains possession pending payment, it has sufficient interest to support a valid insurance with Coverall. However, if the goods are destroyed after risk has passed to Mitzi, the indemnity principle precludes Carb obtaining a double recovery—from Mitzi and from Coverall.

It is interesting to compare the position under a life insurance policy with that under a marine insurance policy. Life Insurance Act 1945 s 86 requires that Carb have an insurable interest in Jim Handy's life when it obtains a policy on his life, but does not require that Carb's interest continue until Jim dies nor is assignment to a party without an insurable interest precluded. The life policy is not confined to a pure indemnity. Under Marine Insurance Act 1909 ss 10–12 Carb need only have an expectation of acquiring an interest in a shipment of goods to insure them during sea transit, but generally cannot recover under the policy unless it has acquired that interest at the time of loss.

WHAT IS THE INDEMNITY PRINCIPLE?

Castellain v Preston
English Court of Appeal (1883) 11 QBD 380

Brett LJ: In this case the action is brought by the plaintiff as representing an insurance company against the defendants in respect of money which has been paid by that company to the defendants on account of the loss by fire of a building. The defendants were the owners of property consisting partly at all events of a house, and the defendants had made a contract of sale of that property with third persons, which contract upon the giving of a certain notice as to the time of payment would oblige those third persons, if they fulfilled the contract, to pay the agreed price for the sale of that property, a part of which was a house, and according to the peculiarity of such a sale and purchase of land or real property the vendees would have to pay the purchase-money, whether the house was, before the date of payment, burnt down or not. After the contract was made with the third persons, and before the day of payment, the house was burnt down. The vendors, the defendants, having insured the house in the ordinary form with the plaintiff's company, it is not suggested that upon the house being burnt down the defendants had not an insurable interest. They had an insurable interest, as it seems to me, first, because they were at all events the legal owners of the property; and, secondly, because the vendees or third persons might not carry out the contract, and if for any reason they should never carry out the contract, then the vendors, if the house was burnt down, would suffer the loss. Upon the happening of the fire the defendants made a claim on the insurance company represented by the plaintiff, and were paid a certain sum which represented the damage done to the house. After that, the contract of sale between the defendants and the third persons, the vendees of the property, was carried out, and the full amount of the purchase-money was paid by the third persons to the defendants notwithstanding the fire. Under those circumstances the plaintiff representing the insurance company brings this action;

I do not say that he brings it to recover back the money which has been paid by the insurance company (for that expression of opinion would rather interfere with the form of the action), but he brings the action in respect of that money.

The question is whether this action is maintainable. The case was tried before Chitty J, and he, in a very careful and elaborate judgment (1882) 8 QBD 613 at 615, has come to the conclusion that the insurance company cannot recover against the defendants in respect of the money paid by them. It seems to me that the foundation of his judgment is this, that he considers that the doctrine of subrogation of the insurer into the position of the assured is confined within limits, which prevent it from extending to the present case. I must now consider whether I can agree with him.

In order to give my opinion upon this case, I feel obliged to revert to the very foundation of every rule which has been promulgated and acted on by the courts with regard to insurance law. The very foundation, in my opinion, of every rule which has been applied to insurance law is this, namely, that the contract of insurance contained in a marine or fire policy is a contract of indemnity, and of indemnity only, and that this contract means that the assured, in case of a loss against which the policy has been made, shall be fully indemnified, but shall never be more than fully indemnified. That is the fundamental principle of insurance, and if ever a proposition is brought forward which is at variance with it, that is to say, which either will prevent the assured from obtaining a full indemnity, or which will give to the assured more than a full indemnity, that proposition must certainly be wrong.

In the course of this discussion many propositions and rules well known in insurance law have been glanced at. For instance, to speak of marine insurance, the doctrine of a constructive total loss originated solely to carry out the fundamental rule which I have mentioned. It was a doctrine introduced for the benefit of the assured; for, as a matter of business, a constructive total loss is equivalent to an actual total loss; and if a constructive total loss could not be treated as an actual total loss, the assured would not recover a full indemnity. But grafted upon the doctrine of constructive total loss came the doctrine of abandonment, which is a doctrine in favour of the insurer or underwriter, in order that the assured may not recover more than a full indemnity. The doctrine of constructive total loss and the doctrine of notice of abandonment engrafted upon it were invented or promulgated for the purpose of making a policy of marine insurance a contract of indemnity in the fullest sense of the term. I may point out that the doctrine of notice of abandonment is most difficult to justify upon principle; it was introduced, rather as a matter of justice in favour of the underwriters, so as to prevent the assured from obtaining by fraud more than a full indemnity. That doctrine is to a certain extent technical, that is to say, although the assured has in reality suffered a constructive total loss, and although he is upon general principles entitled to recover, nevertheless he must fail unless he has given a notice of abandonment. I suppose that the doctrine of notice of abandonment was originally introduced by merchants and underwriters, and afterwards adopted as part of the law as to marine insurance; but at first sight it seems a mere encroachment of the judges.

I have mentioned the doctrine of notice of abandonment for the purpose of coming to the doctrine of subrogation. That doctrine does not arise upon any of the terms of the contract of insurance; it is only another proposition which has been adopted for the purpose of carrying out the fundamental rule which I have mentioned, and it is a doctrine in favour of the underwriters or insurers in order to prevent the assured from recovering more than a full indemnity; it has been adopted solely for that reason. It is not, to my mind, a doctrine applied to insurance law on the ground that underwriters are sureties. Underwriters are not always sureties. They have rights which sometimes are similar to the rights of sureties, but that again is in order to prevent the assured from recovering from them more than a full indemnity. But it being admitted that the doctrine of subrogation is to be applied merely for the purpose of preventing the assured from obtaining more than a full indemnity, the question is, whether that doctrine as applied in insurance law can be in any way limited. Is it to be limited to this, that the underwriter is subrogated into the place of the assured so far as to enable the underwriter to enforce a contract, or to enforce a right of action? Why is it to be limited to that, if when it is limited to that, it will, in certain cases, enable the assured to recover more than a full indemnity? The moment it can be shewn that such a limitation of the doctrine would have that effect, then, as I said before, in my opinion it is contrary to the foundation of the law as to insurance, and must be wrong. And, with the greatest deference to my Brother Chitty, it seems to me that that is the fault of his judgment. He has by his judgment limited this doctrine of subrogation to placing the insurer in the position of the assured only for the purpose of enforcing a right of action, to which the assured may be entitled. In order to apply the doctrine of subrogation, it seems to me that the full and absolute meaning of the word must be used, that is to say, the insurer must be placed in the position of the assured. Now it seems to me that in order to carry out the fundamental rule of insurance law, this doctrine of subrogation must be carried to the extent which I am now about to endeavour to express, namely, that as between the underwriter and the assured the underwriter is entitled to the advantage of every right of the assured, whether such right consists in contract, fulfilled or unfulfilled, or in remedy for tort capable of being insisted on or already insisted on, or in any other right, whether by way of condition or otherwise, legal or equitable, which can be, or has been exercised or has accrued, and whether such right could or could not be enforced by the insurer in the name of the assured by the exercise or acquiring of which right or condition the loss against which the assured is insured, can be, or has been diminished. That seems to me to put this doctrine of subrogation in the largest possible form, and if in that form, large as it is, it is short of fulfilling that which is the fundamental condition, I must have omitted to state something which ought to have been stated. But it will be observed that I use the words "of every right of the assured". I think that the rule does require that limit. In *Burnand v Rodocanachi* (1882) 7 App Cas 333 the foundation of the judgment to my mind was, that what was paid by the United States government could not be considered as salvage, but must be deemed to have been only a gift. It was only a gift to which the assured had no right at any time until it was placed in their hands. I am aware that with regard to the case of reprisals, or that which a person whose vessel had been captured got from the English government by a way of reprisal, the sum received has been stated to be, and perhaps in one sense was, a gift of his own government to himself, but it was always deemed to be capable of being brought within the range of the law as to insurance, because the English government invariably made the "gift", so invariably, that as a matter of business it had come to be considered as a matter of right. This enlargement, or this explanation, of what I consider to be the real meaning of the doctrine of subrogation, shews that in my opinion it goes much further than a mere transfer of those rights which may at any time give a cause of action either in contract or in tort, because if upon the happening of the loss there is contract between the assured and a third person, and if that contract is immediately fulfilled by the third person, then there is no right of action of any kind into which the insurer can be subrogated. The right of action is gone; the contract is fulfilled. In like manner if upon the happening of a tort the tort is immediately made good by the tort feasor, then the right of action is gone; there is no right of action existing into which the insurer can be subrogated. It will be said that there did for a moment exist a right of action in favour of the assured, into which the insurer could have been subrogated. But he cannot be subrogated into a right of action until he has paid the sum insured and made good the loss. Therefore innumerable cases would be taken out of the doctrine, if it were to be confined to existing rights of action. And I go further and hold that if a right of action in the assured has been satisfied, and the loss has been thereby diminished, then, although there never was nor could be any right of action into which the insurer could be subrogated, it would be contrary to the doctrine of subrogation to say that the loss is not to be diminished as between the assured and the insurer by reason of the satisfaction of that right. I fail to see at present if the present defendants would have had a right of action at any time against the purchasers, upon which they could enforce a contract of sale of their property whether the building was standing or not, why the insurance company should not have been subrogated into that right of action. But I am nor prepared to say that they could be, more particularly as I understand my learned Brother, who knows much more of the law as to specific performance than I do, is at all events not satisfied that they could. I pass by the question without solving it, because there was a right in the defendants to have the contract of sale fulfilled by the purchasers notwithstanding the loss, and it was fulfilled. The assured have had the advantage therefore of that right, and by that right, not by a gift which the purchasers could have declined to make, the assured have recovered, notwithstanding the loss, from the purchasers the very sum of money which they were to obtain whether this building was burnt or not. In that sense I cannot conceive that a right, by virtue of which the assured has his loss diminished, is not a right which, as has been said, affects the loss. This right which was at one time merely in contract, but which was afterwards fulfilled, either when it was in contract only, or after it was fulfilled, does affect the loss; that is to say, it affects the loss by enabling the assured, the vendors, to get the same money which they would have got if the loss had not happened.

[His Lordship then referred to various passages in the judgment of Chitty J and concluded at 392:] The contract in the present case, as it seems to me, does enable the assured to be put by the third party into as good a position as if the fire had not happened, and that result arises from this contract alone. Therefore, according to the true principles of insurance law, and in order to carry out the fundamental doctrine, namely, that the assured can recover a full indemnity, but shall never recover more, except, perhaps, in the case of the suing and labouring clause under certain circumstances, it is necessary that the plaintiff in this case should succeed. The case of *Darrell v Tibbitts* (1880) 5 QBD 560 has cut away every technicality which would prevent a sound decision. The doctrine of subrogation must be carried out to the full extent, and carried out in this case by enabling the plaintiff to recover.

[**Cotton LJ** and **Bowen LJ** delivered judgments to similar effect. Compare the comments upon the judgment of Bowen LJ made by Lord Reid and Lord Pearce in *Hepburn v A Tomlinson (Hauliers) Ltd*, pp 246 and 249, *supra*.]

Judgment reversed.

British Traders' Insurance Co Ltd v Monson
High Court of Australia (1964) 111 CLR 86; [1964] ALR 845

[On 6 November 1961 Lindsay John Monson entered into an agreement to lease about seven acres of land with buildings on it for one year from that day, and amongst other provisions the agreement contained an option for Monson to purchase the premises for the sum of £2358 5s 0d at any time during the term of the tenancy or any renewal thereof. There were no terms that obliged Monson to repair damage by fire or to have the property insured, and in the event of total destruction of the dwelling house by fire Monson was to have the choice of terminating the tenancy or of continuing in possession of the land at a reduced rental. This agreement was entered into by Monson after he had discovered that he could not at that time obtain sufficient money to purchase the property and after negotiations for purchasing it directly had been discontinued by him. But when on or about 2 November 1961 Monson signed the proposal form for a policy of fire insurance in the presence of the agent of British Traders' Insurance Co Ltd both he and the agent had believed that within the next few days he would purchase the property, and the lessors cancelled the fire insurance policy which they had previously had. The policy of insurance as issued was dated 9 November 1961, and was expressed to be in force from 6 November 1961.]

Kitto, Taylor and **Owen JJ:** This appeal arises out of an action upon a policy of insurance. By the policy the appellant company agreed in consideration of a premium that if the property described in a schedule, or any part of it should be destroyed or damaged by inter alia fire before a stated time the company would pay to the insured named in the schedule the value of the property at the time of the happening of its destruction or the amount of such damage or at its option reinstate or replace the property or any part thereof. There followed a proviso that the liability of the company should in no case exceed in respect of each item the sum expressed in the schedule to be insured thereon or in the whole the total sum insured thereby. The schedule named as the insured the respondents "for their respective rights and interests", and it described the property insured as consisting of several items of which it is necessary only to mention a dwelling and the furniture contained therein. The dwelling and the furniture were destroyed by fire before the stated time.

At the trial certain questions which we have not now to consider were decided in favour of the respondents, and judgment was given in their favour of £600. That amount represented the value of the furniture only. Nothing was allowed in respect of the dwelling. This was because the trial judge held that the respondents had effected the insurance with no intention of protecting anyone's interest but their own as owners, that therefore they could not recover anything other than an indemnity against any loss as owners, and that in fact they had suffered no such loss as they had no such interest. The facts were that the female respondent had no interest at all in the property, and the male respondent had only an interest under an agreement for a term of one year, which entitled him in the event of the dwelling being totally destroyed

Contracts of Insurance

by fire either to determine the tenancy or to continue it at such reduced rental as should be agreed or settled by arbitration. He was not bound to insure the dwelling or to repair it in case of damage by fire. Notwithstanding that the respondents had represented themselves in the proposal as owners of the property, for reasons which it is not now material to mention the contract of insurance remained in full force and effect at all material times, and we doubt whether the learned trial judge was right in denying that the male respondent was entitled to recover the loss, if any, which he had sustained as a tenant. However, it is unnecessary to consider this matter for no claim was made either prior to or in the course of the proceedings that the male respondent had suffered any loss as tenant and no evidence was adduced to suggest that this had occurred. What is contended is that on the terms of the policy the respondents were entitled to recover the whole amount for which the dwelling was insured, even though the result be that they must account for it to the owner.

On appeal to the Full Court of the Supreme Court the respondents' contention was upheld by a majority of the judges. One line of reasoning which was sustained commenced by construing the policy as containing an unqualified promise by the company to pay the respondents in the event that happened the full amount of the sum insured; and on this basis it was said, in answer to the appellant's insistence that a policy of fire insurance is only a contract of indemnity against loss, that according to undoubted authorities on the subject a party insured may in some circumstances recover more than the value of his insurable interest and that the most cogent of all categories of such circumstances must be that in which the parties have by express words so contracted. It is convenient to deal first with this way of putting the case for the respondents. Its fault lies, we think, not in the fact that it begins with the policy, but in the fact that it gives the policy a meaning which neither general understanding nor the law of insurance will support. It concentrates attention upon the words of obligation: "if the property insured ... be destroyed ... by fire ... the Company will pay to the Insured the value of the property ..." If those words be read in isolation from their context, no doubt the obligation is to pay the full value of the property, regardless of the quantum of loss sustained by the respondents by reason of the destruction by fire. But the all-important fact is that they are words in a document possessing unmistakably and on its face a character which flatly contradicts the notion that the obligation of the company is to pay more than the amount of the respondents' loss. It is issued by an insurance company. It is headed "Fire Insurance Policy". All its provisions, even the very words that are relied upon for their literal meaning, are characteristic of fire insurance policies. It is far too late to doubt that by the common understanding of business men and lawyers alike the nature of such a policy controls its obligation, implying conclusively that its statement of the amount which the insurer promises to pay merely fixes the maximum amount which in any event he may have to pay, and having as its sole purpose, and therefore imposing as its only obligation, the indemnification of the insured, up to the amount of the insurance, against loss from the accepted risk. Brett LJ in *Castellain v Preston* (1883) 11 QBD 380 at 386 said that the contract "means" that the assured, in case of a loss against which the policy has been made, shall be fully indemnified, but shall never be more than fully indemnified. Lord Esher MR said in *Dane v Mortgage Insurance Corp* [1894] 1 QB 54: "By the law of insurance, though the underwriter directly promises to pay on a certain event, the contract is treated as one of indemnity" (at 61). There are undoubtedly cases in which the amount payable in respect of the insured's interest in the property may exceed the marketable value of that interest, but that occurs only where full indemnification to the insured would not be achieved by paying him the amount of the value: *Castellain v Preston* at 400. Hence, if in the present case the lease to the male respondent had contained a covenant by him to make good damage by fire, no doubt the whole amount of the insurance would have been recoverable; but the reason would have been that the fire had cast upon him a liability of at least that amount.

The case of a valued policy is special, but it throws no doubt upon the general principle. In such a case the application of the principle is affected by the agreement of the parties on value in the same way as any obligation to indemnify may be affected by an agreed pre-estimate of the value of property: *Irving v Manning* (1847) 1 HLC 287 at 307; 9 ER 766 at 775. The agreement in the case of a valued policy is as to the value of the subject matter, not the amount of the loss; and its effect upon the assessment of the amount payable to the insured is not that the process is to be directed to anything other than the indemnification of the insured, but only that the assessment of his loss must proceed on the basis of the agreed valuation of the property: *Elcock v Thomson* [1949] 2 KB 755. It may be mentioned that in the course of the argument a somewhat faint attempt was made to suggest that the policy here should be construed as a valued policy. It plainly is not, but even if the value of the dwelling were to be taken as having been agreed at the figure appearing in respect of it in the schedule the answer to the present problem would be unaffected.

To that problem no approach can be valid which fails to accept as its first step that a policy showing, as the policy here shows unmistakably, that it is intended as a policy of fire insurance must be construed as a contract for indemnification only. The celebrated judgments in *Castellain v Preston* show that that is the fixed and central point to which all else in the policy is subordinate. It could not be otherwise, for as Lord Cockburn CJ said in charging the jury in *Chapman v Pole* (1870) 22 LT 306 at 307, the law will not allow of gambling in the form of insurance. It was said in the Supreme Court in the present case that *Castellain v Preston* was a case of subrogation, and that until the question of subrogation arises the principle that a contract of insurance is a contract of indemnity is wrongly invoked to diminish a lawful contract to something less than is provided for by its express terms. With respect, we think this is a mistake. *Castellain v Preston* of course was not a case of subrogation in respect of an outstanding right of action and one might almost wish that some other word had been used as the label of a right which exists when it is too late for subrogation in the ordinary sense. The insured had been paid a sum of money under the policy on the footing that that was the amount of his loss. He had later received from a third party, under a contract with respect to the property, a payment which eliminated the loss. The judgments explain with care how large is the right of an insurer to be placed in the position of the insured in relation to both his rights against third parties and the fruit of those rights. The decision, following *Darrell v Tibbitts* (1880) 5 QBD 560, was that the insured was accountable to the insurer for the amount which the third party had paid him. This was because the insurer's obligation had been only to indemnify the insured against his loss, and the payment originally made to the insured had been made not because it was in fact required for indemnification but because of a mutual assumption, which had turned out to be erroneous, that it was required for indemnification. The money had to be brought to account by the insured because it diminished "the loss against which the insurance office merely undertook to indemnify them": at 397. "The policy", as Cotton LJ said, "is really a contract to indemnify the person insured for the loss which he has sustained ... and from that it follows, of course, that as it is only a contract of indemnity it is only to pay that loss which the assured may have sustained ...": at 393. If the insured in that case had received the payment from the third party while still unpaid by the insurer, and had thereafter sued the insurer on the policy, we should be of opinion, notwithstanding the doubt suggested in *MacGillivray on Insurance Law*, 5th ed, 1961, para 1798, that the fact of his having received the payment from the third party would have constituted a bar to his claim, as distinguished from affording the insurer a right by way of cross-action to have him account for the amount so received: see *Morgan v Price* (1849) 4 Ex 615; 154 ER 1360; *Bruce v Jones* (1863) 1 H & C 769; 158 ER 1094; *Yorkshire Insurance Co Ltd v Nisbet Shipping Co Ltd* [1962] 2 QB 330.

We turn to the other line of reasoning by which the decision against the respondents was supported in the Supreme Court. It consists of two propositions. The first is that a person who has an insurable interest in property, however limited that interest may be, is entitled to insure the whole property for its full value against destruction by fire. This may be conceded; but the second proposition we cannot concede. It is that where a person with only a limited interest does insure the whole property, he is necessarily entitled, if the property is destroyed, to recover on the policy the full value of the property up to the amount of the insurance, though he must account to the other persons interested in the property for the excess over what is required to indemnify him against his own loss. In support of this second proposition two lines of argument are employed. One is based upon s 83 of the Act 14 Geo III c 78, the Fires Prevention (Metropolis) Act 1774 (Imp), which the Supreme Court assumed, no doubt correctly, to have been in force in Tasmania at the material time. (See now s 90E of the Conveyancing and Law of Property Act 1884 (Tas) inserted by s 7 of the amending Act No 72 of 1962.) The section authorises an insurer of buildings against fire, upon the request of any person interested in the building or upon certain grounds of suspicion, to cause the insurance money to be laid out, as far as it will go, towards rebuilding, reinstating or repairing the building. The argument is that since a person with a limited interest may under this provision find his insurance moneys applied to the reinstatement of the building he will not be placed by the insurance in as good a position as he was in before the fire, unless those moneys are equal to the full value of the building. A passage is quoted from para 474 of the 5th edition of *MacGillivray on Insurance Law*, the quotation ending with the statement that such a person "can only secure a certain indemnity to himself by insuring up to the full value of the property, and he has therefore an insurable interest up to that amount". This is true because he has an insurable interest to the extent of any indemnification he may require. But when one turns to consider what indemnification, as things turn out, he in fact *does* require, different answers must be given according as the laying out of the insurance moneys in reinstatement is or is not insisted upon by other persons interested or by the insurer. Indeed, *MacGillivray* goes on to say, immediately after the passage quoted: "If reinstatement is claimed by the company or is insisted on by some third party interested, the company will then be liable to reinstate the property up to the full amount of the insurance. On the other hand, if the company elects to pay in cash and no demand is made by any third party for reinstatement, the company may probably refuse to pay more than the value of the assured's insurable interest calculated independently of the peculiar interest given by the statute." The suggestion here made is in our opinion correct, for only by accepting it is the basic principle of insurance law fully observed. In the present case, where there is no question of reinstatement being required either by the insurer or by any third person, we find nothing in the statutory provision to assist the respondents.

The other line of argument depends upon treating an intention to insure the entire property as identical with an intention to insure the property for the benefit of all persons interested in it. What is said is that if a person having only a limited interest insures the property for its full value "so as to cover all beneficial interests in it" he may recover the full value of the property, and hold the excess over the amount of his own pecuniary loss as trustee for the other persons interested. But it is necessary to define what is meant by saying "so as to cover all beneficial interests in it". No doubt in the normal case, where the person taking out the insurance knows that his own interest in the property is only partial, to say that he insures so as to cover all beneficial interests is the same as saying that he intends his insurance to be for the benefit of all who have beneficial interests in the property. But suppose an exceptional case. Suppose that the insured expects soon to acquire the full beneficial interests in the property and takes out the insurance for his own protection only, having no intention that it shall enure for anyone's benefit but his own. In a sense it is true even in such a case that he insures "so as to cover all beneficial interests in the property"; but only in the sense that he insures so as to cover all beneficial interests for his own benefit. The present case is in fact of this kind. The evidence, even the evidence of the male respondent himself, proved beyond question that neither of the respondents had any intention of insuring for anyone's benefit but their own. It is not only that the schedule described them as being the insured "for their respective rights and interests", and said nothing as to any other rights or interests; though we ourselves should regard that as of great significance. But the fact established by the oral evidence is that when making the proposal for the insurance they expected to be the owners of the entirety by the time the policy issued, and that was the only reason why they insured for the full value. They believed they would need protection for themselves as sole owners of the building, and had no thought of providing protection for anyone but themselves. The male respondent was asked in cross-examination "When you signed the proposal you told Knight (the insurance inspector) you had bought the property". He replied, "Yes". Then he was asked, "What interest do you think you covered?" and he said, "Myself and my wife's". In answer to further questions he said he definitely did not think he had taken the insurance out for anybody else, and that he thought his wife and he would receive payment in the event of fire, but not anybody else. Later he said that he had said he was insuring his own and his wife's interest, and added that he thought he had bought the property and that he intended to insure "the full valuation of it". The trial judge was satisfied with this evidence, for he said in his reasons for judgment that the male respondent had conceded that he intended only to insure the interest of himself and his wife.

It was not suggested in the judgments below, nor is it suggested by the respondents here, that the respondents may recover upon the policy any amount in respect of the loss sustained by the lessor, on the footing that he was an undisclosed principal for whom they took out the policy as agents. They were not authorised by him to insure the property on his behalf, and since they neither intended to insure it as his agents nor professed to be doing so there could be no question of ratification. Nor was there a purported ratification. What is suggested is that the respondents may recover in respect of the lessor's loss and so as to hold the proceeds for his benefit, on the footing of a trusteeship arising from the intention which they had to insure the entire beneficial interest in the property. But once it is appreciated that this intention to cover the entire beneficial interest was not an intention to provide any benefit for the lessor, the case of a trust for him collapses. Whether the respondents would have been entitled to succeed even if they had intended the insurance to be for the benefit of the lessor as well as themselves we are not called upon to decide. The case of *Green v Russell* [1959] 2 QB 226 would suggest that they would not. But clear it is that in the absence of an intention to benefit the lessor by the taking out of the policy the suggested trust for him could not arise: cf *Kauter v Hilton* (1953) 90 CLR 86 at 100, and therefore the principle of indemnity prevents the recovery or retention from the insurer of more than the amount of the loss caused to the male respondent in respect of his interest in the property: *Castellain v Preston* (1883) 11 QBD 380 at 398, 399; *Hordern v Federal Mutual Insurance Co of Australia Ltd* (1924) 24 SR (NSW) 267 at 274; 41 WN (NSW) 54 at 55; *Portavon Cinema Co Ltd v Price and Century Insurance Co Ltd* [1939] 4 All ER 601.

Accordingly we are of opinion that the appeal should succeed ...

[**Menzies J** delivered judgment to the similar effect. **Windeyer J** reached a similar result but did not refer to the Fires Prevention (Metropolis) Act 1774 (Imp).]

Appeal allowed.

With the above cases compare *Ziel Nominees Pty Ltd and Anor v VACC Insurance Co Ltd and Anor* (1976) 50 ALJR 106.

THE QUANTUM OF COVER AND AVERAGE

How does the indemnity principle apply in the case of overinsurance or underinsurance? Coverall would generally refuse to insure Carb for any greater amount than Carb's potential loss. The simple commercial reason is the moral hazard that Carb might be tempted to seek to profit by precipitating the event covered by the insurance. For example, fire insurance is always limited to a strict indemnity because the moral hazard is great, and will be so construed even in the absence of express provision in the policy: *Macaura v Northern Assurance Co Ltd* [1925] AC 619.

If Carb insures goods valued at $10,000 with Coverall for an amount of $20,000 and a premium appropriate to $20,000 cover, should Coverall be obliged to pay more than $10,000 if the goods are totally destroyed? See *British Traders' Insurance Co Ltd v Monson*, p 254, *supra*. Note also in that case the nature of an agreed value policy which could in some instances result in Carb obtaining more than a full indemnity. Some insurance companies will issue agreed value policies for comprehensive motor vehicle insurance based upon the market value of the vehicle at the commencement of the risk. The value is then accepted as the basis for indemnity in the event of total loss despite possible depreciation within the period of insurance. The agreed value is normally reviewed annually.

The Marine Insurance Act 1909 specifically recognises agreed value insurance: see ss 33–34.

In life and personal injury insurance, provided the necessary insurable interest is held when the contract is made, there is no requirement that the insurance be limited to pure indemnity. Carb can insure its key employee's life or limbs for any amount and recover the full sum insured without proving loss or damage of that amount.

If Carb underinsures goods valued at $20,000 for the sum of $10,000, and incurs loss in respect of them to the extent of $10,000, it might expect to be indemnified by Coverall for the full $10,000. Since this would enable Carb to save premium through underinsuring and carrying itself only the less hazardous risk of total loss, insurance companies invariably include some form of average clause in indemnity policies. A typical pro rata average clause reads:

Contracts of Insurance

Wherever a sum insured is declared to be subject to Average, if the property covered thereby shall, at the breaking out of any fire or at the commencement of any destruction of or damage to such property by any other peril hereby insured against, be collectively of greater value than such sum insured, then the Insured shall be considered as being his own insurer for the difference and shall bear a rateable share of the loss accordingly.

The same result will apply automatically under a marine policy by virtue of Marine Insurance Act 1909 s 87:

Where the assured is insured for an amount less than the insurable value, or, in the case of a valued policy, for an amount less than the policy valuation, he is deemed to be his own insurer in respect of the uninsured balance.

Insurance companies have been criticised for undue reliance upon average provisions with the result that the company may waive the clause in appropriate cases of non-marine insurance claims.

THE DOCTRINE OF CONTRIBUTION

There is no statutory restriction upon Carb insuring against the same risk with several companies, say Coverall and All Risks Insurance Co. Carb can claim on Coverall and/or All Risks up to the total amount of its loss but the general principle of indemnity precludes recovery of more than a full indemnity—except of course in life or personal injury policies. This is the reason why Coverall would ask Carb in the proposal form and in the claim form whether it had insured with any other insurer.

Some insurance policies contain clauses precluding double insurance, that is, insurance of the same interest against the same risk. In the absence of such a preclusion, the doctrine of contribution based upon the equitable principle of pro rata sharing, will require Coverall and All Risks to indemnify Carb against loss in the ratio of the amount of their respective insurances. If Carb's aggregate cover under policies with Coverall and All Risks is less than the full insurable value, a partial loss requires the concurrent application of the doctrines of contribution and average (if marine policy or stipulated). If Coverall pays more than its proportionate share, it can recover a pro rata contribution from All Risks. The right of contribution is codified in Marine Insurance Act 1909:

86 (1) Where the assured is over-insured by double insurance each insurer is bound as between himself and the other insurers, to contribute rateably to the loss in proportion to the amount for which he is liable under his contract.

(2) If any insurer pays more than his proportion of the loss, he is entitled to maintain an action for contribution against the other insurers, and is entitled to the like remedies as a surety who has paid more than his proportion of the debt.

DOCTRINES OF ABANDONMENT AND SUBROGATION

If the insured property is totally destroyed so that it cannot be repaired Carb is entitled to cash payment of its full value or the amount of the insurance whichever is the less. If the estimated cost of repairs exceeds the repaired value, Coverall may treat the case as one of total loss and pay the full value of the original goods. In marine insurance Carb can give Coverall a notice of abandonment in respect of a constructive total loss and claim the full value: Marine Insurance Act 1909 ss 66–68. In each case where Coverall agrees to accept a claim for a total loss, it is entitled to the damaged goods as salvage, or to deduct their value from the payment; otherwise, Carb would receive more than a full indemnity. This general rule is again codified in Marine Insurance Act 1909 ss 69(1) and 85(1).

The doctrine of subrogation adopts an analogous approach in relation to rights of action whereby the insured can recoup his loss. The fact that Carb's loss is caused by the negligence of X, or that X is obliged to pay Carb the balance of purchase-money for goods over which Carb has retained its insurance, does not in any way preclude Carb from claiming under its policy with Coverall. However, having paid Carb's claim, Coverall is entitled to take the benefit of Carb's rights to seek recovery from X. For example, in *Hepburn v A Tomlinson (Hauliers) Ltd*, p 245, *supra*, once the insurer Hepburn had paid Tomlinson's claim, from whom would it seek recovery? Compare *Castellain v Preston*, p 251, *supra*.

The same principle has been applied to recover from an employee for negligence which resulted in the insurance company accepting the insured employer's vicarious liability for injuries received by another employee in the course of his employment: *Lister v Romford Ice and Cold Storage Co Ltd* [1957] AC 555. However, the benefit must be enforceable by legal action and concomitant to the loss. Thus a gift to Carb to assist it through difficult times resulting from a fire is not subject to subrogation by Coverall. And "if one of two unique china bases is insured and destroyed, it does not avail the underwriter that by the destruction, the second vase has become more unique and more valuable": *City Taylors Ltd v Evans* (1922) 91 LJKB 379 at 385, per Scrutton LJ.

A corollary of the above doctrine is that the insured, Carb, must not compromise or release its rights against the third party, X, or else it will be liable to Coverall to the extent of the diminution of those rights: *Boag v Standard Marine Insurance Co Ltd* [1937] 2 KB 113; [1937] 1 All ER 714. Coverall has no direct right of action against X, but upon payment of Carb's claim, Carb is obliged to lend its name to such proceedings. Coverall will usually stipulate in its policy that Carb shall allow proceedings to be brought in its name (and sometimes prior to payment of Carb's claim); an equity court will compel Carb to do so provided Coverall agrees to indemnify it for costs: *John Edwards & Co v Motor Union Insurance Co Ltd* [1922] 2 KB 249 at 254. If Coverall recovers more from X than its indemnity to Carb, it must pay Carb any excess after recouping itself: *Goole & Hall Steam Towing Co Ltd v Ocean Marine Insurance Co Ltd* [1928] 1 KB 589 at 598. The marine insurer's subrogation rights are codified in the Marine Insurance Act 1909 s 85.

ASSIGNMENT OF INSURANCE POLICIES

Subject to any restrictions in the policy and the statutory provisions referred to below, the insured can transfer the chose in action representing its interest in an insurance policy to another person. Under the Life Insurance Act 1945 s 87, the benefit of a life policy should be transferred in the form set out in the Fifth Schedule to the Act. Provided the assured had the requisite interest when the policy issued, there is no requirement that the assignee have an insurable interest.

Assignments of marine policies are governed by Marine Insurance Act 1909 ss 56 and 57 which facilitate the transfer of insurance documents under a cif contract:

56 (1) A marine policy is assignable unless it contains terms expressly prohibiting assignment. It may be assigned either before or after loss.

(2) Where a marine policy has been assigned so as to pass the beneficial interest in the policy, the assignee of the policy is entitled to sue thereon in his own name; and the defendant is entitled to make any defence arising out of the contract which he would have been entitled to make if the action had been brought in the name of the person by or on behalf of whom the policy was effected.

(3) A marine policy may be assigned by indorsement thereon or in other customary manner.

57 Where the assured has parted with or lost his interest in the subject-matter insured, and has not, before or at the time of so doing, expressly or impliedly agreed to assign the policy, any subsequent assignment of the policy is inoperative:

Provided that nothing in this section affects the assignment of a policy after loss.

In New South Wales the benefit of a fire policy may be assigned with the consent of the insurer in the following manner under the Insurance Act 1902:

14 (2) Such assignment shall be in the words or to the effect following, namely, "I, AB, of, etc, do hereby assign unto CD the within policy of insurance on [*here describe property insured, etc*]. In witness whereof, etc."

QUESTIONS

Question 12

(1) Distinguish between the requirement of insurable interest and the indemnity principle. What purposes are served by each principle and are they in any way similar? Illustrate by reference to cases.

(2) Under what circumstances does the principle of indemnity apply to contracts of insurance? Explain which types of insurance are not regulated by the indemnity principle and why this is so.

Question 13

Carb Pty Ltd sold 10,000 carburettors to Mitzi Co for $300,000 cif Tokyo net cash against documents. Carb's manufacturing costs including overheads plus freight and insurance were $245,000. Prior to shipment Carb obtained a marine insurance policy over the goods from Coverall Insurance Ltd for $300,000. Carb was designated as the insured under the policy which it intended to assign to Mitzi on payment. The consignment was lost at sea before Carb had tendered the documents to Mitzi, which has now refused to pay. Carb does not wish to prejudice its good commercial relationship with Mitzi and agrees to claim on the policy rather than require Mitzi to pay. Carb lodges a claim with Coverall for $300,000.

Advise Coverall whether, and to what extent, it is obliged to meet the claim.

Question 14

The Sale of Land (Amendment) Act 1982 (Vic) s 35(1) provides:

35 (1) During the period between the making of a contract for the sale of land and the purchaser becoming entitled to possession or to the receipt of rents and profits pursuant to the terms of the contract, any policy of insurance maintained by the vendor in respect of any damage to or destruction of any part of the land agreed to be sold pursuant to the contract shall in respect of the said land, to the extent that the purchaser is not entitled to be indemnified under any other policy of insurance, enure for the benefit of the purchaser as well as for the vendor and the purchaser shall be entitled to be indemnified by the insurer under any such insurance policy in the same manner and to the same extent as the vendor would have been if the land had not been subject to the contract.

What is the purpose of this section? What effect will it have on conveyancing transactions and the insurance industry? Could this effect have been achieved in any other way?

Question 15

(1) Carb Pty Ltd allowed Al Chemist, a Professor of Chemistry, to conduct experiments with engine fuels at its Ryde factory. Al was not employed by Carb but the company hoped to benefit from his research. Carb agreed with Al in writing that in consideration of his carrying out the experiments the company would not hold Al responsible for any loss or damage resulting from his negligence.

Carb already held a fire insurance policy on its factory, plant and equipment with Coverall Insurance Ltd for $700,000. However, after making the above arrangement with Al, Carb proposed for and obtained a further fire policy on factory, plant and equipment with All Risks Insurance Ltd for an additional $200,000. Carb provided each company with a full explanation of its manufacturing and research operations including Al's experiments but did not mention the written agreement with Al Chemist.

Six months later a fire resulting from Al's negligence caused damage to plant and equipment which cost $180,000 to rectify. A valuation made for income tax purposes immediately prior to the fire estimated the current value of factory, plant and equipment at $1 million.

Assuming that neither policy contained an average clause, advise Carb of its rights to recover from Coverall and All Risks.

(2) What difference would it make if both policies contained average clauses?

(3) What difference would it make if Carb had made the written agreement with Al after the fire rather than before it?

(4) What difference would it make if the value of the factory, plant and equipment as at the date of the fire was $800,000?

SECTION 5: INSURANCE CLAIMS

What happens after Carb Pty Ltd has suffered loss as a result of an event covered by insurance? In order to succeed in its claim against Coverall Insurance Ltd, it may be necessary to prove insurable interest and full disclosure prior to contract. In addition the policy, like most contracts, will contain terms and conditions, with which Carb must comply if it is to enforce the contract. Carb or its lawyer should carefully check the terms of the policy immediately the casualty occurs.

Some conditions may require Carb to take some positive action, such as notifying Coverall if Carb commences activities which materially increase the risk, or insures the same risk with another company: see eg, *Steadfast Insurance Co Ltd v F & B Trading Co Pty Ltd* (1971) 125 CLR 578; [1972] ALR 287. Such a requirement may apply prior to and quite independently of a casualty or claim. If such a condition is construed as a condition precedent to recovery, failure to comply would preclude Carb from indemnity under the policy; whereas if it is regarded only as a collateral warranty, Carb would merely be liable in damages for any extra expense incurred by Coverall as the result of the breach.

The general law does not require notification of a claim within any stipulated period, except under the Marine Insurance Act 1909 s 68, where a notice of abandonment must be given with reasonable diligence after receipt of reliable information of the loss. However, most policies specifically require notification of a claim to be given promptly, and may also lay down other preconditions to a right of recovery under the policy. One striking illustration is that of notification of death prior to burial/cremation as a condition precedent to claiming a double benefit for death by accident under a life policy.

In practice, the insurer will sometimes waive full compliance with procedural policy conditions. Such waiver can also be implied from conduct. Again if Coverall represents to Carb that it will not insist upon compliance with policy conditions and Carb relies upon this assurance, Coverall will be estopped from doing so: *Craine v The Colonial Mutual Fire Insurance Co Ltd* (1920) 28 CLR 305.

As a contract of adhesion, these procedural preconditions invariably protect the insurance company and raise issues as to whether they go further than necessary for the protection of the insurer. New South Wales and Victoria have legislated to protect the insured in these circumstances: see Insurance Act 1902 (NSW) s 18, p 226, *supra*, and compare Instruments Act 1958 (Vic) s 27.

It is the practice of insurance companies to carefully compare claim forms with the proposal made prior to issue of the policy. Any inconsistencies may indicate a failure to make an initial full disclosure. We have already noted, p 208, *supra*, that the *uberrimae fidei* doctrine applies to claims as well as pre-contract disclosures.

Contracts of Insurance

SUBMISSION OF CLAIMS TO ARBITRATION

A common provision in insurance policies, as well as in construction and other commercial contracts, requires any disputes arising under the policy to be referred to arbitration. The courts will not allow their jurisdiction to be excluded in relation to an existing cause of action: *Compagneides Messageries Maritimes v Wilson* (1954) 94 CLR 577. However, an appropriately drafted condition can stipulate that, until the dispute has been referred to arbitration, no cause of action shall arise under the policy. This is known as a *Scott v Avery* clause after the case in which it received judicial recognition: (1856) 5 HLC 811; 10 ER 1121. Where court proceedings are brought in derogation of the clause, the court may grant a stay of proceedings until the arbitration has been held: *Heyman v Darwins Ltd* [1942] AC 356; [1942] 1 All ER 337; *Wadsley v City Mutual Life Assurance Society Ltd* [1971] VR 140. The requirement of arbitration is also often combined with a time limit within which the submission to arbitration must be brought: eg, *Gosford Meats Pty Ltd v Queensland Insurance Co Ltd* (1970) 72 SR (NSW) 547 in which the following typical clause was considered:

All differences arising out of this Policy shall be referred to the decision of an arbitrator to be appointed in writing by the parties in difference or if they cannot agree upon a single arbitrator to the decision of two arbitrators, one to be appointed in writing by each of the parties within one calendar month after having been required in writing so to do by either of the parties or, in case the arbitrators do not agree, of an umpire appointed in writing by the arbitrators before entering upon the reference. Then the umpire shall sit with the arbitrators and preside at their meetings. The making of an award shall, subject to any relevant statutory provisions to the contrary, be a condition precedent to any right of action against the company; but if such action be not commenced within one year of the making of an award, the right of action shall be deemed to be abandoned and released. After the expiration of one year after the accrual of the cause of action the company shall not be liable in respect of any claim therefor unless such claim shall in the meantime have been referred to arbitration.

The effect of the *Scott v Avery* clause has been negated by legislation in New South Wales and Victoria, but this does not cover most marine or life insurance: see Insurance Act 1902 (NSW) s 19 and Instruments Act 1958 (Vic) ss 28, 29.

LAW REFORM

Australian Law Reform Commission
Discussion Paper No 7, 1978

66 While the jurisdiction of the courts may not be entirely ousted (*Scott v Avery* (1856) 5 HLC 811) it may be contractually subjected to prior arbitration. Although clauses of this type are found in a large number of policies it has been the practice of many insurers in recent years not to rely on them. The Insurance Council of Australia has recommended to its members the abandonment of arbitration provisions. Some states have already restricted the use of these clauses. They are generally ineffective in New South Wales (Insurance Act 1902 s 19), Victoria (Instruments Act 1958 s 28(2)), Queensland (Insurance Act 1960-68 s 21A) and South Australia (Arbitration Act 1891 1974 s 24a). However, cases still occur where insurers seek to rely on arbitration as a condition precedent to recovery: *Parr v Rural Agents Pty Ltd* [1975] 2 NSWLR 247.

In Australia, arbitration proceedings have tended to become excessively formal. Often, they involve considerable expense and delay. They may discourage a claimant from pressing his claim and may equally discourage an insurer from offering settlement on a claim which it regards as being at all doubtful. Even when the costs of the arbitration are guaranteed by the insurer itself, it seems preferable to allow the insured to take his dispute straight to court. Agreements to arbitrate should be effective, if at all, only when made after a particular loss has occurred.

QUESTION

Question 16

What purposes are served by procedural conditions precedent to recovery under insurance policies? How justifiable are these conditions, and what reforms would you suggest to alleviate any hardship?

FURTHER READING

General

Australian Law Reform Commission, Discussion Paper No 7, Insurance Contracts.
Australian Law Reform Commission, Insurance Contracts, ALRC 20, 1982.
Sutton, *Insurance Law in Australia and New Zealand*, 1980.

Section 1: The Function of Insurance Contracts

Bamford, "Rights and Duties of Insurance Brokers" (1976) *Lloyd's M & CLQ* 59.
North and South Trust Co v Berkeley [1971] 1 WLR 47; [1971] 1 All ER 980.
Norwich Fire Insurance Society Ltd v Brennans (Horsham) Pty Ltd [1981] VR 981.
Norwich Winterthur Insurance (Australia) Ltd v Con-Stan Industries of Australia Pty Ltd [1981] 2 NSWLR 879.
Wilson v Avec Audio-Visual Equipment Ltd [1974] 1 Lloyd's Rep 81.

Section 2: The Uberrimae Fidei Doctrine and Construction of Insurance Contracts

English Law Reform Committee, Fifth Report on Conditions and Exceptions in Insurance Policies, Cmnd 62, 1957.
Hasson, "Misrepresentation and Non-disclosure in Life Insurance" (1975) 38 *MLR* 87.
Latimer, "Good Faith in Insurance Contracts" (1980) 8 *ABLR* 37.
Marene Knitting Mills Pty Ltd v Greater Pacific General Insurance Ltd (1976) 11 ALR 167.
O'Hare, "Materiality and the Insurance Contract" (1971) 2 *ACLR* 230.
Stone v Reliance Mutual Insurance Society Ltd [1972] 1 Lloyd's Rep 469.

Section 3: Insurable Interest

Cassidy, "The Insurance of Land and Buildings the Subject of a Contract of Sale" (1971) 45 *ALJ* 30.
Walker, "Insurance and the Sale of Land" (1981) 9 *ABLR* 148.

Section 4: The Indemnity Principle and its Applications

Barnett Ltd v National Insurance Co of New Zealand Ltd [1965] NZLR 874.
Hobbs v Marlow [1977] 2 All ER 241.

CHAPTER 7

Financing Transactions: Lending on the Security of Goods

"Men lend their money to traders upon mortgages or consignments of goods because they suspect their circumstances, and will not run the risque of their general credit."

Lord Mansfield
Fox v Devonshire (1759) 2 Burr 931 at 942

Section 1: The Function of Credit Transactions
Section 2: Types of Security Interests in Personal Property
Section 3: Perfection of Security Interests in Goods
Section 4: The Insolvent Debtor and Bankruptcy Proceedings
Section 5: Fraudulent Dispositions, Preferences and Floating Charges
Section 6: Money-lending, Hire-purchase and Consumer Credit Legislation

Chapters 7 to 11 deal with various financing transactions secured and unsecured. Chapters 7 and 8 are concerned with lending on the security of goods, Chapter 9 with the assignment by way of sale or security of the proceeds of sales of goods in the form of book debts and other accounts receivable and hire-purchase paper. Chapters 10 and 11 move on to unsecured transactions involving financing and payments by negotiable instruments. Chapter 10 covers bills of exchange, promissory notes and letters of credit. The special relationship of banker and customer, the banking system and rules relating to cheques are considered in Chapter 11.

In the present chapter, the first section will provide an overview of credit transactions, using our prototype transaction to illustrate their purpose and to identify the roles of the respective parties. In Section 2 the various types of security interests are classified by their essential elements, while Section 3 examines the requirements for perfection of these interests at general law and under the Bills of Sale Act and National Companies Code (hereinafter NCC). Section 4 provides an introduction to bankruptcy procedure and considers the impact of the Bankruptcy, Property and Conveyancing Acts on fraudulent and preferential dispositions, as well as on after-acquired property and future advance clauses in floating charges. Section 5 deals with the effects of state moneylending, hire-purchase and consumer credit legislation, concentrating specifically on the New South Wales position.

SECTION 1: THE FUNCTION OF CREDIT TRANSACTIONS

The purchase or development of any property or commercial project can be financed in a number of ways. It may be paid for from existing funds, either in cash or by bill of exchange or cheque. The other main alternative is to use borrowed funds. A background knowledge of sources and types of finance may be obtained from standard commercial and accounting texts. For present purposes the following brief outline will suffice.

The main sources of commercial finance are:

(1) Trading banks which normally lend on commercial projects over relatively short periods of from six months to five years depending on the nature of the project.

(2) Finance companies which lend on short terms at comparatively high rates of interest.

(3) Merchant banks and other companies which extend credit by discounting commercial bills of exchange.

(4) Trade creditors who supply goods and services on extended credit terms.

(5) Public investors who subscribe for shares and debentures in public companies usually through the medium of the stock exchange.

The type of financing will be related to the degree of commercial risk involved, the type of collateral available and the amount of control to be retained by the owners. Commercial finance may be classified in the following ways:

(1) As *equity* (eg, share capital) where the investor has a direct participatory interest in the profitability of the enterprise since the return on his investment (dividends) and its capital value will closely reflect the success or failure of the enterprise; or as *debt*, (eg, fixed interest loans and debentures) where the investor is a creditor entitled to repayment of his capital with interest but whose rate of return does not normally relate directly to the profitability of the enterprise. An important factor in arranging the capital requirements of a commercial enterprise is the ratio between equity and debt. Shareholders in a company are investors in but not creditors of the company.

(2) As *short*, *medium* or *long* term loans or debts. A loan for anything up to three years would normally be regarded as short, from three to five or seven years as medium. Medium and long term loans are usually secured. Interest rates vary according to the length of the loan and other factors.

(3) As *secured* or *unsecured*. The lender will naturally require some assurance that the loan will be repaid. This may consist of a verbal promise, a simple IOU, a monthly credit account or a complex loan agreement. These are all examples of *unsecured* loans.

In many instances the lender will require further assurance of repayment in the form of *security*. This may consist of a mortgage or charge over the specific assets being acquired with the loan monies, or over some other property. Or it could be achieved by the physical deposit of the property itself as in the case of a pledge to a pawnbroker. Consumer finance is usually in the form of short term loans (except for housing loans which can extend up to 30 years and are invariably secured on the family home). Banks, finance companies and credit unions will make unsecured loans (personal loans) to individuals with a satisfactory credit rating. Consumer loans secured by hire-purchase agreement, credit sale contract, or bill of sale over chattels or second mortgages over real estate are more common.

THE FUNCTION OF STOCK-IN-TRADE FINANCING

Industrial expansion in Western countries has required the aggregation of vast amounts of capital. Because most manufacturers and distributors do not possess such capital, financial institutions perform the necessary function of financing the manufacture and distribution of goods. At a consumer level, the goods being financed are often used as collateral for the advance of credit. In a manufacturing setting, the financing transaction is typically a revolving one in which a loan secured upon materials is used to finance operations, and the proceeds of sale are used to finance the purchase of further materials.

Lending on the Security of Goods

Secured stock-in-trade financing can be considered as performing four functions: economic, security, marketing and remedial. The *economic function* refers to the concept of the free-enterprise system requiring that, in the main, the forces of competition in the market should determine the most efficient utilisation of resources; therefore a manufacturer of a product which is in demand in the marketplace should be assisted to maximise his production by using his stock-in-trade as collateral. The *security function* merely ensures that in the event of a default, the financier will have a preferred claim to the stock (and its proceeds) over the claims of other creditors or the debtor's trustee in bankruptcy. The *marketing function* requires that because of the nature of their relationship, the financier positively requires the debtor to dispose of the collateral and to apply the proceeds in reduction of its indebtedness to the financier and/or replenishing its stock. The *remedial function* is merely the corollary of the security function whereby on default the secured creditor can exercise its ultimate remedies over the collateral to achieve repayment. However, the creditor does not desire nor intend to utilise these remedies except as a last resort, and since a default sale will often result in a smaller total return to all creditors—the other creditors have an interest in the manner in which the secured creditor's rights are exercised: see generally Peden, *Stock-in-Trade Financing,* 1974, pp 4–7.

WHAT IS A SECURITY?

A practical definition of a security is: "an interest vested in a person called 'the creditor' in certain property owned by another called 'the debtor', whereby certain rights are made available to the creditor over such property in order to satisfy an obligation personally owed or recognised as being owed to the creditor by the debtor or some other person": Sykes, *The Law of Securities,* 3rd ed, 1978, p 11 (hereinafter *Sykes*).

The term will be used in this sense in these chapters. However, it should be noted that although the security itself is neither a piece of property nor a piece of paper the term is also sometimes used in other contexts to mean either:
- (a) the real or personal property over which the secured creditor claims rights (more accurately described as collateral);
- (b) the documents by which such rights are granted; or
- (c) documents issued by corporations, the state or its instrumentalities evidencing financial obligations, such as shares, debentures, bonds and inscribed stock.

SECURED AND UNSECURED CREDITORS

The essential characteristic of a secured creditor is that he has rights *in rem* against specific or general assets of the borrower. The coverage and nature of those rights will vary with the type of security and collateral: see Section 2, *infra*. In other words the secured creditor will normally be entitled to have his debt satisfied out of the proceeds of the debtor's specific or general assets in priority to the claims of other creditors. If the collateral is inadequate to satisfy the secured debt the creditor may still claim for the balance against the debtor personally but will then be competing directly with the debtor's other unsecured creditors. The same principles apply in general following the bankruptcy of the debtor.

POLICY ISSUES RAISED BY CONFLICTING CLAIMS IN SECURED CREDIT TRANSACTIONS

In order to illustrate the nature of the conflicting claims and to focus attention on possible solutions the following fact situation is suggested:

In order to finance the company's present and future expansion, Carb Pty Ltd obtained from City Bank an agreement to establish a continuing line of credit in favour of Carb whereby City Bank advanced $100,000 to Carb on execution of the agreement and undertook to provide further annual advances of $50,000 for the next three years provided Carb did not breach the agreement by attempting to create any charge competing with the undermentioned charge in favour of City Bank. In consideration of the loan agreement Carb gave City Bank a charge over Carb's present and future assets. The charge prohibited Carb from disposing of or creating without City Bank's consent any subsequent charge ranking in priority to or *pari passu* with the charge to City Bank, but specifically authorised Carb to sell its engines in the ordinary course of its business.

City Bank omitted to register the charge.

Six months later, in order to generate more working capital, Carb borrowed further funds from Easy Finance on the security of a mortgage over present and future stocks of engines, which Easy Finance registered.

Two months later Carb purchased:

(1) 10,000 components from Comp Co on extended credit and gave Comp a fixed charge over the 10,000 components for $7000 being the balance of purchase-money.

(2) 20,000 widgets from Widg Co for $20,000 cash all of which was advanced by Squeeze who took a floating charge over the 20,000 widgets and all similar components which Carb might acquire in the future.

(3) Nuts from Nut Co on secured credit, bolts from Bolt Co on secured credit and silicon spray from Sil Co on secured credit. Carb used these materials to manufacture more engines.

Carb sold:
(a) two engines to Speed for cash, but Speed returned one as defective;
(b) 300 engines to Greatparts Ltd on 60 days open credit;
(c) the entire balance of its stock of engines to Bestcars Ltd at cost price and accepted in full satisfaction of the purchase price a release of an outstanding debt which it owed Bestcars. Carb also hired one engine to Driver (value $10,000) who had an option to purchase the engine at any time during the hiring period.

Carb is in substantial default in paying its debts to City Bank, Easy Finance, Squeeze and each supplier.

Sue Quick has obtained a substantial judgment against Carb in a tort action and is seeking to levy execution on Carb's assets and to petition for its winding up.

QUESTIONS

Question 1

Prepare a list of the competing claims which arise out of the above fact situation. Identify as many as you can of the policy issues created by these conflicting claims or priorities. Do not at this stage attempt to resolve these conflicts by allocating priorities—that is a pleasure in store for you in subsequent questions.

Question 2

What factors affect the levels of interest rates in Western economies? Is there likely to be a difference between interest rates charged by a finance company in lending to a manufacturer, a retailer or a consumer? Why?

SECTION 2: TYPES OF SECURITY INTERESTS IN PERSONAL PROPERTY

As indicated in Section 1, a security interest in property confers on the secured creditor a cluster of proprietary rights *in rem*—in the specific collateral but amounting to something less than ownership of the full legal and equitable title. In Anglo-Australian law a variety of different methods of obtaining security over goods have developed which confer varying rights upon the secured creditor. The orthodox classification is into three categories: mortgages, possessory securities and hypothecations. See eg, *Sykes*, pp 12-17. However, the actual rights, obligations and incidents of security interests do not fit easily or precisely into these classifications, and each type of security device has to be examined in detail to determine the rights which it confers vis-à-vis the parties to it and others affected by it.

Superimposed on the common law principles is a matrix of disuniform state legislation regulating bills of sale, moneylending, hire-purchase, crop and wool liens and stock mortgages. Second, in 1971 the Law Council of Australia prepared a comprehensive report on Consumer Credit Laws known as the Molomby Report which recommended substantial and comprehensive reform in this area. Its proposals were accepted in principle by the Standing Committee of Commonwealth and State Attorneys-General. As a result the following statutes were introduced: Consumer Transactions Act 1972 (SA), Consumer Credit Act 1981 (NSW) and in Victoria the Credit Act 1981, Goods (Sales and Leases) Act 1981 and the Chattel Securities Act 1981. The other states have not as yet moved very far towards implementing the Molomby Committee's proposals. Because of this lack of uniformity among the states it is proposed to deal with these topics in a fairly general manner concentrating on general principles and policy issues with examples drawn from some existing statutes.

The following outline of the various forms of chattel security is based primarily on the common law which is unlikely to be drastically changed by legislation. They are of course affected by existing legislation which is considered in succeeding sections.

Legal mortgage: a transfer of owner Carb's whole legal title, subject to proviso for redemption. Delivery of possession is unnecessary, hence the potential for secrecy.

Legal mortgagee's powers. (1) As owner of legal title, can seize on default, and sell, or foreclose.

(2) Any express powers conferred by the mortgage.

(3) Where by deed (as is usual), additional statutory powers eg, Conveyancing Act 1919 (NSW) ss 7 (definitions of mortgage and property), 109 including powers to sell, insure, and appoint a receiver of the income. Compare in other states: Vic, Property Law Act 1958 ss 18, 101(1)(a); SA, Law of Property Act 1936 ss 7, 47(1)(a); WA, Property Law Act 1969 ss 7, 57(1)(a); Tas, Conveyancing and Law of Property Act 1884 ss 2, 21(1)(a).

Equitable mortgage: may be created in three distinct ways:

(1) An assignment by way of security of an equitable interest in goods (eg, beneficiary's interest under a will, or mortgagor's equity of redemption). Writing is required for validity in all states except Queensland. For example, Conveyancing Act 1919 (NSW) s 23C(1)(c) provides:

A disposition of an equitable interest or trust subsisting at the time of the disposition, must be in writing signed by the person disposing of the same or by his will, or by his agent thereunto lawfully authorised in writing.

(Vic, Property Law Act 1958 s 53(1)(c); SA, Law of Property Act 1936 s 29(1)(c); WA, Property Law Act 1969 s 34(1)(c); Tas, Conveyancing and Law of Property Act 1884 s 60(2)(c).)

(2) An agreement *for value* to give a legal mortgage over specific existing goods will constitute a present equitable security over those goods: eg, in consideration of

a present loan advance Carb delivered share certificates to City Bank and promised to execute a legal mortgage at a future date.

(3) An agreement *for value* to transfer future goods (ie, not yet in existence or owned by the mortgagor Carb). This third type of equitable mortgage has created some difficulties in determining what is necessary for the security to take effect: see *Holroyd v Marshall,* and *Akron Tyre Co Pty Ltd v Kittson* below.

Equitable mortgagee's powers. (1) No power to seize or sell simply by virtue of equitable title.

(2) Upon default, the right to apply to the court for an order for sale, appointment of a receiver, specific performance or foreclosure.

(3) Where by deed, the same statutory powers as for a legal mortgage by deed.

Holroyd and Others v Marshall and Others
House of Lords (1861) 10 HLC 191; 11 ER 999

[Taylor, the tenant of a cloth mill, was financially embarrassed, sold his machinery at auction to A P and W Holroyd who did not remove it but agreed to sell it back to Taylor for £5000 such sum to remain owing to the Holroyds upon the security of an indenture of mortgage. The mortgage also provided: "all machinery, implements, and things which, during the continuance of this security, shall be fixed or placed in or about the said mill, buildings, and appurtenances, in addition to or in substitution for the said premises, or any part thereof, shall, during such continuance as aforesaid, be subject to the trusts, powers, provisos, and declarations hereinbefore declared and expressed concerning the said premises; and the said James Taylor, his executors, etc, will at all times, during such continuance as aforesaid, at the request, etc of the said Holroyds, their executors, etc, do all necessary acts for assuring such added or substituted machinery, implements, and things, so that the same may become vested accordingly."

The deed, which did not contain any express licence to seize after-acquired property, was registered as a bill of sale. Holroyds complained to Taylor that he had sold some of the machinery whereupon he furnished them on 1 March 1860 with an account of the old machinery sold and of the new machinery substituted for it. On 2 April 1860, Holroyds served on Taylor a demand for repayment of the £5000 and interest. On 14 April 1860, Marshall, Sheriff of York, formally seized (but did not remove) all the machinery and effects in the mill under a writ of execution sued out on a judgment recovered by a creditor Preller against Taylor. Holroyds nevertheless proceeded to sell all the original and added and substituted machinery under the powers contained in their mortgage. The sheriff then took forcible possession of the substituted machinery and effects, and resold it. He did not interfere with the sale of the original machinery.

Lord Campbell held that Preller was entitled to the added and substituted machinery. Holroyds appealed to the House of Lords.]

Lord Chancellor (**Lord Westbury**) [after stating the facts of the case (4 August 1862), said:] My Lords, the question is, whether as to the machinery added and substituted since the date of the mortgage the title of the mortgagees, or that of the judgment creditor, ought to prevail. It is admitted that the judgment creditor has no title as to the machinery originally comprised in the bill of sale; but it is contended that the mortgagees had no specific estate or interest in the future machinery. It is also admitted that if the mortgagees had an equitable estate in the added machinery, the same could not be taken in execution by the judgment creditor.

The question may be easily decided by the application of a few elementary principles long settled in Courts of Equity. In equity it is not necessary for the alienation of property that there should be a formal deed of conveyance. A contract for valuable consideration, by which it is agreed to make a present transfer of property, passes at once the beneficial interest, provided the contract is one of which a Court of Equity will decree specific performance. In the language of Lord Hardwicke, the vendor becomes a trustee for the vendee; subject, of course, to the contract being one to be specifically performed. And this is true, not only of contracts relating to real estate, but also of contracts relating to personal property, provided that the latter are such as a Court of Equity would direct to be specifically performed.

A contract for the sale of goods, as, for example, of 500 chests of tea, is not a contract which would be specifically performed, because it does not relate to any chests of tea in particular; but a contract to sell 500 chests of the particular kind of tea which is now in my warehouse in Gloucester, is a contract relating to specific property, and which would be specifically performed. The buyer may maintain a suit in equity for the delivery of a specific chattel when it is the subject of a contract, and for an injunction (if necessary) to restrain the seller from delivering it to any other person...

There can be no doubt, therefore, that if the mortgage deed in the present case had contained nothing but the contract which is involved in the aforesaid covenant of Taylor, the mortgagor, such contract would have amounted to a valid assignment in equity of the whole of the machinery and chattels in question, supposing such machinery and effects to have been in existence and upon the mill at the time of the execution of the deed.

But it is alleged that this is not the effect of the contract, because it relates to machinery not existing at the time, but to be acquired and fixed and placed in the mill at a future time. It is quite true that a deed which professes to convey property which is not in existence at the time is as a conveyance void at law, simply because there is nothing to convey. So in equity a contract which engages to transfer property, which is not in existence, cannot operate as an immediate alienation merely because there is nothing to transfer.

But if a vendor or mortgagor agrees to sell or mortgage property, real or personal, of which he is not possessed at the time, and he receives the consideration for the contract, and afterwards becomes possessed of property answering the description in the contract, there is no doubt that a Court of Equity would compel him to perform the contract, and that the contract would, in equity, transfer the beneficial interest to the mortgagee or purchaser immediately on the property being acquired. This, of course, assumes that the supposed contract is one of that class of which a Court of Equity would decree the specific performance. If it be so, then immediately on the acquisition of the property described the vendor or mortgagor would hold it in trust for the purchaser or mortgagee, according to the terms of the contract. For if a contract be in other respects good and fit to be performed, and the consideration has been received, incapacity to perform it at the time of its execution will be no answer when the means of doing so are afterwards obtained.

Apply these familiar principles to the present case; it follows that immediately on the new machinery and effects being fixed or placed in the mill, they became subject to the operation of the contract, and passed in equity to the mortgagees, to whom Taylor was bound to make a legal conveyance, and for whom he, in the meantime, was a trustee of the property in question.

There is another criterion to prove that the mortgagee acquired an estate or interest in the added machinery as soon as it was brought into the mill. If afterwards the mortgagor had attempted to remove any part of such machinery, except for the purpose of substitution, the mortgagee would have been entitled to an injunction to restrain such removal, and that because of his estate in the specific property...

Lord Wensleydale acquiesced in the judgment proposed.

Lord Chelmsford (at 215): ... The question in the case is, whether the appellants, who have an equitable title as mortgagees of certain machinery fixed and placed in a mill, of which the mortgagor, James Taylor, was tenant, are entitled to the property which was seized by the sheriff, under two writs of execution issued against the mortgagor, in priority to those executions, or either of them?

The title of the appellants depends upon a deed dated 20 September 1858. [His Lordship here stated the bill of sale and the other facts of the case: see *ante*.] The machinery sold by the sheriff was more than sufficient to satisfy the first execution, and the appellants claiming a preference over both executions, contend that the possession taken by them on the 30 April entitled them, at all events, to priority over the second execution of the 11 May. The great question, however, is, whether they are entitled to a preference over the first execution by the mere effect of their deed? or whether it was necessary that some act should have been done after the new machinery was fixed or placed in the mill, in order to complete the title of the appellants?

It was admitted that the right of the judgment creditor, who has no specific lien, but only a general security over his debtor's property, must be subject to all the equities which attach upon whatever property is taken under his execution. But it was said (and truly said) that those equities must be complete, and not inchoate or imperfect or, in other words, that they must be actual equitable estates, and not mere executory rights.

What, then, was the nature of the title which the mortgagees obtained under their mortgage deed? If the question had to be decided at law, there would be no difficulty. At law an assignment of a thing which has no existence, actual or potential, at the time of the execution of the deed, is altogether void: *Robinson v Macdonnell* 5 Maule and Sel 228. But where future property is assigned, and after it comes into existence, possession is either delivered by the assignor, or is allowed by him to be taken by the assignee, in either case there would be the *novus actus interveniens* of the maxim of Lord Bacon, upon which Lord Campbell rested his decree, and the property would pass.

It seemed to be supposed upon the first argument that an assignment of this kind would not be void in law if the deed contained a licence or power to seize the after-acquired property. But this circumstance would make no difference in the case... The decree appealed against proceeds upon the ground, not indeed that an assignment of future property, without possession taken of it, would be void in equity (as the cases to which I have referred show that it would be at law), but that the equitable right is incomplete and imperfect unless there is subsequent possession, or some act equivalent to it to perfect the title.

In considering the case, it will be unnecessary to examine the authorities cited in argument, to show that if there is an agreement to transfer or to charge future acquired property, the property passes, or becomes liable to the charge in equity, where the question has arisen between the parties to the agreement themselves. In order to determine whether the equity which is created under agreements of this kind is a personal equity to be enforced by suit, or to be made available by some act to be done between the parties, or is in the nature of a trust attaching upon and binding the property at the instant of its coming into existence, we must look to cases where the rights of the third persons intervene.

The respondents, in support of the decree, relied strongly on what was laid down by Baron Parke in *Mogg v Baker* 3 Mee and Wels 195 at 198, as the rule in equity which he stated he had derived from a very high authority, "that if the agreement was to mortgage certain specific furniture, of which the corpus was ascertained, that would constitute an equitable title in the defendant, so as to prevent it passing to the assignees of the insolvent, and then the assignment would make that equitable title a legal one; but if it was only an agreement to mortgage furniture to be subsequently acquired, or" (the word "or" is omitted in the report) "to give a bill of sale at a future day of the furniture and other goods of the insolvent, then it would cover no specific furniture, and would confer no right in equity". The meaning of these latter words must be that there would be no complete equitable transfer of the property, because there can be no doubt that the agreement stated would create a right in equity upon which the party entitled might file a bill for specific performance.

This point is so clear that it is almost unnecessary to refer to the observations of Lord Eldon, in the case of the ship *Warre* 8 Price 269, n, in support of it. It must also be observed, that the proposition in *Mogg v Baker* hardly reaches the present question, because it is not stated as a case of an actual transfer of future property, but as an agreement to mortgage, or to give a bill of sale at a future day. The only equity which could belong to a party under such an agreement would be to have a mortgage or a bill of sale of the future property executed to him. It does not meet a case like the present, where it is expressly provided that all additional or substituted machinery shall be subject to the same trusts as are declared of the existing machinery.

Under a covenant of this description to hold that that trust attaches upon the new machinery as soon as it is placed in the mill, is to give an effect to the deed in perfect conformity with the intention of the parties, and, as, by the terms of the deed, Taylor was to remain in possession, the act of placing the machinery in the mill would appear to be an act binding his conscience to the agreed trust on behalf of the appellants, and nothing more would appear to be requisite, unless by the established doctrine of a Court of Equity some farther act was indispensable to complete their equitable title.

The judgment of Lord Campbell resting, as he states, upon Lord Bacon's maxim, determines that some subsequent act is necessary to enable "the equitable interest to prevail against a legal interest subsequently bona fide acquired". It is agreed that this maxim relates only to the acquisition of a legal title to future property. It can be extended to equitable rights and interests (if at all) merely by analogy; but in thus proposing to enlarge the sphere of the rule, it appears to me that sufficient attention has not been paid to the different effect and operation of agreements relating to future property at law and in equity. At law property, non-existing, but to be acquired at a future time, is not assignable; in equity it is so. At law (as we have seen), although a power is given in the deed of assignment to take possession of after-acquired property, no interest is transferred, even as between the parties themselves, unless possession is actually taken; in equity it is not disputed that the moment the property comes into existence the agreement operates upon it.

[His Lordship then dealt with several earlier cases and continued at 220:] Whatever doubts, therefore, may have been formerly entertained upon the subject, the right of priority of an equitable mortgagee over a judgment creditor, though without notice, may now be considered to be firmly established; and, according to the opinion of Lord St Leonard's, "any agreement binding property for valuable consideration" will confer a similar right...

But if it should still be thought that the deed, together with the act of bringing the machinery on the premises, were not sufficient to complete the mortgagee's title, it may be asked what more could have been done for this purpose. The trustee could not take possession of the new machinery, for that would have been contrary to the provisions of the deed under which Taylor was to remain in possession until default in payment of the mortgage money after a demand in writing, or until interest should have become in arrear for three months; and in either of these events a power of sale of the machinery might be exercised. And if the intervenient act to perfect the title in trust be one proceeding from the mortgagor, what stronger one could be done by him than the fixing and placing the new machinery in the mill, by which it became, to his knowledge, immediately subject to the operation of the deed?

I asked Mr Amphlett, upon the second argument, what *novus actus* he contended to be necessary, and he replied "A new deed". But this would be inconsistent with the terms of the original deed, which embraces the substituted machinery, and which certainly was operative upon the future property as between the parties themselves. And it seems to be neither a convenient nor a reasonable view of the rights acquired under the deed, to hold that for any separate article brought upon the mill a new deed was necessary, not to transfer it to the mortgagee, but to protect it against the legal claims of third persons.

But if something was still requisite to be done, and that by the mortgagor, I cannot help thinking that the account delivered by Taylor to the mortgagees of the old machinery sold, and of the new machinery which was added and substituted, was a sufficient *novus actus interveniens*, amounting to a declaration that Taylor held the new machinery upon the trusts of the deed...

I think that the account delivered by Taylor to the mortgagees of the whole machinery which was added and substituted, was a sufficient *novus actus interveniens*, amounting to a declaration that Taylor held the new machinery upon the trusts of the deed, the only act which could be done by him in conformity with it; and it is difficult to understand for what other reason such an account should have been rendered. As between themselves, it is quite clear that a new deed of the added and substituted machinery was unnecessary, no possession could be delivered of it, because it would have been inconsistent with the agreement of the parties; and anything, therefore, beyond this recognition of the mortgagee's right appears to be excluded by the nature of the transaction.

Order of Lord Campbell reversed.

See also *Tailby v Official Receiver* (1888) 13 App Cas 523 (HL) and *King v Greig* [1931] VLR 413.

Akron Tyre Co Pty Ltd v Kittson
High Court of Australia (1951) 82 CLR 477

Latham CJ: This is an appeal from a judgment of the Supreme Court of Victoria (Fullagar J) in an action in which the plaintiffs (three individuals and a company) claim damages for wrongful conversion of motor vehicle tyres. His Honour gave judgment for the plaintiffs for £716 11s 3d, the estimated value of 46 motor tyres.

The plaintiff company, The Economic Cash Buying Co Pty Ltd, let to one C V Vale a number of motor trucks, equipped with tyres, under hire-purchase agreements. As the result of transactions between the parties the three individual plaintiffs later let certain of the trucks to Vale under hire-purchase agreements. The hire-purchase agreements (not under seal) were in the same form in all cases. They provided that the hirer should be at liberty at any time to determine the hiring by returning the goods in good order, repair and condition. The documents, therefore, did not require registration under the legislation relating to bills of sale: Instruments Act 1928 Pt VI ss 27–55; *Helby v Matthews* [1895] AC 471. Vale took tyres off the vehicles and sold them (46 in number) to the defendant appellant company. The plaintiffs did not satisfy the learned trial judge that the tyres of which Vale so disposed were the tyres which were originally on the vehicles. The defendant contended, in the first place, that the plaintiffs had no property in substituted tyres and that the hire-purchase agreements did not apply to them. Secondly, the defendant contended that if any provision in the hire-purchase agreements is to be construed so as to give a title in those tyres to the plaintiffs, the agreements are assurances of personal chattels within the meaning of s 30 of the Instruments Act 1928, and that, as the hire-purchase agreements were not filed as bills of sale under that Act, they are void, at least in so far as they might otherwise operate as an assurance of personal chattels which were not capable of identification at the time when the agreements were made.

There is no evidence as to Vale's title to the tyres which he put on the trucks. But he had possession of them. There is no evidence of title in any other person (for example, there is no evidence that he obtained them under a hire-purchase agreement) and therefore it is to be presumed that Vale had a title to the tyres which he placed on the trucks.

The hire-purchase agreements contained cl 12, which was in the following terms: "Any accessories or goods supplied with or for or attached to or repairs executed to the goods shall become part of the goods." ("The goods" were the motor trucks with tyres on them to which the hire-purchase agreements applied.)

In an action of conversion the plaintiff must prove that he has an immediate right to possession of the goods in question. He must establish a legal right. An equitable right to the enforcement of a trust in respect of chattels will not support a claim for conversion. It is not disputed that Vale had made default under the hire-purchase agreement and that the bailment to him thereunder was determined. The plaintiffs were entitled to take possession of the trucks. They contend that the tyres which Vale had placed on the trucks and subsequently removed and sold to the defendant had become the property of the plaintiffs either by virtue of the terms of cl 12 of the agreement or by virtue of the doctrine of *accessio* at common law. If this is the case the tyres, when they were put on the trucks by Vale, became part of the trucks which were bailed to Vale and he had no right to dispose of them and the plaintiffs should succeed.

Fullagar J held that though cl 12 could not affect the rights of any third party (in this case no rights of any third party were in question) it had the effect of passing the property in the substituted tyres to the owner of the vehicles as soon as they were attached to the trucks. His Honour therefore found it unnecessary to consider the argument that the tyres became part of the vehicles under the doctrine of *accessio*. I also find it unnecessary to consider that doctrine.

The appellant has contended that cl 12, upon its true construction, applies only to things which were supplied by the hirer with the vehicle or had been attached to the vehicle when the hire-purchase agreement was made and to repairs to the goods which had been executed at that time. In other words, the appellant contends that the clause has no reference to future attachments, etc. Under cl 1(a) the hirer agrees to maintain the goods in good order, repair and condition. The hirer was therefore under an obligation to replace worn-out parts and accessories. Under cl 1(b) the hirer agreed to pay when due all moneys payable by him to any person in respect of any accessories or chattels supplied with or for or attached to or in respect of any repairs executed to the goods. This clause uses the same words as are to be found in cl 12.

I agree with the construction of the clause adopted by Fullagar J. It would have hardly any operation in the case of attachments and repairs if it were limited to goods actually attached to the vehicles or incorporated in the vehicles in some way (as in the case of repairs) at the time when the hire-purchase agreement was made. Such things would have already become part of the goods hired and no special provision would be needed in order to bring about the result that they were subject to the terms of the hiring. There is no reason why the clause should not apply both to accessories supplied with the vehicles but not part of them, and to accessories afterwards attached to the vehicles. The object of cl 12 appears to me plainly to be to provide that replacements and attachment of accessories to the vehicle shall bring about the result that by the agreement of the parties the replacements and attachments become part of the vehicles themselves. The words "shall become" are capable of this meaning and they should, in my opinion, be so construed.

A simple assignment of "future property", ie of property which does not exist or in which the assignor at the time of the assignment has no proprietary interest, is completely nugatory at law. At law it is an assignment of nothing. In equity also it is, at the time when it is made, completely ineffective as an assignment of anything. As Jessel MR said in *Collyer v Isaacs* (1881) 19 Ch D 342 at 351, "A man cannot in equity, any more than at law, assign what has no existence" or, I add, "anything which he does not own". But a man may bind himself by a contract for valuable consideration to assign goods which he may thereafter acquire. If he makes such a contract and subsequently delivers the goods to the "assignee" or does some other act which, having regard to the terms of the contract, plainly shows an intention to pass the property, then the property will pass at law by reason of such act: see *Lunn v Thornton* (1845) 1 CB 379; 135 ER 587. That case shows that, if there is an "assignment" of after-acquired goods, the mere acquisition of the goods by the assignors will not pass the property at law. But it is otherwise if there be "some new act" done by the assignor "in furtherance of the original disposition": CB at 387. In the present case there was such a "new act", namely, the attachment of the tyres to the trucks, which were the subject matter of the hire-purchase agreements. Building contracts provide an example of the application of this principle. The property in things brought on to land for building purposes may, if the building contract so provides, pass to the building owner even before they are incorporated in the building: see *Reeves v Barlow* (1884) 12 QBD 436, cited by my brother Williams, and other cases cited in *Halsbury's Laws of England*, 2nd ed, Vol III, pp 298, 299, and in *Benjamin on Law of Sale of Personal Property*, 7th ed, 1931, pp 140 *et seq*. It was argued for the appellant that property in personal chattels could be transferred only by deed, delivery of possession, or contract of sale or exchange. But the cases mentioned establish that the terms of a contract may be such that when a person acquires property and does "some new act" which the contract contemplates, the property in goods may be effectively transferred.

In the present case cl 12 is in the terms of the contract. It is not an assignment—it is an agreement, made for value, that the property in accessories etc shall pass when they are attached to the trucks.

It is not necessary, therefore, for the plaintiffs to rely upon the equitable doctrine which interprets an "assignment" of future property when made for value as constituting in equity, though not at law, a contract to assign. In such a case the assignee will acquire an equitable interest in the property when it comes into the ownership of the assignor and a court of equity will treat his legal interest as subject to a trust for the assignee: *Holroyd v Marshall* (1862) 10 HLC 191; 11 ER 999; *Tailby v Official Receiver* (1888) 13 App Cas 523, and see *Joseph v Lyons* (1884) 15 QBD 280. As already stated, the application of such a doctrine would not give to the plaintiffs the right to immediate possession, which, as they were not in possession of the tyres at the time of the alleged conversion, they must establish in order to succeed in an action of conversion.

Thus, as between the parties, an agreement that property in chattels shall pass upon an act in pursuance of the intended disposition being done by the owner of the chattels, the chattels being then in existence, will give an immediate right to the possession of the property (subject to the terms of, eg any hire-purchase agreement between the parties) when that act is done. Accordingly, as an agreement, cl 12 was effective as between the parties to pass the property in the tyres in question unless it was rendered invalid by the legislation relating to bills of sale.

[His Honour then considered and rejected the appellant's argument that cl 12 was an assurance of personal chattels under Instruments Act 1928 s 30 and was therefore void for non-registration as a bill of sale. He concluded that the plaintiffs had established their case, and the appeal should be dismissed.

Williams and **Kitto JJ** delivered a joint judgment to similar effect.]

Appeal dismissed.

Equitable charge: owner Carb retains legal and equitable *title*, but confers on chargee certain rights in relation to the goods exercisable upon default which are automatically extinguished upon repayment without the need for a reconveyance.

Equitable chargee's powers. (1) The same as for equitable mortgagee except that chargee cannot foreclose because he never had any title.

(2) Where by deed, the same statutory powers as for a legal mortgage, since the respective statutes define a mortgage to include a charge.

A common form of security given by corporations is a floating charge over all or a substantial amount of the corporation's assets. The characteristics of a floating charge have been summarised as:

(a) a charge on a class of assets of a company present and future;
(b) the class of assets is one which, in the ordinary course of business of the company, would be changing from time to time; and
(c) the charge contemplates that, until some future step is taken by those interested in the charge, the company may carry on its business in the usual way as far as concerns the particular class of assets: *Re Yorkshire Woolcombers' Association Ltd* [1903] 2 Ch 284 at 295, per Romer LJ.

Thus the floating charge provides a form of cross-over security whereby present and future advances can be secured over present and after-acquired property. The charge floats over rather than attaches to the specific goods, leaving the company free to sell stock-in-trade in the usual way at any time until the charge crystallises. The powers of a chargee under a floating charge are similar to those under an equitable charge outlined above, but invariably the floating charge will expressly define the defaults which will automatically crystallise the charge, and empower the chargee to enforce the security by seizing the property or appointing a receiver.

Pledge: a possessory security entitling the pledgee to retain possession until the pledgor tenders to him the amount due. Delivery of possession to the pledgee is essential to constitute the pledge. The pledgee cannot foreclose because he lacks any legal or equitable title to the goods. What is the nature of his interest?

The Odessa
Privy Council [1916] 1 AC 145

[In the course of delivering the judgment of the Privy Council, **Lord Mersey** stated that the right of a pledgee to sell is better described as a "special interest" rather than a "special property". He continued at 158-9:]

If it were not for the somewhat unfortunate peculiarity of English terminology involved in the established use of the words "special property" when "special interest" would seem better, it is difficult to see how an argument could be maintained which would effectively distinguish pledge from lien for present purposes.

The very expression "special property" seems to exclude the notion of that general property which is the badge of ownership. If the pledgee sells he does so by virtue and to the extent of the pledgor's ownership, and not with a new title of his own. He must appropriate the proceeds of the sale to the payment of the pledgor's debt, for the money resulting from the sale is the pledgor's money to be so applied. The pledgee must account to the pledgor for any surplus after paying the debt. He must take care that the sale is a provident sale, and if the goods are in bulk he must not sell more than is reasonably sufficient to pay off the debt, for he only holds possession for the purpose of securing himself the advance which he has made. He cannot use the goods as his own. These considerations show that the right of sale is exercisable by virtue of an implied authority from the pledgor and for the benefit of both parties. It creates no jus in re in favour of the pledgee; it gives him no more than a jus in rem such as a lienholder possesses, but with this added incident, that he can sell the property motu proprio and without any assistance from the court.

Pledgee's powers. (1) To sell on default.

(2) To assign provided assignment is not repugnant to the terms of the pledge: *Donald v Suckling* (1866) LR 1 QB 585; *Johnson v Stear* (1863) 15 CB (NS) 330; 143 ER 812.

(3) To retain possession and in some circumstances to use the goods provided this does not injure or deplete them.

(4) By virtue of his possessory rights to sue third parties in detinue or conversion.

Lien: a possessory security entitling the lienee to retain possession until the owner tenders the amount due. A lien may arise by operation of law (statute, common law or usage) without any express agreement. No property passes to the lienee, and the lien will terminate if possession is lost, or if the lienee wrongfully uses or disposes of the goods.

Lienee's powers. (1) Merely to retain possession.

(2) At common law, the lienee has no right of assignment, nor power of sale: *Mulliner v Florence* (1878) 3 QBD 484.

(3) A number of special statutes have conferred specific powers of sale upon lienees: eg, Disposal of Uncollected Goods Acts in Victoria, New South Wales, Queensland and Western Australia; see generally Peden, "Lienee's Statutory Power of Sale" (1968) 6 *Uni of Q LJ* 24.

Hire-purchase or leasing agreement: traditionally these arrangements do not "create" a security, but ensure that the owner retains full legal and equitable title to the goods until the hirer/lessee has completed all payments under the agreement. Since the hirer/lessee has possession and "apparent ownership" of the goods, the potential exists for abuse and for fraud on a bona fide purchaser. These principles remain valid in those states which retain the Uniform Hire-purchase Acts, but have been altered drastically in the new Consumer Credit legislation in South Australia, New South Wales and Victoria: see Section 5, *infra*.

Owner's powers. Subject to the provisions of hire-purchase and consumer credit legislation (where applicable):

(1) To repossess and sell upon default.

(2) To sue hirer/lessee or bona fide purchaser in detinue or conversion following wrongful detention.

(3) To sue hirer for deficiency of payments under the agreement.

QUESTION

Question 3

On 27 April Carb Pty Ltd executed an agreement with City Bank whereby Carb "charged all the company's present and future plant and equipment" to the bank in return for a $150,000 loan. On 6 June Carb ordered two new machinery presses at a cost of $200,000 each, payable on delivery. One press was delivered, installed and paid for on 1 July, but the second was delayed due to a strike on the waterfront. Carb was not obliged to advise City Bank of this acquisition and did not do so. On 30 July Carb defaulted in payment of an interest instalment to the bank, and the next monthly interest instalment was received by the bank two weeks late. On 1 September in order to pay its employees' wages and rent due on the factory premises Carb resold the first of the presses to Greatparts. On 2 September City Bank appointed Ray Seever as receiver of Carb's assets and business. On 15 September the second press was delivered to Carb's premises but before it could be installed it was seized by the bailiff under a writ of execution issued on a District Court judgment in favour of Sue Quick.

Advise Ray Seever in relation to the Bank's rights to recover the two presses. (At this stage, ignore bills of sale and companies legislation.)

SECTION 3: PERFECTION OF SECURITY INTERESTS IN GOODS

In general, each of the above security devices takes effect in accordance with the parties' intentions: eg, in the case of a mortgage or charge at the time of delivery of the executed documents in exchange for the loan advance or other consideration, in the case of a pledge upon delivery of possession of the goods. A lien is effective when the goods are in the lienee's possession and he has provided the work, service or other consideration which generates the indebtedness upon which entitlement to the lien depends.

In some instances, the security is required to be in writing, for example, an equitable mortgage or charge which comes within the terms of Conveyancing Act 1919 (NSW) s 23c(1)(c) or corresponding provisions in other states. Similarly, a sale of goods, credit sale contract, consumer loan contract or hire-purchase agreement should comply with the formal requirements of Sale of Goods Act 1923 (NSW) s 9, Consumer Credit Act 1981 (NSW) ss 24, 35 or Hire-purchase Act 1959 (Qld) s 3 or corresponding provisions in other states.

When Carb gives City Bank a security interest which has taken effect under the general law as above described, it is generally valid and binding as between Carb and City Bank. However, the security interest may not be *perfected*, that is, it may remain open to challenge by third parties; it may be valid for some purposes or against some parties but not against others. These challenges will be examined as follows:

(a) invalidation for non-registration under bills of sale and companies legislation: in this section;

(b) dispositions in fraud of creditors: in Section 5;

(c) claims to after-acquired property and tacking of future advances: in Section 5;

(d) special statutory provisions in moneylending, consumer credit and hire-purchase legislation: in Section 6;

(e) claims of bona fide purchasers for value: in Chapter 8.

EFFECT OF BILLS OF SALE ACTS ON SECURED TRANSACTIONS

The general purpose of the Bills of Sale Acts and Div 9 of the National Companies Code is to preclude a debtor such as Carb from covertly placing its assets beyond the reach of its general unsecured creditors, such as its trade suppliers or judgment creditors (eg Sue Quick), by transferring them or giving security over them while retaining possession. Similar purposes underlie Bankruptcy Act 1966 (Cth) ss 120–122, the fraudulent conveyance provisions in state Acts such as Conveyancing Act 1919 (NSW) s 37A and NCC ss 451, 452. All of these sections which are considered later, attack transactions designed to defraud creditors or to prefer one creditor at the expense of others. None of these Acts is designed specifically to affect the rights and obligations *inter se* of debtor Carb and secured creditor City Bank, nor to deal comprehensively with the problems of competing secured creditors. However, the NCC contains a system for regulating priorities between charges (s 204 and Schedule 5) which will be examined further in Chapter 8.

With these general propositions in mind, read the central provisions of the Bills of Sale Act 1898 (NSW) ss 3, 4, 5.

Corresponding provisions in other states are: Vic, Instruments Act 1958 Pt VI ss 32–58 to be repealed by Chattel Securities Act 1981 (not yet proclaimed); Qld, Bills of Sale and Other Instruments Act 1955 ss 6–7; SA, Bills of Sale Act 1886 ss 2, 28; WA, Bills of Sale Act 1899 ss 3, 5, 25, 27; Tas, Bills of Sale Act 1900 ss 4, 5; ACT, Instruments Ordinance 1933 ss 8, 9.

In Victoria, the proposed repeal of the Instruments Act Pt VI by the Chattels Securities Act 1981 will have the result of no longer requiring chattel securities to be registered except those given prior to the commencement of the new Act. Subsequent

goods mortgages would not be invalid for non-registration, although they would still remain subject to
  (a) challenge under the Bankruptcy Act ss 120–122 or NCC ss 451, 452 where applicable;
  (b) extinguishment by the claims of bona fide purchasers: Chattel Securities Act 1981 ss 8, 11.

However, registration under the voluntary registration scheme for motor cars, trailers and motor boats will protect the secured creditor's interest from extinguishment: see p 359, *infra*.

Other provisions dealing with traders' bills and priorities between competing ordinary bills are considered on pp 357–9, *infra*.

A perusal of these provisions will indicate that the Act only strikes at transactions effected through documents which come within the definition of bill of sale and involve personal chattels as defined. In addition, note that securities given by companies are not included, *Braithwaite v W A McArthur Ltd* (1898) 19 LR (NSW) Eq 158; but see NCC Div 9. A mortgage over land and fixtures is not a bill of sale: Conveyancing Act 1919 s 109A. A security which is valid under the Bills of Sale Act may yet be attacked under Bankruptcy Act ss 120–122 and/or Conveyancing Act s 37A or vice versa. The two types of legislation are not mutually exclusive: see Section 5, *infra*.

The application of the Bills of Sale Act 1898 (NSW) hinges upon three central issues:
  (a) whether the security comes within the definition of bill of sale (s 3) and confers a power to seize (s 4);
  (b) whether the goods are personal chattels (s 3);
  (c) whether the necessary connection between the "bill" and the security exists.

Akron Tyre Co Pty Ltd v Kittson
High Court of Australia (1951) 82 CLR 477

[For facts see p 273, *supra*.]

Latham CJ (at 485): It was argued for the appellant that cl 12, if it operated, was an assurance of personal chattels within the meaning of s 30 of the Instruments Act 1928, which provides inter alia that no bill of sale made either absolutely or conditionally whereby the grantee or holder has power to seize or take possession of any property and effects comprised in the bill of sale shall be operative or have any validity at law or in equity until it has been filed in the manner provided by the Act. Section 27 defines "bill of sale" as including, inter alia, assurances of personal chattels. The same section provides as follows: "'Personal chattels' includes goods furniture fixtures and other articles capable of complete transfer by delivery (either at the time of the making or giving of a bill of sale of the personal chattels specified in the bill or at any time thereafter)." It is contended for the appellant that the result of these provisions is that any document which operates to give property in chattels, whether legal or equitable (*Bank of Victoria Ltd v Langlands Foundry Co Ltd* (1898) 24 VLR 230), even though there are no chattels at the time which answer the description contained in the document, is a bill of sale and must be registered in order to be valid; that is, that the definitions quoted show that what are known as assignments of future property and also agreements to assign such property fall within the provisions of the statute.

[His Honour then proceeded to reject the appellant's argument on the grounds that the Act as drafted did not apply to bills of sale which dealt solely with after-acquired chattels. The reasons included that after-acquired chattels could not be specified in the bill of sale, nor could they be described or their situation set forth as required by s 30(2) of the Act.]

Price v Parsons
High Court of Australia (1936) 54 CLR 332

[The main joint judgment was delivered by Rich, Dixon and McTiernan JJ, and was to the similar effect on each of the issues determined by Starke J in the shorter judgment extracted below. The joint judgment also dealt in more detail with the constitutional relationship between the NSW Bills of Sale Act and the Commonwealth Bankruptcy Act. The facts appear from the following judgment.]

Starke J: Appeal from an order of the Federal Court of Bankruptcy declaring two documents, dated 12 and 15 January 1934, respectively, invalid against the trustee of the bankrupt estate of Cecil Charles Green, because they had not been registered pursuant to the provisions of the Bills of Sale Act 1898 of New South Wales. The appellant, Price, was also ordered to pay to the trustee the sum of £299 9s, the value of the goods covered by the documents.

Green had carried on the business of a garage proprietor at Casino in New South Wales, under the name of "Reliance Motors". In January 1934 he was indebted to Westcott Hazell Ltd in the sum of £299 9s for goods supplied, and the appellant Price was under liability to the company in respect of half that amount as a *del credere* agent. The company advised Price of the amount of Green's indebtedness and that he was in default. Price saw Green about the matter. Price deposed: "He" (Green) "was averse to a bill of sale so there was only one way that I could see in which I could help him out, and I proposed to buy portion of his plant and pay him cash for it. He picked out the articles he would sell and wrote them down and made the account up and I gave him my cheque for the amount." The account is dated 12 January 1934. It debits to Price the value of particular items of machinery, amounting in the aggregate to £299 9s, and is receipted "Paid, C Green". This is one of the documents that have been declared invalid. The cheque for £299 9s found its way to Westcott Hazell & Co Ltd. Price did not take possession of the goods. After the account was made out, Green suggested that he should hire the goods from Price, otherwise he could not carry on his business. Price agreed, and Green paid him £5 "as a deposit until he signed the hire-purchase agreement, or rather a premium". On 15 January a hire-purchase agreement was executed. It is in the usual form. Price is described as "owner" and Green as "hirer". The owner agrees to let and the hirer to hire the particular items of machinery set forth in the account of 12 January 1934 at a rent of £5 per week for a term of 64 weeks. It provides that the hirer may purchase the goods for the total amount of the rent and premium payable under the agreement. It stipulates that until the hirer exercises and completes his option to purchase, the goods shall remain the property of the owner and the hirer shall be a bailee thereof. It enables the owner to retake possession of the goods of the hirer if the hirer make default under it or become bankrupt. It also enables the hirer to determine the hiring by returning the goods to the owner. This is the other document that has been declared invalid.

It is said, truly enough, that "an ordinary ... hiring agreement, containing a licence on default to retake goods which are not the property of the hirer until all the instalments are paid, is not a bill of sale": *Ex parte Crawcour; Re Robertson* (1878) 9 Ch D 419; *McEntire v Crossley Brothers Ltd* [1895] AC 457; *Baldwin's Law of Bankruptcy,* 10th ed, 1910, p 402. And further, that "an agreement to hire back with an option of repurchase after a bona fide sale, independently complete apart from any document" does not fall within the Act: *Manchester, Sheffield, and Lincolnshire Railway Co v North Central Wagon Co* (1888) 13 App Cas 554; *Baldwin's Law of Bankruptcy,* pp 402, 403. But the manifest purpose of the parties in the present case was to secure a sum of money. The sale to Price, though in terms absolute, was always subject to the right of Green to hire back the goods with an option to repurchase or perhaps one may say to redeem them. There was never any intention to give Price any right of property in the goods independently of the terms of the hiring agreement. The sale and hiring were all part of one transaction. Still, as Bowen LJ observed in *North Central Wagon Co v Manchester, Sheffield, and Lincolnshire Railway Co* (1887) 35 Ch D 191, the Bills of Sale Act has not struck at transactions but at documents which constitute an assurance of personal chattels. "If a person could make his transaction complete and effective in law or in equity without the document, the Act could do nothing to affect his rights, and did not purport to do anything to affect his rights": at 207. Now it is argued that the documents of 12 and 15 January 1934 do not, nor does either of them, constitute an assurance of personal chattels within the meaning of the Bills of Sale Act. It may be open to question whether the document of 12 January 1934 would itself have required registration as a bill of sale: see and cf *Ex parte Cooper; Re Baum* (1878) 10 Ch D 313; *Woodgate v Godfrey* (1879) 5 Ex D 24; *Marsden v Meadows* (1881) 7 QBD 80. But the answer to the argument is contained in a judgment of Lindley LJ in *Re Watson; Ex parte Official Receiver in Bankruptcy* (1890) 25 QBD at 39, 40:

"If the conclusion is arrived at that the hiring agreement was a real letting out of goods by the real owner of them, then it is not a bill of sale; but if, as in this case, the supposed hirer is the real owner of the goods, then it has at least the effect of a licence to seize the goods of the borrower of the money as a security for the loan. If the effect of the document is that the lender of the money, and supposed lessor of the goods, can make a title to them by means of the document by estoppel or otherwise, then the document will amount to an assurance within the Bills of Sale Act. The document either amounts to a licence to seize the goods, or, if the lender can make a title to them by the document, then it is an assurance of goods, so that either way it is a bill of sale within the Act." The receipted account of 12 January 1934 and the hire-purchase agreement of 15 January 1934 record the transaction between the parties, and the only title that Price, the appellant, can make to the goods, is by means of and through these documents. They constitute, for the reasons given by Lindley LJ at 39, 40, an assurance of personal chattels or a bill of sale within the meaning of the Bills of Sale Act. The fifth section of the Act provides that no bill of sale shall have any validity as against the official assignee or trustee of a bankrupt estate unless it is duly registered in accordance with the Act. The documents were not registered in accordance with the Act...

The provisions of s 5 of the Bills of Sale Act 1898 of New South Wales, prima facie, therefore, avoided the documents of 12 and 15 January 1934 as against the trustee in bankruptcy appointed under the federal law. The title of the appellant, Price, to the goods particularised in these documents is destroyed as against the trustee in bankruptcy, and prima facie vests in the trustee in bankruptcy by force of that law: see Bankruptcy Act 1924-1933 ss 66, 90, 103. The provisions of s 91(e) of the Act would be inapplicable.

Some other facts, however, require consideration. In June of 1934 the appellant, Price, discussed with Green his financial position. Green's creditors were pressing him. The upshot of the discussion was that Green gave leave to the appellant to take or seize the goods particularised in the documents of 12 and 15 January 1934. On 15 June 1934 Green gave a written authority to the appellant as follows: "I hereby request you to take possession of the goods covered by my hire-purchase agreement with you, it being my desire to determine such agreement under cl 2(b)." The appellant took possession of the goods accordingly and had them removed to other premises. Employees of Green (who had removed the goods for the appellant) desired however to start on their own account another motor business. They requested the appellant to hire the goods to them, which he agreed to do. The appellant and the employees of Green accordingly executed within a few days a hire and purchase agreement in the ordinary form. According to the appellant, he got the goods and disposed of them. He got £275 for them, besides what Green had paid him on hire, that is £45. The evidence, however, does not make it clear whether the appellant received the £275 from the employees of Green or from some other disposition of the goods. But I take it that the money was paid by the employees of Green. It was argued that in obtaining possession of the goods the appellant acquired a title to them which he could maintain without reliance on the documents of 12 and 15 January 1934. But he acquired such possession under and by virtue of the documents which are avoided: possession so obtained creates no independent source of title: *Re Wetherill* (1907) 7 SR (NSW) 337; 24 WN (NSW) 75; *Re Catip; Malick v Lloyd* (1913) 16 CLR 483; (1912) 12 SR (NSW) 552; 29 WN (NSW) 146; *Kent v Parer* [1922] VLR 32; 43 ALT 128; *King v Greig; Rechner, claimant* [1931] VLR 413 at 425, 426...

The order under appeal finds the value of the goods covered by the documents of January 1934, and seized by the appellant, to be £299 9s. The appellant asserts he only got £275 for them, besides £45 which Green paid him for hire. In the absence of any countervailing evidence, I think it should be assumed that the proceeds of the goods represented their value; the price or sum obtained is in this case the only reliable evidence of value. The order against the appellant should be reduced to £275, but otherwise the appeal should be dismissed.

Re Vital Learning Aids Pty Ltd and the Companies Act
Supreme Court of New South Wales, Equity Division [1979] 2 NSWLR 442

[The company by oral agreement engaged the defendant (respondent) as its customs agent to procure entry into Australia from time to time of goods purchased abroad. Prior thereto the customs agent had furnished the company with certain of its standard documents containing its "trading conditions" including one which provided that "All goods (and documents relating to goods) should be subject to a particular and general lien for monies due either in respect of such goods or for any particular or general balance or other monies due from" the company to the agent. The agreement between the parties was that each contract between them would contain such a term. On arrival of goods in Australia, the agent cleared them through customs and retained possession of them.]

Kearney J (at 443): This is a summons by the liquidator of Vital Learning Aids Pty Ltd (in liq) ("the company") for an order under s 245(1) of the Companies Act 1961, requiring the defendant (respondent), as an agent of the company, to deliver to the liquidator certain personal property comprising educational equipment, held by the respondent, to which the company is prima facie entitled.

A preliminary point has been argued on the basis of a statement of facts agreed for the purpose of such argument. The point so raised for determination is whether the general lien created in favour of the respondent in accordance with such facts constitutes a charge requiring registration pursuant to s 100 of the Companies Act, and whether failure to register the same renders any security conferred by such general lien over the above mentioned chattels void as against the applicant, as liquidator of the company.

[His Honour referred to the facts and pleadings and continued at 445:] The applicant submits shortly that the document containing the clause creating the lien is one which evidences a charge, and that the respondent must necessarily rely on such document in order to establish its claim. The submission then proceeds that the instrument which so exists is one which gives to the respondent a right to seize the subject goods, and accordingly falls within the terms of a bill of sale requiring registration in order to be effective as against the applicant. It is further submitted, in support of this claim, that the goods would not have necessarily passed into the possession of the respondent by virtue of the agency agreement between them, but that it required the document containing the relevant provisions to enable the respondent to justify its possession of the goods. While the applicant recognises that the transaction was in the nature of a pledge, nevertheless, the applicant relies upon the refinements affecting a transaction in the nature of a pledge which, in certain circumstances, render the transaction as a whole one which falls within the definition of a bill of sale. The applicant refers in particular to the passages in the judgment of Rowlatt J in *Wrightson v McArthur and Hutchisons (1919) Ltd* [1921] 2 KB 807 at 815: "The special property of a pledgee, as shown by Bowen LJ in the judgment already referred to, exists by virtue of the act of delivery, not by virtue of the document. The point is neatly illustrated by the observations of Lord Parker in *Dublin City Distillery v Doherty* [1914] AC 823 at 855, where he lays it down that where no possession physically is given to complete a common law pledge, but a document is used to pass the possession and complete the pledge, such document is within the definition, unless, of course, it falls within the special exceptions named at the end of the section. It is often said generally that a pledge is not within the definition — indeed Mr Hawke said so frequently in the course of the argument — but, as Lord Parker's dictum shows, that general statement is not accurate. What is accurate is that where the passing of property, special or general, is effected by actual delivery of possession (as truly enough it usually but not invariably is in cases of pledge) any accompanying document does not have the effect of any such instrument as is described by the section."

The applicant, therefore, says that, without the document which is necessarily involved in order to effectuate the agreement between the parties, the respondent would have no title to the possession founding its claim to a lien and that, accordingly, the transaction involves a charge falling within the terms of s 100(3)(c)(i) of the Companies Act so as to entitle the applicant to the order sought.

For the respondent there were two principal submissions. The first was that the contract between the parties was wholly oral. It is said, in this regard, that the document referred to is merely the source from which are derived the relevant words constituting the term of the oral contract creating the lien; in other words, the contents of the document comprising the subject words are imported into the oral contract and thereby become simply a term orally agreed between the parties as part of their bargain. The respondent then submits that, the transaction being wholly oral, the Bills of Sale Act has no application, and reliance is placed upon the decision of Collingwood J in *Waight v Waight and Walker* [1952] 2 All ER 290 at 292, where his Lordship said: "It was further contended that, even if it were a genuine transaction, it should have been registered as a bill of sale and was void for want thereof. In my opinion, this transaction was not affected by the Bills of Sale Acts. This was a simple pledge in which immediate possession of the car was transferred to the pledgee and the transaction was complete without any writing, and the fact that the registration book was also handed over does not bring it within the Acts. The whole transaction was one of pledge, and the Acts have no application to a pledge as distinguished from an assurance or licence to take possession. The Acts are aimed at documents, not at transactions. They do not forbid a loan on the security of chattels; they merely provide that, if the transaction be recorded in writing, it shall be void unless made in the prescribed form and registered."

As further limb of this argument, the respondent says that, even if the applicant's contention were accepted that the oral transaction was "evidenced by" the document involved, this document does not contain any reference to the particular goods the subject of the transaction between the parties. It is then submitted that the document is, therefore, deficient as lacking an essential element which would enable it to qualify as a bill of sale with respect to the subject goods . . .

The second submission of the respondent is that, in any event, the nature of the transaction between the parties is entirely one of pledge; and does not involve any question of a license to seize and take possession of the subject goods. It is submitted that possession was obtained by the respondent through the terms of the agency agreement, and it was only upon such possession being so obtained that the subject term creating the lien commenced to take effect so as to create the lien and grant the power of sale. The respondent refers in this regard to the decision of the Court of Appeal in *Ex parte Hubbard: Re Hardwick* (1886) 17 QBD 690 at 697, in which Lord Esher MR said: "If these documents gave the grantee a right *to take possession* of goods, even though it was a right to take immediate possession, then, as we held in *Ex parte Parsons* (1886) 16 QBD 532, they would be within the Act. But a right to take possession means a right to take it whether the grantor likes it or not. If the real transaction does not depend on the power of the one party to take possession against the will of the other, but on the one voluntarily giving and the other receiving possession — if the transaction does not begin at all until the grantor voluntarily gives possession of the goods to the grantee — that is not an 'authority or licence to *take* possession of personal chattels'."

Further reference is made to the statements in the judgment of Bowen LJ, as follows (at 698): "There are two well-known and entirely distinct kinds of transaction. There is a mortgage of chattels, when there is no delivery of the chattels to the mortgagee, but the general property in them passes to him by the mortgage deed. There is another entirely distinct transaction, which was known to the Romans, and has been long familiar to English law, the transaction of a pawn or pledge, where there must be a delivery of the goods pledged to the pledgee, but only a special property in them passes to him, in order that they may be dealt with by him, if necessary, to enforce his rights — the general property in the goods remaining in the pledgor. A special property in the goods passes to the pledgee in order that he may be able — if his right to sell arises — to sell them. In all such cases there is at common law an authority to the pledgee to sell the goods on the default of the pledgor to repay the money, either at the time originally appointed, or after notice by the pledgee. If the pledge is accompanied by a written document, still the essence of the transaction is that actual possession of the goods should be given to the pledgee. Would you expect the document to give the pledgee a right to take possession of the goods? On the contrary, you would only expect that it would regulate the terms on which they were to be held and applied by him"; and (at 699): "It was next argued by Sir H Davey that these documents are 'licences to take possession of personal chattels as security for a debt'. Are they licences to take possession at all? By that expression is meant a licence which gives an option to the licensee to leave the possession of the goods with the licensor or to take it from him. It seems to me that only such documents can fall within this definition as are consistent with the possession of the goods remaining with the grantor, and that, if it was never intended that the possession should remain with him, but it was intended that the possession should at once be given to the grantee, it is impossible to say that the definition applies."

[His Honour referred to the House of Lords' decision in *Great Eastern Railway v Lord's Trustee* [1909] AC 109 and continued at 448:] In my opinion, the submissions made on behalf of the respondent constitute a correct analysis of the situation created pursuant to the transaction as formulated in the agreed statement of facts. I consider that the agreement between the parties was one which was wholly oral. The mere fact that their oral agreement contained reference to certain terms which are to be found in a document does not have the effect of rendering their agreement partly documentary nor, in my opinion, does it, in the present case, enable such document to be relied on as evidencing a charge effective in the present instance. There are two grounds for this. First, the document is, in my view, not in the category of material evidencing the parties' wholly oral contract; secondly, the charge which it is submitted is evidenced by such a document is not, in my view, adequately evidenced, by reason particularly of the absence of any reference to the subject goods. I do not consider that the introductory words of the subject condition referring to "all goods" is adequate for this purpose. Even if this wording would enable extrinsic evidence to be given to identify the subject goods, this would also have the effect of excluding the provisions of the Bills of Sale Act, which require the charge constituting a bill of sale to be constituted in essential respects by the document.

I agree also with the second submission of the respondent that, on the facts of the present case, the goods were in fact taken into the possession of the respondent pursuant to the agency agreement; it was only upon such possession being obtained that the relevant term commenced to operate so as to create the lien with its concomitant power of sale. It may well be that the company had the power to prevent the goods coming into the possession of the respondent. This did not, of course, occur in the present case. If it had, the result would simply be that the subject term of the agreement between the parties would not have any operation. It is obviously a term which is conditioned upon the respondent receiving possession by the voluntary act of the company, and then having its rights as specified to detain the goods and, if necessary, in reliance upon the security afforded by its lien, to sell the goods.

Accordingly, I declare that the general lien created in the manner described in the agreed statement of facts did not constitute a charge requiring registration pursuant to s 100 of the Companies Act ...

Order accordingly.

With the above case may be compared *Re MacKay* (1972) 20 FLR 147; *Boydell v James* (1936) 36 SR (NSW) 620; *Re James O'Mara* (1924) 24 SR (NSW) 352; and *Stoneleigh Finance Ltd v Phillips* [1965] 2 WLR 508.

Effect of the National Companies Code Pt iv Div 9

In relation to secured transactions involving a company's assets, the NCC performs a similar function to ss 4 and 5 Bills of Sale Act, *supra,* but casts its net wider by including floating charges and charges on some choses in action (goodwill, industrial property and book debts). Furthermore, there is no requirement of a power to seize and the obligation to register applies even when the collateral does not remain in the possession of the company.

The most notable features of Div 9 are as follows:

Section 200 lists the charges required to be registered, but excepts charges and liens arising by operation of law, pledges of personal chattels or marketable securities, certain charges in relation to negotiable instruments or documents of title to goods, transfers of goods in the ordinary course of business, charges on land or fixtures (where included in a charge on land to which they are affixed).

Section 201 requires a company which creates a registrable charge to ensure that notice thereof is lodged with the National Companies and Securities Commission (NCSC) within 45 days.

Section 202(1) requires similar notice where a company acquires property that is subject to a registrable charge.

Section 205(1) provides that a registrable charge is void as a security as against the liquidator or official manager unless a notice was lodged with the NCSC under ss 201 or 202 within the relevant period (usually 45 days) or not later than six months before the commencement of the winding up or appointment of the official manager.

An unregistered but registrable charge will not be void for all purposes (s 200(10)) but will be deferred in priority under s 204 and Schedule 5 as to which see p 360, *infra*.

Section 206 provides for notice to be given to the commission upon the assignment and variation of charges.

Section 207 deals with the satisfaction of, and release of property from charges. The chargee is required to give the company a memorandum of satisfaction within 14 days after receiving the company's request for him to do so: s 207(1).

Section 208(1) provides that where a notice in respect of a charge on property is required to be lodged under ss 201, 202 or 206(2) the notice may be lodged by the company or any interested person.

Section 209 provides a company is to keep documents relating to charges and a register of charges.

Section 211 provides that where a company, a recognised company or a recognised foreign company transfers, assigns or gives security over a personal chattel within the meaning of the Bills of Sale Act 1898 (NSW) and notice in respect of that transfer, assignment or giving of that security is required to be lodged with the commission under Div 9, the document need not be registered under the Bills of Sale Act unless it is made or given jointly with another person or persons one or more of whom is not a company, a recognised company or a recognised foreign company.

Under the code registration is only required in one state or territory; ie Div 9 and Schedule 5 apply to:

(a) charges on property, wherever situate, of companies incorporated in the home jurisdiction: s 199(7);
(b) charges on property within Australia of foreign companies formed overseas and registered in the home jurisdiction: s 199(9); and
(c) charges on property within the home jurisdiction of registered foreign companies formed in a non-participating state or territory: s 199(8).

In the United States, the Uniform Commercial Code deals comprehensively with all security interests in personal property by requiring such interests to be perfected by the secured creditor in most instances either by filing a financing statement or taking possession of the goods. Compare the Australian bill of sale with the following code definition in UCC art 1.201(37):

"Security interest" means an interest in personal property or fixtures which secures payment or performance of an obligation. The retention or reservation of title by a seller of goods notwithstanding shipment or delivery to the buyer (Section 2-401) is limited in effect to a reservation of a "security interest". The term also includes any interest of a buyer of accounts or chattel paper which is subject to Article 9. The special property interest of a buyer of goods on identification of such goods to a contract for sale under Section 2-401 is not a "security interest", but a buyer may also acquire a "security interest" by complying with Article 9. Unless a lease or consignment is intended as security, reservation of title thereunder is not a "security interest" but a consignment is in any event subject to the provisions on consignment sales (Section 2-326). Whether a lease is intended as security is to be determined by the facts of each case; however, (a) the inclusion of an option to purchase does not of itself make the lease one intended for security, and (b) an agreement that upon compliance with the terms of the lease the lessee shall become or has the option to become the owner of the property for no additional consideration or for a nominal consideration does make the lease one intended for security.

QUESTIONS

Question 4

(1) *Briefly* compare and contrast the main features of the following secured

transactions: legal mortgage; equitable mortgage; equitable charge; pledge; lien; and floating charge over a company's present and future assets.

(2) Consider whether, and in what circumstances, each of the above secured transactions require registration under the Bills of Sale Act.

(3) How do the NCC provisions for registration of charges over a company's property differ from the requirements of the Bills of Sale Act? What do each of these sets of provisions seek to achieve? How effective are they? Will a security given over a lathe of Carb Pty Ltd require registration under both the Bills of Sale Act and the NCC?

Question 5

Jim Handy urgently needed $20,000 cash. He approached financier Squeeze and offered to pledge his Mercedes car valued at $30,000 as security for a loan. Squeeze agreed to loan Jim $20,000 provided the legal title to the car was transferred to him by way of security. Jim then pointed out that he would need to continue to use his car, whereupon it was verbally agreed that in consideration of a loan of $20,000 legal title should pass to Squeeze and that Jim would have a lease of the car at $300 per month with an option to repurchase the car for $22,000 at any time within 12 months. Squeeze thereupon gave Jim a cheque for $20,000. The next day, Jim thought it would be wise to put something in writing and wrote to Squeeze stating: "I hereby transfer my car to you, subject to my option to repurchase for $22,000 within 12 months." One month later, the car was seized by the bailiff in execution of a judgment against Jim in favour of Sue Quick. Can Squeeze reclaim the car from the sheriff?

Would it make any difference to your answer if the car belonged to Carb Pty Ltd and the company entered the same transaction with Squeeze?

SECTION 4: THE INSOLVENT DEBTOR AND BANKRUPTCY PROCEEDINGS

In this section it is intended to examine briefly some of the procedural aspects of bankruptcy and its relationship to the recovery of unsecured debts. These materials should be read in conjunction with the next section which includes specific provisions of the bankruptcy and companies legislation on fraudulent dispositions, preferences and charges given by insolvent persons or companies.

PURPOSES OF BANKRUPTCY LAW

In contrast with the pre-bankruptcy law of debt which concentrated solely on punishment of and recovery from debtors and made no distinction between honest and dishonest debtors, the modern law of bankruptcy seeks to fulfil the following objectives:
  (a) to ensure that when a debtor is unable to satisfy his creditor's claims, such property as he has is distributed rateably amongst his general (ie unsecured) creditors;
  (b) to define the rights of creditors to share in such distribution;
  (c) to discharge the honest debtor from further liability after all provable debts have been satisfied so far as possible: *Page v Commonwealth Life Assurance Society Ltd* (1936) 36 SR (NSW) 85 at 97, per Jordan CJ; and *Storey v Lane* (1981) 55 ALJR 608 at 611, per Gibbs CJ and at 613–4, per Aickin J.

How effectively is the law achieving these objectives? Are there differences between the situations of insolvent consumers and insolvent businesses? In 1976 the Australian Law Reform Commission commenced an investigation of particular

The Law Reform Commission:
Insolvency: The Regular Payment of Debts, Report No 6, 1977
1 Bankruptcy and Insolvency: the Need for Change
Introduction

problems of consumer debtors, including whether bankruptcy is an appropriate solution in the case of insolvent consumers.

1 Under the Constitution of the Commonwealth of Australia, a power to make laws "with respect to... bankruptcy and insolvency"[1] is vested in the Commonwealth Parliament. On 10 May 1976, the Attorney-General referred to the Law Reform Commission certain questions concerning the present law on bankruptcy and insolvency. The first question asked of the commission was: "whether the Bankruptcy Act in its application to small or consumer debtors makes adequate provision to enable such debtors to discharge or compromise their debts from their present or future assets or earnings." This question is not directed at narrow legal issues. There is worldwide concern with the social problems which arise from the extensive use which is now made of credit for the sale and purchase of consumer goods.[2] In Australia alone, thousands of persons annually become unable to pay their current instalment debts.[3]

2 Insolvency, that is, inability to pay debts as they fall due, may result from a sudden change of financial circumstances brought about by unemployment or illness. Alternatively, it may simply result from over-commitment of periodical income. For a sudden change in financial circumstances neither creditor nor debtor is normally to be blamed. In many cases of overcommitment, on the other hand, both must take some responsibility. Sales and advertising practices inevitably contribute to this overcommitment. Creditors rely, to a considerable extent, upon the ability of consumers to make dispassionate and realistic assessments of the variety of products put before them, and of the credit arrangements available to them. Some consumers are unable to make these judgments as effectively as many others. They are unskilled in budget planning and make errors in their assessment of their capacity to repay. The widespread advertising of goods and of credit available for their purchase only adds to their difficulties. When they become insolvent, they are equally unskilled in solving their own problems. When their insolvency worsens, other social problems may arise. They need help, but often seek it only when their financial positions have become hopeless and rearrangement of their debts has become impossible. In some cases, bankruptcy becomes inevitable.

3 In cases of overcommitment, as in cases of a sudden change in financial circumstances, the law must achieve a fair balance between the interests of the creditor and the debtor. It must uphold the general principle that debts which have been fairly incurred should be paid. But it must also deal humanely with those who suffer from overburdening debts. It must recognise that most insolvent debtors are honest and wish to pay their debts if they can. It must also recognise that their failure to seek help usually indicates ignorance, shame or embarrassment, not fraud or dishonesty. The law must provide procedures to assist insolvent debtors to rearrange their debts. It must endeavour to minimise needless collection expenses, particularly in the recovery of debts through the courts. It must enhance, rather than impede, opportunities for the financial rehabilitation of insolvent debtors. For those in particular who have little prospect of making substantial repayment, it must find a dignified means of discharge from their debts in bankruptcy. There can be little doubt that the present law, which has remained basically unaltered since enactments in the nineteenth and early twentieth centuries, fails to achieve these aims. Valuable reform of insolvency laws, in particular, has already taken place in the United States and Canada. Expert committees have recently recommended further legislative change in each of those countries. Our own law, too, must be restructured if it is to serve the needs of Australia's consumer credit-based society in the final quarter of the twentieth century.

. . .

---

[1] s 51(xvii).

[2] United States Bankruptcy Commission, Report (1973); Canadian Study Committee on Bankruptcy and Insolvency Legislation, Report (1970); Crowther Committee on Consumer Credit, Report (1971), Cmnd 4596.

[3] Exact statistics are not available. For figures concerning default, judgment debt recovery and bankruptcy, see paras 4, 5, 6 below.

7 A proper consideration of the issues raised by the Attorney-General's first question is dependent upon a full appreciation of the role played by bankruptcy in the recovery of debts, and of the relationship between bankruptcy laws and laws otherwise dealing with the recovery of debts, particularly judgment debts. Bankruptcy is the final procedure provided by the law for dealing with the problem of non-payment of debts. Like some aspects of insolvency, it is governed by Commonwealth law.[4] It is a procedure under which the affected individual is made subject to a number of disabilities and title to his property passes to the Official Receiver for eventual distribution between his creditors. Detailed provisions are contained in the Bankruptcy Act 1966, which is, however, not concerned solely with bankruptcy. It also contains procedures for composition of debts, deeds of arrangement and deeds of assignment which are properly regarded as laws concerned with insolvency rather than bankruptcy. Unlike laws with respect to bankruptcy, insolvency laws do not result in a change of status. In common with bankruptcy, however, they are concerned with a debtor's total financial situation and are aimed at ensuring equitable treatment of his creditors.

8 Bankruptcy laws are used both by debtors and creditors. Debtors who go bankrupt on their own petitions sometimes do so in order to escape from state and territorial debt recovery procedures which preserve close links with nineteenth century models. South Australia, for example, still maintains imprisonment as a sanction for failure to attend an examination hearing and it is to the retention of debt-related imprisonment that the high rate of bankruptcy in that state is often attributed.[5] Of non-business debtors who go bankrupt probably 90 per cent do so on their own petitions. Creditors rarely bring petitions against non-business debtors, partly because of the costs involved, partly because credit providers believe it may provide bad publicity and detrimentally affect future business.[6] The insolvency procedures in the Bankruptcy Act are available only to debtors. For reasons which are subsequently explained,[7] these are rarely used by non-business debtors. The main legal experience of the vast majority of insolvent non-business debtors is in relation to state and territorial judgment recovery.

9 State and territorial judgment debt recovery laws, unlike bankruptcy and insolvency laws, are primarily concerned with each individual debt and the recovery of that debt for the benefit of the individual creditor. The debt of a given creditor is treated separately from those of other creditors, and the judgment creditor has priority over one who has not yet obtained a judgment in his favour. State and territorial debt recovery laws differ considerably, one from another. In some states, debt-related imprisonment orders are an important factor in judgment debt recovery,[8] in others they have been abandoned. In some states, garnishment of wages, or attachment of wages at their source, is a central mode of judgment debt recovery;[9] in South Australia, on the other hand, it is specifically forbidden.[10] When, as often happens, a debtor moves from one state or territory to another, the Service and Execution of Process Act 1903 (Cth) provides a means of enforcement of the judgment debt in accordance with the procedures available in the second jurisdiction.

Different Aims

10 Inevitably, there is a conflict of aims between bankruptcy and insolvency laws, on the one hand, and judgment debt recovery laws, on the other. Some of these conflicts are identified and resolved in the Bankruptcy Act itself. For example, warrants or writs of

---

[4] The power is exercised in the Bankruptcy Act 1966 (Cth). Some state laws are preserved by that Act: s 9(1).

[5] Kelly, 92-3; Judge J M White; Fair Dealings with Consumers (1975) 53. Although less than 10 per cent of the South Australian non-business bankruptcies sampled in a survey by the commission were reported to have resulted from recovery action, this undoubtedly underestimates the real significance of the threat of imprisonment. The relevance of the latter is reported only when the fact is volunteered by the bankrupt.

[6] Further details of this survey are presented in Chapter 4.

[7] See paras 27, 28 below.

[8] eg SA, Local & District Criminal Courts Act 1972; Vic, Imprisonment of Fraudulent Debtors Act 1958.

[9] eg NSW, Courts of Petty Sessions (Civil Claims) Act 1970; District Court Act 1973; Vic, Magistrates (Summary Proceedings) Act 1975.

[10] Mercantile Law Act 1936 s 18.

execution or distress are available under state and territorial laws in favour of individual judgment creditors. As the execution creditor is entitled to priority, this procedure may substantially lessen the likelihood of recovery by other creditors. Recognising this difficulty, the Bankruptcy Act requires certain execution creditors to hand over to the trustee in bankruptcy the proceeds of execution for equal distribution among all creditors.[11] Similarly, at the time when a person becomes bankrupt he may be subject to an order either in respect of his property, under a warrant of execution, or even in respect of his person, under a procedure commonly known as "imprisonment of fraudulent debtors". The Bankruptcy Act provides a means for obtaining discharge of any such order, and a stay of any civil action pending against one who has petitioned in bankruptcy or against whom a petition has been presented.[12] Indeed, the Act specifically provides that when a debtor becomes bankrupt, it ceases to be competent for a creditor to enforce any remedy against the person or property of the debtor, or to commence legal proceedings against him, in respect of a provable debt.[13]

11 Conflict between the policies which lie behind debt recovery laws on the one hand, and bankruptcy and insolvency laws on the other, is not a recent phenomenon. The original purpose of the early bankruptcy statutes was to ensure for creditors a more effective means of recourse against a debtor's property than was provided by execution at common law. The debtor who was made bankrupt did not obtain discharge of his debts. To the extent that his debts were not satisfied by distribution of the proceeds of his property, they remained debts in respect of which execution might subsequently be had, or in respect of which the debtor might simply be imprisoned, since these were the two debt recovery procedures known to the common law.[14] But bankruptcy proceedings could only be instituted by creditors, and then only against traders. Creditors who preferred common law remedies might imprison a debtor, either before or after judgment. Against a non-trader, imprisonment was the only remedy in cases where execution had been, or was likely to be, unsuccessful.

Fourteenth Annual Report on the Operation of Bankruptcy Act 1966 for the year ended 30 June 1981

Causes of business bankruptcies, being bankruptcies of employers and persons engaged in a trade, business or profession on their own account during the year ended 30 June 1981

	Major cause	Contributing causes
1. Lack of sufficient initial working capital	471	315
2. Lack of business ability, acumen, training or experience resulting in such matters as under-quoting, mistakes in estimating, lack of supervision and failure to assess potential of business or to detect misrepresentations	664	390
3. Failure to keep proper books of account and costing records	18	75
4. Economic conditions affecting industry including competition and price cutting, credit restrictions, fall in prices, increases in charges and other overhead expenses, high cost of repairs and maintenance of equipment and changes in the character of business location (by-pass roads)	538	357
5. Seasonal conditions including floods and droughts	27	39
6. Excessive interest payments on hire purchase and loan moneys and capital losses on repossessions	206	148
7. Inability to collect debts due to disputes, faulty work or bad debts	63	71
8. Excessive drawings including failure to provide for taxation either personal or wage tax deductions	140	63
9. Gambling or speculation	16	15
10. Personal reasons including ill health of self or dependents, domestic discord and other personal reasons	133	128
11. Other business reasons or reasons unknown	132	50
	2408	

[11] s 118.
[12] s 60.
[13] s 58(3).
[14] W Holdsworth, *History of English Law*, 7th ed, 1956, VIII, pp 230-3.

Causes of non-business bankruptcies being bankruptcies of wage and salary earners, pensioners, and all other persons having no remunerative employment during the year ended 30 June 1981

	Major cause	Contributing causes
1. Excessive use of credit facilities including presure selling, losses on repossessions and high interest payments	1096	300
2. Liabilities incurred on guarantees	205	43
3. Unemployment	576	368
4. Gambling, speculation and extravagance in living	109	47
5. Absence of health insurance or extensive ill health	167	133
6. Adverse litigation	102	39
7. Domestic discord	168	133
8. Other causes or cause unknown	323	170
	2746	

Bankruptcy Business "Gets Softer Option" from Part 10
Report in *The Australian,* 12 October 1981

Business people faced with bankruptcy should try ways of arranging matters other than by creditor or debtor petitions, a federal minister said yesterday.

Far better use could be made of Pt 10 of the Bankruptcy Act, he said.

The Minister for Business and Consumer Affairs, Mr Moore, said that since 1929-30, when the Depression took its heaviest toll, there had been a decline in bankruptcy matters under Pt 10.

Of all the issues under the Bankruptcy Act, Pt 10 had fallen from 60.24 per cent in 1930-31 to 10.88 per cent in 1980-81.

He said the drop had left little understanding of Pt 10, which allowed debtors to enter schemes of arrangements with creditors which were legally binding on all parties.

This avenue provided for release from liability of the debtor without the procedural formalities of bankruptcy and eventual discharge.

Mr Moore listed the following questions which people could consider when thinking of bankruptcy:

Would there be some psychological advantages for the debtor if he was not declared bankrupt?

This could help creditors when the debtor, realising there was a solution short of bankruptcy, took steps to put his affairs in order sooner than was otherwise possible.

Would a Pt 10 administration be quicker?

This would mean an earlier dividend for creditors and a quicker release for the debtor.

Would a Pt 10 administration be more economical to administer, therefore providing a higher return for creditors?

A lump sum composition, for example, was usually quicker and cost less to administer under Pt 10.

Was the particular case one where there would be advantages in the greater flexibility of Pt 10?

Under Pt 10, the debtor and the creditors had the opportunity of working out an arrangement to their satisfaction.

This was particularly relevant where the debtor had a potentially profitable business.

Mr Moore said the Official Trustee in Bankruptcy might not always have the staff to supervise the continued operations of the business.

In any event he was limited to carrying on the bankrupt's business only "for the beneficial disposal or winding up".

OUTLINE OF BANKRUPTCY PROCEDURE

Bankruptcy law in Australia is entirely the creature of statute although there is a substantial gloss of case law interpreting the series of statutes which have covered the topic. Since the Commonwealth exercised its constitutional power under s 51(xvii) of the Constitution, the federal legislation has superseded the previous state legislation to the extent of any inconsistency. Jurisdiction in bankruptcy matters is primarily exercised by the Federal Court of Australia constituted under the Federal Court of Australia Act 1976.

Bankruptcy proceedings are commenced by the filing of a petition. Let us assume that Jim Handy is insolvent and Easy Finance is one of his creditors. The petition can be presented by creditor Easy or by debtor Jim himself: ss 43, 55. The differing procedure on each is outlined below. Creditor Easy's petition must be founded upon one of the acts of bankruptcy (s 40) which are considered later. Where the requirements of s 43 are satisfied on the presentation of a creditor's petition, the court will make a sequestration order against the estate of debtor Jim.

The effect of the sequestration order is that:
(a) Jim becomes a bankrupt: s 43(2);
(b) Jim's property vests in the Official Trustee in Bankruptcy: s 58(1);
(c) Proceedings by Easy and all other creditors are stayed (s 58(3)), except that secured creditors may realise or otherwise deal with their security and except for maintenance agreements and orders: s 58(5), (5A).

Following sequestration, the Official Trustee will summon a meeting of creditors (s 64) which may appoint a committee of inspection to advise and superintend the trustee: s 70. Bankrupt Jim may be publicly examined before the Registrar as to his assets and affairs (s 69), and must co-operate with the trustee by furnishing information and documents and attending meetings: s 77. Creditors will lodge proofs of their debts with the Official Trustee (s 82), who will decide whether to admit them: s 83.

The property available to the Official Trustee will include all property:
(a) previously owned by Jim during the period of "relation back", that is, from the time of commission of the earliest act of bankruptcy committed by him within six months immediately preceding the date on which Easy's petition was presented or Jim's own application for sequestration was made: s 115(1);
(b) which devolves upon Jim after the commencement of the bankruptcy: s 116(1);
(c) which was the subject of a voluntary settlement, fraudulent disposition, or voidable preference: ss 120-122 and see pp 300-22, *infra*.

The Official Trustee is required to distribute from the bankrupt's estate dividends amongst creditors who have proved their debts: s 140. Such distribution must be in accord with the order of payment of debts in ss 108-114.

Jim may apply to the court for an order of discharge from bankruptcy at any time after his public examination is concluded or dispensed with. The court will take into account a report of the Official Trustee and Jim's general conduct of his financial affairs: s 150. The Official Trustee or a creditor can object to Jim's discharge, but in the absence of any such objection, he will be automatically discharged upon the expiration of three years from the date of bankruptcy: s 149. The effect of discharge is, subject to a few exceptions, to release Jim from all his debts: s 153.

DEBTOR'S PETITION

The procedure on debtor Jim's own petition differs from that on a creditor's petition in a number of ways:
(a) it is more of an administrative procedure than an adversary one, because, once Jim presents his petition accompanied by his verified statement of affairs, he automatically becomes bankrupt from the date the Registrar accepts the petition;
(b) it is not necessary to establish an act of bankruptcy or even Jim's insolvency;

(c) creditors are not involved in the proceedings until after Jim has become a bankrupt.

CREDITOR'S PETITION

The substantive requirements for presentation of creditor Easy's petition are set out in ss 43 and 44. Note that a creditor's petition cannot be presented unless the debtor owes at least $1000 to the petitioning creditor(s) as a liquidated sum and the petition is founded upon an act of bankruptcy committed within six months before presentation of the petition: s 44(1).

A secured creditor may petition or join in a petition but, unless he surrenders his security, the debt owing to him is deemed to be only such amount as exceeds the value of his security.

At the hearing of the petition the court will require proof of the matters in ss 43 and 44, of the service of Easy's petition on Jim and that the debt(s) on which Easy relies is still owing. Since a creditor's petition is presented for the benefit of all creditors and not only for the petitioner, the court will allow another creditor(s) to whom $1000 is owing to be substituted for the petitioning creditor(s) if the petition is not prosecuted with due diligence: s 49. For similar reasons, a petition cannot be withdrawn without leave of the court (s 47(2)), since the court will not allow its process to be used for the purpose of obtaining an advantage for one creditor, nor allow the petition to be withdrawn if there are other creditors willing to take it up: *Re a Debtor* (1930) 2 ABC 164; and *Re Mann* [1958] 1 WLR 1272 at 1274.

The onus rests on the petitioning creditor Easy to prove that a debt of at least $1000 is owing to it at both the presentation of and the hearing of the petition. The debt must be a liquidated sum and not merely a cause of action for damages for an unascertained amount. If Jim pays part of the debt after presentation of the petition but before the hearing, so that less than $1000 remains owing to Easy, the court has no jurisdiction to make a sequestration order (s 52), unless another creditor(s) to whom $1000 is owing is substituted as petitioner(s). Easy may quite properly refuse to accept part payment, or even full payment, since, if Jim is made bankrupt on Easy's or another creditor's petition or on Jim's own petition presented within six months of that payment, it will be void as against the trustee in bankruptcy and recoverable as a preference: s 122. For a criticism of this position which allows the debtor to use the Act as a means of frustrating the petitioning creditor, see (1970) 44 *ALJ* 392.

Normally proof by Easy of the above matters would result in the making of a sequestration order under s 52(1). However, the court does have a discretion to dismiss the petition if it is satisfied that (a) Jim is able to pay his debts (see later as to the test of solvency), or (b) for other sufficient cause a sequestration order ought not to be made: s 52(2). The court retains a discretion to investigate whether the debtor does owe $1000 to Easy even where Easy has a prior judgment from another court: *Wren v Mahoney* (1972) 126 CLR 212; [1972] ALR 307, discussed in Goldring, "Going Behind a Judgment" (1973) 47 *ALJ* 377. The court also has the power to dismiss a petition if it has been used as a means of extorting payment from Jim or for other sufficient cause if it finds that the court's process is being abused: *Rozenbes v Kronhill* (1956) 95 CLR 407.

ACTS OF BANKRUPTCY

There are 14 separate acts of bankruptcy set out in s 40(1) any one of which may be used to found a creditor's petition. These must be read in detail and the following notes merely illustrate some of the more common grounds:

Section 40(1)(a): conveyance or assignment for benefit of creditors generally. While a deed of assignment in favour of creditors under Pt X remains in force, no creditor can petition on this ground. To satisfy s 40(1)(a) the assignment must be of virtually the whole of the debtor Jim's property, and be for the benefit of his creditors generally and not merely some of, or a special class of, his creditors. A creditor who is a party to a deed which is not in conformity with Pt X, or who has assented to or acquiesced in it (eg, by lodging a proof of debt with the trustee (*Re Pinfold* (1961) 19 ABC 45)) cannot rely upon the deed as an act of bankruptcy to found his own petition.

Section 40(1)(b): conveyance etc that would, on bankruptcy, be void against trustee. The various dealings are defined in ss 120-122 which are examined on pp 300-22. The relevant time limit is that the conveyance etc occurred within six months prior to presentation of the petition; thus a settlement made 18 months previously could not be an available act of bankruptcy, but nevertheless can itself be avoided under s 120.

Section 40(1)(c): departure from Australia, house, business etc with intent to defeat/delay creditors. The intent must be proved but the standard of proof is only that the requisite intent was the most probable explanation of the debtor's conduct: it is the actual or implied intent rather than the actual effect which is relevant: *Barton v Deputy Commissioner of Taxation* (1974) 131 CLR 370, which also illustrates the practice of substituting another creditor where the original petitioning creditor is paid after presentation of his petition. It is sufficient if the intent is to defeat or delay any creditor (not merely the petitioner) and that intent need not be the debtor's sole intention.

Section 40(1)(d): execution against the debtor. This act of bankruptcy, like the failure to comply with a bankruptcy notice, is regarded as one of the indicia of insolvency, notwithstanding that the execution was for a small judgment debt. Section 40(1)(d) should be read in conjunction with ss 118-119. The purpose of this ground is to enable creditors other than the judgment creditor who is levying execution to force a sharing of the debtor's property in bankruptcy rather than the judgment creditor obtaining an advantage.

Sections 40(1)(e) and (f) also indicate an admission of insolvency.

Section 40(1)(g): failure to comply with a bankruptcy notice. This is by far the most important act of bankruptcy since approximately 95 per cent of creditors' petitions are founded on this ground. The requirement for proof of this act of bankruptcy will be examined under the following headings:

(1) The creditor has obtained a final judgment or order on which execution has not been stayed.

(2) A bankruptcy notice issued by the Registrar has been served on the debtor.

(3) The debtor has not within the specified time either complied with the notice, or satisfied the court that he has an appropriate counterclaim, set-off or cross demand.

Any creditor can present a petition on this ground and not only the creditor who issued and served the bankruptcy notice.

FINAL JUDGMENT OR ORDER

A "creditor" entitled to issue a bankruptcy notice must hold and be entitled to enforce a final judgment or order; the term includes an assignee who has obtained an assignment of a judgment debt: *Nirens v Fowler Asphalt Pty Ltd* (1966) 9 FLR 255; *sub nom Re Nirens* [1967] ALR 364.

A final judgment is one which determines the rights of the parties in such a way that it cannot be raised again, even if a right of appeal may have been available. Note the extention resulting from the deeming provisions in s 40(3). Normally, a judgment debtor is entitled to apply to the court which awarded the judgment against him to stay execution of the judgment so that he can appeal or apply for time to pay by instalments. Such a stay of proceedings precludes issue or service of a bankruptcy notice based on that judgment.

ISSUE AND SERVICE OF BANKRUPTCY NOTICE: S 41

Under s 41 the Registrar will issue a bankruptcy notice in the prescribed form on application by a judgment creditor who satisfies s 41(3). Bankruptcy is a serious matter affecting the personal status of the individual and the courts have insisted upon strict compliance with all substantive and formal aspects of issue and service of the bankruptcy notice.

BANKRUPTCY NOTICE
Bankruptcy Act 1966

BANKRUPTCY DISTRICT OF THE STATE OF NEW SOUTH WALES AND THE AUSTRALIAN CAPITAL TERRITORY.   No. E 1234 of 1984

Re: JAMES HANDY.

To: (a) ..... JAMES HANDY of 10 Gearway, Ryde ..... Company Director .....

WHEREAS (b) ..... Easy Finance Limited ..... of 300 George Street, Sydney .....

(hereinafter referred to as "the judgment creditor") has claimed the sum of $ ..... 5,000 ..... together with interest thereon at the rate of ... ten (10) ... per centum per annum from ..... 15 January, 1984 ..... (here insert date of judgment) which at the date of issue of this Notice amounts to $ ..... 83-33 ..... making a total of $ ..... 5,083-33 ..... is due by you to him under a final **Judgment** ~~order~~ obtained by him against you in the .....

..... District Court of New South Wales at Sydney .....

on the ..... 15th ..... day of ..... January ..... 1984, being **a judgment** ~~an order~~ the execution of which has not been stayed:

THEREFORE TAKE NOTICE that within ..... fourteen ..... days after service of this notice on you, excluding the day on which this notice is served on you, you are required—

(a) to pay the sum of $ 5,083-33 ..... so claimed by the judgment creditor to the Registrar of the District Court of New South Wales, ... 225 Macquarie St, Sydney, ... or

(b) to secure the payment of the sum referred to in the last preceding paragraph to the satisfaction of the Federal Court of Australia or the judgment creditor .....

..... or compound the sum so specified to the satisfaction of the judgment creditor (or his agent):

AND FURTHER TAKE NOTICE that if, within the period set out above, you fail either to comply with either of the above-mentioned requirements of this notice or to satisfy the Federal Court of Australia that you have a counter-claim, set-off or cross demand equal to or exceeding the sum specified in paragraph (a) of this notice, being a counter-claim, set-off or cross demand that you could not have set up in the **action** ~~proceeding~~ in which the **judgment** ~~order~~ was obtained, you will have committed an act of bankruptcy on which bankruptcy proceedings may be taken against you.

DATED this   fifteenth   day of   March   , 1984.

Deputy Registrar.

NOTE: If you have a counter-claim, set-off or cross demand equal to or exceeding the sum specified in paragraph (a) of this notice, being a counter-claim, set-off or cross demand that you could not have set up in the action/proceeding in which the judgment/order was obtained, you may, under subsection (7) of section 41 of the Bankruptcy Act 1966, within the period set out above, file an affidavit to that effect, and, if you do so, the time for complying with the requirements of this notice shall be deemed to have been extended until the Court determines whether it is satisfied that you have such a counter-claim, set-off or cross demand.

This notice was issued on the application of ..... Lit, E. Gate, Solicitor for ..... the judgment creditor ..... whose address for service is ..... 10 Court Square, Sydney .....

Re Long; Ex parte Fraser Confirming Pty Ltd
Court of Insolvency, exercising Federal Jurisdiction in Bankruptcy
(1975) 12 SASR 130

[Application to set aside bankruptcy notice.]

Walters J: In this matter, a creditor's petition has been presented by Fraser Confirming Pty Ltd seeking an order for the sequestration of the estate of a certain Arthur Joseph Long. The act of bankruptcy on which the petition is founded is the failure of the debtor to comply with the requirements of a bankruptcy notice issued out of this court on 8 April 1975. Particulars of the act of bankruptcy are set forth in the petition in this form:

"The debtor within six months before the presentation of the petition committed the following act of bankruptcy: that he failed either to comply on or before 30 April 1975 with the requirements of a bankruptcy notice duly served upon him on 16 April 1975 or to satisfy the court that he had a counterclaim set-off or cross demand equal to or exceeding the sum specified in paragraph (a) of the said bankruptcy notice"...

Before the day appointed for the hearing of the petition, the debtor filed a notice of his intention to oppose the petition on the ground of irregularity of service of the bankruptcy notice. The application came on before me prior to the hearing of the petition and, by consent of counsel for the parties, it was treated as an application to set aside the bankruptcy notice for want of due service.

On the hearing of the application, counsel for the petitioner relied upon an affidavit of service of a licensed process server who had deposed that on "Wednesday 16 April 1975 at 5.45 o'clock in the afternoon, [he] served Arthur Joseph Long with a copy of the bankruptcy notice by delivering it to him *personally* at his address at 480 Kensington Road, Wattle Park" (italics added) and that "[he] identified the person so served as the said Arthur Joseph Long as he had admitted to [him] that he was the said Arthur Joseph Long referred to in the said bankruptcy notice". In other respects the affidavit of service complied with r 122 of the Bankruptcy Rules in that it exhibited a copy of the bankruptcy notice and proved that the deponent had attained the age prescribed by the rule.

Evidence was then adduced of the debtor who asserted that the bankruptcy notice had never been served upon him personally, as deposed to by the process server, and that the bankruptcy notice and its contents did not come to his knowledge until upwards of eight to ten days after the alleged date of service. He said that he first learned of the existence of the bankruptcy notice on an occasion when he attended at the office of his solicitor, who then informed him that the notice had come into his possession. The evidence of the debtor was supported by the testimony of his wife who said that whilst she had been preparing a meal at about 6.00 pm on 16 April 1975, a person called at her home at 480 Kensington Road, Wattle Park and inquired for her husband. On informing him that her husband was not at home, this person handed her a document which, though she did not examine it, appeared to be "an official document"; and he asked her to give it to her husband. According to her evidence, she placed the document on a sideboard, and when her husband returned home for his meal, a short time later, she forgot to mention the document to him. Having had his meal, her husband left the premises in order to return to his place of business where, as it appears, he was engaged in supervising a discotheque until the early hours of the next day. She did not see her husband on the morning of that day. But on that same day, having seen the document where she had left it on the previous evening, she took it into her husband's place of business and handed it to a female member of the office staff. It would appear that the document remained in the office until it was taken by a member of the staff to the office of the debtor's solicitor, from whom the debtor subsequently learned of its existence.

I accept, though with some hesitation, the evidence of the debtor that the bankruptcy notice was not brought to his knowledge or attention until he consulted his solicitor, some eight to ten days after the document had been delivered to his wife. But I see no reason to reject the wife's story that when the document was handed to her by the process server, she was not informed that it was a bankruptcy notice; that she did not hand it to her husband or bring it to his knowledge or attention on 16 April 1975, or indeed at any time prior to the consultation with his solicitor. Her explanation for her failure to tell her husband that the document had been handed to her is not incredible; she claimed that she "had had three operations recently; [her] nerves [were] not all that good", and that she left business matters to her husband.

At the close of the evidence in support of the debtor's application, the petitioner's counsel stated that the process server was in attendance at court and was available to give evidence, but that it was not proposed to call him. Counsel went on to say: "I do not intend to call him. I am content to accept that the bankruptcy notice was served on Long's wife and that it found its way into Long's solicitor's office within a week of 16 April, and that Long was told by his solicitor, around that time, the nature of the document and ... that it was a bankruptcy notice." In the light of that intimation, and recognising the import of the contents of the affidavit of the process server, I was not disposed to call him of my own motion.

In default of oral evidence of the process server, and taking into account the evidence of the debtor and his wife, and, more especially, the concession made by the petitioner's counsel, I find that the bankruptcy notice was not served personally on the debtor at any time prior to the issue of the petition, and that the notice did not come to his knowledge or attention until about eight or ten days after the process server had delivered it to the debtor's wife on the evening of 16 April 1975.

Having made these findings, it becomes necessary to decide whether the bankruptcy notice was duly served on the debtor, and whether non-compliance with its requirements affords an act of bankruptcy sufficient to found the petition.

The Bankruptcy Rules contain an express direction as to service of a bankruptcy notice; service must be personal service, unless the provisions of s 309(2) of the Bankruptcy Act are availed of for the purpose of substituted service in a suitable case: cf rr 15, 16 and 123; s 309.

In my view, the issue of a bankruptcy notice is a proceeding in bankruptcy. The notice brings in train the processes of bankruptcy; and to enable an act of bankruptcy, based on failure to comply with the requirements of the notice to be available as a ground for a creditor's petition, it is essential, in my opinion, to prove that notice was duly served in accordance with the statutory rules, and further to prove a non-compliance with the requirements of the notice. In this context, I apply the observations of Harman J *In Re A Debtor; Ex parte The Debtor v Bowmaker Ltd* [1951] Ch 313 at 318, where his Lordship said: "A bankruptcy notice, being the document which sets in motion the whole process leading to bankruptcy (which is in the nature of a criminal matter), must be very strictly and narrowly construed on the footing that it is a penal matter."

Admittedly his Lordship was there speaking of an invalid bankruptcy notice, but I think his observations are equally apposite to the need for strict compliance with the formalities of service of a bankruptcy notice...

In taking the view that strict compliance with the rules prescribing the method of service of a bankruptcy notice must be insisted upon, I draw support from the rule laid down by the Divisional Court in *Re Collier; Ex parte Dan Rylands Ltd* (1891) 64 LT 742 at 743, where Cave J observed: "Due service of a bankruptcy notice is necessary in order to constitute an act of bankruptcy, and it is more important that the rules and regulations should be properly complied with in the case of a bankruptcy notice than in the case of a petition for adjudication. When an act of bankruptcy has been committed, then the petition is a less formal matter, and one as to which it is not necessary to take exactly the same view. Very soon after the Act of 1883 came into operation several cases were brought before the courts with reference to a bankruptcy notice, and on more than one occasion the Court of Appeal have expressed the opinion that, since the commission of an act of bankruptcy was a serious matter, and involved consequences of what have been called a penal nature, it was important to see that the necessary preliminaries have been complied with." ...

Reference may also be made to the decision of the Court of Appeal in *Re A Debtor* [1939] 1 Ch 251. There it was held that the handing of a bankruptcy petition to the debtor in a sealed envelope was not good service, for the reason that, as the petition was in a sealed envelope which bore no reference, and called no attention, to its contents, the debtor could have had no knowledge of what was contained in the envelope. In delivering his judgment (in which other members of the court concurred), Sir Wilfrid Greene MR stressed the necessity for "great strictness" in observing the directions prescribed by the relevant English Bankruptcy

Rules for service of a bankruptcy petition. His Lordship said: "It is no exaggeration to say that the practice in regard to writs and the requirements of the law in regard to the service of writs are, and have always been, regarded as matters *strictissimi juris*. In the case of the service of a bankruptcy petition, I can see nothing in the section and rules which can fairly be construed as relaxing the strict requirements which are to be found in the case of service of writs and other documents under the Rules of the Supreme Court": at 256-7...

In seeking to uphold the validity of the bankruptcy notice, counsel for the petitioner relied upon the decision of Philip J in *Re J Goldberger; Ex parte JJ Williams (Murwillumbah) Pty Ltd* [1908] QWN 41. In that case, the learned judge held that if a bankruptcy notice had been served on the debtor's wife, and had been handed by her to the debtor on the day of service and he had read it on the same day, no substantial injustice had been done, and that sequestration proceedings based on the bankruptcy notice were not invalidated. It was argued before me that in the light of the decision in *Goldberger's* case, I should find that in the circumstances proved in evidence, no substantial injustice, prejudice or embarrassment had been caused to the debtor, and that the bankruptcy notice was not invalidated by irregularity in the service of it.

However, it is plain that the facts appearing in *Goldberger's* case are distinguishable from those proved in the present case... With all deference to the learned judge, I venture to say that since he expressly found that the bankruptcy notice was served personally on the debtor, his remarks with regard to the validity of service on the debtor, through the medium of his wife, may be treated as *obiter*. However that may be, the weight of the authorities, to which I have referred earlier in these reasons, persuades me that if the decision in *Goldberger's* case [1958] QWN 41 is pertinent to the facts established in the present case, I should respectfully decline to follow it. In this connection, it is to be noticed that the learned authors of *McDonald, Henry and Meek's Australian Bankruptcy Law and Practice*, 4th ed, 1968, p 85, express the view that "the correctness of this decision [in *Goldberger's* case] is doubtful".

I have come to the conclusion that the failure of the petitioner to prove personal service of the bankruptcy notice on the debtor is not a formal defect, or an irregularity, which can be corrected by bringing it "within the umbrella" of s 306 of the Act. In this context, I think I may suitably apply the words of Bowen LJ in *Re Howes; Ex parte Hughes* [1892] 2 QB 628 at 632: "I do not regard this as a mere technical matter, for bankruptcy proceedings are of a peculiar character. They involve quasi-penal consequences to the debtor, and it is essential that all those forms, the object of which is to prevent injustice, should be strictly followed."

It is my opinion that the want of personal service of the bankruptcy notice on the debtor makes the petition founded on it a nullity, despite the debtor's subsequently acquired knowledge of the existence of the notice and even though there is no proof of substantial injustice having been done to him by the defect in service.

I cannot regard the conditions of s 40(1)(g) and s 41(1) and (4) of the Act as being satisfied. The bankruptcy notice is bad for want of regularity in the service of it. The petition on which it is founded fails *in limine*. The debtor is entitled to have the notice set aside and the petition dismissed. I order accordingly.

Having made the finding that the bankruptcy notice was not served on the debtor personally, I feel constrained to direct the Registrar in Bankruptcy to invite the attention of the Attorney-General for the Commonwealth to my reasons for judgment and, in particular, to the affidavit sworn by the process server on 9 May 1975 and filed in this court on 20 May 1975.

Petition dismissed.

Compare *Re Fairlie* (1969) 14 FLR 65; [1969] ALR 701 and in relation to service of the petition, see *Re Leppard* (1974) 25 FLR 158; [1975] Qd R 71; 5 ALR 556; *Re Florance* (1979) 36 FLR 256.

HAS THE DEBTOR COMPLIED WITH NOTICE OR SATISFIED COURT OF COUNTERCLAIM, SET-OFF OR CROSS DEMAND?

In order to comply with the notice, Jim must pay or secure the debt to the satisfaction of the court or Easy within the time specified in the notice. Alternatively, Jim may satisfy the court that he has a counterclaim, set-off or cross demand equal to or exceeding the sum payable under Easy's judgment. The procedure is set out in s 41(7). The counterclaim must be an existing one which is effective at the date of the application to set aside the bankruptcy notice and it must be against the judgment creditor personally in his own right and not in some other capacity (eg, as a trustee of an estate). Each of these points is illustrated in *Ebert v Union Trustee Co of Australia Ltd* (1960) 104 CLR 346; [1960] ALR 691 in which the High Court also laid down the further requirement that "the debtor must show that he has a prima facie case, even if then and there he does not adduce the admissible evidence which would make out a prima facie case before a court trying the issues that are involved in his counterclaim, set-off or cross demand". See also *James v Abrahams* (1981) 34 ALR 657.

The terms "counterclaim" and "set-off" require that there be a measurable claim for payment of money, although "cross demand" does embrace claims for unliquidated damages in tort (eg, slander: *Re Judd* (1924) 24 SR (NSW) 537) but not for declarations or determinations (eg of the validity of a will: *Ebert's* case). The counterclaim must be one that Jim could not have set up in the original action against him. Basically, this would be confined to:

(a) "One which, from point of time, or from its nature, or from absence of empowering provisions, or from positive inhibition so to do, could not be set up in the particular case in which judgment was obtained": *Re Stokvis* (1934) 7 ABC 53 at 57, per Lukin J; or

(b) Where at the time when the judgment was obtained, the cause of action had not arisen, or Jim had not then obtained an assignment of a debt due by Easy, but did so prior to his application to set aside the bankruptcy notice: *Re a Debtor* [1914] 3 KB 726.

DISTRIBUTION TO CREDITORS

The Official Trustee in Bankruptcy has the duty of actually collecting together Jim's property. This is essentially a practical business matter in which the Official Trustee has the assistance of various statutory powers: eg Jim's statement of affairs (ss 54-55), public examination of Jim (s 69), obtaining other information (s 81) and freezing of bank accounts (s 125). When he has collected Jim's assets, the Official Trustee will distribute them amongst the creditors who have proved their debts (s 140) in accordance with the statutory order of payment of debts set out in ss 108 and 109. The procedure for proof of debts is laid down in ss 82-107. The general principle is, of course, pro rata distribution amongst all unsecured creditors: s 108. However, there are a number of important qualifications upon s 108 including the priority payments for costs and expenses of the petitioning creditor and trustee, wages, income tax (but only in respect of instalment deductions and withholding tax) and other items listed in s 109; and the deferral of payments to the debtor's spouse, claims for interest in excess of 12 per cent pa, and for payments under void settlements and by trustees of earlier bankruptcies: ss 111, 112 and 120.

In addition, it is important to note that a secured creditor, having realised his security, can prove for any remaining unpaid balance of his debt. Alternatively, he may surrender his security to the Trustee, and prove for the whole of his debt: s 90. As the Trustee realises Jim's property, he will distribute dividends to those creditors whose proofs of debts have been accepted: s 140. Before distributing the final dividend he must warn all creditors who have not proved their debts to do so since the payment of the final dividend will be made to those creditors who have proved their debts and will debar all further claims: s 145. Jim's discharge likewise discharges him from all debts provable in the bankruptcy: s 153.

Lending on the Security of Goods

INSOLVENT COMPANIES

The legal rules and procedures for dealing with insolvent companies draw upon and resemble in a general way those applicable to bankruptcy. Although the Commonwealth's constitutional power to make laws with respect to bankruptcy and insolvency would cover winding up of insolvent companies, the Commonwealth has not sought to exercise that power. Bankruptcy Act s 7(2) provides that a sequestration order shall not be made against, or a debtor's petition presented by, a corporation.

The National Companies Code (NCC) therefore governs winding up proceedings. If we assume now that it is Carb Pty Ltd which is being wound up rather than Jim Handy being made bankrupt, the following differences from bankruptcy law will be relevant:

(1) Carb, being a company, may be compulsorily wound up by the court on the petition of its creditors, members etc where it is insolvent, has failed to commence business, becomes unmanageable, or is being conducted in an oppressive manner, or the number of its members falls below the statutory minimum: NCC ss 359, 364. Alternatively, the members of a solvent company can effect a *voluntary* winding up by special resolution without court approval: s 392. In neither case is there any need to prove the equivalent of an act of bankruptcy.

(2) Upon commencement of the winding up, Carb's assets will not be vested in the company's liquidator except in the rare situation where he finds it necessary to apply to the court for such a vesting order: s 374(2). On the other hand, the liquidator will exercise the powers previously given to the board of directors including those of administering and controlling the company's property and activities: s 374(1).

(3) Upon the conclusion of the winding up, Carb is dissolved and thereby ceases to exist: s 411. There is no procedure corresponding to the discharge of a bankrupt individual. However, the procedure for appointment of receivers and managers (Pt X), and for appointment of an official manager (Pt XI) for the purpose of providing an opportunity for the company to trade its way out of difficulties is analogous to the procedure for deeds of arrangement and assignment under Pt X of the Bankruptcy Act.

Notwithstanding the above differences, the liquidation of Carb corresponds to bankruptcy proceedings in the following respects:

(1) The liquidator can claim property previously owned by Carb during the period between the presentation of the petition for compulsory winding up and the winding up order: ss 365, 368. The purpose and effect is similar to the doctrine of relation back in bankruptcy.

(2) NCC s 438 expressly adopts in the case of winding up of insolvent companies the Bankruptcy Act provisions relating to secured and unsecured creditors, provable debts etc.

(3) NCC s 451 expressly avoids any transaction involving Carb's property which would have been void or voidable in the case of a bankrupt individual; eg ss 118, 120–122 and see pp 300–22, *infra*.

QUESTIONS

Question 6

(1) What is the purpose of bankruptcy and insolvency legislation, and how effective is that legislation?

(2) In what respects does the law distinguish between insolvent individuals and companies? Are further reforms necessary to deal with consumer debtors?

(3) When an individual or company becomes insolvent, is sequestration or liquidation always the best course of action? What other alternatives are available, and in what respects, if any, may they be preferable?

Question 7

Jim Handy purchased a yacht from W Indy for $2800 which he paid by cheque. Jim went sailing next day and the yacht sank in a storm. Jim believed it could have been saved if it had not leaked so badly from faulty caulking. He therefore stopped payment of his cheque and consistently refused to pay Indy.

Indy served Jim with a default summons issued by the District Court, Sydney, and when Jim ignored it, obtained a judgment by default for $2800 plus $150 costs. Before the time for application to set aside the judgment had expired, Indy obtained the issue of a bankruptcy notice against Jim demanding payment of $2950 by 1 June 1984. Indy called at Jim's home one Saturday morning and asked for Jim. Mary told Indy that Jim was in the shower and did not want to see Indy anyway, whereupon Indy handed the bankruptcy notice to Mary and requested her to give it to Jim.

Jim seeks your advice. He is concerned about his business reputation, but also considers Indy took him down. He believes he could prove the yacht was faulty. He is willing to pay Indy $2000 in order to dispose of the matter but not more than that amount, although he has ample funds to do so.

SECTION 5: FRAUDULENT DISPOSITIONS, PREFERENCES AND FLOATING CHARGES

As mentioned above, in addition to the Bills of Sale Acts and s 205 NCC, where dispositions or charges given by a debtor such as Carb over its assets would prejudice the claim of other creditors, the trustee in bankruptcy or company liquidator or official manager to those assets, they may be invalidated under one or more of the following provisions:

(1) State fraudulent disposition statutes derived from the early Imperial statute 13 Eliz c 5.

(2) Commonwealth Bankruptcy Act s 121 which also avoids fraudulent dispositions where the debtor becomes bankrupt.

(3) Bankruptcy Act s 122 and NCC s 451 which avoid dispositions and payments by insolvent debtors having the effect of giving a particular creditor a preference.

(4) NCC s 452 which avoids a floating charge given by an insolvent company to the extent that it would give the secured creditor a preference.

FRAUDULENT DISPOSITIONS

The Imperial statute 13 Eliz c 5 and state legislation derived from it render every alienation (which includes a mortgage or other encumbrance) of property made with intent to defraud creditors voidable at the instance of any person thereby prejudiced. For example, an unsecured creditor Sue Quick could be prejudiced by Carb disposing of its assets while insolvent. Conveyancing Act 1919 (NSW) s 37A is typical of these provisions:

37A (1) Save as provided in this section, every alienation of property ... made with intent to defraud creditors, shall be voidable at the instance of the person thereby prejudiced.

(2) This section does not affect the law of bankruptcy for the time being in force.

(3) This section does not extend to any estate or interest in property aliened to a purchaser in good faith not having, at the time of the alienation, notice of the intent to defraud creditors.

(Compare Vic, Property Law Act 1958 s 172; Qld, Property Law Act 1974 s 228; SA, Property Law Act 1936 s 86; WA, Property Law Act 1969 s 89; Tas, Conveyancing and Law of Property Act 1884 s 40.)

Where a debtor has been made bankrupt, or a company placed in liquidation, the Official Trustee in Bankruptcy or liquidator can use these provisions to recover assets disposed of by the debtor. However, the provisions apply whether or not bankruptcy or liquidation has taken place.

If an individual debtor is made bankrupt, all his assets (with minor exceptions) at the date of sequestration become automatically vested in the Official Trustee: Bankruptcy Act 1966 ss 58, 116. When a company such as Carb is wound up, its assets do not vest in the liquidator but he assumes control over the company and its property (NCC ss 374, 396) and dispositions of or levies against Carb's assets are void (NCC ss 368, 401) as from the commencement of the winding up (NCC ss 365, 393).

In addition the Official Trustee can recover other assets under various sections of the Bankruptcy Act, the most important of which are ss 121 and 122 which also apply to companies in liquidation by virtue of NCC s 451.

Note that some of the cases extracted below were decided under the previous Bankruptcy Act 1924 s 95 which corresponded to the present s 122 and that where the cases refer to s 293 Companies Act 1961, you should now read s 451 Companies Code 1981.

The gist of both Conveyancing Act s 37A and Bankruptcy Act s 121 is the need to prove intent to defraud creditors. Cases decided under one section are useful in applying the other. There is no limit on the time period between the fraudulent disposition and the application to have it set aside. Section 121 should be read in conjunction with s 6:

6 A reference in this Act to an intent to defraud the creditors of a person or to defeat or delay the creditors of a person shall be read as including an intent to defraud, or to defeat or delay, any one or more of those creditors.

The combination of s 6 with s 121 raises interesting questions as to the relationship of s 121 with s 122. Can a transfer of a debtor's property to one creditor be in fraud of his other creditors under s 121? If so, what is the purpose of s 122? If not, what is the purpose of s 6?

What are the criteria for determining an intent to defraud?

Re Barnes: Ex parte Stapleton; Barnes & Anor
Supreme Court of Queensland, exercising Federal Jurisdiction in Bankruptcy
(1961) 19 ABC 126

Gibbs J: This motion is brought by Leslie Thomas Stapleton, the trustee of the property of Edgar John Barnes, a bankrupt, against the bankrupt and Nellie May Barnes, who is the mother of the bankrupt, for the following relief in respect of an auxiliary motor vessel named "Syren" and having registered number 10367, together with all fittings, sails and gear aboard the said vessel:
  (a) a declaration that such property vested in and belonged to the applicant as such trustee as aforesaid;
  (b) a declaration that the respondent Nellie May Barnes is trustee of such property for the applicant;
  (c) an order that such respondent do execute a transfer of such property to the applicant on such terms and conditions as may be declared by the court; and
  (d) an order vesting such property in the applicant as such trustee.

[His Honour then set out the grounds expressed in the notice of motion upon which the trustee sought to recover the vessel as the property of the bankrupt.]

In effect, the notice of motion seeks a declaration that the transfer of the property was an alienation made with intent to defraud creditors within the meaning of s 46 of the Mercantile Acts 1867 to 1896, which reproduces the English statute 13 Eliz 1 c 5, [see now Property Law Act 1974 s 172] or that it was an act of bankruptcy under s 52(b) of the Bankruptcy Act 1924-1960 [see now Bankruptcy Act 1966 s 40(1)(b)] with the result that the property vested in the applicant by the operation of the doctrine of relation back. If the applicant makes out his case that the bankrupt and Nellie May Barnes conspired or combined to defraud the bankrupt's creditors, or in other words that the transaction involving the transfer of the property was entered into by both parties with the actual intention of defrauding creditors, the applicant will, in the circumstances of this case, be entitled to a declaration under either statute . . .

The bankrupt presented a debtor's petition on the 24 February 1961, and a sequestration order was made on the 28 February 1961. The transactions which the applicant now seeks to impeach occurred on the 24 January 1961. On that date the bankrupt was in serious financial difficulties. He was the lessee and licensee of an hotel at Ipswich, but he had given a bill of mortgage over the lease and a collateral bill of sale over the furniture, plant and stock-in-trade of the hotel to Deposit and Investment Co Ltd to secure repayment of a debt which, at that date, amounted to about £3000. He had made default in payment of principal and interest under the mortgage and had, in addition, made default in payment of the rent owing to his lessor. In addition, he owed substantial sums to other creditors, including £1300 to the Bulimba Brewery and £700 to one, Hooper. His total liabilities to his unsecured creditors amounted to about £3000.

Some time in January 1961, the bankrupt left the hotel in charge of a manager and sailed from Brisbane to Mooloolaba on the motor vessel which is the subject of this motion. After his departure from the hotel, and on or about the 17 January 1961, the mortgagee exercised its powers under the mortgage and entered into possession of the hotel and, to use the bankrupt's words, "took over everything". The mortgagee subsequently exercised its power of sale, the result of which was to discharge the bankrupt's indebtedness to the mortgagee and to leave available for the bankrupt or his creditors a small surplus, possibly of a few hundred pounds. In January 1961, however, the bankrupt did not know what, if any, surplus would result from the sale of the assets. Apart from his right to any surplus, the bankrupt had virtually no assets except the property now in question. When he presented his petition, he showed his assets as amounting to £2 8s 11d.

On the 24 January 1961, the bankrupt sold the motor vessel, together with radio, sails and equipment, to Nellie May Barnes for the sum of £800. On the same day, an indenture was made between Nellie May Barnes and the bankrupt whereby Nellie May Barnes agreed to lease to the bankrupt, who agreed to take and rent from her, the vessel together with its sails, radio and fittings for the term of 10 years commencing from the twenty-fifth day of January 1961, at a rental of £600 payable in advance by a payment of £300 on the signing of the indenture and the balance of £300 on 1 July 1961.

Nellie May Barnes drew a cheque for £800 in purported payment of the purchase price, but although the bankrupt gave her a receipt for this sum she, in fact, handed it to her solicitors who gave a receipt to the bankrupt for it. On the following day, after the solicitors had time to clear the cheque, they gave to Nellie May Barnes a cheque for £299 19s 3d (being £300 less 9d stamp duty) and gave to the bankrupt a cheque for £487 7s 3d (being £487 8s 6d less 1s 3d stamp duty). The balance of the £800 comprised £10 10s solicitors' costs and £2 1s 6d being the amount which the solicitors estimated would be payable as stamp duties.

On the same day, the 25 January 1961, the bankrupt cashed the cheque for £487 7s 3d and gave portion of the proceeds to Nellie May Barnes. The evidence does not clearly show what was the exact sum which he handed to her. In the evidence at her examination under s 80, in a number of places, she said that she was handed £300 and in another place she said she was given £285. In her oral evidence she mentioned the sum of £287 and since the evidence is clear that on the following day the bankrupt handed her £200, it is probable that £287 was the amount handed to her. In addition, the bankrupt gave her a cheque for £15.

On the following day, the 26 January 1961, the bankrupt handed to Nellie May Barnes the sum of £200. Her evidence is that the bankrupt asked her to mind £200 and to pay £15 to Mrs Geddes to whom he owed it for wages. On this occasion the bankrupt had driven to his mother's house in company with Mrs Geddes, who was present in the house when the bankrupt handed over the sum of £200. Nellie May Barnes paid Mrs Geddes the £15 and banked the balance, £185, in her own account. Subsequently, after the bankrupt was arrested on 7 February 1961, she drew £100 from the account to pay to the solicitors who were to act for him. She gave evidence that she kept the bankrupt for five months after his release from arrest, and suggests that the balance of the £200 was expended in that way.

Lending on the Security of Goods

Both respondents explain the transactions between them as arising out of the bankrupt's need for money. Their version is that the bankrupt wished to borrow £200, but that when Nellie May Barnes refused to lend him this sum without security, he offered to sell her the vessel, and it was agreed that he should sell it to her for £800 and lease it back for £600. The explanation suggested for the return of the £200 to Nellie May Barnes is that the bankrupt, who was living on the vessel, had not the means to keep it safe there; therefore, it is said, he gave it to her to mind for him. It is suggested that there was a genuine arrangement between a mother and her son designed to make money available to the latter. However, although the avowed object of the transaction was to make money available to the bankrupt, the actual result was that within two days virtually all the money which Nellie May Barnes had paid to her solicitors was back in her hands again, although it is true that out of the money she then paid £15 to Mrs Geddes. It was, of course, involved in the nature of the transactions that the possession of the vessel should be retained by the bankrupt.

The first question that arises is whether the evidence establishes that the transfer of the property by the bankrupt was fraudulent. Actual fraud, that is an actual intention to defeat or defraud creditors, must be established, and whether the existence of such an intention should be inferred from the circumstances is a question of fact. In my opinion, the only inference that can be drawn from the facts is that the bankrupt entered into these transactions with the intention of retaining for himself the benefit of the possession of the vessel and its fittings, sails and gear, and at the same time preventing that property from being taken for the benefit of his creditors in the bankruptcy that he must have known was inevitable.

In para 6 of his affidavit the bankrupt swore: "At that time I was licensee of an hotel and had some trading debts, but could, if not pressed for immediate payment of debts not then due, have paid all my debts from the said hotel business. The hotel business was on the market for sale and the value of my assets, excluding the boat, exceeded the value of my liabilities."

This evidence is untrue. The bankrupt was obviously pressed for payment of debts that were due for payment and he could not pay them. In fact, the value of his assets was considerably less than the amount of his liabilities. The bankrupt obviously was fully aware of his own financial plight. He knew that the mortgagee had entered into possession. He was virtually penniless; indeed he said that while on the vessel he lived mainly on oysters he gathered from the rocks. The reason he gave why he did not tell Nellie May Barnes anything about his financial affairs was because: "I did not want her to know I was in such a bad way, mainly. Normally, a person does not want his mother to know he is as bad as I was."

In this desperate financial situation, the fact that he agreed to pay in advance 10 years' rent for the vessel is itself evidence that the transactions were not bona fide. The conclusive fact, so far as the bankrupt is concerned, however, is the return of the £200 to Nellie May Barnes. The bankrupt's evidence was that he wanted "a loan of £200 which was to cover cheques which I had drawn and which were 'bouncing' ". If this were true, his aim in getting £200 was to bank it, and there is no explanation, consistent with his account being true, of why he returned the money to Nellie May Barnes.

There remains the question whether Nellie May Barnes was privy to the fraud. There is no evidence that she was aware of the full extent of the bankrupt's financial difficulties. She gave evidence that she knew that he had had considerable sums of money in the past, that she had seen little of him recently before the 24 January 1961, and that she believed he was in good financial position. Her evidence on this as on other matters, is contradictory and unreliable. [Following an examination of the evidence his Honour concluded:] I have no hesitation in finding that on 24 January 1961, Nellie May Barnes knew that the bankrupt had no ready money.

The explanations that she gave, in the course of her s 80 examination, as to the making of the decision to lease the vessel to the bankrupt, and as to the premature payment of the second sum of £300 or thereabouts in respect of the rental of the vessel, seem to me quite unconvincing. The crucial fact, however, is that on 26 January 1961, the bankrupt paid her back the sum of £200. Her case is that she entered into these transactions, with their attendant trouble and cost in solicitors' fees and duties, simply to make money available to her son, but in fact he did not keep the money. It is true that £15 was paid to Mrs Geddes, but it is significant that the evidence of Nellie May Barnes is that this was paid, not by the bankrupt, who was in Mrs Geddes' company, but by Nellie May Barnes. This indicates that the parties regarded the £200 as being in the disposition of Nellie May Barnes. It is also true that at a later date, sometime after the arrest of the bankrupt on 7 February 1961, Nellie May Barnes drew £100 from her account to pay the solicitors who were engaged to attempt to secure the bankrupt's release from his arrest. The notes of her examination under s 80 contain this evidence: "Is that the position, that he didn't specifically say 'Draw £100 out of that £200', but you told him the solicitor wanted £100 and he said, 'This will have to be paid'?" ... "Yes. He said 'Pay it'."

The fact that this £100 was paid under the spur of necessity at some later time does not lead me to conclude that the parties treated the money which Nellie May Barnes paid into her bank as belonging to the bankrupt. The return to Nellie May Barnes of the money that it was the whole object of the transactions to provide for the son, provides, in the absence of any convincing explanation, strong ground for inferring that both parties to the transactions regarded them as mere shams.

On the evidence, it seems to me that only one inference can be drawn, and that is that Nellie May Barnes knew that the transactions were mere shams designed to preserve the vessel and its fittings, sails and gear for the benefit of the bankrupt at the expense of his creditors.

... In the present case on the evidence, I have concluded that no other inference should be drawn than that both respondents entered into the transactions with the intent of defrauding the creditors of the bankrupt. If the applicant was required to establish fraud beyond all reasonable doubt, he has discharged his burden.

I find, therefore, that the transfer of the property was effected by the bankrupt for the purpose of defrauding his creditors and that Nellie May Barnes was privy to the fraud. There has therefore been a fraudulent conveyance within the meaning of s 46 of the Mercantile Acts. I further find that the sale of the property constituted an act of bankruptcy within s 52(b) of the Bankruptcy Act, and that Nellie May Barnes did not purchase the property in good faith...

I declare that the following property, namely an auxiliary motor vessel named "Syren" and having registered number 10367, together with all fittings, sails and gear aboard the said vessel vested in and belonged to the applicant as trustee of the property of Edgar John Barnes, a bankrupt.

I declare that the respondent, Nellie May Barnes, is trustee of such property for the applicant.

I order that the respondent, Nellie May Barnes, do execute any transfers necessary to be executed for the purpose of transferring such property to the applicant.

I order that the respondent, Nellie May Barnes, pay to the applicant his costs of and incidental to this application to be taxed.

Earlier cases have tended to distinguish between:

(1) *Voluntary dispositions (gifts)*, where the donor's intention is primary, and where it is easier to infer an intention to defraud if the donor is, or is likely to become, insolvent and the necessary consequence is to defraud creditors: *Freeman v Pope* (1870) LR 5 Ch App 538 and *Williams v Lloyd* (1934) 50 CLR 341 provide illustrations.

(2) *Dispositions for value*, where the intention of both parties must be examined since s 121(1) and (2) protect a disponee for valuable consideration who acted in good faith. The consideration need not be full consideration but must be more than nominal. Adequacy of consideration will also be relevant to the question of intent to defraud and good faith. A charge to secure existing debts may be regarded as supported by valuable consideration, provided the creditor can show that it was obtained in return for a promise of forebearance: *Glegg v Bromley* [1912] KB 474.

A number of factors have acquired the quality of badges of fraud particularly in relation to voluntary dispositions:

    (a) the generality of the gift—that is, the inclusion therein of all the grantor's property;

    (b) the grantor's continuance in possession;

    (c) secrecy of the gift;

(d) that it was made *pendente lite*;
(e) that there was a trust between the parties for the grantor's benefit;
(f) unusual statements in the conveyance as to its having been made honestly, truly and bona fide;
(g) a general power of revoking the conveyance;
(h) that it contains false recitals, or false statements as to the consideration;
(i) that the consideration is grossly inadequate.

(See May, *Fraudulent and Voluntary Dispositions,* 3rd ed, 1908, p 71, referring to *Twyne's* case (1601) 3 Co Rep 80a; 76 ER 809.)

Where the disposition by the debtor is held to be fraudulent, subsequent purchasers/encumbrancees in good faith and for value will nevertheless be protected by s 121(2): compare *Brady v Stapleton* (1952) 88 CLR 322.

VOIDABLE PREFERENCES

Section 122 of the Bankruptcy Act, which also applies to insolvent companies by virtue of NCC s 451, is more frequently used than s 121, even though it reaches back only as far as transactions taking place within six months prior to presentation of the bankruptcy or winding up petition. The reason is that it is not necessary to prove fraudulent intent on the debtor's part since s 122 requires only that the transfer, payment, etc has the proscribed effect.

Payment to a judgment creditor or sheriff on his behalf may be attacked as a preference under s 122 as well as under s 118. However, payments of rates and taxes are protected by the combined effect of s 122(2)(a) and (4)(b). Unless the payment, etc is in favour of an *existing creditor* it is not a preference: *Robertson v Grigg* (1932) 47 CLR 257 at 271, per Dixon J. A transaction voidable under s 122 will also be an act of bankruptcy under s 40(1)(b) and enable the Official Trustee to claim all property of the bankrupt from that point of time under the doctrine of relation back: s 115.

The section requires proof that the debtor is unable to pay his debts as they become due from his own money. Can Carb Pty Ltd be insolvent in this sense if its balance sheet shows an excess of assets over liabilities? Is access to temporary loan funds relevant? In *Sandell v Porter* (1966) 115 CLR 666 at 670, Barwick CJ said:

> An essential step in making out that a payment is a preference within s 95 is to establish by evidence to the satisfaction of the court that the payer was at the time of the payment insolvent. Insolvency is expressed in s 95 as an inability to pay debts as they fall due out of the debtor's own money. But the debtor's own monies are not limited to his cash resources immediately available. They extend to monies which he can procure by realisation by sale or by mortgage or pledge of his assets within a relatively short time — relative to the nature and amount of the debts and to the circumstances, including the nature of the business, of the debtor. The conclusion of insolvency ought to be clear from a consideration of the debtor's financial position in its entirety and generally speaking ought not to be drawn simply from evidence of a temporary lack of liquidity. It is the debtor's inability, utilising such cash resources as he has or can command through the use of his assets, to meet his debts as they fall due which indicates insolvency. Whether that state of his affairs has arrived is a question for the court and not one as to which expert evidence may be given in terms though no doubt experts may speak as to the likelihood of any of the debtor's assets or capacities yielding ready cash in sufficient time to meet the debts as they fall due.

Compare the statements of Barwick CJ and Taylor J in *Rees v Bank of NSW*, pp 315 and 317, *infra*.

The two most difficult aspects of s 122 are:
(a) proof of the effect of giving a preference, particularly in relation to running accounts; and
(b) the protective provision in s 122(2)(a).

"Having the Effect of Giving a Preference"

Repayment of part or all of an existing debt obviously gives the creditor an advantage, whereas the payment for goods or services presently supplied does not do so, and is also protected by s 122(2). Where there is a series of payments which are integrated as part of an entire transaction, the overall effect must be examined rather than one payment in isolation. A number of questions arise in this situation:

(1) What nexus is necessary to convert a series of payments into integrated steps of a single transaction?

(2) What is the quantum of the preference in the case of a running account? At what points are the account balances to be compared?

(3) If one security is taken for past debts and also for present or future advances, is the security void in toto?

A number of the leading cases, including *Richardson v Commercial Banking Co of Sydney Ltd, Rees v Bank of NSW,* and *Queensland Bacon Pty Ltd v Rees* are summarised in the following case:

Re Weiss; Ex parte White v John Vicars & Co Ltd
Federal Court of Bankruptcy [1970] ALR 654

Gibbs J: The applicant, Ian Eaglie White, is the trustee of the estate of Geza Weiss (the bankrupt) who became bankrupt on 26 June 1962 on his own petition which was presented on 25 June 1962. The application is for declarations and consequential orders against the respondent, John Vicars & Co Ltd. The declarations sought are that a bill of sale dated 24 January 1962 and registered on 23 May 1962, given by the bankrupt to the respondent, is void against the applicant as such trustee as a preference, priority or advantage under s 95(1) of the Bankruptcy Act 1924, as amended, and that the following payments made by the bankrupt to the respondent are void against the applicant as such trustee as preferences, priorities or advantages under s 95(1):

15 January 1962	£3000 0 0
8 March 1962	£1567 16 10
8 March 1962	£2909 19 9
16 April 1962	£2500 0 0
18 May 1962	£2500 0 0
23 May 1962	£2500 0 0

The applicant seeks orders that the respondent pay to the applicant the amount realised on the sale of the property comprised in the bill of sale or, alternatively, the fair value of such property and the amount of £14,977 16s 7d, or, alternatively, the total of the amount of such of the said payments as the court declares to be void . . .

It is conceded that in the present case at all times on and after 25 December 1961 (the date of the commencement of the period of six months before the presentation of the petition) the bankrupt was unable to pay his debts as they became due from his own money.

The six payments which the applicant seeks to recover were clearly payments in favour of a creditor. The question, however, is whether they (or any of them) had the effect of giving the creditor a preference, a priority or an advantage over the other creditors. There is no doubt that considered in isolation the effect of each payment was to give the respondent a preference, but on behalf of the respondent it is submitted that the payments formed part of a connected series of purchases and payments, whose combined effect was not to give a preference to the respondent.

The net effect of the transactions between the respondent and the bankrupt may be seen by comparing the total amount paid to the respondent on and after each relevant date with the value of the goods delivered to the bankrupt on and after that date. When the figures are examined they reveal the position to have been as follows:

Date	Amount paid on and after date shown	Goods delivered on and after date shown
15 January 1962	£14,977 16 7	£16,911 1 5
8 March 1962	£11,977 16 7	£12,657 7 2

16 April 1962	£7,500 0 0	£644 13 5
18 May 1962	£5,000 0 0	£95 4 5
23 May 1962	£2,500 0 0	£72 15 6

It is clear that for the purpose of deciding whether a payment is void within s 95(1) of the Bankruptcy Act it is the effect in fact of the making of the payment that is decisive. It is also clear that in some cases, where the payment forms part of a wider transaction, or where it is sufficiently connected with other items in a running account, it is the effect of the whole transaction, of all the connected items, that has to be regarded. That this is so was recognised by Lukin J in *Re Patullo; Ex parte Official Receiver* (1931) 3 ABC 197, a case in which the bankrupt purchased goods from the respondent on monthly account and made certain payments on account; the balance of the account increased from month to month since the value of new purchases exceeded the amount of payments made. Lukin J held that there was no preference...

The question was considered by the High Court in *Richardson v Commercial Banking Co of Sydney Ltd* (1952) 85 CLR 110; [1952] ALR 315, a case in which deposits were made by a debtor to his bank account pursuant to an arrangement (which was carried out) that the bank would, so far as the deposits permitted, honour cheques which the debtor had given or was about to give. The court held that (except in the case of one item paid in as the account was closed) there was no preference. In the judgment of the court the following appears (CLR at 132): "In considering whether the real effect of a payment was to work a preference its actual business character must be seen and when it forms part of an entire transaction which if carried out to its intended conclusion will leave the creditor without any preference priority or advantage over other creditors the payment cannot be isolated and construed as a preference." Later in the judgment the court went on to say (at 133): "A running account of any debtor who has reached insolvency must present difficulties under s 95. A debtor who pays something off his grocer's account in order to induce the shop keeper to give him further supplies of groceries can hardly be held, as it seems to us, to give the grocer a preference, if that was the clear basis of the payment. If the grocer credited the money as a payment for the future deliveries instead of the past deliveries of groceries he would in the end be in exactly the same position and yet he could not be attacked as having received a preference. But without stating any principle with an application beyond the facts of this case, it is enough to decide that the payments into the office account possessed in point of fact a business purpose common to both parties which so connected them with the subsequent debits to the account as to make it impossible to pause at any payment into the account and treat it as having produced an immediate effect to be considered independently of what followed and so to be adjudged a preference." From this passage it appears that the mere fact that a payment is in discharge of an existing or past indebtedness does not necessarily mean that its effect has to be considered in isolation (see also *Queensland Bacon Pty Ltd v Rees* (1966) 115 CLR 266 at 284; [1966] ALR 855 at 860-1) and, further, that in deciding whether payments are so integrally connected with counter-payments that the ultimate effect of the course of dealings has to be considered to determine whether the payments are preferences it is necessary to look at their business purpose or business character: see also *Rees v Bank of New South Wales* (1964) 111 CLR 210 at 221-2; [1965] ALR 139 at 144.

In *Queensland Bacon Pty Ltd v Rees,* the High Court had to consider a case in which payments of money were made by a retail company to wholesalers upon running accounts during periods when goods were supplied by the wholesalers to the company. The majority of the court (Barwick CJ and Kitto J) held that the payments in question (with one exception) were received in good faith within s 95(2) of the Bankruptcy Act, but the learned Chief Justice was further of the view that, at least in three of the four cases before the court, there was a preference only to the extent to which the debit to the company in the running account had been reduced by the combined effect of the debits and credits from the date of the first impugned payment to the date of liquidation. Kitto J did not find it necessary to consider this question, but Menzies J who dissented, held that the payments made by the company were preferences. Barwick CJ held that the net effect of the operations on the running account was the determinant of the fact and extent of the preference in those cases where the basis of the payments made to reduce the indebtedness on the account was the continuance of the supply of goods by the wholesaler to the company: see 115 CLR at 285, 290 and 300 and cf 297. In that case there was no binding agreement that the company's order would be accepted or that payment according to the agreed terms for goods already delivered would entitle the company to obtain further supplies on credit, but Barwick CJ held that it was not necessary that the ensuring of further supplies should be an express purpose of the payment. He said, at 285-6: "But, although in one of the quotations I have made from *Richardson's* case (1952) 85 CLR at 133, it was said that the stated basis of the payment should be 'clear', the court in so expressing itself was not, in my view, limiting the type of situation to which its remarks were addressed to those occasions on which the payment was made under express arrangements for a continuance of supply. In my opinion, it is enough if, on the facts of any case, the court can feel confident that implicit in the circumstances in which the payment is made is a mutual assumption by the parties that there will be a continuance of the relation of debtor and creditor in the running account, so that, to use the expressions employed in *Richardson's* case, 'it is impossible' — I interpolate, in a business sense — 'to pause at any payment into the account and treat it as having produced an immediate effect to be considered independently of what followed . . .'." In the three cases in which he held that no preferences had been made, Barwick CJ had regard to the net effect of the operations from the date of the first impugned payment to the date of the commencement of the liquidation because, in the circumstances of the case, no fact or event existed or occurred between those limiting dates to warrant any different conclusion being drawn between one payment and another. However, the learned Chief Justice said (at 282): "But there will be occasions when there will be such facts or events intervening between the first payment which is impugned and the commencement of the liquidation as will require the limiting dates to be different, the terminal date for consideration of the state of the running account being for that reason earlier than the date of the commencement of the liquidation." Menzies J in holding that the payments were preferential, placed reliance on the fact that the parties anticipated that the monthly payments required to be made would exceed the value of the goods that would in the ordinary course be supplied monthly, so that as time went on the account would be reduced: see at 315. He said that the court in *Richardson's* case, in the passage already cited, "had in mind a case where the payments to be made would not exceed the value of the groceries to be supplied", and went on to say: "In the present case it seems to me that it was intended that, upon each occasion in the future when the appellant was to receive a cheque from its debtor, its position would be improved, notwithstanding current supplies and that the object of the arrangement was to bring about a reduction of an existing liability": see at 317.

In the present case, although it is possible to say that some of the payments (particularly those made on and before 8 March 1962) were in discharge of an identifiable past indebtedness, the account kept by the respondent (Exhibit 10) was in the ordinary form of a running account in which debits and credits are recorded chronologically and in which payments are not shown as attributable to any particular deliveries but are brought generally into credit. Of the first three impugned payments (one made on 15 January 1962 and two on 8 March 1962) it seems to me clearly appropriate to say (in the words of Barwick CJ in *Queensland Bacon Pty Ltd v Rees* (CLR at 283 and 286; ALR at 860 and 862)) that each was "a payment on account of a 'running' indebtedness, the payment not in anywise intended or understood to end the relationship of the debtor and creditor, but rather to ensure its continuance", and that "implicit in the circumstances in which the payment is made is a mutual assumption by the parties that there will be a continuance of the relationship of buyer and seller with resultant continuance of the relation of debtor and creditor in the running account". The payments were made to reduce a past indebtedness, but they were made on the clear assumption that further supplies of cloth would be delivered in the future on credit in accordance with the arrangement on which the running account was operated. Of course, there was no express agreement that cloth would be supplied provided that payments were made and withheld if payments ceased, but it is quite clear that both parties contemplated that further deliveries would be made if the payments were made and it is a proper inference that they understood that, although the respondent was not insisting on prompt payment in strict accordance with the agreed terms of credit as a condition precedent to delivery, the continuance of some payments was necessary to ensure future deliveries. Not only is this the proper inference to be drawn from the circumstances of the case but the witnesses in evidence agreed that this was so. [Evidence from Hoar, the secretary of the respondent company and the bankrupt was cited to support the view that the payments were made to ensure continuance of supply of the goods.] On behalf of the applicant some reliance was placed on the submission that the respondent, having accepted the orders placed by the bankrupt, was contractually bound to deliver the goods. Therefore, it was said, the payments were not made to ensure the continuance of supply because the respondent was bound to perform its contract or pay damages for its breach whether the payments were made or not. However, whether or not the respondent was legally obliged to continue deliveries even if payments completely failed (and it is unnecessary to examine the legal position in this regard) from a business point of view the payments made were connected with future deliveries. If the bankrupt had ceased to pay, the respondent might well have decided that it was better to face the hazards of possible litigation than to supply large quantities of goods to a buyer who was apparently unlikely to pay for them.

Each of the three payments of £3000, £1567 16s 10d and £2909 19s 9d was made in reduction of a running account and the basis of the payments was the continuance of the supply of cloth to the bankrupt. Moreover, the parties must have assumed, when each of these payments was made, that the value of the goods to be supplied on and after the date of each payment would exceed the amount of the payment, and this was in fact the case. On any view, the question whether any of these payments was preferential in effect can only be determined by looking at the net effect of the series of payments and deliveries on the running account, and when this is done it is clearly seen that none of these payments had the effect of giving a preference to the respondent.

By the time the payment of 16 April 1962 was made the position had changed. Of the orders previously placed and accepted, only a few remained to be fulfilled, and of the orders placed on 16 March 1962, and not accepted, most were for delivery in August and the quantities which the parties contemplated supplying before that date under those orders were quite small. It appears from Exhibits 14 and 15 that goods delivered on and after 16 April 1962, pursuant to orders placed before March, amounted to about £528, and goods delivered on and after that date pursuant to orders placed in March amounted to about £116. On the other hand, the parties intended substantial payments to be made, since if the promises made by the bankrupt on 3 April 1962 had been fulfilled, a total of £20,000 would have been paid to the credit of the account during April and May. In other words, when the three final payments each of £2500 were made, the parties contemplated that the payments to the credit of the account would greatly exceed the deliveries, and that the debit balance on the account would be substantially reduced. It is true that the parties contemplated some further deliveries on the account, but these were to be insignificant in comparison with the value of the goods supplied until, after an interval of a few months, deliveries were again resumed. It would seem to me that if the views of Menzies J were accepted the payments on and after 16 April 1962 would have to be held to be preferences. However, in the circumstances in which the High Court was divided I ought, I think, to follow the judgment of the learned Chief Justice. I have considered whether, on that view, it would be right to regard the running account as having had an earlier terminal date than the date of the bankruptcy, but it seems to me that the three final payments were still made on a running account on the basis of the continuance of supply, even though it was contemplated that, for a time at least, the value of the goods to be supplied would not be large in itself or as great as the amount of the payments to be made. In my opinion these payments also cannot be considered in isolation, and it is the net effect of the operations from the first impugned payment to the date of the bankruptcy that determines the fact and the extent of preference. However, when the applicant trustee fails in his challenge to the validity of the earlier payments, he is entitled, in the alternative, to choose a later date as the starting point of the examination of the net effect of the operations on the account. In *Rees v Bank of New South Wales* (1964) 111 CLR 210 at 221; [1965] ALR 139 at 143, Barwick CJ said: "In my opinion the liquidator can choose any point during the statutory period in his endeavour to show that from that point on there was a preferential payment..." In the present case, having failed in his challenge to the payments made on 15 January and 8 March, the applicant can impugn the payment of 16 April and claim that the net effect of payments on and after that date was to give a preference. In the circumstances that I have mentioned the change in the situation that had occurred by 16 April 1962, provides abundant justification for taking that date as the starting point of an examination of the account. When that is done, it is seen that during the period on and from 16 April 1962, payments amounted to £7500 and deliveries to £644 13s 5d and that the payments had the effect of giving a preference to the extent of £6855 6s 7d.

The question remains whether this preference is protected by s 95(2) of the Act, but that may conveniently be postponed until a similar question that arises in relation to the execution of the bill of sale, whose date of course is earlier than that of the payments that I have found to be preferential, has been considered.

To say that the earlier payments were not preferences is not the end of the matter so far as the payments made on 8 March 1962 are concerned. I am about to turn to the challenge which is made to the validity of the bill of sale. If that challenge were to succeed, and the bill of sale were held to be void as a preference, the results would be that the execution of the bill of sale would be held to have amounted to the commission of an act of bankruptcy within s 52(c) [1966 Act s 40(1)(b)], and that the bankruptcy of the debtor would, under s 90 [1966 Act s 115], be deemed to have relation back to and to commence at 24 January 1962. The further consequence would be that all payments made by the bankrupt to the respondent after the date of the act of bankruptcy would be void as against the trustee unless they were protected by the provisions of s 96 [1966 Act s 123]: see *Radio Corp Pty Ltd v Bear* [1962] ALR 42; (1961) 108 CLR 414 at 422 and 430, and *Re Levine* (1942) 13 ABC 37. It was conceded in the present case that the respondent could not claim the protection of s 96 because if the execution of the bill of sale amounted to the commission of an act of bankruptcy the respondent at the time of the payments had notice of that act of bankruptcy. If, therefore, the execution of the bill of sale was an act of bankruptcy, all payments made after 24 January 1962 would be recoverable by the applicant whether they were preferences or not.

The bill of sale was, of course, a conveyance or transfer of property, it was made in favour of a creditor and at first sight it would appear incontestable that it had the effect of giving that creditor a preference, a priority or an advantage over the other creditors. However, it was submitted on behalf of the respondent that the respondent was at the time of the execution of the bill of sale already secured by an equitable mortgage, which had been created either in August 1961, or at the latest in November 1961, and that the bill of sale was not a preference, for it gave to the respondent no greater interest in the bankrupt's property than the respondent already had. In support of this submission reliance was placed on the decision of the High Court in *Burns v Stapleton* (1959) 102 CLR 97. [His Honour then referred to the facts in that case.] The decision is clear authority for the proposition that the execution of a formal mortgage document giving security over property which is already subject to an equitable mortgage in favour of the mortgagee in respect of the same debt is not a preference. The question, however, is whether in the present case there did come into being any equitable mortgage in favour of the respondent at any time before the execution of the bill of sale.

It has long been settled that a contract for valuable consideration and capable of specific performance by which it is agreed to mortgage property creates an equitable mortgage of that property: see *Holroyd v Marshall* (1861) 10 HLC 191 at 209; 11 ER 999 at 1006; *Tebb v Hodge* (1869) LR 5 CP 73 at 80; and *Palmer v Carey* [1926] AC 703 at 706-7; [1926] All ER Rep 650. On behalf of the applicant it was submitted that in the present case the parties did not, at any time before 24 January 1962, enter into a binding agreement for the giving of a bill of sale. It was submitted that neither party entered into any anterior contract containing the terms and conditions expressed in the written bill of sale and that neither side intended to contract otherwise than by means of the instrument which was eventually signed and that, on the authority of *Neill v Hewens* (1953) 89 CLR 1, and *Hircock v Farrelly* [1960] Qd R 26, no contract was ever made.

[His Honour then considered the evidence relating to the question whether there was any previous equitable mortgage in the form of an oral agreement to give a bill of sale, and continued:] It is true that on 20 November 1961, after the parties had reached agreement on certain issues, the bankrupt said that on his return to Brisbane he would sign the bill of sale. However, there was no consideration for this promise. It cannot be said that the consideration was an agreement to accept the orders and supply the goods, for the orders had already been accepted and the goods were in the course of being supplied. The bankrupt's remark was merely a statement of his intention that he would bring the negotiations to finality by signing the bill. I am unable to find any anterior oral contract to give a bill of sale over the assets that were subsequently made subject to the written bill of sale. There were a number of binding agreements to supply the goods and no doubt these were entered into on the assumption that some sort of security would be given, but it was not a term of any of those agreements that the price of the goods should be secured by a bill of sale over the relevant assets. It seems to me that *Burns v Stapleton* is distinguishable on the ground that in the present case there was no binding agreement to give a bill of sale and that on ordinary principles it must be held that no equitable mortgage resulted.

It follows therefore that, in my opinion, the effect of the execution of the bill of sale on 24 January 1962 was to give the respondent a preference, a priority or an advantage over the other creditors. The question that then arises is whether the transaction is protected by s 95(2) which provides that nothing in the section shall effect, inter alia, the rights of a purchaser, payee or encumbrancer for good faith, and for valuable consideration and in the ordinary course of business.

In the present case the respondent was an encumbrancer for valuable consideration; it is enough to refer to the promise to forbear to sue which was good consideration: see *Glegg v Bromley* [1912] 3 KB 474; [1911-13] All ER Rep 1138. Moreover, in my opinion, the bill of sale was given "in the ordinary course of business". The meaning of that expression has been considered in a number of cases in the High Court. The various tests that have been suggested have recently been collected in the judgments in *Taylor v White* (1964) 110 CLR 129, and I need not restate them at length although I shall use the words of some of them. It seems to me that, where a trader who seeks to be supplied with goods on credit promises to give security for payment of the price, and is allowed to incur a debt for the price of the goods on the faith of that promise, even though the promise is not legally binding, the subsequent execution of a bill of sale for the purpose of giving effect to the earlier arrangement is "a fair transaction, and what a man might do without having any bankruptcy in view"; it falls into place as "part of the undistinguished common flow of business done", "calling for no remark and arising out of no special or particular situation". In accordance with ordinary business standards it would be honest and fair for the parties in that situation to execute a bill of sale. It would, of course, have been different if the execution of the bill of sale had been postponed to confer some advantage on the trader, for example, to prevent the possible damage to his credit that might result from the registration of a bill of sale or from the knowledge that it had been executed but that did not occur in the present case.

The question then arises whether the bill of sale was executed in good faith. If the respondent knew or suspected that the bankrupt was insolvent it would not have acted in good faith: see *Queensland Bacon Pty Ltd v Rees* (CLR at 287; ALR at 863). However, it is clear that the respondent did not know or suspect the insolvency of the bankrupt and the very fact that it continued to supply goods to the value of £16,911 strongly supports this conclusion. It then becomes necessary to consider whether the case comes within s 95(4)... This sub-section casts no onus on the creditor; its effect is that, if the court is positively satisfied that the circumstances of the payment justify the inference by it that the creditor knew or had reason to suspect the insolvency and the preference, the court is precluded from finding good faith: *Queensland Bacon Pty Ltd v Rees* CLR at 287. To satisfy the sub-section, "it is not enough that the circumstances are such as to lead to the inference that the creditor had reason to suspect that the debtor might be insolvent. The words of the sub-section, to my mind, are quite clear that it is the fact of actual insolvency which must be known or suspected. To be insolvent, the debtor must be unable, as distinct from being merely unwilling, to pay his debts as they fall due. It is one thing to suspect a man's solvency in the sense that one doubts whether he is solvent or insolvent. It is another thing to suspect that he is in fact insolvent. It is of the latter suspicion that s 95(4), in my opinion, speaks": *Queensland Bacon Pty Ltd v Rees*, CLR at 291-2, per Barwick CJ. "The notion which 'reason to suspect' expresses in sub-s (4), is, I think, of something which in all the circumstances would create in the mind of a reasonable person in the position of the payee an actual apprehension or fear that the situation of the payer is in actual fact that which the sub-section describes — a mistrust of the payer's ability to pay his debts as they become due and of the effect which acceptance of the payment would have as between the payee and the other creditors": CLR at 303, per Kitto J.

In the present case the respondent knew in August that the bankrupt then had other creditors. Hoar knew from what he had been told and from what he had seen that the bankrupt's stocks were worth about £18,000, and since, up to that time, the stock supplied by the respondent would not have exceeded about £6560 the balance must have come from other suppliers. The bankrupt had said that his creditors at 30 June 1961 totalled £14,700 and that he had paid off £6000 during July. This meant, of course, that the bankrupt's creditors amounted to over £8000. The respondent did not thereafter, at any time before the execution of the bill of sale, expressly inquire whether these creditors had been paid, but some undated notes (Exhibit 24) made by Hoar show clearly that in November Hoar mentioned the possibility of another creditor obtaining judgment against the bankrupt, and Hoar admitted in cross-examination that at the time when the bill was signed he would have assumed that there were other creditors and indeed that, in the circumstances, it would have been impossible for the respondent to be the only creditor. The respondent certainly had reason to suspect that there were other creditors, and must have suspected that the conversion of the respondent's unsecured debt into a debt secured by the bill of sale would have had the effect of giving the respondent a preference over those other creditors: see *Downs Distributing Co Pty Ltd v Associated Blue Star Stores Pty Ltd* (1948) 76 CLR 463 at 481. The question remains whether it can be inferred that the respondent had reason to suspect that the bankrupt was unable to pay his debts as they became due. It is the circumstances under which the bill of sale was executed that must support this inference, although those circumstances would include the respondent's knowledge of anterior events: see *Queensland Bacon Pty Ltd v Rees* CLR at 292.

On this issue the applicant in argument placed great reliance on the dishonour of the cheques given by the bankrupt in payment of his account. In *Queensland Bacon Pty Ltd v Rees*, the majority of the High Court rejected the view that the giving by a retailer to his wholesale supplier of a cheque that was dishonoured (it not being suggested that the dishonour was due to error or mere formal deficiency) necessarily gave reason to suspect that the retailer was insolvent. Barwick CJ after mentioning the evidence that in one of the cases the marking on the dishonour indicated that arrangements to put the drawer in funds were in train and that payment on representation was probable, went on to say (CLR at 293): "It is, to my mind, too narrow a view of insolvency to say that the dishonour of the cheque in such circumstances gave reason to suspect that the debtor was insolvent. The general restriction of credit then present must have affected a great number of quite solvent people who would find themselves temporarily short of cash and under a necessity to make arrangements to cover the 'short fall' in their overdraft accommodation. The appellant had every reason, in my opinion, to think, in the circumstances, that the debtor whom he understood to have a large, valuable, saleable and well-managed stock would be in a position speedily to make arrangements to remedy what appeared to the appellant to be his temporary lack of liquidity. I would not wish to minimise the significance of the issue of a cheque by a trader which is dishonoured by his banker — particularly by a trader whose credit is focal to his survival in business. That the dishonour calls for inquiry and probably some action is undoubted and, in some circumstances, it may provide ground for suspicion of insolvency. But, here in the circumstances, I have outlined, although it indicated a lack of liquidity, it did not, in my respectful opinion, indicate insolvency." Kitto J (CLR at 302) said: "In many situations, of course, the dishonour of a cheque, unless otherwise explained, carries a strong suggestion of insolvency; but in others it may indicate, to those who are constantly dealing with the drawer and know the general course he is pursuing in his business, no more than a policy of wringing the last ounce of credit out of everyone who can be fobbed off with promises."

In the present case, when the bill of sale was executed on 24 January 1962, eight cheques had been given to the respondent by the bankrupt in payment of his account. Of these, one had been post-dated and four dishonoured. Of the four dishonoured cheques, one had been replaced by other cheques, another had been paid without notice of dishonour having been given, and a third (drawn on 23 November 1961) had been paid after a delay of about six weeks. The fourth cheque (that drawn on 1 December 1961) remained unpaid although the bankrupt had said that it would be met and it was in fact subsequently paid. The length of time for which the cheques drawn on 23 November 1961 and 1 December 1961 had remained dishonoured would, it seems to me, have given considerable cause for disquiet to a reasonable creditor in the position of the respondent. This disquiet might have been increased by the knowledge that the bankrupt had only recently been bankrupt, and that his income tax returns had not been submitted for four years. It must have been thought somewhat surprising, also, that the bankrupt had no overdraft. On the other hand, at that time credit restrictions had caused difficulties to traders generally, and the bankrupt had explained that he sometimes had difficulties in collecting debts. He had substantial stocks of cloth, although it was true that it was not all capable of immediate realisation; some of it at least had to be made into garments before it could be sold. Moreover, the fact of the execution of the bill of sale itself gave no additional reason to suspect that the bankrupt was insolvent; it was executed to give effect to an arrangement made some months before and the delay in its execution was apparently quite unconnected with any financial difficulties on the part of the bankrupt. Whether the circumstances were such that there was reason to suspect insolvency is a question of degree, but in the present case, although it is clear that a reasonable man in the position of the respondent might have doubted whether the bankrupt was insolvent or not, I am not satisfied that the circumstances in which the bill of sale was executed justify the inference that the respondent had reason to suspect that the bankrupt was in fact insolvent.

In reaching this conclusion I cannot ignore that, on 24 January 1962, the respondent was giving and intended to give further credit to the bankrupt, and apparently did not suspect insolvency for, although the question is an objective one, it is legitimate in deciding it to have regard to the contemporaneous view of a businessman, who had seen the bankrupt's stocks and was familiar with the trade: see *Queensland Bacon Pty Ltd v Rees* CLR at 300-1.

I hold that the respondent took the bill of sale in good faith and for valuable consideration and in the ordinary course of business and that the bill of sale accordingly is not void as against the applicant.

I may now return to the question whether the preference that resulted from the making of the three payments each of £2500 is protected by s 95(2) and it is convenient to pass immediately to the questions raised by s 95(4).

It is unnecessary to repeat the account of what had occurred before 24 January 1962, and it is sufficient to recommence the narrative of events after the execution of the bill of sale. At the conversation on 24 January 1962, after the execution of the bill of sale, the bankrupt promised that the cheque for £1567 16s 10d would be paid on 25 January 1962, that a cheque for £2909 19s 9d would be paid on 15 February 1962 and that the sum of £14,762 would be paid during the months of February, March and April. In fact, the cheque for £1567 16s 10d was not paid until 8 March 1962, and the cheque for £2909 19s 9d drawn on 12 February 1962, was dishonoured on 16 February but paid on 8 March 1962. As to the proposed payment of the indebtedness of £14,762, nothing was paid in February, but one cheque for £2500 had been drawn on 23 March 1962, dishonoured, and then paid on 16 April, and another cheque for £2500 which had been drawn on 30 March 1962 had been dishonoured and not paid. Thus, by 16 April 1962, there had been three further notices of dishonour, and further failures by the bankrupt to keep his promises as to payment.

On 3 April 1962 there had occurred the conversation in the course of which the bankrupt had said that the outstanding cheques would be paid in April — and, of course, the payment on 16 April partly fulfilled this promise — and that he would pay another £5000 in April and £10,000 in May. The bankrupt had then said that he still had creditors amounting to £7500 so that, accepting this figure, it is clear that no great reduction had been made in the indebtedness which he owed to his other creditors since July 1961. Moreover, Tanner [an accountant called as a witness by applicant trustee White] had given Hoar the balance sheet as at 30 June 1961 (Annexure "A" to Tanner's affidavit), which showed sundry creditors at that date as £35,391 18s 11d and this was inconsistent with what the bankrupt had said earlier. Although the respondent was still supplying goods, in dwindling quantities, to fulfil existing orders, no further orders were being accepted. Hoar had requested that the bankrupt's accounts be written up. Optimism had evaporated; if suspicion had not taken its place, at least the number of occasions on which cheques had been dishonoured and the bankrupt had failed to pay in accordance with his promises provided grounds for suspicion.

The circumstances of the two final payments even more strongly justify the inference that the respondent had reason to suspect the bankrupt's insolvency. It was by then quite apparent that the debtor's various promises of payment had been broken, and the fact that the four cheques bearing different dates were sent under cover of one letter, although it might have been unimportant under different circumstances, became rather more suspicious when viewed in the light of a history of dishonoured cheques and delayed payments. After 23 May no further deliveries were made to the bankrupt.

I am satisfied that the three cheques, each for £2500, paid respectively on 16 April 1962, 18 May 1962, and 23 May 1962, were all paid under such circumstances as to lead to the inference that the respondent had reason to suspect that the debtor was unable to pay his debts as they became due and that the effect of the payments would be to give it a preference over the other creditors. It follows that these payments, to the extent to which they had the effect of giving a preference, are void as against the applicant. The applicant is accordingly entitled to recover £6855 6s 7d which I have held is the amount of the preference which resulted from these payments...

I order the respondent to pay to the applicant the sum of £6855 6s 7d.

Declaration and orders accordingly.

Bankruptcy Act s 122 applies directly to dispositions by companies by virtue of NCC s 451 so that decisions under both Acts are based on the same principles. The application of s 122 in a case involving the liquidation of a company is illustrated in *Re Discovery Books Pty Ltd* (1972) 20 FLR 470, and *Rees v Bank of NSW*, below.

A transfer of goods to an existing creditor for less than full consideration may also constitute a preference under s 122 eg, *Radio Corp Pty Ltd v Bear* (1961) 108 CLR 414. Similarly, a mortgage or charge in favour of an existing, but previously unsecured, creditor will give that creditor a priority or advantage which is voidable under s 122 unless for fresh consideration eg, *Burns v Stapleton* (1959) 102 CLR 97; and *Re Weiss,* p 306, *supra.*

TRANSACTIONS PROTECTED BY S 122(2)

As mentioned earlier, the intention of the debtor is irrelevant under s 122 and payments for the concurrent supply of goods or services normally confer no advantage on the payee. Accordingly, s 122(2) contains an important protection for creditors who receive goods, payments or security from a debtor, and also for those acquiring title through or under such creditors. As might be anticipated, the creditor must establish that he took with the three elements of good faith, valuable consideration and in the ordinary course of business. The onus of proof is on the creditor or person taking through him: s 122(3). These three elements are considered in the cases which follow. These cases were decided under ss 95 and 96 of the Bankruptcy Act 1924 which are now represented by ss 122 and 123 of the present Act. Conveyances, transfers, payments etc made pursuant to a maintenance agreement or order are also protected under s 122(2). Note that s 122(4)(c) precludes the creditor proving good faith if the circumstances indicate that it knew or had reason to suspect both the debtor's insolvency and the preferential effect of the payment, transfer or charge. This is an objective test according to the standards of the ordinary reasonable man: *Downs Distributing Co Pty Ltd v Associated Blue Star Stores Pty Ltd* (1948) 76 CLR 463.

Where the preference takes the form of repayment of a previous loan or indebtedness, that debt is itself valuable consideration: *Taylor v White* (1964) 110 CLR 129. In other cases, such as where the debtor gives a mortgage or charge, valuable consideration must be proved, eg, the agreement to continue to supply goods, or to forbear to sue for immediate repayment of the loan: *Glegg v Bromley* [1912] 3 KB 474; *Re Weiss,* p 306, *supra.*

Rees v Bank of New South Wales
High Court of Australia (1964) 111 CLR 210

Barwick CJ: The appellant, liquidator of Hennessy's Self Service Stores Pty Ltd (the company) sought of the Supreme Court of Queensland an order that a sum of money, "representing moneys of the company paid to the respondent bank" (the bank) "by deposit to the overdrawn account of the company between 1 December 1960 and the commencement of the liquidation, 10 February 1961, to the extent that they were not disbursed by the Bank in that period in honouring cheques of the company drawn on that account, constituted a preference, priority or advantage" within the meaning, and void by reason, of the Companies Acts 1931-1960 of the State of Queensland, and for consequential orders for payment of such sum by the bank to the liquidator.

Section 275 of the Companies Acts 1931-1960, which because of s 2 of the Companies Act of 1961 of the State of Queensland and the date of the presentation of the petition, still governs the matter, requires that the question be determined in accordance with the provisions of s 95 of the Bankruptcy Act 1924-1960 (Cth), the date of the presentation of the petition being taken to correspond with the presentation of a bankruptcy petition for the purposes of applying that section.

The Supreme Court refused the order which the appellant sought. The primary judge found that deposits and withdrawals had taken place between 1 December 1960 and 8 February 1961 to the extent necessary to effect an overall reduction in the company's overdrawn account to the claimed extent: that throughout the period of these operations the company was unable to pay its debts as they became due: that to the extent of the reduction in the account in the period the bank obtained a preference, priority or advantage: that the transactions (meaning the payments in and withdrawals) took place in the ordinary course of business.

As the challenged transactions took place within six months of the presentation of the petition to wind up the company, the primary judge entered on the question whether the transactions were in good faith, properly regarding the bank as bearing the onus of proof in this respect. No express finding was made that there was valuable consideration for the transactions, apparently this being assumed by the parties and by the judge; and I think, in this case, rightly so. His Honour accepted the view that the bank had been bona fide in receiving and applying the payments in question and accordingly refused the liquidator's application.

The material facts of the matter are recited in the judgment of my brother Taylor and I have no need to repeat them in any detail. It would appear that his Honour the primary judge accepted the view that the bank, through the officers concerned, genuinely believed throughout the period that the company was carrying trading stocks well in excess of the amount of its liabilities, that the company's current financial difficulties were associated with seasonal requirements of its business, the slow movement of some parts of its stocks, and the incautious and accelerated rate of the expansion of its business.

His Honour makes no reference in his reasons for judgment to the imperative provisions of sub-s (4) of s 95 of the Bankruptcy Act (Cth). But for that sub-section, I would not disturb his Honour's finding of bona fides in the bank in connection with the transactions in question. But in my opinion the inference that the bank at least had reason to suspect that the company throughout the period of the payments was unable to pay its debts and that the effect of the payments, as they were to be applied by the bank, would be to give the bank a preference, priority or advantage over the other creditors is inevitable. That the bank bears the onus of negativing such an inference makes the result of this appeal even more certain.

The respondent's counsel submitted that, because the bank held the beliefs, which the primary judge accepted it did hold, as to the extent of the company's trading stock and of the causes of its current embarrassments, it could not be said either to know or to have reason to suspect the company's insolvency — its inability to meet its debts as they became due. But this submission springs from a basic misconception and is not borne out by the judgments of this court to which my brother Taylor refers. It is quite true that a trader, to remain solvent, does not need to have ready cash by him to cover his commitments as they fall for payment, and that in determining whether he can pay his debts as they become due regard must be had to his realisable assets. The extent to which their existence will prevent a conclusion of insolvency will depend on a number of surrounding circumstances, one of which must be the nature of the assets and in the case of a trader, the nature of his business. Here the company's business was the sale of foodstuffs through a number of retail outlets. The asset whose value was said to negative a conclusion of insolvency, or at any rate to obviate the suspicion of it, was its trading stock of foodstuffs. In the ordinary course of the company's business this asset was not available to be realised except by means of retail sales through its various shops. It is possible, of course, in a business such as that of the company for excess stocks to be realised otherwise than through the channels of the company's retail business: but, although there had been an abortive negotiation for a total takeover of the company's business, no proposal to realise surplus stock by some bulk disposal for cash was in contemplation. The bank was not contemplating that the company intended to liquidate its business but to carry it on. Indeed the bank with a degree of sympathy was assisting the company to carry on the business. The stock in trade was clearly not an asset which was available to be realised to meet current debts except in the ordinary course of the company's business, a course which had proved itself inadequate. In this connection, the test applied by Lindley LJ in *Ex parte Russell; Re Butterworth* (1882) 19 Ch D 588, in determining whether a voluntary settlement by a trader was made at a time when he was able to pay his debts without the aid of the settled property, namely, that the trader should be able to pay his debts in the way he is proposing to pay them, ie in the ordinary course of his business, if he is intending to continue it, is instructive.

The bank in this case knew that the company was overtrading, that its only source of money to meet its current trading debts was the takings of its shops, that the whole of the takings were being deposited to the overdrawn account, and that the company's trading debts were not being currently met. However acceptable the motive of the bank in endeavouring to keep the company afloat, by proving its belief that the company had an excess of trading stock over those debts of which the bank was aware, it cannot escape the conclusion that, at the least, it had reason to believe that the company was insolvent. Clearly that stock, in the company's circumstances, was not within the category of realisable assets to which Isaacs J refers in *Bank of Australasia v Hall* (1907) 4 CLR 1514 at 1543.

I agree with my brother Taylor in thinking that the proper inference from the facts is that there was an arrangement between the company and the bank, made at the end of November 1960 through Mr Hennessy for the company and Mr Connors for the bank, with at least the tacit approval of Mr Barton, that the whole takings of the shops should be banked to the credit of the overdrawn account and that the bank should apply so much of the deposits as it determined up to a maximum of £7000 per month in permanent reduction of the company's indebtedness to the bank, the bank deciding, no doubt after consultation with the company, which of the cheques drawn by the company in payment of its trading debts should be met from the account. Such an arrangement with a company in this company's position, however beneficial it might prove to the interest of the company and to its other creditors, both in continuing to provide an outlet for their goods and in providing the company with time for recovery, could only be made with safety to the bank if made in consultation with the company's other creditors. To make and implement it without such consultation meant that if the company failed within the statutory time, the bank must be taken to have accepted the reduction of its overdraft with at least a suspicion, but I think with knowledge, of the insolvency of the company and that that reduction as it took place involved a preference, priority or advantage in favour of the bank over other creditors whose debts were not being met. That consequence follows in this case.

Some reference was made in argument to the decision in *Richardson v The Commercial Banking Co of Sydney Ltd* (1952) 85 CLR 110 which was sought to be used to support the submission that here, because the bank was honouring cheques drawn on the company's account during the period and doing so in consultation with the company, no part of the payments retained by the bank during the period were liable to attack as preferences. But in my opinion *Price's* case (1952) 85 CLR 110 has no relevance to the resolution of this. In *Price's* case except for the receipt of the cheque of £390, the bank's indebtedness was not permanently reduced. In the judgment of the court there appears this passage, both significant to the decision of that case and indicative of its irrelevance to this: ''The burden of showing that a preference resulted is upon the Official Receiver, and we know that in the result there was none actually enjoyed by the bank. To infer that at a point the bank obtained one but that it was freely sacrificed by the spontaneous making of further advances by honouring cheques would we think be wrong. The true reading of the circumstances, we feel little doubt, is that the deposits were made on the footing that so far as the respective deposits would carry, the cheques coming in would be honoured, if it was not decided in consultation that to dishonour them was a safe and better course.'': at 135.

In this case the challenge is not to individual payments as was the case with the cheque for £390 in *Price's* case nor was there an account in liquidation as in *Docker's* case (1938) 10 ABC 198. But at the time of the receipt of each deposit during the relevant period, the bank was able to retain at least some portion of it in permanent reduction of its account. What part it did retain can be determined by taking the total intake into the account during the period and deducting the outgo. It is unnecessary to endeavour to assign this remainder to particular deposits, for the position as to the bank's knowledge in relation to the company's solvency and in relation to the effect of any permanent reduction in the company's indebtedness to the bank was the same throughout the period. Nor is there any need to analyse the course of the overdrawn account during the period to determine whether a preference which had been obtained at one point of time was foregone by the making of further advances which for the time being may have exceeded the extent of the preference. It is sufficient in the circumstances of this case to take the overall effect of the deposits and the withdrawals in the period.

It was also said in argument for the bank that it was not permissible for the liquidator to choose a date within the period of six months and to make a comparison of the state of the overdrawn account at that date and its state at the date of the commencement of the winding up. It was submitted that the proper comparison was between the debit in the account at the commencement of the statutory period of six months and the debit at the commencement of the liquidation — a comparison which in this case would result in a materially lesser figure than that reached by taking the liquidator's comparison. In my opinion the liquidator can choose any point during the statutory period in his endeavour to show that from that point on there was a preferential payment and I see no reason why he should not choose, as he did here, the point of the peak indebtedness of the account during the six months period.

I am therefore of opinion that, accepting all the findings of the primary judge except his finding as to the bona fides of the bank, the deposits to the company's account during the period 1 December 1960 to 8 February 1961, to the extent that they were applied in permanent reduction of the bank's debt, were not received bona fide by the bank within the meaning of the statute because at the time of their receipt the bank had at least reason to suspect that the company was unable to pay its debts as they became due, and that the effect of the receipt of that money applied as the bank proposed to apply it would be to give the bank a preference, priority or advantage over other creditors.

I would for these reasons allow this appeal.

Taylor J [discussed the facts and continued at 229:] It was contended before us on the appeal, although somewhat faintly, that we should differ from the learned judge of first instance and hold that it has not been established that at the material time, which I take to be on and after 1 December 1960, the company was unable to pay its debts as they became due. But, in my view, the conclusion to which his Honour came on this point is inescapable and it is unnecessary to discuss it separately from the main point in the case.

On this point I commence by referring to the case of *Bank of Australasia v Hall* (1907) 4 CLR 1514 where the question arose whether the evidence established that at the time when the debtor had given a security to his creditor he was unable to pay his debts as they became due from his own moneys. On this question Griffith CJ said: "It was suggested, but the argument was not pressed, that the debtor's affairs should be regarded from the point of view of a balance sheet of assets and liabilities. This is not what the statute says. It has always been interpreted in Queensland to mean what it says, and the only English reported case on the point, *Re Washington Diamond Mining Co* [1893] 3 Ch 95, is to the same effect. The question is not whether the debtor would be able, if time were given him, to pay his debts out of his assets, but whether he is presently able to do so with moneys actually available. The most favourable construction that can be put on the words 'his own moneys' is that they include any moneys of which the debtor can obtain immediate command by sale or pledge of his assets": at 1528.

With this statement Barton J entirely agreed whilst Isaacs J said: "The Act requires the debtor to be able to pay his debts as they become due. This does not mean that he is always bound to keep by him in cash a sum sufficient to meet all his outstanding indebtedness however distant the date of payment may be. If at the time he makes the assignment, the debtor's position is such that he has property either in the form of assets in possession or of debts, which if realised would produce sufficient money to pay all his indebtedness, and if that property is in such a position as to title and otherwise that it could be realised in time to meet the indebtedness as the claims mature, with money thus belonging to the debtor, he cannot be said to be unable to pay his debts as they become due from his own moneys. In other words, if the debtor can, by sale or mortgage of property which he owns at the time of the assignment, change the form of the property into cash wholly or partly but sufficient for the purpose of paying his debts as they become due, that requirement of the section is satisfied": at 1543. In the light of these pronouncements it was, to my mind, clearly proved that the company was at all material times unable to pay its debts as they became due. However, the main question is whether the arrangement was made, and the subsequent transactions between the company and the respondent took place, under such circumstances as to lead to the inference that the respondent knew or had reason to suspect that the company was unable to pay its debts as they became due and that the effect of the various transactions would be to give the respondent a preference, priority or an advantage over the creditors. To my mind the answer to this question must be in the affirmative for the evidentiary matters which so plainly establish that the company was unable to pay its debts as they became due were matters within the knowledge of the respondent's responsible officers. It was conceded in evidence that it was found to be "impracticable" for the company to observe the instruction given in September 1960 to reduce its overdraft by £3000 per month and that instead of the company's indebtedness to the respondent being reduced to £17,000 by the end of October 1960 it had risen to £22,655. Then, in the circumstances already related, it further increased to £41,316 on 21 November 1960 and the company's promise to reduce the indebtedness by £10,000 within a week or 10 days was not honoured. Instead, by 1 December 1960 the overdraft had risen to £44,694 and this occurred notwithstanding the dishonour of cheques drawn on the account in November for a total amount approximating £35,000. These cheques had obviously been drawn to pay trade debts and it was about as clear as it could be that the company was unable to meet its debts out of its resources. It was about this time that the arrangement in question was made and from then onward the chief manager required a daily return to be made as to the state of the account. From 1 December 1960 onward there was constant consultation between the respondent and Hennessy as to which of the company's cheques should be honoured and which should be dishonoured. It must, I think, have been apparent by 1 December 1960 that the company was quite unable to meet its debts as they became due but the learned trial judge found that the respondent held the opinion at this time that "behind these cheques there was a very substantial margin of realisable stock". No doubt this belief, if it existed, was induced, as his Honour found, by misstatements by Hennessy as to the value of stock in hand from time to time and by its lack of knowledge of two trade debts aggregating nearly £52,000. But we do not know what Connors believed as to the value of the stock on hand for he was not called as a witness. We do know, however, that promises from time to time to provide him with copies of the company's accounts were not kept, and this, in the circumstances of the case, afforded some grounds for apprehension. Further the features of the case upon which the learned judge founded his decision sink into comparative insignificance when regard is had to the failure on the part of the company, obviously through inability, to meet the respondent's demands to reduce its overdraft by £3000 as from October 1960 and the further failure of the company to make good its promise of 21 November to reduce its overdraft by £10,000 within a week or 10 days. When there is added to these matters the evidence concerning the inability of the company to provide funds to meet the cheques which were dishonoured in November 1960 no doubt can exist that the payments made to the account between 1 December 1960 and 8 February 1961, and which were made subject to the arrangement in question, were made under such circumstances as to lead to the inference that the respondent knew or had reason to suspect that the debtor was unable to pay its debts as they became due and that the effect of the payments would be to give it a preference over other creditors to the extent which the arrangement envisaged.

As already appears the attack which is made is not made in respect of any specific payments to the credit of the account. What is said is that the arrangement was made on the basis that the company would continue to pay the whole of its takings to the credit of its account with the respondent and that the latter should be entitled during each of the three succeeding months — December 1960 and January and February 1961 — to retain in permanent reduction of the company's indebtedness to the respondent so much of the amounts deposited in each of those months, not exceeding £7000 per month, as it should think fit. It is, I think, of no consequence that no individual deposit is attacked or can itself be attacked as a preference; it is sufficient for the appellant to show that the company paid moneys into the hands of the respondent partly in order that it might in some limited fashion be permitted to continue trading and partly in permanent reduction of its overdraft indebtedness. To my mind the payments made in pursuance of an agreement to this effect are void to the extent to which they were, consistently with the arrangement in question, appropriated by the respondent in permanent reduction of the overdraft.

For these reasons I am of the opinion that the order of the Supreme Court should be set aside and that it should be declared that of the moneys deposited to the credit of the company's account with the respondent between 1 January 1960 and 8 February 1961 the sum of £20,292 constituted a preference and, therefore, that such payments were to that extent void as against the liquidator. Further an order should be made that the respondent pay this sum to the liquidator.

[**Kitto J** delivered judgment to similar effect.]

Appeal allowed with costs.

Re Bird (as Trustee of the Estate of Arcadiou); Ex parte M & G Casabene & Sons
Federal Court of Australia (1979) 39 FLR 281

C A Sweeney J: In this application, as amended by leave, Alex Neville Bird, as trustee of the estate of Yiangos Arcadiou, a bankrupt, seeks the following directions and orders: "(a) That payment made by the bankrupt to the respondent on 7 October 1976 for $4000 and on 4 February 1977 for $2500 are void as against the applicant as trustee of the property of the bankrupt as being payment having the effect of giving the respondent a preference, priority or advantage over creditors of the bankrupt, or, alternatively, by virtue of the bankruptcy of the bankrupt having been deemed to have relation back to date 20 September 1976. (b) An order that the respondent pay to the applicant the sum of $6500."

[After considering earlier decisions under s 95 of the Bankruptcy Act 1924, his Honour continued at 286:] Section 122 is one of the provisions of the Act, under which antecedent transactions may be avoided, which are based upon the cardinal principle of administration in bankruptcy, namely, equality between the creditors, which could be simply frustrated in the absence of such provisions.

A creditor, who has received a payment in respect of which a party seeking to avoid it has proved the facts set out in sub-s (1) may escape such an order if he proves that he is a payee in good faith and for valuable consideration and in the ordinary course of business: see sub-ss (2) and (4). In the course of deciding whether he has done so, the court must, of course, give a meaning to the expression "payee in good faith". It is not left at large in doing so, but must bear in mind the provisions of sub-s (4).

That sub-section does not purport to offer an exhaustive definition of the expression "purchaser, payee or encumbrancer in good faith". There may well be facts relevant to the issue of whether a person answers that description, which arise apart from the specific terms of sub-s (4)(c). In respect of such facts, the burden of proof plainly rests upon the payee. In my opinion, sub-s (4)(c) does not displace or qualify the application of that burden of proof in respect of the matters to which it refers. The burden of proof cast upon the payee remains upon him in all matters relevant to the issue of his being a payee in good faith and, if he is to succeed, his proof must be such as to negative the inference set out in sub-s (4)(c).

The question whether a person is a payee in good faith and for valuable consideration and in the ordinary course of business within the meaning of s 122(2)(a) involves the consideration of matters which are often found in practice to be especially within the knowledge of such a person, and sub s (3) plainly imposes the burden of proving the matters referred to in sub-s (2)(a) upon him.

The circumstances under which a payment is made to a creditor which fall for consideration in the decision of the questions set out in sub-s (4)(c) are expressed to be critical to a finding that a creditor is a payee in good faith, and they are also often especially within his knowledge.

The view of the section which I have earlier expressed is, in my opinion, to be preferred to a construction of it under which a creditor would bear the burden of proving that he is a payee in good faith, but would not be called upon to negative the matters which, in effect, disqualify him from being so regarded.

The view which I have taken of the construction of s 122 is, I believe, consistent with the general course of the authorities cited above. (See *S Richards & Co Ltd v Lloyd* per Rich and Dixon JJ (1933) 49 CLR 49 at 60; *Burns v McFarlane* per Rich, Dixon and McTiernan JJ

(1940) 64 CLR 108 at 124; *Rees v Bank of New South Wales* per Barwick CJ (1964) 111 CLR 210 at 217, and *Queensland Bacon Pty Ltd v Rees* per Gibbs J in the Supreme Court of Queensland exercising federal jurisdiction (1966) 115 CLR 266 at 280. The view expressed by Barwick CJ in *Queensland Bacon Pty Ltd v Rees* at 286 appears, with respect, to be inconsistent with these authorities.

The question arises whether the respondent has discharged the burden of proving that the payment received in October 1976 was made under such circumstances as to lead to the inference that it knew or had reason to suspect that the bankrupt was unable to pay his debts as they became due from his own money and that the effect of the payment would be to give him an advantage over other creditors, within the meaning of s 122(4)(c).

[His Honour then considered the meaning of, and authorities on the words "unable to pay his debts as they become due from his own money" and continued at 289:] Section 123 protects certain transactions against the operation of the doctrine of relation back if, as is provided in sub-s (1):

"(e) the transaction took place on or before the date on which the debtor became a bankrupt;

(f) the person, other than the debtor, with whom it took place, did not, at the time of the transaction, have notice of the presentation of a petition against the debtor; and

(g) the transaction was in good faith and in the ordinary course of business."

Sub-section (2) places the burden of proving those matters upon the person who relies on the validity of the transaction.

Sub-section (3) provides: "For the purposes of sub-section (1) of this section, a transaction shall not be deemed not to have been in good faith and in the ordinary course of business by reason only that, at the time of the transaction, the person, other than the debtor, with whom it took place had notice of the commission of an act of bankruptcy by the debtor."

. . .

Under cross-examination, Mr Casabene agreed that by September 1976 he was seriously concerned by the failure of the bankrupt to pay any part of the money he owed, but he said: "I know he will pay me." He wanted the bankrupt to pay him the whole amount due, but on 7 October 1976 he received a payment of $4000, leaving a balance of $1338. He sometimes waited a couple of hours the catch the bankrupt on a building site to repeat his request for payment and kept pressure on him "all the time". The bankrupt would reply: "Don't worry — money is coming."

Other contractors told Mr Casabene in 1976 that the bankrupt was slow to pay but that he would pay, although he always paid in arrears and kept people waiting a long time before paying . . .

The bankrupt had been informed before the work commenced that the respondent's terms would be "strictly 30 days for settlement of accounts". Invoices for the work done in May were prepared on 3 June 1976, and shortly thereafter were delivered to the bankrupt. Accounts rendered were also sent. Invoices in respect of the August work were delivered to the bankrupt shortly after 8 September, which was the date they bore, together with a further account rendered for the May work.

Despite the repeated urgings of Mr Casabene, and more than one call at the bankrupt's home, no payment was received until about 7 October.

"In approximately August of 1976 in spite of having received no payment at all to that time" Mr Casabene accepted instructions from the bankrupt to carry out further work, for which invoices were made out on 8 September 1976, totalling $3954.

The nature of the test to be applied in construing the words "the creditor had reason to suspect" was considered by Latham CJ in *Downs Distributing Co Pty Ltd v Associated Blue Star Stores Pty Ltd (in liq)* (1948) 76 CLR 463 as follows: "It was argued that the words 'the creditor had reason to suspect' meant that the creditor had in his mind some knowledge or belief which to him amounted to reason to suspect; in other words, that the test was a subjective test. In my opinion there is no reason for interpreting the words of the section in this way, and there is every reason for interpreting them as referring to an objective test. The sub-section refers to 'such circumstances as to lead to' one or other of two inferences: either first, that the creditor knew certain facts; or secondly, that the creditor had reason to suspect the existence of certain facts. The provision as to the creditor 'knowing' adopts a subjective criterion—applied by inference made by the court. The other provision as to the circumstances leading to an inference that the creditor had 'reason to suspect' relates in my opinion to what may, by way of comparison, be described as an objective test. It is intended to deal with circumstances such that an inference can fairly be drawn by a court that there was reason to suspect, whether or not in fact the mind of the creditor consciously adverted to the significance with respect to the financial position of the debtor of the matters mentioned in the sub-section. In my opinion a transaction falls within sub-s (4), so that a creditor is excluded from the category of a creditor dealing in good faith under sub-s (2)(b), if, whatever the creditor may think or believe with respect to the circumstances of a transaction, those circumstances are such as to lead to an inference by the court that there was reason to suspect according to the standards of an ordinary reasonable man that the debtor was unable to pay his debts as they became due, and that the effect of the transaction would be to give the creditor a preference over other creditors'': at 475-6.

Williams J said: "His Honour found that the circumstances were such as to lead to the inference that the managing director of the defendant had reason to suspect these matters. It was contended for the appellant that in drawing such an inference the court should have regard to the mentality of the particular creditor. But, in my opinion, the circumstances to which the sub-section refers are such circumstances as would lead a reasonable business man to suspect these matters": at 480.

In *Queensland Bacon Pty Ltd v Rees* Barwick CJ said: "The question of what inference should be drawn from all these circumstances is a question for the court. But the inference being sought is the inference which a reasonable business man in the situation ought to draw. It must be remembered that trading of the kind with which these applications are concerned is, as of present times, predominantly carried on by means of extensive credit and that overdraft accommodation supplements that credit to furnish the circulating capital. Consequently, liquidity can be lost overnight upon a reduction of overdraft limits. Whether this spells insolvency must be determined, it seems to me, by the speed with which assets of a readily realisable kind can be turned into cash. That time will be relative at least to the nature or extent of the indebtedness. Although in the full knowledge of all the facts the company was insolvent, his Honour found that the circumstances did not lead to the conclusion that the appellant knew of that insolvency. The question remains what is the proper inference which the court thinks a reasonable and prudent businessman should draw from those circumstances": at 296.

Kitto J observed: "As in the other three cases, there is great need to keep steadily in view what the precise inference is to which sub-s (4) refers. It is an inference which the court draws from the circumstances known to the creditor at the time when he accepted the payment. It is an inference that the creditor at that time had reason for an actual suspicion of a particular state of facts, that is to say a ground which a reasonable man in his position would have considered sufficient to raise in his mind a real suspicion that the state of facts existed. I venture to repeat that the state of facts consists of two elements. The first is an actual inability on the part of the payer to pay his debts as they became due, as distinguished from a reluctance to accommodate his wider purposes to the limitations of his resources. The second is that the effect of the payment, ie its ultimate, substantial effect, would be that the payee would be in a better position vis-à-vis the other creditors than he would have been if the company's assets had been converted and distributed amongst all the creditors in a due course of winding up": at 312.

Applying the test which the authorities require, I am satisfied that had the respondent been paid in late August or early September 1976, it would have been a payee in good faith and that it would have negatived the inference that it knew or had reason to suspect that the bankrupt was unable to pay his debts as they became due from his own money, and that the effect of the payment would be to give it a preference, priority or advantage over other creditors.

It is true that "about September 1976" Mr Casabene told the bankrupt that the respondent would do no more work for him "until such time as a substantial payment had been received", but I am inclined to the view that this circumstance is not fatal to the respondent's case. It is a nice question, but, on balance, I am satisfied that the respondent has discharged the burden of proving, in respect of the payment of $4000 made on 7 October 1976, that it was a payee in good faith and that it has negatived the inference referred to in s 122(4)(c). The work for which that payment was made had been carried out in May 1976, so that payment was overdue but not to a serious extent.

There being no challenge to the fact that the payment to the respondent was for valuable consideration, it remains to be seen whether it has made out the additional requirement that the payment was made in the ordinary course of business. The tests to be applied have been laid down in *Downs Distributing Co Pty Ltd v Associated Blue Star Stores Pty Ltd (in liq)* where Rich J cited the observation in *Burns v McFarlane* that the expression "ordinary course of business" does not require "an investigation of the course pursued in any particular trade or vocation and it does not refer to what is normal or usual in the business of the debtor or that of the creditor": (1940) 64 CLR 108 at 125. Rich J went on to say: "It is an additional requirement and is cumulative upon good faith and valuable consideration. It is, therefore, not so much a question of fairness and absence of symptoms of bankruptcy as of the everyday usual or normal character of the transaction. The provision does not require that the transaction shall be in the course of any particular trade, vocation or business. It speaks of the course of business in general. But it does suppose that according to the ordinary and common flow of transactions in affairs of business there is a course, an ordinary course. It means that the transaction must fall into place as part of the undistinguished common flow of business done, that it should form part of the ordinary course of business as carried on, calling for no remark and arising out of no special or particular situation": (1948) 76 CLR 463 at 476–7. In *Robertson v Grigg* Evatt J said: "The ordinary course of business is not, I think, to be related to any special business carried on by either debtor or creditor, but is concerned with the character of the impeached transaction itself": (1932) 47 CLR 257 at 273.

In my opinion, the respondent has established that the October payment was made in the ordinary course of business, as that expression has been construed.

The debate upon the effect of s 123 upon the October payment was narrowed by concessions made in the course of argument. Mr Irlicht conceded that the respondent had established that the transaction in question took place before the date on which the debtor became a bankrupt (see s 123(1)(e)) and that the respondent did not, at the time of the transaction, have notice of the presentation of a petition against the debtor: see s 123(1)(f). It was Mr Irlicht's contention that the respondent had failed to show that the transaction was in good faith and in the ordinary course of business: see s 123(1)(g). In my opinion, the respondent has discharged the burden of proving that the transaction met the requirements of s 123(1)(g) for the reasons which I have earlier set out in relation to s 122, bearing in mind, of course, that s 123 does not contain any provision such as that found in s 122(4)(c).

As the respondent has succeeded in its defence to both bases upon which the application in respect of the October payment of $4000 was founded, the application fails in relation to it.

I turn now to consider the payment of $2500 made by the bankrupt to the respondent on 4 February 1977. By that date, Mr Casabene had made many demands upon the bankrupt for payment, including a call to his home on Christmas Eve which he made "to abuse him as to why he let me down, did not pay me the money to pay my men". At that date, the amount owed to the respondent was long overdue in circumstances which in my opinion, would have caused a reasonable businessman in the position of the respondent to have reason to suspect the matters specified in s 122(4)(c)(i) and (ii). It is not merely a case, in my opinion, in which the respondent has failed to negative the inference that it had reason to suspect those matters, but rather one in which the evidence establishes affirmatively that the inference should be drawn . . .

Declaration and order accordingly.

The wide scope of Bankruptcy Act s 123 (replacing s 96 of previous Act) should be noted. It protects dealings by a debtor *before* the day of bankruptcy (ie, during the period of relation back under s 115) of the kind described in s 123 provided the other party had no notice of the presentation of the petition and the transaction was in good faith and in the ordinary course of business. Cases interpreting these terms in s 122 are relevant, but note that the other party's knowledge of the commission of an act of bankruptcy will not of itself preclude a finding of good faith and ordinary course of business: s 123(3); see generally *Griffiths v G W J Blackman &*

Co Pty Ltd (1972) 21 FLR 142. A transaction which is caught by the other specific avoidance provisions in ss 118–122 is not protected by s 123.

FLOATING CHARGES

We noted the characteristics of a floating charge on p 276, *supra*. The critical issues in relation to avoidance by Carb's liquidator of a floating charge given by Carb in favour of City Bank will be:

(a) when will the charge crystallise;
(b) to what extent can City Bank claim after-acquired property; and
(c) to what extent can City Bank claim priority under the charge for advances made to Carb after the execution of the charge.

These issues are especially pertinent in relation to fluctuating collateral such as Carb's stock-in-trade. Section 122 of the Bankruptcy Act will apply by virtue of NCC s 451. In addition NCC s 452 applies specifically to floating charges given by companies (see below). With NCC s 452 may be compared the approach of the High Court in *Burns v Stapleton* (1959) 102 CLR 97 where it held a mortgage given by an individual debtor to secure both past indebtedness and a fresh advance constituted a preference, *but only to the extent of the past indebtedness*.

The predecessor sections of Companies Act 1961 (s 294) and UK Companies Act 1948 (s 322) were considered in *Re Dittmer Gold Mines Ltd (No 1)* [1954] St R Qd 255 and in *Re Yeovil Glove Co Ltd* [1965] 1 Ch 148 respectively. The policy underlying these sections is considered below.

Peden: Stock-in-Trade Financing
1974, pp 15–16, 41–4

Ideally, a single master agreement should provide an effective cross-over security whereby both present and future advances should be secured by all stock, present and future, financed by the financier who made those advances.

The wide reach of such a security interest raises other policy questions. First, in the hands of a monopolistic lender, it could be used to tie the borrower in such a way as to prevent him obtaining finance from other sources. An equitable balance must be reached by regulation to prevent the secured creditor from over-reaching with respect to after-acquired stock, future advances and proceeds. This regulation should conform to—rather than dictate to—economically sound and functional business trends and practices. It is possible to frame suitable curbs upon the over-reaching creditor without destroying the floating nature of the stock-in-trade security. For example, other creditors who provide fresh stock to the borrower or finance its acquisition can be given a prior claim to the fresh stock.

Second, there are sound economic and business reasons for granting a financier the same priority in respect of future periodic advances as was available for the first advance. From the borrower's side, the prospects of obtaining a later repayment date are improved and loan capital will not normally attract interest until the loan is utilised, and future advances may also be negotiated at current interest rates. The confirmation of future funds enables the borrower to proceed confidently. The advantages to the lender are even greater. Administrative costs of negotiating and documenting a new transaction for each advance are avoided. The prospect of a continuing, favourable outlet for investment funds is created. Increments in value of collateral may provide increased security under an after-acquired property clause. The major countervailing considerations are protection of the borrower's right to obtain finance from other sources and adequate warning to other prospective lenders of the potential quantum of future advances...

The legal principles relating to the floating charge comply substantially with the policy of validation of stock-in-trade securities in Objective D. Thus, a single document provides a cross-over security whereby present and future advances can be secured by present and after-acquired stock. However, this charge only creates an equitable interest in after-acquired goods which floats over rather than "attaches" to the specific chattels. At general law, attachment only occurs when, upon the debtor's default, the chargee enforces its security by appointing a receiver or seizing the chattels, or the debtor ceases business or goes into liquidation, thereby crystallising the charge. Of course, by the time one of these events occurs the debtor's stock may be reduced to a low level, taken in execution by a judgment creditor or made the subject of a subsequent specific fixed charge. In any of these situations, the floating charge will be defeated.

In practice, the chargee will attempt to avoid this result by defining in the charge the circumstances which will cause the charge automatically to crystallise into a fixed charge. For example, by providing that entry of judgment or issue of execution against the debtor company will cause the charge to crystallise, the floating charge can probably prevail over the levying judgment creditor: *Davey & Co v Williamson & Sons Ltd* [1898] 2 QB 194; *Evans v Rival Granite Quarries Ltd* [1910] 2 KB 979. However, this point is not free from doubt because leading authorities have disagreed on the question whether default alone will suffice to crystallise the charge: Gower, *Modern Company Law*, 3rd ed, 1969, p 420-1. Compare Pennington, *Company Law,* 2nd ed, 1967, p 344-5. The courts will construe any automatic crystallisation provision strictly (*Government Stock Investment Co v Manila Railway Co* [1897] AC 81 at 87) and may refuse to apply it unless the chargee has actively intervened to enforce its charge. It is for the courts, rather than the charge, to say whether a charge continues to float or has become fixed: *Re Yorkshire Woolcombers' Association Ltd* [1903] 2 Ch 284 at 295. Automatic crystallisation could also have drastic and unforeseen consequences such as freezing all the assets upon a minor default (Sher & Allan, "Financing Dealers' Stock-in-Trade" (1965) 1 *NZULR* 371 at 418; *N W Robbie & Co Ltd v Witney Warehouse Co Ltd* [1963] 1 WLR 1324), unless the chargee is given power to waive such default. The winding up of a corporation definitely crystallises any floating charges created by it so that a registered charge will be upheld against the liquidator in respect of assets covered by the charge at the date of winding up, subject to the provisions governing fraudulent transfers, preferential claims, voidable preferences and floating charges created within six months preceding the winding up.

Fraudulent transfers are declared void against the liquidator by s 121 of the Commonwealth Bankruptcy Act 1966, which also applies to companies and is unlimited as to time. The states have their own versions of this provision which are based on the Elizabethan Fraudulent Conveyances Act 1571 13 Eliz c 5 and operate irrespective of bankruptcy or insolvency proceedings.

Preferential claims are created by s 292(1) of the Uniform Companies Act [see now NCC s 441] for inter alia the petitioning creditor's and liquidator's costs and expenses, for employees' wages, annual and long service leave pay, local rates and taxes. These are to be paid in priority to all unsecured creditors and also have priority over the holders of debentures under any floating charge created by the company.

Voidable preferences are subject to two provisions. [The substance of s 122 Bankruptcy Act 1966 and s 294 Uniform Companies Act (now s 452 NCC) is then set out.]

The combined effect of these two sections appears to uphold the basic purpose of the floating charge while precluding over-reaching by, or preferential treatment of, the chargee. The *general* provision implies that, in the absence of a de facto preference or intent to prefer, the after-acquired property secured by a transfer initially created outside the preference period cannot be claimed by the trustee. The *specific* provision adopts an economic analysis approach rather than rigid legalism of requiring a one-for-one matching of new and old collateral. What is crucial is whether the secured creditor has increased the aggregate value of the collateral subject to its floating charge during the six months prior to liquidation. To the extent that it has, but only to that extent, should the charge be regarded as preferential. This so-called two-point rule is also pragmatic because it is relatively simple to apply. It satisfies the fifth policy in Objective D. However, it is anomalous that it is confined to floating charges since it would seem equally appropriate to fixed charges.

The other feature of the cross-over security, namely the right to tack future advances, is available with the floating charge. However, while the common law has developed rules dealt with hereunder regulating priorities between competing security holders, there is some doubt as to the effectiveness of future advance clauses against judgment creditors. Where a charge which secures a current account specifies the maximum amount of further advances, there is a danger of subordination of the charge under the first-in-first-out rule of *Clayton's* case (1816) 1 Mer 572; 35 ER 781, or the theory that a charge is automatically discharged when it no longer secures any current obligation.

It is important to understand the interrelationship of s 451 and s 452 of the Companies Code. This relationship was considered by Marks J in *Cosmas Fish Processors International Pty Ltd v Hoffman Nominees Pty Ltd* [1982] 1 ACLC 52 at 58:

> I do not consider that s 294 constitutes an exclusive code for undue preferences in respect of floating charges. In my opinion the word "charge" in s 293 is capable of including a floating charge (see definitions of "charge" in s 5: *Gas Light Improvement Co v Terell* (1870) 10 LR Eq 168; *Re Jackson v Bassford Ltd* (1906) 2 Ch 467). I think it clear that ss 293 and 294 are directed primarily at rendering specified types of transactions void or invalid as undue preferences. Section 294, in my view, catches floating charges where s 293 may not. Section 293 has to be read in conjunction with ss 121 and 122 of the Bankruptcy Act. Section 294 renders holders of floating charges unable to avail themselves of any of the Bankruptcy Act exceptions to the undue preference rules incorporated by s 293, and are confined to the exception contained within s 294 itself. The result is that a particular "charge" may be an undue preference by virute of s 293 irrespective of s 294, and if not by s 293 it may be by s 294.

QUESTIONS

Question 8

Jim Handy obtained from his uncle, Tom, in July 1982 a loan to help him meet various payments that were due. This loan was unsecured. Due to further financial problems Jim sought to liquidate some of his assets. One of these was a campervan valued at $18,000. Tom was nearing the age of retirement and was in the market for such a vehicle for touring Australia in retirement. Tom agreed to purchase the campervan from Jim for $16,000 on the basis that Jim would continue to have the use of the vehicle until Tom retired, or until Tom should resell the vehicle (in which later event Tom promised that he would allow Jim one-third of any excess over $16,000 received). In June 1983 Tom retired and paid Jim $16,000 from which Jim immediately repaid Tom the $14,000 which he owed to Tom at that time.

On 1 August 1983 Jim paid his accountant, Will Balance, $350 for a bill relating to the preparation of his income tax return. Jim had also sought Balance's advice in relation to managing his debt and liquidity problems. On 4 August Jim received a third "account rendered" for Balance's professional charges of $800 in relation to this advice. On the account Balance added a threat of legal action unless the debt was paid within seven days. On 8 August Jim paid Balance's account of $800.

On 10 August, Jaye Walker obtained a judgment for $25,000 against Jim in relation to a personal injury claim for damages. A writ of execution has not yet been sought.

On 1 September, Jim failed to comply with a bankruptcy notice previously served on him by Forceful Manufacturers. On 1 November Forceful presented a petition for Jim's bankruptcy and a sequestration order was made against his estate on 1 April 1984.

(1) Advise Tom as to his rights to retain the campervan and the payment of $14,000 received by him from Jim.

(2) Advise the trustee of his rights to recover the amounts of $350 and $800 Jim paid to Will Balance.

(3) Advise Jaye Walker on her right to recover her judgment debt and the procedure she should follow.

(4) Advise the trustee of his right to claim any money or assets received by Jaye Walker if she had issued a writ of execution, and Jim had forestalled the execution by paying Jaye $25,000 on 12 August.

Question 9

Carb Pty Ltd had a long standing credit arrangement with Pressure Sales Co whereby it could purchase goods on a 45 day account. Industrial action by Carb's employees and a flood of imports resulting in falling sales has caused Carb considerable financial difficulty in meeting its payments both to Pressure Sales and other creditors. However, Carb had some investments in other companies which it could have realised but was reluctant to do so because of the adverse effect this would have on its cash flow. The total amount owing to Pressure Sales on 1 May 1983 was $40,000. Carb also owed money to other creditors.

On 6 May 1983 Carb sought further supplies of goods and placed a $5000 order on its account with Pressure Sales which accepted the order, but told Carb that it required Carb to reduce the outstanding balance of its account. Carb did forward a cheque for $2000 but this cheque was dishonoured. Events of the following week caused Carb to take certain drastic steps. A number of creditors demanded payment, causing Carb to realise its investments in other companies, plus a number of other assets. However, it was still unable to meet the demands of all creditors without selling some major items of its production plant.

On 1 June 1983 Carb placed another order with Pressure Sales for $15,000. This time Pressure Sales demanded certain terms, namely, (a) payment of one-third of the price in cash and (b) an agreement to repay the total debt at a rate of $10,000 per month.

Another of Carb's creditors was Suburban Bank, which in 1980 had loaned Carb $100,000 on the security of the deposit of the deeds to Carb's warehouse property. Carb was two months in arrears in its payment of interest to the bank, but on 10 June 1983 obtained a further advance from Suburban of $30,000 on overdraft which it secured by a floating charge over all Carb's present and future property. At the same time Suburban took a registered mortgage over Carb's warehouse property in respect of the $100,000 previously loaned to Carb.

Carb used the overdraft to pay on 10 June a number of creditors, including Pressure Sales to whom it paid $15,000, representing one-third of the price of goods ordered on 1 June and $10,000 off the original debt. On 20 June Pressure Sales delivered further goods to Carb at the price of $12,000 for which part payment of $4000 was made.

On 30 June Carb paid $10,000 to Pressure Sales. No goods were ordered in July, but a payment of $10,000 was made on 31 July leaving a balance of $33,000 owing.

On 2 August a burglary occurred at Carb's warehouse and all stock was stolen, plus $15,000 worth of machinery. Carb was unable to continue its business as the insurance company only paid $40,000 in total as the plant was underinsured. The land and warehouse are valued at $50,000 and remaining plant and fittings at $15,000.

On 26 August Pressure petitioned for the winding up of Carb Pty Ltd and on 1 May 1984 by order of the Supreme Court of NSW the company was wound up.

Col Lector was appointed liquidator of Carb and seeks your advice in relation to the rights of:
  (a) Suburban Bank—to claim the insurance proceeds, land, warehouse, and plant and fittings;
  (b) Pressure Sales—to retain the payments received by it from Carb.

SECTION 6: MONEY-LENDING, HIRE-PURCHASE AND CONSUMER CREDIT LEGISLATION

For present purposes it is only intended to note the more important features of state legislation which regulate consumer credit transactions. The money-lending legislation is non-uniform and therefore only a brief overview will be given. The hire-purchase legislation was uniformly adopted in 1960 but diverse amendments and particularly the enactment of Consumer Credit Acts in South Australia, Victoria and New South Wales have qualified the previous uniform pattern. The money-lending, hire-purchase and consumer credit legislation all confer general powers to re-open harsh and unconscionable transactions.

MONEY-LENDING ACTS[1]

These Acts apply to loans made by a money-lender defined in most instances as a person who carries on the business of money-lending or who holds himself out as doing so. In some states it also includes a person who lends at a rate exceeding a specified percentage. Each of the Acts contains general exemptions in respect of pawnbrokers, bankers and insurance companies. The legislation provides for compulsory licensing of money-lenders and aims to regulate the business of money-lending and thereby protect borrowers by having the money-lender comply with requirements as to maximum rates of interest, ensuring agreements are in writing and signed etc.

HIRE-PURCHASE ACTS[2]

A hire-purchase agreement is a method of carrying out a consumer sale but, like a conditional sale, it also achieves a security function. This may be illustrated from our original example of, say, an agreement whereby Easy Finance supplies a vehicle to Driver on hire-purchase.

Under this agreement Easy enjoys a degree of protection against:
(a) Driver's general creditors including judgment creditors, provided it is not held to be a sham for a loan (see *Price v Parsons*, p 279, *supra*);
(b) Driver's trustee in the event of his bankruptcy, provided also that it is not a sham for a loan;
(c) claims by purchasers or assignees from Driver: see HPA s 9 (all citations to sections in Qld Act);
(d) claims by a repairer to a lien in respect of work done on the vehicle: s 31.

The extent of protection of the secured creditor depends partly upon the common law principle of *nemo dat quod non habet*: since Driver has no proprietary rights to the vehicle but only a right to possession and option to purchase, no one taking through him can acquire any greater rights. On the other hand, the HPA has qualified Easy's "security rights" in a number of respects listed briefly below, but perusal of the sections is recommended:

(1) Easy would be precluded from enforcing the agreement in full, or in some instances from recovering the terms charges, if it fails to comply with HPA requirements as to:
 (a) giving Driver a First Schedule Notice prior to entering the agreement: s 3(1) and First Schedule;
 (b) the detailed contents of the agreement and its execution: s 3(2);

---

[1] Qld, Moneylenders Act 1916; SA, Moneylenders Act 1940; WA, Money Lenders Act 1912; Tas, Lending of Money Act 1915; ACT, Money Lenders Ordinance 1936.
[2] Qld, Hire-Purchase Act 1959; WA, Hire-Purchase Act 1959; Tas, Hire-Purchase Act 1959; ACT, Hire-Purchase Ordinance 1961.

(c) providing Driver with details of his outstanding obligations under the agreement and a copy of the agreement: ss 4, 7 and Second Schedule;
(d) execution by a guarantor before a prescribed witness (as to enforcement against the guarantor): s 19;
(e) not exceeding the maximum rate of terms charges: s 29;
(f) payment of the prescribed minimum deposit: s 25.

(2) Driver has a statutory right to assign his rights under the agreement notwithstanding any prohibition thereon in the agreement: ss 9 and 33(1)(i).

(3) Driver has statutory rights to complete the agreement early or voluntarily return the vehicle prior to completion: ss 11 and 12.

(4) Easy is obliged to give Driver notice (normally 21 days) in the form of the Third Schedule prior to repossessing the vehicle on Driver's default: s 13.

(5) Driver has a statutory right to reinstate the agreement, or to introduce a purchaser for the vehicle following repossession, and Easy is correspondingly precluded from reselling in the meantime: s 14.

(6) The calculation of rebates and the total amount recoverable under the agreement are defined: s 15.

(7) The court is empowered to re-open harsh and unconscionable agreements and grant relief on just terms: s 28.

(8) A repairer of the vehicle has a statutory lien notwithstanding any prohibition on creation of such a lien: s 31 and see Chapter 8.

(9) Easy is precluded from repossessing goods such as a stove or oil heater if they have been affixed to a dwelling house or residence after same is acquired by a bona fide purchaser of the land without notice: s 32 and see Chapter 8.

(10) Easy cannot contract out of the provisions of the Act: s 33.

CONSUMER CREDIT ACT 1981 (NSW)

This Act follows the general lines of the recommendations contained in the Report on Fair Consumer Credit Laws by the Committee of the Law Council of Australia (Molomby Committee 1972). Similar recommendations by the Crowther Committee in England resulted in the enactment of the English Consumer Credit Act 1974. The Crowther Committee identified the following defects in the previous credit laws and Australian reformers have echoed their comments:

i. It lacks any functional basis: distinctions between one type of transaction and another are drawn on the basis of legal abstractions rather than on the basis of commercial reality (4.2.2–5).

ii. It fails to distinguish consumer from commercial transactions (4.2.6).

iii. There is an artificial separation between the law relating to lending and the law relating to security for loans (4.2.7).

iv. There is no rational policy relating to third party rights (4.2.8–9).

v. Many statutes have an excess of technical detail (4.2.10–14).

vi. There is no consistent policy in relation to sanctions for infringement (4.2.15).

vii. In general, there is a failure to provide just solutions to common problems (4.2.16).

(Consumer Credit, Vol 1, para 1.3.6 (1971) Cmnd 4596—the cross-references are to other parts of the report.)

It was the recommendation of the Molomby Committee and strong desire of the finance industry that whatever reforms were enacted would be adopted uniformly throughout Australia. Precedents for such united action existed in the near uniform Hire Purchase Acts 1960, and Companies Acts 1961. However, South Australia moved unilaterally to introduce its Consumer Credit Act and Consumer Transactions Act in 1972. Ten years later New South Wales and Victoria enacted far more complex but closely similar Credit Acts.

The Victorian legislative scheme differs from that in New South Wales in that

Victoria also enacted a Goods (Sales and Leases) Act 1981 which extends consumer protection provisions to consumer sales and leases (cf NSW Sale of Goods Act Pt VIII). In addition, Victoria enacted the Chattel Securities Act 1981 which repealed the provisions of the Instruments Act 1958 dealing with bills of sale (cf Bills of Sale Act 1898 (NSW)). No similar change has been made in New South Wales although Pt IV of the Consumer Credit Act 1981 (NSW) does include in s 105 provisions similar in some respects to the Victorian Chattel Securities Act.

The broad objectives of the new legislation have been stated to include:

(a) To establish a qualified and effective administration to supervise the credit industry through an overall licensing system for persons who provide credit under credit sales or continuing credit contracts, or who make loans at rates exceeding 14 per cent, and to assist users of credit who may encounter difficulties or problems in the use of credit.

(b) To equate all the various forms under which credit may be provided so that the rules applicable will be essentially the same and will govern the substance rather than the form of the transaction.

(c) To apply in a more extensive and sophisticated way the type of regulation and protection (that at present exists in relation to hire purchase) to all forms of credit, including implied purchase leasing arrangements which are used as an alternative to loans and instalment purchases.

(d) To make provision for the disclosure of the actual cost of credit in dollars and cents and in the form of a statutorily determined annual percentage rate. As the basis for determining that rate will be the same in respect of most forms of credit, it will be possible to compare the cost of credit more easily.

(e) In Victoria to abolish the concept of a legal interest being created in goods as a security and to substitute for bills of sale a system that will enable equitable charges to be created in goods to secure debts and other obligations; which interests may be defeated by a bona fide purchase of the goods for value by a person without notice of the secured interest (New South Wales would also protect the interest of a bona fide purchaser).

(f) In Victoria to extend additional protection to what might roughly be described as consumer transactions, ie transactions involving goods and services of a value not more than $15,000 or of a kind normally used for personal domestic or household use or consumption, in particular by incorporating into such sales and leases provisions relating to fitness and quality of the goods and services which cannot be excluded by the supplier.
(Levine J, CCH Consumer Sales and Credit Reporter ¶20-100.)

It should be noted that the ambit of the New South Wales Act is confined to consumer credit transactions, and commercial arrangements such as bill facilities, documentary letters of credit, stock-in-trade financing and factoring of trade debts are not covered: see definition of "credit" in Consumer Credit Act 1981 s 5(1).

The main thrust of the Act (sections are cited to the New South Wales Act) is to regulate three categories of transaction:

(1) credit sales contracts, whereby goods or services are provided of not more than $15,000 cash price, or farm machinery or commercial vehicles irrespective of price, provided a credit charge is imposed—see s 29(1) and definition of "credit sale contract" in s 5, which includes hiring and leasing agreements and hire-purchase (s 14) but excludes continuing credit contracts and lay-by sales (s 15);

(2) continuing credit contracts where the maximum amount owing will not exceed $15,000 and the interest rate charged exceeds 14 per cent pa; bank overdraft facilities are excluded—see s 54 and definition of "continuing credit contract" in ss 5(1) and 53;

(3) loans where the amount financed is $15,000 or less and interest is charged at an annual percentage rate exceeding 14 per cent pa and loans secured by a mortgage over a commercial vehicle or farm machinery—see s 29(2) and definition of "loan contract" in s 5(1).

In each case the Act only applies to credit provided *by credit providers* (defined in s 5(1)) in the course of business and loans *to bodies corporate* are exempt from most parts of the Act.

Each transaction is considered briefly below but attention is directed to the relevant sections of the Act.

Credit sales contracts. These are defined to include sales on credit, whether supplied by the seller or a third party. Thus, they cover transactions traditionally classified as conditional sales, credit-sale agreements and hire-purchase, leasing and hiring agreements. They also include contracts for the supply of services where credit is provided. Consequently, from the date on which the relevant parts of the Consumer Credit Act are proclaimed, the Hire-Purchase Act and the Credit-sale Agreements Act will be repealed. The Lay-by Sales Act 1943 will continue in force.

Amongst the important provisions regulating credit sale contracts are:

(a) *Section 14* which abolishes the concept of hire-purchase in relation to contracts for the hiring of goods with an option to purchase or other title retention devices where the cash price of the goods is not more than $15,000 or the goods are, or include, a commercial vehicle or farm machinery in relation to which the cash price exceeds $15,000: s 14(1). Whatever property interest the supplier has in the goods will be deemed to pass immediately to the hirer (debtor) upon delivery of the goods or the making of the contract, whichever last occurs: s 14(4)(e). Additionally, a goods mortgage back to the supplier will automatically arise: s 14(4)(f). A provision in a hiring agreement giving the supplier a right to seize or a power of sale is void: s 14(4)(g).

Section 14 covers, inter alia:
(1) agreements which oblige the hirer to purchase the goods but reserve title to the seller until payment is complete (traditionally called "conditional sale agreements");
(2) agreements which give the hirer an option to purchase the goods (previously "hire-purchase agreements"); and
(3) straight hiring agreements coupled with an informal arrangement express or implied that at the end of the hiring the hirer will buy the goods for a residual value (known as "implied purchase leases" or "wink and nod" agreements): see s 14(3).

(b) *Section 21* which protects a buyer of goods or services who indicates his need for the extension of credit before entering the contract; s 22 which prevents a supplier requiring a buyer to obtain credit from a specified person. Each section is designed to encourage a buyer to shop around for the best credit terms;

(c) *Sections 24–27* which impose joint and several liability upon a "linked credit provider" (defined in s 5(1)) in conjunction with the actual supplier of the goods or services for misrepresentation, breach of contract or failure of consideration under the main contract for sale of goods or supply of services. The link between the credit provider and supplier must satisfy the test of "linked credit provider" and "tied loan contract" in ss 5(1) and 13(1). These provisions should be examined in more detail in connection with the material in Chapter 9, Section 4: Financing through Chattel Paper on pp 410–15.

(d) *Sections 29–52* which regulate the terms and conditions of credit sale and loan contracts in the consumer area.

(e) In Victoria only, the Goods (Sales and Leases) Act 1981 was enacted concurrently with the Credit Act 1981 (Vic). It introduced mandatory implied terms into contracts for the *sale or lease of goods* dealing with title, freedom from encumbrances, correspondence with description and sample, fitness for purpose and merchantable quality, and into contracts for the supply of *services* that they will be rendered with due care and skill, will be reasonably fit for the normal purposes and

any particular purpose disclosed by the buyer, and where sold after a demonstration, will correspond with the service demonstrated. There are no corresponding provisions in the New South Wales Act, presumably because similar mandatory conditions were implied into consumer sales by the insertion of Pt VIII in the Sale of Goods Act (NSW) in 1975. However, the Sale of Goods Act (NSW) implied conditions do not apply to leases of goods or contracts for the supply of services. The mandatory implied terms in the Trade Practices Act 1974 do apply to:
 (a) leases of goods—by virtue of the broad definition of "supply" in s 4(1);
 (b) contracts for the supply of services: s 74.
However, these terms are generally confined to the supply by a corporation in the course of a business to a consumer.

Continuing credit contracts. These involve the provision of revolving or open-ended credit by a credit provider or another person to a debtor in the course of a business. The credit may be in respect of payment for goods or services or may be paid as cash advances: see s 53, and definition of credit in s 5(1). The definitions cover revolving credit accounts issued by individual retailers to customers and also third party credit cards such as Bankcard and American Express Cards. These are dealt with on p 416. By virtue of the definition of "credit" in s 5(1), floor-planning, stock-in-trade financing and bill facilities are excluded from the definition of "continuing credit contract".

A tied continuing credit contract entered into by a linked credit provider is treated like a tied loan contract: s 13(2). Hence the credit provider (card issuer) is jointly and severally liable to the buyer in respect of misrepresentation, breach of contract or failure of consideration in relation to the contract of sale: s 24(1). However, a third party credit card such as Bankcard would appear to be exempted from s 24 by virtue of s 24(14) and s 53(1)(b).

Loan contracts. These are defined in s 5(1) in terms which are somewhat broader than loan arrangements as defined in the current money-lending legislation. They may include, for example, a purchase of a bill of exchange at a discount. They are, however, confined to loans made by a person or corporation in the course of business to an individual borrower; ie loans to corporations are excluded. The detailed provisions regulating loan contracts are contained in ss 29–52 and cover such matters as:
 (a) pre-contract written disclosure of credit charges, annual percentage rate, instalments, commission charges, security taken (ss 30–31; 37–39);
 (b) provision for debtor to be given a copy of loan contract (ss 32–33), mortgage (s 49) and financial details (ss 50, 51);
 (c) matters to be included in loan contract (s 35);
 (d) forfeiture of credit charges (interest) where certain provisions of the Act are breached (s 46) and criminal penalties for breach (s 47).

Most of these requirements apply similarly to the provision of credit under a credit sale contract. Special provisions apply to agreements for store credit certificates (ss 41–45).

Mortgages and security interests. Mortgage is defined in s 5(1) to include a goods mortgage and a mortgage as used in the Conveyancing Act 1919: see definition in s 7(1) of that Act. Security interest is defined widely to cover all types of consensual securities as well as a *lien,* which secures payment of a debt or money or other obligation. The definition includes reservation of an interest in goods. Some leases or contracts for hiring of goods are excluded from the definition but are deemed by s 14 to be credit sale contracts coupled with a goods mortgage back to the credit provider as explained above.

The following important changes have been introduced by the Consumer Credit Act:

(1) hire-purchase agreements have been abolished in the sense that they are now deemed to be credit sales under which property must pass to the consumer upon making of the contract or delivery of the goods (s 14(4)(e)) coupled with goods mortgages back to the credit providers (s 14(4)(f));

(2) goods mortgages must be in writing (s 95);

(3) provisions in goods mortgages purporting to confer a right of entry upon premises for the purpose of repossession are void, and such entry is prohibited except under a court order (ss 97 and 98);

(4) restrictions are imposed upon giving of a blanket mortgage over all property and/or assets (s 101) or over after-acquired property (s 102) unless the qualifications in s 103 are met;

(5) there is protection for farmers from repossession and sale by a mortgagee of farm machinery whereby the mortgagor farmer can apply to the Credit Tribunal for an order restraining repossession for up to 12 months to enable the farmer to repay or remedy any default under the mortgage (s 119);

(6) loan commitments can be varied (s 79) or postponed (s 120);

(7) statutory protection is provided for bona fide purchasers of goods from a mortgagor or person in possession through the mortgagor thereby extinguishing the claim of the mortgagee's security interest (s 105). This provision follows the approach of s 36 of the Consumer Transactions Act 1972 (SA). It may in practice be coupled with a system of title insurance to cover the mortgagee's interest. Section 105(4) makes provision for the establishment of a registration system for mortgagee's interests. Registration could then constitute constructive notice and preclude a prospective purchaser qualifying for protection under s 105. A penalty is also imposed for attempts to defraud a mortgagee by disposing of goods subject to a mortgage: s 106(1) and (2). These provisions should be considered in greater detail in the context of the priority conflicts outlined in Chapter 8.

The other provisions of Pt V of the Act represent a re-drafting of the provisions of the hire purchase legislation involving little substantive change and may be compared with the summary on pp 327-8, *supra*. These sections are designed to protect the consumer borrower (mortgagor) by:

• requiring notice prior to repossession and sale (ss 111, 116);

• allowing the mortgagor to introduce a buyer for the goods following repossession (s 116(2));

• protecting the mortgagor's right to assign the goods with the mortgagee's consent, such consent not to be unreasonably withheld (s 106);

• permitting the debtor to pay out the contract early (s 109);

• permitting the mortgagor to return the goods and require the mortgagee to resell them (s 110);

• protecting the mortgagor's right to redeem the goods prior to resale (s 117);

• protecting the mortgagor's "equity" in respect of instalments of purchase price or mortgage repayments made prior to termination by the formula for calculating the "net balance due" (ss 107, 113), requiring statements as to the net balance due (s 108) and requiring the mortgagee to account for the proceeds of sale (s 118).

Other noteworthy aspects of the Act include:

• credit providers are generally required to be licensed (s 163); generally money lent by an unlicensed credit provider need not be repaid, nor does any credit charge under the contract need to be repaid (s 184). See generally ss 163-195;

• advertising the availability of credit is regulated (s 125) and credit hawking is prohibited (s 126);

- certain contracts can be re-opened if considered unjust, harsh or oppressive (see ss 147, 148, 149, 151). These sections do not affect the operation of the Contracts Review Act 1980 (NSW);
- provision is made for dealing with situations where there has been unjust conduct by a credit provider (ss 238–241);
- "contracting out" of the Act is prohibited and is made an offence (ss 160, 161);
- where more than 75 per cent of the total amount financed under the credit contract to which a goods mortgage relates has been repaid, the mortgagee is not entitled to repossess the goods without an order of the Tribunal or a request from the mortgagor to exercise a power of sale under s 110 (s 114).

The above synopsis provides no more than a general outline of the provisions of the Act. There is no substitute for grappling with the intricacies of the Act yourself.

QUESTION

Question 10

On 1 September Jim Handy visited the showroom of Bestcars Ltd. He negotiated to purchase a tractor for $30,000 and a utility for $14,000. When he told the sales manager, Will Bye, that he wished to trade in his old Holden station wagon and that he only had $2000 cash and would require finance for the balance, Bye

(a) agreed to allow Jim $3000 trade-in allowance provided Jim agreed to an increase in the sale price of the utility to $15,000;

(b) assured Jim that finance could be obtained provided Jim agreed to apply for credit to Bestcars Credit Corp Ltd (hereafter BCC). BCC had no legal relationship to Bestcars Ltd but Bestcars referred many customers to BCC for finance.

Jim delivered his Holden to Bestcars and paid $2000 deposit.

Jim's application for finance was approved by BCC with whom he entered into a sale agreement whereby he undertook to pay the balance of purchase-money of $40,000 and interest at 20 per cent per annum by 36 monthly instalments. The agreement provided that title would not pass to Jim until the final instalment was paid.

Jim paid five monthly instalments and then suffered financial difficulties and fell behind in his payments. BCC threatened to repossess the vehicles. Jim seeks your advice. He tells you that he probably cannot meet future instalments and thinks it may be wise to extricate himself from the agreement. Jim recalls receiving some papers from BCC but does not remember what they were and cannot find them; nor does he know how much he owes BCC.

BCC has a reputation for toughness, and Jim is fearful he may be overcharged.

Advise Jim as to all his rights and obligations. Explain to him alternative options which are available and which course or courses of action you would recommend and why.

FURTHER READING

General

Peden, *Stock-in-trade Financing,* 1974, especially pp 4–7.

Sykes, *The Law of Securities,* 3rd ed, 1978.

Section 3: Perfection of Security Interests in Goods

Begg, "The Registration of Security Interests in Chattels" (1981) 55 *ALJ* 649.

Section 4: The Insolvent Debtor and Bankruptcy Proceedings
Baxt & Harding, "The Bankruptcy Act, 1966" (1966) 40 *ALJ* 202.
Levin, "The Bankruptcy Amendment Act 1980" (1981) 55 *ALJ* 301.
Lewis's Australian Bankruptcy Law, 7th ed, 1978.
O'Hare, "Bankruptcy Reforms in Australia and the USA" (1979) 7 *ABLR* 332.

Section 6: Money-lending, Hire-purchase and Consumer Credit Legislation
Cullen & Baxt (eds), *Consumer Credit: The Challenges of Change,* 1973.
Dutney, "Chattel Securities Bill (Victoria) and Part VII of Credit Bill (Vic) (Property Mortgages)" (1979) 9 *Qld Law Soc J* 235.
Goldring, "The Consumer Credit Bill (NSW)" (1981) 6 *Legal Service Bulletin* 209.
Goldring & Maher, *Consumer Protection Law in Australia,* 2nd ed, 1983.
McGarvie & Begg, "The Implementation of Fair Consumer Laws" (1971) 45 *ALJ* 708.
MacGillivray, "Proposed Consumer Credit Legislation—The Credit Bill" (1979) 9 *Qld Law Soc J* 227.
O'Hare, "Credit Bills" (1981) 9 *ABLR* 257.
Peden & Seidler, "Form and Substance in Commercial Leasing of Equipment" (1980) 54 *ALJ* 251, 309.
Report on Fair Consumer Credit Laws by Committee of the Law Council of Australia (Molomby Committee) 1972.

CHAPTER 8

Priorities in Relation to Chattel Securities

"This is another case where one of two innocent persons has to suffer for the fraud of a third. It will no doubt interest students and find its place in the textbooks."

Lord Denning MR
Lewis v Averay [1972] 1 QB 198 at 203

Section 1: The Nemo Dat Rule and Protection of Bona Fide Purchasers
Section 2: Priority Conflicts between Competing Secured Creditors
Section 3: Financing Farm Products

In this chapter we turn to the priority conflicts (a) between secured creditors and bona fide purchasers of goods subject to a security interest (Section 1) and (b) between various kinds of secured creditors *inter se* (Section 2). In many cases the conflict will arise because of the dishonesty or insolvency of the principal debtor and will call for a determination of which of two comparatively innocent parties is to pay for the default of a third party. The financing of farm products involves special problems which are raised separately in Section 3.

SECTION 1: THE NEMO DAT RULE AND PROTECTION OF BONA FIDE PURCHASERS

As the basis for discussion we shall adopt the fact situation developed in Chapter 7 in which Carb gave various charges to City Bank, Easy Finance and various suppliers, and then resold engines to various purchasers.

The starting point for consideration of conflicting claims by previous owners or secured creditors as against a bona fide purchaser from either a debtor or thief is the rule *nemo dat quod non habet* which establishes that no one can give a better title than he himself has.

It is important to distinguish between the following situations:

(1) Where Carb's title is subject to a prior encumbrance, such as the floating charge to City Bank or a fixed charge to Comp Co.

(2) Where Carb's title is defective either because it never acquired title due to the supplier Comp Co withholding title under conditional sale (or hire-purchase in those states where same remains applicable) or because Carb has already sold the same goods to someone else, for example, to Easy Finance under a floor plan arrangement.

The common law and statutory provisions have not clearly distinguished these two situations and the legal principles discussed below overlap. For example, City Bank may finance Carb's stock acquisitions through a floating charge while Easy Finance may use a floor plan whereby it retains title and lets the goods to Carb on hire-purchase. While the commercial purpose and effect may be similar, different legal principles will apply which sometimes lead to inconsistent legal results. The Bills of Sale legislation and NCC Pt IV Div 9 considered in Chapter 7 are not specifically addressed to the question of the claims of bona fide purchasers. On the other hand, the Consumer Transactions Act 1972 (SA) s 36, Consumer Credit Act 1981 (NSW) s 105 and Chattel Securities Act 1981 (Vic) ss 8-11 and Pt III provide important statutory exceptions to the *nemo dat* rule and have been created specifically to protect bona fide purchasers from defects in title of the kind described in (2) above.

PROTECTION FROM PRIOR ENCUMBRANCES

What general policies should guide the resolution of the conflict between a secured financier (especially of stock-in-trade) and a buyer? There is a strong public policy in favour of preserving the viability of the market place and satisfying the expectations of buyers by ensuring that purchasers who acquire goods in good faith and for value in the ordinary course from merchants selling stock take free from floating security interests. Further, it is obviously unreasonable to expect commercial or consumer buyers to check public records for security agreements covering stock-in-trade. And, since consumers possess less expertise in business than merchants, they are entitled to a greater degree of protection.

However, such policy reasons for protecting good faith purchasers of stock regardless of the seller's insolvency or default under a stock-in-trade security do not apply with the same force where the purchaser seeks protection against a claim not created by the seller. In the case of a prior defect in the seller's title caused by fraud or theft, there are no special reasons for preferring the purchaser's claim to that of the true owner. In the absence of negligence or conduct of the owner contributing to the fraud or theft, there is no compelling reason to deny his claim, even as against his seller.

To what extent does Australian law meet these policy objectives? In relation to corporate floating charges, recognition of the notion that a security over stock should not preclude a bona fide purchaser for value from acquiring goods free from that security is achieved by reliance upon the licence conferred by the floating charge to sell and pass title in the ordinary course of business until crystallisation of the charge. Unless a purchaser has *actual* notice that the sale is in violation of the floating charge the chargee is estopped from denying the dealer's authority to sell the stock. Australian law recognises that it is impractical for a purchaser to be affected by constructive notice of a stock-in-trade encumbrance; for it has been held that there is no general doctrine of constructive notice in relation to commercial transactions: *Manchester Trust v Furness* [1895] 2 QB 539 at 545; *Re Valletort Sanitary Steam Laundry Co Ltd* [1903] 2 Ch 654; *Port Line Ltd v Ben Line Steamers Ltd* [1958] 2 QB 146 at 167; *Owens v Harris Bros* (1932) 34 WALR 110 at 118. There is no specific principle in our law that recognises the distinction between consumer sales and bulk transactions between merchants, but the limitation on the dealer's authority to sell only in the ordinary course of business will normally prevent a dealer effectively disposing of collateral in a bulk sale to another merchant.

In relation to antecedent claims to which the dealer is not a party but which create defects in title, the law differs between the respective states. The *nemo dat* rule applies to protect the prior owner or encumbrancee, except in Victoria, Tasmania, South Australia and Western Australia, where the Sale of Goods Acts retain the outmoded English principle of sale in market overt: Vic, s 28(1); Tas, s 27(1); SA, s 22; WA, s 22.

The Bills of Sale legislation is disuniform across Australia. Its primary purpose is simply the avoidance of secret charges. In the case of registered bills, the purchaser must rely either on the dealer's statutory power to sell in the ordinary course of business under the Factors Acts or his ostensible authority to sell. In either case this power is dependent upon the purchaser having no notice of any restriction on the dealer's authority to sell. In the case of unregistered bills, the purchaser has additional protection in some states by virtue of the total invalidation of the bill: NSW, s 5c (traders' bills); Tas, s 5; Qld, s 7(1); WA, s 27.

In a floor plan situation, a bona fide purchaser is protected either under the Factors Acts or by the doctrine of estoppel whereby the dealer, having been permitted to sell in its own name, acquires an ostensible authority to continue to do so, provided the purchaser has no actual knowledge of any limitation or revocation of the dealer's authority to sell.

As previously mentioned the Molomby Committee recommended comprehensive reforms in this area. The Consumer Transactions Act 1972 (SA) s 36 and the Consumer Credit Act 1981 (NSW) s 105 and the Chattel Securities Act 1981 (Vic) ss 8-11 and Pt III provide important statutory exceptions to the *nemo dat* rule by protecting bona fide purchasers for valuable consideration who purchase from a mortgagor (or other persons in prescribed circumstances) goods which are subject to a security interest of which the purchaser is unaware. Each section operates to confer on the purchaser a good title to the goods free from the security interest, but the wording of each section varies substantially.

In those states where the Uniform Hire-Purchase Acts still apply, purchasers of goods subject to existing hire-purchase or leasing agreements are not protected from residual claims of the finance company, nor is there any public registration system whereby a prospective purchaser could ascertain the existence of these encumbrances. While there is virtually unanimous agreement that consumer purchasers should obtain clear title to chattels acquired from a dealer for value and in good faith, this solution merely moves the risk of loss back on to the finance industry. The result in South Australia was a system of title insurance which in turn has led to an increase in conversions and higher insurance premiums which are ultimately passed on to the consumer.

The Molomby Committee suggested that encumbrances over identifiable goods such as motor vehicles and boats should be recorded in a register indexed by reference to the goods. A security interest "perfected" by registration would then prevail over a bona fide purchaser, since the prospective purchaser could search the register before acquiring the goods.

A registration system would involve substantial administrative expense, and no such register has as yet been established in any Australian state. However, such a register is to be provided under the Chattel Securities Act 1981 (Vic) and the way has been left open for such a system under the Consumer Credit Act 1981 (NSW) s 105(4). It has been suggested that registration of goods of less than $1500 may not be warranted.

For a detailed discussion of the policy issues involved see Peden, *Stock-in-Trade Financing*, 1974, especially pp 19-20, 50-6 and 186-91.

PROTECTION FROM OTHER DEFECTS IN TITLE: EXCEPTIONS TO NEMO DAT RULE

The common law *nemo dat* rule is codified in Sale of Goods Act 1923 (NSW) (hereinafter SGA):

26 (1) Subject to the provisions of this Act, where goods are sold by a person who is not the owner thereof and who does not sell them under the authority or with the consent of the owner, the buyer acquires no better title to the goods than the seller had, unless the owner of the goods is by his conduct precluded from denying the seller's authority to sell.

(2) Nothing in this Act shall affect —
(a) the provisions of the Factors (Mercantile Agents) Act, 1923;

(b) the validity of any contract of sale under any special common law or statutory power of sale, or under the order of a court of competent jurisdiction.

(Vic, ss 26, 27; Qld, s 24; SA, s 21; WA, s 21; Tas, s 26; ACT, s 26.)

However, as the section indicates, the rule is qualified by other provisions of the Act, the common law doctrine of estoppel, the factors legislation and other special powers of sale. This dichotomy was epitomised by Denning LJ in *Bishopsgate Motor Finance Corp Ltd v Transport Brakes Ltd* [1949] 1 KB 322 at 336-7:

> In the development of our law, two principles have striven for mastery. The first is for the protection of property: no one can give a better title than he himself possesses. The second is for the protection of commercial transactions; the person who takes in good faith and for value without notice should get a better title. The first principle has held sway for a long time, but it has been modified by the common law itself and by statute to meet the needs of our times.

Most of the cases in this area concern a conflict between an honest owner and a bona fide purchaser as to which shall bear the loss occasioned by the fraud of a rogue who has purported to sell the owner's goods to the purchaser. Both parties would have actions against the rogue but he is usually unavailable and/or insolvent. From the materials which follow, you should form your own view as to whether the pendulum has swung far enough or too far in favour of the bona fide purchaser. What general principles or policies should guide the solution of this conflict?

For convenience, the main exceptions to the *nemo dat* rule are listed in the order in which they are considered hereunder:

(a) the common law principles of estoppel, ostensible ownership and agency preserved by SGA s 26;

(b) sale by mercantile agent in the ordinary course of business: Factors (Mercantile Agents) Act 1923 (NSW) s 5;

(c) sale by owner with voidable title: SGA s 27;

(d) sale by seller continuing in possession after prior sale: SGA s 28(1), with which compare a resale by a seller exercising its power of sale under SGA s 50(2);

(e) sale by buyer in possession when title reserved to seller under conditional sale agreement: SGA s 28(2);

(f) sale by a mortgagor of goods subject to a security interest to a purchaser in good faith, for value and without notice of the security interest: Consumer Credit Act 1981 (NSW) s 105; Consumer Transactions Act 1972 (SA) s 36; Chattel Securities Act 1981 (Vic) ss 8, 11 and Pt III;

(g) sale in market overt or under special powers of sale;

(h) the common law doctrines of fixtures and accession.

Before considering these exceptions, two general points should be made. (1) Frequently a buyer in defending its title to goods may simultaneously rely on several alternative exceptions, but in order to succeed only one need be established. (2) These exceptions are concerned with protecting the title of the buyer or subsequent encumbrancees against the original owner (note, eg, the heading above SGA s 26 "Transfer of Title"), which should be distinguished from SGA ss 21-25 headed "Transfer of *property* as between seller and buyer" which were previously considered in Chapter 4.

COMMON LAW PRINCIPLES OF ESTOPPEL, OSTENSIBLE OWNERSHIP AND AGENCY PRESERVED BY SGA s 26

Motor Credits (Hire Finance) Ltd v Pacific Motor Auctions Pty Ltd
High Court of Australia (1963) 109 CLR 87

Taylor J: In the commercial cause out of which this appeal arises the appellant sued the respondent for the return of 20 second-hand motor vehicles which it alleged had been wrongfully detained by the respondent. At the trial the appellant abandoned its claim with respect to four of the vehicles and, as an alternative to the return of the remaining 16, it claimed to recover their value and damages for detention.

The motor vehicles in question had never been in the possession of the appellant but the points of claim filed by it in the action show briefly how the claim arose. It was alleged that on 2 November 1960 and at all material times the motor vehicles were the absolute property of the plaintiff and that, on that date, they were in the possession of a company, Motordom Pty Ltd (hereinafter referred to as Motordom) as bailee for the plaintiff and not otherwise. It was further alleged that on that date Motordom had no authority to sell the vehicles but that, nevertheless, it did, without any such authority, purport to sell them to the defendant whereupon the latter took possession of them. Subsequently the appellant made a demand for the return of the vehicles but the demand was not complied with. In answer to the claim the respondent denied the appellant's title to the vehicles and also denied Motordom's alleged lack of authority to make the sale in question. Additionally, the respondent alleged, in effect, that the appellant had held out and represented Motordom as the owner of the vehicles or as a person having full power and authority to sell them to a purchaser and that the respondent dealt with Motordom on the faith of such representation. Other subsidiary matters were raised by way of defence and to these reference will presently be made.

As its name implies, the appellant is a finance house and it was part of its business to provide accommodation to motor vehicle dealers pursuant to what we were told is called in the trade a "floor plan" or "display agreement". It had entered into such an agreement in writing with a dealer named Webb who, in the course of his business, both bought from and sold to the respondent motor vehicles from time to time. Broadly the purpose of such agreements is to provide dealers with finance to enable them to carry on the business of buying and selling motor vehicles. The agreement which the appellant made with Webb seems to be more or less in a common form and in it the appellant is described as "the company" and the dealer is described as "the agent". It recites that the company, at the request of the agent, had agreed to permit the agent to acquire motor vehicles on its behalf and to sell such vehicles on behalf of the company upon the terms therein set out. The ensuing terms relate both to the purchase of new vehicles and second-hand vehicles but we need make no reference to the provisions of the agreement in so far as they are concerned solely with new vehicles. By cl 1 the agent was authorised to purchase such types of motor vehicles and cycles and in such quantity as the company might from time to time in writing authorise. The agent was to be at liberty to purchase used goods either in the name of the company or in the name of the agent without disclosing the agency. By cl 3 the company was bound to pay to the agent 90 per cent of the purchase price or trade-in allowance paid or allowed in respect of any second-hand vehicle but this provision was subject to the company's right in any particular case to have an assessment made of the fair wholesale value of any such vehicles. Pending resale the agent was to keep all such vehicles in good order and condition and upon resale he was bound to account for the sale price in the manner specified by cl 5. By this clause the agent agreed that as from the date of the acquisition "any goods purchased in pursuance hereof shall be on hire and the possession of the agent shall be as bailee only". Nevertheless he was to be at liberty to sell such goods on behalf of the company. In respect of cash sales and hire-purchase transactions not arranged through the company the agent was bound to account to the company immediately thereafter. In the case of hire-purchase transactions arranged through and accepted by the company, the agent was bound to account for the deposit received in accordance with the terms of the clause. Clause 6 provided that the agent or the company might at any time respectively return or require the return of any vehicles and the agent undertook on demand forthwith to deliver up possession of the vehicles demanded. Further the company was to be at liberty to take possession of any vehicles subject to the agreement without previous notice. The final clause of the agreement related to what was called rental or hiring and it provided in effect for a stipulated interest charge on the amount paid or allowed by the company in connection with the purchase or trading-in of any particular vehicle calculated in respect of the period elapsing between its purchase or trade-in and its subsequent resale.

Prior to the transactions with which we are immediately concerned, Webb had carried on business for some time under the trade name of Motordom. But before the material date the company known as Motordom Pty Ltd was incorporated and it took over Webb's business. He, however, was in control of the company and he continued to manage and control the business. No fresh display agreement was entered into between Motordom and the appellant but there was abundant evidence to show, and the learned trial judge found, that the course of business between them indicated that they assumed a business association more or less on the basis of the arrangement which the earlier written agreement had created between Webb and the appellant. We should, however, mention that the terms of the written agreement seem never to have been strictly adhered to. Indeed, there was one important departure, for Webb, and later Motordom, adopted the practice of purchasing vehicles without any prior authority from the appellant, in writing or otherwise, and according to the learned trial judge, Webb, and Motordom after its incorporation, did not buy on behalf of the appellant but on their own behalf. The course of dealing between the appellant and Motordom was fully discussed by the learned trial judge and it is unnecessary to traverse the same ground in detail. But apparently what happened was that Motordom exercised its own judgment in selecting and purchasing motor vehicles and some of these never became subject to the display agreement. Nevertheless a great many of the vehicles were, subsequently to their purchase, said to be accepted as being subject to the display agreement. What happened was that as vehicles "on display" were sold they would be replaced by other vehicles which Motordom had purchased. Proposals for this purpose were sometimes made by telephone, sometimes in the course of a personal call by Webb at the offices of the appellant and sometimes personally when the appellant's representative visited Motordom's premises. The proposals would be reported to the acceptance manager of the appellant and upon any proposal being accepted a cheque would be made out and forwarded to Motordom accompanied by a list of the accepted vehicles. A number of these lists was tendered in evidence; they refer to the display plan, specify the make and registered numbers of the vehicles accepted and the amounts to be paid in respect of each. After a review of the evidence concerning the numerous dealings between the appellant and Motordom the learned trial judge said that he was satisfied that, at all times prior to 2 November 1960, "it was clear that the course of business was such that when Motordom bought a vehicle it did so on its own account and not as agent for the plaintiff, so that title to that vehicle thereupon passed to Motordom". Upon a careful examination of the evidence this finding of fact was, we think, inevitable. However, the appellant sought to overcome the difficulty presented by this finding by contending that, upon the evidence, it was clear that when a vehicle was subsequently accepted as subject to the display plan and an advance or payment made in respect of it, the title passed to it. As his Honour said it was the claim of the appellant "that when a request was made to it to put any such vehicle on display plan, this constituted an offer to sell that vehicle to the plaintiff upon the terms with which, by reason of the previous arrangements and the course of dealing, the parties were familiar, and that thereupon, when the plaintiff accepted this offer, the title passed to the plaintiff". Nevertheless his Honour was of the opinion that "assuming that the plaintiff then acquired a valid title to such a vehicle, Motordom had the right to retain it in its possession and had a general authority to resell it in its own name and at such price as it should decide, and a right to receive the purchase money and to retain it, subject only to its obligation to account to the plaintiff in the manner specified in the display agreement". His Honour observed that the evidence relating to the terms of the arrangement between the appellant and Motordom was not very clear but, nevertheless, he was prepared to hold that it was "the intention of the parties, when cars were brought into the arrangement, that the general property in those cars should pass to the plaintiff".

With this brief account in mind it is convenient to come to the transaction or transactions which took place on the night of 2 November 1960. During the previous week three cheques of Motordom which had been given by that company to the respondent in payment for vehicles purchased from it, had been dishonoured. These cheques were for £6965, £2535 and £3790 respectively. For a few days the respondent appears to have thought that Motordom's difficulties were only of a temporary nature and that the total sum involved, namely £13,290, would shortly be paid. But by 2 November 1960 it seemed to have become more or less generally known in the trade that Motordom was in serious financial trouble and on the afternoon of that day Webb was summoned to see the respondent's general manager, Crealey. Upon the evidence which the learned trial judge accepted it is quite clear that at this stage the respondent was intent upon obtaining satisfaction from Motordom that day. For this purpose the proposal was made to Webb that he should sell some of Motordom's stock at its various yards to the respondent and, if the outstanding cheques were met upon re-presentation, the respondent would return the cars to Motordom. Webb agreed and the details of what occurred that evening are set out in the learned trial judge's reasons: "A party from the defendant's office, and Webb, then went to several yards, and cars were selected and listed, and prices put against them by Guest. After some discussion about the prices Webb said that he would definitely be taking the cars back, and Crealey then agreed to adopt the prices which Motordom had paid for the cars when it acquired them. There was an arrangement that the defendant would hold the cars, to redeliver them to Motordom, if the money was found. The total amount due to the defendant had been calculated at £16,510. It seems that there was some additional debt, apart from the cheques abovementioned. After 29 cars had been listed, it seems that an upwards adjustment of the price assigned for some of them took place, in order that the total price would come up to £16,510. For each vehicle declarations were obtained, signed by Webb, reciting a sale of the vehicle at a specified price and stating that the vehicle was the seller's sole property, free from any other interest, and that the seller had good right and title to sell it. A cheque which the defendant's accountant, Skinner, had taken with him, was completed in favour of Motordom, for £16,510, and was signed for the defendant by Crealey and Skinner. On the back of it was written, 'Please pay to order of Pacific Motor Auctions Ltd', and this was signed by Webb. The cheque was handed back to the defendant's representatives. The cars were taken away and were subsequently resold by the defendant. The dishonoured cheques of Motordom were not met and on each of them is endorsed the words, 'Payment stopped'": (1962) 79 WN (NSW) at 689.

The news of Motordom's difficulties had also reached the appellant during the afternoon of 2 November and thereupon the appellant's manager communicated with Webb by telephone and expressly revoked his authority to deal with cars which were the property of the appellant. This occurred several hours before Webb's nocturnal dealings with the respondent. It should perhaps also be mentioned that the respondent was not the only motor dealer in attendance upon Webb's premises on that night; representatives of another motor-dealing firm were also present and there is evidence which shows that on that night many of the cars which had been in the yards were disposed of, leaving only a relatively small number of less valuable vehicles. Webb, it remains to be said, was not called as a witness at the trial and it was said during the course of argument that at the time of the trial his whereabouts were unknown.

In the result the learned trial judge dealt with the case on the assumption, which I think he rightly made, that the appellant had established its title to the subject vehicles and that it had, in the circumstances disclosed by the evidence, an immediate right to possession upon which to found its claim. However, he held that in the circumstances as they appeared to him the appellant was estopped from denying that Motordom had authority to sell the vehicles to the respondent. In so deciding his Honour appears to have felt constrained by the decision in *Eastern Distributors Ltd v Goldring (Murphy, Third Party)* [1957] 2 QB 600 and he concluded, upon the authority of that case, that it was an immaterial consideration that the transaction of 2 November 1960 was not in the ordinary course of Motordom's business and that its only purpose was to secure and ultimately to discharge Motordom's outstanding indebtedness to the respondent. But, with respect to the learned judge, I do not regard the *Eastern Distributors* case as requiring or leading to any such conclusion. In the first place there was not in that case any suggestion that the transaction there in question was not in the ordinary course of the dealer's business. But, secondly, it is of vital importance to notice that case was essentially one of ostensible ownership; it was a case where, in the language of Devlin LJ (as he then was) "Coker (the dealer) represented that the car was his, and Murphy (the owner) was privy to that representation being made; so neither can be heard to say that Coker had not a *good title* to transfer to the plaintiffs": [1957] 2 QB 600. The italics are mine and serve to emphasise the fact that the case was primarily one of ostensible ownership and not one of ostensible agency. There has been, as is pointed out in *Ewart on Estoppel,* 1900, p 238 *et seq,* considerable confusion between these two subject matters of estoppel and it is of importance to observe that if a person deals with an ostensible owner no question can arise concerning the extent of that person's authority to deal on behalf of a principal. On the contrary, if he deals with an ostensible agent the question of the extent of the latter's apparent authority is a very material matter. As *Ewart* puts it, in the former case "some person has appeared to be the owner of property when in reality he was not", whilst in the latter type of case "some person has appeared to have authority to do something, when in reality he has not". Accordingly, in the latter case, it is essential to determine what apparent authority an ostensible agent has...

In my view the present case is not one of ostensible ownership. It is, of course, true that Webb, on behalf of Motordom, falsely represented that the vehicles which he purported to sell to the respondent were Motordom's sole and absolute and unencumbered property and free from any charge or other adverse interest whatsoever and that no person or corporation had any right title or interest therein. But this was Webb's representation and there is not the slightest evidence to suggest that he was authorised by the appellant to make the representation or to show that it was made with the latter's knowledge or consent. It is again true that the respondent was not informed of the revocation of Motordom's authority and that the appellant's vehicles still remained in the possession of that company. But, as the learned trial judge found, the respondent knew that Motordom had obtained "floor plan accommodation" from the appellant and that the limit of such accommodation had in October 1960 been increased by £5000. With its knowledge of the manner in which business was conducted in the trade this was the clearest intimation to the respondent that Motordom was dealing in cars which, although in its possession, were not its property and, that being so, we can see no grounds upon which it can be asserted that Motordom's possession of the vehicles in question gave rise to a case of ostensible ownership. The mere fact that the goods of one person are seen to be in the possession of another does not, of itself, create a situation of ostensible ownership. If it were otherwise the owner of a vehicle who had lent it to another might find himself estopped from asserting his title against an innocent purchaser from the latter. The same situation would also arise where the hirer of goods under a hiring agreement had fraudulently disposed of the goods to an innocent purchaser. Many other illustrations might be given but, nevertheless, possession may be given in such circumstances as to make it appear that the person in possession is the owner. For instance, if a vehicle were delivered to a person who happened to be a dealer in motor vehicles in order that he might place it among his stock for sale he would appear to be the owner to any person not knowing the true facts. In the present case, however, it was about as clear as it could be to the respondent that Motordom was dealing in vehicles of which it had possession but which were not its property. Accordingly, the circumstances of its possession were not such as to lead the respondent to suppose that the vehicles in question were the property of Motordom.

Subject to one matter which I shall presently mention, the case therefore comes back to one of ostensible authority. As was found below there is every reason for thinking that notwithstanding the revocation of its authority to deal with the appellant's cars, circumstances continued to exist at the relevant time which would have made it appear to any person dealing with Webb in the ordinary course of business that he continued to have authority to sell the vehicles which remained in his possession. But the transaction in this case was of a very special character and it is that transaction with which we are immediately concerned. As already appears it was not a transaction in the ordinary course of business; it was in effect a forced sale of a substantial part of Motordom's stock which, it seems, secured a limited right of redemption to Motordom and it was entered into purely for the purpose of providing security or ultimately discharging Motordom's debt to the respondent. To me it seems quite clear that if Webb's authority had not been revoked it would not have extended to authorise this present transaction and I can see no reason for supposing that, in the circumstances as they existed on the night of 2 November 1960, he appeared to have a wider authority than that which he would actually have possessed if his authority had not been revoked. This being so I am of the opinion that this issue should have been decided in favour of the appellant...

The next matter was concerned with s 28 of the Sale of Goods Act, the respondent contending that this was a case where Motordom having sold to the appellant the vehicles which were "accepted" for the purposes of the display plan continued in possession of them and that pursuant to that section the transaction of 2 November 1960 was effective to transfer the title to the vehicles to the respondent. There is, however, substantial authority for the proposition that this section has no application where the character of a seller's possession has changed and he does not remain in possession merely as seller but by virtue of his rights as a bailee: *Staffs Motor Guarantee Ltd v British Wagon Co Ltd* [1934] 2 KB 305 and *Eastern Distributors Ltd v Goldring (Murphy, Third Party)* [1957] 2 QB 600 at 613, 614. I see no reason to dissent from the statement of the principle in those cases and this contention of the respondent must therefore be rejected...

For the reasons given the appeal should be allowed and a new trial ordered for the assessment of damages.

Owen J [stated the facts and continued at 102:] As stated above, the learned trial judge proceeded upon the basis that the effect of the "display plan" arrangement between the plaintiff and Motordom was to vest in the plaintiff as purchaser from Motordom the title to cars originally bought by Motordom on its own behalf and subsequently accepted by the plaintiff for inclusion in the "display plan" arrangement, such cars thereafter being held by Motordom as a bailee from the plaintiff for the purposes of resale on the terms of that arrangement. That being so, the question is whether the plaintiff, to adopt the words of s 26(1) of the Sale of Goods Act, "is by its conduct precluded from denying" Motordom's authority to deal with the 16 cars in question in the way in which it did. There can be no doubt that had Motordom sold the cars in the ordinary course of its business, the defendant would have got a good title to them notwithstanding the fact that the plaintiff had revoked Motordom's authority to sell. The case would then have fallen within the terms of s 5 of the Factors Act. But the transaction between Motordom and the defendant was not one in the ordinary course of Motordom's business as a dealer in cars and that section cannot therefore operate. Nor can the defendant rely upon s 28(1) of the Sale of Goods Act since Motordom was not in possession of the goods merely as the seller of them to the plaintiff but as a bailee under the "display plan" arrangement: *Staffs Motor Guarantee Ltd v British Wagon Co Ltd; Eastern Distributors Ltd v Goldring (Murphy, Third Party)*. It was necessary, therefore, for the defendant to show that it had been induced by the plaintiff's conduct to believe that Motordom was entitled to deal with the cars in a manner which was outside the ordinary course of a dealer's business. Motordom professed to sell the cars as the owner of them but there is nothing in the evidence which would justify the conclusion that in the particular transaction with which this case is concerned the plaintiff was privy to that representation. In that respect the facts differ from those in the *Eastern Distributors* case. There Murphy, the owner of the vehicle, agreed that another person, Coker, should pretend to the plaintiff, a hire purchase company, that he, Coker, owned the vehicle in order to induce the plaintiff to buy it from Coker and the plaintiff, in reliance upon the representation that Coker was the owner, bought the vehicle. But that is not this case. By allowing the cars which it owned to be in the possession of Motordom the plaintiff unquestionably held that company out as having authority to sell them in the ordinary course of its business as a dealer and, for the purposes of such sales, to represent that it was the owner of cars sold. And any such sale would have been effective to pass title to an innocent purchaser notwithstanding the revocation of Motordom's authority since a purchaser of goods from one whose business it is to buy and sell goods of that description is entitled to assume that the seller has authority to sell, in the ordinary course of his business, goods of that description which are in his possession. But a purchaser is not entitled to assume that the seller has authority to deal with such goods otherwise than in the ordinary course of business unless there be some further act by the true owner leading the purchaser to believe that the seller is clothed with authority to enter into such a transaction.

In the present case I can see nothing to support such a conclusion and thus preclude the plaintiff from denying Motordom's authority to deal with the cars in the way in which it did. In other words, the plaintiff did no more than hold out Motordom as having authority to dispose of its cars in the ordinary course of its business as a dealer.

It should be added that counsel for the defendant submitted that under the terms of the "display plan" arrangement, the purported revocation by the defendant of Motordom's authority was ineffective. I am unable to agree with the submission but, even if it were so, the defendant's position would not be thereby bettered since the actual authority conferred upon Motordom was, in my opinion, one which did no more than authorise sales in the ordinary course of Motordom's business as a dealer...

The appeal should be allowed and the cross-appeal dismissed.

[**McTiernan J** (dissenting) agreed with the judgment of the trial judge Walsh J and considered that the appeal and cross appeal should be dismissed.]

Appeal allowed with costs.

Pacific Motor Auctions then appealed to the Privy Council, which reversed the decision of the High Court on the application of SGA s 28(1) (see p 348, *infra*) but did not consider the question of estoppel.

Compare *General Distributors Ltd v Paramotors Ltd* [1962] SASR 1 in which a dealer held a car under a floor plan arrangement with the appellant General Distributors who may "have been estopped from denying [the dealer] Beesley's authority to sell and deliver the car to a customer entering his showroom, seeing it there, and purchasing it in good faith": per Napier CJ at 16. However, the sale to another dealer at the latter's premises on the pretext that it was not the type of vehicle that Beesley could easily sell was held to be outside the ordinary course of his business and raised no estoppel against the appellant.

In *Lloyds & Scottish Finance Ltd v Williamson* [1965] 1 WLR 404, the plaintiff owner authorised a dealer to sell its vehicle knowing that the dealer probably would sell as principal and therefore impliedly authorised it to do so. The dealer held itself out to the buyer and sold to him as apparent owner. Accordingly, the buyer obtained a good title at common law even though the sale was not in the ordinary course of business and the dealer did not account to the plaintiff for the proceeds of sale.

SALE BY MERCANTILE AGENT

Factors (Mercantile Agents) Act 1923 (NSW)

3 In this Act, unless the context or subject-matter otherwise requires —
"Mercantile agent" means a mercantile agent having in the customary course of his business as such agent authority either to sell goods, or to consign goods for the purpose of sale, or to buy goods, or to raise money on the security of goods.

5 (1) Where a mercantile agent is entrusted as such with the possession of any goods or the documents of title to goods, any sale pledge or other disposition of the goods made by him in the ordinary course of business of a mercantile agent shall, subject to the provisions of this Act, be as valid as if he were expressly authorised by the owner of the goods to make the same:

Provided that the person taking under the disposition acts in good faith, and has not at the time of the disposition notice that the person making the disposition has not authority to make the same.

(2) Where a mercantile agent so entrusted continues in possession of goods or of the documents of title to goods, any sale pledge or other disposition, which would have been valid if the entrusting had continued, shall be valid notwithstanding the determination thereof, provided that the person taking under the disposition has not at the time thereof notice of such determination.

(Vic, Goods Act ss 65, 67; Qld, Factors Act ss 2, 3; SA, Mercantile Law Act ss 3, 4; Tas, Factors Act ss 3, 5; ACT, Mercantile Law Ordinance ss 4, 6; WA, the English Factors Act 1889 ss 1, 2 apply.)

The main issues which arise under these provisions are:
  (a) whether the person effecting the sale, pledge or other disposition is a mercantile agent: it is the nature of what the agent is required to do rather than the length of time he has been carrying on business which is important. "The business of a mercantile agent, like any other, must have a beginning, and it cannot be that the first transaction in such a business is not within the protection of the statute": *Mortgage Loan & Finance Co of Australia Ltd v Richards* (1932) 32 SR (NSW) 50 at 58, per Halse Rogers J;
  (b) whether the agent has been entrusted as such and by or on behalf of the owner;
  (c) whether the sale, etc was made by the agent in the ordinary course of business as a mercantile agent;
  (d) whether the buyer, pledgee, etc took in good faith and without notice of the lack of actual authority.

Priorities in Relation to Chattel Securities

Roache v Australian Mercantile Land & Finance Co Ltd (No 2)
New South Wales Court of Appeal (1966) 67 SR (NSW) 54

[Kennedy, who was a stock and station agent known to the appellant Roache, pretended he was purchasing lambs from them on behalf of a wholesale butcher and meat exporting company. In reality he had no authority whatsoever from the company and the lambs were sent to the defendant as if they were Kennedy's own property. The defendant sold them at auction and accounted for the proceeds to Kennedy. The defendant relied on s 5 of the Factors (Mercantile Agents) Act 1923 (NSW) as a defence. The principal question was whether Kennedy had the sheep in his possession with the consent of the owner.

In the course of his judgment **Holmes JA** said:] The case is one of those in which the problem posed involves the determination of which of two innocent people is to suffer for the wrong of a third party...

The principle of the common law was, and still is, *nemo dat quod non habet*. The history of agency has involved a series of departures from this principle, designed of course to prevent the obvious stagnation of commerce which would have resulted from its strict application. People dealing with agents would always be at peril if they were confined to having to discover and observe the actual authority of the agent and not be entitled to rely upon the agent's ostensible authority. From early times therefore exceptions upon the common law rule were engrafted in favour of persons dealing with brokers or factors. The principle is stated quite clearly by Lord Ellenborough as long ago as 1812 in *Pickering v Busk* (1812) 15 Ea 38 at 43; 104 ER 758 at 760: "Strangers can only look to the acts of the parties, and to the external indicia of property, and not to the private communications which may pass between a principal and his broker: and if a person authorise another to assume the apparent right of disposing of property in the ordinary course of trade, it must be presumed that the apparent authority is the real authority. I cannot subscribe to the doctrines, that a broker's engagements are necessarily and in all cases limited to his actual authority, the reality of which is afterwards to be tried by the fact. It is clear that he may bind his principal within the limits of the authority with which he has been apparently clothed by the principal in respect of the subject matter; and there would be no safety in mercantile transaction if he could not. If the principal send his commodity to a place, where it is the ordinary business of the person to whom it is confided to sell, it must be intended that the commodity was sent thither for the purpose of sale... The case of a factor not being able to pledge the goods of his principal confided to him for sale though clothed with an apparent ownership, has been pressed upon us in the argument, and considerably distressed our decision. The court however will decide that question when it arises, consistently with the principle on which the present decision is founded. It was a hard doctrine when the pawnee was told that the pledger of the goods had no authority to pledge them, being a mere factor for sale; and yet since the case of *Paterson v Tash* (1743) 2 Str 1178; 93 ER 1110 that doctrine has never been overturned"...

It is significant however that in the two cases to which I have referred the court has been concerned with the authority of a person who was an agent and what his ostensible authority was. There was no question that the person concerned was not an agent of the owner.

It seems to me that this view was maintained in the cases to which we have been referred and many of which were given a close examination, indeed a closer examination than I think is called for for the purposes of this judgment. For example, in *Baines v Swainson* (1863) 4 B & S 270; 122 ER 460 and *Oppenheimer v Frazer and Wyatt* [1907] 1 KB 519 there was a bailment by the owner with the mercantile agent, even though the entrusting was induced by a fraudulent representation. The contrast is to be seen in cases like *Hardman v Booth* (1862) 1 H & C 803; 158 ER 1107 and *Lake v Simmons* [1927] AC 487. I think it was this kind of distinction which was present in the mind of Blackburn J when he gave his opinion as one of the judges summoned to the House of Lords in *Hollins v Fowler* (1875) LR 7 HL 757: "My Lords, it appears from the statement in the case that Fowlers, the plaintiffs had delivered into the actual custody of Bayley, a broker, 13 bails of cotton, their property, they believing they had sold those bails to Seddon, through Bayley as Seddon's broker, after they had refused to trust Bayley himself; and believing that Bayley was the agent of Seddon to receive delivery; so that Fowlers thought they were transferring the property to Seddons either to purchase or to take delivery.

"Under such circumstances the property and legal right to the possession remained in

Fowlers and Bayley could not (except by a sale in market overt) confer on anyone, however innocent, a title superior to his own. He could not do it under the Factors Acts, because he was not entrusted by the plaintiffs as their agents": at 762.

It will be observed that Blackburn J, in dealing it is true with the question of whether an auctioneer had converted goods delivered to him for sale by a broker, also distinguished the case of a delivery to the auctioneer by a factor and that he did it upon the basis that the owner of the goods had not entrusted that factor as his agent. The illustration by Blackburn J is really the very case we have in hand. Furthermore Blackburn J went on to say that in his opinion the decision in *Hardman v Booth* was correct...

In all of these cases however the point is that the owner of the goods however he was deceived was constituting, he thought, the rogue albeit a mercantile agent or factor, as his agent. The question that ultimately arose in each of them, therefore, was whether a purchaser from the agent was entitled to rely upon the agent's ostensible authority. It was clear, however, that the owner had intended to confer upon the agent some authority and consequently the cases fitted into the pattern under which protection was given to a person who took from a factor and who was entitled to rely upon the factor's ostensible authority, so long as he acted without notice and in good faith. These cases have nothing to do with the problem here in hand it seems to me, for the very reason that Roache and Mrs Roache never at any time handed over possession of the lambs to Kennedy so that Kennedy could deal with those lambs as their agent...

On this view of the matter I do not think that the sheep were entrusted to Kennedy by Roache or that they were in Kennedy's possession with the consent of Roache. On that view the Act has nothing to do with the case at all...

It follows therefore that the defence under s 5 of the Factors (Mercantile Agents) Act 1923, as a matter of law cannot succeed, and that the appeal be allowed with costs.

I agree with Jacobs JA that there should be a verdict and judgment for the plaintiff for $2470.88 and costs.

[**Jacobs JA** delivered judgment to similar effect. **Moffitt AJA** agreed with the judgment of Jacobs JA.]

Appeal allowed with costs.

Reference may also be made to *Raffoul v Esanda Ltd* (1970) 72 SR (NSW) 633; *Suttons Motors Pty Ltd v Hollywood Motors Pty Ltd* [1971] VR 684 and *Magnussen v Flanagan* [1981] 2 NSWLR 926.

SALE BY OWNER WITH VOIDABLE TITLE
Sale of Goods Act (NSW) s 27

27 Where the seller of goods has a voidable title thereto, but his title has not been avoided at the time of sale, the buyer acquires a good title to the goods, provided he buys them in good faith and without notice of the seller's defect of title.

(Vic, s 29; Qld, s 25; SA, s 23; WA, s 23; Tas, s 28; ACT s 27.)

This section requires a number of questions to be answered:

(1) When is a seller's title void as distinct from being merely voidable?

(2) If a rogue obtained goods by misrepresenting himself as somebody else and passing a valueless cheque, his purported title may be void *ab initio* for mistake if his identity is an essential element in making the contract: *Ingram v Little* [1961] 1 QB 31 (CA). However, there is a presumption that where a contract is made face to face, a mistake as to identity or attributes of the rogue renders the contract and therefore the title merely voidable so that he can confer a good title on a bona fide purchaser: *Phillips v Brooks* [1919] 2 KB 243; *Lewis v Averay* [1972] 1 QB 198 (CA).

(3) How does the original seller effectively rescind the voidable contract with the rogue?

Car and Universal Finance Co Ltd v Caldwell
English Court of Appeal [1965] 1 QB 525

[Caldwell advertised his Jaguar car for sale and sold it to a rogue Norris in exchange for a cheque for £965. When Caldwell presented the cheque to the bank at 10 am next morning it was dishonoured and he immediately notified the police and Automobile Association of the fraud and sought their assistance to recover the vehicle. Norris resold the car to Motobella Co Ltd who being aware of the defect in title, in turn resold the vehicle and it passed through several transactions until the plaintiffs Car and Universal Finance Co Ltd purchased it in good faith and without notice of the defect in title. Caldwell obtained a judgment by default against Motobella Co Ltd pursuant to which the sheriff seized the car in execution. The plaintiffs brought an interpleader summons to determine whether they were entitled to the vehicle. Denning MR, sitting as an additional judge of the Queen's Bench Division, held that Caldwell had effectively rescinded the contract of sale with Norris. The plaintiff appealed.]

Sellers LJ: This appeal raises a primary point in the law of contract. The question has arisen whether a contract which is voidable by one party can in any circumstances be terminated by that party without his rescission being communicated to the other party. Lord Denning MR has held in the circumstances of this case that there can be rescission without communication where the seller of a motor car, who admittedly had the right to rescind the contract of sale on the ground of fraudulent misrepresentation, terminated the contract by an unequivocal act of election which demonstrated clearly that he had elected to rescind it and to be no longer bound by it. The general rule, no doubt, is that where a party is entitled to rescind a contract and wishes to do so the contract subsists until the opposing party is informed that the contract has been terminated. The difficulty of the seller in this case was that, when he learnt of the fraud and, therefore, ascertained his right to terminate the bargain, he could not without considerable delay find either the fraudulent buyer or the car which had been sold...

An affirmation of a voidable contract may be established by any conduct which unequivocally manifests an intention to affirm it by the party who has the right to affirm or disaffirm. Communication of an acceptance of a contract after knowledge of a fundamental breach of it by the other party or of fraud affecting it is, of course, evidence establishing affirmation but it is not essential evidence. A party cannot reject goods sold and delivered if he uses them after knowledge of a right to reject, and the judgment cites a case where an instruction to a broker to resell was sufficient affirmation of the contract in question even though that conduct was not communicated. It may be said that a contract may be more readily approved and accepted than it can be terminated where a unilateral right to affirm or disaffirm arises. The disaffirmation or election to avoid a contract changes the relationship of the parties and brings their respective obligations to an end, whereas an affirmation leaves the contract effective though subject to a claim for damages for its breach. Where a contracting party could be communicated with, and modern facilities make communication practically worldwide and almost immediate, it would be unlikely that a party could be held to have disaffirmed a contract unless he went so far as to communicate his decision so to do. It would be what the other contracting party would normally require and unless communication were made the party's intention to rescind would not have been unequivocally or clearly demonstrated or made manifest. But in circumstances such as the present case, the other contracting party, a fraudulent rogue who would know that the vendor would want his car back as soon as he knew of the fraud, would not expect to be communicated with as a matter of right or requirement, and would deliberately, as here, do all he could to evade any such communication being made to him. In such exceptional contractual circumstances, it does not seem to me appropriate to hold that a party so acting can claim any right to have a decision to rescind communicated to him before the contract is terminated. To hold that he could would involve that the defrauding party, if skilful enough to keep out of the way, could deprive the other party to the contract of his right to rescind, a right to which he was entitled and which he would wish to exercise, as the defrauding party would well know or at least confidently suspect. The position has to be viewed, as I see it, between the two contracting parties involved in the particular contract in question. That another innocent party or parties may suffer does not in my view of the matter justify imposing on a defrauded seller an impossible task. He has to establish, clearly and unequivocally, that he terminates the contract and is no longer to be bound by it. If he cannot communicate his decision he may still satisfy a judge or jury that he had made a final and irrevocable decision and ended the contract. I am in agreement with Lord Denning MR who asked [1965] 1 QB 525 at 531 "How is a man in the position of Caldwell ever to be able to rescind the contract when a fraudulent person absconds as Norris did here?" and answered that he can do so (at 532) "... if he at once, on discovering the fraud, takes all possible steps to regain the goods even though he cannot find the rogue nor communicate with him".

[His Lordship then discussed the well-known case of *Scarf v Jardine* (1882) 7 App Cas 345 and continued:]

In the case of an innocent misrepresentation, in circumstances which would permit the party misled to rescind, the other party would not deliberately avoid communication (for that would seem to negative innocence) and circumstances would be rare where communication could not be readily made in one way or another. If communication were possible, it is difficult to see how there could be rescission without communication, and the inference would be that the contracting parties require communication of termination. Special circumstances may arise and call for future consideration but I do not think the comparison made in argument on behalf of the plaintiffs between innocent and fraudulent misrepresentation invalidates the judgment of Lord Denning MR. It has to be recognised that in transactions such as this where fraud intervenes, some innocent party may have to suffer, and it may well be that legislation is overdue to do justice between the victims of fraud and to apportion in some way the loss. In the present case, however, I can see nothing unjust in the loss falling on G & C Finance (against whom the plaintiffs can claim redress), who made the minimum inquiries, who bought a car, which, apparently, they never saw and hired it out to a man, of whose existence and identity they did not know, and who may well have been fictitious, rather than that the loss should fall on the defendant, who acted immediately and did all in his power to retract the transaction.

I would dismiss the appeal on this issue and that is sufficient to decide the appeal in the defendant's favour...

[**Upjohn** and **Davies LJJ** delivered judgment to similar effect.]

Appeal dismissed with costs.

SECOND SALE BY ORIGINAL SELLER

We have already noted that when a buyer defaults, the unpaid seller has a statutory power of sale under SGA s 50(2) which will protect the second buyer even if he is aware of the first sale: see pp 133–5, *supra*. Conversely, where Carb sells to Easy Finance which advances the purchase price under a floor plan arrangement, Carb will retain possession for the purposes of final sale. If Carb fails to reimburse Easy Finance from the ultimate proceeds of the sale to second buyer Driver or Bestcars Ltd, can Easy Finance recover from these buyers? Easy Finance may be estopped from denying Carb's authority to sell (see *Pacific Motor Auctions* case, p 338, *supra*), or Driver and Bestcars may rely on SGA s 28(1) which provides:

28 (1) Where a person having sold goods continues or is in possession of the goods or of the documents of title to the goods, the delivery or transfer by that person or by a mercantile agent acting for him of the goods or documents of title under any sale pledge or other disposition thereof to any person receiving the same in good faith and without notice of the previous sale shall have the same effect as if the person making the delivery or transfer were expressly authorised by the owner of the goods to make the same.

(Vic, s 30; Qld, s 27(1); SA, s 25(1); WA, s 25(1); Tas, s 30(1); ACT, s 29(1).)

Pacific Motor Auctions Pty Ltd v Motor Credits (Hire Finance) Ltd
Privy Council (1965) 112 CLR 1

[For the facts, see p 338, *supra*.]

Lord Pearce [delivered the judgment of their Lordships. After stating the facts and reviewing the decisions in the lower courts, he continued at 198:] The point under s 28(1) turns on the construction of the words "where a person having sold goods continues or is in possession of the goods". Are those words to be construed in their full sense so that wherever a person is found to be in possession of goods which he has previously sold he can, whatever be the capacity in which he has possession, pass a good title? Or is some, and if so what, limitation to be placed on them by considering the quality and title of the seller's possession at the time when he sells them again to an innocent purchaser?

Section 28(1) does not limit its effect to a sale "made in the ordinary course of business" as does s 5 of the Factors (Mercantile Agents) Act 1923 and the corresponding English provision. But Mr Newton for the respondent urged their Lordships to limit the application of s 28(1) in a like manner, since Motordom was in fact a mercantile agent and therefore it was not right to attribute to it a wider authority than was provided by the section particularly directed to its activity. Their Lordships are unable to accept this view. Section 28(1) is not limited to any particular class of seller; it applies to a purchase from any kind of seller made in good faith and without notice of the previous sale.

[Lord Pearce then examined the history of s 28(1) and its antecedents and concluded it was intended as a protection to innocent purchasers in cases where estoppel gave insufficient protection.]

The first reported question that arose about the construction of those same words is to be found in *Mitchell v Jones* (1905) 24 NZLR 932, a case under the New Zealand Sale of Goods Act 1895. There the owner of a horse sold it to a buyer and some days later obtained it back from him on lease. Then, having possession of the horse in the capacity of lessee, he sold it a second time to an innocent purchaser. The Full Court held that the innocent purchaser was not protected. Stout CJ said: "The point turns on how the words 'or is in possession of the goods'... are to be construed... The meaning is—first, that if a person sells goods and continues in possession, even though he has made a valid contract of sale, provided that he has not delivered them, he may to a bona fide buyer make a good title; and, secondly, the putting-in of the words 'or is in possession of the goods' was meant to apply to a case of this character: if a vendor had not the goods when he sold them, but they came into his possession afterwards, then he would have possession of the goods, and if he sold them to a bona fide purchaser he could make a good title to them. He would be in the same position as if he had continued in possession of the goods when he made his first sale. In such a case as that he could make a good title to a bona fide purchaser. That is not this case. In this case the person who sold the goods gave up possession of them, and gave delivery of them to the buyer. The relationship, therefore, of buyer and seller between them was at an end. It is true that the seller got possession of the goods again, but not as a seller. He got the goods the second time as the bailee of the buyer, and as the bailee he had no warrant, in my opinion, to sell the goods again, nor could he make a good title to them to even a bona fide purchaser": at 935. And Williams J said that the section "does not apply where a sale has been absolutely final by delivery and possession has been obtained by the vendee": at 936. It has not been doubted in argument nor do their Lordships doubt that that case was rightly decided.

In 1934, however, MacKinnon J, founding on that case, put a further gloss on the statutory provision in *Staffs Motor Guarantee Ltd v British Wagon Co Ltd* [1934] 2 KB 305. In April one Heap agreed with a finance company to sell his lorry to it and then to hire it from the company on hire purchase terms. He filled up a proposal form which was accepted, and a hire purchase agreement dated 2 May was signed. During the term of the hiring he sold it to an innocent purchaser. It seems that there was an interval between the agreement to sell and the hire purchase agreement, but it does not appear from the report that there was any physical delivery or interruption of Heap's physical possession. MacKinnon J held that "Heap's possession of the lorry" (at the time of the second sale) "was not the possession of a seller who had not yet delivered the article sold to the buyer, but was the possession of a bailee under the hire purchase agreement": at 314. Although the sale had not been completed by physical delivery nor had there been interruption of the seller's physical possession, he held that the case was covered by the principle in *Mitchell v Jones*.

[His Lordship then referred to several other English decisions and continued at 202:] There is thus no case which holds that the section does not apply where after the sale the seller simply attorns to the buyer and holds the goods as his bailee.

It is plainly right to read the section as inapplicable to cases where there has been a break in the continuity of the physical possession. On this point their Lordships accept the observations of the learned judges in *Mitchell v Jones* as to the words "or is" which are the sole grounds for any doubt on this point. But what is the justification for saying that a person does not continue in possession where his physical possession does continue although the title under or by virtue of which he is in possession has changed? The fact that a person having sold goods is described as *continuing* in possession would seem to indicate that the section is not contemplating as relevant a change in the legal title under which he possesses. For the legal title by which he is in possession *cannot* continue. Before the sale he is in possession as an owner, whereas after the sale he is in possession as a bailee holding goods for the new owner. The possession continues unchanged but the title under which he possesses has changed. One may perhaps say in loose terms that a person having sold goods continues in possession as long as he is holding because of and only because of the sale; but what justification is there for imposing such an elaborate and artificial construction on the natural meaning of the words? The object of the section is to protect an innocent purchaser who is deceived by the vendor's physical possession of goods or documents and who is inevitably unaware of legal rights which fetter the apparent power to dispose. Where a vendor retains uninterrupted physical possession of the goods why should an unknown arrangement, which substitutes a bailment for ownership, disentitle the innocent purchaser to protection from a danger which is just as great as that from which the section is admittedly intended to protect him?

Since the original provision under the Factors Act 1877 (s 3) dealt only with the continuing in possession of documents of title to goods, it seems clear that it was intending merely to deal with the physical possession of the documents and it did not intend that a consideration of the legal quality of the possession of the documents should have any relevance. When the Factors Act 1889 (s 8) added continuance in possession of the goods themselves to continuance in possession of the documents, it can hardly be suggested that the word "possession" was intended to have any more esoteric meaning in relation to goods than it had in relation to documents of title. Moreover such a construction would be in direct conflict with the definition (s 1(2) of the Factors Act 1889) whereby "a person shall be deemed to be in possession of goods or of the documents of title to goods where the goods or documents are in his actual custody or are held by any other person subject to his control or for him or his benefit". When s 8 of the Factors Act 1889 came to be enacted again as s 25(1) of the Sale of Goods Act 1893, the identical words cannot have been intended to bear a different meaning from that which by definition they bore under the 1889 Act.

[His Lordship then referred further to the history of the section and continued at 204:] The climate of legislative opinion was at the time of the passing of the 1877 and 1889 Factors Acts favourable to legislation which would prevent the buyers or others from being misled by an apparent possession of goods which was belied by legal transactions which were unknown to the world at large. In 1878 the Bills of Sales Act destroyed the validity of assignments and the like without delivery unless registered and in 1883 the Bills of Sale (Amendment) Act made similar provisions in respect of agreements to secure money on goods remaining in the apparent possession of the borrower...

There is therefore the strongest reason for supposing that the words "continues in possession" were intended to refer to the continuity of physical possession regardless of any private transactions between the seller and purchaser which might alter the legal title under which the possession was held.

Their Lordships do not think that such a view of the law which they believe parliament to have intended could in practice create any adverse effect. It would mean that when a person sells a car to a finance house in order to take it back on hire-purchase the finance house must take physical delivery if it is to avoid the risk of an innocent purchaser acquiring title to it. But in any event such arrangements where there is no delivery are not without some jeopardy owing to the Bills of Sale Acts.

It seems to their Lordships that *Staffs Motor Guarantee Ltd v British Wagon Co Ltd* [1934] 2 KB 305 (and *Eastern Distributors Ltd v Goldring (Murphy, Third Party)* [1957] 2 QB 600 in so far as it followed it), was wrongly decided. Even if it were rightly decided, it would not cover the facts of this case. For even assuming that a separate agreement of bailment, following a sale, without any break in the seller's physical possession, were sufficient to break its continuity for the purposes of the section, here there was no such separate bailment. Motordom's continued physical possession was solely attributable to the arrangement which constituted the sale. It was a term of the sale by Motordom to the respondent that Motordom should be entitled to retain possession of the cars for the purpose of selling them to customers. Motordom only received 90 per cent of the price on the sale to the respondent, and it cannot be argued that the sale ended at that stage. It would be absurd to suppose that either party intended Motordom to sell its stock for 90 per cent of its value without getting a right to any further benefit. The transaction by which Motordom sold the cars to the respondent was inextricably mixed with Motordom's right to keep the cars for display at its premises. In their Lordships' opinion Motordom, having sold the goods whose ownership is disputed, continued in possession of them . . .

Their Lordships will therefore humbly advise Her Majesty that the appeal should be allowed, the order of the High Court dated 28 August 1963 set aside with costs and the order of the Supreme Court of New South Wales dated 25 July 1962 restored. The respondent must pay the costs of this appeal.

Compare *Mercantile Credits Ltd v F C Upton & Sons Pty Ltd* (1974) 48 ALJR 301 (HC).

RESALE BY BUYER IN POSSESSION

We have already noted in Chapter 2 the important legal distinction between a conditional sale and a hire-purchase agreement. In each the seller retains title but:
 (a) if Easy Finance hires an engine to Carb with an option of purchase, Carb has no power to pass title to a third person Driver (*Helby v Matthews* [1895] AC 471), whereas:
 (b) if Easy Finance enters into a conditional sale agreement with Carb which agrees to buy and obtains possession of the engine, Carb can pass title to Driver notwithstanding Easy Finance's reservation of title: *Lee v Butler* [1893] 2 QB 318.

The difference is that only in the second example is Driver protected by SGA ss 28(2) and (3) which provide:

28 (2) Where a person having bought or agreed to buy goods obtains with the consent of the seller possession of the goods or the documents of title to the goods, the delivery or transfer by that person or by a mercantile agent acting for him of the goods or documents of title under any sale pledge or other disposition thereof to any person receiving the same in good faith and without notice of any lien or other right of the original seller in respect of the goods shall have the same effect as if the person making the delivery or transfer were a mercantile agent intrusted by the owner with the goods or documents of title.

(3) In this section the term "mercantile agent" means a mercantile agent having in the customary course of his business as such agent authority either to sell goods, or to consign goods for the purpose of sale, or to buy goods, or to raise money on the security of goods.

(Vic, s 31; Qld, s 27(2); SA, s 25(2); WA, s 25(2); Tas, s 30(2); ACT, s 29(2). Note also that in some circumstances the Consumer Credit Act 1981 (NSW), Consumer Transactions Act 1972 (SA) and Victorian Credit Act 1981 and Chattel Securities Act 1981 will also be applicable: see discussion p 352, *infra*.)

To obtain the protection of s 28(2) Driver would have to establish that:
 (a) Carb had agreed to buy;
 (b) Carb obtained lawful possession with Easy Finance's consent and possession must be referable to the contract although it need not have been in the capacity of a buyer: *Langmead v Thyer Rubber Co Ltd* [1947] SASR 29;
 (c) P obtained delivery of the goods or a transfer of documents of title to them in good faith without notice of Easy Finance's rights.

A further difficulty is the meaning of the terms in s 28(2) "shall have the same effect as if the person making the delivery or transfer were a mercantile agent intrusted by the owner with the goods or documents of title". Since a delivery or transfer by a mercantile agent will only pass title when he acts in the ordinary course of business of a mercantile agent, how can Carb so act unless it is a mercantile agent? In *Langmead v Thyer Rubber Co Ltd* [1947] SASR 29 at 39, Reed J observed that sub-s (3) of s 25 (NSW s 28(2)) of the Sale of Goods Act defines "mercantile agent" in the same words as are used in s 3 of the Mercantile Law Act 1936 (NSW Factors

(Mercantile Agents) Act 1923 s 3). He further observed that a sale by a mercantile agent is not valid under s 4 of that Act (NSW s 5) unless it is made by him "when acting in the ordinary course of business of a mercantile agent". He continued:

Section 25(2) of the Sale of Goods Act contains no stipulation that any sale etc under which goods are delivered or transferred must, in order to be effective, be made in any particular manner, such as in the course of the business of a mercantile agent. The meaning of s 25(2) appears to be that where, for example, a sale by a person who has bought or agreed to buy goods has taken place, if the conditions therein stated are satisfied, the delivery or transfer of the goods is to have the same effect as if a sale of the goods had been legally effected by a mercantile agent, ie, made by him when acting in the ordinary course of business as a mercantile agent.

Compare that passage with the decision of the English Court of Appeal in *Newtons of Wembley Ltd v Williams* [1965] 1 QB 560 where Sellers LJ said at 574-5:

Before one takes too favourable a view for the sub-buyer and too harsh a view against the true owner of the goods as to the cases where s 9 [NSW SGA s 28(2)] can be invoked, one must remember that it is taking away the right which would have existed at common law, and for myself I should not be prepared to enlarge it more than the words clearly permitted and required. It seems to me that all that s 9 can be said clearly to do is to place the buyer in possession in the position of a mercantile agent when he has in fact in his possession the goods of somebody else, and it does no more than clothe him with that fictitious or notional position on any disposition of those goods. Section 2(1) [NSW Factors (Mercantile Agents) Act s 5(1)] makes it clear that the sub-buyer from a mercantile agent, to whom that section applies, has in order to obtain the full advantage of the sub-section, to establish that the mercantile agent was acting in the ordinary course of business. It is said that that is a somewhat vague phrase, and we have been referred to some authorities with regard to that. It may be that in some cases precisely what is in "the ordinary course of business" of a mercantile agent may call for some special investigation, but on the face of it it seems to me that it envisages a transaction by a mercantile agent and is to be derived from such evidence as is either known to the court or established by evidence as to what would be the ordinary course of business.

[And Pearson LJ added at 578-9:] This problem then arises: if a person is not in fact a mercantile agent, how can he be acting in the ordinary course of business of a mercantile agent? It seems on the face of it to be an impossible position, and, therefore, I was tending to the opinion for some time that those words simply could not be applied to the s 9 position of a buyer, at any rate if the buyer was not a mercantile agent. However, that problem arises from the absence of a sufficient definition of how wide the hypothesis is to be, and one does have this provision, that the transaction shall have the same effect as if the buyer were a mercantile agent. I suppose it follows that when one is applying the hypothesis in s 2 one assumes that he is a mercantile agent: if he has a business it is assumed to be the business of a mercantile agent; or the other way of putting it is that the transaction will be validated if this buyer is doing something which would constitute acting in the ordinary course of business if he were a mercantile agent.

SALE OF GOODS SUBJECT TO A SECURITY INTEREST

Consumer Credit Act 1981 (NSW)

105 (1) Subject to this section, where the mortgagee under a goods mortgage is not in possession of goods that are subject to the mortgage and a person who does not carry on a trade or business of dealing in goods of the same class or kind purchases (otherwise than at a sale in execution of a judgment or order of a court) an interest in the goods from—
    (a) the mortgagor; or
    (b) a person other than the mortgagor who is in possession of the goods in circumstances where the mortgagor has lost his right to possession of the goods or is estopped from asserting his title to the goods against the purchaser,
for value, in good faith and, when he pays the purchase price or first pays any part of the purchase price, without notice of the security interest of the mortgagee in the goods, the purchaser acquires the interest purchased free from that security interest.

(2) For the purposes of subsection (1), a purchase of an interest in goods is not a purchase of that interest for value, in good faith and without the notice referred to in that subsection where—
(a) the purchaser and the seller are members of the same household;
(b) the purchaser and the seller are corporations that, by section 6(5) of the Companies Act 1961 are, for the purposes of that Act, deemed to be related to each other; or
(c) either the purchaser or the seller is a corporation and the other of them is a natural person who, within the meaning of the Companies Act, 1961, is a director or officer of the corporation,
unless it is proved beyond reasonable doubt that it is such a purchase.

(Vic, Chattel Securities Act ss 8, 11 and Pt III; SA, Consumer Transactions Act s 36.)

Note that this exception to the *nemo dat* rule protects consumer purchasers but not dealers acquiring goods, or encumbrancees: see *Gurr v Esanda Ltd* (1982) ASC ¶55-6. Section 105(4) envisages the establishment of a system for registering the mortgagee's interest under a goods mortgage, and, if implemented, would presumably treat registration as constructive notice to a prospective purchaser.

Section 106 imposes criminal sanctions against persons who assign, sell or dispose of goods the subject of a regulated goods mortgage, or who attempt to do so, or by any other means defraud or attempt to defraud the mortgagee. However, an assignment is permitted with the mortgagee's consent, which shall not be unreasonably withheld.

SALE IN MARKET OVERT OR UNDER SPECIAL POWERS OF SALE

Market overt. The Goods Act 1958 (Victoria) s 27 provides:

27 (1) Where goods are sold in market overt according to the usage of the market the buyer acquires a good title to the goods provided he buys them in good faith and without notice of any defect or want of title on the part of the seller.
(2) Nothing in this section shall affect the law relating to the sale of cattle.

(Compare Tas, s 27(1); SA, s 22; WA, s 22; market overt does not apply in NSW (SGA s 4(2)), nor in Qld (*Sorley and Stirling v Surawski* [1953] St R Qd 110) or ACT (see Sutton, *Sales and Consumer Law,* 3rd ed, 1983, pp 355-6).)

The concept of market overt dates from early times when public marketplaces were commonly created by special statute or charter. It is not particularly appropriate to modern commerce, although produce and livestock markets would normally meet the criteria that the market must be appointed as a public market by custom, statute or local authority and be open to all persons.

Statutory powers of sale. In addition to an unpaid seller's power of sale under SGA s 50(2), other statutory powers of sale confer specific protection for the buyer: eg NSW, Pawnbrokers Act 1902 s 17, Warehousemen's Liens Act 1935 s 6, Liquor Act 1912 s 73, Disposal of Uncollected Goods Act 1966 ss 5, 10, 11 and 18 and corresponding provisions in other states: see generally, Peden, "Lienee's Statutory Power of Sale" (1968) 6 *Uni of Qld LJ* 24.

Where a sheriff or bailiff sells under a writ of execution, he usually only warrants to sell the right, title and interest (if any) of the judgment debtor. Whether such a sale will cure any such defect will depend on the terms of the particular statute: see eg, Goods Act 1963 s 83A (Vic). Where the writ of execution has been issued by Sue Quick against Carb's assets and delivered to the sheriff for execution, a sale by Carb prior to the sheriff's levy will be protected by SGA s 29 (Vic, s 82; Qld, s 28; SA, s 26; WA, s 26; Tas, s 31; ACT, s 30).

COMMON LAW DOCTRINES OF FIXTURES AND ACCESSION

These doctrines apply to conflicts with bona fide purchasers and also to conflicts between secured creditors and will therefore be examined in Section 2.

QUESTIONS OF LAW REFORM

The above materials indicate the difficulty of resolving the conflicting claims of owner, secured creditor and bona fide purchaser. Reference has been made to some of the Molomby Committee's recommendations and their partial implementation in recent credit legislation in New South Wales, South Australia and Victoria. The exceptions to the *nemo dat* rule have been discussed. Should the *nemo dat* rule be replaced, perhaps by the principle of French law *possession vaut titre*? Or should the exceptions to the *nemo dat* rule be extended? Would greater protection of innocent purchasers have any effect on the incidence of property theft and fraud? If a central register of security interests in chattels is utilised how is it to operate and who is to administer it? Should special rules apply to motor vehicles? These are some of the more important policy questions which as yet remain unanswered.

QUESTIONS

Question 1

Jim Handy bought a vintage Bentley for $18,000 at an auction sale conducted by Bestcars Ltd. He paid the price but left the car with Bestcars after arranging for them to repaint it silver grey. Two weeks later due to a mistake by Bestcars, the Bentley was sold by auction for $13,500 to Dealer who paid the $13,500 and took delivery.

In response to Dealer's advertisement for sale of the Bentley, Slick came to Dealer's premises on 5 May and, using an assumed name, agreed to buy the Bentley for Dealer's asking price of $16,000. Contrary to his usual practice, Dealer accepted a cheque from Slick in full payment and Slick drove off in the Bentley. Dealer banked the cheque on 6 May and was advised by his bank on 10 May that the cheque had been dishonoured because it was a forgery.

Meanwhile on 8 May Slick resold the Bentley from his home for $14,000 in a private sale to Driver who had no knowledge of the previous transactions. Slick has disappeared.

(1) Advise Jim Handy whether he can recover the Bentley from Driver or damages from anyone else.

(2) What difference, if any, would it make to your advice if either (a) Slick had resold to Driver on 15 May rather than on 8 May? or (b) Driver had bought the car at a sale where it was auctioned on instructions from Slick?

Question 2

Carb Pty Ltd entered into an agreement with Easy Finance which provided inter alia:

(1) Carb may apply to Easy Finance for finance in connection with second-hand engines purchased as stock for reconditioning and sale.

(2) On approval of an application Easy Finance shall advance to Carb 90 per cent of the price paid by Carb, whereupon title shall pass to Easy Finance.

(3) Carb shall retain possession of such stock and may sell same in its own name at prices determined by it, but on completion of any sale Carb shall account to Easy Finance for so much of the proceeds as equal the amount previously advanced by Easy Finance.

(4) Carb shall pay Easy Finance a rental equal to two per cent per month for the period it retains possession of such engines.

(5) Easy Finance reserves the right to cancel Carb's authority and repossess any engines at any time and without prior notice.

On 3 June, Easy Finance heard that Carb was in financial difficulty and immediately notified Carb that its authority to deal with 100 engines the subject of their agreement was withdrawn. Later that day Bestcars Ltd prevailed upon Carb to sell the entire balance of its stock of engines, including the above 100, at cost price of $30,000 and in part satisfaction of the purchase price to set off an amount of $10,000 which Carb owed Bestcars on a previous transaction. Bestcars handed Carb cheques for $20,000 and $10,000 and Carb returned the second cheque to Bestcars, who then took possession of the engines. Bestcars was aware of the agreement between Carb and Easy Finance but did not know of the revocation of Carb's authority.

Assuming Carb is now insolvent, discuss Easy Finance's rights against Bestcars.

Question 3

"This is another case where one of two innocent parties has to suffer for the fraud of a third. It will no doubt interest students and find its place in the textbooks": [1972] 1 QB 203. These words of Lord Denning typify the conflict between the interests of owner and bona fide purchaser. Do the exceptions to the *nemo dat* rule achieve a fair balance between these interests or what reforms would you recommend?

Question 4

Various proposals have been made for the creation of registers of ownership and security interests over motor vehicles and other chattels. What purposes would these proposals serve and are they feasible?

SECTION 2: PRIORITY CONFLICTS BETWEEN COMPETING SECURED CREDITORS

In this section we will examine the various conflicting claims to priority between different classes of secured creditors: see Question 1 in Chapter 7. What policy objectives should be sought in resolving these conflicts and how appropriate are the solutions under the present Australian law? Consider the following statement of suggested policies:

Peden: Stock-in-Trade Financing
1974, pp 16–17

E—Competing security interests in stock-in-trade

Where separate financiers claim security interests in the same stock-in-trade, it is essential that legal rules should be available to resolve the conflict. If these rules are designed with a view to conforming with business patterns and are clear, the parties will generally regulate their own activities so as to avoid conflict. The same general policy reasons for public notification of a security interest referred to under the last heading are equally applicable to competing security interests, and therefore favour a general priority rule based upon the time of filing public notice, or its equivalent—the taking of possession. Certain qualifications upon this general rule are required to take account of special situations.

First, the need to prevent a first financier over-reaching by blanketing the borrower's after-acquired stock has been noted. A typical situation based upon the prototype transaction arises where a manufacturer or merchant creates a floating charge over stock-in-trade in favour of A and then finances through B the acquisition of future stocks which are also covered by the after-acquired property clause in A's floating charge. This gives rise to a direct conflict especially where A makes future advances under the original charge but subsequent to B's advance. The floating charge should be deferred to the subsequent financier of specific assets. This solution preserves the borrower's freedom to utilise alternative financing to acquire fresh stocks. A subsidiary consequence is the preferential treatment which will often result to distributors and financiers of new goods, thereby paying lip-service to the need to increase gross national product.

Second, we have already noted under the previous heading that in appropriate circumstances a financier should be able to tack future advances onto an existing loan to achieve the same priority. This is appropriate where the debtor has no collateral except work in progress which increases in value as it proceeds towards completion. The financier may only be willing to make advances as the collateral increases in value, yet the borrower needs from the outset a commitment—or at least the expectation—of the availability of the future advances. However, the financier again must be restrained from over-reaching the borrower or his other creditors. There is little danger of this where the financier is obliged to make the future advances since the borrower and subsequent creditors can ascertain their position. However, the law should not allow a situation to arise whereby a subsequent creditor is misled, or is unable to ascertain the extent of the first financier's ultimate encumbrance.

Third, special rules will be necessary to determine the interests of secured creditors with separate claims to stock which has been mixed, commingled or processed so as to make physical separation impracticable. The guiding principle here should be to prevent the situation arising in the first instance, and failing that, to reach an equitable compromise based upon the proportionate amount which the obligation secured upon each ingredient bears to the sum of the obligations secured upon all ingredients.

The present Australian law will be examined in the following order:
(a) the general law rules for determining priority between two secured creditors claiming non-possessory securities over the same collateral;
(b) the effect of bills of sale legislation upon these basic general law rules;
(c) priorities under the Chattel Securities Act 1981 (Vic);
(d) priorities under the National Companies Code;
(e) special rules in relation to tacking of future advances;
(f) conflicts between possessory securities (pledge and lien) and the owner or non-possessory secured creditor;
(g) conflicts involving the common law doctrines of fixtures and accession and relevant statutory provisions.

At this stage we are not dealing with questions of validity of securities as against unsecured creditors, trustees in bankruptcy, company liquidators or bona fide purchasers all of which have been considered earlier. In view of special priority problems with farm products it is also desirable to treat these separately in Section 3.

GENERAL LAW PRIORITY RULES

The bills of sale legislation is primarily concerned with invalidation of unregistered securities as against trustees in bankruptcy and judgment creditors. Subject to varying provisions in some states' Bills of Sale Acts dealt with later, they do not purport to regulate priorities between competing secured creditors. Accordingly, the starting point for determining priorities is the following common law principles:
(a) where the equities are equal, the security created first in time will prevail;
(b) where the equities are equal, the law prevails.

Applying these principles to our fact situation:

(1) If Carb first grants to City Bank and subsequently to Easy Finance charges which each purport to create legal interests, Bank will prevail under Principle (a). Of course, if Bank's is a valid legal security, it follows that Easy's security can only create an equitable interest, and Bank's legal interest prevails by virtue of Principle (b) as well.

However, if Bank by gross negligence or fraud had induced Easy to accept Carb's security, the equities would not be equal, and Easy's equitable interest would prevail.

(2) If Carb grants equitable securities to Bank and subsequently to Easy, Bank being the first in time will prevail (Principle (a)).

(3) If Carb first grants an equitable security to Bank and subsequently gives Easy a legal security, Easy will prevail provided it had no notice of Bank's prior equitable security when it acquired its own (Principle (b)).

In the case of a prior floating charge to Bank and a subsequent specific charge to Comp Co over Carb's present assets, Comp will prevail for either of two reasons. First, since Bank's floating charge is necessarily equitable only, Comp will prevail under Principle (b) if it takes a legal security without notice of Bank's floating charge: *Re Hamilton's Windsor Ironworks* (1879) 12 Ch D 707; *Governments Stock Co Ltd v Manila Railway Co Ltd* [1897] AC 81. Second, even if Comp's is an equitable charge, it may prevail on the basis that a prior uncrystallised floating charge confers on Carb an implied licence to continue to deal with its assets in the ordinary course of business.

NO COMMON LAW DOCTRINE OF CONSTRUCTIVE NOTICE

The above principles recognise that subsequent chargees Easy and Comp can only prevail if they take without notice of any restriction upon Carb's licence to deal with or create subsequent charges ranking in priority to or *pari passu* with the floating charge: *English & Scottish Mercantile Investment Co v Brunton Ltd* [1892] 2 QB 700. At general law, registration of a bill of sale or company security is not deemed to be constructive notice of its existence or contents: *Manchester Trust v Furness* [1895] 2 QB 539 at 545. If Easy or Comp in fact searches and discovers the existence but not the contents of Bank's charge before taking its own security, it is doubtful if it is then placed on notice of any restriction contained in it: see Peden, *Stock-in-Trade Financing*, p 45. Contrast the position under the Queensland Bills of Sale and Other Instruments Act of 1955, where s 8 makes registration of a bill of sale constructive notice of its existence and contents to all persons except the grantee of any prior registered bill relating to the same goods. There is no corresponding provision in other states.

PURCHASE MONEY SECURITY INTEREST

In our original fact situation, Comp Co took a fixed charge not over Carb's existing stock but over the very components which Comp itself sold to Carb. Similarly, Squeeze advanced to Carb the full purchase price to enable Carb to acquire *new* stock (20,000 widgets) from Widg Co. In each case there are English decisions in relation to real estate which prefer the subsequent specific mortgagee on the basis that the purchaser (here Carb) never received the full legal title because it remained subject to the rights of the unpaid seller (Comp) or mortgagee (Squeeze) from the outset: *Wilson v Kelland* [1910] 2 Ch 306; *Re Connolly Brothers Ltd (No 2)* [1912] 2 Ch 25.

It is instructive to compare the above position with the rules of priority by notice filing and the concept of purchase money security interests under the Uniform Commercial Code. See in particular ss 9–107, 9–302, 9–312.

PRIORITIES UNDER BILLS OF SALE LEGISLATION

Some states have provisions in their bills of sale legislation which determine priorities between competing securities. However, they are not comprehensive and far from uniform. After a brief interstate comparison, attention will be focused on the New South Wales provisions.

The respective Acts only apply to registrable bills (see pp 278–9, *supra*). Since bills confined to after-acquired goods are not registrable in Tasmania and South Australia, such a bill will be valid in those states without registration, but being equitable only will be deferred to a subsequent specific charge taken without notice. In the case of registrable bills:

(1) In Tasmania, a bill is totally void against all persons unless registered within 30 days: s 5. The Act is silent as to priorities for registered bills so they rank from date of execution under the general law rule.

(2) In New South Wales (for traders' bills) a bill is invalid for all purposes until registered, but when registered, priorities are determined by that date rather than the date of execution: NSW, s 5c and *Franov v Deposit & Investment Co Ltd* (1962) 108 CLR 460.

(3) In Victoria, under the Instruments Act 1958 ss 33 and 35, a similar result applies as for traders' bills in New South Wales. However, when the Chattel Securities Act 1981 is proclaimed to come into force, it will repeal those parts of the Instruments Act which regulate bills of sale. As to the effect of the Chattel Securities Act on priority between competing securities, see p 359, *infra*.

(4) In South Australia, Western Australia, Queensland and New South Wales (ordinary bills), an unregistered bill remains valid *inter partes*, but priorities are determined according to date of registration: SA, s 18; WA, s 34; Qld, s 7(2)(b); NSW, s 5A. These provisions would appear to preclude the possibility of a subsequent purchase-money secured creditor gaining priority over a prior registered bill. However, note that because there is some overlap between the Bills of Sale Act 1898 (NSW) and the Consumer Credit Act 1981 (NSW), amendments to the former Act are likely but the details of such amendments are not available at time of writing.

PRIORITIES UNDER BILLS OF SALE ACT 1898 (NSW)

Trader's bills. By amendments in 1938, the New South Wales Act introduced the distinction between trader's bills and ordinary bills. "Trader" is defined as "a person engaged or about to engage in the business of selling by retail any goods, wares or merchandise but does not include a farmer ... or a company ... " "Trader's bill of sale" means "a bill of sale made or given by way of security by a trader the personal chattels comprised in or made subject to which are or include plant, fixtures, and fittings and/or goods, wares, or merchandise which, at the time of the making or giving of the trader's bill of sale are owned and used or intended to be used, or which are to be thereafter acquired and when so acquired will be owned and used or intended to be used, by the trader in or in connection with the business in which he is engaged or about to engage".

The following details of the legislative scheme should be noted:

(1) To be filed or recorded in accordance with the Act *as a trader's bill*, the necessary statutory declaration must be furnished and annexed to the bill as required by s 5B(1).

(2) The trader's bill must be *lodged* for registration within 15 days after it was executed (s 5c(2)(b)), and if no caveat is entered under s 5G by any unsecured creditor objecting to its being filed, it will be *filed or recorded* 14 days after lodgment: ie, there is a distinction between *lodgment* and *filing/recording* 14 days later.

(3) The trader's bill only takes effect as regards trade goods when it is filed/recorded: see *Franov v Deposit & Investment Co Ltd* (1962) 108 CLR 460. If properly advised, what procedure should Deposit & Investment Co Ltd have taken to avoid what happened in the above case?

(4) A trader's bill which also includes *non-trade goods* is effective in respect of the non-trade goods as soon as it is lodged: ss 5c(5) and 5B(4).

(5) If the trader's bill is invalidated for non-lodgment, all moneys "secured thereby" become immediately repayable: s 5c(4).

Ordinary bills. Section 5A(1) requires the grantor of an ordinary bill of sale to furnish a statutory declaration indicating his interest in the goods and whether or not there is any money owing in respect of the purchase or upon the security of the goods. By virtue of s 5A(3) the reward for complying with s 5A(1) is that the

declaration is deemed to be conclusive evidence in favour of the grantee of the truth of the facts stated in the declaration provided:
(a) the grantee did not know the facts were false;
(b) no prior bill over the same goods and containing a similar declaration had been recorded under the Act;
(c) s 5A(3) is made subject to s 5A(6) so that if the grantor is not the "true owner" of the goods the declaration under s 5A(3) will not deem him to be so.

Some doubt surrounds the meaning of "true owner" in s 5A(6). Does the grantor *still* remain the "true owner" after he has granted the first bill of sale? Does it make a difference if the first bill is a legal mortgage or an equitable security? If the grantor is no longer the true owner then s 5A(3) will have very little scope for operation. Note carefully the invalidating effect of s 5A(4) on a grantee who does not comply with ss 5A(1) and (2) or who knows the declaration is false. The section operates in favour of prior security holders and in favour of the unpaid seller to the grantor of the goods comprised in the bill of sale even though he holds no security over the goods.

Section 5A does not apply to trader's bills of sale: s 5A(7).

PRIORITIES UNDER THE CHATTEL SECURITIES ACT 1981 (Vic)

Victoria is the only state as yet to enact a Chattel Securities Act 1981 by way of partial implementation of the Molomby Committee Report. The commencement of the Act has not yet been proclaimed, but when it does come into force, it will repeal those parts of the Instruments Act which regulate bills of sale and will introduce a concept of security interests. All non-possessory security interests (ie, goods mortgages and charges but not pledges or possessory liens) are given the effect of statutory charges: s 5.

The Act provides a voluntary system for registration of non-possessory security interests, and of the interest of the lessor or owner of goods the subject of a lease or hire-purchase agreement: s 16. The registration system only applies to motor cars and trailers with provision for extension of the system to motor boats: s 13.

The Act does not invalidate an unregistered security interest, lease or hire-purchase agreement, nor does it specifically determine priorities by the date of registration. Priorities between competing security interests would therefore be determined by the general law principles referred to on p 356, *supra*, subject to the following qualifications:

(1) Where goods subject to a mortgage, lease or hire-purchase agreement become fixtures to land, the rights of the security holder are protected against a purchaser or mortgagee of the land, but the owner or mortgagee of the goods may not be able to retake possession of the goods: s 7.

(2) The interest of a goods mortgagee, lessor or owner of goods subject to a hire-purchase agreement may be extinguished by a purchaser in good faith for value and without notice of the prior interest: ss 8, 9, 10. These provisions only apply where the purchase price of the goods does not exceed $15,000 or they comprise a commercial vehicle or farm machinery. If the purchaser is a member of the seller's household, or a related corporation, or the seller and purchaser are related by one being a director or officer of the other, the purchaser must prove beyond reasonable doubt that the purchase is for value in good faith and without notice. A purchaser who is a person who carries on a trade or business in which he deals in goods of the kind acquired cannot obtain the protection of ss 8, 9 or 10 unless Pt III applies (ie unless the goods are a motor car, trailer or motor boat and the prior interest is not registered).

(3) Although the point is not free from doubt, it is probable that a subsequent security holder or encumbrancee would not qualify as a purchaser under ss 8, 9 or 10.

(4) Registration under s 16 of a security interest of a lessor or of an owner under hire-purchase in respect of a motor car, trailer or motor boat would appear to constitute constructive notice and prevent a bona fide purchaser acquiring clear title under ss 8, 9 or 10, except in the case of a security interest of a dealer to which s 23 applies.

PRIORITIES UNDER THE NATIONAL COMPANIES CODE (NCC)

The NCC deals with priorities between competing registrable charges (as enumerated in s 200(1)) on the property of a company. Section 204(1) provides that subject to that section priorities between registrable charges are to be determined according to the provisions of Schedule 5 of the Act. However, the order of priorities is subject to any express or implied consent given by a chargee whose charge would otherwise be entitled to priority that varies those priorities and any agreement between chargees that affects those priorities: s 204(2). By s 204(3) the holder of a registered floating charge is deemed to have consented to that charge being postponed to a subsequent registered fixed charge that is created before the floating charge becomes fixed, unless the creation of the subsequent fixed charge contravened a provision of the instrument or resolution creating or evidencing the floating charge, and a notice in respect of the floating charge indicating the existence of that provision was lodged with the commission under ss 201, 202 or 206 before the creation of the subsequent registered charge.

Schedule 5 sets out the priorities between registrable charges. Clause 1 deals with the priority accorded to a registered charge on property of a company. Clause 2 deals with the priority accorded to an unregistered charge on property of a company. Clause 3 deals with the effect of Schedule 5 on the equitable doctrine of tacking, to be discussed, *infra*. Clause 4 provides that a reference to a person having notice includes a person having constructive notice ("constructive notice" is given the same meaning as at general law).

Note that because Schedule 5 extends only to registrable charges, priorities between charges which are not registrable, and between one which is and one which is not, are left to be determined by general law.

TACKING OF FUTURE ADVANCES

The practical commercial reasons for future advance lending were referred to on p 323, *supra*. Does the Australian law allow City Bank to obtain the same priority for future advances made to Carb as it enjoyed in respect of its original loan, and yet prevent Bank from:
- (a) over-reaching Carb by blanketing its assets so as to preclude access to alternative financing from Easy Finance or Comp Co even in respect of fresh collateral; or
- (b) misleading these subsequent creditors?

The answer varies according to whether the common law rules apply, or the statutory provisions adopted only in Victoria and Tasmania; or whether the provisions of NCC s 204 and Schedule 5 apply.

At common law, Bank's first charge will retain priority for future advances over the intervening charges of Easy or Comp in the following cases:

(1) Where Bank's charge is a legal interest and Bank had no notice of the intervening charges when it made the future advances. This rule is based on the second common law principle preferring a legal interest obtained without knowledge of the prior equitable interest.

(2) Where Bank's charge, whether legal or equitable, envisages or requires further advances which are again made when Bank had no notice of the intervening interests: *Hopkinson v Rolt* (1861) 9 HLC 513; 11 ER 829; *West v Williams* [1899] 1 Ch 132. This rule is based on the contract for future advances.

Although registration of Easy and Comp's intervening charges does not constitute constructive notice to Bank, it is normal practice for intervening chargees automatically to notify all prior chargees. This would preclude Bank from obtaining any priority for future advances even when obligatory. Therefore, in practice, Bank would typically have included in its floating charge a prohibition on Carb granting subsequent charges. Bank could then respond to Easy or Comp's notice by calling in Carb's debt without making the future advances. In that event, Carb's only means of obtaining outside financing would be to pay off Bank (perhaps incurring penal interest or extra charges) or to induce the three creditors to enter an agreement regulating the permissible degree of tacking.

The United Kingdom, Victoria and Tasmania have legislated in similar terms to reduce these adverse effects on debtor and original chargee.

Conveyancing and Law of Property Act 1884 (Tas)

38(1) After the commencement of this Act, a prior mortgagee shall have a right to make further advances to rank in priority to subsequent mortgages (whether legal or equitable)—
  (a) if an arrangement has been made to that effect with the subsequent mortgagees;
  (b) if he had no notice of such subsequent mortgages at the time when the further advance was made by him; or
  (c) whether or not he had such notice as aforesaid, where the mortgage imposes an obligation on him to make such further advances,
whether or not the prior mortgage was made expressly for securing further advances.

(2) Where the prior mortgage was made expressly for securing a current account or other further advances, a mortgagee in relation to the making of further advances shall not be deemed to have notice of a mortgage merely by reason that it was registered, if it was not registered at the date of the original advance or when the last search, if any, by or on behalf of the mortgagee was made, whichever last happened.

(3) Save in regard to the making of further advances as aforesaid, the right to tack is hereby abolished; but this provision shall not affect any priority in respect of further advances made without notice of a subsequent incumbrance or by arrangement with the subsequent incumbrancer.

(Compare Property Law Act 1958 (Vic) s 94.)

As mentioned under the previous heading, tacking is dealt with in cl 3 of Schedule 5 of the NCC. The clause uses the terminology of "present" and "prospective" liabilities, which are defined in s 199. The Eggleston Committee Report (para 57) contained the following comment on who should bear the onus of obtaining priority:

> It seems to us to be reasonable to provide that if the instrument creating the charge expressly provides for the making of further advances, the holder of a registered charge should be entitled to the benefit of the security in respect of further advances, even if they were made after he received notice, by registration or otherwise, of a subsequent interest, unless he has agreed not to exercise the right. A person who proposed to advance money on the security of a second mortgage of personal property, and who was aware of the existence of a registered charge providing for further advances, would then be required to protect himself by obtaining the agreement of the first mortgagee that the second charge should rank before any advances made by the holder of the earlier charge after the date of the second mortgage.

This recommendation was adopted in Schedule 5 cl 3(4)(d): if the lender is obliged to make further advances then all such advances are accorded the same priority as the initial liability regardless of whether the chargee has actual knowledge or not of any other charge.

Provision is also made for advances which the lender was not obliged to make:

cll 3(2), 3(3) and 3(4). The rationale behind these provisions seems to be that due to the obligations imposed by ss 201 and 202 to describe the nature of the liability secured, a subsequent chargee can reasonably be expected to take steps to secure that charge.

COMPETING CLAIMS WITH POSSESSORY SECURITIES

The two typical forms of possessory security are pledge and lien. Neither requires registration under the bills of sale legislation because the goods do not remain in the debtor's possession. Similarly, a pledge of a personal chattel or marketable security, and a charge or lien over property arising by operation of law do not require registration under the NCC: ss 200(1)(b) and 200(1)(a) respectively. However, a lien or charge on a crop, a lien on wool or a stock mortgage do require registration under the NCC: s 200(1)(h).

Since possession is an essential element of each security, it is unlikely that there will be a direct conflict between creditors claiming possessory securities of pledge or lien. In each case if Jim Handy having either pledged his car to Squeeze for a loan, or left it with mechanic Wrench for repairs, subsequently regains possession lawfully, the rights of Squeeze or Wrench to the goods will be at an end, save in very exceptional circumstances. Examples of such exceptional cases are:

In respect of a lien. *Albemarle Supply Co Ltd v Hind Co* [1928] 1 KB 307, where the lienee allowed the hirer to have possession under a special arrangement and for a limited temporary purpose. Scrutton LJ said at 318:

> The plaintiffs [hire-purchase company] next contended that any lien was lost because the cabs went out of the possession of the [defendant lienee's] garage each day to ply for hire. The defendant proved an agreement with Botfield [hirer] at a time when the lien existed, that the cabs should go out for hire each day on the terms that they should be returned to the garage each night, the lien continuing while the cabs were in possession of the garage. I do not think any plying for hire under this agreement prevented the lien, if any, from continuing, and in my view repair of a damaged cab, though it may be described as "maintenance", gave rise to a repairer's lien.

In respect of a pledge. *Reeves v Capper* (1838) 5 Bing (NC) 136; 132 ER 1057, where the first pledgees (shipowners) allowed the pledgor (ship's captain) the use of his chronometer which he had pledged to them, for the purposes of a voyage. It was held that this "gave him no interest in the chronometer, but only a licence or permission to use it, for a limited time, whilst he continued as their (the pledgee's) servant, and employed it for the purpose of navigating their ship". The case may be regarded as exceptional, and distinguished on the basis that the captain had mere custody — not possession — on behalf of the pledgees who retained constructive possession.

Conflicts between non-possessory and possessory security interests are determined by the normal rule that the security created first in time will prevail. Thus if Easy Finance holds a prior security in the form of bill of sale or hire-purchase agreement over Jim Handy's vehicle, it will take priority over a subsequent possessory security such as a pledge to Squeeze or lien to repairer Wrench unless an estoppel can be proved. This will depend on whether Jim has any authority — actual, implied or ostensible — under the prior security to create such a possessory security so as to bind the owner or prior secured creditor such as Easy. The lien or pledge is obviously enforceable against Jim since he was privy to its creation, but if he defaults in paying Squeeze or Wrench, can they maintain their pledge or lien as against Easy Finance?

By way of introduction to this type of conflict, review the outline summary of liens and hire-purchase agreements in Chapter 7, and note the following points regarding liens. Liens may be classified according to their origin (common law, contract or statute) and according to their scope or extent (general or particular liens).

Common law liens. These arise by operation of the common law—no agreement is necessary. There are three kinds:

Artificer's lien: any person such as Wrench who by his labour, skill or materials has improved a chattel bailed to him for that purpose is automatically entitled to a lien for the cost of such improvements. However, storage or mere maintenance is not regarded as improving the chattel. At common law, only the owner or someone acting on his authority can authorise the work.

Innkeeper's lien: an innkeeper has a lien over goods brought to his inn by a guest. In New South Wales, by virtue of Innkeeper's Act 1968 ss 6(a) and 8, the lien will not extend to any vehicle, horse or other live animal, or equipment of a traveller. Unlike the artificer's lien, the innkeeper can assert his lien over goods carried by the guest even though they belong to a third party: *Mulliner v Florence* (1878) 3 QBD 484.

Common carrier's lien: a common carrier has a lien over goods consigned to him for carriage, and like the innkeeper, he can assert his lien over goods so consigned as against the true owner even though he has neither authorised nor consented to their carriage.

The right of the innkeeper and common carrier to maintain a lien against the owner of goods who is not privy to the circumstances giving rise to the lien originally arose as a compensation to innkeepers and common carriers for the strict liability which the common law imposed on them in respect of loss or damage to the goods. Each of the common law liens is a particular lien only (see below) unless there is a specific agreement for a *general* lien.

Contractual liens. Contractual liens arise either by common usage in particular trades or callings, or by express agreement. Usage has implied that bankers, solicitors, factors, stockbrokers, and insurance brokers are entitled to a lien over their clients' goods and documents held by them in connection with their professional relationship to their client. Each lien is a *general* lien (see below). Similarly, usage confers on a warehousekeeper a *particular* lien (and arguably a *general* lien) over goods deposited with him; and accountants have a *particular* lien in respect of clients' books. Any of the liens arising by usage can of course have their incidents varied by specific agreement in individual cases; eg, a warehousekeeper can contract for a general lien. And a person who would not at common law or by general usage be entitled to any lien (eg, parking lot proprietor) may establish such a lien by contract.

Statutory liens. A number of statutes specifically create a right of lien, or codify an existing common law lien, or confer additional powers (eg, a power of sale) which did not exist at common law.

Examples from New South Wales statutes include:
(a) unpaid seller's lien and power of sale: Sale of Goods Act 1923 s 50;
(b) innkeeper given a power of sale: Liquor Act 1912 s 73;
(c) warehousemen given a power of sale: Warehousemen's Liens Act 1935 s 6;
(d) general statutory power of sale conferred on many bailees for reward and lienees: Disposal of Uncollected Goods Act 1966 s 5.

General and particular liens. A *general lien* entitles the lienee to retain possession of goods as security for payment of all monies owing by the owner of the goods on all accounts however arising. A *particular lien* only entitles the lienee to retain possession of the goods as against payment of those charges arising in relation to those goods. Thus, the distinction goes to the question of what amounts must be tendered to the lienee to obtain release of the security.

AUTHORITY TO CREATE LIENS

We now return to the question of the authority of a non-owner, usually a bailee, to authorise the performance of work on goods so that the contractor acquires a lien enforceable against the owner or secured creditor.

Lombard Australia Ltd v Wells Park Motor Pty Ltd
Supreme Court of Victoria [1960] VLR 693

[Dodkin was the assignee of a hire-purchase agreement in respect of a car originally entered into between the plaintiff finance company and one Hills as hirer. The agreement provided that the hirer should not sell, assign, sublet, pledge or mortgage the goods or his interest under the agreement; that he should not create or allow to be acquired any lien on the goods; that he should, at his own expense, keep the goods and all parts thereof in good repair and condition and working order; that he should not have any authority to pledge the credit of the owner or to create any lien on the goods for repairs or otherwise; and that nothing contained in the agreement should be deemed to create any such authority.

Shortly after Dodkin acquired the car it broke down some miles from Frankston, and at Dodkin's request, on 27 November 1959, the defendant company towed it to its garage and arranged for its repair. The defendant was not aware that the car was subject to a hire-purchase agreement. The hire-purchase agreement was terminated in February 1960, and the plaintiff sought to repossess the car from the defendant's garage. The defendant had not been paid for the repairs by Dodkin and refused to release the car as it claimed a lien in respect of the towing and repairs.]

Herring CJ [having referred to the evidence, continued:] The question I have to decide is whether the lien that the defendant relied upon is one that can be enforced against the plaintiff, and I have had a very interesting argument presented to me. A number of cases have been referred to, both cases in England and one particular case in Australia: *Fisher v Automobile Finance Co of Australia Ltd* [1928] VLR 131; (1928) 41 CLR 167; 34 ALR 363. That case was tried originally in the County Court and then went on appeal first to the Full Court of Victoria and then on to the High Court; and as I understand the matter, that case really determines the case that is before me. In *Fisher's* case the plaintiff finance company brought an action against Fisher claiming delivery of a Chevrolet motor truck and £110 as damages for the conversion or, alternatively, for detention. The plaint alleged that the plaintiff was at all times material owner of the truck and entitled to possession of it, and that the defendant, having the truck in his possession, custody or control, had wrongfully converted it to his own use and/or had wrongfully refused or neglected to deliver it to the plaintiff when demanded. At the trial, one defence raised was that the defendant was entitled to retain possession under a lien for work and labour done and materials supplied in connection with the vehicle. The facts were that one Brander had hired this Chevrolet motor truck under a hire-purchase agreement from the plaintiff company and one of the terms of that agreement (cl 3) was that the hirer should throughout the term of the agreement at his own expense in all things, take proper care of the said motor vehicle and keep the said motor vehicle in good order and condition and should make good all damage to the said motor vehicle during the continuance of the hiring whether by fire or accident or otherwise. Clause 6 provided "that the hirer shall not have or be deemed to have any authority to pledge the owner's credit for any repairs to the said motor vehicle or to create a lien thereon in respect of such repairs, or in respect of any other matter, but if the said motor vehicle shall require to be repaired, the hirer shall allow the owner's nominee to execute the repairs at the hirer's expense and the owner shall be entitled to possession of the said motor vehicle for such purpose".

The County Court judge upheld the lien and entered judgment for the defendant. He considered that his decision was supported by the case of the *Albemarle Supply Co Ltd v Hind & Co* [1928] 1 KB 307; [1927] All ER Rep 401 . . .

Then *Fisher's* case came on appeal to the Full Court and the Full Court, consisting of Mann J (as he then was), McArthur J and Wasley AJ allowed the appeal of the plaintiff company and entered judgment for the plaintiff for delivery up of the truck. The ratio I think of the judgment of the court, which was delivered by Sir Frederick Mann, is to be found at the bottom of [1928] VLR 137, where his Honour said: "The point is that the person who does work upon the chattel can succeed only upon showing an authority from the owner to the person who has left the chattel in question. Of course, that authority may be proved by showing an express agreement or an implied agreement, or the principal may be estopped by his conduct from denying an authority. But in one or other of those ways authority must, in our opinion, be established." What his Honour is saying is that in order to justify a lien for repairs on a motor car, for example, or any other article for that matter, and maintain it against the owner of the goods, a repairer has got to show an authority from the owner to the person who has left the chattel in question. And then, as he says, you may find an express agreement conferring that authority, or an implied agreement, or it may be that the principal is estopped by his conduct from denying that the intermediary had an authority.

Well now, in *Fisher's* case, where was the authority to be found? In cl 3, to which I have referred, there was the obligation upon the hirer to keep the motor vehicle in good order and condition, and from an obligation of that kind the courts in England have been prepared to imply an authority to create a lien. The first of the cases is *Keene v Thomas* [1905] 1 KB 136. In that case, there was a hiring of a dog-cart, and the dog-cart was damaged, and the hirer took the dog-cart in for repairs to a repairer, and the repairer claimed a lien as against the owner, and that lien was upheld. The decision of the divisional court was based upon the fact that the agreement cast an obligation upon the hirer to keep the dog-cart in good repair. That case was followed in *Green v All Motors Ltd* [1917] 2 KB 625. That was a case where a motor car, the subject of a hire-purchase agreement, was during the currency of the agreement damaged by an accident, and the hirer, who was under an obligation imposed by the hire-purchase agreement to keep the car in good repair and working condition, sent it to the defendants to be repaired. The defendants were informed that the car was held on a hire-purchase agreement. Later, when the plaintiff, the owner, terminated the agreement and demanded the car from the defendants, the defendants claimed a lien and refused to deliver up the car. It was held that they had a lien on the car as against the plaintiff for the cost of the repairs. *Keene v Thomas* was followed and approved and it was impossible, I think, really to distinguish the two cases. The ground of the decision in *Keene v Thomas* applied also in *Green v All Motors Ltd*. Swinfen Eady LJ, I think, went a little further than the court had gone in *Keene v Thomas* and so, I think, did Scrutton LJ, though it was not strictly necessary for them to do so in order to determine the case. Bankes LJ was more cautious. At [1917] 1 KB 632, he said: "In *Keene v Thomas* the point, as stated by Lord Alverstone CJ, was 'whether the man who made the bargain with the repairer had authority from the plaintiff to make such a bargain'. That is the first point to be decided. The question, therefore, is whether on 31 October, when Price made the bargain with the defendants for the repair of the motor car, he had authority from the plaintiff to do so." His Lordship went on: "In my opinion he clearly had authority—unless the plaintiff had determined the hire-purchase agreement before that date." The authority was to be found in the fact that there was this obligation to keep the car in repair. As I say, Swinfen Eady LJ I think went further; so did Scrutton LJ, because he said, *ibid*, at 633: "The hirer of a chattel is entitled to have it repaired so as to enable him to use it in the way in which such a chattel is ordinarily used. The hirer was therefore entitled, without any express authority from the owner, to have the motor car repaired so as to enable him to use it as a motor car is ordinarily used." And then he went on, a few lines lower down: "In the present case the hirer of the car had the express duty imposed upon him of keeping the car in repair, and therefore of having it repaired when necessary. That makes this case similar to *Keene v Thomas,* which was a decision of a divisional court. Accordingly the hirer had by contract a duty as well as a right, until the hire was terminated, to have the car repaired, with the ordinary consequence of giving the repairer a lien on the car for the proper cost of the repairs."

There, it will be seen, Scrutton LJ talks not only about the duty to repair, which was the basis, as I understand it, of the decision in *Keene v Thomas,* but also about the right of the hirer to repair, and the question has been raised in this case as to how far Scrutton LJ's dictum about the right of the hirer to have the vehicle repaired so as to enable him to use it as a motor car is ordinarily used, gives him a right to create a lien as against the owner. In neither of these cases to which I have referred—*Keene's* case and *Green's* case—was there any express limitation in the terms of the hiring agreement upon the right of the hirer to create a lien.

There was, in *Fisher's* case such a limitation in cl 6, to the terms of which I have already referred. There was not only the restriction, the provision that the hirer should not have or be deemed to have any authority to pledge the owner's credit for any repairs or create a lien, but the agreement went on to provide that "if the motor vehicle shall require to be repaired, the hirer should allow the owner's nominee to execute the repairs at the hirer's expense", and actually the hirer, in *Fisher's* case, broke that provision, because he did not allow the owner's nominee to execute the repairs. Instead he took the car to Fisher to be repaired and, as I understand the facts of the case, the restriction upon the right of the hirer to create a lien prevented Fisher in that case from relying upon the terms of the agreement as constituting an implied authority. If he sought to rely upon the provisions of cl 3 with its obligation upon the hirer to keep the motor vehicle in good order and condition, he was faced with the other provision in cl 6 which said, despite that, there was to be no authority to create a lien. And so, once it was made clear by Mann J in the passage I have read from his judgment, that you have to find authority somewhere from the owner, authority had to be looked for, apart from the agreement. It had to be sought somewhere else and as I understand it, authority was sought to be based upon the contention that the owner had assented to a full continuous user by the hirer and that, from this user, with the assent of the owner, an authority from the owner to create a lien could be inferred. The owner had put the motor car in the uncontrolled use of the hirer and so had assented to a position which might induce others to act accordingly. This was the way it was put and depended I think, really upon the right that Scrutton LJ had mentioned in *Green's* case, based on the fact that the hirer had the uncontrolled use of the motor vehicle. I think there was support for the view put to be found in the statements by Swinfen Eady LJ and Scrutton LJ, and possibly a statement also of Collins J, in *Singer Manufacturing Co v London and South Western Railway Co* [1894] 1 QB 833.

Great reliance in the Full Court was placed on *Albemarle Supply Co Ltd v Hind & Co* [1928] 1 KB 307; [1927] All ER Rep 401, in the Court of Appeal. This was a case in which there was a contractual limitation of authority to create a lien. There was in the hiring agreement, which related to several taxicabs, an obligation to keep the taxicabs, the subject matter of the hire-purchase agreement, in repair and, at the same time, there was a contractual limitation of authority so far as the creation of liens was concerned, in very much the same terms as the limitation of authority in the present case, to which I have already referred and which is to be found in cl 2(a) of the hire-purchase conditions. This contractual limitation of authority was not communicated to the repairer of the taxicabs in the *Albemarle* case. The lien he claimed was upheld.

Mann J, in dealing with the *Albemarle* case, conceded that there were passages in the judgments of each of the Lord Justices which gave colour to some of the broad propositions that had been laid down, or had been submitted by counsel to the Full Court. One of the propositions that his Honour contended had been stated too broadly was the proposition that, if one gives to another the right to use a chattel, that right necessarily carries with it the right to repair the chattel, or to have it repaired by other people, and allow the parties who repair it to acquire a lien upon it in respect of the work so done. Mann J recognised that there were statements in *Albemarle's* case which gave colour to that particular broad proposition, but he then went on to say that, if you understood the case properly, you would find that there was evidence upon which the court could properly conclude that the owner had held out the hirer as having authority to do what he had in fact done, and that which he had done for years, and that was to take the taxicabs to a particular repairer and be responsible, as indeed the defendant in that case had been responsible, for many years, for keeping them in good order and condition. In that case, the taxis had been under hire-purchase agreement for some years, they had been stabled—that was the word that was used, I think, whether it is the correct expression or not—at Hind & Co's garages, and had been kept in repair by Hind & Co, and they knew they were owned by the plaintiff, and they were entitled to assume, so the Full Court thought on the evidence, that Botfield, the hirer, had the authority to have them dealt with in the way they had been dealt with by Hind & Co. And so Mann J said that he thought that, when you understood the circumstances and facts of the *Albemarle* case, there was nothing really inconsistent with the view that he had expressed that, before you can enforce your lien, before a repairer can enforce his lien against the owner of the goods, he has got to show that, by some agreement express or implied or some estoppel, that authority was conferred, or that the principal was estopped by his conduct from denying that he had given authority.

Priorities in Relation to Chattel Securities

When the matter came before the High Court on appeal, this issue was very clearly raised, and the argument that was put on this matter by Sir Owen Dixon, then Mr Owen Dixon KC, appeared in *Fisher v Automobile Finance Co of Australia Ltd* (1928) 41 CLR 167 at 172. He put it in this way: "Where the true owner put the truck into the hands of a bailee for his use extending over a considerable period of time, the person in possession has a necessary authority to put the chattel into the possession of a third person to have it repaired by him, and that authority is uncontrollable by a special agreement unknown to the repairer. The right to create the lien rests on ostensible authority rather than upon ostensible ownership. The agreement between the parties is of importance only to show that the owner has assented to the user, and so assented to a position which imports authority. Full continuous user with the consent of the owner constitutes an authority. When the owner of a chattel puts another in uncontrolled use of a chattel he assents to a position which may induce others to act accordingly, and in such an event the owner will be bound." That was the argument that was put for the appellant before the High Court and it was rejected by all members of the High Court. Knox CJ, Gavan Duffy and Starke JJ gave one joint judgment in which they say (at 174): "The rule of law is that an artificer's lien arises only when 'the work in respect of which the charges arose was done by the order or at the request of the owner or some person authorised by him'." After referring to several cases, they then say that *Keene v Thomas, Green v All Motors Ltd* and *Albemarle Supply Co Ltd v Hind & Co* are all cases in which such an authority was inferred. "The learned judges of the Supreme Court", they then go on to say, "declined to draw any such inference in the circumstances of the present case, and, in our opinion, they were right". So what they were saying was that the Supreme Court was right in refusing to draw any inference of authority in the circumstances of the case, and, therefore, they were saying that they were supporting the view, I think, that had been put below that you could not properly draw an inference of authority from the mere fact that the hirer had the uncontrolled right to use the motor car; that you had to show something more than that. And if you looked at the agreement, in order to find an implied authority, you were confronted at once with the limitation upon the authority which appeared in the agreement. In other words, you could not look at that agreement and say: "Well now, from this agreement, from the terms of this agreement, requiring the motor vehicle to be kept in repair, we can imply an authority to create a lien", because that clause had to be looked at in its setting, and part of the setting was a definite provision saying that no authority is conferred by these provisions to create a lien. And it is interesting, I think, in this connection to refer to what was said by Sargant LJ, in the *Albemarle* case [1928] 1 KB 307 at 320, where he referred to the existence in the agreement in that case of the special clause, preventing the hirer from creating any lien for repairs. He said that the existence in the agreement of that special clause does not, in his judgment, operate to the prejudice of the defendants in the absence of their knowledge of that clause. But then he goes on: "The result might be otherwise if (as is not the case) the defendants had to rely upon any authority specially given to the hirer by the agreement. In that case, the special authority could hardly be invoked except subject to the special limitation"...

So far as I am concerned, of course, I am bound by the decision of the High Court in *Fisher's* case and I think that it negatives the proposition that you can spell out of the mere fact that the hirer has the full and uncontrolled use of the motor car — any right to create a lien. And so when you look at the facts of the present case, there is no foundation, I think, for the lien sought to be made out. There is admittedly no express authority. When you look for an implied authority and turn to the agreement, you find the requirement to keep the motor vehicle in good repair and condition and working order. In the same clause, however, it is provided quite definitely that "the hirer is to have no authority to create any lien on the goods for repairs or otherwise. And nothing herein contained, shall be deemed to create any such authority." It is made as clear as words can make it, that there is to be no implied authority from the obligation to keep the goods in repair, and so you are thrown back on the fact that the hirer had full, continuous, uncontrolled user of the chattel to base your lien upon and as I say, I think that *Fisher's* case makes it quite clear that you cannot found a lien on that basis alone. You have got to have something else, to constitute an apparent or an ostensible authority. And there was nothing else here because, admittedly, the repairer did not know that the motor car was the subject of a hire-purchase agreement. It did not know that

Dodkin was not the owner, and I think, for these reasons, the plaintiff must succeed. The lien is not made out.

One further case might be mentioned and that is *Bowmaker Ltd v Wycombe Motors Ltd* [1946] KB 505; [1946] 2 All ER 113. There a motor car was the subject of a hire-purchase agreement. The hirer was put in possession, he did not keep up his payments, and the agreement was terminated. After the agreement had been terminated, he took the motor car along to a repairer to repair it, it was repaired, the repairer claimed a lien for the work he had done, and it was held by the court, quite rightly, if I may say so with respect, that he was not entitled to the lien because any authority that the hirer might have had over the motor car had been terminated. In the course of his judgment, Lord Goddard CJ referred to the *Singer Manufacturing Co* case and the *Albemarle* case and reiterated, I think, the dicta to which reference has already been made, and though it was quite unnecessary for him to say anything about the matter at all, I think he does give support to the wider view which was put by Scrutton LJ and Swinfen Eady LJ in the course of their judgments in the cases to which I have referred, the view which has been, I think, so far as Australia is concerned, rejected by the Full Court of this state and the High Court.

Mr Hewitt, for the defendant sought to rely upon the fact that part of the moneys for which a lien was sought was the cost of towing the vehicle from the place where it had broken down to the garage, and he sought to rely upon the analogy of an agency by necessity and suggested that this might strengthen the position of the repairer. I cannot see how one can distinguish between the cost of the towing and the repairs, for this purpose. Indeed, it may be that the lien sought to be raised cannot be raised in any event for towing costs, but I do not have to decide that point. It is sufficient for me to say that I think that in order to establish the lien or whatever it is, an authority has to be shown, and that authority is not shown in this case for the reasons that I have given. Nor, in my opinion, is the plaintiff estopped from saying that he had given no authority.

The result is, I think, that there must be judgment in this action for the plaintiff for the recovery of the vehicle. The plaintiff also claims damages for the retention of the vehicle for which Mr McGarvie is asking £15. This seems to me to be a reasonable figure and so I will make an order for the return of the vehicle and fix the damages at £15 . . .

Judgment for the plaintiff.

Compare the decision of the English Court of Appeal in *Tappenden v Artus and Rayleigh Garage Ltd* [1964] 2 QB 185.

Where the person authorising the work is a hirer under a hire-purchase agreement, the above cases must be read subject to the relevant provisions of the Uniform Hire-Purchase legislation, where applicable, eg Hire-Purchase Act 1959 (Qld) s 31, Hire-Purchase Act 1959 (WA) s 26, Hire-Purchase Act 1959 (Tas) s 35.

In South Australia, the Consumer Transactions Act 1972 s 37 provides similar protection for a workman who does work on goods comprised in a consumer lease or consumer mortgage. Under each of these Acts, the worker will not be affected by constructive notice of a prohibition in the agreement merely because he knows the goods are subject to a hire-purchase agreement or consumer mortgage. What is the purpose of these sections? Can a finance company effectively give notice to prospective lienees? These issues will not arise in relation to credit sales under the Consumer Credit Act 1981 (NSW) or Credit Act 1981 (Vic) because the buyer-debtor acquires the property in the goods upon delivery and therefore has full authority to create a lien: s 14.

Somewhat analogous conflicts can arise where goods are affixed to land or buildings, or incorporated as components in a machine or vehicle, or mixed with other goods. For example, Carb may install in its factory (mortgaged to City Bank) new equipment acquired on lease from Trident Co or subject to a separate charge to Easy Finance. Or it may utilise components acquired subject to separate charges to Nut Co, Bolt Co and Sil Co in the manufacture of its engines.

Priorities in Relation to Chattel Securities

WHEN DO CHATTELS BECOME FIXTURES?

We referred in Chapter 1 to a number of practical situations where the answer to this question will be significant. In *Australian Provincial Assurance Co Ltd v Coroneo* (1938) 38 SR (NSW) 700 at 712–13 Jordan CJ provided this answer:

A fixture is a thing once a chattel which has become in law land through having been fixed to land. The question whether a chattel has become a fixture depends upon whether it has been fixed to land, if so for what purpose. If a chattel is actually fixed to land to any extent, by any means other than its own weight, then prima facie it is a fixture; and the burden of proof is upon anyone who asserts that it is not: if it is not otherwise fixed but is kept in position by its own weight, then prima facie it is not a fixture; and the burden of proof is on anyone who asserts that it is: *Holland v Hodgson* (1872) LR 7 CP 328 at 335. The test of whether a chattel which has been to some extent fixed to land is a fixture is whether it has been fixed with the intention that it shall remain in position permanently or for an indefinite or substantial period: *Holland v Hodgson* at 336, or whether it has been fixed with the intent that it shall remain in position only for some temporary purpose: *Vaudeville Electric Cinema Ltd v Muriset* [1923] 2 Ch 74 at 87. In the former case, it is a fixture, whether it has been fixed for the better enjoyment of the land or building, or fixed merely to steady the thing itself, for the better use or enjoyment of the thing fixed: *Holland v Hodgson*; *Reynolds v Ashby & Son* [1904] AC 466; *Colledge v H C Curlett Construction Co Ltd* [1932] NZLR 1060; *Benger v Quartermain* [1934] NZLR s 13. If it is proved to have been fixed merely for a temporary purpose it is not a fixture: *Holland v Hodgson* at 337; *Vaudeville Electric Cinema Ltd v Muriset*. The intention of the person fixing it must be gathered from the purpose for which and the time during which user in the fixed position is contemplated: *Hobson v Gorringe* [1897] 1 Ch 182; *Pukuweka Sawmills Ltd v Winger* [1917] NZLR 81. If a thing has been securely fixed, and in particular if it has been so fixed that it cannot be detached without substantial injury to the thing itself or to that to which it is attached, this supplies strong but not necessarily conclusive evidence that a permanent fixing was intended: *Holland v Hodgson; Spyer v Phillipson* [1931] 2 Ch 183 at 209–10. On the other hand, the fact that the fixing is very slight helps to support an inference that it was not intended to be permanent. But each case depends on its own facts. In *Pukuweka Sawmills Ltd v Winger* at 90, 91, 120, a bush tramway introduced on the land for the temporary purpose of removing logs in the course of timbergetting and clearing, and capable of being moved from place to place, was held not to be a fixture; notwithstanding that a relatively secure degree of fixation was necessary whilst the tramway was in use in any particular place. On the other hand, a wooden building, resting on land by its own weight but brought there for the purpose of being permanently used as a dwelling house, was held in *Reid v Smith* (1905) 3 CLR 656 to be a fixture.

The above passage was approved and applied in *Kay's Leasing Corp Pty Ltd v CSR Provident Fund Nominees Pty Ltd* [1962] VR 429 at 432–4, per Adam J. See also *Grigor v International Harvestor Co of Australia Pty Ltd* [1942] St R Qd 238.

Where the conflict concerns goods let on hire-purchase which have become fixtures in a dwelling house, the common law principles are qualified by the Uniform Hire-Purchase Acts (where applicable): see Hire-Purchase Act 1959 (Qld) s 32; Hire Purchase Act 1959 (WA) s 27; Hire-Purchase Act 1959 (Tas) s 36. Under these sections, is a sale on hire-purchase of a full prefabricated home with installation of services an agreement in relation to goods? Is the house when erected affixed to a dwelling house, and can a sale of such a house be a conversion of the "goods" which were the subject of the original hire-purchase agreement? See *Stanley Thompson Investments Pty Ltd v Nock and Kirby Finance Co Pty Ltd* [1969] NSWR 345; Baxt, "When is a house not a home... Fixtures under the Hire-Purchase Act" (1970) 2 *ACLR* 59. Again, these issues will not arise in relation to credit sales of goods under the Consumer Credit Act 1981 (NSW) or Credit Act 1981 (Vic) because property will pass upon delivery and prior to installation. Note, however, Chattel Securities Act 1981 (Vic) s 7.

THE DOCTRINES OF CONFUSION AND ACCESSION

The Australian law differs from the original Roman law concepts of confusion and accession. *Confusion* is the inextricable mixing of goods so that they cannot be separately identified as where fungible commodities such as wheat or wine are pooled for marketing. If the two parcels are mixed through the negligence of one owner, the other innocent owner is entitled to the whole, unless this will result in substantial injustice: *Sandeman & Sons v Tyzack & Branfoot Steamship Co Ltd* [1913] AC 680 at 695. In the case of consensual or accidental mixture, the general rule is the equitable principle that the former owners share in proportion to their respective contributions to the mixture: *Farnsworth v Federal Commissioner of Taxation* (1949) 78 CLR 504 at 510. Only where the amount of each contribution cannot be ascertained will the result be equal division. Where the goods over which one contributor or chargee holds a security are pooled, the charge can only amount to an equitable charge on the bulk and therefore is subject to deferment in favour of a subsequent legal charge over the whole commingled goods: *Farnsworth's* case at 518.

Accession covers the joinder of two distinct items into a single chattel. Where the original components such as nuts, bolts and silicon spray are the property of, or subject to charges to, different parties, Carb, Nut Co, Bolt Co and Sil Co, the doctrine of accession may result in one owner or chargee having a prior claim to the entire new product. Where applicable, the doctrine of accession precludes apportionment and awards to the owner/chargee of the principal component title or security in the entirety. Therefore, where applicable it can pass a title which is freed of prior defects or encumbrances in title and constitutes a further common law exception to the *nemo dat* rule: see Section 1, p 338, *supra*.

In what circumstances will the doctrine apply? How is the principal component to be determined?

Rendell v Associated Finance Pty Ltd
Supreme Court of Victoria (Full Court) [1957] VR 604

O'Bryan J [delivered the following written judgment of the court:] This was an order nisi made returnable before the Full Court to review an order made on 7 March 1957 by a court of petty sessions at Shepparton whereby the defendants were ordered to pay to the complainant the sum of £53 with costs fixed at £21 1s 6d. The complainant's particulars of claim demanded payment of this sum under a contract alleged to have been made between him and the defendants or one of them, and in the alternative as damages for conversion or detention of a motor engine.

The magistrate found in favour of the complainant in conversion and made the order in his favour against both defendants on that ground.

The relevant facts were as follows. On 8 September 1952, the complainant Rendell bought from a person not concerned in this litigation a Chevrolet car engine No BFR511572. It was what is called in the motor trade "a Chevrolet short motor". It was reconditioned and installed by Rendell in his 1942 Chevrolet truck. After using it for about two years, during which time his truck did about 12,000 miles, he removed it from his own truck and hired it to one R L Pell, of Kyabram, under the terms of a hire-purchase agreement dated 2 September 1955. That agreement contained terms now familiar in hire-purchase agreements. It provided, inter alia, that the hirer should pay £20 for the option of purchasing the engine and £8 2s 6d each week for its hire. Until the exercise of the option of purchase, the engine was to remain the absolute property of the complainant Rendell. The hirer, Pell, agreed not to sell or encumber or dispose of the engine or any interest therein and not to part with personal control of it. Rendell was given the right without notice to put an end to the hiring and to take possession of the engine if the hirer, inter alia, made default in punctual payment of any hire payment or failed to observe or perform any of the agreements or conditions contained in the agreement and on his part to be observed and performed. In fact Pell never did exercise the

Priorities in Relation to Chattel Securities

option to purchase the engine, but he parted with possession of it in circumstances now about to be related. Before entering into this hiring agreement, Pell had early in August 1955 taken a Chevrolet 1942 utility truck on hire-purchase terms from the defendant finance company. That agreement was also in a form common to this type of transaction. The trader who introduced the business to the finance company was the defendant Connley, who gave a guarantee in writing to the finance company for the due performance by Pell of all obligations imposed upon him by the hire-purchase agreement.

It is not necessary to refer in detail to the terms of this agreement. It contained a clause entitling the finance company to repossess the hired truck upon breach by Pell of any of the provisions of the agreement. It also contained this clause: "Any accessories or goods supplied with or for or attached to or repairs executed to the goods shall become part of the goods." The motor engine in this truck when Pell took delivery of it under his hire-purchase agreement was No BFR484451. At some date after 2 September 1955 (the evidence did not disclose precisely when), Pell replaced this engine by the one which he had hired from Rendell. Rendell did not assist in this operation, but he became aware of the fact shortly after it had been done. If engine No BFR511572 had been Pell's own engine, by attaching it to the hired truck he would have passed his right of ownership therein to the defendant company, by reason of the condition contained in his hire-purchase agreement with the defendant company: see *Akron Tyre Co Pty Ltd v Kittson* (1951) 82 CLR 477. But as he had no greater rights in it than that of hirer, the clause in his agreement with the defendant company that accessories or goods attached to the hired truck should become part of the truck, could not operate *proprio vigore* to pass the property in the engine to the company: see *Akron Tyre* case at 483, 485, and 489.

Pell did not keep up his payments for the hire of the truck, and the defendant Connley, acting with the authority and on behalf of the defendant company, repossessed the truck on 15 February 1956. At that time, neither Connley nor the company knew that Pell had substituted a different engine in the truck for that which was in it when in August 1955 he had taken possession of it under his hiring agreement. Connley, after repossession, kept the truck, with engine No 511572 attached to it, in his own yard. At first, he so held the truck on behalf of the finance company.

On 13 March the finance company made a demand upon Connley for payment to them of the sum of £236 18s 6d (less £39 if paid before a certain date). The demand was made pursuant to Connley's guarantee of the due performance by Pell of his obligations under his hire-purchase agreement with the company. Connley paid the net amount of this demand, ie £197 18s 6d to the company on 15 May, and it was mutually agreed between Connley and the company that in consideration of this payment the property in the truck (including Rendell's engine) should pass to Connley, who thereafter retained possession thereof in his own right and not on behalf of the company . . .

The first ground of the order *nisi* is that the magistrate should have held that the engine, in consequence of its having been installed by Pell in the motor truck, became the property of the defendant company and had prior to any act of conversion by the defendants ceased to be the property of the complainant.

Mr McInerney contended that this was so, not by reason of any agreement between Pell and the finance company, but because the engine when attached as an accessory to the truck lost its identity as an engine and became part of the truck to which it was attached, so that the property in it passed to the owner of the truck. He contended that this happened by operation of law under the doctrine of accession of title, which he claimed applied to the facts in this case as part of English law which it has adopted from the Roman law. The second ground of the order *nisi,* which is really complementary to the first, is that the magistrate was wrong in holding, if he did so hold, that the doctrine of accession could not apply, because Pell did not have any title to the engine. The fact that Pell did not have a title to the engine is not necessarily an answer to the defendant's claim, because the fundamental notion of this doctrine is that property may pass under it by the act of a stranger and without the consent of the original owner. When the doctrine operates, it does so by force of law and not by agreement; it may do so contrary to the wishes of the owner, and it may be the act of a wrongdoer which brings the doctrine into operation.

Mr McInerney's contention was that the title to a chattel is divested if it has been incorporated into a principal chattel, so that it has ceased, from a practical point of view, to exist as a separate entity, and has become instead an integral part of the principal chattel, and that in determining whether it has so become an integral part of the principal chattel, the question whether it can be detached therefrom without permanent or serious injury to the principal chattel is a useful but not a conclusive test. He contended that if the union occurs in such a way that what is produced is a new chattel identical in kind with only one of the pre-existing chattels, you have accession, and the ownership of the chattel whose identity is lost passes to the owner of the principal chattel, and he submitted that is what happened in this case — that is that the engine, having been attached as a working unit in this motor truck, has lost its identity as a motor engine and has become part of the truck itself. The contention was supported by the citation of passages in various commentaries on Roman law, eg *Sohm's Institutes of Roman Law*, 3rd ed, pp 323-7; Moyle, *The Institutes of Justinian*, 1883 ed, book 2, title 1, s 26, p 41.

[O'Bryan J then explained the preference of the common law for treating these questions in a pragmatic manner from the viewpoint of the law of tort, rather than the Roman law of acquisition of ownership by *accessio, specificatio* and *confusio*, which proceed from the point of view of the law of property. He continued:]

The views of the commentators on Roman law in relation to problems such as arise in this case cannot therefore be trusted as necessarily supplying reliable guidance.

In most cases, if the plaintiff's interests alone are looked at, conversion which sounds in damages will give him a complete remedy. The same applies to detinue because the power of the court to order specific restitution of chattels is discretionary and not a matter of right. Such an order may be refused altogether or made only on such terms as to the court seems necessary to do complete justice between the parties: *Whiteley Ltd v Hilt* [1918] 2 KB 808 at 818, and at 824. If, for instance, the defendant has since taking the property increased its value by his own labour or materials, the plaintiff is entitled to recover as damages only its original and not its present value: *Reid v Fairbanks* (1853) 13 CB 692; *Clerk and Lindsell on Torts*, 11th ed, pp 463-4. The difficulty is that the owner of a chattel when it has been incorporated into another chattel may claim an interest in the combined chattel. Prima facie he would appear to have a right to take his own, and the question thus arises how both interests are to be protected. If the chattels can be severed without damage to either chattel, there would appear to be no necessity to invoke any doctrine of accession of title by reason of the annexation of the goods of the one to that of the other. But in some cases severance from a practical point of view may be impossible, eg the mixture of liquids, the sewing of cotton or accessories into a garment, the painting of a picture on the canvas of another, the laying of planks in a ship, or the building of bricks into a wall. In such cases, English lawyers called in Roman law to their aid. But fundamentally the transfer of property in chattels in English law depends upon intention and consent. Transfer by operation of law is resorted to only in circumstances of necessity, and whether those circumstances exist must be determined in each case as it arises. And in determining the existence of necessity, the injury caused by severance is, no doubt, a material consideration. In *Sandeman and Sons v Tyzack and Branfoot Steamship Co Ltd* [1913] AC 680 at 694-5, after considering the legal consequences of the goods of A becoming indistinguishably and inseparably mixed with the goods of B in circumstances in which the principles governing the resultant effect upon property rights are clear, Lord Moulton went on to say: "The fact is that the conclusions of the courts in such cases, though influenced by certain fundamental principles, have been little more than instances of cutting the Gordian knot — reasonable adjustments of the rights of parties in cases where complete justice was impracticable of attainment. I doubt whether even the fundamental principles enunciated above would be strictly adhered to in extreme cases where they would lead to substantial injustice." In *Re Oatway* [1903] 2 Ch 356 at 359 Joyce J observed: "It is a principle settled as far back as the time of the Year Books that, whatever alteration of form any property may undergo, the true owner is entitled to seize it in its new shape if he can prove the identity of the original material: see *Blackstone* vol II, p 405, and *Lupton v White* (1808) 15 Ves 432. But this rule is carried no farther than necessity requires, and is applied only to cases where the compound is such as to render it impossible to apportion the respective shares of the parties." Both these passages strongly suggest that the fundamental principle in English law in relation to the passing of property by reason of the annexation of one chattel to another looks to the necessity of the occasion.

Priorities in Relation to Chattel Securities

Two Australian decisions of strong persuasive authority in relation to accessories added to a motor vehicle were brought to our attention. In *Bergougnan v British Motors Ltd* (1929) 30 SR (NSW) 61, the Full Court of New South Wales had to consider the question whether the property in motor tyres belonging to A which had been put into a motor lorry belonging to B, passed to B. It was held that the tyres did not so merge into the motor lorry so that the ownership in them passed to the owner of the lorry. The basis of the decision appears to have been that there was no change of ownership because they were readily identifiable and could be detached without damage to the lorry. There was, however, no real discussion of the doctrine of accession, but this absence is readily explainable on the view that the facts did not require resort to such a doctrine.

The same question in relation both to tyres and other accessories which had been attached to a motor prime-mover trailer was considered again by the Full Court of New South Wales in *Lewis v Andrews and Rowley Pty Ltd* (1956) 73 WN (NSW) 670. Ferguson J in a judgment in which Roper CJ in Eq concurred, emphasised at the outset that it is a general rule of English law that property in chattels is transferred only when the owner so intends; that the doctrine of accession is an exception to that rule, but that doctrine is only applied where the circumstances require its application. He rejected the submission that if the attached articles are essential to the operation of the vehicle, they became, when affixed, incorporated with it so that the property in them thereby passes to the owner of the vehicle. In his opinion the doctrine of accession is applied only as a matter of practical necessity. He accordingly held that the property in those accessories which were readily identifiable and could be detached from the vehicle without damage thereto did not pass to the owner of the vehicle. He also expressed the opinion that once it was proved that the articles claimed belonged to the plaintiff at the time when they were attached to the vehicle and that he intended to retain his ownership therein, it was for the defendant on proper evidence to establish that the property in them had passed to the owner of the vehicle. Manning J dissented from the view of the majority. In his opinion, different principles apply both to the case of chattels affixed to real property and to cases on the passing of property in contracts for work and labour done and materials supplied. He regarded the state of affairs where accessories are attached to a motor vehicle for the purpose of enabling the vehicle to operate as such, as falling into a third group of cases, viz, those relating to chattels which had been bound together, and to which the doctrines adopted from the Roman law have been applied.

He agreed that such authority as does exist regarding this third class of case is somewhat unsatisfactory. After discussing some of the cases and rejecting detachability as the test to determine whether property passes or not, he said (at 677): "In my opinion, the test may be stated as follows: 'Has the chattel which has been added to or incorporated in another chattel ceased to exist as a separate chattel?'" He added that "in cases of the kind now under consideration, the owner of a chattel will not normally lose his title to it except by operation of law or by an act or an agreement on his part by which he intends to divest himself of it. But if he so acts in relation to his chattel that he annexes it to or incorporates it into some other chattel, he will be presumed conclusively to have intended to divest himself of it providing: (1) that the incorporation or annexation results in the chattel ceasing to exist as a separate chattel, and (2) that he ceases to be entitled to possession of the new chattel, and (3) that his action was wrongful as against the person lawfully in possession." It must be remembered that he was discussing a case in which the plaintiff had himself attached to the property of the defendant the chattels which he sought to recover. On the question of onus of proof, Manning J was of the opinion that once it was established that the chattel had been incorporated in or annexed to another chattel, then unless the consequences were apparent or a matter of common knowledge, the plaintiff having asserted his claim was bound to prove that at the material time, the goods claimed continued to have a separate existence.

The test propounded by Manning J would in many cases be very difficult of application. Take the instance of a battery or a fan belt or a wireless set put into a motor car. Does the incorporation or annexation of these chattels result in their ceasing to have a separate existence? If it does, garage proprietors could not safely lend batteries to car owners while the owner's battery is being recharged. Yet such chattels lose their identity just as much and as little as does an engine, for all are capable of ready annexation and detachment. And what of wheels and tyres? Is a spare wheel or tyre in a different position from one attached as a running unit to the car?

Manning J, with the other members of the court, rejected as incorrect the test applied in the Canadian case, *Regina Chevrolet Sales Ltd v Riddell* [1942] 3 DLR 159 (see per Ferguson J at 672 and per Manning J at 677). In that case the question was whether the property in tyres which were attached to a truck passed to the truck owner. The Court of Appeal of Saskatchewan held that they did because they were an integral part of the truck necessary for its proper working and for that reason, when used to equip the truck, became by accession the property of the person who has the property in the truck. If that test is rejected, the question "has a particular accessory been so attached to a principal chattel that it has ceased to exist as a separate chattel?" is not made any more easy of answer.

... We consider the test laid down by Ferguson J (in which Roper CJ in Eq concurred) is the proper one to apply in this class of case in which accessories in the nature of spare parts are attached to a motor vehicle. Prima facie the property in the accessory does not pass to the owner of the vehicle if the owner of the accessory did not intend it to pass. It is for the defendant by proper evidence to show that the necessity of the case requires the application of principles whereby the property is deemed to pass by operation of law. The accessories continue to belong to their original owner unless it is shown that as a matter of practicability they cannot be identified, or, if identified, they have been incorporated to such an extent that they cannot be detached from the vehicle.

It is clear in this case that the plaintiff was the owner of the engine when it was annexed to the truck and that he intended to retain the property in the engine until Pell exercised his option to buy it. In our opinion, he is entitled to rely on the presumption that he continued to remain the owner, so that in the absence of evidence to the contrary the engine continued to belong to him, which, in this case, would require evidence from the defendants that as a matter of practicability it had been so attached to the truck that it could not be detached therefrom. But even if the ultimate onus was on the plaintiff, as Mr McInerney contended, to prove that at the date of conversion he was still entitled to possession of the engine, or in other words to prove that its manner of annexation did not as a matter of justice require that it should remain where it was, so that the property in it should be deemed to have passed to the owner of the truck, the proper inference from the meagre material placed before the magistrate was that it had not been so annexed or attached but could be detached without difficulty or harm to anything. It had been placed upon the complainant's own Chevrolet 1942 truck and had apparently been removed from it without difficulty. The truck hired to Pell was also a Chevrolet 1942 model. Moreover, we think the court should take judicial notice of the fact that in these days it is common practice to replace motor engines which are the worse for wear by new or reconditioned engines of the same make and year of manufacture. This is done without damage either to the engine or the motor vehicle. This is an age when automobile parts are generally standardised and interchangeable, at all events in the case of motor vehicles of the same make and year of manufacture. The court should not shut its eyes to what is common knowledge.

For these reasons we are of opinion that the property in the engine remained throughout the property of the complainant, Rendell, and that the magistrate arrived at the correct decision in this regard. Nothing that we have said is intended to cover a case where the plaintiff's chattel has been annexed to another by his authority, either express or implied, or where his conduct is such as to estop him from contending that he is still entitled to his chattel. These are questions which do not arise in this case.

[The court then considered and rejected the argument on behalf of Connley that Rendell had agreed to Connley selling the vehicle with Rendell's engine in it. It was further argued on behalf of Connley that, although he took possession of Rendell's engine, he did not then know that it was in the truck, and therefore could not be presumed to have intended to convert it. The court concluded at 612-13:] This principle, however, does not help the defendants in this case. On the evidence as it stands, the proper inference is that Connley, when he took possession of the motor truck, knew that it had an engine in it, and intended to repossess the whole vehicle including the engine. He intended to repossess the truck under a claim of right for the person whom he believed to be the true owner, namely the finance company. As the evidence stands, it is proper also to infer that he intended to exercise dominion over the whole truck, including its engine. It does not matter that he was mistaken as to what engine was attached to the truck or that he believed the finance company to be the owner of that engine.

Priorities in Relation to Chattel Securities

The wrong of conversion does not involve any element of dishonesty in the tort feasor. The attempt to apply the principle of *Fouldes v Willoughby* (1841) 8 M & W 540 to the facts of this case is to confuse an intention to take possession of the goods and to exercise a dominion over them, with the mistaken belief as to their identity or ownership. "In order to amount to a conversion the act done with respect to the chattel must have been one of wilful and wrongful interference": *Salmond on Torts,* 10th ed, p 287; *Fleming on Torts,* p 60; *Clerk and Lindsell on Torts,* 11th ed, p 422. Here the evidence disclosed an intentional taking of the engine with the truck. If that is so, Connley's interference with the engine was done at his peril. "Persons dealing with property in chattels or exercising acts of ownership over them do so at their peril": per Cleasby B in *Fowler v Hollins* (1872) LR 7 QB 616 at 639. Connley's mistaken belief that the engine in the truck belonged to the company on whose behalf he repossessed it, avails him nothing: *Fowler v Hollins* (1875) LR 7 HL 757. Nor does it avail him that in repossessing the truck he was acting not on his own behalf, but on behalf of the finance company. This is clear from what was said by Alderson B in the passage just cited: "When, therefore, a man takes that chattel either for the use of himself or of another it is a conversion." As the engine in February 1956, when the truck was repossessed by Connley, still belonged to Rendell, Connley was therefore guilty of a conversion of the engine, and as he was then acting with the authority and on behalf of the finance company, the company is also liable for his acts as their agent...

Order nisi discharged.

QUESTIONS

Question 5

On 6 September, Carb Pty Ltd borrowed $50,000 from Easy Finance on the security of a floating charge over all Carb's present and future property. The charge included the following clause: "Carb Pty Ltd is prohibited from creating any subsequent charge over any of its present or future assets during the currency of this charge." On 9 September, Easy Finance lodged at the National Companies and Securities Commission a notice containing the prescribed particulars of its charge. However, due to an oversight by Easy Finance the notice did not refer to the clause quoted above.

On 21 October, Carb Pty Ltd purchased 10,000 components from Comp Co on six months credit and gave a fixed charge over these components to Comp Co to secure the unpaid purchase price of $10,000. Comp Co omitted to register the charge.

On 1 November, Carb Pty Ltd purchased $25,000 worth of widgets from Widg Co. The purchase price was advanced to Carb by Squeeze who took a floating charge over all Carb's present and future assets. That night at a dinner party Squeeze overheard a conversation in which Comp Co's general manager told a business colleague that Comp Co had taken a charge over Carb's assets. On 4 November, Squeeze lodged notice of its charge with the commission.

On 10 December an order was made for the winding up of Carb Pty Ltd, and Col Lector was appointed as liquidator.

Discuss the priorities as between the charges held by Easy Finance, Comp Co and Squeeze.

What difference would it make if either
(a) notice of Comp Co's charge had been lodged with the commission on 25 October, or
(b) the dinner party and conversation overheard by Squeeze took place on 22 October?

Question 6

(1) On 7 August, Carb Pty Ltd borrowed $25,000 from City Bank secured by a floating charge over all of Carb's present and future stock-in-trade.

On 14 August, Carb Pty Ltd purchased 5000 $1 widgets from Widg Co and in return for extended credit gave Widg Co a fixed charge over the widgets supplied.

On 21 August, City Bank was asked to loan a further $20,000 to Carb Pty Ltd.

Assume you have been requested to advise City Bank. Under what circumstances can City Bank obtain the same priority in respect of the proposed future advances as it enjoyed in respect of its original loan? In your answer consider City Bank's position alternately

(a) at common law;
(b) under the National Companies Code;
(c) where the credit is being extended by the Bank and Widg Co to Jim Handy as an individual rather than to Carb Pty Ltd, and the transactions take place in Tasmania and are governed by Tasmanian law.

(2) What purposes are served by future advance lending? What should the law seek to achieve in this area? Is this result best achieved under the common law principles or under the respective statutory rules?

Question 7

Mary Handy needed a new electric kiln for her pottery business which she conducted in the basement of the Handy's home which was registered in Jim and Mary's joint names.

She approached Squeeze for the necessary finance. On 1 March, at his suggestion, she sold her sports car to Squeeze in order to provide the necessary downpayment on the kiln, and entered into a lease agreement with Squeeze in respect of both the sports car and kiln.

The lease provided inter alia:

"(1) The term of this lease is three years and the lessee shall have an option to extend the term for a further three years.

"(2) The lessee shall not create any lien over the goods.

"(3) The lessor shall be entitled to repossess the goods if the lessee defaults in payment of any rental instalment.

"(4) Any replacement parts hereafter attached to the goods shall become a part thereof."

After Squeeze delivered the kiln, Mary had it built into the basement wall with the flue extending out through the roof.

On 1 July Jim and Mary Handy mortgaged their home to City Bank.

By 30 November, Mary was substantially in arrears in her lease payments to Squeeze, and Jim and Mary had defaulted under their mortgage to City Bank.

Jim borrowed Mary's sports car in December for a weekend trip to the Bathurst races. The engine overheated as the car climbed the Blue Mountains. Fearing that the engine might seize, Jim called the Bathurst Sporting Car Club, which sent a truck to tow the vehicle 120 km to Bathurst. While staying at the Club's premises for the weekend, Jim arranged for the Club's mechanic to replace the faulty radiator. Jim also ordered a radio, new seat belts and reclining seats to be installed in Mary's car as surprise Christmas presents for her.

At the end of the weekend, the club manager handed Jim the following bill:

To towing charges (120 km)	$60
Supply and fit radiator	150
Supply and install radio, seat belts and seats	900
Two nights accommodation and meals	120
	1230

Jim requested that this amount be added to his monthly account, picked up the car keys and was walking towards the car, when Squeeze suddenly appeared and stated that he was repossessing the car. The Club manager immediately intervened and demanded back the keys and car as security for payment of the $1230 bill.

Assuming Jim and Mary are insolvent, discuss the respective claims of
(a) Jim, Mary, City Bank and Squeeze to the kiln; and
(b) Jim, Mary, Squeeze and the Bathurst Sporting Car Club to the sports car and its accessories.

SECTION 3: FINANCING FARM PRODUCTS

As outlined on p 144, *supra,* rural production still accounts for a very substantial proportion of Australia's GNP. The financing of farmers' production costs presents some special challenges which call for separate treatment from other forms of collateral. Farm produce may be broadly compared to other forms of stock-in-trade in that it is produced for sale and changes its content, in the case of livestock by natural increase and death as well as by purchase and sale. On the other hand, farmers hold livestock for longer periods than most merchants retain stock. In addition, the financing of crops and wool clips must conform to the seasonal processes of growing, harvesting, lambing and shearing.

Inherent in the nature of rural production is the potential for conflicting claims such as:
(a) a livestock financier's claim to progeny under an after-acquired property clause as against a subsequent specific loan on the security of newborn lambs, calves, etc;
(b) a sheep lienee's claim in respect of the annual wool clip as against a purchaser or mortgagee of the sheep;
(c) a crop lienee's claim as against a purchaser or mortgagee of the land on which the timber, crops or fruit are growing prior to harvesting.

METHODS OF FARM FINANCING

Students from country areas may be well aware of the typical methods of farm financing, but they are outside the normal experience of many students and lawyers. Normally the initial financing of rural properties is carried by trading banks or insurance companies which take a first mortgage over the farm itself. Livestock financing is provided by pastoral houses, wool brokers and the Commonwealth Development Bank, which would take a second mortgage over the farm, as well as a stock mortgage, which is generally regarded as a makeweight rather than a primary security. Similarly, liens on annual crops are used as a means of short-term seasonal financing usually carried by trading banks. Australia's wool clip is also handled on a seasonal basis; in this case the financing is carried by wool brokers who take a wool lien over the annual wool clip, thereby obtaining the business of handling and selling the clip and ensuring direct reimbursement of loans from the proceeds of sale.

THE LEGAL BASIS FOR FARM FINANCING

The fluctuating nature of farm produce makes it difficult to obtain an adequate security at common law, yet the aggregate value of Australia's crops in the ground and livestock on the hoof is enormous. It is not surprising therefore that although non-registration will result in varying degrees of invalidity, the pattern of legislation has been to facilitate farm credit by improving the legal quality of the available security interest rather than the invalidation of secret securities. While the general pattern is similar in the various states, the legislation is far from uniform; therefore, for present purposes it is intended to provide a general descriptive outline with examples from particular states where appropriate. The relevant legislation in each state is: NSW, Liens on Crops and Wool and Stock Mortgages Act 1898; Vic, Instruments Act 1958; Qld, Bills of Sale and Other Instruments Act 1955; SA, Liens on Fruit Act 1923 and Stock Mortgages and Wool Liens Act 1924; WA, Bills of Sale Act 1899; Tas, Stock, Wool and Crop Mortgages Act 1930; ACT, Instruments Ordinance 1933. For a detailed analysis, see Sykes, *The Law of Securities,* 3rd ed, 1978, Chapters 13 and 17.

CROP LIENS

A mortgage over a crop, presently growing or in prospect, is valid at common law, but is a weak security because it is merely equitable until the crop is harvested, and is liable to be defeated by a sale or mortgage of the land. Should a crop mortgage be registered as a bill of sale? The answer will generally depend upon the definition of "personal chattels" or "chattels" in the bills of sale legislation. In Western Australia, where there is no statutory crop lien, an assignment of a growing crop apart from the land requires registration under Bills of Sale Act 1899-1971 s 5. In the other states, provision has been made for statutory liens or mortgages over crops although the South Australian Act (Liens on Fruit Act 1923) is confined to growing fruit. Most of the statutes prescribe a standard simple form of crop lien: see, eg, Schedule 2 of the New South Wales Act.

The main advantage of the statutory lien or mortgage is that by virtue of the statute it is virtually equivalent to a legal mortgage provided the crop has actually been sown and registration requirements are fulfilled. In some states it can also be given by the holder of the land—ie, the person in exclusive possession, which includes a lessee of the land, but not a share-farmer unless the proprietor were joined as a co-lienor (eg, NSW s 4). Under the New South Wales Act, upon default of the lienor, the crop lienee is empowered to enter, harvest, carry away and sell the crop (s 5).

The main priority conflicts in relation to crop liens and their resolution under the New South Wales Act are:

(1) The crop lienee will be absolutely protected from the lienor's trustee in bankruptcy, unsecured creditors and purchasers of the land provided the crop lien is registered within 30 days: ss 4 and 5.

(2) The registered crop lien is also protected from claims of the lienor's landlord or real estate mortgagee subject to payment out of the proceeds of the crop of up to one year's arrears of rent (s 9) or mortgage interest (s 7) if same is owing by the lienor.

(3) Priorities between competing registered crop liens are determined by the date of execution rather than registration: *A-G for NSW v Hills & Halls Ltd* (1923) 32 CLR 112.

WOOL LIENS

Apart from statute a purported mortgage over wool growing on the sheep's back would at best be an equitable interest only and since it would be defeated by any dealing with the sheep, would not really be feasible. It is doubtful if it would require registration under bills of sale legislation since wool on the sheep's back is not capable of independent transfer by delivery. (See also Bills of Sale Act 1898 (NSW) s 14.) The purpose of the wool liens legislation is to facilitate the creation of a valid security over the wool clip prior to shearing. A simple form is prescribed in Schedule 3 of the New South Wales Act.

Under the New South Wales and Victorian Acts the lien is limited to one year's duration and hence a new lien would have to be given each year. The wool lienee is entitled upon the owner's default to take possession of the sheep, to wash and shear them and to add the expenses of washing, shearing and transporting the wool to the amount secured by the lien (NSW s 12(2)).

The main priority conflicts and their resolution under the New South Wales Act are:

(1) The wool lienee will be absolutely protected from the lienor's trustee in bankruptcy and unsecured creditors provided the wool lien is registered within 30 days: s 11.

(2) The registered wool lien will also be protected against purchasers or subsequent mortgagees of the sheep: s 11.

(3) Priorities between competing registered wool liens in New South Wales are probably determined by the date of execution on the analogy to crop liens pursuant to *A-G for NSW v Hills & Halls Ltd* (1923) 32 CLR 112. However, it is arguable that it is impossible to grant a valid second wool lien on the ground that the grazier is no longer the "owner" or "proprietor" of the wool after the statutory title has passed to the first lienee: see discussion in *Sykes,* 3rd ed, pp 528-9. In Victoria, Queensland and South Australia, priorities are determined by date of registration; and in Tasmania, a subsequent wool mortgagee could obtain priority by first registration unless affected by notice of the prior lien: Vic, s 76; Qld, ss 7(2)(b), 34; SA, s 25; Tas, s 11 and Bills of Sale Act 1900 s 36.

(4) Conflict between a prior mortgagee of the sheep and subsequent wool lienee raises again the question whether a grazier who has given a stock mortgage over his flock remains the "owner" or "proprietor" of the sheep capable of granting a wool lien. The Acts suggest a solution by providing for the mortgagee of the sheep consenting to the granting of a subsequent wool lien: NSW, s 14; Vic, s 77; Qld, s 29; SA, s 9; WA, s 45; Tas, s 11; ACT, s 28. In the absence of such consent, the wool lienee has at best an equitable charge at general law which does not attract the protection of the Acts. Under the Queensland and South Australian Acts, a subsequent lien without the consent of the sheep mortgagee is void: Qld, s 29; SA, s 9.

STOCK MORTGAGES

Livestock, like other chattels, can be the subject of a legal mortgage. However, by statute such a security is required to be separately registered in all states, except that in Western Australia it is registered as a bill of sale, and in Queensland it is registered in the same manner as a bill of sale although regarded as a separate instrument. It appears that dual registration is not required: see eg, Bills of Sale Act 1898 (NSW) s 14. The definition of stock varies between the states: eg, in New South Wales it is confined to sheep, cattle and/or horses; in South Australia pigs, goats, camels, mules and donkeys are also included. In New South Wales mortgages of sheep, cattle and/or horses may be registered under either Act, while securities over other stock such as pigs, goats and poultry should be registered under the Bills of Sale Act to avoid invalidation. In either case, a stock mortgage will normally include the same type of provisions as a bill of sale. The statutes in some states confer additional statutory rights but the New South Wales Act adds little, and in any event, additional provisions can be stipulated in the mortgage itself.

The main purpose of registration is to avoid invalidity under bills of sale legislation. In some states after-acquired stock including progeny is automatically deemed to be covered by the stock mortgage: Vic, s 75; WA, s 38; Tas, Bills of Sale Act 1900 s 35. But in New South Wales after-acquired stock must be expressly claimed. The mortgagee's title to after-acquired stock is on general principle merely equitable, but the Queensland Act confers a legal title in respect of progeny: s 27. In most states, priorities in respect of stock mortgages are dealt with in a similar manner to ordinary bills of sale. Thus, in New South Wales an unregistered stock mortgage is invalidated as against judgment creditors (s 4) and the trustee in bankruptcy (s 5) but not as regards bona fide purchasers. Priorities between two competing stock mortgages will be governed by date of registration in Queensland, South Australia and Western Australia, while registration under the Bills of Sale Act (NSW) offers the priority advantages of s 5A considered on p 358-9, *supra*.

QUESTION

Question 8

What is the nature and purpose of crop and wool liens? What is the effect obtained by registering a lien under the relevant statutes?

FURTHER READING

Section 1: The Nemo Dat Rule and Protection of Bona Fide Purchasers

Begg, "The Registration of Security Interests in Chattels" (1981) 55 *ALJ* 649.

Cullen & Baxt (eds), *Consumer Credit: The Challenges of Change*, 1973.

McGarvie & Begg, "The Implementation of Fair Consumer Laws" (1971) 45 *ALJ* 708.

O'Hare, "Credit Bills" (1981) 9 *ABLR* 257.

Peden, "Lienee's Statutory Power of Sale" (1968) 6 *Uni of Qld LU* 24.

Peden, *Stock-in-Trade Financing*, 1974, esp pp 19-20, 50, 54, 56, Appendix pp 186-91.

Peden, "Title Problems in Relation to Chattels—Proposals for a Registration System for Motor Vehicles in Australia" (1968) 42 *ALJ* 239.

Peden & Seidler, "Form and Substance in Commercial Leasing of Equipment" (1980) 54 *ALJ* 251 at 309.

Report on Fair Consumer Credit Laws by Committee of the Law Council of Australia (Molomby Committee) 1972.

Sutton, *Sales and Consumer Law in Australia & New Zealand*, 1983, Chapters XIV-XVII.

Sutton, "The Motor Credits Case" (1965) 39 *ALJ* 233.

Section 2: Priority Conflicts between Competing Secured Creditors

Guest, "Accession and Confusion in the Law of Hire-Purchase" (1964) 27 *MLR* 505.

Nicholson, "Accessory Clauses in Motor Vehicle Hire-Purchase Agreements" (1966) 39 *ALJ* 408.

Peden, "The Creation of Common Law Liens" (1969) 18 *Int & Comp LQ* 129.

Tyree, "Priorities under Section 5A, Bills of Sale Act, 1898" (1983) 21 *Law Soc J* 19.

Section 3: Financing Farm Products

Atkins, R J, *Bills of Sale, Liens and Stock Mortgages in New South Wales*, 2nd ed, 1939.

Else-Mitchell, "Liens on Crops and Wool—A Critical Review of the Legislation" (1939) 13 *ALJ* 270.

Hennessy, "Chattel Mortgages in NSW" (1960) 34 *ALJ* 72.

Sykes, "Crop and Wool Lien Complexities" (1959) 33 *ALJ* 46.

CHAPTER 9

Lending on the Security of Proceeds: Assignment of Choses in Action and Chattel Paper; Credit Cards

"No man's credit is as good as his money."
E W Howe

Section 1: An Overview of Credit Practices involving Proceeds
Section 2: Requirements for Valid Assignments
Section 3: Priorities between Competing Claims
Section 4: Financing through Chattel Paper
Section 5: Arrangements with Credit Cards

In this chapter, the scene moves to the further stage where the borrower, whether he be manufacturer, wholesaler or retailer (in our story, Carb Pty Ltd) has sold goods from stock in circumstances where the buyers normally will take title clear of Carb's secured creditors. In return Carb will have received proceeds of sale which may vary in form. They may have been:
  (a) cash;
  (b) cheques, bills of exchange or promissory notes;
  (c) unsecured book debts payable at 30, 60 or 90 days;
  (d) credit sales or hire-purchase agreements (chattel paper);
  (e) right to payment of the sale price duly discounted by a credit card issuer such as Bankcard.

Each of these forms of proceeds, with the exception of cash, comes within the legal classification of choses in action which was explained in Chapter 1. If Carb has used these proceeds as a source of finance, it will have assigned the choses to its lender in one form or another. Thus, the legal context in which this chapter is set, concerns:
  (a) the requirements for a valid assignment of various types of choses in action (Section 2); and
  (b) the rules governing priorities between competing claims thereto (Sections 3-5).

SECTION 1: AN OVERVIEW OF CREDIT PRACTICES INVOLVING PROCEEDS

DEFINITION AND TYPES OF CHOSES IN ACTION

By definition a chose in action is an intangible incorporeal bundle of rights, often represented by a piece of paper. Students unfamiliar with commercial dealings normally find these intangible concepts somewhat unreal and difficult to comprehend. Therefore a brief outline of credit practices seems warranted. Students taking courses in commerce, accounting or economics may find assistance in some of their business texts. The primary definition of a chose in action is any right which is enforceable by action. Although many rights such as debts or rights of action for breach of contract cannot be reduced into physical possession, other rights, such as shares, debentures and bills of exchange are represented by documents evidencing the underlying obligation which may be transferred by physical delivery of the document.

Choses in action can also be divided into legal choses and equitable choses.

Legal choses in action are those which can be recovered or enforced by action at common law, and include debts, contractual rights, rights to damages in tort, and company shares.

Equitable choses in action are those which could previously only be enforced in the equity jurisdiction, and include an interest in a trust fund, in a deceased estate or in a partnership, or the beneficial interest in company shares where the legal interest is held by a trustee or nominee.

Future chose in action is a term used to describe the mere possibility or expectancy of becoming entitled to a chose in action at a future time; for example, a shareholder's right to dividends prior to any recommendation of declaration of a dividend; or the expectation of next-of-kin to a share in the intestacy of a person still living. Distinguish a presently vested right to receive payment in the future, such as future instalments of rent under a valid lease, which is a present chose in action.

Apart from a general floating charge which usually covers a company's total assets, the intangible assets most commonly assigned by way of security are:
(a) debts, especially current unsecured accounts receivable (see below);
(b) shares and other securities issued by companies (Section 2);
(c) contract rights, including right to payment under credit sale or hire-purchase agreements or goods mortgages coupled with property rights in the goods (see Section 4);
(d) policies of insurance and assurance (see p 260, *supra*);
(e) negotiable instruments, including bills of exchange, promissory notes and cheques (see Chapters 10 and 11).

METHODS OF FINANCING BOOK DEBTS

Factoring has been defined as "a continuing legal relationship between a financial institution (the "factor"), and a business concern (the "client") selling goods or providing services to trade customers (the "customers") whereby the factor purchases the client's book debts either without or with recourse to the client, and in relation thereto controls the credit extended to customers and administers the sales ledger": Biscoe, *Law and Practice of Credit Factoring*, 1975, p 3.

It should be noted that factoring has not been developed in this form in relation to debts owed by *consumers*. The reasons are primarily the small average amount of each consumer debt which increases administrative overheads and the difficulty of obtaining adequate credit information on individual consumers where they have no direct contractual relationship with the factor. Accordingly, consumer financing normally takes the form of a retailer's own unsecured monthly credit account, a credit card scheme (eg, unsecured credit extended by Bankcard) or hire-purchase, credit sale or goods mortgage (secured credit from a finance company). Note that except in the case of the retailer's own credit account, the credit contract is normally made directly between the financial institution and the consumer, although the retail trader may introduce them and also be a party to an agreement with the financial institution.

Factoring of trade debts can take a variety of forms (using Biscoe's terminology):

Non-recourse factoring. The client assigns absolutely to the factor debts which the factor approves. The factor carries the risk that the customer will be financially unable to pay and has no recourse to the client.

Recourse factoring. The client assigns debts to the factor which the factor collects from the customer. However, the ultimate credit risk remains with the client to whom the factor has recourse in respect of debts which a customer fails to pay for any reason.

Confidential factoring. The client assigns debts and the credit risk to the factor (ie, without recourse), but no notice of the assignments is given to customers from whom the client continues to collect the debts as agent for the factor. An Australian illustration of confidential factoring is given in *G E Crane Sales Pty Ltd v Commissioner of Taxation* (1971) 126 CLR 177, where Menzies J outlined the process at 181-2.

Invoice discounting. Resembles confidential factoring in that the financier purchases debts from the client who collects them as agent for the financier without notification to the customer. However, the financier will have recourse to the client, and the client may choose to assign some debts but not others.

For a detailed description of current English practices, see *Biscoe*, Ch 1. The Australian pattern is developing along similar lines although factoring is a more recent innovation here.

BENEFITS OF FACTORING

Factoring can offer considerable advantages to small and medium-sized businesses especially if they are expanding and therefore need cash flow. These advantages may include insulation from bad debt losses, accelerated cash flow, improved efficiency and more management time for production, sales and planning, improved credit rating and an increased return on invested funds. It has also been claimed that an efficient system of factoring has macro-economic significance in "the stabilising influence on industry of authoritative and judicious credit control; the promotion of the efficiency and profitability of the medium and small firm; and facilitation of expansion of such firms thereby promoting employment and the growth of the Gross National Product": *Biscoe*, p 27. It is equally important that the legal framework facilitates rather than hinders commercial financing.

SECTION 2: REQUIREMENTS FOR VALID ASSIGNMENTS

The requirements for valid assignments will be dealt with in the following order:
(a) legal choses in general;
(b) equitable choses;
(c) statutory requirements for specific choses: book debts, shares, insurance policies and industrial property.

Not every chose in action is assignable: a chose may be unassignable on the grounds of public policy (interests in bare rights to litigate); or prohibited by statute (certain pensions), or because it is a contract for personal skill and confidence. See Starke, *Assignment of Choses in Action in Australia*, 1972, Ch 7.

ASSIGNMENT OF LEGAL CHOSES

Cash is not a chose in action, although it shares with bills of exchange and cheques the quality of free negotiability. Cash is of course transferable by delivery. *Negotiable instruments* (bills of exchange, cheques and promissory notes) are legal choses in action; since they enjoy the distinctive quality of negotiability and the applicable law has been codified in the Bills of Exchange Act, they will be dealt with separately in Chapters 10 and 11. A *debt* is an ascertained sum of money which is actually payable, or will become payable in the future by reason of a present obligation: *Webb v Stenton* (1883) 11 QBD 518 at 526-8. A debt is a typical form of legal chose in action and will be used as the focus for examining the requirements for assignment.

Let us assume as a basic illustration that Carb Pty Ltd sold 3000 carburettors to Greatparts Ltd for $30,000 on open credit. In consideration of a loan of $20,000 Carb (assignor) assigned to Factors Ltd (assignee) the debt owed to it by Greatparts (debtor).

In the nineteenth century, a legal chose in action (other than assignments by or to the Crown, and transfers of negotiable instruments) was not recognised by the common law because of the procedural difficulty that, although the assignment conferred rights upon the assignee directly, it created no direct obligation from the debtor to the assignee. In our illustration, Greatparts had no direct contract or obligation to Factors. In practice, the difficulty would have been overcome in one of three ways:

(a) Factors could insist on Carb acting as its agent to recover the debt from Greatparts, or better still, appointing Factors under a power of attorney to do so;

(b) Factors could obtain Greatparts' agreement to pay Factors in exchange for a release of its obligation to pay Carb (ie, a novation of the original obligation); or

(c) in appropriate cases the equity courts would specifically enforce the equitable obligation involved in the assignment of the legal chose, for example, by requiring Carb to allow its name to be used in an action to recover the debt owed by Greatparts.

ASSIGNMENT OF LEGAL CHOSES AT LAW

To avoid these cumbersome procedures, a simple statutory form of legal assignment for debts and other legal choses in action has been provided by legislation in each state. The Australian enactments are based on s 25 of the Judicature Act 1873 (UK), and the legislation in the respective states adopts a similar form: NSW, Conveyancing Act 1919 s 12; Vic, Property Law Act 1958 s 134; Qld, Property Law Act 1974 s 199; SA, Law of Property Act 1936 s 15; WA, Property Law Act 1969 s 20; Tas, Conveyancing and Law of Property Act 1884 s 86; ACT, Law of Property (Miscellaneous Provisions) Ordinance 1958 s 3 (applying NSW Conveyancing Act s 12).

It should be noted that these sections do not apply to assignments of:

(a) shares which are regulated by the Companies Code (ss 178, 183, 184);

(b) life insurance policies (Life Insurance Act 1945 (Cth) ss 87-91: see p 260, *supra*);

(c) marine insurance policies (Marine Insurance Act 1909 (Cth) s 56: see p 260, *supra*);

(d) fire policies (Insurance Act 1902 (NSW) ss 14, 16: see p 261, *supra*).

In reading the section note that the essential elements are:

(i) the assignment must be absolute (not purporting to be by way of charge only);

(ii) the assignment must be in writing and signed by the assignor;

(iii) express written notice of assignment must be given to the debtor, trustee or other person from whom the assignor was entitled to claim the debt or chose in action. Such notice may be given by the assignor or assignee.

The section does not explicitly state whether it applies to the following:

(a) an outright mortgage of a legal chose in action (as distinct from a charge which is expressly excluded);
(b) an assignment of part of a chose in action or of a future chose;
(c) an assignment by way of gift;
(d) an assignment of which the assignee (Factors) has not been notified, even though the debtor (Greatparts) has received notice.

These questions must be answered from the case law.

Durham Brothers v Robertson
English Court of Appeal [1898] 1 QB 765

[The defendant entered into a building contract on 1 April 1895, with contractors, Smith & Co, under which it was stipulated that the contractors should build certain houses which were to be leased to them at a ground-rent of £150. One of the clauses of the contract gave the contractors the option of paying an additional ground-rent of £60 in consideration of which they were to receive from the defendant a sum of £1080. On 19 August of the same year the contractors wrote to the plaintiffs in the following terms: "Re Building Contract of Middle Class Dwellings situate on the west side South Lambeth Road. In consideration of money advanced from time to time we hereby charge the sum of £1080, being the agreed price for the sale of £60 per annum ground-rent which will become due to us from John Robertson, Esq, of No 73, Rosendale Road, West Dulwich, on the completion of the above buildings as security for the advances, and we hereby assign our interest in the abovementioned sum until the money with added interest be repaid to you." The plaintiffs gave notice of the assignment to the defendant, the John Robertson named therein, and this action was brought against him to recover the amount which it was alleged had, in the events that happened, become due. The defence was a denial that the amount ever became payable to the contractors under their building contract, and, secondly, that there was no valid assignment of the sum within s 25, sub-s (6), of the Judicature Act 1873 (NSW Conveyancing Act s 12).

The learned judge gave judgment for the plaintiffs on both points.

The defendant appealed.

The arguments on the question of fact whether the amount became payable and so much of the judgments as related to that question are omitted.]

Chitty LJ [stated the facts, quoted the letter and continued at 769:] Now the document divides itself into two parts. First, there is a charge upon £1080 for the advances; and, secondly, there is an assignment of the interest of Smith & Co in the £1080 in terms not absolute, but until the happening of an event, namely, the repayment of the advances with interest. On repayment of the advances and interest the assignment, according to the import of the document, comes to an end.

Dealing with the case apart from the Judicature Act, there is here unquestionably a valid equitable assignment. To operate as an equitable assignment no particular form of words is required in the document: an engagement or direction to pay, out of a debt or fund, a sum of money constitutes an equitable assignment, though it does not operate as an assignment of the whole fund or debt. A mere charge on a fund or debt operates as a partial equitable assignment. As is well known, an ordinary debt or chose in action before the Judicature Act was not assignable so as to pass the right of action at law, but it was assignable so as to pass the right to sue in equity. In his suit in equity the assignee of a debt, even where the assignment was absolute on the face of it, had to make his assignor, the original creditor, party in order primarily to bind him and prevent his suing at law, and also to allow him to dispute the assignment if he thought fit. This was *a fortiori* the case where the assignment was by way of security, or by way of charge only, because the assignor had a right to redeem. Further, the assignee could not give a valid discharge for the debt to the original debtor unless expressly empowered so to do. The original debtor, whether he admitted the debt or not, was not concerned with the state of the accounts between the assignor and the assignee where the debt was assigned by way of security; and the rule was that where he did not dispute the debt he should have his costs of suit out of the debt; he was regarded in the light of a stakeholder. It is unnecessary to cite authorities in support of any of the above propositions.

Now it was in order to afford some remedy for this state of the law that sub-s 6 was passed.

It is plain on reading it that it does not apply to every case of equitable assignment of a debt or chose of action.

Two matters, as is apparent on the face of it, had to be regarded: first, the simplifying the remedy in favour of the assignee; and, secondly, the protection of the original debtor.

[The Lord Justice then quoted the section and continued at 771:] To bring a case within the sub-section transferring the legal right to sue for the debt and empowering the assignee to give a good discharge for the debt, there must be (in the language of the sub-section) an absolute assignment not purporting to be by way of charge only. It is requisite that the assignment should be, or at all events purport to be, absolute, but it will not suffice if the assignment purport to be by way of charge only. It is plain that every equitable assignment in the wide sense of the term as used in equity is not within the enactment. As the enactment requires that the assignment should be absolute, the question arose whether a mortgage, in the proper sense of the term, and as now generally understood, was within the enactment. In *Tancred v Delagoa Bay and East Africa Railway* (1889) 23 QBD 239 there was an assignment of the debt to secure advances with a proviso for redemption and reassignment upon repayment. It was there held by the Divisional Court (disapproving of a decision in *National Provincial Bank v Harle* (1881) 6 QBD 626) that such a mortgage fell within the enactment. It appears to me that the decision of the Divisional Court was quite right. The assignment of the debt was absolute: it purported to pass the entire interest of the assignor in the debt to the mortgagee, and it was not an assignment purporting to be by way of charge only. The mortgagor-assignor had a right to redeem, and on repayment of the advances a right to have the assigned debt reassigned to him. Notice of the reassignment pursuant to the sub-section would be given to the original debtor, and he would thus know with certainty in whom the legal right to sue him was vested. I think that the principle of the decision ought not to be confined to the case where there is an express provision for reassignment. Where there is an absolute assignment of the debt, but by way of security, equity would imply a right to a reassignment on redemption, and the sub-section would apply to the case of such an absolute assignment. In a well-known judgment of the Exchequer Chamber in *Halliday v Holgate* (1868) LR 3 Ex 299, the late Willes J, in delivering the judgment of the court, distinguished between lien, pledge, and mortgage, and spoke of a mortgage as passing the property out and out. A mortgage is not mentioned in the enactment; but where there is an absolute assignment of the debt, the limiting words as to a charge only are not sufficient to exclude a mortgage ...

The assignment before us complies with all the terms of the enactment save one, which is essential: it is not an absolute but a conditional assignment. The commonest and most familiar instance of a conditional assurance is an assurance until J S shall return from Rome. The repayment of the money advanced is an uncertain event, and makes the assignment conditional. Where the Act applies it does not leave the original debtor in uncertainty as to the person to whom the legal right is transferred; it does not involve him in any question as to the state of the accounts between the mortgagor and the mortgagee. The legal right is transferred, and is vested in the assignee. There is no machinery provided by the Act for the reverter of the legal right to the assignor dependent on the performance of a condition; the only method within the provisions of the Act for revesting in the assignor the legal right is by a retransfer to the assignor followed by a notice in writing to the debtor, as in the case of the first transfer of the right. The question is not one of mere technicality or of form: it is one of substance, relating to the protection of the original debtor and placing him in an assured position.

It is necessary to refer to *Brice v Bannister* (1878) 3 QBD 569. In that case there was an assignment of £100 out of money due or to become due to the assignor under a contract to build a ship, with an express power to give a good discharge to the debtor. Lord Coleridge CJ held that the assignment was within s 25. [The majority view of the Court of Appeal was that the letter was a good equitable assignment. See also *Ex parte Nichols* (1883) 22 Ch D 782 at 787, per Lindley LJ.] The decision of Lord Coleridge CJ in *Brice v Bannister*, that the case fell within s 25 appears to me to be open to question. The assignment purported to be by way of charge only. It was a direction to pay the £100 out of money due or to become due. No doubt it purported to be a charge of an unredeemable sum of £100; but still it was a charge. The section speaks of an absolute assignment of any debt or other chose in action. It does not say "or any part of a debt or chose in action". It appears to me as at present advised to be questionable whether an assignment of part of an entire debt is within the enactment. If it be, it would seem to leave it in the power of the original creditor to split up the single legal cause of action for the debt into as many separate legal causes of action as he might think fit. However, it is not necessary to decide the point in the present case, and I leave it open for future consideration.

The result then, thus far, is this: the plaintiffs' assignment is not within the Act, and they had no legal right to sue for it. The assignment, however, is a valid equitable assignment, but by way of security only, and without power to give a valid discharge to the debtor. No relief can be given to the plaintiffs in this action as it is constituted. It is admitted as between the parties to this action that considerably less than £1080 is due to the plaintiffs in respect of their advances. In the absence of Smith & Co the amount due from them to the plaintiffs cannot be ascertained. An account taken in this action of the advances would not bind Smith & Co. Nor could the matters in question, on the footing that the plaintiffs have a mere equitable assignment, be finally determined in the absence of George Tapley Smith, who has or seems to have had an adverse claim to the £1080 under the documents of 18 August 1896. Mr Jelf [for the plaintiffs] was unquestionably right when he admitted that the plaintiffs' case failed unless it came within s 25.

The result is that the plaintiffs fail in the action. The appeal must be allowed, and judgment entered for the defendant.

[**A L Smith LJ** agreed with the judgment of Chitty LJ.

Collins LJ agreed with the judgment of Chitty LJ except that he pronounced no opinion on the question whether an assignment of part of a debt was within the section.]

Appeal allowed.

An example of the problems provided by the statutory method of assignment under s 12 of the Conveyancing Act 1919 (NSW) is the case of *Grey v Australian Motorists and General Insurance Co Ltd* [1976] 1 NSWLR 609. The appellant assigned to a finance company the rights to payment under a number of contracts for repair. The respondent refused to pay the appellant alleging that the company was not liable to pay the repairer due to the assignment of the debts to the finance company. The form of assignment provided for the signature of the finance company as assignee, but there were no such signatures on the documents. The court was required to consider the meaning of "absolute" in s 12 of the Conveyancing Act and the requirements as to notice to the assignee. These two issues overlapped considerably. Samuels JA held that s 12 provided all that was necessary to complete a statutory assignment; as this did not include notice to the assignee it was not required for an effective assignment. As the assignment was valid between assignor and assignee without notice to the debtor, and there was nothing in the operative part of the document which made its operation conditional upon some future event, such as a signature, there was sufficient evidence to show a valid statutory assignment. Mahoney J delivered a judgment to similar effect.

Conversely, Glass JA held that the agreement was conditional and required the signature of the finance company. The assignment was subject to a condition precedent which had not been fulfilled. Having reached this conclusion there was no need to consider the issue of notice.

See also *International Leasing Corp (Vic) Ltd v Aiken* (1966) 85 WN (Pt 1) (NSW) 766 at 793, per Asprey JA; *Rekstin v Severo Sibirsko etc and Bank of Russian Trade Ltd* [1933] 1 KB 47; *Curran v Newpark Cinemas Ltd* [1951] 1 All ER 295; *Standing v Bowring* (1885) 31 Ch D 282; *Hughes v Pump House Hotel Co Ltd* [1902] 2 KB 190; *Anning v Anning* (1907) 4 CLR 1049; *Norman v Commissioner of Taxation*, p 389, *infra*; *Shepherd v Commissioner of Taxation*, p 396, *infra*.

ASSIGNMENT OF LEGAL CHOSES IN EQUITY

Prior to introduction of the statutory mode of assignment, legal choses could be assigned *only* in equity. Legal choses can now be assigned under the statute. Where the statutory requirements are not fulfilled (eg, the assignment is conditional, by way of charge or of part only of a legal chose) can the assignment still be effective in equity? See *Norman v Federal Commissioner of Taxation* (1963) 109 CLR 9 at 29, per Windeyer J, p 392, *infra*. The requirements for a valid equitable assignment of a legal chose must be considered in two distinct situations—where the assignment is supported by valuable consideration, and where it is not.

Where there is valuable consideration. Here equity previously enforced such an assignment as an agreement or contract to assign and it continues to do so, even where s 12 is available but has not been complied with; that is, s 12 is not the exclusive or mandatory mode of assigning legal choses.

Where there is no valuable consideration (ie, a gift of a legal chose). As with an *inter vivos* gift of any form of property, the donor must take the appropriate steps to divest himself of that property. Where there is no contract which equity can enforce, equity will not assist a volunteer (the donee) unless the donor has done everything necessary to complete the gift.

Milroy v Lord
Court of Appeal in Chancery (1862) 4 De G F & J 264; 45 ER 1185

Turner LJ (at 274-5): I take the law of this court to be well settled, that, in order to render a voluntary settlement valid and effectual the settler must have done everything which, according to the nature of the property comprised in the settlement, was *necessary to be done* in order to transfer the property and render the settlement binding upon him. He may of course do this by actually transferring the property to the persons for whom he intends to provide, and the provision will then be effectual, and it will be equally effectual if he transfers the property to a trustee for the purposes of the settlement, or declares that he himself holds it in trust for those purposes; and if the property be personal, the trust may, as I apprehend, be declared either in writing or by parol; but, in order to render the settlement binding, *one or the other* of these modes must, as I understand the law of this court, be resorted to, for *there is no equity in this court to perfect an imperfect gift*. The cases I think go further to this extent, that if the settlement is intended to be effectuated by one of the modes to which I have referred, the court *will not give effect to it by applying another of those modes*. If it is intended to take effect by transfer, the court will not hold the intended transfer to operate as a declaration of trust, for then every imperfect instrument would be made effectual by being converted into a perfect trust. [Emphasis added.]

Milroy v Lord does not answer the following questions:

(1) Must the donor himself do everything which is necessary to be done to transfer the property or only those things which are essential that he do because no one else can do them for him?

(2) What is it necessary for the donor to do under the statutory provisions of the Conveyancing Act (NSW) s 12 and corresponding provisions in other states?

There has been considerable academic and judicial debate on these important questions. The High Court divided in *Anning v Anning* (1907) 4 CLR 1049 with (a) Griffith CJ holding that an assignment was complete in equity (even if all the requirements at law had not been completed) provided that all that remained to be done *could* be done by the donee (even though it could also be done by the donor); (b) Higgins J holding that property did not pass until the donor had done all that was *in his power* to do in order to complete the gift; and (c) Isaacs J holding that the assignment was not effectual until all the statutory requirements including notice had been fulfilled. Queensland has adopted a statutory solution: see Property Law Act 1974 s 200, quoted on p 400, *infra*.

The issue has been raised in cases involving choses in action (*Re Rose dec'd (No 1)* [1949] Ch 78; *Re Rose dec'd (No 2)* [1952] Ch 499; *Norman v Commissioner of*

Taxation—judgment of Windeyer J below; *Olsson v Dyson* (1969) 120 CLR 365 at 385-7, per Windeyer J); and involving real property (*Brunker v Perpetual Trustee Co Ltd* (1937) 57 CLR 555 at 600-2, per Dixon J; *Taylor v Deputy Commissioner of Taxation* (1969) 43 ALJR 237 at 239).

Norman v Federal Commissioner of Taxation
High Court of Australia (1963) 109 CLR 9; [1964] ALR 131

Menzies J: This is a case stated by Taylor J pursuant to s 198 of the Income Tax and Social Services Contribution Assessment Act 1936-1958 upon an appeal by H A Norman (the taxpayer) in respect of his income tax assessment for the year ended 30 June 1958.

The only questions argued were whether it was the taxpayer or his wife who derived two items of income, one consisting of £450 interest paid by a partnership and the other of £460 paid as dividends by about twenty companies in which the taxpayer was a shareholder at the time when the dividends were declared and paid to him. The taxpayer claimed that neither of these sums should be regarded as his income contending that on 21 December 1956 he had voluntarily but effectively assigned them to his wife. The Commissioner contested the effectiveness of the assignment.

The assignment relied upon was a deed executed both by the taxpayer and his wife whereby the taxpayer purported to assign to her four descriptions of income for terms having different starting points but all ending on 30 June 1958. [No question arose as to the first two.] The third was the interest on the sum of £3000 being part of a sum deposited by the taxpayer on loan at interest with a firm consisting of Sale Service Ltd and Car X'Change Ltd which in the year of income amounted to £450. This is one item in dispute. The fourth comprised dividends from shares transferred to the taxpayer by the trustees of one or other of the two estates already mentioned subsequently to the execution of the deed of assignment. In the year of income dividends from these shares amounted to £460. This is the other item in dispute ...

It is convenient to deal with the two items in dispute separately.

The sum of £3000 deposited with the firm was part of a larger sum covered by two agreements of loan, the first dated 7 July 1953 and the second 30 June 1955. The second agreement was in substitution for the first but embodied the earlier agreement's terms and conditions except that the rate of interest was raised from 12 per cent to 15 per cent per annum. The borrowing firm consisted of two family companies in each of which the taxpayer was interested both as shareholder and director. On 21 December 1956 the taxpayer was a creditor of the firm in a sum of £4669 so that what was assigned by the deed of gift was the interest on part of a debt of a larger amount. The debt was for no fixed term and the firm was at liberty to repay it or any part of it at any time without notice. The lender was required to give 18 months' notice if he should require payment of the debt or any part of it and in that event interest was from the date of the notice reduced to 1½ per cent per annum. No notice in writing of the assignment was given to the firm. It is common ground that the assignment did not operate as a legal assignment of interest or the taxpayer's right to it, and the real question is whether there was an effectual equitable assignment of a right to interest. I do not think there was because what was assigned was not an existing right but was no more than a right which might thereafter come into existence and so could not be effectually assigned in equity without consideration.

In general future property was not assignable at common law: *Lunn v Thornton* (1845) 1 CB 379; 135 ER 587 but in equity after-acquired property was assignable for value according to the principles stated by Lord Macnaghten in *Tailby v Official Receiver* (1888) 13 App Cas 523 but only for value notwithstanding the assignment was by deed: *Re Ellenborough* [1903] 1 Ch 697. If then interest that may arise under a contract has the character of a future rather than an existing right, the deed, lacking consideration, was not effective to entitle the assignee to the interest in question as and when it became due and payable. I regard interest which may accrue in the future upon an existing loan repayable without notice as having the character of a right to come into existence rather than of a right already in existence and I do not regard *Earle (G & T) Ltd v Hemsworth RDC* (1928) 44 TLR 758; (1928) 140 LT 69, upon which Mr Bright for the taxpayer relied, as any authority to the contrary. [His Honour then demonstrated that *Earle's* case dealt only with a presently existing debt payable at a future date which was held assignable at law.] What was said in *Horwood v Millar's Timber and Trading*

Co Ltd [1917] 1 KB 305 has application here. There, the question of the assignability of wages to be earned arose and Warrington LJ, speaking, I think, without any reference to the Judicature Act s 25(6), said: "The assignment with which we have to deal is not the assignment of an actual debt, not the assignment of a chose in action which is in existence, but the assignment of a chose in action, wages which a man is going to earn, which may hereafter come into existence. Now the effect of that is nothing more than to create a contractual obligation between the two parties. That was stated by Lord Macnaghten in his speech to the House of Lords in *Tailby v Official Receiver* (1888) 13 App Cas 523 in these terms: 'It has long been settled that future property, possibilities and expectancies are assignable in equity for value. The mode or form of assignment is absolutely immaterial provided the intention of the parties is clear. To effectuate the intention an assignment for value, in terms present and immediate, has always been regarded in equity as a contract binding on the conscience of the assignor and so binding the subject matter of the contract when it comes into existence, if it is of such a nature and so described as to be capable of being ascertained and identified': at 543. In other words, the real effect of such an assignment where property is not in existence, is that it is carried into effect not because it passes the property, but because it is a contractual obligation binding upon the assignor, and one which can be specifically enforced if the contract and the subject matter of it are sufficiently definite": at 314, 315. Under the contract of loan now under consideration, there was no liability for or right to interest until it began to accrue in an annual period and in 1956 the borrowers were under no liability for and the lender had no right to interest for 1958. It is not that interest for 1958 was not payable in 1956; it is that in 1956 interest for 1958 was nothing but an expectancy. It appears to me that the entries which were made in the books of the firm, clearly enough with the approval of both the assignor and the assignee, accorded with the true legal position in that the taxpayer was credited with all interest falling due upon his loan and his account was then debited and his wife's account was then credited with so much of the interest as was interest upon £3000 of the debt. To put it shortly, there were gifts of interest paid but not a gift of interest to be paid.

The conclusion I have just stated makes it unnecessary for me to consider whether, if at the time of the deed the taxpayer had a right to future interest that was capable of assignment without consideration, the deed constituted a complete and perfect transfer of that right to his wife so that the second principle stated by Dixon J in *Comptroller of Stamps (Vic) v Howard-Smith* (1936) 54 CLR 614 at 622 would apply. See too *Re Rose; Midland Bank Executor and Trustee Co Ltd v Rose* [1949] Ch 78; *Re Rose; Rose v Inland Revenue Commissioners* [1952] 1 Ch 499 ...

Dixon CJ [delivered a judgment to the similar effect as Menzies J. The Chief Justice did, however, disagree with Menzies J, as to the effectiveness of the assignment of future interest. Dixon CJ concluded that because the future interest was merely an expected right there could not be a satisfactory divestment of the future accrual by way of gift. He also stated at CLR 16:] As to the question of the alleged assignment of the interest, I have had the advantage of reading the discussion contained in the judgment of Windeyer J of the whole subject of voluntary equitable assignments and I do not know that there is anything contained in it with which I am disposed to disagree. In the conclusion, however, that in this case there was an effectual equitable assignment of the future interest I cannot agree. I think that such a conclusion must be reached in order to support an answer favourable to the taxpayer of so much of the question in the case stated as relates to the sum of £450 (sc interest). It appears to me that the future interest was the merest expectancy or possibility, having no existence in contemplation of law. After all, it must be remembered that to escape the obligation of including the interest in his assessable income the taxpayer must show that by 1 July 1957 he had denuded himself of all right to the interest. That, I think, could not be correct. After all, there was no more than an expected right with respect to the sums and I do not think the necessary divestment of the future accrual could be made by way of gift ...

[**Owen J** agreed with the judgment of Menzies J.]

Windeyer J: The ultimate question is this case is whether before 1 July 1957 the taxpayer had effectually assigned his right to receive certain moneys that would otherwise have been receivable by him and been part of his income for the year ending on 30 June 1958. [His Honour then briefly restated the facts.]

Lending on the Security of Proceeds

(i) As to attempted assignment of things not yet in existence:

As it is impossible for anyone to own something that does not exist, it is impossible for anyone to make a present gift of such a thing to another person, however sure he may be that it will come into existence and will then be his to give. He can, of course, promise that when the thing is his he will make it over to the intended donee. But in the meantime he may change his mind and when the times comes refuse to carry out his promise, even though it were by deed. A court of law could not compel him to perform it. A court of equity would not. Courts of equity never had the objections to all agreements about future interests that, until the seventeenth century, were deeply rooted in the common law. Equity did not share the view that such agreements were void on the ground of maintenance. But things not yet in existence could only be the subject of agreement, not of present disposition. And, in relation to promises and agreements, equity has been faithful to its maxim that it does not come to the aid of volunteers. For equity a deed does not make good a want of consideration.

If we turn from attempted gifts of future property to purported dispositions of it for value, the picture changes completely. The common law objection remains. But in equity a would-be present assignment of something to be acquired in the future is, when made for value, construed as an agreement to assign the thing when it is acquired. A court of equity will ensure that the would-be assignor performs this agreement, his conscience being bound by the consideration. The purported assignee thus gets an equitable interest in the property immediately, the legal ownership of it is acquired by the assignor, assuming it to have been sufficiently described to be then identifiable. The prospective interest of the assignee is in the meantime protected by equity. [His Honour then cited various English authorities to support this principle.] These cases, however, are really beside the point in this case. We are concerned here with a purported gift, not with an assignment for value . . .

(ii) As to assignment of choses in action:

Assignment means the immediate transfer of an existing proprietary right, vested or contingent, from the assignor to the assignee. Anything that in the eye of the law can be regarded as an existing subject of ownership, whether it be a chose in possession or a chose in action, can today be assigned, unless it be excepted from the general rule on some ground of public policy or by statute. But a mere expectancy or possibility of becoming entitled in the future to a proprietary right is not an existing chose in action. It is not assignable, except in the inexact sense into which, again to use Maitland's words, lawyers slipped when it is said to be assignable in equity for value.

The distinction between a chose in action, which is an existing legal right, and a mere expectancy or possibility of a future right is of cardinal importance in this case, as will appear. It does not, in my view, depend on whether or not there is a debt presently recoverable by action because presently due and payable. A legal right to be paid money at a future date is, I consider, a present chose in action, at all events when it depends upon an existing contract on the repudiation of which an action could be brought for anticipatory breach.

The common law doctrine that debts and other choses in action were not assignable never applied to Crown debts; and, by the influence of the law merchant, bills of exchange and promissory notes were outside it. And it was never accepted in equity . . .

What had happened was that the common law rule came to be circumvented in various ways. One was by novation. Another was by the assignor giving a power of attorney to the assignee to sue the debtor at law in the assignor's name, without having to render an account: the history of this has been narrated at length by Mr Bailey in learned articles in the *Law Quarterly Review* Vols 27 and 28. And courts of equity would come to the assistance of the assignee if the assignor refused to do whatever was necessary to enable the assignee to get the benefit of the assignment. Thus a recalcitrant assignor would be required, on having an indemnity for his costs, to permit his name to be used in an action to recover the debt; or an assignor would be restrained from receiving the debt for himself, as for example in *L'Estrange v L'Estrange* (1850) 13 Beav 281; 51 ER 108. Because the assistance of equity was available, it was generally not needed. The common law courts recognised that an assignee might sue in the assignor's name . . . Therefore, as the Chief Justice observed during the hearing of this case, it is somewhat misleading to say, as is often said, that before the Judicature Act the common law would not allow assignments of legal choses in action. Long before 1873 the development of common law processes and the impact of equity had pushed the common law prohibition of the assignment of choses in action back into history. Nevertheless the original doctrine survived, to this extent that, until the Judicature Act 1873 s 25(6), and the corresponding statutory provisions in Australia and elsewhere came into operation, an assignee of a legal debt could not in his own name bring an action against the debtor to recover the debt. The original creditor must be the plaintiff on the record. He remained in law the owner of the chose in action. What the provision of the Judicature Act 1873, did was to render unnecessary the previous circumlocutions. Debts and other legal choses in action were made directly assignable by the statutory method. But this, while it simplified assignments, has not simplified the law surrounding them, as the argument in this case showed.

It is settled that any assignment that satisfies the requirements of the statute is valid and fully effectual although it be voluntary. That is to say the law now provides a means whereby the legal owner of a chose in action may make a complete and perfect gift of it. That being so, and as equity does not perfect an imperfect gift, can there ever now be an effectual voluntary assignment unless all the statutory requirements are met? The question is not an easy one if a purely logical answer be sought. Equity intervened to assist the assignments of choses in action because they were not assignable at law. Now that they are, why, it may be asked, should equity aid imperfect attempts at voluntary assignments of them. On the other hand, it can be urged that the statute provides a method or machinery whereby assignment may be effected, but that it does not detract from the validity of any transaction that would have been effective in equity it if had occurred before the statute came into operation. There is some authority for the latter proposition; see eg *German v Yates* (1915) 32 TLR 52. And Lord Macnaghten's well-known words in *William Brandts' Sons & Co v Dunlop Rubber Co* [1905] AC 454 are sometimes invoked in support of it: "Why that which would have been a good equitable assignment before the statute should now be invalid and inoperative because it fails to come up to the requirements of the statute, I confess I do not understand. The statute does not forbid or destroy equitable assignments or impair their efficacy in the slightest degree": at 461. But this was said in reference to an assignment for value. I do not think that his Lordship's remarks should be read as qualifying the principle that equity does not perfect imperfect voluntary assignments. If an attempt is made to assign, by way of gift, a chose in action assignable under the statute, then, as I see the matter, the requirements of the statute cannot be ignored; for the general rule of equity is that an effective assignment occurs only if the donor does all that, according to the nature of the property, he must do to transfer the property to the donee. But the weight of authority is, I think in favour of the view that in equity there is a valid gift of property transferable at law if the donor, intending to make, then and there, a complete disposition and transfer to the donee, does all that *on his part* is necessary to give effect to his intention and arms the donee with the means of completing the gift according to the requirements of the law: see *Brunker v Perpetual Trustee Co (Ltd)* (1937) 57 CLR 555, per Dixon J at 600-2; *Re Smith* (1901) 84 LT 835; *Re Rose* [1949] Ch 78; *Re Rose* [1952] 1 Ch 499. I think therefore that, if a man, meaning to make an immediate gift of a chose in action that is his, executes an instrument that meets the requirements of the statute and delivers it to the donee, actually or constructively, he has put it out of his power to recall his gift. It is true that until notice is given to the debtor or person against whom the chose is enforcable at law, all the requirements of the statute have not been complied with. But the notice can be given by the donee; and, if the donee has express or implied authority to give it, I think that equity would not allow the donor to deny the right of the donee to do so and so intercept his gift. I reach this conclusion with some hesitation, for it involves some departure from the majority view in *Anning v Anning* (1907) 4 CLR 1049. But it accords, it seems to me with general principle. For these reasons I consider that, if the debt that the deed in this case purported to assign had been an existing chose in action assignable by the statutory procedure, the only question would be whether the assignor had purported to make an absolute assignment of it, and whether he did all that on his part had to be done to that end. The difficulty is that, as will appear, what it was sought to assign was part only of a prospectively larger debt.

(iii) As to assignments of part of a debt:

It has been held that the statutory method of assignment is not available for the assignment of parts of debts or choses in action: *Williams v Atlantic Assurance Co* [1933] 1 KB 81; *Re Steel Wing Co Ltd* [1921] 1 Ch 349 ... The conclusion does not depend simply on a literal interpretation of the statutory language and of the phrase "absolute assignment". Before the statute an assignee was permitted to bring his action at law in the name of the assignor when he was seeking to recover a whole debt assigned to him. If a debt had been broken into parts this procedure was not appropriate. A creditor cannot recover a debt piecemeal in a court of law. Therefore, when part of a debt was assigned, proceedings to enforce the assignment had to be brought in a court of equity. And the assignee, not the assignor, would be the plaintiff in the suit. The assignor (the creditor) as legal owner, the debtor and any assignees of other parts of the debt were all necessary parties, so that all the obligations of the debtor and the rights of all persons interested in the fund might be established by the decree. This was the rule of the Chancery Court. It is still the law: see *Performing Right Society Ltd v London Theatre of Varieties Ltd* [1924] AC 1 at 14, 20, 30, 31. As an assignment of part of a debt is still necessarily an equitable assignment, the question arises can it be made by way of gift; and, if so, how?

(iv) As to whether consideration is required for the equitable assignment of a chose in action not assignable at law:
One might have expected that this would long ago have been authoritatively settled. But the question is, according to *Halsbury*, 3rd ed, Vol 4, p 495, "uncertain" ...

There are several senses in which the phrase "equitable assignment" may be used; and the question, Is consideration necessary for an equitable assignment?, does not admit of a single short answer covering all of them.

If the interest to be assigned is a creature of equity, such as the beneficial interest of a cestui que trust, then, apart from any statutory provisions, an assignment of it can, of course, only be effected in equity; for the common law does not know it. Any present assignment of such an interest, that is to say of a chose in equity, is therefore necessarily an equitable assignment. Such an assignment can be by way of gift; and, except that writing is required by s 9 of the Statute of Frauds, no formality is necessary beyond a clear expression of an intention to make an immediate disposition. In short, there is no reason at all why a person should not give away any beneficial interest that is his: the classic statement is that of Knight Bruce LJ in *Kekewich v Manning* (1851) 1 De GM & G 176; 42 ER 519; see too *Re McArdle (dec'd)* [1951] 1 Ch 669. It is, of course, necessary that the transaction should take the form of, and be intended as, an immediate transfer of the beneficial interest of the assignor, as distinct from an agreement to assign it. The distinction is critical, for consideration is always necessary to attract the support of equity to a transaction that is a contract rather than a conveyance. The judgment of Stuart VC in *Voyle v Hughes* (1854) 2 Sm & G 18; 65 ER 283, puts all this clearly.

Turning, from assignments that are equitable because the property assigned is a chose in equity, to assignments that are equitable because the property assigned is a legal chose in action not assignable except by the aid of equity: It has been said that historically there could be no equitable assignment of a debt except for value. Whether this be correct or not as a general proposition, it never meant that there must be consideration as now understood in the law of contract. An assignment in satisfaction, or part satisfaction, of an antecedent debt was taken in equity as made for value. And this was what had happened in case after case appearing in the reports in which assignments were upheld in equity before the Judicature Act. Whether equity would then give any aid to an assignment of a chose in action made for no value at all, but as a pure gift, is less clear. There are in the reports categorical statements each way, extending over two centuries or more.

[His Honour then cited a number of English cases.] Sir Frederick Jordan, in his *Chapters on Equity in New South Wales* said that "although the authorities were in an unsatisfactory state, the better opinion appears to be that any sufficiently clear expression of intention to assign a legal chose in action which was not assignable at law was sufficient to assign it in equity, although there were no consideration ..." This view was taken in New Zealand, by Barrowclough CJ, in *Pulley v Public Trustee* [1956] NZLR 771. In *Liverpool & London and Globe Insurance Co v Hartley & Ford* [1927] VLR 523 at 529 Cussen J tended somewhat to the opposite opinion. But strictly that case was one of the assignment of a possibility; and there is no doubt at all that consideration is necessary for the assignment of a possibility or expectancy — the distinction, as stated above, being between an implied agreement to assign something that may never come into existence and a present disposition of property in existence: see *Re Ellenborough* [1903] 1 Ch 697 ...

Professor Keeton, in the work to which I have referred above, after surveying the authorities, said: "As far as the actual decisions are concerned, they support as a whole the proposition that an assignment of a chose in action in equity before 1873 was effective if it were either accompanied by consideration or was under seal and was absolute in form, so that the assignor was as fully divested of the property as it was possible for him to be ... The requirement of a seal in an equitable assignment seems distinctly anomalous and would appear to be an acceptance of the common law rules as to assignments between assignor and assignee": p 197.

It seems to me that, in principle, so far as a deed has any efficacy in connection with equitable assignments, it is not that a deed takes the place of valuable consideration where that is needed to attract the aid of equity. Rather it is that, in cases where value is not so required but a clear expression of intention is, the delivery of a deed couched in terms of present gift manifests, in the best possible way, the intention of the assignor to make an immediate and irrevocable transfer.

[His Honour then examined the reasons for the intervention of equity in assignments of choses in action. One reason was that equity held men to the agreements and promises made for value. The other rationale is based on the analogy of a trust. An assignment amounted in nature to a declaration of trust and allowed the use of the assignee's name to recover the debt.]

An agreement to assign will be effective as an equitable assignment if it be for value; for then equity looks on that as done which ought to be done. But this does not mean that there cannot be in equity an actual assignment of a chose in action as distinct from an agreement to assign. I think there can, and that it can be by way of gift. In such a case equity enforces the assignment, not by compelling the assignor to do something, but by refusing to allow him to act in a way inconsistent with what he has done, that is by restraining him from derogating from his gift. His conscience becomes bound, not by value received, but because, as between him and the assignee, his gift was complete.

This view of the matter is in accordance with the decision of the Court of Appeal in *Re Patrick* [1891] 1 Ch 82, a case concerning a voluntary settlement by which the settlor assigned certain debts to trustees before the Judicature Act 1873, came into operation. The court, consisting of Lindley, Bowen and Fry LJJ, held that there had been a complete assignment of the debts. The decision has been somewhat depreciated by text-writers, because Lindley LJ said that the assignment of the debts was complete "within the principle of *Kekewich v Manning* (1851) 1 De GM& G 176; 42 ER 519 which is the leading case on this subject": at 87; and it has been pointed out that *Kekewich v Manning* was a case of the assignment of an equitable chose, not of a legal chose in action. But, as between assignor and assignee, does that make any difference? Why should consideration be said to be necessary to bind the conscience in the one case when it is not necessary in the other? Before 1873 a chose in equity and a chose in action were both transferable in equity and only in equity. The assignments were alike made effective because of the remedies that a court of equity could provide. To speak of equity not perfecting an imperfect gift seems beside the point where no gift could be made except in equity. To say that the donor must do everything that according to the nature of the property is necessary to transfer it means little when it is in law not transferable; for equity looks to the intent not the form. These considerations have added weight in the case of part of a debt; for a part of a debt never was assignable so as to be recoverable at law even in an indirect way. It being necessary for the decision of this case to come to a conclusion on a vexed question, my conclusion is that the deed that the taxpayer executed did not fail becaue it was voluntary. The whole of a debt being now voluntarily assignable under the statute, it would be a strange anomaly if a part could not be the subject of voluntary equitable assignment. To say, "you can give away the whole, but you cannot give away a part, for a part you must get a price" would seem to contradict commonsense. And I do not think it necessary to do so.

(v) As to the facts:

It is convenient to consider separately the two sums in question, the amount of £450 first, that being the first matter dealt with in the stated case.

The sum of £450 (interest on money lent). The deed of 21 December 1956 states: "The assignor doth hereby transfer and assign all his right title and interest in and to—... (b) all

Lending on the Security of Proceeds

the interest derived from the assets or investments specified in the second schedule hereto for a period commencing on the 1st day of July 1957 and ending on the 30th day of June 1958 unto the assignee for her own use and benefit absolutely ..."

[His Honour then referred to other terms of the deed and a similar previous transaction and continued at CLR 36:] No notice of the deed of 21 December was expressly given to the partnership or to its member companies, as had been done in the case of the 1955 deed. Apparently this was overlooked on the second occasion. Probably, if it was thought of at all, it was dismissed as an insignificant formality, because those concerned with the direction of the affairs of the partnership business knew all about the matter ... It would be unreal in the circumstances to suppose that the companies constituting the partnership should be considered as having had no notice of the deed. They had, and they acted upon it, in the sense that, when the interest upon money lent by the taxpayer fell due on 30 June 1958, an amount of £450 (being 15 per cent of £3000) was shown in the books of the partnership as credited to the taxpayer's account, then debited to his account and credited to the account of his wife in the same way as was done in earlier years while the 1955 deed was current.

Nevertheless, no express notice in writing of the assignment has ever been given to the partnership, as is required by the Law of Property Act 1936 (SA) s 15, corresponding with s 25 of the Judicature Act 1873. The legal right to a debt passes only from the date of such notice; so that there never was as between the taxpayer and his wife a legal assignment of the debt.

Moreover, quite apart from the absence of a notice in writing, this assignment is of a part of a debt. The deed, it is true, speaks of "interest derived from the sum of three thousand pounds deposited". But there was no separate fund of £3000 in which the taxpayer had an interest; and at all relevant times the amount owing to him by the partnership exceeded £3000. The transactions between him and the partnership were simply those of lender and borrower. The legal relationship they created was that of creditor and debtor. All that, on any view, the deed assigned was therefore £450 out of a prospectively larger sum for interest that would become due on 30 June 1958. As the statute is not applicable to an assignment of a part of a debt, it becomes unnecessary to consider whether an instrument which is to "cease, determine and be of no effect upon the death of the assignor or assignee" is an "absolute assignment" within the meaning of the statute.

But, said the taxpayer, I do not rely upon the deed as effecting an assignment by virtue of the statute; my case is that there was an effectual assignment in equity. To this the Commissioner made two answers. First that there cannot be a voluntary assignment of an existing legal chose in action. As to that, for the reasons I have given, I do not agree. Secondly it was said a thing which is not yet in existence cannot be the subject of an equitable assignment except for consideration. That, as I have said, is undoubtedly so. It is true too that the interest, to the extent of £450, that the deed assigned was not due and payable at the date of the deed. But a contract to pay a sum of money on a future day, call it interest or what you will, calculable in amount according to conditions presently agreed, is in my view a presently existing chose in action. As between the parties to a contract of money lent at interest the borrower is simply a debtor who must pay a sum or sums (called interest) that he has, for good consideration (the forbearance of the creditor) contracted to pay to his creditor at the time or times stipulated. Why should not the creditor before the date when this debt becomes due and payable, assign his right to receive payment on the due date? He could assign the whole under the statute: *Walker v Bradford Old Bank Ltd* (1884) 12 QBD 511. Why not part in equity? What he assigns is not, it seems to me, a right to arise in the future but a present contractual right to be paid at a future date a sum of money, to be calculated in the agreed manner: cf *Lett v Morris* (1831) 4 Sim 607; 58 ER 227. In *Brice v Bannister* (1878) 3 QBD 569, Lord Coleridge CJ said "that a debt to become due is a chose in action, is clear" at 573. Interest on money lent is recoverable by action at law as a debt separate from the principal, as the common indebitatus count for interest shows: see *Halsbury*, 3rd ed, Vol 27, p 12.

But it was urged this case is not like a case of a loan for a fixed term. What was owing might, it is pointed out, have been repaid by the partnership, or reduced below £3000, after the date of the deed of assignment and before 1 July 1957. As a matter of law, no doubt that is so. But it does not, I think, follow that the taxpayer had for that reason no assignable right. He had a present right to be paid interest at a future date on the money he had lent, unless in the meantime the loan was repaid. The taxpayer assigned the benefit of this contract, to the extent of £450 to become due conditionally in 1958, to his wife by the deed of 1956. I consider that the deed was an effectual equitable assignment. It operated, I think, upon its delivery as a deed. The assignee had notice of it and assented. It was valid and binding as between assignor and assignee. In so far as any notice to the debtor, the partnership, was necessary to perfect it in equity as against the debtor, the companies had sufficient notice of it and acted accordingly.

The sum of £460 (dividends from companies). I turn now to the second matter, the sum of £460. This arises under provisions of the deed whereby the taxpayer purported to assign "all his right title and interest in and to all the interest dividends and other income to which the assignor may be entitled arising from the estates and investments and assets specified in the first schedule hereto for a period commencing on 1st day on January 1957 and ending on the 30th day of June 1958".

[His Honour then discussed the facts and concluded at CLR 40:] It comes back to this: Is a dividend that may become payable in the future upon shares presently held something that can be assigned in equity? Is it a present chose in action or a mere possibility? Is it property in existence, or something not in existence and therefore not capable of being assigned in the absence of consideration? I think it is the latter. The court will not compel directors to declare a dividend: *Bond v Barrow Haematite Steel Co* [1902] 1 Ch 353. A dividend is not a debt until it is declared. Until then it is in the eye of the law a possibility only. When it is declared it becomes a debt for which a shareholder who is on the register at the date of the declaration may sue. The companies paid the dividends to the registered holder of the shares, the taxpayer. They knew nothing of the purported assignment. Depending perhaps in some cases on their articles of association, they might have paid the dividends directly to the taxpayer's wife had they been directed by him to do so. But, in the absence of consideration, such a direction would have been merely a revocable mandate, not an assignment. Dividends that may be declared are to my mind quite unlike the interest that will become due according to an existing contract of loan if the loan be not repaid.

I agree in the conclusions of McTiernan J both as to the sum of £450 and the sum of £460, and for substantially the same reasons as he has expressed. I have elaborated my reasons on some aspects because of the arguments addressed to us.

I have not considered the effect of s 260 of the Income Tax Assessment Act on these transactions. The Commissioner has not thought fit to rely upon it; and, although it was adverted to, its application was not argued. I therefore say nothing about it.

I would answer the questions asked (a) Yes, subject to any question that may arise under s 260 of the Act; (b) No.

[**McTiernan J** delivered a judgment to the similar effect as Windeyer J.]

Question in the case stated answered as follows: The learned judge hearing the appeal would, upon the facts appearing in the case stated, be neither bound nor at liberty to hold that (a) the said sum of £450 (interest), or (b) the said sum of £460 (dividends) did not constitute assessable income of the appellant in respect of the income year which ended on 30 June 1958.

Shepherd v Federal Commissioner of Taxation
High Court of Australia (1965) 113 CLR 385

Barwick CJ: The taxpayer is the grantee of letters patent in respect of improved castors. He granted a licence to a manufacturer in Victoria to manufacture the castors upon terms inter alia that the licensee covenanted to pay him monthly during the continuance of the licence a royalty of five per cent of the gross sale price of castors manufactured by or on behalf of the licensee which had been sold during the preceding month.

On 23 July 1957, whilst both the letters patent and the licence to manufacture were in force, the taxpayer executed a deed poll in the following terms: "I George Frederick Shepherd of 11 Manor St Brighton in the State of Victoria Engineer Do Hereby Assign absolutely and unconditionally to the persons hereinafter named and described and in the proportions hereinafter specified all my right title and interest in and to an amount equal to ninety per centum of the income which may accrue during a period of three years from the date of this assignment from royalties payable by Mark Cowen of 370 Orrong Road Caulfield in the said State manufacturer under a Deed made on the twelfth day of March 1954 between myself the

Lending on the Security of Proceeds

said George Frederick Shepherd and the said Mark Cowen in respect of a license granted by me to the said Mark Cowen to make use exercise and vend castors under and in accordance with the Inventions protected by Letters Patent [in respect of three specific registered patents for castors.]

"The names and descriptions of the persons to whom my right title and interest in such income is assigned and the proportions in which the amount of ninety per centum of such income is assigned are:" [the names and addresses of five assignees and their respective shares of the royalty income were then set out.]

Thereafter the taxpayer informed the licensee of the "arrangements", meaning the provisions of the deed poll. He directed the licensee that each royalty payment due under the licence should be divided into six parts and to pay the persons named in the deed poll the appropriate proportion of the royalties set opposite their names therein. The taxpayer arranged at the same time that the licensee should pay the royalties quarterly rather than monthly as provided by the licence.

The payments by the licensee to the recipients of these respective percentages of the amounts of royalty payable under the licence apparently commenced in September 1957 and continued thereafter. Such payments were effected by not negotiable cheques drawn in favour of the named persons for the appropriate amount sent to the taxpayer and by him forwarded to the persons concerned.

The total amount which became payable under the licence for royalties during the financial year commencing on 1 July 1958 was £7030; £999 thereof being paid to the taxpayer and the balance to the persons named in the deed poll in the manner described.

The Commissioner assessed the taxpayer in respect of the income year 1958-59 upon the full sum of £7030 as income derived by him. The taxpayer objected to that assessment claiming that £6031, being the total of the amounts paid to the donees by the licensee, was not income derived by him during the year of income.

The questions upon which the Taxation Board of Review seeks answers are: "1 Whether the taxpayer by the deed referred to in para 5 hereof effectively assigned to the persons named therein in the proportions therein set forth, all his right title and interest in and to an amount being 90 per centum of the royalties which in fact accrued during the period of three years from 23 July 1957 under the agreement made on 12 March 1954 referred to in para 2 hereof. 2 Whether the sum of £6031 or some and what part thereof, referred to in para 9 hereof formed part of the taxpayer's assessable income for the year ended 30 June 1958."

The Commissioner's principal contention is that the gift was a gift of part of the taxpayer's income to be derived from royalties. The income was thus first derived by the taxpayer and then, pursuant either to a voluntary promise so to do, or to a voluntary assignment of the royalties themselves, portions of his income were handed over to the donees. The taxpayer on the other hand contends for an immediate gift of parts of his right to the royalties.

The answers to the questions asked by the Taxation Board of Review turn, in my opinion, exclusively upon the construction of the deed poll. The licensee was under promise to pay royalties to the taxpayer. That promise in its entirety would have been assignable at law pursuant to the provisions of s 134 of the Property Law Act 1958 (Vic). But part of it could not be so assigned, nor could the royalties as after acquired property be assigned at law. Thus, whether the deed poll be construed as an attempted assignment of part of the promise to pay royalties or an attempted assignment of part of the royalties themselves when received, it will in either case be ineffective at law. In my opinion, the deed poll is not capable of being regarded as or as containing a covenant by the taxpayer to pay money in the future to the named persons, the amount to be paid being quantified in relation to the amount of royalties recieved by the taxpayer. The function of the expression "an amount equal to" in the operative words of the deed poll is not, in my opinion, to make the purported assignment a covenant to pay money but, as I shall mention later, its purpose, in my opinion, is to work out the fraction of the right to royalties which in total is being assigned to the donees. Indeed, I see in the employment of the words "an amount equal to" an indication that it is the right to the royalties rather than the royalties as after acquired property which is the subject matter of the assignment. There is therefore no need to consider whether the principle that a person with whom or for whose benefit a covenant is made in a deed poll may recover at law upon the covenant though neither a party to nor a signatory of it would be applicable to this deed if on its proper construction it contained a covenant to pay money to the named persons.

In my opinion, the situation of the deed poll is that it is ineffective at law to confer on any of the named persons any legal right whether to any part of the promise to pay royalties or of the royalties themselves when received.

However, a part or parts of a chose in action can be assigned in equity. In my opinion, if the assignment of a part of the chose in action consisting of the promise to pay royalties is complete, it is effective to vest the appropriate part of the right equitably in the assignee, whether or not the assignment is for consideration or by way of gift. It is only if the donee needs the assistance of equity to complete the gift, as distinct from enforcing the right given, that he can be met with the defence that equity will not assist a volunteer. Here, if there was an immediate gift of a proportion of the right to the royalties, the donees need seek no assistance. If the deed upon its true construction evidences an intention presently to assign part of the right, the assignment would be complete within the doctrines of equity. If, on the other hand, the deed purports to assign the stated proportion of the royalties as after-acquired property the assignment would be ineffective in equity for want of consideration. The question therefore, in my opinion, is a narrow one, namely, whether upon its true construction the deed purports to assign part of the right to the royalties or of the royalties themselves as after-acquired property.

Nothing, it seems to me, turns on the fact that the taxpayer himself obtained or transmitted the cheques to the donees. Such a course is quite consistent with either construction of the deed poll, ie either construing it as an immediate gift of a part of the chose in action or as a gift of the royalties themselves as and when received.

The task in construing the deed is to find the meaning intended by the taxpayer as expressed. No form of words is required for an equitable assignment but it is necessary to find the expression of an intention to assign. The deed does purport in terms presently to assign its subject matter and to do so absolutely and unconditionally. In describing what he considered he had done by the operative words of the deed, the taxpayer in the second paragraph of the deed, speaks of the persons "to whom my right title and interest ... is assigned". The difficulty in the case arises in the description of the subject matter of the gift. That description begins with the words "all my right title and interest in and to" which words are appropriate to the assignment of a chose in action as distinct from its ultimate produce. But the words that follow create the problem, "an amount equal to 90 per centum of the income which may arise during a period of three years from the date of this assignment"...

As I have mentioned, the dominant consideration is the intention of the taxpayer as expressed in the deed. The expressed indications of an intent presently to assign portions of his right to royalties are strong enough, in my view, to overbear any contrary indication which might possibly be derived from the words which I have just discussed. These clumsy expressions are used, in my opinion, as I have said, in an endeavour to attain the two desiderata of a gift of part only of the right and only for a limited period of years. They are not in any case really so inappropriate to a present gift of a part of the right to royalties that they should be allowed to dominate the construction and to displace the evident intention expressed in the earlier part of the deed.

I have come to the conclusion that upon the true construction of the deed poll the taxpayer did thereby equitably assign to the named donees the stated proportions of his right during the ensuing three years to royalties from the licensee under the licence to manufacture the patented article.

[His Honour considered the application of *Norman v Federal Commissioner of Taxation* (1963) 109 CLR 9 and distinguished it in a similar manner to that adopted by Kitto J below.]

Accordingly, in my opinion, the questions asked by the reference by the Taxation Board of Review should be answered: 1 Yes. 2 No.

Kitto J [set out the facts and continued at CLR 394:] The terms of the deed poll have been set out and I shall not repeat them. The deed exhibits in its operative words, and underlines twice later, the intention of effecting an immediate alienation of property presently existing, presently belonging to the assignor, and consisting of a right, title and interest in respect of royalties to become payable by Cowen under the licence agreement. The suggestion has been offered that nevertheless the operation of the deed on its true construction is not that of an assignment but is that of a covenant to pay an amount to be calculated by applying 90 per cent to the total of the royalties in the three-year period. If this were in truth its operation the consequence would necessarily be that the royalties themselves would have been the income of the appellant; but the suggested construction does not appear to me to give the deed its true effect. The force of the contention lies in the presence of the words "an amount equal to", which may be thought to show that the intention was to make over a sum of money measured by reference to the royalty income but not necessarily forming part of if, and thus to create though somewhat clumsily, a mere money obligation. But the subject of the right which the appellant had in respect of the three-year period under his agreement with Cowen was correctly described by the use of the indefinite article; it was "an amount" and not the royalty income itself. Consequently an assignment of 90 per cent of the right in respect of the period, or (what comes to the same thing) an assignment of the right to an amount equal to 90 per cent of the royalty income of the period, might be expressed, without inaccuracy, as an assignment of the right to be paid an amount out of that income equal to 90 per cent thereof. That, it seems to me, is what the collocation of words means. To construe what purports to be an assignment of property as a covenant to make payments seems to me a step which only compelling circumstances or a compelling context could justify, and I do not think that it can be right to take that step in the present case. It would mean doing no little violence to the language of the instrument, and the probabilities seem to me to be against it. After all, a person whose intention it was to undertake a future pecuniary obligation, equal to a percentage of his royalty income in a future period but to be met out of his resources generally, would not be very likely to choose the language of assignment to express that intention, or even, I should have thought, to choose a deed poll rather than a deed inter partes as the appropriate instrument for the purpose.

On behalf of the Commissioner the contention was made that if the deed be construed as intending an assignment it should be held to have been ineffectual on the ground that in respect of the royalties to become payable by Cowen the appellant had no more than a mere expectancy or possibility such as cannot be assigned either at law or in equity: *Re Ellenborough* [1903] 1 Ch 697. In support of this contention reliance was placed upon the decision which this court gave in *Norman v Federal Commissioner of Taxation* in relation to a purported voluntary assignment of what was described in the relevant deed as the assignor's right, title and interest in and to the interest payable by a firm in respect of a sum of £3000 being portion of a larger sum that had been deposited by the assignor with the firm and was still outstanding at the date of the assignment. That case, however, stands in clear contrast with the case that is before us. The deposit had been made under an agreement which provided that the firm might repay the money or any part of it at any time without notice, but that the taxpayer should not be entitled to require payment except upon eighteen months' notice. As it turned out, the money was not repaid before the end of the relevant year of income, so that interest in accordance with the agreement became payable and was paid in respect of that year. The interest was held to be the assignor's income, on the ground that the attempt to assign the right to receive it was void as being an attempt to assign, without valuable consideration, property not presently in existence. To understand the ground of decision it is necessary to remember that in respect of the future year the loan agreement recorded the terms which apply to the relationship of borrower and lender so long as such a relationship should exist, but it left the borrower free to decide whether such a relationship should exist in the relevant year. It gave the lender no right in any possible event to insist upon there being a loan in existence in that year. In the present case the situation at the date of the assignment was exactly the opposite. There existed at that time a contractual relationship between the appellant and Cowen which by its terms must continue throughout the ensuing three years, whether Cowen should wish it to continue or not. The appellant, therefore, had a vested right in respect of those three years. It might indeed become divested, for the licence agreement provided for cesser of Cowen's liability to pay royalties if the letters patent should not be maintained or should be declared void; but the right existed, though it was thus subject to defeasance by events not within the control of Cowen. It is true also that what the appellant's right under the licence agreement would yield in royalties in those years — indeed, whether it would yield any royalties at all in those years — no doubt depended upon contingencies partly within the control of Cowen. It was for him to decide how many castors, if any, he would manufacture in accordance with the appellant's inventions and try to sell. Market conditions would then determine how successful his efforts to sell would be. But whatever he might do or desire to do, the existence of the appellant's contractual right would be unaffected, though the quantum of its product might be. The tree, though not the fruit, existed at the date of the assignment as a proprietary right of the appellant of which he was competent to dispose; and he assigned 90 per cent of the tree. The case is of the general class of which *Brice v Bannister* (1878) 3 QBD 569 is an example, and may be usefully compared with *Bergmann v Macmillan* (1881) 17 Ch D 423 and *Hughes v Pump House Hotel Co Ltd* [1902] 2 KB 190.

The intention being to assign a part only of a chose in action—only 90 per cent of it and for a limited period—the assignment had of necessity to be equitable: *Re Steel Wing Co Ltd* [1921] 1 Ch 349. So far as the formal means employed is concerned there can be no doubt as to its sufficiency, for all that is required for an equitable assignment is a manifestation by the assignor of an intention to transfer the chose in action to the assignees in a manner binding upon himself, as distinguished from an intention merely to give a revocable mandate while retaining ownership of the chose in action: *Milroy v Lord* (1862) 4 De GF & J 264 at 274; 45 ER 1185 at 1189. Construed in the sense I have indicated, the deed in the present case manifests unequivocally the intention to make an assignment. To construe it as intending a revocable mandate would be impossible. But we have been invited to hold that an equitable assignment of existing property is ineffectual unless for valuable consideration. The general question was discussed by Windeyer J in his dissenting judgment in *Norman v Federal Commissioner of Taxation* at 30-4, where the proposition now contended for was rejected. I agree in the views which his Honour expressed in this portion of his judgment, as, apparently, did Dixon CJ in that case. We are not here considering a purported equitable assignment of a legal chose in action capable of assignment at law. The consideration which is necessary to attract the jurisdiction of equity to perfect an imperfect assignment is not necessary where the only possible assignment is equitable and the assignor has done all that could be done by him to perfect an equitable assignment.

In the result, I am of opinion that when the distribution of royalty moneys were made amongst the five persons nominated as assignees the moneys each received were the fruits of an undivided share of a contractual right which share had become beneficially his or her own property. Accordingly I would hold that the royalty moneys which were paid to the five persons, up to ninety per cent of the whole, were not assessable income of the appellant.

I would answer the questions asked in the case stated: (1) Yes; (2) No.

[**Owen J** (dissenting) held that on the construction of the deed poll, the appellant had covenanted to pay named persons *an amount equal* to 90 per centum of the income which might accrue from royalties payable to him, but that he did not assign a contractual right to receive any part of that income.]

Questions asked in the reference answered as follows: 1 Yes. 2 No.

See also *Williams v Commissioner of Inland Revenue* [1965] NZLR 395; *McLeay v Commissioner of Inland Revenue* [1963] NZLR 711; *Everett v FTC*, p 401, *infra*. Compare the statutory solution adopted under Property Law Act 1973 (Qld):

200 (1) A voluntary assignment of property shall in equity be effective and complete when, and as soon as, the assignor has done everything to be done by him that is necessary in order to transfer the property to the assignee—
  (a) notwithstanding that anything remains to be done in order to transfer to the assignee complete and perfect title to the property; and
  (b) provided that anything so remaining to be done is such as may thereafter be done without intervention of or assistance from the assignor.

(2) This section is without prejudice to any other mode of disposing of property, but applies subject to the provisions of this and of any other Act.

ASSIGNMENT OF EQUITABLE CHOSES

By definition an equitable chose can be assigned *only in equity*. At general law the only requirement for a valid equitable assignment of an equitable chose is that the assignor Carb clearly expresses its intention to assign; no specific form of words is necessary and there need be no consideration. However, where the assignment is of an existing equitable interest or trust held by a trustee for the assignor Carb the assignment must be in writing and signed by Carb or its agent authorised in writing: Conveyancing Act 1919 s 23C(1)(c), which provides:

23C (1) Subject to the provisions of this Act with respect to creation of interests in land by parol—
. . .
    (c) a disposition of an equitable interest or trust subsisting at the time of the disposition, must be in writing signed by the person disposing of the same or by his will, or by his agent thereunto lawfully authorised in writing.

(Vic, Property Law Act 1958 s 53(1)(c); Qld, Property Law Act 1974 s 11(1)(c); SA, Law of Property Act 1936 s 29(1)(c); WA, Property Law Act 1969 s 34(1)(c); Tas, Conveyancing and Law of Property Act 1884 s 60(2)(c).)

An example of an equitable chose in action is an interest in a partnership. A partner's interest in a partnership is a chose in action assignable in whole or in part: *Hocking v Western Australian Bank* (1909) 9 CLR 738. However, the Partnership Act 1892 (NSW) s 31 (Vic, 1958 s 35; Qld, 1891 s 34; SA, 1891 s 31; WA, 1895 s 42; Tas, 1891 s 36; ACT, Partnership Ordinance 1963 s 36) regulates the right of an assignee of a share in a partnership. Specific assets of a partnership are not assignable, but only future rights to anticipated income, as well as the net residue of capital resulting from the sale of assets on the termination of the partnership.

The nature of the interest in a partnership requires that the assignment be made in writing: Conveyancing Act 1919 (NSW) s 23C(1)(c).

A number of problems arise with such an assignment. For example, can the interest be assigned under s 12 of the Conveyancing Act? What is the nature of the interest assigned? Can a portion of the interest be assigned?

Commissioner of Taxation v Everett
High Court of Australia (1979) 143 CLR 440

[On 1 July 1966 the respondent became a partner in a legal firm by acquiring a 13 per cent interest in the business. No formal partnership agreement was executed; however, a document described as "Heads of Agreement" was initialled by the partners and regulated their relationship. It provided that the respondent had a 13 per cent interest in the capital and income of the firm. On 7 January 1969 the respondent entered into a deed with his wife whereby for a consideration of $3832.50 he conveyed and assigned to her $6/13$ths of his interest. The wife's only entitlement was to receive the portion of the share of profits, and any other moneys to which the respondent would otherwise have been entitled, had the assignment not been made. Notice of the assignment was given by the respondent to his partners and the assignment was accepted by the members of the firm.

For the tax year ended 30 June 1973 the Commissioner assessed the respondent on the basis of including the assigned income as his income, which meant an increase in assessable income of $11,185. The respondent appealed to the Supreme Court of New South Wales where Meares J upheld the appeal, reducing the taxable income by the assigned amount. On appeal the majority of the Full Court of the Federal Court affirmed the judgment of Meares J. The Commissioner appealed to the High Court, where he submitted that the right of the respondent to receive his proportion of partnership profits was a right separate and severable from his share in the partnership and that this right did not flow from, nor was it the result of, that share.]

Barwick CJ, Stephen, Mason and **Wilson JJ** [delivered a joint judgment in the course of which they said at 447:] A partner's interest in the partnership is a chose in action assignable in whole or in part: *Hocking v Western Australian Bank* (1909) 9 CLR 738 at 743. The better opinion seems to be that, though the interest of a partner is an equitable interest, it may be assigned under s 12 of the Conveyancing Act 1919 (NSW), as amended, the counterpart of s 25(6) of the Supreme Court of Judicature Act 1873 (UK), now s 136 of the Law of Property Act 1925 (UK). The interest, being a chose in action, falls within the expression "debt or other legal chose in action" because the section, in providing that notice shall be given to a trustee "as a person liable in respect of such debt or other legal chose in action", appears to contemplate the assignment by a beneficiary of an equitable chose in action against a trustee. There would be no point in referring to a trustee if the section made provision only for the assignment by strangers to the trust of debts owing by, and choses against, persons who happen to be trustees. The expression "legal chose in action" may be read as "lawfully assignable chose in action". See generally O R Marshall, *Assignment of Choses in Action*, pp 162-8 and the cases there cited; Meagher, Gummow & Lehane, *Equity—Doctrines and Remedies*, paras 605-8; *Re Pain; Gustavson v Haviland* [1919] 1 Ch 38 at 44.

However, the weight of authority is against the view that part of a debt or a chose in action can be assigned under that section: *Re Steel Wing Co* [1921] 1 Ch 349; *Williams v Atlantic Assurance Co Ltd* [1933] 1 KB 81 at 100, 108; *Walton & Sullivan Ltd v J Murphy & Sons Ltd* [1955] 2 QB 584; *Norman v Federal Commissioner of Taxation* (1963) 109 CLR 9 at 29; *Shepherd v Federal Commissioner of Taxation* (1965) 113 CLR 385 at 390, 396. Consequently, the assignment in the present case had effect as an equitable assignment.

[Their Honours then discussed the different forms of property and continued at 450:]

The distinction between present property and future property or mere expectancy gives rise to some borderline cases. For present purposes the point to be made is that an equitable assignment of present property for value, carrying with it a right to income generated in the future, takes effect at once whereas a like assignment of mere future income, dissociated from the proprietary interest with which it is ordinarily associated, takes effect when the entitlement to that income crystallises or when it is received, and not before.

Thus, in *Norman's* case it was held that an assignment of the assignor's right to future interest and future dividends was an assignment of a mere expectancy, there being no certainty that interest would be earned or dividends declared. But subsequently, in *Shepherd's* case, an assignment of the taxpayer's right, title and interest under a licence agreement to 90 per cent of the income which might accrue for three years by way of royalties proportioned to the number of products manufactured was held by majority (Barwick CJ and Kitto J, Owen J dissenting) to be an assignment of an existing chose in action and not of a mere expectancy. In this case there is no need to explore the grounds advanced in *Shepherd's* case for distinguishing *Norman's* case. The fineness of that distinction is beside the point here.

[Their Honours concluded that the assignment was of present property with a right to a share of future income. The assignment was effective at once, and conferred an immediate equitable entitlement on the assignee wife. The assignment effectively vested the right to future income in the wife. The appeal should therefore be dismissed.

Murphy J (dissenting) held that the case concerned taxation rather than equity. The income derived under the partnership agreement was characterised as income derived through personal exertion, and hence could not be diverted for tax purposes by the mechanism used in this case. He placed considerable emphasis on the need to ensure that taxpayers pay on the basis of financial capacity and to prevent the use of devices to avoid taxation. In his view the appeal should be allowed.]

Appeal dismissed with costs.

See also *McLeay v Commissioner of Internal Revenue* [1963] NZLR 711 and *Hocking v Western Australian Bank* (1909) 9 CLR 738.

Will a failure to comply with s 23C(1)(c) be fatal where valuable consideration is provided for the assignment or will it operate as an agreement to assign enforceable in equity? See *Oughtred v Internal Revenue Commissioners* [1960] AC 206 and Meagher, Gummow and Lehane, *Equity—Doctrines and Remedies*, 1975, pp 187-90. Notice to the trustee or debtor Greatparts is not necessary to the validity of an equitable assignment. However, it is highly desirable for the assignee Factors to give notice to Greatparts in order to preserve Factors' priority under the rule in *Dearle v Hall*. (See Section 3.)

ASSIGNMENT OF SO-CALLED FUTURE CHOSES

It is impossible either at law or in equity for Carb to assign a chose in action which is not in existence or acquired by Carb at the date of the purported assignment: *Holroyd v Marshall*, p 270, *supra*, and *Akron Tyre Co Ltd v Kittson*, p 273, *supra*. However, an agreement by Carb to assign to Factors future debts either absolutely or by way of charge will operate as a contract to assign when the debts arise and are acquired by Carb provided Factors furnishes consideration for the agreement. As to the distinction between a mere expectancy (sometimes called a future chose) and a presently existing right to receive payment in the future, see *Norman v Federal Commissioner of Taxation*, p 389, *supra*; *Commissioner of Taxation v Everett*, p 401, *supra*; *Federal Commissioner of Taxation v Betro Harrison Constructions Pty Ltd* (1978) 20 ALR 647.

STATUTORY REQUIREMENTS FOR ASSIGNMENTS OF SPECIFIC CHOSES

We have already noted that there are special statutory provisions regulating the assignment of company shares and various types of insurance policies. In addition, Commonwealth legislation provides for the assignment (which includes mortgage) of patents (Patents Act 1952 ss 23, 152); trade marks (Trade Marks Act 1955 s 82), industrial designs (Designs Act 1906 ss 16, 38), and copyright (Copyright Act 1968 s 196). Each of these provides for a comparatively simple form of assignment signed by the assignor and, except for copyright, for registration of same. These incorporeal rights do not qualify as personal chattels and so are not affected by the bills of sale legislation, but a charge given by Carb on a patent or licence under a patent, on a trade mark, or on a copyright or a licence under a copyright must be registered under the Companies Code s 200(1)(e) to avoid invalidation in the event of Carb's liquidation.

Book debts. The financing of Carb's book debts can be achieved by Factors either taking a mortgage or charge over the debts or by purchasing the debts with or without recourse. Whether such arrangement should be registered will depend upon (a) the meaning of "book debts"; (b) whether the assignment is by way of charge or outright sale; (c) whether it is given by a company such as Carb or an unincorporated trader/partnership:

(1) A book debt is defined in s 200(4) of the Companies Code as a debt due or about to become due to the company on account of or in connection with a profession, trade or business carried on by the company. Included in this statutory definition are future book debts. See also *Robertson v Grigg* (1932) 47 CLR 257 at 266, per Gavan Duffy CJ and Starke J; and Mason, "Company Charges — Registration of Book Debts" (1970) 2 *ACLR* 47.

(2) A mortgage or charge given by a company such as Carb to Factors over its present and/or future book debts should be registered under the Companies Code in order to avoid invalidation by Carb's liquidator in the event of winding up: ss 200(1)(f), 205. However, failure to register the charge will not render it invalid inter partes or for other purposes, although it may affect its priority in relation to other company charges: s 204 and Schedule 5.

(3) In most states, neither absolute assignments nor mortgages of book debts by unincorporated traders/partnerships require to be registered. The exceptions are Bills of Sale Act 1899 (WA) s 5 and Instruments Act 1958 (Vic) s 84. The Bills of Sale and Other Instruments Act 1955 (Qld) s 24 provides for the *optional* registration of assignments of book debts but no consequence follows from non-registration. The repealing of the doctrine of reputed ownership under the Bankruptcy Act 1924 by the current Act means this section has little importance today.

In practice, most factoring of book debts in Australia is carried out by way of purchase rather than charge in order to avoid where possible the publicity of registration. Is the legal distinction between a sale and a mortgage/charge of book debts logical or consistent with the functions of the two transactions?

In the United States, sales of and security interests in accounts receivable are treated in the same way and a financing statement must be filed: UCC ss 9-102(1)(b) and 9-302. The official comment to s 9-102 reads:

> Commercial financing on the basis of accounts and chattel paper is often so conducted that the distinction between a security transfer and a sale is blurred, and a sale of such property is therefore covered by subsection (1)(b).

The filing requirement was adopted "on the theory that there is no valid reason why public notice is less appropriate for assignments of accounts than for any other type of nonpossessory interest": comment to s 9-302.

QUESTIONS

Question 1

Explain the purpose and methods of financing book debts. Identify any practical or legal difficulties which might hinder the use of accounts receivable as collateral?

Question 2

In *Milroy v Lord*, p 388, *supra*, Turner LJ stated that "in order to render a voluntary settlement valid and effectual the settler must have done everything which, according to the nature of the property comprised in the settlement, was necessary to be done in order to transfer the property and render the settlement binding upon him".

Explain how this principle has been applied in Australia to the *voluntary* assignment of
(a) legal choses in action; and
(b) equitable choses in action.

Question 3

Discuss the effect of the following transactions:

(1) Jim Handy offered to assist one of Carb's suppliers named Bob Broke who was in financial difficulty. In return for new capital and technology supplied by Jim, Bob made Jim an equal partner in his business. Within two years the business was again flourishing and Jim was receiving a share of the sizable profits.

On the advice of his accountant, Jim executed a deed whereby he assigned
  (a) in consideration of $5000 a one-half share of his interest in the partnership to his adult daughter Suzy;
  (b) without consideration a one-quarter share of his interest in the partnership to his infant son Colin.

(2) On 1 July 1982 Carb Pty Ltd made a loan of $40,000 to Gaskets Ltd to assist it in developing a new sealant in which Carb was interested. The loan agreement stated that the loan was for a maximum of 10 years but provided that the capital could be repaid in full at any time after six months from the date of the agreement, or by instalments of $5000 at a time. The agreement provided inter alia:
  (a) The loan of $40,000 shall be repaid on or before 30 June 1992. The borrower may repay the principal sum in full at any time after 1 January 1983, or may repay the same by instalments of $5000 at a time.
  (b) The principal sum or so much thereof as shall remain outstanding shall bear interest at the rate of 15 per cent per annum and shall be paid by quarterly instalments.

On 1 July 1983 when no principal had been repaid, Carb Pty Ltd assigned by deed of gift to Jim Handy and Mary Handy a one-third share each in the interest accruing or to accrue on the loan to Gaskets Ltd. A copy of the deed was forwarded by Jim to Gaskets Ltd.

(3) On their twentieth wedding anniversary Jim Handy presented to Mary Handy as a gift a card on which appeared the words: "To Mary—With love from Jim. I hereby give you to use as you please
(a) my interest in the estate of my Aunt Jessie;
(b) my entitlement as residuary beneficiary under the will of my mother Mabel."
The entire card had been printed in gold by a calligrapher friend of Jim's.
At that time
(a) Aunt Jessie had died intestate and Jim was entitled as one of her next-of-kin to a one-quarter share of her undistributed estate.
(b) Mabel was quite ill and died three weeks after Jim and Mary's anniversary, leaving her entire estate to Jim.
(c) Jim was under pressure from his bank and other creditors whose debts he could not meet.

SECTION 3: PRIORITIES BETWEEN COMPETING CLAIMS

In the illustration provided on p 384, *supra*, Carb assigned to Factors the $30,000 debt owed to Carb by Greatparts. The main claimants who may challenge the rights of the assignee Factors are:
(a) the debtor, Greatparts;
(b) competing assignees, for example, Factors and City Bank;
(c) Carb's execution creditors or liquidator (or trustee in bankruptcy of an individual assignor).
Each of these claims will be examined in turn.

DEFENCES OR COUNTERCLAIMS BY THE DEBTOR

If Greatparts disputes that it owes Carb $30,000 or alleges a counterclaim against Carb, can it dispute Factors' right to recover the full $30,000? Is there a difference between a counterclaim that the $30,000 has been incorrectly calculated, a claim that the carburettors supplied by Carb are defective, or a claim against Carb which is unrelated to the original contract of sale? Does it make a difference if Carb assigns the debt to Factors before it was aware of Greatparts' counterclaim? Can Greatparts counterclaim against Factors for more than $30,000?

The basic rule is stated by James LJ in *Roxburghe v Cox* (1881) 17 Ch D 520 at 526:

> Now an assignee of a chose in action, according to my view of the law, takes subject to all the rights of set-off and other defences which were available against the assignor, subject only to this exception, that after notice of an assignment of a chose in action the debtor cannot by payment or otherwise do anything to take away or diminish the rights of the assignee as they stood at *the time of the notice*. [Emphasis added.]

The principle that the assignee takes subject to equities can also be seen as an application of the more general principle *nemo dat quod non habet*. Thus, as between successive assigns of a chose in action, defects in title are transmitted: see *Southern British National Trust Ltd (in liq) v Pither* (1937) 57 CLR 89 at 112, per Dixon J. Unlike the transfer of title to chattels there are no statutory exceptions to the *nemo dat* rule as applied to assignments of choses in action. Thus, if B obtains an assignment of a chose in action from A by fraud, B cannot confer on C any better title than he himself had. However, the doctrine of estoppel could enable C to obtain a title free of the defects in B's title if A had invested B with the indicia of ownership, for example, by holding him out as the ostensible owner: *Southern British National Trust Ltd (in liq) v Pither* at 112-13.

One difficulty with the rule in *Roxburghe v Cox* is that there is no real definition of the word "equities". In *Clyne v Deputy Commissioner of Taxation* (1981) 55

ALJR 552, Mason J stated that "equities" is a word of general expression, which includes defences which would have been available to the debtor in an action brought against him by the assignor as well as set-offs and counterclaims. A contract between the assignor and the debtor may exclude the right of set-off. This is one way to avoid the rule in *Roxburghe v Cox*. If this step is not taken any assignee will always take subject to any defence or set-off available to the debtor at the time when notice of assignment is given, provided they arise out of the same contract and there is a sufficient nexus between the rights assigned and the cross-claim or set-off: see *Business Computers Ltd v Anglo-African Leasing Ltd* [1977] 1 WLR 578 and *Provident Finance Corp Pty Ltd v Hammond* [1978] VR 312.

It follows from these cases that there are several advantages for Factors in giving notice to Greatparts of Carb's assignment to it. Notice will prevent Greatparts actually paying Carb the $30,000 or negotiating a release. In the absence of such notice, payment by Greatparts to Carb of $30,000 would give Greatparts a valid discharge against any claim by Factors. However, on receipt of a valid notice, Greatparts should pay Factors and thereby acquire a release from its original debt to Carb. The position is exactly the same in respect of an equitable assignment and a statutory assignment under Conveyancing Act (NSW) s 12 and corresponding provisions in other states. Section 12 expressly preserves "all equities which would have been entitled to priority over the right of the assignee if this Act had not been passed"; but it also enables the debtor Greatparts to give a good discharge without the concurrence of the assignor Carb. Since the assignee Factors is entitled to the benefit of Carb's original rights, it follows that any waiver or release by Greatparts of potential rights against Carb may also be availed of by Factors: *Re Blakely Ordnance Co; Ex parte New Zealand Banking Corp* (1867) 3 Ch App 154 at 159-60; *Higgs v Assam Tea Co* (1869) LR 4 Exch 387. In some cases the debtor may not be able to rely on an undisclosed equity. Should the debtor's conduct be intended to lead an assignee into the belief or assumption that the assignment will be free of equities then his conduct will prevent him from relying on that equity, eg *Mangles v Dixon* (1849) Mac & G 437 at 466.

COMPETING ASSIGNEES

In general it does not make any difference in the resolution of competing assignments whether they are outright assignments by way of sale (eg, factoring) or securities, except that a floating charge by Carb to City Bank may allow Carb to continue to dispose of book debts in the ordinary course of business. Thus, a subsequent assignment of specific existing debts to Factors will gain priority over a prior floating charge provided the subsequent assignee Factors takes without notice of any restriction upon Carb's licence to deal with its assets in priority to the floating charge: *English & Scottish Mercantile Investment Co v Brunton Ltd* [1892] 2 QB 700. See discussion regarding constructive notice, p 357, *supra*. However, this common law position may be displaced where the competing assignments constitute registrable charges over assets of a company such as book debts which fall within the ambit of the Companies Code s 200(1), in which case the priority rules in s 204 and Schedule 5 of the code will apply: see p 360, *supra*.

In contrast to dealings with real estate and choses in possession, when competing assignments of choses in action arise, the time of executing an assignment, the distinction between legal and equitable interests and the doctrine of the bona fide purchaser are largely displaced by the principal priority rule called:

The Rule in Dearle v Hall
High Court of Chancery (1828) 3 Russ 1 at 23, 29; 38 ER 475 at 483-5

Sir Thomas Plumer MR: It is true that a chose in action does not admit of tangible actual possession ... But ... in the case of a chose in action, you must do everything towards having possession which the subject admits; you must do that which is tantamount to obtaining possession, by placing every person, who has an equitable or legal interest in the matter, under an obligation to treat it as your property. For this purpose, you must give notice to the legal holder of the fund, in the case of a debt for instance, notice to the debtor is, for many purposes tantamount to possession. If you omit to give that notice, you are guilty of the same degree and species of neglect as he who leaves a personal chattel to which he has acquired a title, in the actual possession, and under the absolute control of another person ...

What opportunities of fraud would be afforded, if a party, who, having obtained an equitable conveyance, conceals it from every body, and lies by for years, while intermediate transactions are taking place, could at any time come forward with his secret deed, and say to a subsequent purchaser, who had advanced his money in ignorance of the existence of such a claim, "My deed is in date prior to yours; and, therefore, whatever may have been my negligence, or your diligence, the property belongs to me." Good sense, reason, authority, and equity are all on the other side.

The effect of the rule may be summarised:

As between two equitable assignees, the subsequent will prevail over the former if notice of his assignment is first given to the debtor or trustee, provided that he gave value for the assignment and he did not know of the prior assignment when he acquired his own interest.

The rule originally applied only to equitable choses in action, but it is now applied equally to legal choses such as trade debts. The rule is specifically preserved in relation to assignments of legal choses under Conveyancing Act (NSW) s 12 and corresponding provisions in other states by the express provision that the assignee takes subject to the equities. Thus, although an assignment under s 12, eg to Factors, gives a legal title, it remains subject to prior equities and the doctrine of bona fide purchaser does not apply. An earlier equitable assignee, eg City Bank, will therefore prevail over the later legal assignee Factors if:

(a) the equitable assignee City Bank was the first to give notice to the debtor Greatparts; or
(b) Factors did not give value for its assignment; or
(c) Factors was aware of the earlier equitable assignment to City Bank prior to completion of its own assignment by giving notice to Greatparts.

The presence of *any one* of these alternatives will defeat Factors. In the situation in (c) Factors might nonetheless prevail as an equitable assignee thus: an assignment to it for value will make it an equitable assignee though it has not given notice to Greatparts. The fact that Factors came to know of the earlier equitable assignment after it acquired its own equitable assignment and before notice to Greatparts will not defeat its equitable assignment, provided always that its assignment is the first to be notified to Greatparts.

CONSTRUCTIVE KNOWLEDGE AND ACTUAL NOTICE

It is important to distinguish:

(1) *The knowledge of an assignee* (eg, Factors) that a chose in action has previously been assigned which will preclude it obtaining priority for its assignment (ie, a shield which prevents Factors utilising the rule in *Dearle v Hall*: see *Re Hamilton's Windsor Ironworks* (1879) 12 Ch D 707 at 711). However, Factors will not be denied the benefit of *Dearle v Hall* if it obtained knowledge of City Bank's prior assignment after obtaining its own but before giving notice to Greatparts: *Re Holmes* (1885) 29 Ch D 786; *Mutual Life Assurance Society v Langley* (1886) 32 Ch D 460 at 468. Here the equitable doctrine of constructive notice is applicable so that when Factors is aware of particular facts which would put a person of normal intelligence upon enquiry it will be deemed to have such knowledge as that enquiry would have yielded. It would seem that registration of City Bank's floating charge including a

claim to book debts would constitute constructive notice to Factors of the existence of the charge: see Companies Code Schedule 5 para 4. Would Factors receive constructive notice of such an assignment if the charge is registered by lodgment under s 201(1) of the prescribed notice but same omits any reference, for example, to book debts? Of course, if Factors in fact searched the register it would be affected by such knowledge as it actually acquired.

(2) *The knowledge of the debtor Greatparts or trustee* (informal notice) of a prior assignment (to City Bank) which will preclude a subsequent assignee (Factors) from gaining priority by being the first to give express notice (in the sense used in (3) below). This knowledge of debtor Greatparts or trustee is again a shield which prevents Factors utilising the rule in *Dearle v Hall*. Knowledge for this purpose need not come from the assignor Carb or assignee City Bank, and may be quite informal provided it is such that an ordinary businessman would treat as reliable: *Arden v Arden* (1885) 29 Ch D 702 at 708; *Ipswich Permanent Money Club Ltd v Arthy* [1920] 2 Ch 257.

(3) *The express notice to the debtor Greatparts or trustee* which subsequent assignee Factors must give first in order to gain priority over prior assignee City Bank by using *Dearle v Hall* as a sword. However, remember that for Factors to do so, it must not itself have prior knowledge of the kind described in (1); and the debtor Greatparts or trustee must not have prior knowledge of the kind described in (2).

The express notice described in (3) need not be in writing but it must be actually and directly communicated to the debtor/trustee. Note that, *quite apart from* the rule in *Dearle v Hall*, the notice required to constitute a statutory assignment under Conveyancing Act s 12 and corresponding provisions in other states must be express *and in writing.*

CLAIMS BY THE ASSIGNOR'S EXECUTION CREDITORS, LIQUIDATOR OR TRUSTEE IN BANKRUPTCY

If Sue Quick has a judgment debt owing to her by Carb, she can garnishee or attach debts or other choses in action owing by a third party such as Greatparts to Carb provided Carb has not already effectively assigned or otherwise disposed of them. As we noticed in the income tax cases concerning assignment, *Norman's* case and *Shepherd's* case, the question is whether the assignor has effectively dispossessed himself of the right to deal with or receive the benefit of the chose in action. Accordingly, except where Carb is being wound up (see below), it is not essential that an assignment to Factors has been fully completed under Conveyancing Act s 12 or that notice has been given to debtor Greatparts provided the assignment is valid as between Carb and Factors. *Dearle v Hall* only regulates priorities between competing assignments. Hence, a valid assignment which takes effect in equity before a garnishee order is served on debtor Greatparts will place the chose in action outside the range of execution creditor Sue Quick.

Similarly, in the case of the winding up of Carb (or bankruptcy of an individual), an assignment by Carb of a chose in action which is effected prior to "the commencement of the winding up or bankruptcy" remains valid subject to the following:

(1) The doctrine of relation back, whereby the commencement of the winding up dates from the resolution to wind up or presentation of the petition (Companies Code ss 365, 368) and the bankruptcy can be deemed to extend as far back as six months prior to presentation of the petition (Bankruptcy Act 1966 ss 115, 116).

(2) Invalidation of a charge given by a company (or individual in Victoria or Western Australia) over its book debts unless registered within 45 days under the Companies Code s 201 (or Bills of Sale Act (WA) 1899 s 5; Instruments Act 1958 (Vic) s 84).

(3) The provisions of the Conveyancing and Property Acts, Bankruptcy Act and Companies Act dealing with dispositions in fraud of creditors and preferences outlined in Chapter 7, Section 5.

Where creditor Sue Quick has attached a debt owing by Greatparts to Carb, she is not entitled to retain the benefit of the attachment as against Carb's liquidator unless she has completed the attachment by actual receipt of the debt before the commencement of the winding up, or receiving notice of a meeting having been called for voluntary winding up of Carb: Companies Code s 455. However, a right of action of a bankrupt to recover damages for personal injuries or wrongs to himself or a member of his family or in respect of the death of a member of his family is specifically excluded from the trustee in bankruptcy by Bankruptcy Act s 116(2)(g); and see s 118(10).

It should be noted that the doctrine of reputed ownership which still applies under the Bankruptcy Act 1914 (UK) s 38(c) was abolished by the Bankruptcy Act 1966 (Cth) so that notice to the debtor of Greatparts or trustee is not necessary to defeat the trustee in bankruptcy provided the assignment of the chose in action was effective in equity prior to the commencement of the bankruptcy.

QUESTIONS

Question 4

On 10 January Carb Pty Ltd executed a floating charge in favour of City Bank over its stock-in-trade and book debts. City Bank did not register the charge.

On 1 September Carb Pty Ltd sold 2000 carburettors to Greatparts for $40,000 on 60 days credit. As Carb had a liquidity problem it accepted an offer on 10 September from Sponge that it should assign Greatpart's debt to him for $38,000. Carb made the assignment on the same day in return for a cheque which in fact Sponge had stolen from his employer. On 11 September Sponge sought to reassign the debt to Easy Finance. Easy Finance then contacted Greatparts who confirmed that the debt had not been paid but advised that because of some minor defects they intended to seek a reduction of $1000 in the price. Thereupon Easy finance paid Sponge $35,000 for the further assignment of the debt. Sponge cashed Easy Finance's cheque and disappeared.

The cheque Sponge had given to Carb was presented for payment on 14 September, but was dishonoured because Sponge's employer had stopped the cheque. Realising the vulnerability of Carb's position, Jim Handy immediately notified Greatparts to refrain from paying the debt to Sponge. Greatparts replied that in tests conducted on 13 September the carburettors had proved to be totally useless and could only be used for scrap metal. It therefore intended to counterclaim $32,000 damages as a set-off against the contract price.

Jim Handy then negotiated a compromise on behalf of Carb whereby Greatparts agreed to reduce its counterclaim to $15,000 and Carb agreed to accept $25,000 in full settlement provided same was paid within 14 days.

Before Carb received payment, several of its creditors filed applications in the Supreme Court to wind up Carb.

Advise Easy Finance of its rights to recover the $40,000 debt from Greatparts. Consider all possible defences which may be raised against its claim.

Question 5

Easy Finance loaned Carb Pty Ltd $30,000 secured by a deed by which Carb assigned to Easy Finance all its existing and future book debts. The deed provided:

"(1) Carb hereby covenants to forward promptly to Easy Finance copies of all its sales invoices.

(2) Easy Finance shall be entitled to collect all debts from Carb's customers until the loan of $30,000 and interest are repaid."

While the loan was still current, Carb sold 500 carburettors to Greatparts for $20,000 on 90 days credit. Greatparts was a notoriously slow payer. Carb's directors assumed that Easy Finance would not be interested in collecting this debt, and therefore decided to discount it with Factors Ltd in order to obtain cash which was urgently needed in Carb's business.

On 2 June, Factors' credit manager telephoned Greatparts whose bookkeeper, being unaware of the assignment to Easy Finance, assured Factors that the $20,000 was owing to Carb and was unencumbered. On 4 June, Factors obtained from Carb a written assignment of the $20,000 debt in return for $18,000 immediate cash settlement. On 10 June, Factors served written notice on Greatparts of its assignment and requested payment at the expiration of the 90 day credit period.

Greatparts seeks your advice. There is some doubt as to the true factual position and you are asked to advise Greatparts whether it should pay Easy Finance or Factors in each of the following alternative situations:

- (a) On 7 June Greatparts heard from a reliable independent source that Carb had assigned all its book debts to Easy Finance; or
- (b) On 8 June Factors learned of the prior assignment to Easy Finance; or
- (c) Easy Finance notified Greatparts on 14 June for the first time of its claim to the debt. Greatparts then advised Factors of Easy Finance's claim, this being the first knowledge which Factors had received of the earlier assignment.

Question 6

What is the rationale underlying the rule in *Dearle v Hall*? Can you devise an alternative rule or scheme which would better serve the business community? Compare and contrast your suggestions with the rule in *Dearle v Hall*.

SECTION 4: FINANCING THROUGH CHATTEL PAPER

A common form of financing consumer goods is a credit sale by a retailer, or either a goods mortgage or hire-purchase agreement contracted by the consumer with a retailer or finance company. For example, Carb may arrange to sell an engine to Driver which is financed on hire-purchase by Easy Finance. In the USA, these agreements are called chattel paper which correctly conveys the concept of a monetary obligation (chose in action owed by Driver) coupled with a security interest in the specific consumer goods which may be repossessed in the event of default.

In Australia, the most typical form of consumer credit financing is a tripartite arrangement, in which retailer (Carb) negotiates a sale to consumer (Driver) which is then directly financed by a finance company (Easy Finance). In this transaction the effect of the legal documentation is really that Carb sells not to Driver but to Easy, which in turn lets the goods on hire-purchase to Driver so that there is no need for Carb to assign the hire-purchase paper. The position is different under the Consumer Transactions Act 1972 (SA), and will also change in New South Wales and Victoria when the new consumer credit legislation comes into force. This legislation provides that under a consumer credit sale, the property interest of the supplier in the goods shall pass to the consumer, and the consumer is deemed to have entered into a goods mortgage back to the supplier. This deemed security interest, or an actual written goods mortgage to an outside financier, will thus replace the present form of hire-purchase agreement whereby the financier reserves title to the goods as its security: see SA, Consumer Transactions Act 1972 s 24; NSW, Consumer Credit Act 1981 s 14; Vic, Credit Act 1981 s 14.

In contrast, the English pattern is for the retailer to write its own hire-purchase agreements and then assign a batch of them *en masse* to a finance company under a "block discounting" arrangement. This practice is possible but less common in Australia. Each method achieves the same result: Carb receives cash, Driver his goods, and Easy its chattel paper. Each method throws up similar policy issues:

(1) Should Easy, which may have had little or nothing to do with the sale negotiations and know even less about the quality of the goods, be responsible for defective goods or other breaches of contract by Carb? On the other hand, should a fly-by-night retailer of shoddy goods (surely not Carb!) be entitled to wash its dirty chattel paper by selling it to a financier—particularly if the two are associated companies?

(2) Should the transaction be registered either as a bill of sale, or as an assignment of book debts?

(3) Should Easy, as assignee of Carb's hire-purchase agreement with Driver, be entitled to priority over a prior floating charge, eg in favour of City Bank, which purports to encumber all Carb's stock-in-trade and the proceeds of sale thereof?

LIABILITY OF FINANCIERS: TIED LOANS

At common law, we have noted that in general an assignee of Carb's total rights under the hire-purchase agreement, credit sale, goods mortgage or of the simple debt itself, takes subject to the equities. Thus Driver could raise against Easy a counterclaim for defective goods by way of set-off against Easy's claim for payment. This proposition is subject to three qualifications:

(1) Driver could use the counterclaim only as a shield, not as a sword; ie, he could not recover greater damages from Easy than necessary to extinguish the original purchase price.

(2) If Driver had agreed not to raise such claims against an assignee of Carb, he would be bound by that agreement: *Re Blakely Ordnance Co* (1867) 3 Ch App 154 at 159-60; conversely, a restraint on assignment of Carb's contractual rights may prevent Easy enforcing its purported rights as assignee: *Helstan Securities Ltd v Hertfordshire CC* [1978] 3 All ER 262.

(3) If Driver had given Carb negotiable promissory notes by way of collateral, and Easy qualified as a holder in due course of those notes, it would take free of Driver's equities against Carb (see Chapter 10).

In Australia, the common law solutions outlined above have been substantially modified by legislation. First, the Hire-Purchase Acts (HPA) of the various states impose a direct liability upon the finance company where it is the "owner" of the goods. In the Queensland Act, for example, note:

(a) the statutory warranties in s 5(1), (2) and (3) which are not excludable except in the limited circumstances of s 5(3); see also s 33(1)(i);
(b) the statutory power to join, and impose liabilities on, the manufacturer even though he is not a party to the agreement, nor liable under the common law principles of negligence;
(c) the remedies are specifically geared to a tripartite transaction involving dealer, owner (finance company) and hirer, and impose direct liability on the owner (ss 5(1), (2), (3) and 6(1)(a)), as well as on the dealer (s 6(1)(b)), while providing for the owner to seek indemnity from the dealer (ss 5(4) and 6(3)).

Second, the Consumer Transactions Act 1972 (SA) and the corresponding legislation in New South Wales and Victoria yet to be proclaimed has or will abolish the concept of hire-purchase in those states, but expressly provides for recovery from a linked credit provider. The "linked credit provider" is defined similarly in each statute.

Consumer Transactions Act 1972 (SA)

5 In this Act, unless the contrary intention appears—

"linked consumer credit contract" means a consumer credit contract made by a consumer with a credit provider in respect of a consumer contract with a supplier who is in relation to that credit provider a linked supplier:

"linked supplier" in relation to a credit provider means a supplier who introduces a consumer to a credit provider or who takes any part in negotiations leading to the formation of a credit contract between that credit provider and a consumer and, without limiting the generality of the foregoing, includes—
  (a) a supplier who by agreement or arrangement (whether formal or informal) with a credit provider refers applicants for credit to that credit provider;
  (b) a supplier who has available for use by those who may seek credit documents intended to be used as contracts with, or offers or applications to, the credit provider; or
  (c) a supplier on whose premises any contract with, or offer or application to, the credit provider is signed by the consumer in pursuance of an arrangement between the supplier and the credit provider, or in circumstances from which the existence of such an arrangement between the credit provider and the supplier might reasonably be inferred,
and "linked credit provider" has a correlative meaning:

13 (1) Where a consumer is entitled to recover damages against a supplier under or in respect of a consumer contract or any breach thereof, or any representation or warranty made in the course of, or in connection with, negotiations leading to the formation of the contract, he shall be entitled to recover those damages from—
  (a) the supplier; or
  (b) subject to this section a linked credit provider (not being a supplier in respect of the consumer contract) who provided credit in respect of the consumer contract.

(2) Where judgment is sought against a credit provider for the recovery of damages in pursuance of this section, the action must be brought against the supplier and the credit provider unless the supplier is insolvent, or there is no reasonable prospect of serving process upon him, in which event the action may be brought against the credit provider alone.

(3) A judgment shall not be given against a credit provider under this section for an amount exceeding the amount of the principal advanced under the consumer credit contract and of the costs (if any) awarded against the credit provider.

(4) Where judgment is given in favour of the plaintiff in an action in which the supplier and the credit provider are joined as parties, the plaintiff shall not proceed to enforce the judgment against the credit provider unless he has by notice in writing served upon the supplier demanded satisfaction of the judgment and the supplier has not, at the expiration of thirty days from the date of service of the notice, satisfied the judgment.

(5) A credit provider against whom any amount has been recovered under this section, may recover that amount, as a debt due to him, from the supplier.

(Compare NSW, Consumer Credit Act 1981 ss 5, 13, 24; Vic, Credit Act 1981 ss 5, 13, 24.)

On the other hand, the Commonwealth Trade Practices Act 1974 (TPA) specifically excluded the financier from liability for breach of the implied conditions of correspondence with description and sample, of merchantable quality and fitness for purpose provided the conditions in s 73 were met. Section 73 applies only to leases, hiring and hire-purchase contracts, and thus the extent of the application of this section to transactions in New South Wales, Victoria and South Australia may be restricted through the abolition of hire-purchase transactions in these states.

Is there an inconsistency between TPA s 73 and the respective provisions in the state HPA and Consumer Transactions Act 1972 (SA)? If so, does the Commonwealth Act prevail under s 109 of the Constitution or are the state Acts saved by TPA s 75(3)? See *General Motors Acceptance Corp v Credit Tribunal* (1977) 137 CLR 545.

It should be noted that all of the above provisions deal with a situation where the financier is linked to the consumer sale by providing financial assistance directly to the consumer. They do not cover the situations where Carb sells to Driver on hire-purchase or in return for bills of exchange or promissory notes which it then discounts to Easy Finance in situations where the general law would insulate Easy from Driver's counterclaims. The Rogerson Committee considered these questions:

Report on the Law Relating to Consumer Credit and Money-lending, 1969
Chapter XVI—Assignment of credit grantors' rights in consumer credit transactions

Assignments

From the consumer's point of view, there are two dangers in assignments by credit grantors of their rights in consumer credit transactions. First, the assignment may prejudice defences or claims which the consumer has against the assignor. Secondly, the personality of the credit grantor may be important to the consumer, eg, the credit grantor may have the reputation of being considerate in cases of hardship whereas an assignment by the credit grantor of his rights to another may foist a person of an entirely different character on to the consumer. It would obviously be pointless to require that before an assignment be made, the consumer's consent must be obtained, because in many cases a consumer would be unable to make an informed evaluation of the character or likely behaviour of the assignee.

Because of these considerations, we think that there is a strong case to be made for prohibiting such assignments, except perhaps in exceptional cases where, for example, a retailer who has been carrying his own finance becomes financially distressed and needs to sell his outstandings. In this case assignment could be permitted with the approval of the Commissioner.

If this is thought too radical a proposal, we feel that at the very least the law should make it clear that assignees should take the rights assigned subject to all defences and claims that the consumer may have had against the original credit grantor.

[The committee stated that there was a need to preserve the position under the general law, that an assignee takes subject to all claims and defences of the consumer. The use of "cut-off clauses" which provide in the original credit contract that the consumer will not pursue claims against an assignee should be prevented.]

We note that the present Australian Hire-Purchase Acts partly achieve this end by defining "owner" as including not only the person letting or selling the goods under a hire-purchase agreement, but also his assignees. This provision is not entirely satisfactory in that while it makes clear that assignees of the owner take subject to the owner's statutory obligations under the Act, it does not also make clear whether assignees take subject to all claims of the hirer or buyer arising under or out of the contract, eg, actions for breach of contractual terms, or claims to relief for misrepresentation. This ought to be clearly provided for. Section 2.404 (alternative A) of the United States Uniform Consumer Credit Code seems to us a useful guide as to how this might be achieved, viz:

"With respect to a consumer credit sale or consumer lease, other than a sale or lease primarily for an agricultural purpose, an assignee of the rights of the seller or lessor is subject to all claims and defenses of the buyer or lessee against the seller or lessor arising out of the sale of lease notwithstanding an agreement to the contrary, but the assignee's liability under this section may not exceed the amount owing to the assignee at the time the claim or defense is asserted against the assignee. Rights of the buyer or lessee under this section can only be asserted as a matter of defense to or set-off against a claim by the assignee."

Promissory notes

A question related to that of assignments arises in the case of promissory notes issued to the credit grantor by the consumer in connection with the latter's instalment obligations under a consumer credit contract. Should these be negotiated to a holder in due course, it is likely that the latter will take free of equities arising between consumer and credit grantor and will be able to enforce the notes against the consumer regardless of defences the consumer might have had against the credit grantor, had there been no negotiation. Submissions we received suggest that promissory notes are not in common use in Australia in the present context, but nevertheless they have posed considerable problems in a number of overseas jurisdictions and it seems desirable to anticipate and provide for these problems here.

Some attempt to do this has been made in the present Hire-Purchase Acts. [The Report then set out the relevant section (NSW, s 39; Vic, s 31; Qld, s 36; SA, s 31; WA, s 31; Tas, s 40; see also Consumer Credit Act 1972 (SA) ss 49, 50).]

Some disadvantages of this provision are, first, that it requires the consumer to pay up in the first instance regardless of his ultimate liability. This may cause hardship and embarrassment to him. Secondly, to reimburse himself, he is required to proceed against the owner, which may be costly, inconvenient and, in the case of a fly-by-night or insubstantial credit grantor, sometimes worthless. Thirdly, the section does not make it clear that "the liability of the hirer under the agreement" is arrived at, for these purposes, by deducting any rights, set-offs and counterclaims which the hirer might have against the owner, from the total amount otherwise payable. This clearly ought to be the position.

A much more radical approach to the problem has been taken in legislation in some other jurisdictions where it is proposed that promissory notes issued in connection with a consumer credit sale be prohibited (see eg, Section 2.403 Uniform Consumer Credit Code; see also the recommendation to this effect of the Royal Commission on Credit in Nova Scotia, p 407). For reasons which we have set out above in relation to assignments, we think that there is much merit in these proposals and we recommend their adoption. We would, however, go further and extend them to cover the case of post-dated cheques used to serve the function of promissory notes.

Again if these proposals are thought too radical, at the very least the law ought to make it clear that transferees of promissory notes and post-dated cheques in these circumstances should take subject to all rights which the consumer has against the original credit grantor. The Select Committee of the Ontario Legislature on Consumer Credit has recently recommended provisions to this effect (paras 138-50).

We think, however, that there is need to go further than this. The Ontario Committee's recommendations, while perhaps reasonable enough in respect of the first transferee from the seller, who is likely to know of the circumstances in which the promissory note was issued, would seem less reasonable in the case of holders of the note further stages removed, whose rights would be very much at hazard. We consider a more complete solution to the problem to be that suggested by Goode and Ziegel, *Hire-Purchase and Conditional Sale*, p 112. The authors propose that legislation should provide that all promissory notes (we would also include post-dated cheques) given in respect of a consumer credit sale should bear a statement to that effect (eg, "Consumer Note. Subject to Equities"), in default of which they should be void except as against a holder in due course, and that the holder of any promissory note containing such a statement should take the note subject to all defences of which the buyer under the associated transaction may be entitled to avail himself . . .

We realise that there may be constitutional difficulties in the way of the states enacting such a provision, in which event it would be necessary for the Commonwealth to amend the Commonwealth Bills of Exchange Act 1909-1958.

In Victoria, the "more radical position" has been adopted, and the Credit Act 1981 (Vic) s 124 directly prohibits the taking of a bill of exchange or promissory note by a credit provider. The approach in New South Wales is less radical. The Consumer Credit Act 1981 (NSW) s 124(1) provides that the bill of exchange or promissory note shall bear a prescribed notice, and this must comply with the legibility provisions in s 154 of the Act. Failure to comply with s 124(1) will render the credit provider liable to pay any excess: s 124(3). The Consumer Credit Act 1972 (SA) s 50 imposes on the credit provider liability for any excess on the amount payable under the contract.

The Molomby Committee in its report on Fair Consumer Credit Laws (1972) recommended that the supplier should remain primarily liable but that linked financiers should be jointly liable under tied loans but would be entitled to an indemnity from the supplier: Ch 5.4. For a general commentary on the above proposals, see J Llewellyn in *Consumer Credit—The Challenges of Change*, eds Cullen & Baxt, 1973, pp 43-5.

REGISTRATION OF ASSIGNMENTS OF CHATTEL PAPER

The second issue concerning registration of the assignment turns on what is transferred. Where title to the goods, the subject of hire-purchase, are charged by way of security to Easy Finance, they would appear to remain chattels capable of transfer by delivery and hence registration as a bill of sale would be required despite decisions to the contrary in *Motor Credits Ltd v Wollaston* (1929) 29 SR (NSW) 227; and *Blackwood's Ltd v Chartres* (1931) 31 SR (NSW) 619. If the goods had been sold by Carb under conditional sale (as distinct from hire-purchase), the title assigned to Easy would be no more secure than that of Carb, and would therefore be subject to the risk of Driver reselling to a bona fide purchaser under Sale of Goods Act (NSW) s 28(2) and corresponding provisions in other states.

An assignment by Carb of its hire-purchase agreements, including the right to receive instalments of hiring charges, would require registration under the Companies Code s 200(1)(f) if it were constructed in the form of a charge over the company's general book debts: see also Companies Code s 211. We have already noted that registration does not necessarily constitute notice and in order to preserve its rights under the rule in *Dearle v Hall* against another assignee, Easy Finance should notify Driver and other hirers.

PRIORITY CONFLICTS OVER PROCEEDS OF STOCK-IN-TRADE

The third issue concerns the potential conflict between a stock-in-trade financier (eg, in the form of a floating charge to City Bank) and an assignee of chattel paper or accounts receivable by Carb as proceeds of its stock-in-trade. Although this conflict has been much debated in the United States, it has not to date received much attention in Australia for two reasons:

(1) The rule in *Dearle v Hall* makes it virtually impossible for City Bank to obtain an effective security over Carb's future book debts.

(2) The prevalent practice of finance companies (eg, Easy Finance) acquiring goods directly from retailers (Carb) and letting them on hire-purchase to consumers (Driver) results in the retailer receiving cash proceeds rather than chattel paper. Since the cash proceeds will normally lose their identity when mixed with Carb's general funds it will again be impossible for City Bank to trace and attach these proceeds under its floating charge. For a general discussion of the doctrine of tracing, see Hanbury & Mandsley, *Modern Equity*, 11th ed, 1981, pp 663-75. Peden, *Stock-in-Trade Financing*, 1974, pp 17-19, 48-9 outlines a number of important policy considerations in relation to the securing of proceeds of sale from stock-in-trade, as well as discussing the implications of the rule in *Dearle v Hall* for this type of transaction.

QUESTIONS

Question 7

Carb Pty Ltd purchased new retail premises with the aid of a loan from Easy Finance. One condition of the loan agreement was that Carb would refer customers requiring credit to Easy and would display brochures advertising Easy's credit plans.

Thereafter Carb was approached by three new customers:

(1) Driver wished to purchase a new engine on extended credit. Carb agreed to sell to him for $8000 an engine manufactured by Carb and referred him to Easy to obtain finance. The result was that Carb sold the engine to Easy which let it on hire for three years to Driver with an option to purchase. While $6000 was still owing under the hiring agreement, the engine seized due to faulty manufacture.

(2) Strong was likewise referred by Carb to Easy to obtain finance for the acquisition of an engine manufactured by Biltwell Ltd which Carb had in stock. Carb sold the engine to Easy which leased it to Strong for three years at a monthly

rental of $100. Easy's finance manager told Strong informally that the company would negotiate to sell the engine to him for its residual value after the end of the three year term. Within six months of taking possession, the engine exploded due to a faulty valve and destroyed Strong's garage and half his house.

(3) Speed was interested in Carb's new super sports engine. Jim Handy clinched the sale when he assured Speed that the engine would produce 130 bhp at 6000 rpm and would only consume one litre of petrol per 10 kilometres in Speed's car. Speed agreed to purchase the engine for $12,000 plus interest at 15 per cent per annum by 36 monthly instalments. The contract provided inter alia:

"(a) The property in the goods shall only pass to the buyer when the purchase price has been paid in full;
(b) the buyer shall not be entitled to bring any action for breach of condition or warranty against any assignee of this agreement."

At Carb's insistence Speed signed 36 promissory notes in respect of the 36 instalments due under the contract. One month later Carb experienced liquidity problems, and without notice to Speed, assigned the contract and indorsed 10 of the promissory notes to Easy Finance in return for payment of $5000.

Speed refused to pay any further instalments because the engine did not perform in accordance with Jim Handy's assurances.

Carb Pty Ltd is now in liquidation.

Advise Driver, Strong and Speed of their rights against all parties.

Question 8

How effectively can a floating charge secure proceeds of sale of retailers' stock, such as cash, cheques, accounts receivables and chattel paper? Outline the position under current Australian law and assess whether it is responsive to commercial needs.

SECTION 5: ARRANGEMENTS WITH CREDIT CARDS

The use of single store credit cards is common and generally well understood. Retail stores which offer 30 day and revolving credit accounts normally sell goods to their approved customers on an unsecured basis, so that property in the goods passes unconditionally to the customer at the point of sale. If the goods prove defective the customer has a direct right of cross-action against his seller-creditor which often facilitates a compromise. If the credit extends more than one month beyond the billing date interest is charged.

The retailer could in theory factor these consumer book debts but, as explained at the commencement of this chapter, the small amount of the average consumer's monthly account with a retail store renders such an arrangement uneconomic. Where high priced consumer durables are sold on credit, security is usually taken in the form of a credit sale, hire-purchase agreement or goods mortgage dealt with in the previous section.

Third party credit card arrangements raise further issues.

W J Chappenden: Bank Credit Cards
(1973) 5 *Comm Law Assoc Bull* 19

Two and three party credit (or charge) card schemes have been operating in Australia for some years. Examples of two party schemes are those run by some large departmental stores. These allow selected customers to obtain goods or services at departments of the store on production of a charge card issued by the store and to pay a single sum on receipt of an account at the end of a month or other period. Examples of three party schemes are those operated by Diner's Club and American Express. These allow cardholding members to obtain goods and services from merchant members of the schemes on production of their credit cards

Lending on the Security of Proceeds

and to pay single bills presented by the card issuing organisation at the end of a given period. The merchants' accounts, less an agreed discount, are paid by the card-issuer...

This article describes in Part 1 the main features of the new [Bankçard] scheme and in Part II considers some unsolved legal problems involved in charge card operations.

Part 1 — The Scheme

Outline of the scheme

Each bank in the scheme will issue credit cards to selected customers. A cardholder to whom a card is issued may purchase goods and services on credit from any merchant who has joined the scheme. The customer will produce his credit card and sign a sales slip for each purchase that he makes. The merchant supplying the goods or service will then pay the sales slip into his own bank account very much as if it were cash and receive a credit for the face value of the slip less a discount. Slips will be sent by the depository bank to a service bureau[4] set up by the banks and there charged to the cardholder's account. An account will be sent to the cardholder each month and the cardholder will make payment to his own bank. The service bureau will also adjust accounts between the banks...

The issuing bank and the cardholder

Each bank will issue its own cards. It will select from its existing customers those to whom the facility is to be offered and will send cards to them without a request by the bank's customer. Customers to whom cards have not been issued and new customers will be able to apply for cards if they want them.

Where a card is sent to a customer it will probably be accompanied by a statement of the terms on which the card is offered. The card may be expected to carry a declaration that it is issued on the terms of the statement and a warning that the cardholder has a specified liability for purchases made with the card if it is lost or stolen. The card may also be expected to show the date of expiry, the cardholder's name, address and account number and have a space for the cardholder's signature. The customer is, of course, free to reject the card but will accept it if he signs and uses it.

A number of terms are common in American and British schemes and it is known that many of the terms or variations on them will appear in the Australian scheme. They include:

1 An undertaking by the customer not to exceed his credit limit. The credit limit will vary from customer to customer and in the USA does not usually exceed $(US)1000. The credit is a revolving credit so that if a cardholder has a credit limit of $500 and has spent $100 he has an effective credit limit of $400 until the $100 is paid when the limit is re-established as $500.

2 An authorisation by the customer to the bank to pay merchants for all purchases made with the card.

3 An undertaking to notify the bank in writing if the card is lost or stolen. The customer will be liable for unauthorised purchases made with the card before the bank receives notice but only up to a certain figure. This figure has not been announced but the corresponding figure in England is £50 and an equivalent figure can be expected here.[5]

4 An undertaking to reimburse the bank for all payments made to merchants by the bank in respect of the customer's purchases. The customer will be able to choose between paying the account within 25 days of the date of the statement[6] and paying it in instalments over a period. If the first alternative is chosen, no charge will be made for credit so that a customer will have up to 55 days free credit. If the second alternative is chosen the customer will be charged interest. A rate of one and one half per cent on the monthly balance is charged by the UK banks.

5 An undertaking by the customer not to raise against the bank any defence or counterclaim which he could raise against the merchant. The function of this clause will be considered in Part II.

---

[4] Called Charge Card Services Ltd.
[5] Legislation is likely to fix the limit at £30 in the UK. Reform of the Law on Consumer Credit (1973) Cmnd 5427.
[6] Not, it will be noticed, 25 days of the date of receipt of the notice. A correspondent of the London Times reported that he received a statement 23 days after its date giving him two days in which to pay. *Times*, 3 October 1973.

The merchant and the depository bank

A merchant participating in the scheme has rights and obligations under his agreement with the bank at which he deposits his sales slips. A number of rights and obligations are common in the USA and the UK and similar provisions can be expected in Australia. The provisions are:

1 The merchant must sell goods and services to all persons presenting credit cards of any bank in the scheme at the price at which he sells such goods and services for cash.

2 The merchant must obtain the cardholder's signature on a sales slip for each purchase and compare the signature on the slip with the signature on the card.

3 The merchant must confirm the sale with the service bureau if it is above a specified figure.

4 The merchant must deposit sales slips within a certain time of the sale. The merchant will be credited with the value of the sale less a discount. The rate of discount will probably vary with the type of goods or services sold and will be within the range of two to seven per cent.[7] The bank will reserve the right to refuse a slip and to "charge back" a slip for which credit has been given in certain circumstances. These include cases where:
   (a) There is a dispute between the cardholder and the merchant arising out of the sale.
   (b) The sales slip exceeds the specified figure and the sale was not cleared with the service bureau.
   (c) The sale was made after the date of expiry shown on the card.
   (d) The sale was made against a counterfeit card or a card which appeared on a stop-list.
   (e) The sales slip is not signed or the signature is illegible.

5 The merchant must not give refunds in cash to a cardholder but must complete and deposit a refund slip so that a credit will in due course be made to the cardholder's account.

6 The merchant must follow good sales practices and allow credit for items returned by cardholders. Whether or not such a term is expressly included in the agreement between merchant and bank it is clear that banks will keep a watchful eye on their merchants and will exclude merchants against whom complaints are made by cardholders.

Merchant and cardholder

It may be concluded that, with the obvious difference that the merchant looks primarily to the bank for payment, the contract between cardholder and merchant is the same as if the customer had paid cash. Thus, if the customer has obtained goods by the production of his card there will be a contract of sale of goods between customer and merchant and the transaction will be covered by the Sale of Goods Act. If the goods are defective the customer will have the same rights against the seller as any purchaser under the Act.

A point of some interest is whether if the merchant fails to obtain payment from the bank, for example, because the customer's signature is illegible, he can proceed against the customer. It is submitted that in such a case the customer would be liable. The transaction between the merchant and the cardholder will be subject to an implied term that the customer will pay if the bank does not.

Advantages and disadvantages

The cardholder receives a number of advantages from the scheme. He need carry less cash; the loss or destruction of a charge card is less detrimental than the loss of a full wallet; a credit card is acceptable where a personal cheque is not; the cardholder receives an itemised statement of his purchases periodically; the cardholder receives a period of free credit. On the debit side the card induces improvident spending and the customer cannot obtain the discounts he might be able to negotiate for cash payments.

The advantages to the merchant are that his book keeping is simpler, his risk of bad debts less and the costs less than if he financed his own credit sales; he receives virtually immediate reimbursement for his advances; he handles and carries less cash than he would otherwise do which reduces the risk of losses due to theft; he makes sales to persons who would not have dealt with him if he had stayed outside the scheme. The disadvantages to the merchant are

---

[7] "The merchant charge in a bank card scheme almost never exceeds 5 per cent and the average is probably nearer 3 per cent or 2 per cent" Blackwell Credit Cards and the Banks, 1972 *Journal of the Institute of Bankers* 226, 227.

that the clerical work involved is greater than in cash sales and, of course, he must allow a discount to the bank.

The advantages to the banks are the discounts allowed by merchants and the interest charges paid by cardholders who do not settle immediately. Another advantage is that the scheme introduces to banks persons who would not have taken up accounts apart from the scheme. On the other hand the banks bear the risk of bad debts and most of the risks of unauthorised use of lost cards. Again, the capital cost of establishing the scheme is immense and the scheme will have to operate for a substantial period before the banks obtain a real return.

It may be wondered whether charge cards have advantages and disadvantages for persons who do not have cards. It is generally accepted that the level of prices will gradually rise to cover the discount allowed by the merchant to the bank, but, on the other hand, persons able to pay cash may be able to negotiate a discount with a merchant equivalent to the merchant's discount to the bank.

Part II — Legal Problems

Two problems involved in the use of credit cards have been much discussed by lawyers. They are:

1 Can a cardholder raise against the issuing bank defences which he could have raised against the merchant?

2 What is the extent of the liability of a cardholder for purchases made with his card which he did not authorise?

Availability of defences

A person who buys goods on credit and finds they are not in accordance with the contract before he pays for them is in a good tactical position in law. He will simply refuse to pay until the defect is put right. If the supplier sues, the buyer will set up the breach of contract by the seller as a defence. If, on the other hand, the purchaser has paid for the goods before he discovers the defect he will have to take the initiative. If the seller is unco-operative the buyer will have no remedy but to sue. If the amount involved in the sale is small it will simply not be worth the buyer's while to go on. Again, if the buyer and seller live far apart it will be too much trouble for the purchaser to pursue his remedies.

These facts make it important to know whether the cardholder can refuse to pay the bank for goods and services in respect of which the merchant is in breach of contract or whether he must pay the bank and then proceed against the merchant.

The contracts between (i) the bank and the merchant and (ii) the bank and the cardholder may make some provisions for such cases. The cardholder may agree not to raise against the bank defences he could have raised against the merchant and the bank may reserve the right against the merchant to refuse credit for, or to charge back, items about which the cardholder and the merchant are in dispute. The result of these clauses is to allow the bank a very considerable discretion in cases of customer/merchant disputes and, as the body of case law on this topic is virtually non-existent, it may be assumed that the banks exercise their discretion generously in the interests of cardholders.

For a number of reasons, however, it is necessary to know what the law would be if the contract were silent on the question.

The answer to the question depends largely on how a wider question is to be answered. The wider question is the basic one: What is the nature of the credit card transaction? Two theories[8] have been put forward to answer the question. They may be called:

(i) the assignment theory; and

(ii) the direct obligation theory.

The *assignment theory* is that there is a simple sale of goods or services by the merchant to the cardholder on credit and that the right to receive payment for the goods or services is then assigned by the merchant to the bank. If this theory is sound, the bank takes the merchant's rights against the cardholder subject to any rights the cardholder has against the merchant.

---

[8] See Maffley and McDonald, the "Tripartite Credit Card Transaction: A Legal Infant" (1960) 48 *California Law Rev* 459.

The *direct obligation theory* is that the cardholder is a borrower from the bank. The bank agrees to lend sums to the cardholder up to an agreed limit so that he may make purchases from merchant members of the scheme. The amount of the loan is to be paid direct by the bank to the merchants. If this theory is correct the customer will not be able to raise defences against the bank merely because he could have raised them against the merchant. The bank's rights against the cardholder are original rights under the contract to lend and not rights derived from the contract between the merchant and the customer. Even on this theory, however, the customer will not necessarily be liable to the bank for every item which the merchant notifies to the bank. The terms of the contract will describe exactly what the cardholder must pay for but it is certain that he will not have to pay for items notified to the bank in error or where there is fraud by the merchant's servants.

Which of the two theories, assignment or direct obligation, is the right one has not been settled by any court in the USA, the UK or elsewhere but it is probably true to say that the direct obligation theory is generally accepted as being the one the courts will follow in the UK and in Australia.[9]

It may be asked whether if the defences of the consumer are not preserved at common law, they should be preserved by statute. There are arguments for and against. Those who advocate that the defences of the cardholder should not be good against the bank argue that if the customer can refuse to pay the bank on an allegation of breach of contract by the merchant, the unscrupulous cardholder would exploit the advantage. They go on to say that if the bank could be made liable, the costs of the scheme would increase. Further, they point out, the banks are not experts in the sale of goods and (non-banking) services and cannot supervise all their merchants. Those who argue that the defences should be good against the bank point to the ease with which the bank can charge back disputed items. They suggest that the dishonest customer will soon be identified and can be excluded from the scheme. Similarly "bad" merchants can soon be weeded out and the bank is in a better position to bring pressure to bear on a defaulting merchant.

In the USA the advocates of the view most favourable to the cardholder are tending to prevail and a number of States have introduced legislation to preserve the cardholder's rights subject to certain limitations, for example, the cardholder must have made an honest attempt to settle with the merchant. However, no such protection can be expected in Australia or the UK. The British government's White Paper[10] makes no mention of the topic in its proposals for legislation and the Molomby Report recommendations would not lead to statutory preservation of the cardholder's defences in Australia.

Liability for unauthorised purchases

Although the matter is not settled beyond doubt, it is likely that a cardholder is not liable to pay for purchases made with his card which he has not authorised unless either he is in some way at fault or the matter is regulated by contract.[11] An example of fault by the cardholder would be where the cardholder knew that purchases were being made by an unauthorised person but did not notify the bank.

The contract between the cardholder and the bank will seek to regulate the matter. It will provide that the customer must pay for all purchases made with his card until he notifies the bank in writing that the card has been lost or stolen. Until the bank receives such notice the cardholder will be required to pay for unauthorised purchases up to a certain ceiling. If reasonable steps are taken to bring the term to the customer's notice it will settle most questions of liability for unauthorised purchases.

There is, however, an area in which problems may still arise. If the merchant has been negligent in allowing a person to make purchases with a card which is not his own, will such negligence prevent the bank from relying on the clause imposing liability on the cardholder?

An example of the kind of problem involved is found in the American case of *Gulf Refining Co v Williams Roofing Co*[12] where the plaintiff issued a number of credit cards to the

---

[9] See Report on Fair Consumer Credit Laws (The Molomby Report) p 41 n 2 Crowther Report on Consumer Credit (UK) Chapter 6.12.3.
[10] Reform of the Law on Consumer Credit (1973) Cmnd 5427 (UK).
[11] 15 *American Law Reporter* 3d 1086 (1967).
[12] (1945) 186 SW 2d 790.

defendant for use by his employees. The defendant typed across the face of the cards "Good for Truck Only". One of the cards came into the hands of a rogue who made over two hundred purchases with it before the defendant notified the card-issuer. The imposter was not driving a truck when he made his purchases and there was evidence that the merchants who supplied him knew that he was not entitled to the card. The contract between the plaintiff and the defendant provided that the defendant should be liable for unauthorised purchases made with the card before its loss was reported. The court held that the cardholder need not pay for the purchases. The merchants could not have enforced the purchases against the defendant and the card-issuer could not be in a stronger position.

Whether the result would be the same in Australia depends to an extent on whether Australian courts adopt the assignment theory or the direct obligation theory of the credit card transaction. If, as seems likely, the direct obligation theory were adopted, the decision would probably be against the defendant.

The practice of sending unsolicited credit cards referred to in the above article is now prohibited by Trade Practices Act 1974 s 63A. For an expanded version of this discussion see Chappenden, "Credit Cards: Some Legal Problems" (1974) 48 *ALJ* 306.

QUESTION

Question 9

(1) Jim and Mary Handy were returning from a picnic in the country in Jim's vintage touring car when Jim noticed that the steering mechanism was somewhat stiff. He pulled into a local garage where the proprietor Wrench removed the steering wheel and greased the mechanism.

Wrench charged Jim $20 for his services and Jim asked if Wrench would accept payment on Mary's American Express card as Jim had no cash or credit cards with him. Wrench prepared the American Express voucher for the amount of $20, and as Mary was making a phone call, Jim signed the voucher for her.

The Handys resumed their journey but after travelling two kilometres the steering wheel jammed causing the car to crash into a stone fence. Jim walked back to Wrench's garage and angrily demanded that he tow the car to Jim's home. Wrench did so and then demanded $200 for towing charges. Jim refused to pay.

Mary immediately telephoned American Express Co, notified it of Wrench's faulty work and requested that the voucher for $20 should not be paid.

Subsequent investigations proved that Wrench had failed to reassemble the steering mechanism correctly thereby causing it to jam. Repairs to the car's bodywork cost Jim $3000.

Analyse the respective relationships between Jim, Mary, Wrench and American Express and advise Jim and Mary of their rights and obligations.

(2) Assume now that Mary had not notified her complaint to American Express before Wrench presented his sales voucher on which he had added a separate item "Towing $200", and had received payment of $209 representing the face value of the voucher less the normal five per cent discount.

FURTHER READING

Section 1: An Overview of Credit Practices Involving Proceeds

Biscoe, *Law and Practice of Credit Factoring,* 1975.

Starke J G, *Assignment of Choses in Action in Australia,* 1972.

Section 2: Requirements for Valid Assignments

Cullity & Ford, "Gifts of Future Income from Choses in Action" (1966) 30 *The Conveyancer* 286.

Johnson, "Accounts Receivable Financing in Canada: Nature of the Charge and Rights of Priority" (1981) 15 *UBCLR* 87.

McKay, "Some Aspects of the Alienation of Income for Taxation Purposes" (1974–75) 6 *NZULR* 1.

Zines, "Equitable Assignments: When Will Equity Assist a Volunteer" (1965) 38 *ALJ* 337.

Section 3: Priorities Between Competing Claims

Begg, "The Registration of Security Interests in Chattels" (1981) 55 *ALJ* 649.

Kloss, "Assignments Without the Consent of the Debtor" (1979) 43 *Conv (NS)* 261.

McLauchlan, "Priorities—Equitable Tracing Rights and Assignments of Book Debts" (1980) 96 *LQR* 90.

Section 4: Financing through Chattel Paper

Luntz, "Section 73 of the Trade Practices Act and the Liability of Financiers for Defective Products" (1975) *ABLR* 90.

Mason & Butler, "The Trade Practices Act 1974 and the Possible Inconsistency Therewith of Certain State Laws Dealing with Consumer Protection" (1975) 49 *ALJ* 539.

Section 5: Arrangements with Credit Cards

Chappenden, "Credit Cards: Some Legal Problems" (1974) 48 *ALJ* 306.

Corkery, "Credit Cards in New Zealand: Some Potential Problems" (1977) *NZLJ* 30.

Sharma, "Credit Cards in Australia: Some Predictable Legal Problems" (1972) 3 *Lawasia* 106.

CHAPTER 10

Financing Through Negotiable Instruments, Promissory Notes and Letters of Credit

"Creditors have better memories than debtors."
English Proverb also attributed to Benjamin Franklin

Section 1: The Origin, Purpose and Function of Negotiable Instruments
Section 2: Transfer and Negotiation of Bills of Exchange
Section 3: Rights and Liabilities of Parties and Discharge
Section 4: Financing International Transactions: Letters of Credit

In Chapters 10 and 11 our focus moves away from the security aspects to the modes of payment in sales and financing transactions. In the present chapter, Sections 1 to 3 deal with the functions, characteristics and methods of transferring, enforcing and discharging the most typical negotiable instruments — bills of exchange. Much of this law is codified in the Bills of Exchange Act (Cth) and constant reference will be made to relevant sections. The same basic principles apply to promissory notes. The final section will build upon the discussion of import and export sales in Chapter 5 and address the particular problems associated with financing international transactions. The other common form of negotiable instrument, the cheque, is examined in Chapter 11 in the context of the Australian banking system and banker-customer relations.

SECTION 1: THE ORIGIN, PURPOSE AND FUNCTION OF NEGOTIABLE INSTRUMENTS

In mediaeval Europe there was considerable opportunity for trade between merchants from different countries, and Italian bankers loaned money to merchants and the nobility throughout Europe. Payment for these transactions in gold, silver or local currency was both inconvenient and subject to the dangers of theft, loss and counterfeiting, and therefore the merchants developed their own customs and usages for acknowledging and meeting their monetary obligations. These consisted of written orders from a creditor to his debtor directing payment to a third party to whom the creditor himself owed an obligation. By mercantile custom these orders themselves were transferable, and became known as bills of exchange.

Since bills could also be used as a means of acknowledging a debt payable at a future time, they became useful devices for financing loans. While loaning of money at interest was forbidden as usury, a bill of exchange could be transferred (discounted) for less than its face value at maturity, the amount of the discount representing the "interest" for the use of funds advanced prior to the date of payment of the bill.

The mercantile usages associated with negotiable instruments were incorporated into English law as part of the law merchant (see Chapter 1), and formed the basis for the codification in the English Bills of Exchange Act 1882 which was followed in the Bills of Exchange Act 1909 (Cth). This process of codification and the relationship between the previous common law and the statute is similar to the Sale of Goods legislation: see pp 15–16, *supra*. Today bills of exchange continue to perform these dual functions:

(1) As a mode of payment usually at a specified future date; they have traditionally been most common in external trade where payment is often deferred. They are also used in domestic transactions although cheques are used in the majority of transactions which call for prompt payment.

(2) As a means of financing through the system of discounting commercial bills in the short-term money market.

COMPARISON WITH OTHER CHOSES IN ACTION

You will recall the illustration in Chapter 9 of the assignment of a legal chose (p 384, *supra*): In consideration of a loan Carb Pty Ltd assigned to Factors Ltd the $30,000 unsecured debt owed to it by Greatparts Ltd.

Prior to enactment of the Conveyancing Act 1919 (NSW) s 12 and corresponding provisions in other states, this assignment would not have conferred on Factors a direct right to sue Greatparts at common law for $30,000 if Greatparts did not pay. Further, Factors would have no recourse to Greatparts in equity if Greatparts paid Carb prior to Factors giving Greatparts notice of the assignment. After the passing of these statutes, Factors still took its assignment under s 12 "subject to the equities", viz subject to (a) any competing assignment which was entitled to priority under the rule in *Dearle v Hall*, and (b) any counterclaim which Greatparts might have been entitled to set up against Carb in mitigation or total extinguishment of the debt. We also noted the potential for a similar defence to that in (b) being raised against finance and credit card companies as assignees of chattel paper or accounts receivable.

It would obviously simplify these assignments and make the underlying obligations more saleable if the financial institution which was being asked to buy them could be assured it was acquiring title free of such competing claims or counterclaims. On the darker side, this raises the worrying spectre of a "get rich quick" purveyor of shoddy goods disappearing immediately after discounting a wad of credit obligations to an associated financier tarred with the same brush which would seek to shelter under the umbrella of negotiability. The public clearly is entitled to some protection from this type of activity and the new Credit Acts in New South Wales and Victoria go some distance towards achieving this end. Conversely, should a financier who is truly independent of the seller of shoddy goods and accepts the assignments in good faith be held responsible? If the law does not facilitate the ready assignability of such commercial obligations, may not the cost of borrowing be increased and in turn passed on to the consumer?

It was as the result of considerations such as these that the fourteenth century merchants devised the concept of instruments which would enjoy the quality of negotiability provided certain conditions were satisfied. These customs evolved in the special mercantile courts, were incorporated into the common law and eventually codified in the Bills of Exchange Act.

In contrast to Factors' position as assignee of a chose in action, where it is the *holder in due course* of a negotiable instrument whereby Greatparts has undertaken to pay Carb, the instrument has the following qualities which are the hall marks of negotiability:

(1) Title can be passed by Carb to Factors simply by delivery of the instrument (when payable to bearer) or by valid indorsement on and delivery of the instrument (when payable to order).

(2) Assignee Factors can in its own name directly sue the debtor Greatparts (or any other party liable on the instrument, such as Carb if it has indorsed the instrument).

(3) Assignee Factors takes free of prior equities provided it acquires the instrument bona fide for value and without notice of any defect in title.

(4) Notice to the original debtor Greatparts is unnecessary to protect Factors' rights.

(5) Consideration for the assignment is presumed.

For further reference see discussion of the rights of a holder in due course, p 444, *infra*; *London Joint Stock Bank v Simmons* [1892] AC 201 and Riley, *Bills of Exchange in Australia,* 3rd ed, 1976, pp 5–8.

Although the term "negotiable" is sometimes used as a synonym for transferable, it should be clear that in the term "negotiable instrument" it connotes a narrower technical meaning. Only those instruments which were recognised as negotiable under the law merchant or have had that quality conferred by statute (eg, promissory notes) qualify.

From the materials which follow it will be apparent that the following enjoy these qualities of negotiability: bills of exchange, cheques (except when crossed "not negotiable"), promissory notes, bank notes and coins in current use, and securities payable to bearer.

SECTION 2: TRANSFER AND NEGOTIATION OF BILLS OF EXCHANGE

Sections 2 and 3 of this chapter will deal with the substantive law and practice regarding bills of exchange and promissory notes. The Bills of Exchange Act 1909 (BEA) is the first and most important source of our current law on bills of exchange, promissory notes and cheques, and a brief introduction to the Act should preface detailed examination of the substantive law.

THE CONSTITUTIONAL POSITION

The Commonwealth Constitution s 51 (xvi) empowers the federal parliament to make laws with respect to "Bills of exchange and promissory notes". BEA was enacted under that power. Since it followed closely the English Act of 1882 drafted by Sir Mackenzie Chalmers, it not only ensured cohesion within Australia but also a high degree of uniformity with other common law countries most of which also copied the English Act. What kind of a code is BEA, does it cover every aspect of negotiable instruments and what is its relationship to state laws?

Stock Motor Ploughs Ltd v Forsyth
High Court of Australia (1932) 48 CLR 128

Starke J: The appellant brought an action in the Supreme Court of New South Wales upon two promissory notes given by the respondent to it. The respondent by his plea alleged that the promissory notes were given as collateral security for two instalments payable under a hire-purchase agreement made between the appellant and himself, and that the action was commenced without leave of the court, contrary to the provisions of the Moratorium Act 1930-1931 of New South Wales. This Act in effect prohibits, without leave of the court mentioned in the Act, calling up or demanding or bringing action to recover hire-purchase money or any instalments thereof (ss 4, 11(1) and 20). The Supreme Court resolved that this was a good plea, and reversed an order striking it out. From this decision an appeal was brought to this court, which also granted leave to appeal.

The decision, it was contended, was wrong for two reasons—one that the provisions of the Moratorium Act did not extend to obligations on collateral securities, the other that the provisions of the Moratorium Act were inconsistent with a law of the Commonwealth, namely, the Bills of Exchange Act 1909-1912, and to the extent of the inconsistency were invalid (Constitution s 109).

In my opinion, the former reason was completely and satisfactorily disposed of in the Supreme Court by Harvey CJ in Eq. The hire-purchase agreement and the promissory notes secured the same hire-purchase money; it was one debt or sum of money secured by two separate or collateral promises, the performance of either of which fulfilled or satisfied the other. In short, the commencement of the action on the note is a demand for payment of the purchase-moneys or instalments due and payable under the hire-purchase agreement.

The latter reason raises a more difficult question, but I agree with the conclusion reached by the Supreme Court that there is no inconsistency between the provisions of the Moratorium Act and the Bills of Exchange Act. It should not be forgotten that the enactment of a moratorium for New South Wales is within the constitutional power of that state. The only question is whether there is an inconsistency, a contrariety, or an opposition between the state law—or the provisions of that law relevant to the case in hand—and the federal law.

Sometimes such inconsistency is found because the federal power has set up a uniform and exclusive rule or code relating to a subject matter within its jurisdiction and no room is left for the operation of state law. But that is not the case here, for the Bills of Exchange Act does not provide a complete and exclusive code in relation to bills of exchange and promissory notes. It is only necessary to refer to s 5 preserving the rules of common law; to the provisions as to capacity and authority of parties (Pt II Div 2) and as to the consideration of the bill (Pt II Div 3); and to the absence of any provisions as to property in bills, as to equitable rights, limitations, and so forth. All these subjects must be governed by the laws of the states within their several territorial limits, for the federal power has not been exercised upon them in relation to bills of exchange and promissory notes.

Is there any inconsistency between the Moratorium Act and any particular provision of the federal Act? The only material provisions are, I think, those contained in ss 43, 62, 94 and 95. The effect of these provisions is that the maker of a promissory note engages that he will pay it according to its tenor, and that the holder may sue on the note in his own name and recover the amount thereof and interest thereon. The sections set forth the obligations arising *ex contractu* on the making of an instrument within the definition of a promissory note (s 89). But the statement and enactment of those obligations does not prescribe, define, or deal with the time within which they may be exercised, or how and in what manner they may be suspended. Such matters rest upon the agreement of the parties or the action of a competent legislature. Where the federal power has not acted, the competent legislatures are necessarily the states, within their territorial limits.

The appeal ought, in my opinion, to be dismissed.

[**Gavan Duffy CJ, Evatt** and **McTiernan JJ** delivered judgments to similar effect.

Dixon J agreed that the provisions of the Moratorium Act applied to the action against the hirer Forsyth on the promissory notes but considered them to be inconsistent with the Bills of Exchange Act and to that extent invalid.]

Appeal dismissed.

The majority opinions in *Stock Motor Ploughs Ltd v Forsyth* were applied in *YZ Finance Co Pty Ltd v Cummings* (1964) 109 CLR 395 where the High Court unanimously held that s 24(1) of the Money-lenders and Infants Loans Act 1942 (NSW) (now Money-lending Act), which prohibits a money-lender who has taken security suing to recover a loan other than by enforcing his security, was not inconsistent with BEA. Similar questions may arise where the holder of a bill of exchange or promissory note given by a hirer or debtor seeks to enforce it in circumstances which contravene hire-purchase or consumer credit legislation. The Credit Act 1981 (Vic) s 124 has taken the most radical approach by prohibiting absolutely the taking of a bill of exchange or promissory note in discharge or security

THE BILLS OF EXCHANGE ACT

The BEA is virtually the bible of negotiable instruments law; students should initially skim through the whole Act to gain an overview of its structure and contents, and refer to it constantly in working with the following materials. The importance of careful attention to every word of the statute was emphasised by Lord Herschell in *Vagliano's* case (p 16, *supra*) and should not be ignored. This basic structure of the Act is:

Part II (ss 8–77A) covers bills of exchange;
Part III (ss 78–88E) applies only to cheques;
Part IV (ss 89–95) applies only to promissory notes.

Cheques are a species of bill of exchange so that most of the general provisions of Pt II *also apply* to cheques. Since cheques involve special relationships between banker, customer and payee and the special provisions of Pt III, they are covered separately in the next chapter. In England and New Zealand, Cheques Acts introduced further specific provisions for cheques and similar legislation has been recommended in Australia: see Chapter 11.

Subject to minor modifications, the general provisions of the Act relating to bills of exchange apply equally to promissory notes. Cases involving one type of negotiable instrument are for many purposes equally applicable to others and a number of the cases extracted involve promissory notes: eg, *Stock Motor Ploughs Ltd v Forsyth*, p 425, *supra*; *Arab Bank Ltd v Ross*, p 444, *infra*; *Stenning v Radio & Domestic Finance Ltd*, p 447, *infra*; *Douglas v Tiernan*, p 449, *infra*; *Automobile Finance Co of Australia Ltd v Law*, p 451, *infra*. For further brief comments on promissory notes see p 454, *infra*.

WHAT IS A BILL OF EXCHANGE?

The Bills of Exchange Act s 8 provides the following exclusive definition:

8(1) A bill of exchange is an unconditional order in writing addressed by one person to another, signed by the person giving it, requiring the person to whom it is addressed to pay on demand, or at a fixed or determinable future time, a sum certain in money to or to the order of a specified person, or to bearer.

Unless each element is satisfied, the instrument will not qualify as a bill or attract the provisions of the Act. Examine the following specimens carefully.

(A) Bill of exchange payable on demand prior to acceptance:

$3000	Duty Stamp	Carb House Gcarway Sydney 2 April 1984
On demand pay Mitzi Co or order the sum of Three Thousand dollars value received		
To Easy Finance George Street, Sydney		Carb Pty Ltd *J. Handy* Director

(B) Time bill of exchange after acceptance:

Front

| Accepted. Payable at Suburban Bank Ryde Bestcars Ltd *Will M. Buy* 15 February 1984 | $5000 Three months after sight pay Carb Pty Ltd or order the sum of Five Thousand dollars value received

To Bestcars Ltd
North Road
Ryde | Duty Stamp | Motorway Wollongong 1 February 1984

Greatparts Ltd
W. Lever.
General Manager |

Back (with two indorsements)

Pay Factors Ltd or order
  Carb Pty Ltd
  J. Handy

Pay Commercial Bank or order
  Factors Ltd
  B. W. K. Dett.

(C) Contrast the structure of an ordinary cheque:

| Duty Stamp | NOT NEGOTIABLE | COUNTRY BANK WESTERN BRANCH | 1 June 1984 |

Pay Carb Pty Ltd   or bearer
the sum of Eight hundred dollars $800.00.

Bourke Motors
Dusty String.

(D) and promissory note:

No. **44**   Duty Stamp   Due **1 June, 1984**

$ **1,000-00**   **1 March, 1984**

~~On demand~~ / .... **Three** .... Months after date

Promise to pay **Squeeze**

or order the sum of **One thousand dollars**

(**$1,000-00**)   Value received

Payable at **Sydney Bank, Head Office, Sydney**   *Jim Handy.*

428

Check whether each has all the necessary characteristics of a bill of exchange. What differences do you notice between the structure of the respective documents? Is the promissory note a bill of exchange, and if not, why not? What is meant by an unconditional order?

Rosenhain and Another v Commonwealth Bank of Australia
High Court of Australia (1922) 30 CLR 46

Knox CJ, **Gavan Duffy** and **Starke JJ**: The Commonwealth Bank brought an action against the appellants upon a document, drawn by Caravel Co Inc in New York upon the appellants Rosenhain & Co in Melbourne, substantially in the following terms: "Documents against acceptance—New York, 30 December 1920—Sixty days after sight ... pay to the order of Caravel Co Inc one thousand four hundred and seventy-one pounds ten shillings and sevenpence (sterling), value received, with interest at the rate of 8 per cent per annum until arrival of payment in London to cover, and charge same to account of—Caravel Co Inc, Henry Bront, Asst Treasurer—To Rosenhain & Co, 563 Bourke Street, Melbourne, Australia—Thru London Joint City and Midland Bank." The words "Documents against acceptance" were typewritten at the top of the document outside a marginal black line which surrounded the other writing upon it. The document was indorsed in blank by the Caravel Co Inc, and ultimately by various indorsements to the Commonwealth Bank. The document was presented to Rosenhain & Co, who wrote across its face "Sighted 28/2/21 and accepted payable at the Royal Bank of Australia Ltd Melbourne as £1471 10s 7d plus interest at 8 per cent per annum." It was at a later date presented for payment, but was not paid. The Bank subsequently, on 17 October 1921, issued its writ under the Instruments Act, as already mentioned, and claimed against the appellants £1565 15s 7d as the indorsee of a bill of exchange ... An appearance was entered by the defendants in the action without prejudice to an application on their part to set aside the writ and the service thereof, upon the ground that the action commenced by the writ was not an action upon a bill of exchange within the meaning of the Instruments Act. Schutt J heard the motion but dismissed it; and from this dismissal an appeal has been brought, by leave, to this court.

The matter which requires decision is of no little commercial importance for it turns upon the question whether the document on which the bank founds its claim is or is not a bill of exchange. If it is, the bank must, it is admitted, succeed; if it is not, the bank cannot succeed, and the appellants will be in a position to force an investigation of the accounts and cross-claims between them and the Caravel Co Inc.

Now, the term "bill of exchange" is defined, both in the Instruments Act and in the Bills of Exchange Act 1909 in the same words as are contained in the Bills of Exchange Act 1882 of Great Britain: "A bill of exchange is an unconditional order in writing addressed by one person to another signed by the person giving it requiring the person to whom it is addressed to pay on demand or at a fixed or determinable future time *a sum certain in money* to or to the order of a specified person or to bearer." "The sum payable by a bill is a sum certain ... although it is required to be paid ... with interest": see Instruments Act 1915 (Vic) ss 4, 10: Bills of Exchange Act 1909 ss 8, 14.

The distinction between interest recoverable under the contract and as part of the debt and interest recoverable as damages must be borne in mind. The Bills of Exchange Acts themselves recognise the distinction: see Instruments Act (Vic) s 10; Bills of Exchange Act ss 14 (3), 62. Clearly the interest dealt with in s 10 of the Instruments Act and in s 14 of the Bills of Exchange Act is that required by the contract to be paid. Clearly also these sections are dealing with the certainty of the sum payable. So far as that sum is concerned, certainty is not destroyed because a definite rate of interest is not specified. The same conclusion seems to have been reached before the Act (see *Warrington v Early* (1853) 2 El & Bl 763), possibly because the promise implied by the law was to pay a reasonable rate of interest, understood, in England at all events, from usage or the custom of merchants, or because of the usury laws or the practice of the Courts, as £5 per centum: see *Byles on Bills*, 15th ed, p 444; *Chalmers on Bills of Exchange*, 8th ed, p 30; *Halsbury's Laws of England*, Vol II, p 468.

The "sum certain" must, however, if the document is to constitute a bill of exchange, be payable on demand, or at a fixed or determinable future time. "Certainty," as Ashhurst J said in *Carlos v Fancourt* (1794) 5 TR 482 at 486, "is a great object in commercial instruments;

and unless they carry their own validity on the face of them, they are not negotiable". Now, the document under consideration did not fix a "determinable future time" for payment of the sums mentioned therein, but a fixed time, namely, "sixty days after sight". Consequently the sum must be certain at this fixed time if it is to conform to the provisions of the Bills of Exchange Acts. But clearly the sum was not certain on that date, nor could it be made certain from anything appearing on the face of the document; for interest was to run on from the time fixed for payment, namely, "sixty days after sight" "until arrival of payment in London," and it was quite uncertain, both on the face of the document and in fact, when this event would happen, or indeed whether it would happen at all.

If it be suggested that the document was payable "at a determinable future time", the uncertain contingency on which it became payable can be demonstrated from decided cases. Thus a document expressed to be payable "thirty days after the arrival of the ship Paragon at Calcutta" or "ninety days after sight or when realised" could not be supported as a bill of exchange, for it is quite indefinite "when these uncertain events would probably be reduced to a certainty": *Palmer v Pratt* (1824) 2 Bing 185; *Alexander v Thomas* (1851) 16 QB 333.

Another contention made for the appellants was that the document sued upon was not an unconditional order to pay money because it was conditional upon documents being handed over on acceptance. It is not necessary, having regard to what has been said, to determine what is the legal effect of the words "documents against acceptance" at the top of the document sued upon, and perhaps all the surrounding facts are not available for a proper determination of the question. They may be a direction to the banker who presents the document or a direction to or part of the terms of the transaction with Rosenhain & Co. But, whatever their effect may be, "it does not follow, because the drawee is not bound to accept unless a condition is fulfilled, that, when he has accepted his transferable or negotiable promise to pay is not unconditional. It turns on the terms of his promise to pay": *Guaranty Trust Co of New York v Hannay & Co* [1918] 2 KB at 666, per Scrutton LJ. And with the citation of this valuable opinion we may leave the point for further consideration in a case where it actually falls for decision ...

Appeal allowed.

PARTIES TO A BILL OF EXCHANGE

It is important to understand the names given to the parties to a bill and the economic relationship which they bear to each other: only then will the legal rules governing transfer, negotiation, and the liability of the parties make sense for you.

In specimen A on p 427, it is assumed that Carb intended to fulfil an obligation to pay Mitzi $3000, and requested Easy Finance to accept the liability to pay Mitzi by advancing $3000 on Carb's behalf. Easy Finance is not liable on the bill until it accepts it.

In specimen B, it is assumed that Bestcars was indebted to Greatparts in the amount of $5000, and that Greatparts is likewise indebted to Carb for a similar amount. Greatparts could have assigned Bestcars' debt (a chose in action) to Carb. Instead Greatparts (the creditor) drew the bill of exchange on Bestcars (which is Greatparts' debtor) payable to Carb (Greatparts' creditor). In technical jargon the *drawer* Greatparts drew a time bill on the *drawee* Bestcars in favour of the *payee* Carb. In practice Greatparts would prepare the bill and send it to Bestcars for acceptance. When Bestcars wrote its acceptance across the bill on 15 February, it also became the *acceptor* and *primarily liable* to pay the bill to the payee Carb, or to whomsoever Carb may transfer the bill called the *holder*.

After signing its acceptance on the bill Bestcars would send it back to Greatparts who would forward it to Carb. By the first indorsement on the back of the bill the *indorser* Carb has transferred its rights to the bill to the *indorsee* Factors (probably under a discounting arrangement so that Carb can obtain immediate payment). The *second indorser* Factors has likewise indorsed the bill to the *second indorsee* Commercial Bank, either by way of assignment or possibly for collection and crediting to Factors' account at Commercial Bank. Bestcars will be required to pay

$5000 to the *holder* Commercial Bank on maturity of the bill three months after acceptance, namely on 15 May or within three days of grace thereafter.

In specimen C, note that with a cheque, the *drawer* Bourke Motors draws on the *drawee* Country Bank, at which Bourke Motors has a current account, but the bank does not accept the cheque and accordingly never becomes obligated to the payee or holder, as did the drawee Bestcars when it accepted the bill of exchange in specimen B. Therefore, the drawer remains the party primarily liable on the cheque although it will have a right to insist that its bank pay the cheque provided there are sufficient funds to the credit of its account. In specimen D, Jim Handy, as the *maker* of the promissory note, is the party primarily liable to pay the *payee* Squeeze.

In each specimen, the instrument can be negotiated by the payee or subsequent holder either by indorsement and delivery (in the case of the *order* bills) or by simple delivery (where they are payable to *bearer*).

One of the fundamental concepts in BEA is that of a holder defined in s 4 as:
(a) payee of a bill or note in possession of it; or
(b) the indorsee (ie, under a valid—not a forged or unauthorised indorsement) who is in possession of it; or
(c) the bearer, who is defined as the person in possession of a bill or note which is payable to bearer.

The important related definitions of holder for value and holder in due course and their respective rights are considered on pp 441-2, *infra*.

ACCEPTANCE

We noted above that Bestcars accepted Greatparts' bill by signing its name on the bill and returning it to Greatparts. This is in accord with s 4 which defines acceptance as "an acceptance completed by delivery or notification". Acceptance is the signification by the drawee of his assent to the order of the drawer (s 22) and must be written on the bill and completed by delivery or notification (s 4). An acceptance may be general (ie, unqualified) or may be qualified, for example, as to the prior fulfilment of condition, or as to time or place of payment (s 24). The acceptance must clearly indicate a promise to pay the bill: see generally *Smith v Commercial Banking Co of Sydney Ltd* (1910) 11 CLR 667.

NEGOTIATION OF A BILL

BEA s 36 provides:

36(1) A bill is negotiated when it is transferred from one person to another in such a manner as to constitute the transferee the holder of the bill.

In this context, negotiation means transfer and hence it is necessary to ascertain what bills (and cheques) are transferable and the method of transfer. Section 13 distinguishes between:

(1) Non-transferable bills—ie, bills which prohibit transfer. Note that the reference in s 13(1) to "not negotiable" means in this context not transferable.
Example: Pay Taxation Department only.
(2) Transferable bills which consist of:
(a) bearer bills—ie, originally payable to bearer, on which the only or last indorsement is in blank: s 13(3). These are transferable simply by delivery: s 36(2).
Examples: Pay J Handy or bearer; or
           Pay J Handy or order
Indorsement: (signed) J Handy.
(b) order bills—ie, payable to order, or to a particular person without words prohibiting transfer: ss 13(4) and (5). These are transferable by the holder's indorsement and delivery: s 36(3).

Examples: Pay J Handy or order;
Pay to the order of J Handy; or
Pay J Handy.

The distinction between transferability as illustrated above, and negotiability, in the sense of the quality of passing a better title than the transferor had, is illustrated by the fact that a transferable cheque payable to bearer or to order can be crossed "not negotiable": see s 87 and pp 504-5, *infra*.

INDORSEMENTS

Indorsement means the transfer of a bill, cheque or promissory note by the transferor (indorser) signing his name on it and delivering it to the indorsee. Further details are specified in s 37. We have noted that indorsement is necessary for the transfer of an order bill or note but is not required for one payable to bearer. An indorsement will normally fulfil a second function, namely, to make the indorser liable on the instrument except in the case of indorsement "without recourse". Sometimes a person not otherwise a party to or liable on a bill may agree to guarantee payment by indorsing it as an accommodation party to assist another party to the bill. For example, in specimen B, Factors might request Mary Handy to add her indorsement in her personal capacity to that of Carb Pty Ltd.

Other types of indorsements include:

(1) Indorsement in blank, which specifies no indorsee, and converts an order bill to one payable to bearer: s 39(1).

(2) Special indorsement, which specifies the indorsee, eg, Pay J Handy, or Pay J Handy or order: s 39(2).

(3) Restrictive indorsement, which restricts further transfer, eg, Pay J Handy only; or merely authorises another to deal with the bill on behalf of the indorser, eg, Pay Commercial Bank for collection for account of Factors Ltd: ss 40, 41.

(4) Sans Recours or "without recourse" indorsement, which effectively transfers an order bill but negatives the liability of the indorser on the bill, eg, Carb might hand its solicitor a cheque for payment of stamp duty but payable to "AD Visor or order", which the solicitor might indorse: Pay Stamp Commissioner or order, sans recours (signed) AD Visor: see s 21.

EFFECT OF FORGED OR UNAUTHORISED SIGNATURES

Much of the ligitation regarding negotiable instruments arises out of an instrument having been signed without capacity, without authority or by simple forgery. As to lack of capacity or general authority, see BEA ss 27, 30 and 31. Fundamental to an understanding of negotiation of, and liability under, a bill, cheque or note are BEA ss 28 and 29.

An analysis of these and related sections indicates that a forged or unauthorised signature cannot:

(a) make liable the person whose signature it purports to be (s 28); or
(b) pass any rights to the bill to any party taking it through the forged/unauthorised signature or subsequent thereto; or
(c) convert an order bill into a bearer bill.

However, s 29 recognises three types of exceptions:

(1) Where the person whose signature has been written without authority adopts or ratifies it as his own.

(2) Where the person against whom it is sought to enforce the bill is precluded from setting up the forgery or lack of authority: see *Greenwood v Martins Bank Ltd* [1933] AC 51, below.

(3) Where s 29 is qualified by another section of the Act. There are a number of relevant sections: ss 12(3), 59(b)(i), 60(2)(b) and 65 which will be dealt with below,

Ratification and Estoppel

What is the difference between ratification and estoppel? Can a forgery be ratified? In what circumstances will a person be estopped from setting up a forgery?

Greenwood v Martins Bank Ltd
House of Lords [1933] AC 51

Lord Tomlin: My Lords, on 6 March 1926, the appellant, who was carrying on a dairyman's business at Blackpool, opened with the respondents at their branch in Clifton Street, Blackpool, a joint account in the name of himself and his wife. It was arranged with the respondents that cheques on this account should bear the signatures both of the appellant and of his wife.

On 8 November 1928, the appellant opened a further banking account in his own name at the same branch of the respondents' bank. Cheques upon this account were to bear the signature of the appellant alone.

The passbooks and chequebooks in respect of these accounts were kept by the appellant's wife, who gave her husband a cheque from the chequebook when he asked for it.

In October 1929, the appellant asked his wife to bring him a cheque, saying that he wanted to draw £20 from his separate account with the respondents, whereupon the appellant's wife informed the appellant that there was no money in the bank and told him that she had used the money to help her sister in legal proceedings relating to a house and had drawn it out. The appellant thereupon asked her who had forged his name and she would not tell him. She begged the appellant not to inform the respondents of the forgeries until her sister's case was over. In the hope of a favourable result to the sister's action and for his wife's sake the appellant said nothing to the respondents.

On 5 June 1930, the appellant discovered that there were no legal proceedings instituted by his wife's sister and that his wife had deceived him. Thereupon the appellant informed his wife that he would go at once to the respondents. He returned to the house that evening without having gone to the bank. On his return his wife shot herself.

After his wife's death the appellant ascertained that he had been debited by the respondents in his separate account with the sum of £410 6s in respect of forged cheques.

At this time the appellant was not aware that anything irregular had occurred in connection with the joint account of himself and his wife.

On 19 August 1930, the appellant began an action against the respondents in the King's Bench Division, Preston District, for a declaration that he was entitled to be credited by the respondents with the sum of £410 6s with which he alleged they had wrongfully debited him.

In their defence the respondents denied forgeries and alternatively pleaded that they were caused to pay the money by reason of the appellant's own negligence and, further that he was estopped from saying that the respondents paid the money wrongfully or without his authority or that the signatures on the cheques were placed there without his authority. At the trial ratification, adoption and estoppel were all relied upon by the respondents.

The action was tried at the Manchester Assizes on 12 May 1931, before Mr Commissioner du Parcq KC (now du Parcq J), and in the course of the trial the following facts with regard to the separate account were admitted or proved, namely:

(1) Between 14 November 1928, and 20 October 1929, the appellant's wife, Emma Greenwood, drew 44 "order" cheques upon the appellant's separate banking account and forged the name of the appellant as drawer of the said cheques. The value in the agregate of such cheques was the sum of £410 6s. Forty-two of such cheques were expressed to be in favour of a non-existent person, Emily Greenwood, and in the remaining two of them, dated respectively 14 January 1929, and 16 May 1929, the name of the payee inserted was "Emma Greenwood". The cheques purported to be endorsed by the drawees, but by whom the endorsements were made was not proved.

(2) The forged cheques were presented for payment, and through the negligence of the respondents' officials in failing to detect that the signatures thereon were not genuine, were

honoured and paid. The respondents debited the appellant's account with sums amounting in all to £410 6s in respect of such cheques.

(3) Some of the cheques were presented for payment by the appellant's wife in person and others by some other woman who was not definitely identified. It did not appear how many or which of the cheques were presented by the appellant's wife.

(4) The appellant did not give the respondents any information in regard to the matter until after his wife's death, and until after her death the respondents remained in ignorance of the forgeries. It further appeared in the course of the proceedings and the appellant then for the first time became aware that there had been grave irregularities in connection with the joint account and that his wife had drawn upon that account by eleven cheques to which she had forged his name, and that she had closed the account by drawing out the balance with a cheque signed by herself alone and, notwithstanding the absence of the appellant's signature, honoured by the respondents ...

Now it may be said at once that there can be no question of ratification or of adoption in this case. The necessary elements for ratification were not present, and adoption as understood in English law requires valuable consideration, which is not even suggested here.

The sole question is whether in the circumstances of this case the respondents are entitled to set up an estoppel.

The essential factors giving rise to an estoppel are I think:

(1) A representation or conduct amounting to a representation intended to induce a course of conduct on the part of the person to whom the representation is made.

(2) An act or omission resulting from the representation, whether actual or by conduct, by the person to whom the representation is made.

(3) Detriment to such person as a consequence of the act or omission.

Mere silence cannot amount to a representation, but when there is a duty to disclose deliberate silence may become significant and amount to a representation.

The existence of a duty on the part of the customer of a bank to disclose to the bank his knowledge of such a forgery as the one in question in this case was rightly admitted.

The respondents' case is that the duty ought to have been discharged by the appellant immediately upon his discovery in October 1929, and that if it had been then discharged they could have sued the appellant's wife in tort and the appellant himself would have been responsible for his wife's tort. They claim that his silence until after his wife's death amounted in these circumstances to a representation that the cheques were not forgeries and deprived the respondents of their remedy.

The appellant, on his part, says: (1) that there was no representation express or implied; (2) that the respondents' omission to sue and any resulting loss was the consequence of their own initial negligence and was not due at any rate exclusively to the appellant's omission; and (3) that there was in fact no loss or detriment, because the only remedy of the respondents against the appellant's wife would have been in contract and not in tort, and because such a remedy would have been fruitless against the wife and the appellant would not have been responsible.

Now the evidence of the respondents' cashier, which was accepted by the learned commissioner, was that the appellant after his wife's death said to the respondents' officials "that he had known about it since last October, that he did not wish to cause any bother and he did not want to give his wife away".

The appellant's silence, therefore, was deliberate and intended to produce the effect which it in fact produced—namely, the leaving of the respondents in ignorance of the true facts so that no action might be taken by them against the appellant's wife. The deliberate abstention from speaking in those circumstances seems to me to amount to a representation to the respondents that the forged cheques were in fact in order, and assuming that detriment to the respondents followed there were, it seems to me, present all the elements essential to estoppel. Further, I do not think that is is any answer to say that if the respondents had not been negligent initially the detriment would not have occurred. The course of conduct relied upon as founding the estoppel was adopted in order to leave the respondents in the condition of ignorance in which the appellant knew they were. It was the duty of the appellant to remove that condition however caused. It is the existence of this duty, coupled with the appellant's deliberate intention to maintain the respondents in their condition of ignorance, that gives its significance to the appellant's silence. What difference can it make that the condition of ignorance was primarily induced by the respondents' own negligence? In my judgment it can make none. For the purposes of the estoppel, which is a procedural matter, the cause of the ignorance is an irrelevant consideration.

[His Lordship then held that the respondent bank had suffered loss or detriment as the result of the plaintiff's failure to disclose the forgeries which prevented the bank suing the plaintiff or his wife in tort prior to her death when its action against the plaintiff for the wife's tort abated. He therefore held that the appeal failed. The other members of the House of Lords concurred in the judgment of Lord Tomlin.]

Order of the Court of Appeal affirmed and appeal dismissed.

STATUTORY QUALIFICATIONS OF s 29

BEA s 12 provides:

12(1) Where a bill is not payable to bearer, the payee must be named or otherwise indicated with reasonable certainty.

(2) . . .

(3) Where the payee is a fictitious or non-existing person, the bill may be treated as payable to bearer.

Since a bearer bill can be negotiated without indorsement, a forged or unauthorised indorsement is irrelevant to the passing of rights to the bill, as it is with a bearer bill. What is the meaning of "fictitious or non-existing person" in s 12(3), and whose intention is to be examined in answering this question?

In *Bank of England v Vagliano Bros* [1891] AC 107, the House of Lords considered a case in which a fraudulent clerk employed by Vagliano Bros concocted purported bills of exchange on which he forged the signature of a foreign correspondent Vucina who had previously drawn bills on Vagliano in the course of trade. The clerk inserted the name "Petridi & Co or order" as payee and procured the genuine acceptance of Vagliano of the forged "bills". After forging the indorsement of Petridi & Co, he cashed the bills with the Bank of England which was acting as Vagliano's banker and debited its account. When sued by Vagliano, the bank's defence was that the payee was fictitious and the bills could therefore be treated as payable to bearer. A majority of the House of Lords held that it was immaterial whether Vagliano as the acceptors of the bill knew that Petridi was an existing firm. The bills were treated as payable to bearer because the drawer (in this case the fraudulent clerk) never intended Petridi & Co to have any right to the bills and inserted the payee's name by way of pretence only. The decision was followed in *Clutton v Attenborough & Son* [1897] AC 90.

Vinden v Hughes
King's Bench Division [1905] 1 KB 795

[The plaintiffs Vinden & Rogers employed a clerk Cross whose regular duty was to fill up cheques payable to the order of the plaintiffs' customers, have them signed by the plaintiffs and post them to the customers. Between 1901 and 1903 Cross filled up 27 cheques to the order of various known customers, had them signed by the plaintiffs, misappropriated them, forged the payees' indorsements and cashed them with the defendant Hughes, a local shopkeeper, who took the cheques in good faith.]

Warrington J: The question I have to decide in this case is, what is the true construction of s 7, sub-s 3, of the Bills of Exchange Act 1882 (Aust BEA s 12(3)), applied to the facts of this particular case; that is to say, in other words, I have to decide whether in the case before me the payees of certain cheques were fictitious or non-existing persons within the meaning of that 3rd sub-section.

[The learned judge shortly stated the facts as above and continued:]

On these facts I have now to decide whether the defendant Hughes is liable for the moneys which he thus paid to Cross . . .

Is the person whose name was inserted in each of these cheques by Cross a "fictitious" person within the meaning of the Bills of Exchange Act? I thought at one time the case was covered by the second branch of the judgments in *Bank of England v Vagliano Brothers* [1891]

AC 107. I will come back to that presently, merely saying in passing that on further consideration I do not think those judgments do cover this case. Independently of authority, what am I to say is meant by "fictitious"? It seems to me this at all events must be true. It cannot be fictitious in the abstract. You must look at the circumstances of the particular case, and say whether the name of the person inserted in the bill is the name of a fictitious person having regard to all those circumstances.

In this case let us consider what was the position of Mr Vinden when he signed these cheques. It was not a fiction to him then. It was intended to be, and was to him at that moment, a perfectly real transaction. He believed that he owed the sum of money represented by the cheque to the person whose name appeared upon it, and he signed the cheque in that belief. It was only when he discovered that he had been imposed upon by his clerk that there was, I will not say a fiction, but that there was anything that was not real and in accordance with his intention. I think I am entitled to say that the fraud perpetrated upon him has really nothing to do with the construction of the Act of parliament, and that what one has to look at (and the only thing one has to look at for the purpose of construing that Act) is the state of things at the time the cheque was drawn. At the time the cheque was drawn he intended to pay (I will take the first one on the list) "T H Graves" the sum of £29. T H Graves, by the way, is not a non-existent person. I should have said on that that T H Graves is not a "fictitious" person.

[His Honour then distinguished *Clutton v Attenborough & Sons* [1897] AC 90 on the grounds that it dealt with a non-existent person.]

Now does *Bank of England v Vagliano Brothers* carry it any further, or rather, is that case any authority on the particular question which I have to decide? In *Bank of England v Vagliano Brothers* the facts were very special and very peculiar; the document with which the House of Lords had to deal was a document purporting to be drawn by a drawer, really accepted by an acceptor, and in favour of a real payee — that is to say, not a non-existing payee. I say advisedly purporting to be drawn by a drawer, because it was not drawn at all, the name of the drawer being forged. The two learned Lords whose judgments have been most relied upon in this case were Lord Halsbury and Lord Herschell. I think it is enough for me to refer to what Lord Herschell says on the question raised in the present case as to the meaning of the word "fictitious". One must bear this in mind — that in the case with which he had to deal, there being no drawer in fact, the use of a name as payee was a mere fiction, although the payee actually existed. I think all the expressions which have been referred to in his judgment in support of the defendant's case here are explained by that fact, and I think he is not dealing with the case of the drawer of the document intending to issue the document, and intending to issue it with the name of the particular payee upon it, that payee not being non-existent. On p 152 he says this, and this is a passage which was relied upon as summing up what he means: "Do the words, 'where the payee is a fictitious person', apply only where the payee named never had a real existence? I take it to be clear that by the word 'payee' must be understood the payee named on the face of the bill; for of course by the hypothesis there is no intention that payment should be made to any such person. Where, then, the payee named is so named by way of pretence only, without the intention that he shall be the person to receive payment, is it doing violence to language to say that the payee is a fictitious person? I think not. I do not think that the word 'fictitious' is exclusively used to qualify that which has no real existence. When we speak of a fictitious entry in a book of accounts, we do not mean that the entry has no real existence, but only that it purports to be that which it is not — that it is an entry made for the purpose of pretending that the transaction took place which is represented by it." Then again, later on, he says: "It seems to me, then, that where the name inserted as that of the payee is so inserted by way of pretence only, it may, without impropriety, be said that the payee is feigned or pretended, or, in other words, a fictitious person." Now those passages which I have read, which were the passages mainly relied upon by the defendant, would be satisfied entirely by the case in which the drawer drawing the cheque puts into it the name of the person who exists, but whose name is inserted by mere pretence. In the present case let us test it. Take those words of Lord Herschell. Did Mr Vinden draw this cheque in favour of T H Graves and the others as a mere pretence? It is impossible to come to that conclusion on the facts of this case. It was not a mere pretence at the time he drew it. He had every reason to believe, and he did believe, that those cheques were being drawn in the ordinary course of business for the purpose of the money being paid to the persons whose names appeared on the face of those cheques. That seems to me really to answer the defendant's case. I confess that I was much impressed by those passages in Lord Herschell's judgment and in Lord Halsbury's judgment; but when you come to see what it is they are directing their minds to, I think one appreciates that they are not really expressions which govern, or were intended in any way whatever to govern, such a case as that which I have now before me.

I come to the conclusion, therefore, that ... the payees in these cases are not fictitious or non-existing persons; that the bills, therefore, cannot be treated as payable to bearer; that the forged indorsement, therefore, did not entitle the defendant to receive payment of the amounts of the cheques; and that accordingly he is liable to the plaintiffs for the loss that has been sustained ...

The result will be that there will be judgment for the plaintiffs for the amount claimed, less the £20 paid into court, and costs.

The present state of the authorities has been summarised as follows:

Byles: Bills of Exchange
24th ed, 1979, p 27

The result of the cases appears to be that in determining whether a payee is fictitious or not, the intention of the drawer of the bill is decisive.[1] If he inserted the name as a mere pretence, to give colour to the instrument, the payee is fictitious, notwithstanding that he in fact exists[2]; he is just as much a fictitious person as Richard I in Ivanhoe. If, on the other hand, the drawer intended his named payee to receive his money the payee is not fictitious, notwithstanding the fact that the drawer was deceived into drawing the instrument by a third person who intended to misappropriate the instrument, and to further his intention fraudulently represented to the drawer, contrary to the fact, that the payee was entitled to the sum specified in the instrument. Though the transaction is in fact fictitious, the drawer believes it to be real.[3] The drawer is intending to write history, not romance.

In the case of a non-existing person the intention of the drawer is immaterial. If the payee is in fact not a real person, the subsection applies even though the drawer believed him to be a real person and intended him to receive payment under the instrument.[4]

The liabilities of the acceptor, drawer and indorsers of a bill are specified in ss 59 and 60 of the Act. These sections do not contradict s 28 by making a person liable on a bill where he has not signed it, but preclude another party (acceptor/indorser) from pleading the absence or lack of genuineness of prior parties' signatures as a means of avoiding the acceptor's or indorser's own liability. Each section operates only in favour of a holder in due course, which raises a problem of circularity since a subsequent party cannot strictly qualify as a holder in due course unless he is a holder and the document is a bill of exchange. The very absence or invalidity of prior signatures on the bill may prevent the document being a bill of exchange (s 8) and would preclude him qualifying as a holder: s 29. Thus, ss 59(b)(i) and 60(2)(b) require for their application the assumption of the very facts which they are intended to establish. How can the "holder" pull himself up by his own bootstraps? In *Vagliano's case*, Lord Halsbury LC said ([1891] AC 107 at 116, 120):

---

[1] It has been held in America that the intent of the drawer of a cheque in inserting the name of a payee is the sole test of whether the payee is a fictitious person: *Snyder v Corn Exchange Nat Bank* (1908) 221 Penn Rep 599 at 606, where the decision in the *Vagliano* case is referred to; and the later cases cited in Beutel's *Brannan*, 7th ed, 1948, p 324. Section 3-111 of the Uniform Commercial Code sets out what instruments are payable to bearer; the section contains no reference to fictitious payees, which is now in s 3-405 dealing with indorsements by impostors.

[2] *Bank of England v Vagliano* [1891] AC 107; see also *Edinburgh Ballarat Gold Quartz Mine Co v Sydney* (1891) 7 TLR 656.

[3] *North and South Wales Bank v Macbeth* [1908] AC 137.

[4] *Clutton v Attenborough* [1897] AC 90.

I have designedly avoided calling these documents bills of exchange. They were nothing of the sort. But if they got into the hands of an innocent owner for value without notice, Vagliano would undoubtedly have been responsible upon them; for he had given them a genuineness as against himself by accepting them ...

For reasons I have already given, it seems to me difficult to treat them as bills of exchange at all; but as against the person now insisting on their possessing the quality of such instruments, and remembering that it was his act by which they were put into circulation in that character, it does not seem unreasonable that, applying the doctrine of estoppel to him, one may consider whether as against him they may not possess qualities which, in their inception, they did not possess.

Riley suggests (p 142) that the circularity problem can be resolved because the estoppel under s 60(2)(b) "does not constitute a real exception to the general rule that a person in possession of a bill under a forged endorsement cannot be a holder in due course. That term is used here to indicate that if a person takes the bill under the conditions prescribed by s 34 he has a right of recourse by estoppel against one who endorsed after the forged endorsement; but it does not mean that payment to him by the drawee or acceptor would be a valid discharge of the bill" under s 64: see Section 3, *infra*, re discharge.

QUESTIONS

Question 1

(1) Discuss the development and characteristics of modern negotiable instruments. Compare them to other methods of assigning property rights.

(2) "The Bills of Exchange Act is a comprehensive and exclusive code covering all aspects of negotiable instruments." Discuss this broad proposition indicating any necessary qualifications.

Question 2

Which of the following documents qualify as bills of exchange? Give your reasons. What is the significance of establishing that an instrument is a bill of exchange?

(a)

I, Jim Handy owe you Silas Squeeze One thousand dollars ($1000.00) which is payable on 7 October 1985.

Jim Handy

(b)

WITHDRAWAL FORM   CITY SAVINGS BANK
                                  HEAD OFFICE

Please pay One hundred and fifty dollars $150.00
receipt whereof is hereby acknowledged

J. Handy

Account No: 123-4567   Depositor's Signature

Note: Depositor's passbook must accompany withdrawal form.

Financing Through Negotiable Instruments, etc

(c)

```
AUSTRALIAN DOLLAR TRAVELLERS CHEQUE          No JH 78-123-789
J. Handy                          Perisher Valley NSW 1 July 1984
(Signature)

              FIRST CITY BANK OF AUSTRALIA

      Pay to the order of   The Bellevue Motel
                               (Payee)
   when countersigned below by the person whose signature appears above
   the sum of
   ONE HUNDRED DOLLARS in Australian Currency (A $100) or equivalent
   in local currency at current buying rate for bankers' cheques in Sydney

                                          R. E. Liabell

      (countersignature)                  General Manager
                                          First City Bank of Australia
                                          Sydney, NSW
```

(d)

```
Duty
Stamp              SUBURBAN BANK LIMITED
                         Ryde, NSW
                                                     1 May 1984

Pay Carb Pty Ltd                                  or bearer
The sum of Two thousand dollars      $2000.00

                                  Suburban Bank Limited
                                  Bill Dollar       Manager
                                  Will Balance     Accountant
```

Question 3

What type of instrument is illustrated below? In each case indicate (a) the correct role of each party (eg drawer, acceptor, etc) and (b) what are the requirements for a valid negotiation of the instrument?

(1)

```
Duty
Stamp              CITY BANK                     2 April 1984


         Pay Cash or bearer                      $100.00
         The sum of One hundred dollars


                                          Carb Pty Ltd
                                          J. Handy
                                          Director
```

(2) Same as (1) except substitute "order" for "bearer"
(3)

$3000   Duty Stamp   Carb House
Gearway
Sydney
2 April 1984

Three months after sight pay to the order of Widg Co the sum of Three thousand dollars value received.

To Financiers Ltd
O'Connell Street
Sydney

Carb Pty Ltd
J. Handy
Director

---

(4) Same as (3) except delete "to the order of".
(5) Same as (4) except add words "not negotiable" immediately after "Widg Co".

SECTION 3: RIGHTS AND LIABILITIES OF PARTIES AND DISCHARGE

For the purposes of this section we shall use the bill of exchange in specimen B, p 428, *supra*, as a basic illustration. It is most important to distinguish between three types of liability in relation to such bills:

(1) The liability which Greatparts, Bestcars and Carb undertook when they became parties to the bill by signing it, in their respective capacities of drawer, acceptor and indorser. This section is primarily concerned with this kind of liability and the manner in which that liability is discharged.

(2) The liability of a person who converts a bill of exchange by misappropriating it or the proceeds thereof. Thus, if a rogue Sly steals the bill from Factors, he can never acquire a good title to it, and is liable to the true owner of the instrument, Factors, in an action for conversion in the same way as if he had stolen a motor car. Similarly, if Sly negotiates the bill to a third party Beer, he having taken through a thief can likewise be sued by the owner Factors in conversion unless:

(a) he qualifies as a holder in due course; or
(b) the bill has been discharged; or
(c) where the third party is a bank, it can establish one of the statutory defences in ss 65, 86, 88B or 88D, which will be dealt with in Chapter 11.

(3) The liability of a customer to his bank with respect to the manner in which he issues cheques and the corresponding liability of the bank to its customer with respect to the manner in which it handles the customer's cheques. The special duties arising out of the banker–customer relationship will also be considered in Chapter 11.

LIABILITY OF RESPECTIVE PARTIES ON A BILL

In Section 2 we examined the negative provisions in ss 28 and 29 to the effect that no person is liable on a bill who has not signed it, and that a forged or unauthorised signature is of no effect. We now examine the positive side, namely, the nature of the liability and the order of liability which the respective parties undertake when they sign a bill of exchange. These are set out in ss 59–61 which should be carefully

Financing Through Negotiable Instruments, etc

read. Taking specimen B above as your example, work out the obligations undertaken by each of the parties and fill in the blank spaces:

Primary liability, s 59(a): acceptor .... engages to pay holder ....

Secondary liability, s 60(1)(a): drawer .... engages to pay holder .... if acceptor........................... fails to do so.

Tertiary liability, s 60(2)(a): 1st indorser .... engages to pay holder .... if acceptor........................... and drawer .... fail to do so.

Quaternary liability, s 60(2)(a): 2nd indorser .... engages to pay holder .... if acceptor ...., drawer ...., and 1st indorser .... fail to do so.

While title to the above bill ran "down" the line from payee to the final indorsee (holder), the claim of liability ran back "up" the line in the sense that if the bill were dishonoured by the acceptor, the holder could sue all the prior parties liable on the bill, the second indorser could sue the first indorser, drawer and acceptor; and so on. We noted on p 432, *supra,* that a person not otherwise a party to a bill may sign it to "back" another party, and thereby incur the liability of an indorser, and is sometimes described as quasi-indorser: s 61. The one person can be a party to the same bill in several capacities; for example, drawer Greatparts, could draw a bill on the drawee–acceptor Bestcars in which it designated itself as payee also. Problems can arise as to the order and capacity in which parties signed a bill which in turn affect their respective liabilities.

For examples involving indorsements by directors of companies where the issue of whether they had indorsed in their personal capacity so as to become personally liable, or only in a representative capacity on behalf of their companies see *H Rowe & Co Pty Ltd v Pitts* [1973] 2 NSWLR 159; 22 FLR 333 and *Rolfe Lubell v Keith* [1979] 1 All ER 860. For a comprehensive discussion of the first case and the law and practice of indorsements, see Chappenden, "*H Rowe & Co Pty Ltd v Pitts*: Old and New Problems as to Bills of Exchange" (1975) 49 *ALJ* 173. As to the effect of a conditional indorsement, and the need for an indorsement to be completed by delivery, see BEA ss 26 and 38 and *Laney v Gates* (1935) 35 SR (NSW) 372.

RIGHTS OF HOLDERS AND HOLDERS IN DUE COURSE

The definition of holder was noted on p 431, *supra.* The related concepts of holder for value and holder in due course are covered in BEA ss 32 and 34 which are central provisions deserving careful study together with s 43 which sets out the rights and powers of a holder.

Let us take the illustration on p 428 of the specimen B bill of exchange and assume that the acceptor Bestcars dishonoured it by failing to pay it at maturity on 15 May. As a holder of the bill Commercial Bank will want to sue some or all of the parties liable on the bill—Bestcars, Greatparts, Factors and Carb. In order to succeed a holder must prove its entitlement to the bill and that consideration has been given for it. Assistance is provided by s 32(1)(b) which treats an antecedent debt or liability as good consideration (this would not be sufficient consideration to sue on an ordinary contract), and also by s 35 which raises a rebuttable presumption that: "Every party whose signature appears on a bill is *prima facie* deemed to have become a party thereto for value."

Note that the holder Bank need not have itself given value for the bill in order to sue on the bill (s 32(2)), but in order to obtain the benefits of a holder in due course, it must itself provide value and take in good faith. What consideration is needed to satisfy s 32(1)?

Walsh, Spriggs, Nolan and Finney v Hoag & Bos Pty Ltd
Supreme Court of Victoria (Full Court) [1977] VR 178

[The appellants, solicitors for the Logan family, drew a cheque on their trust account payable to the respondents, estate agents, in discharge of the liability of the Logans for commission on the sale of land. The cheque was delivered to the agents. At the request of the Logans, the solicitors subsequently stopped payment of the cheque. The estate agents succeeded in an action against the solicitors for payment of the cheque. The solicitors appealed on the ground that there was no consideration for the cheque under BEA s 32(1).]

Lush J [stated the facts, quoted s 32(1) and continued at 186:] A bill of exchange represents a new promise to pay independent of any contractual undertakings which may have preceded it. The action on the bill is brought on this new promise and it must be for this new promise that consideration is given. Consideration must, in the general law of contract, move from the promisee to the promisor in respect of the promise.

In the case of bills of exchange it is not essential that consideration should move from the holder (ie the payee, indorsee or bearer) to the party sued, but it may move or have moved from some other party to the bill or from a stranger to the bill. See *Wragge v Sims Cooper & Co (Australia) Pty Ltd* (1933) 50 CLR 483, per Dixon J at 492-3. Where, however, the holder is in fact the person alleged to be supplying the consideration the ordinary analysis applies and it must appear that consideration was given and that it was given in the relevant sense to the promisor, being an immediate party, in respect of the promise.

Consideration lies in detriment to the promisee or benefit to the promisor. (The word "detriment" is used in the special sense given to it in the law of consideration: see *Salmond and Williams, Contracts*, p 112.) An antecedent debt does not constitute consideration under the general law of contract, but in giving effect to the exception now embodied in para (b) it is appropriate to direct attention to both the detriment and the benefit aspects of consideration. Relating the concepts of detriment and benefit to an antecedent debt, the payee/creditor may be regarded as sustaining detriment if a cheque is accepted as conditional payment of the debt, because when the condition is fulfilled and the cheque is honoured his right will be extinguished. On the other hand, the drawer of the cheque may, conditionally, on its honouring, receive a benefit by the release by payment of his liability. *Currie v Misa* (1875) LR 10 Ex 153 was the case which before the Bills of Exchange Act 1882 (UK) established that, as an exception to the general law, an antecedent debt was good consideration for a bill of exchange. The majority judgment said at 164: "The security is offered to the creditor and taken by him as money's worth, and justice requires that it should be as truly his property as the money which it represents would have been his had the payment been made in gold or a Bank of England note. And, on the other hand, until it has proved unproductive, the creditor ought not to be allowed to treat it as a nullity, and to sue the debtor as if he had given no security." The last sentence indicates that the effect of the receipt of the bill on the creditor's rights was regarded as a significant factor.

In the great majority of cases, a cheque is given both to provide payment for the payee-creditor and to obtain release of a debt owed by the drawer, but as a matter of principle the antecedent debt should be regarded as supplying consideration if the cheque is given in conditional payment of the debt and if it is given in circumstances such that, when honoured, it will terminate the payee's right to the debt, even though it is not drawn by the debtor. In *Salmond and Williams*, pp 112-13 it is said that benefit to the promisor is an accidental and inessential feature of consideration and that detriment, "present or contemplated", to the promisee is the invariably essential element of consideration, a proposition which is in itself related to the rule that consideration must move from the promisee.

If there are difficulties in the application of principles taken from the general law of consideration to the statutory case of an antecedent debt, they may be accepted: since an antecedent debt must for present purposes be accepted as a form of consideration, it is proper to relate it to both detriment and benefit aspects of consideration. It is not sufficient to regard it as capable of supplying consideration only if it confers a benefit on the promisor by conditionally releasing his obligation.

Where the drawer does not get the benefit of conditional release, as when he is not the debtor, the payee will suffer conditional detriment only if payment, when made, will discharge the debt and in the absence of some circumstances additional to the fact of the debt and the fact of payment by a person not the debtor the debt will not be discharged by the payment. As regards the debtor, the payment is *res inter alios acta*. If he is sued for the debt he may be able to plead payment, by ratification. But he may not wish to do so because of factors affecting his relationship with either drawer or payee, such as the state of account between him and either of them and in any case they may by agreement cancel the payment transaction at any time before it has been ratified: *Leake on Contracts*, 6th ed, p 666; *Belshaw v Bush* (1851) 11 CB 191; *Walter v James* (1871) LR 6 Ex 124. Payment by a third party without any actual or professed authority has been held inoperative to discharge the debtor: *Leake*, p 666 ...

In the present case the appellants, at the time the cheque was given, had at least ostensible and probably actual implied authority to make the payment on behalf of the Logans and were in effect making the payment out of moneys of the Logans in their hands, for which they were accountable to the Logans.

The decision in *Oliver v Davis* [1949] 2 KB 727 is generally regarded as establishing that a debt due by A to the payee of a cheque is not consideration under s 32(1)(b) for a cheque drawn by B. In *Ayers v Moore* [1940] 1 KB 278; [1939] 4 All ER 351 an action by the payee of bills of exchange against the acceptor, whose acceptance had been procured by fraud of the drawer, who was indebted to the payee, Hallett J at 282 may have been expressing a different view when he said: "Here there is unquestionably on the accepted facts an antecedent debt or liability ... Although there may have been no express agreement to forbear. I think that in the present state of the authorities there can be no doubt there was sufficient consideration for the giving of the bills. I think that the bills operated as a conditional payment of part of the past debt, and, therefore, even without an express agreement, that point fails" (ie the point that there was no consideration).

Denning LJ, in *Oliver v Davis* at 742-3 said that if this passage contains anything to the contrary of the proposition that para (b) does not apply to a promise to pay on antecedent debt of a third party, he could not agree with it.

Somervell LJ, in the same case said (at 741) that the natural meaning of the expression "antecedent debt" in para (b) was that it meant a debt due from the person who gives the negotiable instrument in question and if there were doubt then it was resolved by *Crears v Hunter* (1887) 19 QBD 341, a decision on the common law before the Bills of Exchange Act 1882 (UK).

Evershed MR's judgment is expressed in less absolute terms. The Master of the Rolls said (at 735-6) that he thought that the "antecedent debt" was a debt of the promisor or drawer of the bill and while "on the facts of this case it may not be strictly necessary to express a concluded view on that matter" the case of *Crears v Hunter* "strongly supported" that view. "This at any rate is plain—that if the antecedent debt or liability of a third party is to be relied upon as supplying 'valuable consideration for a bill', there must at least be some relationship between the receipt of the bill and the antecedent debt or liability. And for practical purposes it is difficult to see how there can be any distinction between a case in which there is a sufficient relationship for this purpose between the bill and the antecedent debt or liability and the case in which, as a result of that relationship, there is in the ordinary sense a consideration passing from the payee to the drawer of the bill. Otherwise the creditor might recover both on the debt from the third party and on the cheque from the drawer." Beside these observations should be placed those of Somervell LJ (at 742) that in the case of a negotiable instrument given in respect of the debt of a third party consideration of the kind referred to in para (a) must be found ...

Wragge v Sims Cooper & Co (Australia) Pty Ltd lends support to the conclusion here reached. Just as in that case Starke J at 488 and Dixon J at 492 considered it useful to describe the effect of the transaction under consideration in terms postulating an indorsement by the creditor to the payee or a drawing by the creditor on the debtor accepted by the debtor in favour of the payee, so in this case it is useful to say that on the date the cheque sued upon was drawn the exact result of the transaction carried out would have been achieved if the Logans had drawn a bill on the appellants, which they had accepted, in favour of the respondent. In this situation, no question of lack of consideration would have arisen.

Further, the conclusion reached in the present case is consistent with the observations already referred to of Dixon J concerning situations in which consideration moves from a stranger to the bill. If the existence of an antecedent debt between the drawer as debtor and a stranger can constitute consideration under para (b), it would appear logical that an antecedent debt existing between the payee as creditor and a stranger may also provide consideration. In the former case it is the notion of benefit to the debtor which supplies the consideration. In the latter it is the notion of detriment to the creditor by extinguishment of his right.

The appeal should be dismissed.

[**Young CJ** and **Jenkinson J** delivered judgments to the same effect.]

Appeal dismissed.

Further illustrations of the principles that consideration must be provided, but not necessarily by the holder himself are *Sharp v Ellis; Re Edward Love & Co Pty Ltd* [1972] VR 137; *Diamond v Graham* [1968] 2 All ER 909; and *Bonior v A Siery Ltd* [1968] NZLR 254.

HOLDER IN DUE COURSE

Assuming that Commercial Bank became a holder for value of the bill of exchange and there is no defect in title which can be raised in opposition to its rights as holder, it will succeed in suing all prior parties under the general principles of contract. It will not have to rely specifically on the special protection available to a holder in due course. However, if there is some defect in the title of one of the previous parties it will be a great advantage to the bank to establish that it satisfies the conditions of s 34 and is entitled as a holder in due course to the benefits enumerated in BEA s 43 which should be read carefully.

In order to qualify as a holder in due course, the bank must establish that:

(1) It is a holder: s 4. If the bank has taken the bill under or through a forged indorsement (eg, Carb's) it cannot be a holder in due course as against any party whose liability on the bill was incurred prior to the forgery. The original payee (Carb) also will not qualify as a holder in due course because the term implies a party to whom the bill has been negotiated rather one to whom it was originally issued: *Jones (RE) Ltd v Waring & Gillow Ltd* [1926] AC 670.

(2) The bill is complete and regular on the face of it.

(3) It became the holder before the bill was overdue or had been dishonoured.

(4) It took the bill in good faith and for value and without notice of any defect in title.

Several important issues here include:

(a) When is a bill complete and regular on its face, and what are the rights of a holder of a bill which is not complete and regular?

(b) What is meant by good faith, is it negated by negligence or notice, and upon whom is the onus of proving the presence or absence of good faith?

Arab Bank Ltd v Ross
English Court of Appeal [1952] 2 QB 216; [1952] 1 All ER 709

Appeal from McNair J.

The plaintiffs, the Arab Bank Ltd, of Jerusalem, claimed that they were the holders in due course of two promissory notes dated 12 July 1946, made by the defendant Ross, each for £10,000 and payable on demand on 1 July 1947, and 31 December 1947. The payees were "Fathi and Faysal Nabulsy Company", a firm registered in Palestine, of which Fathi and Faysal Nabulsy were the two partners. The notes were alleged to have been given in pursuance of an agreement between Ross and the payee firm as part of the purchase price for shares in the Lostock Hall Spinning Co Ltd. By the statement of claim it was alleged that the notes had been duly indorsed by the Nabulsys to the order of the plaintiffs.

By his defence the defendant alleged that he had been induced to make or deliver the notes by the fraud of the payees, in that the shares were at that time charged to the Arab National Bank Ltd, who held the certificates and blank transfers to secure the payees' overdraft of £25,000, and the payees knew that they were not in a position to sell or transfer the shares; that in order to secure the certificates the defendant had had to pay £20,000 to the Arab National Bank Ltd; that the plaintiffs were not holders in due course of the notes but merely agents for collection on behalf of the payees; that the plaintiffs had knowledge of the fraud on the part of the Nabulsys and therefore had not taken the notes in good faith; and further, that as the Nabulsys were directors of the plaintiff bank the plaintiffs were affected with notice of the fraud.

McNair J held that it had not been proved that the share certificates were deposited with the National Bank at or before the date of the agreement; that even if they had been this was not inconsistent with ability to pass a good title; that there was nothing in the evidence to show that the issue of the notes was affected with fraud, duress or illegality within the meaning of s 30(2) of the Bills of Exchange Act 1882 [Aust, s 35(2)]; that the plaintiff bank had discounted the notes for value and it was not established that they had acted otherwise than in good faith and without any notice of any defect in the bills; and that the plaintiffs were not affected by any knowledge possessed by the Nabulsys, by reason of the fact that they or their firm were directors of the bank.

During the hearing before the judge counsel for the defendant sought to raise a further point, which had not been pleaded in the defence, viz, that the notes when taken by the plaintiffs were not complete and regular on their face, because whilst the notes were payable to "Fathi and Faysal Nabulsy Company", the indorsement was "Fathi and Faysal Nabulsy", the word "company" being omitted; and therefore the plaintiffs could not succeed as holders in due course by reason of s 29(1) of the Bills of Exchange Act 1882 [Aust, s 34(1)].

The judge, while ruling that this point should have been pleaded, and refusing leave to amend the defence, nevertheless allowed it to be argued as a point of law. He held, however, that the signature of the names of the two partners by the hand of the one partner Faysal was the known and recognised signature of the partnership and would leave nobody in any reasonable doubt that the named payee intended to pass property in the notes to the bank. In his opinion the notes were complete and regular on their face.

The judge therefore gave judgment for the plaintiffs, and the defendant appealed.

Denning LJ: The first question in this case is whether the Arab Bank Ltd were holders in due course of the promissory note, and that depends on whether, at the time they took it, it was "complete and regular on the face of it" within s 29 of the Bills of Exchange Act 1882. Strangely enough, no one doubts that the "face" of a bill includes the back of it. I say strangely enough, because people so often insist on the literal interpretation of Acts of parliament, whereas here everyone agrees that the literal interpretation must be ignored because the meaning is obvious. The meaning is that, looking at the bill, front and back, without the aid of outside evidence, it must be complete and regular in itself.

Regularity is a different thing from validity. The Act itself makes a careful distinction between them. On the one hand an indorsement which is quite invalid may be regular on the face of it. Thus the indorsement may be forged or unauthorised and, therefore, invalid under s 24 of the Act [Aust, s 29], but nevertheless there may be nothing about it to give rise to any suspicion. The bill is then quite regular on the face of it. Conversely, an indorsement which is quite irregular may nevertheless be valid. Thus, by a misnomer, a payee may be described on the face of the bill by the wrong name, nevertheless, if it is quite plain that the drawer intended him as payee, then an indorsement on the back by the payee in his own true name is valid and sufficient to pass the property in the bill (*Leonard v Wilson* (1834) 2 Cr & M 589; *Bird & Co v Thomas Cook & Son Ltd* [1937] 2 All ER 227; *Hadley v Henry* (1896) 22 VLR 230), but the difference between front and back makes the indorsement irregular unless the payee adds also the misnomer by which he was described on the front of the bill. This is what he eventually did in *Leonard v Wilson*.

Regularity is also different from liability. The Act makes a distinction between these two also. On the one hand a person who makes an irregular indorsement is liable thereon despite the irregularity. Thus, if a payee, who is wrongly described on the front of the bill, indorses it in his own true name, the indorsement is irregular, but he is liable to any subsequent holder and cannot set up the irregularity as a defence; or, if he is rightly described on the front of the bill, but indorses it in an assumed name, the indorsement is irregular but he is liable thereon as if he had indorsed it in his own name: see s 23(1) and s 55(2) of the Act [Aust, ss 28(a), 60(2)]. Conversely, a regular indorsement will not impose liability if it is forged or unauthorised. Thus, where a firm is the payee, but is described in an unauthorised name which is substantially different from its real name, an indorsement by one partner in that name does not impose liability on the other partners: *Kirk v Blurton* (1841) 9 M & W 284. It would be otherwise if the name was substantially the same: *Forbes v Marshall* (1855) 11 Ex 166.

Once regularity is seen to differ both from validity and from liability, the question is when is an indorsement irregular? The answer is, I think, that it is irregular whenever it is such as to give rise to doubt whether it is the indorsement of the named payee. A bill of exchange is like currency. It should be above suspicion. But if it is asked: When does an indorsement give rise to doubt? I would say that that is a practical question which is, as a rule, better answered by a banker than a lawyer. Bankers have to consider the regularity of indorsements every week, and every day of every week, and every hour of every day; whereas the judges sitting in this court have not had to consider it for these last 20 years. So far as I know the last occasion was in *Slingsby's* case [1932] 1 KB 544.

The Law Merchant is founded on the custom of merchants, and we shall not go far wrong if we follow the custom of bankers of the City of London on this point. [His Lordship then discussed the evidence provided by London bankers that they would not accept such an indorsement.]

The truth is, I think, that the bankers adopted this strict attitude both in their own interests and also in the interests of their customers. It would be quite impossible for them to make inquiries to see that all the indorsements on a bill are in fact genuine; but they can at least see that they are regular on the face of them: see *Bank of England v Vagliano* [1891] AC 107 at 157, per Lord Macnaghten. That is some safeguard against dishonesty. It is a safeguard which the bankers have taken for the past 120 years at least, and I do not think we should throw any doubt today on the correctness of their practice ... The word "company" in this case is not, however, mere description. It is part of the name itself. It was suggested that an indorsement in Arabic letters would be regular. I cannot accept this view. The indorsement should be in the same lettering as the name of the payee; for otherwise it could not be seen on the face of it to be regular. My conclusion is, therefore, that this promissory note, when it was taken by the Arab Bank Ltd, was not complete and regular on the face of it. They were not, therefore, holders in due course ...

Now I must come to the pleadings. The Arab Bank Ltd claimed that they were "holders in due course." They have failed to make good that claim because the indorsement was not regular on the face of it. But nevertheless it is, I think, open to them to claim as "holders." The difference between the rights of a "holder in due course" and those of a "holder" is that a holder in due course may get a better title than the person from whom he took, whereas a holder gets no better title. In this regard a person who takes a bill which is irregular on the face of it, is in the same position as a person who takes a bill which is overdue. He is a holder but not a holder in due course. He does not receive the bill on its own intrinsic credit. He takes it on the credit of the person who gives it to him: cf *Brown v Davies* (1789) 3 TR 80 at 82 per Buller J. He can sue in his own name, but he takes it subject to the defects of title of prior parties: see s 38 of the Act [Aust, s 43] ...

Thus the plaintiffs here who have alleged that they are "holders in due course", can rely on the more limited allegation that they are "holders"; because the greater allegation of "holders in due course" includes the lesser allegation of "holders". Upon these pleadings I think the plaintiffs were clearly entitled to rely on the fact that they were "holders" and the defendants have to meet a claim on that footing ... The result is that no defect has been shown to exist in the title of the Nabulsy brothers. There is no answer to the plaintiffs' claim as holders, and the appeal must be dismissed.

[**Somervell** and **Romer LJJ** delivered judgments to similar effect.]

Appeal dismissed.

NOTICE AND GOOD FAITH

The concepts of notice and good faith are related. In *London Joint Stock Bank v Simmons* [1892] AC 201 at 221, Lord Herschell said:

One word I would say upon the question of notice, and being put upon inquiry. I should be very sorry to see the doctrine of constructive notice introduced into the law of negotiable instruments. But regard to the facts of which the taker of such instruments had notice is most material in considering whether he took in good faith. If there be anything which excites the suspicion that there is something wrong in the transaction, the taker of the instrument is not acting in good faith if he shuts his eyes to the facts presented to him and puts the suspicions aside without further inquiry.

And in *Jones v Gordon* (1877) 2 App Cas 616 at 628-9 Lord Blackburn said:

Farther, my Lords, I think it is right to say that I consider it to be fully and thoroughly established that if value be given for a bill of exchange, it is not enough to shew that there was carelessness, negligence, or foolishness in not suspecting that the bill was wrong, when there were circumstances which might have led a man to suspect that. All these are matters which tend to shew that there was dishonesty in not doing it, but they do not in themselves make a defence to an action upon a bill of exchange. I take it that in order to make such a defence, whether in the case of a party who is solvent and *sui juris*, or when it is sought to be proved against the estate of a bankrupt, it is necessary to shew that the person who gave value for the bill, whether the value given be great or small, was affected with notice that there was something wrong about it when he took it. I do not think it is necessary that he should have notice of what the particular wrong was. If a man, knowing that a bill was in the hands of a person who had no right to it, should happen to think that perhaps the man had stolen it, when if he had known the real truth he would have found, not that the man had stolen it, but that he had obtained it by false pretences. I think that would not make any difference if he knew that there was something wrong about it and took it. If he takes it in that way he takes it at his peril.

But then I think that such evidence of carelessness or blindness as I have referred to may with other evidence be good evidence upon the question which, I take it, is the real one, whether he did know that there was something wrong in it. If he was (if I may use the phrase) honestly blundering and careless, and so took a bill of exchange or a bank-note when he ought not to have taken it, still he would be entitled to recover. But if the facts and circumstances are such that the jury, or whoever has to try the question, came to the conclusion that he was not honestly blundering and careless, but that he must have had a suspicion that there was something wrong, and that he refrained from asking questions, not because he was an honest blunderer or a stupid man, but because he thought in his own secret mind — I suspect there is something wrong, and if I ask questions and make farther inquiry, it will no longer be my suspecting it, but my knowing it, and then I shall not be able to recover — I think that is dishonesty. I think, my Lords, that that is established, not only by good sense and reason, but by the authority of the cases themselves.

In this connection, note the terms of BEA s 96: "A thing is deemed to be done in good faith, within the meaning of this Act, where it is in fact done honestly whether it is done negligently or not."

Stenning v Radio and Domestic Finance Ltd
Supreme Court of New Zealand [1961] NZLR 7

[The appellant entered into a conditional purchase agreement with Ronald Jorgensen (trading as "Metropolitan Motors") for the purchase of a Ford motor car. The agreement breached the Hire Purchase and Credit Sales Stabilisation Regulations 1957, in that the stipulated deposit of £167 10s being one half of the cash price was not in fact paid as stated in the agreement.

The appellant gave 12 promissory notes to the dealer Jorgensen, signed by the appellant as maker and these were subsequently indorsed by Jorgensen when he discounted the conditional purchase agreement and promissory notes with the respondent finance company. Jorgensen failed to paint the car or warrant its fitness and the appellant refused to accept the defective vehicle or to pay any instalments under the agreement.

The respondent sued the appellant in the Magistrate's Court for the balance of £189 14s 11d payable under the agreement; or alternatively upon the collateral promissory notes. The magistrate entered judgment for the respondent company pursuant to the provisions of the conditional purchase agreement.

One of the grounds of appeal was:

"(3) That the respondent company stands in no better position as holder of the collateral promissory notes than as assignee of the conditional purchase agreement."]

Richmond J [after dealing with earlier submissions turned to the third submission at 17:]

The promissory notes were originally made payable to "Metropolitan Motors", being the name under which Jorgensen was trading. Jorgensen clearly had a defective title to the notes within the meaning of s 29(2) of the Bills of Exchange Act 1908 [Aust, s 34(2)] as he had obtained the promissory notes for an illegal consideration. The question accordingly arises whether or not the respondent company was a holder in due course of the notes because if it was, then by virtue of s 38(b) of the Bills of Exchange Act [Aust, s 43(1)(b)] it would hold the notes "free from any defect of title of prior parties". The position will be otherwise if the respondent company is merely a holder for value. A holder for value may sue on a note in his own name: s 38(a) and may in certain circumstances confer a good title if he negotiates the note or obtains payment thereof: s 38(c). A holder for value is also able to sue the maker of the note notwithstanding as between the maker and the payee no consideration was given: s 27(2). A holder for value, however, as opposed to a holder in due course, takes subject to any defect of title affecting the title of the payee of the note from whom he acquired the note by endorsement, other than the defect, if one can call it such, of mere absence of consideration.

In the present case, the respondent company had no notice of the fact that the promissory notes were given by the appellant for an illegal consideration. This fact, however, will not assist the respondent company unless all the requirements of s 29 [Aust, s 34] of the Bills of Exchange Act 1908 (which defines the expression "holder in due course") are satisfied. [His Honour then quoted the section.]

Section 29(1)(b) stipulates that the holder, at the time the bill was negotiated to him, should have no notice of *any* defect in the title of the person who negotiated it. In the present case the respondent company had no notice of the illegality but the wording of s 29 is such that in my opinion the respondent company, if it had notice of *some* other defect in Jorgensen's title, will fail to qualify as a holder in due course.

In the present case, the respondent company obtained the promissory notes by endorsement contemporaneously with the assignment of the conditional purchase agreement. The respondent company was of course aware of the contents of the conditional purchase agreement, including the provisions of cl 2 whereby the appellant undertook if called upon to "execute promissory notes each to the amount of the said monthly or weekly instalment as the case may be *for the purpose of the better securing to the owner the said weekly or monthly instalments* and such promissory notes shall be deemed to be collateral to and co-existent with this Agreement". The respondent therefore knew that, on the face of the agreement, Jorgensen's right to enforce payment of the notes was to some greater or lesser extent dependent on the continued existence of the appellant's liability to meet the instalments under the conditional purchase agreement. Clearly, for example, Jorgensen could not have taken action on a promissory note representing an instalment that had already been paid. The question then is whether knowledge that Jorgensen did not have an unrestricted right to sue on the notes in all circumstances amounts to knowledge of a "defect in title" within the meaning of s 29(1)(b).

This restriction on the right of Jorgensen to sue on the notes does not fall within the illustrations of defective title given by s 29(2). If then the only types of "defect in title" contemplated by the Bills of Exchange Act are those enumerated in s 29(2), clearly the respondent company must be a "holder in due course". It seems to me however that s 29(2) is merely an enumeration of certain matters which amount to a defect in title without purporting to be exhaustive. So far as I have been able to discover there is very little authority bearing on this matter. Indeed, the only decided case from which I have been able to derive any assistance is *Brennan v Pitt Son and Badgery Ltd* (1899) 20 NSWLR (Eq) 179. In that case the plaintiff, being indebted to one Burcher, executed in favour of Burcher two promissory notes and a mortgage. The mortgage was expressed to be collateral security for the due payment of the promissory notes and interest and any other sums that might be advanced. At a later date Burcher sub-mortgaged his mortgage to the defendants, Pitt Son and Badgery Ltd, and at the same time endorsed over to them the two promissory notes. The question arose whether the defendant company, as holder of the promissory notes, was entitled to sue on the notes without regard to the actual state of accounts between the plaintiff and Burcher. The judgment of the court was delivered by Owen J. The following passage occurs in the judgment: "But in the present case the promissory notes and the mortgage remain in the hands of the assignee, and the assignee in taking the assignment of the mortgage and endorsement of the promissory notes, knew that they represented the same transaction, and were security for the same debt. The endorsee, therefore, was not a purchaser for value without notice": at 191.

It appears to me to be implicit in the judgment in *Brennan v Pitt Son and Badgery Ltd* that the Full Court in that case regarded knowledge on the part of the defendent company that the promissory notes were collateral security only as amounting to knowledge of a defect in title on the part of Burcher. For similar reasons, I conclude that the respondent company in the present case was not a holder in due course and accordingly holds the promissory notes subject to the same taint of illegality as affected them in the hands of Jorgensen. I add that I have found this question a difficult one, and have arrived at the foregoing conclusion with some hesitation.

So far I have treated the promissory notes as having been given for an illegal consideration. I am of opinion however that, even if the respondent company was a holder in due course, it could not, in the circumstances of the present case, enforce payment of the notes against the appellant. In *Byles on Bills of Exchange*, 21st ed, p 138, attention is drawn by the learned author to the importance of distinguishing between illegality which avoids a negotiable security in the hands of any holder and illegality which merely shifts on to the holder of the instrument the onus of proving that he is a holder in due course.

[His Honour then reviewed the history of English statutory provisions prohibiting the giving of negotiable instruments for illegal purposes and concluded that the promissory notes in the present case were not merely given for an illegal consideration but were themselves given in contravention of the Hire Purchase Regulations. He concluded at 20-1:] If the promissory notes are to be allowed to have effect independently from the conditional purchase agreement, then, in my opinion, they would directly or indirectly defeat the operation of the Hire Purchase Regulations by permitting the payee or holder to enforce payment of a debt incurred under an agreement rendered illegal and void by the regulations. As, in my opinion, the making of notes was in direct contravention of a statutory prohibition I consider that they were at all times absolutely null and void and incapable of any legal effect and remained so in the hands of the respondent company even if, contrary to the views which I have expressed earlier in this judgment, the respondent company was a holder in due course.

Appeal allowed.

Comparable Australian cases are: *Automobile Finance Co of Australia Ltd v Henderson* (1928) 23 Tas LR 9; *Scottish Loan & Finance Co Ltd v Payne* (1935) 52 WN (NSW) 175.

Douglas v Tiernan
Supreme Court of New South Wales (1931) 32 SR (NSW) 149

Harvey J: In this case we think there will have to be a new trial. The plaintiff, Ross Douglas, sued the defendant, James Tiernan, on a promissory note which had been given by Tiernan to one Arthur Franklin, in connection with a land transaction, and had been endorsed by Arthur Franklin to the plaintiff.

The defence pleaded by the defendant was that the note had been obtained from him by fraud, and that the plaintiff had notice of the fraud when it was endorsed to him. The plaintiff simply proved the endorsement of the note to him and closed his case, and the defendant thereupon established that the note had been obtained from him by fraud and misrepresentation. That position was not disputed by the plaintiff's counsel, and it then brought into play the provisions of s 35 of our Bills of Exchange Act, which is the same as s 30 of the English Bills of Exchange Act of 1882. The effect of that section seems to have been definitely determined by the case of *Tatam v Haslar* (1889) 23 QBD 345 ...

It is now established by that case that as soon as fraud is shown to affect the bill in question the onus is thrown upon the party suing upon the bill of establishing affirmatively that he has given value for the bill, and that he gave value in good faith. Both those facts must be proved by the plaintiff ...

The account which was given by the plaintiff of the way in which he had taken the note was not a very clear or definite statement of the facts. The jury might have accepted his statement; they might, on the other hand, have decided that it was given in such an unreliable way that they could not accept it as a true statement of what his state of mind was. It was obviously a question for the jury ...

I think his Honour was in error in taking the case away from the jury, and that he should have left it to them, explaining to them that the onus lay on the plaintiff of establishing affirmatively to their satisfaction that he had taken a note under circumstances which established his bona fides.

[**Halse Rogers** and **Stephen JJ** concurred.]

Appeal upheld, new trial ordered.

DISCHARGE OF A BILL OF EXCHANGE

Where there are no hitches, a bill of exchange such as specimen B on p 428, *supra*, will be paid by the acceptor (Bestcars) to the true owner or his agent on his behalf (Commercial Bank on its own account or on behalf of Factors). In the case of a cheque as in specimen C, payment will be made by the drawee bank called the paying bank (Country Bank) on which the drawer (Bourke Motors) drew the cheque. In specimen D, the maker Handy will pay the payee Squeeze. In each case payment to the owner will discharge the bill, cheque or promissory note. This means that all rights to sue on the bill, cheque or note are extinguished.

However where there is a defect in the title of the person to whom the drawee/acceptor/maker pays, we must look more closely at the Act to determine whether the instrument is discharged. The fundamental provision is BEA s 64.

64(1) A bill is discharged by payment in due course by or on behalf of the drawee or acceptor.

"Payment in due course" means payment at or after maturity of the bill to the holder thereof in good faith and without notice that his title to the bill is defective.

Under s 64 it is the drawee/acceptor who must act in good faith and without notice. "Payment in due course" includes but does not require payment to a holder in due course; but it does require payment to a holder. Thus, payment to a person who takes under or through a forged indorsement can never constitute discharge by payment in due course.

Although discharge precludes anyone suing on the bill, cheque or note, it does not prevent the true owner suing a wrongdoer for conversion of the instrument or its proceeds. For example, if a thief steals specimen C from the payee Carb and the Country Bank pays the bearer cheque in due course, it will be discharged so that Carb cannot sue Bourke Motors, but Carb will be entitled to sue by way of an action in conversion the thief (if available), and possibly the bank which collected the $800 for him.

If the cheque had been an order cheque on which the thief forged Carb's indorsement s 64 would not apply. However, where a bill payable to order is drawn on a bank (including an order cheque which by definition is always drawn on a bank) which pays it in good faith and in the ordinary course of business to someone who took under or through a forged indorsement, the bank receives special protection under s 65. Compare ss 86 and 88B in relation to cheques which are discussed in Chapter 11.

Where a negotiable instrument is received in payment of a debt, it is presumed to be accepted conditionally and merely on account of the debt which is not considered to be satisfied until the instrument is honoured by actual payment. A creditor might accept a cheque or note in full satisfaction and take the risk of non-payment on himself but this would require a specific agreement or special circumstances: *Armco (Aust) Pty Ltd v Federal Commissioner of Taxation* (1948) 76 CLR 584 at 609-10; *Tilley v Official Receiver in Bankruptcy* (1960) 103 CLR 529; [1961] ALR 83.

Other means by which bills and cheques are discharged are where the acceptor becomes the holder (s 66), waiver (s 67), cancellation (s 68) and alteration (s 69). Section 69 entitles a holder in due course to enforce a materially altered bill, where the alteration is not apparent, but only to the extent of the amount for which it was originally issued prior to the unauthorised alteration. When is an alteration material and when is it apparent?

Automobile Finance Co of Australia Ltd v Law
High Court of Australia (1933) 49 CLR 1

Gavan Duffy CJ, Rich, Dixon and **McTiernan JJ:** The question in this case is whether a holder in due course of a promissory note is entitled to recover upon it from the maker although after its issue some writing was added without the maker's consent. The note was made payable at a fixed future time to a specified payee or his order. It was upon a stamped printed form which, at the side of the place of signature, bore the words "Payable at". The body was filled up in handwriting which was not that of the maker; and, in another hand clearly distinguishable from the first, and in a darker ink, the words "Commercial Banking Co of Sydney Hamilton Vic" appeared after "Payable at". The note in this condition was negotiated to the present holder who took it in good faith and for value. But it was established by evidence that when the maker signed the note and delivered it to the payee it bore no writing after the printed words "Payable at", and that the name of the bank was placed there by a clerk of the payee without the maker's authority. [Their Honours then quoted BEA s 69.]

In the County Court, Judge Macindoe held that the promissory note thus had been materially altered and that the alteration was apparent, and, therefore, that the note was avoided even in the hands of a holder in due course. He said that it was obvious from an examination of the note itself that the place of payment was filled in by some person other than the maker, or the person who filled in the rest of the note; that both the handwriting and the ink were different, and he concluded from those circumstances that it was apparent that an alteration in a material particular had been made.

On appeal to the Supreme Court, the Full Court, consisting of Mann ACJ, Lowe and Gavan Duffy JJ, affirmed this judgment. Upon the question whether the instrument bore an apparent alteration, Mann ACJ said that an alteration was apparent on the face of a bill within the meaning of the section, if a man scrutinising the bill, which he is asked to take for business purposes, would by ordinary caution be led to question the authority of any part of it; applying that test, he thought the payee of this note as a prudent man, should have been led at once to question the authority of this part of the note. He said the question was whether it raised a reasonable doubt of material alteration. We are unable to agree with this opinion. We assume that the clerk who filled up the blank after the printed words "Payable at" thereby made a material alteration in the promissory note, but we cannot think that the alteration is apparent within the meaning of the enactment. That meaning, in our opinion, requires that it should be apparent upon inspection of the bill that its text has undergone a change. The document itself must show that some revision of the text has taken place, and its appearance must be consistent with the revision having occurred after completion or issue, though it may also be consistent with its having occurred before completion. Inspection of the document must show that something has been done to it as and for an alteration of that which otherwise was, or was to become, the instrument. In *Leeds Bank v Walker* (1883) 11 QBD 84 at 90, Denman J speaks of "some incongruity on the face of the note". In *Woollatt v Stanley* (1928) 138 LT 620, Salter J makes the test of apparency whether the alteration is of such a kind that it would be observed and noticed by an intending holder scrutinising the document with reasonable care. This does not mean merely that what has been substituted or added should be visible to him upon reasonable examination, but that the fact that it was put there as an addition or substitution will thus be seen. The question, which was put and answered in the Full Court, namely, whether a scrutiny of the bill would lead a prudent man to question the authority of any part of it, does not seem to us to be the same thing. We cannot but think that it tends to substitute inference or suspicion as to the origin of a part of the document for its actual objective state or condition as seen on inspection. Moreover, such a test does not direct the mind to what the state or condition must show, namely, that something has been done to the document in order to alter its tenor.

In the present case all that appears is that the main part of the printed form was filled up in one hand and a subsidiary part in another hand and in different ink. We cannot see how this makes it apparent that the subsidiary part was filled up as an alteration. If a manifest difference in handwriting in parts of an otherwise regularly completed bill amount to an apparent alteration, it is difficult to see what useful operation would remain to sub-s 2 and the proviso to sub-s 3 of s 25. Under these provisions, if a bill is wanting in any material particular, the person in possession has a prima facie authority to fill up the omission in any way he thinks fit, and, although he exceed his actual authority, a subsequent holder in due course may enforce it according to its tenor. It is clear that, if the material particular is supplied in another handwriting, the case is not one of an apparent alteration avoiding the bill. Perhaps there is something to be said in the present case for the view that the existence of a blank after the uncancelled printed words "Payable at" operated as prima facie authority to supply the place of payment, but, in any case, when the space was filled up, it was not, in our opinion, an apparent alteration of the note.

For these reasons we think the appeal should be allowed.

The County Court judgment should be discharged and in lieu thereof judgment should be entered for the appellant, the plaintiff, for £64 and interest from 15 January 1933.

Starke J [briefly referred to the facts and arguments and concluded at 12:] In the view I take of the case, it is unnecessary to determine whether the note had or had not been materially altered, for the alteration, if there were one, is not apparent. The proviso to the Act, as I construe it, requires that the alteration be visible or apparent, as an alteration or change in the very words or figures originally written or printed in the document, upon its inspection. It is not enough to say that a prudent businessman would be put upon inquiry, or that his suspicions would be aroused by the form of the document. The alteration may be by addition, interlineation, or otherwise, but it must be visible as an alteration, upon inspection. The alteration in the present case is not "apparent" in the sense indicated, and the appeal should therefore, in my opinion be allowed.

Evatt J [stated the facts and continued at 13:] The two main questions in this case depend upon the meaning and application of s 69 of the Bills of Exchange Act 1909, for, by s 95, the provisions of the Act affecting bills, including those contained in s 69, apply with the necessary modifications to promissory notes.

(1) The first question is whether the subsequent insertion of the place of payment of the note without the maker's assent is a "material alteration" . . .

In the case of a bill, s 69(2) expressly provides that the addition of a place of payment without the acceptor's consent is a material alteration. It seems to me that there is every reason for applying to notes the rule as to material alteration in bills, so that by direct force of s 95(2), whereby the maker of a note is deemed to correspond with the acceptor of a bill, "the addition of a place of payment without the *maker's* assent" is a material alteration. This is the result of substituting the word "maker" for the word "acceptor" in s 69(2) . . .

(2) The next question, and the one most debated before us, is whether the plaintiff succeeded in establishing that the alteration in the note was "not apparent".

[His Honour then considered various authorities and concluded at 17-19:] Further, I think that Mann ACJ states the rule of law with substantial accuracy thus: "The word 'apparent' must be given some narrower meaning than one which would limit the exception to cases in which the face of the bill shows that the alteration had been made at a particular time. The way in which the question has been approached by the courts shows that. The cases on this question show that the way to approach the matter is to regard 'apparent' as referring to a case in which the person concerned is put upon inquiry, and should have his suspicions aroused": [1933] VLR at 367.

I think that this conclusion is right. My reasons for accepting it may be summed up as follows:

(1) The proviso to s 69(1) which deals with the rights of a holder in due course, postulates

that, although a bill or note is "complete and regular on the face of it" (s 34(1)), it may contain an apparent alteration.

(2) A promissory note does not require the inclusion within it of any place of payment, so that its presence is not inconsistent with its having been added after delivery.

(3) Section 69(2) definitely postulates that an "alteration" may consist of an "addition of a place of payment".

(4) In such a case the "alteration" would take the form of an insertion of additional words.

(5) Section 69 postulates that any and every kind of "alteration" to a bill or note *may* be "apparent".

(6) Therefore an insertion of words indicative of a place of payment may be an "apparent" alteration.

Leaving out such an extreme case as *Koch v Dicks* [1933] 1 KB 307, where the fact of alteration is openly asserted and authenticated, it would seem to follow that the typical case where an alteration by addition would be "apparent" is the case of an obvious change in handwriting. In the present instance there is the appearance not only of a very distinct change of handwriting and ink, but also of a serial number in the changed handwriting and ink. I do not think that the intention of the code was to protect holders in due course in every case where the material alteration consisted of the addition of a place of payment. A contrary intention is to be implied from s 69.

I am inclined to think that, behind the suggestion that the alteration to the note in suit is not apparent, lies the assumption either that it is not an alteration at all or else that, in any event, many persons proposing to discount it would be willing to encounter the extremely slight risk of the alteration's having been unauthorised. But the first assumption is contrary to s 69(2), and the second assumption is quite irrelevant because an alteration is apparent if always observed, whatever action may subsequently be taken by the observer.

I conclude that the plaintiff has entirely failed to prove that the "material alteration" to the note on which he sued was "not apparent", and that the appeal should be dismissed.

Appeal allowed.

DUTIES OF THE HOLDER: PRESENTMENT, NOTICE OF DISHONOUR AND PROTEST

In order to exercise and preserve his rights against various parties to a bill of exchange, the holder may have to fulfil a number of procedures, including presentment for acceptance and payment, issuing notices of dishonour and noting and protesting the dishonour. These matters are regulated by BEA Div 5 ss 44–57. A brief illustration from specimen B on p 428, *supra,* must suffice for present purposes.

The drawee Bestcars might dishonour the bill in two ways: by refusing to accept it, or by refusing to pay it after having accepted it. If it refuses to accept, it is of course not liable on the bill (s 28) but may thereby breach its contract with Greatparts.

Presentment for acceptance. Under s 44, the holder Commercial Bank only need present the bill to Bestcars for acceptance in the three cases where the bill:

(a) is payable "after sight", in order to fix the date of maturity;

(b) expressly stipulates that it shall be presented for acceptance; or

(c) is drawn payable elsewhere than at Bestcars' residence or place of business.

If Bank fails to present the bill for acceptance or negotiate it within a reasonable time, drawer Greatparts and any prior indorser will be discharged: s 45. The reason for this rule is that until a bill is presented for acceptance Greatparts and indorser Carb will not know whether drawee Bestcars is going to accept it and hence will not know whether they themselves are likely to have to pay it. Section 46 lists the rules for presentment for acceptance. Section 47 provides that if a drawee refuses to accept the bill, the person presenting it must treat it as dishonoured or his rights against the drawer and indorsers are forfeited. Bank treats it as dishonoured by noting and protesting it or issuing a notice of dishonour: s 53.

Presentment for payment. If Bestcars dishonours the bill when it is presented for acceptance, an immediate right of recourse against drawer Greatparts and indorser Carb accrues to holder Bank, and presentment for payment is not necessary: s 48. However, where Bestcars accepts the bill, Bank must promptly present the bill to Bestcars for payment at maturity (s 50) except where presentment is excused by special circumstances: s 51. Failure to present the bill immediately it falls due will discharge Greatparts and Carb: s 50(1).

Notice of dishonour. On dishonour by non-acceptance or non-payment, holder Bank must issue a notice of dishonour to Greatparts and Carb in order to make them liable on the bill: s 53. The reason is simply to inform them that they may be held liable to pay the bill dishonoured by Bestcars, and failure to give prompt notice to any party will discharge it from liability (s 53) except where notice or delay is excused under s 55, or the notice is lost or delayed in the post: s 54(o). The notice must comply with the formalities in s 54.

Noting and protesting. These are formal procedures to facilitate proof of dishonour. They are required in case of a foreign bill (one which is not either drawn and payable within Australasia, or drawn within Australasia upon some person resident therein: s 9(1)). It is not necessary to note or protest an inland (local) bill, but the holder may choose to do so. The procedure involves formal presentation of the bill by a notary public or his clerk to the drawee for acceptance or payment, and recording of the drawee's response in the notary's register. The protest is the certificate issued by the notary summarising the formal demand and response: s 56. The Bills of Exchange Act s 100 and the Second Schedule provide a simpler method of protest without use of a notary.

Since cheques are not accepted, there is no need to note or protest their dishonour and it would normally be superfluous to give notice of dishonour to the drawer himself. As to promissory notes, see below.

PROMISSORY NOTES

Notes are dealt with in Pt IV of BEA. We have already compared the specimen form of note with those of a bill and cheque: pp 427-8, *supra*. The definition of bill in s 8 should also be compared with that of promissory note in s 89:

89(1) A promissory note is an unconditional promise in writing made by one person to another, signed by the maker, engaging to pay, on demand or at a fixed or determinable future time, a sum certain in money, to or to the order of a specified person, or to bearer.

Promissory notes are used in commerce as a convenient method of establishing an obligation between two parties for payment of a fixed sum, with interest if desired, at a fixed future time. They are easily negotiated and can be enforced without the need to prove the terms of the contract (eg, of sale) out of which the debt arose. A holder in due course takes free of prior equities or counterclaims.

Subject to certain modifications, the general provisions of the Act relating to bills apply equally to notes. For example, the requirements for indorsement and negotiation, rights of a holder in due course, and liability of the parties correspond: see s 95 and *Automobile Finance Co of Australia Ltd v Law* per Evatt J, p 451, *supra*. The maker is the party primarily liable and then each indorser in turn. The holder of a note should present it to the maker for payment at maturity. A note payable on demand, which has been indorsed, must be presented to the maker for payment within a reasonable time of indorsement, or else the indorser is discharged: s 92(1). As there is no drawee or acceptor, there is no need to present for acceptance, or protest a dishonoured note: s 95.

Financing Through Negotiable Instruments, etc

QUESTIONS

Question 4

On June 1 Jim Handy handed his wife Mary three cheques:

Cheque No 1 for $1500 was drawn by Carb Pty Ltd in favour of Mary Handy. This represented the half-yearly interest payment on a loan of $20,000 by Jim to Carb Pty Ltd. Jim had requested Carb to issue the cheque to Mary as he believed this would form part of her taxable income rather than his.

Cheque No 2 for $200 payable to "Jim Handy or bearer" which Jim had received as a gift from his Aunt Jessie and in exchange for which Mary paid Jim $200 in cash.

Cheque No 3 for $100 drawn by Design Ltd in favour of "Jim Handy or order" which Jim indorsed to Mary and presented to her as a birthday gift. The cheque was an advance payment to Jim for some consulting work which Jim subsequently performed for Design Ltd.

On June 2 Jim and Mary had a serious argument as a result of which Jim arranged for Carb Pty Ltd, Aunt Jessie and Design Ltd to stop payment of the three cheques before Mary had banked them.

Discuss Mary's rights against all parties.

Question 5

Jim Handy employed his niece Honor Trew as a clerk on a very low wage. When she was short of money, Honor occasionally forged Jim's signature on cheques drawn on City Bank and made them payable to herself. The manager at City Bank became suspicious and phoned Jim to ask if the cheques paid to Honor were signed by him. Not wanting to cause a family scandal, Jim assured the manager that all was well. Honor continued to forge cheques for a further two months. When she had accumulated $10,000 she left for Venezuela, leaving no forwarding address. Realising that he could not recover his money from Honor, Jim sued the bank for paying the forged cheques. Advise City Bank.

Question 6

For some months Carb had been supplying Bestcars Ltd with a fuel filter to modify their engines. Greatparts Ltd supplied several of the necessary component parts to Carb. On each occasion payment was arranged by Carb drawing bills on Bestcars payable to Greatparts Ltd.

Greatparts Ltd's bookkeeper Shrewd prepared a bill purporting to be drawn by Carb Pty Ltd in the following form, and forged Jim Handy's signature:

$3000	Duty Stamp	Ryde 1 August 1984

Thirty days after sight pay Greatparts Coy or order the sum of Three Thousand Dollars

To Bestcars Ltd
North Road,
Ryde

Carb Pty Ltd
J. Handy
Director

Shrewd sent the bill to Bestcars together with a forged invoice on Carb's letterhead for $3000 which directed Bestcars to send the bill after acceptance to Greatparts. Believing the documents to be genuine, Bestcars' manager accepted the bill for Bestcars before forwarding it to Greatparts.

Shrewd then forged the following indorsement on the back of the bill:

Pay Jetaway Trips Ltd
Greatparts Ltd
per W. Leaver

Shrewd used the bill to pay for a one way ticket to Venezuela which would normally cost $1500. Jetaway discounted the bill with Easy Finance.

Bestcars discovered the fraud and refused to honour the bill on due date. Advise Easy Finance of its rights against all parties.

Question 7

(1) Greatparts Ltd drew the following bill of exchange on Bestcars Ltd for the price of parts supplied by it to Bestcars. Greatparts owed Handy $2000 and intended to use the bill to pay off part of its debt to Handy.

$950	Duty Stamp	Liverpool, 1 July 1984

Ninety days after date pay J Handy the sum of Nine hundred and fifty   dollars

To Bestcars Ltd
North Road,
Ryde

Greatparts Ltd
W. Lever
General Manager

Bestcars accepted the bill and Greatparts sent it to Handy on 15 July. Handy had no prior experience with such instruments and asked Slick to assist him. Slick fraudulently induced Handy to indorse the bill in blank and to give it to him, ostensibly for the purpose of collecting the proceeds for Handy.

However, Slick altered the amount of the bill to $950,000 which alteration was not apparent because of the spaces left when the bill was originally drawn. Slick also wrote above Handy's indorsement "Pay to the order of Factors Ltd" and used the bill to pay a debt owed by Slick to that Company and then disappeared.

Factors Ltd in turn indorsed the bill to Bill Discounts Ltd a merchant banking house, which agreed to buy the bill at a discounted figure of $915,000. When Bill Discounts presented the bill to Bestcars on 2 October payment was refused.

Advise Bill Discounts of its rights against all parties.

(2) What difference would it make to your advice if either
(a) Bill Discounts presented the bill to Bestcars on 3 October; or
(b) the bill had been drawn on Sydney Bank, Head Office rather than Bestcars and was payable on demand; and if instead of inducing Handy to indorse the bill, Slick had himself forged Handy's indorsement?

Financing Through Negotiable Instruments, etc

SECTION 4: FINANCING INTERNATIONAL TRANSACTIONS: LETTERS OF CREDIT

This topic could alone embrace several volumes covering the law and practice of international exchange and forward exchange contracts, foreign currency loans, export credit insurance and exchange control regulations. For present purposes, it is intended to build upon the previous sections of this chapter coupled with the treatment of international sales in Chapter 5, and focus attention upon the use of bills of exchange, and particularly documentary letters of credit as methods of paying for, and financing, international transactions.

The following discussion is based upon the illustration of an international sale developed in Chapter 5. Carb contracted to sell 20,000 carburettors cif Yokohama for $200,000 to be paid in this case 90 days after the shipping documents arrived in Japan. Assume Carb has never had such a large order and lacks the capital to finance it.

Several alternatives are available in this situation. Carb may be able to arrange a bank loan secured on its existing assets. When the goods are shipped, the 90 day bill of exchange (in commercial and bankers' language commonly called a draft) could be discounted with Carb's bank in order to repay the loan. In this case, Carb's contract with Mitzi would provide for the acceptance of the 90 day bill of exchange for $200,000 on receipt of shipping documents comprising shipped bill of lading, marine insurance policy, invoice, inspection certificates and, where appropriate, a certificate of origin, and export and import licences. Carb would deliver the goods to a ship bound for Yokohama and send by airmail to its agent or bank's representative in Yokohama the abovementioned documents with a bill of exchange drawn by Carb on Mitzi for $200,000. The bill of lading might be attached to the bill of exchange (then called a documentary bill) to ensure that the buyer did not receive the bill of lading until it accepted the bill of exchange.

However, until Mitzi does accept the bill of exchange, there is no certainty that it will honour its obligations under the contract and accordingly no worthwhile collateral which Carb can use as a security for its bank loan to finance the manufacture of 20,000 carburettors. Conversely, Mitzi would not be willing to commit itself to signing a negotiable bill of exchange until it received confirmation that goods conforming to the contract had actually been shipped. See, eg, *Henry Dean & Sons (Sydney) Ltd v O'Day Pty Ltd,* p 156, *supra.* This gap between seller and buyer can be filled by the documentary letter of credit, which has been described as "a great financing system in the development of overseas trade" and "the crankshaft of modern commerce". The following is typical of how a confirmed irrevocable documentary credit would be used.

The contract of sale from Carb to Mitzi would require that Carb could ship the goods at any time from 1 May to 1 July 1984 cif Yokohama and payment by Mitzi to be by opening a confirmed irrevocable credit in Sydney for $A200,000 in favour of Carb and utilisable by drawing a 90 day bill of exchange against delivery of shipping documents comprising shipped bill of lading, marine insurance policy, inspection certificate, etc. In compliance with the contract, Mitzi must establish (normally through its bank, called issuing bank, eg, Tokyo Bank) at a bank in Sydney (if it is not a branch of Tokyo Bank, it will be its correspondent bank in Sydney, called the intermediary bank, eg, Sydney Bank) in favour of Carb (called the beneficiary) a documentary letter of credit for $200,000. Tokyo Bank must undertake not to revoke the credit. In order to be doubly sure of the value of the credit, Carb has stipulated that it be a confirmed, as well as irrevocable, credit. This requires the intermediary bank, now called confirming bank (Sydney Bank), not only to advise Carb that the credit has been established but also to confirm the credit by undertaking to fulfil the provisions for payment by, for example, accepting a bill of exchange drawn by Carb on Sydney Bank.

Since the contract of sale provided for a 90 day bill, neither Tokyo Bank, Sydney Bank nor Mitzi will actually have to pay cash for three months after acceptance of the bill. By this time the goods should have arrived in Yokohama and Mitzi may even have resold them. When Sydney Bank does accept the bill drawn by Carb, it holds as security the shipping documents representing the goods. On the other hand, even before shipment Carb has available an irrevocable promise to pay backed by substantial banks. Carb can use this letter of credit to obtain from its own bank, City Bank, pre-shipment finance with which to meet production costs. After shipping the goods it can discount with City Bank the bill which Sydney Bank accepted in return for the shipping documents.

The above example is based on the analysis in Weaver & Craigie, *The Law Relating to Banker and Customer in Australia,* 1975, p 733. There are, of course, a number of possible variations (see pp 462-6, *infra*) but this example was intended to provide you with some feel for the commercial realities which underlie the legal forms and rules. It should be clear from the above illustration that the primary function of the documentary credit is to enable trading banks to lend their name and credit standing to the transaction thereby overcoming "lack of knowledge of, or of confidence in, one of the parties to the transaction by the other, or uncertainty regarding a political situation in the country of the buyer": *Paget's Law of Banking,* 9th ed, 1982, p 529.

Why must Mitzi establish the credit in favour of Carb by the first available shipping date?

Pavia & Co SPA v Thurmann-Nielsen
English Court of Appeal [1952] 2 QB 84; [1952] 1 All ER 492

Thurmann-Nielsen agreed to sell and Pavia & Co agreed to buy a quantity of Brazilian groundnuts, shipment from Brazil as to one-half at any time between 1 February and 30 April, and as to the balance at any time between 1 March and 31 May at sellers' option cif Genoa. On 9 February the sellers had asked the buyers to open the credit under the two contracts and continued to press them to do so throughout February and March. The buyers repeatedly told the sellers that the credit would be available in a few days' time but it was not in fact made available until 22 April 1949. The sellers' bankers in Brazil refused to agree to the goods being sent to the port of shipment unless and until they were satisfied that a credit as stipulated in the contract had been opened by the buyers in the sellers' favour. The sellers dispatched about 675 tons after 22 April 1949, but never shipped the balance of about 2325 tons. They subsequently brought arbitration proceedings, claiming damages for breach of contract by the buyers in failing to open the credit.

At the hearing by the board of an appeal from the umpire's award awarding damages to the sellers, it was contended for the buyers that their obligation under the contracts was confined to providing the credit in time only to be available against presentation of documents.

For the sellers it was contended that the credit required under the contracts must be made available to them throughout the whole of the shipping period, or, alternatively, as soon as possible from the beginning of the period or within a reasonable time from that beginning. On a submission from the arbitrators to the court on this issue, McNair J gave judgment for the sellers. The buyers appealed.

Denning LJ: The sale of goods across the world is now usually arranged by means of confirmed credits. The buyer requests his banker to open a credit in favour of the seller, and in pursuance of that request the banker, or his foreign agent, issues a confirmed credit in favour of the seller. This credit is a promise by the banker to pay money to the seller in return for the shipping documents. Then the seller, when he presents the documents, gets paid the contract price. The conditions of the credit must be strictly fulfilled, otherwise the seller would not be entitled to draw on it.

The question in this case is this: In a contract which provides for payment by confirmed credit, when must the buyer open the credit? In the absence of express stipulation, I think the credit must be made available to the seller at the beginning of the shipment period. The reason is because the seller is entitled, before he ships the goods, to be assured that, on shipment, he will get paid. The seller is not bound to tell the buyer the precise date when he is going to ship; and whenever he does ship the goods, he must be able to draw on the credit. He may ship on the very first day of the shipment period. If, therefore, the buyer is to fulfil his obligations he must make the credit available to the seller at the very first date when the goods may be lawfully shipped in compliance with the contract. I agree with the answer given by McNair J. The appeal should be dismissed.

[**Somervell LJ** delivered judgment to the same effect. **Roxburgh J** agreed.]

Appeal dismissed.

Is the same reasoning applicable to an fob contract?

Ian Stach Ltd v Baker Bosley Ltd
Queen's Bench Division [1958] 2 QB 130; [1958] 1 All ER 542

In July 1956, the plaintiffs, Ian Stach Ltd, steel merchants, contracted with the defendants, Baker Bosley Ltd, for the sale to them of 500 metric tons of ship plates of West German origin at the price of $205 per metric ton. Both parties were middlemen under a string of contracts. The plaintiffs, while negotiating the contract with the defendants, at the same time entered into a contract with their suppliers, Amalgamated Exporters (Steel and Machinery) Ltd, for the purchase of 600 metric tons of ship plates at $190 per metric ton, of which the 500 tons to be sold to the defendants was to form a part. The contract between the plaintiffs and the defendants was signed on 10 July 1956, and provided for the goods to be delivered fob Benelux port (probably Amsterdam/Rotterdam), destination Canada. Delivery was to be August/September 1956, and payment by confirmed irrevocable letter of credit divisible and transferable and assignable to the plaintiffs' nominees in Western Germany. The plaintiffs undertook to establish a two per cent performance bond immediately they received a pre-advice from the defendant's bank that the letter of credit was being established. In a letter of 12 July 1956, the plaintiffs informed the defendants that delivery would be made by their suppliers to Rotterdam or Amsterdam as the defendants required; that it was the defendants' responsibility to obtain shipping space; that calling forward instructions should be sent as soon as possible; and that they were urgently awaiting either a pre-advice from the defendants' bank that the credit was being established or else the actual credit itself. The defendants, however, who were experiencing difficulty in obtaining a letter of credit from their own buyers, failed to establish the credit. In a letter of 8 August 1956, the plaintiffs requested the defendants "to open immediately your letter of credit covering this order, as the mills are pressing us for this most energetically". As the defendants still failed to do so, the plaintiffs informed them on 14 August that as they had failed to adhere to the conditions of the contract they would be held responsible for the consequences. In the events which happened the defendants never in fact opened the letter of credit in favour of the plaintiffs.

[The plaintiffs resold the steel at a lower price and sued the defendants for the difference of £1964 as damages for breach of contract, alleging an implied term that the defendants would establish the letter of credit not later than 1 August 1956, or, alternatively, forthwith upon being thereafter called on to do so.]

Diplock J: This case raises the question: at what time under an fob contract, where payment is by confirmed credit, must the buyer open the credit? International trade has to an increasing extent over the last 30 or 40 years been financed by bankers' confirmed credits. So much so that the classic fob and cif contracts of the textbooks providing for cash or acceptance against documents without the intervention of the banker are now probably the exception rather than the rule ... The relevant facts are fairly short. Both the plaintiffs and the defendants are merchants dealing in steel, among other metals. As each knew, neither of them was a manufacturer or stockist or a user of steel: they were both middlemen. The sums involved in contracts which they had on hand at any particular time were large, and, as is usual in the trade, beyond their own financial resources. Their method of carrying on business, again usual in the trade, was to enter into practically simultaneous contracts of purchase and sale, and to rely upon the banker's credits opened by the buyers to enable them to pay the purchase price to the person from whom they had in turn bought.

Where, as in the present case, there is a string of merchants' contracts between the manufacturer or stockist and the ultimate user, the normal mechanism for carrying out the various contracts is the familiar one which was intended to be used in this case: the ultimate user, under the terms of his contract of sale, opens a transferable, divisible credit in favour of his seller for his purchase price: his seller in turn transfers so much of the credit as corresponds to his own purchase price to his seller or, more probably, if his own contract with another merchant also calls for a transferable, divisible credit, procures his own banker to issue a back-to-back credit — that is to say, he lodges the credit in his favour with his own banker, who in his turn issues a transferable, divisible credit for the amount of his purchase price to his own seller; and so on, through the string of merchants, until the banker of the last merchant in the string issues the credit in favour of the actual manufacturer or stockist. The reason why they issue fresh credits is that in banking practice a transferable credit is regarded as transferable once only, and also as is obvious in this sort of trade, it is deisred, naturally enough, by any merchant in the string to conceal from his buyer and his seller who his own customer is. That is the way, as both parties to the present transactions knew, in which this type of business is normally carried on.

[His Lordship referred to the facts and continued at QB 139:] The first question that I have to decide is: When was it the duty of the defendants to open the letter of credit or to forward the banker's pre-advice? — that alternative having been put forward in the letter of 12 July 1956.

As has been pointed out in numerous cases, the commercial purpose of a banker's confirmed credit is more than a mere method of payment: it creates a direct liability upon the banker independent of the contract of sale, and is an undertaking by the banker that if the seller presents the required documents in the required time he will receive payment of the contract price. The commercial importance of this independent undertaking constituted by opening a confirmed credit is illustrated in a recent case in the Court of Appeal — *Hamzeh Malas & Sons v British Imex Industries Ltd* [1958] 2 QB 127 — where the Court of Appeal refused an injunction to restrain the defendants from making use of the credit. I need merely refer to a passage in the judgment of Jenkins LJ, where he says at 129: " ... it seems to be plain enough that the opening of a confirmed letter of credit constitutes a bargain between the banker and the vendor of the goods, which imposes upon the banker an absolute obligation to pay, irrespective of any dispute there may be between the parties as to whether the goods are up to contract or not. An elaborate commercial system has been built up on the footing that bankers' confirmed credits are of that character, and, in my judgment, it would be wrong for this court in the present case to interfere with that established practice. There is this to be remembered, too. A vendor of goods selling against a confirmed letter of credit is selling under the assurance that nothing will prevent him from receiving the price. That is of no mean advantage when goods manufactured in one country are being sold in another. It is, furthermore, to be observed that vendors are often reselling goods bought from third parties. When they are doing that, and when they are being paid by a confirmed letter of credit, their practice is — and I think it was followed by the defendants in this case — to finance the payments necessary to be made to their suppliers against the letter of credit. That system of financing these operations, as I see it, would break down completely if a dispute as between the vendor and the purchaser was to have the effect of freezing, if I may use that expression, the sum in respect of which the letter of credit was opened."

A letter of confirmed credit constitutes a direct undertaking by the banker that the seller, if he presents the documents as required in the required time, will receive payment; and where there is provision that under a contract a confirmed credit is to be provided, then as was pointed out by Devlin J in *Sinason-Teicher Inter-American Grain Corp v Oilcakes and Oilseeds Trading Co Ltd* [1954] 1 WLR 935 at 939; [1954] 2 All ER 497 that undertaking from the banker should be obtained before the seller embarks upon those operations which lead directly to the performance of his obligations under the contract.

There is clear authority binding upon me that in cif contracts the confirmed credit must be opened at latest by the beginning of the shipment period. That was decided by the Court of Appeal in *Pavia & Co SPA v Thurmann-Nielsen* [1952] 2 QB 84; [1952] 1 TLR 586; [1952] 1 All ER 492 where Somervell LJ said (QB at 88): "I think when a seller is given a right to ship over a period and there is machinery for payment, that machinery must be available over the whole of that period"; and Denning LJ put the matter succinctly in the following words ...

[His Lordship then quoted the second paragraph from the judgment of Denning LJ extracted p 459, *supra*.] That, I think, is as far as the binding authorities upon cif contracts go.

It is, however, to be observed that in the *Sinason-Teicher* case in the Court of Appeal, Denning LJ said this (WLR at 1400): "We were referred to *Pavia & Co SPA v Thurmann-Nielsen*. I agree with what Devlin J said about that case. It does not decide that the buyer can delay right up to the first date for shipment. It only decides that he must provide the letter of credit at latest by that date. The correct view is that, if nothing is said about time in the contract, the buyer must provide the letter of credit within a reasonable time before the first date for shipment. The same applies to a bank guarantee: for it stands on a similar footing."

I think that those observations, although entitled to great respect, are obiter, and they were not necessary for the decision in that case — as indeed appears from the judgment of Devlin J (WLR at 939) in the lower court, where he refers to the matter and says it is unnecessary to decide it. Neither of the other Lords Justices appears to me to express any view on the matter.

Those being the cases upon cif contracts, Mr Kerr, to whom for his researches among the case law I am much indebted, has drawn my attention to five cases which concern fob contracts.

[His Lordship then referred to five cases involving contracts on special fob terms which indicated a shipping date or otherwise specified the date for opening the credit. His Lordship continued at QB 142:] The distinction between those cases and the present case is that this is a classic fob contract in that the buyer is entitled to call for shipment at any time within the shipping period and up to the end of the shipping period. The authority for that (if any be wanted) is to be found in *J & J Cunningham Ltd v Robert A Munro & Co Ltd* (1922) 28 Com Cas 42. So it is said that there is a distinction to be drawn between a cif contract and a classic fob contract and a distinction to be drawn between a classic fob contract and those fob contracts which were the subjects of the cases to which Mr Kerr referred, namely, that in the classic fob contract, where the buyer can dictate the date of shipment, the seller is not obliged to commence any of the operations directed to performing his obligations under the contract until he has had shipping instructions or calling forward instructions from the buyer. It is urged by Mr Lawson that, applying the ratio decidendi in the cif contract cases — the *Pavia* line of cases — the time at which the confirmed credit must be opened is a reasonable time before the shipping instructions take effect. The rival contention by Mr Kerr is that the credit must be opened a reasonable time (as he put it) before the earliest shipping date; but in his reply he was prepared to put it as at latest by the earliest shipping date. Mr Lawson, on the other hand, says that it must be a reasonable time before the actual shipping date.

There is no authority which guides me in this matter. It seems to me, however, that the contention for which Mr Kerr argues is the sensible one, and, since it is the sensible one, and since there is no authority to the contrary, the one which I am inclined to hold, and do hold, is good law.

I am fortified in this view by the fact that it is quite apparent from the correspondence and from the conduct of the parties in this case (and, so far as one can see, from that of the parties to the other contracts) that it is their view that that was the requirement of the contract. It seems to me that, particularly in a trade of this kind, where, as is known to all parties participating, there may well be a string of contracts all of which are financed by, and can only be financed by, the credit opened by the ultimate user which goes down the string getting less and less until it comes to the ultimate supplier, the business sense of the arrangement requires that by the time the shipping period starts each of the sellers should receive the assurance from the banker that if he performs his part of the contract he will receive payment. That seems to me at least to have the advantage of providing a definite date by which the parties know they have to fulfil the obligation of opening a credit.

The alternative view put forward by Mr Lawson, namely, that the credit has to be opened a reasonable time before the actual shipping date, seems to me to lead to an uncertainty on the part of the buyer and seller which I should be reluctant to import into any commercial contract ...

It seems to me that in a case of this kind, and in the case of an ordinary fob contract financed by a confirmed banker's credit, the prima facie rule is that the credit must be opened at latest (and that is as far as I need go for the purposes of this case) by the earliest shipping date. In that way one gets certainty into what is a very common commercial contract. In any other way one can, I think, only get a position in which neither buyer nor seller knows what his rights are until all the facts have been ascertained, and one, and possibly two or three, courts have directed their minds to the question whether in all the circumstances that was a reasonable time for the credit to be opened.

I therefore hold that it was the duty of the defendants under this contract to open their letter of credit or to get a banker's pre-advice of it by 1 August 1956, at the latest...

Judgment for the plaintiffs.

TYPES OF LETTERS OF CREDIT

An initial distinction should be made between (a) open or clean letters of credit issued to travellers and (b) bankers' commercial or documentary letters of credit.

Open letters of credit are issued by banks to their customers to enable the customers to obtain cash when travelling. The letter may be addressed to other branches of the bank or another specific bank authorising that bank to cash cheques or drafts for the customer; or it may be a circular letter of credit with a similar authorisation to the establishing bank's agents throughout the world. Neither form places any contractual obligation on the other banks to comply with the request for funds. Travellers' letters of credit are very convenient but are less popular today because they have been the vehicle for some frauds perpetrated by forgery and have tended to be superseded by travellers' cheques.

Bankers' documentary letters of credit were comprehensively described at the beginning of this section, and should be examined in the light of *The Uniform Customs and Practice for Documentary Credits (UCP)*, published by the International Chamber of Commerce. This document provides a standard set of rules to govern the interpretation, application and general usages of bankers' documentary credits. UCP do not have statutory effect, but are invariably incorporated by express reference into the special conditions of the letter of credit as in the specimen on p 464, *infra*. Accordingly, the exporter and importer of goods should take the UCP into account when preparing their contract of sale. The current 1974 edition of UCP (containing amendments to provide for container shipping documents) is available from the overseas or international departments at the head offices of the trading banks or from the International Chamber of Commerce (Publication No 290). Further revisions of UCP have been drafted by the International Chamber of Commerce but have not been finalised at the date of writing.

UCP contains the following definition of a documentary credit:

(a) These provisions and definitions and the following articles apply to all documentary credits and are binding upon all parties thereto unless otherwise expressly agreed.

(b) For the purposes of such provisions, definitions and articles the expressions "documentary credit(s)" and "credit(s)" used therein mean any arrangement, however named or described, whereby a bank (the issuing bank), acting at the request and in accordance with the instructions of a customer (the applicant for the credit):

    (i)   is to make payment to or to the order of a third party (the beneficiary), or is to pay, accept or negotiate bills of exchange (drafts) drawn by the beneficiary, or

    (ii) authorises such payments to be made or such drafts to be paid, accepted or negotiated by another bank, against stipulated documents provided that the terms and conditions of the credit are complied with.

The documentary credit involves at least three parties:

(a) the applicant for credit (in our example Mitzi);

(b) the applicant's bank called the issuing bank (Tokyo Bank);

(c) the beneficiary of the credit (Carb) and in some cases another bank, namely the advising or confirming bank (Sydney Bank).

An illustration of an irrevocable credit is shown on p 464, *infra*. This credit constitutes a promise by Tokyo Bank (issuing bank) to pay the beneficiary Carb. The credit may be drawn in a form which allows Carb to assign it. It may call for confirmation by a confirming bank (confirmed irrevocable credit); or it may be available to Carb to draw a bill of exchange (draft) on the issuing bank, which is called a negotiation credit, whereby the bank engages to pay the drawer Carb or subsequent bona fide holders to whom Carb may negotiate the draft.

The distinction between revocable and irrevocable credits and the incidents of an irrevocable confirmed credit are set out in Articles 1-3 of UCP:

Article 1
  (a) Credits may be either:
    (i) revocable, or
    (ii) irrevocable.
  (b) All credits, therefore, should clearly indicate whether they are revocable or irrevocable.
  (c) In the absence of such indication the credit shall be deemed to be revocable.

Article 2
A revocable credit may be amended or cancelled at any moment without prior notice to the beneficiary. However, the issuing bank is bound to reimburse a branch or other bank to which such a credit has been transmitted and made available for payment, acceptance or negotiation, for any payment, acceptance or negotiation complying with the terms and conditions of the credit and any amendments received up to the time of payment, acceptance or negotiation made by such branch or other bank prior to receipt by it of notice of amendment or of cancellation.

Article 3
  (a) An irrevocable credit constitutes a definite undertaking of the issuing bank, providing that the terms and conditions of the credit are complied with:
    (i) to pay, or that payment will be made, if the credit provides for payment, whether against a draft or not;
    (ii) to accept drafts if the credit provides for acceptance by the issuing bank or to be responsible for their acceptance and payment at maturity if the credit provides for the acceptance of drafts drawn on the applicant for the credit or any other drawee specified in the credit;
    (iii) to purchase/negotiate, without recourse to drawers and/or bona fide holders, drafts drawn by the beneficiary, at sight or at a tenor, on the applicant for the credit or on any other drawee specified in the credit, or to provide for purchase/negotiation by another bank, if the credit provides for purchase/negotiation.
  (b) An irrevocable credit may be advised to a beneficiary through another bank (the advising bank) without engagement on the part of that bank, but when an issuing bank authorises or requests another bank to confirm its irrevocable credit and the latter does so, such confirmation constitutes a definite undertaking of the confirming bank in addition to the undertaking of the issuing bank, provided that the terms and conditions of the credit are complied with:
    (i) to pay, if the credit is payable at its own counters, whether against a draft or not, or that payment will be made if the credit provides for payment elsewhere;
    (ii) to accept drafts if the credit provides for acceptance by the confirming bank, at its own counters, or to be responsible for their acceptance and payment at maturity if the credit provides for the acceptance of drafts drawn on the applicant for the credit or any other drawee specified in the credit;
    (iii) to purchase/negotiate, without recourse to drawers and/or bona fide holders, drafts drawn by the beneficiary, at sight or at a tenor, on the issuing bank, or on the applicant for the credit or on any other drawee specified in the credit, if the credit provides for purchase/negotiation.
  (c) Such undertakings can neither be amended nor cancelled without the agreement of all parties thereto. Partial acceptance of amendments is not effective without the agreement of all parties thereto.

Teaching Materials and Cases on Commercial Transactions

Irrevocable Documentary Credit—available by acceptance
Tokyo Bank Limited International Division

Telephone 28465 Telex TB007

Original

Date 1 May, 1984

IRREVOCABLE DOCUMENTARY CREDIT	Credit number	
	of issuing bank	of advising bank
	97531	86420
Advising bank	Applicant	
Sydney Bank Limited Head Office George Street Sydney	Mitzi Co Tarumi-Ku Tokyo	
Beneficiary	Amount	
Carb Pty. Limited 10 Gearway Ryde. N.S.W.	Two hundred thousand dollars ($200,000-00) Australian currency	
	Expiry Date 31 July, 1984	
	at the counters of: Sydney Bank, Head Office	

Dear Sir(s)
We hereby issue in your favour this documentary credit which is available by acceptance of your draft at Sydney Bank Limited, Head Office, Sydney drawn on Sydney Bank Limited accompanied by the following documents: shipped bill of lading
marine insurance policy
commercial invoice
inspection certificate by Natsun Cars
Australian export licence
covering
200 cases automotive carburettors

Each draft accompanying documents must state: "Drawn under credit No. 97531/of Tokyo Bank Ltd and No. 86420 of Sydney Bank Limited (advising bank)".

Despatch/Shipment from Sydney to Yokohama	Partial shipments	Transhipments

Special conditions:

We hereby engage that drafts drawn in conformity with the terms of this credit will be duly accepted on presentation and duly honoured at maturity.	Advising bank's notification
Yours faithfully Tokyo Bank Limited International Division Countersigned J. Yamamura	Sydney Bank Limited Head Office, Sydney Will Cash Manager 8 May, 1984. Place, date, name and signature of advising bank.

Except so far as otherwise expressly stated, this documentary credit is subject to the "Uniform Customs and Practice for Documentary Credits" (1974 Revision) International Chamber of Commerce (Publication No. 290). This document conforms with the standard form No. 2 of the I.C.C.

A number of variations on this basic form of documentary credit are in common use. These include:

Transferable credits which state that they are transferable and entitle the beneficiaries to nominate third parties as substituted beneficiaries. These are described in UCP:

Article 46

(a) A transferable credit is a credit under which the beneficiary has the right to give instructions to the bank called upon to effect payment or acceptance or to any bank entitled to effect negotiation to make the credit available in whole or in part to one or more third parties (second beneficiaries).

(b) The bank requested to effect the transfer, whether it has confirmed the credit or not, shall be under no obligation to effect such transfer except to the extent and in the manner expressly consented to by such bank, and until such bank's charges in respect of transfer are paid.

(c) Bank charges in respect of transfers are payable by the first beneficiary unless otherwise specified.

(d) A credit can be transferred only if it is expressly designated as "transferable" by the issuing bank. Terms such as "divisible", "fractionnable", "assignable", and "transmissible" add nothing to the meaning of the term "transferable" and shall not be used.

(e) A transferable credit can be transferred once only. Fractions of a transferable credit (not exceeding in the aggregate the amount of the credit) can be transferred separately, provided partial shipments are not prohibited, and the aggregate of such transfers will be considered as constituting only one transfer of the credit. The credit can be transferred only on the terms and conditions specified in the original credit, with the exception of the amount of the credit, of any unit prices stated therein, and of the period of validity or period for shipment, any or all of which may be reduced or curtailed. Additionally, the name of the first beneficiary can be substituted for that of the applicant for the credit, but if the name of the applicant for the credit is specifically required by the original credit to appear in any document other than the invoice, such requirement must be fulfilled.

(f) The first beneficiary has the right to substitute his own invoices for those of the second beneficiary, for amounts not in excess of the original amount stipulated in the credit and for the original unit prices if stipulated in the credit, and upon such substitution of invoices the first beneficiary can draw under the credit for the difference, if any, between his invoices and the second beneficiary's invoices. When a credit has been transferred and the first beneficiary is to supply his own invoices in exchange for the second beneficiary's invoices but fails to do so on first demand, the paying, accepting or negotiating bank has the right to deliver to the issuing bank the documents received under the credit, including the second beneficiary's invoices, without further responsibility to the first beneficiary.

(g) The first beneficiary of a transferable credit can transfer the credit to a second beneficiary in the same country or in another country unless the credit specifically states otherwise. The first beneficiary shall have the right to request that payment or negotiation be effected to the second beneficiary at the place to which the credit has been transferred, up to and including the expiry date of the original credit, and without prejudice to the first beneficiary's right subsequently to substitute his own invoices for those of the second beneficiary and to claim any difference due to him.

Article 47

The fact that a credit is not stated to be transferable shall not affect the beneficiary's rights to assign the proceeds of such credit in accordance with the provisions of the applicable law.

Back-to-back credits which are used to finance string contracts where the same goods are sold or resold by middlemen in the type of situation described in *Ian Stach Ltd v Baker Bosley Ltd*, p 459, *supra*. The irrevocable credit opened by the ultimate purchaser (eg, buyer from Mitzi) in favour of Mitzi can be used by Mitzi as backing for the issuance by Tokyo Bank of a similar irrevocable credit in favour of Carb.

Red clause credits which are used where the buyer agrees to assist the seller in obtaining pre-shipment finance. The credit contains a special clause printed in red in which the buyer as applicant for the credit (Mitzi), authorises the issuing bank

(Tokyo Bank) to request the advising bank (Sydney Bank) to advance to the beneficiary Carb part or all of the credit on overdraft prior to shipment. It is intended that the advance will be repaid from the proceeds of drawings when the goods are actually shipped, but in the meantime, the applicant Mitzi (and, in the case of an irrevocable credit, the issuing Tokyo Bank) guarantee repayment of the advances and interest thereon.

Standby letters of credit are a more recent development in international commerce designed to perform the function normally performed by a contract of guarantee or performance bond in domestic transactions. Under the so-called standby credit, the issuing bank undertakes to pay a specified sum to the beneficiary of the credit if the principal fails to perform his contractual obligations. This is in contrast to the normal letter of credit which constitutes a promise to pay *upon due performance,* eg, upon delivery of bill of lading, insurance policy and other documents specified in the letter of credit.

In the international context, the principal will often deal directly with his local bank (the "opening bank") which will in turn instruct the "issuing bank" in the beneficiary's country to issue the standby credit to the beneficiary.

For a fuller description of the various types of credits, see *Weaver & Craigie,* pp 733-9, or Gutteridge & Megrah, *The Law of Bankers' Commercial Credits,* 6th ed, 1979, Ch 2, and specimen forms in Appendix D.

THE LEGAL BASIS FOR AN IRREVOCABLE CREDIT

In UCP art 3, *supra,* an irrevocable credit is described as a "definite undertaking" which "can neither be amended nor cancelled without the agreement of all parties thereto". When UCP are incorporated into buyer Mitzi's irrevocable (or irrevocable and confirmed) letter of credit, the issuing Tokyo Bank is presumably bound to its customer Mitzi, and it is said a bank which revoked such a credit would do so at its peril. However, a number of questions remain:

(1) On what basis in law can Carb as beneficiary of the credit claim that the credit is irrevocable in its favour? Can Mitzi, which originally applied for the credit to be issued, request issuing Tokyo Bank to revoke the credit—perhaps because Carb's goods are defective?

(2) Assuming the irrevocable credit cannot be revoked without the beneficiary Carb's concurrence, at what point in time does it become irrevocable?

Urquhart Lindsay & Co Ltd v Eastern Bank Ltd
King's Bench Division [1922] 1 KB 318

Rowlatt J: In this case the essential facts are few and simple. The plaintiffs in this country arranged with the Benjamin Jute Mills, Calcutta, to manufacture and ship to them over a series of months a quantity of machinery, at prices mentioned in a pro forma invoice; subject however to a stipulation not infrequently insisted upon by manufacturers at the date when the arrangement was made, that should the cost of labour or wages advance there would be a corresponding advance in the prices to be paid by the buyers. The goods were to be paid for by means of a confirmed irrevocable credit to be opened by the buyers in favour of the plaintiffs with a bank in this country, who were to pay the plaintiffs for each shipment as it took place. In pursuance of this arrangement the defendant bank at the instance of the buyers issued to the plaintiffs a document the terms of which I need not rehearse in detail, it being sufficient to state that the defendants undertook up to a certain amount and within a certain limit of time to pay the plaintiffs, against bills drawn upon the buyers accompanied by corresponding invoices and shipping documents, the amount of such invoices. This credit was by its terms to be irrevocable and the invoices were to be for machinery. There can be no doubt that upon the plaintiffs acting upon the undertaking contained in this letter of credit consideration moved from the plaintiffs, which bound the defendants to the irrevocable character of the arrangement between the defendants and the plaintiffs; nor was it contended before me that this had not become the position when the circumstances giving rise to this action took place.

Having received the letter of credit, the plaintiffs proceeded to manufacture the machinery and actually shipped two instalments of it, receiving payment from the defendants under the letter of credit against bills accompanied by invoices and other documents called for by that instrument. Before the third shipment was made the buyers, finding that the plaintiffs were including in their invoices an addition to the prices originally quoted, in respect of an alleged rise in the cost of wages or materials, instructed the defendants only to pay so much of the next invoices as represented the original prices. These instructions (very unfortunately, as I think, from many points of view) the defendants obeyed. The plaintiffs however refused to part with the documents representing their goods unless they received the full amount of the invoices; and upon the defendants maintaining their position cancelled the contract as to further shipments, as upon a repudiation by the buyers, and have brought this action against the defendants, claiming as damages the loss on material thrown on their hands, and loss of profit; in other words, the same damages as they would claim against the buyers on their repudiation of the contract. After the action had been commenced the defendants paid to the plaintiffs the amount of the invoices, the original refusal of which had caused the dispute.

In my view the defendants committed a breach of their contract with the plaintiffs when they refused to pay the amount of the invoices as presented. Mr Stuart Bevan contended that the letter of credit must be taken to incorporate the contract between the plaintiffs and their buyers; and that according to the true meaning of that contract the amount of any increase claimed in respect of an alleged advance in manufacturing costs was not to be included in any invoice to be presented under the letter of credit, but was to be the subject of subsequent independent adjustment. The answer to this is that the defendants undertook to pay the amount of invoices for machinery without qualification, the basis of this form of banking facility being that the buyer is taken for the purposes of all questions between himself and his banker or between his banker and the seller to be content to accept the invoices of the seller as correct. It seems to me that so far from the letter of credit being qualified by the contract of sale, the latter must accommodate itself to the letter of credit. The buyer having authorised his banker to undertake to pay the amount of the invoice as presented, it follows that any adjustment must be made by way of refund by the seller, and not by way of retention by the buyer.

[His Lordship then discussed the measure of damages.]

Judgment for plaintiffs.

The irrevocability of a letter of credit was likewise upheld in *Hamzeh Malas & Sons v British Imex Industries Ltd* [1958] 2 QB 127; [1958] 1 All ER 262 where the Court of Appeal refused to extend an interim injunction to restrain the defendant sellers from drawing on a letter of credit or receiving payment from the bank which had issued the credit. The basis of the decision is indicated by Jenkins LJ in the passage already quoted in *Ian Stach Ltd v Baker Bosley Ltd*, p 459, *supra*. However, Sellers LJ did point out that the court might well grant such an injunction where there was evidence of a fraudulent transaction.

A G Davis: Commercial Letters of Credit
(1965) 5 *Syd LR* 14 at 14-18

First then, as to the operation of commercial letters of credit, which Lord Chorley, *Law of Banking*, 4th ed, 1960, p 179 has aptly described as the crankshaft of modern commerce. Almost without exception, they arise out of a contract for the sale of goods, the seller usually being in one country and the buyer in another, though in the United States, internal letters of credit, that is, those in which the seller carries on business in one state and the buyer in another, are not unknown. One of the terms of the contract for the sale of goods is that the buyer will pay the purchase price by means of a letter of credit. Usually there will be some description of the type of letter of credit, whether revocable or irrevocable, confirmed or unconfirmed. I shall explain some of these terms later. In order to carry out his side of the contract, the buyer will go to his banker to procure the issue by him, the banker, of a letter of credit in favour of the seller. But before the banker will issue the letter of credit, he will get his customer, the buyer, to complete and sign an application to open a documentary credit. This is a most important document from the point of view of both the buyer and the banker. In it the buyer will instruct the banker as to what documents he is to receive on the buyer's behalf, in compliance with the contract for the sale of the goods. Must the insurance be covered by a policy of insurance or is a certificate sufficient? Must the bills of lading be "shipped" bills of lading or will a "received for shipment" bill of lading suffice? Are partial shipments allowed? Is transhipment allowed? I must say that it is only with the development of the law relating to commercial letters of credit that these details have been worked out. In the early type of letters of credit, careless phrases such as "bills of lading" "insurance cover" and the like were used and the courts have been concerned to determine what the parties really intended. But more and more these details are being looked after...

But to get back to the application made to the bank to issue the letter of credit: after detailing the documents required and the goods which they are intended to cover, the buyer agrees that, in consideration of the bank issuing the letter of credit, the bank shall have a pledge on all goods and documents of title over the goods which are delivered into the possession of the bank or its correspondents as a result of the opening of the credit. In addition, as might well be expected, there is a further clause exonerating the bank from liability for any error, fault, or mistake in the description, quantity, quality or delivery of the goods concerned.

Now this application for the issue of a letter of credit is a most important document. It is, of course, a contract between the buyer and the bank, supported by adequate consideration. The bank will depart from the terms of this application—sometimes called a letter of request, only at its peril. If the application calls for a full-set of bills of lading, it is no good for the banker to accept one or two. Quite an amount of the litigation which has arisen out of letters of credit, has involved the duty of the bank under the terms of the letter of request.

Being satisfied that the letter of request is all in order and being satisfied as to the credit-worthiness of his customer, the bank will issue the letter of credit. I shall not, at the moment, complicate the matter by making reference to correspondent or confirming bankers who will normally carry on business in the seller's country. For the sake of simplicity, I shall merely state that in the letter of credit which the issuing banker—for our purposes—sends direct to the seller, the banker authorises the seller to draw on him, at sight or at so many weeks or months after sight on account of the goods the subject of the contract of sale for the sum which represents the purchase price of the goods.

This does create one of the most difficult theoretical problems concerning commercial letters of credit—a problem which, however, does not seem to have worried the courts. As I have mentioned, in the case or an irrevocable letter of credit—I shall not mention here the revocable letter of credit which is rarely used—the issuing banker gives an unqualified promise to the beneficiary of the credit—the seller—that he will meet the seller's drafts provided they are accompanied by the documents specified in the letter of credit. But normally the beneficiary will be unknown to the issuing banker. He is known only as the person that his customer has named as the seller in whose favour the letter of credit is to be issued. It would be begging the question to say that there is no contract between them. But certainly there is no consideration moving from the seller to the banker sufficient to support a simple contract. Yet it is recognised throughout the common law world that the banker's promise is absolute; he cannot withdraw from it with impunity... it has been sought to uphold the banker's duty by saying that when the seller "acted on the promise" contained in the letter of credit, whatever that may mean, consideration moved from the seller and thereafter the banker could not revoke his promise. Of course, it may be said that in acting on the banker's promise, the seller was not doing anything more than he was bound to do under his contract with the buyer and, as we all know, there is much doubt whether a promise to perform or the performance of a duty towards a third party, already existing, does constitute consideration. But let us look at the authorities.

[The author then referred to the judgment of Rowlatt J in *Urquhart Lindsay* case extracted on p 466, *supra*.]

What "acting on the undertaking" meant Rowlatt J did not say. But in the circumstances, as the contract was to "manufacture and deliver", the beginning of the manufacturing would seem to be an acting on the undertaking sufficient to constitute consideration.

The particular document discussed in *Dexters Ltd v Schenker & Co* was not in form a letter of credit, but it was treated as such. The defendants wrote to the plantiffs as follows: "Re 10 tons vegetable grease for Messrs Astra . . . we beg to inform you that today we have received the amount of . . . (£700 odd) for the above consignment. We request you to arrange shipment of this parcel by earliest occasion and let us have your shipping advice, stamped and signed B/L and certificate of insurance as soon as possible. At once after receipt of the goods at Rotterdam we will transfer the abovenamed amount to you": (1923) 14 Lloyd LR 586.

The defendants refused to pay on the ground that the goods were not as described in the contract. They also pleaded absence of consideration moving from the seller but abandoned this plea during the argument. Greer J said: "Now it is clear that, until the plaintiffs got a form of banker's credit which would comply with the terms of the contract, they were not bound to send the goods forward at all; and therefore, not having got the banker's credit, until there was a substituted arrangement for some other credit elsewhere, they were under no obligation to anybody to send forward the goods. Therefore, it is quite clear that there was a full and ample consideration for this undertaking, and I am not surprised that Mr Wallington (counsel for the defendants) withdrew the contention which appears in the pleadings that there was no consideration": (1923) 14 Lloyd LR 586.

Authority, such as there is, in the United States, is to the like effect. In *Moss v Old Colony Trust Co* (1923) 140 NE 803 a Buenos Aires merchant sought to recover from the bank damages against the bank because it refused to accept and pay four drafts drawn by the plaintiff under an irrevocable letter of credit issued by the defendants in his favour. Dealing with the effect of such a letter of credit Rugg CJ said: "A letter of credit is an offer by a bank or other financial agency to be bound to the person to whom it is directed, when accepted and acted upon by the latter according to its stipulations . . . The letter of credit, when so accepted and acted upon by the person in whose favour it is issued, becomes a contract between them wholly independent of the relations between the writer of the letter of credit and its customer": (1923) 140 NE 803.

On the authorities, therefore, it would seem that once the seller has "acted upon" the banker's promise, whether by beginning manufacture, shipping goods or doing any other act contemplated by the original contract between buyer and seller, there is a binding contract and the banker repudiates it only at his peril. At least, it seems, he cannot plead absence of consideration.

STRICT COMPLIANCE WITH THE DOCUMENTARY CREDIT

The terms of the documentary credit are designed to protect both buyer and seller. The buyer is entitled to receive through the issuing or advising bank all the shipping documents in proper form which he has specified in the contract of sale with the seller and in the documentary credit issued by his bank. The seller is correspondingly guaranteed that he will be paid if he presents those specified documents to the advising bank. Export transactions involving documentary credits operate by using documents representing the goods rather than by delivery of the goods themselves.

Great importance therefore attaches to the description of the documents in the sale contract and documentary credit, the legal interpretation of those descriptions and strict compliance with them. The requirements for various standard documents— shipping documents, marine bills of lading, insurance policies, invoices, are set out in UCP Section C, which includes in arts 14–33 standard requirements for shipping documents, namely various types of bills of lading and combined transport documents, insurance documents and commercial invoices.

Much litigation has turned upon the question whether the documents tendered under a documentary credit comply with its terms. "The conditions of the credit must be strictly fulfilled, otherwise the seller would not be entitled to draw on it": Denning LJ in the *Pavia* case quoted on p 458, *supra*. The issuing or confirming bank is obliged to honour the credit when the seller tenders conforming documents. This will occur in the great majority of cases. However, various problems may arise including:

(1) The documents may not conform to the conditions of the credit in some minor respect; or a document may be ambiguous. How closely must the documents conform?

(2) The bank may overlook a deficiency in the documents and pay out on the credit. What is its position?

(3) The bank may suspect that the documents have been obtained by fraud, or are forged. Is it obliged to pay? Is it responsible to its customer, the buyer, if it does pay?

(4) The buyer may request the bank not to pay, and furnish some evidence to the bank as to the invalidity of the documents. Should the bank act as judge between the rival claims of buyer and seller?

A G Davis: Commercial Letters of Credit
(1965) 5 *Syd LR* 14 at 18–20

But the seller, for his part, must strictly comply with the terms of the letter of credit if he is to hold the banker liable on it. As has been mentioned, the letter of credit will stipulate what documents must accompany the seller's drafts. These, for the protection of the banker against claims by his customer, must comply exactly with those specified in the letter of request. The banker can seek reimbursement from his customer only if he has complied with the customer's mandate. Therefore, if the buyer has told the banker that among the accompanying documents is to be a certificate of quality signed by X, then such a document must be specified in the letter of credit and accompany the seller's draft. It is no good forwarding a certificate signed by Y, even though, in the particular trade, Y may be more expert than X.

I had what, to me, is an amusing illustration of this point some years ago. A New Zealand merchant had sold some butter — not a large quantity, measured in hundredweights, to an importer in Cuba. The terms were so much a hundredweight cif Havana. According to the terms of the sales contract the seller's drafts had to be accompanied by a certificate of quality authenticated by the Cuban consul in New Zealand. A letter of credit issued by a Cuban bank had been confirmed by an Auckland bank; that is to say, the Auckland bank, the correspondents of the Cuban bank, had, in broad terms, guaranteed the Cuban bank's letter of credit. But no one could find a Cuban consul in New Zealand so the New Zealand merchant thought it would do just as well if he got the certificate of quality from the United States consul. This was some years before the Castro regime. The geography of the foreign exchange clerk at the bank must have been a bit weak. Apparently he thought Cuba was part of the United States. In any event he accepted the United States certificate as complying with the terms of the letter of credit. Then the Foreign Manager came on the scene. Checking through what I suppose is the documents register, he found that the terms of the letter of credit had not been complied with in that an ineffective certificate of quality had been accepted and forwarded to Havana along with the other documents; and, what was more important immediately, the seller, the Auckland merchant, had been paid for the butter. His drafts had been met. That was where I came in and my advice was asked. From the legal point of view I could only advise that the bank would be liable if the Cuban bank refused to accept their drafts. But from a practical point I advised the bank to "wait and see". For one thing the Auckland merchant was a customer — and a good customer — of the bank; secondly, like the nurse's baby in "Midshipman Easy", the amount involved was small and, finally, the Cuban bank and the Cuban merchant might accept a United States consular certificate as the equivalent of one issued by a Cuban consul. The outcome was entirely satisfactory. No one seems to have noticed the error. The Havana bank met the Auckland bank's draft. The Auckland Foreign Manager heaved a sigh of relief and the Auckland merchant was told to expunge from any future contracts for the sale of butter to Cuba any reference to a Cuban consul or a Cuban consular certificate.

But a large amount of litigation has arisen out of allegations that incorrect documents have been tendered and accepted in purported performance of the duties of the seller, on the one hand, and of the banker, on the other. It works both ways. The seller, on his part, must tender to the issuing banker or to his correspondent, documents which comply *exactly* with those specified in the letter of credit. The issuing banker must, in the letter of credit, specify exactly what documents the seller must tender and this list must correspond exactly with those specified by the buyer in his letter of request.

The necessity for *exact* compliance was stressed by the English Court of Appeal in *Rayner v Hambros Bank* [1943] KB 37. The letter of credit, issued in favour of the plaintiffs, called for an invoice and bills of lading covering a shipment of "Coromandel groundnuts". The plaintiffs presented an invoice for "Coromandel groundnuts" and bills of lading describing the goods not as "Coromandel groundnuts" but as "machine-shelled groundnut kernels. Country of origin, British India". In the margin of the bills of lading were the marks: "OTC CRS Aarhus". The defendant bank refused to meet drafts drawn under the letter of credit on the ground that the letter of credit called for an invoice and bills of lading both covering a shipment of "Coromandel groundnuts". The bills of lading did not prescribe the goods in those terms. In an action against Hambros, evidence was given before the trial judge, Atkinson J and accepted by him (a) that "machine-shelled groundnut kernels" are the same commodity as "Coromandel groundnuts" and would be understood to be so in the trade in London; and (b) that the marginal mark on the bills of lading "CRS" was short for "Coros" or "Coromandels" and would be universally understood to be so in the trade in London. Atkinson J gave judgment for the plaintiffs, holding that the documents tendered covered "in the customary way" the goods mentioned in the letter of credit. His decision was unanimously reversed by the Court of Appeal. MacKinnon LJ quoted Bailhache J in *English, Scottish and Australian Bank Ltd v Bank of South Africa*: "It is elementary to say that a person who ships in reliance on a letter of credit must do so in exact compliance with its terms. It is also elementary to say that a bank is not bound or indeed entitled to honour drafts presented to it under a letter of credit unless those drafts with the accompanying documents are in exact accord with the credit as opened": (1922) 13 Lloyd LR 21.

And, added MacKinnon LJ: "The words in that bill of lading clearly are not the same as those required by the letter of credit ... I think on pure principle that the bank were entitled to refuse to accept this sight draft on the grounds that the documents tendered, the bill of lading in particular, did not comply exactly with the terms of the letter of credit which they had issued": [1943] KB at 40.

Dealing with that part of Atkinson J's judgment in which he said that "a sale of Coromandel groundnuts is universally understood to be a sale of machine-shelled kernels", MacKinnon LJ said (at 41): "... when Atkinson J says that it is 'universally understood', he means that these gentlemen from Mincing Lane have told him: '... We understand that 'Coromandel groundnuts' are machine-shelled groundnut kernels, and we understand when we see 'CRS' that that means 'Coromandels'.' ... I think that is a perfectly impossible suggestion ... it is quite impossible to suggest that a banker is to be affected with knowledge of the customs and customary terms of every one of the thousands of trades for whose dealings he may issue letters of credit."

Goddard LJ was, as usual, forthright. He said: "I protest against the view that a bank is to be deemed affected by knowledge of the trade of its various customers."

Judgment was consequently given for the defendants.

Assuming, although the matter is not free from doubt, that the relationship between the issuing banker and the beneficiary is contractual, it can readily be appreciated that, as in many cases arising out of contracts, one of the important questions is: how is this contract to be construed? What do the words of the contract mean? It certainly is amazing how businessmen — bankers also — can make their contracts in such ambiguous terms, leaving it to the courts to try to determine what they meant. Letters of credit suffer from this vice, as reference to a few of the decided cases will show.

Recent illustrations of disputes regarding the conformity of documents with the terms of documentary credits include: *Commercial Banking Co of Sydney Ltd v Jalsard Pty Ltd* [1973] AC 279; [1972-73] ALR 559; 46 ALJR 436 (Privy Council on appeal from NSW Supreme Court), where the bank had paid on the strength of certificates of inspection which certified as to the packing of the goods but not as to their quality. Since the plaintiff buyer's application for the letter of credit merely specified a certificate of inspection, the bank was held to have acted on a reasonable interpretation of this ambiguous description. See also *Gian Singh & Co Ltd v*

Banque de l'Indochine [1974] 1 WLR 1234; [1974] 2 All ER 754; and Notes in (1973) 47 *ALJ* 268, and (1976) 50 *ALJ* 478, 534.

United City Merchants (Investments) Ltd v Royal Bank of Canada
House of Lords [1982] 2 WLR 1039

Lord Diplock: My Lords, this appeal, which is the culmination of protracted litigation, raises two distinct questions of law which it is convenient to deal with separately. The first, which I will call the documentary credit point, relates to the mutual rights and obligations of the confirming bank and the beneficiary under a documentary credit. It is of general importance to all those engaged in the conduct and financing of international trade for it challenges the basic principle of documentary credit operations that banks that are parties to them deal in documents only, not in the goods to which those documents purport to relate. The second question, which I will call the Bretton Woods point, is of less general importance. It turns upon the construction of the Bretton Woods Agreements Order in Council 1946 and its application to the particular fact of the instant case...

A Peruvian company, Vitrorefuerzos SA ("the buyers") agreed to buy from the second appellants ("the sellers") plant for the manufacture of glass fibres ("the goods") at a price of $662,086 fob London for shipment to Callao. Payment was to be in London by confirmed irrevocable transferable letter of credit for the invoice price plus freight, payable as to 20 per cent of the invoice price upon the opening of the credit, as to 70 per cent of the invoice price and 100 per cent of the freight on presentation of shipping documents and as to the balance of 10 per cent of the invoice price on completion of erection of the plant in Peru.

The buyers arranged with their Peruvian bank, Banco Continental SA ("the issuing bank") to issue the necessary credit and the issuing bank appointed the respondents, Royal Bank of Canada ("the confirming bank") to advise and confirm upon its own behalf the credit to the sellers. The confirming bank duly notified the sellers on 30 March 1976 of the opening of the confirmed irrevocable transferable letter of credit. So far as concerned the 70 per cent of the invoice price and 100 per cent freight there was nothing that was unusual in its terms. It was expressed to be subject to the Uniform Customs and Practice for Documentary Credits (1974 revision) of the International Chamber of Commerce ("the Uniform Customs") and to be available by sight drafts on the issuing bank against delivery inter alia of a full set "on board" bills of lading evidencing receipt for shipment of the goods from London to Callao on or before a date in October 1976, which was subsequently extended to 15 December 1976...

The goods, which had to be manufactured by the sellers, were ready for shipment by the beginning of December 1976. It was intended by the loading brokers acting on behalf of Prudential Lines Inc ("the carriers") that they should be shipped on a vessel belonging to the carriers (*American Legend*) due to arrive at Felixstowe on 10 December 1976. (The substitution of Felixstowe for London as the loading port is immaterial. It was acquiesced in by all parties to the transaction.) The arrival of *American Legend* at Felixstowe was cancelled and another vessel, *American Accord,* was substituted by the loading brokers: but its date of arrival was scheduled for 16 December 1976, one day after the latest date of shipment required by the documentary credit. The goods were in fact loaded on *American Accord* on 16 December 1976; but the loading brokers, who also acted as agents for the carriers in issuing bills of lading, issued in the first instance a set of "received for shipment" bills of lading dated 15 December 1976, and handed them over to the sellers in return for payment of the freight. On presentation of the shipping documents to the confirming bank on 17 December that bank raised various objections to their form, of which the only one that is relevant to the documentary credit point was that the bills of lading did not bear any dated "on board" notation. The bills of lading were returned to the carriers' freight brokers who issued a fresh set bearing the notation, which was untrue: "These goods are actually on board 15 December 1976. E H Munday and Co (Freight Agents) Ltd as agents." The amended bills of lading together with the other documents were re-presented to the confirming bank on 22 December 1976, but the confirming bank again refused to pay on the ground that they "had information in their possession which suggested that shipment was not effected as it appears in the bill of lading".

The learned judge after a careful hearing, lasting for no less than 30 days, held that Mr Baker, the employee of the loading brokers to the carriers who was in charge of the transaction on their behalf, had acted fraudulently in issuing the bills of lading bearing what was to his knowledge a false statement as to the date on which the plant was actually on board *American Accord*. The judge held, however, that neither the sellers (nor their transferee) were parties or privies to any fraud by Mr Baker; at the time of both presentations of the shipping documents to the confirming bank on 17 and 22 December 1976, they bona fide believed that the plant had in fact been loaded on *American Accord* on or before 15 December 1976, and that the annotation on the reissued bill of lading, stating the goods to be actually on board at that date, was true...

The documentary credit point

My Lords, for the proposition upon the documentary credit point, both in the broad form for which counsel for the confirming bank have strenuously argued at all stages of this appeal and in the narrower form or "halfway house" that commended itself to the Court of Appeal, there is no direct authority to be found either in English or Privy Council cases or among the numerous decisions of courts in the United States of America to which reference is made in the judgments of the Court of Appeal in the instant case. So the point falls to be decided by reference to first principles as to the legal nature of the contractual obligations assumed by the various parties to a transaction consisting of an international sale of goods to be financed by means of a confirmed irrevocable documentary credit. It is trite law that there are four autonomous though interconnected contractual relationships involved. (1) The underlying contract for the sale of goods, to which the only parties are the buyer and the seller; (2) the contract between the buyer and the issuing bank under which the latter agrees to issue the credit and either itself or through a confirming bank to notify the credit to the seller and to make payments to or to the order of the seller (or to pay, accept or negotiate bills of exchange drawn by the seller) against presentation of stipulated documents; and the buyer agrees to reimburse the issuing bank for payments made under the credit. For such reimbursement the stipulated documents, if they include a document of title such as a bill of lading, constitute a security available to the issuing bank; (3) if payment is to be made through a confirming bank the contract between the issuing bank and the confirming bank authorising and requiring the latter to make such payments and to remit the stipulated documents to the issuing bank when they are received, the issuing bank in turn agreeing to reimburse the confirming bank for payments made under the credit; (4) the contract between the confirming bank and the seller under which the confirming bank undertakes to pay to the seller (or to accept or negotiate without recourse to drawer bills of exchange drawn by him) up to the amount of the credit against presentation of the stipulated documents.

Again, it is trite law that in contract (4), with which alone the instant appeal is directly concerned, the parties to it, the seller and the confirming bank, "deal in documents and not in goods", as art 8 of the Uniform Customs puts it. If, on their face, the documents presented to the confirming bank by the seller conform with the requirements of the credit as notified to him by the confirming bank, that bank is under a contractual obligation to the seller to honour the credit, notwithstanding that the bank has knowldge that the seller at the time of presentation of the conforming documents is alleged by the buyer to have, and in fact has already, committed a breach of his contract with the buyer for the sale of the goods to which the documents appear on their face to relate, that would have entitled the buyer to treat the contract of sale as rescinded and to reject the goods and refuse to pay the seller the purchase price. The whole commercial purpose for which the system of confirmed irrevocable documentary credits has been developed in international trade is to give to the seller an assured right to be paid before he parts with control of the goods that does not permit of any dispute with the buyer as to the performance of the contract of sale being used as a ground for non-payment or reduction or deferment of payment.

To this general statement of principle as to the contractual obligations of the confirming bank to the seller, there is one established exception: that is, where the seller, for the purpose of drawing on the credit, fraudulently presents to the confirming bank documents that contain, expressly or by implication, material representations of fact that to his knowledge are untrue. Although there does not appear among the English authorities any case in which this exception has been applied, it is well established in the American cases of which the leading or "landmark" case is *Sztejn v J Henry Schroder Banking Corp* (1941) 31 NYS 2d 631. This judgment of the New York Court of Appeals was referred to with approval by the English

Court of Appeal in *Edward Owen Engineering Ltd v Barclays Bank International Ltd* [1978] QB 159, though this was actually a case about a performance bond under which a bank assumes obligations to a buyer analogous to those assumed by a confirming bank to the seller under a documentary credit. The exception for fraud on the part of the beneficiary seeking to avail himself of the credit is a clear application of the maxim ex turpi causa non oritur actio or, if plain English is to be preferred, "fraud unravels all". The courts will not allow their process to be used by a dishonest person to carry out a fraud.

The instant case, however, does not fall within the fraud exception. Mocatta J found the sellers to have been unaware of the inaccuracy of Mr Baker's notation of the date at which the goods were actually on board *American Accord*. They believed that it was true and that the goods had actually been loaded on or before 15 December 1976, as required by the documentary credit.

Faced by this finding, the argument for the confirming bank before Mocatta J was directed to supporting the broad proposition: that a confirming bank is not under any obligation, legally enforceable against it by the seller/beneficiary of a documentary credit, to pay to him the sum stipulated in the credit against presentation of documents, if the documents presented, although conforming on their face with the terms of the credit, nevertheless contain some statement of material fact that is not accurate. This proposition which does not call for knowledge on the part of the seller/beneficiary of the existence of any inaccuracy would embrace the fraud exception and render it superfluous.

My Lords, the more closely this bold proposition is subjected to legal analysis, the more implausible it becomes; to assent to it would, in my view, undermine the whole system of financing international trade by means of documentary credits.

It has, so far as I know, never been disputed that as between confirming bank and issuing bank and as between issuing bank and the buyer the contractual duty of each bank under a confirmed irrevocable credit is to examine with reasonable care all documents presented in order to ascertain that they appear *on their face* to be in accordance with the terms and conditions of the credit, and, if they do so appear, to pay to the seller/beneficiary by whom the documents have been presented the sum stipulated by the credit, or to accept or negotiate without recourse to drawer drafts drawn by the seller/beneficiary if the credit so provides. It is so stated in the latest edition of the Uniform Customs. It is equally clear law, and is so provided by art 9 of the Uniform Customs, that confirming banks and issuing banks assume no liability or responsibility to one another or to the buyer "for the form, sufficiency, accuracy, genuineness, falsification or legal effect of any documents". This is well illustrated by the Privy Council case of *Gian Singh & Co Ltd v Banque de l'Indochine* [1974] 1 WLR 1234, where the customer was held liable to reimburse the issuing bank for honouring a documentary credit upon presentation of an apparently conforming document which was an ingenious forgery, a fact that the bank had not been negligent in failing to detect upon examination of the document.

It would be strange from the commercial point of view, although not theoretically impossible in law, if the contractual duty owed by confirming and issuing banks to the buyer to honour the credit on presentation of apparently conforming documents despite the fact that they contain inaccuracies or even are forged, were not matched by a corresponding contractual liability of the confirming bank to the seller/beneficiary (in the absence, of course, of any fraud on his part) to pay the sum stipulated in the credit upon presentation of apparently conforming documents. Yet, as is conceded by counsel for the confirming bank in the instant case, if the broad proposition for which he argues is correct, the contractual duties do not match. As respects the confirming bank's contractual duty to the seller to honour the credit, the bank, it is submitted, is only bound to pay upon presentation of documents which not only appear on their face to be in accordance with the terms and conditions of the credit but also do not in fact contain any material statement that is inaccurate. If this submission be correct, the bank's contractual right to refuse to honour the documentary credit cannot, as a matter of legal analysis, depend upon whether *at the time of the refusal* the bank was virtually certain from information obtained by means other than reasonably careful examination of the documents themselves that they contained some material statement that was inaccurate or whether the bank merely suspected this or even had no suspicion that apparently conforming documents contained any inaccuracies at all. If there be any such right of refusal it must depend upon whether the bank, when sued by the seller/beneficiary for breach of its contract to honour the credit, is able to prove that one of the documents did in fact contain what was a material misstatement.

It is conceded that to justify refusal the misstatement must be "material" but this invites the query: "material to what?" The suggested answer to this query was: a misstatement of a fact which if the true fact had been disclosed would have entitled the buyer to reject the goods; date of shipment (as in the instant case) or misdescription of the goods are examples. But this is to destroy the autonomy of the documentary credit which is its raison d'être; it is to make the seller's right to payment by the confirming bank dependent upon the buyer's rights against the seller under the terms of the contract for the sale of goods, of which the confirming bank will have no knowledge.

Counsel sought to evade the difficulties disclosed by an analysis of the legal consequences of his broad proposition by praying in aid the practical consideration that a bank, desirous as it would be of protecting its reputation in the competitive business of providing documentary credits, would never exercise its right against a seller/beneficiary to refuse to honour the credit except in cases where at the time of the refusal it already was in possession of irrefutable evidence of the inaccuracy in the documents presented. I must confess that the argument that a seller should be content to rely upon the exercise by banks of business expediency, unbacked by any legal liability, to ensure prompt payment by a foreign buyer does not impress me; but the assumption that underlies reliance upon expediency does not, in my view, itself stand up to legal analysis. Business expediency would not induce the bank to pay the seller/beneficiary against presentation of documents which it was not legally liable to accept as complying with the documentary credit unless, in doing so, it acquired a right legally enforceable against the buyer, to require him to take up the documents himself and reimburse the bank for the amount paid. So any reliance upon business expediency to make the system work if the broad proposition contended for by counsel is correct, must involve that as against the buyer, the bank, when presented with apparently conforming documents by the seller, is legally entitled to the option, *exercisable at its own discretion and regardless of any instructions to the contrary from the buyer,* either (1) to take up the documents and pay the credit and claim reimbursement from the buyer, notwithstanding that the bank has been provided with information that makes it virtually certain that the existence of such inaccuracies can be proved, or (2) to reject the documents and to refuse to pay the credit.

The legal justification for the existence of such an independently exercisable option, it is suggested, lies in the bank's own interest in the goods to which the documents relate, as security for the advance made by the bank to the buyer, when it pays the seller under the documentary credit. But if this were so, the answer to the question: "to what must the misstatement in the documents be material?" should be: "material to the price which the goods to which the documents relate would fetch on sale if, failing reimbursement by the buyer, the bank should be driven to realise its security". But this would not justify the confirming bank's refusal to honour the credit in the instant case; the realisable value on arrival at Callao of a glass fibre manufacturing plant made to the specification of the buyers could not be in any way affected by its having been loaded on board a ship at Felixstowe on 16 December instead of 15 December 1976.

My Lords, in rejecting this broad proposition I have dealt with it at greater length than otherwise I would have done, because it formed the main plank of the confirming bank's argument on the documentary credit point before Mocatta J—who, however, had no hesitation in rejecting it, but found for the confirming bank on the Bretton Woods point. It formed the main ground also in the confirming bank's notice of cross-appeal to the Court of Appeal upon which the confirming bank would seek to uphold the judgment in its favour if the sellers' appeal should succeed upon the Bretton Woods point. It was not until half-way through the actual hearing in the Court of Appeal that the notice of cross-appeal was amended to include a narrower proposition referred to as a "half-way house" which the Court of Appeal accepted as being decisive in the confirming bank's favour. This rendered it unnecessary for that court to rule upon the broad proposition that I have so far been discussing, although Stephenson LJ indicated obiter that for his part he would have rejected it. In the confirming bank's argument before this House a marked lack of enthusiasm has been shown for reliance on the "half-way house" and the broad proposition has again formed the main ground on which the confirming bank has sought to uphold the actual decision of the Court of Appeal in its favour on the documentary credit point.

The proposition accepted by the Court of Appeal as constituting a complete defence available to the confirming bank on the documentary credit point has been referred to as a "half-way house" because it lies not only half way between the unqualified liability of the confirming bank to honour a documentary credit on presentation of documents which upon reasonably careful examination appear to conform to the terms and conditions of the credit, and what I have referred to as the fraud exception to this unqualified liability which is available to the confirming bank where the seller/beneficiary presents to the confirming bank documents that contain, expressly or by implication, material representations of fact that to his own knowledge are untrue; but it also lies half way between the fraud exception and the broad proposition favoured by the confirming bank with which I have hitherto been dealing. The half-way house is erected upon the narrower proposition that if any of the documents presented under the credit by the seller/beneficiary contain a material misrepresentation of fact that was *false to the knowledge of the person who issued the document* and intended by him to deceive persons into whose hands the document might come, the confirming bank is under no liability to honour the credit, even though, as in the instant case, the persons whom the issuer of the document intended to, and did, deceive included the seller/beneficiary himself.

My Lords, if the broad proposition for which the confirming bank has argued is unacceptable for the reasons that I have already discussed, what rational ground can there be for drawing any distinction between apparently conforming documents that, unknown to the seller, in fact contain a statement of fact that is inaccurate where the inaccuracy was due to inadvertence by the maker of the document, and the like documents where the same inaccuracy had been inserted by the maker of the document with intent to deceive, among others, the seller/beneficiary himself? Ex hypothesi we are dealing only with a case in which the seller/beneficiary claiming under the credit *has* been deceived, for if he presented documents to the confirming bank with knowledge that this apparent conformity with the terms and conditions of the credit was due to the fact that the documents told a lie, the seller/beneficiary would himself be a party to the misrepresentation made to the confirming bank by the lie in the documents and the case would come within the fraud exception, as did all the American cases referred to as persuasive authority in the judgments of the Court of Appeal in the instant case.

The American cases refer indifferently to documents that are "forged or fraudulent", as does the Uniform Commercial Code that has been adopted in nearly all states of the United States of America. The Court of Appeal reached their half-way house in the instant case by starting from the premiss that a confirming bank could refuse to pay against a document that it knew to be forged, even though the seller/beneficiary had no knowledge of that fact. From this premiss they reasoned that if forgery by a third party relieves the confirming bank of liability to pay the seller/beneficiary, fraud by a third party ought to have the same consequence.

I would not wish to be taken as accepting that the premiss as to forged documents is correct, even where the fact that the document is forged deprives it of all legal effect and makes it a nullity, and so worthless to the confirming bank as security for its advances to the buyer. This is certainly not so under the Uniform Commercial Code as against a person who has taken a draft drawn under the credit in circumstances that would make him a holder in due course, and I see no reason why, and there is nothing in the Uniform Commercial Code to suggest that, a seller/beneficiary who is ignorant of the forgery should be in any worse position because he has not negotiated the draft before presentation. I would prefer to leave open the question of the rights of an innocent seller/beneficiary against the confirming bank when a document presented by him is a nullity because unknown to him it was forged by some third party; for that question does not arise in the instant case. The bill of lading with the wrong date of loading placed on it by the carrier's agent was far from being a nullity. It was a valid transferable receipt for the goods giving the holder a right to claim them at their destination, Callao, and was evidence of the terms of the contract under which they were being carried.

But even assuming the correctness of the Court of Appeal's premiss as respects forgery by a third party of a kind that makes a document a nullity for which at least a rational case can be made out, to say that this leads to the conclusion that fraud by a third party which does not render the document a nullity has the same consequence appears to me, with respect, to be a non-sequitur, and I am not persuaded by the reasoning in any of the judgments of the Court of Appeal that it is not.

Upon the documentary credit point I think that Mocatta J was right in deciding it in favour of the sellers and that the Court of Appeal were wrong in reversing him on this point.

[His Lordship then considered the Bretton Woods point and concluded that to the extent that the contracts did not offend exchange control regulations the plaintiffs' (sellers') claim was enforceable. Accordingly the appellants were entitled to payment for that part of the purchase price which was not a monetary transaction in disguise.

Lords Fraser, Russell, Scarman and **Bridge** concurred.]

Appeal allowed.

See also *Establissment Esefka International Austalt v Central Bank of Nigeria* [1979] 1 Lloyd's Rep 445.

SECURITY OVER DOCUMENTS AND GOODS

Documentary credits can be used not only to pay for imported goods but also to finance their purchase with borrowed funds secured on the shipping documents. In the illustration at the beginning of this section, Mitzi obtained a documentary credit from Tokyo Bank to finance the purchase of carburettors from Carb. Upon honouring that credit Tokyo Bank would receive the shipping documents and hold them as security for the advance. If Mitzi became bankrupt, the bank could realise on its security. However, when the goods arrived in Yokohama, the bank would probably release the documents to Mitzi to enable it to obtain delivery from the ship and resell. In return, if it followed English and Australian practice, the bank would take from Mitzi a trust receipt under which Mitzi would pledge the shipping documents, the goods and the proceeds of sale to the bank for repayment of the bank's loan and undertake to reimburse the bank from the proceeds of sale.

The trust receipt is an incongruous and potentially vulnerable security, lacking the element of continuous possession normally required for a valid pledge. However, it is not normally registered as a bill of sale or charge over the goods, nor as a charge over proceeds in the form of book debts in the case of a corporate customer: see, eg, Companies Code s 200(2)(c). When the bank redelivers the documents to the customer for the purpose of collecting the goods, the bank may be faced with challenges to its security in various situations.

(1) Mitzi may be put into liquidation while in the possession of the documents or the goods: see *Re Allester Ltd* [1922] 2 Ch 211, which also provides an illustration of the trust receipt. See also *Official Assignee of Madras v Mercantile Bank of India Ltd* [1935] AC 53 (PC).

(2) Mitzi may pledge the goods a second time to another institution to obtain a second advance. In this situation, will the redelivery to the pledgor for the limited purpose of obtaining possession of the goods on the bank's behalf estop it from maintaining its prior security as against the second pledgee? See *Mercantile Bank of India Ltd v Central Bank of India Ltd* [1938] AC 287. On the other hand, if the pledgor Mitzi is a mercantile agent, as will often be the case, will the provisions of the Factors legislation be applicable when the bank entrusts Mitzi with possession of the documents of title for the purpose of collecting the goods? See *Lloyds Bank Ltd v Bank of America National Trust and Savings Association* [1938] 2 KB 147, and see pp 344-8, *supra*.

(3) Where the bank releases the documents to Mitzi with express authority to sell, a bona fide buyer takes free of any claim by the pledgee-bank, even if Mitzi does not sell as a mercantile agent, and the bank will be left to its claim against Mitzi in respect of the proceeds of sale.

INSURING AGAINST THE BUYERS' DEFAULT

Certain risks inherent in export sale transactions cannot be avoided or covered by commercial insurance. They comprise (a) commercial risks, such as the insolvency of the overseas buyer; and (b) political risks, such as foreign governments' expropriation, or embargo on importation of the goods or blockage of foreign exchange. In order to ensure that Australian exporters were not deterred by such risks, the Australian government in 1957 established the Export Payments Insurance Corporation, subsequently renamed Export Finance and Insurance Corporation (EFIC). Its function is to encourage and expand trade with countries outside Australia by providing a specialised range of insurance and guarantee facilities not normally obtainable from commercial insurers.

EFIC is designed to be financially self-sustaining. Insurance is not automatically granted on all export contracts; a proposal must be submitted as for ordinary commercial insurance. However, if the particular risk is declined by EFIC the government itself may underwrite the export sale where it is important to the national interest, for example, to develop a new market or improve Australian trade relations.

EFIC offers insurance against each of the risks mentioned above, and its policies usually cover 90-95 per cent of an exporter's losses. It will also enter into guarantees to Australian commercial lending institutions in respect of loans to finance Australian exports made to either the exporters or the foreign buyer. Credit terms offered in the competitive market for selling capital goods can be as important to the buyer as the quality or price of the goods. Guarantees by EFIC therefore can be a crucial factor in negotiating a sale.

EXCHANGE CONTROL

Exchange control and the related controls on imports and exports are intended to control the flow of capital to and from Australia so as to protect the currency and Australia's overseas reserves. Exchange control has important economic consequences: externally, it affects Australia's balance of payments and exchange rates; internally, it has an effect on money supply, availability of capital, and interest rates. The principal controls are contained in the Banking (Foreign Exchange) Regulations made under the Banking Act 1959 (Cth). The regulations are quite detailed and complex and only a broad outline is attempted here of some provisions affecting import and export transactions. Since the Foreign Exchange Regulations are subject to amendment from time to time and the practice of the Reserve Bank under the regulations can change at short notice, the latest amendments should always be checked before entering a financial commitment with a foreign party.

The regulations affect the financing of imports into Australia as well as direct and portfolio foreign investments by Australian residents. Many of the regulations and rulings are designed to prevent currency speculation (eg, in anticipation of a devaluation) disguised as a current import or export transaction, which in genuine cases would not normally be restricted.

Where goods are imported, the necessary foreign currency must be purchased from a trading bank and used only for the stated purpose. Normally the goods must be paid for within a period of six months of arrival in Australia and the bank must receive proof that the goods have arrived. Similarly, the foreign currency proceeds from Australian export sales must be sold to a bank in Australia and the system is policed by requiring the export documents to be handled through a bank.

Banking (Foreign Exchange) Regulations

16(1) A person shall not export goods unless—

(a) payment of an amount equal to the export value of the goods has been or is to be received in Australia—
  (i) in such currency;
  (ii) in such manner; and
  (iii) within such period, before or after the date of exportation of the goods,
as the bank for the time being has approved; or
(b) the authority of the Bank for the export has been obtained.
(2) ...
(3) ...

17 Where foreign currency representing the proceeds of sale of goods that have been or are to be exported is received, the owner of the goods shall, unless otherwise authorized by the Bank, as soon as is reasonably practicable, sell that foreign currency, or procure the sale of that foreign currency, to a bank in Australia for Australian currency at a rate of exchange fixed or authorized by the Bank and in force for the time being.

Approval of transactions covered by the regulations must be obtained when the contract is made; retrospective approval will not be granted. Since a transaction which has not been approved is illegal, the courts have no power at common law to enforce it or grant other civil relief. At common law the transaction is invalid: *Sykes v Stratton* [1972] 1 NSWLR 145. The unenforceability of such a transaction has been used as a means of avoiding liability in quite unwarranted situations: eg, *TM Duche & Sons (UK) Ltd v Walworth Industries (Aust) Pty Ltd* [1962] SR (NSW) 165; 79 WN (NSW) 27. For a critical appraisal of the civil consequences of the Regulations see Gerard Horton, "Australian Exchange Control—Its Civil Consequences" (1973) 47 *ALJ* 124.

Since these decisions and Horton's article, and presumably as a result of them, reg 45 has been introduced and amendments made to the Banking Act.

Banking (Foreign Exchange) reg 45

45 No act or thing done, or contract or other transaction entered into, is invalid or unenforceable by reason only that the provisions of these Regulations have not been complied with.

This regulation does not apply to any transaction the validity of which was questioned in any proceedings prior to 3 December 1974. It is also subject to the following provision:

Banking Act 1974 (Cth)

5(1) No act or thing done, and no contract or other transaction entered into, before the commencement of this Act, shall be deemed to be, or ever to have been, invalid or unenforceable by reason only that a provision of the Banking (Foreign Exchange) Regulations has not been complied with, but the foregoing
  (a) does not apply to any act, thing, contract or other transaction the validity of which, has, before 3 December 1974, been called in question, for that reason, in any proceedings, whether or not the proceedings have been completed before that date, except proceedings in which the court holds that it is just and equitable that the act, thing, contract or other transaction should be treated as being valid; ...

These provisions were considered in *Talga Ltd v MBC International Ltd* (1976) 8 ALR 269; 50 ALJR 619 in which the Full High Court upheld the validity of Banking Act 1974 s 5 and held a loan agreement valid notwithstanding breaches of the regulations. In the course of his judgment at the original hearing which was later approved by the Full Court on appeal, Gibbs J said at 625:

That provision [Banking (Foreign Exchange) Regulation 45] does not apply to agreements made before the amending regulation was enacted, but the opening words of s 5(1) lay down a similar rule with regard to agreements entered into before the commencement of the Act. To that general rule there is an exception intended to prevent the provisions of s 5 from applying to transactions whose validity has been called in question, for the reason that a provision of the regulations has not been complied with, in proceedings commenced before 3 December 1974. That exception is itself subject to an exception; the general rule expressed in the opening words of s 5(1) does apply if in the proceedings the court holds that it is just and equitable that the transaction should be treated as valid. The provisions of s 5(1) clearly show, what was already apparent from the words of reg 8 themselves, that the regulations are designed, not for the protection of individuals but to enable certain financial transactions to be controlled in the public interest. Section 5(1) gives no guide to the court in making its decision whether or not it is just and equitable that a transaction should be treated as being valid and in my opinion confers on the court the widest discretion to reach its decision in the light of all the circumstances of the case. It is, in my opinion, necessary that the court shall make its decision in respect of each transaction separately.

QUESTIONS

Question 8

(1) On 1 May 1984 Carb Pty Ltd contracted to sell 20,000 carburettors to Mitzi Co of Tokyo for $300,000 fob Sydney. Payment was to be by establishment of an irrevocable documentary credit. The contract required delivery Sydney during the period of 60 days commencing 1 September 1984.

By 15 June Carb had received no advice of the opening of the credit. Carb cabled Mitzi to open the credit immediately and sent reminder cables on 22 and 30 June. Mitzi's only reply was a letter dated 3 July advising that the credit would be established by 30 July. Carb was under great pressure to complete orders under other more profitable contracts and had not commenced manufacturing Mitzi's order. It is doubtful if Carb can have the order ready by 1 September.

It is now 10 July and Carb seeks your advice as to its position at this stage.

(2) Assume now that Carb received advice from Sydney Bank, Head Office, on 30 July that Tokyo Bank on behalf of Mitzi Co had established an irrevocable credit at Sydney Bank confirmed by Sydney Bank in favour of Carb for $300,000; and that Mitzi had arranged for carriage of the consignment on *SS Maru* departing Sydney 15 October for Yokohama and required Carb to deliver on board.

On 1 August Carb seeks your advice.

Question 9

Carb Pty Ltd entered into a contract on 1 September to purchase from Anglo-Eastern Oil Co 10,000 barrels of Iranian light crude oil cif Sydney for $300,000 payment to be by irrevocable documentary credit for $300,000 in London confirmed by Commerce Bank, incorporating UCP provisions and providing for drawing a 60 day draft against delivery of the following shipping documents: shipped bill of lading, insurance policy, commercial invoice, certificate of inspection and origin by the Chief Engineer of Goodlube Ltd.

Carb requested Sydney Bank to establish the letter of credit in London. On 5 September Commerce Bank, London, advised Anglo-Eastern that Sydney Bank on behalf of Carb had established an irrevocable credit at Commerce Bank confirmed by Commerce Bank in favour of Anglo-Eastern for $300,000 requiring acceptance of a 60 day draft on presentation of the shipping documents listed above.

Anglo-Eastern, who were not producers but rather dealers in the spot market for petroleum products bought the necessary oil from Sheik Abdulla and established their own letter of credit back-to-back with Carb's credit.

Following an OPEC meeting on 10 September, world oil prices fell dramatically; Carb could now buy the same volume of product in Kuwait for $200,000. Carb now wishes to instruct Sydney Bank to cancel the credit. Advise Carb.

What difference would it make to your advice if the oil had already been loaded on board *Endeavour II* and Anglo-Eastern presented to Commerce Bank, London, the documents listed in each of the following alternative factual situations:

(1) shipped bill of lading, insurance policy, commercial invoice identifying 10,000 barrels of Iranian light crude oil, and certificate of inspection and origin; or

(2) the same documents as in (1) but Carb had received reliable information that the certificate of inspection and origin certifying as to the quality and origin of the oil had been honestly but negligently prepared by the Chief Engineer of Goodlube Ltd and the product was in fact Russian heavy crude; or

(3) the same facts as in (1) but the certificate had been forged by Sheik Abdulla without any knowledge of Goodlube or Anglo-Eastern;

(4) the same facts as in (1) but the certificate had been forged by Anglo-Eastern;

(5) the same facts as in (1) but the invoice did not specify 10,000 barrels or Iranian light crude.

Question 10

(1) The documentary letter of credit has been called "the crankshaft of modern commerce". Do you agree?

(2) Consider the advantages and disadvantages of the use of the irrevocable letter of credit.

(3) Carb Pty Ltd is considering exporting steel products to Pacifica, a South Pacific nation, with a reputation for political upheavals, economic instability and shady entrepreneurs. What can Carb do to minimise the risks of trading with Pacifica?

If Carb proceeds to trade with Pacifica, briefly outline the type of restrictions on exchange control it is likely to encounter in Australia.

FURTHER READING

Sections 1, 2 and 3: Bills of Exchange

Chappenden & Bilinsky, *Riley's Bills of Exchange,* 3rd ed, 1976.

Rajanayagam, *The Law Relating to Negotiable Instruments in Australia,* 1980.

Walker, "The Australian Revival of the Bill of Exchange" (1978) 52 *ALJ* 244.

Other works which relate specifically to Banking Law are listed at the end of Chapter 11 but will also be relevant to the present chapter.

Section 4: Financing International Transactions: Letters of Credit

Edwards, "The Role of Bank Guarantees in International Law" (1982) 56 *ALJ* 281.

Ellinger, *Documentary Letters of Credit — A Comparative Study,* 1970.

Ellinger, "Fraud in Documentary Credit Transactions" (1981) *J Bus Law* 258.

Fraser, "The Banking (Foreign Exchange) Regulations and Australia's Treaty Obligations under the International Monetary Fund Agreement" (1980) 8 *ABLR* 168.

Gutteridge & Megrah, *The Law of Bankers' Commercial Credits,* 6th ed, 1979.

International Chamber of Commerce, Uniform Customs and Practice for Documentary Credits (1974 revision) — a new revision is in course of preparation.

Leighton, "Exchange Control in Australia" (1976) 8 *Comm Law Assoc Bull* 47.

Purvis & Darvas, *Commercial Letters of Credit, Shipping Documents and Termination of Disputes in International Trade,* 1975.

Reserve Bank of Australia, *Exchange Control,* 1980.

Sexton, "Tightening the Foreign Exchange Net" (1975) 3 *ABLR* 254.

Tedeschi, "Recent Changes to Exchange Control Provisions" (1982) 20 *Law Soc J* 151.

CHAPTER 11

The Banker-Customer Relationship and the Banking System

"A banker is a fellow who lends his umbrella when the sun is shining and wants it back the minute it begins to rain."

Mark Twain

Section 1: The Australian Banking System, and the Use of Cheques
Section 2: Duties of Paying Bank and its Customer at Common Law
Section 3: Duties of Collecting and Paying Banks and Pt III Bills of Exchange Act

Taking the general principles relating to bills of exchange outlined in Chapter 10 as a base, this chapter will examine the rules and practices of the Australian banking system with particular focus on the most common form of bill of exchange—the cheque. Section 1 provides an overview of the legislative basis for the Australian banking system, the different types of banks, the main functions of the trading banks, and the system for drawing, depositing, clearing and paying cheques. This will form a useful introduction to Section 2, which covers the relationship at common law between banks and their customers, and Section 3 which deals with the particular duties of banks when collecting and paying cheques, and the statutory protections for banks under Pt III of the Bills of Exchange Act (BEA).

SECTION 1: THE AUSTRALIAN BANKING SYSTEM, AND THE USE OF CHEQUES

Every year, over 1000 million cheques are drawn and paid through the Australian banking system. Although there are other modes of making payments, such as credit cards (see pp 416–21, *supra*), and some predictions and developments overseas suggest the expansion of computerised systems of credit transfers, the cheque remains the most common method of payment in commercial and many consumer transactions.

BEA Pt III applies exclusively to cheques, which are defined as follows: "A cheque is a bill of exchange drawn on a banker payable on demand": s 78(1).

Thus, all cheques are bills of exchange, and except as otherwise provided in Pt III, "the provisions of this Act applicable to a bill of exchange payable on demand apply to a cheque": s 78(2). However, not all bills of exchange are cheques and in addition to the differences of form noted on pp 427–8, *supra*, note the following points:

(1) A cheque is always drawn on a bank but is not accepted by the bank, and it involves a special relationship between the bank and its customer.

(2) A cheque is payable on demand; no days of grace are available; noting and protesting are unnecessary.

(3) The use of the banking system and cheques is so widespread in the general consumer community, as well as in business, that it raises different policy issues from those concerning *commercial* bills of exchange and letters of credit. In 1964 the Manning Committee recommended introduction of a separate Cheques Act and successive drafts have been prepared but not yet enacted.

(4) The privilege of conducting current cheque account banking business is a monopoly conferred only upon banks authorised under Pt II of the Banking Act 1959 (Cth). These banks and savings banks are afforded special statutory protections under the Bills of Exchange Act Pt III, in relation to the collection of cheques.

WHAT IS "A BANK" OR "BANKING BUSINESS"?

The Commonwealth has power under Constitution s 51(xiii) to make laws with respect to "banking other than State banking; also State banking extending beyond the limits of the State concerned, the incorporation of banks, and the issue of paper money". It is to be expected that the Commonwealth government would use this power to regulate the banking system since it is a useful and flexible medium for controlling the money supply. Thus the Reserve Bank of Australia controls the lending policies of the banks and also requires a stipulated percentage of funds deposited with the banks to be placed with the Reserve Bank or invested in government securities.

However, there are constitutional limits on these powers. For example, the states have full powers to create their own state-owned banks (eg, State Bank of NSW, State Bank of Victoria, Rural Industries Bank of Western Australia) and these cannot be subjected to different Commonwealth regulations than those applying to the rest of the banking system; nor could the Commonwealth prohibit state or private banks from conducting banking business for a state or its instrumentalities: *Melbourne Corp v The Commonwealth* (1947) 74 CLR 31; [1947] ALR 377. Similarly, the Commonwealth's attempt to destroy the private banking system by nationalising all banks except state banks was held to be unconstitutional in *Bank of NSW v The Commonwealth* (1948) 76 CLR 1 (HC); [1948] ALR 89; (1949) 79 CLR 497 (PC); [1948] ALR 606.

The primary function of banks in a commercial or economic sense is the borrowing and lending of money and an economist examining these activities would tend to group banks, building societies, finance companies, merchant banks and perhaps insurance companies and credit unions within the same general category. On the other hand, because of the statutory descriptions of banks and banking business in the Australian Constitution, Banking Act, and Bills of Exchange Act, the lawyer must look carefully at the specific functions of each institution to determine whether it is governed by particular legislation.

Apart from state banks, the Commonwealth has plenary powers with respect to banks and banking: see Banking Act 1959 (Cth) ss 5-11.

The term "banking business" is not defined in the Act, but has been considered by the courts: see below. Whether a body corporate or group of individuals are carrying on banking business will determine whether they are in breach of the Banking Act. However, the test of whether a body corporate is *a bank* for all purposes raises different questions. For example, in the BEA s 4 defines "banker" as including "a body of persons whether incorporated or not, who carry on the business of banking". Is this a wider concept than that of a "bank" under the Banking Act? Can a corporation claim the protection of the Bills of Exchange Act without being an authorised bank under Pt II of the Banking Act? A number of cases have discussed the concept of banking business. In *Australian Independent Distributors Ltd v Winter & Ors* (1965) 112 CLR 443 the High Court considered whether the activities of the Adelaide Co-operative Society Ltd, registered as a Provident Society, was carrying on the business of banking. Kitto, Taylor and Owen JJ said at 452:

> What constitutes "the business of banking" was considered by this court in *Commissioners of the State Savings Bank of Victoria v Permewan, Wright & Co Ltd* (1914) 19 CLR 457. The question was whether the Commissioners of the Savings Bank were "bankers" within the meaning of s 88 of the Commonwealth Bills of Exchange Act 1909 and s 83 of the Victorian Instruments Act 1890. In each Act "banker" was defined to include persons "who carry on the business of banking". Griffith CJ was of opinion that the commissioners were not carrying on such a business because depositors, other than Friendly Societies, could not operate upon their accounts by cheque. The majority of the court took the opposite view and, in the course of his judgment, Isaacs J said: "That expression 'business of banking', or an equivalent as 'business of bankers', 'business as bankers', and 'business of a banker', has been of constant use in English legislation... the phrase was continued in the English Bills of Exchange Act 1882, on which Australian Acts have been modelled. This indicates a constant signification of the term 'banking' as a business. The fundamental meaning of the term is not, and never has been, different in Australia from that obtaining in England. Various writers attempt various definitions, more or less discordant, and many of them referring to functions that are now very common and convenient, and even prominent, as if they were indispensable attributes. The essential characteristics of the business of banking are, however, all that are necessary to bring the appellants within the scope of the enactments; and these may be described as the collection of money by receiving deposits upon loan, repayable when and as expressly or impliedly agreed upon, and the utilisation of the money so collected by lending it again in such sums as are required. These are the essential functions of a bank as an instrument of society. It is, in effect, a financial reservoir receiving streams of currency in every direction, and from which there issue outflowing streams where and as required to sustain and fructify or assist commercial, industrial or other enterprises or adventures. If that be the real and substantial business of a body of persons, and not merely an ancillary or incidental branch of another business, they do carry on the business of banking (1914) 19 CLR at 470, 471."

> With this statement Gavan Duffy and Rich JJ, agreed and in *Melbourne Corp v The Commonwealth* (1947) 74 CLR 31 it was quoted with approval by Rich J at 64, 65.

> If that definition is applied to the present case, as we think it should be, it is apparent that the second of these essential characteristics is absent. The power to lend money conferred upon the society by r 7 was limited to the making of loans to its members to enable them to acquire land or buildings to be used for residential or business and residential purposes and in fact none of the society's moneys was used for the making of loans for that or any other purpose. Having regard to that circumstance, Chamberlain J held, and rightly held, that the society had not carried on "the business of banking" and had not therefore contravened either s 5(1)(II) of the Industrial and Provident Societies Act or s 7 of the Banking Act.

> We were referred, however, to *Re The Bottomgate Industrial Co-operative Society* (1891) 65 LT (NS) 712 in which Smith J with whom Mathew J agreed, speaking of the prohibitions against carrying on "the business of banking" contained in the Industrial and Provident Societies Acts of 1862 and 1876, expressed the view that it was not necessary "in order to constitute a banking business prohibited by the statute, that the society should carry on every part of a business carried on by some bankers; it is sufficient to bring the business within the prohibition, if the society carried on what is a principal part of the business of a banker, viz, receiving money on deposit, allowing the same to be drawn against as and when the depositor desires, and paying interest on the amounts standing on deposit". There is no doubt that the receipt of money on deposit capable of being drawn against by the depositor is a common feature of the business of banking but, as Griffith CJ pointed out in *Permewan, Wright's* case, transactions of that kind are frequently carried on in Australia by commercial institutions "whom no one would think of calling bankers": at 464.

A similar issue arose for decision in England in *United Dominions Trust Ltd v*

The Banker-Customer Relationship and the Banking System

Kirkwood [1966] 2 QB 431; [1966] 1 All ER 968, which concerned the question whether the finance company UDT which habitually borrowed and loaned money was "bona fide carrying on the business of banking" so as to be exempt from the provisions of the English Moneylenders Acts. In the course of his judgment in the Court of Appeal, Lord Denning MR said (at QB 445-7):

The characteristics of banking
  Seeing that there is no statutory definition of banking, we must do the best we can to find out the usual characteristics which go to make up the business of banking. In the eighteenth century, before cheques came into common use, the principal characteristics were that the banker accepted the money of others on the terms that the persons who deposited it could have it back again from the banker when they asked for it, sometimes on demand, at other times on notice, according to the stipulation made at the time of deposit; and meanwhile the banker was at liberty to make use of the money by lending it out at interest or investing it on mortgage or otherwise. Thus, Dr Johnson in 1755 in his dictionary defined a "bank" as a "place where money is laid up to be called for occasionally" and a "banker" as "one that traffics in money, one that keeps or manages a bank". Those characteristics continued for a long time to dominate thought on the subject. Thus, in 1914, Isaacs J in the High Court of Australia said ((1915) 19 CLR 457 at 470, 471) that: "The essential characteristics of the business of banking ... may be described as the collection of money by receiving deposits on loan, repayable when and as expressly or impliedly agreed upon, and the utilisation of the money so collected by lending it again in such sums as are required": see *State Savings Bank of Victoria Commissioners v Permewan Wright & Co Ltd* (1915) 19 CLR 457; [1915] VLR 81.
  You will notice that those characteristics do not mention the use of cheques, or the keeping of current accounts. Accordingly, we find in the courts cases in which a company was held to carry on the business of banking even though it issued no cheques and kept no current accounts but only issued deposit receipts, repayable on notice (see *RE Shields' Estate, Bank of Ireland (Governor & Co), Petitioners* [1901] 1 IR 172) or only kept deposit accounts from which the depositors could withdraw their money on demand or on notice, this being on production of a passbook, not by cheque: see *RE Bottomgate Industrial Co-operative Society* (1891) 65 LT 712 (DC); *State Savings Bank of Victoria Commissioners v Permewan Wright & Co Ltd*. If that were still the law, it would mean that the building societies were all bankers.
  The march of time has taken us far beyond those cases of 50 years ago. Money is now paid and received by cheque to such an extent that no person can be considered a banker unless he handles cheques as freely as cash. A customer nowadays who wishes to pay money into his bank takes with him his cash and the cheques, crossed and uncrossed, payable to him. Whereas in the old days it was a characteristic of a banker that he should receive *money* for deposit, it is nowadays a characteristic that he should receive *cheques for collection* on behalf of his customer. How otherwise is the customer to pay his money into the bank? It is the only practicable means, particularly in the case of crossed cheques. Next, when a customer wishes to withdraw the money which he has deposited or to pay his creditors with it, he does it in most cases by drawing a cheque on the bank. Occasionally he does it by a draft on the bank or a written order. Whereas in the old days he might withdraw it on production of a passbook and no cheque, it is nowadays a characteristic of a bank that the customer should be able to withdraw it by cheque, draft or order. This view has gradually gained acceptance: see *RE District Savings Bank Ltd; Ex parte Coe* (1861) 3 De GF & J 335, per Turner LJ at 338; *RE Shields' Estate,* per Lord Ashbourne.
  In 1924 Atkin LJ gave a modern picture of a characteristic banking account in *Joachimson v Swiss Bank Corp*: "The bank undertakes to receive money and collect bills for its customer's account. The proceeds so received are not to be held in trust for the customer, but the bank borrows the proceeds and undertakes to repay them. The promise to repay is to repay at the branch of the bank where the account is kept, and during banking hours. It includes a promise to repay any part of the amount due against the written order of the customer addressed to the bank at the branch ... bankers never do make a payment to a customer in respect of a current account except on demand.": [1921] 3 KB 110 at 127; 37 TLR 534 ...
  There are, therefore, two characteristics usually found in bankers today: (i) They accept money from, and collect cheques for, their customers and place them to their credit; (ii) They honour cheques or orders drawn on them by their customers when presented for payment and

debit their customers accordingly. These two characteristics carry with them also a third, namely: (iii) They keep current accounts, or something of that nature, in their books in which the credits and debits are entered.

Those three characteristics are much the same as those stated in *Paget's Law of Banking*, 6th ed, 1961, p 8: "No one and nobody, corporate or otherwise, can be a 'banker' who does not (i) take current accounts; (ii) pay cheques drawn on himself; (iii) collect cheques for his customers."

TYPES OF BANKS AND BANKING SERVICES

Since 1959, the trading bank and savings bank activities of Australian banks have been separated, and each separate corporation is authorised to carry on only its own particular kind of banking: Banking Act 1959 s 9 and First Schedule.

Trading banks provide a number of general services for their customers including:
(a) basic services: cheque and interest bearing deposit accounts, personal loans, safe custody and night safe, bank opinions and periodical payments;
(b) general finance: for capital goods, property, farm development, bridging loans;
(c) merchant banking: short/medium term loans, standby facilities, acceptance, indorsement and discounting commercial bills;
(d) international banking: finance for exports/imports, provision of foreign currency, overseas remittances, trade enquiries;
(e) investment: portfolio management and advice, purchase/sale of investments, retirement funds;
(f) other general services including arrangement of insurance, travel and economic research and information.

In this chapter we will be primarily concerned with the duties and functions of banks in relation to cheques.

Savings banks provide interest bearing savings accounts, investment and special purpose savings accounts, housing loans, and loans to semi-government bodies and schools.

Merchant banks are often associated with share-broking firms, and the trading banks. They provide finance for the development of new businesses and products either in the form of equity capital or loans. They also factor book debts, deal in securities and the short-term money market. These "banks" have received individual exemptions under Banking Act s 11 from the general prohibition against non-banks carrying on banking business: s 8. However, this does not entitle them to carry on the *general business* of banking (eg, cheque accounts) nor to describe themselves as banks: s 66.

Finance companies have traditionally provided finance for the purchase of motor vehicles and other consumer goods, particularly by way of hire-purchase. In more recent times they have diversified their lending to include business and lease finance, mortgages on commercial property and homes, and some discounting of bills of exchange and factoring of book debts. Higher interest rates paid by finance companies on their public borrowings and charges by them on loans reflect the greater risks involved. Many of the larger finance companies are owned or partly owned by banks.

Building societies were founded for the purpose of providing finance for home building, largely through the investments of their members. However, the higher interest rates offered to investors have witnessed a substantial growth in these societies to the point where they are serious competitors with savings banks for general savings and investments even by those not seeking a housing loan.

Other financial institutions which play important roles as channels for investment and/or providers of loans include credit unions, cash management trusts, unit trusts and mutual funds, life and general insurance companies, pastoral and wool broking companies, and factoring companies. We have noted that banks are regulated under the Banking Act and insurance companies under the Life Insurance Act or Insurance Act (see pp 199–200 and 483, *supra*). In addition to state legislation for specific types of institutions such as the Building and Co-operative Societies Act 1901, Permanent Building Societies Act 1967 and Credit Union Act 1969 in New South Wales and similar legislation in other states, the Financial Corporations Act 1974 (Cth) provides comprehensive regulations over all corporations which are in the business of providing finance. This covers all the institutions described above, except banks, life and general insurance companies which are specifically exempted by s 8(2). The Australian government has in recent times given consideration to the implications of structural changes in the banking and general financial sectors including increasing the number of banks allowed to operate in Australia.

For further descriptions of the functions of banks and other financial institutions, see Weerasooria & Coops, *Banking Law and Practice in Australia*, 1976, Pt I.

WHO IS A CUSTOMER?

This question is important because of the special relationship and duties which arise between a bank and its customer at general law, and particularly the statutory protections available to a bank in dealing with its "customer's" cheques. However, the BEA contains no definition of a "customer", and the determination will depend upon the application of the common law decisions to the facts of each case. What kind of relationship must be established and how long need it subsist?

Commissioners of Taxation v English Scottish & Australian Bank Ltd
Privy Council [1920] AC 683

[Note that their Lordships' judgment which is reproduced in full at this point deals also with the right of the owner of a cheque to sue a collecting bank in conversion and the statutory defences available to the bank under the BEA which are considered in Section 3, *infra*.

The judgment of their Lordships was delivered by **Lord Dunedin:**] On 6 June 1917, Mr A Friend, York Street Sydney, put a cheque drawn by himself on the Australian Bank of Commerce for £786 18s 3d into an envelope, along with some other cheques drawn by other members of his family, and addressed the envelope to the Commissioners of Taxation, George Street North, Sydney. He gave the envelope to a clerk to deliver, and the envelope was duly delivered by being placed in a box put for the purpose of receiving such letters in the Taxation Department. The cheque was in payment of an assessment for income tax and was in the following terms: "Pay 053 or bearer the sum of £786 18s 3d." It was crossed with the word "Bank", that is to say, generally not specially. The figures "053" correspond with the final figures on the number of the cheque, and this method of filling up a bearer cheque seems to be a common habit in Sydney. Attached to the assessment notice sent to Mr Friend there is the following instruction: "Collectors will not call for payment of taxes, but the taxpayer should (a) pay the tax at the Taxation Office, George Street North, Sydney, in cash or bank notes, cheques, or postal notes, payable in New South Wales; or (b) remit the same to the Commissioners at Sydney, by bank draft, payable on demand, or cheque, crossed, and marked 'Commissioners of Taxation—not negotiable'—payable in NSW; or by Post Office money order, or by postal note, marked 'Commissioners of Taxation—not negotiable'."

It is, therefore, to be observed that in making his payment by means of a bearer cheque delivered at the office Mr Friend was acting in strict accordance with the instructions issued. The cheque in question was stolen by some person unknown and was never cashed by the Commissioners of Taxation.

On 7 June a man who gave his name as Stewart Thallon entered the head office of the respondents' bank at Sydney and stated that he wished to open an account. He was received by the accountant of the bank, who went through the usual procedure of taking his name and address, which he gave at certain well-known residential chambers in Sydney, and making him sign the signature-book. Being asked how much he wished to bank, he replied "£20" and handed that sum in bank notes to the accountant. The accountant filled up a "paid-in" slip and handed it and the money to the teller. Thallon said he would take a cheque-book and was given one, the charge being debited to his account. He then told the accountant that every cheque he signed for cash would be accompanied by an order to pay, and the accountant added a note to that effect to be entered in the ledger account. A ledger account was opened in the ordinary form, but no inquiry was instituted to check the authenticity of the address.

On 8 June the cheque in question was handed in with a pay-in slip to be credited to Thallon's account, which was done. Later in the same day the cheque was cleared in the ordinary manner and was paid by the Australian Bank of Commerce. On 9, 11 and 12 June three cheques for £483 16s 6d, £260 10s 0d and £50 12s 6d, respectively, drawn by Thallon, were presented for payment by persons each accompanied with an order signed by Thallon to pay. No more was ever seen of Thallon; no person of that name lived at the address given and it may be taken as certain that the name of Thallon was an assumed one.

The present action was raised by the Commissioners of Taxation against the English, Scottish and Australian Bank, the ground of liability being conversion of the cheque. The defence was s 88 of the Bills of Exchange Act 1909 (Cth), which enacts as follows: "(1) Where a banker in good faith and without negligence receives payment for a customer of a cheque crossed generally or specially to himself, and the customer has no title or a defective title thereto, the banker shall not incur any liability to the true owner of the cheque by reason only of having received such payment. (2) A banker receives payment of a crossed cheque for a customer within the meaning of this section notwithstanding that he credits his customer's account with the amount of the cheque before receiving payment thereof."

There was originally another defence, that the bank was a holder for value, but this was decided adversely to the respondents and is not now insisted on. The appellants' reply to the plea founded on s 88 was twofold. They said, first, that in the circumstances Thallon was not a customer, and secondly, that the bank had been guilty of negligence in receiving payment.

The action was tried before Pring J who sustained the defence, holding that in the sense of the Act Thallon was a customer and that no negligence in the circumstances had been proved against the bank. On appeal to the Supreme Court for New South Wales the decision was upheld by a majority, Sly J dissenting. Appeal being taken to this board, both the points above stated were argued by the appellants. Both the questions, namely, Who is a customer? and, What is negligence? were the subjects of discussion in the case of *Kendall v London Bank of Australia* (1918) 18 SR (NSW) 394, and the learned judges in the Appellate Court import by reference their opinions in that case, which was decided on the same day as the present case.

As regards the first point, namely, whether Thallon was a customer in the sense of the Act, their Lordships do not think it necessary to say much. As to this, there is unanimity among all the learned judges who tried both cases, the facts in *Kendall's* case, so far as this point is concerned, being practically the same. Their Lordships are of opinion that the word "customer" signifies a relationship in which duration is not of the essence. A person whose money has been accepted by a bank on the footing that they undertake to honour cheques up to the amount standing to his credit is, in the view of their Lordships, a customer of the bank in the sense of the statute, irrespective of whether his connection is of short or long standing. The contrast is not between an habitué and a newcomer, but between a person for whom the bank performs a casual service, such as, for instance, cashing a cheque for a person introduced by one of their customers, and a person who has an account of his own at the bank. Thallon was, therefore, a customer, though one of short standing: see the opinion of Lord Davey in *Great Western Ry Co v London and County Banking Co* [1901] AC 414.

The remaining point is, was there negligence on the part of the bank in collecting the cheque? Their Lordships say "in collecting the cheque", because that is in a slightly different phrase what the statute says, "without negligence receives payment for a customer". It is not a question of negligence in opening an account, though the circumstances connected with the opening of an account may shed light on the question of whether there was negligence in collecting a cheque. In the case of *Commissioners of State Savings Bank v Permewan, Wright & Co* (1914) 19 CLR 457 at 478 in the High Court of Australia, Isaacs J says: "Apart from the well-established rule that whether or not the evidence establishes that a person acts without negligence is a question of fact, the legal principles found in *Morison v London County and Westminster Bank* [1914] 3 KB 356, and relevant to the present, are (1) that the question should in strictness be determined separately with regard to each cheque; (2) that the test of negligence is whether the transaction of paying in any given cheque was so out of the ordinary course that it ought to have aroused doubts in the bankers' mind, and caused them to make inquiry." If there be inserted after the words "given cheque" the words "coupled with the circumstances antecedent and present", their Lordships think this is an accurate statement of the law.

The question is necessarily a question of fact. If the case has been tried by a jury, it would be for the jury to determine under proper direction whether the bank had been negligent or not. It follows that, being a question of fact, it is really impossible to lay down rules or statements which will determine what is negligence and what is not ... Each case must be determined on its own circumstances. In view, however, of what was said in the decision of the High Court of Australia abovementioned, their Lordships feel bound to say that they cannot agree with the view of the learned Chief Justice in that case where he says that the care to be taken is not less than a man invited to purchase or cash such a cheque for himself might reasonably be expected to take. This seems to their Lordships to apply an inapposite standard, for the simple reason that it is no part of the business or ordinary practice of individuals to cash cheques which are offered to them, whereas it is part of the ordinary business or practice of a bank to collect cheques for their customers. If, therefore, a standard is sought, it must be the standard to be derived from the ordinary practice of bankers, not individuals. Their Lordships think, therefore, that the evidence of bank officials in *Kendall v London Bank of Australia* as to the practice of banks was rightly tendered and received, as indeed the court in that case decided.

Coming now to the reasons alleged for holding the learned trial judge to have been wrong in holding no negligence proved, they really amount to this, that the bank ought not to have collected a cheque for a customer who was of such recent introduction and about whom they knew nothing. There was, however, nothing suspicious about the way the account was opened. A customer, however genuine and respectable, could hardly, assuming him to start with a deposit of £20 in cash, have opened it in any other way. Was then the fact that a cheque was paid into that account for collection one day after the account was opened a circumstance of an unusual character calculated to arouse suspicion and provoke inquiry? For if it was laid down that no cheque should be collected without a thorough inquiry as to the history of the cheque, it would render banking business as ordinarily carried on impossible: customers would often be left for long periods without available money. Now if the cheque here had been for some unusually large sum, perhaps suspicion might have been aroused. This is really a question of degree, and their Lordships cannot say that the trial judge was wrong in thinking that £743 was not a sum of such magnitude as to create the duty of inquiry.

If the cheque had been in different form, things might well have been otherwise. Their Lordships cannot help remarking that to a certain extent the appellants have themselves to thank for what has happened, owing to the terms of their instructions. If they had insisted that in the case of payments made at the office, as they did insist in the case of drafts sent by post, the cheques should be made payable to the Commissioners of Taxation, then there would have been something on the face of the cheque to arouse inquiry. The fact that the cheque was to bearer distinguishes this case from *Commissioners of State Savings Bank v Permewan, Wright & Co.* In that case, in the case of 36 cheques, the cheques were drawn in favour of the commissioners, or had such markings on them as showed that they were drawn for the purpose of paying duties. This was held, their Lordships think rightly, to be a circumstance which ought to have put the bank on inquiry when such cheques were presented by a private individual ... There was here no note of warning of any kind on the cheque, and accordingly the conditions which arose in that case do not apply.

Their Lordships will therefore humbly advise His Majesty to dismiss the appeal with costs.

When a customer opens a bank account, some form of identification is usually required. In the case of an account for a business or company, the bank may require references. A company such as Carb Pty Ltd should be required to produce its certificate of incorporation, and a copy of the resolution authorising its officers (eg, directors Jim and Mary Handy) to sign cheques drawn or indorsed on behalf of the company.

THE BANK'S CLEARING SYSTEM

The legal duties owed by banks in paying and collecting cheques will be easier to grasp if the basic pattern of the system for clearing and paying cheques is understood. Cheques received by banks for collection which were drawn on other banks are sent to the main capital city office of the collecting bank, which takes them to a central clearing house for exchange several times daily with other participating banks. The amounts of the cheques are totalled to derive net balances owing between the respective banks, which are then settled by the banks drawing cheques on Exchange Settlement Accounts maintained by each bank with the Reserve Bank. Similar exchanges are effected in some country centres where all the local banks meet to exchange local cheques.

The system may be illustrated by the following simplified example: Carb sold 500 carburettors to Bourke Motors and received the following cheque in payment:

On 5 May Jim Handy took the cheque to City Bank, Ryde branch and deposited the cheque for the credit of Carb's account. Before doing so, he wrote on the back of the cheque "Carb Pty Ltd" and Mary and Jim both signed the indorsement. The Ryde branch (collecting bank) sent the cheque to City Bank's Head Office in Sydney which processed it through the Central Clearing House to the Country Bank which in turn forwarded it to its Bourke branch (paying bank) for clearance against Bourke Motors' account. Although City Bank would credit Carb's ledger balance with the $10,000 deposit on 5 May, the proceeds of the cheque would not be available for Carb to draw upon until sufficient time (perhaps five working days) had elapsed for Country Bank to clear the cheque or notify City Bank if it was dishonoured on arrival at the Bourke Branch.

As technology has developed, the banks have attempted to automate their operations particularly by the use of computers. At the present time, in order to ensure protection against forgeries, etc, it is necessary for every cheque to be moved physically from the branch of the bank at which it is paid in to the branch of the bank on which it is drawn. Naturally, the banks are anxious to minimise the administrative costs of such operations involving hundreds of millions of cheques each year. It is understood that they are developing technical methods, and seeking amendments in the law, to facilitate clearances at a distance "by remote control". For further descriptions of the clearing system, see Weerasooria & Coops, *Banking Law and Practice in Australia,* 1976, Pt I, pp 39-40, 46-9.

QUESTIONS

Question 1

Lord Denning in *Kirkwood's* case pp 485-6, *supra,* listed the requirements of "banking business". Are the state savings banks carrying on "banking business" under that definition? Do they qualify as bankers under the Banking Act and the BEA? Compare the position under the English and Australian law.

Question 2

The City Cash Management Trust is owned by City Bank and Coverall Insurance Ltd in equal shares. The Trust operates deposit accounts for investors, and also makes loans to companies and individuals. Investors can deposit directly with the Trust cash or cheques which are credited through the Trust's account with City Bank.

The volume of the Trust's operations have expanded due to the high interest rates which it offers investors, but the bank charges, federal government tax on cheques and state government duty are proving to be very heavy. In order to reduce these charges, the Trust wishes to arrange to collect cheques deposited with it directly from the drawers' respective banks.

The Trust also believes it can obtain a competitive advantage if it allows its customers to use its facilities for payment of their regular bills. It plans to do this by providing its customers with either
   (a) cheque forms which they can draw as authorised signatories on the Trust's bank account with City Bank up to the limit of their credit with the Trust; or
   (b) cheque forms which they can draw directly on the Trust which would then undertake to pay the amount of such cheques to the banks collecting them.

Advise the Trust in relation to these proposals. Do you foresee any legal or practical difficulties in their implementation. Would the Trust incur any risks?

Question 3

Snatch stole four cheques from a postbox. Each was payable to a separate payee or bearer. The following day she opened two separate accounts with two of the cheques at different branches of City Bank in the assumed names of the respective payees of those cheques. The cheques were for amounts of $20 and $400 respectively. Three days later when the cheques had been cleared she withdrew the proceeds and closed the accounts.

Fearing detection, she hurried to Pacific Bank where she arranged for an air booking and travellers cheques for a trip to Venezuela. When the travel officer requested payment, Snatch produced the two remaining stolen cheques for $200 and $400 respectively. The travel officer arranged for them to be cashed by the bank's teller and the proceeds to be applied in payment for the air tickets and travellers cheques, which Snatch took with her on the afternoon flight for Caracas.

Are the respective banks likely to be entitled to any protection if sued by the owners of the respective cheques? If not, are there any precautions which the banks might have taken to avoid liability?

Would your answer differ if Snatch had maintained accounts with each of the banks for the three years preceding the above incidents.

SECTION 2: DUTIES OF PAYING BANK AND ITS CUSTOMER AT COMMON LAW

In this section, we deal with the paying bank's duty to its customer (as drawer of a cheque), which is almost exclusively determined by the common law. The duties owed to the true owner of a cheque by both paying and collecting banks, which are substantially qualified by statute, are considered in Section 3.

The reciprocal duties of a paying bank and its customer (Carb) in relation to the operation of a cheque account may be briefly summarised:
   (1) The bank is obliged to meet Carb's mandates (ie, pay its cheques) with due care

and in strict compliance with the mandate, provided it is clear and unambiguous, and there are sufficient funds in the account or appropriate arrangements have been made for an overdraft.

(2) Carb is subject to the correlative duty to act carefully in drawing its cheques in a form which is free of ambiguity and so as not to mislead the bank: *Joachimson v Swiss Bank Corp* [1921] 3 KB 110 at 127, per Atkin LJ.

It follows that a customer will not be responsible for cheques on which his signature is forged or which are otherwise issued without his authority, and the bank is not entitled to debit his account with amounts paid out on such cheques. However, Carb is obliged to inform the bank immediately it becomes aware, or even has reasonable grounds to suspect, that this situation has arisen. If it fails to do so, it may be estopped from denying the validity of any mandates forged or altered thereafter: see *Greenwood v Martins Bank Ltd*, p 433, *supra*.

The above formulations lead to a number of further questions which call for a more detailed examination of judicial decisions. For example:

(1) Does the customer have a positive duty to take precautions against fraudulent alteration of the cheque after it leaves his hands? Does leaving a blank space in a cheque which is otherwise complete, of itself, constitute a breach of the customer's duty?

(2) Can the customer's duty be reduced to a firm definition in the abstract, or will it vary with the facts and course of dealing between the bank and each customer? What importance should be attached to the instructions given by the bank to its customer both personally and on the cover of the chequebook?

(3) What is the effect of the customer's negligence in drawing the cheque? Does it exempt the bank from its correlative duty in paying the cheque, or can the customer recover from the bank if its negligence has contributed to the loss?

(4) Is there a valid distinction between the customer's negligence in drawing a cheque (eg, signing in blank, or leaving large gaps in a signed cheque) and negligence in the conduct of the customer's business or affairs (eg, careless selection of staff, or leaving a chequebook in an unsafe place)?

Commonwealth Trading Bank of Australia v Sydney Wide Stores Pty Ltd and Another
High Court of Australia (1981) 55 ALJR 574

Gibbs CJ, Stephen, Mason, Aickin, Wilson and **Brennan JJ**: The issue here is whether this court should adhere to its decision in *Marshall v The Colonial Bank of Australasia* (1904) 1 CLR 632, which was affirmed on appeal by the Privy Council [1906] AC 559, or whether we should follow the later decision of the House of Lords in *London Joint Stock Bank v Macmillan and Arthur* [1918] AC 777 and apply the principle which it enunciated that the drawer of a cheque will be responsible for any loss caused by his drawing of a cheque in such a manner as to facilitate a fraudulent alteration of the cheque.

The first respondent sued the paying bank (the appellant) and the collecting bank (the second respondent) in respect of certain cheques drawn on its account with the appellant. The first respondent then had in its employ a man named Prior. From time to time it became necessary for the first respondent to draw cheques in favour of an organisation called "Computer Accounting Services" with which it had dealings. The cheques were made out "Pay CAS or order". The first respondent in its statement of claim and the appellant in its defence alleged that Prior altered the cheques in question so as to make them read "Pay CASH or order" simply by adding the letter "H" after the letters "CAS".

In its statement of claim the first respondent alleged that the appellant in breach of its contractual duty failed to exercise reasonable care in that notwithstanding that each of the cheques bore the words "Pay CASH or order", each of them was crossed, each bore the words "Not Negotiable" and "A/c Payee Only", each cheque was for a large amount and the appellant failed to make enquiries of the first respondent before paying the cheques.

Paragraph 5 of the appellant's defence pleaded:

"In answer to the whole of the statement of claim, the second defendant says:

(a) the plaintiff was its customer.

(b) as such customer the plaintiff owed a duty of care to the second defendant in relation to the drawing of cheques upon it.

(c) the plaintiff acted negligently in relation to the subject cheque.

[Their Honours then referred to the pleadings and the decision of Rogers J at the original hearing in the Supreme Court of NSW, as well as the history of prior conflicting decisions. They continued at 576:] In that case [*Young v Grote* (1827) 4 Bing 253; 130 ER 764] Y, a customer of a banker delivered to his wife printed cheques signed by himself, but with blanks for the sums, requesting his wife to fill the blanks up according to the exigency of his business. She caused one to be filled up with the words "fifty pounds" and the figures "2s 3d", the "fifty" being commenced with a small letter, and placed in the middle of a line, the figures 50.2.3. were also placed at a considerable distance from the printed pound sign. In this state she delivered the cheque to her husband's clerk to receive the amount. He inserted at the beginning of the line in which the word "fifty" was written, the words "Three hundred and", and the figure "3" between the pound sign and the "fifty". The banker having paid the £350.2.3. it was held that the loss must fall on the customer.

The judgments of the Court of Common Pleas have generated great controversy as to what was the ground of the decision. Best CJ said ((1827) 4 Bing at 258; 130 ER at 766) "if it be the fault of the customer that the banker pays more than he ought, he cannot be called upon to pay again". He quoted Pothier's statement that, if a banker has been led into error by the fault of a drawer, the drawer not having taken care to write his letter of mandate so as to prevent falsification, for instance if he wrote in figures the sum drawn by the letter and someone added a zero, the drawer would be bound to indemnify the banker for the loss he had sustained. The other members of the court were not so explicit. Burrough and Gaselee JJ found that Y was bound to bear the loss because he was guilty of negligence. Park J alone of the four judges, though agreeing that the drawer was guilty of negligence, put the decision on another ground, saying that Y left the cheques to be filled up by his wife and when filled up by her, they became his genuine orders. It seems that the majority decided the case on the ground that Y had delegated the drawing of the cheque to his wife and that she was guilty of negligence in drawing the cheque in such a way as to facilitate the fraudulent alteration of the amount of the cheque which would not have been made but for the careless manner in which the cheque was drawn. So understood, the principle according to which the case was decided stands as an apparent exception to the general rule that the banker is only entitled to make debits to the customer's account in accordance with the customer's authority.

In the cases which followed there was much discussion as to what was the precise ground of decision in *Young v Grote*. The discussion invariably proceeded on the footing that the case was correctly decided. As Lord Finlay LC noted in *Macmillan* (at 795), the correctness of the decision was accepted by judges of great distinction, notably Parke B, Pollock CB and Lord Cranworth LC. The cases in which *Young v Grote* was accepted were examined in detail by Lord Finlay LC in *Macmillan*. There is no point in our repeating that examination here. It is sufficient for us to say that various views were expressed as to the true foundation of the doctrine. Some said that it is but an instance of the general principle that as between two persons, he whose negligence enabled the fraud to be committed must bear the loss: *Ex parte Swan* (1859) 7 CB (NS) 400 at 400; 141 ER 871 at 887; *The Mayor, Constables & Co of Merchants of the Staple of England v The Governor and Co of the Bank of England* (1887) 21 QBD 160 at 167; *London and South Western Bank v Wentworth* (1880) 5 Ex D 96 at 105. Some thought that the drawer is estopped by this negligence from disputing the authority of the banker to pay: *Bank of Ireland v Trustees of Evans' Charities* (1855) 5 HLC 389 at 413-44; 10 ER 950 at 960; *Orr & Barber v Union Bank of Scotland* (1854) 1 Macq 513 at 523; *Ex parte Swan* (1859) 7 CB (NS) at 431-2; 141 ER at 884; contra Earl of Selborne LC in *Bank of England v Vagliano Bros* [1891] AC 107 at 126. Others asserted that the payment is allowed so as to avoid circuity of action, the customer being liable to the bank for his negligence: *Swan v The North British Australasian Co* (1863) 2 H & C 175 at 189-90; 159 ER 73 at 79. And Parke B in *Robarts v Tucker* [1851] 16 QB 560 at 580; 117 ER 994, at 1002, considered that a person who drew a cheque in blank gave "authority to any person in whose hands it was to fill up the cheque in whatever way the blank permitted".

It was in 1873 that discordant voices first expressed the view that the maker of an instrument was under no duty not to facilitate a forgery. In *Société Générale v The Metropolitan Bank (Ltd)* (1873) 27 LT (NS) 849, a case of fraudulent alteration of foreign bills, the Court of Common Pleas held that the defendant indorser was not liable on a bill in which the word "eight" had been written in a blank before the word "days" and subsequently, after the indorsement the letter "y" had been added to the word "eight", there being a space between "eight" and "days". Bovill CJ said (at 856): "Parties cannot prevent forgery being committed; they must use reasonable care not to afford opportunities for it, and if space is left for a word or a figure to be introduced, and if such word or figure is introduced, I cannot think that a jury would come to the conclusion that the maker of the instrument in its original form would be guilty of negligence."

Brett J said (at 857-8): "I not only protest that there was no negligence, but say that no judge ought to leave to the jury the fact as evidence of negligence. But there is no duty on anyone to suppose that those, against whose character there is no imputation, will commit forgery whenever the opportunity arises."

Later in *Baxendale v Bennett* (1878) 3 QBD 525 a case involving the acceptance of a bill in blank, the acceptor having authorised the drawer to fill in his name as drawer, Brett LJ (at 533-4) thought that the authority of *Young v Grote* (1827) 4 Bing 253; 130 ER 764, had been undermined by the observations made in *Bank of Ireland v Trustees of Evans' Charities* (1855) 5 HLC 389; 10 ER 950. Subsequently as Lord Esher MR in *Scholfield* in the Court of Appeal [1895] 1 QB 536 at 543 he described *Young v Grote* as "the front of bad argument" and the other member of the majority Rigby LJ at 556, considered that the principle of *Young v Grote* should not be followed.

It was in the light of this history that the House of Lords gave its decision in *Scholfield*. There a bill for £500 was presented for acceptance with a stamp of a much larger amount than was necessary and with spaces left. The acceptor wrote his acceptance and handed the bill to the drawer, who fraudulently filled up the spaces and turned it into a bill for £3500. It was held, affirming the Court of Appeal, that the acceptor owed no duty of precaution to the plaintiff, a bona fide holder for value and was guilty of no negligence. Lord Halsbury LC considered that the doctrine that "giving opportunity for forgery" affects the validity of the forged instrument formed no part of English law. He rejected the principle enunciated by Pothier and appears to have concluded that *Young v Grote*, was wrongly decided. He said (at 352):

"My Lords, this very case has in almost precisely similar circumstances been already decided in the *Adelphi Bank v Edwards* (not reported; the facts, the decision and the grounds thereof are stated in the judgment of Lord Watson, p 540), and I regret very much that that case has not been reported. I entirely concur with what Lindley LJ said in that case, that it was wrong to contend that it is negligence to sign a negotiable instrument so that somebody else can tamper with it; and the wider proposition of Bovill CJ in a former case, *Société Générale v Metropolitan Bank* 27 LT (NS) 849 at 856, that people are not supposed to commit forgery, and that the protection against forgery is not the vigilance of parties excluding the possibility of committing forgery, but the law of the land."

It is noteworthy, however, that of their Lordships who constituted the House of Lords on this occasion, the Lord Chancellor was alone in his dissatisfaction with *Young v Grote*. Lord Watson stated that the doctrine Pothier had no application outside the relationship of banker and customer (pp 534-9). He accordingly distinguished *Young v Grote*. Lord Shand and Lord Davey were of the same opinion. The other members of the House distinguished *Young v Grote*. Not all the Law Lords appear to have appreciated that there is a contractual relationship between the drawer of a cheque and his paying bank which imposes on the drawer a duty of care to that bank and that this relationship distinguishes the drawing of a cheque from the acceptance of a bill.

Unlike *Scholfield, Marshall* involved cheques and the relationship between banker and customer. In *Marshall* the plaintiffs brought an action to recover a balance in their account with the defendants. The defence was that there was no balance, five cheques having been drawn by the signatories to the account which, when paid, were for sums which in the aggregate amounted to the balance sought to be recovered by the plaintiffs. The plaintiffs were not familiar with accounts and left the clerical work in connection with the estate to their co-executor who filled out the cheques in his own handwriting and sent them to the plaintiffs for signature. After the cheques had been signed by the plaintiffs their co-executor fraudulently altered them to larger amounts and obtained the full amounts from the defendant. He was enabled to do so by reason of the circumstance that the cheques when initially drawn left a space between the pound symbol and the first figure appearing thereafter and left a space before the commencement of the statement of the amount in writing.

Griffith CJ who delivered the judgment of this court acknowledged that as the relationship of banker and customer was contractual there was an implied mutual obligation on each party not to do anything which would hamper the other party in performing the contract or would delay him in performing it.

The question for decision was therefore whether there was evidence of breach of duty. On this aspect of the case Griffith CJ rejected the proposition that *Young v Grote* affirmed the doctrine of Pothier that if the banker has been led into error by the fault of the drawer, the drawer not having taken care to write the draft in such a manner as to prevent falsification, the drawer must indemnify the banker. He thought that the judgments did not support this view and that each of the judges relied on other circumstances as establishing the default of the drawer. He noted that the authority of *Young v Grote* had been confined, especially by *Scholfield v Earl of Londesborough* [1895] 1 QB 536, to the proposition that the drawer of a cheque may, by his negligence in connection with drawing it, disentitle himself to complain that the banker has paid a larger sum upon it than the drawer intended (at 651-2). The Chief Justice went on to say (at 660): "... authority cannot be inferred merely from the existence of blank spaces in the document. It may well be that the existence of blank spaces, combined with other circumstances, either intrinsic to the document or extrinsic, may be evidence of delegated authority to fill them up. But the mere existence of a blank is not sufficient."

In affirming the decision of the High Court the Judicial Committee held that *Scholfield* was the governing authority not *Young v Grote*. Like the High Court, their Lordships considered that the authority of *Young v Grote* had been confined by *Scholfield*. They acknowledged that the contractual relation existing between a banker and his customer differentiated the case from that of the acceptor and the holder of a bill. Yet they thought that the duty that subsists between customer and banker is substantially the same as that which exists between the acceptor and the holder of a bill, though they declined to offer an abstract definition of the duty. Sir Arthur Wilson, who delivered the judgment of the Judicial Committee, having quoted the penultimate paragraph in the speech of the Lord Chancellor in *Scholfield*—the paragraph which we have set out earlier—went on to enunciate "... the proposition that, whatever the duty of a customer towards his banker may be with reference to the drawing of cheques, the mere fact that the cheque is drawn with spaces such that a forger can utilise them for the purpose of forgery is not by itself any violation of that obligation": at 568.

With great respect, we think that several criticisms must be made of the judgments, both in this court and in the Privy Council, in *Marshall*. Those judgments clearly were influenced by the speech of the Lord Chancellor in *Scholfield*, and it does not appear to have been appreciated that Lord Halsbury's views were not shared by the other members of the House. In the first place, those judgments did not acknowledge that the contractual relationship between customer and banker distinguished the drawing of a cheque from the acceptance of a bill of exchange, and consequently failed to give effect to the important consequences of the distinction. The existence of the contractual relationship which is the foundation for imposing a duty on the customer in relation to the drawing of his cheque is absent in the case of the acceptor of a bill. In the second place, the judgments failed to recognise that the decision in *Young v Grote* had been followed in many cases and that the principle that the drawer of a cheque was guilty of negligence vis-à-vis his banker in so drawing a cheque as to facilitate forgery had been accepted in many cases. It is right to say that there was a long-standing controversy as to the precise effect of the decision in *Young v Grote,* but that controversy, as we have seen, related to the theoretical basis for the doctrine, not to the existence of the doctrine itself. In the third place, the judgments support the view expressed by Bovill CJ and Brett J in *Société Générale,* and by the Lord Chancellor in *Scholfield,* that it is not the duty of a drawer of a cheque to guard against the possibility of a forgery, that this is a matter best left to the criminal law. This view does not conform to modern notions of the duty of care and the standard of care expected of the reasonable man. It is now well settled that the reasonable man should in appropriate circumstances take account of the possibility that others will break the law and act accordingly.

Subject to some qualification these criticisms form the main thrust of the speeches in *Macmillan*. To them we should add three comments. One is that it seems fair as between banker and customer that the customer should bear responsibility for the loss when it is his careless drawing of the cheque that facilitates that loss through forgery. No heavy burden is placed on the drawer. He is merely required to exercise care when drawing the cheque. The second comment is that the *Marshall* view imposes a considerable burden on bankers without their having any very satisfactory means of protecting themselves. The *Macmillan* view promotes the negotiability of cheques by affording banks, which have to determine the authenticity of many cheques in a short period of time, the assurance that the drawer by his negligence may not increase the risk of loss through fraudulent alteration without being responsible for the consequences. The final comment is that there is no convincing distinction between a case where the careless drawing of the cheque facilitates loss by fraudulent increase in the amount of the cheque and the case where the customer draws his cheque in blank and his agent exceeds his authority by filling in a cheque for a larger amount than that authorised by the drawer, in which event the drawer is responsible—see the speech of Lord Shaw of Dunfermline in *Macmillan* at 826–7.

It is significant that in other jurisdictions the principle enunciated by *Macmillan* has been adopted. The existence of the duty on the part of the drawer of a cheque has been affirmed in Canada [citation of cases]. In the United States of America the existence of a similar duty has been generally, but not universally, acknowledged though in some instances the rule has been affected by statute [citation of cases].

Macmillan dealt with the drawing of a cheque in such a manner as to facilitate by forgery an increase in the amount for which it was drawn. The judgments contain nothing which restricts the duty or its scope to the possibility of loss by such means, that is, the filling in of gaps created by the manner in which the amount has been written in words and figures. But there is no occasion to pursue the question whether the duty of care extends to the drawing of a cheque in such a manner as not to facilitate a fraudulent alteration in the name of the payee, a question of the kind that arose in *Slingsby v District Bank Ltd* [1932] 1 KB 544. We have merely to decide whether the primary judge was correct in following *Marshall* in preference to *Macmillan,* a matter which he determined as a question of law at the threshold of the case. The primary judge was, of course, bound to follow *Marshall.* We are at liberty to depart from it. For the reasons already given the principle enunciated in *Macmillan* is to be preferred to that stated in *Marshall.*

The question of law submitted for determination by this court may be answered by saying that, arising from the contract between banker and customer, there is a duty upon the customer to take usual and reasonable precautions in drawing a cheque to prevent a fraudulent alteration which might occasion loss to the banker.

Whether the respondent was in breach of its duty by neglecting some usual and reasonable precaution in the drawing of the cheques is a question of fact and is one of the issues to be determined by the tribunal of fact.

We would allow the appeal and remit the matter to the Supreme Court.

Murphy J: The question is whether a bank customer who (innocently) draws a cheque so negligently as to facilitate a forgery should be liable for loss to the bank caused by the forgery. The answer involves issues of precedent, modern theories of negligence, and social policy. The precedent, which bound the trial court, is that in *Marshall v The Colonial Bank of Australasia Ltd* (1904) 1 CLR 632; [1906] AC 559, in which the Privy Council affirmed the decision of this court, that the drawer is not liable. That decision is out of line with modern developments of general principles of care applicable in tort and contract.

In terms of social policy, there is a real question whether it would be better to let the loss continue to fall on the banking industry. Although the standard of care habitually observed by cheque drawers may fairly be described as low, I am not satisfied that any considerable burden has been imposed on banks by the application of the *Marshall* decision. If in practice, the losses, which to individual bank customers would be onerous, are cumulatively only slight for the banking system in comparison with the vast amount of business done by cheque, a sensible system of loss spreading would be to continue as before. Further if the cumulative losses are now slight, it would be absurd to impose a standard of care such that every drawer of cheques would have to regard employees and associates as potential forgers. However, this branch of the law can be brought into harmony with other areas (and with the law on this subject in other countries) and undesirable social consequences also avoided, by adoption of a standard of care which would not require us to turn into a suspicious society.

The *Marshall* case should be over-ruled, and in accordance with modern doctrines of care, the negligent drawer should be liable, but no high standard of care should be required. I agree with the proposed order.

Appeal allowed.

In 1964, the committee appointed to review the Bills of Exchange Act, under the Chairmanship of Manning J of the New South Wales Supreme Court, prepared a report, recommending substantial reform of the Act, and annexed a draft Cheques Act. The committee's recommendations regarding indorsements and crossed cheques were implemented in 1971, but the remainder of the report is still under consideration. Among other recommendations, the report suggested (paras 241-5) the enactment of a section in the Cheques Act in the following terms:

Clause 13: A customer of a bank, who draws a cheque on such bank, owes a duty to the bank to take reasonable care in drawing such cheque so as not to facilitate the making of an unauthorised addition or alteration thereto.

Kepitagalla Rubber Estates Ltd v The National Bank of India Ltd
King's Bench Division [1909] 2 KB 1010

[The secretary of the plaintiff company, named Talbot, forged the signatures of two of the company's directors upon seven cheques which purported to have been drawn by the directors on behalf of the company. The cheques were drawn on the defendant bank which paid them across the counter to Talbot who absconded with the proceeds. Talbot forged some of the signatures with the aid of a rubber stamp representing the signature of one of the directors. The forgeries extended over a period of two months, during which time the directors did not examine the bank pass book nor the company's cash book. The bank debited the company's account with the amount of the cheques.

The plaintiffs sued to recover the moneys so debited as money had and received by the defendants to the use of the plaintiffs. In its defence the bank alleged inter alia that the plaintiffs had by their conduct and neglect misled the defendants and caused or permitted them to be misled into paying the cheques.]

Bray J [stated the facts and the nature of the action and continued. The defendants] contended, first, that it was the duty of the plaintiffs to them, as their bankers and as part of the contract between them, (a) to use reasonable care in the issuing of mandates to the defendants, and (b) in the carrying out of their business relating to the issuing of mandates, and if they delegated these duties to another, they must use reasonable care to supervise the execution of the duties and to prevent the delegation from being abused. I think the cases established the first part of this proposition. [His Honour then cited a number of cases including *Bank of England v Vagliano* [1891] AC 107.]

I should come to the same conclusion apart from authority. It seems to me to be clearly the duty of a person giving a mandate to take reasonable care that he does not mislead the person to whom the mandate is given. That, as has been pointed out, is the duty as between a principal and his agent: *Ireland v Livingston* (1872) LR 5 HL 395; and although the relationship between a customer and his banker is not that of principal and agent, the same considerations would seem to apply. The customer is asking the bank to do something. Surely he should take care that his request is made in such a way as not to mislead his banker. Now, assuming this to be the duty, has it been broken in this case? [His Honour then reviewed the evidence and concluded:] In truth, the plaintiffs have done no acts whatever in relation to the issuing of the mandate, and, further, there is no evidence to shew that the bank were misled by any conduct on their part. If the duty is only to take reasonable care in issuing a mandate it is impossible for me to find a breach of that duty.

Therefore it is that the defendants go further and say that there is a duty "to use reasonable care in the carrying out of their business relating to the issuing of mandates". This is a very vague statement of the duty. What is meant, I suppose, is that, beyond the care which must be taken in the transaction itself, a customer must, in the course of carrying on his business, take reasonable precautions to prevent his servants from forging his signature, or, if the customer be a company, the directors must take reasonable precautions to prevent the company's servants from forging their signatures. Now is there any authority for this proposition? I can find none. [His Honour then discussed a number of previous cases and continued:] Without referring in detail to these cases, they can be summed up by saying that they lay down most clearly that the negligence must be in or immediately connected with the transaction itself and must have been the proximate cause of the loss...

I think Mr Scrutton's contention equally fails when it is considered apart from authority. It amounts to a contention on the part of the bank that its customers impliedly agreed to take precautions in the general course of carrying on their business to prevent forgeries on the part of their servants. Upon what is that based? It cannot be said to be necessary to make the contract effective. It cannot be said to have really been in the mind of the customer, or, indeed, of the bank, when the relationship of banker and customer was created. What is to be the standard of the extent or number of the precautions to be taken? Applying it to this case, can it be said to have been in the minds of the directors of the company that they were promising to have the passbook and the cash book examined at every board meeting, and to have a sufficient number of board meetings to prevent forgeries, or that the secretary should be supervised or watched by the chairman? If the bank desire that their customers should make these promises they must expressly stipulate that they shall. I am inclined to think that a banker who required such a stipulation would soon lose a number of his customers. The truth is that the number of cases where bankers sustain losses of this kind are infinitesimal in comparison with the large business they do, and the profits of banking are sufficient to compensate them for this very small risk. To the individual customer the loss would often be very serious; to the banker it is negligible...

Judgment for the plaintiffs.

What is the appropriate form of action where the bank has debited its customer's account with the amount of a cheque paid without proper authority? In *National Bank of New Zealand Ltd v Walpole and Patterson Ltd* [1975] 2 NZLR 7 at 12, Richmond J said in the New Zealand Court of Appeal:

I am unaware of any other case in which such a claim has been based on the notion of damage caused by wrongful debiting as opposed to an action in debt (whether for money lent or for money had and received). When a banker pays out on a cheque he is not thereby paying away funds of the customer. The money or credits used by the banker to meet a cheque are his own. If the banker has no valid mandate from his customer then he has no authority to debit the payment in current account as between himself and his customer. If the banker makes an unauthorised debit entry the customer does not thereby suffer a loss equivalent to the amount of the cheque. The wrongful debit entry may cause the banker to dishonour a subsequent valid cheque and in that case the customer will have his remedy for the wrongful dishonour. Again, if the customer demands payment from the banker of the true amount standing to his credit then the unauthorised debit entry cannot avail the banker as a defence. But in my opinion it is quite fallacious to found a claim on the proposition that the making of a wrongful debit entry results in a loss to the customer of an equivalent amount.

Would an action in conversion be appropriate in these circumstances? If not, whom might the customer sue for conversion?

THE BANK'S DUTY TO PAY A PROPER MANDATE

The relationship between customer and banker is both one of creditor and debtor, and also of principal and agent. Thus, assuming Carb's account with City Bank is in credit, the bank as Carb's debtor, and also as its agent, is obliged to pay Carb's cheques promptly and in accordance with its directions. The same applies to the extent of an approved overdraft. It follows that a bank which, through a mistake, erroneously fails to honour its customer's cheque, may be sued by the customer for damages: *Gibbons v Westminster Bank Ltd* [1939] 2 KB 882. If customer Carb is engaged in a business, it is entitled to recover without proof of special damages, but a person not so engaged must prove special damages. In either case, a claim for defamation can be added if the customer's reputation (eg, for honesty and credit rating) has been injured by the wrongful dishonour of the cheque. However, the bank is not obliged to pay a cheque *pro tanto* where there are insufficient funds in the account or overdraft limit to meet the cheque in full.

We noted earlier that since the bank is obliged to pay its customer's cheques without delay, it is entitled to expect that its customer will frame the mandate in an unambiguous form. Failure to do so will entitle the bank to refuse or delay payment pending further authorisation or clarification.

The bank has no authority to pay its customer's cheque or debit his account where:
(a) his signature has been forged, even though the forgery could not reasonably be detected because it is cleverly executed: compare BEA s 29; or
(b) he has countermanded payment by means of a "stop-order"; or the customer has died and the bank has notice thereof: BEA s 81.

Commonwealth Trading Bank v Reno Auto Sales Pty Ltd
Supreme Court of Victoria [1967] VR 790

Gillard J: On Saturday, 27 November 1965, one Rainer Hans Gossler arranged to purchase a motor car from the defendant Reno Auto Sales Pty Ltd. He gave the defendant as a deposit on the transaction an open cheque for £250, drawn on the plaintiff at its Newport branch. On the Sunday Gossler repented of his bargain and instructed his wife to instruct the plaintiff on the Monday to cancel his cheque. Somewhere between 9.00 am and 9.30 am Mrs Gossler rang the Newport branch and spoke to a Miss Sturdy, who at the time was a machinist/typist, whose duty it was to answer the telephone. Mrs Gossler in evidence gave an account of the conversation she had with Miss Sturdy.

[His Honour then set out the evidence given by Mrs Gossler and Miss Sturdy to the effect that Mrs Gossler had told Miss Sturdy to hold the cheque until her husband came into the bank that afternoon to cancel the cheque. She gave Miss Sturdy details of the number, amount and payee of the cheque. Miss Sturdy stated that she did not do anything about the cheque nor tell anyone else in the bank because Mrs Gossler had not wanted the cheque stopped and she thought that Mr Gossler would come in to stop payment before the cheque was presented. His Honour continued at 791:] In the report made by the bank manager, the account given to him by Mrs Gossler in the afternoon was recorded as follows: "Mrs Gossler told me she had rung the bank at 9.00 am that day at her husband's request, had spoken to a girl on our staff and had asked that the cheque be held up, and had said that her husband would let us know definitely later in the day whether or not it was to be stopped. She had impressed on the girl the cheque was to be held up and the girl had assured her that it would be." In that state of the evidence it is very difficult to deduce precisely what instructions were given by Mrs Gossler to Miss Sturdy. Obviously something was said about holding up the cheque, but equally clearly, it never occurred to Miss Sturdy that Mrs Gossler was instructing the bank to stop payment, and on that account she did not pass on the information to those whose duty it would be to pay cheques.

On the Monday, also, Gossler returned the motor car to the defendant, and in the afternoon with his wife attended the bank to give a written countermand of payment of the cheque. In the meantime, however, shortly after 9.30 in the morning, the cheque had been presented and was collected over the counter at the Newport branch by a representative of the defendant. Because of the state of Gossler's account, the cheque was only paid after the teller had queried the condition of the account, and had conferred with the manager thereon. Neither of them knew anything of the message received by Miss Sturdy. It should also be here observed that Gossler's account has not been debited by the plaintiff with payment of the cheque. In these proceedings the plaintiff now sues the defendant for repayment of the moneys collected, as money had and received, on the basis that Gossler's cheque had been paid by it to the defendant under an alleged mistake of fact...

When a customer of a bank delivers a cheque to a third party in satisfaction of a contractual obligation by the customer to the third party, the cheque purports to be prima facie an absolute payment: see Blackburn J, in *Pollard v Bank of England* (1871) LR 6 QB 623 at 630. It is, however, now established that the delivery of such a cheque is a conditional payment, or to be more technically accurate, it is a conditional satisfaction: see Dixon CJ, in *Tilley v Official Receiver in Bankruptcy* (1960) 103 CLR 529 at 533; [1961] ALR 83 at 85 . . .

Since a cheque is a revocable mandate, and does not constitute an assignment of the customer's funds, and there being no contractual relationship between the bank and the third party, the bank owes no duty to the third party receiving the cheque and seeking payment. Accordingly, the third party can obtain no legal redress against and from the bank if payment were refused by the bank: see *Schroeder v Central Bank of London (Ltd)* (1876) 34 LT 735. Hence, in this case, the plaintiff was, *quoad* the defendant, quite entitled to refuse to pay Gossler's cheque. The plaintiff's duty was to Gossler alone. The cheque constituted a mandate to the plaintiff to use a portion of Gossler's funds held by the plaintiff in payment of the cheque and in complete satisfaction of Gossler's legal obligation to the defendant, which was conditionally satisfied by the delivery of the cheque. The duty and authority of the plaintiff to and by Gossler to pay the cheque might be determined at any time by an appropriate countermand of payment.

The relationship between a bank and its customer lies in a contract, and although primarily the contractual relationship so constituted is that of debtor and creditor, nevertheless when the bank is called upon to pay its customer's cheque, it is acting as an agent of its customer for the specific purpose of using his funds to pay his cheque: see *Westminster Bank Ltd v Hilton* (1926) 136 LT 315. The bank, being an agent for a specific purpose, is required to act on a customer's instructions, but in the interests of all parties such instructions should be clear and unambiguous so as not to mislead the bank or its servants as to the customer's intentions: see per Fletcher Moulton LJ, in *Curtice v London City & Midland Bank Ltd* [1908] 1 KB 293 at 299. If a countermand of payment is desired by the customer, it should be communicated quite unequivocally to the relevant person in the bank, who may be expected to make payment or supervise such payment. As Cozens-Hardy MR said in Curtice's case at 298: "Countermand is really a matter of fact. It means much more than a change of purpose on the part of a customer. It means, in addition, a notification of that change of purpose to the bank. There is no such thing as a constructive countermand in commercial transactions of this kind." See also *Hilton's* case.

When his Lordship there refers to a notification of that change of purpose to the bank, it seems to me that where the bank is a corporate body, acting through its servants, it must mean a notification to an authorised servant of the bank, who can prevent payment being made on the cheque.

On the evidence I have heard, I am not satisfied that the message received by Miss Sturdy from Mrs Gossler constituted a countermand by Gossler of the payment of his cheque. The conversation deposed to by both the ladies was, in my view, extremely ambiguous. On the face of the most favourable view to the plaintiff, the plaintiff, *quoad* Gossler, would not have been safe in acting upon the telephone message to refuse payment. If the manager or the teller had known of the message, neither of them could have safely acted upon the view that payment was stopped. Miss Sturdy says she did not regard the payment as being stopped and I am of the same opinion.

It has, however, been urged by Mr Forsyth that even if payment were not stopped, the cheque was to be "held up", and the manager would never have approved payment, nor would the teller ever have paid the cheque, until some investigation had been made as to the authenticity and the substance of the telephonic message: cf Lord Dunedin in *Hilton's* case at 316.

The manager and the teller may well have thought it desirable to investigate the message, but so equivocal was the message they would have been under no legal obligation to do so, and they would have been under no obligation to stop payment as the result of such ambiguous directions: see *Curtice's* case and *Hilton's* case.

Undoubtedly payment was made by the teller and authorised by the manager to the defendant in ignorance of the message. If the manager had had notice of it, I believe he would not have authorised payment, but that he would have made inquiries. I think this is the proper inference to draw from his evidence. The crucial question then arises whether payment was made under such a mistake of fact as to enable the plaintiff to recover from the defendant on the count of money had and received.

[His Honour then discussed the authorities on the recovery of money paid under mistake and concluded that the plaintiff was not entitled to succeed on this ground.]

Judgment for the defendant.

For a critical comment on this case, see Luntz, "The Bank's Right to Recover on Cheques Paid by Mistake" (1968) 6 *MULR* 308.

BANKS' OTHER DUTIES

Of course banks do owe other duties to their customers apart from honouring their cheques. For example, banks are obliged to maintain secrecy in relation to their customers' accounts, their transactions with the bank and any information acquired as the result of the banker–customer relationship: *Tournier v National Provincial and Union Bank of England* [1924] 1 KB 461. Like any other professional, the banker owes a duty of care to his customer in giving advice and information and for the safe custody of any documents or other valuables committed to his care. However, these duties may be subject to statutory provisions, such as the powers of the Commissioner of Taxation under ss 263 and 264 of the Income Tax Assessment Act 1936: see *Commissioner of Taxation v Australia & New Zealand Banking Group Ltd* (1979) 53 ALJR 336; *O'Reilly v Commissioners of the State Bank of Victoria* (1983) 83 ATC 4156. See generally Weerasooria and Coops, *Banking Law and Practice in Australia,* 1976, Chs 16, 23, 24.

QUESTIONS

Question 4

Carb Pty Ltd opened a new account at City Bank. Carb instructed the bank that only cheques signed by a director and the secretary of the company should be paid. Specimen signatures were furnished by Jim Handy (director) and Mary Handy (secretary). As a precaution against fraud Carb further directed the bank not to cash any cheques for amounts exceeding $3000 unless personally presented by Jim or Mary.

The company appointed a new bookkeeper Stan Upright who had a reputation for honesty. Shortly thereafter Mary left on a well deserved six week holiday. Before she left she signed 20 blank cheque forms Nos 40501 to 40520 in respect of the new account and left the chequebook in Jim's custody.

After Mary's departure, Jim partially filled in cheque no 40501 as follows:

Pay Cash   or bearer
The sum of $90

As he was in a hurry, Jim countersigned the cheque and handed it to Upright with the request that he complete it and use the $90 to purchase postage stamps for the business. Jim left the chequebook lying on his desk.

While Jim was away, Upright took the chequebook, and wrote cheque No 40502 for $2000 payable to himself. He forged Jim's signature on the cheque by accurately tracing the imprint made on cheque No 40501 which Jim had signed with a sharp ball point pen.

Upright also filled in cheque No 40503 for $2480 payable to Manana Airlines. He was disturbed before he could copy Jim's signature, so he took the cheque as it was and immediately left the company's premises.

Upright added the figures "50" and the words "Nine thousand and fifty dollars" to cheque No 40501, and cashed it and No 40502 at City Bank. He used No 40503, which only bore Mary's signature, to pay Manana Airlines for a ticket to Brazil and caught the afternoon flight. He has not been seen since.

Jim did not notice the missing cheques until three days later by which time cheque No 40503 had been cleared by City Bank.

Advise Carb of its rights against City Bank in respect of each cheque.

Question 5

The inconsistency between *Marshall's* case and *Macmillan's* case has caused much confusion in banker-customer relationships. To what extent, if at all, has this situation been clarified?

Who should bear the loss in cases of forgery of cheques? Consider both social and commercial needs.

Question 6

(1) Following discovery of Upright's fraud in Question 4, the manager of City Bank instructed the ledger keeper not to pay Carb's cheques in future without reference to him. Due to a misunderstanding by the ledger keeper, City Bank dishonoured with the answer "unpaid" Carb's genuine cheque for $2600 in payment of its monthly interest installment on a business loan from Easy Finance. Advise Carb of its rights against City Bank.

(2) What difference would it make to your advice in the following alternative situations:
  (a) City Bank had dishonoured the cheque with the answer "refer to drawer—insufficient funds", and when Easy Finance queried the answer, the ledger keeper had referred to Carb's cheques as "rubbery"? or
  (b) There had been only $2500 in Carb's account when Easy Finance presented Carb's cheque to City Bank? or
  (c) Jim Handy had telephoned City Bank before Easy Finance presented the cheque, and said to the receptionist "I'm uncertain about payment of that cheque—please hold it for a while"?

(3) If Jim wishes to stop payment of the cheque, what should he do?

SECTION 3: DUTIES OF COLLECTING AND PAYING BANKS AND PT III BILLS OF EXCHANGE ACT

In Section 2 we considered the duty owed by a paying bank, City Bank, to its customer Carb in respect of cheques drawn on Carb's cheque account. We did not examine there the position where the bank pays not to the true owner but to someone who has no title to the cheque such as a thief. What duty does City Bank owe to the true owner of the cheque in this situation? Again, if the proceeds of the cheque are collected for the thief by another bank (say, Country Bank) does it also owe a duty to the true owner? In this section we will examine:
  (a) the nature of the duties owed by collecting and paying banks to the true owner;
  (b) the form and effect of various crossings on cheques;
  (c) the effect of the statutory defences available to collecting and paying banks under BEA; and
  (d) the position in relation to so-called "bank cheques".

Let us take a simple illustration as the basis for our discussion:

In payment of insurance premium, Carb Pty Ltd drew the following cheque and mailed it to Coverall Insurance Ltd in accordance with Coverall's instructions.

```
┌─────────────────────────────────────────────────────────────────┐
│  Duty   │N│P│                                                   │
│  Stamp  │E│A│           CITY BANK           1 June 1984          │
│         │G│Y│           RYDE BRANCH                              │
│         │O│E│                                                    │
│         │T│E│                                                    │
│      Pay Cove rall Insurance Ltd ................... or order    │
│      The sum of Eight thousand dollars ........... $8000.00      │
│                                                                  │
│         │N│A│                        Carb Pty Ltd                │
│         │O│C│                                                    │
│         │T│C│                    J. Handy  M. Handy              │
│         │ │O│                        Directors                   │
└─────────────────────────────────────────────────────────────────┘
```

The cheque was intercepted in the mail by a dishonest postman Stamper who forged the following indorsement on the back of the cheque:

> Pay J. Stamper or order
> Coverall Insurance Ltd
>
> *J. Jones*
>   Director

Stamper then deposited the cheque in his account with Country Bank which collected it, whereupon Stamper withdrew $8000 and decamped.

These facts raise a number of questions as to the rights and liabilities of the parties. The following checklist (excuse the pun) is suggested as a convenient method of approaching problems of this kind:

(1) Is the instrument a bill of exchange (s 8)? Is it a cheque (s 78)? Is it payable to order or bearer?

(2) Is the cheque crossed? Is it "negotiable"? If so, what consequences?

(3) Who owns the cheque? Has the owner received payment? If not, then whom can he sue? How does he frame his cause(s) of action?

(4) What defences may be available to the defendants? What must be proved to make good those defences?

BANKS' DUTIES AT COMMON LAW

We observed in Chapter 8 that where a motor car is stolen and then bought or otherwise converted, no matter how innocently, by a third party who takes from or through the thief, at common law the third party will be liable to the owner. Will the same reasoning apply to Country Bank which has collected and paid the proceeds of the cheque to Stamper who has no title? If so, what is the cause of action? In *Lloyds Bank Ltd v The Chartered Bank of India, Australia and China* [1929] 1 KB 40 at 55-6 Scrutton LJ in the English Court of Appeal said:

> Conversion primarily is conversion of chattels, and the relation of bank to customer is that of debtor and creditor. As no specific coins in a bank are the property of any specific customer there might appear to be some difficulty in holding that a bank, which paid part of what it owed its customer to some other person not authorised to receive it, had converted its customer's chattels; but a series of decisions binding on this court, culminating in *Morison's* case [1914] 3 KB 356 and *Underwood's* case [1924] 1 KB 775, have surmounted the difficulty by treating the conversion as of the chattel, the piece of paper, the cheque under which the money was collected, and the value of the chattel converted as the money received under it:

see the explanation of Phillimore LJ in *Morison's* case 378. The plaintiffs' case as to conversion was rested on these authorities, and the trial judge adopted it.

Compare *Commissioners of Taxation v ES & A Bank Ltd*, p 487, *supra*; *Commissioners of the State Savings Bank of Victoria v Permewan, Wright & Co Ltd*, p 512, *infra*; *Marfani & Co Ltd v Midland Bank Ltd*, p 520, *infra*.

Coverall's action for conversion of the cheque or its proceeds should not be confused with an action (a) by a holder suing the drawer or indorser *on* a dishonoured cheque; or (b) by the drawer against the paying bank for wrongfully paying his cheque contrary to the mandate.

CROSSINGS ON CHEQUES

The form in which a cheque is drawn will be very relevant in determining whether a particular person acquired title to it or is liable for conversion of it. Only a document which qualifies as a bill of exchange will attract the provisions of BEA. Only cheques are covered by Pt III of BEA, and cheques payable to order must be indorsed in order to transfer title. In addition cheques may be crossed in order to hamper their negotiation by unauthorised persons. BEA provides for general and special crossings and the "not negotiable" crossing. The main provisions are ss 82, 83, 85 and 87.

The crossings may be illustrated thus:

General crossings   Special crossings

| | | BANK | | NOT NEGOTIABLE | | | COUNTRY BANK | | COUNTRY BANK BOURKE BRANCH NOT NEGOTIABLE |

These crossings can be used on cheques payable to order or bearer. The words "not negotiable" can be added to any cheque which is crossed (either generally or specially). Section 85 imposes on the paying bank a statutory duty *to the true owner* to obey the crossings on the cheque. This is in addition to the duty which the paying bank owes *to its customer* to obey his mandate as part of the common law obligations of the banker-customer relationship: see pp 491-2, *supra*. The most important practical consequence of crossing a cheque is that it cannot be cashed across the counter at the bank on which it is drawn but must be collected through a bank account.

"NOT NEGOTIABLE" CHEQUES

The Bills of Exchange Act ss 82 and 83 provide for the addition of the words "not negotiable" to a crossed cheque. The words should be placed between the parallel lines on the front of the cheque. Their effect is prescribed by s 87, which does not prevent a cheque crossed "not negotiable" being transferred in a similar way to an

The Banker-Customer Relationship and the Banking System

uncrossed cheque. Contrast the position of a non-transferable cheque drawn payable to "Taxation Department only" under s 13(1): see p 431, *supra*.

The two most important consequences of the "not negotiable" crossing are:

(1) Since it lacks the quality of negotiability, the transferee can acquire no better title than the person from whom he acquired it; however, since it is legally transferable, "so long as there is no defect of title, or failure of consideration, the cheque may pass from hand to hand just as if it was an open cheque or a simply crossed cheque, and each successive holder acquires full rights and title thereon": *Paget's Law of Banking*, 9th ed, 1982, p 205.

(2) It acts as a warning to anyone accepting payment by a transfer of a "not negotiable" cheque, or to a collecting bank accepting it for collection, that if the title is defective, it can acquire no better title and may be liable to the true owner in conversion: see *Commissioners of State Savings Bank of Victoria v Permewan, Wright & Co Ltd*, p 512, *infra*.

"Account Payee" Crossing

The words "account payee", "account payee only", or "account J. Smith" are often added to the crossing on a cheque. Although they are not recognised by BEA, they have a legal and practical significance, which was summarised by the Privy Council in *Universal Guarantee Pty Ltd v National Bank of Australasia Ltd* (1965) 65 SR (NSW) 102 at 106, on appeal from the Supreme Court of New South Wales.

(1) A crossing means that the paying bank paying the cheque to a banker in good faith and without negligence has the protection of s 86 of the Bills of Exchange Act 1909-1958 of the Commonwealth of Australia.

(2) The words "not negotiable" do not prevent the cheque from being negotiated but mean that the holder of the cheque cannot have and is not capable of giving a better title to the cheque than that of the holder from whom he obtained it (s 87 of the Bills of Exchange Act 1909-1958).

(3) The addition of the words "a/c payee" or "a/c payee only" refer to the payee named in the cheque and not the holder at the time of presentation, *House Property Co of London Ltd v London County and Westminster Bank* (1915) 84 LJKB 1846, but they do not prevent, at law, the further negotiability of the cheque. The words merely operate as a warning to the collecting bank that if it pays the proceeds of the cheque to some other account it is put on inquiry and it may be in a difficulty in relying on any defence under s 88 of the Act in an action against it for conversion of the cheque: per Scrutton LJ in *Underwood (AL) Ltd v Bank of Liverpool and Martins* [1924] 1 KB 775 at 793. These words do not cast on the paying bank, paying the cheque to a banker, any additional obligation to satisfy itself that the collecting bank is collecting it on behalf of the named payee. That is entirely the responsibility of the collecting bank.

The Manning Committee considered the effect of these crossings in its report. In relation to references in the following extracts from the report and in cases extracted later it should be noted that s 88 of the Act has now been replaced by s 88D.

Manning Committee Report

[The Committee analysed the existing law and practice in relation to the "account payee only" crossing, and concluded:]

85 Having in mind also the great volume of cheques amounting to a substantial portion of 69,000,000 per annum which are not paid to the credit of the named payee, the committee believes that the introduction of a provision giving the crossing "account payee only" the force of making a cheque non-transferable, would result in far more inconvenience to a large volume of people, particularly those in humble circumstances who have no bank accounts, than it would be worth in the matter of giving drawers of cheques protection additional to that which is already available to them by using the "not negotiable" crossing.

86 The committee therefore recommends that statutory recognition of the crossing

"account payee only" to give it the force of making a cheque a non-transferable instrument, be not given.

87 The committee considers that having indicated that, in its view, the crossing "account payee only" is not, in practice, giving drawers of cheques significantly more protection than the "not negotiable" crossing, and having recommended against amending the Act to give the crossing the protection by way of non-transferability, which the committee believes many drawers consider they obtain by using the crossing, it is only logical for the committee to recommend an amendment of the Act which will have the effect of causing the use of the crossing to be discontinued.

PROTECTION OF COLLECTING AND PAYING BANKS UNDER BEA

Prior to 1971, banks' statutory protection was contained in ss 64, 65 and 86 (paying bank) and 88, (collecting banks) and the cases decided prior to this time will refer to those sections. In 1964, the Manning Committee had recommended the enactment of a Cheques Act to expand the protection available to banks under these sections. For a critical and at times amusing commentary on the report, see Riley (1965) 1 *Fed L Rev* 183. Although the implementation of the full report is still awaited, the Bills of Exchange Act 1971 repealed s 88 (collecting banks) and replaced it with ss 88D and 88E. It also added s 88B (further protection for paying banks) and s 88C (unindorsed order cheque as evidence of receipt). A useful summary of the effect of the amendments is contained in (1971) 45 *ALJ* 321 and 635. Some assistance in understanding the background and purpose of the amendments may be obtained from the legislators.

Hansard Report of House of Representatives, May 1970
Bills of Exchange Bill 1970
Second Reading

Mr Hughes (Berowra, Attorney-General)—I move: That the Bill be now read a second time.

This Bill is designed to amend the provisions of the Bills of Exchange Act relating to cheques and bank drafts. The main purpose of the Bill is to do away with the necessity for indorsements on order cheques and bank drafts that are paid into the account of the payee. It will benefit the public and relieve bankers of much of the unproductive work at present involved in examining indorsements. The Bill will effect other incidental improvements in the law relating to cheques. Before proceeding to deal with the substance of the Bill, I should explain that it will be an interim measure pending the introduction of a comprehensive Cheques Bill to codify the civil law relating to cheques, of which the Governor-General made mention in opening the last parliament . . .

[The Attorney-General then referred to the Manning Committee Report and explained that some of its recommendations required modification to take account of fundamental changes taking place in banking procedures, particularly in the use of computers and centralisation of the process of presentation and clearance of cheques.]

I turn now to consider the main purpose of the Bill which is, as I have said, to do away with unnecessary indorsement of cheques. It may assist honorable members if I give some figures that bear upon this matter. Estimates I have been able to obtain indicate that over 800 million cheques are issued annually in Australia and that about one-quarter or approximately 200 million are order cheques. Cheques drawn on the Reserve Bank are invariably payable to order; these include cheques for social service payments, repatriation payments and income tax refunds. The Department of Social Services alone, I understand, issues some two million cheques each fortnight. In addition, cheques drawn by state governments and by companies are usually payable to order. At present, all these cheques have to be indorsed by the payees and examined by bankers.

It is estimated that over two million order cheques are dishonoured annually for lack of indorsement or for irregular indorsement. It is also estimated that at least three-quarters of all cheques drawn are deposited to the credit of the payee so, in the great majority of cases where cheques are returned for indorsement, no question of title to the cheque is involved. The dishonour of a cheque in these cases does not safeguard the drawer or true owner. It is a great inconvenience to the private individual and to commercial firms and also involves the banker in much unproductive work. In the United Kingdom a solution to the problem of unnecessary indorsement of cheques was attempted in the Cheques Act 1957. It is a different solution to that proposed in this Bill and I think that I should take a moment or two to explain why I propose in this Bill a different solution.

[The Attorney-General referred to the history and basic approach of the Cheques Act (UK) which differed from the recommendations of the Mocatta Committee Report of 1956.]

The Manning Committee, having considered all these matters and having heard submissions from all interested parties, concluded that the original recommendation of the Mocatta Committee should be followed—that is, that the necessity for indorsement should be done away with only in the case of cheques paid into the account of the payee. The government has accepted this recommendation. The matter that was decisive in its decision was that the examination by banks of the regularity of indorsements of negotiated cheques is a valuable protection to drawers and the true owners of cheques. I have dealt at some length with the reasons why this Bill provides a different solution from that which the United Kingdom Act provides. It will, however, provide the same practical benefits as a matter of law as are provided in the United Kingdom by a combination of law and banking practice.

In summary, the effect of the indorsement provisions of the Bill will be as follows: A customer of a banker will not need to indorse an order cheque paid into his account if he is the payee; only those cheques that have been negotiated to third parties will require indorsement. A banker paying a cheque drawn on him by a customer will only have to examine a cheque for indorsement where he pays it over the counter. A banker with whom cheques are deposited by a customer will now only have to examine the face of each cheque to ascertain whether it is to be paid into the account of the payee and, if so, he will not have to turn over the cheque to look at the back and compare the indorsement with the name of the payee. The principal provisions that give effect to the proposed alteration of the law concerning indorsement are new ss 88B and 88D contained in cl 5 of the Bill. The former deals with the responsibility of a banker paying a cheque drawn on him by a customer, commonly called a "paying banker", and the latter deals with a banker who receives payment for a customer, commonly called a "collecting banker". These provisions will also extend to bank drafts, which include what are commonly called "bank cheques".

I shall now deal with the provisions of proposed new s 88B. Section 65 of the present Act protects a banker who pays a cheque bearing a forged indorsement or an indorsement made without authority if he acts in good faith and in the ordinary course of business. Section 86 protects a banker against a common law claim for conversion in respect of a crossed cheque where he pays the cheque to another banker in good faith and without negligence. Failure to examine order cheques for indorsement would be contrary to the ordinary course of business under s 65 and would constitute evidence of negligence under s 86. Accordingly, to obtain the protection of ss 65 and 86 a paying banker must examine order cheques for indorsement. If the proposed alteration of the law concerning indorsements is made, a paying banker will not know whether a cheque has been paid into a payee's account with the collecting banker or into some other account. Proposed new s 88B will, therefore, relieve a paying banker of the responsibility for ensuring the regularity of indorsement of all order cheques paid to a collecting banker and leave that responsibility to be discharged by the collecting banker alone. A paying banker will, however, continue to be responsible for ensuring the regularity of an indorsement on an order cheque that he pays over the counter.

The purpose of new s 88D is, firstly, to do away with the necessity for a collecting banker to examine for indorsement order cheques that are paid into the account of the payee, and, secondly, to extend to uncrossed cheques the protection afforded by s 88 to a collecting banker in the case of crossed cheques. At present, under s 88 of the Act, a collecting banker who receives payment of a crossed cheque in good faith and without negligence is protected against the common law liability for conversion to which he is subject if his customer had no title or a defective title to the cheque. A banker, like anyone else who deals with property inconsistently with the rights of the true owner, is liable to the true owner in an action for conversion. To bring himself within the protection of the section, a collecting banker must examine an order cheque to verify the indorsement; to receive payment of a cheque bearing an irregular indorsement would be evidence of negligence on his part.

Under the proposed provision, a collecting banker must continue to examine negotiated order cheques to bring himself within the protection of the provision. Much of the benefit of doing away with the necessity for indorsement on order cheques paid into a payee's account would be lost if collecting bankers were to insist on indorsement where there were minor discrepancies between the name of the payee appearing on the cheque and the name of the customer's account. The proposed s 88D provides, therefore, that where the name of the payee on the cheque is so similar to the name of the customer that it would be reasonable for the collecting banker to assume that the customer is the person intended by the drawer to be the payee, the banker need not concern himself with the absence of or irregularity in indorsement.

It is important that the proposed change in the law relating to indorsements should be introduced without affecting the position of persons under other provisions of the Act or under the common law. The Bill contains two proposed provisions directed to that end: Proposed new s 88C, which is intended to preserve the value of paid order cheques as evidence of receipt of the amount of the cheque, and proposed new s 88B, which is intended to preserve the rights that a collecting banker now has as a holder for value under s 32 in respect of indorsed order cheque. So far as evidence of receipt is concerned, the drawer of an indorsed order cheque, under the existing law, can use it after payment by his banker as evidence, although it is not conclusive evidence, of receipt by the payee of the amount of the cheque. In fact, a paid indorsed order cheque is as good evidence of the payment of money as the simple receipt of the kind sometimes printed on the back of cheques.

If the proposed change in the law concerning indorsements is effected, there is no reason why a paid unindorsed order cheque would have any less value as evidence of payment than a paid indorsed order cheque now has. Proposed new s 88C ensures that this will be so by providing that an order cheque that appears to have been paid by the banker on whom it is drawn is evidence of the receipt by the payee of the sum payable by the cheque. This provision will, I believe, be useful for auditors and others required to satisfy themselves that the payee has in fact received the amount of the cheque. This provision will extend to a bank draft. The purpose of new s 88E is to ensure that a collecting banker who at the present time has the rights of a holder for value in respect of an indorsed cheque will not be prejudiced by the proposed change in the law to do away with the necessity for indorsement on cheques payable to order that are paid into the payee's account.

The reason why a collecting banker now requires an indorsement on a cheque payable to order is to establish himself as a holder for value, thus enabling him to sue on the cheque in his own right. In order that a collecting banker will continue to have the rights of a holder for value in respect of cheques that will not in future be indorsed because they will be collected for the payee, new s 88E provides that the banker will have the rights of a holder that he would have had if the payee had indorsed it in blank.

DEFENCES OF A COLLECTING BANK

As indicated above, anyone who receives a cheque to which he has no title can be sued by the owner in conversion, subject to two distinct lines of defence:

(a) he qualifies as a holder in due course; or
(b) being a bank, it satisfies all the elements of s 88D.

Holder in due course defence. (See p 441, *supra*.) In order for Country Bank to qualify as a holder in due course, it is necessary (i) to acquire the cheque from someone who already qualifies as a holder (which Stamper does not); (ii) by means of a valid transfer (including indorsement in the case of an order cheque); (iii) in good faith; (iv) for value, and (v) without notice of any defect in title: s 34. In the case of a "not negotiable" cheque, any defect in title will also preclude a subsequent holder qualifying as a holder in due course.

A bank which collects an order cheque for its customer may be assisted by s 88E since it will not be prevented from qualifying as a holder in due course by the customer failing to indorse the cheque provided:

(a) the customer is the payee of the cheque (which Stamper was not);
(b) the bank gave value, or has a lien, on the cheque.

When does a bank "give value" for a cheque, and can it claim the protection of a holder in due course when it is also acting as its customer's agent for collection of the cheque?

Barclays Bank Ltd v Astley Industrial Trust Ltd
Queen's Bench Division [1970] 2 QB 527; [1970] 1 All ER 719

[Mabon's Garage Ltd (M), garage proprietors, had a large overdraft at the plaintiff bank. The bank received five cheques to the value of £2850 drawn by the defendant company payable to M in respect of hire-purchase transactions purporting to have been effected by M. As the result of receiving these cheques for collection to the credit of M's account, the bank decided to pay two cheques drawn on the account by M, and amounting to £345 which the bank would otherwise have dishonoured because of the extent of M's existing overdraft. The hire-purchase transactions were subsequently found to have been fraudulent. M's directors were convicted and M went into liquidation. The defendant countermanded payment of the cheques for £2850 which were dishonoured on presentation. The bank sued the defendants on the basis that it was a holder in due course of the cheques. Milmo J held that the plaintiff bank was not aware of M's fraud and had no reason to suspect any defect in M's title to the cheques. The relevant provisions of the English statutes are Bills of Exchange Act s 2, definition of holder; ss 27(1)(b), (3); 29(1); 30(2) and Cheques Act 1957 s 2. (Equivalent provisions in BEA 1909 (Cth) are ss 4, 32(1)(b), (3), 34(1), 35(2), 88E).]

Milmo J [stated the facts and continued at QB 536:] The plaintiffs contended that they were holders in due course of the cheques sued upon and were entitled to recover from the defendants the amount thereof . . .

It was the plaintiffs' case that the cheques were complete and regular on the face of them and that they became the holders of them before they were overdue and that the cheques had not previously been dishonoured. They said that they had taken the cheques in good faith and that at the time when the cheques were negotiated to them they had no notice of any defect in the title of Mabon who negotiated them. I find all these matters established. The substantial issue was whether the plaintiffs had taken the cheques for value within the meaning of s 29(1)(b) and the plaintiffs contended that they had done so on five grounds which to some extent overlapped.

These grounds may be summarised as follows:

(1) That on 19 November when the cheques were handed to the plaintiffs, there was an antecedent debt in the form of an overdraft owing by Mabon to the plaintiffs and exceeding the amount of the cheques, and that by virtue of s 28(1)(b) of the Bills of Exchange Act 1882, this was valuable consideration for the cheques.

(2) That the cheques were handed over by Mabon, a debtor, to the plaintiffs, their creditor, and there being no agreement to the contrary, the cheques must be treated as a conditional payment pro tanto of the debt, the condition being that the cheques should be honoured on presentation and that pending dishonour the plaintiffs' right to sue for so much of the debt as was covered by the cheques was suspended. In support of this contention the plaintiffs relied, inter alia, upon *Currie v Misa* (1875) LR 10 Exch 153 and *McLean v Clydesdale Banking Co* (1883) 9 App Cas 95.

(3) That the plaintiffs as Mabon's bankers had by implication of law a lien on cheques coming into their possession from Mabon to the extent of Mabon's indebtedness to them at the time and that, therefore, by virtue of s 27(3) of the Bills of Exchange Act 1882, the plaintiffs were deemed holders of the cheques for value to the extent of Mabon's overdraft which at the time was £4673.

(4) That on 19 November, after the receipt of the five cheques, the plaintiffs gave Mabon credit against these cheques by paying the two Mabon cheques for amounts totalling £345 upon which they had deferred a decision and that the plaintiffs would not have honoured these cheques if they had not received the defendants' cheques.

(5) That the plaintiffs gave value for the five cheques sued upon by honouring on 18 November cheques for a total of £2763 drawn by Mabon relying upon the promise of Mabon's directors that the plaintiffs would receive these five cheques on the following day.

The defendants conceded that the plaintiffs had a lien on the five cheques. Their case was that the plaintiffs took the cheques merely as Mabon's agents for collection and that having taken the cheques as agents for collection they could not have taken them for value within the meaning of s 29(1)(b) and therefore could not be holders in due course. The basic proposition contended for on behalf of the defendants was that under the Bills of Exchange Act 1882, a distinction has to be drawn between a holder for value on the one hand and a holder who has given value or taken for value on the other and that it is only a holder who has given value or taken for value who can be a holder in due course.

I am unable to accept the contention that a banker cannot at one and the same time be an agent for collection of a cheque and a holder of that cheque for value. It seems to me that the language of s 2 of the Cheques Act 1957, negatives this proposition since it presupposes that a banker who has been given a cheque for collection may nevertheless have given value for it. It is, moreover, a commonplace occurrence for a banker to allow credit to a customer against an uncleared cheque. A banker who permits his customer to draw £5 against an uncleared cheque for £100 has given value for it but it is to be said that in consequence he is no longer the customer's agent for the collection of that cheque? I readily accept that if a banker holds a cheque merely—and I emphasise the word "merely"—as his customer's agent for collection he cannot be a holder for value and still less a holder in due course; but that is an entirely different proposition.

The principal point which I have to determine in this case is whether the expressions "holder for value", "holder who has given value", and "holder who has taken for value", where they occur in the Bills of Exchange Act 1882, bear different meanings. In s 2 of the Act "holder" is defined and in s 29(1) there is a definition of "holder in due course" which was not an expression which was in common use, if it was in use at all, prior to the passing of the Act which, of course, purports to be a codifying enactment and not legislation which fundamentally changes the pre-existing law. Prior to the passing of the Act the expression "bona fide holder for value without notice" was widely used in judgments, in legal textbooks and in legal parlance to describe what the Act now calls a "holder in due course". The expression "holder for value" is freely used in the Act but with the possible exception of s 28(2) one looks in vain to discover what the rights of the holder for value are if they differ in any way from those of a "holder who has given value" or a "holder who has taken for value". My attention was not drawn to any authority which defined the rights of a "holder for value" as distinguished from a "holder who has given value" or a "holder who has taken for value" or in which it was held that a "holder for value" within the meaning of the Bills of Exchange Act 1882, is in any weaker or different position from a holder who has given value or taken for value.

On the other hand, light is thrown upon the matter by the speech of Lord Atkin in *Midland Bank Ltd v Reckit* [1933] AC 1 at 18 where, referring to two cheques which, unlike the other cheques which were the subject matter of the claim, were not marked "not negotiable", he said: "... the bank claim to be holders in due course to the extent of the overdraft existing when they were paid in. That they were holders for value to that extent is, I think, true whether the value is said to be the payment of the antecedent debt (the overdraft), or to be the lien to the extent of the overdraft" (referring to s 27(3) of the Bills of Exchange Act 1882).

This passage of Lord Atkin was obiter dicta but I think it plainly shows that he took the view that a person who by virtue of s 27(3) is deemed to be a "holder for value" is in the same position as a person who "took for value" within the meaning of s 29(1) . . .

In my judgment the holder of a cheque who has a lien on it is by virtue of s 27(3) deemed to have taken that cheque for value within the meaning of s 29(1)(b) to the extent of the sum for which he has a lien. I, therefore, hold that when these five cheques were delivered to the plaintiffs by Mabon's directors on 19 November, the plaintiffs thereupon acquired a lien upon them to the extent of Mabon's overdraft which then stood at £4673, and that although the cheques were delivered, inter alia, for collection, the plaintiffs were holders of the cheques and by reason of s 27(3) are deemed to have become holders for value to the extent of £4673. The plaintiffs took the cheques in good faith and without notice of any defect in Mabon's title and the conditions in s 29(1) to make them holders in due course have been satisfied.

I think that the plaintiffs are also entitled to succeed on at least two other grounds, and quite independently of s 27(3). In my view, the necessary implication of what occurred between Mr Ashenden and the Mabon directors was that the plaintiffs impliedly agreed to accept the five cheques in conditional reduction of Mabon's overdraft, the condition being that the cheques should not be dishonoured on presentation. To this extent the plaintiffs agreed to treat the five cheques as cash...

Another ground upon which I hold that the plaintiffs on 19 November gave value for the cheques is that they paid the two cheques for a total of £345 drawn by Mabon which they would not have done unless they had received the defendants' cheques. There are passages in two of the judgments in the Court of Appeal in *Westminster Bank Ltd v Zang* [1966] AC 182, which support this view. Admittedly they did not constitute any part of the ratio decidendi but I believe them to be sound law. Danckwerts LJ said at 206, 207: "If the bank did in fact allow the customer to draw against this cheque before it was cleared, I cannot see why that did not amount to giving value... I do not find anything in those cases which prevents the liberty given by a bank to draw against a particular uncleared cheque being value."

Salmon LJ said, at 210: "An obvious way of becoming a holder for value is to give value by honouring a cheque drawn against an uncleared cheque whether or not there is an antecedent contract to do so. Whether the bank has honoured a cheque drawn against uncleared effects is a matter of fact"...

Judgment for the plaintiffs with costs.

COLLECTION BY BANKER FOR A CUSTOMER IN GOOD FAITH AND WITHOUT NEGLIGENCE: BEA s 88D

The more usual defence for a collecting bank is s 88D (previously s 88). It is important to understand the various elements of this section.

(1) The bank must be collecting for a customer: *Commissioners of Taxation v ES & A Bank Ltd,* p 487, *supra.* The bank can plead this defence even though it has credited the customer's account and allowed him to draw against the cheque prior to clearance: see s 88D(1)(a)(ii). In that situation, the bank may simultaneously rely on s 88D and the defence of holder in due course.

(2) The bank must act in good faith: this is not usually an issue. Good faith is quite distinct from the question whether the bank has been negligent: see s 96 and pp 446–50, *supra.*

(3) The bank must act without negligence: this is a mixed question of fact and law, and raises a number of questions as to what are the indicia of negligence. The duty of care owed by the collecting bank to the true owner of the cheque is a common law duty enunciated in the cases, except to the extent that s 88D(2) and (3) have modified that duty in respect of indorsements. The more important issues include:

(a) does the duty only arise when the bank is asked to collect the cheque in question, or are earlier circumstances, including those surrounding the opening of the account also relevant? Is there any difference between the English and Australian law and practice in this regard? See *Kendall v London Bank of Australia Ltd*, p 517, *infra*; *Marfani & Co Ltd v Midland Bank Ltd,* p 520, *infra.*

(b) How closely must the bank examine its customers' background, and how fully should it monitor its business operations? And do different principles apply to a trust account operated by, say, a real estate agent, a solicitor or a stock broker? See *Day v Bank of NSW* (1978) 19 ALR 32.

(c) What features of the cheque should put the bank upon enquiry? For example, the nature of the payee: *Commissioners of State Savings Bank of Victoria v Permewan, Wright & Co Ltd,* p 512, *infra*; *Commercial Bank of Australia Ltd v Flannagan* (1932) 47 CLR 461; the relationship or connection of payee or person presenting the cheque for collection to the drawer or indorser: *Orbit Mining & Trading Co Ltd v Westminster Bank Ltd* [1963] 1 QB 794; [1962] 3 All ER 565; the amount of the cheque in relation to the general operation of the account.

(d) What effect do various crossings have on the duty of the collecting bank? For example, "not negotiable": *Commissioners of State Savings Bank of Victoria v Permewan, Wright & Co Ltd,* p 512, *infra*; "account payee only": *Universal Guarantee Pty Ltd v National Bank of Australasia Ltd,* p 505, *supra.*

(e) What is the effect of absence of, or irregularity in, an indorsement? See s 88D(2) and (3).

Before extracting the relevant cases on the negligence questions, three other points should be noted. First, where the same bank (including different branches of the same bank) is both the paying and collecting bank, it is entitled to the protection of s 88D provided it was not negligent in performing its function as collecting bank. However, it cannot rely upon the due care which it exercises as paying bank to exonerate it from a claim of negligence in its capacity of collecting bank: *Carpenters' Co v British Mutual Banking Co Ltd* [1938] 1 KB 511. Second, a collecting bank's defence of contributory negligence by the true owner of the cheque was accepted in one New Zealand and one English case as a ground for apportionment of damages recoverable in conversion from a collecting bank: *Helson v McKenzies (Cuba Street) Ltd* [1950] NZLR 878; and *Lumsden & Co v London Trustee Savings Bank* [1971] 1 Lloyd's Rep 114. However, these decisions have been criticised (O'Hare (1971) 45 *ALJ* 694), and rejected by Samuels J in *Wilton v Commonwealth Trading Bank of Australia* [1973] 2 NSWLR 644 and by the Full Court of South Australia in *Day v Bank of NSW* (1978) 19 ALR 32; and in *Grantham Homes Pty Ltd v Interstate Permanent Building Society Ltd* (1979) 37 FLR 191. Third, s 88D(4) will enable a bank which collects for its customer a "bank cheque" (treated as equivalent to a cheque: s 88A) issued by itself to qualify for protection in its capacity as collecting bank.

Commissioners of the State Savings Bank of Victoria v Permewan, Wright & Co Ltd
High Court of Australia (1914) 19 CLR 457

Appeal from the Supreme Court of Victoria.

An action was brought in the Supreme Court by Permewan, Wright & Co Ltd against the Commissioners of the State Savings Bank of Victoria, whereby the plaintiffs sought to recover from the defendants the sum of £1545 11s 11d damages for the conversion by the defendants of 58 cheques drawn by and on behalf of the plaintiffs on the Royal Bank of Victoria. Alternatively, the plaintiffs claimed the same amount received by the defendants in respect of the same cheques as money had and received by them to the use of the plaintiffs. The plaintiffs also claimed £400 as damages in the nature of interest. The cheques in question had been handed to one Charles Heath, a clerk of the plaintiffs, for the purpose only of paying customs duties in respect of goods of their customers, but were fraudulently paid in by him for collection to his own account at a branch of the State Savings Bank; the amounts of them were passed to his credit, and that bank received payment of them from the Royal Bank. All the cheques were crossed and marked "not negotiable". Of 22 of the cheques some were payable to a number or bearer, and marked "Duty" or "Duties" and others were payable to "Duties" or bearer. The other 36 cheques were payable in one or other of the following manners: to "HM Customs" or bearer; to "Duty" or bearer, and specially marked "for Duty only"; to a number or bearer and specially marked "HM Customs Duty"; to "HM Customs Duty" or bearer; to "HM Customs" or bearer and specially marked "HM Customs Duty".

Madden CJ gave judgment for the plaintiffs and the defendants appealed to the High Court.

Griffith CJ [dealt with the question whether the defendants (appellants) were bankers, and then continued at 466:] Section 88 of the Bills of Exchange Act exonerates from liability a banker who in good faith and without negligence receives payment for a customer of a cheque crossed generally or specially to himself, and to which the customer has no title or a defective title. The cheques in respect of which this action is brought were all payable to bearer and crossed generally, with the words "not negotiable" added. The effect of these words is that a person taking the cheque has not and cannot give a better title to it than that which the person from whom he took it had: s 87.

Negligence means, in my opinion, the omission to take such reasonable care as a banker charged with the duty of collecting a crossed cheque for a customer ought to take for the protection of the true owner, having regard to the circumstances under which it is presented for collection. In my opinion the care to be taken is not less than a man invited to purchase or cash such a cheque for himself might reasonably be expected to take. The relevant circumstances include the general character of the banking operations carried on by the banker, the nature of the account of the customer who asks to have the cheque collected for him, and all such information as the banker possesses as to the customer's title to the cheque, whether that information is derived from extrinsic sources or from the cheque itself.

I have already stated the character of the operations carried on by the defendants. The account of their customer Heath was opened in October 1898 by a deposit of £8 0s 10d. Two additional deposits of £1 17s 6d and £3 3s were made before the end of July 1899, at which time he had a balance of £3 13s 5d. On 1 August 1899 he made a deposit of £42 18s by cheque, and before the end of the year made a further deposit of £3 10s. His balance was then £1 7s 6d. His operations on the account during the years 1900–06 were of a similar kind. Withdrawals were, with very rare exceptions, of round sums of small amount. The account was not in any sense an ordinary business account, by which I mean an account on which a trader operates by cheques for the purpose of his business.

On 28 November 1907 the first of the cheques in question, which was for £35 14s 8d was lodged with the defendants for collection. On 5 February following another cheque drawn by the plaintiffs for £94 12s 1d was similarly lodged. Between that date and 20 May 1912 56 other cheques of the plaintiffs, making in all a total sum of £1545 11s 11d, were lodged. Between November 1907 and May 1912 only 16 cheques drawn by persons other than the plaintiffs were deposited, all except two being of small amount. Withdrawals were made in the same manner as before, ie, almost entirely in round sums.

I now turn to the information disclosed by the cheques themselves. I have stated that they were all marked "not negotiable". The words were in fact boldly printed across the cheques between two lines also printed. Mr Starke contended, with some courage, that these words upon a cheque made payable to bearer are negligible for the purpose of s 88. I cannot accept this view. In my opinion the words "not negotiable" on a crossed cheque are a danger signal held out before every person invited to deal with it, and are equivalent to saying "Take care: this cheque may be stolen". I think, further, that they indicate that the drawer of the cheque (whether, as in this case, the words are printed upon it or are written) intended that the person to whom it was to be handed or sent should apply it to some specific purpose and no other. A reasonably careful man to whom such a cheque is tendered should therefore examine the cheque to see whether there is anything upon its face to indicate such a purpose. If there is not, it may be that he may safely rely on the honesty of the bearer; but, if there is, it is his duty to make inquiries, and if he fails to do so he cannot claim to have acted without negligence.

To apply these principles I will take as an illustration a cheque for £50 4s 9d, drawn on 4 November 1911. The form of the cheques was: "Pay HM Customs or bearer", and between the crossing lines was written "HM Customs Duty". I put myself in the place of an ordinary person to whom such a cheque is presented with a request to cash it or purchase it. He would see, first of all, that the person presenting the cheque might have no title to it, and would naturally ask himself whether there was anything on its face to show the purpose to which the drawer intended it to be applied, or otherwise to cast any doubt on the title of the person presenting it to him. He would find upon it words indicating prima facie that the cheque was intended by the drawer to be applied in payment of customs duty and for no other purpose. If he knew, further, as the defendants did, that the drawers were customs agents who would in the ordinary course of their business give crossed cheques for that purpose, the inference would be almost irresistible. Under these circumstances the ordinary person would certainly feel called upon in his own interests to make inquiry as to the bearer's title. It was suggested that the defendants might, if they had considered the matter at all, have thought that the cheque represented money entrusted to Heath by the plaintiffs for disbursements in payment of customs duties on their behalf. Having regard to the nature of his account, I do not think that they could have thought anything of the kind. But the main argument for the defendants was that bankers are not bound to have regard to anything written on the face of a cheque which is not expressly authorised by the Act to be so written, except in the single instance of such words as "Account of AB" or "Credit AB" or some plain statement of want of title.

And all the witnesses called by them not only admitted that they followed this practice, but insisted that they were right in doing so. They do not even pretend to have exercised any care at all. With regard to this cheque, therefore, I think that negligence is clearly established as against the defendants.

The question of negligence with regard to the other cheques depends on the same principles, although the words written upon their face were not always the same. For instance, the cheque first stolen was drawn in favour of a number "or bearer", with the word "Duty" written within the crossing lines in red ink. It was suggested that the word "Duty" was ambiguous, and could not give rise to a suspicion that the cheques were intended to be applied in payment of Crown duties. In my opinion, the word "Duty" would suggest to any reasonable person addressing his mind to the matter that the cheque was to be applied either in payment of federal customs duty or state stamp or probate duty, which are the only Crown duties payable in Victoria, and, if he knew, as the defendants did, that plaintiffs were customs agents, that it was to be applied in payment of customs duties...

An argument was addressed to us to the effect that even if the defendants were guilty of negligence in respect to the earlier cheques they were excused from taking care with respect to the later ones by the plaintiffs' default in not sooner finding out Heath's fraud and warning them. If the defendants had in fact applied their minds to the point, and if the plaintiffs ought to have discovered the fraud, the argument might have some weight. But the defendants' case is that they did not, and were not bound to, examine the cheques at all, or take any notice of what they call irrelevant words written on their face. They were not, therefore, misled by any inaction of the plaintiffs. Nor is there any foundation for the suggestion that the plaintiffs ought to have discovered the fraud. In Australia it is not, as in England, the practice for bankers to return their customers' cheque to them with the passbook, and the only information that the plaintiffs could derive from their passbook was that the cheques had been debited to their account. Heath's frauds were so cunningly devised that the plaintiffs' principals obtained the goods in respect of which the duties were payable, and recouped to the plaintiffs the duties for which the cheques were drawn. This argument therefore fails.

In my judgment the defendants, even if they are bankers, have not brought themselves within the protection of s 88 as to any of the cheques.

In my opinion, therefore, the appeal fails as to the whole case.

Isaacs J [considered the question whether the appellants were bankers and then continued at 473:] Then comes the second question, whether they have discharged themselves of their prima facie obligation to pay over the money claimed to the true owners of the cheques. In other words, have they established that they received payment of the various cheques without negligence? Good faith is not challenged. As to negligence, it is requisite in the first place, in view of the course the argument has taken to get a clear conception of the relation of s 88 to the other sections of the Act...

In 1852, when there was yet no legislation touching the crossing of cheques, *Bellamy v Marjoribanks* (1852) 7 Ex 389 was decided. From that case it appears that the practice of crossing cheques began in the clearing house, and was a device voluntarily adopted by the bank clerks who wrote their firm's name across the cheques sent to the clearing house, so as to facilitate the making up of accounts there as between the banks themselves. Even that was a modern expedient, apparently in the beginning of the nineteenth century. Then merchants themselves adopted the practice of crossing their cheques—whether intended to go through the clearing house or not—by writing across it the name of a banker or the words "and Co".

This practice became a recognised custom by 1828 to this extent, that bankers generally refused to pay such a cheque except to a banker, the known object of the drawer being to facilitate the tracing of the cheque and its payment, by relying on the probity and high regard for honourable dealing which bankers proverbially exhibit, and the consequent practical obstacle this presented to a dishonest holder of a cheque so crossed, when asking the drawee to pay it. But the crossing did not restrict the absolute negotiability of the cheque, and this is the central point of the situation. At common law a cheque was inherently negotiable. Negotiability in its full sense means capability of being transferred by delivery or indorsement so as to give a good title to the instrument to the transferee, taking bona fide and for value, thereby constituting him the true owner, notwithstanding any defect of title in the transferor.

The Banker-Customer Relationship and the Banking System

And at common law, any restriction of this complete negotiability was incompatible with the notion of a cheque...

The crossing was a protection and safeguard, but to *the owner of the cheque*, whoever he might be; and if the banker, seeing this crossing, were still to pay it to a private holder, the circumstance of his so paying it would be strong evidence of negligence in an action against him.

Three points must be here noted: (1) That the duty of care was one imposed by the common law, in view of the custom of crossing cheques, recognised by bankers as indicating a desire or expectation by the drawer that the drawee would pay it only to or through a banker. (2) That this indication of desire and expectation was not a direction, restraining negotiability, for that was legally impossible. It operated as a *caution* to the banker, and he was liable for negligently failing to comply with the caution. (3) That the protection was only in favour of the true owner, whoever he might be.

[His Honour then dealt with further legislative amendments in England.]

Once more parliament intervened in 1876 by passing the Act 39 & 40 Vict c 81, which codified the law of crossed cheques up to that time, and, to meet the omission pointed out by Lord Cairns, modified the common law still further by providing that a person taking a cheque crossed generally or specially, and bearing in either case the words "not negotiable", should not have or be capable of giving a better title than his transferor had. This did what some judges had said was conceptionally impossible, namely, make a cheque not completely negotiable and still leave it a cheque.

The immediate object of doing that was to protect the real and rightful owner from theft and fraud by increasing the responsibility of the paying banker. But the effect of it at common law was also to make every person who wrongfully dealt with the cheque liable for conversion. Observe it required no special legislative direction for that purpose. Liability was a common law consequence, as soon as the instrument was made "non-negotiable" by law, and was proved not to have been parted with by its owner. Aimed directly at such a case as *Smith v Union Bank of London* (1875) 1 QBD 31, so as to make the paying bank liable for a manifest breach of duty to obey the direction on the face of the cheque, it had the indirect but inevitable consequence of making a collecting bank liable for conversion, however innocent and careful it or its customer might be. The legislature therefore added—not a new duty, not a statutory obligation, as it seems to me, with very great respect to the view taken in *Paget* (pp 257-8) —but a statutory qualification of a rigorous common law rule of absolute liability.

All persons other than a collecting banker still remained subject to that rule of liability, because they were unnamed, showing that it is not the statute that creates the liability. The collecting banker, however, if he could show good faith and due care, was permitted to relieve himself from his prima facie responsibility. The due care was necessarily referable to the same object as the primary responsibility, namely, the rights of the true owner. The rightful owner's protection was diminished in this respect for the sake of general financial business, represented by banking transactions. So far as this was necessary the exemption existed; but not beyond. And necessity went no further than honesty and ordinary care for the true owner's interests.

This law is, with one modification and some immaterial verbal changes, in force now. The conditions of exemption now are that (1) a banker alone is relieved; (2) the banker must be the banker who "receives payment", that is, the collecting banker; (3) payment must be received for a "customer"; (4) the payment must be received in good faith and without negligence; and (5) the banker must merely have received payment for the customer—which now includes crediting the customer's account with the amount of the cheque before actual receipt of payment...

The words "non-negotiable", though restricting the negotiability of the cheque in the sense I have mentioned, are not prohibitive of payment to a person other than the "named payee or bearer"; they are consistent with such payment provided there is no bad faith or negligence. Consequently their mere presence cannot determine the question of negligence. That must depend, like every other case of negligence at common law, on the fair examination of the circumstances as they appeared at the time.

Cases have been cited, the latest of which is *Morison v London County and Westminster Bank* [1914] 3 KB 356. But, except for their affirmance of some principle of law, they are no precedent for any other case. Apart from the well established rule that whether or not the evidence establishes that a person acts without negligence is a question of fact, the legal principles found in *Morison's* case and relevant to the present are: (1) that the question should in strictness be determined separately with regard to each cheque; (2) that the test of negligence is whether the transaction of paying in any given cheque was so out of the ordinary course that it ought to have aroused doubts in the banker's mind, and caused them to make inquiry; (3) that the absence of any complaint over a sufficient period may in certain circumstance be in itself a fact which, as to later cheques, outweighs other facts that in themselves are some evidence of negligence; and (4) that the third principle operates, not merely if suspicion has in fact been previously excited in the bankers' mind, but also if it ought to have been; that is, as to each cheque you regard in considering the question of negligence all the circumstances existing at that time.

Those principles are found particularly in the judgments of Lord Reading CJ and Phillimore LJ.

[His Honour then referred to the fact that the collecting bank was a savings bank used by small depositors rather than a commercial bank dealing with a current or trading account.]

It appears to me, therefore, that what might in the case of an account current in a commercial bank pass as an ordinary payment in of a cheque, subject to a business adjustment between the depositor and the drawer of the cheque, might well be so far out of the ordinary course of a savings bank deposit as to excite suspicion or raise a demand for inquiry in the minds of the officials. What would be ordinary elsewhere might be extraordinary there. Consequently I am not satisfied that the appellants as to the first 22 cheques, which, like the rest, are all crossed "not negotiable" were, in the first instance, free from negligence.

The cheques specially crossed "Duty" or "Duties" could not well be supposed to be savings. Cheques for "duties" are not given until they are wanted for immediate payment. They had obviously to be accounted for; they were manifestly not accounted for in that account, as an inspection of the items clearly shows. And it is sufficiently improbable that they would have been accounted for or adjusted in some other account in some other bank, while these particular cheques were paid into this bank, to call for some inquiry. "Duties" means some liability to government and *par excellence* customs duties, particularly when paid in by a depositor who describes himself as "Shipping Agent". I do not forget the word "bearer"; but that does not obliterate the word "Duties", and the crossing indicates that negotiability in its full sense does not exist, and should put the bank on the alert.

One important feature of the case in favour of the appellant bank is this—there never was any complaint by any person that Heath had improperly appropriated a single cheque...

Now, in view of the common law liability in favour of the true owner arising from the "caution" of mere crossing, referred to in the earlier cases, and the still more stringent endeavour to protect the "true owner", whoever he might be, by the words "non-negotiable", the presence and connotation of the word "duties", the knowledge of who and what Permewan, Wright & Co were, and the business they did, and the manifest state of Heath's account, were not outweighed by the circumstances of the opposite scale of non-complaint ... on the whole, the appellants have not satisfied my mind that they took care and acted with caution, or did more than take the risk, and let the true owner, whoever he might be, look after himself and take his chance; and so, as Blackburn J said in 1875 in the passage I have quoted from *Smith v Union Bank of London* (1875) LR 10 QB 291 at 297, "they incur a liability to the true holder of the cheque, whoever he may be". The respondents are the "true owner", and to them the bank is responsible. If that is so, as to the earliest cheque, the following 21 are more difficult to justify, and the further subsequent ones from their more definite and stringent form, are *à fortiori* instances.

It was contended that the knowledge of the appellant's clerks, though acquired in the course and for the purpose of the bank's business, should not be imputed to the bank so as to make it responsible for the act of its other clerks, who had not personally that knowledge. I am unable to entertain that objection. The knowledge of a clerk acquired in the way mentioned is the knowledge of the bank. It is his duty to communicate it to his principals ... Looking at the various cheques, either singly or as part of a series, I arrive at the conclusion that the appellants are justly held liable for all the cheques, and that this appeal should be dismissed with costs.

[**Gavan Duffy**, **Rich** and **Powers JJ** delivered judgments to similar effect on the negligence question, but held that the 22 cheques payable to a number or bearer, or to Duties or bearer had been collected without negligence.]

Decision of the Supreme Court of Victoria varied.

London Bank of Australia Ltd v Kendall
High Court of Australia (1920) 28 CLR 401

Isaacs and **Rich JJ:** The respondent, Kendall, sued the appellant for wrongfully converting a cheque. The defence was twofold, namely, first, that Kendall was not the true owner of the cheque, and, next, that the cheque was collected by the bank without negligence, and for one Howard, a customer, and therefore that the bank was protected by s 88 of the Commonwealth Bills of Exchange Act 1909. The trial took place before Pring J without a jury, and the learned judge found (1) that Kendall was the true owner, and (2) that, though Howard was a customer, the bank was negligent in respect of the collection of the cheque. His Honour gave judgment for the present respondent for the amount of the cheque, £83 8s 9d, and costs. On appeal to the Full Court, the Chief Justice and Sly J held that the judgment was right, and accordingly (Ferguson J dissenting) the appeal was dismissed. This court gave special leave to appeal from that decision on the ground that important questions of law and banking practice were involved.

... Before us, it was contended (1) that Kendall was not the true owner of the cheque at the time the bank collected it, and (2) that the bank was not negligent in respect of the collection.

[Their Honours then discussed the duty of an appellate court in relation to findings of fact, and continued at 409:]

(2) *True Owner*—The facts material to the question of true ownership of the cheque are as follows: It was proved that the plaintiff drew the cheque on 5 June 1917. It was crossed, but simply by two parallel transverse lines. His clerk enclosed it in an envelope, which was addressed "Commissioners of Taxation", and posted it in a street pillarbox. The cheque was sent as in payment of income tax, of which notice of assessment had been received. The notice stated that cheques posted should be crossed and marked "Commissioners of Taxation—not negotiable". Had that direction been followed, the cheque would have been at the risk of the commissioners so far as the respondent is concerned, and probably would never have gone astray. But the cheque never reached the commissioners' hands, and was never accepted by them. Not having seen sent in the form directed, the sending of the cheque was a mere offer of the cheque by Kendall to the commissioners, which, until accepted, remained his.

(3) *Negligence*— ... The test of whether, in the absence of precautions, the banker has been negligent in any particular case is now finally settled by the *English, Scottish and Australian Bank* case 36 TLR 305 to be this: Was the transaction of paying in the given cheque, coupled with the circumstances antecedent and present, so out of the ordinary course that it ought to have aroused doubts in the bankers' minds and caused them to make inquiry? As Lord Dunedin says at 306, "the question is necessarily a question of fact". And, as we are reminded by the same judgment, "it is really impossible to lay down rules or statements which will determine what is negligence and what is not. Each case must be determined on its own circumstances". It is very distinctly pointed out in the case just referred to (1) that "it is not a question of negligence in opening an account, though the circumstances connected with the opening of an account may shed light on the question of whether there was negligence in collecting a cheque".

(4) *Need for Inquiry*—The opening of the account in this case is a very material antecedent circumstance, and it should be carefully noted. [Their Honours then set out the circumstances of the opening of the account.] An account was opened in the books of the bank in which, under date 5 June 1917, A S Howard was credited with £209 1s 8d. The next day, all the cheques having been collected without any objection, Howard (as we may call him) drew a cheque for £206, payable to "Cash or Bearer", and it was paid over the counter. This left the account in credit £3 1s 8d.

We may stop there for a moment in order to estimate these antecedent circumstances because the payment in of the Kendall cheque took place just afterwards. How did the matter present itself to the bank, or rather how ought it to have presented itself to the bank? Howard, as he called himself, was, at the opening of the account, utterly unknown to the bank, and he brought no credentials. He said he was an indent merchant or agent, but produced no confirmation of his statement, and gave no further information as to the nature of his business. He said he had had a bank account in Adelaide, but he neither mentioned, nor was asked, the name of the bank, nor whether it was represented in Sydney, nor when he closed his account there. He stated he had no bank account in Sydney, but he did not state how long he had been in Sydney. On the Tuesday he presented cheques, one of which was dated 31 May, the Thursday before, possibly reaching him about Friday—all of the cheques crossed generally, three of them containing the words "not negotiable". Those words, while not preventing transferability of the cheques, prevented negotiation; and so there was one possibility more that the person holding such a cheque was not the true owner: his transferor might not have had a title. As to how he came to have so many cheques crossed "Bank" and "not negotiable" while having no bank account, and how, having no bank account, he was carrying on his business, no inquiry whatever was made. Now, the mere fact that a cheque is crossed, even including the words "not negotiable", is not sufficient to establish negligence in the absence of inquiry. A customer satisfactorily established may well pay in such a cheque without raising any cause for doubt. But, as Lord Sterndale observed in *Crumplin's* case 109 LT at 858, "the taking of a cheque crossed 'not negotiable' is one matter which must be taken into consideration along with all the other matters surrounding the transaction".

Was the transaction of 5 June itself so far in the ordinary course of banking business as to arouse no doubt in the mind of an ordinary prudent banker? It would be strange to us if it were. Having regard to the fact that the deposit of such cheques may take place late one day and the payment out to the depositor of the collected proceeds of the cheques may take place next day, it is very little more protection to the true owner than if the cheques were open. Sir John Paget, in the second edition of his work on banking (p 262), says: "Banks have sometimes put forward, as evidence that they exercised due caution about the collection of a cheque, the fact that, before crediting it, they inquired from the paying bank whether it would be paid on presentation. It is obvious that such a proceeding affords no safeguard to the true owner. The paying banker could have no means of knowing in whose hands the cheque might be; the inquiry, so far as he is concerned, only relates to the state of his customer's account."

Now, if such an inquiry, followed, as it is assumed to be, by actual payment on presentation —for otherwise the question would not arise—is no safeguard, it is *a fortiori* no safeguard simply to present the cheque without any preliminary warning. That is how we view the matter, apart from direct evidence of the usual course of banking business. We are of opinion that even without such evidence, and simply testing the matter by the ordinary risks of human nature, operating on the opportunities afforded by such instruments and banking facilities, that in the circumstances as they appeared to the bank on 5 June, the bank would be justly put on inquiry. The account as opened was suspicious: the customer was not merely unknown, but was doing something that needed some explanation in the absence of which the bank ran the risk of being made a necessary but unquestioning intermediary in a fraud. At that moment it must be borne in mind that "Howard" was not a customer, and that the bank owed him no duty whatever. Up to that point there was therefore no conflict of obligation; there was simply a conflict of duty to the "true owner" and the interest of the bank itself in obtaining a new customer. Where a customer is once properly established, his convenience and the bank's general duty towards him are additional elements in the situation, and of more or less relative force according to the circumstances. Lord Dunedin gives effect to this consideration in a passage in the judgment in the *English, Scottish and Australian Bank* case 36 TLR at 306, where it is said: "For if it was laid down that no cheque should be collected without a thorough inquiry as to the history of the cheque, it would render banking business as ordinarily carried on impossible; *customers would often be left for long periods without available money*." Here, however, the matter was uncomplicated by any such consideration. The bona fides of the bank is undoubted; but it did not give the matter sufficient consideration.

[Their Honours then referred to evidence given by officers of the appellant bank, and of other banks operating in Sydney and concluded:] There can be no doubt that, in any event, the opening of the account was contrary to good banking practice, and that practice is founded on a reasonable regard for the interests of persons otherwise likely to be prejudiced by the conjoint operations of strangers and the banks themselves.

Then, was this unsatisfactory state of affairs cleared up by subsequent events, or was it not darkened by them? The cheques were cleared next day, and the proceeds credited to Howard's account. "Howard" drew £206 as stated. He did not ask for a draft to send abroad; he did not give a cheque to a business firm: he simply drew out over the counter all but £3 1s 8d of the amount deposited the day before. This reduced the account practically to a nominal account; the bank being made the statutory instrument of an unknown person to collect the cheques he brought in. Then, immediately after, a further transaction took place, involving the Kendall cheque. "Howard" deposited four further cheques. [Their Honours then described three other crossed cheques.] The fourth was the cheque sued for, dated 5 June, drawn on the Union Bank of Australia Ltd, Sydney, payable to "50 or Bearer" for £83 8s 9d and simply crossed with two lines. It is therefore seen that on 6 June we have not merely to consider the payment in of the Kendall cheque. That cheque must be considered with all the "circumstances antecedent and present". The summation is: that the transaction of paying in that cheque to an account which originated in such manner as to make its character suspicious, to begin with, which was carried on in such manner as not to dissipate but to deepen suspicion, if only the bank had given the matter reasonable thought, and which, having been reduced to the position of a mere nominal account, was being in effect reinstated by the batch of cheques of which the Kendall cheque was one, was of such a character as to put the bank upon inquiry.

Reference to *Crumplin's* case 109 LT at 858 col 2 will show that in the opinion of Lord Sterndale the fact of opening an account with a small sum, or of soon drawing it down to practically nothing, is a material consideration in connection with such a question as the present. We hold, then, that the bank was put on inquiry with reference to the collection of the Kendall cheque.

(5) *Proper Inquiry*—Learned counsel on both sides dealt with the question of what inquiry should have been made in order to test the problem of negligence. This, like the question of negligence in general, is purely dependent on the circumstances. The only guiding principle is that, where doubt is once aroused as to the nature and true ownership of the cheque, the nature and extent of the inquiry proper to allay it must be measured by what, in the circumstances, a fair-minded banker, paying due regard to the reasonable exigencies of banking business in relation to the person depositing the cheque, would consider it prudent to do in order to protect the interests of the true owner whoever he might be. The practice of the three banks mentioned indicates a very fair and efficient means where a stranger, unvouched for, proposes to create the relation of banker and customer for the first time. It was urged that to permit an unknown man to open an account with cash one day and next day to pass without inquiry a crossed cheque was not very different in effect from passing the cheque without question at the inception of the account. From the standpoint of the true owner that may be so; but from the standpoint of the bank it is not so. Once, as in *Commissioners of Taxation v English, Scottish and Australian Bank* (*Thallon's* case) 36 TLR 305, an account is established apparently satisfactorily, the relation of banker and customer is created, and a duty has arisen on the part of the banker towards his customer which cannot be entirely ignored. Inquiry as to the respectability of an intended customer who proposes to open an account with a protected cheque is shown to be ordinary English banking practice, and by two banks, one certainly, and the other probably, identical with banks carrying on business in Australia (*Ladbroke & Co v Todd* (1914) 30 TLR 443). It is a definite step to be so far satisfied with the respectability and status of a stranger as to be willing to create the relative duties and obligations of banker and customer. Once that situation is satisfactorily created, while the bank may in a case like *Thallon's* not unreasonably consider itself free from negligence if it refrains from hampering its customer, its position is altogether different where the circumstances are as they exist here. Though the relation has been created, yet if not entirely satisfactory to begin with, time or events or both may so operate as to remove all doubt or so far to lull suspicion as to justify the bank in treating the account as reliable. (See *Ross v London County Westminster and Parr's Bank* [1919] 1 KB 678 at 687.) Neither time nor events have so operated here. On the contrary, as we have said, later events added to the need of caution.

Coming to the conclusions (1) that the bank has not sustained the onus of establishing the absence of negligence and (2) that the facts affirmatively considered establish there was negligence, we hold that the appellant is not within the protection of s 88.

The appeal is dismissed with costs.

Gavan Duffy J: I agree that the appeal should be dismissed.

Appeal dismissed with costs.

Marfani & Co Ltd v Midland Bank Ltd
English Court of Appeal [1968] 2 All ER 573

Having as instructed drawn a crossed cheque for £3000 in favour of Eliaszade [E] with whom the plaintiff company had business dealings, and having got it signed by the company's Pakistani managing director, who then went abroad, Kureshy [K] the Pakistani office manager of the company, went to a branch of the defendant bank where considerable business was done with Pakistanis. He called himself E and sought to open a new account in that name. He told the securities officer, who had authority to open new accounts, that he was thinking of going into business as a restaurateur, signed the particulars required by the bank with the name of E, and gave two restaurateurs as referees. He paid in £80 on 24 January 1966, to open the account and said that the majority of the funds would come later, and the following day he paid in the £3000 cheque, which he had endorsed (unnecessarily) in the name of E, together with £35 9s 6d in cash. The bank had the cheque specially cleared the same day without being asked to, and credited the proceeds to the new account in E's name, although they would not have allowed the account to be operated without a satisfactory reference. On 26 January 1966, the bank was visited by Mr Ali, one of the referees (the other did not reply to the bank's inquiry), a Pakistani who had been known to the bank since about 1961, had had an account with them for some years and had previously introduced satisfactory Pakistani customers to the bank. He told the bank's branch manager that E (as K was known to both of them) had been known to him "for some time" (he was not asked how long), that he, Mr Ali, believed that E intended starting a restaurant and that in Mr Ali's opinion he (ie K known as E) was all right for the conduct of a bank account. Mr Ali had in fact known K for only a month as a customer at his restaurant and was in no position to vouch for his trustworthiness or even his identity. Payments out of the account started at the end of January 1966; viz, a few days after Mr Ali's reference was given. All the money in K's account was withdrawn in the course of the first week of February 1966, and he left for Pakistan. The plaintiff company brought an action for conversion of the £3000 cheque against the defendant bank.

[Nield J gave judgment for the defendant bank, holding that it was protected by s 4 of the Cheques Act 1957 (Aust, BEA s 88D) since it acted in accordance with the ordinary practice of careful bankers and had discharged the onus of disproving negligence. The plaintiff company appealed to the Court of Appeal.]

Diplock LJ [referred to the facts and continued:]

At common law one's duty to one's neighbour who is the owner, or entitled to possession, of any goods is to refrain from doing any voluntary act in relation to his goods which is a usurpation of his proprietary or possessory rights in them. Subject to some exceptions which are irrelevant for the purposes of the present case, it matters not that the doer of the act of usurpation did not know, and could not by the exercise of any reasonable care have known, of his neighbour's interest in the goods. This duty is absolute; he acts at his peril.

A banker's business, of its very nature, exposes him daily to this peril. His contract with his customer requires him to accept possession of cheques delivered to him by his customer, to present them for payment to the banks on which the cheques are drawn, to receive payment of them and to credit the amount thereof to his own customer's account, either on receipt of the cheques themselves from the customer, or on receipt of actual payment of the cheques from the banks on which they are drawn. If the customer is not entitled to the cheque which he delivers to his banker for collection, the banker, however, innocent and careful he might have been, would at common law be liable to the true owner of the cheque for the amount of which he receives payment, either as damages for conversion or under the cognate cause of action, based historically on assumpsit, for money had and received.

So strict a liability, so absolute a duty, on bankers would have discouraged the development of banking business. It was accordingly progressively mitigated by statute, first by s 82 of the Bills of Exchange Act 1882, then by the Bills of Exchange (Crossed Cheques) Act 1906, and finally by s 4 of the Cheques Act 1957, which is the current statute with which we are concerned, and sub-s (1) of which reads as follows: "(1) Where a banker, in good faith and without negligence—(a) receives payment for a customer of an instrument to which this section applies; or (b) having credited a customer's account with the amount of such an instrument, receives payment thereof for himself, and the customer has no title, or a defective title, to the instrument, the banker does not incur any liability to the true owner of the instrument by reason only of having received payment thereof."

Sub-section (2) provides that the section applies inter alia to cheques...

The only respect in which this substituted statutory duty differs from a common law cause of action in negligence is that, since it takes the form of a qualified immunity from a strict liability at common law, the onus of showing that he did take such reasonable care lies on the defendant banker. Granted good faith in the banker (the other condition of the immunity) the usual matter with respect to which the banker must take reasonable care is to satisfy himself that his own customer's title to the cheque delivered to him for collection is not defective, ie, that no other person is the true owner of it. Where the customer is in possession of the cheque at the time of delivery for collection, and appears on the face of it to be the "holder", ie, the payee or indorsee or the bearer, the banker is, in my view, entitled to assume that the customer is the owner of the cheque unless there are facts which are known, or ought to be known, to the banker which would cause a reasonable banker to suspect that the customer is not the true owner.

What facts ought to be known to the banker, ie, what inquiries he should make, and what facts are sufficient to cause him reasonably to suspect that the customer is not the true owner, must depend on current banking practice, and change as that practice changes. Cases decided 30 years ago, when the use by the general public of banking facilities was much less widespread, may not be a reliable guide to what the duty of a careful banker, in relation to inquiries and as to facts which should give rise to suspicion, is today.

The duty of care owed by the banker to the true owner of the cheque does not arise until the cheque is delivered to him by his customer. It is then, and then only, that any duty to make inquiries can arise. Any antecedent inquiries that he has made are relevant only in so far as they have already brought to his knowledge facts which a careful banker ought to ascertain about his customers before accepting for collection the cheque which is the subject matter of the action, and so have relieved him of any need to ascertain them again when the cheque which is the subject matter of the action is delivered to him. What the court has to do is to look at all the circumstances at the time of the acts complained of, and to ask itself were those circumstances such as would cause a reasonable banker possessed of such information about his customer as a reasonable banker would possess, to suspect that his customer was not the true owner of the cheque...

In all actions of the kind with which we are here concerned, the banker's customer has in fact turned out to be a fraudulent rogue, and attention is naturally concentrated on the duty of care which was owed by the banker to the person who has in fact turned out to be the true owner of the cheque. We are always able to be wise after the event, but the banker's duty fell to be performed before it, and the duty which he owed to the true owner ought not to be considered in isolation. At the relevant time the banker was entitled to take into consideration the interests of his customer who, be it remembered, would in all probability turn out to be honest, as most men are, and his own business interests, and to weigh these against the risk of loss or damage to the true owner of the cheque in the unlikely event that he should turn out not to be the customer himself...

From the practical point of view of foreseeable loss to the true owner, it seems to me to make no difference whether the banker has received payment of the cheque or not, so long as he retains the payment in his own hands and it is capable of being followed and recovered from him by the true owner. The relevant time for determining whether the banker has complied with his duty of care towards the true owner of the cheque is, in my opinion, the time at which the banker pays out the proceeds of the cheque to his own customer, and so deprives the true owner of his right to follow the money into the banker's hands.

The question in this case, therefore, is whether the defendant bank have proved that by 2 February when they started to pay out the proceeds of the cheque to Kureshy, they had taken all reasonable care to ascertain that he was the true owner of the cheque. This is to be judged by the practice of careful bankers... It seems a reasonable inference that what the defendant bank did in the present case was in accordance with current banking practice. The judge accepted that it was, and counsel for the plaintiff company has not sought to argue the contrary. What he contends is that this court is entitled to examine that practice, and to form its own opinion whether it does comply with the standard of care which a prudent banker should adopt. This is quite right, but I venture to think that this court should be hesitant before condemning as negligent a practice generally adopted by those engaged in banking business.

Counsel for the plaintiff company ... submits that the defendant bank, before opening the account, ought to have required Kureshy to produce some document to identify himself, ought to have inquired the name of his previous employer (he had told them that he was not employed) and about previous banking accounts held by him.

The defendant bank's answer was that they regarded a trustworthy reference as more reliable than inquiries made of the customer himself. It is to be borne in mind that, whatever inquiries it might be prudent for the bank to make for their own purposes, the only inquiries which they were under any duty to the plaintiff company to make were inquiries directed to discovering whether their new customer might use the account for the fraudulent purpose of cashing cheques belonging to other people. The purpose of such inquiries would be to find out (a) whether the customer was a fraudulent rogue, and if so (b) whether he would be likely to have opportunities of dishonestly obtaining other people's cheques, and in particular those of the plaintiff company. As a matter of commonsense, a person who is opening a bank account for a dishonest purpose is unlikely himself wittingly to give any information calculated to disclose his dishonest purpose. He will be prepared with appropriate answers to lull suspicion. It may be that a searching interrogation would reveal inconsistencies or improbabilities in his story, but a bank cannot reasonably be expected to subject *all* prospective customers to a cross-examination, which cannot fail to give the impression that the bank doubts their honesty, and which would be understandably resented by the 999 honest potential customers, on the off chance of detecting the thousandth dishonest one. If there is some other independent and apparently trustworthy source from which the honesty of the potential customer may be verified, to rely on this source of information is not only less likely to damage the bank's own business by driving away honest customers than interrogation of the customer himself, but is also more likely to result in the successful detection of the occasional dishonest one.

Counsel for the plaintiff company placed great reliance on the speech of Lord Wright in *Lloyds Bank Ltd v E B Savory & Co* [1932] All ER Rep 106; [1933] AC 201 as authority for the proposition that it is the duty of a banker, when opening a new account, to ascertain the name of the customer's or customer's spouse's employers, in addition to obtaining suitable references. Lord Wright went further than the other members of the three to two majority, Lord Buckmaster and Lord Warrington, both of whom considered that such inquiries might be dispensed with if an apparently reliable and trustworthy reference were obtained. That case, as all other cases, depended on its own particular facts. The frauds had gone on for a very long time. There were many other matters calculated to arouse suspicion in the social conditions of the 1920s. It was decided on expert evidence, not of what is now current banking practice, but of what it was nearly 40 years ago. I find in it no more than an illustration of the application of the general principle that a banker must exercise reasonable care in all the circumstances of the case.

Counsel for the defendant bank argued that, in any event, on the facts now known to us, none of the proposed inquiries would have resulted in any suspicion of Kureshy's honesty. He had prepared his scheme too well. Failure to make them was not causative of the loss. There are dicta, which can be found collected in *Baker v Barclays Bank, Ltd* [1955] 2 All ER 571 at 582–4, which suggest that, even if it could be proved that a failure to make a particular inquiry which a prudent banker would have made, had no causative effect on the loss sustained by the true owner, the banker would, nevertheless, be disentitled to the protection of s 4 of the Cheques Act 1957. For my part I think that these dicta are wrong; but it is obviously difficult to prove so speculative a proposition as what would have happened if inquiries had been made which were not made, and I do not think that the defendant bank has sustained the onus of proving it here. I prefer to put it in the alternative way which I have already indicated. It does not constitute any lack of reasonable care to refrain from making inquiries which it is improbable will lead to detection of the potential customer's dishonest purpose, if he is dishonest, and which are calculated to offend him and maybe drive away his custom if he is honest.

I turn next to the criticisms of the defendant bank's acceptance of Mr Ali's reference. We must resist the temptation of hindsight. We know now (as the defendant bank did not) that Mr Ali's knowledge of Kureshy was brief and scanty. He was in no position conscientiously to vouch for Kureshy's trustworthiness, or even his identity. Were the defendant bank acting prudently in relying on what Mr Ali told them about their new customer who called himself Eliaszade? Their new customer was a Pakistani, a close community who in England keep themselves to themselves. The most reliable source of information about him would be likely to be a fellow Pakistani whom the defendant bank could reasonably regard as trustworthy. Mr Ali was a Pakistani of substance, a restaurateur and thus likely to know about other Pakistanis in the same line of business. He had been a valued customer of the defendant bank for some six years. He had introduced a number of other Pakistanis as customers, and all of these had proved satisfactory. The bank had no reason to doubt Mr Ali's honesty, conscientiousness or candour, or to suppose that he would vouch for the trustworthiness of a customer unless he had reasonable grounds for doing so. I do not think that there was any lack of reasonable care on the part of the defendant bank in accepting and acting on Mr Ali's reference. It is to be noted that what he said about Eliaszade confirmed what Kureshy had said about himself two days before. There was no inconsistency between them.

The only criticism which has given me trouble is that, on being told by Mr Ali that he had known Eliaszade "for some time", the bank manager did not ask Ali how long he had known him. We know now that had that inquiry been made and answered truthfully, it would have disclosed that Mr Ali was in no position to vouch for Eliaszade's trustworthiness, and the bank would have been under a duty to make further inquiries before allowing this new customer to draw on his account; but this again is hindsight. The real question is: given their knowledge of Mr Ali as a valued customer, and their experience of him as a reliable referee for Pakistani customers, ought his use of the imprecise expression "some time" to have aroused their suspicion that his knowledge of Eliaszade might be insufficient to enable him to express a reliable view of Eliaszade's trustworthiness? Should it have led them to inquire further as to the facts on which that knowledge was based? This, I think, was very much a matter for the judge, who saw and heard Mr Ali as well as the bank witnesses. I agree with his conclusion [1967] 3 All ER at 975 that the defendant bank, in acting without further probing on the information given to them by Mr Ali as to their customer's trustworthiness, were not in breach of their duty to the plaintiff company to take reasonable care in relation to the plaintiff company's cheque which Kureshy had delivered to them for collection...

I would dismiss the appeal.

[**Danckwerts LJ** and **Cairns J** delivered judgments to similar effect.]

Appeal dismissed.

DEFENCES OF A PAYING BANK

A paying bank is liable to be sued in the following situations:
(a) by its customer the drawer if it disobeys his mandate: see Section 2, *supra*;
(b) by the true owner of a cheque which the bank has paid to someone else in contravention of the crossing: s 85(2).

Both of these situations should be distinguished from the case where the paying bank dishonours a cheque and (i) its customer sues the bank for breach of the bank's contract with its customer, or (ii) the holder or holder in due course sues the drawer or indorser *on* the dishonoured cheque, but cannot sue the bank on the cheque. Why not?

Where City Bank as the paying bank has paid a cheque to Country Bank which is collecting for Stamper who has no title, it may be sued by the true owner Coverall. In defence City Bank may rely on one or more of the statutory defences in BEA ss 64, 65, 86 and 88B. These provisions complement each other but also overlap so that several may apply concurrently.

(1) Payment in Due Course: BEA s 64

(See p 450, *supra*.) The definition of "payment in due course" requires payment to a *holder* by the drawee (here City Bank) which must act in due course. This does *not* mean the person receiving payment must be a holder in due course. Payment in due course discharges the cheque; ie, no one, including the true owner, can sue on it, although a separate right of action in conversion can be brought against the person or bank receiving payment if its title is defective.

(2) Payment by the Bank of Order Bill or Cheque Under Forged Indorsement: BEA s 65

Where a purported transfer of an order cheque is effected under a forged indorsement as in our illustration, the cheque is not discharged by payment under s 64. However, where City Bank pays in good faith and in the ordinary course of business, s 65 *deems* it to have paid in due course, thus protecting it from the true owner Coverall as well as from the drawer Carb. The section does not apply to order cheques which have not been indorsed or are irregularly indorsed. It appears that s 65 applies to cheques paid to another bank through the banking system as well as to those made by the paying bank over the counter: *Australian Mutual Provident Society v Derham* (1979) 39 FLR 165. In that case it was also held that failure of the paying bank to concern itself with the possible liability of the drawer for stamp duty on the cheque did not prevent the payment of the cheque being in the ordinary course of business.

(3) Payment by the Bank of Crossed Cheque: BEA s 86

The bank is required to act in good faith and *without negligence,* which is a stricter test than "in the ordinary course of business" under s 65: *Carpenters' Co v British Mutual Banking Co Ltd* [1938] 1 KB 511; [1937] 1 All ER 183. The bank must pay in accordance with the crossing but this does not require it to be satisfied that a cheque crossed "account payee only" is being collected for the account of the payee: *Universal Guarantee Pty Ltd v National Bank of Australasia Ltd*, p 505, *supra*. The section provides protection to the drawer Carb *qua* the payee Coverall if the payee has received the cheque. This was not available under s 65, but otherwise the section adds nothing to s 65.

(4) Payment by the Bank of Crossed or Uncrossed Cheque: BEA s 88B

This provision, added in 1971, is considerably wider than s 86 in that it applies to *uncrossed* cheques and to unindorsed and irregularly indorsed cheques. In the absence of s 88B it would have been both negligent and outside the ordinary course of business to pay to another bank an order cheque which was unindorsed or irregularly indorsed, and hence ss 65 and 86 would not have applied. As to the meaning of irregular indorsement, see *Slingsby v District Bank Ltd* [1932] 1 KB 544 (CA). *Semble*, indorsement without authority includes a forged indorsement: *Australian Mutual Provident Society v Derham, supra*.

The Relationship of Drawer and Payee

In the normal situation, the payee Coverall or its indorsee would receive payment of Carb's cheque which would be discharged under s 64 and Carb's obligation to Coverall would be satisfied. However, what is Carb's position *qua* Coverall where Coverall does not receive payment due to intervention by a rogue Stamper? Sections 65 and 88B may protect City Bank from actions by Carb or Coverall even though the cheque is not discharged. However, the question whether Carb obtains a discharge *qua* Coverall is determined by the agreement between them as to the mode of payment and by s 86.

If Coverall has instructed Carb to post the cheque then it is posted at Coverall's risk: *Channon v English, Scottish & Australian Bank* (1918) 18 SR (NSW) 30. A request to post can be implied from the payee's request to *remit* the cheque but not merely from the fact that the drawer has posted cheques on previous occasions. The drawer must draw and dispatch the cheque in the stipulated manner in order to pass the risk of loss to the payee: *London Bank of Australia Ltd v Kendall*, p 517, *supra*.

Section 86 provides drawer Carb with a statutory discharge *qua* Coverall provided the cheque is crossed, has come into Coverall's hands and is paid by City Bank in good faith and without negligence. It appears that the cheque will be deemed to have come into the payee's hands on being posted in accordance with his instructions as explained above. As the true owner, Coverall would then be entitled to sue Stamper and Country Bank in conversion: *London Bank of Australia Ltd v Kendall*, p 517, *supra*.

Conclusion

This section may conveniently be summarised by answering the questions originally posed in our factual illustration (pp 502-3, *supra*):

(1) The instrument is a cheque payable to order. Therefore the provisions of BEA apply; it can only be transferred by proper indorsement.

(2) The cheque is crossed, with the addition of "account payee only" and is not negotiable. Therefore no one can obtain a better title who takes through Stamper. All the provisions of BEA Pt III will be available.

(3) Coverall is the true owner of the cheque because it instructed Carb to send it by mail. Coverall has not been paid, and can sue Stamper (if he can be found), Country Bank and City Bank in conversion. Assuming City Bank has paid in good faith and without negligence Carb obtains a discharge of its indebtedness to Coverall which cannot sue Carb for the debt: s 86.

(4) Stamper is a thief and has no defence. He is not a holder since the cheque is payable to order: s 4; therefore he cannot be a holder in due course even if he satisfied the other requirements of value and good faith.

Country Bank is not a holder in due course because Stamper was not a holder, it did not give value for the cheque (s 34), Coverall's indorsement was forged (s 29), and the cheque is "not negotiable" (s 87). Country Bank received payment for a customer and may seek to rely on s 88D, but would have great difficulty rebutting the claim of negligence because of the absence of any explanation why Stamper was depositing a cheque payable to Carb Pty Ltd, the amount of the cheque, "not negotiable" crossing, and "account payee only" crossing.

City Bank has paid the crossed cheque to another banker as required by s 85(2)(b) and will raise defences under:

Section 65 — payment in good faith in ordinary course of business despite forged indorsement;

Section 86 — payment of crossed cheque in good faith and without negligence; as to paying bank's duty on "account payee only crossing": see *Universal Guarantee Pty Ltd v National Bank of Australasia Ltd*, p 505, *supra*;

Section 88B — payment in good faith and without negligence — available even if cheque uncrossed and not indorsed.

Note that s 64 is not available because payment was not made to a holder.

If the facts were changed so that Carb discovered Stamper's theft before City Bank paid the cheque and effectively countermanded payment, neither Stamper nor anyone taking through him could sue Carb on the cheque.

Brief Excursus on Bank Cheques

A bank cheque does not come within the s 8 definition of "bill of exchange", but see ss 10(2) and 65(2). However, it has been equated to an ordinary cheque by s 88A, and the 1971 amendments specifically extended protection to a bank paying and collecting drafts drawn upon itself: ss 88B(2) and (3), 88C(2), 88D(4).

A bank cheque is normally regarded as the equivalent of cash, but if it is crossed "not negotiable" the title of the holder may be defective. Although a bank will honour its own bank cheques in virtually every case, it has been held entitled to dishonour without liability to the payee where there was a total failure of the consideration for the issue of the bank cheque: *Sidney Raper Pty Ltd v Commonwealth Trading Bank of Australia & Ors* [1975] 2 NSWLR 227; (1975) 25 FLR 217, noted (1976) 50 *ALJ* 529.

It appears that a bank owes a duty to use reasonable care in securing its blank printed forms of bank cheques since the community places trust in a bank cheque and would not suspect that it had been forged. The duty which has been described as one of "high but reasonable care" was held not to have been breached in *Capri Jewellers Pty Ltd v Commonwealth Trading Bank of Australia* (unreported) noted in [1973] ACLD 152. And in *John's Period Furniture Pty Ltd v Commonwealth Savings Bank of Australia* (1980) 24 SASR 224 a bank which failed to notify the police or any other person that bank cheque forms had been stolen from its safe was not liable to a retailer who accepted them with forged signatures.

For further discussion on bank cheques see Weerasooria & Coops, *Banking Law and Practice in Australia*, 1976, pp 158-63. Would travellers' cheques be treated in the same way?

QUESTIONS

In the following *separate* fact situations, discuss the rights and liabilities of each party and both paying and collecting banks.

Question 7

After serving a jail sentence for assault, Bill Sly obtained a position as night security officer with Suburban Bank. He used his position to obtain a key to a locked cabinet from which he stole a blank form of bank cheque. The next day the bank manager discovered the theft and immediately notified all branches of Suburban Bank not to honour this particular cheque, but took no further action.

A week later Sly forged the signatures as drawers of two of the bank officers whose names he knew, and filled in the amount of $10,500 and the payee Uptown Jewellers on the bank cheque form which he then used to purchase a gold bracelet from that firm. Sly disappeared and Uptown Jewellers deposited the cheque into its account with City Bank for collection. Suburban Bank refused payment of the cheque.

Question 8

(1) Carb Pty Ltd obtained from City Bank a crossed bank cheque payable to "B Slee or order" for $250. Carb posted the cheque to Barry Slee in payment of consulting fees due to him. Bill Sly intercepted the cheque in the mail, indorsed the back of the cheque "B Sly" and deposited the cheque in his account with Federal Bank. As the cheque was a bank cheque, Federal Bank allowed Sly to withdraw all funds from the account including the uncollected proceeds of the cheque for $250. Sly then disappeared. The cheque was paid by City Bank in the normal manner.

(2) What difference would it make to the rights and liabilities of all parties if:
  (a) Slee had specifically requested Carb to hold the cheque at its premises for him to collect; or
  (b) learning that the cheque had gone astray in the mail, Carb had requested City

The Banker-Customer Relationship and the Banking System

Bank not to pay the cheque; and Sly, after adding his indorsement as in (1) above, had cashed the cheque with bookmaker Betts who deposited it into his account at City Bank.

Question 9

(1) Will Forge was the internal accountant of Carb Pty Ltd and an authorised signatory on its bank account. At the company's direction, he drew a company cheque on its current account with City Bank, Eastwood Branch, in favour of Mary Handy in payment of an annual dividend:

Duty Stamp	CITY BANK EASTWOOD BRANCH	10 August 1984

Pay Mary Handy .... or bearer
The sum of Six thousand
three hundred dollars $6300.00

ACCOUNT PAYEE ONLY

Carb Pty Ltd

W. Forge

Forge gave the cheque to Jim Handy who as the second authorised signatory co-signed it as drawer and handed it back with the request that Forge deposit it for him in Jim and Mary Handy's joint account at City Bank, Eastwood Branch. However, Forge pocketed the cheque while he went to the Ryde Branch of City Bank and opened a current account in his own name with a $50 cash deposit. He gave his occupation as accountant of Carb Pty Ltd. Later the same day Forge wrote "Mary Handy" on the back of the cheque and paid it into his own new account. When the cheque had been cleared, Forge cashed a cheque for $6000 on his new account and absconded to a South American republic which had no extradition treaty with Australia.

(2) What difference, if any, would it make to your answer if:
(a) it had been an order cheque? or
(b) the words "not negotiable" had been written in the crossing? or
(c) City Bank, Ryde Branch, had allowed Forge to withdraw $6000 from his new account before the proceeds of the cheque had been cleared? or
(d) City Bank, Ryde Branch, had cashed the cheque for Forge?

Question 10

Explain the roles of both paying and collecting banks in the process of handling cheques. Outline the extent of statutory protection afforded to both banks illustrating your answer by reference to decided cases. Your answer should also include an explanation of the purpose of the 1971 amendments to the Bills of Exchange Act, and show how it increased the banks' protection.

FURTHER READING
General
Paget's *Law of Banking*, 9th ed, 1982.
Report of the Committee to Review the Bills of Exchange Act 1909–1958 (Manning Committee) 1964.
Weaver & Craigie, *The Law Relating to Banker and Customer in Australia*, 1975.
Weerasooria & Coops, *Banking Law and Practice in Australia*, 1976.

Section 1: The Australian Banking System, and the Use of Cheques
Note (1979) 7 *ABLR* 167.
Santow, "The Role of Merchant Banks in Australia" (1973) 1 *ABLR* 321.
Yango Pastoral Co Pty Ltd v First Chicago Australia Ltd (1978) 53 ALJR 1.

Section 2: Duties of Paying Bank and its Customer at Common Law
Coleman, "Negligence in Drawing Cheques; *Commonwealth Trading Bank of Australia v Sydney Wide Stores Pty Ltd*" (1981) 9 *ABLR* 376.
Commercial Bank of Australia Ltd v Younis [1979] 1 NSWLR 444.
Ryan v Bank of New South Wales [1978] VR 555.

Section 3: Duties of Collecting and Paying Banks and Pt III Bills of Exchange Act
"Banker and Customer—Cheques Crossed 'Account Payee only'" (1978) 52 *ALJ* 287.
Davies, "The Effect of Crossing a Cheque 'A/c Payee only'" (1967) 7 *Aust Lawyer* 33.
Ellinger, "The Collection and Payment of Cheques" (1969-70) 9 *WALR* 101.
Frolich, "Travellers' Cheques and the Law in Australia" (1980) 54 *ALJ* 388.
Karkar, "The 'Not Negotiable' Crossing of Cheques" (1976) 4 *ABLR* 4.
Makin, "The Australian Bank Cheque—Some Further Legal Aspects" (1976) 3 *Monash ULR* 66.
Weerasooria, "The Australian Bank Cheque—Some Legal Aspects" (1975) 2 *Monash ULR* 180.

Index

Banker and customer — see also Cheques,
  Bills of Exchange
  Australian banking system 482-90
  bank
    defined 483-6
    services 486-7
    types of 486-7
  Bankcard 416-21
  bank cheques 525
  clearing system 489-90
  collecting bank 502-23
    duties 503
    statutory defences 508-23
  credit cards 416-21
  customer
    definition 487-9
    duties 491-8
  exchange control 478-80
  international transactions 457-8
  letters of credit — see also **Credit transactions** 457-77
  Manning Committee Report 497, 505-6
  paying bank
    duties 491-501
    statutory defences 523-5
  regulation of banks 483-6
Bankruptcy
  acts of 292-3
  bankruptcy notice 294-8
  distribution to creditors 298
  petition 291-2
  procedure 290-9
  purposes 286-90
  reform 287-9
  statistics 289-90
  voidable transactions — see also
    Secured transactions 278-85, 300-25
Bills of exchange
  acceptance 431
  alteration 451-3, 497
  cheques — see **Cheques**
  constitutional position 425-7
  definition 427-30
  discharge 440, 450-3

  dishonour 454
  estoppel 433-5
  fictitious payee 435-8
  forged signature 432-3
  forms 427-9
  good faith 446
  holder
    definition 430-1
    duties 453-4
    rights 441-53
  holder in due course 430-1, 441-53
  indorsements 432
  liabilities of parties 440-1
  negotiation 431-8
  notice 446, 453
  noting 454
  parties to 430-1
  presentment 453-4
  protest 454
  ratification 433-5
  transfer 431-8
  unauthorised signature 432-3
Book debts — see **Choses in action**
Business organisations — see also **National Companies Code**
  insolvent companies 299
  partnership
    assignment of interest 401-2

Carriage of goods
  air, by 168-9
  bailment 163-8
  land, by 168
    common carrier 168
  sea, by 169-91
    bills of lading 169-70
      construction 174-9
      exemption clauses 179-89
    charterparties 169
    containerisation 189-91
    Hague Rules 171-9
Cheques — see also **Negotiable instruments**
  account payee cheques 505-6
  bank cheques 525
  clearance 489-90
  crossings on cheques 504-6
  definition 482

Cheques — cont
  drawer/payee relationship 524–5
  forms 428
  not negotiable cheques 504–5
  payment in due course 524
  payment of 524
  statutory provisions 504–5
Choses in action
  book debts
    assignment 382–3, 403
    definition 403
  chattel paper 410–15
  choses in possession distinguished 5
  debts 384
  definitions 381
  equitable choses
    assignment 400–2
    definition 382
  factoring book debts 382–3, 403
  financing methods 382–3, 410–15
  future choses 382, 402
  legal choses
    assignment 383–400
      at law 384
      in equity 387
    definition 381
  partnership interest 401
  priorities
    chattel paper, in 415
    competing assignments 406
    counterclaims 405
    Dearle v Hall, rule in 406
    notice, effect of 407
Codification 15
Commercial law
  codification 15
  definition 4
  history 2–4
  nature 5
  policy considerations 6
  practice 7
  reform 6
  sources 6
  transactions, prototype 8
Constitutional law
  bills of exchange, on 425–7
  Commonwealth powers 5–6
Consumer Credit Acts
  bills of sale 329
  chattel paper 414
  chattel security 278, 329
    priorities 359
  continuing credit contract 331
  credit provider 329
  credit sales contract 329
  fixtures 368
  implied terms 330

  linked credit provider 412
  loan contracts 331
  mortgage 331
  purchaser protection 352
  reform 331
  registration 337
  security interest 331
  tied loans 411
Consumer protection
  consumerism 6
  credit — see **Credit transactions**
  legislation, scope of 35
Contracts
  acceptance 10
  cif 150
  consideration 10
  construction, rules of 11
  credit — see **Credit transactions, Consumer Credit Acts**
  definition 19
  fob 147
  formal requirements 27
  formation 19
  frustration 103
  fundamental breach 11
  insurance — see **Insurance**
  privity of 179–89
  representations 10
  sale — see **Sale of goods**
  tied loan contracts 411–13
  work and labour 21–4
Credit transactions — see also **Secured transactions**
  continuing credit contracts 331
  credit cards 416–21
  credit sales contract 330
  function of 265–7
  hire purchase 327–8
    assignment by owner 413
    rights and duties 327
  international 457–80
  letters of credit 457–77
    compliance with 469–77
    form 464
    legal basis 466–9
    types of 462–6
    Uniform Customs and Practices 462–5, 472–7
  linked credit provider 411
  loan contracts 331
  moneylending legislation 327
  mortgages 331
  negotiable instruments, finance by 414
  proceeds, loan on 381
  promissory notes, finance by 414, 423
  statutory requirements 27, 328–33
  tied loan contracts 411

Index

Environmental protection 6
Export sales — *see* **International sales**

Hire purchase — *see* **Credit transactions, Secured transactions, Consumer protection**

Import sales — *see* **International sales**
Insurance
    abandonment 259
    arbitration
        of claims 262
        reform 263
    assignment 260, 384
    average 258-9
    broker, duties to insurer, proponent 201-7
    claims 262
        arbitration of 262
        procedure 262
    contribution 259
    Export Finance and Insurance Corporation 478
    function 197-8
    good faith — *see also uberrimae fidei* doctrine 207-43
    indemnity 250-62
        amount of cover 258-9
        average 258-9
        definition 251-8
        insurable interest, and 251
    insurable interest 243-50
        indemnity, and 251
        life insurance 243-4
        marine insurance 243
        other types of insurance 244
        re-insurance 207
    life insurance, insurable interest 243-4
    marine insurance, insurable interest 243
    representative, relationship with insurer, proponent 201-7
    risks, types of 198-201
    subrogation 259-60
    uberrimae fidei doctrine 207-43
        common law duty 207-22
        cover note 238-41
        disclosure to agent 228-38
        materiality 208-28
        statutory qualifications 211-13, 222, 226, 238
        terms of policy 222-8

International sales
    characteristics of 143
    conflict of law rules 193
    contracts

        carriage, of 163-93
        cif 150
        fob 147
    exchange control 478-80
    Export Finance and Insurance Corporation 478
    finance of — *see also* **Credit transactions** 457-80
    insurance for export payments 199, 478
    international law of 193-6
    significance of 143
    uniform law of 194-6

Manufacturer's liability 79

National Companies Code
    book debts 403
    charges 284
    floating charges 323
    insolvent companies 299
    priorities 284, 360
Negotiable instruments — *see also* **Cheques, Bills of exchange**
    comparison with other choses in action 424
    origin 423
    promissory notes 413-14, 428, 454
    purpose 423

Partnership — *see* **Business organisations**
Promissory notes — *see* **Negotiable instruments**
Property
    passing, time of 83-102
    personal property — *see also* **Sale of goods** 5
        choses in action 5
        choses in possession 5
        fixtures 20, 369
    real property
        personalty compared 5
        profit à prendre 19

Remedies
    breach, for 14
    buyer's — *see* **Sale of goods**, remedies of buyer
    quantum meruit 31
    seller's — *see* **Sale of goods**, remedies of seller

Sale of goods
    acceptance of goods 14
        as evidence 27-9
        as performance 111-29
    codification 15

Sale of Goods — *cont*
    commercial aspects 11–15
    consumer credit agreements 24
    consumer sales 19, 35–7
    delivery of goods 14, 111
    earnest 29
    equipment, supply and erection 21
    equitable rules 16
    export sales — *see* **International sales**
    fixtures 20
    formalities 27–33
    goods
        conformity of 40
        definition 19
        delivery 27
        receipt 27
        severability 31
        specific 24
        unascertained 24
    hire purchase 24–6
    historical aspects 15
    implied terms 35
        description 40–5, 51–5
        examination 72
        fitness 40, 45–51, 56–67
        freedom from encumbrances 38
        merchantable quality 40, 45–55, 67–8, 72–9
        quiet possession 38–9
        sale, right of 37–8
        sample, correspondence with 40, 43–5
        title 37–9
    import sales — *see* **International sales**
    manufacturer's liability 79
    memorandum 30
    part payment 29
    performance 83, 111–29
        by acceptance 112–29
        by delivery 111
        by payment 111
    property, time of passing 83–102
    quantum meruit 31
    remedies of buyer 133–5, 138–41
        damages, for breach of warranty 141
        late delivery, for 140
        non-delivery, for 140
        specific performance 138–40
    remedies of seller 130–8
        damages 135–8
        lien 130–2
        personal action for price 135
        resale 133–5
    risk, passing of 83, 102–10
    self-service stores, in 43
    severability 31
    stages of 12
    Statute of Frauds 27–33
        reform of 31–3
Secured transactions — *see also* **Credit transactions**
    bankruptcy, effect on
        bill of sale 278
        floating charge 284, 323–5
        fraudulent dispositions 300–5
        preferences 305–14
        protection from 314–23
        voluntary dispositions 304
    bills of sale
        hire purchase as 279–81
        invalidation 278–81
        priorities 358
    charge
        equitable 275
        floating 278
        priorities 284, 360
        registration 281–5
    choses in action, over 381–409
    consumer credit contracts
        bills of sale 278
        chattel paper 414
        fixtures 369
        lien 368
        security interest 331
    definition 267
    dispositions
        for value 304
        fraudulent 300
        voluntary 304
    farm product financing 377–80
        crop liens 378
        legal basis 377
        methods 377
        stock mortgages 379
        wool liens 378
    fraudulent dispositions 300
    goods, perfection of interest in 278
    hire purchase 277
        bill of sale, as 279–81
        chattel paper 410–15
        fixtures 369
        lien 368
    lease 277
    letters of credit 457–77
    lien 277, 362–8
        authority to create 364–8
        common law 363
        contractual 363
        crop 378
        general 363
        particular 363
        statutory 363
        unpaid seller's 130–2
        wool 378

Index

Secured transactions — *cont*
  mortgage
    equitable 269–75
    legal 269
    stock 379
  nemo dat rule and exceptions 335, 337–54
    common law estoppel 338–44
    factors legislation 344–6
    market overt 353
    mercantile agent 344–6
    reform 354
    resale by buyer 351–2
    resale by seller 348–51
    security interest 352–3
    statutory powers of sale 353
    voidable title 346–8
  perfection of 278–85
  personal property, interests in 268–77
  pledge 276, 362
  priorities — *see also* nemo dat rule and exceptions
    accession 353, 370
    bills of sale legislation 357–9
    bona fide purchaser protection 336–54
    charges 360
    chattel paper, in 410–15
      consumer credit contracts 359
    chattel securities, between stock-in-trade purchasers 336, 415
    choses in action, in 405–9
    confusion 370
    fixtures 353, 369
    floating charge 335, 360
    future advance lending 360
    general law rules 356
    law reform 354
    National Companies Code 284, 360
    purchase money security interest 357
    secured creditors, interests in stock-in-trade 355–6
    tacking of future advances 360
  proceeds, in — *see* **Choses in action**
  trust receipt 477

Trade practices — *see also* **Consumer protection**
  generally 8
  implied terms 37
  manufacturer's liability 79–80
  misrepresentation 128
  tied loans 412